LINDLEY

&

BANKS

ON

PARTNERSHIP

AUSTRALIA
The Law Book Company
Brisbane · Sydney · Melbourne · Perth

CANADA
Carswell
Ottawa · Toronto · Calgary · Montreal · Vancouver

Agents
Steimatzky's Agency Ltd., Tel Aviv;
N.M. Tripathi (Private) Ltd., Bombay;
Easten Law House (Private) Ltd., Calcutta;
M.P.P. House, Bangalore;
Universal Book Traders, Delhi;
Aditya Books, Delhi;
Macmillan Shuppan KK, Tokyo;
Pakistan Law House, Karachi, Lahore.

LINDLEY

&

BANKS

ON

PARTNERSHIP

SEVENTEENTH EDITION

BY

R. C. I'ANSON BANKS, LL.B.

of Lincoln's Inn, Barrister

LONDON
Sweet & Maxwell
1995

"A Treatise on the Law of Partnership, including its application to Companies," first edition (in two volumes) by Nathaniel Lindley, afterwards Lord Lindley, M.R., and a Lord of Appeal ... 1860
Second Edition by the Author ... 1867
Third Edition by the Author ... 1873
Fourth Edition by the Author ... 1878
The work was divided in *Lindley on Companies* (one volume) and *Lindley on Partnership* (one volume), each by the Author in ... 1888
Sixth Edition by the Hon. W. B. Lindley ... 1893
Seventh Edition by Judge the Hon. W. B. Lindley and T. J. C. Tomlin ... 1905
Eighth Edition by Judge the Hon. W. B. Lindley and A. Andrews Uthwatt ... 1912
Ninth Edition by Judge the Hon. W. B. Lindley ... 1924
Tenth Edition by Judge the Hon. W. B. Lindley ... 1935
Eleventh Edition by Henry Salt, K.C., and Hugh E. Francis ... 1950
Twelfth Edition by Ernest H. Scamell ... 1962
Thirteenth Edition by Ernest H. Scamell ... 1971
Fourteenth Edition by Ernest H. Scamell and R. C. I'Anson Banks ... 1979
Fifteenth Edition by Ernest H. Scamell and R. C. I'Anson Banks ... 1984
Sixteenth Edition by R. C. I'Anson Banks ... 1990
Seventeenth Edition by R. C. I'Anson Banks ... 1995

Published in 1995 by
Sweet & Maxwell Limited of
South Quay Plaza, 183 Marsh Wall,
London E14 9FT.
Computerset by PB Computer Typesetting
Pickering, N. Yorks.
Printed in Great Britain by
The Bath Press, Bath, Avon

No natural forests were destroyed to
make this product; only farmed
timber was used and re-planted.

ISBN 0421-48260-5

A catalogue record for this book is
available from the British Library

PREFACE

"The operation was successful — but the patient died"

Anon.

Such was the risk when, in the last edition, I embarked on the radical surgery which I perceived to be necesary in order to invigorate this work to meet the needs of the partnership practitioner in the 1990s. However, the reception which that edition received both from reviewers and from those who have had occasion to dip into its contents would seem to demonstrate that the patient not only survived the operation, but is enjoying a new and well deserved lease of life. In order to consolidate that position, I have in this edition continued with the restoration process and readers will now find that further quotations from Lord Lindley's 5th edition and his Supplement on the Partnership Act 1890 have been included, particularly in the chapters which make up Part One (The Nature of a Partnership). However, on this occasion, few structural changes have been necessary.

Although there has been a steady flow of partnership or partnership-related cases since 1990, landmark decisions have been relatively few in number. Worthy of particular note were *Hadlee v. The Commissioners of Inland Revenue* [1993] A.C. 524 and *Gray v. I.R.C.* [1994] S.T.C. 360 (concerning the nature of partnership share), *Re Sutherland & Partners' Appeal* [1994] S.T.C. 387 (concerning the authority of a partner to conduct proceedings against the wishes of his co-partners, albeit that the Court of Appeal's ultimate decision was disappointingly narrow in scope) and *Faulks v. Faulks* [1992] 15 E.G. 82 (concerning the status of milk quota as a partnership asset). Equally, the potential significance of some decisions has been downgraded by the inadequacy of the published report: see, for example, *Re C. & M. Ashberg, The Times*, July 17, 1990.

Yet the relative dearth of English authorities has in many ways been compensated by a veritable cornucopia of New Zealand decisions (both old and new) to which my attention was drawn by Dick and Anne Webb, whose interest and enthusiasm I gratefully acknowledge. In some areas, the courts of that country have addressed issues which remain relatively untouched here, *e.g.* the vexed question of the right of an expelled partner to a fair hearing.

The seemingly unstoppable drive towards a European superstate has caused me to broaden the scope of the existing section on European partnerships in order to provide a more comprehensive overview of the comparative laws in the various jurisdictions. I have also sought to analyse the difference between a partnership and the recently introduced European Economic Interest Grouping or EEIG.

The new regime of partnership taxation introduced by the Finance Act 1994, which is due to be supplemented in the forthcoming Finance Act 1995, has necessitated a major overhaul of Chapter 34, a task complicated by the fact that, during the initial "run in" period, both old and new regimes are operating side by side. The opportunity has been taken to incorporate additional Revenue material in Appendix 6, particularly in relation to continuance elections, although these will become extinct under the new regime.

Limited partnerships continue to be something of a minority interest (although, in comparative terms, the number on the register has soared in recent years). However, one aspect which cannot be ignored is the status of such a partnership as a collective investment scheme for the purposes of the Financial Services Act 1986.

As important as the inclusion of the decided cases and new statutory materials is a proper understanding of some of the old "chestnuts" that, from my own experience, still tend to perplex practitioners; amongst those revisited in this edition are the effect of (and some of the anomalies created by) sections 38 and 43 of the Partnership Act 1890 and the manner in which a partnership contract can be repudiated. Equally, account must be taken of what might be styled partnership practice, which can evolve speedily to accommodate partners' needs: by way of example, what is in this work styled a power of suspension (but is now coming to be known, more colloquially, as a "garden leave" clause) has been encountered in partnership agreements for some years but has enjoyed such an explosion of popularity since I completed this edition, that it can now truly be regarded as a common form provision.

As always, I must record a number of debts of gratitude:

— My practice manager, Kim Pangratis, for her constant encouragement (and frequent cups of tea and coffee).
— The editorial staff of Sweet & Maxwell, for their patience and good humour in the face of many slipped deadlines.
— Numerous clients, who (whether they knew it or not) were kept waiting while proofs were read, etc.
— My sons, Oliver and Freddie, who seemed to grow up so much whilst I was locked away and who accepted my unavailability with relative and quiet(ish) stoicism.
— Most importantly, the one person without whose support and forbearance, this edition would, quite literally, never have been produced, namely by beloved wife, Susie. I can never adequately express my thanks to her but I will continue to try.

The law is, so far as possible, stated as at July 1, 1994. Regrettably, it was not possible to take account of the passage of the Trade Marks Act 1994 (which eliminates the distinction between trade and service marks) or the consolidating Value Added Tax Act 1994. Although this edition was delayed in the hopes that the Insolvent Partnerships Order 1994 (S.I. 1994 No. 2421) would be available, in the event it was not produced until September 1994, far too late to be reflected in the text. Nevertheless, it has been possible to reproduce the main body of the Order itself (even if not the voluminous Schedules) in Appendix 7 for reference purposes.

Finally, it is in many ways pleasing to note that, at long last, partnership law is coming to be widely recognised as a specialist subject in its own right and not merely as a relatively unimportant adjunct to·company law. Yet, the siren voices advocating a move away from partnership towards incorporation are, as I write this Preface, once more being heard. Perhaps the true flexibility and benefits of the partnership relation have yet to be fully understood, because they are so easily obscured by the spectre of unlimited liability. Only time will tell. It is my firm belief that this work and the law of partnership are assured of a future extending far into the 21st Century.

R.C. I'ANSON BANKS   January 15, 1995
48 Bedford Row
London WC1

TABLE OF CONTENTS

Part One

THE NATURE OF PARTNERSHIP

Part Two

FORMATION OF PARTNERSHIP BY FORMAL AGREEMENT

Part Three

THE RIGHTS AND OBLIGATIONS OF PARTNERS AS REGARDS THIRD PARTIES

Part Four

THE RIGHTS AND OBLIGATIONS OF PARTNERS
BETWEEN THEMSELVES

Part Five

DISSOLUTION AND WINDING-UP

Part Six

LIMITED PARTNERSHIPS

Part Seven

TAXATION

APPENDICES

TABLE OF CASES

TABLE OF STATUTES

TABLE OF STATUTORY INSTRUMENTS

Bold type indicates where references are set out in full

RULES OF THE SUPREME COURT

Bold type indicates where references are set out in full

TABLE OF SECURITIES AND INVESTMENT BOARD RULES

Part One

THE NATURE OF PARTNERSHIP

CHAPTER 1

INTRODUCTION

1. ORIGIN OF THE LAW OF PARTNERSHIP

UNTIL the Partnership Act of 1890, the law of partnership was to be **1–01** found almost exclusively in legal decisions and in textbooks; few Acts of Parliament related directly to partnerships as opposed to what were then styled "joint stock companies". The law of partnership was, on the whole, a good example of judge-made law, developing slowly with the growth of trade and commerce and representing generally perceived views of justice. On the other hand, it suffered from the laws against usury, from what previous editors called "unsound views of political economy" (culminating in *Waugh v. Carver*,[1] and not rectified until reviewed by the House of Lords in *Cox v. Hickman*[2]) and from the parallel systems of law and equity which prevailed until 1875, when the Judicature Acts came into operation.

It was those Acts which, by merging the administration of law and equity, greatly facilitated the legislative revision and improvement of various branches of the law, including partnership which had begun as an off-shoot of the law of contract but, by 1890, had become a virulent plant in its own right.

Limited partnerships

Prior to January 1, 1908, when the Limited Partnerships Act 1907 **1–02** came into force, only one kind of partnership was known to English law, namely the "general" partnership, in which the liability of every partner for the debts and obligations of the firm was unlimited. The Limited Partnerships Act 1907 introduced a second kind of partnership, called limited partnership, in which the liability of one or more (but not all) of its members could be limited.

Although limited partnerships are the creation of the 1907 Act and are subject to its express provisions, they are otherwise governed by the Partnership Act 1890 and the general rules of equity and common law applicable to partnerships. For this reason, the law applicable to

---

[1] (1793) 2 H.Bl. 235.
[2] (1860) 8 H.L.C. 268.

such partnerships is considered separately, after the treatment of general partnerships.[3]

2. THE PARTNERSHIP ACT 1890

Background to the Partnership Act 1890

1-03   In 1879, Sir Frederick Pollock drew a Bill for the consolidation and amendment of the law of partnership which was brought into the House of Commons in 1880 and again, with modifications, in 1882, 1883, 1884 and 1889. Ultimately, in its amended form, it was taken up by the Government of the day and, although altered in many respects, that bill was the foundation of the Act now known as the Partnership Act 1890.

Act not a complete codification

1-04   The Act is not (and does not purport to be) a complete code of partnership law; thus, it contains no provision relating to goodwill, to the administration of partnership assets in the event of a partner's death or bankruptcy[4] or, indeed, to the manner in which legal proceedings can be brought by and against a firm. Moreover, section 46 preserves the pre–existing rules of equity and common law, except in so far as they are inconsistent with the Act's express provisions. Although the Act did endeavour (for the most part successfully) to reduce an amorphous mass of largely uncorrelated case law into a series of authoritative propositions, it was, in the words of Lord Lindley, "not a perfect measure, nor even so good as Parliament might have made it."[5]

Alterations in the law

1-05   In real terms, the Partnership Act 1890 introduced no great change in the law. Apart from introducing a number of minor amendments and removing certain doubts, the only significant development lay in the new procedure for making a partner's share available for the payment of his separate judgment debts.[6]

---

[3] See Pt. 6, *infra*, paras. 28–01 *et seq.*

[4] Or, for that matter, on the occurrence of any other event which will dissolve the firm: see ss.32–35, *infra*, paras. A1–33 *et seq.* Note, however, the provisions of ss.38, 39 and 44, *infra*, paras. A1–40, A1–41, A1–45. As to the position where one or more of the partners (or the firm itself) is insolvent, see Chap. 27, *infra*, paras. 27–01 *et seq.*

[5] Perhaps one of the Act's greatest failings lay in the provisions of s.42, which caused both Lord Lindley and the editor of the 6th edition of this work to question the value of a judgment for an account of profits thereunder: see *infra*, para. 25–26.

[6] See the Partnership Act 1890, s.23(2), *infra*, para. A1–24. Although no doubt welcome at the time, this procedure is now only rarely used by creditors.

Structure of the Act

The Act is divided into five parts, headed as follows: **1–06**

1. Nature of partnership, sections 1–4.
2. Relations of partners to persons dealing with them, sections 5–18.
3. Relations of partners to one another, sections 19–31.
4. Dissolution of partnership and its consequences, sections 32–44.
5. Supplemental, sections 45–50.

The first four parts correspond with the four books into which the pre-1890 editions of this work were subdivided. The division is a natural one which has, in the main, been adopted in all previous editions of this work and which is followed in the present edition.

Definitions of "partnership" and "firm": the conceptual problem

Partnership

The basic definition of the term "partnership" is contained in **1–07** section 1 and at its very heart lie the words "carrying on a business with a view of profit"; however, the definition is further refined by section 2, which sets out those circumstances in which profits may be shared by persons who are *not* members of a partnership.

Pre–Act definitions: quasi–partnership

Before the Act, partnership was defined in various ways but there **1–08** was no authoritative definition of the word. Persons might not be partners and yet incur liabilities as if they were: in pre-1890 editions of this work, the term "quasi–partner" was used when referring to such persons, in order to distinguish them from "true" partners. Although apt, this term did not find its way into section 14, which specifically provides for liability on the basis of "holding out," or indeed any other section of the Act and it was accordingly abandoned in subsequent editions.

The firm

The expression "firm" is defined in s.4(1). This definition **1–09** highlights a feature which is peculiar to the English law of partnership and which, in turn, distinguishes it from the laws of Scotland[7] and of

---

[7] See the Partnership Act 1890, s.4(2), *infra*, para. A1–05. A recent graphic illustration of the operation of this section may be found in *Arif v. Levy & McRae*, 1992 G.W.D. 3–156.

other EU countries,[8] *i.e.* a refusal to recognise the firm as an entity separate and distinct from the partners who compose it. Notwithstanding a number of inroads in recent years,[9] this feature remains as central to the law of partnership as it was in Lord Lindley's day. Thus, as no one can owe money to himself, it was held (and would still be held)[10] that no debt could exist between any member of a firm and the firm itself and, whilst the courts of equity would, in winding up the affairs of a firm, treat it as the debtor or creditor of its members (as the case might be), this was only for book-keeping purposes, so as to enable accounts to be settled between the partners.

This failure to accord recognition to "the firm" had for many years prior to 1890 been perceived as a defect in the law of partnership[11] and, in his supplement on the Partnership Act, Lord Lindley appears to have regretted that the Act did not, in this respect, seek to assimilate the English and Scots law. Had it done so, the procedural difficulties which can attend actions by and against firms, particularly where there has been a change in the partners or where one or more of them are resident abroad, would have been greatly reduced.

1–10   The term "firm" (as defined) seemingly does not include persons liable by reason of holding out (section 14),[12] but this is entirely consistent with the "pure" definition of partnership, which would exclude such persons on the ground that their liability is based on estoppel rather than on actual membership of the firm.

An obvious omission: goodwill

1–11   One aspect of great practical importance (and of no little difficulty) was unfortunately not dealt with in the Act, namely the treatment of goodwill on a general dissolution[13] and, in particular, the extent to which the firm name can continue to be used by the former partners. Sir Frederick Pollock's Bill dealt with this question, as did the Bill which passed through the House of Commons in 1889 and the Bill which was brought into the House of Lords in 1890. However, in the event, the clauses relating to this subject were struck out owing, so Lord Lindley believed, to "differences of opinion, and to the

---

[8] See *infra*, paras. 2–32 *et seq.*

[9] In particular, a firm may now be wound up as an unregistered company under the Insolvency Act 1986: see, *infra*, para. 27–07 *et seq.*

[10] See *infra*, para. 19–05.

[11] In his Supplement on the Act, Lord Lindley noted that, in 1855, the Mercantile Law Amendment Committee had expressed the opinion that it would be "very convenient and useful" to recognise firms as having separate legal personality under English law.

[12] See *Hudgell Yeates & Co. v. Watson* [1978] Q.B. 451, 467, *per* Waller L.J. and note *Re C. & M. Ashberg, The Times*, July 17, 1990. But see also *infra*, para. 12–05.

[13] See, as to the meaning of this expression, *infra*, para. 24–03.

difficulty of arriving at a conclusion which would be acceptable to both Houses of Parliament." The relevant law is, therefore, to be found in the pre- and post-Act decisions (see section 46), so that a number of doubts and difficulties still inevitably persist.

Relevance of pre-1890 law

Cases decided prior to the Partnership Act 1890 must naturally be **1–12** read subject to its provisions. Where those provisions are clear, they must be followed and earlier decisions must not be regarded as binding authorities to be followed in preference thereto.[14] They may, however, be useful in order to explain the history of the Act and to show the state of the law up to that time. Indeed, there is now a more liberal and practical approach towards questions of construction, so much so that the House of Lords has sanctioned reference to some parliamentary materials as an aid to construction where that is necessary to overcome an ambiguity or to avoid an absurd result.[15] Thus, where the provisions of the Act are obscure or do not quite cover a particular case, reference to the previous case law may provide the only authoritative guidance.

---

[14] See the judgment of Lord Herschell in *Bank of England v. Vagliano* [1891] A.C. 107, 144–145; *Herdman v. Wheeler* [1902] 1 K.B. 361, 367, *per* Channell J.; *Hall v. Hayman* [1912] 2 K.B. 5, 12, *per* Bray J.; *Wimble, Sons & Co. v. Rosenberg & Sons* [1913] 3 K.B. 743, 747, *per* Vaughan Williams L.J.; *Despatie v. Tremblay* [1921] 1 A.C. 702, 709. See also *Grey v. I.R.C.* [1960] A.C. 1.

[15] *Pepper v. Hart* [1993] A.C. 593; also *Scher v. Policyholders Protection Board* (No. 2) [1993] 3 W.L.R. 1030. This represented a substantial departure from the previous law: see, for example, *Black-Clawson International Ltd. v. Papierwerke Waldhof-Aschaffenburg A.G.* [1975] A.C. 591; *Davis v. Johnson* [1979] A.C. 264; *Fothergill v. Monarch Airlines Ltd.* [1981] A.C. 251; *Hadmore Productions Ltd. v. Hamilton* [1983] A.C. 191; *M/S Aswan Engineering Establishment Co. v. Lupdine Ltd.* [1987] 1 W.L.R. 1. *Cf. Pickstone v. Freemans plc* [1989] A.C. 66; *Ex p. Factortame* [1990] 2 A.C. 85; *O'Rourke v. Binks* [1992] S.T.C. 703. Note, however, that the *Pepper v. Hart* approach has its limits: see *N.A.P. Holdings U.K. Ltd. v. Whittles* [1993] S.T.C. 592, 602.

CHAPTER 2

DEFINITION OF PARTNERSHIP

1.   THE DEFINITION IN THE PARTNERSHIP ACT 1890

2–01 SECTION 1(1) of the Partnership Act 1890 provides as follows:

> "Partnership is the relation which subsists between persons carrying on a business in common with a view of profit."

From this statutory definition it appears that, before a partnership can be said to exist, three conditions must be satisfied, *i.e.* there must be (1) a business (2) which is carried on by two or more persons in common (3) with "a view of profit."[1] Views differ as to whether a fourth condition should also be imported, namely an agreement to *share* any profits realised.[2] Each of these conditions, actual or supposed, will now be considered in turn.

A.   THE BUSINESS

2–02 By section 45 of the Act, "business" includes "every trade, occupation, or profession."[3] It follows that virtually any activity or venture of a commercial nature, including a "one off" trading venture,[4] will be regarded as a business for this purpose. On the other hand, the mere fact that a particular activity is profitable will

---

[1] As to whether the profit motive is a question of fact or law or both, see *Morden Rigg & Co. & Eskrigge (R. B.) & Co. v. Monks* (1923) 8 T.C. 450, 464, *per* Sterndale M.R.

[2] Sir Frederick Pollock was the main proponent in favour of the fourth condition: see *Pollock on the Law of Partnership* (15th ed.), pp. 9 *et seq.*

[3] See generally, *Smith v. Anderson* (1880) 15 Ch.D. 247, 258, *per* Jessel M.R.; *Newstead v. Frost* [1980] 1 W.L.R. 135 (H.L.). In his Supplement on the Act, Lord Lindley merely opined that "The meaning of the word [*business*] in this Act is very wide, but probably not wider than its ordinary meaning as given in dictionaries." *Cf.* the definition of "business" in the Landlord and Tenant Act 1954, s.23(2); and see also the somewhat exceptional decision in *Three H. Aircraft Hire v. Customs and Excise Commissioners* [1982] S.T.C. 653, discussed *infra*, para. 37–01, n.2. For the meaning of a bequest of a business, or of a partner's share or interest therein, see *Re Rhagg* [1938] Ch. 828, where the authorities are reviewed by Simonds J. In that case it was conceded (rather than held, as stated in the headnote) that the bequest was not adeemed by the supervening accession of the legatee to partnership with the testator in the interval between the date of the testator's will and the date of his death. But the headnote in [1938] 3 All E.R. 314, makes it clear that such concession was made.

[4] *Re Abenheim* (1913) 109 L.T. 219; *Mann v. D'Arcy* [1968] 1 W.L.R. 893; and see also *ibid* s.32.

not of itself turn it into a business: an example of such an activity is to be found in the management of a particular property, which may or may not qualify as a business, depending on the circumstances. This is to an extent emphasised by section 2(1) of the Act which, embodying the effect of a number of earlier decisions, provides:

> "Joint tenancy, tenancy in common, joint property, common property, or part ownership does not of itself create a partnership as to anything so held or owned, whether the tenants or owners do or do not share any profits made by the use thereof."

Equally, an activity which might not ordinarily be classed as a business, e.g. buying, selling and holding investments, may qualify if it is carried on as a commercial venture; a fortiori if a partnership is formed to carry on such an activity.[5]

B.   Two or More Persons Carrying on a Business in Common

If a partnership is to exist, it must be shown that two or more **2–03** persons are carrying on the business. If a group of individuals carry on a business not on their own behalf but on behalf of a third party, they will not be regarded as partners;[6] on the other hand, if a business is run by one or more persons on behalf of themselves and others, a partnership may be held to exist.[7] Thus, a "sleeping partner" may be "carrying on a business" for the purposes of the Act.

By virtue of the Interpretation Act 1978,[8] the word "person" includes "a body of persons corporate or unincorporate" and there is no doubt that a partnership can exist between an individual and a limited company or, indeed, between two or more such companies. In recent years, so called "corporate" partnerships have become popular as a vehicle for companies to pool their resources for a particular project, e.g. oil exploration, or for tax reasons. Further impetus has been given to this trend by the official recognition of the role which such partnerships have to play in the venture capital field (albeit in this case exploiting the advantages of the limited partnership).[9]

---

[5] See *Smith v. Anderson* (1880) 15 Ch.D. 247, 261, *per* Jessel M.R. On the facts, the Court of Appeal held that no association had been formed for the purpose of carrying on a business (within the meaning of the Companies Act 1862, s.4) but that the deed under consideration provided for the management of a trust fund.

[6] See *Holme v. Hammond* (1872) L.R. 7 Ex. 218; *Re Fisher & Sons* [1912] 2 K.B. 491.

[7] See *Cox v. Hickman* (1860) 8 H.L.Cas. 268.

[8] s.5, Sched. 1.

[9] See [1987] S.T.I. 783. See further, as to corporate partnerships, *infra*, paras. 11–02 *et seq.*

2-04   It is perhaps self evident, but nonetheless deserving of specific mention, that the definition of partnership requires the "carrying on" of a business. It naturally follows that a partnership cannot exist before the business is commenced.[10]

It is also a fundamental condition of the definition that the business is carried on by two or more persons "in common," *i.e.* there must be a single business, even if that business is carried on in a number of separate divisions. If, on a true analysis, each supposed partner is carrying on a separate business, as in the case of a mutual insurance society[11] or a genuine share-farming agreement,[12] there can in law be no partnership between them.

C.   "WITH A VIEW OF PROFIT"

2-05   In this element of the definition, by "profit" is meant the net amount remaining after paying out of the receipts of a business all the expenses incurred in obtaining those receipts; this should be contrasted with "gross returns," *e.g.* the royalties received by an author.[13]

The intention to make a profit (even if a profit is not actually realised)[14] lies at the very heart of the partnership relation. As Lord Lindley put it:

> "An agreement that something shall be attempted with a view to gain, and that the gain shall be shared by the parties to the agreement, is the grand characteristic of every partnership, and is the leading feature of nearly every definition of the term."[15]

It is where the profit motive can be identified as subsidiary to some other purpose that difficult questions can arise: in such cases, it is necessary to ask whether there is in fact any genuine "view of profit" at all. Thus, if a partnership is formed with some other predominant motive, *e.g.* tax avoidance, but there is also a real, albeit ancillary, profit element, it may be permissible to infer that the business is

---

[10] See *infra*, paras. 2–09 *et seq*. Note that, in his Supplement on the Act, Lord Lindley questioned whether the statutory definition "went too far ... by making the actual carrying on business (*sic*) a test of partnership." See also *infra*, para. 2–07 n.27.

[11] See *infra*, para. 2–30.

[12] See *infra*, para. 5–19.

[13] See the classic definition of the word "profit" by Fletcher Moulton L.J. in *Re Spanish Prospecting Co. Ltd.* [1911] 1 Ch. 92, 98. See also *Gresham Life Assurance Society v. Styles* [1892] A.C. 309, 322 *et seq.*, *per* Lord Herschell; *Beauchamp v. J. W. Woolworth PLC* [1990] 1 A.C. 478, 489, *per* Lord Templeman. And note *Customs and Excise Commissioners v. Bell Concord Educational Trust Ltd.* [1990] 1 Q.B. 1040.

[14] A court will only dissolve a partnership under s.35(*e*) that if it is incapable of making a profit: see *infra*, para. 24–73. It follows that a partnership which makes a loss will only cease to satisfy the statutory definition if the partners have no *intention* of making a profit.

[15] *Mollwo, March & Co. v. Court of Wards* (1872) L.R. 4 P.C. 419; *R. v. Robson* (1885) 16 Q.B.D. 137.

being carried on "with a view of profit."[16] If, however, it could be shown that the sole reason for the creation of a partnership was to give a particular partner the "benefit" of, say, a tax loss, when there was no contemplation in the parties' minds that a profit (in the sense outlined above) would be derived from carrying on the relevant business, the partnership could not in any real sense be said to have been formed "with a view of profit."

Societies and clubs, the object of which is not to acquire profit, are clearly not partnerships;[17] nor are mutual insurance societies.[18]

D.   A FOURTH CONDITION: DIVISION OF PROFITS?

Before the Partnership Act 1890 it was commonly said to be essential **2–06** for a partnership to have as its object, not only the acquisition, but also the *division* of profit.[19] This approach derived no little support from the terms "partnership" and "partner," which are self-evidently derived from the verb "to part" in the sense of to divide amongst or share.[20] It must, on any footing, be accepted that division of profits amongst the partners has always been (and remains) the general, even if not the universal, object of partnership but this was not perceived as an essential element of the definition under the pre-1890 law. Thus, it is apprehended that persons who carried on a business in all other respects as partners, but with the object not of dividing the profits between themselves but of applying them towards some charitable purpose would have been regarded as partners.[21] In the

---

[16] *Newstead v. Frost* [1980] 1 W.L.R. 135, 140; *cf. Overseas Containers (Finance) Ltd. v. Stoker* [1989] 1 W.L.R. 606. The judicial attitude to tax avoidance schemes has undergone a fundamental change in recent years (see *W. T. Ramsey Ltd. v. I.R.C.* [1982] A.C. 300; *Furniss v. Dawson* [1984] A.C. 474), although subsequent decisions appear to have substantially restricted the scope of the "*Ramsay*" and "*Furniss*" principles: see, for example, *Craven v. White* [1989] A.C. 398; *Shepherd v. Lyntress Ltd.* [1989] S.T.C. 617; *Customs & Excise Commissioners v. Faith Construction Ltd.* [1990] 1 Q.B. 905; *I.R.C. v. Fitzwilliam* [1993] 1 W.L.R. 1189; *cf. Moodie v. I.R.C.* [1993] 1 W.L.R. 266. It is submitted that, in pursuance of such principles, a court could not ignore the existence of a genuine partnership brought into existence as part of a tax avoidance scheme: Millet J. was certainly not prepared to do so in *Ensign Tankers (Leasing) Ltd. v. Stokes* [1989] 1 W.L.R. 1222, 1242–1243 (this argument was not pursued in Court of Appeal at [1991] 1 W.L.R. 341 or in the House of Lords at [1992] 1 A.C. 655). But note the decision in *Gisborne v. Burton* [1989] Q.B. 390, where the Court of Appeal, in effect, extended the application of the *Ramsay* principle outside the sphere of taxation.

[17] See *infra*, para. 2–29.

[18] See *infra*, para. 2–30.

[19] *Pooley v. Driver* (1876) 5 Ch.D. 458, 472, *per* Jessel M.R.; *Mollwo, March & Co. v. Court of Wards* (1872) L.R. 4 P.C. 419.

[20] Lord Lindley made the obvious point that there is more to partnership than merely sharing, since "persons may share almost anything imaginable, and may do so either by agreement amongst themselves or otherwise." It is the realisation and, in general, the sharing *of profits* which is at the heart of partnership.

[21] That this is not so far-fetched as might at first sight appear, see the trust in *R. v. Special Commissioners of Income Tax* [1922] 2 K.B. 729; also *The Abbey, Malvern Wells v. Minister of Local Government and Planning* [1951] Ch. 728. Moreover, the Value Added Tax Tribunal has accepted the correctness of this proposition: *Stephanie A. Manuel t/a Stage Coach Centre for the Performing Arts v. The Commissioners* (LON/90/807) [1992] S.T.I. 47. Note, however, the contrary (*obiter*) view seemingly expressed by Hoffmann J. in *Blackpool Marton Rotary Club v. Martin* [1988] S.T.C. 823, 830–831. The business in question may, of course, be a single adventure.

same way, if two persons purported to carry on business as partners under a firm name, on terms that they were both to contribute capital and share losses equally, but that one of them was to be paid a fixed salary every year irrespective of the venture's profitability, whilst the other took the entirety of the profits (if any), they would, surely, have been treated as partners.[22]

If the above analysis is correct, then the omission of the supposed fourth element from the definition of partnership must have been intentional and accords with the previous law.[23] On the other hand, if in the cases supposed the participants would not have been regarded as partners under the old law, either the Act altered the position or an essential term was omitted from the definition.[24] Faced with these two alternatives, the current editor agrees with previous editors of this work that the omission of the supposed fourth element appears to be a studious one, so that it is not permissible to import it, even if it did previously exist and could otherwise be said to have been saved by section 46 of the Act. In the circumstances, it is submitted that the division of profits is no more than a common incident of the partnership relation, rather than of its very essence.[25]

At the same time, it must be recognised that section 44(a) of the Act does contemplate that if, on a general dissolution, there are sufficient funds available, there will be an ultimate division of the profits for the benefit of all the partners.[26]

Partnership a contractual relationship

2–07   Partnership, although often called a contract, is more accurately described as a relationship *resulting from* a contract. This was made clear in the original statutory definition introduced into the House of

---

[22] In previous editions, reference was at this point made to *Watson v. Haggitt* [1928] A.C. 127, where Haggitt had for two years received a "salary" whilst Watson had drawn all the net profits of the business. However, it appears that there was in reality a sharing of profits in this case: see *ibid.* [1927] N.Z.L.R. 209, 212, *per* Alpers J. And see *Marsh v. Stacey* (1963) 107 S.J. 512, where the junior partner, who was to receive a fixed salary of £1,200 plus one-third of the profits of one branch of the firm, would undoubtedly have been liable as a partner; also *Stekel v. Ellice* [1973] 1 W.L.R. 191.

[23] Similarly, a division of profits was not essential to a joint stock company: *Re Russell Institution* [1898] 2 Ch. 72; *Re Jones* [1898] 2 Ch. 83.

[24] The question arose in *Re Fisher & Sons* [1912] 2 K.B. 491. *Sed quaere*, if it was decided; see *infra*, para. 5–08.

[25] For a criticism of this view, see *Pollock on the Law of Partnership* (15th ed.), pp. 9 *et seq*. The current editor submits (along with previous editors) that Sir Frederick Pollock's criticism does not meet the difficulties discussed in the text. Note, however, that in *Blackpool Marton Rotary Club v. Martin* [1988] S.T.C. 823, 830, Hoffmann J. observed that it is of the essence of the definition of partnership that a business is carried on "with a view to a profit to which the partners will be [*sic*] in some proportion or other each be individually entitled." *Quaere* whether this is in accordance with the authorities.

[26] See *infra*, paras. 25–39 *et seq*. In earlier editions of this work reference was made at this point to s.39, rather than s.44; however the former section contains no reference to profits.

Lords[27] but not, ultimately, in the Act itself. Nevertheless, the origin of the relationship in an agreement, whether express or implied, was clearly established before the Act and may legitimately be inferred from its provisions.[28]

Other definitions

The various comparative definitions of partnership, drawn from a **2–08** number of different legal systems, which appeared in earlier editions of this work, are considered to be of more jurisprudential than practical interest and, given their accessibility in those editions, have not been retained in the present edition.[29] Of greater relevance is the line of the law of partnership in a number of European countries, which is to be found at the end of this Chapter.[30]

2. CONTEMPLATED PARTNERSHIPS

Business not yet commenced

An agreement between two or more persons to carry on business at **2–09** a future time cannot render them partners before they actually start to carry on that business. It is the carrying on of a business, not a mere agreement to carry it on, which is the test of partnership,[31] hence the importance of distinguishing between actual and contemplated partnerships. As Lord Lindley put it:

> "Persons who are only contemplating a future partnership, or who have only entered into an agreement that they will at some future time become partners, cannot be considered as partners before the arrival of the time agreed upon."[32]

He then went on to point out the difficulty of distinguishing between an agreement for an immediate partnership or an agreement for a

---

[27] According to Lord Lindley's Supplement on the Partnership Act, the original definition was: "Partnership is the relation which subsists between persons who have agreed to carry on a business in common with a view of profit." Lord Lindley commented: "This definition was inaccurate, for, as pointed out by Parke J. in *Dickinson v. Valpy* [*(1829) 10 B. & C. 128, 141–2*], persons who have entered into an agreement that they will at some future time carry on business as partners, can *not* be considered as partners until the arrival of that time." This, of course, accords with the present position: see *infra*, paras. 2–09 *et seq.*

[28] See especially ss.1, 2, 19, 24, 32, 33, 40 and 41; and *Davis v. Davis* [1894] 1 Ch. 393. *Cf. Collins v. Barker* [1893] 1 Ch. 578.

[29] See the 15th ed., pp. 16–18; also the observations of Jessel M.R. thereon in *Pooley v. Driver* (1876) 5 Ch.D. 458, 471 *et seq.*

[30] See *infra*, paras. 2–32 *et seq.*

[31] See the statutory definition of partnership, *supra*, paras. 2–01 *et seq.* And see *supra*, paras. 2–04, n.10, 2–07, n.27.

[32] See *Dickinson v. Valpy* (1829) 10 B. & C. 128, 141–142, *per* Parke J. And see, in addition to the cases cited below, *Osborne v. Jullion* (1856) 3 Drew. 596, where the partnership (?) depended on the result of experiments.

future partnership. This difficulty may in practice be compounded where the parties depart from the strict terms of their agreement. If they opt for a future commencement date, but begin to carry on business together at an earlier date, they will be partners as from that earlier date; if they defer the date of commencement, no partnership will come into existence on the date originally chosen. Equally, if one intending partner carries on the business prior to the agreed commencement date without the approval or acquiescence of the others, no immediate partnership will come into existence.

General principle

2–10 So long as an agreement to form a partnership remains executory, no partnership will be created. Subject to the point noted in the previous paragraph, intending partners will retain that status if the chosen commencement date has not yet arrived or if some act still remains to be done before the business can be commenced. Precisely the same principle applies as between the promoters of companies, as will be seen hereafter.

(a) Application of the Principle: Ordinary Partnerships

Share not yet taken

2–11 In *Howell v. Brodie*,[33] the defendant intended to become a partner in a market proposed to be erected and advanced considerable sums of money for that purpose; ultimately, on the completion of the market, he took a one-seventh share in it. The plaintiff builder sought to make him liable for the cost of work and materials employed in erecting the market, on the ground that he was a partner with the person by whom he (the plaintiff) had been employed; however, the court held that no partnership existed until the defendant took up his share, which he did not do until after the plaintiff's period of employment.

Share of profits expected in lieu of salary

2–12 In *Burnell v. Hunt*,[34] A and B agreed that A should take premises and purchase machinery and materials to carry on the business of a silk-lace maker, and that B should manage the business and receive half the profits as soon as any accrued. In the meantime, he was to be paid £2 a week. It was held that, so long as the £2 per week continued to be paid, no partnership existed.[35]

---

[33] (1839) 6 Bing. N.C. 44.
[34] (1841) 5 Jur. 650 (Q.B.). The real point here was whether B had any interest in the goods, which he clearly had not, and would not have had even if there had been profits to divide.
[35] See also *Ex p. Hickin* (1850) 3 De G. & Sm. 662.

Option to become a partner

A person who is contemplating joining another in business may **2–13** agree that the business is initially to be carried on upon terms which do not involve the creation of a partnership, but which confer upon him the right to become a partner, either at a specified time or at a time of his choosing. Such an agreement, if bona fide, and not a colourable device for disguising the existence of an immediate partnership,[36] will not constitute the parties as partners until the option has been exercised.[37] This is illustrated by *Ex p. Davis*,[38] where a creditor had a right to nominate himself as a partner with his debtor but had not exercised the right.

Similarly, in *Gabriel v. Evill*,[39] the defendant agreed to enter into **2–14** partnership with two prospective partners and to bring in £1,000 in cash and £1,000 in goods. It was also agreed that the partnership would have a retrospective commencement date, but the defendant reserved to himself the option of determining at any time within 12 months from that date whether he would become a partner or not. He duly advanced the £2,000, and several other acts were done in pursuance of the agreement, but within the 12 months the defendant exercised his option and declared his intention not to become a partner. It was held that he never did in fact become one, and that he had not incurred any liability as if he had.[40]

In *Price v. Groom*,[41] a debtor carried on business under what was **2–15** then styled an inspectorship deed, which authorised the trustees to carry on the business themselves, and to take the profits, if they chose. Their interest in the profits, however, did not commence until the debtor's interest determined; and it was held that, whilst he carried on the business, there was no partnership between him and the trustees, they and he not being entitled to the profits at the same time.

---

[36] See *Courtenay v. Wagstaff* (1864) 16 C.B.(N.S.) 110.

[37] In the opinion of the current editor, such an option will, in general, be personal to the prospective partner and, thus, not freely assignable, although much will naturally depend on the terms of the agreement. Note also that a mortgagor may give his mortgagee an option to become his partner and, thereupon, to acquire the mortgaged property: *Reeve v. Lisle* [1902] A.C. 461. However, if that arrangement forms part of the original mortgage transaction, it may be regarded as a clog on the equity of redemption: see *Lisle v. Reeve* [1902] 1 Ch. 53, 71 *et seq.*; also *Samuel v. Jarrah Timber and Wood Paving Co. Ltd.* [1904] A.C. 323, 329, per Lord Lindley; *Lewis v. Frank Love Ltd.* [1961] 1 W.L.R. 261.

[38] (1863) 4 De G.J. & S. 523.

[39] (1842) 9 M. & W. 297; also *Ex p. Turquand* (1841) 2 M.D. & D. 339; *Re Hall* (1864) 15 I.Ch.R. 287.

[40] Compare this case with *Jefferys v. Smith* (1827) 3 Russ. 158. There A agreed to purchase B's share in a firm; A acted and was treated as a partner by the other members, but afterwards rescinded the contract with B: it was held that a partnership nevertheless subsisted between A and B's co-partners.

[41] (1848) 2 Ex. 542.

2-16   In *Re Young, ex p. Jones*,[42] A lent B £500 for his business under a
written contract, by the terms of which A was to have sole control
and management of the business, with the option of becoming a
partner within a certain time; in the interim, for the use of his
money, he was to be paid a weekly sum out of the profits of the
business. B was to draw a similar weekly sum. Before the time for
the exercise of the option had expired B became bankrupt. The court
held that A, who had not exercised the option, was not a partner in
the business.[43]

Partnership agreement to be drawn up

2-17   Persons who agree to become partners and who intend to sign a
formal partnership deed may become partners even though they
never sign such a deed.[44] On the other hand, a deed may be prepared
but never acted on, in which case no partnership will be created.[45]
But if the parties agree that they are not to become partners until
they have signed such a deed, the partnership will not commence
until that condition has been performed, unless they can be shown to
have waived the need for such performance. Thus, in *Battley v.
Lewis*,[46] two persons had agreed to become partners as from a future
date, on terms to be embodied in a deed to be executed on that date.
In fact, the deed was executed, in an amended form, but on a later
date. It was nevertheless held that the partnership began on the
original date. Significantly, the parties had in fact commenced
business as partners on that date, so that it was wholly immaterial (as
regards the question before the court) what the *terms* of the
partnership were.

Conditional agreement

2-18   If persons agree to become partners on certain terms and/or with a
view to carrying on a particular business, they cannot be obliged to
enter into partnership on some other terms or with a view to carrying
on some other business; they will only be regarded as partners when
they actually participate in the "new" partnership and thereby
preclude themselves from objecting to the variation of their original
agreement.[47]

---

[42] [1896] 2 Q.B. 484.

[43] As to A's right to prove for the money lent, see *infra*, paras. 5–40 *et seq.*, 27–108.

[44] See *Syers v. Syers* (1876) 1 App.Cas. 174; *Mavor v. Hill* [1952] C.P.L. 472; *Stekel v. Ellice*
[1973] 1 W.L.R. 191. Note also *Walters v. Bingham* [1988] 1 F.T.L.R. 260.

[45] *Alexander Bulloch & Co. v. I.R.C.* [1976] S.T.C. 514.

[46] (1840) 1 Man. & G. 155; and see *Wilson v. Lewis* (1840) 2 Man. & G. 197. *Cf. Ellis v. Ward*
(1872) 21 W.R. 100, where the intended partners quarrelled before they signed the deed.

[47] *Fox v. Clifton* (1830) 6 Bing. 776.

(b) Application of the Principle: Promoters of Companies

Where two or more persons are preparing to set up a company and **2–19** intend to become members of the company after its formation, they will not be regarded as partners if this is their only business association. Admittedly, they may share a common object which is, ultimately, the acquisition of profit, but their immediate object is the formation of the company.[48] On the other hand, persons who together carry on the *business* of promoting companies with a view to making profits therefrom will unquestionably be partners.[49]

Early cases: statutory companies

Two old cases are technically at variance with the above **2–20** propositions, namely *Holmes v. Higgins*[50] and *Lucas v. Beach*.[51] In the former, several persons, who had associated together in order to obtain the Act of Parliament necessary to form a railway company and subscribed money for that purpose, were held to be partners. Similarly, in *Lucas v. Beach*, the court held that persons associated together for the purpose of passing a turnpike Act, who had each subscribed for shares in the tolls from the proposed road, were partners. However, in both of these cases the real question was whether the plaintiff was, by virtue of an implied contract, entitled to recover from the defendants remuneration for services rendered by him for their joint benefit. It was held that he was not. As a result, both cases were thought to be (and, on occasion, cited as) authorities for the proposition that persons engaged in setting up what is now known as a statutory company are partners. Indeed, in *Lucas v. Beach* it was asked in argument, "What is there to prevent a number of individuals from entering into a partnership with the limited object, in the first instance, of procuring an act of Parliament, and with an ulterior object in view when the act has passed?"[52] Lord Lindley had no hesitation in responding thus:

"The answer is, that to call persons so associated partners is to ignore the difference between a contract of partnership and an agreement to enter into such a contract, to confound an agreement with its result, and to hold persons to be partners although they have not yet acquired any right to share profits. It cannot be

---

[48] *Keith Spicer v. Mansell* [1970] 1 W.L.R. 333; also *Wood v. Argyll* (1844) 6 Man. & G. 928; *Hamilton v. Smith* (1859) 5 Jur. (N.S.) 32; *Hutton v. Thompson* (1846) 3 H.L.C. 161; *Bright v. Hutton* (1852) 3 H.L.C. 341.
[49] See *Royal Victoria Palace Syndicate* (1873) 29 L.T. 668; affirmed (1874) 30 L.T. 3.
[50] (1822) 1 B. & C. 74.
[51] (1840) 1 Man. & G. 417; *Barnett v. Lambert* (1846) 15 M. & W. 489 was a similar case.
[52] See also *per* Lord Brougham in *Hutton v. Upfill* (1850) 2 H.L.C. 674, 691–692.

contended that the right to share profits would, under such an agreement as is supposed, accrue before the passing of the act, and if not, how can the parties to such an agreement be *partners* at an earlier period?"[53]

2–21   It is accordingly submitted that Lord Lindley was justified in stating that *Holmes v. Higgins* and *Lucas v. Beach* cannot be relied on as authorities on this issue.[54] They cannot even be reconciled with the later decisions in *Reynell v. Lewis*[55] and *Wyld v. Hopkins*[56] where, following detailed consideration, it was held that no partnership subsisted between persons who had subscribed for the purposes of forming a railway company and of procuring the necessary Act of Parliament. Lord Cranworth subsequently confirmed this to be the correct principle,[57] and there are numerous other decisions to the like effect.[58]

3. ASSOCIATIONS NOT GOVERNED BY THE PARTNERSHIP ACT 1890

Statutory exceptions

2–22   The definition of "partnership" contained in section 1(1) of the Partnership Act 1890,[59] if standing alone, would include not only partnerships in the ordinary sense of the term, but also many companies and associations which differ from ordinary partnerships in certain fundamental respects. The latter are, however, expressly excluded from the ambit of the Act by section 1(2), which provides as follows:

---

[53] When considering the latter part of this passage, the terms of the statutory definition of partnership contained in the Partnership Act 1890, s.1(1) must be borne in mind, since there is now no express requirement that partners must actually *share* profits: see *supra*, para. 2–06.

[54] In editions of this work prior to the 16th the following footnote appeared at this point: "They are authorities for the point actually decided, *viz.* that a person doing work for the joint benefit of himself and others cannot recover compensation from them by virtue of any implied promise to pay him." However, it is submitted that this proposition ignores the finding of partnership in each case which was at the root of the decision. See also, as to the entitlement (or otherwise) of a partner to remuneration *infra*, paras. 20–36 *et seq.*

[55] (1846) 15 M. & W. 517.

[56] *Ibid.*

[57] *Capper's Case* (1851) 1 Sim. N.S. 178.

[58] See *Batard v. Hawes* (1853) 2 E. & B. 287; *Walstab v. Spottiswoode* (1846) 15 M. & W. 501; *Forrester v. Bell* (1847) 10 I.L.R. 555; *Hutton v. Thompson* (1846) 3 H.L.C. 161; *Bright v. Hutton* (1852) 3 H.L.C. 341; *Hamilton v. Smith* (1859) 5 Jur. N.S. 32; *Norris v. Cottle* (1850) 2 H.L.C. 647; *Besley's Case* (1851) 3 Mac. & G. 287; *Tanner's Case* (1852) 5 De G. & Sm. 182. But see also the judgment of Lowry C.J. in *De Pol v. Cunningham* [1974] S.T.C. 487, where assets were jointly owned in equity pending the formation of a limited company. Lowry C.J. (but not the other Lords Justices) concluded that the parties were "bound to be in partnership" (see p. 500). It is thought that this conclusion was not in accordance with authority, or strictly justified on the facts of the case.

[59] See *supra*, para. 2–01.

Partnership Act 1890, section 1(2)

"1.— ... (2) But the relation between members of any company **2–23** or association which is—

(a) Registered as a company under the Companies Acts 1862 or any other Act of Parliament for the time being in force and relating to the registration of joint stock companies;[60] or

(b) Formed or incorporated by or in pursuance of any other Act of Parliament or letters patent, or Royal Charter; or

(c) A company engaged in working mines within and subject to the jurisdiction of the Stannaries[61];

is not a partnership within the meaning of this Act."

There are thus excluded from the Partnership Act 1890 registered companies and incorporated and unincorporated companies which derive special privileges from the Crown or the legislature.

Distinction between corporations and partnerships

A corporation is an artificial person created by special authority[62] **2–24** and endowed with capacity to acquire rights and incur obligations, in order to further or achieve the objects for which it was created.[63] Certainly a corporation is composed of a number of individuals, but the rights and obligations of those individuals are not the same as those of the corporation; nor are the rights and obligations of the corporation exercisable by or enforceable against those individuals, either jointly or separately, but only collectively, as an artificial entity, *i.e.* the corporation enjoys separate legal personality. Civilian lawyers put it in these terms: *Si quid universitati debetur singulis non debetur, nec quod debet universitas singuli debent.*[64] (If anything is owed to an entire body, it is not owed to the individual members, nor do the individual members owe what is owed by the entire body.)

With partnerships, it is the opposite: the firm is not an entity **2–25** distinct from the individuals composing it[65] and the partners

---

[60] See, now, the Companies Act 1985 (as amended).

[61] The Stannaries jurisdiction no longer exists: see the Companies Consolidation (Consequential Provisions) Act 1985, s.28.

[62] *i.e.* by the authority of the law of England, the Crown (*i.e.* royal charter) or Parliament or by prescription.

[63] The corporation's powers will not be unlimited: see, for example, *Hazell v. Hammersmith and Fulham London Borough Council* [1992] 2 A.C. 1.

[64] See also *Re Sheffield and South Yorkshire Permanent Building Soc.* (1889) 22 Q.B.D. 470, 476, *per* Cave J.; *Salomon v. Salomon & Co. Ltd.* [1897] A.C. 22.

[65] *Cf.* the exceptional position of the International Tin Council as an unincorporated association with legal personality: *J.H. Rayner (Mincing Lane) Ltd. v. Department of Trade and Industry* [1990] 2 A.C. 418. And note also *Arab Monetary Fund v. Hashim (No. 3)* [1991] 2 A.C. 114.

collectively cannot acquire rights or incur obligations. The rights and liabilities of a partnership are the rights and liabilities of the partners and are enforceable by and against them individually. The principle is stated by the civilian lawyers thus: *Si quid societati debetur singulis debetur et quod debet societas singuli debent.*[66] (If anything is owed to the partnership, it is owed to the individual members and the individual members owe what is owed by the partnership.) Limited exceptions to this principle are, however, to be found in the statutory provisions governing income tax assessments against a firm[67] and in the insolvency legislation as applied to partnerships.[68]

Companies

(1) *Unincorporated*

2-26 Unincorporated companies were once common and in many ways resembled partnerships. However, Lord Lindley identified the fundamental distinction in these terms:

> " ... a partnership consists of a few individuals known to each other, bound together by the ties of friendship and mutual confidence, and who, therefore, are not at liberty without the consent of all to retire from the firm and substitute other persons in their places; whilst a company consists of a large number of individuals not necessarily nor indeed usually acquainted with each other at all, so that it is a matter of comparative indifference whether changes amongst them are effected or not.[69] Nearly all the differences which exist between ordinary partnerships and unincorporated companies, will be found traceable to the above distinction. Indeed it may be said that the law of unincorporated companies was composed of little else than the law of partnership modified and adapted to the wants of a large and fluctuating number of members."

2-27 Since the Companies Act 1862, unincorporated companies formed for the purpose of carrying on any business that has as its object the acquisition of gain have, with certain exceptions, required to be registered and this remains the position under the Companies Act 1985, although the exceptions are now few in number.[70] Thus, an

---

[66] See *Lloyd v. Loaring* (1802) 6 Ves.Jr. 773; *Beaumont v. Meredith* (1814) 3 V. & B. 180; *Ryhope Coal Co. v. Foyer* (1881) 7 Q.B.D. 485.
[67] But only in the case of firms in existence prior to April 6, 1994: see *infra* paras. 34–05 *et seq.*
[68] See *infra*, paras. 27–08 *et seq.*
[69] See *Smith v. Anderson* (1880) 15 Ch.D. 247, 273, *per* James L.J. and *Re Stanley* [1906] 1 Ch. 131, 134, *per* Buckley J.
[70] See the Companies Act 1985, s.716 (as amended) and the various Partnerships (Unrestricted Size) Regulations made pursuant thereto: see *infra*, paras. 4–28, 4–29, 29–02. *Cf.* the Companies Act 1948, s.434 in its original form.

unincorporated company with more than 20 members would have to be registered;[71] if the number of members is less than 20, it would, generally, be regarded as a partnership within the meaning of the Partnership Act 1890.[72]

(2) *Incorporated*

Lord Lindley defined such companies in the following terms: **2–28**

"Incorporated companies are societies consisting usually of many persons, having transferable shares in a common fund, but incorporated by Royal Charter or by Act of Parliament. They are not pure partnerships, for their members are recognised as an aggregate body; nor are they pure corporations, for their members are more or less liable to contribute to the debts of the collective whole. Incorporated companies are intermediate between corporations known to the common law and ordinary partnerships, and partake of the nature of both; and the law relating to these companies depends as well on the principles which govern ordinary partnerships, as on those which are applicable to corporations strictly so called."[73]

Now such companies are governed by the provisions of the Companies Act 1985 and the Insolvency Act 1986 and there is relatively little scope for the application of partnership principles.[74]

Clubs and societies

It follows from the terms in which partnership is defined by the **2–29** Partnership Act 1890 that societies and clubs, which do not have as their object the acquisition of gain, are not partnerships; consistently with that conclusion, various cases show that their members are not as such liable for each other's acts.[75] Indeed, it has been recognised that an ordinary club is formed on the tacit understanding that its members do not become liable to pay any money beyond the subscription required by its rules.[76] Lord Lindley described it as "a

---

[71] See the Companies Act 1985, s.716(1).

[72] But see, as to mutual insurance companies, *infra*, para. 2–30.

[73] See *Re Accidental and Marine Insurance Corp.* (1870) L.R. 5 Ch.App. 424, 431, *per* Giffard L.J.; also Baird's Case, *ibid.* 725, 734 *et seq.*, *per* James L.J.

[74] Of course, there are still companies which are regarded as quasi-partnerships, to whom some partnership principles may be applied: see *Ebrahimi v. Westbourne Galleries* [1973] A.C. 360 and numerous other cases of that class.

[75] *Flemyng v. Hector* (1836) 2 M. & W. 172; *Caldicott v. Griffiths* (1853) 8 Ex. 898. See also *Todd v. Emly* (1841) 8 M. & W. 505; *The St. James's Club* (1852) 2 De G.M. & G. 383. And see, as to the nature of a club, *Fletcher v. Income Tax Commissioner* [1972] A.C. 414; *Kowloon Stock Exchange v. I.R.C.* [1985] 1 W.L.R. 133.

[76] *Wise v. Perpetual Trustee Co.* [1903] A.C. 139; in the absence of an express power in the rules, the majority cannot even raise the subscriptions so as to bind existing members: *Harington v. Sendall* [1903] 1 Ch. 921. As to the effect of an express power to alter rules, see *Thellusson v. Valentia* [1906] 1 Ch. 480; [1907] 2 Ch. 1; *Doyle v. White City Stadium Ltd.* [1935] 1 K.B. 110.

mere mis-use of words to call such associations partnerships."[77] If members *are* to be made liable, it will be by reason of their own acts[78] or the acts of their agents; in the latter case, the person who seeks to establish liability must prove the agency, since none will be implied by the mere fact of the association.[79] This principle is so clearly established that even the ordinary rule which entitles a trustee to be indemnified by his *cestui que* trust[80] does not apply as between the trustees of the club and individual members.[81]

Societies in which each member acts only for himself

2–30   It has been held that no partnership subsists between the members of a mutual insurance society, in which each member, in consideration of a payment made to him, underwrites a policy for a stipulated sum, on the ground that there is neither community of profit nor community of loss between them. A policy so underwritten in reality comprises a number of separate contracts, whereby each underwriter agrees, on a given event, to pay the whole or a proportionate part of the sum written against his name. In such a society there is no joint property nor do its members enter into any joint contract: each is alone liable to the insured, in accordance with the terms of the contract into which he has entered.[82] Although it was decided that such societies had for their object the acquisition of gain within the

---

[77] See *Blackpool Marton Rotary Club v. Martin* [1988] S.T.C. 823 (this aspect was not pursued in the Court of Appeal: see [1990] S.T.C. 1); also *Todd v. Emly*; *The St. James's Club*; *Wise v. Perpetual Trustee Co.*, *supra*; *R. v. Robson* (1885) 16 Q.B.D. 137. In *Lloyd v. Loaring* (1802) 6 Ves.Jr. 773, the Caledonian Lodge of Freemasons, and in *Silver v. Barnes* (1839) 6 Bing.N.C. 180 and *Beaumont v. Meredith* (1814) 3 V. & B. 180, friendly societies, were called partnerships, but this is incorrect: see *Re Lead Company's Workmen's Fund Soc.* [1904] 2 Ch. 196. In *Minnitt v. Lord Talbot* (1881) L.R.Ir. 1 Ch. 143, persons who had advanced money to add to and improve a club were held to have a lien on the property for their money. See further as to this case, (1881) L.R.Ir. 7 Ch. 407, and the comments thereon in *Wise v. Perpetual Trustee Co.* [1903] A.C. 139, 149, 150; *cf. Wylie v. Carlyon* [1922] 1 Ch. 51, where no lien or charge was created.

[78] As in *Cross v. Williams* (1862) 7 H. & N. 675, where the commandant of a rifle corps was held liable for all uniforms he had ordered; see also *Samuel Bros. Ltd. v. Whetherly* [1907] 1 K.B. 709; [1908] 1 K.B. 184. *Cf. Lascelles v. Rathbun* (1919) 63 S.J. 410, where the commanding officer was not liable for goods supplied for the officers' mess.

[79] This passage (in its original form) was cited with approval by Lord Parker in *London Association for Protection of Trade v. Greenlands Ltd.* [1916] 2 A.C. 15, 39, and by Fraser J. in *Hardie & Lane Ltd. v. Chiltern* [1928] 1 K.B. 663, 690; and see *Wise v. Perpetual Trustee Co.* [1903] A.C. 139. *Cf. Flemyng v. Hector* (1836) 2 M. & W. 172 and *Wood v. Finch* (1861) 2 F. & F. 447 (where the agency was not established) with *Luckombe v. Ashton* (1862) 2 F. & F. 705; *Cockerell v. Aucompte* (1857) 2 C.B.(N.S.) 440; *Burls v. Smith* (1831) 7 Bing. 705; and *Delauney v. Strickland* (1818) 2 Stark. 416, (where it was). In *Luckombe v. Ashton* and *Burls v. Smith*, the defendant was a member of the managing committee. This was not the case in *Cockerell v. Aucompte* or *Delauney v. Strickland*. See also *Thomas v. Edwards* (1836) 2 M. & W. 215.

[80] *Hardoon v. Belilios* [1901] A.C. 118.

[81] *Wise v. Perpetual Trustee Co.* [1903] A.C. 139. As to subrogation, see *Wylie v. Carlyon* [1922] 1 Ch. 51.

[82] See *Strong v. Harvey* (1825) 3 Bing. 304; *Redway v. Sweeting* (1867) L.R. 2 Ex. 400; *Andrews' and Alexander's Case* (1869) 8 Eq. 176; *Gray v. Pearson* (1870) L.R. 5 C.P. 568. As to actions between the members of such societies, see *Bromley v. Williams* (1863) 32 Beav. 177; *Harvey v. Beckwith* (1864) 12 W.R. 819 and 896.

meaning of what is now section 716 of the Companies Act 1985,[83] it is apprehended that, for the above reasons, they are still not partnerships within the meaning of the Partnership Act 1890.

Building Societies, Industrial and Provident Societies and Friendly Societies are all governed by specific statutes and do not require separate consideration.

European Economic Interest Groupings

The European Economic Interest Grouping or EEIG is a creation **2–31** of EC law and was originally introduced in 1985 by means of an EC Council Regulation.[84] It consists of two or more individuals, companies or firms who carry on their principal activity or have their central administration in different Member States[85] and who combine together in order to develop their own respective businesses[86] rather than a joint business.[87] Consistently therewith, an EEIG cannot properly be formed with a view to making a profit for itself,[88] although there is obviously no objection to any incidental profits which may be realised being shared between its members.[89]

An EEIG must be registered in the Member State in which it has its official address[90] and its precise legal status will be determined by the law of the State where it is registered.[91] By virtue of the European Economic Interest Grouping Regulations 1989,[92] an EEIG

---

[83] See the decisions under the corresponding section of the Companies Act 1862 (s.4): *Ex p. Hargrove* (1875) L.R. 10 Ch. 542; *Re Padstow Total Loss Association* (1882) 20 Ch.D. 137. As to mutual loan societies, see *Jennings v. Hammond* (1882) 9 Q.B.D. 225; *Shaw v. Benson* (1883) 11 Q.B.D. 563; *Ex p. Poppleton* (1884) 14 Q.B.D. 379; *Greenberg v. Cooperstein* [1926] Ch. 657. Freehold land societies did not require registration under that Act: *Re Siddall* (1885) 29 Ch.D. 1. See also as to carrying on business for gain, *England v. Webb* [1898] A.C. 758.

[84] Council Regulation 2137/85 of July 25, 1985. The text of this regulation is reproduced in the European Economic Interest Grouping Regulations 1989 (S.I. 1989 No. 638), Sched. 1. For a more detailed consideration of the nature and regulation of an EEIG, see *Palmer's Company Law*, Vol. 2, paras. 16.201 *et seq.*

[85] It follows that an EEIG may not be formed between individuals, etc. based in the *same* member State: Council Regulation 2137/85, Art. 4(2).

[86] The expression used in the Council Regulation 2137/85, Art. 3(1) is "economic activities" rather than "business."

[87] *Ibid.* The activity of the EEIG must be related, but ancillary, to the economic activities of its members and it may not, *inter alia*, exercise any degree of control over its members' own activities or hold any shares in a member undertaking, employ more than 500 persons or be a member of another EEIG: *ibid.* Art. 3(1), (2). It should also be noted that, in the preamble to the Council Regulation, it is stated that "a grouping differs from a firm or company principally in its purpose, which is only to facilitate or develop the economic activities of its members to enable them to improve their own results" and that "by reason of that ancillary nature, grouping's activities must be related to the economic activities of its members but not replace them so that, for example, a grouping may not itself, with regard to third parties, practise a profession, the concept of economic activities being interpreted in its widest sense."

[88] *Ibid.* Art. 3(1).

[89] *Ibid.* Art. 21(1); see also *ibid.* Art. 40. As to the sharing of losses, see *ibid.* Art. 21(2).

[90] *Ibid.* Art. 6. See also *ibid.* Arts. 7, 10, 39(1).

[91] *Ibid.* Art. 1(3). Note that *ibid.* Art. 1(2) provides that an EEIG will, once registered and irrespective of its legal status under the national law concerned, have the capacity to contract and to sue and be sued in its own name.

[92] (S.I. 1989 No. 638). These regulations were made pursuant to the powers conferred by the European Communities Act 1972, s.2(2).

registered in Great Britain[93] will be a body corporate and will thus enjoy separate legal personality.[94] It naturally follows that it cannot exist as a partnership within the meaning of the Partnership Act 1890.[95] If an EEIG registered in some other Member State carries on any activities here,[96] it is considered that an English court would, on normal conflict principles, generally look to its status under the law of the State of registration.[97] However, whilst an EEIG displays many characteristics traditionally associated with partnership under English law,[98] it is doubted whether, given the express requirements of the Council Regulation, it could ever be said to involve "persons carrying on a business in common with a view of profit" in the sense contemplated by the Partnership Act 1890.[99]

4. PARTNERSHIP IN EUROPE

Recognition and nationality of member State partnerships

2–32   Partnership is recognised as a legal relationship throughout Europe and, provided that it has been formed in accordance with the laws of a member State, and has its registered office or principal place of business within the E.C., a firm will be treated for all purposes of E.C. law in the same way as a natural person who is a national of a member State.[1]

Civil and commercial partnerships

2–33   All European jurisdictions, without exception, recognise that partnership is a relationship founded on contract and thus accord partners considerable latitude in the terms which they may adopt. However, the distinction between civil and commercial partnerships,

---

[93] European Economic Interest Grouping Regulations 1989, reg. 9.

[94] *Ibid.* reg. 3.

[95] See the Partnership Act 1890, s.1(2), *supra*, para. 2–23.

[96] The 1989 Regulations do not require an EEIG which has its official address outside the United Kingdom to register under the Companies Act 1985, unless it maintains an establishment in Great Britain: European Economic Interest Grouping Regulations 1989, regs. 9(1), 12(1). See also Council Regulation 2137/85, Arts. 6, 10.

[97] See *ibid.* Art. 2(1). And see, generally, Dicey & Morris, The Conflict of Laws (12th ed., 1993), Chap. 30.

[98] *e.g.* each member must have one vote on all issues (Council Regulation 2137/85, Art. 17(1)); major decisions affecting the EEIG must be taken unanimously (*ibid.* Art 17(2)); members share profits equally in the absence of some other agreement (*ibid.* Art. 21(1)); members are subject to unlimited joint and several liability for debts, but only after the liquidation of the EEIG is completed (*ibid.* Art. 24(1)).

[99] s.1(1), *supra*, para. 2–01. Surely there is in reality no business in common?: see, *supra*, n.87. Moreover, the only legitimate "view of profit" is the profit to be realised by each member of the EEIG from carrying on his or its own business: see Council Regulation 2137/85, Art. 3(1). *Quaere*, could it be argued that there is a sufficient, albeit subsidiary, profit motive?: see further, *supra*, para. 2–05.

[1] European Community Treaty, Art. 58. As to the possibility of partnership involving a breach of *ibid.* Art. 85, see *infra*, para. 8–05.

which is central to many of those jurisdictions, is not recognised by English or, for that matter, Irish law,[2] which is scarcely surprising given their common law origins. Although the distinction is now blurred in some countries, and particularly in France,[3] civil partnerships have traditionally been governed by the civil law as administered by the civil courts, whilst commercial partnerships have been governed by the commercial law as administered by the commercial courts.[4] As will be seen hereafter, the distinction can be important, not only in terms of the formalities of creation but also in terms of the type of partnership vehicle to be adopted.

In some countries, it is possible for prospective partners to opt for **2-34** a commercial partnership irrespective of the nature of the business carried on,[5] but on the whole this is rare. In practice, it is the object with which the partnership was formed which will determine its status. Thus, there are some activities which must be carried on through a civil partnership: these will include most land–based businesses, *e.g.* farming, building development, etc.,[6] the practice of various professions[7] and certain "one off" ventures. On the other hand, where the business involves recognised commercial activities, particularly if they are performed continuously and repeatedly, the firm will almost certainly be treated as commercial,[8] save in those countries where the existence of such a partnership is dependent on the completion of certain formalities.[9]

It would be inappropriate in a work of this nature to engage in a detailed analysis of the law of partnership in other jurisdictions, but an outline of the most common features to be found in civil and commercial partnerships may be of assistance to the reader.[10]

---

[2] Partnerships in Ireland are still governed by the Partnership Act 1890 and the Limited Partnerships Act 1907. It should be noted that the distinction is also seemingly not recognised in Finland and Norway.

[3] Certain laws governing civil and commercial partnerships were assimilated by the Law of January 4, 1978. The Netherlands also appears to be in the process of such an exercise in the course of preparing its new Civil Code.

[4] Of course, there is inevitably a degree of overlap, so that in many cases parts of the civil law will apply to commercial partnerships; on the other hand, the commercial law is rarely, if ever, applied to civil partnerships. Equally, if a civil partnership carries out commercial activities, it may well become subject to the commercial law.

[5] France is the most obvious example, where prospective partners can choose the *société en nom collectif* instead of the *société civile*; Belgium and Spain appear to adopt a similar approach. If there is any doubt as to which vehicle has been chosen, then it will be necessary to look at the objects of the partnership in order to identify whether they are civil or commercial. In Austria and Germany, a partnership may start life as civil prior to the completion of the formalities requisite to qualify as a commercial partnership.

[6] But note that, under the Law of July 13, 1967, the acquisition of land for resale is regarded as a commercial activity in France, although development with a view to the sale of a completed building is not: see the Law of July 9, 1970.

[7] Often referred to as the "liberal" professions, *e.g.* law, accountancy, medicine, dentistry, etc.

[8] See the French Commercial Code, Arts. 1, 632, 633.

[9] See, *infra*, para. 2–39.

[10] For more detailed information the reader is referred to *Maitland-Walker's Guide to European Company Law* (1993); *Joint Ventures in Europe* (Butterworths, 1991); Le Gall and Morel, *French Company Law* (1992).

Civil partnership[11]

2–35 In general, a civil partnership may only be formed if its objects are of a civil, *i.e.* non-commercial, nature as recognised by the laws of the country in question.[12] As a contractual relationship, there are few formalities to be satisfied: the agreement may be written or oral and registration is not required. Equally, the partnership will not enjoy separate legal personality and will not be carried on under a firm name. The exception is the French *société civile* which will, on the completion of certain registration formalities, enjoy such personality.

2–36 With one exception,[13] there is no restriction on the persons who may enter into a civil partnership and the rights and duties of the partners *inter se* will in large measure be determined by the terms of their agreement, whatever its form. As regards liabilities to third parties, each partner will for the most part accept unlimited liability, but not in the sense understood by English law. In the majority of European countries[14] the members of a civil partnership are only liable for their proportionate share of the firm's debts and obligations, whether determined on a *per capita* basis (*i.e.* equally) or pro rata to their capital contributions.[15] Joint and several liability is thus largely unknown.[16] The position is, however, different in Germany, since the members of a *Gesellschaft des bürgerlichen Rechts* will be jointly and severally liable to a third party in respect of contractual or tortious claims, but only if they *all* entered into the contract or committed the wrong; otherwise, the liability will fall only on those partners who did contract or commit the wrong. Whether they will have any right of contribution from their co-partners will depend on the terms of the partnership agreement. The position appears to be broadly the same in the case of a Dutch *maatschap*, save that each partner is only required to bear his share of the liability.

 The dissolution of a civil partnership is brought about in much the same way as in the case of a commercial partnership, and reference should be made to paragraph 2–42, *infra*.

---

[11] *i.e* the *Bürgerlich rechtliche Erwerbgesellschaft* (Austria), *société civile* (Belgium, France and Luxembourg), *burgerlijke venootschap* (Belgium), *Gesellschaft des bürgerlichen Rechts* (Germany), *società semplice* (Italy), *maatschap* (the Netherlands), *sociedades civis* (Portugal), *société simple* (Switzerland). The *enkelt bolag* in Sweden would also seem to fall within this class.

[12] See, *supra*, para. 2–34.

[13] In Italy, the courts have ruled that a corporation may not be a partner in any form of partnership, whether civil or commercial.

[14] *i.e.* in Austria, Belgium, France and Luxembourg. The position in Portugal is less clear.

[15] The basis of division varies from country to country, although most permit the partners to alter the incidence of any liability as between themselves.

[16] But there appears to be such liability in Italy and Switzerland. *Cf.* the position under English and Irish law, as set out in the Partnership Act 1890, s.9.

Commercial partnership

In most European jurisdictions, there are three basic species of **2–37**
commercial partnership,[17] namely:

   (i)   the undisclosed or "secret" partnership;
  (ii)   the general partnership;
 (iii)   the limited partnership.

Before considering each species in turn, it should be noted that both
individuals and corporations may enter into partnership, save in Italy
where corporate partnerships are not permitted.[18] It is, however, a
requirement of French law that each partner should be qualified to
act as a trader or *commerçant*;[19] Greece imposes an equivalent
requirement. Moreover, with the exception of Austria,[20] there is no
limitation on the number of persons who may enter into a single
partnership.

   (i)   *The undisclosed or "secret" partnership.*[21] The distinctive **2–38**
characteristic of this type of partnership is, as the name implies, that
its existence remains undisclosed *vis-à-vis* third parties. It naturally
follows that a third party will have no remedy against the partnership
or against any member thereof other than the partner(s) with whom
he was directly concerned. This is so even if the latter disclose the
existence of the partnership without their co-partners' knowledge.
Only in France is this principle departed from, where the partners
can authorise each other to disclose the existence of the partnership
to third parties, thereby rendering it a *société en participation
ostensible.* As a result, they will all be jointly and severally liable for
the firm's debts and obligations.

---

[17] In Austria, an additional form of partnership (the *Erwerbsgesellschaft*) was introduced in 1990 for the benefit of small traders (as opposed to merchants). This type of partnership may be created in either a general form (*offene Erwerbsgesellschaft*) or a limited form (*kommandit Erwerbsgesellschaft*). Such partnerships are subject to similar registration requirements as those applicable to general and limited partnerships.

[18] Some countries, *e.g.* Austria, merely prohibit some foreign corporations from entering into partnership.

[19] As defined by the French Commercial Code, Art 1.

[20] An undisclosed partnership (*stille Gesellschaft*) in Austria may only have two partners. If the participation of more than two partners is required, a series of separate partnerships will have to be created. Ireland has similar size restrictions to those which apply to English partnerships (as to which see, *infra*, paras. 4–27 *et seq*.) but, as already noted, Irish law does not recognise the distinction between civil and commercial partnerships.

[21] The *stille Gesellschaft* (Austria, Germany), *société en participation* (France), *afanis eteria* (Greece), *stille selskap* (Norway), *cuentas en participación* (Spain). The *association en participation* in Belgium shares the same characteristics as the above forms of partnership, but is governed solely by the Civil Code. The *stille vennootschappen* will be recognised as a civil partnership in the Netherlands under the terms of the new Dutch Civil Code.

By its very nature, the creation of an undisclosed partnership is not attended with any formality nor is any form registration required. In no jurisdiction is legal personality conferred on such a partnership.

2-39   (ii) *The general partnership.*[22] There are two common features shared by such partnerships, namely the unlimited liability of each partner for the debts and obligations of the firm (even if, in some instances, a creditor must first look to the firm's assets) and, save only in Sweden, the need for some form of registration and/or public notification. However, the precise formalities of creation differ widely. In France, it is necessary to have a written partnership agreement for registration purposes;[23] similarly in Belgium, Greece, Italy, Luxembourg, the Netherlands and Norway. In other countries, an oral agreement will suffice.[24] Again, in some instances registration/public notification will be a prerequisite to the creation of a commercial partnership,[25] whilst in others a failure to satisfy such requirements, though attended by certain penalties, will not affect the existence of the partnership.[26] In France, Belgium, Greece and Norway, registration will also confer separate legal personality on the firm;[27] in Sweden, such personality is obtained on *formation* of the partnership and not solely by reason of registration.

2-40   A general partnership will carry on business under a name which will be entered in the relevant register. That name will normally comprise the names of all the partners or include the name of at least one partner,[28] together with some general indication that other partners do exist, *e.g.* by adding the words "and Company" or some other recognised reference to the type of partnership in question.[29] Subject to the terms of the agreement, all partners will be entitled to take part in the management of the business and to bind the firm, save in France and Luxembourg where a manager is usually appointed to undertake this function.[30]

---

[22] The *offene Handelsgesellschaft* (Austria, Germany), *venootschap onder firma* (Belgium, the Netherlands), *société en nom collectif* (Belgium, France, Luxembourg, Switzerland), *interessentskab* (Denmark), *avoin yhtiö* (Finland), *omorrithmos eteria* (Greece), *società in nome colletivo* (Italy), *ansvarlige selskaper* (Norway), *sociedades em nome colectivo* (Portugal), *sociedad colectiva* (Spain), *handelsbolag* (Sweden), *kollektivgesellschaft* (Switzerland).

[23] Thus, the agreement must be produced for the purposes of registration tax and deposited, along with certain other documents, with the registrar of the local Commercial Court; thereafter, registration in the Registry of Commerce and Companies must be obtained.

[24] *i.e.* in Austria, Denmark, Finland, Germany, Sweden and Switzerland.

[25] *i.e.* in Belgium, Germany, Greece, Luxembourg and Norway. It should be noted that in Austria and Germany, the firm may, nevertheless, qualify as a civil partnership prior to registration; in other countries, *e.g.* Greece, a *de facto* general partnership may exist, but only for the protection of third parties.

[26] *i.e.* in Austria, Denmark, Finland, Italy, the Netherlands, Sweden and Switzerland.

[27] Under the terms of the proposed new Dutch Civil code, so–called "public" partnerships (*openbare vennootschappen*) will also enjoy separate legal personality.

[28] In Finland the trade name of a firm may not include the name of any person who is not a partner; moreover, fictitious names are not permitted in Greece.

[29] *e.g.* in France, the name must indicate that the firm is a *société en nom collectif.*

[30] In practice, the manager may, but need not, be one of the partners.

As already noted, the liability of the partners in respect of the **2–41** debts and obligations of the firm is joint and several and, save in Sweden, actions by and against the firm can be brought in the firm name, whether or not the firm itself enjoys separate legal personality. In some countries, incoming partners are, somewhat surprisingly, liable for debts and obligations incurred *before* they joined the firm.[31]

The transfer of shares in a general partnership and the introduction of new partners will be governed by the terms of the agreement; otherwise it will be dependent upon the consent of all the partners being obtained.

Dissolution of a general partnership may be brought about in a **2–42** number of ways, which are broadly comparable to the events which can give rise to a dissolution under English law.[32] They may briefly be summarised as follows:

(1) the death or bankruptcy of a partner (subject to any agreement to the contrary);

(2) the insolvency of the firm;

(3) the expiration of a fixed term;

(4) the completion (or total failure) of a particular venture;

(5) where no period is specified in the agreement, on the requisite period of notice being given by one or more of the partners;

(6) where all the partners agree to dissolve/pass a resolution dissolving the firm;

(7) where the number of partners is reduced to one;[33]

(8) under French and Greek law, where one or more of the partners ceases to have capacity to act as a trader; or

(9) where a court of competent jurisdiction orders the firm to be dissolved.[34]

In addition, partners may themselves legislate for other circumstances in which their partnership is to be terminated.

(iii) *The limited partnership.*[35] The limited partnership is recog- **2–43** nised in all European countries. Although similar to a general

---

[31] *i.e.* Austria, France, Greece, Sweden and Switzerland.

[32] See, *infra*, paras. 24–04 *et seq.*

[33] In France, a period of grace (1 year) is allowed in which an additional partner or partners can be recruited; even then, a dissolution will only occur if the Court so orders. The period of grace in Italy is 6 months.

[34] Different rules apply in the case of an undisclosed partnership, *e.g.* the death of a secret partner will not normally dissolve the firm.

[35] The *kommanditgesellschaft* (Austria, Germany, Switzerland), *gewone commanditaire venootschap* (Belgium, the Netherlands), *société en commandite simple* (Belgium, France, Luxembourg), *kommanditselskab* (Denmark), *kommanditityhtiö* (Finland), *eterorrithmos eteria* (Greece), *società in accomandita semplice* (Italy), *kommandittselskab* (Norway), *sociedades em comandita* (Portugal), *sociedad comanditaria* (Spain), *kommanditbolag* (Sweden), *société en commandite* (Switzerland).

partnership in terms of the formalities of creation,[36] its distinctive feature, as in English law, is the presence or one or more limited partners, whose liability for the firm's debts and obligations is limited to the amount of their capital contributions, and one or more general partners, whose liability is unlimited. Only in Italy are companies prevented from entering into such a partnership, whilst in Switzerland such a restriction only applies in the case of the general partner[37]: it follows that, by employing a limited company as a sole general partner, full limitation of liability can be achieved in other jurisdictions.[38] It should also be noted that, under French and Greek law, the limited partners need not have the capacity to act as traders. The firm's entry in the relevant register will inevitably specify the quantum of the limited partners' capital contributions.

2–44   In France and Belgium there are two types of limited partnership, namely the *société en commandite simple*[39] and the *société en commandite par actions*[40]; a similar distinction is drawn in various other countries.[41] Since the latter form is more analogous to a company, it is not further considered here. The principle feature of the former is that the limited partners may not take part in the management or conduct of the affairs of the partnership on penalty of forfeiting their limited status. A similar penalty is imposed on a limited partner in most other jurisdictions, apart from Germany and Switzerland,[42] although Austria does appear to permit limited partners to participate in *internal* management.

2–45   The transfer of limited partners' shares will normally be governed by the terms of the agreement; in the absence of any such provision, the consent of all the partners must normally be obtained.[43] Any such transfer of the share of a limited partner will, of course, need to be registered.

Broadly speaking, a limited partnership may be dissolved in the same way as a general partnership,[44] although the death or bankruptcy of a limited partner will rarely, of itself, cause a dissolution.

---

[36] See, *supra*, para. 2–39.

[37] In Austria, a *foreign* limited company can only be a general partner if it maintains a branch there.

[38] In Austria and Germany, such a partnership will attract the special designation "GmbH & Co. KG".

[39] Also known in Belgium as *gewone commanditaire venootschap*.

[40] Also known in Belgium as *commanditaire vennootschap op aandelen*.

[41] *i.e.* Denmark, Greece, Italy, Luxembourg, Portugal and Spain.

[42] The limited partners will, however, forfeit that status if they represent themselves as general partners.

[43] In Italy, the consent of those partners holding a majority of the partnership capital will be sufficient.

[44] See, *supra*, para. 2–42.

Chapter 3

GENERAL NATURE OF A PARTNERSHIP

1. THE COMMERCIAL AND LEGAL VIEWS

The commercial view

Partners are, in both commercial and legal terms, collectively **3–01** referred to as "a firm,"[1] but with very different underlying perspectives.[2] Thus, the usual commercial view of partnership, as reflected in the approach of most accountants, involves treating a firm in much the same way as a company, *i.e.* as an entity distinct from its members and with independent rights and obligations.[3] As a consequence, in drawing up partnership accounts, where money is due to or from a partner he will normally be shown as a creditor or debtor of the *firm* and not as a creditor or debtor of his co-partners.[4]

Consistently with its perceived status as a separate entity, there is a **3–02** tendency to regard a firm's rights and obligations as unaffected by any change in its membership: in effect, the rights and obligations of the "old" firm prior to the change are automatically deemed to have been assumed by the "new" firm. Lord Lindley summarised the thinking which lies at the heart of the commercial view in the following terms:

> "The partners are the agents and sureties of the firm: its agents for the transaction of its business; its sureties for the liquidation of its liabilities so far as the assets of the firm are insufficient to meet them. The liabilities of the firm are regarded as the liabilities of the partners only in case they cannot be met by the firm and discharged out of its assets."

---

[1] Partnership Act 1890, s.4. See, as to the effect of this section under Scots law (where the firm has separate legal personality), *Jardine-Paterson v. Fraser*, 1974 S.L.T. 93 (Ct. of Sess.).

[2] In drawing a distinction between the two views, which he styled the mercantile and the legal, Lord Lindley acknowledged his obligations to Cory's *Treatise on Accounts* (Pickering, 2nd ed., 1839) and to a paper by J. M. Ludlow entitled "On the mercantile notion of the firm, and the need of its legal recognition," in the 2nd vol. of the Papers read before the Juridical Society, p. 40.

[3] See *supra*, para. 2–24.

[4] A recent (albeit ultimately unsuccessful) example of this approach can be seen in *MacKinlay v. Arthur Young McClelland Moores & Co.* [1990] 2 A.C. 239.

3-03   This attitude is, if anything, encouraged by certain attributes displayed by a majority of firms, ranging from the adoption of a distinctive name which is unrelated to the names of the partners to the maintenance of a separate bank account in the firm name. Because of these attributes, changes in a firm tend to have no visible effect on its existence or on the continuity of its business; in short, partners may come and go but the firm *appears* to go on.

The legal view

3-04   The legal view of a firm is very different: in English law, the firm is not generally recognised as an entity distinct from the partners composing it.[5] Admittedly, in taking partnership accounts and in administering partnership assets, the courts have to some extent adopted the commercial view; moreover, actions may be brought by or against partners, and income tax assessments may in some cases be raised, in the firm name.[6] However, apart from these few exceptions, the general rule holds good; thus, a firm as such cannot be a tenant and claim protection under Part II of the Landlord and Tenant Act 1954.[7] Lord Lindley stated the orthodox legal view as follows:

> "The law, ignoring the firm, looks to the partners composing it; any change amongst them destroys the identity of the firm; what is called the property of the firm is their property, and what are called the debts and liabilities of the firm are their debts and their liabilities. In point of law, a partner may be the debtor or the creditor of his co-partners, but he cannot be either debtor or creditor of a firm of which he is himself a member."[8]

---

[5] See *Meyer & Co. v. Faber (No. 2)* [1923] 2 Ch. 421; *Ex p. Gliddon* (1884) 13 Q.B.D. 43; *Hoare v. Oriental Bank Corporation* (1877) 2 App.Cas. 589; see also *Ex p. Corbett* (1880) 14 Ch.D. 122, 126, *per* James L.J.; *Sadler v. Whiteman* [1910] 1 K.B. 868, 889, *per* Farwell L.J. (affirmed [1910] A.C. 674); *R. v. Holden* [1912] 1 K.B. 483. As to Scotland, see the Partnership Act 1890, s.4(2); *Jardine-Paterson v. Fraser*, 1974 S.L.T. 93 (Ct. of Sess.); note also *Arif v. Levy & McRae* 1992 G.W.D. 3–156.

[6] As to actions, see R.S.C. Ord. 81, reproduced *infra*, paras. A2–09 *et seq.* As to income tax assessments in the case of firms in existence prior to April 6, 1994, see the Income and Corporation Taxes Act 1988, s.111 and *infra*, paras. 34–05 *et seq.* An intermediate position is achieved under the Value Added Tax Act 1973: see *infra*, para. 37–06. Note also that a firm as such may now be appointed as a company auditor (Companies Act 1989, s.26(1), (2)) and an insolvent partnership may be wound up as an unregistered company (see *infra*, paras. 27–09 *et seq.*).

[7] *Kissane & Clarke v. Jones*, September 26, 1975, and March 1, 1976, unreported, discussed at (1976) 120 S.J. 827, 850. *Cf.* the position in Scotland: *Jardine-Paterson v. Fraser*, 1974 S.L.T. 93 (Ct. of Sess.).

[8] *Green v. Hertzog* [1954] 1 W.L.R. 1309. See also Lord Cottenham's judgment in *Richardson v. The Bank of England* (1838) 4 My. & Cr. 165, 171, 172; *De Tastet v. Shaw* (1818) 1 B. & A. 664; *Lee v. Neuchatel Asphalte Co.* (1886) 41 Ch.D. 1. And see *Ellis v. Kerr* [1910] 1 Ch. 529; *Napier v. Williams* [1911] 1 Ch. 361, as to the invalidity of covenants entered into by a man with himself and others jointly before the alteration of the law by the Law of Property Act 1925, s.82. In *Rye v. Rye* [1961] Ch. 70, 78, Lord Evershed M.R. expressed the view that, whilst partners may be able to grant a lease to themselves, they cannot make any covenants therein which are enforceable. *Cf.* Lord Ratcliffe's analysis in the House of Lords at [1962] A.C. 496, 512.

It should be added to the above proposition that a partner cannot be employed by his own firm, for no man can employ himself.[9]

Status and liability of a partner

Also central to an understanding of the law of partnership is the **3–05** dual capacity in which a partner acts, *i.e.* both as a principal and an agent. Lord Lindley explained:

"As a principal [a member of an ordinary partnership[10]] is bound by what he does himself and by what his co-partners do on behalf of the firm,[11] provided they keep within the limits of their authority; as an agent, he binds them by what he does for the firm, provided he keeps within the limits of his authority."

Thus, where a partner receives money belonging to the firm, he will do so both as principal (*i.e.* for himself) and as agent for his co-partners; in those circumstances, he cannot be treated as having received the money in a fiduciary capacity.[12]

However, as Lord Lindley took care to point out, it is wrong to regard a partner as a mere surety for the firm's debts[13]: as a principal, he is personally liable to meet those debts, whether or not they could be met out of the partnership assets.[14]

2. STATUS OF FIRM IN SPECIFIC CONTEXTS

(a) Firm name

It is important to identify the precise significance of a firm name **3–06** since, as previously noted,[15] it represents an attribute which tends to encourage the commercial rather than the legal view of a firm. Lord Lindley put it in this way:

---

[9] On this basis, it was held in *Ellis v. Joseph Ellis & Co.* [1905] 1 K.B. 324 that a partner who worked for the partnership at a weekly wage was not entitled to compensation under the Workman's Compensation Act 1897. It follows that such a partner's "salary" will inevitably be treated as part of his profit share for tax purposes: *MacKinlay v. Arthur Young McClelland Moores & Co.* [1990] 2 A.C. 239, 249C. Note, however, that in *Rowley Holmes & Co. v. Barber* [1977] 1 W.L.R. 371, it was held that a legal executive in his capacity as executor of a deceased sole proprietor of a firm of solicitors *could* employ himself for redundancy payment purposes.

[10] It is presumed that by this expression, Lord Lindley referred to a partnership governed by the general law (rather than by some special contractual arrangement), since it is difficult to see what other form of partnership could have existed at that time. Now, of course, there exists the limited partnership, in which the limited partners have *no* authority to bind the firm: see the Limited Partnerships Act 1907, s.6(1) and *infra*, paras. 30–01 *et seq.*

[11] Ironically, the use of the expression "the firm" in this context itself gives succour to the commercial view.

[12] *Piddocke v. Burt* [1894] 1 Ch. 343.

[13] See *supra*, para. 3–02.

[14] Until the law was altered by the Partnership Act 1890, s.23, the property of the firm was, of course, liable to be seized for the private debts of any of the partners composing it.

[15] See *supra*, para. 3–03.

"... the name under which a firm carries on business is in point of law a conventional name applicable only to the persons who, on each particular occasion when the name is used, are members of the firm."[16]

Once this point is understood, the fallacy of the commercial view becomes apparent. The firm name is a convenient method of describing a group of persons associated together in business: no more and no less.

It follows that confusion will inevitably arise where an individual "A" trades under the name "A & Co." or continues to trade in the name of a former firm, either because he has become the sole continuing partner or because he is otherwise to be regarded as its successor, *e.g.* following a purchase of its goodwill. In such cases A is, and at all times remains, a sole proprietor and no question of partnership arises. When applied to such a person, the term "sole partner," although used in common parlance, is both inappropriate and misleading.[17]

3–07 When a firm is referred to by its name or trading style, evidence is admissible to show who in fact was a member of the firm at the relevant time.[18] If a number of people carry on business under such a name or style, anything which they may do in that name or style will be just as effective as if their individual names had been used. An obvious example of this is the use of firm names on bills of exchange and promissory notes; indeed, more formal instruments will be valid, even though some of the executing parties are described as "A & Co."[19] Partners may also be registered as shareholders in the firm name,[20] but they cannot insist on being so registered.[21]

---

[16] See the Partnership Act 1890, s.4(1). A firm is usually described in legal proceedings as "XYZ & Co. (a Firm)" or "XYZ & Co. (sued as a firm)"; alternatively, the form "X, Y and Z trading as XYZ & Co." may be used.

[17] *Alexander Mountain & Co. v. Rumere* [1948] W.N. 243, reversed (on the facts) at [1948] 2 K.B. 436; *Oswald Hickson Collier & Co. v. Carter Ruck* [1984] A.C. 720 note; *Re C. & M. Ashberg, The Times*, July 17, 1990. See also *W. Hill & Son v. Tannerhill* [1944] K.B. 472 (C.A.), where Hill, trading without partners as W. Hill & Son, issued a writ in the supposed firm name contrary to what was then R.S.C. Ord. 48A (see now R.S.C. Ord. 81, r. 1 *infra*, para. A2–09). The relevant limitation period having expired, it was held that Hill might nevertheless amend the writ by substituting himself as plaintiff. Note also the decisions in *Harold Fielding Ltd. v. Mansi* [1974] I.C.R. 347; *Allen & Son v. Coventry* [1980] I.C.R. 9; *Jeetle v. Elster* [1985] I.C.R. 389.

[18] *Carruthers v. Sheddon* (1815) 6 Taunt. 15; *Bass v. Clive* (1815) 4 M. & S. 13; *Stubbs v. Sargon* (1838) 3 My. & Cr. 507; also *Latouche v. Waley* (1832) Hayes & Jones (Ir.Ex.) 43.

[19] See further *infra*, paras. 12–163 *et seq*.

[20] *Weikersheim's Case* (1873) L.R. 8 Ch.App. 831.

[21] *Re Vagliano Anthracite Collieries Ltd.* [1910] W.N. 187, where the definition of "person" contained in the Interpretation Act 1889, s.19 (now the Interpretation Act 1978, Sched. 1), was not adverted to. Note also that, in *Dunster's Case* [1894] 3 Ch. 473, the Registrar of Joint Stock Companies appears to have insisted that the company's memorandum of association could not properly be signed in a firm name; it is assumed that a similar attitude would still be adopted.

Effect of change in the partners

Because the firm name represents no more than a convenient **3–08** means of describing the partners who for the time being make up the firm, whenever the partners change that name must take on a new meaning. This can lead to a number of complications, as the following examples (which are, for convenience, arranged in alphabetical order) demonstrate:

Advances to a firm

An authority given to trustees to lend money to a firm would not, **3–09** as a general rule, authorise a loan to the continuing partners after one partner has died or retired.[22]

Authority given to or on behalf of firm

An authority given to two partners to take out insurance in their **3–10** names does not authorise them to insure in the names of themselves and a third party whom they have subsequently taken into partnership.[23] Similarly, if a firm, A, B and C, has an agent D, and C retires, D may continue to be the agent of the firm but he will in reality be the agent of A and B, but not of C.[24]

Business Names Act 1985

If there is a change of partners and the new firm continues to use **3–11** the old name, this will often bring the firm within the scope of the Business Names Act 1985. As a result it may be necessary to apply to the Secretary of State for written approval of the name,[25] and to ensure that the requisite information is included on all documents issued by the firm and that a suitable notice is displayed in the partnership premises.[26]

---

[22] See *Fowler v. Reynal* (1851) 3 Mac. & G. 500; *Re Tucker* [1894] 1 Ch. 724, affirmed [1894] 3 Ch. 429; *Smith v. Patrick* [1901] A.C. 282.

[23] *Barron v. Fitzgerald* (1840) 6 Bing.N.C. 201. But of course a continuance of the authority may be inferred from subsequent dealings with the new firm. See *Pariente v. Lubbock* (1856) 8 De G. M. & G. 5.

[24] See *Jones v. Shears* (1836) 4 A. & E. 832.

[25] Business Names Act 1985, ss.2(1), (3); also the Company and Business Names Regulations 1981 (S.I. 1981 No. 1685), as amended by the Company and Business Names (Amendment) Regulations 1982 (S.I. 1982 No. 1653) and the Company and Business Names (Amendment) Regulations 1992 (S.I. 1992 No. 1196). It is doubtful whether the provisions of *ibid.* s.2(2) will apply in such circumstances: see further, *infra*, para. 3–31.

[26] *Ibid.* s.4. See also *infra*, para. 3–32.

Conveyance to a firm

3–12 In *Wray v. Wray*,[27] it was held that a conveyance of freeholds to "William Wray in fee simple" passed the legal estate to the persons who were at the date of the conveyance the members of the firm which traded under that name.[28]

Employees of firm

3–13 A change in the firm will not generally affect the employees' continuity of employment for the purposes of the Employment Protection (Consolidation) Act 1978.[29] This is so even where the partnership is dissolved but the employment is continued by one of the former partners.[30]

Executorships and trusteeships

3–14 Where a testator appoints a firm—such as a firm of solicitors—to be the executors and/or trustees of his will, only partners at the time the will was made can act;[31] partners admitted subsequently are only eligible if the testator has framed the appointment in such a way as to include them.[32]

Legacy to a firm

3–15 If a legacy is left to a firm, the legacy is, in the absence of a contrary intention, payable to those partners who were members of the firm at the date of the will.[33] Moreover, if a legacy is left to the

---

[27] [1905] 2 Ch. 349.

[28] See also *Maugham v. Sharpe* (1864) 17 C.B.(N.S.) 443 (a mortgage); *Brutton v. Burton* (1819) 1 Chit. 707 (a warrant of attorney); *Evans v. Curtis* (1826) 2 C. & P. 296 (an agreement for a lease); *Moller v. Lambert* (1810) 2 Camp. 548 (a bond); *Gorrie v. Woodley* (1864) 17 I.C.L.R. 221 (a guarantee); *Latouche v. Waley* (1832) Hayes & Jones (Ir.Ex.) 43; also *infra*, paras. 14–30 *et seq.* For the effect of a conveyance to partners under the post-1925 law, see *Re Fuller's Contract* [1933] Ch. 652 and the Law of Property Act 1925, s.34(2); also *infra*, para. 18–30.

[29] Sched. 13, para. 17; *Harold Fielding Ltd. v. Mansi* [1974] I.C.R. 347; *Allen & Son v. Coventry* [1980] I.C.R. 9; *Jeetle v. Elster* [1985] I.C.R. 389; see also an article at 136 N.L.J. 353; *cf. Brace v. Calder* [1895] 2 Q.B. 253, considered *infra*, para. 3–39; *Briggs v. Oates* [1990] I.C.R. 473. The employees' rights would also now seem to be protected by the Transfer of Undertakings (Protection of Employment) Regulations 1981.

[30] *Jeetle v. Elster supra.* Note, however, that the partner who continued Mrs. Elster's employment had acquired premises and equipment from the firm; *cf.* the position in *S.I. (Systems and Instruments) v. Grist & Riley* [1983] I.C.R. 788 (which did not concern a firm). See also, as regards the effect of a general dissolution, *Tunstall v. Condon* [1980] I.C.R. 786; *Briggs v. Oates* [1990] I.C.R. 473; and *infra*, para. 25–02.

[31] However, if there are more than four of such partners, they cannot all accept the appointment: Trustee Act 1925, s.34(2); Supreme Court Act 1981, s.114(1).

[32] See *Re Horgan* [1971] P. 50.

[33] See *Stubbs v. Sargon* (1838) 3 My. & Cr. 507; *Re Smith* [1914] 1 Ch. 937. In *Mayberry v. Brooking* (1855) 7 De G. M. & G. 673, a legacy of a debt due to A was held to pass A's interest in a debt due to him and his co-partners. *Cf. Ex p. Kirk* (1877) 5 Ch.D. 800.

"representatives" of an old firm, it will be payable to the personal representatives of the last survivor of the partners of that firm, and not to its successors in business.[34]

Offices and appointments held by firm

If a firm is by name appointed to a particular office, it is the **3–16** partners at the time of such appointment who will, in law, fill that office, since the firm, as such, cannot.[35] Equally, the rights annexed to that office will only be exercisable by such partners and not, in the absence of some contrary intention, by partners admitted subsequently[36] or, for that matter, by a successor to the firm's business.[37] However, there are occasional exceptions to this principle: thus, the Companies Act 1989 now permits a firm *as such* to be appointed as a company auditor[38] and, moreover, provides for such an appointment to devolve on a successor firm[39] or a sole continuing "partner,"[40] provided that the eligibility conditions are satisfied.[41]

The mere fact that an office cannot be held by a firm will not, of itself, prevent it being held *on behalf* of the partners for the time being, so that it can, effectively, be treated as partnership property.[42]

Rights in and to firm name

Unless it forms part of the goodwill of the firm (as will usually be **3–17** the case),[43] there is no proprietary right in a firm name;[44] nor, apart from certain statutory restraints and questions of passing off,[45] is there any restriction on partners' freedom to adopt the name of their

---

[34] *Leak v. M'Dowall* (1863) 3 N.R. 185; *Kerrison v. Reddington* (1847) 11 I.Eq.R. 451. And see *Greville v. Greville* (1859) 27 Beav. 594.

[35] *De Mazar v. Pybus* (1799) 4 Ves.Jr. 644. And see, as to Scotland, *Kirkintilloch Equitable Co–operative Society Ltd. v. Livingstone*, 1972 S.L.T. 154 (Ct. of Sess.). In New Zealand it has been held that a firm cannot be appointed to act as director or secretary of a company: *Commercial Management Ltd. v. Registrar of Companies* [1987] N.Z.L.R. 744. *Semble*, the position is the same under the Companies Act 1985: see, in particular, *ibid.* ss. 286, 293, 294.

[36] See *Barron v. Fitzgerald* (1840) 6 Bing.N.C. 201; *Stevens v. Benning* (1855) 1 K. & J. 168.

[37] *Hole v. Bradbury* (1879) 12 Ch.D. 886; *Robson v. Drummond* (1831) 2 B. & Ad. 303; see also *infra*, para. 3–37.

[38] Companies Act 1989, s.26(1), (2).

[39] A firm will only be treated as a successor firm for this purpose if it has substantially the same members as the original firm and if it succeeded to the whole or substantially the whole of that firm's business: *ibid.* s.26(3)(*a*), (4).

[40] *Ibid.* s. 26(3)(*b*), (4). The expression "sole partner" is, of course, something of a misnomer: see *supra*, para. 3–06.

[41] *Ibid.* s.25.

[42] See further, *infra*, para. 18–42.

[43] Lord Lindley observed "The name by which a firm is known is not of itself the property of the firm ...". Moreover, it does not necessarily follow that goodwill (and any associated name) will always be partnership property, see, for example, *Miles v. Clark* [1953] 1 W.L.R. 537, noticed *infra*, para. 18–35.

[44] See *infra*, para. 3–21; but note the decision in *Barr v. Lions* 1956 S.L.T. 250, where a Scots court appears to have accepted the propriety of a transfer of a business name independently of goodwill.

[45] See *infra*, paras. 8–10 *et seq.*, 8–17 *et seq.*

choice.[46] Indeed, they may adopt more than one name, even though neither the Partnership Act 1890 nor the Business Names Act 1985 seem to contemplate this possibility.[47] However, whether or not the firm name is a partnership asset,[48] it would seem that a partner may not make use of it in order to secure some private benefit for himself.[49]

Passing off

3-18   A firm may not adopt a name similar to that of another firm or comprising a name or description of goods or services which has become identified with, and indicative of, goods produced or services supplied by another firm, in such a way as to pass itself off as being, or its goods or services as produced or supplied by, that other firm.[50] Equally, there can be no objection to a person carrying on a business in his own name or in a name which he, either alone or in partnership with others,[51] has acquired by reputation;[52] it follows that partners cannot be restrained from adopting a firm name which genuinely seeks to identify the membership of the firm, merely on the ground that it is so similar to the name of an established firm that mistakes are almost certain to arise.[53] *Per contra*, if the name is adopted dishonestly and with an intention to mislead members of the public,[54] when its use can be restrained.[55]

---

[46] See also *infra*, paras. 5–54 *et seq.*

[47] See the Partnership Act 1890, s.4(1). As to the position under the Business Names Act 1985, see *infra*, para. 3–29.

[48] See *supra* n.43.

[49] Partnership Act 1890, s.29; *Aas v. Benham* [1891] 2 Ch. 244; and see *infra*, paras. 16–08 *et seq.* Semble, the application of this section is not dependent on establishing that the firm name is partnership property.

[50] As to the basic requirements for a passing-off action, see *Erven Warnink B.V. v. J. Townend & Sons (Hull) Ltd.* [1979] A.C. 731 and the earlier cases cited therein; also *Reckitt & Colman Products Ltd. v. Borden Inc.* [1990] 1 W.L.R. 491; *County Sound plc v. Ocean Sound Ltd.* [1991] F.S.R. 367. It should be noted that a passing-off action may be brought in England to protect the goodwill of a foreign business, where that goodwill prospectively extends to England: *Maxim's Ltd. v. Dye* [1977] 1 W.L.R. 1155; *cf. Anheuser–Busch Inc. v. Budejovicky Budvar N.P.* [1984] F.S.R. 413. See also *My Kinda Bones Ltd. (T/A Chicago Rib Shack) v. Dr. Pepper's Stove Co. Ltd. (T/A Dr. Pepper's Manhattan Rib Shack)* [1984] F.S.R. 289.

[51] *Fine Cotton Spinners and Doublers' Assoc. Ltd. v. Harwood Cash & Co. Ltd.* [1907] 2 Ch. 184, 188, *per* Joyce J.

[52] *Jay's Ltd. v. Jacobi* [1933] Ch. 411; *Habib Bank Ltd. v. Habib Bank A.G. Zurich* [1981] 1 W.L.R. 1265.

[53] *Turton v. Turton* (1888) 42 Ch.D. 128; *Tussaud v. Tussaud* (1890) 44 Ch.D. 678; *Saunders v. Sun Life Assurance Co. of Canada* [1894] 1 Ch. 537; *Burgess v. Burgess* (1853) 3 De G.M. & G. 896. See also *Lee v. Popeck* (1967) 111 S.J. 114 (solicitor practising under the name of Tringhams and also under his own name, David Lee, held not entitled, in interlocutory proceedings, to an injunction restraining two solicitors from practising under the name of David Leigh & Co.). But see *Legal and General Assurance Society v. Daniel* [1968] R.P.C. 253.

[54] *Teofani & Co. Ltd. v. A. Teofani* [1913] 2 Ch. 545; *Holloway v. Holloway* (1800) 13 Beav. 209; *Croft v. Day* (1843) 7 Beav. 84; *Lewis's v. Lewis* (1890) 45 Ch.D. 281; *J. & J. Cash Ltd. v. Cash* [1902] W.N. 32.

[55] In editions of this work prior to the 15th, there appeared at this point extensive references to the right of a firm to prevent persons registering a company to carry on a rival business under a name identical or similar to the firm name. These have not been retained, but are to be found in the 15th ed. at pp. 40, 41.

Firm name as a trade or service mark

Although a monopoly in an ordinary English word cannot be **3–19**
acquired merely by assuming it as a trade name,[56] a firm name may
be registered as a trade or service mark for particular classes of goods
or services if "represented in a special or particular manner."[57]
Provision is made to prevent the improper registration of the same
trade or service mark by several persons.[58]

It should be noted that a trade or service mark can be registered in
the joint names of the partners, provided that no partner is entitled,
as against his co-partners, to use it otherwise than for partnership
purposes.[59]

Under the Trade Marks Act 1938, a registered trade or service **3–20**
mark is assignable and transmissible, whether or not in connection
with the goodwill of a business and whether relating to some or all of
the goods or services in respect of which it is or was registered, save
where the result would be that more than one person would at
common law or by registration have exclusive rights to use similar
trade or service marks in respect of the same kind of goods or
services, and the use would be liable to cause deception or
confusion.[60] Assignment or transmission for use in different parts of
the United Kingdom is not permissible unless approved by the
registrar.[61] Unlike the position under the earlier law,[62] if on a
dissolution all the partners are equally entitled to the goodwill of the
firm, they cannot, even by agreement, insist on a trade or service
mark belonging to the firm being registered in their *respective*

---

[56] *Aerators Ltd. v. Tollitt* [1902] 2 Ch. 319. The Copyright Acts have no application to mere
names: see *Maxwell v. Hogg* (1867) L.R. 2 Ch. 307.

[57] Trade Marks Act 1938, ss.3, 9 (as respectively amended, in relation to service marks, by the
Trade Marks (Amendment) Act 1984, Sched. 1, paras. 1, 6). See also *Registrar of Trade Marks v.
W. and G. Du Cros* [1913] A.C. 624; *British Milk Products Co.'s Application* [1915] 2 Ch. 202;
Edgar Staines v. Victor La Rosa [1953] 1 W.L.R. 474. As to the circumstances under which a
surname will be registered, see *Teofani & Co. Ltd. v. A. Teofani* [1913] 2 Ch. 545, 567 *et seq.*; *R.
J. Lea Ltd.'s Application* [1913] 1 Ch. 446.

[58] Trade Marks Act 1938, s.12 (as amended by the Trade Marks (Amendment) Act 1984, Sched.
2, para. 2 and, in relation to service marks, by *ibid.* Sched. 1, para. 8).

[59] *Ibid.* s.63 (as amended, in relation to service marks, by the Trade Marks (Amendment) Act
1984, Sched. 1, para. 23).

[60] *Ibid.* s.22(1), (2) (as amended, in relation to service marks, by the Trade Marks (Amendment)
Act 1984, Sched. 1, para. 12).

[61] *Ibid.* s.22(4), (6) (as respectively amended by the Trade Marks (Amendment) Act 1984, Sched.
2, para. 3 and, in relation to service marks, by *ibid.* Sched. 1, para. 12).

[62] In earlier editions of this work, the old law was summarised thus: "In any case where, by
reason of a dissolution of partnership or otherwise, a person who was entitled to more than one
registered trade mark ceased to carry on business, and the goodwill of the business did not pass to
one successor but was divided, the registrar might, except in the case of associated trade marks,
formerly have permitted an apportionment of his registered trade marks among the persons in fact
continuing the business, subject to such conditions and modifications, if any, as he might think
necessary in the public interest." This proposition rested on the Trade Marks Act 1905, s.23, as
amended by the Trade Marks Act 1919, s.12, Sched. 2, and superseded and repealed by the Trade
Marks (Amendment) Act 1937, s.7, and the Trade Marks Act 1938, s.70 and Sched. 4.

names.[63] If they cannot agree to vest the trade or service mark in one or more of themselves (jointly if more than one), it must be realised for the benefit of all the partners.

Assignment of firm name

3–21   An assignment of the right to use a firm name in gross will not confer on the assignee any rights connected with the use of that name as against third parties; *per contra*, if it is assigned in conjunction with the business or part of the business.[64] A firm may, however, agree to confer on a third party the right to use the firm name in connection with his business and, if that agreement is not tainted by a fraudulent intention to deceive the public, it will be perfectly valid as between the parties.[65]

If, following the dissolution of a firm, its business is wholly discontinued, the old firm name may be adopted by another trader,[66] provided he does not thereby expose the members of the former firm to any risk of liability.[67] The position as between the partners following a dissolution will be noticed hereafter.[68]

Change in firm name

3–22   The rights and liabilities of a firm will not in general be affected by a change in its name, unless that change is also accompanied by a change in its members. Admittedly, a change of name will be of significance to the partners where the old name is registered as a trade or service mark or where it effectively represents the firm's goodwill, but otherwise a mere change of name will mean no more than a change in the label by which they are collectively known. Equally, one partner does not have power to bind his co-partners by using a name under which they do not carry on business together, unless they have expressly or impliedly sanctioned its use.[69]

---

[63] See the Trade Marks Act 1938, ss.22–25 and *Re Ehrmann's Application* [1897] 2 Ch. 495 (a decision under the Patents, Designs and Trade Marks Act 1883). It is considered that the latter decision was not affected by the Trade Marks Act 1905, s.20 (as amended), nor by the Trade Marks Act 1938, s.12(3). But see also the Trade Marks Act 1938, s.22(4) (as amended) and *R. J. Reuter Co. v. Muhlens* [1954] Ch. 50.

[64] *Thorneloe v. Hill* [1894] 1 Ch. 569; *Kingston Miller & Co. Ltd. v. Thomas Kingston & Co. Ltd.* [1912] 1 Ch. 575, 581, 582, *per* Warrington J. But *cf. Barr v. Lions*, 1956 S.L.T. 250; and see *infra*, para. 10–156.

[65] See *Coles (J. H.) Proprietary Ltd. v. Need* [1934] A.C. 82. If the agreement amounts to a revocable licence and such licence is revoked, the firm can obtain an injunction against the licensee to restrain continued use of the firm name: *ibid.*

[66] *Pink v. Sharwood (No. 2)* (1913) 109 L.T. 594.

[67] See *Townsend v. Jarman* [1900] 2 Ch. 698, and other cases of that class, noticed *infra*, paras. 10–162 *et seq.*; and see *infra*, paras. 5–54 *et seq.*

[68] See *infra*, paras. 10–160 *et seq.*

[69] See *Kirk v. Blurton* (1841) 9 M. & W. 284 and the other cases of that class noticed *infra*, paras. 12–160 *et seq.*

A change of name may, nevertheless, necessitate an application to the Secretary of State for approval of the new name under the Business Names Act 1985[70] and may also bring within the scope of the Act a firm to which its provisions formerly did not apply.[71]

Change in a partner's name

A change in the name of a partner will not normally have any **3-23** impact on the firm name, unless it causes the Business Names Act 1985 to apply and thus, conceivably, necessitates approval for the continued use of the name being sought from the Secretary of State.[72] However, such approval would not in any event be required in relation to a name which was lawfully used by the firm immediately prior to February 26, 1982.[73]

Business Names Act 1985

Reference is made throughout this work to the application of the **3-24** Business Names Act 1985 to partnerships and, for convenience, a connected account of its main provisions will be given at this point. The Act consolidated the provisions of Part II of the Companies Act 1981, which had in turn repealed and replaced the Registration of Business Names Act 1916,[74] and forms part of the legislative framework controlling the use of (*inter alia*) firm names.[75]

Firms, persons and corporations affected

By section 2 of the Act, the following firms, persons and **3-25** corporations are subject to its controls:

---

[70] ss.2(1), 3; also the Company and Business Names Regulations 1981 (S.I. 1981 No. 1685), as amended by the Company and Business Names (Amendment) Regulations 1982 (S.I. 1982 No. 1653) and the Company and Business Names (Amendment) Regulations 1992 (S.I. 1992 No. 1196). The 1981 and 1982 regulations were originally made pursuant to the Companies Act 1981, s.31(1) but continue to have effect under the 1985 Act: Interpretation Act 1978, s.17(2)(*b*).

[71] As a result, the requisite information would have to be included on the firm's business letters and other documentation and displayed in the partnership premises: Business Names Act 1985, s.4.

[72] *Ibid.* ss.2(1), 3; also the Company and Business Names Regulations 1981 (as amended): see *supra*, n. 70. In the case of a change of name by a woman in consequence of marriage, the position is effectively the same as it was under the Registration of Business Names Act 1916: see *Seymour v. Chernikeef* [1946] K.B. 434.

[73] Business Names Act 1985, ss.2(3), 8(1).

[74] Neither the Companies Act 1981 nor the Business Names Act 1985 replaced the registration requirements contained in the 1916 Act, and to that extent have been said to afford less protection. For an outline of the position under the 1916 Act, the reader is referred to the 14th ed. of this work, pp. 38–45.

[75] The provisions relating to company names, which formerly appeared in the Companies Act 1981, ss.22–27, are to be found in the Companies Act 1985 and fall outside the scope of the present work. It may, however, be noted that s.714(1) of the 1985 Act requires the Registrar of Companies to keep an index of, *inter alia*, the names of all limited partnerships.

1. Every partnership[76] which has a place of business in Great Britain and which carries on business[77] in Great Britain under a name which does not consist of the surnames of all partners who are individuals and the corporate names of all partners who are bodies corporate, without any addition other than the forenames of the individual partners or the initials thereof or, where there are two or more individual partners with the same surname, the addition of the letter "s" at the end of that surname.[78] It is also permissible to add to the firm name an indication that the business is carried on in succession to a former owner of the business.[79]

    If, on a change in the members of a partnership to which the section originally did not apply, there is no longer the necessary correlation between the firm name and the surnames of the current partners, then the section may become applicable and affect the continued use of that name.[80]

3-26   2. Every individual who has a place of business in Great Britain and who carries on business in Great Britain under a name which does not consist of his surname without any addition other than his forename or the initial thereof,[81] or an indication that the business is carried on in succession to a former owner of the business.[82]

3. Every company capable of being wound up under the Companies Act 1985 which has a place of business in Great Britain and which carries on business in Great Britain under a

---

[76] Partnership is expressed to include a foreign partnership (Business Names Act 1985, (s.8(1)), but is not otherwise defined. *Cf.* the position under the equivalent Manx legislation: *Buckmaster and Moore v. Fado Investments* [1986] P.C.C. 95. It is unclear whether the partnership is the "person" referred to in the Act, or whether that expression is intended to denote each partner individually. Whilst the latter would appear to be intended (since it would avoid the partnership being treated as an entity distinct from the partners composing it), a number of anomalies do nevertheless arise: see *infra*, paras. 3–31, n. 95; 3–33, n. 7; 3–34, n. 12.

[77] Business includes profession: *ibid.* s.8(1). As to the general meaning of the word, see *Smith v. Anderson* (1880) 15 Ch.D. 247, 258, *per* Jessel M.R.

[78] *Ibid.* s.1(1)(a), (2)(a). Surname in relation to a peer or person usually known by a British title different from his surname means the title by which he is known, and initial includes any recognised abbreviation of a name: *ibid.* s.8(1). The addition of the words "and Co." would clearly constitute an improper addition for these purposes: see *Evans v. Piauneau* [1927] 2 K.B. 374, 377 (a decision under the Aliens Restriction (Amendment) Act 1919—now repealed).

[79] *Ibid.* s.1(2)(c).

[80] See *infra*, para. 3–31 *et seq.*

[81] Business Names Act 1985, s.1(1)(b), (2)(b). It is submitted that, by virtue of s.6(c) of the Interpretation Act 1978, the use of more than one forename or initial will not constitute an improper addition for the purposes of subs. (2)(b), but this should be compared with the more precise provisions of the Registration of Business Names Act 1916, s.1(6). Under the latter Act, if any Christian name or initial was added to the surname, *all* the Christian names or initials had to be added to escape the need for registration: *Brown v. Thomas and Burrows* (1922) 39 T.L.R. 132; *Limond v. Bernthal*, 1953 S.L.T. (Sh.Ct.) 97. Whether there is a similar requirement under the 1985 Act is unclear, but it is tentatively thought not.

[82] Business Names Act 1985, s.1(2)(c).

name which does not consist of its corporate name without any addition, other than an indication that the business is carried on in succession to a former owner of the business.[83]

Approval of names

Where section 2 applies, no business can be carried on in Great **3–27** Britain under a name which would be likely to give the impression that the business is connected with Her Majesty's Government or with any local authority, or which includes any word or expression for the time being specified in regulations made under the Act, without first obtaining the written approval of the Secretary of State.[84] Where, however, a business was carried on under a lawful business name[85] immediately before February 26, 1982,[86] and continues thereafter to be carried on under the same name, no approval is required.[87]

It should be noted that where the firm name comprises the **3–28** surnames of some (but not all) of the partners, approval will have to be sought if any one or more of those surnames consist of a word specified in the regulations.[88]

Where it is necessary to obtain the approval of a name, the persons proposing to use it, *i.e.* in the case of a firm all the partners, must first approach any "relevant body" specified for that purpose,[89] with a view to ascertaining whether that body has any objection to the proposed name.[90] There must then be submitted to the Secretary of State, apparently as part of the application for approval,[91] a statement that such a request has been made of the relevant body concerned, together with a copy of any response received.[92]

---

[83] *Ibid.* s.1(1)(c) and (2)(c). Note also the powers of the Secretary of State in relation to the names of overseas companies under the Companies Act 1985, s.694.

[84] Business Names Act 1985, ss.2(1), 3; see also the Company and Business Names Regulations 1981 (S.I. 1981 No. 1685), as amended by the Company and Business Names (Amendment) Regulations 1982 (S.I. 1982 No. 1653) and the Company and Business Names (Amendment) Regulations 1992 (S.I. 1992 No. 1196). The 1981 and 1982 regulations were originally made pursuant to the Companies Act 1981, s.31(1) but continue to have effect under the 1985 Act: Interpretation Act 1978, s.17(2)(b). There is no provision as to the precise manner in which an application is to be made to the Secretary of State.

[85] A lawful business name is a name under which the business was carried on without contravening s.2(1) of the Act or s.2 of the Registration of Business Names Act 1916: s.8(1).

[86] This was the day originally appointed for the coming into force of the Companies Act 1981, s.28(5): see the Companies Act 1981 (Commencement No. 3) Order 1982 (S.I. 1982 No. 103).

[87] Business Names Act 1985, s.2(3).

[88] *e.g.* Duke or King: see Column (1) of the Schedule to the Company and Business Names Regulations 1981 (as amended).

[89] Business Names Act 1985, s.3(1)(b). See also Column (2) of the Schedule to the Company and Business Names Regulations 1981 (as amended).

[90] Business Names Act 1985, s.3(2)(a).

[91] This is by no means clear. It might be possible to supply the necessary statement after submitting the application to the Secretary of State without strictly contravening the provisions of the subsection.

[92] Business Names Act 1985, s.3(2)(b).

Same firm using two or more names

3-29   In the case of a firm which carries on business under more than one name, approval may have to be sought in respect of each such name, but there would otherwise appear to be no restriction on the number of names which may be employed.

Two or more firms with the same name

3-30   There is no limit on the number of firms which can carry on business under the same name, and it is thought that more than one firm may, in theory at least, apply for, and obtain approval from the Secretary of State in respect of an identical name.[93]

Effect of changes in the partners

3-31   Where approval of a firm name has been sought and obtained, and there is a subsequent change in the constitution of the firm, whether by the death, retirement or expulsion of an existing partner or the admission of a new partner, the position is far from clear. It is submitted that the departure of an existing partner will not affect the validity of the approval previously obtained by all the partners and that continued use of the firm name after the change is permissible.[94] However, the admission of a new partner will unquestionably require a fresh approval to be sought, seemingly by the new partner alone.[95] Such approval should be obtained before the new partner is admitted to the firm, since it is doubtful whether he can be regarded as a transferee of the business and thereby seek to defer the need for approval for 12 months.[96]

In the case of a firm which carries on business under a name which initially does not attract the application of the Act, a change of partners may well bring the firm within its scope and, moreover,

---

[93] It is by no means clear whether the Secretary of State will seek to refuse approval on the ground that some other partnership is carrying on business under the same name, but it is thought that any such refusal might be open to challenge.

[94] If, however, the partnership is the "person" referred to in the Business Names Act 1985, s.1(1), then a change of partners will bring a new firm into existence and fresh approval for the continued use of the name will be required: see *supra*, para. 3–25, n. 76.

[95] This view is advanced on the assumption that the "person" referred to in *ibid.* s.1(1) is each separate partner rather than the partnership: see *supra*, para. 3–25, n. 76. In that event the existing partners will already have obtained the requisite approval, and will not be obliged to make any further application. If, on the other hand, the partnership is the "person," an entirely fresh approval will be required on behalf of the "new" enlarged firm.

[96] *Ibid.* s.2(2) provides that no approval need be sought for the continued use of a name by a person to whom the business has been transferred on or after February 26, 1982 and who continues to carry on the business under the same name during the period of 12 months beginning with the date of the transfer. Since the new partner will, at most, be the transferee of a share or interest in the partnership business, it is considered that this subsection may be inapplicable, although the point is eminently arguable.

require approval to be sought from the Secretary of State, if the existing firm name is to continue unchanged.[97]

Information to appear on business letters, etc.

Every partnership[98] to which section 2 of the Act applies must state **3–32** in legible characters on all its business documentation[99] the name of each partner and the address within Great Britain at which any document can be effectively served on him.[1] The only exception to this requirement consists of documents issued by a firm with more than 20 partners[2] which maintains at its principal place of business a list of all the partners' names, provided that none of their names appear in the document (otherwise than in the text or as a signatory) *and* the document states in legible characters the address of the firm's principal place of business and that the list of names is open to inspection there.[3] Any person is entitled to inspect that list during office hours.[4]

In addition to the above (and irrespective of the size of the firm), any person with whom anything is done or even discussed in the course of the partnership business is entitled to request, and must be supplied with, a written notice containing a list of the names and addresses of all the partners.[5]

A notice containing the names and addresses of all the partners must also be displayed in a prominent position, in any premises where the partnership business is carried on and to which the customers of, or suppliers of goods or services to, the business have access.[6]

Penalties

Failure to obtain any requisite approval from the Secretary of State **3–33** for the use of a firm name or, without reasonable excuse, to include the necessary information on all the firm's business documentation, to display the necessary notice in the partnership premises, to supply a

---

[97] See *supra*, para. 3–27.

[98] See *supra*, para. 3–25, n. 76.

[99] *i.e.* all its business letters, written orders for goods or services to be supplied to the business, invoices and receipts issued in the course of the business and written demands for payment of debts arising in the course of the business.

[1] Business Names Act 1985, s.4(1)(a). And see also the (1982) 79 L.S.Gaz. 85.

[2] As to the types of firm which can be formed with more than 20 partners, see *infra*, paras. 4–27 *et seq.*

[3] Business Names Act 1985, s.4(3).

[4] *Ibid.* s.4(4).

[5] *Ibid.* s.4(2). The notice may need to be in a form specified in regulations made under the Act: *ibid.* s.4(5). As yet, no such regulations have been made.

[6] *Ibid.* s.4(1)(b). The notice may need to be in a form specified in regulations under the Act: *ibid.* s.4(5). Again, no regulations have yet been made.

list of the partners' names and addresses on request or to permit inspection of a list of those names and addresses maintained at the partnership premises constitutes an offence, in respect of which all the partners might be liable to a fine on summary conviction.[7]

Disability of firms in default

3–34   In addition to the penalties which may be imposed for breach of a firm's obligations under the Act,[8] the firm will be subject to a general disability as regards contracts entered into whilst the breach continues.[9] Thus, if at the time of the breach the firm entered into a contract in the course of its business, and the partners subsequently commence proceedings to enforce rights arising out of that contract, they may find those proceedings summarily dismissed if the defendant[10] can show that, by reason of the breach, he has been unable to pursue a claim against the firm arising out of the contract or that he has suffered some financial loss in connection therewith.[11] This would appear to be the position even though the breach was the fault of only one partner and unknown to the other partners.[12] However, the court is given a residual discretion to permit the proceedings to continue, if it would be just and equitable so to do.[13]

   The disability imposed by the Act is limited to the firm itself; it has no application to persons claiming under it, *e.g.* a trustee in bankruptcy or liquidator.[14]

---

[7] *Ibid.* ss.2(4), 4(6), (7), 7. It is again unclear whether the "person" committing the offence is the partnership or the individual partners concerned: see *supra*, para. 3–25, n. 76 and para. 3–31, n. 95. If it is the former, then it would seem that all the partners will be liable even in respect of a breach of which they have no knowledge. If it is the latter, then only the partner or partners responsible would appear to be liable. As to the liability of officers and members in respect of offences committed by a body corporate, see *ibid.* s.7(4), (5). This will, of course, be of relevance in the case of a corporate partnership, as to which see, generally, *infra*, paras. 11–02 *et seq.*

[8] See *supra*, para. 3–33.

[9] *i.e.* a breach of *ibid.* s.4(1) or (2). Of course, if the partnership does not fall within the scope of *ibid.* s.1(1), there can be no breach of these provisions.

[10] The vague expression "the defendant" is not expressly limited to contracting parties. It is, however, doubtful whether a non-contracting party could ever be in a position to invoke the section.

[11] *Ibid.* s.5.

[12] This again highlights the anomaly referred to *supra*, in para. 3–25, n. 76; 3–31, n. 95; 3–33, n. 7. If the "person" for the purposes of the section is each partner individually, then are the proceedings to be dismissed only as against the partners responsible for the breach? This is obviously not the intention, and it is thought that the section can only be applied if the entire proceedings are dismissed, thereby penalising all the partners for breaches committed by some of their number.

[13] It is submitted that the court will be likely to approach the exercise of this discretion in a manner similar to that adopted in relation to the Registration of Business Names Act 1916, s.8. Relief under that section was granted where a foreign name had been wrongly spelt (*Hawkins v. Duché* [1921] 3 K.B. 226), and where the defaulter (the plaintiff) did not know of the Act or the need for registration thereunder, and the defendant knew he owned the business and was not misled (*Weller v. Denton* [1921] 3 K.B. 103). See also *Re Oxley* [1932] W.N. 271; *Lawrence Vanger & Co. v. Company Developments (Property Division) Ltd.* (1977) 244 E.G. 43. And see *Buckmaster and Moore v. Fado Investments* [1986] P.C.C. 95 (a decision under the equivalent Manx legislation, but concerning an English partnership).

[14] See *Hawkins v. Duché, supra.*

(b) Legal Proceedings

The complications which formerly resulted from the refusal of the law **3–35**
to recognise the firm as a separate entity are of largely historical
interest.[15] Partners can now sue, and be sued, in the firm name,[16]
although this has in no way affected their individual liability to satisfy
judgments against the firm. Bankruptcy has, of course, always
presented its own peculiar problems.[17]

Nevertheless, a continuing, and graphic, illustration of such refusal
may be found in the rule that, for taxation purposes, if London and
country firms of solicitors share a common partner, the former will
not be entitled to agency fees when acting for the latter, but will
rather be treated as acting on its own account.[18]

(c) Contractual Rights and Liabilities

Effect of change in the partners

Where there is a change in the partners, the members of the "new" **3–36**
firm may quite properly agree with the members of the "old" firm
that the partnership should be treated as continuing and that all
existing rights and obligations should be effectively taken over by the
new firm. However, so far as concerns third parties, such an
agreement is *res inter alios acta*, unless they consent to be bound
thereby.[19]

It naturally follows that any contract into which the firm has **3–37**
entered may be determined or breached by such a change. If, on its
true construction, the contract is framed solely by reference to an
existing firm, it will be determined by any change in its members.
This is illustrated by the decision in *Tasker v. Shepherd*,[20] where two
partners appointed an agent for four and a half years and one of
them died before the expiration of that period. It was held that the
surviving partner need no longer employ the agent's services, since
the appointment was only by reference to the existing partnership,
the contract being for a term of four and a half years but only if the
parties should live that long. Similarly, if the contract is of a personal

---

[15] In essence those complications were that (1) a firm could not sue or be sued otherwise than in
the names of the partners composing it, (2) an action could not be brought by the firm against a
partner, or by a partner against the firm and (3) one firm could not bring an action against another
if they both shared one or more partners in common.

[16] See R.S.C. Ord. 81, *infra*, para. A2–09 *et seq.*

[17] None more so than under the new insolvency legislation: see *infra*, paras. 27–01 *et seq.*

[18] *Re Borough Commercial and Build. Soc.* [1894] 1 Ch. 289.

[19] See *infra*, paras. 13–24 *et seq.*

[20] (1861) 6 H. & N. 575; and see, generally, *I.R.C. v. Graham's Trustees*, 1971 S.L.T. 46;
Kirkintilloch Equitable Co-operative Society Ltd. v. Livingstone, 1972 S.L.T. 154.

character, which is only to be performed by the individual partners who have entered into it or is otherwise dependent on their particular attributes, a change in the firm will determine the contract by rendering its performance impossible.[21]

3–38   If, on the other hand, it can be inferred that the contract is to be performed by the firm as from time to time constituted, then a change in the partners will not *per se* determine the contract or constitute a breach of it. However, this is a pure question of construction in relation to each individual contract, and no general principles can usefully be formulated.[22] However, as was made clear by Scott J. in *Briggs v. Oates*,[23] in approaching the question of construction the size of the firm will often be a material consideration.

Right to damages: Brace v. Calder

3–39   Where a change in the partners determines a contract which is not, in its terms, conditional on the continued existence of the firm, the change may also constitute a breach of contract for which the partners will be liable in damages. Thus in *Brace v. Calder*,[24] a firm of four partners agreed to employ the plaintiff as a branch manager for two years, but before the two years had expired, two of the partners retired. The continuing partners were willing to employ the plaintiff on the same terms as before, but the plaintiff declined and sued the four original partners for breach of contract. The court held that the engagement of the plaintiff was for a fixed term of two

---

[21] *Robson v. Drummond* (1831) 2 B. & Ad. 303. As a rule, contracts of agency are of such a character: see *Brace v. Calder* [1895] 2 Q.B. 253, *infra*, para. 3–39; *Friend v. Young* [1897] 2 Ch. 421, 429, *per* Stirling J. Similarly, in the case of contracts between an author and publisher: *Stevens v. Benning* (1855) 1 K. & J. 168; *Hole v. Bradbury* (1879) 12 Ch.D. 886; *Griffith v. Tower Publishing Co. Ltd.* [1897] 1 Ch. 21. And see also *Kemp v. Baerselman* [1906] 2 K.B. 604 (contract to supply goods); *Graves v. Cohen* (1929) 46 T.L.R. 121 (owner and jockey). As to contracts which are *not* of a personal character, see *Messager v. British Broadcasting Co.* [1929] A.C. 151; *Phillips v. Alhambra Palace Co.* [1901] 1 K.B. 59; *John Brothers Abergarw Brewery Co. v. Holmes* [1900] 1 Ch. 188; *Tolhurst v. Associated Portland Cement Manufacturers Ltd.* [1903] A.C. 414; *British Waggon Co. v. Lea* (1880) 5 Q.B.D. 149; *Re Worthington* [1914] 2 K.B. 300. Note that, even where the contract is personal and has been determined, an obligation to continue payments for services previously rendered may still remain: *Wilson v. Harper* [1908] 2 Ch. 370; *cf. Sales v. Crispi* (1913) 29 T.L.R. 491.
[22] See *Briggs v. Oates* [1990] I.C.R. 473, 481, *per* Scott J.; *Jardine-Paterson v. Fraser*, 1974 S.L.T. 93. Of course, in Scotland a firm is a separate legal entity: Partnership Act 1890, s.4(2).
[23] [1990] I.C.R. 473, 482.
[24] [1895] 2 Q.B. 253. *Quaere*, if the plaintiff would have been entitled to damages if the contract had been determined by the death of one of the partners: see *ibid*. p. 261, *per* Lopes L.J. *Brace v. Calder* was followed in *Briggs v. Oates* [1990] I.C.R. 473. As to the effect of a *general* dissolution, see *Tunstall v. Condon* [1981] I.C.R. 786 and *infra*, para. 25–02. Note also, in this context, that account must be taken of certain statutory provisions affecting employees' rights: see the Employment Protection (Consolidation) Act 1978, Sched. 13, para. 17, considered in *Allen & Son v. Coventry* [1980] I.C.R. 9 and *Jeetle v. Elster* [1985] I.C.R. 389; *cf. Harold Fielding v. Mansi* [1974] I.C.R. 347; and see the Transfer of Undertakings (Protection of Employment) Regulations 1981 (S.I. 1981 No. 1794).

years[25] and that the retirement of the two partners determined the contract and constituted a breach of contract or wrongful dismissal, for which the four partners were liable in damages; however, as the continuing partners were willing to employ the plaintiff on the same terms as before, he was only entitled to nominal damages.[26]

Insurance policies

A contract of insurance is a personal contract and, unless it is **3-40** assignable without the consent of the insurers (as in the case of marine insurance) or, on its true construction, it is to continue notwithstanding a change in the firm, the admission of a new partner will, in the absence of such consent, terminate it.[27] Nevertheless, in the case of a third party motor insurance policy, it has been held that, where a new partner was admitted before an accident, the insurers were not thereby relieved of their liability to indemnify the persons who were partners when the policy was effected, provided that they retained their undivided interest in the insured vehicle.[28]

(d) Partnership Disabilities

Disabilities of one partner affect the firm

The disability of one partner will affect the whole firm, so that the **3-41** legal capacity of the firm will be no greater than that of the partner with the *least* legal capacity.[29] This proposition stems from the

---

[25] As to when a discontinuance of a business will amount to a breach of contract entered into for a fixed term, *cf.* the cases in which an obligation to continue the business was implied (*Re R. S. Newman Ltd.* [1916] 2 Ch. 309; *Ogdens Ltd. v. Nelson* [1905] A.C. 109; *Turner v. Goldsmith* [1891] 1 Q.B. 544; *Telegraph Despatch Co. v. Maclean* (1873) L.R. 8 Ch. 658; *M'Intyre v. Belcher* (1863) 14 C.B.(N.S.) 654) with those in which it was not (*Hamlyn & Co. v. Wood & Co.* [1891] 2 Q.B. 488; *Re Railway and Electrical Appliances Co.* (1888) 38 Ch.D. 597; *Rhodes v. Forwood* (1876) 1 App.Cas. 256; *Casajee Nanabhoy v. Lallbhoy Vullubhoy* (1876) L.R. 3 Ind.App. 200, and *Bovine Ltd. v. Dent* (1905) 21 T.L.R. 82). And see *L. French & Co. Ltd. v. Leeston Shipping Co. Ltd.* [1922] 1 A.C. 451 (determination of a charter); also *cf. Turner v. Sawdon & Co.* [1901] 2 K.B. 653 and *Konski v. Peet* [1915] 1 Ch. 530 (where it was held there was no obligation to supply the plaintiff with work) with *Herbert Clayton, etc. Ltd. v. Oliver* [1930] A.C. 209; *Devonald v. Rosser* [1906] 2 K.B. 728; *Re Rubel Bronze & Metal Co. and Vos* [1918] 1 K.B. 315 (where it was held that there was such an obligation). As to the rules for determining what terms, if any, are to be implied, see generally *The Moorcock* (1889) 14 P.D. 64; *Liverpool City Council v. Irwin* [1977] A.C. 239; *Chitty on Contracts* (26th ed.), paras. 901 *et seq.*

[26] As to the measure of damages where a subsequent offer is unreasonably refused, see also *Payzu Ltd. v. Saunders* [1919] 2 K.B. 581; as to whether a refusal is unreasonable, see *Yetton v. Eastwoods Froy* [1967] 1 W.L.R. 104. And see also *Re Foster Clark's Indenture Trusts* [1966] 1 W.L.R. 125 and *supra*, n. 24.

[27] See the Australian case of *Maxwell v. Price* [1959] 2 Lloyd's Rep. 352.

[28] *Jenkins v. Deane* (1933) 150 L.T. 314; and see an article in 177 L.T. 415. Semble, the policy would be terminated by the death, retirement or expulsion of a partner on the principles discussed *infra*, paras. 3-43 *et seq.*

[29] Illustrations of this doctrine will be found *infra*, paras. 14-60 *et seq.* See also the following cases concerning solicitors: *Duke of Northumberland v. Todd* (1878) 7 Ch.D. 777; *Re Borough Commercial and Building Society* [1894] 1 Ch. 289 (noticed *supra*, para. 3-35); *Rakusen v. Ellis, Munday & Clarke* [1912] 1 Ch. 831; *David Lee & Co. (Lincoln) Ltd. v. Coward Chance* [1991] Ch. 259; *Re a Firm of Solicitors* [1992] 1 Q.B. 959. And note *Re Scientific Investment Pensions Plan, The Times*, December 10, 1992.

general rule that no person can by an agent do anything which he cannot do himself; it follows that, whilst each member of a firm may be a principal as regards his own conduct, he is also the agent of his co-partners and, therefore, he cannot do for the firm what they cannot do. However, this rule does not extend to *physical* capacity, since there can be no objection to an agent doing on his principal's behalf what that principal is himself physically unable to do. Thus, in *Newstead v. Frost*,[30] it was held that a partnership between Mr. David Frost and a Bahamian company could validly carry on the business of exploiting Mr. Frost's talent as a television personality with a view to sharing the profits therefrom, even though the company itself was incapable of appearing on television.

3–42   There are a number of statutory disabilities which will affect not only the firm but also each partner in his private capacity, *viz.*:

Auditors: By the Companies Act 1989, s.27(1) a firm will be ineligible for appointment as the auditor of a company if any partner is an officer or employee of that company.[31]

County Courts: By the County Courts Act 1984, s.13(1), no officer of a county court may either by himself or his partner be directly or indirectly engaged as solicitor or agent for a party in proceedings in that court.[32]

Insolvency: The Insolvency Rules 1986[33] restrict (even if they do not in all cases actually prohibit) the partners of a liquidator or trustee in bankruptcy or of a member of a liquidation or creditors' committee from doing various acts which they would otherwise be free to do.

Investment business: By rules made by the Securities and Investment Board under the Financial Services Act 1986,[34] a partner may be prevented from effecting a transaction on his own account which he could properly effect if he was not a partner.

Mental Health Act 1983:   By the Mental Health Act 1983, s.12(5), certain persons and their partners are disqualified from signing medical recommendations for the admission of patients.

Solicitors Act 1974:   By the Solicitors Act 1974, s.38(1), it is unlawful for a solicitor who is a justice of the peace for any area, and

---

[30] [1980] 1 W.L.R. 135 (H.L.).
[31] The appointment of a firm as a company auditor is authorised by the Companies Act 1989, s.26(1). See also *supra*, para. 3–16.
[32] See *R. v. Skierski* [1959] C.L.Y. 623.
[33] rr. 4.128(3), 4.149, 4.170, 6.139(3), 6.147, 6.165; Insolvency Act 1986, s.435.
[34] Financial Services (Conduct of Business) Rules 1990, rr. 5.15, 5.20, 5.21, 14.01, 14.03.

for any partner of his, to act in connection with any proceedings before the justices for that area.[35]

(e) Sureties and Securities

Sureties: effect of change in the partners

It is a fundamental principle of the law of suretyship, that any act 3–43 on the part of the principal creditor which alters the risk of the surety without his consent, discharges him from future liability.[36]

Sureties to a firm

It follows that, where a person acts as surety *to* a firm, it is 3–44 essential to ascertain whether or not in so doing he has agreed to act as surety to the firm as from time to time constituted. If he did, a subsequent change in its membership will obviously not discharge him from liability.[37] However, if there was no such agreement, his liability will continue only so long as the firm remains unchanged. This is recognised by the Partnership Act 1890, s.18, which provides as follows:

> "18. A continuing guaranty or cautionary obligation given either to a firm or to a third person in respect of the transactions of a firm is, in the absence of agreement to the contrary, revoked as to future transactions by any change in the constitution of the firm to which, or of the firm in respect of the transactions of which, the guaranty or obligation was given."[38]

---

[35] A limited number of exceptions to the general prohibition are set out in *ibid.* subss. (2)–(4).

[36] See as to sureties, *Holme v. Brunskill* (1877) 3 Q.B.D. 495; also *Bank of India v. Trans Continental Commodity Merchants Ltd.* [1982] 1 Lloyd's Rep. 506. As to the discharge of apprentices and their sureties by a change in the firm to which they are bound, see *Lloyd v. Blackburne* (1842) 9 M. & W. 363; *R. v. St. Martin's* (1835) 2 A. & E. 655.

[37] *Pease v. Hirst* (1829) 10 B. & C. 122; *Metcalfe v. Bruin* (1810) 12 East 400; and see *Barclay v. Lucas* (1783) 1 T.R. 291, note; *Kipling v. Turner* (1821) 5 B. & A. 261. In *Pariente v. Lubbock* (1856) 8 De G.M. & G. 5, an authority to a firm of consignees to recognise the consignor's son as his agent was held to continue, notwithstanding changes in the firm, as long as the consignor continued his business connections with the firm.

[38] This section replaced the Mercantile Law Amendment (Scotland) Act 1856, s.7 and the Mercantile Law Amendment Act 1856, s.4 (repealed by Partnership Act 1890, s.48). The latter section provided as follows: "No promise to answer for the debt, default or miscarriage of another made to a firm consisting of two or more persons, or to a single person trading under the name of a firm, and no promise to answer for the debt, default, or miscarriage of a firm consisting of two or more persons, or of a single person trading under the name of a firm, shall be binding on the person making such promise in respect of anything done or omitted to be done after a change shall have taken place in any one or more of the persons constituting the firm or in the persons trading under the name of a firm, unless the intention of the parties that such promise shall continue to be binding notwithstanding such change shall appear either by express stipulation or by necessary implication from the nature of the firm or otherwise." See, as to the position under that Act, *Backhouse v. Hall* (1865) 6 B. & S. 507. In his Supplement on the Partnership Act 1890, Lord Lindley commented "The wording of the present section [*i.e.* s.18] differs considerably from that of the previous acts, but so far at least as relates to England, it does not appear to have introduced any alteration in the law."

3-45   In such a case, whatever may be the cause of the change in the firm, *e.g.* the death,[39] retirement[40] or expulsion of an existing partner, or the introduction of a new partner,[41] it will immediately put an end to the surety's future liability, since his position and risk are thereby fundamentally altered; even though he may not suffer as a result, he can quite properly say *non hoec in foedera veni* (*i.e.* this is not what I agreed). However, his liability in respect of a debt already accrued and ascertained is not affected, even by a transfer of the debt, whether by assignment or novation, from the old to the new firm.[42]

Sureties for a firm

3-46   The same principles apply in a case where a person acts as surety for the conduct of a firm, as is demonstrated by the Partnership Act 1890, s.18.[43] However, the mere fact that a person has agreed to act as surety for another does not necessarily mean that he has agreed to act as surety for his conduct *as a partner*, still less for the conduct of him and his co–partners.[44]

Securities: effect of change in the partners

3-47   Analogous questions arise in relation to securities. Thus, if a banking firm is given security for future advances and there is then a change in the members of the firm, the security will prima facie extend only to those advances which are made before the change.[45] Again, if a partner pledges his own property for future advances to be made to the firm and then dies, an advance made after his death to the surviving partners will not be chargeable against the property pledged.[46] Similarly, if a person deposits deeds as a security for advances to be made to him, the security does not cover advances made to him and his partners.[47]

---

[39] *Holland v. Teed* (1848) 7 Hare 50; *Strange v. Lee* (1803) 3 East 484; *Weston v. Barton* (1812) 4 Taunt. 673; *Pemberton v. Oakes* (1827) 4 Russ. 154; *Simson v. Cooke* (1824) 1 Bing. 452; *Chapman v. Beckington* (1842) 3 Q.B. 703; *Backhouse v. Hall* (1865) 6 B. & S. 507.

[40] *Myers v. Edge* (1797) 7 T.R. 254; *Dry v. Davy* (1839) 10 A. & E. 30; and see *Solvency Mutual Guarantee Co. v. Freeman* (1861) 7 H. & N. 17.

[41] *Wright v. Russel* (1774) 2 Wm.Bl. 934.

[42] *Bradford Old Bank v. Sutcliffe* [1918] 2 K.B. 833.

[43] As to the position before the Act, see *Bellairs v. Ebsworth* (1811) 3 Camp. 53; *University of Cambridge v. Baldwin* (1839) 5 M. & W. 580; *Simson v. Cooke* (1824) 1 Bing. 452. Also *Dance v. Girdler* (1804) 1 Bos. & Pull. N.R. 34. *Cf. Universal Co. v. Yip*, June 18, 1986 (C.A.T. No. 581), [1987] C.L.Y. 1845, where, exceptionally, liability under the guarantee continued notwithstanding the fact that the firm had been taken over by a limited company. As to policies of insurance, see *supra*, para. 3–40.

[44] *London Assurance Co. v. Bold* (1844) 6 Q.B. 514; *Montefiore v. Lloyd* (1863) 15 C.B.(N.S.) 203, where the partnership was known to the surety.

[45] See *Ex p. Kensington* (1813) 2 V. & B. 79, 83, *per* Lord Eldon.

[46] *Bank of Scotland v. Christie* (1841) 8 Cl. & F. 214.

[47] *Ex p. M'Kenna* (1861) 3 De G.F. & J. 629; *Ex p. Freen* (1827) 2 Gl. & J. 246; also *Chuck v. Freen* (1828) 1 Moo. & M. 259. These cases turned on the terms of the memoranda of deposit, and on the circumstances under which the securities were given.

Equitable mortgages

Different principles applied in the case of equitable mortgages, but **3–48** it has now been held that a mortgage by deposit of title deeds can no longer be created in the face of the strict requirements of section 2 of the Law of Property (Miscellaneous Provisions) Act 1989[48] accordingly the following authorities must be approached with caution. Nevertheless, it has been held that an equitable mortgage by deposit of title deeds could be extended, even by parol, to cover advances made after a change in the firm with which the deeds have been deposited.[49] Moreover, although a legal mortgage could not be converted into an equitable mortgage by parol,[50] it might be so converted by a written agreement; thereafter, it might, as an equitable mortgage, become available as a security for advances made after a change in the firm to which the legal mortgage was originally given.[51] On this basis, Lord Lindley observed:

> "Owing to these doctrines a security given to a firm for advances to be made by it, is, upon a change in the firm, readily made a continuing security; and a slight manifestation of intention on the part of the borrower that it should so continue, will enable the new firm to hold the securities until the advances made by itself as well as those made by the old firm have been repaid."[52]

Lien of solicitors

The lien which a firm of solicitors has on the papers and deeds, **3–49** etc., of its clients is not lost by a mere change in the firm.[53] However, that lien only attaches where such papers have come into the possession of the persons to whom the client is *legally* indebted; it follows that, if papers only come into the possession of a firm after the admission of a new partner[54] or the retirement or expulsion of an existing partner,[55] they cannot be retained on account of a debt due before the change. Lord Lindley went on to observe:

---

[48] *United Bank of Kuwait plc v. Sahib*, *The Times*, July 7, 1994. See also *Emmet on Title* (19th ed.), para. 25–116; *Snell's Equity* (29th ed.), p. 445; *cf.* the preface to Cousins, *The Law of Mortgages*.

[49] See *Ex p. Lloyd* (1824) 1 Gl. & J. 389; *Ex p. Lane* (1846) De G. 300; also *Ex p. Nettleship* (1841) 2 Mont.D. & De G. 124.

[50] *Ex p. Hooper* (1815) 2 Rose 328. The position would, of course, be no different under the Law of Property (Miscellaneous Provisions) Act 1989, s.2.

[51] *Ex p. Parr* (1835) 4 D. & C. 426.

[52] See *Ex p. Kensington* (1813) 2 Ves. & Bea. 79; *Ex p. Marsh* (1815) 2 Rose 240; *Ex p. Alexander* (1824) 1 Gl. & J. 409; *Ex p. Lloyd* (1838) 3 Deac. 305.

[53] *Pelly v. Wathen* (1849) 7 Hare 351. The point was left open on appeal: see (1851) 1 De G.M. & G. 16.

[54] *Re Forshaw* (1847) 16 Sim. 121; *Pelly v. Wathen*, *supra*.

[55] *Vaughan v. Vanderstegen* (1854) 2 Drew. 409.

"The death of a partner is not, however, it is conceived, equivalent to retirement, for the survivors become the legal creditors; and there is, therefore, no reason why they should not have a lien for a debt due to them and their deceased partner on papers coming into their possession after his death."

The dissolution and winding up of a solicitors' partnership discharges the partners from any obligation to act for a former client;[56] any lien they may have on his papers will naturally be subject to the client's right to insist on those papers being handed over to a fresh solicitor, albeit subject to the lien, to enable any pending business to be completed.[57]

The difficulties discussed above will not, of course, arise when the court exercises its statutory powers under section 73 of the Solicitors Act 1973.[58]

(f) Revenue Law

Effect of change in the partners

3–50   For income tax purposes, any change in the firm will result in the cessation of the old firm and the creation of a new one, unless the partners elect to treat the partnership as continuing.[59] On the other hand, for the purposes of value added tax, any change in the firm will, in general, be ignored for registration purposes, unless it will result in a complete identity of partners as between two formerly separate partnerships.[60]

---

[56] Subject to the application of the Partnership Act 1890, s.38, *infra*, paras. 13–64 *et seq.*
[57] *Griffiths v. Griffiths* (1843) 2 Hare 587; *Rawlinson v. Moss* (1861) 7 Jur. (N.S.) 1053.
[58] See, generally, *Fairfold Properties Ltd. v. Exmouth Docks Co. Ltd. (No. 2)* [1993] Ch. 196.
[59] Income and Corporation Taxes Act 1988, s.113. See further, *infra*, paras. 34–45 *et seq.*
[60] Value Added Tax Act 1983, s.30(1). See further, *infra*, paras. 37–02 *et seq.* Note, however, that the change in the firm must be notified: see *infra*, para. 37–07.

CHAPTER 4

CAPACITY OF PARTNERS

1. CAPACITY

IN the normal course, there is nothing to prevent the creation of a **4-01** valid partnership between persons who are of full age and mental capacity. Admittedly there are cases in which, by virtue of some statutory provision, one or more of the partners are required to possess a specific qualification, particularly in the case of certain trades and professions,[1] but otherwise, there is no class of persons, other than alien enemies,[2] who are *per se* incapable of becoming partners.[3] This is so even in the case of undischarged bankrupts, although they may suffer from certain disabilities which will, ultimately, affect their ability to participate fully in the firm's activities.[4] Whilst physical incapacity may affect the rights of the partners *inter se*, it is irrelevant to the formation or continuance of a partnership.[5]

Even where one or more of the partners is under 18 or suffering **4-02** from a mental disorder, the partnership will not be null and void, although the incapacity may affect the partners' respective rights and duties[6] and, in some cases, lead to a dissolution of the firm.[7]

Questions of incapacity can conveniently be considered under the following headings: (*a*) aliens; (*b*) minors; (*c*) mentally disordered persons; (*d*) husbands and wives; (*e*) companies; (*f*) bankrupts and disqualified persons; and (*g*) trustees, personal representatives and nominees.

(a) Aliens[8]

An alien who is not an enemy has full capacity to enter into a **4-03** partnership and will be bound by its terms,[9] subject only to questions

---

[1] See *infra*, paras. 8–15 *et seq.*
[2] See *infra*, paras. 4–04 *et seq.*
[3] Formerly the clergy and convicts were subject to disabilities in terms of their capacity to contract, but these have long since been swept away. The status of partners subject to a disqualification order under the Company Directors Disqualification Act 1986 is unclear: see *infra*, para. 4–24.
[4] See *infra*, paras. 4–22, 4–23.
[5] See *Newstead v. Frost* [1980] 1 W.L.R. 135 (H.L.).
[6] See *infra*, paras. 4–07 *et seq.*
[7] See *infra*, paras. 4–11, 4–13, 4–14.
[8] This somewhat archaic expression is still in common usage and is, indeed, defined by the British Nationality Act 1981, s.50(1), in the following terms: "a person who is neither a Commonwealth citizen nor a British protected person nor a citizen of the Republic of Ireland." See also the Status of Aliens Act 1914, s.27(1).
[9] Co.Lit. 129b; Bac.Ab. Alien D.

of diplomatic or sovereign immunity.[10] However, an enemy alien is in a very different position.

Alien enemies

4–04 The expression "alien enemy" has a special meaning, namely a person who is either resident[11] or carrying on business in a country which is at war with the United Kingdom. Such a person's country of birth and personal attitude are wholly irrelevant[12]: either he is resident or carrying on business in such a country or he is not. Thus, a foreigner who resides in the United Kingdom and enters into partnership here will not become an alien enemy on the outbreak of war between the United Kingdom and his native country, unless he returns to reside or carry on business in that country.[13] His position will be the same if he is resident in an allied or neutral country.[14] Conversely, a United Kingdom citizen who resides or carries on business in a country with whom the United Kingdom is at war will be just as much an alien enemy as the nationals resident there.[15]

Effects of war

4–05 Where a state of war exists between the United Kingdom and another country, all commercial and other dealings with alien

---

[10] The diplomatic immunity accorded to a diplomatic agent by the Diplomatic Privileges Act 1964 does not extend to actions relating to professional or commercial activities exercised by the diplomatic agent in the United Kingdom which are outside his official functions: *ibid.* Sched. 1, Art. 31. As to the definition of a diplomatic agent, see *ibid.* s.2(1) and Sched. 1, Art. 1(*e*). Even if the immunity conferred by the Act applies, it may be expressly waived by the sending state or by the initiation of proceedings by the diplomatic agent: *ibid.* Sched. 1, Arts. 31(1), 32(2), (3). Waiver does not imply waiver of immunity in respect of the execution of the judgment, for which a separate waiver is necessary: *ibid.* Art. 32(4). It should also be noted that sovereign immunity, which was previously absolute, is now severely restricted, and is only available in respect of acts of a governmental, as opposed to commercial, nature: State Immunity Act 1978, s.3; *Amalgamated Metal Trading v. Department of Trade and Industry, Financial Times,* February 28, 1989. As to proceedings between partners where a state is a member of a U.K. partnership, see *ibid.* s.8.

[11] The word "residence" in the Trading with the Enemy Act 1939, s.2(1)(*b*) which defines "enemy" as "any individual resident in enemy territory," means *de facto* residence, irrespective of the circumstances: *Vamvakas v. Custodian of Enemy Property* [1952] 2 Q.B. 183.

[12] See *Johnstone v. Pedlar* [1921] 2 A.C. 262; also *Porter v. Freudenberg* [1915] 1 K.B. 857, and the cases cited therein; *Re Duchess of Sutherland, Bechoff & Co. v. Bubna* (1915) 31 T.L.R. 248 and 394 and (1921) 65 S.J. 513; *Janson v. Driefontein Consolidated Mines Ltd.* [1902] A.C. 510; *W. L. Ingle Ltd. v. Mannheim Insurance Co.* [1915] 1 K.B. 227.

[13] See the cases in n. 12, *supra*; also *Wells v. Williams* (1697) 1 Ld.Ray. 282, in which it was held that the defendant could not rely on his supposed status as an alien enemy by way of defence to an action brought by a foreigner resident here, even though a state of war did exist. An alien who is a subject of an enemy state and who resides in the U.K. may, however, be liable to seizure, imprisonment, and deportation, under statutory or common law powers.

[14] *Re Duchess of Sutherland, Bechoff & Co. v. Bubna* (1915) 31 T.L.R. 248 and 394 and (1921) 65 S.J. 513.

[15] As to residence in the enemy country, see *M'Connell v. Hector* (1802) 3 Bos. & Pul. 113; *O'Mealey v. Wilson* (1808) 1 Camp. 482; *cf. Roberts v. Hardy* (1815) 3 M. & S. 533 and *Ex p. Baglehole* (1812) 18 Ves.Jr. 525; as to carrying on business there, see *The Jonge Klassina* (1804) 5 Rob.Chr. 297; *The Indian Chief* (1801) 3 Rob.Chr. 12; *The Portland* (1800) 3 Rob.Chr. 41. Note also, as to the position of a partner who remains in England, *The Anglo–Mexican* [1918] A.C. 422; *The Lutzow* [1918] A.C. 435; *The Manningtry* [1916] P. 329. As to a partner who is an enemy subject in a neutral country, see *The Hypatia* [1917] P. 36.

enemies are, in the absence of a Crown licence, contrary to public policy and illegal.[16] It follows that, if such a licence is not held, any contract entered into with an alien enemy will, save in very exceptional circumstances, be void *ab initio*.[17] Equally, any contract which remains executory on the outbreak of war will be automatically terminated if its further performance will require dealings with alien enemies;[18] this will be so even if the contract contains a provision suspending such performance for as long as the war continues.[19] However, in this case the illegality does not render the contract void *ab initio* but merely makes further performance impossible, so that the rights of the contracting parties are unaffected to the extent that they accrued *before* the war.[20]

An alien enemy may not, in the absence of a licence granted by the Crown, bring an action in the United Kingdom,[21] but there are no restrictions on proceedings brought *against* such a person. As a defendant, the alien enemy may appear in the proceedings and will be in the same position as any other defendant.[22]

The property of an alien enemy may be confiscated at the **4–06** discretion of the Crown, and will generally be vested in a custodian

---

[16] *Ertel Bieber & Co. v. Rio Tinto Co.* [1918] A.C. 260; *Re Badische Co. Ltd.* [1921] 2 Ch. 331; *Tingley v. Müller* [1917] 2 Ch. 144; *Halsey v. Lowenfeld* [1916] 2 K.B. 707; *Robson v. Premier Oil & Pipe Line* [1915] 2 Ch. 124; *R. v. Kupfer* [1915] 2 K.B. 321. The restrictions imposed by the common law are supplemented by statute: see for example the Trading with the Enemy Act 1939, s.1 (as amended by the Emergency Laws (Miscellaneous Provisions) Act 1953, s.2, Sched. 2), which provides that it is an offence to trade or attempt to trade with the enemy.

[17] In *Tingley v. Müller* [1917] 2 Ch. 441, a contract entered into after the outbreak of war by a British subject with a German (acting through another British subject pursuant to an irrevocable power of attorney granted before the war), was held to be valid since its performance did not necessitate any dealings with the enemy.

[18] *Re Coutinho, Caro & Co.* [1918] 2 Ch. 384; *Halsey v. Lowenfeld* [1916] 2 K.B. 707; *Duncan, Fox & Co. v. Schrempft & Bonke* [1915] 3 K.B. 355; see also the cases cited in n. 16, *supra*. If the contract only remains executory to the extent of a payment falling to be made by the enemy, such payment can be recovered during the war: *ibid.*; *Clapham S.S. Co. v. Naamlooze, etc. Rotterdam* [1917] 2 K.B. 639; *W. L. Ingle Ltd. v. Mannheim Insurance Co.* [1915] 1 K.B. 227. Leases and other contracts which confer rights of property are not terminated: *Halsey v. Lowenfeld, supra*; *London & Northern Estates Co. v. Schlessinger* [1916] 1 K.B. 20. As to arbitration clauses, see *Dalmia Dairy Industries Ltd. v. National Bank of Pakistan* [1978] 2 Lloyd's Rep. 223.

[19] *Ertel Bieber & Co. v. Rio Tinto Co.* [1918] A.C. 260; *Re Badische Co. Ltd.* [1921] 2 Ch. 331; *Naylor, Benzon & Co. v. Krainische Industrie Gesellschaft* [1918] 2 K.B. 486; *Clapham S.S. Co. v. Naamlooze, etc. Rotterdam* [1917] 2 K.B. 639; *Zinc Corpn. v. Hirsch* [1916] 1 K.B. 541. *Fried. Krupp Akt. v. Orconera Iron Ore Co.* (1919) 88 L.J.Ch. 304; *cf. Zinc Corpn. Ltd. v. Skipwith* (1914) 31 T.L.R. 106, as to a provision to resume trading operations after the war. *Quaere*, whether a clause of the type referred to in the text might operate if the suspension of the contract and the preservation of the parties' respective obligations thereunder would not be detrimental to this country or of advantage to the enemy.

[20] See *Ertel Bieber & Co. v. Rio Tinto Co.* [1918] A.C. 260, 268, *per* Lord Dunedin, as applied in *Helbert Wagg & Co.'s Claim* [1956] Ch. 323 and considered in *Arab Bank v. Barclays Bank (Dominion, Colonial and Overseas)* [1954] A.C. 495 (where it held that a right to be paid a credit balance on a current account is an accrued right which is suspended, but not abrogated, by the outbreak of war); see also *Naylor, Benzon & Co. v. Krainische Industrie Gesellschaft* [1918] 1 K.B. 331, 345, *per* McCardie J.; *Zinc Corpn. v. Hirsch* [1916] 1 K.B. 541, 556, *per* Swinfen Eady L.J.; *Chandler v. Webster* [1904] 1 K.B. 493; *Sovfracht (V/O) v. Van Udens Scheepvaart en Agentuur Maatschapp (N.V. Gebr.)* [1943] A.C. 203.

[21] *Porter v. Freudenberg* [1915] 1 K.B. 857. Note, however, *The Mowe* [1915] P. 1.

[22] *Porter v. Freudenberg, supra*, at pp. 880 *et seq.*; *Robinson & Co. v. Continental Insurance Co. of Mannheim* [1915] 1 K.B. 155.

during the war.[23] The disposition of such property will be provided for by the peace treaty.[24]

It naturally follows from the foregoing that a partnership between a resident British citizen or subject (or a resident alien) and an alien enemy is incapable of creation or, if validly created before the outbreak of war, of further continuation thereafter.[25] In the latter case, the dissolution of the firm will be automatic and is in no way dependent on the partners' knowledge of the illegality.[26] This, of course, assumes that the United Kingdom is one of the bellicose nations; under English law different principles apply to commercial disputes between members of warring nations if the United Kingdom is in the position of a neutral.[27]

(b) Minors

4-07 A minor, *i.e.* a person under the age of 18,[28] may enter into partnership[29] but will, as a general rule, incur no liability to his partners or to third parties whilst he remains under age. When he attains 18, or even before, he may, if he chooses, repudiate the agreement,[30] but his partners will now seemingly have two options. They may either seek a restitution order under the Minors' Contracts Act 1987[31] or proceed to apply the whole of the partnership property, which naturally includes the minor's share, in payment of the firm's debts and liabilities.[32] Equally, a creditor of the firm who has obtained judgment against the firm in the proper form[33] may levy

---

[23] *Re Ferdinand ex–Tsar of Bulgaria* [1921] 1 Ch. 107; *Porter v. Freudenberg, supra*, at p. 869. Unless the Crown's power of confiscation is exercised, the enemy holds his property subject to all its obligations which may be enforced against him during the war if their performance does not involve trade or other dealings with the enemy: *Halsey v. Lowenfeld* [1916] 2 K.B. 707; *London & Northern Estates Co. v. Schlesinger* [1916] 1 K.B. 20.

[24] *Daimler Co. v. Continental Tyre etc. Co.* [1916] 2 A.C. 307; *Hugh Stevenson & Sons v. Aktiengesellschaft etc.* [1918] A.C. 239; *Tingley v. Müller* [1917] 2 Ch. 144; *Ottoman Bank v. Jebara* [1928] A.C. 269.

[25] Partnership Act 1890, s.34; *R. v. Kupfer* [1915] 2 K.B. 321; *Hugh Stevenson & Sons v. Aktiengesellschaft etc., supra*; *Rodriguez v. Speyer Bros.* [1919] A.C. 59. The decision in *Feldt v. Chamberlain* (1914) 58 S.J. 788 cannot be regarded as good law. See also *infra*, para. 24–34.

[26] See *Hudgell Yeates & Co. v. Watson* [1978] Q.B. 451 (solicitor failing to renew his practising certificate).

[27] Thus, an award under an arbitration clause contained in a contract between two belligerent states (India and Pakistan) was held to be valid and enforceable in England: *Dalmia Dairy Industries Ltd. v. National Bank of Pakistan* [1978] 2 Lloyd's Rep. 223. Equally, there can be no objection to persons resident in a neutral country forming a partnership in order to trade with the belligerent nations: *Ex p. Chavasse* (1865) 4 De G.J. & S. 655; *The Helen* (1801) 3 Rob.Chr. 224.

[28] Family Law Reform Act 1969, s.1.

[29] In *Re A. and M.* [1926] Ch. 274, the only two partners were both minors. See also, *Alexander Bulloch & Co. v. I.R.C.* [1976] S.T.C. 514 (where two minors were held not to be partners on the particular facts of the case).

[30] See *infra*, paras. 4–11, 4–12.

[31] s.3.

[32] See *Lovell v. Beauchamp* [1894] A.C. 607.

[33] *i.e.* on a judgment "against the defendant firm other than A B a minor" obtained in an action against the firm in the firm name. See the cases in the next note and *infra*, para. 14–19. If the action is not brought against the firm in the firm name, the minor partner ought not to be joined as a defendant: see the cases cited *infra*, n. 35; also *infra*, para. 14–44.

execution against such property, but not against the separate property of the minor.[34]

Lord Lindley explained the rationale behind the minor partner's **4–08** freedom from liability for partnership debts in these terms:

"The irresponsibility of an infant for the debts of a partnership of which he is a member is an obvious consequence of his general incapacity to bind himself by contract, and does not require to be supported by any special authority.[35] It might, perhaps, be thought that an infant who held himself out as a partner would be liable to persons trusting to his representations if they did not know him to be under age; but this is not so[36] . . .".

It is thus clear that, in a case of holding out,[37] the third party would not, prior to the Partnership Act 1890, have been entitled to proceed against the minor partner, even if he did not appear to be under age. There is no reason to suppose that the Act altered the law in this respect.

Torts

Just as a minor is not responsible for the torts of his agent, a minor **4–09** partner cannot be held liable for the misconduct of his co-partners.[38] He is, however, liable for his own torts, including fraud and negligence, although the standard of care expected of him in relation to the latter will vary according to his age. It follows that, subject to the latter factor, there may be some scope for an action for negligent mis-statement[39] in respect of representations made by a minor partner, whether to his co-partners or to third parties dealing with the firm. Whether such an action will lie principally depends on whether the cause of action is in substance contractual, or is so directly connected with the contract as to amount to an indirect method of enforcement. In either of the above cases, *e.g.* where a minor's negligent mis-statement has induced a third party to enter into

---

[34] *Lovell v. Beauchamp* [1894] A.C. 607; *Harris v. Beauchamp* [1893] 2 Q.B. 534.

[35] Lord Lindley nevertheless cited *Chandler v. Parkes* (1800) 3 Esp. 76; *Jaffray v. Frebain* (1803) 5 Esp. 47; *Gibbs v. Merrill* (1810) 3 Taunt. 307; and *Burgess v. Merrill* (1812) 4 Taunt. 468, which "show that an infant partner ought not to be joined as a defendant in an action against the firm."

[36] See *Price v. Hewitt* (1853) 8 Ex. 146; *Johnson v. Pye* (1665) 1 Sid. 258; Vin.Ab. Enfant, H.2, pl. 16; *Glossop v. Colman* (1815) 1 Stark 25; *Green v. Greenbank* [1816] 2 Marsh. 485.

[37] See *infra*, paras. 5–43 *et seq.*

[38] Lord Lindley added "The irresponsibility of an infant as a partner, seems therefore to be complete, except in cases of fraud." There is now more than one such exception, as appears from the text.

[39] See generally, as to such actions, *Hedley Byrne & Co. Ltd. v. Heller & Partners* [1964] A.C. 465; *Mutual Life and Citizens Assurance Co. Ltd. v. Evatt* [1971] A.C. 793; *Esso Petroleum Co. Ltd. v. Mardon* [1976] Q.B. 801. But see also *Argy Trading Development Co. Ltd. v. Lapid Developments Ltd.* [1977] 1 W.L.R. 444.

partnership with him as a result of which that third party suffers damage, no action would be allowed.[40] *Per contra*, if the minor's tortious act, although concerned with the subject-matter of the contract, is in truth independent of it.

Fraud

4–10 The liability of a minor who perpetrates a fraudulent act no longer varies solely according to the relief sought, since a restitution order may now be made in all cases.[41] Nevertheless, equitable relief, *e.g.* rescission[42] or an injunction,[43] will seemingly be granted more readily than other forms of relief, although the limits are not clearly defined.[44]

An example of the type of attitude likely to be adopted by the courts is, perhaps, to be found in a number of cases decided under the old bankruptcy laws. The general principle was that a minor could not be made bankrupt, even on his own petition, in the absence of debts for necessaries supplied to him or other debts which were legally enforceable against him.[45] However, if a minor, having fraudulently represented himself as of full age and thereby obtained credit from third parties, were subsequently made bankrupt, the adjudication would not be annulled and his deceived creditors would be paid out of his estate.[46] It may be that the position remains the same under the Insolvency Act 1986.[47]

Repudiation by minor

4–11 Whilst a minor partner is, in general, free from liability in respect of partnership debts, he cannot insist, as against his co-partners, that in taking the partnership accounts he must be credited with his due share of any profits, but not be debited with his due share of any losses. He must either repudiate the whole agreement or abide by its

---

[40] See *R. Leslie Ltd. v. Sheill* [1914] 3 K.B. 607, 620, *per* Kennedy L.J.

[41] Minors' Contracts Act 1987, s.3. And see *Wright v. Snowe* (1848) 2 De G. & Sm. 321.

[42] *Lemprière v. Lange* (1879) 12 Ch.D. 675.

[43] *Woolf v. Woolf* [1899] 1 Ch. 343, where a minor was restrained from carrying on his business in such a way as to represent it as the plaintiff's.

[44] See *R. Leslie Ltd. v. Sheill* [1914] 3 K.B. 607, where most of the earlier cases, including *Stocks v. Wilson* [1913] 2 K.B. 235, are considered. The minor may also be required to pay the costs of the action: *ibid.*; see also the cases in the previous two notes.

[45] *Re A. and M.* [1926] Ch. 274; *Lovell v. Beauchamp* [1894] A.C. 607; *Ex p. Jones* (1881) 18 Ch.D. 109; *Ex p. Henderson* (1798) 4 Ves.Jr. 163; *Ex p. Lees* (1836) 1 Deac. 705; *Belton v. Hodges* (1832) 9 Bing. 365; *Re a Debtor* [1950] Ch. 282.

[46] See *Ex p. Watson* (1809) 16 Ves.Jr. 265; *Ex p. Bates* (1841) 2 M.D. & D. 337; *Ex p. Unity Banking Association* (1858) 3 De G. & J. 63. A receiving order was set aside in *Stocks v. Wilson* [1913] 2 K.B. 235. Observations on the old bankruptcy cases are contained in that decision and in *R. Leslie Ltd. v. Sheill* [1914] 3 K.B. 607.

[47] This Act repealed and replaced the Insolvency Act 1985, which had itself replaced the Bankruptcy Act 1914 with a new regime of personal insolvency. The 1986 Act contains no provisions relating to minors but, by virtue of the Insolvency Rules 1986 (S.I. 1986 No. 1925), r. 7.51, R.S.C. Ord. 80 is applicable in the case of insolvency proceedings against a minor.

terms, and it is only under the agreement that he can claim any share of the profits.[48]

A minor partner may repudiate the partnership contract either before or within a reasonable time after he has attained 18.[49] His right to recover any money paid (or property transferred) under that contract will depend on whether he has received any benefit out of the partnership, as Lord Lindley explained:

"If [the minor] avoids the contract, and has derived no benefit from it, he is entitled to recover back any money paid by him in part performance of it[50]; but he cannot do this if he has already obtained advantages under the contract, and cannot restore the party contracting with him to the same position as if no contract had been entered into."[51]

Equally, the other partners may now seek a restitution order against the minor in respect of any property which he may have acquired under the contract.[52]

A minor partner who decides to exercise his right of repudiation on coming of age should do so promptly and unequivocally, since a person who retains a share in a partnership cannot rid himself of its incidental obligations[53] and will, moreover, risk liability for debts incurred after that date by reason of the doctrine of holding out.[54] This is well illustrated by the decision in *Goode v. Harrison*,[55] where the minor partner was known to be a member of the firm. After he had attained full age he did not expressly either affirm or disaffirm the partnership, and he was held liable for debts incurred subsequently by his co-partners. It follows that, if he is to avoid any risk of liability, a minor who has represented himself as a partner must, when he comes of age, ensure that he is not held out as a partner thereafter.   **4–12**

---

[48] See *Lovell v. Beauchamp* [1894] A.C. 607, 611; *London & N.W.Ry. v. McMichael* (1850) 5 Ex. 114.

[49] Co.Lit. 380b; *Newry and Enniskillen Railway v. Coombe* (1849) 3 Ex. 565; *Dublin and Wicklow Railway v. Black* (1852) 8 Ex. 181. In some cases a minor cannot repudiate a contract before he comes of age, unless it is to his benefit to do so: see *Waterman v. Fryer* [1922] 1 K.B. 499; *Roberts v. Gray* [1913] 1 K.B. 520. A contract of partnership is not one of such cases: see *Cowern v. Nield* [1912] 2 K.B. 419, 422, *per* Phillimore J.

[50] *Corpe v. Overton* (1833) 10 Bing. 253; *Steinberg v. Scala (Leeds) Ltd.* [1923] 2 Ch. 452.

[51] *Holmes v. Blogg* (1818) 8 Taunt. 5087; *Ex p. Taylor* (1856) 8 De G.M. & G. 254; *Valentini v. Canali* (1889) 24 Q.B.D. 166; *Steinberg v. Scala (Leeds) Ltd.* [1923] 2 Ch. 452; *Pearce v. Brain* [1929] 2 K.B. 310. *Hamilton v. Vaughan-Sherrin Electrical Engineering Co.* [1894] 3 Ch. 589 cannot be relied upon: see *Steinberg v. Scala (Leeds) Ltd.*, *supra*.

[52] Minors' Contracts Act 1987, s.3.

[53] See *London & North-Western Railway v. McMichael* (1850) 5 Ex. 855; *Cork and Bandon Railway v. Cazenove* (1847) 10 Q.B. 935; *Ebbett's Case* (1870) L.R. 5 Ch.App. 302. Cf. *Baker's Case* (1870) L.R. 7 Ch.App. 115.

[54] Partnership Act 1890, s.14, *infra*, paras. 5–43 *et seq*.

[55] (1821) 5 B. & A. 147.

(c) Persons Suffering from Mental Disorder

4–13 A contact entered into by a person suffering from mental disorder will be binding on him so long as (1) the other contracting party acted bona fide and was unaware of his incapacity[56] and (2) a receiver had not, at that time, already been appointed[57] or Court of Protection proceedings commenced.[58] It necessarily follows that, subject to those two conditions, such a person may enter into a valid contract of partnership and, thereby, assume all the rights and liabilities which normally attend that relationship. However, it should be noted that, whether the contract is *per se* voidable or not, the Judge of the Court of Protection[59] is empowered, in the course of administering the property and affairs of a patient,[60] *inter alia* to give directions for the carrying out of any contract entered into by him and, indeed, for the dissolution of any partnership of which he is a member.[61]

4–14 Similar principles apply in the case of a supervening mental disorder affecting a member of an existing firm. Thus, it is clear that a partner's mental incapacity will not, of itself, dissolve the firm or, indeed, affect his continuing entitlement to a share of the partnership profits.[62] The corollary is, of course, his continuing responsibility for the debts and liabilities of the firm.[63] However, in such a case, account must again be taken of the overriding powers exercisable by the Court of Protection.[64]

(d) Husband and Wives

4–15 Married women were formerly subject to wide ranging disabilities in terms of their legal capacity, but those disabilities have long since been removed.[65] Nevertheless, the involvement of a married woman in a business with her husband may still have certain specific consequences.

Loans

4–16 If a wife lends money to her husband, or vice versa, and a bankruptcy order is subsequently made against the borrower, the

---

[56] See *Hart v. O'Connor* [1985] A.C. 1000, P.C., where the earlier cases (particularly *Imperial Loan Co. v. Stone* [1892] 1 Q.B. 599 and *Molton v. Camroux* (1849) 4 Ex. 17) are considered.
[57] Pursuant to Mental Health Act 1983 s.99.
[58] See *Re Marshall* [1920] 1 Ch. 284; also *Re Walker* [1905] 1 Ch. 160. And see Heywood & Massey, *Court of Protection Practice* (12th ed.), p.227.
[59] As to the meaning of this expression, see the Mental Health Act 1983, s.94(1), as amended by the Public Trustee and Administration of Funds Act 1986, s.2(2).
[60] This expression is defined in the Mental Health Act 1983, s.94(2).
[61] See *ibid.* s.96(1).
[62] *Jones v. Noy* (1833) 2 M. & K. 125.
[63] *Sadler v. Lee* (1843) 6 Beav. 324. At this point Lord Lindley, referring to *Sadler v. Lee*, unaccountably mentioned only the continuing liability of the incapacitated partner for the "subsequent misconduct of the other members."
[64] See the Mental Health Act 1983, s.96(1).
[65] See as to these disabilities, the 14th ed. of this work, at pp. 60–63.

lender will be postponed to all the borrower's other creditors.[66] As under the previous law, it would seem that if the borrower is a member of a firm and the money is lent for the purpose of its business, upon the firm being wound up as an unregistered company,[67] the lender will be postponed to the borrower's separate creditors *and* to the joint creditors of the firm.[68] However, a loan to a firm of which the bankrupt spouse was a member will be repayable out of its assets like any other partnership debt, even though that spouse's separate creditors may thereby be preferred.[69]

Partnerships between husband and wife

Husbands and wives frequently enter into partnership together **4–17** although, as in the case of other contractual obligations, the court may be less ready to *infer* the existence of that relationship.[70] Equally, where a partnership is found to exist, the court will not ignore the matrimonial background. Thus, in *Bothe v. Amos*,[71] where the partnership was tied in closely with the marital relationship, the break up of the marriage in effect put an end to the partnership.

It should also be noted that, on the termination of the marriage, the spouses' respective rights in and to the partnership business may fall to be dealt with by the Family Division under the wide jurisdiction exercised over the property rights of husband and wife.[72]

Contributions to spouse's business

Although not strictly relevant to the law of partnership, brief **4–18** mention may also be made in this connection of the interest which a husband or wife may acquire as a result of contributions to the success of a business carried on by his or her spouse. Thus, where a

---

[66] Insolvency Act 1986, s.329. The predecessor of this section (the Bankruptcy Act 1914, s.36) treated a loan made by a husband differently from a loan made by a wife, but the distinction has, for obvious reasons, not been preserved. The current section also applies where the creditor marries the debtor before the commencement of the bankruptcy.

[67] See further, *infra*, paras. 27–07 *et seq*.

[68] See *Ex p. Neilson and Craig v. The Trustee* [1929] 1 Ch. 534.

[69] *Ex p. Nottingham* (1887) 19 Q.B.D. 88 (a decision under the Married Women's Property Act 1882, s.3), which is thought still to be good law; see also *Ex p. Neilson and Craig v. The Trustee*, *supra*.

[70] *Parrington v. Parrington* [1951] W.N. 534; *Nixon v. Nixon* [1969] 1 W.L.R. 1676; *Simon v. Simon* (1971) 115 S.J. 673; *Re Cummins* [1972] Ch. 62; *Britton v. The Commissioners* (1986) V.A.T.T.R. 209. It is submitted that the court's reluctance to infer the existence of a partnership will often stem from a failure specifically to raise the question for determination; in *Re John's Assignment Trusts* [1970] 1 W.L.R. 955, Goff J. found the conclusion that a partnership existed inescapable: see *ibid*. p.960. Note, also, *Saywell v. Pope* [1979] S.T.C. 824. And see *Butler v. Butler* (1885) 16 Q.B.D. 374; *Burgess v. Florence Nightingale Hospital for Gentlewomen* [1955] 1 Q.B. 349; *Behrens v. Bertram Mills Circus* [1957] 2 Q.B. 1.

[71] [1976] Fam. 46. *Quaere*, was the court fully seised of the partnership issue?

[72] See further, *infra*, para. 24–44.

wife has worked for many years without wages and has thereby assisted her husband to build up a valuable business, the court will be likely to hold that she has acquired an interest therein, or in some asset purchased out of the profits thereof.[73]

(e) Companies

General principle

4–19   Lord Lindley summarised the position in these terms:

"There is no general principle of law which prevents a corporation from being a partner with another corporation or with ordinary individuals, except the principle that a corporation cannot lawfully employ its funds for purposes not authorised by its constitution."[74]

This is still the position,[75] save that the Companies Act 1989 has effectively swept away the *ultra vires* doctrine: now the validity of anything which a company may do can no longer be questioned on the ground that it is not authorised by its memorandum.[76] Nevertheless, viewed from a purely internal perspective, a company's ability to enter into partnership will for the most part depend on the terms of its memorandum and articles, as illustrated by the decision in *Newstead v. Frost*,[77] where it was held that the word "all kinds of financial ... or other operations" in a company's memorandum authorised it to carry on a business in partnership. However, it is a relatively simple matter to amend the memorandum so as to ensure that a partnership venture is duly authorised.[78]

---

[73] See *Nixon v. Nixon* [1969] 1 W.L.R. 1676; *Muetzel v. Muetzel* [1970] 1 W.L.R. 188; *Simon v. Simon* (1971) 115 S.J. 673; *Re Cummins* [1972] Ch. 62. The principles enunciated in the above cases might conceivably be applied so as to confer on a wife an interest in a partnership business carried on by her husband and others, but surely that interest would be merely derivative (*i.e.* it would form part of the husband's share) and would not affect the other partners' entitlements. Such interest would, in any event, be subject to any provisions affecting the husband's share which may be contained in the partnership agreement, *e.g.* accruer on retirement or death.

[74] At this point Lord Lindley referred to *Gill v. The Manchester, Sheffield etc., Railway Co.* (1873) L.R. 8 Q.B. 186 "as to one company being the agent of another, if not its partner." He went on "Having regard ... to this principle [*i.e. the second principle in the quotation set out in the text*], it may be considered as prima facie *ultra vires* for an incorporated company to enter into partnership with other persons", citing in support two American cases, *Sharon Coal Corp. v. Fulton Bank*, 7 Wend. 412; *Catskill Bank v. Gray*, 14 Barb. 479). This cannot, on any footing, now be regarded as an accurate statement of the law: see *infra.*

[75] See, for example, *Hugh Stevenson & Son v. Aktiengesellschaft, etc., Industrie* [1918] A.C. 240; *Newstead v. Frost* [1980] 1 W.L.R. 135 (H.L.). And see *infra,* paras. 11–02 *et seq.*

[76] Companies Act 1985, s.35(1) (as substituted by the Companies Act 1989, s.108(1)). See also *ibid.* ss.35A, 35B (as added by the Companies Act 1989, s.108(1)); and note the provisions of *ibid.* s.322A (as added by the Companies Act 1989, s.109(1)).

[77] [1980] 1 W.L.R. 135, 141.

[78] Companies Act 1985, ss.4 (as substituted by the Companies Act 1989, s.110(2)), 5. Note also the latitude conferred by a "general commercial company" objects clause: see *ibid.* s.3A (as prospectively inserted by the Companies Act 1989, s.110(1)).

A company is a person within the meaning of that word in section **4–20** 1(1) of the Partnership Act 1890.[79]

Enemy companies

In the event of war, whilst the question whether a company is to be **4–21** regarded as an enemy will prima facie be determined by reference to its country of incorporation, the ultimate test is one of control. In order to identify the seat of control, the "corporate veil" may be lifted in order to see whether the company's agents or the persons in *de facto* control of its affairs, whether authorised or not, are resident in an enemy country or, even if not so resident, are taking the side of, or are otherwise themselves controlled by, the enemy.[80] It is only on the latter question that it is necessary to enquire whether or not the shareholders themselves are enemies. However, if the country of incorporation is England, the company will remain English and control by the enemy will not exonerate it from the operation of English law.[81]

(f) Bankrupts and disqualified persons

The Partnership Act 1890 provides that the bankruptcy of a partner **4–22** will dissolve the firm, but this may be overridden by agreement.[82] There is, as such, no statutory or other prohibition on a bankrupt becoming or remaining a partner, although account must be taken of section 360(1) of the Insolvency Act 1986, which is in the following terms:

"The bankrupt is guilty of an offence if—

(a) either alone or jointly with any other person, he obtains credit[83] to the extent of the prescribed amount[84] or more without giving the person from whom he obtains it the relevant information about his status; or

(b) he engages (whether directly or indirectly) in any business under a name other than that in which he was adjudged

---

[79] Interpretation Act 1978, s.5, Sched. 1. As to local authorities, see *Jones v. Sec. of State for Wales* (1974) 28 P. & C.R. 280.

[80] See *Daimler Co. Ltd. v. Continental Tyre Co.* [1916] 2 A.C. 307, 345–346, *per* Lord Parker; *Kuenigl v. Donnersmarck* [1955] 1 Q.B. 515; *The Hamborn* [1919] A.C. 993; *Re Badische Co.* [1921] 2 Ch. 331, 338–342 and 365–372, *per* Russell J.; also *The Roumanian* [1915] P. 26. The question whether a company is to be regarded as an enemy is distinct from the question whether it is trading with the enemy: see *Re Hilckes* [1917] 1 K.B. 48.

[81] *Kuenigl v. Donnersmarck* [1955] 1 Q.B. 515.

[82] Partnership Act 1890, s.33(1). See further, *infra*, para. 24–22.

[83] Two instances in which the bankrupt is treated as having obtained credit are set out in subs. (2). Note also *R. v. Smith* (1915) 11 Crim.App.R. 81; *R. v. Hartley* [1972] 2 Q.B. 1; *R v. Miller* [1977] 1 W.L.R. 1129 (decisions under the Bankruptcy Act 1914, s.155).

[84] Currently £250: The Insolvency Proceedings (Monetary Limits) Order 1986 (S.I. 1986 No. 1996), Art. 3, Sched., Pt. II.

bankrupt without disclosing to all persons with whom he enters into any business transaction the name in which he was so adjudged."

4–23 It is considered that, consistently with the position under the equivalent section of the Bankruptcy Act 1914,[85] no offence would be committed under limb (*a*) of the section if the bankrupt obtains credit for a third party, *e.g.* his partner;[86] if, however, he obtains credit on behalf of the *partnership* of which he is a member, it will be obtained jointly and an offence will be committed. As to limb (*b*), it is thought that a bankrupt could not properly enter into or join a partnership which carries on business in any name other than his own, unless the bankruptcy is disclosed to every person dealing with the firm.[87]

In addition to his liability to be prosecuted under the section, a bankrupt cannot enforce any agreement entered into in breach of its provisions.[88]

Disqualification orders

4–24 Where an insolvent partnership is wound up as an unregistered company, the court may in certain circumstances make an order against one or more of the partners under the Company Directors Disqualification Act 1986.[89] Such an order will seemingly prohibit those partners from entering into partnership during the period of disqualification, without the leave of the court.[90] However, it is questionable whether contravention of such an order would, as such, render the firm illegal.[91]

(g) Trustees, personal representatives and nominees

Trustees and personal representatives

4–25 A trustee or personal representative may clearly enter into partnership, although he will be personally liable for any debts and liabilities thereby incurred.[92] Whether he will be entitled to an indemnity out of the trust fund or estate will, in essence, depend on

---

[85] Bankruptcy Act 1914, s.155(a). Note, however, that in a number of cases, the courts have stressed that the Insolvency Act 1986 introduced a new insolvency regime, so that cases decided under the 1914 Act may have no or only limited relevance: see *infra*, para. 27–110, n. 93.

[86] *R. v. Godwin* (1980) 71 Cr.App.R. 97. *Per contra*, if credit is obtained for a company which is in reality the bankrupt's alter ego: *ibid.*

[87] It is submitted that a partnership formed with the intention of committing an offence under the above section would prima facie be illegal.

[88] *De Choisy v. Hynes* [1937] 4 All E.R. 54 (a decision under the Bankruptcy Act 1914, s.155).

[89] See *infra*, para. 27–64.

[90] Company Directors Disqualification Act 1986, s.1.

[91] See *ibid.* s.15 and *infra*, para. 27–64, n. 33.

[92] See *infra*, paras. 26–27 *et seq.* Also *Muir v. City of Glasgow Bank* (1879) 4 App.Cas. 337.

whether his activities constitute a breach of trust.[93] It might be thought obvious that the trustee or personal representative will not thereby constitute his beneficiaries as partners,[94] but the Department of Trade and Industry has expressly confirmed that, in the case of limited partnerships in the venture capital field,[95] "where one of the partners ... is the trustee of an unauthorised unit trust for exempt funds the partner concerned will be regarded as a single partner for the purposes of the 20 partner limit." Why it was thought necessary to obtain such confirmation is unclear.

Nominees

The position of a nominee is more difficult. It is submitted that, in **4-26** the case of a bare nominee whose status is known to and accepted by his co-partners, the true partner will be the nominee's principal. Equally, if the other partners insist on contracting with the nominee as principal, albeit that he so contracts for the ultimate benefit of his own principal, it is difficult to see how the latter could be regarded as a partner.[96]

2. THE SIZE RESTRICTIONS

Position at common law

Apart from statute, there is no limit to the number of persons who **4-27** may be members of a partnership.[97]

Statutory restrictions

Although there have in the past been a number of statutory **4-28** limitations on the size of partnerships, attended with various penalties, the only present restriction is to be found in section 716 of the Companies Act 1985, which is of general application.[98] That section (so far as relevant) provides as follows:

"(1) No company, association, or partnership consisting of more than 20 persons shall be formed for the purpose of carrying on any business that has for its object the acquisition of gain by the

---

[93] See *infra*, paras. 26–33 *et seq.*

[94] See *Smith v. Anderson* (1880) 15 Ch.D. 247. And see, generally, *infra*, paras. 26–37 *et seq.*

[95] See the Statement issued by the British Venture Capital Association on May 26, 1987.

[96] See, generally, the judgments of the Court of Appeal in *Smith v. Anderson* (1880) 15 Ch.D. 247. And see also, for an analogous situation, *infra*, para. 12–174.

[97] The supposed illegality of partnerships so large as to be incapable of suing and being sued was, however, discussed in *Lindley on Companies* (6th ed.), Vol. I, pp. 180 *et seq.*

[98] *Cf.* the Companies Act 1948, s.429 which (in its original form) applied different restrictions in the case of banking partnerships.

company, association, or partnership, or by its individual members, unless it is registered as a company under this Act, or is formed in pursuance of some other Act of Parliament,[99] or of letters patent.

(2) However, this does not prohibit the formation—

(a) for the purpose of carrying on practice as solicitors, of a partnership consisting of persons each of whom is a solicitor[1];

(b) for the purpose of carrying on practice as accountants, of *a partnership which is eligible for appointment as a company auditor under section 25 of the Companies Act 1989*[2];

(c) for the purpose of carrying on business as members of a recognised stock exchange,[3] of a partnership consisting of persons each of whom is a member of that stock exchange[4];

(d) for any purpose prescribed by regulations (which may include a purpose mentioned above), of a partnership of a description so prescribed."[5]

4–29   In addition to the exemptions conferred by the section itself, the following professional firms are exempted from the operation of section 716(1), pursuant to a series of rules, some of which were originally made under section 120 of the Companies Act 1967[6]:

(i) partnerships of surveyors, auctioneers, valuers, estate agents, land agents, and estate managers, where not less than three-quarters of the total number of partners are members of one or more of the relevant professional bodies;[7]

---

[99] A limited partnership is formed "in pursuance of some other Act," *i.e.* the Limited Partnerships Act 1907. The restrictions applicable to such partnerships are contained in the Limited Partnerships Act 1907, s.4(2) and the Companies Act 1985, s.717 (as amended). See *infra*, para. 29–02.

[1] This expression is defined in relation to England and Wales, as a solicitor of the Supreme Court: *ibid.* subs. (3) (as substituted by the Companies Act 1989, Sched. 19, para. 15(3)). The Act does not require a solicitor to hold a practising certificate, even though that is a prerequisite of practice: see the Solicitors Act 1974, s.1(c); also *infra*, para. 8–43.

[2] The italicised words were substituted by the Companies Act 1989 (Eligibility For Appointment as Company Auditor) (Consequential Amendments) Regulations 1991 (S.I. 1991 No. 1997), reg. 2, Sched., para. 53(3).

[3] The expression "recognised stock exchange" is defined in the Companies Act 1985, s.716(4) (as substituted by the Companies Act 1989, Sched. 19, para. 15(3)).

[4] This paragraph was formerly followed by a definition of "recognised stock exchange" (as inserted by the Financial Services Act 1986, Sched. 16, para. 22) but this definition was omitted by the Companies Act 1989, Sched. 19, para. 15(2). See also the preceding note.

[5] This paragraph was added by the Companies Act 1989, Sched. 19, para. 15(2). It seems unlikely that this amendment will herald a general relaxation in the size restrictions *beyond* the professional or quasi-professional spheres.

[6] Those regulations made prior to the Companies Act 1985 must be treated as made under *ibid.* s.716(1)(d): Interpretation Act 1978, s.17(2)(b); Companies Consolidation (Consequential Provisions) Act 1985, s.31(2), (11).

[7] The Partnerships (Unrestricted Size) No. 1 Regulations 1968 (S.I. 1968 No. 1222), reg. 1(b), Sched. The specified bodies set out in *ibid.* Sched., Pt. II are the Royal Institution of Chartered Surveyors, the Chartered Lands Agents' Society, the Chartered Auctioneers' and Estate Agents' Institute and the Incorporated Society of Valuers and Auctioneers. It should, however, be noted that the Chartered Land Agents' Society and the Chartered Auctioneers' and Estate Agents' Institute have since amalgamated with the Royal Institution of Chartered Surveyors.

(ii) partnerships of actuaries, where all the partners are Fellows of either the Institute of Actuaries or the Faculty of Actuaries;[8]

(iii) partnerships of what are styled building designers,[9] where not less than three-quarters of the partners are either registered under the Architects (Registration) Act 1931[10] or are recognised by the Engineering Council[11] as a chartered engineer or by the Royal Institution of Chartered Surveyors as a chartered surveyor;[12]

(iv) partnerships of loss adjusters, where not less than three-quarters of the total number of partners are members of the Chartered Institute of Loss Adjusters;[13]

(v) partnerships of insurance brokers, where all the partners are registered as such or are enrolled bodies corporate;[14]

(vi) partnerships of town planners, where not less than three-quarters of the partners are members of the Royal Town Planning Institute;[15]

(vii) multi-national partnerships formed between solicitors and registered foreign lawyers;[16]

(viii) stockbroking partnerships which are, on formation, member firms of the London Stock Exchange by virtue of having succeeded to the business of other member firms;[17]

(ix) partnerships of consulting engineers, where the majority of the partners are recognised by The Engineering Council as chartered engineers;[18]

(x) partnerships of patent agents, where each partner is a registered patent agent[19] or, in the case of a firm comprising

---

[8] The Partnerships (Unrestricted Size) No. 2 Regulations 1970 (S.I. 1970 No. 835), reg. 2.

[9] This expression does not denote a specific profession or qualification, but represents a compendious reference to those professions involved in building design.

[10] At the time of writing it seems possible that this Act will be repealed in the near future.

[11] The reference to the Engineering Council was substituted for a reference to the Council of Engineering Institutions by the Partnerships (Unrestricted Size) No. 4 (Amendment) Regulations 1992 (S.I. 1992 No. 1438), reg. 2.

[12] The Partnerships (Unrestricted Size) No. 4 Regulations 1970 (S.I. 1970 No. 1319), reg. 2 (as amended).

[13] The Partnerships (Unrestricted Size) No. 5 Regulations 1982 (S.I. 1982 No. 530), reg. 2.

[14] The Partnerships (Unrestricted Size) No. 6 Regulations 1990 (S.I. 1990 No. 1581), reg. 2(1).

[15] The Partnerships (Unrestricted Size) No. 7 Regulations 1990 (S.I. 1990 No. 1969), reg. 2. All the partners must, in fact, be individuals holding corporate membership of the Institute: *ibid.* reg. 3.

[16] The Partnerships (Unrestricted Size) No. 8 Regulations 1991 (S.I. 1991 No. 2729), reg. 2. As to the definition of a multi–national partnership, see the Courts and Legal Services Act 1990, s.89(9). And see, generally, the Solicitors' Practice Rules 1990 as amended by the Multi-National Legal Practice Rules 1991.

[17] The Partnerships (Unrestricted Size) No. 9 Regulations 1992 (S.I. 1992 No. 1028), reg. 2(1). The London Stock Exchange is defined in *ibid.* reg. 2(2) as the International Stock Exchange of the United Kingdom and the Republic of Ireland.

[18] The Partnerships (Unrestricted Size) No. 10 Regulations 1992 (S.I. 1992 No. 1349), reg. 2. These regulations revoked the former Partnerships (Unrestricted Size) No. 3 Regulations 1970 (S.I. 1970 No. 992).

[19] The Partnerships (Unrestricted Size) No. 11 Regulations 1994 (S.I. 1994 No. 644), reg. 2 (1)(a), (2)(a). These regulations revoked the Partnerships (Unrestricted Size) No. 1 Regulations 1968 (S.I. 1968 No. 1222), reg. 1(a).

both patent agents and trade mark agents, where each partner is duly registered[20] *and* at least one quarter of the partners are patent agents;[21] and

(xi) partnerships of registered trade mark agents, where each partner is a registered trade mark agent[22] or, in the case of a firm comprising both trade mark agents and patent agents, where each partner is duly registered[23] *and* at least one quarter of the partners are registered trade mark agents.[24]

4–30   A partnership contravening the above restrictions would be illegal and thus incapable of creation or, in the case of an existing firm, of continued existence.[25] One way of avoiding this result might be the creation of one or more "parallel" partnerships, although care must be taken to avoid complete identity between the members thereof.[26] Alternatively, it may be possible to resort to trustee or, perhaps, nominee partners.[27]

---

[20] See the Copyright, Designs and Patents Act 1988, ss.275, 282; Register of Patent Agents Rules 1990 (S.I. 1990 No. 1457); Register of Trade Mark Agents Rules 1990 (S.I. 1990 No. 1458).

[21] The Partnerships (Unrestricted Size) No. 11 Regulations 1994, reg. 2(1)(c); Patent Agents (Mixed Partnerships and Bodies Corporate) Rules 1994 (S.I. 1994 No. 362), r. 3(a), (b).

[22] The Partnerships (Unrestricted Size) No. 11 Regulations 1994, regs. 2(1)(b), (2)(b).

[23] See *supra*, n. 20.

[24] The Partnerships (Unrestricted Size) No. 11 Regulations 1994, reg. 2(1)(c); Registered Trade Mark Agents (Mixed Partnerships and Bodies Corporate) Rules 1994 (S.I. 1994 No. 363), r. 3.

[25] See *infra*, para. 8–46.

[26] But note, in this context, the Value Added Tax Act 1983, Sched. 1, para. 1A, considered *infra*, para. 37–10.

[27] See *supra*, paras. 4–25, 4–26.

CHAPTER 5

RULES FOR ASCERTAINING THE EXISTENCE OF A PARTNERSHIP

1. GENERAL OBSERVATIONS

THE ultimate test of the existence of a partnership is by reference to **5-01** the statutory definition set out in section 1 of the Partnership Act 1890,[1] as supplemented by the rules set out in section 2. Although the earlier cases, on which those sections were based, may be of relevance, they cannot take precedence over the provisions of the Act itself.

Partnership Act 1890, section 2

This section provides as follows: **5-02**

"2. In determining whether a partnership does or does not exist, regard shall be had to the following rules:

(1) Joint tenancy, tenancy in common, joint property, common property, or part ownership does not of itself create a partnership as to anything so held or owned, whether the tenants or owners do or do not share any profits made by the use thereof.

(2) The sharing of gross returns does not of itself create a partnership, whether the persons sharing such returns have or have not a joint or common right or interest in any property from which or from the use of which the returns are derived.[2]

(3) The receipt by a person of a share of the profits of a business is prima facie evidence that he is a partner in the business but the receipt of such a share, or of a payment contingent on or varying with the profits of a business, does not of itself make him a partner in the business; and in particular—

(a) The receipt by a person of a debt or other liquidated amount by instalments or otherwise out of the accruing profits of a business does not of itself make him a partner in the business or liable as such:

---

[1] See *supra*, paras. 2–01 *et seq*.
[2] There may be an intermediate position between sharing (net) profits and sharing gross returns, *e.g.* where the expenses of only one of the parties is to be deducted in computing the profits: see the various decisions concerning arrangements between publishers and authors cited *infra*, para. 5–30, n. 88.

(b) A contract for the remuneration of a servant or agent of a person engaged in a business by a share of the profits of the business does not of itself make the servant or agent a partner in the business or liable as such[3]:

(c) A person being the widow or child of a deceased partner, and receiving by way of annuity a portion of the profits made in the business in which the deceased person was a partner, is not by reason only of such receipt a partner in the business or liable as such:

(d) The advance of money by way of a loan to a person engaged or about to engage in any business on a contract with that person that the lender[4] shall receive a rate of interest varying with the profits, or shall receive a share of the profits arising from carrying on the business, does not of itself make the lender a partner with the person or persons carrying on the business or liable as such. Provided that the contract is in writing, and signed by or on behalf of all the parties thereto:

(e) A person receiving by way of annuity or otherwise a portion of the profits of a business in consideration of the sale by him of the goodwill of the business is not by reason only of such receipt a partner in the business or liable as such."

The three basic rules embodied in the section will be considered in detail in subsequent parts of this Chapter.

Application of section 2

5–03   With one exception (the receipt of a share of profits), the above rules are formulated as negative propositions and merely establish the evidential weight to be attached where the particular facts of a case precisely duplicate those set out in the section. However, it will rarely, if ever, be possible to divorce those facts from the surrounding circumstances so as to permit the statutory rules to be applied in their pure form, as Lord Lindley explained in his Supplement on the Partnership Act 1890:

"The rules contained in this section only state the weight which is to be attached to the facts mentioned, when such facts stand alone. Those facts, when taken in connection with the other facts of the case, may be of the greatest importance, but when there are other

---

[3] Paragraphs (b) to (e) respectively re-enacted, with slight modifications, Bovill's Act (28 & 29 Vict. c.86), ss.2, 3, 1 and 4.

[4] *Not* a third party: *Re Pinto Leite and Nephews* [1929] 1 Ch. 221.

facts to be considered this section will be found to be of very little assistance."

In cases of the latter type, the statutory rules in effect give way to a principle so fundamental that it is not expressly stated in the Act itself,[5] namely that, in Lord Lindley's original formulation:

"in determining the existence of a partnership ... regard must be paid to the true contract and intention of the parties as appearing from the whole facts of the case. Although this principle is no longer expressed it is still law."[6]

Construction of agreement

Any agreement must be construed as a whole: the mere fact that **5-04** the parties describe themselves as partners is not conclusive,[7] nor does the use of the word "syndicate" imply the existence of a partnership.[8] On the other hand, the parties may agree to share profits and losses, but at the same time declare that they are *not* to be partners: it will then be for the court to identify their real status. Although a declaration against partnership will be ineffective when all the indicia of partnership are present,[9] it may affect the interpretation of other clauses and, thereby, rebut inferences which could otherwise be drawn from them if they stood alone. Thus, such a declaration may be of particular significance where the nature of the relationship does not appear clearly from the remainder of the agreement. In *Adam v. Newbigging*,[10] Lord Halsbury summarised the position as follows:

"If a partnership in fact exists, a community of interest in the adventure being carried on in fact, no concealment of name, no

---

[5] In his Supplement on the Act, Lord Lindley pointed out that this principle was expressly stated when the Bill was first introduced into the House of Lords.

[6] See the Partnership Act 1890, s.46, and *Davis v. Davis* [1894] 1 Ch. 393; *Re Beard & Co.* [1915] Hansell Bank.Rep. 191; *Walker West Developments Ltd. v. F. J. Emmett Ltd.* (1978) 252 E.G. 1171; *Saywell v. Pope* [1979] S.T.C. 824. Lord Lindley observed that this principle had been recognised ever since *Cox v. Hickman* (1860) 8 H.C.L. 268; see also *Badeley v. Consolidated Bank* (1888) 38 Ch.D. 238, 258, *per* Lindley L.J.; *Hawksley v. Outram* [1892] 3 Ch. 359; *Mollwo, March & Co. v. Court of Wards* (1872) L.R. 4 P.C. 419; *Pooley v. Driver* (1876) 5 Ch.D. 458; *Walker v. Hirsch* (1884) 27 Ch.D. 460; *Ross v. Parkyns* (1875) 20 Eq. 331; *Trower & Sons v. Ripstein* [1944] A.C. 254.

[7] See *Goddard v. Mills, The Times*, February 16, 1929; *Newstead v. Frost* [1980] 1 W.L.R. 135 (H.L.); *H.E. the Minister of Public Works of the Government of Kuwait v. Sir Frederick Snow & Partners* [1981] Com.L.R. 103; *Norton Warburg Holdings Ltd. v. Perera* (1982) 132 N.L.J. 296.

[8] *Tyser v. The Shipowners Syndicate (Reassured)* [1896] 1 Q.B. 135.

[9] See *Adam v. Newbigging* (1888) 13 App.Cas. 308, 315, *per* Lord Halsbury; *Ex p. Delhasse* (1878) 7 Ch.D. 511; *Moore v. Davis* (1879) 11 Ch.D. 261 (where there was only a qualified declaration against partnership; had it been unqualified, the outcome might have been different: see the observations of Wrottesley J. in *Fenston v. Johnstone (Inspector of Taxes)* (1940) 23 T.C. 29). See also *Weiner v. Harris* [1910] 1 K.B. 285, 290, *per* Cozens-Hardy M.R.; *Pooley v. Driver* (1876) 5 Ch.D. 460; *Fenston v. Johnstone (Inspector of Taxes), supra; Stekel v. Ellice* [1973] 1 W.L.R. 191. And see *Horne v. Pollard and Anderson* [1935] N.Z.L.R. s. 125.

[10] (1888) 13 App.Cas. 308, 315.

verbal equivalent for the ordinary phrases of profit or loss, no indirect expedient for enforcing control over the adventure will prevent the substance and reality of the transaction being adjudged to be a partnership; and I think I should add, as applicable to this case, that the separation of different stipulations of one arrangement into different deeds[11] will not alter the real arrangement, whatever in fact that arrangement is proved to be, and no 'phrasing of it' by dexterous draftsmen, to quote one of the letters, will avail to avert the legal consequences of the contract."

5–05   In *Weiner v. Harris*[12] Cozens-Hardy M.R. was more forceful:

"Two parties enter into a transaction and say 'It is hereby declared there is no partnership between us.' The Court pays no regard to that. The Court looks at the transaction and says 'Is this, in point of law, really a partnership?' It is not in the least conclusive that the parties have used a term or language intended to indicate that the transaction is not that which in law it is."

5–06   If the agreement is not in writing the intention of the parties must naturally be ascertained from their words and conduct.[13] Moreover, in construing any agreement, account must be taken of any subsequent modifications which may have been introduced by the parties, whether intentionally or unintentionally.[14]

Labelling: joint ventures, etc.

5–07   Equally, it is not possible to avoid partnership by describing the relationship between the participants in some other way, *e.g.* as joint venturers; the label will be ignored and the court will look to the substance of the transaction rather than its outward form.[15] Conversely, it cannot automatically be assumed that the participants in a transaction described as a joint venture do *not* each intend to carry on their own separate businesses: such situations are by no means unknown, *e.g.* share farming and oil exploration ventures.[16] In

---

[11] *Cf. Lewis v. Frank Love* [1961] 1 W.L.R. 261.

[12] [1910] 1 K.B. 285, 290.

[13] However, the evidence will frequently be insufficient to prove that a partnership exists: see, for example, *Swiss Air Transport Co. Ltd. v. Palmer* [1976] 2 Lloyd's Rep. 604. And see also *Eames v. Stepnell Properties Ltd.* [1967] 1 W.L.R. 593; *Scott v. Ricketts* [1967] 1 W.L.R. 828; *Johnston v. Heath* [1970] 1 W.L.R. 1567; *Vater v. Tarbuck* (1970) 214 E.G. 267.

[14] Partnership Act 1890, s.19. See also *infra*, paras. 10–10 *et seq.*

[15] See *Paterson v. McKenzie* [1921] G.L.R. 43; *Canny Gabriel Castle Jackson Advertising v. Volume Sales (Finance)* (1974) 131 C.L.R. 321.

[16] See further, as to share farming agreements, *infra*, para. 5–19. Another example cited in earlier editions of this work is that of underwriters assuming a fractional proportion of an insurance liability under the terms of a single policy (albeit dependent on the precise terms of that policy): *Tyser v. Shipowners Syndicate (Reassured)* [1896] 1 Q.B. 135. Similarly, the joint ownership and operation of a ship would not necessarily create a partnership.

all such cases the court must carefully scrutinise the parties' arrangements in order to ascertain their true intentions.

2. CO-OWNERSHIP

Co-owners not necessarily partners

As is clearly established by section 2(1) of the Partnership Act **5–08** 1890, a partnership will not necessarily subsist between the co-owners of property, whatever the manner of their acquisition, unless that was their original intention.[17] An illustration of this principle may perhaps be found in *Re Fisher & Sons*,[18] albeit that the true basis for the decision is unclear. On the other hand, if premises are purchased by, and vested in, co-owners who subsequently carry on a business from those premises, there may be a partnership in the business, even if there is none in the premises.[19]

Co-ownership and partnership compared

The principal differences between co-ownership and partnership[20] **5–09** may be summarised as follows:

1. Co-ownership does not necessarily result from an agreement. Partnership is the result of an express or implied agreement, even in those cases where the creation of a partnership was not intended.[21]

---

[17] See the Partnership Act 1890, s.2(1); also *Kay v. Johnston* (1856) 21 Beav. 536. Whether the co-owners intend to become partners may, of course, be doubtful: see, for example, *Sharpe v. Cummings* (1844) 2 Dowl. & L. 504; *Wilson v. Holloway* [1893] 2 Ch. 340; *Davis v. Davis* [1894] 1 Ch. 393; *National Insurance Co. of New Zealand Ltd. v. Bray* [1934] N.Z.L.R. s. 67. See also *George Hall & Son v. Platt* [1954] T.R. 331, and the judgment of Lowry C.J. in *De Pol v. Cunningham* [1974] S.T.C. 487 (where the issue was not clearly defined). And see *infra*, paras. 5–10 et seq.

[18] [1912] 2 K.B. 491. In that case, a testator, who carried on business alone under the name E. W. Fisher & Sons, by his will appointed his wife and two other persons as his executors and trustees, and empowered them to carry on his business for the benefit of his wife for life. Following his death in 1903, the three executors continued to carry on the business in the old name and were still doing so in 1911, although the terms of the will and the manner in which the business was carried on are not apparent from the report. Phillimore J. held that the executors were clearly joint debtors, but were not partners, and did not elaborate further. The precise basis for the decision is thus unclear: the significant factor may have been the absence of any sharing of profits, the entirety being paid to the wife. Alternatively, it may have been that the executors were merely co-owners, there existing no other contractual relationship between them. Yet still they were held jointly liable, almost as if they were partners. Perhaps the explanation was that, by trading under a firm name, they had held themselves out as partners under the Partnership Act 1890, s.14.

[19] *Re John's Assignment Trusts* [1970] 1 W.L.R. 955.

[20] A number of other differences once existed: see further, the 15th ed. of this work, at pp. 79–81.

[21] Lord Lindley put it more laconically: "Co-ownership is not necessarily the result of agreement. Partnership is". But see also, in this context, *supra*, para. 2–07.

2. Co-ownership does not necessarily involve a community of profit or of loss. Partnership, to a greater or lesser extent, does.[22]

3. One co-owner can, without the consent of the others, transfer his interest (or, in the case of land, his equitable interest) to a third party, who will thereafter stand in his shoes so far as concerns the other co-owners.[23] A partner will rarely, if ever, have such an extensive freedom.[24]

4. One co-owner is not as such the agent, real or implied, of the other co-owners.[25] A partner is the agent of his co-partners, at least so far as concerns activities falling within the scope of the partnership business.[26]

5. One co-owner has no lien on the jointly owned property for outlays or expenses or for the other co-owners' shares of a joint debt. A partner does enjoy such a lien.

6. One co-owner may in general compel a sale of jointly owned land.[27] A partner has no such right during the subsistence of the partnership, notwithstanding the existence of an express or statutory trust for sale.[28] However, on a dissolution a partner is usually entitled to have all the partnership property sold, whether land or not, and the proceeds applied in the manner laid down in the Partnership Act 1890.[29]

7. Co-ownership does not necessarily have as its purpose the realisation of gain. Such a purpose is of the very essence of partnership. It follows that the remedies by way of account and otherwise which one co-owner has against the others differ in many important respects from, and indeed are less

---

[22] Again, Lord Lindley put this proposition shortly, viz.: "Co-ownership does not necessarily involve community of profit or of loss. Partnership does." This goes too far: community of loss is not referred to in the statutory definition of partnership (Partnership Act 1890, s.1(1)) and, indeed, will not always be present: see infra, paras. 5–16, 5–65, 5–66.

[23] It would seem, however, that an ordinary co-owner's freedom to dispose of his share could be restricted by agreement: see Caldy Manor Estate v. Farrell [1974] 1 W.L.R. 1303. It should be noted that, where such a transfer is made by a joint tenant, the joint tenancy will be severed and the third party will only become a tenant in common (or, in the case of land, a tenant in common in equity) with the other owners.

[24] See the Partnership Act 1890, s.31(1), considered infra, paras. 19–59 et seq.

[25] Cf. Fairclough v. Berliner [1931] 1 Ch. 60; Gill v. Lewis [1956] 2 Q.B. 1; Jacobs v. Chaudhuri [1968] 2 Q.B. 470. And see the Landlord and Tenant Act 1954, s.41A (as inserted by the Law of Property Act 1969, s.9).

[26] See the Partnership Act 1890, s.5, considered infra, paras. 12–02 et seq.

[27] See the Law of Property Act 1925, ss.26(3), 30(1). And see, generally, Re Mayo [1943] Ch. 302; Bull v. Bull [1955] 1 Q.B. 234; Jones v. Challenger [1961] 1 Q.B. 176; Cullingford v. Cullingford (1967) 204 E.G. 471; Re John's Assignment Trusts [1970] 1 W.L.R. 955; Williams v. Williams [1976] Ch. 278; Re Holliday [1981] Ch. 405; Dennis v. MacDonald [1982] Fam. 63; Stott v. Ratcliffe (1982) 126 S.J. 310; Re Citro [1991] Ch. 142 and other cases of that class.

[28] See Re Buchanan-Wollaston's Conveyance [1939] Ch. 738.

[29] See infra, paras. 19–04 et seq., 23–179 et seq. However, the effect of the Law of Property Act 1925, s.26(3) on partnership land which is held upon a statutory trust for sale has yet to be considered by the courts. Technically, a partition would be possible under ibid. s.28(3) (as amended by the Mental Health Act 1959, Sched. 7) if all the partners consent. As to chattels, see ibid. s.188. See also infra, paras. 23–183, 23–184.

extensive than, those which one partner has against his co-partners.[30]

Co-owners sharing profits, produce or gross returns

Where co-owners share the profits realised by the employment of **5–10** their joint property, their relationship may appear to be almost indistinguishable from partnership. In such a case, the question will be whether, having regard to all the circumstances, an agreement for a partnership should be inferred, even if this is not susceptible of an easy answer.[31]

If each co-owner merely receives his due share of the produce or **5–11** gross returns derived from the employment of the joint property, no partnership will be created.[32] Thus, if one co-owner of a house agrees to leave its general management to the other, on terms that the latter will lay out his own money on necessary repairs and then arrange for the house to be let, recouping himself out of the rent, the co-owners will not be partners even though they divide the net rent equally between them.[33] The same can be said of the co-owners of a racehorse, who share both winnings and expenses,[34] and, in general, of the co-owners of a ship.[35]

Equally, if the co-owners convert the produce or gross returns into **5–12** money, use that fund in order to defray the cost of obtaining such produce or returns, and ultimately divide the net profits, a partnership may be created, albeit only in relation to those profits and *not* in relation to the property itself. However, the distinction between such cases and those considered in the preceding paragraph is obviously a fine one.

---

[30] Note that in *Roderick v. Mark*, December 14, 1981 (unreported), Mr. Julian Jeffs Q.C., sitting as a Deputy High Court Judge in the Chancery Division, followed certain obiter remarks of Lord Denning M.R. in *A. E. Jones v. F. W. Jones* [1977] 1 W.L.R. 438, 442, and held that a partnership of doctors was liable to account to a co-owner (who was not a member of the partnership) for the notional rent received by the partnership in respect of the jointly owned premises pursuant to the then National Health Service (General Medical and Pharmaceutical Services) Regulations 1974 (see now the National Health Service (General Medical Services) Regulations 1992). Since, however, both counsel conceded the principle of a co-owner's right to an account, it is thought that the point is still technically open to argument. Any reader interested in this issue should consider Lord Lindley's own analysis of the position, which is to be found in the 5th ed. of this work at pp. 57, 58.

[31] See, for example, *Fenston v. Johnstone (Inspector of Taxes)* (1940) 23 T.C. 29.

[32] Partnership Act 1890, s.2(3); also *infra*, paras. 5–15 *et seq.*

[33] *French v. Styring* (1857) 2 C.B.(N.S.) 357, 366, *per* Willes J. See also *Lyon v. Knowles* (1864) 3 B. & Sm. 556; *London Financial Assoc. v. Kelk* (1884) 26 Ch.D. 107.

[34] *French v. Styring, supra; quaere*, whether in this case there was a partnership in the profits. It would seem not: the agreement was to divide the winnings as gross returns.

[35] *Helme v. Smith* (1831) 7 Bing. 709; *Ex p. Young* (1813) 2 V. & B. 242; *Ex p. Harrison* (1814) 2 Rose 76; *Green v. Briggs* (1848) 6 Hare 395; also *Att.-Gen. v. Borrodaile* (1814) 1 Price 148. Equally, the co-owners *may* be partners: *Campbell v. Mullett* (1819) 2 Swan. 551; *The James W. Elwell* [1921] P. 351, 368–369, *per* Hill J.

Joint purchase of goods for re-sale or division

5–13   If several persons together purchase goods intending to re-sell them and to divide the profits, a partnership will almost inevitably be created.[36] However, if their intention is to divide those goods between themselves, they will not be partners nor liable as such. Thus, in *Coope v. Eyre*,[37] A agreed to purchase oil with a view to dividing it between himself and others, each of them paying him their due proportion of the purchase price. A purchased the oil and then went bankrupt. The vendor sought to make the other parties to the agreement liable for the purchase price, but he failed, it being held that A purchased as a principal and not as an agent and since there was no community of profit or loss, the persons among whom the oil was to be divided could not be made liable as partners or "quasi-partners" (*i.e.* partners by holding out). A similar result was achieved in *Hoare v. Dawes*,[38] notwithstanding Lord Mansfield's early doubts, and in *Gibson v. Lupton*.[39]

Co-owners of mines

5–14   Privately owned mines and quarries, although rarely encountered today,[40] represent a special class of jointly owned property; as such, they were accorded detailed consideration in earlier editions of this work. That account does not appear in the present edition.[41]

Although the co-owners of a mine or quarry may be partners and the mine or quarry may be partnership property, neither is a necessary incidence of co-ownership, for the reasons discussed above.[42] Nevertheless, it will be difficult, if not impossible, for those co-owners actually to work the mine or quarry without entering into partnership, at least as to the profits realised.[43]

3. SHARING GROSS RETURNS

5–15   The distinction between sharing gross returns and sharing profits was well established before the Partnership Act 1890 and is, of course, preserved in section 2(2).

In order to appreciate the distinction, it is necessary to understand what is meant by the terms "profits," "losses" and "returns." Lord Lindley explained the distinction in this way:

---

[36] *Reid v. Hollinshead* (1825) 4 B. & C. 867; *Oppenheimer v. Frazer and Wyatt* [1907] 2 K.B. 50.
[37] (1788) 1 H.Bl. 37.
[38] (1780) 1 Doug. 371.
[39] (1832) 9 Bing. 297.
[40] Most mines were nationalised by the Coal Industry Nationalisation Act 1946.
[41] For a detailed consideration of the position, see the 15th ed. of this work at pp. 82 *et seq.*
[42] See *supra*, paras. 5–08 *et seq.*
[43] See *Jefferys v. Smith* (1820) 1 Jac. & W. 298; *Crawshay v. Maule* (1818) 1 Swan. 495; *Faraday v. Wightwick* (1829) 1 R. & M. 45.

"Profits (or net profits) are the excess of returns over advances [*i.e. expenses*]; the excess of what is obtained over the cost of obtaining it.[44] Losses, on the other hand, are the excess of advances over returns; the excess of the cost of obtaining over what is obtained. Profits and net profits are for all legal purposes synonymous expressions; but the returns are often called gross profits; hence it becomes necessary to call profits net profits in order to avoid confusion."

Notwithstanding that admonition, the expression "profits," meaning net profits as opposed to gross returns, is conventionally used, in this work and elsewhere.

Persons who share gross returns and their attendant expenses or **5–16** the difference between them (whether a positive or negative sum), necessarily share both profits and losses: profits, if the returns exceed the expenses; losses, if those expenses exceed the returns. But persons who merely share the profits, *i.e.* the excess of the returns over the expenses, do not necessarily share losses, at least as between themselves.[45] This is because those profits may be shared by persons who have made no contribution towards the expenses; indeed such persons may be entitled to an express indemnity against losses, as in the case of the so-called "salaried" partner.[46]

Implications of sharing gross returns

Where the receipt of gross returns is dependent on incurring **5–17** expenditure, those returns will obviously include a profit element (assuming that a profit has been made), but will not include losses. This is because a loss will result only if the expenses exceed the returns, and this will not occur because the expenses are borne by those incurring them and are not payable out of the returns. That is not to say that the recipient of a share of the returns may not himself make a loss, but it is not a *shared* loss. It follows that, if gross returns are to be divided irrespective of a venture's profitability, the division will involve only an incidental sharing of profits rather than a sharing of profits in the true sense.

---

[44] For a discussion of the meaning of "profits," see *Re Spanish Prospecting Co. Ltd.* [1911] 1 Ch. 91. See also *Gresham Life Assurance Society v. Styles* [1892] A.C. 309, 322 *et seq.*, *per* Lord Herschell; *Beauchamp v. F. W. Woolworth PLC* [1990] 1 A.C. 478, 489, *per* Lord Templeman. And note *Customs and Excise Commissioners v. Bell Concord Educational Trust Ltd.* [1990] 1 Q.B. 1040.

[45] *Per contra*, perhaps, as regards third parties: see *infra*, paras. 5–32 *et seq.*

[46] See further, *infra*, para. 5–65.

On the other hand, if the persons who share the gross returns also share the attendant expenses, a sharing of both profits and losses will necessarily be involved.[47]

Lord Lindley's view

5–18   Although this was the distinction which was seen to be of significance prior to, and consequently preserved in, the Partnership Act 1890,[48] and which accounts for the rule that the receipt of a share of profits is prima facie evidence of partnership whilst the sharing of gross returns is not,[49] Lord Lindley questioned its reasonableness "at least where there is any community of capital or common stock." He observed that:

"the rule itself is probably attributable less to the difference which exists between net profits and gross returns than to the doctrine which so long confused the whole law of partnership in this country, and according to which all persons who shared profits incurred liability as if they were really partners. When this doctrine was rife, the distinction between sharing net profits and gross profits (*i.e.* returns) had considerable practical value; but ... the doctrine in question is now wholly exploded, and the distinction alluded to is of little importance."[50]

Share farming agreements

5–19   Notwithstanding Lord Lindley's doubts, a resurgence of interest in the significance of the distinction has been generated by the comparatively recent innovation of the share farming agreement, whereby a land owner and a working farmer combine their resources with a view to sharing the ultimate produce in agreed proportions.[51] In theory, each is carrying on a wholly separate business, so that

---

[47] But *cf.* the position of co–owners discussed *supra*, paras. 5–10 *et seq.*
[48] See Partnership Act 1890, s.2(2), (3), *supra*, para. 5–02.
[49] This rule appears clearly from the decisions in *Gibson v. Lupton* (1832) 9 Bing. 297 and *French v. Styring* (1857) 2 C.B.(N.S.) 357.
[50] Further illustrations of the rule, to which reference was made in some detail in earlier editions of this work, are to a greater or lesser extent to be found in *Sutton & Co. v. Grey* [1894] 1 Q.B. 285; also *Lyon v. Knowles* (1864) 3 B. & S. 556; *Cox v. Coulson* [1916] 2 K.B. 177, 181, *per* Swinfen Eady L.J.; *Montagu Stanley & Co. v. J. C. Solomon Ltd.* [1932] 2 K.B. 287. Similarly in the old cases concerning whaling voyages: *Wilkinson v. Frasier* (1802) 4 Esp. 182; *Mair v. Glennie* (1815) 4 M. & S. 240; *Perrott v. Bryant* (1836) 2 Y. & C.Ex. 61; *Stavers v. Curling* (1836) 3 Bing.N.C. 355. And note also *Steel v. Lester* (1878) 3 C.P.D. 121, 128, *per* Lindley J.; *The Riverman* [1928] P. 33, 38, *per* Hill J. See further, the 15th ed. of this work at p. 88, n. 92.
[51] The land owner will usually supply both land and fixed equipment, whilst the farmer will physically carry out the farming operations, using his own labour and machinery. *Cf.* the position in *George Hall & Son v. Platt* [1954] T.R. 331.

there is no "business in common," let alone one carried on "with a view of profit."[52] Provided that the share farming agreement reflects this and the participants adhere to its strict terms, no partnership should result, even though the superficial appearance may at times suggest otherwise.[53]

4. SHARING PROFITS

Scope of Section 2(3) of the Partnership Act 1890

In seeking to identify the consequences which may flow from the **5–20** sharing of profits, section 2(3) of the Partnership Act 1890[54] performs two inter-related, but nevertheless distinct, functions. First, it defines the extent to which profit sharing may be treated as evidence of a partnership as between actual or potential partners; secondly, it defines the extent to which the recipient of a profit share can, on that ground alone, be affixed with liability by a third party *as if* he were a partner. The formulation of the general rule at the beginning of the subsection appears to be confined in its application to the former function, whilst the specific rules contained in paragraphs (a) to (e) are, by the addition of the words "or liable as such", equally applicable to both.

In the following consideration of the subsection and its history, the two functions will be treated separately under the headings (a) sharing profits as evidence of partnership; and (b) sharing profits as a ground of liability.

(a) Sharing Profits as Evidence of Partnership

The statutory rule

The general rule, which is set out in the opening words of section **5–21** 2(3) of the Partnership Act 1890, is in the following terms:

"The receipt by a person of a share of the profits of a business is prima facie evidence that he is a partner in the business, but the receipt of such a share, or of a payment contingent on or varying

---

[52] See Partnership Act 1890, s. 1(1), *supra*, paras. 2–01 *et seq.*
[53] See the Australian case of *Cribb v. Korn* (1911) 12 C.L.R. 205, where it was held that no partnership resulted from such an agreement. This case demonstrates that share farming agreements have been familiar for many years in Australia. They have also been widely used in America and New Zealand: see *Stratton's Joint Ventures in Farming* (1981) and *Stratton, Gregory and Williams' Share Farming* (2nd ed., 1985), both published by the Country Landowner's Association.
[54] See *supra*, para. 5–02.

with the profits of a business, does not of itself make him a partner in the business".

This rule predated the 1890 Act and had been the subject of detailed analysis by the Court of Appeal in *Badeley v. Consolidated Bank.*[55] In that case, Lord (then Lord Justice) Lindley himself summarised the position as follows[56]:

> "It is no longer right to infer either partnership or agency from the mere fact that one person shares the profits of another. It may be, and probably it is true, that if all that is known is that one person carries on a business and shares the profits of that business with another, prima facie those two are partners, or prima facie the person carrying on the business is carrying it on as the agent of the person with whom he shares his profits. That may be true, and I think is true even now; but when you have a great deal more to consider it appears to me to be a fallacy to say that you are to proceed upon the idea that sharing profits prima facie creates a partnership or an agency, and that prima facie presumption has to be rebutted by something else."

Lord Lindley was in fact critical of the terms of section 2(3) as an attempt to embody the existing rule in a statutory form and, in his Supplement on the Act, commented:

> "The first clause of this sub-section is not well expressed, and indeed appears to contain a contradiction in terms, for if the receipt of a share of the profits of a business is prima facie evidence of partnership, it necessarily follows that the receipt of such a share, if that is the only fact in the case, must of itself be sufficient to establish a partnership. The effect of the receipt of a share of profits in determining the existence or non-existence of a partnership was very carefully considered by the Court of Appeal in the recent case of *Badeley v. Consolidated Bank* (1888),[57] and it

---

[55] (1888) 38 Ch.D. 238; *cf. Pooley v. Driver* (1876) 5 Ch.D. 458. See also *Re Young* [1896] 2 Q.B. 484, noticed *supra*, para. 2–16; and note the old building society cases: *Brownlie v. Russell* (1883) 8 App.Cas. 235; *Tosh v. North British Building Society* (1886) 11 App.Cas. 489; *Auld v. Glasgow, Working Men's Building Society* (1887) 12 App.Cas. 197.

[56] (1888) 38 Ch.D. 238, 258; also *ibid.* pp. 250 (*per* Cotton L.J.), 262 (*per* Bowen L.J.).

[57] See also *Mollwo March & Co. v. Court of Wards* (1872) L.R. 4 P.C. 419, 433. In the main work Lord Lindley also cited, in this context, the Irish case of *Barklie v. Scott* (1827) 1 Hud. & Br. 83. There a father paid a sum of money as his son's share of the capital of a partnership, it being agreed that during the son's minority the profits should be accounted for to the father; it was held that the father was not himself a partner since that was clearly not the parties' intention. *Cf. Reid's Case* (1857) 24 Beav. 318, where the father who had transferred shares into his minor son's name was held to be a contributory. Equally, there were dicta the other way: see, for example, *Heyhoe v. Burgh* (1850) 9 C.B. 431; *Fox v. Clifton* (1832) 9 Bing. 115; *Ex p. Langdale* (1811) 18 Ves.Jr. 300.

is conceived that this sub-section does not alter the law stated in that case."

Confirmation of the correctness of Lord Lindley's approach is to be found in the judgment of North J. in *Davis v. Davis*[58]:

"Adopting then the rule of law which was laid down before the Act, and which seems to me to be precisely what is intended by section 2, sub-section 3, of the Act, the receipt by a person of a share of the profits of a business is prima facie evidence that he is a partner in it, and, if the matter stops there, it is evidence upon which the Court must act. But, if there are other circumstances to be considered, they ought to be considered fairly together; not holding that a partnership is proved by the receipt of a share of profits, unless it is rebutted by something else; but taking all the circumstances together, not attaching undue weight to any of them, but drawing an inference from the whole."[59]

Illustrations of the statutory rule

There are obviously abundant examples of the application of the 5–22 rule in cases decided both before and after the passing of the 1890 Act.

Thus, ignoring for the present section 2(3)(b),[60] it was frequently held prior to the 1890 Act that employees who were remunerated by reference to the profits of a business were not partners therein, at least where it appeared from the agreement that no partnership was intended.[61] Indeed, the comparative popularity of this device may, in some measure, have contributed to the gradual introduction and recognition of the concept of "salaried" partnership, which in general involves an employee being held out as a partner[62] and remunerated

---

[58] [1894] 1 Ch. 393, 399.

[59] See also *Walker West Developments Ltd. v. F. J. Emmett Ltd.* (1979) 252 E.G. 1171, 1173, *per* Goff L.J.; *Saywell v. Pope* [1979] S.T.C. 824.

[60] See *supra*, para. 5–02.

[61] *Ex p. Tennant* (1877) 6 Ch.D. 303; *Ross v. Parkyns* (1875) L.R. 20 Eq. 331; *Trower & Sons v. Ripstein* [1944] A.C. 254; *Rawlinson v. Clarke* (1846) 15 M. & W. 292; *Stocker v. Brockelbank* (1851) 3 Mac. & G. 250; *Shaw v. Galt* (1863) 16 I.C.L.R. 357; *Radcliffe v. Rushworth* (1864) 33 Beav. 484 (where there was a holding out and a deed executed by the alleged partners, in which they were described as carrying on business together). See also *Geddes v. Wallace* (1820) 2 Bli. 270; *R. v. Macdonald* (1861) 7 Jur.(N.S.) 1127, where an employee remunerated by a share of profits was convicted of embezzlement, which he could not then have been if he had been a partner (*cf.* the position now, as considered in *R. v. Bonner* [1970] 1 W.L.R. 838); *Withington v. Herring* (1829) 3 Moo. & Pay. 30. Moreover, the Employment Protection (Consolidation) Act 1978 expressly contemplates the remuneration of employees in this way: see *ibid.* s.144(2) and *Goodeve v. Gilsons* [1985] I.C.R. 401. In *Marsh v. Stacey* (1963) 107 S.J. 512, a person who was admittedly a junior partner was entitled to "be paid a fixed salary of £1,200 as a first charge on the profits" but in one year the profits were not sufficient to pay that sum to him. The Court of Appeal held that he was not entitled to have the deficiency made good by the other partner. See also *Thompson Brothers & Co. v. Amis* [1917] 2 Ch. 211, a decision on the former excess profits duty.

[62] Partnership Act 1890, s.14: see *infra*, paras. 5–43 *et seq.*

by a fixed salary and/or a share of profits, but denied many of the rights and duties normally associated with partnership, *e.g.* an obligation to contribute capital and to share losses and a right to participate fully in the management of the firm.[63] Equally, such an employee may be a partner in the true sense, if he enjoys a share of profits and an interest in the partnership capital,[64] although this would, to say the least, be unusual.

5–23   Another illustration of the rule can be seen in the case of the vendor of a business who receives a share of profits as consideration for the sale, *i.e.* a case now falling within section 2(3)(a) of the 1890 Act.[65] Similarly, where a trader and his customers enter into an agreement under which the trader is to distribute a part of his profits to the customers in proportion to the purchases made by them, no partnership is created.[66]

Agreements to share profits and losses

5–24   An agreement to share profits and losses, in the sense of making good the losses if any are sustained, may be said to be character-istic—if not of the essence[67]—of a partnership contract. As Lord Lindley explained:

"Whatever difference of opinion there may be as to other matters, persons engaged in any trade, business, or adventure upon the terms of sharing the profits *and* losses arising therefrom, are necessarily to some extent partners in that trade, business or adventure".[68]

---

[63] See generally, as to such partners, *Stekel v. Ellice* [1973] 1 W.L.R. 191; and note that in *Casson Beckman & Partners v. Papi* [1991] BCLC 299, the court was content, at the parties' invitation, not to draw any distinction between an employee and a salaried partner. See also *infra*, para. 5–65.

[64] See *Reid v. Hollinshead* (1825) 4 B. & C. 867; *Ex p. Chuck* (1832) 8 Bing. 469; *Gilpin v. Enderby* (1824) 5 B. & A. 954. In such a case, an express term in the agreement negativing any implication of partnership may be ineffective *vis-à-vis* third parties, such as the Inland Revenue: see *Fenston v. Johnstone* (1940) 23 T.C. 29, where there was held to be a partnership and not merely remuneration for management services. The managing partner put up no capital and contributed no assets, but he was to share in profits and losses arising in the development or sale of certain land. See also *Tate v. Charlesworth* (1962) 106 S.J. 368. *Cf. Walker v. Hirsch* (1884) 27 Ch.D. 460.

[65] See *Hawksley v. Outram* [1892] 3 Ch. 359; also *Re Young* [1896] 2 Q.B. 484, noticed *supra*, para. 2–16. And see *Pratt v. Strick* (1932) 17 T.C. 459.

[66] See *Ogdens Ltd. v. Nelson* [1905] A.C. 109 (where the existence of a partnership was not suggested).

[67] See *supra*, para. 2–06 and *infra*, paras. 5–27 *et seq.*

[68] Lord Lindley went so far as to add "nor is the writer aware of any case in which the persons who have agreed to share profits and losses have been held *not* to be partners." He found no difficulty in reconciling the decisions in *Mair v. Glennie* (1815) 4 M. & S. 240 (on the basis that "the expression 'profit or loss' seems to have been used for gross returns") and *Geddes v. Wallace* (1820) 2 Bli. 270 (where "the arrangement as to profit and loss did not apply to the person as to whom the question of partnership or no partnership was raised").

Only one case, *Re Jane*,[69] is in any real sense inconsistent with the above proposition.

Thus, if it is to retain its true meaning, the description "partners" **5–25** must, almost as a matter of course, be applied to persons who agree to share profits and losses, whether or not they have themselves used that word.[70] However, it is not the necessary corollary of such an agreement that each party will enjoy all the rights and privileges normally associated with partnership, *e.g.* a right to participate in the management of the business,[71] to dissolve the firm,[72] or to share in the value of goodwill on a dissolution. Rather, the partners' rights and duties will in each case be determined by the terms of their agreement or, in the absence of any such agreement, by the 1890 Act itself.[73]

At the same time, it may be inappropriate to describe as partners **5–26** persons who have agreed to share profits and losses if there is no general obligation to *make good* the losses. For example, where a selling agent agrees to share the profits and losses realised on his sales, it may be intended that he should be paid by a share of profits, with the losses of one year merely being deducted from the gains of another. If this is the true intention, he will not be in partnership with the vendor.[74] Similarly, there may be an agreement involving some, but not all, losses being made good but disclosing an intention not to create a partnership. In such a case, unless there are other circumstances inconsistent with that avowed or apparent intention, there will be no partnership.[75] This is illustrated by the decision in

---

[69] (1914) 110 L.T. 556. In that case two partners, J. and W., agreed to dissolve partnership on September 20, 1909 and, on that date, W assigned his share and interest in the partnership to J. The deed of dissolution provided that an account should be taken on December 31, 1909, that W.'s share when ascertained was to be credited to him in the books of the firm and to remain as a loan to the firm for 10 years, bearing interest, and that if, on taking the account, there was found to be an insufficiency of assets to meet the liabilities, W. was to pay J. half the deficit. J. continued to carry on the business and was adjudicated bankrupt in January 1910. It was held by the Court of Appeal that the partnership terminated on September 20, 1909, though the final account was not to be taken until December 31. The precise point decided was that moneys standing to the credit of the current account of the firm on November 4 formed part of J.'s separate estate, and that the bank had no right to set this off in discharge of a debt due in respect of money advanced by them to the firm; it was not decided that W. was not liable for debts incurred between September 20 and December 31.

[70] See *Green v. Beesley* (1835) 2 Bing. N.C. 108; *Brett v. Beckwith* (1856) 3 Jur.(N.S.) 31; also *Greenham v. Gray* (1855) 4 I.C.L.R. 501; *Fenston v. Johnstone* (1940) 23 T.C. 29.

[71] As in *Walker v. Hirsch* (1884) 27 Ch.D. 460 (where, ultimately, no partnership was found to exist).

[72] See, as to this, *Moore v. Davis* (1879) 11 Ch.D. 261 and *Pawsey v. Armstrong* (1881) 18 Ch.D. 698, in both of which it was held that there *was* a right to dissolve. *Quaere* whether *Pawsey v. Armstrong* went too far: see *Walker v. Hirsch, supra*. Of course the court's jurisdiction to dissolve a firm under the Partnership Act 1890, s.35 will continue to be exercisable on the application of any partner, irrespective of the terms of the agreement.

[73] *Walker v. Hirsch, supra*; Partnership Act 1890, ss.24 *et seq.*

[74] See, however, *Fenston v. Johnstone* (1940) 23 T.C. 29, *supra*, para. 5–22, n. 64.

[75] See *Walker v. Hirsch* (1884) 27 Ch.D. 460; *Sutton & Co. v. Grey* [1894] 1 Q.B. 285.

English Insurance Co. v. National Benefit Assurance Co. (Official Receiver)[76] where two insurance companies ("English" and "National") entered into an agreement, styled a "participation" agreement, which in essence provided as follows: National were to be entitled to and had to accept a quota participation equal to a one-eighth share of all risks arranged by English through their marine department. The participation was to be equal to 50 per cent. of the share retained by English at their own risk of all marine insurance accepted on or after a certain date, but with a maximum limit on any one ship. The liability of the two companies was to commence automatically at the same time, the expressed intention being that they should participate *pari passu* in all the marine insurances accepted by English. National were to be entitled to a proportionate part of the net premiums and other benefits received by English and were to bear their proportionate share of all losses. English were alone to settle all claims which might arise under their policies, and National were to be bound thereby. English were to receive from National a commission on the net premiums paid to them in respect of their participation and on their profits under the agreement. The House of Lords decided that the agreement amounted to a contract of re-insurance[77] and did not create a partnership between the two companies. The true meaning of the agreement was that English were to carry on their business as principals and that National were, as between themselves and English, to receive a proportion of the premiums paid to English less commission and were, in consideration of such receipt, to indemnify English against a proportion of the losses suffered by that company as principals.[78]

Loans and other agreements where no sharing of losses

5–27   Persons who agree to share the profits of a venture are prima facie partners, even though they may also have agreed between themselves that they will not be liable for losses beyond the amount of their respective contributions.[79] Indeed, so strong is the inference of partnership where there is a sharing of profits that a provision expressly negativing the sharing of losses as to one or more of the parties may be insufficient to displace it. Thus, notwithstanding certain observations of Lord Loughborough in *Coope v. Eyre*,[80] there

---

[76] [1929] A.C. 114.
[77] The contract was invalid for non-compliance with the requirements of the Stamp Act 1891 and the Marine Insurance Act 1906. For similar cases, see *Re Home and Colonial Ins. Co.* [1930] 1 Ch. 102; *Re National Benefit Ass. Co.* [1931] 1 Ch. 46; *Motor Union Ins. Co. v. Mannheimer Versicherungsgesellschaft* [1933] 1 K.B. 812.
[78] [1929] A.C. 121, *per* Lord Hailsham L.C.
[79] *Brown v. Tapscott* (1840) 6 M. & W. 119.
[80] (1788) 1 Bl.H. 48. Lord Loughborough is reported to have said: "In order to constitute a partnership, communion of profits and loss is essential."

is nothing to prevent one or more partners from agreeing to indemnify the others against losses, or to prevent full effect from being given to a partnership agreement containing such an indemnity.[81]

However, if it were agreed that one or more of the parties should **5–28** be indemnified not only in respect of losses beyond the amount of his or their contributions, but also in respect of the loss of those contributions themselves, there would, as to such parties, exist a contract of loan rather than partnership.[82] The mere fact that there may, in such circumstances, be a sharing of profits as between lender and borrower does not make them partners or liable as such,[83] and the old cases where the contrary was found, in order to avoid the consequences of the strict application of the usury laws, are no longer good law.[84]

Equally, a dormant partner, by which is meant a partner (in the **5–29** true sense of that word) who is not known and does not appear to be a partner, cannot escape liability by seeking to masquerade as a mere lender of money.[85] In each case, his status will depend on a careful analysis of the purported "loan" agreement and the rights and duties which attach to him thereunder. All too often, the dividing line between loan and partnership will be a fine one. As Lord Lindley explained:

"The right of a lender is to be repaid his money with such interest or share of profits as he may have stipulated for; and his right to a share of profits involves a right to an account and to see the books of the borrower, unless such right is expressly excluded by agreement. If however a lender stipulates for more than this (*e.g.* for a right to control the business or the employment of the assets or to wind up the business) or if his advance is risked in the business or forms part of his capital in it, he ceases to be a mere lender and becomes in effect a dormant partner."[86]

---

[81] See *Bond v. Pittard* (1838) 3 M. & W. 357 (two solicitors, one of whom was not to be liable for losses, were held to be partners for the purpose of suing for fees); also *Geddes v. Wallace* (1820) 2 Bli. 270; *Walker West Developments Ltd. v. F. J. Emmett Ltd.* (1979) 252 E.G. 1171.

[82] See Pothier, *Contrat de Société*, ss.21 and 22. Compare *Pooley v. Driver* (1876) 5 Ch.D. 458 and *Badeley v. Consolidated Bank* (1888) 38 Ch.D. 238.

[83] Partnership Act 1890, s.2(3)(d); however, there must be a written agreement if that paragraph is to apply: see *infra*, paras. 5–39, 5–41.

[84] See *Bloxham v. Pell* (1775) cited 2 Wm.Bl. 999; *Fereday v. Hordern* (1821) Jac. 144; *Gilpin v. Enderby* (1824) 5 B. & A. 954; see also *Ex p. Notley* (1833) 3 Dea. & Ch. 367.

[85] See *Pooley v. Driver* (1876) 5 Ch.D. 458.

[86] Compare *Mollwo March & Co. v. Court of Wards* (1872) L.R. 4 P.C. 419; *Re Young* [1896] 2 Q.B. 484; *Pooley v. Driver, supra.* See also *Re Beard & Co.* [1915] Hansell Bank.Rep. 191, where one person guaranteed another's business account in return for a share of profits.

Agreements where no joint property

5–30   As is self evident from section 1(1) of the Partnership Act 1890,[87] partnership does not require the presence of any jointly owned or partnership property. Lord Lindley put it thus;

> "It is not ... essential to the existence of a partnership, that there shall be any joint capital or stock. If several persons labour together for the sake of gain, and of dividing that gain, they will not be partners the less on account of their labouring with their own tools".[88]

5–31   Equally, where one person owns property and the other possesses a particular skill, they may agree that the latter should have control of the property for their mutual benefit and that they should divide the profits derived from its employment between themselves. In such cases, it may be no easy task to identify whether or not a partnership has been created: everything will depend on the terms of the parties' agreement and on their underlying intentions.[89]

(b)   Sharing Profits as a Ground of Liability

The original doctrine

5–32   The origins of the controversial and uncompromising doctrine that the recipient of a share of the profits of a business is liable for its debts and obligations, just as if he were a full partner, may perhaps be traced to a decision of Lord Mansfield.[90] However its first

---

[87] See *supra*, paras. 2–01 *et seq.*

[88] See *Formont v. Coupland* (1824) 2 Bing. 170; *Lovegrove v. Nelson* (1834) 3 M. & K. 1; *French v. Styring* (1857) 2 C.B.(N.S.) 357; also *Meyer v. Sharpe* (1813) 5 Taunt. 74; *Smith v. Watson* (1824) 2 B. & C. 401; *Steel v. Lester* (1878) 3 C.P.D. 121; *Miles v. Clarke* [1953] 1 W.L.R. 537; also the cases cited *supra*, para. 5–18, n. 50. The dictum of Lord Cairns L.C. in *Syers v. Syers* (1876) 1 App.Cas. 174, 181, to the effect that a partnership in profits is a partnership in the assets by which they are made is, in the words of Lord Lindley, "by no means universally true." Lord Lindley also referred in this context to the following cases concerning authors and publishers: *Gale v. Leckie* (1817) 2 Stark. 107; *Gardiner v. Childs* (1837) 8 C. & P. 345; *Venables v. Wood* (1839) 3 Ross L.C. on Com.Law. 529; *Reade v. Bentley* (1857) 3 K. & J. 271 and (1858) 4 K. & J. 656; *Wilson v. Whitehead* (1837) 10 M. & W. 503. Lord Lindley added that *Venables v. Wood, supra,* "is an authority for the proposition that authors and publishers are not partners at all, and *quaere* whether this is not the correct doctrine?" No partnership was created in *Kelly's Directories Ltd. v. Gavin and Lloyds* [1902] 1 Ch. 630; see also *Abrahams v. Herbert Reiach Ltd.* [1922] 1 K.B. 477, 482, *per* Atkin L.J.

[89] See *Stocker v. Brocklebank* (1851) 3 Mac. & G. 250, where it was clear that no partnership was intended; *Walker v. Hirsch* (1884) 27 Ch.D. 460; *Re Young* [1896] 2 Q.B. 484; also *Pawsey v. Armstrong* (1881) 18 Ch.D. 698. *Cf.* the Irish case of *Greenham v. Gray* (1881) 4 L.R. Ir. 501, where a partnership was held to exist, even though the assets used to carry on the business belonged to one partner. It seems that in this instance the plaintiff intended to create a partnership, whilst the defendant did not. And see also *Fenston v. Johnstone* (1940) 23 T.C. 29; *George Hall & Son v. Platt* [1954] T.R. 331. And see *supra*, para. 5–17.

[90] *Bloxham v. Pell* (1775), cited at 2 Wm.Bl. 999.

formulation is traditionally ascribed to De Grey C.J. in the later case of *Grace v. Smith*,[91] where he sought to distinguish between the position of such a person and that of a mere lender thus:

"Every man who has a share of the profits of a trade, ought also to bear his share of the loss. And if any one takes part of the profit, he takes a part of that fund on which the creditor of the trader relies for his payment. If any one advances or lends money to a trader, it is only lent on his general personal security. It is no specific lien upon the profits of the trade, and yet the lender is generally interested in those profits; he relies on them for repayment. And there is no difference whether that money be lent *de novo*, or left behind in trade by one of the partners who retires; and whether the terms of that loan be kind or harsh, makes also no manner of difference. I think the true criterion is to inquire whether Smith [*the defendant*] agreed to share the profits of the trade with Robinson [*the continuing partner*], or whether he only relied on those profits, as a fund of payment: a distinction, not more nice than usually occurs in questions of trade or usury. The jury have said this is not payable out of the profits, and I think there is no foundation for granting a new trial."[92]

Eighteen years later, the doctrine was emphatically approved in **5–33** *Waugh v. Carver*[93] and, although criticised by Lord Lindley among others,[94] held sway until the decision of the House of Lords in *Cox v. Hickman*.[95]

In earlier editions of this work, the state of the law prior to *Cox v. Hickman* was analysed in some detail but, given its lack of current practical relevance, that analysis has not been retained.[96] Suffice it to say that the harshness of the doctrine led the courts to draw subtle distinctions between the sharing of profits on the one hand and the sharing of gross returns and the payment of sums computed by reference to profits on the other.[97]

---

[91] (1775) 2 Wm. Bl. 998.
[92] *Ibid.* p.1000. It was this judgment, rather than the decision in the case, that was regarded as the authority for the proposition referred to in the text.
[93] (1793) 2 H.Bl. 235.
[94] See the 15th ed. of this work at pp. 98, 99.
[95] (1860) 8 H.L.C. 268.
[96] See the 15th ed. of this work at pp. 99 *et seq.*
[97] See for example, *Benjamin v. Porteus* (1796) 2 H.Bl. 590; *Dry v. Boswell* (1808) 1 Camp. 330; *Ex p. Hamper* (1811) 17 Ves.Jr. 403, 412, *per* Lord Eldon L.C.; *Ex p. Rowlandson* (1811) 1 Rose 89; *Ex p. Langdale* (1811) 18 Ves.Jr. 300; *Ex p. Watson* (1815) 19 Ves.Jr. 459; *Mair v. Glennie* (1815) 4 M. & S. 240 (the expression "profits or loss" in this case being equivalent to gross returns); *Pott v. Eyton* (1846) 3 C.B. 32; *Heyhoe v. Burgh* (1850) 9 C.B. 431, 440, 444, *per* Coltman J..

The position following Cox v. Hickman

5–34   In *Cox v. Hickman*,[98] the House of Lords effectively decided that persons who share the profits of a business do not incur any liability as partners *unless* they personally carry on the business or it is carried on by others as their real or ostensible agents. Although *Waugh v. Carver*[99] and the other cases were technically distinguished, they were in effect overruled. Lord Lindley summarised the position thus:

> "In fact, although the House of Lords in deciding *Cox v. Hickman*, professed to overrule no previous authority, the effect of that decision has unquestionably been to put a great branch of partnership law on a substantially new footing."

5–35   He then observed that the decisions in *Kilshaw v. Jukes*,[1] *Re English and Irish Church and University Insurance Society*,[2] *Bullen v. Sharp*,[3] *Holme v. Hammond*[4] and *Mollwo, March & Co. v. Court of Wards*[5] conclusively showed that analysis to be correct. Indeed, those cases went some way towards establishing a general principle that a person who does not hold himself out as a partner is not liable to third parties for the acts of persons whose profits he shares, unless he and they are really partners *inter se*, or unless they are his agents,[6] which is a doctrine that was firmly established by the House of Lords in *Gosling v. Gaskell*.[7]

5–36   It goes almost without saying that where parties *intentionally* enter into partnership, albeit for a limited purpose beneficial to themselves, they may find that they are treated as partners for more general purposes. This was the position before the Partnership Act 1890[8] and remains so thereafter.

---

[98] (1860) 8 H.L.C. 268. See also *Price v. Groom* (1848) 2 Ex. 542; *Re Stanton Iron Co.* (1855) 21 Beav. 164; *Gosling v. Gaskell* [1897] A.C. 575; and see *Owen v. Body* (1836) 5 A. & E. 28; *Janes v. Whitbread* (1851) 11 C.B. 406.

[99] (1793) 2 H.Bl. 235.

[1] (1863) 3 B & S. 847.

[2] (1862) 1 Hem. & M. 85. *Cf. Re Albion Life Assurance Society* (1880) 16 Ch.D. 83.

[3] (1865) L.R. 1 C.P. 86.

[4] (1872) L.R. 7 Ex. 218.

[5] (1872) L.R. 4 P.C. 419. *Cf. Pooley v. Driver* (1876) 5 Ch.D. 458; *Pratt v. Strick* (1932) 17 T.C. 459.

[6] As in *Steel v. Lester* (1878) 3 C.P.D. 121. See also *Associated Portland Cement Manufacturers Ltd. v. Ashton* [1915] 2 K.B. 1.

[7] [1897] A.C. 575; followed in *Sowman v. David Samuel Trust Ltd.* (*In liquidation*) [1978] 1 W.L.R. 22. See also *Badeley v. Consolidated Bank* (1888) 38 Ch.D. 238; *Hawksley v. Outram* [1892] 3 Ch. 359; and see Baron Bramwell's judgment in *Bullen v. Sharp* (1865) L.R. 1 C.P. 86, 125 *et seq.*; *Holme v. Hammond* (1872) L.R. 7 Ex. 218; *Mollwo March & Co. v. Court of Wards* (1872) L.R. 4 P.C. 419; *Ex p. Tennant* (1877) 6 Ch.D. 303.

[8] See *Pooley v. Driver* (1876) 5 Ch.D. 458.

Statutory modifications of the common law

Bovill's Act was passed in 1865 in order to remove any **5-37** presumption of partnership or of liability as a partner in four specific cases, which were substantially re-enacted in the Partnership Act 1890, section 2(3)(b) to (e).[9] However, this subsection went further than Bovill's Act, first in establishing the general statutory principle that the receipt of a share of profits does not *of itself* constitute a partnership, even though it is prima facie evidence thereof[10] and, secondly, by providing that the repayment of a debt out of profits does not of itself make the recipient a partner or liable as such.[11]

Although the various cases referred to in paragraph (a) to (e) of **5-38** section 2(3) to an extent illustrate the general statutory principle, they at the same time *expressly* negative the liability of persons entering into contracts or arrangements of the types described therein.[12] It follows that, should the conditions stated in any of those paragraphs not be entirely satisfied, there will be the normal prima facie inference of partnership resulting from the sharing of profits but it will still be necessary to consider all the circumstances in order to determine whether or not a partnership actually exists.[13] Equally, it is clear that a person who is in truth a partner, albeit dormant, cannot avoid liability merely by purporting to satisfy the letter of those conditions.[14]

In only one case, set out in paragraph (d), is there a requirement **5-39** for a written contract, signed by or on behalf of the parties. In some ways it is surprising that the same requirement was not applied throughout the subsection, although its value is, on a true analysis, doubtful, as Lord Lindley explained in his Supplement on the Act:

"If it is law that a contract not within this sub-section is admissible as evidence to show the terms on which the loan is made,[15] and there appears to be nothing in this act to exclude such evidence, it is difficult to see the utility of the proviso to the present sub-section. Whether the contract is or is not within the sub-section,

---

[9] These cases formed ss.1–4 of Bovill's Act (28 & 29 Vict. c. 86). However, that Act left various types of agreement wholly untouched, *e.g.* those considered in *Waugh v. Carver* (1793) 2 H.Bl. 235; *Cheap v. Cramond* (1821) 4 B. & A. 663; *Smith v. Watson* (1824) 2 B. & C. 401; *Cox v. Hickman* (1860) 8 H.L.C. 268.

[10] See *supra*, paras. 5–21 *et seq.*

[11] Partnership Act 1890, s.2(3)(a). This is the type of agreement considered in *Cox v. Hickman* (1860) 8 H.L.C. 268.

[12] See *supra*, para. 5–03.

[13] *Ibid.* See also *supra*, paras. 5–21 *et seq.*

[14] See *Ex p. Delhasse* (1878) 7 Ch.D. 511; also *Syers v. Syers* (1876) 1 App.Cas. 174; *Pooley v. Driver* (1876) 5 Ch.D. 458. Cf. *Mollwo, March & Co. v. Court of Wards* (1872) L.R. 4 P.C. 419; *Ex p. Tennant* (1877) 6 Ch.D. 303.

[15] Lord Lindley based this proposition on *Pooley v. Driver* (1876) 5 Ch.D. 458, a decision under Bovill's Act (which required the contract to be in writing but not signed).

when its terms are once proved its real effect must be considered, and if on the construction of the contract the relation between the parties is that of debtor and creditor, there is nothing in this act or the general law to change this relation into the different relation of partners. If this be so, the only advantage of a signed contract appears to be that such a contract is more easily proved than a verbal or unsigned contract."[16]

Where a contract provides that a person will receive a fixed sum "out of the profits" of a business, that is equivalent to a contract that he will receive "a share of the profits" for the purposes of both this section and section 3.[17] However, where money is advanced on terms that a third party will receive a share of profits, neither section will apply.[18]

Partnership Act 1890, section 3

5–40   Section 3 of the Partnership Act 1890[19] must be read in conjunction with section 2(3). It is framed in the following terms:

"3. In the event of any person to whom money has been advanced by way of loan upon such a contract as is mentioned in the last foregoing section, or on any buyer of a goodwill in consideration of a share of the profits of the business, being adjudged a bankrupt, entering into an arrangement to pay his creditors less than [one hundred pence][20] in the pound, or dying in insolvent circumstances, the lender of the loan shall not be entitled to recover anything in respect of his loan, and the seller of the goodwill shall not be entitled to recover anything in respect of the share of profits contracted for, until the claims of the other creditors or the borrower or buyer for valuable consideration in money or money's worth[21] have been satisfied."

This section applies not only to loans to partners but extends also to loans to individuals and to companies.[22] It causes the lender to be

---

[16] At that stage, it had not, of course, been decided that the Partnership Act 1890, s.3 was equally applicable to written and unwritten contracts (see *infra*, para. 5–41) and Lord Lindley perceived a possible advantage to the creditor whose agreement was *not* reduced to writing.

[17] *Re Young* [1896] 2 Q.B. 484. Note that the share of profits payable to a lender could not be deducted in estimating the profits of the firm for the purposes of the former excess profits duty: *Walker v. Commissioners of Inland Revenue* [1920] 3 K.B. 648.

[18] *Re Pinto Leite and Nephews, ex p. Visconde de Olivaes* [1929] 1 Ch. 221.

[19] This section was a substantial re-enactment of Bovill's Act (28 & 29 Vict. c. 86), s.5, which was probably the only section of that Act which introduced a change in the law; see the following decisions thereunder: *Ex p. Taylor* (1879) 12 Ch.D. 366; *Ex p. Corbridge* (1876) 4 Ch.D. 246.

[20] The words in square brackets were substituted by virtue of Decimal Currency Act 1969, s.10.

[21] As to the meaning of this expression, see *Midland Bank Trust Co. Ltd. v. Green* [1981] A.C. 513 (a decision under the Land Charges Act 1972, s.4(b)).

[22] *Re Leng* [1895] Ch. 652; *Re Theo Garvin Ltd.* [1969] 1 Ch. 624; *cf. Re Rolls Royce Ltd.* [1974] 1 W.L.R. 1584 And note the terms of the Insolvent Partnerships Order 1986, art. 10(7); see *infra*, paras. 27–85, 27–108.

treated as a deferred creditor but seemingly does not deprive him of the right to retain any security he may have taken for the advance,[23] nor of the right to foreclose on such security.[24]

Equally, if a loan is made to a trader pursuant to an agreement **5-41** under which the interest is intended to vary according to the profits of his business, but which is drafted in such a way as to be unintelligible, that agreement will be treated as void and the lender will be allowed to prove in competition with the other creditors for the amount of his loan.[25]

However, if a loan is made to a firm on terms that the lender will share the profits of the business, and the partners subsequently dissolve the firm and one of their number continues to carry on the business and *de facto* takes over the loan (*i.e.* without any form of novation), but is then bankrupted, the section will apply and the lender will not be permitted to compete with his other creditors.[26]

It is clear from section 2(3)(d) that a loan on terms that the lender will be entitled to a share of profits does not *per se* constitute a partnership if the agreement is in writing and signed by both the borrower and the lender.[27] What, however, is the position if there is no writing,[28] or if the writing is not signed? Is the lender a partner with the borrower and, if not, can the lender compete with the borrower's other creditors in the event of his bankruptcy?[29] As already noted,[30] the answer to the first of these questions is dependent on an analysis of all the circumstances and upon the real intention of the parties. As to the second, the courts have, as might be expected, construed section 3 in such a way as to avoid placing a lender under an oral agreement in a better position than one under a written agreement and held that in neither case can he compete with the other creditors.[31]

It is not considered that the application of section 3 could be **5-42** avoided by the device of splitting the loans, *e.g.* by lending the same person a small sum in consideration of a large share of profits, and a large sum at a low fixed rate of interest. In such a case it is submitted that a court would either hold the lender liable as a partner or apply the section to both loans. Where, however, in the ordinary course of

---

[23] *Ex p. Sheil* (1877) 4 Ch.D. 789.
[24] *Badeley v. Consolidated Bank* (1888) 38 Ch.D. 238. *Quaere* whether he has a right to present a petition for an insolvency order: see the arguments presented under the old bankruptcy law in *Re Miller* [1901] 1 K.B. 51.
[25] *Re Vince* [1892] 2 Q.B. 478. See also *Re Gieve* [1899] W.N. 41, 72.
[26] *Re Mason* [1899] 1 Q.B. 810.
[27] See *supra*, para. 5–02.
[28] See, as to this, *Pooley v. Driver* (1876) 5 Ch.D. 458.
[29] See s.3.
[30] See *supra*, para. 5–21.
[31] *Re Fort* [1897] 2 Q.B. 495. *Cf. Re Vince* [1892] 2 Q.B. 478.

business dealings a person makes a loan falling within the section and then bona fide makes another loan to the same borrower upon different terms, he can prove for the second loan in competition with the other creditors, even though he cannot compete in respect of the original loan.[32] On the other hand, if a lender who is entitled to a share of profits agrees to the substitution of a fixed rate of interest, his loan will remain within the ambit of the section, so that he cannot prove in competition with the other creditors unless, on a true analysis, the old loan has been repaid and a new loan made on different terms.[33]

5. PARTNERSHIP BY ESTOPPEL

Doctrine of holding out

5–43   The doctrine that a person who holds himself out as a partner will be liable as such to all persons who rely on his representation was well established long before the Partnership Act 1890 and was in truth no more than an illustration of the general principle of estoppel by conduct.[34] The Act now provides as follows:

"14.—(1) Every one who by words spoken or written or by conduct represents himself, or who knowingly suffers himself to be represented, as a partner in a particular firm, is liable as a partner[35] to any one who has on the faith of any such representation given credit to the firm, whether the representation has or has not been made or communicated to the person so giving credit by or with the knowledge of the apparent partner making the representation or suffering it to be made.

(2) Provided that where after a partner's death the partnership business is continued in the old firm-name, the continued use of that name or of the deceased partner's name as part thereof shall not of itself make his executors or administrators estate or effects liable for any partnership debts contracted after his death."

In order to establish liability under the section, the plaintiff must in essence prove (a) a holding out, (b) reliance thereon and (c) the

---

[32] See Ex p. Mills (1873) 8 Ch.App. 569; Re Mason [1899] 1 Q.B. 810.

[33] Ex p. Taylor (1879) 12 Ch.D. 366; Re Stone (1886) 33 Ch.D. 541; Re Hildesheim [1893] 2 Q.B. 357; Re Mason [1899] 1 Q.B. 810. Cf. Re Abenheim (1913) 109 L.T. 219, where there was a new agreement and the lender was entitled to prove in competition with other creditors; Re Slade [1921] 1 Ch. 160, decided under the Married Women's Property Act 1882, s.3.

[34] See in particular Waugh v. Carver (1793) 2 H.Bl. 235; Dickinson v. Valpy (1829) 10 B. & C. 128. Scarf v. Jardine (1882) 7 App.Cas. 345 was the last important case on this subject before the Act of 1890. See also De Berkom v. Smith (1793) 1 Esp. 29; Ex p. Matthews (1814) 3 V. & B. 125; Ex p. Watson (1815) 19 Ves.Jr. 459; Ford v. Whitmarsh (1840) Hurl. & Walm. 53. As to partnership by estoppel inter partes, see Holiday Inns Inc. v. Broadhead (1974) 232 E.G. 951.

[35] As to the nature of the liability so incurred, see infra, para. 13–04.

consequent giving of credit to the firm. These requirements will now be considered in turn.

(a) Holding Out

Question of fact or law?

The Court of Appeal has decided that the existence of a **5–44** partnership raises a mixed question of both law and fact, requiring an inference to be drawn from the primary facts found by the trial judge.[36] By analogy, it is considered that holding out can no longer be regarded as a pure question of fact,[37] since in order to determine that a person has been held out as a partner it will be necessary to find the existence of an apparent (as opposed to a real) partnership.

Form and time of representation

As is apparent from section 14(1), the holding out need not take **5–45** any particular form: it may be express or implied, and made orally, in writing or by conduct or by any combination of the three. Moreover, a person may hold himself out as a partner (or be so held out by others) without his name being revealed, so that if, with his authority, he is referred to as a person who does not wish to have his name disclosed, he will be liable to third parties who give credit to the firm in reliance on that representation.[38]

However, there can be no liability on the basis of holding out unless the relevant representation was made *before* the credit was given.[39]

Unauthorised holding out

Where a person has not held himself out but has been held out by **5–46** others, their authority to do so may be called into question. In such a case, express authority is not necessary since implied authority may be inferred.[40] Thus, if the person held out has signed or allowed his

---

[36] *Keith Spier Ltd. v. Mansell* [1970] 1 W.L.R. 333, 335, *per* Harman L.J. This accords with Lord Lindley's views: see *infra*, para. 7–16.

[37] Note, however, that Lord Lindley had observed "Whether a defendant has or has not held himself out to the plaintiff is in every case a question of fact, not a question of law ...". He then referred to *Wood v. Duke of Argyll* (1844) 6 Man. & G. 928; *Lake v. Duke of Argyll* (1844) 6 Q.B. ·477 .

[38] *Martyn v. Gray* (1863) 14 C.B.(N.S.) 824. See also *Maddick v. Marshall* (1864) 17 C.B.(N.S.) 829.

[39] *Baird v. Planque* (1858) 1 F. & F. 344.

[40] See *Wood v. Duke of Argyll* (1844) 6 Man. & G. 928; *Lake v. Duke of Argyll* (1844) 6 Q.B. 477; *Spooner v. Browning* [1898] 1 Q.B. 528. And see *Fox v. Clifton* (1830) 6 Bing. 776; *Edmundson v. Thompson* (1861) 2 F. & F. 564.

name to appear on documents or other materials prepared for public consumption,[41] or has made or authorised representations as to his position, albeit not intended for repetition,[42] that may be sufficient to affix him with liability.

Knowingly suffering a holding out

5–47   Liability can arise under section 14 of the Partnership Act 1890 where a person "knowingly suffers" himself to be held out as a partner, although the precise scope of this limb remains unclear. Certainly, it has been held that a retiring partner cannot be said to have knowingly suffered himself to be represented as a partner merely because he did not take care at the time of his retirement to ensure that all notepaper bearing his name as a partner had been destroyed, where the firm subsequently, without his knowledge or authority, used that notepaper to place an order.[43] By way of contrast, where under the old law[44] a partner had failed to inform the Registrar of Business Names of the dissolution of his partnership, he was held liable (on the basis of holding out) to a subsequent creditor of his former partner, who had continued the business, on the ground that the creditor had seen the registration certificate in the name of the two partners.[45] The dividing line is thus a fine one, as is illustrated by the following unresolved problem: Will a person who has not authorised others to hold him out as a partner but who, knowing that they are in fact holding him out, makes no attempt to stop them incur any liability under the section? Will he knowingly suffer himself to be held out if he merely protests? Must he go further and advertise his true position or apply for an injunction?[46] In view of the imprecision inherent in the section, prudence would seem to dictate the immediate commencement of proceedings if the objections are ignored.[47]

---

[41] *Collingwood v. Berkeley* (1863) 15 C.B.(N.S.) 145 (a decision relating to company prospectuses); also *Maddick v. Marshall* (1864) 17 C.B.(N.S.) 829. *Cf. Fox v. Clifton* (1830) 6 Bing. 776.

[42] *Martyn v. Gray* (1863) 14 C.B.(N.S.) 824.

[43] *Tower Cabinet Co. v. Ingram* [1949] 2 K.B. 397. See also *Jackson v. White and Midland Bank* [1967] 2 Lloyd's Rep. 68.

[44] The former Registration of Business Names Act 1916 was repealed by the Companies Act 1981. See now the Business Names Act 1985, considered *supra*, paras. 3–24 *et seq.*

[45] *Bishop v. Tudor Estates* [1952] C.P.L. 807.

[46] See *Barton v. Reed* [1932] 1 Ch. 362, 375 *et seq.*, *per* Luxmoore J.; also *Atkin v. Rose* [1923] 1 Ch. 522; *Berton v. Alliance Economic Investment Co.* [1922] 1 K.B. 761; *Elders Pastoral Ltd. v. Rutherford*, noted at [1991] N.Z.L.J. 73; and note *Wilson v. Twamley* [1904] 2 K.B. 99; *Bryant v. Hancock & Co.* [1898] 1 Q.B. 716, affirmed at [1899] A.C. 442. Before the Act authority, express or implied, was necessary.

[47] As in *Walter v. Ashton* [1902] 2 Ch. 282. As to the right to an injunction when there is any risk of liability, see *ibid.*; also *Gray v. Smith* (1889) 43 Ch.D. 208; *Thynne v. Shove* (1890) 45 Ch.D. 577; *Burchell v. Wilde* [1900] 1 Ch. 551; *Townsend v. Jarman* [1900] 2 Ch. 698.

Effect of fraud

If a person has been induced to hold himself out (or to allow **5–48**
himself to be held out) as a partner by fraud or by a promise of
freedom from liability, he will remain fully liable under the section to
third parties who have relied on the representation. So far as such
third parties are concerned, the fraud or promise is strictly *res inter
alios acta*.[48]

(b) Reliance

It need hardly be stated that, in order to establish liability under the **5–49**
section, a third party must show that he was aware of the holding
out; if he was ignorant of it, he cannot have been misled or otherwise
have acted "on the faith" of the representation.[49] However, a
question of some difficulty may arise when, knowing of the holding
out, the third party is in possession of information which indicates
that the person held out is not in truth a partner.

A person held out as a partner will be liable whether or not he
shares the profits or losses of the business,[50] and there would seem to
be no logical reason why his liability should be negatived or in any
way affected merely because the third party knows that he shares
neither and, indeed, (if such be the case) that he is entitled to a full
indemnity from the persons who make use of his name. In the words
of Lord Lindley:

"His name does not induce credit the less on account of his right
to be indemnified by others against any loss falling in the first
instance on himself; and although, in the case supposed, he cannot
be believed to be a *partner*, the lending of his name does justify
the belief that he is willing to be responsible to those who may be
induced to trust him for payment."[51]

On this basis, a "salaried" partner[52] could not reasonably expect to **5–50**
escape liability even if, unusually, he is known to enjoy that status.[53]

---

[48] See *Ex p. Broome* (1811) 1 Rose 69; *Ellis v. Schmoeck* (1829) 5 Bing. 521; *Collingwood v. Berkeley* (1863) 15 C.B.(N.S.) 145; *Maddick v. Marshall* (1864) 16 C.B.(N.S.) 387 and (1864) 17 C.B.(N.S.) 829.

[49] See *Vice v. Anson* (1827) 7 B. & C. 409; *Pott v. Eyton* (1846) 3 C.B. 32; *Hudgell Yeates & Co. v. Watson* [1978] Q.B. 451.

[50] *Ex p. Watson* (1815) 19 Ves.Jr. 459. See also *Kirkwood v. Cheetham* (1862) 2 F. & F. 798, where A was B's agent and held himself out as B's partner; both A and B were held to be liable for goods supplied to A for B. Cf. *Hardman v. Booth* (1862) 1 Hurl. & Colt. 803.

[51] See *Brown v. Leonard* (1816) 2 Chitty 120, noticed *infra*, para. 5–59.

[52] See further, *infra*, paras. 5–65, 5–66.

[53] What, in any event, is a third party to assume on learning of the salaried partner's status? After all, some salaried partners may, for whatever reason, not be given a full indemnity against debts, etc.

However, there may be exceptional cases where the information available to the third party is of such a nature that liability will be avoided, and the decision in *Alderson v. Pope*[54] may represent an example of just such a case. Lord Ellenborough is reported to have held:

"that where there was a stipulation between A, B and C, who appeared to the world as co-partners, that C should not participate in the profit and loss, and should not be liable as a partner, C was not liable as such to those who had notice of this stipulation, and that notice to one member of a firm was notice to the whole partnership."

Since the above represents the entirety of the report, the precise significance of the words "should not be liable as a partner" is unclear. Lord Lindley's analysis was as follows:

"If these words meant that C was to be indemnified by A and B ... the decision was erroneous.[55] But if they meant that C could not be liable at all to third parties for the acts of A and B, then the question would arise whether this was not altogether inconsistent with C's conduct ...".

5–51   In the latter case, the decision would be in accordance with section 8 of the Partnership Act 1890, and in no way inconsistent with the principle discussed in the preceding paragraph, since the creditors will have had notice not only that C should not participate in profits (which, it is submitted, would be strictly irrelevant) but also that he should *not be under any liability as a partner*.

(c) The Giving of Credit

5–52 This expression is not defined in section 14 of the Partnership Act 1890, and it is submitted that it should not be construed in a technical or restrictive sense but as describing any transaction with the firm. Thus, in *Lynch v. Stiff*[56] the High Court of Australia held, on the equivalent wording of the Partnership Act 1862 (New South Wales), that a client had given credit to a supposed firm of solicitors by entrusting the firm with his money for investment purposes. Indeed, it is thought that there could even be an effective holding out *vis-à-vis*

---

[54] (1808) 1 Camp. 404n. But note the terms of the Partnership Act 1890, s.8, considered *infra*, paras. 12–154 *et seq.*

[55] Lord Lindley justified this conclusion by reference to his previous observations, which have already been set out *verbatim*.

[56] [1943] 68 C.L.R. 428. The expression pre-dated the Partnership Act 1890: see, for example, *Dickinson v. Valpy* (1829) 10 B. & C. 128, 141, *per* Parke J.

the Inland Revenue and the Commissioners of Customs and Excise,[57] which illustrates one of the frequently unappreciated risks undertaken by unwary salaried partners.[58]

Inchoate partnerships, etc.

A person who holds himself out as willing to *become* a partner **5–53** does not thereby incur any liability to third parties.[59] There is no justification for extending the liability of persons who have represented themselves as partners to those who merely indicate their intention to enter into partnership at some future time.[60] This is implicit in the decisions in *Bourne v. Freeth*[61] and *Keith Spicer Ltd. v. Mansell*.[62]

Use of firm name after change in firm: outgoing partners

It often happens that, after the dissolution of a partnership, one or **5–54** more of the former partners continue to carry on the business under the old name; *a fortiori* in the case of a technical dissolution resulting from the retirement or expulsion of a partner. In applying the doctrine of holding out in such cases, it must be remembered that, until he has notice to the contrary, a person who deals with a firm after a change in its constitution is entitled to treat as partners all apparent members of the old firm and all persons whom he knows to have been members of the old firm.[63] Notice in the *Gazette* is sufficient notice in the case of persons who have had no dealings with the firm prior to the change but, in the case of those who have had such dealings, actual notice must be proved.[64] However, no notice of retirement is necessary in order to prevent a partner, who is not known to the person dealing with the firm to have been a partner, from becoming liable for debts contracted after his retirement.[65] This

---

[57] It might, however, be argued that there is no reliance by the Commissioners of Customs and Excise, given the registration requirements contained in the Value Added Tax Act 1983 and the regulations made thereunder (as to which, see *infra*, paras. 37–06 *et seq.*). Otherwise, see *ibid.* s.30(5).

[58] See further, as to such partners, *infra*, paras. 5–65, 5–66.

[59] See *Floydd v. Cheney* [1970] Ch. 602.

[60] Lord Lindley put it thus: "Although a person who represents himself to be a partner is properly held liable as a partner to persons who have acted on the faith of his being so, it would be in the highest degree unjust to confound a representation by a person that he intended to become a partner with a representation that he was one in point of fact, and to hold him as much liable to third parties for the one representation as for the other."

[61] (1829) 9 B. & C. 632. See also *Reynell v. Lewis* and *Wyld v. Hopkins* (1846) 15 M. & W. 517. Cf. *Martyn v. Gray* (1863) 14 C.B.(N.S.) 824.

[62] [1970] 1 W.L.R. 333.

[63] Partnership Act 1890, s.36; *Tower Cabinet Co. v. Ingram* [1949] 2 K.B. 397; also *Evans v. Drummond* (1801) 4 Esp. 89; *Farrar v. Deflinne* (1844) 1 Car. & K. 580; *Scarf v. Jardine* (1882) 7 App.Cas. 345, 349, *per* Lord Selborne L.C.; and see *infra*, paras. 13–42 *et seq.*

[64] See the cases cited in the preceding note; also *Pillani v. Motilal* (1929) 45 T.L.R. 283.

[65] Partnership Act 1890, s.36(3); *Carter v. Whalley* (1830) 1 B. & Ad. 11; *Elders Pastoral Ltd. v. Rutherford*, noted at [1991] N.Z.L.J. 73.

will be the position even if a person dealing with the firm discovers that he was a partner after the date of his retirement, because the date from which section 36(3) of the Partnership Act 1890 operates is the date of the retirement.[66]

5–55   A retiring partner may, nevertheless, remain liable for debts contracted in the course of completing a particular transaction commenced prior to the date of his retirement, irrespective of the above principles,[67] on the basis that, having authorised his co-partners to act as his agents, he is estopped from denying the agency as against persons who, without notice of the revocation of that authority, have acted on the footing that the agency continued.[68]

The current editor's view is that the position will be the same in the case of any other outgoing partner.[69]

Continued use of firm name

5–56   If the firm name does not disclose the fact that the retiring partner is member of the firm, the continued use of that name after his retirement will not, as a matter of fact, involve any holding out, otherwise than to persons who knew of his former connection with the firm.[70] Equally, if the firm name consists only of the surname of the retiring partner, followed by the words "and Co.," the continued use of that name will not, under ordinary circumstances, represent the retiring partner to be a continuing member of the firm and thereby expose him to liability.[71]

5–57   On the other hand, if the firm name indicates that the retiring partner *is* a member of the firm, the continued use of that name will inevitably represent him as still being such a member and, if he omits to give due notice of his retirement, his liability will continue.[72] If, however, he does give such notice, but authorises or "knowingly suffers"[73] his former partners to carry on business under the old name, it is doubtful whether or not he will thereby incur liability on the basis of holding out. Although the answer to this question depends on the true construction of sections 14 and 36 of the

---

[66] *Tower Cabinet Co. v. Ingram* [1949] 2 K.B. 397.

[67] *Court v. Berlin* [1897] 2 Q.B. 396.

[68] *Scarf v. Jardine* (1882) 7 App.Cas. 345, 349, (*per* Lord Selborne), 357 (*per* Lord Blackburn). See also the Partnership Act 1890, s.5 and *infra*, paras. 12–02 *et seq*.

[69] The Partnership Act 1890 s.36(3) refers only to death, bankruptcy and retirement, whilst *ibid.* subss. (1) and (2) are of general application. It is considered that retirement must for these purposes be construed widely, so as to include any form of departure, whether voluntary or compulsory.

[70] See the cases cited *supra*, para. 5–54, n. 63.

[71] *Burchell v. Wilde* [1900] 1 Ch. 551; *Townsend v. Jarman* [1900] 2 Ch. 698.

[72] Partnership Act 1890, s.36.

[73] As to the meaning of this expression, see *supra*, para. 5–47.

Partnership Act 1890,[74] the following pre-1890 cases may give some indication of the possible outcome.[75]

In *Williams v. Keats*,[76] after a partner had retired and notice **5–58** thereof had been given by advertisement in the *Gazette*, a bill of exchange was accepted by his co-partner in the names of himself and his former partner. Both partners' names still remained painted up over their old business premises. Lord Ellenborough held that the retired partner was liable on the bill notwithstanding the advertisement, since there was no evidence to show that the plaintiff in fact knew of his retirement.[77] Significantly, the only evidence that the retired partner had authorised the continued use of his name was the fact that he had not prevented it.[78] *Dolman v. Orchard*[79] was a similar case, although it appears that there was no advertisement; nevertheless, the verdict favoured the retiring partner.

In *Brown v. Leonard*,[80] the plaintiff sued on a promissory note **5–59** made in the name of Spring, Leonard and Bush. Before the note was made Bush had retired from the firm; moreover, he had informed the plaintiff of that fact before he accepted the note, but added that his name was to continue to be used for a certain time following the retirement. Bush was held liable on the note, notwithstanding his retirement, although he does seem to have undertaken that the note would be provided for.

In *Newsome v. Coles*,[81] a firm comprising a father, Thomas Coles, **5–60** and his three sons carried on business under the name of Thomas Coles & Sons. Thomas Coles died, but the three sons carried on the partnership business under the old name for several years. The firm was then dissolved. The business was thereafter carried on by one of the sons under the old name, the other sons having established a new business. The dissolution was advertised in the *Gazette* and notice was sent to all persons who had previously had dealings with the firm. The plaintiff did not know of the dissolution and had had no previous dealings with the firm, but he sought to make all three sons liable on a bill of exchange accepted after the dissolution by the one who had continued to trade under the old name and who had accepted the bill in that name. The other sons, however, had never

---

[74] In this connection, see the cases cited *supra*, para. 5–56, n. 71.
[75] As to how far they may be used for the purposes of construing the Act, see *Bank of England v. Vagliano* [1891] A.C. 107, 145, *per* Lord Herschell. See also *supra*, para. 1–12, n. 14.
[76] (1817) 2 Stark. 290.
[77] It appears from the arguments that the plaintiffs were not old customers of the firm, so that notice in the *Gazette* would now be sufficient notice under the Partnership Act 1890, s.36.
[78] Cf. *Newsome v. Coles* (1811) 2 Camp. 617, *infra*, para. 5–60.
[79] (1825) 2 Car. & P. 104.
[80] (1816) 2 Chitty 120.
[81] (1811) 2 Camp. 617.

held themselves out to the plaintiff as partners in any firm carrying on business under the name of Thomas Coles & Sons and they had done nothing to authorise the use of that name after the dissolution; equally, they did know that the old name was still being used and they had taken no steps to restrain such use. It was held that they were not bound to take such steps and the plaintiff's claim was rejected.[82]

5–61   In *Ex p. Central Bank of London*,[83] John Fraser and William Fraser were partners in a business which was carried on under the name "W. and J. Fraser". John Fraser retired and notice of his retirement was sent to the firm's principal creditors. William, with the consent of John, thereafter continued to carry on the business under the old name and accepted a bill of exchange in that name. The Court of Appeal held that John was not liable to the holder of the bill. This case went further than *Newsome v. Coles*,[84] because John Fraser's name was part of the firm name, and he appears to have consented to, and not merely acquiesced in, the continued use of that name. Moreover the bank, who were holders of the bill, had had no previous dealings with the firm, and it does not appear from the report that notice of the dissolution had been advertised in the *Gazette* or otherwise given to them.

Incoming and outgoing partners: Scarf v. Jardine

5–62   The application of the holding out doctrine becomes more complicated when a new partner is admitted to the firm on or immediately after a partner's retirement and the firm name continues unchanged. This may be illustrated by the following example. Assume that A and B carry on business under the name X & Co. Neither A nor B holds himself out as a member of that firm to anyone who does not know of his connection with it. Thus, if A retires from the firm but gives no notice thereof, he will remain liable to existing customers who know of that connection and continue to deal with the firm on the assumption that he is still a partner; but A will incur no liability to new customers of X & Co. who have never heard of him. If, on A's retirement, C enters into partnership with B, and B and C thereafter carry on business under the name X & Co., even an old customer of X & Co., who continues to deal with the firm and has no notice of A's retirement or C's admission, cannot

---

[82] *Cf. Williams v. Keats, supra,* para. 5–58; and see the terms of the Partnership Act 1890, s.14(1), *supra,* para. 5–43.

[83] [1892] 2 Q.B. 633. The case was decided after the passing of the Partnership Act 1890 but was not a decision under that Act.

[84] Kay L.J. considered the case to be governed by *Newsome v. Coles, supra*: see [1892] 2 Q.B. 633, 639.

truly say that A ever held himself out as a partner with C or with both B and C. Consequently, such an old customer cannot maintain an action against A, B and C jointly for a debt contracted by X & Co. after A's retirement.[85] What he *may* do is either sue A and B, on the ground that he dealt with X & Co. relying on the fact that they were both still members of that firm, or sue B and C, on the ground that they are his real debtors. He must, however, elect between those two options: he may not sue A, B and C on the ground that B and C are in truth the partners of X & Co. and that A is estopped from denying that he is a member of that firm. This was decided in *Scarf v. Jardine*.[86]

On the other hand, if the old customer has no notice of A's **5–63** retirement, but learns that C has become a partner of X & Co., it is submitted that he would be entitled to sue A, B and C jointly for a debt contracted by X & Co. after A's retirement and C's admission.[87]

The position would be different in the above example if A and B carried on business in their own names rather than in the name of X & Co. Thus, again assuming A to have retired but to have given no notice thereof and C to have entered into partnership with B, if the new firm, with A's consent, carries on business under the name A, B and C, A would necessarily hold himself out as being in partnership with B and C and would be estopped from denying it as against anyone dealing with the new firm in reliance thereon.

Position of estate of deceased partner

If a partner dies and the surviving partners carry on the business in **5–64** the old name, they will not thereby impose any liability on the estate of the deceased partner (or on his personal representatives) on the basis of holding out, even when they deal with old customers of the firm who have no notice of the death. This is provided for in section 14(2) of the Partnership Act 1890, although even prior to that Act the holding out doctrine had never been extended to such a case.[88] Even if the deceased partner's personal representative is the surviving partner, the position will be the same: as a general rule a debt contracted by a personal representative in that capacity gives the

---

[85] In recent editions of this work (*i.e.* prior to the 16th ed.) the following additional observations appeared at this point: "To allow him to do so would, indeed, be to give him the best of both worlds of partnership liability—apparent in the case of A and actual in the case of C—and it is appropriate that the customer should not be allowed to have it both ways when dealing with a firm whose name does not point to any specific members."

[86] (1882) 7 App.Cas. 345.

[87] Lord Lindley observed "*Scarf v. Jardine* is not an authority against this proposition, nor are Lord Selborne's observations in that case at 7 App.Cas. 350, as the author understands them." See also *infra*, para. 13–04.

[88] Partnership Act 1890, s.14(2); *Webster v. Webster* (1791) 3 Swan. 490; *Devaynes v. Noble* (*Houlton's Case*) (1816) 1 Mer. 616; *Vulliamy v. Noble* (1817) 3 Mer. 593.

creditor no right of recourse against the assets comprised in the estate.[89]

Salaried partners

5–65   Perhaps the most common case of a deliberate holding out which will be encountered today, particularly in the professions, is that of the so called "salaried partner." By this notoriously vague expression is usually meant a person who, though in reality an employee of the firm remunerated by a fixed or variable salary, is nevertheless held out to clients and to the world as a partner. However, that is not to say that a salaried partner may not be a partner in the true sense, as was made clear by Megarry J. in *Stekel v. Ellice*[90]:

> "Certain aspects of a salaried partnership are not disputed. The term 'salaried partner' is not a term of art, and to some extent it may be said to be a contradiction in terms. However, it is a convenient expression which is widely used to denote a person who is held out to the world as being a partner, with his name appearing as a partner on the notepaper of the firm and so on. At the same time, he receives a salary as remuneration, rather than a share of the profits, though he may, in addition to his salary, receive some bonus or other sum of money dependent upon the profits. *Quoad* the outside world it often will matter little whether a man is a full partner or a salaried partner; for a salaried partner is held out as being a partner, and the partners will be liable for his acts accordingly. But within the partnership it may be important to know whether a salaried partner is truly to be classified as a mere employee, or as a partner.

> "... It seems to me impossible to say that as a matter of law a salaried partner is or is not necessarily a partner in the true sense. He may or may not be a partner, depending on the facts. What must be done, I think, is to look at the substance of the relationship between the parties; and there is ample authority for saying that the question whether or not there is a partnership depends on what the true relationship is, and not on any mere label attached to that relationship."[91]

Consistently with the views expressed in the above passage, few identifiable principles can be derived from the decided cases. In

---

[89] See *Farhall v. Farhall* (1871) 7 Ch.App. 123; *Owen v. Delamere* (1872) 15 Eq. 134; but see *Vulliamy v. Noble* (1817) 3 Mer. 593. And see further, *infra*, paras. 26–26 *et seq.*

[90] [1973] 1 W.L.R. 191, 198D–F, 199G–H.

[91] See further, as to the latter point, *supra*, paras. 5–05 *et seq.*

Burgess v. O'Brien,[92] the Industrial Tribunal took the view that Burgess was a partner, even though he was remunerated by a salary and commission and was not liable to meet any share of losses whereas, in *Briggs v. Oates*,[93] Scott J. appears to have regarded a similar remuneration package as indicative of employment rather than partnership.[94] Equally, in some instances, the courts appear to pay scant regard to a salaried partner's true status.[95]

The possibility that a salaried partner may also be held out to the **5–66** Inland Revenue and to the Commissioners of Customs and Excise, and thereby find himself liable for all the tax due from the firm, has already been noted.[96] He can hardly complain about this once he has accepted the benefit of a Schedule D (rather than a Schedule E) assessment on his partnership remuneration.

Minors

A minor does not incur contractual liability by holding himself out **5–67** as a partner.[97]

Torts

The doctrine of holding out only applies in favour of persons who **5–68** have "given credit to the firm"[98] on the footing that the person whom they seek to make liable is a partner thereof.[99] The doctrine has no wider application, *e.g.* in relation to pure torts which are in no way dependent upon the injured party having had any dealings with or placing trust in the firm. Admittedly, in *Stables v. Eley*,[1] a retired partner, whose name appeared on a cart, was held liable for the negligence of its driver, but the case did not establish any point of principle, as Lord Lindley explained:

"... although in that case there may have been evidence to go to the jury that the defendant was liable, proof by him that the driver was not his servant would have rendered him not liable."[2]

---

[92] [1966] I.T.R. 164. The Tribunal also appears to have been influenced by the very act of holding out, but this cannot be right: see *Briggs v. Oates*, *infra*. And see an article at (1991) 135 S.J. 1058.

[93] [1990] I.C.R. 473. In this case, there was also evidence that Oates did not know that the partnership between Briggs and his existing partner was due to expire *before* the conclusion of Oates' contractual period of employment: *ibid*. p. 475E.

[94] *Ibid*. p. 475D.

[95] See, for example, *United Bank of Kuwait Ltd. v. Hammoud* [1988] 1 W.L.R. 1051.

[96] See *supra*, para. 5–52.

[97] See *supra*, para. 4–08.

[98] See *supra*, para. 5–52.

[99] See *Scarf v. Jardine* (1882) 7 App.Cas. 357.

[1] (1825) 1 C. & P. 614.

[2] As when A's servant was wearing B's livery: *Quarman v. Burnett* (1840) 6 M. & W. 499, 508–509, *per* Parke B.

As observed in previous editions of this work, if the decision went further than this it is wrong, the Court of Appeal having disapproved it as reported.[3] Naturally, the position will be different in the case of professional negligence, negligent mis-statements and analogous forms of tortious liability, where there is ample scope for the application of the doctrine.

Judgment in firm name

5–69   As will be seen hereafter, a judgment obtained against a firm in the firm name may be enforced against a person who has rendered himself liable for the firm's debts by reason of the holding out doctrine.[4]

Business Names Act 1985

5–70   Neither this Act nor its predecessors[5] made any direct alteration in the law on the subject under discussion. However, as has already been seen,[6] the Act does require the names and addresses of the partners in a firm having a place of business and carrying on business in Great Britain under a name which does not consist of the surnames of all the partners (together with any permitted additions)[7] to be shown on all business letters and other documents issued by the firm,[8] and in a notice prominently displayed in the partnership premises.[9] In this way it has had the incidental effect of reducing the risk of liability resulting from an inadvertent holding out.

Outgoing partners

5–71   The presence of a partner's name on the firm's notepaper, etc.,[10] in compliance with the requirements of the Act, obviously provides a ready means whereby the continuing partners may, following his departure from the firm, hold him out as still remaining a member thereof. However, it has already been seen that an outgoing partner is not bound to secure the destruction of all such notepaper and other

---

[3] See *Smith v. Bailey* [1891] 2 Q.B. 403.

[4] See *Davis v. Hyman & Co.* [1903] 1 K.B. 854; also *infra*, paras. 14–89 *et seq.*

[5] The use of business names was originally governed by the Registration of Business Names Act 1916 but that Act was repealed and replaced by a more liberal regime introduced by the Companies Act 1981, Pt. II. The 1985 Act consolidated the relevant provisions of the 1981 Act.

[6] See *supra*, paras. 3–24 *et seq.*

[7] Business Names Act 1985, s.1(2).

[8] *Ibid.* s.4(1)(a). The other documentation referred to in the subsection comprises written orders for goods or services to be supplied to the business, invoices and receipts issued in the course of the business and written demands for payment of debts arising in the course of the business. The only exception to this requirement consists of documents issued by a firm of more than 20 partners, provided that certain conditions are met: *ibid.* s.4(3).

[9] *Ibid.* s.4(1)(b).

[10] See generally, *ibid.* s.4; and see *supra*, para. 3–32.

documentation in order to free himself from potential liability on that account,[11] although it would be otherwise if he authorised its use.[12]

6. GENERAL AND PARTICULAR PARTNERSHIPS

It is now only rarely necessary to draw a formal distinction between **5–72** general and particular partnerships, in the manner traditionally adopted by writers on partnership law.[13] Nevertheless, there are still many cases in which persons enter into a partnership limited to a particular trade, transaction or adventure where the distinction may be of relevance.[14]

Partnership for one transaction

If persons who are not partners in any other business share the **5–73** profits and losses (or merely the profits) of a particular trade, transaction or adventure, they will become partners to that extent and to that extent only.[15] Thus, if two solicitors, who are not partners, are jointly retained to conduct litigation in a particular case, and they agree to share the profit costs arising therefrom, they will become partners only so far as concerns the conduct of that case.[16] In the same way, a partnership may be limited to the purchase and sale of a particular asset,[17] the working of a patent either at large[18] or confined to a particular area,[19] the development of a plot of land,[20] the exploitation of a contract of service[21] or the sowing, cropping, harvesting and sale of a particular crop.[22] In all such cases, the rights and liabilities of the partners are governed by the same principles as apply to general partnerships,[23] albeit that they may be quantitatively (even if not qualitatively) less extensive.

---

[11] *Tower Cabinet Co. v. Ingram* [1949] 2 K.B. 397.

[12] *Ibid.*

[13] This classification can be traced to the following passage in the Digest—"*Societates contrahuntur sive universorum bonorum, sive negotiationis alicujus, sive vectigalis, sive etiam rei unius*" (Partnerships are contracted either in the whole of the goods of the respective partners, or in some particular speculation, or in a state concession or even in a single piece of property): Dig. xvii, tit. 2 (*pro socio*), 1–5 pr. However, save for the purpose noted in the text, Lord Lindley considered such classification "not worth enlarging upon."

[14] These partnerships are referred to in the Partnership Act 1890, s.32(b). See *infra*, paras. 24–07 *et seq.*

[15] See *Re Abenheim* (1913) 109 L.T. 219, 220, *per* Phillimore J.; *Mann v. D'Arcy* [1968] 1 W.L.R. 893; also *De Berkom v. Smith* (1793) 1 Esp. 29; *Smith v. Watson* (1824) 2 B. & C. 401; *Heyhoe v. Burgh* (1850) 9 C.B. 431. See, as to partnerships in profits only, *supra*, paras. 5–30, 5–31.

[16] *Robinson v. Anderson* (1855) 20 Beav. 98 and, on appeal, 7 De G.M. & G. 239; *McGregor v. Bainbrigge* (1848) 7 Hare 164.

[17] *Oppenheimer v. Frazer & Wyatt* [1907] 2 K.B. 50.

[18] *Lovell v. Hicks* (1837) 2 Y. & C.Ex. 472.

[19] *Ridgway v. Philip* (1834) 1 Cr.M. & R. 415.

[20] *Fenston v. Johnstone (Inspector of Taxes)* (1940) 23 T.C. 29; *Walker West Developments Ltd. v. F. J. Emmett* (1979) 252 E.G. 1171.

[21] *E. Rennison & Son v. Minister of Social Security* (1970) 114 S.J. 952.

[22] *George Hall & Son v. Platt* (1954) 47 R. & I.T. 713.

[23] See *Reid v. Hollinshead* (1825) 4 B. & C. 867, and the cases cited *supra*, nn. 15 and 16.

5-74   The scope of any such partnership will naturally depend on the terms of the agreement into which the parties have entered as well as upon their subsequent conduct. This is illustrated by the decision in *J. & J. Cunningham v. Lucas*,[24] where the plaintiffs had purchased potatoes from suppliers in Holland for resale in this country. Originally the potatoes were to be shipped in two vessels, but one vessel was damaged and a larger vessel was substituted. More potatoes were purchased in order to fill the substituted vessel. The plaintiffs claimed that the defendants had agreed to enter into a joint venture whereby all the potatoes would be marketed in this country and the plaintiffs and the defendants would share any loss or profit equally. The defendants claimed that only part of the cargo was agreed to be the subject of the joint venture. McNair J., after considering all the circumstances, held that the plaintiffs had established their claim and directed an account to be taken accordingly.

7. SUB-PARTNERSHIPS

5-75 Lord Lindley defined a sub-partnership as follows:

"A sub-partnership is as it were a partnership within a partnership; it presupposes the existence of a partnership to which it is itself subordinate. An agreement to share profits only constitutes a partnership between the parties to the agreement. If, therefore, several persons are partners and one of them agrees to share the profits derived by him with a stranger, this agreement does not make the stranger a partner in the original firm. The result of such an agreement is to constitute what is called a *sub-partnership*, that is to say, it makes the parties to it partners *inter se*; but it in no way affects the other members of the principal firm."[25]

Thus, a sub-partnership is, conventionally, a partnership in a share of another partnership and, whilst it is of a derivative nature, the sub-partnership normally operates outside the confines of the main partnership.[26] However, there is, in theory, no reason why a sub-partnership should not be formed between a group of partners within

---

[24] [1957] 1 Lloyd's Rep. 416.

[25] This principle was stated thus by civilian lawyers: "*Socius mei socii, socius meus non est*" (The partner of my partner is not my partner).

[26] In *Ex p. Barrow* (1815) 2 Rose 255, Lord Eldon stated the law thus: "I take it to have been long since established, that a man may become a partner with A where A and B are partners and yet not be a member of that partnership which existed between A and B. In the case of *Sir Chas. Raymond* [(1734)], a banker in the city, a Mr. Fletcher agreed with Sir Chas. Raymond that he should be interested so far as to receive a share of his profits of the business, and which share he had a right to draw out from the firm of Raymond & Co. But it was held that he was no partner in that partnership; had no demand against it; had no account in it; and that he must be satisfied with a share of the profits arising and given to Sir Chas. Raymond." See also *Bray v. Fromont* (1821) 6 Madd. 5; *Ex p. Dodgson* (1830) Mont. & Mac. A. 445.

the head partnership, with or without the blessing of the other partners.[27]

In practice, most partnership agreements prohibit the creation of sub-partnerships without the consent of the other partners.[28]

Where a sub-partnership is created, the terms of the head **5–76** partnership will not be incorporated as a matter of implication,[29] so that it cannot be assumed that the sub-partnership will endure for the same term as the head partnership.

It follows from the fact that a sub-partner will not become a partner in the head partnership that he will not be liable to the creditors of that firm; his indirect participation in the profits of the head partnership is naturally not sufficient to found any such liability.[30] Moreover, the sub-partnership and the head partnership will, in the current editor's view, be distinct entities for the purposes of the insolvency legislation.[31]

Arrangements analogous to sub-partnership

It is not unknown in some spheres for all the members of a **5–77** partnership to enter into a series of partnerships with individual third parties regulating the terms on which the main firm's business will be carried on as between those members on the one hand and the third party on the other.[32] On one view this could be regarded as a true sub-partnership if it involves the creation of a partnership in the aggregate shares of the members of the main firm, although it is doubtful whether this will ever be the parties' intention. Equally, a member of Firm A may enter into a wholly separate partnership with third parties (Firm B), but in a representative capacity.[33] In such a case, that partner's share in Firm B will be an asset of Firm A and, to that extent, it could be said that there is a sub-partnership therein.[34]

So-called "group partnerships" will be adverted to hereafter.[35]

---

[27] This might be appropriate in the case of a national firm with an overall profit sharing structure, where individual offices are to be treated as separate "profit centres" with a greater or lesser degree of autonomy.

[28] See infra, para. 10–80.

[29] Frost v. Moulton (1856) 21 Beav. 596.

[30] See generally, supra, paras. 5–32 et seq.

[31] See infra, paras. 27–12, 27–28.

[32] Such a situation is occasionally encountered (particularly in medical partnerships) when a series of "salaried" partners are engaged. In an extreme case, the end result may even be a pyramidal structure, as each salaried partner is required to sanction the admission of subsequent salaried partners. The complications which can ensue are considerable and, accordingly, such an option is not to be commended.

[33] See, as to trustee and nominee partners, supra, paras. 4–25, 4–26.

[34] Unusually, in this case the supposed sub-partnership is created before the main partnership.

[35] See infra, paras. 11–20 et seq.

CHAPTER 6

CONSIDERATION FOR A CONTRACT OF PARTNERSHIP

6–01 An agreement to enter into partnership, like any other contract, must be supported by consideration if it is to be enforceable. However, in a normal case such consideration can readily be found, whether in the form of a contribution of capital or a particular skill, or some act which may result in liability to third parties.[1] Alternatively, it may (and, indeed, frequently will) be represented by the mutual obligations which the parties undertake by entering into partnership together.

6–02 A bona fide contract of partnership is not invalidated by the unequal size or value of the parties' contributions: each must be his own judge of the adequacy of the consideration which he will receive. Vice-Chancellor Wigram put it in this way:

> "If one man has skill and wants capital to make that skill available; and another has capital and wants skill; and the two agree that the one shall provide capital and the other skill, it is perfectly clear that there is a good consideration for the agreement on both sides; and it is impossible for the court to measure the quantum of value. The parties must decide that for themselves."[2]

Sharing of profits but not losses

6–03 It has already been seen that parties may enter into partnership on terms that they will all share the profits, but that losses will be borne by only some of their number.[3] Such an agreement, which amounts to no more than an agreement that some parties will indemnify the others against losses, is not invalid as a *nudum pactum* even where the management of the firm is to be left in the hands of the parties offering the indemnity,[4] although there is one early expression of judicial opinion to the contrary.[5] Lord Lindley pointed out that the

---

[1] See The Herkimer (1804) Stewart's Adm.Rep. 17, 23; *Andersons' Case* (1877) 7 Ch.D. 75.
[2] *Dale v. Hamilton* (1846) 5 Hare 369, 393, *per* Wigram V.-C.
[3] See *supra*, paras. 5–27 *et seq.*
[4] *Geddes v. Wallace* (1820) 2 Bli. 270 is an example of such an agreement. Note also *Walker West Developments Ltd. v. F. J. Emmett Ltd.* (1979) 252 E.G. 1171.
[5] In *Brophy v. Holmes* (1828) 2 Moll. 5, Hart L.C. expressed the opinion that an agreement between A and B that A should advance capital, that B should be sole manager, and that they should divide the profits equally, but that all losses should fall on B was, as regards the last stipulation, void, as being a *nudum pactum*; his Lordship thought that under such an agreement the losses should be borne equally.

fact that the parties indemnified "become, or agree to become, partners is quite sufficient consideration to give validity to a contract that they shall be indemnified."

Premiums

At one time the payment of a premium as part of the consideration **6–04** for entry into partnership was widespread, but such payments are now rarely encountered save, perhaps, in the case of certain "investment" partnerships. Nevertheless, where a premium is due but unpaid, it may be recovered by action, provided that the plaintiff has been ready and willing to take the defendant into partnership as agreed.[6] The return of premiums in the event of the premature termination of the partnership is now governed by the Partnership Act 1890, s.40.[7]

Medical partnerships in the National Health Service

By the National Health Service Act 1977, s.54 and Sched. 10, it is **6–05** an offence for any medical practitioner whose name is entered on any list of medical practitioners undertaking to provide general medical services in the National Health Service to sell the goodwill or any part of the goodwill of his medical practice. It is also an offence for any person to buy such goodwill.[8] This prohibition applies equally to sales and purchases of shares of goodwill as between partners.[9]

However, the Act goes further by providing that where, in **6–06** pursuance of a partnership agreement, any valuable consideration, other than the performance of services in the partnership, is given as consideration for being taken into partnership, there is for the purposes of the section deemed to have been a sale of goodwill by the partner to whom the consideration is given.[10] It follows that the payment of a premium or the imposition on an incoming partner of some particularly onerous obligation unconnected with the practice will almost inevitably involve the commission of an offence. What is less clear is the extent to which the prohibition will affect any of the obligations normally imposed by a partnership agreement. It has been held to have no application in the case of restrictions on competition,

---

[6] *Walker v. Harris* (1793) 1 Anst. 245.
[7] See *infra*, para. 25–06 *et seq*.
[8] National Health Service Act 1977, Sched. 10, para. 1(1).
[9] *Ibid*. Sched. 10, para. 1(8).
[10] *Ibid*. Sched. 10, para. 2(2)(*a*).

whether they be mutual or unilateral.[11] As to other, less controversial provisions, the arguments have been canvassed before the Court of Appeal but, in the event, no judicial opinion has been formally expressed thereon.[12] It is submitted that it could only be argued that an offence has been committed in an exceptional case where the obligations assumed by one or more of the partners are grossly disproportionate to those assumed by the others.[13]

6–07   There will also be a deemed sale of goodwill if a partner, in pursuance of a partnership agreement, performs services for a consideration which is substantially inadequate.[14]

Consideration and inheritance tax

6–08   The existence or adequacy of the consideration given by a partner on his admission to the partnership may be material in determining whether the whole or any part of the share in the partnership assets to which he becomes entitled either immediately or on the death, retirement or expulsion of another partner, is to be treated as a chargeable transfer for the purposes of inheritance tax, albeit potentially exempt and, perhaps, qualifying for 100 per cent relief. This subject is more fully discussed in Part Seven of this work.[15]

---

[11] *Kerr v. Morris* [1987] Ch. 90, overruling *Hensman v. Traill, The Times*, October 22, 1980 and applying the National Health Service Act 1977, Sched. 10, para. 2(4)(a), (5). Note, however, that the Medical Practices Committee (which is charged with the task of certifying whether particular transactions involve a sale of goodwill: see *ibid.* Sched. 10, para. 1(2)) unaccountably takes a different view and seems intent on ignoring this decision: see the Guidance Note issued in May 1992 and entitled "Considerations relating to the prohibition on the sale of goodwill of NHS General Medical Practice in England and Wales." See further the *Encyclopedia of Professional Partnerships*, Pt. 5.

[12] *Kerr v. Morris supra*, at pp. 109G, 115E.

[13] See further, as to the potential application of this prohibition, the *Encyclopedia of Professional Partnerships*, Pt. 5.

[14] National Health Service Act 1977, Sched. 10, para. 2(2)(c).

[15] See *Att.-Gen. v. Boden* [1912] 1 K.B. 539; *Att.-Gen. v. Ralli* (1936) 15 A.T.C. 523; *Perpetual Executors and Trustees Association of Australia v. Taxes Commissioner of Australia* [1954] A.C. 114 (P.C.). Although these are all cases on estate duty, the principles embodied therein are equally applicable to inheritance tax: see further, *infra*, paras. 36–02 *et seq.*

CHAPTER 7

EVIDENCE BY WHICH A PARTNERSHIP MAY BE PROVED

1. INTRODUCTION

UNLIKE the position in most other European jurisdictions,[1] no **7–01** particular formalities attend the creation of a partnership and there is in general no need for a written agreement, much less a deed. Nevertheless, reliance on an oral agreement may, inter alia, present certain problems of proof.[2] Although there is no universal requirement for the registration of partnerships, some firms may, by reason of their size, need to register as companies under the Companies Act 1985[3] or, by choosing to adopt that form, as limited partnerships under the Limited Partnerships Act 1907.[4]

2. PARTNERSHIPS INVOLVING LAND

Law of Property (Miscellaneous Provisions) Act 1989, s.2

The Law of Property (Miscellaneous Provisions) Act 1989, s.2 **7–02** superseded the provisions of the Law of Property Act 1925, s.40 with effect from September 27, 1989.[5] The new section (so far as material) provides as follows:

"2.—(1) A contract for the sale or other disposition[6] of an interest in land[7] can only be made in writing and only by incorporating all the terms which the parties have expressly agreed in one document or, where contracts are exchanged, in each.

(2) The terms may be incorporated in a document either by being set out in it or by reference to some other document.

(3) The document incorporating the terms or, where contracts are exchanged, one of the documents incorporating them (but not necessarily the same one) must be signed by or on behalf of each party to the contract.

---

[1] See *supra*, paras. 2–32 *et seq.*
[2] See *Figes v. Cutler* (1822) 3 Stark. 139.
[3] See *supra*, paras. 4–27 *et seq.*
[4] See *infra*, paras. 29–17 *et seq.*
[5] Law of Property (Miscellaneous Provisions) Act 1989, ss.2(8), 4, 5(3), Sched. 2.
[6] This expression has the same meaning as in the Law of Property Act 1925: Law of Property (Miscellaneous Provisions) Act 1989, s.2(6).
[7] This expression means "any estate, interest or charge in or over land or in or over the proceeds of sale of land": *ibid.*

. . .

(5) This section does not apply in relation to—

(*a*) a contract to grant such a lease as is mentioned in section 54(2) of the Law of Property Act 1925 (short leases);

(*b*) a contract made in the course of a public auction; or

(*c*) a contract regulated under the Financial Services Act 1986;

and nothing in this section affects the creation or operation of resulting, implied or constructive trusts."

7–03   In contrast, the Law of Property Act 1925, s.40 provided as follows:

"40. (1) No action may be brought upon any contract for the sale or other disposition of land or any interest in land, unless the agreement upon which such action is brought, or some memorandum or note thereof, is in writing, and signed by the party to be charged or by some other person thereunto by him lawfully authorised.

(2) This section applies to contracts whether made before or after the commencement of this Act and does not affect the law relating to part performance, or sales by the court."

7–04   The potential application of the latter section (and its predecessor)[8] to agreements for partnership received close judicial attention over the years but, even prior to its repeal, a number of uncertainties still remained. Nevertheless, it is submitted that the cases decided thereunder and Lord Lindley's views thereon are indicative of the approach which the courts are likely to adopt in relation to the new legislation.

Forster v. Hale

7–05   Lord Lindley observed in relation to that part of section 4 of the Statute of Frauds which related to land (which was the precursor of section 40 of the Law of Property Act 1925) that it had been held as follows:

"1. that a partnership constituted without writing is as valid as one constituted by writing[9]; and 2. that if a partnership is proved to exist, then it may be shown by parol evidence that its property consists of land."[10]

---

[8] Statute of Frauds, s.4.

[9] *Essex v. Essex* (1855) 20 Beav. 442.

[10] The Scottish case of *Munro v. Stein* 1961 S.C. 362, noticed *infra*, para. 7–12, is a clear illustration of this second proposition. But see further, *infra*, para. 7–11.

He stated that these propositions had first been clearly laid down in **7–06**
Forster v. Hale,[11] where the plaintiff had attempted to obtain an
account of the profits of a colliery on the ground that it was
partnership property, to which a preliminary objection was taken that
there was no signed writing, such as was then required by the Statute
of Frauds. The Lord Chancellor dealt with this submission as follows:

> "That was not the question: it was whether there was a
> partnership: the subject being an agreement for land, the question
> then is, whether there was a resulting trust for that partnership by
> operation of law. The question of partnership must be tried as a
> fact, and as if there was an issue upon it. If by facts and
> circumstances it is established as a fact, that these persons were
> partners in the colliery, in which land was necessary to carry on
> the trade, the lease goes as an incident. The partnership being
> established by evidence, upon which a partnership may be found,
> the premises necessary for the purposes of that partnership are by
> operation of law held for the purposes of that partnership."[12]

In the event, this ruling had no bearing on the ultimate decision, it **7–07**
being held that the agreement alleged was of such a nature as not to
require a signed writing under the statute.[13] It should also be noted
that the evidence clearly showed a partnership to have existed.[14]

Dale v. Hamilton

The principles canvassed in *Forster v. Hale* were subsequently **7–08**
applied,[15] but not without some hesitation, by Vice-Chancellor
Wigram in *Dale v. Hamilton*.[16] In essence, he held that an agreement
to form a partnership for the purpose of buying, improving and
selling land might be proved by parol; that it might then be shown by
parol that certain land had been bought for the purposes of the
partnership and, consequently, that the plaintiff was entitled to a
share of the profits obtained by its resale. The Vice-Chancellor
directed an issue as to the fact of partnership, but Lord Lindley
opined that:

> "his decision is an authority for the proposition that the Statute of
> Frauds does not preclude a person from establishing by parol an

---

[11] (1800) 5 Ves.Jr. 308.

[12] *Ibid.* p. 309.

[13] *Ibid.* p. 313. The Statute of Frauds, s.4, required written evidence to prove any agreement that was not to be performed within the space of a year.

[14] See also *Dale v. Hamilton* (1846) 5 Hare 369, 386; *Isaacs v. Evans* (1899) 16 T.L.R. 113.

[15] In earlier editions of this work the *Forster v. Hale* principle was described as "carried to its extreme limit"; *quaere* is this right: see *infra*, para. 7–14.

[16] (1846) 5 Hare 369.

agreement to form a partnership for the purpose of buying and selling land at a profit."[17]

7–09   Although an appeal was pursued by both parties, it went off on other grounds[18] and, notwithstanding a reference to a certain degree of "embarrassment" in the court below,[19] has not since been regarded as casting any doubt on the authority of the Vice-Chancellor's decision.[20]

7–10   Lord Lindley regarded the above decision as going a long way towards amending the Statute of Frauds and pointed out that in both of the cases discussed above there was in fact a signed writing showing a trust in the plaintiff's favour which, although relied on by Sir Richard Pepper Arden M.R. in *Forster v. Hale*[21] and by Lord Cottenham in *Dale v. Hamilton*,[22] was, curiously enough, not made the foundation of the decision of the Lord Chancellor in the former case nor considered sufficient by the Vice-Chancellor in the latter.

Caddick v. Skidmore

7–11   Lord Lindley observed that *Dale v. Hamilton* is difficult to reconcile with sound principle or with the later decision in *Caddick v. Skidmore*.[23] There the plaintiff alleged that it had been agreed between him and the defendant that they should become partners in a colliery and share the profits equally, and he sought to enforce that agreement. The defendant denied the alleged agreement and asserted that the true agreement was that the plaintiff and the defendant should share the royalties obtained from the colliery. The defendant also raised the Statute of Frauds as a defence to the plaintiff's claim. In this case no partnership in fact was proved[24] and there was no agreement for a partnership as distinguished from an agreement to share the profits of the colliery in question. The terms of that agreement were not in writing and were in dispute. Under these circumstances the Statute of Frauds was held to provide a good defence. Although both *Forster v. Hale* and *Dale v. Hamilton* were cited to the Court, no reference was made thereto in the Lord Chancellor's judgment.

---

[17] See also *Cowell v. Watts* (1850) 2 H. & Tw. 224.
[18] (1847) 2 Ph. 266.
[19] *Ibid.* pp. 272, 273.
[20] See the cases cited *infra*, para. 7–12.
[21] (1798) 3 Ves.Jr. 696.
[22] (1847) 2 Ph. 266.
[23] (1857) 2 De G. & J. 52.
[24] This was Lord Lindley's view and, on that basis, it is considered that the decision is reconcilable with the other authorities: see *infra*, para. 7–14. However, it is submitted that the judgment of the Lord Chancellor is not wholly clear in this respect.

The later decisions

Notwithstanding the above decision, it is fair to say that the **7–12** authority of *Forster v. Hale* and *Dale v. Hamilton* has never seriously been challenged.[25] The principle was repeated (albeit without reference to either case) in *Essex v. Essex*,[26] and both decisions were approved (*obiter*) by Kekewich J. in *Gray v. Smith*[27] and applied by the same judge in *Re De Nicols*.[28] Moreover, the principle was not questioned by the Privy Council in *Abseculeratne v. Perera*[29] or by the Court of Appeal in *Steadman v. Steadman*,[30] and was accepted and applied in 1987 in an unreported decision of His Honour Judge Baker in *Froley v. Smith*.[31]

It is also interesting to note that a similar attitude appears to be adopted by the courts in Scotland, without reference to the English authorities. Thus in *Munro v. Stein*,[32] Lord Wheatley expressed the following view:

"In my opinion, in deciding the constitution of the partnership and what it comprehended, it is competent to prove by parole evidence what each party was bringing into the partnership estate. A different situation might have arisen if the situation had been that the [*deceased partner in question*] was alleged to have brought heritable property into the partnership agreement after the partnership had been constituted."[33]

It should, however, be noted that in *Isaacs v. Evans*,[34] where there **7–13** was a disputed partnership in a gold mine in Wales, Farwell J. effectively distinguished *Forster v. Hale* on the basis that a partnership had clearly been established in that case and on that footing, following *Caddick v. Skidmore*, allowed a defence raising the Statute of Frauds.

---

[25] Note that the proposition was set out without apparent qualification in Williams, *The Statute of Frauds*, s.4 (1932), p. 25, to which Edmund Davies L.J. referred in his dissenting judgment in *Steadman v. Steadman* [1974] Q.B. 161, 170.

[26] (1855) 20 Beav. 442.

[27] (1889) 43 Ch.D. 208. This case decided that the Statute of Frauds was applicable to an agreement for the retirement of a partner, where that agreement necessarily involved the assignment of his share in any land held by the partnership.

[28] [1900] 2 Ch. 410. This was not, however, a partnership case.

[29] [1928] A.C. 173. Again, this was not a partnership case.

[30] [1974] Q.B. 161. See in particular, *ibid.* p. 183, *per* Scarman L.J. The point was not referred to in the House of Lords: see [1976] A.C. 536.

[31] July 3, 1987. In this case, where H.H. Judge Baker was sitting as a judge of the Chancery Division, there was no dispute as to the existence of the partnership.

[32] 1961 S.C. 362.

[33] *Ibid.* p. 368. In so holding, Lord Wheatley appears to have placed reliance on the provisions of the Partnership Act 1890, s.20(1).

[34] (1899) 16 T.L.R. 113. Decisions along similar lines appear to have been reached by the courts in Australia and New Zealand: see *Meyenberg v. Pattison* (1890) 3 Q.L.J. 184; *Imrie v Nisbet* (1908) 27 N.Z.L.R. 783; *Douglas v. Hill* [1909] S.A.S.R. 28; *Cody v. Roth* (1909) 28 N.Z.L.R. 565. But see further, *infra*, para. 7–14, n. 40.

The principle

7–14   Notwithstanding Lord Lindley's reservations regarding the decision in *Dale v. Hamilton*, it is submitted that there is a logical and consistent principle running through the authorities which, although originally formulated by reference to the Statute of Frauds, was (prior to its repeal) equally applicable to section 40 of the Law of Property Act 1925. That principle may be summarised in the following propositions (which are, for convenience, formulated on the supposition that section 40 remains in force):

1. The section is inapplicable when considering the pure issue of the existence of a partnership.[35]
2. Where an action is brought which is dependent on establishing the existence of a partnership and such existence is admitted, the section will not apply.[36]
3. Where the existence of an alleged partnership is disputed, the court must first determine that issue and may, in a suitable case, be asked to do so as a preliminary point.[37] If the existence of the partnership is proved, then the section will be inapplicable;[38] if its existence cannot be proved, the section will provide a good defence.

It is considered that both *Caddick v. Skidmore* and *Isaacs v. Evans* were, on a true analysis, cases of the latter class.[39] This analysis is also, in fact, confirmed by a number of Australian and New Zealand authorities, albeit by reference to different legislation.[40]

The present position

7–15   It has already been seen[41] that section 2 of the Law of Property (Miscellaneous Provisions) Act 1989, lists a number of express exceptions to the general requirement that all contracts for the sale or other disposition of an interest in land should be reduced to writing and these exceptions should prima facie be treated as exhaustive. However, it has already been held that collateral contracts are

---

[35] *Forster v. Hale* (1800) 5 Ves.Jr. 308.
[36] *Forster v. Hale, supra; Froley v. Smith*, unreported, July 3, 1987.
[37] *Forster v. Hale, supra; Dale v. Hamilton* (1846) 5 Hare 369; *Re De Nicols* [1900] 2 Ch. 410, 417.
[38] *Ibid.*
[39] But see *supra*, para. 7–11, n. 24.
[40] See *Kilpatrick v. Mackay* (1878) 4 V.L.R. (E.) 28; *Ford v. Comber* (1890) 16 V.L.R. 540; *Griffith v. Graham* (1920) 15 M.C.R. 41; *Johnson v. Murray* (1951) 2 W.W.R. (N.S.) 447. *Cf.* the cases cited *supra*, n.34.
[41] *Ibid.* s.2(5) *supra*, para. 7–02. Part performance no longer constitutes such an exception: *cf.* the Law of Property Act 1925, s.40(2), *supra*, para. 7–03.

outside the scope of the section[42] and it is submitted that the propositions formulated above are so fundamental to the law of partnership that they will continue to operate, thereby constituting partnership agreements as a further exception to the strict requirements of the Act. However, until this view is judicially confirmed, the need for a written agreement cannot be over-emphasised.

3. PARTNERSHIPS GENERALLY

A mixed question of law and fact

Lord Lindley pointed out that: **7–16**

"The question whether a partnership does or does not subsist between any particular persons is a mixed question of law and fact, and not a mere question of fact."[43]

This view was, many years later, endorsed by the Court of Appeal.[44] It follows that an appeal will lie on any finding of partnership/no partnership without leave.

Evidence

In considering the evidence which must be adduced in order to **7–17** establish the existence of a partnership, two distinct questions arise, *viz.*:

(*a*) What has to be proved?
(*b*) How it is to be proved?

(a) What has to be proved

It has already been explained that persons who are not in fact in **7–18** partnership together may be held liable as if they were and, conversely, that those who are liable *as if* they were partners may not actually *be* partners.[45] It follows that proof of such liability will

---

[42] *Record v. Bell* [1991] 1 W.L.R. 853; also *Tootal Clothing Ltd. v. Guinea Properties Ltd.* (1992) 64 P. & C.R. 452. And note the approach adopted by Hoffman J. in *Spiro v. Glencrown Properties Ltd.* [1991] Ch. 537.

[43] This statement was in marked contrast to Lord Lindley's expressed view that holding out (or, in the terminology current at the time, *quasi–partnership*) involved a pure question of fact: see *supra*, para. 5–44, n. 37.

[44] See *Keith Spicer Ltd. v. Mansell* [1970] 1 W.L.R. 333. And see *supra*, para. 5–44.

[45] See *supra*, paras. 5–43 *et seq.*

amount to no more than prima facie evidence that a real partnership exists;[46] if it is not even possible to prove such liability, there will necessarily be insufficient evidence to establish the existence of a partnership.[47]

7–19   On this footing, the crucial question is the *purpose* for which the existence of a supposed partnership must be proved: if a third party seeks to make persons liable as partners, then all that must be established is such liability, the existence or otherwise of a true partnership being largely irrelevant.[48] If, on the other hand, it is a question of liability as between the alleged partners, it will be necessary to prove the existence of a partnership in point of fact.[49] It may also be important to identify whether a supposed partnership actually exists or is merely in contemplation.[50]

(b) How is it to be proved

7–20 Although it is outside the scope of this work to consider pure questions of evidence, attention can usefully be drawn to certain evidential points which may arise when attempting to establish the existence of a partnership.

Written agreements and other formal requirements

7–21   A person can obviously be made liable as if he were a partner without the need to produce a copy, or otherwise to prove the existence, of any written partnership deed or agreement into which he may have entered.[51] Moreover, even though some formal step may be required for the creation of a valid partnership by the law of another country,[52] failure to take that step will not prevent persons who in fact trade as partners from being so treated in this country, irrespective of whether the issue arises as between the alleged partners or as between them and a third party.[53]

---

[46] See *Peacock v. Peacock* (1809) 2 Camp. 45; *Davis v. Davis* [1894] 1 Ch. 393, 400, *per* North J.

[47] Lord Lindley put it this: "Proof of such a state of things as is sufficient to establish a *quasi*-partnership is prima facie evidence of a real partnership, but evidence which is insufficient to establish a *quasi*-partnership must, *a fortiori*, fail to establish a real partnership between the same persons."

[48] The position will, of course, be otherwise where it is sought to affix a party with liability on the basis of an act which can only be attributed to him under the Partnership Act 1890, s.5: see *infra*, para. 12–05.

[49] See generally, *supra*, paras. 5–01 *et seq.*

[50] See *supra*, paras. 2–09 *et seq.*

[51] See *Alderson v. Clay* (1816) 1 Stark. 405, where a person was proved to be a member of a company without the production of the company's deed. Note, however, the decision in *Figes v. Cutler* (1822) 3 Stark 139, noticed *infra*, para. 23–194, n. 37.

[52] See, for example, *supra*, paras. 2–32 *et seq.*

[53] *Shaw v. Harvey* (1830) Moo. & M. 526; *Maudslay v. Le Blanc* (1827) 2 C. & P. 409n.; *Mavor v. Hill* [1952] C.P.L. 472; [1952] C.L.Y. 2497.

If counterpart partnership deeds are executed, a partner can be **7–22**
compelled to produced his copy on a *subpoena duces tecum*; where
there is only one deed, it has been held that a partner cannot be
compelled to produce it unless all the other partners are parties to
the action or otherwise consent to its production,[54] but it is doubtful
whether this approach would now be followed.[55]

No written agreement

It has already been seen that partnerships can be, and frequently **7–23**
are, created by parol.[56] It follows that the absence of direct
documentary evidence of an agreement for partnership is not of itself
fatal to the case of a plaintiff who seeks to establish a partnership
between himself and the defendant.[57] In addition to the plaintiff's
oral testimony,[58] the existence of such a partnership will have to be
proved by reference to the parties' conduct and, in particular, to the
way in which they have dealt with each other and with third parties.
However, dealings of the latter type will only be of real evidential
value if they were known to and, thus, conducted with the express or
implied authority of the other alleged partner(s). Such knowledge
may, *inter alia*, be proved by reference to books of account, letters,
admissions and the oral evidence of employees, agents and other
persons.[59]

Retrospective agreements

If partners agree that their partnership is deemed to have begun on **7–24**
a date earlier than its actual date of commencement, proof of that
agreement would not enable a third party to render them liable as
partners in respect of claims attributable to any period prior to the
latter date. As regards the third party, such an agreement is strictly

---

[54] *Forbes v. Samuel* [1913] 3 K.B. 706, 721–724, *per* Scrutton J. (although this was an action to recover a statutory penalty).

[55] See *Macmillan Inc. v. Bishopsgate Investments Trust plc* [1993] 1 W.L.R. 1372. *Cf. Phipson on Evidence* (14th ed.), para. 38–09. And see *infra*, para. 23–102. *Quaere* whether, if a third party has entered into an agreement with the alleged partners, his solicitors can be compelled to produce that agreement: see *Harris v. Hill* (1822) 3 Stark. 140. However, the solicitor to the alleged partners may in any event be required to give evidence, subject to questions of professional privilege or confidence: see *Williams v. Mudie* (1824) 1 Car. & P. 158.

[56] See *supra*, paras. 7–01 *et seq*. And note the decision in *Walters v. Bingham* [1988] 1 F.T.L.R. 260.

[57] If an action is brought by a third party, it is in any event unnecessary to prove the existence of an agreement: see *supra*, para. 7–19.

[58] See *infra*, para. 7–26.

[59] As to the presumption arising from the joint retainer of solicitors, see *McGregor v. Bainbrigge* (1848) 7 Hare 164; *Webster v. Bray* (1849) 7 Hare 159; *Robinson v. Anderson* (1855) 20 Beav. 98 and, on appeal, 7 De G.M. & G. 239. And for cases in which a partnership has been inferred from a number of circumstances, see *Jacobsen v. Hennekenius* (1714) 5 Bro.P.C. 482; *Peacock v. Peacock* (1809) 2 Camp. 45; *Nicholls v. Dowding* (1815) 1 Stark. 81; *Nerot v. Burnand* (1827) 4 Russ. 247, affirmed at (1828) 2 Bli.(N.S.) 215.

res inter alios acta and of no evidential or other value.[60] It is submitted that an admission as to the existence of a partnership which can be explained as referring to such a backdated commencement would be similarly regarded.[61]

Partnership by holding out

7–25   When it is sought to make a person liable on the basis of holding out,[62] evidence must be adduced of:

> (1) his acts or of what has been done by others with his knowledge or consent;
> (2) the plaintiff's reliance on the representation thereby made and
> (3) the "credit" thereby given to the firm.[63]

However, the statements and acts of the defendant's alleged co-partners are not evidence against him until he and they are shown in some way to have been connected with each other.[64]

Acts and evidence of alleged co-partner

7–26   It goes almost without saying that the principle last described does not apply so as to exclude the testimony of a person deposing to the existence of a partnership between himself and another.[65] There are, however, a number of other exceptions, which apply even where a third party alleges the existence of a partnership.

. Thus, if a partnership is alleged to exist between A and B, and A is called to prove it but denies its existence, then, although the person who called A cannot usually adduce evidence to discredit his testimony, he may adduce *other* evidence to show that the partnership does in fact exist.[66]

---

[60] *Wilsford v. Wood* (1794) 1 Esp. 182; *Vere v. Ashby* (1829) 10 B. & C. 288; *Waddington v. O'Callaghan* (1931) 16 T.C. 187; *Saywell v. Pope* [1979] S.T.C. 824. See further, *infra*, paras. 13–18 *et seq.* and, as to the position *vis-à-vis* the Inland Revenue, *infra*, paras. 34–07 *et seq.*

[61] Lord Lindley merely expressed the tentative view that such an admission "might be worth nothing".

[62] Partnership Act 1890, s.14.

[63] See further *supra*, paras. 5–44 *et seq.*

[64] See *Grant v. Jackson* (1793) Peake 268; *Edmundson v. Thompson* (1861) 8 Jur.(N.S.) 235. Lord Lindley went on to observe at this point that "it is obviously reasoning in a circle to infer a partnership from acts of [*the alleged partners*], unless he and they can be connected by other evidence admissible against him."

[65] Such testimony was not excluded even before the alteration of the law relating to the competency of witnesses: *Blackett v. Weir* (1826) 5 B. & C. 385; *Hall v. Curzon* (1829) 9 B. & C. 646.

[66] *Ewer v. Ambrose* (1825) 3 B. & C. 746. Alternatively, application may be made for the witness to be ruled hostile and cross-examination allowed. Note also that previous inconsistent statements, once proved in relation to a hostile witness, are admissible as evidence of any fact stated therein of which direct oral evidence by him would be admissible: see the Civil Evidence Act 1968, s.3.

Moreover, once a prima facie case of partnership has been **7–27** established, one alleged partner's acts will be admissible against the others, as Lord Lindley explained:

"... after sufficient evidence has been given to raise a presumption that several persons are partners, then the acts of each of those persons are admissible as evidence against the others for the purpose of strengthening the prima facie case against them."

This is illustrated by the decision in *Norton v. Seymour*,[67] where, in order to prove a partnership between the defendants Seymour and Ayres, the plaintiff called a witness who gave evidence that Ayres had admitted the partnership in the course of a conversation. The plaintiff then adduced in evidence a circular and invoice issued by Seymour, headed Seymour and Ayres, stating that the business would in future be carried on in those names. Ayres disputed the admissibility of the document, contending that there was no evidence to connect her with it, but the court held it to be admissible on the footing that, before the document was introduced, evidence of a partnership had been given and the document tended to confirm that evidence. A similar approach was adopted in *Nicholas v. Dowding*.[68]

Presumption of continuance of partnership

If there is evidence that a partnership existed at some past date, it **7–28** will be presumed to have continued unless the contrary is proved. Thus, in an action for the price of goods supplied to a firm between June 1893 and February 1894, a letter written by one of the defendants in January 1893 stating that he had dissolved the partnership in April 1892 was held to be evidence that the partnership was still in existence when the goods were supplied, although the statement that the partnership had previously been dissolved was admissible in the defendant's favour.[69]

Business Names Act 1985

The provisions of this Act will often facilitate proof of the existence **7–29** of a partnership, given the obligation imposed on any firm carrying on business under a name which does not merely comprise the surnames of all the partners (together with any permitted additions)[70]

---

[67] (1847) 3 C.B. 792.
[68] (1815) 1 Stark. 81. See also *Alderson v. Clay* (1816) 1 Stark. 405.
[69] *Brown v. Wren Bros.* [1895] 1 Q.B. 390. As the law then stood, it was left to the jury to decide what weight should be attached to the letter.
[70] *Ibid.* s.2. See further, *supra*, paras. 3–25 *et seq.*

to disclose their names not only on all business letters and other documents issued by the firm,[71] but also in a notice prominently displayed in the partnership premises[72] and in a list made available to customers on request.[73]

Usual evidence of partnership

7-30   Certain types of evidence are frequently relied on in order to prove the existence of an alleged partnership and might be termed the "usual" evidence thereof. They are, for convenience, presented in alphabetical order.

(i) *Accounts*,   draft or final, whether prepared for internal use or for production to the Inland Revenue.[74]

(ii) *Admissions*:   A person's admission that he is a member of a particular partnership is evidence of that fact against him[75] and will normally make it unnecessary to prove the execution of a partnership agreement in order to affix him with liability.[76]

However, an admission is by no means conclusive evidence, as was clearly recognised by Parke B. in *Ridgway v. Philip*,[77] when he observed that:

"An admission does not estop the party who makes it; he is still at liberty, as far as regards his own interest, to contradict it by evidence."

In that case, one defendant was allowed to explain an admission that he was in partnership with the other defendants.[78] Similarly,

---

[71] *Ibid.* s.4(1)(a). The other documentation referred to in the subsection comprises written orders for goods or services to be supplied to the business, invoices and receipts issued in the course of the business and written demands for payment of debts arising in the course of the business. The only exception to this requirement consists of documents issued by a firm of more than 20 partners, provided that certain conditions are met: *ibid.* s.4(3).

[72] *Ibid.* s.4(1)(b).

[73] *Ibid.* s.4(2).

[74] Note the scope of the Income and Corporation Taxes Act 1988, s.111 (in its original form), considered *infra*, para. 34–05. And see also, as to the evidential value of accounts, *Barton v. Morris* [1985] 1 W.L.R. 1257, noticed *infra*, para. 18–56, where, however, the existence of the partnership was not in dispute.

[75] *Sangster v. Mazarredo* (1816) 1 Stark. 161; *Studdy v. Sanders* (1823) 2 D. & R. 347; *Clay v. Langslow* (1827) 1 Moo. & M. 45; *Brown v. Wren Bros.* [1895] 1 Q.B. 390, noticed *supra*, para. 7–28. *Cf. Grant v. Jackson* (1793) Peake 268.

[76] *Harvey v. Kay* (1829) 9 B. & C. 356; *Ralph v. Harvey* (1841) 1 Q.B. 845; and see *Tredwen v. Bourne* (1840) 6 M. & W. 461.

[77] (1834) 1 Cromp., M. & R. 415, 417.

[78] See also *Newton v. Belcher* (1848) 12 Q.B. 921; *Newton v. Liddiard* (1848) 12 Q.B. 925 (both cases concerning admissions made by promoters of companies).

where defendants had in a letter referred to D as their "managing partner," they were permitted to adduce evidence showing that he was not in fact their partner.[79] Even the execution of a deed describing a person as a partner will not necessarily be conclusive, even though it will represent strong evidence against him.[80] Where an admission has been based on a false assumption, little weight ought to be attached to it: this seems to have been the true basis for the decision in *Vice v. Anson*.[81]

A clear admission of partnership may be explained as referable only to a partnership for a limited purpose.[82]

(iii) *Advertisements, etc.*: The names of the alleged partners may appear in advertisements,[83] on notices or nameplates inside or outside the partnership premises,[84] or on vehicles.[85]

(iv) *Agreements and other documents*: A partnership may be **7–31** proved by means of a written agreement[86] or by other, less formal, documents, *e.g.* an unsigned memorandum or draft agreement acted on by the partners,[87] or a series of letters. Moreover, an agreement between A and B may disclose a trust for C, and be evidence in his favour that he is a partner.[88] See also Admissions, *supra*.

If it is sought to rely on the terms of a partnership agreement as against a new partner who was not one of the original parties thereto, it will be necessary to prove conduct of such a nature as to show his unequivocal intention to be bound thereby.[89]

---

[79] *Brockbank v. Anderson* (1844) 7 Man. & G. 295. And see *Brown v. Brown* (1813) 4 Taunt. 752; *Mant v. Mainwaring and Hill* (1818) 8 Taunt. 139.

[80] See *Radcliffe v. Rushworth* (1864) 33 Beav. 484; *Empson's Case* (1870) L.R. 9 Eq. 597.

[81] (1827) 7 B. & C. 409; see also *Owen v. Van Uster* (1850) 10 C.B. 318. Lord Lindley questioned whether *Vice v. Anson* was good law, since although the defendant had no legal interest in the mine, she was entitled as a partner to share the profits obtained by working it. He asked rhetorically "And what more was necessary to make her liable to the supplier?"

[82] See *De Berkom v. Smith* (1793) 1 Esp. 29; *Ridgway v. Philip* (1834) 1 Cromp., M. & R. 415.

[83] See *Maudslay v. Le Blanc* (1827) 2 C. & P. 409, note; *Bourne v. Freeth* (1829) 9 B. & C. 632; *Reynell v. Lewis* (1846) 15 M. & W. 517; *Lake v. Argyll* (1844) 6 Q.B. 477; *Wood v. Argyll* (1844) 6 Man. & G. 928. In *Ex p. Matthews* (1814) 3 V. & B. 125, an advertisement of dissolution was relied on. In earlier editions of this work it was observed in the text that "A prospectus or advertisement issued by one person and assented to by another is abundant evidence of a contract upon the terms contained in the prospectus or advertisement": *Fox v. Clifton* (1830) 6 Bing. 776, 797, *per* Tindal C.J.

[84] *Williams v. Keats* (1817) 2 Stark. 290. See also *Pott v. Eyton* (1846) 3 C.B. 32. And note the terms of the Business Names Act 1985: see further, *supra*, paras. 3–32, 7–29.

[85] *Stables v. Eley* (1825) 1 C. & P. 614: see further, *supra*, para. 5–68.

[86] See generally, *supra*, paras. 5–05 *et seq.*

[87] *Worts v. Pern* (1707) 3 Bro.P.C. 548; *Williams v. Williams* (1867) L.R. 2 Ch.App. 294; *Baxter v. West* (1858) 1 Dr. & Sm. 173; *Munro v. Stein*, 1961 S.C. 362. See also *Zamikoff v. Lundy* (1970) 9 D.L.R. (3d) 637 (Ontario C.A.); *Walters v. Bingham* [1988] 1 F.T.L.R. 260; *cf. Firth v. Amslake* (1964) 108 S.J. 198, noticed *infra*, para. 9–13.

[88] As in *Dale v. Hamilton* (1847) 2 Ph. 266. See also *Page v. Cox* (1851) 10 Hare 163; *Murray v. Flavell* (1883) 25 Ch.D. 89; *Byrne v. Reid* [1902] 2 Ch. 735, 744, *per* Stirling L.J.

[89] *Zamikoff v. Lundy* (1970) 9 D.L.R. (3d) 637 (Ontario C.A.). Cf. *Firth v. Amslake* (1964) 108 S.J. 198. See further, *infra*, paras. 9–12, 9–13, 10–215. And note *Walters v. Bingham*, [1988] 1 F.T.L.R. 260.

(v) *Bills, circulars and invoices*: containing the names of the alleged partners.[90]

(vi) *Bills of exchange*: The manner in which bills have been drawn, accepted, or endorsed has frequently been treated as providing evidence of partnership.[91]

(vii) *Draft agreements*: See Agreements, *supra*.

(viii) *Joint bank accounts*: The operation of such accounts in connection with a business may be some evidence of partnership, but is not conclusive, nor even prima facie evidence thereof.[92]

7–32 (ix) *Judgments*: Apart from any question of issue estoppel and the provisions of the Civil Evidence Act 1968,[93] a finding as to the existence of a partnership in one action will not generally be admissible as evidence in a subsequent action.[94]

(x) *Letters and memoranda*: These may show an intention to admit a person to partnership or to give him a share of profits, but must be coupled with evidence that such intention was acted on.[95] See also Admissions, *supra*.

(xi) *Meetings*: Evidence may be adduced to show that parties attended and took part in meetings[96] or required them to be called.[97]

(xii) *Payment of money into court*: When, in an action against alleged partners, they pay money into court, this does not amount to an admission of the partnership alleged to exist between them, but only of their joint liability to the extent of the amount paid in.[98]

---

[90] *Young v. Axtell* (1784) 2 H.Bl. 242; *Norton v. Seymour* (1847) 3 C.B. 792. Note also that, where the Business Names Act 1985 applies, the names of all the partners must in general appear on all documents issued by the firm: see *supra*, paras. 3–32, 7–29.

[91] *Guidon v. Robson* (1809) 2 Camp. 302; *Spencer v. Billing* (1812) 3 Camp. 310; *Gurney v. Evans* (1858) 3 H. & N. 122; *Duncan v. Hill* (1873) 2 Brod. & B. 682.

[92] See *Jackson v. White and Midland Bank* [1967] 2 Lloyd's Rep. 68. Conversely, the absence of a joint bank account may be evidence *against* the existence of a partnership: *Waddington v. O'Callaghan* (1931) 16 T.C. 187; *Saywell v. Pope* [1979] S.T.C. 824, 835, *per* Slade J.

[93] *Ibid*. s.11 (as amended) provides that a conviction is admissible in civil proceedings for the purpose of proving that the offence was committed. This might be relevant where a conviction could only have been obtained on the basis that the defendant was a partner, *e.g.* as in *Clode v. Barnes* [1974] 1 W.L.R. 544 (a decision under the Trade Descriptions Act 1968).

[94] See generally, *Phipson on Evidence* (14th ed.), Chap. 33, and in particular paras. 33–90 *et seq*.

[95] *Heyhoe v. Burgh* (1850) 9 C.B. 431; *Baxter v. West* (1858) 1 Dr. & Sm. 173, where a partnership for seven years was proved by an unsigned memorandum on which the parties had acted.

[96] *Lake v. Argyll* (1844) 6 Q.B. 477; *Wood v. Argyll* (1844) 6 Man. & G. 928. See also *Peel v. Thomas* (1855) 15 C.B. 714.

[97] *Tredwen v. Bourne* (1840) 6 M. & W. 461.

[98] *Charles v. Branker* (1844) 12 M. & W. 743.

(xiii) *Recitals in agreements*.[99]

(xiv) *Registers, etc.*: The entry of the name of a person in a particular register does not, in the absence of some specific statutory provision, affect him unless he can be proved to have authorised the use of his name.[1] Thus, an entry in custom-house books made by one of three alleged partners, to the effect that he and the other two were jointly interested in certain goods, though conclusive as between them and the Crown, was not so as between them and third parties.[2]

(xv) *Releases* executed by all the alleged partners.[3]

(xvi) *Use of property* by several persons jointly.[4]

(xvii) *Witness*: A witness may be asked not only which persons compose a particular firm, but also whether named individuals do so.[5]

---

[99] *Leiden v. Lawrence* (1863) 2 N.R. 283.

[1] *Fox v. Clifton* (1830) 6 Bing. 776. As to the registers of ships, see *Tinkler v. Walpole* (1811) 14 East 226; *Flower v. Young* (1812) 3 Camp. 240; and see *M'Iver v. Humble* (1812) 16 East 169. And as to the register of Hackney Carriage licences, see *Strother v. Willan* (1814) 4 Camp. 24; *Weaver v. Prentice* (1795) 1 Esp. 369.

[2] *Ellis v. Watson* (1818) 2 Stark. 453.

[3] *Gibbons v. Wilcox* (1817) 2 Stark. 43.

[4] *Weaver v. Prentice* (1795) 1 Esp. 369; *Re John's Assignment Trusts* [1970] 1 W.L.R. 955. But see, as to co-owners who are not partners, *supra*, paras. 5–08 *et seq*.

[5] *Acerro v. Petroni* (1915) 1 Stark. 100. Note that in *Burgue v. De Tastet* (1821) 3 Stark. 53, it was held that, to prove a partnership between A in England and B in Spain, it was not enough to show that A once dwelt in a town in Spain, that B resided and carried on business there under the name of A, B & Co., and that there was no-one there of the name of A.

CHAPTER 8

ILLEGAL PARTNERSHIPS

1. WHICH PARTNERSHIPS ARE ILLEGAL

Illegality never presumed

8–01   A partnership cannot be created by, or be continued on the basis of, an illegal contract but such illegality is never presumed: if it is alleged by a party, he must prove its existence. However, if the illegality appears on the face of documents comprised in the court file or otherwise becomes apparent during the course of the hearing, the court will itself take the point, even though it is not relied upon by any party to the proceedings.

8–02   Lord Lindley summarised the evidence necessary to establish the illegality of a partnership in these terms:

"... in order to show that a partnership is illegal it is necessary to establish either that the object of the partnership is one the attainment of which is contrary to law, or that the object being legal, its attainment is sought in a manner which the law forbids. But proof that a firm has been guilty of an illegal act is not sufficient to bring the firm within the class of illegal partnerships; for if this were enough, every partnership which does not pay its debts, or which commits any tort, or is guilty of culpable negligence, would be illegal, which is obviously absurd.[1] Neither does it by any means follow that because one or more clauses in a contract of partnership are illegal the partnership is itself illegal."[2]

Illegality and *ultra vires*

8–03   A clear distinction must be drawn between a partnership which is carried on for illegal purposes and one which is merely void as being *ultra vires* one or more of the partners. A partnership of the latter class, though not *per se* illegal, will clearly be unenforceable. The

---

[1] See *Thwaites v. Coulthwaite* [1896] 1 Ch. 496; also *Armstrong v. Armstrong* (1834) 3 M. & K. 45, 64–65, *per* Brougham L.C.; *Sharp v. Taylor* (1848) 2 Ph. 801; *Brett v. Beckwith* (1856) 3 Jur.(N.S.) 31; *Ex p. Longworth's Executors* (1859) 1 De G.F. & J. 17.

[2] See *R. v. Stainer* (1870) L.R. 1 C.C.R. 230; *Re General Co. for the Promotion of Land Credit* (1870) L.R. 5 Ch.App. 363; *Collins v. Locke* (1879) 4 App.Cas. 674; *Swaine v. Wilson* (1889) 24 Q.B.D. 252; *Gozney v. Bristol Trade and Provident Society* [1909] 1 K.B. 901; *Osborne v. Amalgamated Society of Railway Servants* [1911] 1 Ch. 540; *Russell v. Amalgamated Society of Carpenters and Joiners* [1912] A.C. 421; *McEllistrim v. Ballymacelligott Co-op. Society* [1919] A.C. 548.

most obvious example was formerly the company whose memorandum of association did not permit it to enter into partnership, but the *ultra vires* doctrine has now been largely swept away, particularly as regards dealings with third parties;[3] accordingly, a better example is to be found in the case of local authorities and other statutory bodies who seek to enter into partnership in order to discharge their statutory functions.[4]

General grounds of illegality

Apart from those trades and professions the conduct of which is **8–04** governed by specific statutory restrictions,[5] there are a number of grounds of general application on the basis of which a partnership or some term of the partnership agreement will or may be found to be illegal. For convenience, they will be considered in alphabetical order.

Competition

(A) ARTICLE 85 OF THE EUROPEAN COMMUNITY TREATY

Article 85 renders null and void all agreements between under- **8–05** takings which may affect trade between Member States and which have as their object or effect the prevention, restriction or distortion of competition within the Common Market.[6] As will be seen hereafter,[7] a person who enters into partnership will generally accept an implied (even if not an express) obligation not to compete with the business of the firm; it is therefore arguable that the relationship *per se* involves an agreement in breach of Article 85, given that each of the partners must unquestionably be regarded as a separate "undertaking."[8] The current editor submits that, in an appropriate case,[9] the Commission of the European Communities might well sustain this argument, drawing an analogy between

---

[3] See the Companies Act 1985, s.35(1), 35A, 35B (as substituted by the Companies Act 1989, s.108(1)). See also *supra*, para. 4–19 and *infra*, para. 11–03.

[4] See *Jones v. Secretary of State for Wales* (1974) 28 P. & C.R. 280, where the Court of Appeal considered whether it would be *intra vires* for a local planning authority to enter into a "partnership scheme" with a firm of developers for the redevelopment of a city centre. Whilst it was doubted that the Town and Country Planning Act 1971, s.52 would authorise such a scheme, the court held that it was probably *intra vires*. Note, however, that the expression "partnership" is used loosely in relation to arrangements of this type and may denote something more akin to co-operation rather than partnership in the true sense.

[5] See *infra*, paras. 8–15 *et seq.*

[6] The full text of Article 85 is set out *infra*, paras. A5–01, A5–02. See also *infra*, paras. 10–196 *et seq.*

[7] See *infra*, paras. 16–08 *et seq.*

[8] *Gottfried Reuter v. BASF A.G.* [1976] 2 C.M.L.R. D.44 (76/743/EEC), at D.55, para. [35]. See also *infra*, para. 10–197.

[9] In view of the scope of Article 85, such a case could only occur where the partners enjoy a significant share of the relevant market, which will in practice be comparatively rare.

partnerships and joint ventures. Thus, in *Re Wano Schwarzpulver GmbH*,[10] the Commission held that a joint venture between two corporations for the manufacture and sale of blackpowder involved a breach of the Article and observed:

"Parties who hold significant stakes in a joint venture will not in general within the field of such a joint venture compete with each other's activities or with the activities of the joint venture, even if they are contractually free to do so."[11]

The position is *a fortiori* in the case of a partnership.

(B) COMPETITION ACT 1980

8–06 Similar reasoning to that outlined above might also be applied to the provisions of the Competition Act 1980, which seeks to control "anti-competitive practices" carried on in the United Kingdom.[12] Thus, at least in theory, the mere creation of a partnership between two or more persons might lead to a reference to the Monopolies and Mergers Commission and, ultimately, an order under section 10 of the Act prohibiting the partners from engaging in the anti-competitive practice, *i.e.* the partnership itself.[13]

Criminal element

8–07 A partnership will be illegal if it is formed for the purpose of deriving profit from a criminal offence, *e.g.* from smuggling, robbery, theft, etc.[14] Perhaps the classic illustration of such a partnership is to

---

[10] [1979] 1 C.M.L.R. 403 (78/921/EEC).

[11] *Ibid.* p. 411, para. [29]. See also *Re De Laval-Stork VOF* [1977] 2 C.M.L.R. D.69 (77/543/EEC); *Re the Agreement between the General Electric Co. Ltd. and the Weir Group Ltd.* [1978] 1 C.M.L.R. D.42 (77/781/EEC); *Re the Joint Venture of Amersham Intl. and Buchler GmbH* [1983] 1 C.M.L.R. 619 (82/742/EEC); *Re Agreements between Rockwell Intl. Corp. and Iveco Industrial Vehicles Corp. BV* [1983] 3 C.M.L.R. 709 (83/390/EEC); *Re the Agreement between Volkswagenwerk A.G. and Maschinenfabrick Augsburg-Nurenberg (MAN)* [1984] 1 C.M.L.R. 621 (83/668/EEC), where the parties are referred to as partners, but appear in reality to have been joint venturers; *Carbon Gas Technologie GmbH* [1984] 2 C.M.L.R. 275 (83/669/EEC).

[12] As to the meaning of the phrase "anti-competitive practices" see the Competition Act 1980, s.2(1). And see further *infra*, para. 10–201.

[13] As to the various steps which must be taken before an order can be made under *ibid.* s.10, see *ibid.* ss.3–9 (as amended). Note also, in this context, the power of the Director General of Fair Trading under the Fair Trading Act 1973 to refer a "monopoly situation" (as defined in *ibid.* ss. 6, 7) or a "complex monopoly situation" (as defined in *ibid.* s.11(1)) to the Commission.

[14] See *Biggs v. Lawrence* (1789) 3 T.R. 454 and *Stewart v. Gibson* (1838) 7 Cl. & F. 707, as to smuggling. In the latter case, particular care had been taken to conceal the true nature of the illegal transactions. It does not matter that the crime is to be committed in a foreign, but friendly, country: *Foster v. Driscoll* [1929] 1 K.B. 470, where an agreement between co-adventurers for the export of whisky into the U.S.A., when the prohibition laws were in force in that country, was held to be illegal, those laws not being mere revenue laws. See also the Scottish case *Lindsay v. Inland Revenue*, 1933 S.C. 33. However, the courts will not, in general, enforce the penal, revenue or other public law of another country: see *Att.-Gen. of New Zealand v. Ortiz* [1982] Q.B. 349, and the cases referred to therein (this aspect not being considered by the House of Lords on appeal: see [1984] A.C. 1); *United States of America v. Inkley* [1989] Q.B. 255. See also *Williams and Humbert Ltd. v. W. & H. Trade Marks (Jersey) Ltd.* [1986] A.C. 368.

be found in the curious (and, indeed, notorious) case of *Everet v. Williams*.[15]

Discrimination

It is unlawful[16] for the partners of an existing firm or for persons **8–08** who are proposing to enter into partnership together[17] to discriminate against a woman[18] on the grounds of sex in relation to a position as partner in the firm:

(*a*) in the arrangements made for the purpose of determining who should be offered that position;[19]

(*b*) in the terms on which that position is offered,[20]

---

[15] (1725), 2 *Pothier on Obligations*, by Evans, p. 3, note citing Europ.Mag., 1787, Vol. II, p. 360. Some interesting particulars relating to the case will also be found in 9 L.Q.R. 197. It was an action instituted by one highwayman against another for an account of their spoils. The bill stated that the plaintiff was skilled in dealing in several commodities, such as plate, rings, watches, etc.; that the defendant applied to him to become a partner; that they entered into partnership, and it was agreed that they should equally provide all sorts of necessaries, such as horses, saddles, bridles, and equally bear all expenses on the roads and at inns, taverns, alehouses, markets, and fairs; that the plaintiff and the defendant proceeded jointly in the said business with good success on Hounslow Heath, where they dealt with a gentleman for a gold watch; and afterwards the defendant told the plaintiff that Finchley, in the county of Middlesex, was a good and convenient place to deal in, and that commodities were very plentiful at Finchley, and it would be almost all clear gain to them; and they went accordingly, and dealt with several gentlemen for divers watches, rings, swords, canes, hats, cloaks, horses, bridles, saddles, and other things; that about a month afterwards the defendant informed the plaintiff that there was a gentleman at Blackheath, who had a good horse, saddle, bridle, watch, sword, cane, and other things to dispose of which he believed might be had for little or no money; that they accordingly went and met with the said gentleman, and after some small discourse they dealt for the said horse, etc.; that the plaintiff and the defendant continued their joint dealings together until Michaelmas, and dealt together at several places, *viz.* at Bagshot, Salisbury, Hampstead, and elsewhere to the amount of £2,000 and upwards. The rest of the bill was in the ordinary form for a partnership account. The bill is said to have been dismissed with costs to be paid by the counsel who signed it; and the solicitors for the plaintiff were attached and fined £50 apiece. The plaintiff and the defendant were, it is said, both hanged, and one of the solicitors for the plaintiff was afterwards transported. See *Ashhurst v. Mason* (1875) L.R. 20 Eq. 225, 230, note. The case was referred to by Jessel M.R. in *Sykes v. Beadon* (1879) 11 Ch.D. 170, 195. See also *Jeffrey & Co. v. Bamford* [1921] 2 K.B. 351, 355, *per* McCardie J.; *Foster v. Driscoll* [1929] 1 K.B. 470, 511, *per* Lawrence L.J.

[16] Sex Discrimination Act 1975, s.11(1), as amended by the Sex Discrimination Act 1986, s.1(3). The subsection was formerly inapplicable to firms comprising five or less partners, but is now of general application; *cf.* the Race Relations Act 1976, s.10. As to the consequences of a breach of the subsection, see the 1975 Act, Pt. VII.

[17] Sex Discrimination Act 1975, s.11(2).

[18] Although *ibid.* s.11(1) refers only to a woman, discrimination against a man is equally unlawful: *ibid.* s.2(1). However, it would seem, following the decision of the Court of Justice of the European Communities in *Webb v. Emo Air Cargo (U.K.) Ltd.*, The Times, July 15, 1994 (an employment case), that discrimination against a woman on the grounds of pregnancy may now be regarded as *per* se unlawful. Such discrimination was formerly thought to be permissable in an employment context: *Hayes v. Malleable Working Men's Club and Institute* [1985] I.C.R. 703; *Shomer v. B. & R. Residential Lettings* [1992] I.R.L.R. 317; *Webb v. Emo Air Cargo (U.K.) Ltd.* [1993] 1 W.L.R. 49, H.L. *Cf. Turley v. Allders Department Stores Ltd.* [1980] I.C.R. 66.

[19] There will be no unlawful discrimination in relation to a position as partner under this head where, if it were employment, being a man would be a genuine occupational qualification for the job: *ibid.* s.11(3). As to the meaning of "genuine occupational qualification," see *ibid.* s.7(2).

[20] An exception is afforded where the terms relate to death or retirement, but not expulsion: *ibid.* s.11(4), as amended by the Sex Discrimination Act 1986, s.2(2). Expulsion is now defined in *ibid.* s.82(1A) (as inserted by the Sex Discrimination Act 1986, 2(3)) in such a way as to include any form of compulsory termination, whether on notice or otherwise. *Quaere* to what extent a term applicable only *after* an expulsion, *e.g.* a restraint covenant, would fall within s.11(4)(*a*), since it

continued on next page

(c)   by refusing or deliberately omitting to offer her that position[21]
      or

(d)   where the woman is already a partner, in the way access is
      afforded to any benefits, facilities or services, or by refusing
      or deliberately omitting to afford her such access, by
      expelling[22] her from that position, or by subjecting her to any
      other detriment.[23]

Where an agreement contains a term which is unlawful as a result
of discrimination against a woman, the consequences will depend
upon whether or not she was a party thereto. If she was, the term
will merely be unenforceable against her;[24] if she was not, it will be
void.[25] It follows that a discriminatory provision in a partnership
agreement could not, of itself, render the partnership illegal.

8–09   Discrimination on the grounds of race is similarly unlawful, save
that the restrictions do not apply where the firm (or proposed firm)
consists of five or less partners.[26]

Firm name

8–10   The Business Names Act 1985 prohibits a firm from carrying on
business under a name which does not consist of the surnames of all
the partners (together with any permitted additions)[27] and which
either is likely to give the impression that the business is connected
with Her Majesty's Government or with any local authority, or
includes any word or expression for the time being specified in
regulations made under the Act, unless the prior approval of the
Secretary of State has been obtained.[28] A breach of that prohibition
will result in the commission of an offence, in respect of which all the

---

[20]—*continued from page 131*
does not strictly "provide for" expulsion as required by that paragraph. See generally, as to the
scope of s.11(4), *Roberts v. Cleveland Area Health Authority* [1979] 1 W.L.R. 754; *Duke v. G.E.C.
Reliance Ltd. (formerly Reliance Systems Ltd.)* [1988] A.C. 618 (both decisions under *ibid.* s.6(4),
which is in similar terms).
[21] There will be no unlawful discrimination in relation to a position as partner under this head
where, if it were employment, being a man would be a genuine occupational qualification for the
job: *ibid.* s.11(3). And see n. 19 *supra.*
[22] See, as to the meaning of this expression, *supra,* n. 20.
[23] A provision relating to death or retirement, as opposed to expulsion, cannot be discriminatory:
Sex Discrimination Act 1975, s.11(4), as amended by the Sex Discrimination Act 1986, s.2(2). See
further, *supra,* n. 20.
[24] *Ibid.* s.77(2).
[25] *Ibid.* s.77(1).
[26] Race Relations Act 1976, s.10; *cf.* the Sex Discrimination Act 1975, s.11 (as amended). Note
in particular that the former section, unlike the latter, is potentially applicable to all provisions,
including those relating to death or retirement. As to the consequences of unlawful racial
discrimination on partnership contracts, see the Race Relations Act 1976, s.72.
[27] s.1. See generally, *supra,* paras. 3–24 *et seq.*
[28] *Ibid.* ss.2(1), 3; also the Company and Business Names Regulations 1981 (S.I. 1981 No. 1685)
as amended by the Company and Business Names (Amendment) Regulations 1982 (S.I. 1982 No.
1653) and the Companies and Business Names (Amendment) Regulations 1992 (S.I. 1992 No.
1196).

partners would seem to be liable to a fine on summary conviction.[29] However, provided that the other provisions of the Act are complied with, use of such an unapproved name would not appear to impose any disability on the firm,[30] nor will the firm itself be illegal.

Breach of the other requirements of the Act[31] will attract criminal **8–11** penalties,[32] and may impose certain disabilities on the firm,[33] but again does not appear to affect the legality of the firm.

Apart from the provisions of the 1985 Act and any question of **8–12** fraud,[34] holding out[35] or passing off,[36] there is no general restriction on the use of business names by persons other than bankrupts.[37] Moreover, there may, depending on the circumstances, be no objection to the retention of a firm name by continuing or surviving partners.[38] However, there are numerous statutory restrictions on the adoption of names or titles which imply a professional qualification[39] and, moreover, the governing bodies of the professions frequently prohibit their members from practising under anything other than their own names or an established firm name.[40]

Public policy, etc.

Lord Lindley observed that "a partnership may be illegal upon the **8–13** general ground that it is formed for a purpose forbidden by the

---

[29] Business Names Act 1985, ss.2(4), 7(1), (2). It would seem that each partner commits a separate offence, since each is a "person" for the purposes of s.7(2): see *supra*, para. 3–33, n. 7.

[30] *Ibid.* s.5, which imposes disabilities in relation to certain proceedings, only applies in the event of a breach of s.4(1) or (2).

[31] *i.e. ibid.* s.4, as to which, see *supra*, para. 3–32.

[32] *Ibid.* ss.4(6), (7), 7(1), (2). No offence is committed if a reasonable excuse can be shown: *cf.* s.2(4).

[33] *Ibid.* s.5. In order to invoke the section, the defendant must satisfy certain requirements, and the court before which the proceedings are brought has a residual discretion to permit the proceedings to continue: see *supra*, para. 3–34.

[34] See *Gordon v. Street* [1899] 2 Q.B. 641.

[35] Partnership Act 1890, s.14: see *supra*, paras. 5–43 *et seq.* See also *infra*, paras. 10–162 *et seq.*

[36] See *supra*, para. 3–18.

[37] As to bankrupts, see *supra*, para. 4–22. In earlier editions of this work, consideration was given to the possible illegality resulting from the adoption by a firm of a business name implying incorporation. Lord Lindley concluded that "even if assuming to act as a corporation is an offence at common law, which is very doubtful, the offence is not committed by trading under a name which is by usage as applicable to an unincorporated as to an incorporated body." For further details, the reader is referred to the 15th ed., at p. 147.

[38] See *infra*, paras. 10–159 *et seq.* Lord Lindley wrote: "when a firm has an established reputation and one of its members dies, it is not deemed wrong for the survivors to continue the business under the old name, although, perhaps, the reputation of the firm may have been due mainly, if not entirely, to the ability and integrity of the deceased partner. The legal view of such conduct is in accordance with established usage, and it has been accordingly held not to be illegal for surviving partners to continue to carry on business under the old name." and referred to *Bunn v. Guy* (1833) 4 East 190; *Lewis v. Langdon* (1835) 7 Sim. 421; *Aubin v. Holt* (1855) 2 K. & J. 66; *cf. Thornbury v. Bevill* (1842) 1 Y. & C.Ch. 554). However, the current editor submits that this will only be the position where the business is not or cannot, for whatever reason, be sold; see *infra*, paras. 10–164 *et seq.*

[39] *e.g.* Architects (Registration) Act 1938, s.1; Veterinary Surgeons Act 1966, s.20; Medical Act 1983, s.49; Dentists Act 1984, s.39; Banking Act 1987, s.67; Opticians Act 1989, s.28; Solicitors Act 1974, s.21.

[40] See generally, *infra*, paras. 8–17 *et seq.*; also the *Encyclopedia of Professional Partnerships*.

current notions of morality, religion, or public policy."[41] On that ground, he considered that a partnership formed for the purpose of deriving profit from the sale of obscene or blasphemous prints or books, or for the procurement of marriages[42] or of public offices of trust, would be "undoubtedly illegal."[43]

War

8-14   It has already been seen[44] that a partnership between a resident British citizen or a resident alien and an alien enemy is illegal and incapable of creation or continuation; on the same basis, a partnership formed in order to trade with an enemy nation would clearly be illegal.[45] However, since a neutral may lawfully trade with one of the belligerent nations, a partnership formed for that purpose would be unobjectionable.[46]

Statutory grounds of illegality

8-15   Lord Lindley stated that "a partnership is also illegal if formed for a purpose forbidden by statute, although independently of the statute there would be no illegality."[47] Of course, any question of illegality will depend on the construction of the particular statute concerned. Thus, in the case of the statutory prohibitions on the conduct of certain professions by unqualified persons, the mere entry into partnership of such a person may or may not result in an illegality, according to the terms of the relevant prohibition.[48] In this connection Lord Lindley observed:

"With reference however to those statutes which prohibit unqualified persons from carrying on certain trades or businesses,

---

[41] See *Bowman v. Secular Society* [1917] A.C. 406; *Rodriguez v. Speyer Bros.* [1919] A.C. 59; *Lemenda Trading Co. Ltd. v. African Middle East Petroleum Co. Ltd.* [1988] Q.B. 448 and the cases there cited.

[42] *Semble* this would not apply to an ordinary dating agency.

[43] See *Chitty on Contracts* (26th ed.), paras. 1133 *et seq.* As to the sale of offices, see *Sterry v. Clifton* (1850) 9 C.B. 110; as to associations formed with a view to disseminating irreligious views, see *Pare v. Clegg* (1861) 29 Beav. 589; *Thornton v. Howe* (1862) 8 Jur.(N.S.) 663. Note also the decision in *Herring v. Walround* (1682) 2 Ch.Ca. 110, where it seems to have been held that an agreement to share the profits derived from the public exhibition of a "human monster" (apparently Siamese twins) was illegal. On the basis that he was not aware of any similar case, Lord Lindley opined that "the decision ... would not probably now be followed upon grounds of public policy."

[44] See *supra*, para. 4-06 and *infra*, para. 24-34.

[45] See *supra*, para. 4-05. Although the decision in *Feldt v. Chamberlain* (1914) 58 S.J. 788 would seem to support a contrary view, it cannot be regarded as good law.

[46] *Ex p. Chavasse* (1865) 4 De G.J. & S. 655; *The Helen* (1801) L.R. 1 Adm. & Ecc. 1.

[47] Lord Lindley then discoursed on the former distinction that was taken between *mala prohibita* and *mala in se*, pointing out that it had long ceased to be recognised as of any value for legal purposes: see *Aubert v. Maze* (1801) 2 Bos. & Pul. 371. This passage has not been retained.

[48] See *infra*, paras. 8-30, 8-40, 8-43, 8-47.

it may be observed that such statutes are not infringed by an unqualified person who does nothing more than share the profits arising from those trades or businesses, if they are in fact carried on by persons who are duly qualified.[48a] The unqualified person is not within the mischief of the statutes in question, and the partnership of which he is a member is not therefore illegal."[49]

The current editor considers that, as it stands, this statement is too widely drawn, since it takes no account of the agency which exists between partners, which will cause each partner's acts to be attributed to the other partners.[50]

Equally, although a statute may appear to prohibit certain activities **8-16** and impose a penalty for failure to observe its provisions, it does not follow that conduct which would attract the penalty is necessarily illegal.[51] If the statute can genuinely be classed as prohibitory,[52] as will be the case if the penalty is imposed for the protection of the public,[53] then such conduct will be illegal. *Per contra* if, on a true construction of the statute, the penalty merely represents, as Lord Lindley put it, "the price of a licence for doing what the statute apparently forbids."[54] Thus, in *Brown v. Duncan*,[55] it was held that a partnership of distillers was not illegal, even though one partner carried on business as a retail dealer in spirits within two miles of the distillery (contrary to the Duties on Spirits Act 1823, ss.132, 133) and was not registered as a member of the firm in the excise books (as required by the Excise Licences Act 1825, s.7). Lord Lindley did, however, doubt whether the statutes in question were properly construed by the court.

The following alphabetical list of businesses and professions contains the most important examples of partnerships whose legality is or may be affected by statute:

[48a] *Cf.* the Dentists Act 1984, ss.40, 41, noticed *infra*, para. 8–30.

[49] *Raynard v. Chase* (1756) 1 Burr. 2.

[50] See, in particular, *Hudgell Yeates & Co. v. Watson* [1978] Q.B. 451, noticed *infra*, para. 8–43.

[51] *S.C.F. Finance Co. Ltd. v. Masri (No. 2)* [1987] Q.B. 1002; *Phoenix General Insurance Co. of Greece S.A. v. Halvanon Insurance Co. Ltd.* [1988] Q.B. 216; *Re Cavalier Insurance Co. Ltd.* [1989] 2 Lloyd's Rep. 430; also *R. v. Hall* [1891] 1 Q.B. 747; *R. v. Kakelo* [1923] W.N. 220; and the other cases in the next two notes.

[52] *Phoenix General Insurance Co. of Greece S.A. v. Halvanon Insurance Co. Ltd.*, *supra*; *Re Cavalier Insurance Co. Ltd.*, *supra*; also *Bartlett v. Vinor* (1692) Carth. 252; *Cope v. Rowlands* (1836) 2 M. & W. 149; *Taylor v. The Crowland Gas and Coke Co.* (1854) 10 Ex. 293; *Melliss v. Shirley Local Board* (1885) 16 Q.B.D. 446; *Whiteman v. Sadler* [1910] A.C. 514; *Cornelius v. Phillips* [1918] A.C. 199.

[53] *Victorian Daylesford Syndicate v. Dott* [1905] 2 Ch. 624, 629, *per* Buckley J.; *Anderson Ltd. v. Daniel* [1924] 1 K.B. 138; also *Law v. Hodson* (1809) 11 East 300; *Little v. Poole* (1829) 9 B. & C. 192. The illegality may arise in connection with the performance of the contract: see *Anderson v. Daniel* [1924] 1 K.B. 138.

[54] *S.C.F. Finance Co. Ltd. v. Masri (No. 2)* [1987] Q.B. 1002; also *Johnson v. Hudson* (1809) 11 East 180; *Swan v. The Bank of Scotland* (1835) 2 Mont. & Ayr. 661; *Smith v. Mawhood* (1845) 14 M. & W. 452.

[55] (1829) 10 B. & C. 93; and see *Smith v. Mawhood* (1845) 14 M. & W. 452.

Accountants

8–17   Any person who acts as a company auditor[56] whilst ineligible for appointment to such an office[57] commits an offence.[58] Moreover, an auditor who becomes ineligible during his term of office must forthwith vacate that position.[59] Eligibility is dependent on the prospective auditor maintaining membership of a recognised super-visory body[60] and satisfying that body's own eligibility test.[61] A firm may be appointed as an auditor[62] and changes in the firm will, in general, be ignored, provided that its eligibility is unaffected.[63]

Since audit work forms only one element of an accountancy practice, it is submitted that acceptance of an audit appointment by an ineligible firm could not of itself render the firm illegal unless, exceptionally, the firm was formed with the intention of committing such an offence.[64]

Bankers

8–18   The restrictions on banking businesses are now contained in the Banking Act 1987.[65] By that Act, it is an offence for any person other than an institution authorised by the Bank of England,[66] a person exempted from its provisions[67] or, within certain limits, a European institution[67a] to accept a deposit in the course of carrying on a "deposit–taking business."[68] Only a partnership formed under

---

[56] See, as to the meaning of this expression, the Companies Act 1989, s.24(2).

[57] See generally, as to eligibility, *ibid.* ss. 25(1), 27.

[58] *Ibid.* s. 28(1), (3). It is a defence for the appointee to prove that he "did not know and had no reason to believe that he was, or had become ineligible for appointment": *ibid.* s.28(5). Certain transitional provisions were contained in the Companies Act 1989 (Commencement No. 12 and Transitional Provision) Order 1991 (S.I. 1991 No. 1996), Art. 4 (although this article is clearly misnumbered).

[59] *Ibid.* s.28(2), (3). And see the preceding note.

[60] See, as to the meaning of this expression, *ibid.* s. 30; also *ibid.* Sched. 1, Pts. I, II. Recognition has been accorded to the Institute of Chartered Accountants in England and Wales, the Institute of Chartered Accountants of Scotland, the Institute of Chartered Accountants in Ireland and the Chartered Association of Certified Accountants.

[61] Companies Act 1989, s.25(1). As to individuals originally authorised pursuant to the Companies Act 1967, s. 13(1), see *ibid.* ss. 25(3), 34(1).

[62] *Ibid.* ss. 25(2), 26(2).

[63] *Ibid.* s. 25(3)–(5). See also *supra*, para. 3–16.

[64] Even then the position is not entirely free from doubt: see *Dungate v. Lee* [1969] 1 Ch. 545, *infra*, para. 8–21; *S.C.F. Finance Co. Ltd. v. Masri (No. 2)* [1987] Q.B. 1002.

[65] This Act repealed and replaced the Banking Act 1979.

[66] See as to the manner in which such authorisation may be obtained, *ibid.* ss.8 *et seq* (as amended).

[67] *Ibid.* s.4, Sched. 2. (as amended).

[67a] See the Banking Coordination (Second Council Directive) Regulations 1992 (S.I. 1992 No. 3218), regs. 3(1), 5–7 (as amended, in the case of reg. 5, by the Banking Coordination (Second Council Directive) (Amendment) Regulations 1993 (S.I. 1993 No. 3225), reg. 2(e), (f)). Note also the power of the Bank of England under *ibid.* regs. 9 *et seq.*

[68] Banking Act 1987, s.3(1), (2). The expression "deposit-taking business" is defined in *ibid.* s.6. See also *S.C.F. Finance Co. Ltd. v. Masri (No. 2)* [1987] Q.B. 1002.

the laws of the United Kingdom or of a member state of the EC may apply for such authorisation,[69] and it will not be granted if (*inter alia*) the business is under the effective control of only one individual partner or the firm's initial capital falls below the prescribed minimum.[70] Authorisation, once granted, may, (and, in certain circumstances, must) be revoked[71] or restricted[72]: the dissolution of a firm is one of the events in which its authorisation *may* be revoked.[73] Moreover, a new partner can only be admitted to an authorised firm after the Bank of England has been notified and taken no objection;[74] any other change in the constitution of the firm must be notified within 14 days.[75]

A partnership which is authorised may describe itself as an **8–19** authorised institution,[76] and adopt a name or description indicating that it is a bank or banker or carrying on a banking business,[77] provided that, in the case of a banking *name* only, the partnership was formed under the laws of the United Kingdom and the necessary capital requirements are satisfied.[78] The direct or indirect use of any of those expressions by an unauthorised person will, save in a very limited number of cases,[79] constitute an offence.[80]

An authorised partnership carrying on a deposit–taking business is **8–20** subject to the same size restrictions as any other firm[81] and, if it is not registered under the Companies Act 1985, may be wound up as an unregistered company on a petition presented by the Bank of England.[82]

---

[69] See *ibid.* s.8(1) (as amended by the Banking Coordination (Second Council Directive) Regulations 1992, reg. 2.5), and the definition of "institution" in *ibid.* s.106(1).

[70] See *ibid.* s.9(2), Sched. 3, paras. 2, 6 (as substituted by the Banking Coordination (Second Council Directive) Regulations 1992, reg. 27(4)). Various other detailed requirements are set out in Sched. 3 (as amended).

[71] *Ibid.* s.11 (as amended by the Banking Coordination (Second Council Directive) Regulations 1992, reg. 28). See also *ibid.* s.12A (as added by *ibid.* reg. 29).

[72] *Ibid.* s.12.

[73] *Ibid.* s.11(9)(a).

[74] *Ibid.* ss.21(1) (as amended by the Banking Coordination (Second Council Directive) Regulations 1992, reg. 31(1)), (2), (5), 22 (as amended by the Banking Coordination (Second Council Directive) Regulations 1992, reg. 31(2)), 23. Contravention of these provisions is an offence: *ibid.* s.25(1). There is no power to object to an *existing* partner, analogous to that contained in *ibid.* s.24. But see *ibid.* s.11(1)(a), Sched. 3, para. 1.

[75] *Ibid.* ss.36, 105(3)(a).

[76] *Ibid.* s.18, read subject to the Banking Coordination (Second Council Directive) Regulations 1992, Sched. 8, para. 6.

[77] *Ibid.* ss.67(1), 69(1), read subject (in the case of the latter subsection) to the Banking Coordination (Second Council Directive) Regulations 1992, Sched. 8, para. 18.

[78] *Ibid.* s.67(2)(b).

[79] *Ibid.* ss.68, 69(2)–(8), read subject to the Banking Coordination (Second Council Directive) Regulations 1992, Sched. 8, paras. 18, 19.

[80] *Ibid.* s.73.

[81] See *supra*, para. 4–28.

[82] Banking Act 1987, s.92(1), (2); Insolvent Partnerships Order 1986 (S.I. 1986 No. 2142), Art. 8(1).

It is considered that a partnership formed with the *intention* of carrying on the business of deposit–taking without the requisite authorisation would be illegal; *per contra*, if the original intention is to carry on some other business, in the course of which the partnership will incidentally accept deposits.[83]

Bookmakers

8–21   Although bookmakers are required to hold a bookmaker's permit and to renew it with effect from June 1 each year,[84] it was held in *Dungate v. Lee*[85] that, in the case of a partnership, it is sufficient if one of the partners holds such a permit, unless there was from the outset a common intention that the other partners would also act as bookmakers. It follows that, unless no partner holds a permit, the legality of a bookmaking partnership will depend on the terms of the initial agreement and the intention of the parties. Moreover, if such a partnership is legal upon its creation, it will not become illegal merely because one or more partners who do not hold permits have, at some late stage, purported to act as bookmakers.[86]

Consumer credit businesses

8–22   By the Consumer Credit Act 1974[87] every person, firm or company carrying on a consumer credit business,[88] a consumer hire business,[89] or an ancillary credit business[90] is required to take out a licence issued by the Director General of Fair Trading in respect of the

---

[83] See *S.C.F. Finance Co. Ltd. v. Masri (No. 2)* [1987] Q.B. 1002, 1026 (a decision under the equivalent provisions of the Banking Act 1979). The rights and obligations of the persons making the deposits will not in any event be affected: *ibid.* See now, the Banking Act 1987, s.3(3).

[84] Betting, Gaming and Lotteries Act 1963, s.2, Sched. 1 (as amended).

[85] [1969] 1 Ch. 545 (a decision under the Betting and Gaming Act 1960, s.2).

[86] *Dungate v. Lee* [1969] 1 Ch. 545. See also *Thwaites v. Coulthwaite* [1896] 1 Ch. 496; *Saffery v. Mayer* [1901] 1 K.B. 11; *Brookman v. Mather* (1913) 29 T.L.R. 276; *Keen v. Price* [1914] 2 Ch. 98; *Jeffrey & Co. v. Bamford* [1921] 2 K.B. 351. The cases to the contrary (*Thomas v. Dey* (1908) 24 T.L.R. 272; *O'Connor and Ould v. Ralston* [1920] 3 K.B. 451), and the dictum of Fletcher Moulton L.J. in *Hyams v. Stuart King* [1908] 2 K.B. 696, 718, cannot be relied on. See further *infra*, para. 8–64.

[87] This Act replaced the provisions of the Moneylenders Acts 1900 and 1927, and the Pawnbrokers Act 1872.

[88] Consumer credit business is defined in *ibid.* s.189(1) as "any business so far as it comprises or relates to the provision of credit under regulated consumer credit agreements." See as to consumer credit agreements, *ibid.* s.8(2) (as amended by the Consumer Credit (Increase of Monetary Limits) Order 1983 (S.I. 1983 No 1878)), Sched. 2 and, as to regulated agreements, *ibid.* ss.8(3), 15(2), 82(3) and 189(1). Clearly some sort of "business" as opposed to an isolated series of transactions would need to be shown before a licence is required: see *ibid.* s.189(2); also *Edgelow v. MacElwee* [1918] 1 K.B. 205; *Wills v. Wood* (1984) 128 S.J. 222; *R. v. Marshall* [1990] Crim.App.R. 73.

[89] See as to the meaning of consumer hire business, *ibid.* ss.15 (as amended by the Consumer Credit (Increase of Monetary Limits) Order 1983), 189(1).

[90] An ancillary credit business is defined in *ibid.* s.145 as comprising credit brokerage, debt-adjusting, debt-counselling, debt-collecting, and the operation of a credit reference agency. A number of exceptions are set out in *ibid.* s.146.

activities proposed to be carried on.[91] There are no relevant exceptions to this requirement.[92]

Licences. Two types of licence may be issued under the Act, **8-23** namely a standard licence and a group licence.[93] In the case of a partnership, a standard licence will be issued in the firm name,[94] but will not cover any businesses carried on by the individual partners, for which each will need a separate licence. Once a licence to carry on a particular business has been obtained, all lawful activities done in the course of that business, whether by the licensee or other persons on his behalf, will be covered,[95] unless such activities have been limited by the licence itself.[96] The name specified in a standard licence will be the only name under which the business may be carried on and, when determining whether to grant such a licence, the Director must be satisfied not only that the applicant is a fit person to engage in the activities which it will cover, but also that the name in which it is to be granted is not misleading or otherwise undesirable.[97]

Because a standard licence will be granted in the firm name, **8-24** changes in the constitution of the firm (*e.g.* by death, retirement or otherwise) will not affect the validity of the licence, so long as the business continues to be carried on in that name. However, notice of any such change must be given to the Director.[98] Only when the business ceases to be carried on in the firm name will the licence cease to have effect.[99] It would consequently appear that, if one partnership, A Co., which holds a licence to carry on, say, a consumer credit business under that name, amalgamates with another firm, B Co., which holds a licence to carry on, say, a consumer hire

---

[91] See *ibid.* s.21 (consumer credit business and consumer hire business), as applied by s.147 (ancillary credit business). Obviously no licence will be required if there is no business: see n. 88 *supra.*

[92] See generally, ss.16(1) (as amended), 21(2), (3); also the Consumer Credit (Exempt Agreements) Order 1989 (S.I. 1989 No. 869), as amended.

[93] *Ibid.* s.22(1). In the normal course of events, a standard licence will be applied for. A group licence may only be issued if it appears to the Director that the public interest is better served by so doing than by obliging the persons concerned to apply separately for standard licences: s.22(5). A group licence will be particularly appropriate in the case of the professions: group licences have in fact been granted (*inter alios*) to the Law Society, the Institute of Chartered Accountants in England and Wales and the Chartered Association of Certified Accountants. Note that s.22 must be read subject to the provisions of the Banking Coordination (Second Council Directive) Regulations 1992 (S.I. 1992 No. 3218), reg. 57.

[94] *Ibid.* s.22(4). *Cf.* the Moneylenders Act 1927, s.2(3).

[95] Consumer Credit Act 1974, s.23(1). Thus the activities of employees and agents will be covered by the licence.

[96] *Ibid.* s.23(2).

[97] *Ibid.* ss.24, 25. Note that s.25 must be read subject to the provisions of the Banking Coordination (Second Council Directive) Regulations 1992, reg. 58.

[98] *Ibid.* s.36(2)(c). Notice must also be given of any change in the registered particulars of the firm: *ibid.* s.36(1).

[99] *Ibid.* s.36(5).

business under that name, the new firm, AB Co., may carry on the consumer credit business under the name A Co., or the consumer hire business under the name B Co., but may not carry on either business under any other name. In order to use the name AB Co., a new licence will be required.

8–25   An offence will be committed by each partner if the firm engages in any activity for which it does not hold a valid licence (including an activity falling outside the scope of its licence),[1] if it carries on business under a name not specified in the licence,[2] or if notice is not duly given of any change in the firm's constitution or in the particulars entered in the register.[3] However, the commission of any such offence will not render the partnership illegal.[4] *Quaere* whether there will be any question of illegality if the partnership was formed with the intention of carrying on unlicensed activities.[5]

8–26   *Renewal, variation, suspension and revocation of licences.* A standard licence, once granted, is valid for five years unless suspended, revoked or otherwise determined.[6] A renewal application must be made at the end of that period. On the other hand, a group licence will be granted for a specified or indefinite period and may be renewed either upon application by the licensee or of the Director's own motion.[7]

8–27   Standard licences may be varied upon application of the licensee.[8] Such an application may be made where the firm wishes to extend the scope of its business, *e.g.* where the licence covers a consumer credit business and it is also desired to carry on a credit brokerage business, or where it is desired to carry on the existing business under another name. In certain circumstances, the licence may be compulsorily varied at the insistence of the Director.[9]

---

[1] *Ibid.* ss.39(1), 167, Sched. 1. Note that s.39(1) must be read subject to the provisions of the Banking Coordination (Second Council Directive) Regulations 1992, reg. 5, as amended by the Banking Coordination (Second Council Directive). (Amendment) Regulations 1993 (S.I. 1993 No. 3225), reg. 2(e), (f).

[2] *Ibid.* s.39(2).

[3] *Ibid.* s.39(3).

[4] This would seem to be the effect of *ibid.* s.170(1).

[5] It is doubtful whether *ibid.* s.170(1) go so far as to negative this argument: see *Dungate v. Lee* [1969] 1 Ch. 545, *supra*, para. 8–21; *S.C.F. Finance Co. Ltd. v. Masri (No. 2)* [1987] Q.B. 1002.

[6] *Ibid.* s.22(1)(a) and the Consumer Credit (Period of Standard Licence) Regulations 1975 (S.I. 1975 No. 2124), reg. 2, as amended by the Consumer Credit (Period of Standard Licence) (Amendment) Regulations 1991 (S.I. 1991 No. 817), reg. 2. The period was originally three years, and had been extended to 10 years by the Consumer Credit (Period of Standard Licence) Amendment Regulations 1979 (S.I. 1979 No. 796) and then 15 years by the Consumer Credit (Period of Standard Licence) (Amendment) Regulations 1986 (S.I. 1986 No. 1016). Note that s.22 must be read subject to the Banking Coordination (Second Council Directive) Regulations 1992, reg. 57.

[7] *Ibid.* s.22(1)(b).

[8] *Ibid.* s.30.

[9] *Ibid.* s.31.

If the Director at any time forms the view that a current licence **8–28** should be revoked or suspended, on the basis that, if the licence had expired at that time, he would have been minded not to renew it, he must give notice to the licensee (or in the case of a group licence give general notice)[10] that he is "minded to revoke the licence, or suspend it until a specified date or indefinitely," stating his reasons therefore and inviting the licensee to make representations.[11] The Director may thereafter proceed to revoke or suspend the licence.[12] If the licence is suspended, the firm can apply to the Director for the suspension to be ended,[13] or, if the period of suspension has not been specified, it may be ended by the Director of his own motion.[14] During a period of suspension, the firm will be treated as if no licence had ever been granted.[15]

In the case of a licence held by an individual, it will be terminated **8–29** by his death, bankruptcy or mental incapacity.[16] As regards licences granted to, *inter alia*, partnerships, other terminating events may be specified by regulations made under the Act.[17] By the Consumer Credit (Termination of Licences) Regulations 1976[18] it is provided that, on the occurrence of any of the terminating events set out in the Schedule thereto,[19] the determination of the licence will in most cases[20] be deferred for a period of twelve months.[21] During the period of deferment, certain persons will be authorised to carry on the business.[22]

A standard licence will also cease to have effect whenever a change in a partnership has the result that the business ceases to be carried on under the name specified in the licence.[23]

---

[10] The Director must also notify the original applicant: *ibid.* s.32(4).

[11] *Ibid.* s.32(1)–(3).

[12] *Ibid.* s.32(1), (5).

[13] *Ibid.* s.33.

[14] *Ibid.* s.32(8).

[15] *Ibid.*

[16] *Ibid.* s.37(1).

[17] *Ibid.* s.37(2).

[18] (S.I. 1976 No. 1002). The Regulations were amended by the Consumer Credit (Termination of Licences) (Amendment) Regulations 1981 (S.I. 1981 No. 614).

[19] The additional "terminating events" specified in the Regulations are as follows: (a) the approval by the court of a composition or scheme of arrangement under the Bankruptcy Act 1914, s.16 (see now the Insolvency Act 1986, s.260) proposed by the licensee (whether the licensee is an individual or a partnership), (b) the registration under the Deeds of Arrangement Act 1914 of a deed of arrangement executed by the licensee (whether the licensee is an individual or a partnership), (c) in the case of a partnership where all the partners are adjudged bankrupt, the date of the last such adjudication, and (d) the relinquishment of the licence by the licensee by notice in writing served on the Director: *ibid.* reg. 2, Sched., Pt. I (as amended).

[20] Where the licence is voluntarily relinquished by the licensee, the period of deferment is one month: *ibid.* reg. 3(2) (as substituted by the Consumer Credit (Termination of Licences) (Amendment) Regulations 1981).

[21] *Ibid.* reg. 3(1) (as substituted by *ibid.*).

[22] *Ibid.* reg. 5, Sched., Pt. I (as amended).

[23] Consumer Credit Act 1974, s.36(5).

Dentists

8–30   Any person, other than a registered dentist, a visiting EEC practitioner[24] or a registered medical practitioner, who carries on, or holds himself out as carrying on or prepared to carry on, the practice of dentistry[25] commits an offence.[26] Moreover, any individual, other than a registered dentist or a registered medical practitioner, who carries on the *business* of dentistry[27] also commits an offence, unless he was carrying on such business on July 21, 1955.[28] The business of dentistry will be treated as carried on if that individual, or a partnership of which he is a member, receives a payment for services rendered in the course of the practice of dentistry by him or a partner of his.[29] It follows that a partnership between a registered dentist and an unqualified person is, almost by definition, illegal.[30] The position will be the same if the name of a qualified partner is for any reason erased from the dentists' register.[31]

It is also an offence for an unqualified person to take or use the title of dentist, dental surgeon or dental practitioner.[32]

Estate agents

8–31   Estate agents first became subject to statutory controls in 1982, with the coming into force of the greater part of the Estate Agents Act 1979.[33]

An undischarged bankrupt is absolutely prohibited from engaging in any form of estate agency work, except as an employee.[34] Moreover, if section 22 of the Act is ultimately brought into force,[35] the Secretary of State will have power, by regulations, to lay down certain minimum standards of competence for persons engaging in

---

[24] See the Dentists Act 1984, s.53(1), Sched. 4.

[25] This expression is defined in *ibid.* s.37.

[26] *Ibid.* s.38.

[27] This expression is defined in *ibid.* s.40.

[28] *Ibid.* s.41.

[29] *Ibid.* s.40(1).

[30] A partnership formed with a view to providing *free* dentistry would not *per se* be illegal, but would it satisfy the test of partnership set out in the Partnership Act 1890, s.1, *i.e.* would there be the requisite "view of profit"? See further, the *Encyclopedia of Professional Partnerships*, para. 4–002.

[31] See, as to the circumstances in which a dentist's name may be so erased, *ibid.* ss.23, 24, 27.

[32] *Ibid.* s.39.

[33] Most of the Act (excluding, *inter alia*, s.22) came into force on May 3, 1982: The Estate Agents Act 1979 (Commencement No. 1) Order 1981 (S.I. 1981 No. 1517).

[34] Estate Agents Act 1979, s.23 (as amended by the Insolvency Act 1985, Sched. 8, para. 33). An undischarged bankrupt may not, however, avoid the section by forming a company and employing himself: s.23(3). A breach of the section constitutes an offence, for which the penalty is a fine.

[35] This now seems unlikely: see the Review of Estate Agency published by the Department of Trade and Industry in June 1989, para. 8.1.

estate agency work.[36] Once those standards have been prescribed, it will be an offence for any partner to engage in such work on the firm's behalf unless the relevant number of partners have attained the required standard.[37] However, it is submitted that contravention of either prohibition would not *per se* render a partnership illegal, unless it were formed with the intention of committing an offence under the Act.

In addition, the Director General of Fair Trading is empowered to **8–32** make orders prohibiting persons from carrying on estate agency work where they have been convicted of certain offences, committed discrimination in the course of estate agency work, failed to comply with certain of their obligations under the Act, or engaged in any other undesirable practices which may be prescribed by the Secretary of State.[38] So far as concerns the latter two grounds, the act of one partner will automatically be imputed to his co-partners, unless they are able to show that it was done without their connivance or consent[39]; on that basis, the Director may take the view that all the partners are unfit to carry on estate agency work and issue orders against each of them. Any person who fails without reasonable excuse to comply with such an order commits an offence,[40] but there would appear to be no reason why such a person should not remain as a partner, provided that he does not *personally* engage in estate agency work.[41] The Director may in certain circumstances make a warning order before making a full order under the Act,[42] and may revoke or vary an order once made on the application of the person to whom it was addressed.[43]

---

[36] *Ibid.* s.22. The regulations may specify certain professional or academic qualifications which are to be taken as evidence of competence: s.22(2). The expression "estate agency work" is not defined in the Act.

[37] s.22(3)(b). Any person convicted will be liable to a fine.

[38] *Ibid.* s.3; and see the Estate Agents (Undesirable Practices) (No. 2) Order 1991 (S.I. 1991 No. 1032); the Estate Agents (Specified Offences) (No. 2) Order 1991 (S.I. 1991 No. 1091), as amended by the Estate Agents (Specified Offences) (No. 2) (Amendment) Order 1992 (S.I. 1992 No. 2833), Art. 2. An order made under the section may prohibit the recipient from doing any estate agency work at all or merely any estate agency work of a particular description (s.3(2)) and may be limited to a particular area within the United Kingdom (s.3(5)). A register of orders made under the Act is to be kept by the Director and is to be open to inspection on payment of the prescribed fee: *ibid.* s.8.

[39] Estate Agents Act 1979, ss.3(3)(c), 31(3).

[40] *Ibid.* s.3(8). The penalty is a fine.

[41] It is assumed that a partner against whom an order had been made would not fall to be treated as a person who had attained the required standard of competence for the purposes of *ibid.* s.22(3)(a), but this is by no means clear. If this is correct, it would seem that the making of an order against one partner might result in a contravention of that subsection by the other partners if they carried on doing estate agency work without admitting another partner who had attained the required standard.

[42] *Ibid.* s.4. If the person to whom the warning order has been addressed fails to comply with its terms, that failure will be conclusive evidence that he is unfit to carry on estate agency work for the purposes of *ibid.* s.3: s.4(3).

[43] *Ibid.* s.6.

The restrictions on the size of partnerships between estate agents are contained in the Companies Acts 1985, and the regulations treated as made thereunder.[44]

Financial services

8–33   By the Financial Services Act 1986,[45] no person may carry on, or purport to carry on, investment business[46] in the United Kingdom unless he is duly authorised so to do[47] or is exempt from the provisions of the Act.[48] Apart from the limited class of persons who are entitled to authorisation as of right,[49] a person wishing to carry on such business will have three choices: he may seek authorisation direct from the Securities and Investment Board ("SIB"),[50] he may join one of the Recognised Self-Regulating Organisations ("SRO"),[51] or he may obtain a certificate issued by a Recognised Professional Body ("RPB").[52]

8–34   *SIB authorisation.*[53]   Such authorisation may be applied for by a firm[54] and will be granted in the firm name, thereby permitting the firm, and any successor, to carry on investment business in that name or (with the SIB's consent) in any other name.[55] One of the factors to be taken into account on such an application will be the identity of the partners;[56] authorisation must in general be granted if they can each be shown to be a fit and proper person to carry on investment business.[57] Although subsequent changes in the constitution of the firm will not affect its authorisation, they must be notified to the SIB.[58] In the case of the admission of a partner, this could in theory lead to the firm's authorisation being withdrawn or suspended, if the

---

[44] See *supra*, paras. 4–28 *et seq.*
[45] s.3. Contravention of the prohibition is an offence: *ibid.* s.4.
[46] This expression is defined in *ibid.* s.1(2), Sched. 1, Part II.
[47] *i.e.* pursuant to *ibid.* Chap. III.
[48] *i.e.* pursuant to *ibid.* Chap. IV.
[49] See *ibid.* ss.22 *et seq.*, 31 *et seq.* (read subject, in the case of *ibid* ss.31, 32, to the Banking Coordination (Second Council Directive) Regulations 1992 (S.I. 1992 No. 3218) reg. 51, Sched. 9, para. 6).
[50] *Ibid.* s.25. The functions of the Secretary of State under this section were transferred to the SIB pursuant to *ibid.* s.114.
[51] *Ibid.* s.7, read subject to the Banking Coordination (Second Council Directive) Regulations 1992, reg. 48(1).
[52] *Ibid.* s.15.
[53] It is understood that applications for such authorisation are regarded more as a "last resort" alternative to membership of an SRO than as an obvious first option: see the *Encyclopedia of Financial Services Law*, para. 2–020.
[54] *Ibid.* s.26(1)(c).
[55] *Ibid.* s.27(6).
[56] *Ibid.* s.27(3)(b).
[57] *Ibid.* s.27(2).
[58] *Ibid.* s.52, read subject to the Banking Coordination (Second Council Directive) Regulations 1992, Sched. 9, para. 32; the Financial Services (Notification) Regulations 1988, reg. 2.05(1). Notification must also be given (*inter alia*) of any application which may be made to dissolve the partnership: *ibid.* reg. 2.03(d).

new partner is not regarded as a fit and proper person.[59] Similar consequences can result if the SIB takes the view that an existing partner no longer satisfies that criterion or if there has been any contravention of the Act.[60] In every case, the SIB must first give written notice of its intention to take such action.[61] An authorisation can only be surrendered if the SIB is agreeable.[62]

Membership of an SRO. Applications for such membership must **8–35** comply with the rules of the relevant SRO, which will in turn reflect the strict requirements of the Act.[63] In each case, it will be necessary to show that the partners are fit and proper persons to carry on investment business of the kind(s) with which the SRO is concerned.[64] Although voluntary termination of membership with a view to avoiding investigation and possible disciplinary proceedings is not permitted, each SRO will inevitably reserve power to terminate such membership in appropriate circumstances.[65]

Certification by a RPB. The issue of such certificates will be **8–36** governed by the rules of the relevant RPB which must comply with the requirements laid down in the Act.[66] In the case of a partnership, the certificate will be issued in the firm name and will authorise the firm, and any successor, to carry on investment business in that name.[67] However, certification will only be possible if the firm is managed and controlled by partners who are each members (or otherwise governed by the rules) of an RPB,[68] and at least one of whom is a member (or governed by the rules) of the RPB issuing the certificate.[69] Moreover, the firm's main business must consist of the practice of the profession(s) concerned.[70]

---

[59] Financial Services Act 1986, s.28(1)(a), read subject to the Banking Coordination (Second Council Directive) Regulations 1992, Sched. 9, para. 5.

[60] *Ibid.* s.28(1).

[61] *Ibid.* s.29.

[62] *Ibid.* s.30.

[63] *Ibid.* s.10(2), (3), Sched. 2, read subject to the Banking Coordination (Second Council Directive) Regulations 1992, Sched. 9, paras. 3, 45. Currently, three self-regulating organisations are recognised under the Act. They are the Investment Management Regulatory Organisation (IMRO), the Securities and Futures Authority (SFA) and the Personal Investment Authority (PIA), which replaces the Financial Intermediaries Managers and Brokers Regulatory Association (FIMBRA) and the Life Assurance and Unit Trust Regulatory Organisation (LAUTRO).

[64] *Ibid.* Sched. 2, para. 1.

[65] See *ibid.* Sched. 2, para. 2, read subject to the Banking Coordination (Second Council Directive) Regulations 1992, reg. 48(2), Sched. 9, para. 45(1). SRO's will normally reserve the right to prohibit a member from engaging in certain types of investment business: see, for example, the decision in *R. v. Life Assurance Unit Trust Regulatory Organisation Ltd.* [1993] Q.B. 17. For the detailed rules made by the various SROs, see the *Encyclopedia of Financial Services Law.*

[66] *Ibid.* s.18(2), (3), Sched. 3.

[67] *Ibid.* s.15(3).

[68] *Ibid.* s.16(2).

[69] *Ibid.* Sched. 3, para. 2(2)(b).

[70] *Ibid.* Sched. 3, para. 2(3).

8–37   An authorised firm which carries on investment business outside the scope of its authorisation does not in general commit an offence,[71] so that questions of illegality will not arise. If an *unauthorised* firm carries on such business, an offence will be committed,[72] but it is considered that there would again be no illegality, save where there was at the outset an intention to commit such an offence; even then, the position is far from clear.[73]

Insurers

8–38   The Insurance Companies Act 1982 prohibits the conduct of insurance business[74] otherwise than by authorised persons[75] and contains no provision which would permit authorisation to be granted to a partnership.[76] However, a limited exemption is afforded in the case of certain classes of general insurance business carried on solely in the course, and for the purposes, of a banking business[77] and in the case of insurance companies whose general business consists of effecting and carrying out certain prescribed types of contract, so long as no other insurance business is carried on.[78]

8–39   Where an unauthorised insurance business is carried on, an offence is committed.[79] However, it is doubted whether a partnership which carries on such a business would *ipso facto* be illegal, unless (perhaps) it were formed with the intention of committing an offence under the Act.[80]

Medical practitioners

8–40   The Medical Act 1983[81] prohibits the recovery in a court of law of any charge for medical advice, attendances, operations, or medicines prescribed or supplied by a person who is not fully registered under

---

[71] See *ibid*. s.3. And see, further, the *Encyclopedia of Financial Services Law*, para. 2–009, where the exceptions are listed.

[72] *Ibid*. ss.3, 4(1).

[73] Note the terms of *ibid*. s.5 and, in particular, s.5(3); see also *Dungate v. Lee* [1969] 1 Ch. 545, *supra*, para. 8–21; *S.C.F. Finance Co. Ltd. v. Masri (No. 2)* [1987] Q.B. 1002.

[74] Insurance business is now classified as either long term or general: *ibid*. s.1, Scheds. 1, 2.

[75] *Ibid*. ss.2(1). This prohibition does not apply to members of Lloyd's: s.2(2)(a).

[76] See *ibid*. ss.7(1), 8(3)(a), 9(1)(a). The expression "body corporate" does not include a Scottish firm: *ibid*. s.96(1).

[77] *Ibid*. s.2(4).

[78] *Ibid*. s.2(5). The particular contracts concerned are those under which the benefits provided by the insurer are exclusively or primarily in kind: see the Insurance Companies Regulations 1981 (S.I. 1981 No. 1654), reg. 23 (as amended), which has effect under this section: Interpretation Act 1978, s.17(2)(b).

[79] *Ibid*. s.14.

[80] This would seem to follow from the Financial Services Act 1986, s.132(6); see also *Dungate v. Lee* [1969] 1 Ch. 545, *supra*, para. 8–21; *S.C.F. Finance Co. Ltd. v. Masri (No. 2)* [1987] Q.B. 1002.

[81] s.46(1). Note that certain medical appointments may also only be held by fully registered practitioners: *ibid*. s.46(2).

the Act.[82] However, whilst this provision might prevent a firm comprising one or more unregistered partners from recovering such charges, it would not make the firm itself illegal.[83]

It is an offence for an unqualified person to take or use certain names or titles which denote or imply a medical qualification[84] or registration under the Act.[85]

Although, in the case of practices carried on within the National **8–41** Health Service, there is an absolute prohibition on actual or deemed sales of goodwill,[86] there is nothing in the relevant legislation which would *per se* render a partnership illegal. Nevertheless, in the course of discharging its obligations thereunder, the Family Health Services Authority may in certain circumstances decline to recognise a firm's existence.[87]

Patent and trade mark agents

Although it is no longer an offence under the Copyright, Designs **8–42** and Patents Act 1988 for unregistered persons to practise as patent agents,[88] a firm may not in general carry on business under any name or description which contains the words "patent agent" or "patent attorney" or otherwise in the course of its business describe itself (or permit itself to be described) as such, unless all the partners are registered patent agents[89] or at least one quarter of them are so registered and the remainder are registered trade mark agents.[89a] It accordingly follows that a partnership would only be illegal if (exceptionally) it were formed with the express intention of carrying on business in breach of the foregoing restriction.

---

[82] As to the meaning of the expression "fully registered," see *ibid.* s.55(1).

[83] *Turner v. Reynall* (1863) 14 C.B.(N.S.) 328, 333, 334, *per* Erle C.J. However, the decision itself, to the effect that the disability imposed by a predecessor of *ibid.* s.46(1) is cured by registration prior to the hearing of the proceedings, was subsequently disapproved: see *Leman v. Houselay* (1874) L.R. 10 Q.B. 66; *Howarth v. Brearley* (1887) 19 Q.B.D. 303; also *De la Rosa v. Prieto* (1864) 16 C.B.(N.S.) 578. And see generally, the *Encyclopedia of Professional Partnerships*, Pt. 5.

[84] *i.e.* physician, doctor of medicine, licentiate in medicine and surgery, bachelor of medicine, surgeon, general practitioner or apothecary.

[85] Medical Act 1983, s.49(1).

[86] National Health Service Act 1977, s.54, Sched. 10. See in particular, *Kerr v. Morris* [1987] Ch. 90; also the *Encyclopedia of Professional Partnerships*, paras. 5–023 *et seq.*

[87] National Health Service (General Medical Services) Regulations 1992 (S.I. 1992 No. 635), reg. 24(4).

[88] s.274. *Cf.* the Patents Act 1977, s.114 (repealed by the 1988 Act).

[89] Copyright, Designs and Patents Act 1988, s.276(2). Note, however, the exceptions set out in *ibid.* ss.277, 278. As to what does *not* amount to describing oneself as a patent agent, see *Graham v. Tanner* [1913] 1 K.B. 17 and *Hans v. Graham* [1914] 3 K.B. 400 (both decisions under the former Patents and Designs Act 1907). As to registration as a patent agent, see the Copyright, Designs and Patents Act 1988, s.275 and the Register of Patent Agents Rules 1990 (S.I. 1990 No. 1457).

[89a] Patent Agents (Mixed Partnerships and Bodies Corporate) Rules 1994 (S.I. 1994 No. 362), r.3(a), (b). These rules were made pursuant to the power conferred by the Copyright, Designs and Patents Act 1988, s.279.

Subject to satisfaction of the above conditions regarding the constitution of a mixed firm, there are no restrictions on the size of patent agents' partnerships.[90]

Similar rules apply to partnerships carrying on practice as registered trade mark agents.[90a]

Solicitors

8-43   In *Hudgell Yeates & Co. v. Watson*[91] it was held that a partner's accidental failure to renew his practising certificate rendered the firm illegal and, thus, immediately caused its dissolution.[92] However, with a view to legalising so-called multi-disciplinary partnerships, the Courts and Legal Services Act 1990 repealed the former prohibition on a solicitor acting as agent for an unqualified person in any action or bankruptcy matter[93] and, at the same time, authorised the creation of partnerships between solicitors and registered foreign lawyers.[94] However, it still remains an offence for any person to act as, or to pretend to be, a solicitor unless he has been admitted as such, his

---

[90] The Partnerships (Unrestricted Size) No. 11 Regulations 1994 (S.I. 1994 No. 644), reg. 2(1)(a) (firms comprising only patent agents), (c) (firms comprising both registered patent agents and registered trade mark agents). These regulations replaced the Partnerships (Unrestricted Size) No. 1 Regulations 1968 (S.I. 1968 No. 1222), reg. 1(a). And see *supra*, para. 4–29.

[90a] A firm may only describe itself as "registered trade mark agent(s)" if all the partners are registered as such (Copyright, Designs and Patents Act 1988, s.283(2)) or if at least one quarter of them are so registered and the remainder are registered patent agents (*ibid*; Registered Trade Mark Agents (Mixed Partnerships and Bodies Corporate) Rules 1994 (S.I. 1994 No. 363), r.3(b)). As to registration as a trade mark agent, see the Copyright, Designs and Patents Act 1988, s.282 and the Register of Trade Mark Agents Rules 1990 (S.I. 1990 No. 1458). Subject to satisfaction of the above condition in the case of a mixed partnership, there are no restrictions on the size of a trade mark agents' partnership: Partnerships (Unrestricted Size) No. 11 Regulations 1994, reg. 2(1)(b) (firms comprising only registered trade market agents), (c) (firms comprising both registered trade mark agents and registered patent agents).

[91] [1978] Q.B. 451; see also *Williams v. Jones* (1826) 5 B. & C. 108; *Scott v. Miller* (1859) Johns. 220. Where parties had entered into a written agreement which contemplated their immediate entry into partnership, parol evidence was not admissible to show that the agreement was only intended to take effect when they had both qualified: *Williams v. Jones, supra*. Even holding out an unqualified person as a partner might, as the law formally stood, have been illegal: *Edmondson v. Davis* (1801) 4 Esp. 14.

[92] By virtue of the Partnership Act 1890, s.34: see *infra*, para. 24–35 *et seq*. The dissolution will occur irrespective of the partners' knowledge or state of mind: *Hudgell Yeates & Co. v. Watson, supra*. In that case the Court of Appeal was, however, prepared to infer the creation of a new partnership between the remaining (qualified) partners. Bridge L.J. even went so far as to suggest that the original partnership was reconstituted as soon as the unqualified partner had renewed his practising certificate (see [1978] Q.B. 462), but such an approach is fraught with difficulty. Since the partners would, almost by definition, not appreciate that there had been any change in the firm, they would not be in a position to submit continuance elections under the Income and Corporation Taxes Act 1988, s.113(2) (if relevant) or, indeed, to give the requisite notification to the Law Society under the Solicitors' Investment Business Rules 1990, r.7(2)(a). See further, the *Encyclopedia of Professional Partnerships*, Pt. 8.

[93] s.66(1), which provides "Section 39 of the Solicitors Act 1974 (which in effect, prevents solicitors entering into partnership with persons who are not solicitors) shall cease to have effect." The power of the Law Society to maintain its professional stance against multi-disciplinary partnerships was preserved by *ibid*. s.66(2). How long that stance will continue is now open to question.

[94] *Ibid*. s.89, Sched. 14. And see the Multi-National Legal Practice Rules 1991 made by the Law Society pursuant to *ibid*. s.89(3).

name is on the roll and he holds a current practising certificate.[95] On that footing, given that each partner unquestionably acts as the agent of his co-partners,[96] it is difficult to see how the creation of a partnership between a solicitor and an unqualified person could be created without such an offence being committed;[97] if that analysis is right, then the creation of such a partnership is still illegal. The current editor is aware of the argument that agency has no relevance in this context, but remains unconvinced as to its validity.[98] Of course, at the present time, the problem is largely academic given that multi-disciplinary partnerships are prohibited by the Solicitors Practice Rules 1990[99] and, moreover, there is now little scope for a partner's inadvertent failure to renew his practising certificate to render him unqualified.[1]

Strict professional rules also limit the extent to which a solicitor can **8–44** share his professional fees with an unqualified person under arrangements falling short of partnership.[2]

A solicitor who carries on one of the specified types of ancillary credit business,[3] and who is not engaging in contentious business,[4] must obtain a licence under the Consumer Credit Act 1974.[5] Moreover, if the firm is to carry on investment business, it must either hold a certificate issued by the Law Society[6] or obtain authorisation in one of the other ways specified in the Financial Services Act 1986.[7]

There are no restrictions on the size of solicitors' partnerships[8] or partnerships between solicitors and registered foreign lawyers.[9]

---

[95] See the Solicitors Act 1974, ss.1, 20, 21. As to what may amount to acting as a solicitor, see *Piper Double Glazing Ltd. v. D.C. Contracts* [1994] 1 W.L.R. 777, 783, *per* Potter J.

[96] Partnership Act 1890, s.5; see in particular *Hudgell Yeates & Co. v. Watson* [1978] Q.B. 451, 461D–G (*per* Bridge L.J.), 467F (*per* Waller L.J.), 471B (*per* Megaw L.J.).

[97] Indeed, in the absence of the Solicitors Act 1974, s.39, would the qualified partners not commit an offence under *ibid.* s.21 as principals in the second degree?

[98] This issue is discussed in greater detail in the *Encyclopedia of Professional Partnerships*, Pt. 8 and in an article by the current editor at (1991) 135 S.J. 696. But see also *Raynard v. Chase* (1756) 1 Burr. 2 and Lord Lindley's view set out *supra*, para. 8–15.

[99] Solicitors' Practice Rules 1990, r.7(6).

[1] See the Solicitors Act 1974, s.14(2), (6) (as substituted by the Courts and Legal Services Act 1990, s.86).

[2] Solicitors' Practice Rules 1990, r.7(1).

[3] *i.e.* credit brokerage, debt-adjusting, debt-counselling, debt-collecting, or the operation of a credit reference agency, as variously defined in the Consumer Credit Act 1974, s.145. There must however be a "business" of the relevant type: see *Wills v. Wood* (1984) 128 S.J. 222; also *Edgelow v. MacElwee* [1918] 1 K.B. 205.

[4] Consumer Credit Act 1974, s.146(2). "Contentious business" is now defined in the Solicitors Act 1974, s.87(1) (as amended).

[5] Consumer Credit Act 1974, s.147, applying Pt. III of the Act (excluding s.40). See further, *supra*, paras. 8–22 *et seq.* Note also the terms of the group licence granted to the Law Society under the Act: see General Notice No. 1011 dated July 26, 1979.

[6] Such certificates are issued pursuant to the Solicitors' Investment Business Rules 1990, r.4 (as amended). See further, the *Encyclopedia of Professional Partnerships*, Pt. 8.

[7] See *supra*, paras. 8–33 *et seq.*

[8] Companies Act 1985, s.716(2)(a). See also *supra*, para. 4–28.

[9] Partnerships (Unrestricted Size) No. 8 Regulations 1991 (S.I. 1991 No. 2729). See also the Courts and Legal Services Act 1990, s.89.

Stockbrokers

8–45   A stockbroking firm must obtain authorisation under the Financial
Services Act 1986 before it can lawfully carry on investment
business,[10] and such authorisation will, in the absence of an
exemption from that requirement, be a pre-requisite to membership
of the International Stock Exchange.[11] There is accordingly no real
scope for questions of illegality to arise.[12]

No size restrictions apply in the case of partnerships between
members of recognised stock exchanges.[13]

Unregistered partnerships, etc.

8–46   By the Companies Act 1985,[14] a firm comprising 20 or more
partners must register as a company under the Act, unless
(exceptionally) it has been formed in pursuance of some other Act or
of letters patent. A firm which fails to register when required so to
do is illegal.[15] However, exemption from this requirement is
conferred on certain professional firms, so long as the partners (or, in
some cases, a specified number of them) hold the prescribed
qualifications.[16] It follows that an obligation to register may arise as
an indirect result of a change in the firm, if that change will either
cause the number of partners to exceed 20 or alter the proportion of
partners holding the requisite qualifications; a similar consequence
may follow where an existing partner becomes unqualified, as a result
of disciplinary proceedings or otherwise.

Veterinary surgeons

8–47   With a few minor exceptions,[17] veterinary surgery may only be
practised by persons who are registered either as veterinary

---

[10] Such authorisation will either be obtained direct from the Securities and Investment Board or
by membership of one of the Recognised Self-Regulating Organisations: see further, *supra*, paras.
8–33 *et seq*. Investment business is defined in the Financial Services Act 1986, Sched. 1, Pt. II (as
amended).
[11] Rules of the International Stock Exchange of the United Kingdom and the Republic of
Ireland, r.110.1. This Exchange has obtained recognition as an investment exchange pursuant to the
Financial Services Act 1986, s.37 and so is itself an exempt person under *ibid*. s.36(1).
[12] See *supra*, para. 8–37.
[13] Companies Act 1985, s.716(2)(c); Partnerships (Unrestricted Size) No. 9 Regulations 1992 (S.I.
1992 No. 1028). See also, *supra*, para. 4–28.
[14] s.716(1): see *supra*, para. 4–28.
[15] *Harris v. Amery* (1865) L.R. 1 C.P. 155; *Smith v. Anderson* (1880) 15 Ch.D. 247; *Jennings v.
Hammond* (1882) 9 Q.B.D. 225; *Re Padstow Total Loss Assoc.* (1882) 20 Ch.D. 137; *Shaw v.
Benson* (1883) 11 Q.B.D. 563; *Ex p. Poppleton* (1884) 14 Q.B.D. 379; *Greenberg v. Cooperstein*
[1926] Ch. 657. *Sykes v. Beadon* (1879) 11 Ch.D. 170, although overruled by *Smith v. Anderson*,
supra, on the need for registration, would have been correctly decided if the association had been
required to register.
[16] See the Companies Act 1985, s.716(2)(d) (as added by the Companies Act 1989, Sched. 19,
para. 15(2)) and the various Partnerships (Unrestricted Size) Regulations considered *supra*, paras.
4–28 *et seq*.
[17] Veterinary Surgeons Act 1966, s.19(4), Sched. 3; the Veterinary Surgery (Exemptions) Order
1962 (S.I. 1962 No. 2557), as amended; the Veterinary Surgery (Exemptions) Order 1973 (S.I. 1973

—*continued on next page*

surgeons[18] or veterinary practitioners.[19] An unregistered person who practises or holds himself out as practising or prepared to practise veterinary surgery[20] or who uses any name or title which implies that he is registered or that he is a practitioner of or qualified to practise veterinary surgery commits an offence.[21]

It is submitted that a partnership between qualified and unqualified persons formed solely with a view to permitting the latter to practise veterinary surgery would clearly be illegal;[22] what is more doubtful is whether an unqualified partner could in any event be regarded as practising veterinary surgery through the agency of his co-partners.[23] If he were, any partnership involving an unqualified person would be *per se* illegal.[24]

2. CONSEQUENCES OF ILLEGALITY

Any event which makes it unlawful for the business of a firm to be **8-48** carried on or for the members of the firm to carry on that business in partnership will cause an immediate dissolution, even if the partners are unaware of the illegality.[25] This is graphically illustrated by the decision in *Hudgell Yeates & Co. v. Watson*,[26] where a partner in a firm of solicitors had accidentally omitted to renew his practising certificate and thus rendered himself unqualified for a period of some seven months.[27] It follows that a partnership which is illegal *ab initio* is strictly incapable of existing, since its dissolution will occur at the very moment of its creation.

---

[17]—*continued from previous page*
No. 308); the Veterinary Surgery (Blood Sampling Order) 1983 (S.I. 1983 No. 6), as amended; the Veterinary Surgery (Epidural Anaesthesia) Order 1992 (S.I. 1992 No. 696). Note also that a visiting EEC veterinary surgeon can render veterinary services on a temporary basis without seeking full registration under the 1966 Act: see the Veterinary Surgeons Qualifications (EEC Recognition) Order 1980 (1980 No. 1951), Art. 5(1).
[18] *i.e.* a person who is duly registered in the register of veterinary surgeons maintained pursuant to the Veterinary Surgeons Act 1966, s.2.
[19] *i.e.* a person who is duly registered in the supplementary veterinary register maintained pursuant to *ibid.* s.8(1). The number of persons who are so registered is, in fact, negligible.
[20] *Ibid.* s.19(1).
[21] *Ibid.* s.20(1), (2), (4). It is also unlawful to apply to any business a description which implies that any person involved therein possesses veterinary qualifications which he does not in fact possess: *ibid.* s.20(3). As to the position of a visiting EEC veterinary surgeon, see the Veterinary Surgeons Qualifications (EEC Recognition) Order 1980, Art. 5(9)(b).
[22] See *Dungate v. Lee* [1969] 1 Ch. 545, *supra*, para. 8–21; *S.C.F. Finance Co. Ltd. v. Masri (No. 2)* [1987] Q.B. 1002.
[23] Partnership Act 1890, s.5. See further, *supra*, para. 8–43, n. 96. *Cf.* the view expressed by Lord Lindley, *supra*, para. 8–15.
[24] It should be noted that, in its Guide to Professional Conduct, the Royal College of Veterinary Surgeons does not appear to recognise this risk, although it does seek to prohibit the formation of partnerships between qualified and unqualified persons on professional grounds. See further the *Encyclopedia of Professional Partnerships*, Pt. 10.
[25] Partnership Act 1890, s.34. See further, *infra*, paras. 24–34 *et seq.*
[26] [1978] Q.B. 451.
[27] *Quaere* whether, as the law now stands, such a partnership would still be regarded as illegal: see *supra*, para. 8–43.

Agreements for partnership

8–49   If a partnership would, once formed, be illegal, any agreement for
its formation must necessarily itself be illegal. On this ground it has
been held that no action lies for the recovery of a premium agreed to
be paid by a prospective partner on being taken into an illegal
partnership.[28] Similarly, no action to enforce such an agreement will
be entertained, irrespective of part performance, as illustrated by the
decision in *Ewing v. Osbaldiston*.[29] In that case, the plaintiff and the
defendant agreed to become partners in a theatre and the plaintiff
advanced certain monies which were, together with other monies
provided by the defendant, applied by the latter in acquiring the lease
of the theatre. However, the defendant procured an assignment of
the lease into his sole name and failed to perform his obligations
under the agreement. The plaintiff commenced proceedings seeking a
declaration that the plaintiff and the defendant were partners in the
theatre and in the lease thereof, an order that the agreement between
them should be performed and, if necessary, dissolution of the
partnership and the taking of the usual accounts. However, the
agreement was illegal, by virtue of the Plays Act 1736, and the action
was dismissed. On appeal it was held that, due to the illegality of the
agreement, the court could not decree its specific performance. The
court also held that, if the plaintiff sought to recover the amount of
his advance, he could not do so in the same proceedings since, even
assuming him to have had a lien on the property acquired (which the
court did not accept), he had not claimed to enforce it therein.

Actions by an illegal partnership

8–50   If a partnership is illegal, its members cannot in general maintain
an action in respect of any transaction tainted with the illegality.[30]
For example, if a partnership is formed in order to sell smuggled
goods, it cannot recover the price of any such goods which it may
have sold.[31] However, an illegal partnership can seemingly prosecute
a person for stealing its property[32] and, moreover, enforce a bequest

---

[28] *Williams v. Jones* (1826) 5 B. & C. 108. And see *Harse v. Pearl Life Assurance Co.* [1904] 1
K.B. 558; also *Duvergier v. Fellows* (1832) 1 Cl. & F. 39. As to whether the illegality of a
partnership can be determined by arbitration pursuant to the terms of the agreement by which it
was constituted, see *Harbour Assurance Co. (U.K.) v. Kansa General International Insurance Co.
Ltd.* [1993] Q.B. 701.

[29] (1837) 2 M. & Cr. 53.

[30] But *cf. S.C.F. Finance Co. Ltd. v. Masri (No. 2)* [1987] Q.B. 1002 and *Phoenix General
Insurance Co. of Greece S.A. v. Halvanon Insurance Co. Ltd.* [1988] Q.B. 216; also *Re Cavalier
Insurance Co. Ltd.* [1989] 2 Lloyd's Rep. 430; *Tinsley v. Milligan* [1994] 1 A.C. 340 (H.L.).

[31] See *Biggs v. Lawrence* (1789) 3 T.R. 454. And see also *Jennings v. Hammond* (1882) 9 Q.B.D.
225; *Shaw v. Benson* (1883) 11 Q.B.D. 563.

[32] See *R. v. Frankland* (1883) L. & C. 276. This would still appear to be the position under the
Theft Act 1968: see generally, as to thefts of partnership property, *R. v. Bonner* [1970] 1 W.L.R.
838. Formerly, a person could be prosecuted for embezzling the funds of an illegal partnership (*R.
v. Tankard* [1894] 1 Q.B. 548), but the offence no longer exists.

in its favour, provided that it is of a beneficial nature and not impressed with any trust.[33]

Actions against an illegal partnership

The illegality of a partnership affords no ground of defence where **8–51** an action is brought against it by a third party, unless that third party was aware of all the facts and is seeking to enforce a transaction which is itself tainted by the illegality.[34] In the latter case, his claim must necessarily be defeated by the operation of the rule *ex turpi causa non oritur actio*.[35] Thus, where partners have been fraudulently induced to join a firm, that fraud is no defence to an action brought by a creditor of the firm,[36] unless the creditor was himself party thereto.[37]

Actions between members of illegal partnership

So far as concerns a member of an illegal partnership, the most **8–52** serious consequence of the illegality is undoubtedly his inability to maintain an action against his co-partners in relation to matters affecting the firm and his interest therein.

Lord Lindley summarised the position thus: **8–53**

"However ungracious and morally reprehensible it may be for a person who has been engaged with another in various dealings and transactions to set up their illegality as a defence to a claim by that other, for an account and payment of his share of the profits made thereby, such a defence must be allowed to prevail in a court of justice. Were it not so, those who—*ex hypothesi*—have been guilty of a breach of the law, would obtain the aid of the law in enforcing demands arising out of that very breach; and not only would all laws be infringed with impunity, but, what is worse, their very

---

[33] See *Bowman v. Secular Society* [1917] A.C. 406, 436–438, *per* Lord Parker. Since the firm is not a legal person, the individual partners are in fact the legatees: see *supra*, para. 3–15.

[34] *Re South Wales Atlantic Steamship Co.* (1876) 2 Ch.D. 763. See also *Newland v. Simons & Willer (Hairdressers) Ltd.* [1981] I.C.R. 521. And note *Phoenix General Insurance Co. of Greece S.A. v. Halvanon Insurance Co. Ltd.* [1988] Q.B. 216; *Re Cavalier Insurance Co. Ltd.* [1989] 2 Lloyd's Rep. 430.

[35] Lord Lindley put it thus: "... the illegality of the firm does not *per se* afford any answer to a demand against it, arising out of a transaction to which it is a party, and which transaction is legal in itself. Unless the person dealing with the firm is *particeps criminis*, there can be no *turpis causa* to bring him within the operation of the rule *ex turpi causa non oritur actio*; and he, not being implicated in any illegal act himself, cannot be prejudiced by the fact that the persons with whom he has been dealing are illegally associated in partnership." In support he cited the judgment of Mellish L.J. in *Re South Wales Atlantic Steamship Co., supra*, and *Brett v. Beckwith* (1856) 3 Jur.(N.S.) 31.

[36] *Henderson v. The Royal British Bank* (1857) 7 E. & B. 356.

[37] See *Batty v. M'Cundie* (1828) 3 C. & P. 203.

infringement would become a ground for obtaining relief from those whose business it is to enforce them. For these reasons, therefore, and not from any greater favour to one party to an illegal transaction than to his companions, if proceedings are instituted by one member of an illegal partnership against another in respect of the partnership transactions, it is competent to the defendant to resist the proceedings on the ground of illegality."[38]

8–54   Illegality will be raised by the court of its own motion if it is clear on the face of the pleadings or documents, or otherwise becomes apparent during the course of the trial. It does not matter that the parties do not themselves seek to rely on the illegality: if all the relevant facts have been adduced and the court is satisfied that no further evidence can cure the illegality, it will decline to interfere.[39] However, the doctrine does not extend so far as to prevent the court from exercising jurisdiction over its own officers.[40]

Examples of illegality between partners

8–55   When partnerships between marine insurers were illegal, it was held that a partner in such a firm, who had personally met all its liabilities, could not recover any contribution from his co-partners.[41] Equally, if one partner received premiums payable under a policy, his partners could not recover their shares from him,[42] even pursuant to an express covenant.[43] An arbitrator's award in favour of one partner was even held to be unenforceable by reason of the illegality.[44] Lord Lindley observed that "[*the foregoing*] cases are of undoubted authority, and are always referred to as such, although the particular ground of illegality on which they rested no longer exists."

---

[38] See *Holman v. Johnson* (1775) 1 Cowp. 341; *Thomson v. Thomson* (1802) 7 Ves.Jr. 470; *Cousins v. Smith* (1807) 13 Ves.Jr. 544; *Sykes v. Beadon* (1879) 11 Ch.D. 170; *Foster v. Driscoll* [1929] 1 K.B. 470. Lord Lindley did in fact go on to observe that "there are indeed some old cases in which this defence was not allowed to prevail; but they have long been overruled." Those old cases were in fact *Dover v. Opey* (1733) 2 Eq.Ca.Abr. 7 and *Watts v. Brooks* (1798) 3 Ves.Jr. 611. It should, however, be noted that a right of contribution which arises under the Civil Liability (Contribution) Act 1978, s.1(1) (as to which see further, *infra*, para. 20–16) where there is no such right under the general law will *not* be affected by the *ex turpi causa non oritur actio* rule: see *K v. P* [1993] Ch. 140. Illegality must always be specifically pleaded: see R.S.C. Ord. 18, r.8(1); also *Shell Chemicals U.K. Ltd. v. Vinamul Ltd. (formerly Vinyl Products Ltd.), The Times*, March 7, 1991.
[39] *Evans v. Richardson* (1817) 3 Mer. 469. *Scott v. Brown Doering & Co.* [1892] 2 Q.B. 724; *Gedge v. Royal Exchange, etc. Corp.* [1900] 2 Q.B. 214; *North-Western Salt Co. v. Electrolytic Alkali Co.* [1914] A.C. 461; *Lipton v. Powell* [1921] 2 K.B. 51; *Rawlings v. General Trading Co.* [1921] 1 K.B. 635; *Chettiar v. Arunsalam Chettiar* [1962] A.C. 294.
[40] *Re Thomas* [1894] 1 Q.B. 747.
[41] *Mitchell v. Cockburn* (1794) 2 H.Bl. 380. See also *Thwaites v. Coulthwaite* [1896] 1 Ch. 496, 501–502, *per* Chitty J.
[42] *Booth v. Hodgson* (1795) 6 T.R. 405. In this case the premiums had been received by two of the partners *qua* brokers.
[43] *Lees v. Smith* (1797) 7 T.R. 338. Such a covenant will itself be tainted by the illegality.
[44] *Aubert v. Maze* (1801) 2 Bos. & Pul. 371.

Although it had been held in two very old cases that one partner **8–56**
might maintain an action for a contribution where he had met the
liabilities of an illegal partnership at the express request of the other
partner, the latter promising to pay his share at a later stage,[45] Lord
Lindley was in no doubt that these decisions had subsequently been
overruled. He cited *De Begnis v. Armistead*,[46] where the plaintiff and
the defendant had entered into an illegal agreement to produce an
opera and to divide the resulting profits. By the agreement, the
plaintiff was required to pay the singers and the defendant to provide
a theatre and to pay the dancers. All the requisite payments were
made in accordance with the agreement, but the concern proved to
be loss making. When an account was prepared in the course of
winding up its affairs, a balance was found to be due to the plaintiff.
When the plaintiff brought proceedings on a bill of exchange given by
the defendant in respect of that balance, he successfully proved that it
was made up of sums which he had paid at the defendant's request. It
was nevertheless held that, by reason of the illegality, the plaintiff
could not recover the balance in question, either on the bill of
exchange or as a simple debt.[47]

In the same way, an action for an account in respect of the dealings **8–57**
and transactions of an illegal partnership cannot be sustained by one
partner against another,[48] nor will an action lie on a settled account
in respect of such dealings and transactions.[49]

Fraud

If a person is induced to enter into an illegal contract by fraudulent **8–58**
misrepresentations, which do not relate to its legality, he can make
no claim under the contract; however, if he is himself unaware of the
illegality, he may recover damages from the person who deceived
him.[50] The position would appear to be the same where he is induced
by the misrepresentations to believe that the contract is legal, when
in fact it is not.[51]

---

[45] See *Faikney v. Reynous* (1767) 4 Burr. 20; *Petrie v. Hannay* (1789) 3 T.R. 418.

[46] (1833) 10 Bing. 107. And see *Fisher v. Bridges* (1854) 3 E. & B. 642.

[47] In fact, the plaintiff did recover £30 which he had loaned to the defendant in order to meet hotel expenses.

[48] *Knowles v. Haughton* (1805) 11 Ves.Jr. 168; *Armstrong v. Armstrong* (1834) 3 M. & K. 45; *Harvey v. Collett* (1846) 15 Sim. 332; also *Farmers' Mart Ltd. v. Milne* [1915] A.C. 106. But see *Greenberg v. Cooperstein* [1926] Ch. 657.

[49] *Re Home & Colonial Insurance Co. Ltd.* [1930] 1 Ch. 102; *Law v. Dearnley* [1950] 1 K.B. 400. And see *Joseph Evans & Co. v. Heathcote* [1918] 1 K.B. 418.

[50] *Shelley v. Paddock* [1980] Q.B. 348; *Saunders v. Edwards* [1987] 1 W.L.R. 1116.

[51] *Re Mahmoud and Ispahani* [1921] 2 K.B. 716; *Burrows v. Rhodes* [1899] 1 Q.B. 816; see also *Haseldine v. Hosken* [1933] 1 K.B. 822. As to the position where the plaintiff can rely on a proprietary right, see *Bowmakers Ltd. v. Barnet Instruments Ltd.* [1945] K.B. 65; *Singh v. Ali* [1960] A.C. 167; *Belvoir Finance Co. Ltd. v. Stapleton* [1971] Q.B. 210; *cf. Chettiar v. Arunsalam Chettiar* [1962] A.C. 294. Note also *Archbolds (Freightage) Ltd. v. S. Spanglett Ltd.* [1961] 1 Q.B. 374.

Concealed illegality

8–59   It is perhaps self evident that the consequences of illegality cannot be avoided by concealing the true purpose for which a partnership was formed.[52] In such a case, whether or not the partnership agreement has been reduced to writing, the illegality may be proved by parol evidence.[53]

Where illegality is not a defence

8–60   Illegality will, in general, only constitute a defence to an action brought by one partner against another if it taints the partnership itself, since that is the contract upon which the plaintiff must rely in order to maintain his claim.[54] There is no general rule that, where money has been illegally obtained, the person in possession must necessarily be permitted to retain it.[55]

8–61   Thus, if A and B are parties to an illegal contract and, in pursuance thereof, B pays money to C for A's benefit, A can recover such money from C.[56] It follows that if two partners, A and B, enter into an illegal agreement with C and, pursuant thereto, C pays money to D for the benefit of A and B, not only can A and B recover this money from D but, if he pays it over to A or B, the recipient must account to the other for his share. This must also be the case if C, instead of paying the money to D, pays it directly to A or B. The principle was summarised by Lord Lindley in these terms:

> "... if an illegal act has been performed in carrying on the business of a legal partnership, and gain has accrued to the partnership from such act, and the money representing that gain has been actually paid to one of the partners for the use of himself and co-partners, he cannot set up the illegality of the act from which the gain accrued as an answer to a demand by them for their shares of what he has received."[57]

On this basis, it was held that a partner was entitled to an account of moneys which had actually come into the hands of his co-partner as a

---

[52] *Armstrong v. Armstrong* (1834) 3 M. & K. 45, 53; *Stewart v. Gibson* (1838) 7 Cl. & F. 707.
[53] See *Collins v. Blantern* (1767) 2 Wils. 341; *Foster v. Driscoll* [1929] 1 K.B. 470.
[54] See *Farmers' Mart Ltd. v. Milne* [1915] A.C. 106, 113, *per* Lord Dunedin; *Euro-Diam Ltd. v. Bathurst* [1990] 1 Q.B. 1; *Re Cavalier Insurance Co. Ltd.* [1989] 2 Lloyd's Rep. 430; *Tinsley v. Milligan* [1994] 1 A.C. 340 (H.L.); *Skilton v. Sullivan, The Times*, March 25, 1994; *cf. Whiteman v. Sadler* [1910] A.C. 514. See also *infra*, para. 20–13.
[55] See, for example, *Re Cavalier Insurance Co. Ltd.*, *supra*; *Tinsley v. Milligan*, *supra*; *cf. Gordon v. Commissioner of Police* [1910] 2 K.B. 1080.
[56] *Tenant v. Elliott* (1797) 1 Bos. & Pul. 3; *Farmer v. Russell* (1798) 1 Bos. & Pul. 296; *Bousfield v. Wilson* (1846) 16 M. & W. 185; *Nicholson v. Gooch* (1856) 5 E. & B. 999.
[57] Lord Lindley stated that this proposition followed from the decisions in *Tenant v. Elliott*, *supra*, and other cases of that class.

result of the employment of a ship in a manner prohibited by the navigation laws.[58]

Equally, if money is paid by A to B to be applied for an illegal **8–62** purpose, A may require B to return the money if B has not already parted with it[59] and the illegal purpose has not been carried out,[60] either wholly or in part.[61]

Illegality set up by personal representatives

The liability of a deceased partner's personal representative to **8–63** account to creditors and beneficiaries for the assets comprised in the estate is not affected by the illegality of any transactions in which the deceased may himself have been involved.[62] In such a case, the maxim *ex turpi causa non oritur actio* clearly cannot defeat the claims of such persons, since the illegality has no bearing thereon. Even if the personal representative was one of the deceased's partners and was himself involved in the illegal transactions, he must account for the deceased's share of the resulting profits, provided that such share has actually been placed to the deceased's credit in the partnership books and has come (or might have come) into the personal representative's hands.[63] On the other hand, if no account has been settled as between the partners in respect of such profits, the personal representative could seemingly rely on the illegality *qua* partner by way of defence to a claim for an account.[64]

---

[58] *Sharp v. Taylor* (1848) 2 Ph. 801; see also *Sheppard v. Oxenford* (1855) 1 K. & J. 491. *Cf. Sykes v. Beadon* (1879) 11 Ch.D. 170.

[59] See *Taylor v. Lendey* (1807) 9 East 49; *Barclay v. Pearson* [1893] 2 Ch. 154 (a decision under the Lottery Acts); also the following cases under the old Gaming Acts (which made gaming contracts void though not illegal): *Varney v. Hickman* (1847) 5 C.B. 271; *Hampden v. Walsh* (1847) 1 Q.B.D. 189; *Taylor v. Bowers* (1876) 1 Q.B.D. 291; *Diggle v. Higgs* (1877) L.R. 2 Ex. 422; *O'Sullivan v. Thomas* [1895] 1 Q.B. 698; *Burge v. Ashley & Smith Ltd.* [1900] 1 Q.B. 744; *Shoolbred v. Roberts* [1900] 2 Q.B. 497; and see *Re Futures Index* [1985] F.L.R. 147. Note also, as to the operation of resulting trusts, *Rowan v, Dann* (1991) 64 P & C.R. 202.

[60] See *Herman v. Jeuchner* (1884) 15 Q.B.D. 561; *Strachan v. Universal Stock Exchange (No. 2)* [1895] Q.B. 697; *Re Futures Index* [1985] F.L.R. 147.

[61] *Kearley v. Thomson* (1890) 24 Q.B.D. 742; *Bigos v. Bousted* [1951] 1 All E.R. 92; also *Ouston v. Zurowski* [1985] 5 W.W.R. 169. *Cf. Hermann v. Charlesworth* [1905] 2 K.B. 123 and *Parkinson v. College of Ambulance* [1925] 2 K.B. 1, where the money was given to a charity. At this point, Lord Lindley also briefly discoursed on the rights of the subscribers to an illegal company in the following terms: "Although, therefore, the subscribers to an illegal company have not a right to an account of the dealings and transactions of the company and of the profits made thereby, they have a right to have their subscriptions returned [*Harvey v. Collett (1846) 15 Sim. 332*]; and even though the moneys subscribed have been laid out in the purchase of land and other things for the purpose of the company, the subscribers are entitled to have that land and those things reconverted into money, and to have it applied as far as it will go in payment of the debts and liabilities of the concern, and then in repayment of the subscriptions. In such cases no illegal contract is sought to be enforced; on the contrary the continuance of what is illegal is sought to be prevented [*Sheppard v. Oxenford (1855) 1 K. & J. 491; Butt v. Monteaux (1854) 1 K. & J. 98. See also Symes v. Hughes (1870) L.R. 9 Eq. 475; Taylor v. Bowers (1876) 1 Q.B.D. 291*].'' See also, as to the taking of accounts in such a case, *Greenberg v. Cooperstein* [1926] Ch. 657.

[62] See *Joy v. Campbell* (1804) 1 Sch. & Lef. 328; *Hale v. Hale* (1841) 4 Beav. 369.

[63] See *Joy v. Campbell, supra.*

[64] See *Ottley v. Browne* (1810) 1 Ball & B. 360; *cf. Sharp v. Taylor* (1848) 2 Ph. 801.

Bookmaking partnerships

8–64   It has already been seen that a partnership between bookmakers will not be illegal if it is to be carried on in a lawful manner, even though one of the partners may have been guilty of some illegal acts in the conduct of the business.[65] The court will accordingly not hesitate to direct an account between partners in such a business, save perhaps in relation to any particular transactions which have been carried out in an illegal manner; moreover, the plaintiff will be entitled to recover any balance of his capital which has not been applied in payment of bets[66] and, it is thought, his share of profits (if any).[67]

8–65   Money lent to a firm of bookmakers to be used as capital in their business is recoverable and a charge on the firm's assets to secure the loan is enforceable: *per contra* if it can be shown that the money was, in fact, knowingly lent for betting purposes.[68]

Criminal liability

8–66   The final, and perhaps the most obvious, consequence of partners engaging in an illegal enterprise is, of course, the risk of criminal prosecution. The sanctions available to the court may include an order for the forfeiture of the partners' interests in assets owned by the firm,[69] although such an order will rarely be made if an innocent partner also has an interest in those assets.[70]

---

[65] *Dungate v. Lee* [1969] 1 Ch. 545: see *supra*, para. 8–20.

[66] See *Thwaites v. Coulthwaite* [1896] 1 Ch. 496; *Keen v. Price* [1914] 2 Ch. 98. As to the illegal transactions in the former case, see [1896] 1 Ch. 501, 502, *per* Chitty J.; but see also *supra*, para. 8–62.

[67] See *Harvey v. Hart* [1894] W.N. 72. A share of profits was not sought in *Keen v. Price, supra*; though it was said in the latter case that the Gaming Act 1892 was overlooked in *Thwaites v. Coulthwaite, supra*, that Act was considered in *Harvey v. Hart*. See also *Bookman v. Mather* (1913) 29 L.T. 276, where the plaintiff recovered on an I.O.U. given to him by the defendant for the balance due to him on an account taken on the dissolution of their betting partnership; *cf. Joseph Evans & Co. v. Heathcote* [1918] 1 K.B. 418, where it was said that an action on an account stated under a contract void as in restraint of trade would not lie.

[68] *Humphery v. Wilson* (1929) 45 T.L.R. 535.

[69] See the Misuse of Drugs Act 1971, s.27 (as amended); Powers of Criminal Courts Act 1973, s.43 (as amended); Criminal Justice Act 1988, ss.71 (as amended), 77. *Quaere*, does a partner have an interest in land owned by the firm for the purposes of the Drug Trafficking Offences Act 1986, s.9(4)(a), (5)(a)? The current editor tentatively submits that he does not.

[70] *R. v. Troth* [1980] Crim.L.R. 249, where an order for the forfeiture of a partner's interest in a tipper lorry owned by a firm, pursuant to the Powers of Criminal Courts Act 1973, s.43, was quashed since the order would be likely to lead to difficulties and might prove so onerous as to be not worth making.

CHAPTER 9

DURATION OF PARTNERSHIP

The normal rule: partnership at will

Under the somewhat misleading rubric "Retirement from partner- **9–01** ship at will," the Partnership Act 1890, section 26(1) provides that:

"(1) Where no fixed term has been agreed upon for the duration of a partnership, any partner may determine the partnership at any time on giving notice of his intention so to do to all the other partners."[1]

In a similar vein is section 32, which states:

"32. Subject to any agreement between the partners, a partnership is dissolved—

. . .

(c) If entered into for an undefined time, by the partner giving notice to the other or others of his intention to dissolve the partnership."

Both sections thus appear to cover the same ground, albeit that only section 32 directly takes account of any contrary agreement which may have been reached between the partners. The difference of wording was regarded as significant in *Moss v. Elphick*,[2] but the current editor submits that both sections must inevitably take effect subject to any such contrary agreement.[3]

Lord Lindley, in a statement of principle formulated prior to the **9–02** Act but which has since received judicial approval,[4] summarised the position thus:

". . . the result of a contract of partnership is a partnership at will, unless some agreement to the contrary can be proved."[5]

---

[1] This was also the position prior to the Act: see *Heath v. Sansom* (1831) 4 B. & Ad. 172, 175, *per* Parke J.; *Frost v. Moulton* (1856) 21 Beav. 596; *Syers v. Syers* (1876) 1 App.Cas. 174.

[2] [1910] 1 K.B. 465. The decision was affirmed on appeal: see [1910] 1 K.B. 846.

[3] Partnership Act 1890, s.19: see further, *infra*, paras. 10–10 *et seq.*

[4] See *Moss v. Elphick* [1910] 1 K.B. 846, 849, *per* Farwell L.J.; *Abbott v. Abbott* [1936] 3 All E.R. 823, 826, *per* Clauson J.

[5] The burden of proof will fall on the party seeking to allege such an agreement: see *Burdon v. Barkus* (1862) 4 De G.F. & J. 42.

Express and implied agreements negativing partnership at will

9–03 In order to negative the implication of a partnership at will, there must be some express or implied agreement that is inconsistent with the right which a partner would otherwise have to determine the partnership by notice. Thus, an express term that "This agreement shall be terminated by mutual arrangement only" will clearly amount to such an agreement[6] and will constitute a partnership for joint lives,[7] unless all the partners agree to dissolve the partnership at some earlier date. Equally, where partners are, following the expiration of a fixed term partnership, negotiating a new agreement and expressly agree to be bound by the terms of a draft "pending the adoption of a new deed," an effective fixed term partnership may be implied.[8]

9–04 Cases where a contrary agreement is sought to be drawn from the conduct of the partners inevitably give rise to difficulty, and Lord Lindley was forced to observe that:

> "it is not possible to lay down any rule by means of which the intention of the partners on this head can be certainly ascertained, where no express agreement has been come to."

Partners have sought to rely on a number of external and internal factors as indicative of their intentions, with varying degrees of success. These will now be considered.

(a) External factors

Debts

9–05 The mere fact that a firm has incurred debts and, indeed, secured them on its assets, does not imply an agreement that the firm will continue until those debts have been paid, for they can equally well be paid after the dissolution of the firm.[9]

---

[6] *Moss v. Elphick* [1910] 1 K.B. 465 and (on appeal) *ibid.* 846. And see *Abbott v. Abbott* [1936] 3 All E.R. 823, where the agreement declared that the death or retirement of any partner should not terminate the partnership and contained various other provisions relating to retirement; also *Wilson v. Kircaldie* (1895) 13 N.Z.L.R. 286, where the partnership was to continue so long as it was profitable; *cf. Arcus v. Richardson* [1933] N.Z.L.R. 348, which seems exceptional. However, it is not considered that, just because certain provisions in an agreement deal specifically with a future period (*e.g.* staged increases in certain partners' profit shares), there is sufficient evidence of an intention that the partnership will endure for that period. Note also *Wheeler v. Van Wart* (1838) 2 Jur. 252.

[7] Note that, in his Supplement on the Partnership Act 1890, Lord Lindley observed: "It is presumed, although there appears to be no decision on the point, that a partnership for the joint lives of the partners is a partnership for a fixed term, which would expire on the death of the partner who first died."

[8] *Walters v. Bingham* [1988] 1 F.T.L.R. 260. See further, as to this case, *infra*, para. 10–22.

[9] See *King v. The Accumulative Assurance Co.* (1857) 3 C.B. (N.S.) 151. *Quaere* whether, if the firm agrees to pay a profit-based annuity to an outgoing partner, it can be implied that the partnership must continue for so long as the annuity is payable: see further, *infra*, para. 10–147.

Employees

The current editor considers that the offer of fixed term contracts **9–06** to employees will not *per se* affect the existence of a partnership at will.[10]

Leases

Similarly, where partners have taken a lease of premises from **9–07** which to carry on the partnership business, there can be no implication that the partnership must necessarily subsist during the term of the lease;[11] indeed such a proposition would in most cases be absurd. The argument was analysed by Lord Eldon in *Crawshay v. Maule*[12] in the following terms:

"Without doubt, in the absence of express there may be an implied contract as to the duration of a partnership, but I must contradict all authority if I say that wherever there is a partnership, the purchase of a leasehold interest of longer or shorter duration, is a circumstance from which it is to be inferred that the partnership shall continue as long as the lease. On that argument the court, holding that a lease for seven years is proof of partnership for seven years, and a lease of fourteen of a partnership for fourteen years, must hold that if the partners purchase a fee simple, there shall be a partnership for ever. It has been repeatedly decided that interests in land purchased for the purpose of carrying on trade are no more than stock in trade."

(b) Internal factors

Continuation after fixed term

Where a partnership, which was originally entered into for a fixed **9–08** term, is continued after its expiry and there is no evidence as to the intended duration of that continuation partnership,[13] it will be treated as a partnership at will rather than as having been renewed for a further fixed term.[14] This emphasises a danger of the fixed term partnership, which is all too often overlooked.

---

[10] See, for example, *Briggs v. Oates* [1990] I.C.R. 473, where the fixed term offered to a salaried "partner" extended beyond the term of the partnership. See, in particular, *ibid.* p. 475, *per* Scott J. Equally, it would seem that this point may not have been addressed directly.

[11] See *Featherstonhaugh v. Fenwick* (1810) 17 Ves.Jr. 298; *Jefferys v. Smith* (1820) 1 Jac. & W. 301; *Alcock v. Taylor* (1830) Tam. 506; *Burdon v. Barkus* (1862) 4 De G.F. & J. 42.

[12] (1818) 1 Swan. 495, 508. See also *Syers v. Syers* (1876) 1 App.Cas. 174, 189, *per* Lord Hatherley.

[13] *e.g.* as in *Walters v. Bingham* [1988] 1 F.T.L.R. 260.

[14] Partnership Act 1890, s.27; and see also *Featherstonhaugh v. Fenwick* (1810) 17 Ves.Jr. 307; *Booth v. Parks* (1828) 1 Moll. 465; *Neilson v. Mossend Iron Co.* (1886) 11 App.Cas. 298. And note *Cuffe v. Murtagh* (1881) 7 Ir.L.R. 411; *Daw v. Herring* [1892] 1 Ch. 284.

Joint adventure

9–09 If a partnership is entered into for a single adventure or undertaking, it will usually be possible to infer an agreement that the partnership is to endure until its completion.[15] In *Reade v. Bentley*,[16] an agreement between a publisher and an author, which required the publisher to defray the expenses of a work written by the author and entitled him to receive a percentage on the gross sales, and which provided that the net profits of each edition should be divided equally between the parties, was held to create an agreement for a joint adventure between the author and the publisher lasting for as long as might be necessary to dispose of a complete edition. The publication of each new edition prolonged the adventure until the completion of that edition; thereafter, either party was free to withdraw.

Sub-partnerships and group partnerships

9–10 In *Frost v. Moulton*,[17] it was held that an agreement by one of two partners to enter into a sub-partnership with a third party did not incorporate any of the terms of the head partnership and, in particular, did not contain an implied term that the sub-partnership should have the same duration as the head partnership.

9–11 In contrast, where a number of existing partnerships agree to form a group partnership[18] which is to endure for a fixed period, the current editor submits that a term must necessarily be implied that each of those existing partnerships will not be determined during that period.[19]

Change in partners

9–12 Where a new partner is admitted to a fixed term partnership, as a matter of law that partnership will determine and a new partnership will be created between the enlarged number of partners.[20] However, whether that new partnership is at will depends on the terms of the original agreement, *i.e.* whether it contemplates the admission of additional partners, and, more importantly, whether the new partner

---

[15] Partnership Act 1890, s.32(b); *Reade v. Bentley* (1858) 4 K. & J. 656; see also *McClean v. Kennard* (1874) L.R. 9 Ch.App. 336.

[16] (1858) 4 K. & J. 656. As to whether such an agreement constitutes a partnership, see *supra*, para. 5–30, n. 88.

[17] (1856) 21 Beav. 596. See generally, at to such partnerships, *supra*, paras. 5–75 *et seq.*

[18] See further, as to these partnerships, *infra*, paras. 11–20 *et seq.*

[19] This would, in turn, require a term to be implied into each existing partnership pursuant to the Partnership Act 1890, s.19.

[20] See *supra*, paras. 3–01 *et seq.*

has expressly or impliedly agreed to be bound either by that or some other agreement.[21]

Thus, in *Firth v. Amslake*,[22] two doctors had, prior to 1958, carried **9–13** on practice in partnership under the terms of a deed which provided for the partnership to continue during their joint lives. In 1958, they agreed in principle with a third doctor that all three would enter into partnership and share profits and losses equally. From May 1959, the three doctors practised together and a draft deed was drawn up but, in the event, never signed because one of the doctors objected to certain of its provisions. In October 1959, the two original partners wrote to the third partner saying that, since agreement could not be reached, the partnership ought to be dissolved as from November 30, 1959. Plowman J. held that, when the third doctor joined the firm in May 1959, the new partnership thereby created, which had superseded the old partnership, was a partnership at will, since no agreement had been reached as to its duration. As a result, that partnership could be (and in fact had been) validly determined by notice.

Dissolution

Whether a partnership has been entered into for a fixed term or is **9–14** merely at will, the right to rescind the agreement for fraud or misrepresentation or to accept a repudiatory breach of the agreement will, in an appropriate case, remain.[23] Similarly, the power of the court (or an arbitrator) to dissolve a firm pursuant to the provisions of the Partnership Act 1890[24] will override any agreement as to duration into which the partners may have reached.[25]

---

[21] *e.g.* there might be some temporary agreement, pending the execution of a formal deed, as in *Walters v. Bingham* [1988] 1 F.T.L.R. 260 (albeit not a case involving the admission of a new partner). See also *Zamikoff v. Lundy* (1970) 9 D.L.R. (3d) 637; and see *infra*, para. 10–215.

[22] (1964) 108 S.J. 198. Note also *Hensman v. Traill, The Times*, October 22, 1980, where the agreement expressly provided for a dissolution on the retirement of a partner.

[23] See *infra*, paras. 23–48, 23–51 *et seq.*, 24–04. As to frustration, see *infra*, para. 24–05.

[24] *Ibid.* s.35: see further, *infra*, paras. 24–39 *et seq.*

[25] See *Syers v. Syers* (1876) 1 App.Cas. 174.

Part Two

FORMATION OF PARTNERSHIP BY FORMAL AGREEMENT

CHAPTER 10

PARTNERSHIP AGREEMENTS

ALTHOUGH the formation of a partnership *may* be unintentional,[1] in **10–01**
the majority of cases the relationship will be entered into by design.
Yet, it is surprising that so many firms, particularly in the
professions, are not governed by a written agreement, whether
because the partners thought it unnecessary or "never got around to
it," or because they allowed their existing agreement to lapse
following the admission of a new partner.[2] In truth, a well drawn
agreement represents the most elementary form of protection for
partners and should, given the fragility of the partnership at will as a
business medium[3] and the increasingly complex financial and
management structures adopted in modern day firms, now be
regarded as indispensable.

In earlier editions of this work, the present chapter was entitled **10–02**
"Partnership Articles," reflecting the common usage of that
expression in Lord Lindley's day. Although references to partnership
articles are still encountered,[4] the correct generic term is now more
properly partnership *agreements*, thus including all forms of documentation, whether under hand or seal.[5]
Before considering the usual clauses found in partnership agreements, it will be useful to set out a number of general principles
governing the construction and application of such agreements.

1. CONSTRUCTION AND APPLICATION OF PARTNERSHIP AGREEMENTS

A partnership agreement, like any other agreement, must be **10–03**
construed according to the normal canons of construction,[6] but it

---

[1] See *supra*, paras. 5–01 *et seq.*
[2] See for example, *Firth v. Amslake* (1964) 108 S.J. 198, *supra*, para. 9–12.
[3] See *infra*, para. 24–10 *et seq.*
[4] In fact, the current editor has adopted this style for one of the precedents in the *Encyclopedia of Professional Partnerships*: see *ibid.* Precedent 2.
[5] Note, as to the execution of deeds, the provisions of the Law of Property (Miscellaneous Provisions) Act 1989, s.1.
[6] Lord Lindley referred in this context to *Story on Partnership*, Chap. 10; *Collyer on Partnership* (2nd ed.), pp. 137 *et seq.* It should also be noted in passing that the Unfair Contract Terms Act 1977, ss.2–4 will not apply to a contract for the formation of a partnership: *ibid.* Sched. 1, para. 1. It is, however, hard to imagine the type of provision which might otherwise have attracted the application of those sections.

should not be assumed that principles developed in relation to commercial contracts will automatically apply.[7] Equally, it is clear that the approach of the court to questions of construction is less rigid than in former times.[8]

There is no general rule that, in construing a document, the same meaning must be assigned to the same expression wherever it occurs: indeed, the usual form of definitions clause adopted in partnership and other agreements will be at pains to make this clear.[9] In practice, such a mechanical approach can only be resorted to in cases of particular difficulty or ambiguity.[10] Similarly, with the *contra proferentem* rule.[11]

The following principles are, however, of particular relevance and importance in the present context:

A. AGREEMENT NOT EXHAUSTIVE

10–04 It would be virtually impossible to draft an agreement which regulates every aspect of the partnership relation, and this was clearly recognised by Lord Lindley when he observed that partnership agreements:

> "are not intended to define, and are not construed as defining, all the rights and obligations of the partners *inter se*. A great deal is left to be understood."

Thus, although the maxim *expressum facit cessare tacitum*[12] naturally applies to such agreements, it will not as a general rule exclude those rights and obligations which are implied by the Partnership Act 1890 or by the general law. In this context, Lord Lindley quoted from the judgment in *Smith v. Jeyes*,[13] where Lord Langdale reportedly said:

---

[7] *e.g.* see *Henry Boot Construction v. Central Lancashire New Town Development Corporation* (1980) 15 Build. L.R. 8, where the *ejusdem generis* rule of construction was held not to apply to commercial contracts. It is thought unlikely that the same approach would be adopted when construing a partnership agreement; *sed quaere.*

[8] See for example, *Re Marr* [1990] Ch. 773, 784, where Nicholls L.J. emphasised that mechanical rules of construction are "out of step" with the modern purposive approach to the interpretation of statutes and documents; also *Bank of Scotland v. Wright* [1991] BCLC 244. And see, as to the *contra proferentem* principle, *Macey v. Qazi, The Times*, January 13, 1987, C.A.

[9] See the *Encyclopedia of Professional Partnerships*, Precedent 1, cl. 1.

[10] *Watson v. Haggitt* [1928] A.C. 127, 131, *per* Warrington L.J. But, for a different approach, see *Smith v. Gale* [1974] 1 W.L.R. 9.

[11] *Macey v. Quazi, The Times*, January 13, 1987, C.A.

[12] *i.e.* The express mention of one thing implies the exclusion of the other: see *Broom's Legal Maxims* (10th ed.), pp. 443 *et seq.*

[13] (1841) 4 Beav. 503, 505. See also, as to the inapplicability of the maxim *expressio unius est exclusio alterius, Nelson v. Bealby* (1862) 4 De G.F. & J. 321; *Browning v. Browning* (1862) 31 Beav. 316.

"The transactions of partners with each other cannot be considered merely with reference to the express contract between them. The duties and obligations arising from the relation between the parties are regulated by the express contract between them, so far as the express contract extends and continues in force; but if the express contract, or so much of it as continues in force, does not reach to all those duties and obligations, they are implied and enforced by the law ... When it is insisted that the conduct of one partner entitles the other to a dissolution, we must consider not merely the specific terms of the express contract, but also the duties and obligations which are implied in every partnership contract."[14]

Equally, where an agreement contains a detailed and seemingly comprehensive set of provisions governing some particular aspect of the firm's affairs, it is still necessary to ensure that the partners have not, by their conduct, inadvertently confined or altogether excluded the application of those provisions.[15]

B. AGREEMENT CONSTRUED BY REFERENCE TO THE PARTNERS' OBJECTIVES

Lord Lindley stated this important principle in the following terms: **10–05**

"The attainment of the objects which the partners have declared they had in view is always regarded as of the first importance. All the provisions of the articles[16] are to be construed so as to advance and not to defeat those objects; and however general the language of partnership articles may be, they will be construed with reference to the end designed and, if necessary, receive a restrictive interpretation[17] accordingly."[18]

The current editor considers that this principle lay behind the decision in *Mann v. D'Arcy*,[19] where Megarry J. held, on purely commercial grounds, that a managing partner had authority to enter into a subsidiary partnership venture with a third party in the course of carrying on the partnership business. Similarly, in *Hitchman v.*

---

[14] And see *Blisset v. Daniel* (1853) 10 Hare 493, 533, *per* Page Wood V.-C.

[15] Partnership Act 1890, s.19: see *infra*, para. 10–10 *et seq.*

[16] *i.e.* the agreement: see *supra*, para. 10–02.

[17] Or, where appropriate, a generous interpretation: see *Hitchman v. Crouch Butler Savage Associates* (1983) 127 S.J. 441, *infra* para. 10–98.

[18] In this context, Lord Lindley referred to *Collyer on Partnership* (2nd ed.), p. 137 and cited the decision in *Chapple v. Cadell* (1822) Jac. 537.

[19] [1968] 1 W.L.R. 893. And see *infra*, para. 12–13.

Crouch Butler Savage Associates Services,[20] the court refused to construe a provision requiring the signature of a particular senior partner to all expulsion notices as applicable to an expulsion notice served on him by the other partners.[21]

C. AGREEMENT CONSTRUED SO AS TO DEFEAT FRAUD

10–06 Lord Lindley observed that:

> "Any provision, however worded, will, if possible, be construed so as to defeat any attempt by one partner to avail himself of it for the purpose of defrauding his co-partner."

Thus, where the agreement provides for the preparation of accounts which are to be signed by the partners and thereafter to be binding on them, a false account knowingly drawn up by one partner will not bind his co-partners if they signed it believing its contents to be correct.[22] In the same way, it would seem that the exercise of a power conferred on a partner will be treated as invalid if it was intended to cover up or avoid the consequences of his own fraud.[23]

D. AGREEMENT CONSTRUED SO AS TO AVOID UNFAIRNESS AND EXPLOITATION

10–07 Lord Lindley's formulation of this principle,[24] which is closely related to that considered in the previous paragraph, was as follows:

> "Every power conferred by the articles[25] on any individual partner, or on any number of partners, is deemed to be conferred with a view to the benefit of the whole concern; and an abuse of such power, by an exercise of it, warranted perhaps by the words conferring it, but not by the truth and honour of the articles, will not be countenanced."

---

[20] (1983) 127 S.J. 441. And see, for further examples, *Sykes v. Land* (1984) 271 E.G. 1265; *Clarke v. Newland* [1991] 1 All E.R. 397 (C.A.), noticed *infra*, para. 10–188, n. 71.

[21] *Cf. Re A Solicitors' Arbitration* [1962] 1 W.L.R. 353 and *Bond v. Hale* (1969) 72 S.R. (N.S.W.) 201, noticed, *infra*, para. 10–98.

[22] See *Oldaker v. Lavender* (1833) 6 Sim. 239. See also the various cases cited *infra*, paras. 10–133 *et seq.* And see *infra*, para. 10–62.

[23] *Walters v. Bingham* [1988] 1 F.T.L.R. 260, 267–268, *per* Browne-Wilkinson V.-C. However, this part of his decision was clearly *obiter*.

[24] He actually headed this section "Articles to be construed so as to defeat the taking of unfair advantages."

[25] *i.e.* the agreement: see *supra*, para. 10–02.

Thus, a power of expulsion or compulsory retirement may not be exercised with a view to securing a financial or other benefit at the cost of the expelled or retiring partner.[26]

E.   AGREEMENT CONSTRUED IN THE FACTUAL MATRIX

In construing a partnership agreement, regard must now be had to **10–08** the factual matrix in which it was executed, as Lord Wilberforce explained in *Reardon Smith Line Ltd. v. Hansen-Tangen*[27]:

"... what the court must do must be to place itself in thought in the same factual matrix as that in which the parties were. All of these opinions seem to me implicitly to recognise that, in the search for the relevant background, there may be facts which form part of the circumstances in which the parties contract in which one, or both, may take no particular interest, their minds being addressed to or concentrated on other facts so that if asked they would assert that they did not have these facts in the forefront of their mind, but that will not prevent those facts from forming part of an objective setting in which the contract is to be construed."

This principle does not, however, enable the court to enquire into the *negotiations* which preceded the agreement[28] or the subjective intentions of the parties.[29] It naturally follows that an earlier draft of the agreement will not be admitted into evidence as an aid to construction.[30]

F.   TERMS IMPLIED TO GIVE THE AGREEMENT BUSINESS EFFICACY

Where necessary, the court will be prepared to imply a term to give **10–09** business efficacy to the agreement into which the partners have entered. In *Miles v. Clarke*,[31] Harman J. employed this principle to

---

[26] See *Blisset v. Daniel* (1853) 10 Hare 493, *infra*, para. 10–100.

[27] [1976] 1 W.L.R. 989, 997. See also *Prenn v. Simmonds* [1971] 1 W.L.R. 1381; *Bunge S.A. v. Kruse* [1977] 1 Lloyds Rep. 492; *Staffordshire Area Health Authority v. South Staffordshire Waterworks Co.* [1978] 1 W.L.R. 1387; *Clarke v. Newland* [1991] 1 All E.R. 397 (C.A.), noticed *infra*, para. 10–188, n. 71.

[28] *Prenn v. Simmonds*, *supra*. As to the circumstances in which the court can look at words *deleted* from a document before it is executed, see *Punjab National Bank v. de Boinville* [1992] 1 W.L.R. 1138 (C.A.).

[29] *Plumb Bros. v. Dolmac (Agriculture)* (1984) 271 E.G. 373.

[30] *National Bank of Australasia v. Falkingham* [1902] A.C. 585, 591, *per* Lord Lindley; *Mercantile Bank of Sydney v. Taylor* [1893] A.C. 317.

[31] [1953] 1 W.L.R. 537, *infra*, para. 18–35. And see, generally, *Chitty on Contracts* (26th ed.), paras. 905 *et seq.*

identify which assets had become the property of the partnership and which had remained in the separate ownership of the partners.

G. Terms Varied by Express or Implied Agreement

10–10 Prior to the Partnership Act 1890, it was well established that any term of a partnership agreement (in Lord Lindley's words "however express") could be abandoned with the consent of all the partners and that such consent might be given expressly or impliedly, *i.e.* by conduct.[32]

This principle which, in the case of written agreements, must be regarded as an exception to the parol evidence rule,[33] was given statutory force by section 19 of the Partnership Act 1890, which provides as follows:

> "19. The mutual rights and duties of partners, whether ascertained by agreement or defined by this Act, may be varied by the consent of all the partners, and such consent may be either express or inferred from a course of dealing."

It goes without saying that no variation will be effective if the consent of *all* the partners is not forthcoming.

Express agreement

10–11   Where the agreement confers power on a majority of partners to vary its terms[34] but does not otherwise specify how such decision is to be taken, notice of the proposed variation and of the meeting at which it is to be considered must be given to all the partners.[35] If the minority are not given an opportunity to be heard, they will not be bound by the variation.[36] Although Lord Lindley appeared to suggest that the majority have power to alter the agreement in *all* cases,[37] he

---

[32] See, generally, *Const v. Harris* (1824) T. & R. 496; *England v. Curling* (1844) 8 Beav. 129; *Somes v. Currie* (1855) 1 K. & J. 605; *Coventry v. Barclay* (1863) 3 De G.J. & S. 320; *Pilling v. Pilling* (1887) 3 De G.J. & S. 162. The rule appears to have been of nineteenth-century origin, since it was not applied in *Smith v. The Duke of Chandos* (1740) Barn. 412.

[33] See *Shore v. Wilson* (1842) 9 Cl. & F. 355, 555, *per* Parke B.; *Angel v. Duke* (1875) 32 L.T. 420. There is no doubt as to the continuing application of the parol evidence rule: *W.F. Trustees Ltd. v. Expo Safety Systems Ltd.*, *The Times*, May 24, 1993 (a decision concerning the construction of conveyancing documents).

[34] See the *Encyclopedia of Professional Partnerships*, Precedent 2, Art. 8.00.

[35] See *Const v. Harris* (1824) T. & R. 496.

[36] *Ibid.* pp. 518, 525, *per* Lord Eldon.

[37] The passage originally read: "If it is proposed to make an alteration in the articles by an agreement which shall be binding on all parties, notice of the proposed change and of the time and place at which it is to be taken into consideration, ought to be given to all the partners. For, even if the change is one which it is competent for a majority to make against the assent of the minority, all are entitled to be heard upon the subject; and unless all have an opportunity of opposing the change, those who object to it will not be bound by the others."

qualified that suggestion in his Supplement on the Partnership Act 1890.[38]

It is doubtful whether such a power could be used to alter the *nature* of the partnership or to bring about its premature determination, although much will depend on its precise terms.[39]

Implied agreement

For the partnership terms to be varied by an implied agreement, **10–12** there must be evidence of a course of conduct adopted by all the partners which is inconsistent with the continued application of those terms. Thus, in *Jackson v. Sedgwick*,[40] Lord Eldon held that the executors of a deceased partner were not entitled to enforce a provision in the agreement entitling them to the payment of an allowance in lieu of profits for the period from the last annual account to the date of death, because the partners had for some years failed to draw up annual accounts and had, moreover, engaged in a business different from that originally contemplated: in those circumstances, adherence to the strict terms of the agreement would clearly have worked an injustice.[41]

Equally, if the agreement provides for the entitlement of a **10–13** deceased partner to be determined by reference to an account similar in form to the firm's annual accounts, any accounting practice habitually adopted by the partners in drawing up such accounts will be applied, even if this will result in a payment to the outgoing partner of more than he would otherwise have been entitled to.[42]

Again, if all the partners agree to contribute towards losses but one is never called on to do so, this may be sufficient to warrant an inference that the original agreement has been varied *vis-à-vis* that partner.[43]

It is, of course, essential to demonstrate that all partners have impliedly accepted the variation. This may be more difficult in a large firm or where there is a dormant partner.[44]

---

[38] Lord Lindley observed "The mutual rights and duties of partners cannot be varied except by the consent of all the partners, and the passage in Lord Eldon's judgment in *Const v. Harris*, in which he says that 'that is the act of the majority which is the act of the majority, provided all are consulted and the majority are acting *bona fide*,' is only true of cases in which the majority has the power of binding the minority." See also (1824) T. & R. 496, 517, *per* Lord Eldon.

[39] See *Morgan v. Driscoll* (1922) 38 T.L.R. 251 (which concerned a power to vary the rules of a voluntary association).

[40] (1818) 1 Swan. 460; also *Simmons v. Leonard* (1844) 3 Hare 581. Cf. *Cruickshank v. Sutherland* (1922) 92 L.J.Ch. 136 and the other cases noticed *infra*, paras. 10–133 *et seq*.

[41] (1818) 1 Swan. 470.

[42] *Ex p. Barber* (1870) L.R. 5 Ch.App. 687. In this case, the partners had adopted the practice of debiting bad debts to the profit and loss account in the year in which they were discovered to be bad.

[43] *Geddes v. Wallace* (1820) 2 Bli. 270.

[44] See *Re Frank Mills Mining Co.* (1883) 23 Ch.D. 52, 56, *per* Jessell M.R.

Admission of new partner

10–14   When a new partner is admitted to a firm on the terms of an existing written agreement,[45] he may in practice not be informed that those terms have subsequently been varied by an implied agreement for the simple reason that the partners themselves are unaware of that fact.[46] In such circumstances, the current editor submits that the original terms will apply, until such time they are again varied by the conduct of all the partners *including* the new partner.

Derivative partner

10–15   If, exceptionally, a partner is brought into the firm derivatively, *i.e.* by taking over the share of an existing partner *in specie*,[47] he will be bound by an amendment to the partnership agreement previously acquiesced in by that partner.[48]

H.   AGREEMENT PRESUMED TO APPLY AFTER EXPIRATION OF FIXED TERM

10–16 Consistently with the pre-existing law,[49] section 27 of the Partnership Act 1890 provides as follows:

> "27.—(1) Where a partnership entered into for a fixed term is continued after the term has expired, and without any express new agreement, the rights and duties of the partners remain the same as they were at the expiration of the term, so far as is consistent with the incidents of a partnership at will.
>
> (2) A continuance of the business by the partners or such of them as habitually acted therein during the term, without any settlement or liquidation of the partnership affairs, is presumed to be a continuance of the partnership."

---

[45] See further, *supra*, paras. 9–11, 9–12.

[46] In the current editor's experience, incoming partners are frequently not even informed about *express* variations which may, for example, be fully documented in partnership minutes. In such cases, the result will technically be the same as that considered in the text. See also *infra*, para. 10–215.

[47] *Cf.* the position under the Partnership Act 1890, s.31, *infra*, paras. 19–59 *et seq*.

[48] See *Const v. Harris* (1824) T. & R. 496, 521, *per* Lord Eldon. Lord Lindley's original formulation of this somewhat obscure proposition was as follows: "It seems that a person who comes into a firm through another who has acquiesced in a variation of the terms of the partnership articles, is bound by that acquiescence, and cannot revert to the original articles." Note also *Zamikoff v. Lundy* (1970) 9 D.L.R. (3d) 637 and *infra*, para. 10–215.

[49] See *Crawshay v. Collins* (1808) 15 Ves.Jr. 218; *Featherstonhaugh v. Fenwick* (1810) 17 Ves.Jr. 298; *Booth v. Parks* (1828) 1 Moll. 465; *Neilson v. Mossend Iron Co.* (1886) 11 App.Cas. 298.

Effect of new agreement

The application of the section is naturally displaced by a new **10–17** agreement, but not by the existence of an unexecuted draft,[50] unless the partners have agreed to be bound by that draft pending the execution of a formal deed[51] or have otherwise acted on the footing that it governs the continuing partnership.[52]

Clauses framed by reference to fixed term partnership

The rule embodied in section 27 will, in an appropriate case, **10–18** enable a provision of the agreement framed solely by reference to the original fixed term to apply after its expiration. Thus, in *Essex v. Essex*,[53] the partners had entered into a fixed term partnership for 14 years and agreed that, if either should die "during the said co-partnership term," the other should be entitled to acquire his share at a certain price. The fixed term expired but the partnership was continued on the old terms. One partner then died. It was held that the survivor was entitled to acquire his share as originally agreed: the court in effect regarded the reference to "the partnership term" as equivalent to "the continuation of the partnership."[54]

This principle will be of considerable importance in the case of any reference in an agreement to an event occurring "during the term" or "during the partnership."[55]

Clauses consistent with partnership at will

In order to ascertain whether a particular clause is capable of being **10–19** carried over into a partnership at will, account must naturally be taken of its precise terms,[56] so that generalisation is difficult. Nevertheless, it has already been seen that a right to acquire an outgoing partner's share can survive the expiration of the fixed term;[57] a similar attitude has been adopted towards a right to acquire a partner's share "after the determination of the partnership."[58]

---

[50] *Neilson v. Mossend Iron Co.*, *supra*. See also *Stekel v. Ellice* [1973] 1 W.L.R. 191.

[51] *Walters v. Bingham* [1988] 1 F.T.L.R. 260.

[52] In such a case, the draft will have effect by virtue of the Partnership Act 1890, s.19, *supra*, para. 10–10.

[53] (1855) 20 Beav. 442; see also *Cox v. Willoughby* (1880) 13 Ch.D. 863; *McLeod v. Dowling* (1927) 43 T.L.R. 655.

[54] Lord Lindley observed that "The expression 'the partnership term' was held equivalent to the time during which the partners continue in partnership without coming to any fresh agreement." However, this is not borne out by the report at (1855) 20 Beav. 442.

[55] But see *Neilson v. Mossend Iron Co.* (1886) 11 App.Cas. 298.

[56] *Essex v. Essex* (1855) 20 Beav. 442, *supra*, para. 10–18; also *King v. Chuck* (1853) 17 Beav. 325; *Cox v. Willoughby* (1880) 13 Ch.D. 863; *McLeod v. Dowling* (1927) 43 T.L.R. 655. *Cf. Cookson v. Cookson* (1837) 8 Sim. 529, which has not been followed.

[57] *Daw v. Herring*, *supra*, explaining *Yates v. Finn* (1875) referred to at 13 Ch.D. 839, 840; *Brooks v. Brooks* (1901) 85 L.T. 453; *M'Gown v. Henderson*, 1914 S.C. 839. See also *Neilson v. Mossend Iron Co.* (1886) 11 App.Cas. 298.

[58] See *Yates v. Finn*, *supra* (as explained in *Daw v. Herring* [1892] 1 Ch. 284); also *Cookson v. Cookson* (1837) 8 Sim. 529 (which has not been followed); *Murphy v. Power* [1923] 1 I.R. 68.

An arbitration clause drawn in wide terms has been held to apply,[59] but it is submitted that such a clause, like any other common form provision, will normally be carried over even if it is in more restricted terms.[60]

Clauses inconsistent with partnership at will

10–20   Although a number of provisions governing the position *following* a dissolution have, with one exception, been held to survive, a different attitude is adopted towards those clauses which relate to the *manner* in which the partnership is to be terminated. Thus, a clause declaring that the partnership should stand dissolved if one partner assigned, mortgaged or disposed of his share without the consent of the other has been held not to survive;[61] similarly in the case of a clause which in effect required each partner to decide whether to carry on the business or to retire and be paid out the value of his share within the "three months before the termination of [the] contract."[62]

The exception to which reference was made in the previous paragraph is a covenant restraining competition, which has been held not to be carried forward into a partnership at will.[63]

Expulsion: the doubtful case

10–21   It was held in *Clark v. Leach*[64] that a power to dissolve a partnership if a partner should "neglect or refuse to attend to the business of the ... partnership" which, if exercised, would entitle the other partners to acquire his share, did not survive the expiration of the initial fixed term. On this basis, it might legitimately be expected that any power of expulsion or compulsory retirement[65] should be similarly regarded; indeed, in his Supplement on the Partnership Act 1890, Lord Lindley pointed out that:

> "It has ... been decided that a right of expulsion cannot be exercised after the expiration of the original term[66]; and it is clear that any clause which prevents a partner from determining the partnership at his will would be inapplicable."[67]

---

[59] *Gillett v. Thornton* (1875) L.R. 19 Eq. 599. See also *Morgan v. William Harrison Ltd.* [1907] 2 Ch. 137.

[60] See *Essex v. Essex* (1855) 20 Beav. 442, 450, *per* Sir John Romilly M.R.

[61] *Campbell v. Campbell* (1893) 6 R. 137 (H.L.).

[62] *Neilson v. Mossend Iron Co.* (1886) 11 App.Cas. 298.

[57] *Hensman v. Traill, The Times,* October 22, 1980. This part of the decision was not overruled in *Kerr v. Morris* [1987] Ch. 90, but its authority is now, perhaps, reduced.

[64] (1863) 1 De G.J. & S. 409. This decision was seemingly approved in an *obiter* part of the judgment of Stirling J. in *Daw v. Herring* [1892] 1 Ch. 284, 290.

[65] See further, as to such powers, *infra*, paras. 10–95 *et seq.*

[66] In support of this proposition, Lord Lindley cited *Clark v. Leach* (1863) 1 De G.J. & S. 409 and *Neilson v. Mossend Iron Co.* (1886) 11 App.Cas. 298.

[67] At this point, Lord Lindley referred to the Partnership Act 1890, s.26 and the decision in *Neilson v. Mossend Iron Co., supra.*

However, in an *obiter* part of his judgment in *Walters v.* **10–22** *Bingham*,[68] Browne-Wilkinson V.-C., after referring to Lord Westbury's decision in *Clark v. Leach*, reportedly observed:

"Lord Westbury said that whether or not the power of expulsion continued to apply depended on the intention of the parties. He held that a 'stipulation so special and extraordinary' and one 'not ordinarily found in contracts of partnership' could not be held to survive. He also relied on the fact that, being a partnership at will, there was no longer any need for a power of expulsion and that the power was in the nature of a power to forfeit.

I do not regard that case a providing binding authority as to the law applicable in a case occurring 120 years later in wholly different circumstances, after the passing of the Partnership Act 1890. In modern professional partnerships with very numerous partners a power of expulsion, far from being 'special and extraordinary,' is commonplace and normal.[69] Indeed, such a power is essential if a total dissolution as between all the partners is to be avoided when it is necessary to get rid of one unsatisfactory partner. Where there is a large number of continuing partners, the power of expulsion is not inconsistent with a partnership at will. Expulsion and dissolution by notice are two different concepts producing different results. In *Clark v. Leach* there were only two partners: therefore whether there were expulsion or dissolution, the whole partnership was at an end. But in large modern partnerships there is a fundamental difference between expulsion (leaving the partnership continuing between the remainder) and dissolution (which puts an end to the whole partnership as between all partners). In large, modern professional partnerships there is no inconsistency between a power of expulsion and a partnership at will."

The following points should be noted in relation to the Vice- **10–23** Chancellor's decision:

1. The Partnership Act 1890 expressly preserved the pre-existing law, save in so far as it was inconsistent with the express provisions of the Act.[70]
2. Although it is correct that a power of expulsion is now commonplace, there is still a clear and fundamental inconsistency between the existence of such an express power and the

---

[68] [1988] 1 F.T.L.R. 260, 268. The Vice Chancellor had, in fact, already held that the partnership was not at will (see *supra*, para. 10–16), so that this point strictly did not require to be decided.
[69] Note that, in the 5th edition of this work, Lord Lindley clearly regarded a power of expulsion as falling within the category "Usual Clauses in Articles of Partnership": see *ibid.* pp. 426 *et seq.*
[70] See *ibid.* s.46.

inherent power of each partner (including a partner proposed to be expelled)[71] to bring about a general dissolution of the partnership at a moment's notice.[72]

3. If there is such an inconsistency, it is difficult to see how it can be removed by the sheer size of the partnership or by the fact that it carries on a professional practice.

4. A power of expulsion is clearly of an expropriatory nature and, on that account, will always be construed strictly.[73] By analogy, the court should be cautious in seeking to extend the scope of such a power beyond the term originally contemplated.

Although the Vice-Chancellor's decision naturally commands great respect, the current editor believes that its basis in law is questionable and should be approached with a degree of caution.

2. USUAL CLAUSES FOUND IN A PARTNERSHIP AGREEMENT

Drafting the agreement

10–24   The remainder of this chapter is devoted to a consideration of those clauses which are commonly encountered in partnership agreements. In terms of subject matter, as opposed to content, these have changed little since Lord Lindley's day[74]; however, there is no such thing as a standard partnership agreement, and it should not be assumed either that each of these "usual" clauses will be required in every case or that their inclusion guarantees the suitability of the agreement.[75]

The potential draftsman should also bear in mind that the majority of the provisions of the Partnership Act 1890 apply unless they are expressly or impliedly excluded by the agreement.[76] In some cases, he may be content with those provisions; in others he may not. Yet he must at the same time have regard to the position of the partners themselves, who may be unfamiliar with the workings of the Act. Lord Lindley made this point in the following passage written prior to

---

[71] Unless such a partner is *in all cases* prohibited from exercising the power because of his duty of good faith: see *Walters v. Bingham* [1988] 1 F.L.T.R. 260, 267. And see *infra*, paras. 10–118, 24–13.

[72] See the Partnership Act 1890, s.26(1), 32(c), *infra*, paras. 24–10 *et seq.*; also *ibid.* s.25, *infra*, para. 24–85. And see *Clark v. Leach* (1863) 1 De G.J. & S. 409, 415, *per* Lord Westbury.

[73] See *infra*, para. 10–98.

[74] Although a few of Lord Lindley's original headings can no longer be regarded as "usual", they have been retained in the interests of completeness.

[75] See, further, the checklist in the *Encyclopedia of Professional Partnerships*, paras. 1–050 *et seq.*

[76] See, in particular, *ibid.* ss.19, 24, 25, 29 and 30.

the Act (thereby incidentally seeming to ignore the use of partnerships in the solicitors' profession):

"In framing articles of partnership, it should always be remembered, that they are intended for the guidance of persons who are not lawyers; and that it is therefore unwise to insert only such provisions as are necessary to exclude the application of rules which apply where nothing to the contrary is said. The articles should be so drawn as to be a code of directions to which the partners may refer as a guide in all their transactions, and upon which they may settle among themselves differences which may arise, without having recourse to Courts of Justice."

The practice of resorting to short form "Heads of Agreement," **10–25** although occasionally required on grounds of expediency, should never be regarded as a long term substitute for a comprehensive agreement. Regrettably, once such heads of agreement are in place, there is an understandable tendency to regard the proliferation of documentation as an unnecessary evil, but this is frequently an economy that partners live to regret.

As in the previous edition of this work, the current editor has not sought to reproduce typical precedents of the "usual" clauses in an attempt to place them in context. The basic content of this chapter is directed towards identifying the purpose and effect of each clause: this is not a drafting work and any standardised form which does not encompass all the variations considered in the text and which is not accompanied by a commentary specifically directed towards the particular form of words used might inadvertently mislead the prospective draftsman.[77]

Form of agreement

Partnership agreements traditionally take the form of a deed,[78] **10–26** although this is not strictly necessary save where the agreement will operate to convey land or an interest in land from one partner to another,[79] where it purports to grant a power of attorney[80] or, more rarely, where a gratuitous benefit is to be conferred on a third

---

[77] However, for the assistance of the reader, footnote references to the *Encyclopedia of Professional Partnerships*, which is a companion to this volume, have been incorporated.

[78] See, as to the formalities for the execution of a deed, the Law of Property (Miscellaneous Provisions) Act 1989, s.1.

[79] Law of Property Act 1925, s.52(2). The proposition in the text is not absolute: it is still possible to prove the existence and terms of a partnership solely on the basis of oral evidence, even where the partnership property consists of land: see *supra*, paras. 7–02 *et seq*.

[80] *e.g.* to sign *Gazette* notices, continuance elections under the Income and Corporation Taxes Act 1988, s. 113(2), etc.: see the Powers of Attorney Act 1971, s.1. See *infra*, paras. 10–205, 10–206.

party.[81] Since consideration will flow from each partner to the other(s),[82] an agreement under hand will normally suffice.[83]

A. PARTIES

10–27 It is always necessary to identify the parties to the agreement and to state whether they will be partners in the true sense (normally styled "equity" partners), partners with only limited rights to participate in profits and in the management of the firm (normally styled "non-equity" or, where appropriate, "salaried" or "fixed share" partners), or mere employees who are to be held out as partners (also misleadingly styled "salaried" partners).[84] In fact, persons falling within the latter class should not be made parties to the agreement at all.

Where the parties are numerous, the modern practice is to schedule their names and addresses, often in such a way as to permit the schedule to be altered in order to accommodate future changes in the firm.[85]

If one partner is to hold a particular position in the firm, *e.g.* "senior partner," "managing partner" or "administration partner," that should be stated in the agreement and provision for the succession of other partners to that position, whether after the expiration of the first holder's term of office or on his departure from the firm, should be made.

B. NATURE OF THE BUSINESS[86]

10–28 Lord Lindley emphasised the need for the agreement to establish the nature of the business to be carried on, explaining:

> "Upon it depends the extent to which each partner is to be regarded as the implied agent of the firm in his dealings with strangers[87]; and upon it also in a great measure depends the power of a majority of partners to act in opposition to the wishes of the minority."[88]

---

[81] See the Law of Property Act 1925, s.56(1) and *infra*, paras. 10–151. But consider also the inheritance tax implications: see *infra*, para. 36–35.

[82] See *supra*, paras. 6–01 *et seq.*

[83] *Quaere*, could there be a partnership under which one or more partners accept no obligations whatsoever? It is thought not, given the definition in the Partnership Act 1890, s.1(1), *supra*, paras. 2–01 *et seq.*

[84] See further *supra*, para. 5–65.

[85] See the *Encyclopedia of Professional Partnerships*, Precedent 2, Art. 1.00.14, Sched. 1.

[86] *Ibid.* Precedent 1, cl. 2.

[87] See the Partnership Act 1890, s.5, *infra*, paras. 12–02 *et seq.*

[88] See *ibid.* s.24(8), *infra*, paras. 15–05 *et seq.*

However, as demonstrated by the arguments advanced in *Nixon v. Wood*,[89] disputes can still arise even where the nature of the business *is* clearly established in the agreement.

C. COMMENCEMENT DATE[90]

It is essential that the commencement date of the partnership is **10–29** established with certainty, since it is only from that date that each partner will be liable for the acts of his co-partners and, thus, for the debts and obligations of the firm.[91]

No commencement date specified

Lord Lindley observed: **10–30**

"Prima facie, articles of partnership, like other instruments, take effect from their date; and if they are executed on the day of their date, and contain no expression indicating when the partnership is to begin, it must be taken to commence on the day of the date of the articles, and parol evidence to show that this was not intended is not admissible."[92]

A deed takes effect at the moment of its execution, irrespective of the date which appears on its face;[93] thus, if it can be demonstrated by extrinsic evidence that the deed was executed on some other date, the partnership will be regarded as commencing on that date,[94] unless the partners were in fact carrying on the business with effect from some earlier date.[95]

Retrospective and future commencement dates

Agreements frequently provide that the partnership is to be **10–31** deemed to have commenced on some past date. If, as will usually be the case, the partners were in fact carrying on business together at that date, the agreement will have retrospective effect as regards them, but not as regards third parties, *e.g.* the Inland Revenue. If, on

---

[89] (1987) 284 E.G. 1055.
[90] See the *Encyclopedia of Professional Partnerships*, Precedent 1, cl. 2.
[91] See *infra*, paras. 13–18 *et seq*.
[92] *Williams v. Jones* (1826) 5 B. & C. 108. If the agreement is not dated, parol evidence is admissible to show that it was not intended to take effect from the time of execution: *Davis v. Jones* (1856) 17 C.B. 625.
[93] *Morell v. Studd & Millington* [1913] 2 Ch. 648.
[94] See *Browne v. Burton* (1847) 17 L.J. Q.B. 49.
[95] In such a case, the actual date of commencement will be provable as a fact independently of the date on which the agreement was executed. See also *supra*, para. 2–09 and *infra*, para. 13–19.

the other hand, no business was carried on at that date, the agreement cannot regulate a non-existent relationship and will, therefore, only have full effect when business is actually commenced.[96] However, it might, depending on its terms, have a limited effect as regards the interim period, *e.g.* so as to deem debts incurred during that period to be liabilities of the partnership.[97]

Similarly, an agreement providing for a *future* commencement date will not prevent the partnership coming into existence at an earlier date, if the partners in fact carry on business together with effect from that date.[98]

Formal agreement to be drawn up

10-32   If prospective partners enter into an interim agreement,[99] intending that a more formal agreement will be prepared and executed in due course, it does not mean that the commencement of the partnership will necessarily be delayed until the formal agreement is in place. Everything will depend on the terms of the interim agreement, assuming it to be binding on the partners.[1]

D. DURATION[2]

10-33 The duration of the partnership must always be stated in the agreement, if the creation of a partnership at will is to be avoided.[3] This usually takes the form of a fixed term of years or a term for the "joint lives" of the partners.[4] On occasion, an unlimited duration is adopted, but the right of each partner to dissolve the firm is expressly excluded.[5]

Since a partnership will normally be dissolved by the death or bankruptcy of a partner,[6] it is essential that this consequence is expressly negatived.[7] At the same time, it should also be confirmed, *ex abundanti cautela*, that the retirement or expulsion of a partner under any power contained in the agreement will not determine the

---

[96] *Vere v. Ashby* (1829) 10 B. & C. 288; *Waddington v. O'Callaghan* (1931) 16 T.C. 187; *Saywell v. Pope* [1979] S.T.C. 824. See also *infra*, paras. 34–12 *et seq.*

[97] No rights against the intended firm would be conferred on third party creditors in such a case.

[98] *Battley v. Lewis* (1840) 1 Man. & G. 155.

[99] *e.g.* heads of agreement, see *supra*, para. 10–25.

[1] See *England v. Curling* (1844) 8 Beav. 129; also *Branca v. Cobarro* [1947] K.B. 854.

[2] See the *Encyclopedia of Professional Partnerships*, Precedent 1, cl. 3.

[3] Partnership Act 1890, ss.26(1), 32(c), *supra*, paras. 9–01 *et seq.* and *infra*, paras. 24–10 *et seq.*

[4] Where the term is referable to the joint lives of the partners, care must be taken to ensure that the relevant lives are those of the *current* partners.

[5] This may be appropriate where one or more of the partners is a company: see further, as to corporate partnerships, *infra*, paras. 11–02 *et seq.*

[6] Partnership Act 1890, s.33(1), *infra*, paras. 24–20 *et seq.*

[7] In the case of bankruptcy, the current editor considers that the effects of *ibid.* s.33(1) will be *impliedly* excluded if there is power under the agreement to expel a bankrupt partner. And see, generally, *William S. Gordon & Co. Ltd. v. Mrs. Mary Thomson Partnership*, 1985 S.L.T. 122.

partnership as regards the continuing partners.[8] However, whilst such express provisions may avoid the worst effects of a dissolution, they cannot as a matter of law prevent there being a *technical* dissolution on any change in the composition of the firm.[9]

If the chosen term expires, but the partnership continues without a new agreement, it will do so as a partnership at will.[10] This will also be the position if a new partner is admitted during the term, unless the existing agreement contemplates the possibility of such admission and the incoming partner agrees to be bound by its terms.[11]

E.   FIRM NAME[12]

It is desirable, but not essential,[13] that the firm name should be **10–34** stated in the agreement, together with the procedure for altering that name.[14] It is also usual to include a reference to the need to comply with the provisions of the Business Names Act 1985,[15] by way of an *aide-mémoire* to the partners.

Use of firm name

Lord Lindley said: **10–35**

"... it should be declared that no partner shall enter into an engagement on behalf of the firm except in its name. Such an agreement is capable of being enforced[16]; and it may be of use in determining, as between the partners, whether a given transaction is to be regarded as a partnership transaction or not."

In practice, such declarations are not normally included in modern agreements, save in relation to cheques.[17]

---

[8] The agreement should also, of course, provide for the acquisition of the outgoing partner's share, so that the point is largely academic. Note the decision in *William S. Gordon & Co. Ltd. v. Mrs. Mary Thomson Partnership*, *supra*.

[9] See *supra*, paras. 3–01 *et seq.* and *infra*, para. 24–02; also *Hadlee v. Commissioner of Inland Revenue* [1989] 2 N.Z.L.R. 447, 455, *per* Eichelbaum J. This issue was not canvassed before the Privy Council: see [1993] A.C. 524.

[10] Partnership Act 1980, s.27, *supra*, para. 10–15 *et seq.*

[11] See *supra*, paras. 9–11, 9–12 and *infra*, para. 10–215.

[12] See the *Encyclopedia of Professional Partnerships*, Precedent 1, cl. 5.

[13] The name may, of course, give some indication of the type of business carried on by the firm and, thereby, assist in identifying the extent of each partner's implied authority pursuant to the Partnership Act 1890, s.5, *infra*, paras. 12–01 *et seq.*

[14] This will usually be dealt with, if at all, in the clauses governing decision making: see *infra*, paras. 10–82 *et seq.*

[15] See *supra*, paras. 3–24 *et seq.* It is not necessary to be too specific as to the requirements of the Act.

[16] See *Marshall v. Colman* (1820) 2 J. & W. 266.

[17] See the *Encyclopedia of Professional Partnerships*, Precedent 1, cl. 6(3).

F. THE PREMIUM

10–36 Although a reference to premiums[18] has been retained, they are now rarely, if ever, encountered and most certainly could not be considered "usual." If a premium is to be paid, the agreement should identify both the time and manner of payment[19] and the circumstances in which it is to be returned, whether on dissolution or otherwise.[20]

G. PARTNERSHIP PREMISES[21]

10–37 It is desirable, but not in all cases essential, to identify the premises from which the firm will carry on business and the manner in which decisions in relation to those and any other premises will in the future be taken.[22]

Premises owned by one or more partners

10–38 What is of greater importance is to ensure that the occupation rights of the firm are clearly established where the premises are to remain in the sole ownership of one or more of the partners. If a lease in favour of the firm is to be granted then it must be in writing.[23]

If the agreement omits any reference to such occupation rights then, in the absence of any other evidence, it will not be assumed, merely because the premises are indispensable to the partnership business, that they belong to the firm[24] or are subject to the firm's right to (i) a lease or tenancy[25] or, where relevant, (ii) an exclusive licence to occupy within the meaning of the Agricultural Holdings Act 1986.[26] It will rather be inferred that each individual partner who

---

[18] This expression is not defined in the Partnership Act 1890: see further, as to its meaning, *infra*, para. 25–06.

[19] *e.g.* if it is payable in instalments, will they continue even if the partnership is dissolved? See also *infra*, para. 25–15.

[20] See the Partnership Act 1890, s.40 and *Handyside v. Campbell* (1901) 17 T.L.R. 623, 624, *per* Farwell J. See also *infra*, para. 25–10.

[21] See the *Encyclopedia of Professional Partnerships*, Precedent 1, cl. 4.

[22] See *Clements v. Norris* (1878) 8 Ch.D. 129.

[23] *Rye v. Rye* [1962] A.C. 496. For a form of lease, see *Key & Elphinstone's Precedents in Conveyancing* (15th ed.), Vol. 1, p. 985. And see, as to the termination of such a lease, *Brenner v. Rose* [1973] 1 W.L.R. 443; *Sykes v. Land* (1984) 271 E.G. 1265; *cf. Featherstone v. Staples* [1986] 1 W.L.R. 861. As to agreements to surrender the lease on dissolution, see *Joseph v. Joseph* [1967] Ch. 78 and *infra*, para. 18–47.

[24] *Eardley v. Broad, The Times*, April 28, 1970 and (1970) 215 E.G. 823. See also *infra*, paras. 18–32, 18–33.

[25] *Rye v. Rye, supra.* A tenancy was inferred in *Pocock v. Carter* [1912] 1 Ch. 663, but this can no longer be considered good law.

[26] *Harrison-Bradley v. Smith* [1964] 1 W.L.R. 456. A contrary view was advanced in *Harrison v. Wing* [1988] 29 E.G. 101, 103, but the point appears not to have been fully argued, since their Lordships make no reference to the decision in *Harrison-Bradley v. Smith*. See also *Bahamas International Trust Co. Ltd. v. Threadgold* [1974] 1 W.L.R. 1514. It is considered that occupation pursuant to such a licence would properly fall to be disregarded for the purposes of the eligibility test under the Agricultural Holdings Act 1986, s.36(3)(b) in relation to *other* land: see *ibid.* Sched. 6, para. 6(1)(e). *Per contra*, perhaps, if the licence cannot be terminated whilst the partnership continues: see an article by Michele Slatter in [1986] Conv. 320.

is not beneficially interested in the premises has been granted a non-exclusive licence to enter them in order to carry on the partnership business.[27] Such licences would seem to be contractual and might, as a matter of implication, not be terminable during the currency of the partnership, particularly if it can be shown that the partnership business can only be carried on from those premises and that the termination of the licences would strike at the substratum of the partnership agreement.[28] In such circumstances the only effective way of determining the licences would be to dissolve the partnership but, even then, they would prima facie continue until the winding-up is complete.[29]

Covenant against assignment, etc.

Where leasehold premises owned by a partner are occupied by the **10–39** firm, there will be no breach of a covenant against assignment, underletting, parting with or sharing possession if that partner merely permits his co-partners to go into occupation for the purposes of carrying on the partnership business.[30] *Per contra* if an assignment of the tenancy to the firm can be inferred or if the covenant prohibits the sharing of occupation.

H. PARTNERSHIP PROPERTY[31]

The agreement should, so far as possible,[32] identify: **10–40**

(a) those assets which constitute partnership property;[33]
(b) those assets which are to be retained in the ownership of a partner but to be used by the firm and, if so, on what basis;[34] and
(c) if partnership money is to be spent on an asset belonging to a partner, whether the firm will be entitled to a lien for its return.[35]

In earlier editions of this work, the view was advanced that the agreement should also record the partners' respective beneficial

---

[27] *Harrison-Broadley v. Smith*, *supra*.
[28] *Cf.* the position where the firm has a tenancy: *Brenner v. Rose* [1973] 1 W.L.R. 443; *Sykes v. Land* (1984) 271 E.G. 1265.
[29] See *infra*, para. 25–03.
[30] *Gian Singh & Co. v. Nahar* [1965] 1 W.L.R. 412 (P.C.) where, however, there appears to have been merely a covenant against assignment and subletting.
[31] *Encyclopedia of Professional Partnerships*, Precedent 1, cl. 8(1).
[32] It is not, of course, feasible to list every item and certain generic descriptions may have to be resorted to.
[33] Note that milk quota is incapable of existing as an asset independently of the land to which it relates: see *Faulks v. Faulks* [1992] 15 E.G. 82, noticed *infra*, para. 18–21.
[34] See, in the case of land, *supra*, para. 10–38.
[35] See *infra*, paras. 18–37 *et seq.*, 20–25, 20–26.

interests in the partnership property. In the current editor's opinion such a provision is neither usual nor necessary, provided that the partners' shares in asset surpluses or capital profits[36] are clearly stated.[37] However, if a partner is to have *no* interest whatsoever in such property, a declaration to this effect should be included, if only for the avoidance of doubt.[38]

Goodwill

10–41   The agreement should establish whether or not goodwill is a partnership asset: although there is something akin to a presumption that it belongs to the firm, this will not always be the case.[39] If the goodwill is to be retained by a particular partner or partners, it should be decided whether any *increase* in its value will also belong to those partners or to the firm and, if the latter, how the firm's entitlement is to be ascertained and realised on a dissolution.

Land[40]

10–42   If one partner is entitled to land which is to be brought into the partnership, it is certainly advisable to ensure that the legal estate is conveyed into the names of at least two of the partners.[41] However, as between the partners themselves, all that is required is a simple declaration in the agreement that the land will constitute partnership property. Such a declaration will take effect under section 53(1)(b) or (c) of the Law of Property Act 1925; the position where there is no written agreement has already been noticed earlier in this work.[42]

Offices and appointments[43]

10–43   Although a particular office or appointment cannot normally itself be regarded as a partnership asset, it may be (and often is) treated as held on the firm's behalf, so that the partner concerned is obliged to account to the firm for any fees or other remuneration received.[44]

---

[36] See, as to these expressions, *infra*, paras. 10–129, 17–05.

[37] See *infra*, para. 10–66. Note, however, that complications may arise where preferential "salaries" are payable to partners as a first charge on profits: see *infra*, para. 10–69 (where the same problem is considered in relation to the sharing of losses).

[38] *e.g.* in the case of a so-called "salaried" partner.

[39] See *Miles v. Clarke* [1953] 1 W.L.R. 537; *Stekel v. Ellice* [1973] 1 W.L.R. 191; see also *infra*, paras. 10–158 *et seq.*, 18–18, 18–35.

[40] See also *supra*, paras. 10–37 *et seq.*

[41] See *supra*, paras. 18–60 *et seq.*

[42] See *infra*, paras. 7–02 *et seq.* Otherwise, it will be necessary to prove that the other partners have acted to their detriment, if the effects of the Law of Property Act 1925, s.53(1)(b) are to be avoided: see *Midland Bank v. Dobson* (1986) 1 F.L.R. 171. And see *Rye v. Rye* [1962] A.C. 496.

[43] See the *Encyclopedia of Professional Partnerships*, Precedent 11, cl.12(1).

[44] See *Smith v. Mules* (1852) 9 Hare 556; *Collins v. Jackson* (1862) 31 Beav. 645; *Casson Beckman & Partners v. Papi* [1991] BCLC 299, 309, *per* Balcombe L.J. and *infra*, paras. 18–19, 18–20. See also *Carlyon Britton v. Lumb* (1922) 38 T.L.R. 298.

Where partners hold such positions, or are likely to do so, their duty to account or their right to retain any fees, etc., should be clearly stated in the agreement. In some cases, it may even be appropriate to require an outgoing partner to relinquish any offices held, with a view to one of the continuing partners seeking to be appointed in his place; however, this is not common.[45] Whether it is more practical merely to require the outgoing partner to employ the services of the firm when carrying out his official duties[46] will ultimately depend on the nature of the office and the propriety of the holder fettering his discretion in this way,[47] but the current editor ventures to suggest that this will rarely provide a satisfactory solution.

Consideration should also be given to the treatment of the office in the event of a general dissolution: it would be possible to legislate in advance for the payment of an agreed sum in consideration of its retention by the then incumbent, thus reflecting the approach likely to be adopted by a court, which was summarised by Lord Lindley as follows:

"If the profits of the office are partnership assets, and the firm is dissolved whilst the office is held by one of its members, the Court, in winding up the partnership, will leave him in the enjoyment of the office, but charge him with its value in his account with the firm."[48]

Trade secrets, etc.

If a partnership is formed with a view to exploiting a new and **10–44** unpatented invention, the agreement should identify whether the invention will belong to the firm or to the partner who discovered it and, if the former, how it is to be treated in the event of a dissolution. Lord Lindley explained the position following a dissolution in these terms:

"... if there be no agreement on the subject, all the parties will have a right to work it, in opposition to each other, there being no ground upon which any of them can be prevented from so doing. If, however, it can be proved by the inventor that his secret was to be kept from his co-partners, or that they, if they discovered it,

---

[45] This is confirmed by the expert evidence (in relation to liquidation appointments) adduced in *Casson Beckman & Partners v. Papi, supra,* at pp. 302b–d, 307b. In the case of an executorship, such a provision would in any event be unworkable and, in the case of a trusteeship, might place the trustee partner in breach of the obligations which he owes to his beneficiaries.

[46] This appears to be a fairly common practice in the accountancy profession, so far as concerns liquidation appointments: see *ibid.* pp.302b–d.

[47] The current editor submits that this would be wholly inappropriate in the case of an executorship or trusteeship, where the primary duty is owed to the relevant estate or trust.

[48] See *Smith v. Mules* (1852) 9 Hare 556. *Cf. Ambler v. Bolton* (1871) L.R. 14 Eq. 427.

were not to make use of their discovery, they will not be allowed to violate the agreement into which they have entered, or the trust reposed in them; and the circumstance that the invention has not been patented will not be material."[49]

To this should be added the qualification that, if the invention is a partnership asset, it may effectively form part of the goodwill of the business, which will fall to be sold on dissolution, thereby precluding the partners from its further exploitation.[50]

I. Income and Liabilities Derived from Previous Business[51]

10–45 Where a new partner is admitted to an existing firm, the agreement should properly establish, on the one hand, his entitlement (if any) to share in profits derived from (i) bills delivered prior to the date of his admission and (ii) work in progress as at that date and, on the other, his obligation to contribute towards debts or liabilities incurred prior to but outstanding at that date.[52] If the finances of the old and new firms are to be kept separate, that fact should be clearly stated.

A clause of the type under consideration will not, of itself, confer any additional rights on or against third parties.[53]

Warranty regarding existing debts

10–46   Where an incoming partner agrees to undertake liability for existing debts, he should prudently require the other partners to warrant that they have made full disclosure of the nature and amount of those debts.

---

[49] See *Morison v. Moat* (1851) 9 Hare 241; and, generally, *Terrapin v. Builders Supply Co.* [1960] R.P.C. 128; *Seager v. Copydex* [1967] 1 W.L.R. 923; *Coco v. A. N. Clark, Engineers* [1968] F.S.R. 415; *Schering Chemicals Ltd. v. Falkman Ltd.* [1982] Q.B. 1; *Fraser v. Thames Television Ltd.* [1984] Q.B. 44. The employment cases are of less relevance in the present context, but see, nevertheless, *Faccenda Chicken Ltd. v. Fowler* [1987] Ch. 117 and the cases there cited. As to the possible remedies where confidential information is shared with an *intending* partner, see *LAC Minerals Ltd. v. International Corona Resources Ltd.* [1990] F.S.R. 441 (Sup.Ct. of Canada).

[50] See *Re Keene* [1922] 2 Ch. 475; also *Trego v. Hunt* [1896] A.C. 7; *Murray v. King* [1986] F.S.R. 116 (concerning a copyright). As to the partners' rights to enforce a sale of the goodwill, see *infra*, paras. 10–160 *et seq.*

[51] See the *Encyclopedia of Professional Partnerships*, Precedent 1, cl. 8.

[52] See generally, as to the significance of such a provision *infra*, paras. 13–28 *et seq.*, 14–48 *et seq. Semble*, there is no presumption that, merely because the assets of the existing firm become assets of the new firm, the former's liabilities are assumed by the latter: see *Creasey v. Breachwood Motors Ltd.* [1992] BCC 638 (where a number of Scots authorities are reviewed). Note, however, that there *is* such a presumption when a partner retires from a firm: see *infra*, para. 10–207. This aspect does not appear to have been explored in the above decision. It should also be noted in this context that it was held in *Robertson v. Brent* [1972] N.Z.L.R. 406 that work in progress does not exist as an asset of a continuing firm, at least in the case of a solicitors' practice, although the current editor doubts the correctness of the decision.

[53] See, in particular, the Partnership Act 1890, s.17(1), *infra*, para. 13–25. In practice, an express assignment of book debts under the Law of Property Act 1925, s.136 is rare: see *infra*, para. 10–204.

In *Walker v. Broadhurst*[54] the incoming partner secured an effective *guarantee* from the father of one of the other partners that the debts did not exceed a stated sum, but this is most unusual.

J. CAPITAL[55]

It is obviously important that the agreement records the amount of **10–47** capital which each partner is required to contribute and the manner in which such capital, once contributed, is to be owned.[56] If the agreement is unclear, the partners might conceivably find that their shares in capital are treated as equal, notwithstanding the fact that their contributions were unequal.[57]

Capital should be stated as a sum of money

Lord Lindley observed: **10–48**

"The capital should be expressed to be so much money; and if one of the partners is to contribute lands or goods instead of money, such lands or goods should have a value set upon them, and their value in money should be considered as his contribution."[58]

This elementary step will ensure that the firm's capital structure is always readily identifiable.[59]

Capital expressed in terms of assets

Nevertheless, agreements will be encountered in which capital is **10–49** treated as synonymous with the partnership assets,[60] so that the value of the firm's capital base, and thus of each partner's contribution, will constantly fluctuate. It follows that, unless the assets are revalued

---

[54] (1853) 8 Ex. 889. Lord Lindley unaccountably referred to this case when dealing with capital.

[55] See the *Encyclopedia of Professional Partnerships*, Precedent 1, cl. 7.

[56] Lord Lindley commented at this point "It by no means follows that the partners are to be entitled to the assets in the proportions in which they contribute to the capital. Indeed, if no express declaration upon the subject is made, the *prima facie* inference is that all the partners are entitled to share the assets (minus the capital) equally, although they may have contributed to the capital unequally." This, in a sense, begs the real question as to how the *capital itself* is to be owned. The surplus assets will normally be shared in the same manner as profits: see *infra*, paras. 10–66, 17–05, 19–18 *et seq*.

[57] See the Partnership Act 1890, ss.24(1), *infra*, paras. 17–08 *et seq*.

[58] Lord Lindley went on, somewhat delphically, "If this be not done, the articles and accounts and the proportions in which profits and losses are to be shared will be less perspicuous and free from doubt than will otherwise be the case." It is unclear whether the profits and losses to which he refers are of an income or capital nature. If the former, the respective size of each partner's capital contribution would normally be irrelevant. See also *infra*, para. 17–01.

[59] See further, *infra*, paras. 17–02 *et seq*.

[60] See for example, *Sykes v. Land* (1984) 271 E.G. 1264. See also *infra*, para. 17–04.

annually,[61] the firm's accounts will never show the true capital position as between the partners.[62] Lord Lindley also pointed out that, where this practice is adopted,

"... the partner who contributes land will generally be inclined to look upon such land as his, and not as part of the common stock."

It is, however, doubted whether many partners would be swayed towards such a view.

Capital contribution in form of debts

10–50   A capital contribution may take the form of good debts owed to a partner, either to a stated value or generally. An example of the former is to be found in *Toulmin v. Copland*,[63] where a partner had agreed to contribute £40,000 of good debts owing by customers of his former firm. Those customers thereafter dealt with the new firm and, in due course, an aggregate sum in excess of £40,000 was received from them. The partner was held to have satisfied his obligation to bring in capital, even though the customers had incurred further debts due to the new firm, since a single continuous account had been maintained in respect of each customer and those payments which were not specifically appropriated to an item in the relevant account were applied to the earliest item therein, *i.e.* the debts originally brought in.

10–51   If, on the other hand, a partner merely agrees to contribute capital in the form of book debts, but not to a stated value, the size of his contribution will, in the absence of some other agreement, depend on the amount which they actually realise. This is illustrated by *Cooke v. Benbow*,[64] where a father had taken his sons into partnership and agreed to contribute all the capital, plant, and stock-in-trade then and usually employed by him in the business. For the purposes of an account drawn up at the commencement of the partnership, the father's book debts were discounted by 20 per cent. but, in the event, almost the full value was realised. The surplus was held to form part of the father's capital and was, therefore, not distributable as profit.

---

[61] Quite apart from the expense, this would have adverse capital gains tax consequences: see *infra*, para. 35–17.
[62] Thus, calculation of interest on capital will be impossible: see *infra*, para. 10–55.
[63] (1834) 2 Cl. & F. 681 and (1838) 7 Cl. & F. 349.
[64] (1865) 3 De G.J. & S. 1. See also *Binney v. Mutrie* (1886) 12 App.Cas. 160.

Capital contribution as a condition precedent

In some cases, a partner's right to participate in profits and his **10–52**
other entitlements under the agreement may be made conditional on
the introduction of his capital contribution, *i.e.* that contribution will
be treated as a condition precedent.[65] However, in practice this is
rare. Thus, in *Kemble v. Mills*,[66] A and B had agreed to become
partners, on terms that A would bring in £2,000 and do certain
things, and B would bring in £5,000. It was held that A could bring
an action in respect of B's failure to bring in the £5,000, even though
he did not prove that he had brought in the £2,000 or that those
things had been done.

Additional capital

A partner cannot normally be required to contribute additional **10–53**
capital, even if upon this depends the continued existence of the
firm.[67] Accordingly, it may in some cases be necessary to provide a
mechanism whereby a binding decision to increase the partnership
capital can be taken, thus forcing each partner to bring in additional
sums. As might be expected, clauses providing for such a decision to
be taken on a majority vote are comparatively rare.

Variable and graduated contributions

It is not uncommon to encounter agreements under which the size **10–54**
of each partner's capital contribution is directly related to the size of
his profit share so that, as the latter varies, so does his contribution.
Such an arrangement will frequently form part of a complex "points"

---

[65] In this connection, Lord Lindley referred to the rules laid down in the "well-known" note to
Pordage v. Cole (1669) 1 Wms.Saund. 320a. Those rules are by no means easy to understand, but
are set out in full for the convenience of the reader: "1. If a day be appointed for payment of
money, or part of it, or for doing any other act, and the day *is* to happen, or *may* happen, *before*
the thing which is the consideration of the money, or other act, is to be performed, an action may
be brought for the money, or for not doing such other act *before* performance; for it appears that
the party relied upon his *remedy*, and did not intend to make the *performance* a condition
precedent; and so it is where *no time* is fixed for performance of that which is the consideration of
the money or other act. 2. When a day is appointed for the payment of money, etc., and the day is
to happen *after* the thing which is the consideration of the money, etc., is to be performed, no
action can be maintained for the money, etc., before performance. 3. Where a covenant goes only
to *part* of the consideration on both sides, and a breach of such covenant may be paid for in
damages it is an independent covenant, and an action may be maintained for a breach of the
covenant on the part of the defendant, without averring performance in the declaration. 4. But
where the mutual covenants go to the *whole consideration* on both sides, they are mutual
conditions, and the performance must be averred. 5. Where two acts are to be done at the same
time, as where A covenants to convey an estate to B on such a day, and in consideration thereof B
covenants to pay a sum of money on the *same day*, neither can maintain an action without showing
performance of, or an offer to perform, his part, though it is not certain which of them is obliged to
do the first act; and this particularly applies to all cases of sale."
[66] (1841) 9 Dow. 446. *Cf. Marsden v. Moore* (1859) 4 H. & N. 500. See also *Stavers v. Curling*
(1836) 3 Bing.N.C. 355.
[67] See *infra*, para. 17–10.

or "lock-step" system for profit sharing,[68] designed to enable incoming partners to fund their contributions out of profits over a set period. Under such a scheme, a partner whose profit share is reduced will naturally receive a partial return of his capital, even though the firm's capital base will remain unchanged.

Interest on capital

10–55   If interest on capital is to be paid, this must be provided for in the agreement.[69] In general, such interest amounts to no more than an allocation of profits and, for that reason, should in the current editor's view properly be included in the clause dealing with profit sharing.[70] Interest paid *irrespective* of the profitability of the firm is unusual.

The importance of ensuring that each partner's capital contribution is stated in cash terms has already been noted.[71] It goes without saying that interest cannot be computed by reference to an indeterminate sum of capital.[72]

Interest on capital should normally be made payable *after* interest on advances.[73]

K.   BANKERS OF THE PARTNERSHIP[74]

10–56 It is usual for the agreement to name the bank (and, where relevant, the particular branch) at which the firm will maintain its account(s), even though that decision could quite properly be taken at a subsequent date.[75] In the case of a large partnership with branch offices nationwide, a number of different banks or branches may be involved; these may conveniently be incorporated in a schedule. Some professions require members to maintain separate client accounts, and this fact will usually be reflected in the agreement.[76]

A clause requiring all partnership moneys not required for current expenses to be paid into the appropriate bank account is traditionally included.[77]

---

[68] See *infra*, para. 10–67.
[69] See the Partnership Act 1890, s.24(4), *infra*, para. 17–13.
[70] See the *Encyclopedia of Professional Partnerships*, Precedent 1, cl. 11(3).
[71] See *supra*, para. 10–48.
[72] Thus, undrawn profits left in the firm and used as a form of circulating capital should not be credited to the partners' capital accounts (a practice which has become increasingly common) unless it is intended thereby to increase the capital base of the firm: see further, *infra*, paras. 17–06, 17–07.
[73] *i.e.* effectively reflecting the precedence accorded to interest on advances by the Partnership Act 1890, s.24(3).
[74] See the *Encyclopedia of Professional Partnerships*, Precedent 1, cl. 6.
[75] *e.g.* pursuant to an express power in the agreement or by a majority decision under the Partnership Act 1890, s.24(8), *infra*, paras. 15–05 *et seq*.
[76] *e.g.* accountants, architects, solicitors, and surveyors. See, further, the *Encyclopedia of Professional Partnerships*.
[77] Where client accounts are maintained, a similar clause relating to clients' money is also generally included.

Cheque signing

It is important to establish each partner's *express* authority to draw **10-57** cheques on the partnership account[78]: thus, the agreement should state whether cheques drawn in the firm name require the signatures of one, two or more partners or, where appropriate, the signatures of one partner and a designated employee.[79] The bank mandate should naturally reflect the terms so agreed. If the mandate permits any one partner to sign cheques and there is no restriction in the agreement, each partner will have authority to issue cheques *vis-à-vis* both the bank and his co-partners.[80]

If the agreement declares that the signature of one partner is sufficient, this will amount to a binding agreement between the partners to arrange and thereafter maintain a continuing mandate in those terms.

Other forms of transfer

Whilst most agreements scrupulously provide for the signing of **10-58** cheques by partners, it is rare to find any clause restricting their authority to initiate transfers between accounts and other similar transactions. This does, however, merit consideration in some cases.[81]

L.   BOOKS AND ACCOUNTS[82]

It is usual to include in the agreement provisions governing both the **10-59** maintenance of the partnership books and the preparation of accounts, either annually or on a more frequent basis.[83] Lord Lindley explained the purpose lying behind such clauses in this way:

"The object of taking partnership accounts is twofold, viz. (1) To show how the firm stands as regards strangers; and (2) To show how each partner stands towards the firm.[84] The accounts,

---

[78] See *infra*, para. 12–51.

[79] Where the firm maintains both an office and clients' account, different cheque signing arrangements may be made for each. Moreover, account may have to be taken of the relevant professional rules: see, for example, the Solicitors' Accounts Rules 1991, r. 8(1). For an illustration of the dangers which can be presented by allowing a single partner to sign cheques on a client account, see *Lipkin Gorman v. Karpnale Ltd.* [1991] 2 A.C. 548.

[80] Since this is, as regards the bank, a case of *express* authority, the firm will be bound even if the cheque is issued otherwise than in the ordinary course of business. However, the position will prima facie be different as between the partners.

[81] See the *Encyclopedia of Professional Partnerships*, Precedent 8, cl. 6(6). Also *infra*, para. 12–51.

[82] See *ibid*. Precedent 1, cll. 9, 10.

[83] The advent of computerisation has greatly facilitated the preparation of so-called "interim" and "management" accounts, although these are rarely prepared more often than on a quarterly basis.

[84] To this list should now, perhaps, be added a third object, namely for the purposes of production to the Inland Revenue: see *infra*, para. 10–61, n. 90.

therefore, which the articles should require to be taken, should be such as will accomplish this twofold object. The articles should consequently provide, not only for the keeping of proper books of account, and for the due entry therein of all receipts and payments, but also for the making up yearly of a general account, showing the then assets and liabilities of the firm, and what is due to each partner in respect of his capital[85] and share of profits, or what is due from him to the firm, as the case may be."

It should be noted that, in the case of certain corporate partnerships, there is now a *statutory* obligation to prepare annual accounts just as if the firm were a company formed and registered under the Companies Act 1985.[86]

Maintenance and custody of books

10–60 As well as requiring the partners to maintain the partnership books, the agreement should also provide where those books are to be kept and record any limitations on the partners' rights of access thereto. The position will otherwise be governed by the Partnership Act 1890.[87] Any unauthorised attempt by a partner to remove the books from the place where they are required to be kept will be restrained by the court.[88] It follows that if a partner is to be permitted to have temporary custody of the books, this must be clearly stated.[89]

Preparation of annual (or other) accounts

10–61 The normal form of clause governing the preparation of partnership accounts will specify (a) the date (or dates) up to which such accounts are to be prepared;[90] (b) by whom;[91] and (c) on what accounting basis, *e.g.* whether goodwill and work in progress are to be valued, whether losses of capital are to be recouped, etc. It may also be desirable to record any unusual expenses which are to be

---

[85] See *supra*, paras. 10–47 *et seq.* and *infra*, paras. 17–02 *et seq.*
[86] See the Partnerships and Unlimited Companies (Accounts) Regulations 1993 (S.I. 1993 No. 1820), regs. 3(1), 4(1)(a). See further, *infra*, para. 22–11.
[87] *Ibid.* s.24(9), *infra*, para. 22–09.
[88] See *Taylor v. Davis* (1842) 3 Beav. 388, note; *Greatrex v. Greatrex* (1847) 1 De G. & Sm. 692.
[89] See *infra*, para. 22–14.
[90] The agreement usually establishes the date up to which the firm will prepare its annual accounts for submission to the Inland Revenue and the manner in which a decision to alter that date can be taken. The date(s) up to which interim accounts are to be prepared are of less significance.
[91] Annual accounts will generally be prepared by the partnership accountants and, where necessary, audited by them. On the other hand, interim accounts will in all probability be prepared internally.

borne by the firm, whether or not these will be deductible against profits.[92]

The partners will usually be required to sign the annual accounts, once they have been approved.[93]

Reopening agreed accounts

It is obviously desirable that, once the annual accounts have been **10–62** approved and signed by the partners, they should be regarded as conclusive: this is normally provided for in the agreement, subject to the proviso that each partner is entitled to have obvious or "manifest" errors corrected within a set period. However, such provisions do not provide absolute finality, as Lord Lindley explained:

> "A provision to this effect is extremely useful, and should never be omitted[94]; but, however stringently it may be drawn, no account will be binding on any partner who may have been induced to sign it by false and fraudulent representations, or in ignorance of material circumstances dishonourably concealed from him by his co–partners.[95] Where, however, all parties act *bona fide*, such clauses are operative; but the usual provision as to manifest errors applies only to errors in figures and obvious blunders, not to errors in judgment, *e.g.* in treating as good debts which ultimately turn out to be bad, or in omitting losses not known to have occurred.[96] All errors are manifest when discovered; but such clauses as those referred to here are intended to be confined to oversights and blunders so obvious as to admit of no difference of opinion."

The circumstances in which a settled account can be re-opened in the absence of such a provision are considered in greater detail hereafter.[97]

Agreed accounts not binding for all purposes

Although an account, once signed and approved, may be binding **10–63** on the partners, it does not follow that it will be binding for all

---

[92] Lord Lindley gave the following examples of unusual allowances: "an allowance for treating customers, for management, for rent, maintenance of servants, etc." It would seem that he must have been contemplating the payment of such allowances to partners, rather than to third parties. With the exception of rent, such allowances are unlikely to be deductible by the firm: see *MacKinlay v. Arthur Young McClelland Moores & Co.* [1990] 2 A.C. 239 and *infra*, para. 34–30. In such a case, they are better expressed as a preferential profit share: see *infra*, para. 10–68.

[93] This will usually be required as a pre-requisite to submitting the accounts to the Inland Revenue.

[94] See *London Financial Ass. v. Kelk* (1834) 26 Ch.D. 107, 151, *per* Bacon V.–C.

[95] See *Oldaker v. Lavender* (1833) 6 Sim. 239; *Blisset v. Daniel* (1853) 10 Hare. 493.

[96] See *Ex p. Barber* (1870) L.R. 5 Ch.App. 687; also *Laing v. Campbell* (1865) 36 Beav. 3 (where there was no agreement).

[97] See *infra*, paras. 23–107 *et seq.*

purposes. Thus, unless the agreement provides otherwise,[98] annual accounts prepared for the purposes of calculating the firm's divisible profits may be of no relevance when calculating the financial entitlement of an outgoing partner.[99] In particular, the fact that goodwill has been treated as valueless in such accounts[1] or that other assets have consistently appeared therein at their original or depreciated book value[2] will not, of itself, necessarily justify the adoption of those accounting practices on the death, retirement or expulsion of a partner; *a fortiori* in the case of a general dissolution.[3]

Equally, the fact that an asset is included in the firm's accounts is not conclusive of its status as a partnership asset.[4]

Failure to sign accounts

10–64 Bona fide accounts drawn up on the usual basis may be binding on a partner even if he has not signed them, provided that he has seen a copy and has not suggested that they are erroneous.[5]

M.   PROFITS AND LOSSES[6]

10–65 The agreement should always record the manner in which profits and losses are to be shared[7]: if it fails to do so, and no other agreement or understanding can be proved, the Partnership Act 1890 will ensure that all profits and losses are shared equally.[8] Even where the partners are content with the position under the Act, it is usual to declare that the sharing ratios are equal.

Capital and income profits and losses

10–66   Profits and losses may be of a capital or income nature.[9] Most firms do not seek to apply different sharing ratios to each class,

---

[98] See *Coventry v. Barclay* (1864) 3 De G.J. & S. 320; *Ex p. Barber* (1870) L.R. 5 Ch.App. 687; also *infra*, para. 10–133.

[99] *Blisset v. Daniel* (1853) 10 Hare 493. *Cf. Coventry v. Barclay, supra.*

[1] *Wade v. Jenkins* (1860) 2 Giff. 509. *Cf. Steuart v. Gladstone* (1878) 10 Ch.D. 626; *Hunter v. Dowling* [1895] 2 Ch. 223, *infra*, para. 10–137.

[2] *Cruickshank v. Sutherland* (1922) 92 L.J.Ch. 136; *Noble v. Noble*, 1965 S.L.T. 415 (Ct. of Sess.); *Clark v. Watson*, 1982 S.L.T. 450 (O.H.); *cf. Thom's Executrix v. Russel & Aitken*, 1983 S.L.T. 335 (O.H.). See further *infra*, para. 10–138.

[3] Any adjustments which have to be made in the event of a dissolution will inevitably distort the position as it appears in the accounts: see *infra*, paras. 25–39 *et seq.*

[4] *Barton v. Morris* [1985] 1 W.L.R. 1257. See further, *infra*, paras. 18–56 *et seq.*

[5] *Coventry v. Barclay* (1864) 3 De G.J. & S. 320, 328, *per* Lord Westbury. See also *Ex p. Barber* (1870) L.R. 5 Ch.App. 687; *Hunter v. Dowling* [1893] 1 Ch. 391 (affirmed [1893] 3 Ch. 212). See also *infra*, para. 10–133.

[6] See the *Encyclopedia of Professional Partnerships*, Precedent 1, cl. 11.

[7] Unaccountably, Lord Lindley did not include this among the "usual" clauses to be found in a partnership agreement.

[8] *Ibid.* s.24(1). See further, *infra*, paras. 19–18 *et seq.*, 20–03 *et seq.*

[9] Capital profits or losses represent the amount by which the value (or net sale proceeds) of the partnership assets exceed or fall short of their book value: see *infra*, para. 17–05. This is not necessarily the same thing as a loss of part of the firm's *fixed* capital, which may have to be made good before any profits are divided: see *infra*, para. 21–03.

although it is prudent to establish the general application of the agreed shares by referring *specifically* to capital profits and losses. However, in some cases the partners may wish to ensure that the greater part, if not the whole, of any capital profit or loss will accrue to a particular partner or group of partners.[10] In such a case, the chosen capital profit sharing ratio will be applied when dividing the surplus assets on a dissolution.[11]

Profit sharing arrangements

Whilst a partner might, typically, expect to be allocated an initial **10–67** share of profits which will remain unchanged as long as the partnership continues,[12] more complex arrangements are now increasingly being adopted, particularly in the professional sphere. A combination of two or more of the following sharing arrangements are, in practice, commonly encountered:

(*a*) preferential "salaries" expressed as a first charge on profits;[13]

(*b*) sharing ratios varying according to the level of the firm's profits, *i.e.* where differing ratios are applied to each tranche of profits;[14]

(*c*) sharing ratios varying according to each partner's age and/or seniority within the firm;[15]

(*d*) sharing ratios directly related to capital contributions;[16]

(*e*) incentive profit pools, consisting of a set proportion of the firm's profits distributable at the discretion of a particular partner or committee of partners;[17]

(*f*) "target" based sharing ratios, which are subject to reduction if the target is not met; and

(*g*) *ad hoc* sharing ratios agreed shortly after the year end.[18]

---

[10] See *infra*, paras. 35–05, n. 11, 36–24 *et seq.*

[11] Partnership Act 1890, s.44(b) *infra*, paras. 25–40 *et seq.*

[12] Barring, of course any change in the composition of the firm, which will, in any event, technically result in the creation of a new partnership: see *supra*, paras. 3–01 *et seq.*

[13] Such a salary may be paid for a number of reasons, *e.g.* where the firm occupies premises owned by a partner, it may represent a payment in lieu of rent. *Cf.* the position of a salaried partner *infra*, para. 10–70. See further, as to the true status of a partner's salary as a share of profits, *MacKinlay v. Arthur Young McClelland Moores & Co.* [1990] 2 A.C. 239, 249A–C.

[14] In such cases, there may well be a residual sharing ratio applied to all profits over a certain figure. This may indicate the manner in which losses are to be shared: but see *infra*, para. 10–69.

[15] Such a scheme will normally be implemented by means of a "points" or "ladder" system (otherwise known as "lockstep"), with each partner progressively acquiring a larger share until a "plateau" share is reached, usually in the age range 40–50. Thereafter, a partner can expect his share gradually to decrease as he nears retirement.

[16] The ownership of capital may itself be tied to a "points" or "lock-step" system, so that alterations in the partners' profits shares will follow automatically.

[17] This device is currently in vogue in mid- to large-sized firms and is often administered by partners dubbed "the three wise men." Equally, complex balloting systems are by no means unknown. Although *potentially* divisive, such schemes seem to cause few problems in practice.

[18] It must be appreciated that, if no agreement is reached, the profits will prima facie be shared equally: Partnership Act 1890, s.24(1). This may constitute an incentive to some partners so to conduct themselves that agreement is impossible. *Quaere*, would this involve a breach of the duty of good faith? Even if it would, surely the court could not dispense with those partners' agreement.

The payment of interest on capital[19] and special allowances to partners[20] may also form part of the overall profit sharing structure, along with the allocation of a particular source of income received by the firm.[21]

10–68   Some agreements provide for a notional deduction to be made from the profit share of a partner who is incapacitated for more than a certain period, that deduction being shared between the other partners as a recompense for the additional workload which they are forced to shoulder. More common, at least in the professions, is a provision entitling the other partners to employ a locum, initially at the firm's expense but, if the partner's incapacity is prolonged, subsequently at his expense.[22]

Losses

10–69   The agreement may provide that losses (whether of an income or capital nature) are to be shared in a different way to profits. On the other hand, if the agreement merely establishes the proportions in which profits are to be shared but does not mention losses, it will be inferred, in the absence of any evidence indicating a contrary intention, that losses are to be borne in the same proportions.[23] This can lead to unforeseen difficulties where the profit shares are not fixed but vary according to the level of profits or where some partners enjoy a preferential or discretionary profit entitlement; if the court is not prepared to infer that losses should be borne in the same way, it may have no alternative but to hold the partners liable in equal shares.[24] Accordingly, it is, in such cases, essential that the agreement deals specifically with the treatment of losses.

"Salaried" partners

10–70   The remuneration of a salaried partner[25] will normally be expressed as a fixed share of profits or merely as a "salary." The agreement should, in either case, clearly establish whether such remuneration is payable irrespective of the firm's profitability and whether the salaried partner will be liable for losses and, if so, to what extent. It

---

[19] See *supra*, para. 10–55.

[20] See *infra*, paras. 20–41, 34–30.

[21] In medical partnerships, it is often provided that certain payments received under the National Health Service, *e.g.* a seniority payment or a notional or cost rent, will be allocated to a particular partner; alternatively, it may be agreed that a particular source of income will not be accounted for by the recipient partners: see the *Encyclopedia of Professional Partnerships*, Precedent 8, cll. 12, 13.

[22] See *ibid.* Precedent 8, cl. 19.

[23] See *Re Albion Life Assurance Society* (1880) 16 Ch.D. 83.

[24] Partnership Act 1890, s.24(1), *infra*, paras. 20–03 *et seq.*

[25] See as to the status of such partners *Stekel v. Ellice* [1973] 1 W.L.R. 191 and *supra*, para. 5–65.

is usual to deal with the latter point by means of an express indemnity.[26]

Provided that the salaried partner's remuneration is stated to be payable out of profits, the court will usually be prepared to infer that it will abate if those profits are insufficient. Thus, in *Marsh v. Stacey*,[27] a partnership deed provided for the payment to a junior partner of a "fixed salary of £1,200 as a first charge on the profits and in addition thereto one-third share of the net profits arising from the Reigate branch" of the firm. For two consecutive years the firm's profits were less than £1,200. The court held that, on a true construction of the deed, the junior partner's salary was only payable out of profits, but would have priority over any payments due to the other partners. Equally, in an appropriate case, the agreement may be construed as providing for a guaranteed salary as well as an indemnity against losses,[28] in which case the supposed "partner" will, it is conceived, be no more than an employee of the firm.[29]

Medical partnerships within the National Health Service

The National Health Service Act 1977 contains stringent prohibi- **10–71** tions on the actual or deemed sale of what may conveniently be styled National Health Service goodwill.[30] Whilst partners are free, within certain limits,[31] to divide their profits in any way they may choose, the Medical Practices Committee, which is effectively charged with the task of policing the statutory prohibitions,[32] have announced that they may treat as evidence of a deemed sale of goodwill the fact that an incoming partner does not reach parity within three years of his admission.[33]

Drawings in anticipation of profits

Since the precise quantum of a partner's share of profits will not be **10–72** known until the partnership accounts have been prepared and approved,[34] the agreement should generally provide for each partner to draw on account of his *anticipated* profit share, whether monthly

---

[26] But see *infra*, para. 20–06.

[27] (1963) 107 S.J. 512. Note that in the Bar Library transcript ([1963] No. 169 at p. 4), the partner in question is not referred to as the "junior" partner.

[28] See *Geddes v. Wallace* (1820) 2 Bli. 270.

[29] He will, nevertheless, be held out as a partner: Partnership Act 1890, s.14.

[30] See the National Health Service Act 1977, s.54, Sched. 10; also *Kerr v. Morris* [1987] Ch. 90.

[31] See the National Health Service (General Medical Services) Regulations 1992 (S.I. 1992 No. 635), reg. 24(4)(b).

[32] See the certification procedure under the National Health Service Act 1977, Sched. 10, para. 1(2). As to the form of the certificate, see the National Health Service (General Medical Services) Regulations 1992, reg. 18, Sched. 7.

[33] See the Guidance Note on the Prohibition on the Sale of Goodwill of NHS Medical Practice in England and Wales, re-issued in May 1992.

[34] See *supra*, paras. 10–59 *et seq*.

or otherwise.[35] The precise amount of such drawings may be stated in the agreement, but will almost inevitably require adjustment if the partnership is to endure for anything other than a short period. Where appropriate, drawings may be directly related to the size of a partner's preferential "salary."[36]

Although it is always desirable to pitch drawings at a level which will ensure that no partner receives more than his ultimate profit entitlement, an unforeseen downturn in profits can undermine even the most conservative of estimates. The agreement should accordingly require any overdrawings to be repaid to the firm within a set period, usually without interest. Although the current editor is aware of cases in which firms have in mid-year been forced to limit, or even to suspend, partners' drawings in order to avoid an imminent financial crisis, it is rare to find such an eventuality specifically addressed in the agreement.

Division of profits and tax provision

10–73   The agreement will normally provide for the ultimate division of profits after the approval of the annual accounts, although this is arguably unnecessary.[37] Moreover, it is increasingly common to find that an income tax retention is made out of each partner's profit share and taken to a reserve or tax account, thus ensuring that funds are available when an assessment is made on the firm or on the individual partners (as the case may be).[38] The current editor apprehends that this trend will continue notwithstanding the fundamental changes in partnership taxation introduced by the Finance Act 1994.

N.   POWERS AND DUTIES OF PARTNERS[39]

Just and faithful clause

10–74   Lord Lindley observed:

> "It is the practice to insert in partnership articles an express covenant by each partner to be true and just in all his dealings with the others. This, however, is always implied[40]; and the clause in question therefore adds little from a legal point of view, although it may serve to remind the partners of their mutual obligations to good faith."

---

[35] This will not always be appropriate, *e.g.* where profits will only be realised at the conclusion of a particular venture.

[36] See *supra*, para. 10–67.

[37] See also *infra*, paras. 21–07, 21–08.

[38] See *infra*, paras. 34–17 *et seq.*

[39] See the *Encyclopedia of Professional Partnerships*, Precedent 1, cll. 12 *et seq.*

[40] See *infra*, paras. 16–01 *et seq.*

Although no longer framed as covenants, such clauses are still found in most agreements.[41]

Attention to partnership affairs

A clause specifying how much time each partner is required to **10–75** devote to the partnership business is vital, even though Lord Lindley put it in less emphatic terms:

"The time and attention which the partners are to give to the affairs of the firm should be expressly mentioned; especially if one of them is to be at liberty to give less of his time and attention than the others."

The mere fact that some partners are devoting all their time and efforts to the success of the partnership business is no guarantee that other partners will do likewise. If an *express* obligation has not been imposed, it may be difficult, if not impossible, to show that a partner's lack of commitment or outside interests involve a breach of some other clause of the agreement.[42] A dissolution under the Partnership Act 1890,[43] even if obtainable, will scarcely represent an attractive remedy.

An obligation on a partner to devote his whole time to the business **10–76** should be accompanied by a prohibition on engaging in other forms of business.[44] Equally, if one partner holds a particular office or appointment to which he is required to devote time during normal working hours, this should be specifically mentioned and, if appropriate, he should be required to account to the firm for any fees or other remuneration derived therefrom.[45]

Lindley also drew attention to the fact that: **10–77**

"Inattention to business by reason of illness is ... no breach of an agreement to attend to it."[46]

The current editor considers that the same principle should, in general, be applied whenever a partner is prevented from fulfilling his

---

[41] A covenant in such terms will not cause any sum due from one partner to another on taking the partnership accounts to be treated as a specialty debt: see *Powdrell v. Jones* (1854) 2 Sm. & G. 305. *Semble*, breach of such a clause gives rise to a claim in damages: see *infra*, para. 16–05.

[42] *Quaere*, can the other partners complain of a breach of that partner's express or implied duty of good faith in such circumstances? As to the possible remedies where wilful inattention to the business can be proved, see *infra*, para. 20–42.

[43] See *infra*, paras. 24–39 *et seq.*

[44] See *infra*, para. 10–78.

[45] See the *Encyclopedia of Professional Partnerships*, Precedent 11, cl. 12(1).

[46] Lord Lindley referred to *Boast v. Firth* (1868) L.R. 4 C.P. 1; *Robinson v. Davison* (1871) L.R. 6 Ex. 269. Neither concerned a partnership.

obligations by any other circumstances beyond his control. However, it may be appropriate, depending on the duration of a partner's incapacity, to impose some form of financial penalty, whether by way of a reduction in his profit share or by forcing him to bear the cost of employing a locum.[47]

Agreement not to carry on other businesses, etc.

10–78   Each partner will normally agree not only that he will devote his whole time to the partnership business but also that he will not engage in any other business, whether or not competing with the firm's business.[48] Such an agreement can be enforced by injunction,[49] but it does not follow that a partner who acts in breach of it will *necessarily* be bound to account to the firm for any profits which he may realise in the course of his outside activities.[50] Thus, a duty to account will in general arise only where the business is of the same nature as firm's business and is carried on in competition with it[51] or where an express provision is included in the agreement.

A similar prohibition will often be imposed in the case of offices and appointments, although it may be necessary to exempt any position held by a partner when the partnership commenced.[52]

Holidays, leave, etc.

10–79   The agreement should state each partner's entitlement to holidays and, where relevant, maternity, sabbatical or other periods of leave.[53] It goes without saying that any obligation to devote time to the partnership business must be read subject thereto.

Restrictions on the authority of partners

10–80   Any restriction on the implied authority of a partner should be specifically mentioned in the agreement.[54] This will usually take the form of a clause prohibiting any partner from doing certain acts

---

[47] See *supra*, para. 10–68.

[48] As to the position in the absence of such a clause, see the Partnership Act 1890, s.30, *infra*, paras. 16–09 *et seq*.

[49] See the first part of the injunction in *England v. Curling* (1878) 8 Beav. 129; also *Whitwood Chemical Co. v. Hardman* [1891] 2 Ch. 416; *Grimston v. Cuningham* [1894] 1 Q.B. 125. *Cf. Davis v. Foreman* [1894] 3 Ch. 654; *Kirchner & Co. v. Gruban* [1909] 1 Ch. 413 (where seemingly negative obligations were held to be of a positive nature); also *Metropolitan Electric Supply Co. Ltd. v. Ginder* [1901] 2 Ch. 799 (the reverse case). See also *infra*, para. 16–31.

[50] *Aas v. Benham* [1891] 2 Ch. 244; also *Dean v. Macdowell* (1878) 8 Ch.D. 345; *Trimble v. Goldberg* [1906] A.C. 494, 500.

[51] See the Partnership Act 1890, s.30 and *infra*, para. 16–31.

[52] See *supra*, para. 10–43.

[53] Regrettably, experience shows that disagreements over the timing of holidays can be extremely divisive. Accordingly, it is in some cases necessary to provide for a particular "pecking" order as between the partners: see, generally, the *Encyclopedia of Professional Partnerships*, Precedent 1, cl. 12, Precedent 2, Art. 7.05.

[54] As to the effect of such a restriction, see the Partnership Act 1890, s.8, *infra*, paras. 12–148 *et seq*.

without the prior consent of the other partners, *e.g.* engaging and dismissing employees,[55] giving guarantees, assigning or charging his share in the partnership, entering into any form of sub-partnership as regards that share[56] and drawing, accepting, or endorsing bills of exchange (other than cheques).[57] Certain of the restrictions may be qualified in such a way that they do not apply to acts done in the usual or ordinary course of business, etc.[58] A partner acting in breach of such a restriction is generally required to indemnify his co-partners against resulting losses.[59]

In giving or withholding their consent to a particular act, the general body of partners must act bona fide in the interests of the partnership but, in the view of the current editor, they will not normally be subject to an implied duty to act reasonably.[60]

Managing and senior partners, etc.

If one partner is to be given special or exclusive authority to carry **10–81** out certain functions in the firm, the limits of that authority should be clearly stated.[61] Contrary to popular belief amongst partners and others, a "senior" partner has no special rights or authority merely because he is the first named in the agreement.[62]

O. DECISION-MAKING[63]

Although it is no longer strictly necessary, where there are more than **10–82** two partners, to confer power on the majority to decide ordinary matters connected with the partnership business,[64] it is still highly desirable that the agreement establishes how decisions on both large and small issues affecting the firm are to be taken. Differing majorities or complete unanimity may be required, depending on the

---

[55] This can be contentious: see *infra*, para. 12–67.

[56] See *supra*, para. 5–75. As to a partner's implied authority to enter into a partnership with a third party in order to further the interests of the main partnership business, see *infra*, paras. 12–13, 12–80.

[57] The agreement should, as a separate matter, establish how and by whom cheques are to be drawn: see *supra*, para. 10–57. And see *infra*, paras. 12–41 *et seq.*, 12–51, 12–175.

[58] See the Partnership Act 1890, ss.5, 7 *infra*, paras. 12–02 *et seq.*, 12–148.

[59] See the *Encyclopedia of Professional Partnerships*, Precedent 1, cl. 15.

[60] See *Price v. Bouch* (1987) 53 P. & C.R . 257 (a decision concerning restrictive covenants); *Imperial Group Pension Trust Ltd. v. Imperial Tobacco Ltd.* [1991] 1 W.L.R. 589, 596F *et seq.*, *per* Browne-Wilkinson V.-C. (a pension fund case).

[61] See also *supra*, para. 10–27 and *infra*, para. 10–87.

[62] Indeed, the senior partner is no longer *per se* responsible for ensuring that the firm delivers an income tax return: see, as to the position prior to the tax year 1996/7 the Taxes Management Act 1970, s.9(2) (as substituted by the Finance Act 1990, s.90(1)) and, as to the position from 1996/97 onwards, *ibid.* s.12AA(2) (as added by the Finance Act 1994, s.184). *Cf.* the original s.9(1) and see *infra*, paras. 34–17, 34–18.

[63] See the *Encyclopedia of Professional Partnerships*, Precedent 1, cl. 17, Precedent 2, cl. 7.11.

[64] See the Partnership Act 1890, s.24(8), *infra*, paras. 15–05 *et seq.*; note also *Falkland v. Cheney* (1704) 5 Bro.P.C. 476.

precise nature of the decision.[65] Particular attention should be paid to those decisions which relate to the nature of the firm's business,[66] the amendment of the agreement,[67] the admission of new partners,[68] the expulsion of a partner,[69] the dissolution of the firm[70] and now, increasingly, a merger with another firm or firms.[71] It is no longer usual to provide how the option of dissolving the firm is to be exercised in the event of a partner suffering his share in the partnership property to be charged for his separate debts,[72] since this will usually be made a ground for expulsion. Some firms may be content for all decisions to be taken on a simple majority vote, particularly where the number of partners is small.

10–83   It is common to find that all decisions relating to the "management and control" of the business are required to be taken on a simple majority vote,[73] even though this expression is notoriously vague.[74] If this device is resorted to, it would be wise to ensure that the more contentious classes of decision are *specifically* referred to and, if necessary, excepted from the scope of the provision.

No majority possible

10–84   Lord Lindley observed:

> "It is difficult to lay down a general rule for the determination of what is to be done if the partners are equally divided. Articles of partnership, as usually drawn, are silent upon this question, but if it were declared that in such a case matters should be left in *statu quo*, probably some little assistance would be given to the preservation of peace and goodwill."

This view is perhaps optimistic in the face of today's commercial pressures, so that it is now sometimes provided that the senior

---

[65] See, for example, the approach adopted in the *Encyclopedia of Professional Partnerships*, Precedent 2.

[66] See the Partnership Act 1890, s.24(8), *infra*, paras. 15–05, 15–09. And see also *Nixon v. Wood* (1987) 284 E.G. 1055.

[67] See *supra*, para. 10–11.

[68] See *infra*, paras. 10–215 *et seq.*

[69] See *infra*, paras. 10–95 *et seq.*

[70] See *infra*, paras. 10–113 *et seq.*

[71] If (as will normally be the case), a unanimous vote in favour of merger is required, one partner will be able to frustrate its implementation, however necessary it may be for the survival of the firm. Equally, whilst a partner may be content that decisions to admit additional partners can be taken on a majority vote, should he really be forced into a wholly different partnership, with, perhaps, a different name and business ethic, against his will?

[72] See the Partnership Act 1890, s.33(2), *infra*, paras. 24–29 *et seq.*

[73] In the case of a large firm, management and control may be vested in a designated managing partner or management/executive committee rather than the general body of partners: see *infra*, para. 10–87.

[74] *Cf.ibid.* s.24(8), *infra*, paras. 15–05 *et seq.*

partner or chairman of the partners' meeting will have a second or casting vote.

In the case of a two man partnership, unanimity will always be required for any decision.[75]

Weighted voting

Where a majority vote is to be taken on a particular issue, it does **10–85** not follow that each partner must have a single vote of equal weight: voting weighted according to seniority or capital contribution/profit share is by no means uncommon, thus permitting a particular cadre of partners to maintain overall control.

Meetings

In medium to large sized firms, it is usual for the agreement to **10–86** contain detailed provisions governing the calling of meetings, quorums, agendas and, where appropriate, proxy voting. It may also be declared that a written resolution signed by the requisite number of partners should be binding on all without the need for a formal meeting to be convened.[76]

Management structures in large firms

In larger professional firms it is now common to find that the **10–87** agreement establishes a complex management structure, usually based around a managing or executive partner/committee and a series of committees/sub-committees charged with diverse responsibilities.[77] Some decisions will be capable of being taken in committee, whilst others will be referred to a full partners' meeting. The managing or executive partner will normally fulfil a co-ordinating role, although he may be responsible for *implementing* decisions once taken.

It is a matter for debate whether such a structure is better implemented on an *ad hoc* basis rather than being the subject of detailed provision in the agreement. In practice, the answer is likely to be dictated by the size of the firm: in a mid-sized firm based around a small number of offices, where the partners are in more or less regular contact, undue formality in the agreement may stultify flexibility in the approach to management. On the other hand, a large

---

[75] But see the decision in *Donaldson v. Williams* (1833) 1 Cromp. & M. 342, considered *infra*, para. 12–67.

[76] This runs counter to the normal principles of partnership law: see *infra*, para. 15–08.

[77] In larger professional firms, the position of "head of department" is gaining in importance and will usually confer on the holder a degree of day to day control over the running of the relevant department, as well as an automatic seat on the firm's management committee.

firm, with, perhaps, a national or multi-national practice, must have
clearly established procedures from the outset, because it will only be
feasible to convene partners' meetings on an infrequent basis.

P. RETIREMENT[78]

(a) Voluntary retirement

10–88 Since there is, as such, no inherent right to "retire" from a
partnership under the Partnership Act 1890 or under the general
law,[79] otherwise than by agreement, it is usually desirable to provide
for the voluntary retirement of partners from the outset. Otherwise,
the only course open to a partner who wishes to leave the firm may
be to bring about a general dissolution.

Retirement will normally be dependent on the service of a written
notice which may only be permitted to take effect on a particular
date, *e.g.* the end of an accounting period.[80] The minimum period of
notice will usually be specified, and will vary according to the trade
or profession concerned.

10–89 With a view to limiting the disruption caused by the retirement of a
partner, some firms restrict the number of partners who may give
notice of retirement at any one time or within a given period. This is
not without risk, since a partner who truly does not wish to remain
with the firm, but who is unable to give notice to retire may vent his
frustrations to the detriment of all the partners.[81]

A retirement notice, once given, cannot be unilaterally withdrawn,[82] although it may be superseded by a general dissolution.[83]

Acquisition of retiring partner's share

10–90 The agreement should provide for the continuing partners to
acquire the retiring partner's share at a valuation or in some other
manner,[84] although a failure to do so will not always result in a
general dissolution.[85]

---

[78] See the *Encyclopedia of Professional Partnerships*, Precedent 1, cll. 18 *et seq.* As to
discriminatory retirement terms, see the Sex Discrimination Act 1975, s.11(4) (as amended by the
Sex Discrimination Act 1986, s.2(2)); *cf.* the Race Relations Act 1976, s.10.
[79] See *infra*, paras. 24–79 *et seq.*
[80] This may well facilitate the calculation of the retiring partner's financial entitlement, by
obviating the need for special "retirement" accounts: see *infra*, paras. 10–133 *et seq.*
[81] *e.g.* by seeking a dissolution under the Partnership Act 1890, s.35.
[82] See *Twogood v. Farrell* [1988] 2 E.G.L.R. 233 (C.A.).
[83] See *infra*, para. 24–16, where the position is considered in relation to dissolution notices.
[84] See *infra*, paras. 10–121 *et seq.*
[85] See *Sobell v. Boston* [1975] 1 W.L.R. 1587. The concept of "retirement" itself connotes the
continuation of the business, which will be impossible if the partnership is placed in *general*
dissolution. See also *infra*, para. 10–166.

If the continuing partners' rights are framed in terms of an option to acquire the retiring partner's share, and the option is exercisable *before* the chosen retirement date, the retiring partner's room for manoeuvre may be severely limited, as Lord Lindley explained:

"If such a clause is acted on, and a partner notifies his desire to retire to his co-partner, and the latter declares his option to purchase the share of the retiring partner, a contract is thereby concluded between them, from which neither can depart without the consent of the other. Consequently, the retiring partner cannot withdraw his notice and dissolve the partnership under some other clause in the deed.[86] Even if the co-partner who is to purchase the other's share infringes the partnership articles, the Court will not willingly interfere and dissolve the partnership; although, if the partner who is to retire conducts himself so as to prejudice the business and exclude the other, the Court will interpose for the protection of the latter; for otherwise the business to which he is shortly to be solely entitled may be entirely ruined."[87]

Power to sell or assign share

Subject to any restriction contained in the agreement,[88] a partner is **10–91** free to sell or otherwise assign his share to a third party, but he will still remain a member of the partnership.[89] In Lord Lindley's day, an express provision permitting such a sale, as a species of retirement, appears to have been common, since he went on to explain:

"If it is provided that a partner may sell his share, and no restrictions are mentioned, he may sell to anyone he likes, even to a pauper[90]; and, on giving his co-partners notice of his withdrawal from the firm, he will cease to be a member thereof as between himself and them; even although the purchaser from him does not come forward to take his place as a partner in the firm.[91]

---

[86] See *Warder v. Stilwell* (1856) 3 Jur.(N.S.) 9; *Homfray v. Fothergill* (1866) L.R. 1 Eq. 567; also *Jones v. Lloyd* (1874) L.R. 18 Eq. 265. It is, however, submitted that the notice could not be withdrawn even *prior* to the service of the option notice: *Warder v. Stilwell, supra.*

[87] See *Warder v. Stilwell, supra.*

[88] It is, in practice, rare to see an agreement which does *not* contain such a restriction: see *supra,* para. 10–80.

[89] Partnership Act 1890, s.31, *infra,* paras. 19–59 *et seq.* See also *infra,* para. 24–77.

[90] See *infra,* para. 19–72. Alternatively, the sale may be to one of the other partners: see *Cassels v. Stewart* (1881) 6 App.Cas. 64.

[91] *Jefferys v. Smith* (1827) 3 Russ. 158. As to the vendor partner's right to an indemnity from the purchaser, see *Dodson v. Downey* [1901] 2 Ch. 620. Previous editors have questioned whether the headnote in this case is supported by the facts or the judgment. The current editor does not share those doubts. See also *infra,* para. 19–67.

It is sometimes declared that a partner who is desirous of retiring shall offer his share to his co-partners before selling it to anyone else."

10–92   A clause of this type would now be wholly exceptional, but might, perhaps, be encountered in a corporate or investment partnership. Nevertheless, the following principles may be drawn from the older cases:

1. Subject to the precise terms of the clause, if the offer is duly made to all the other partners, one or more of them may accept it and acquire the share.[92]
2. A written notice of a partner's wish to dispose of his share may be treated as sufficient even though it is not seen by all the other partners, *e.g.* where it is written in a book which is produced at partners' meetings and which each partner has at all times been at liberty to inspect.[93] However, notice should in general be given to each partner individually.
3. If the other partners decline to purchase the share but seek to frustrate attempts to sell it to a third party by refusing to take that third party into the partnership, they may ultimately be compelled to acquire it at a valuation.[94]
4. The time limit for acceptance of the offer cannot in general be enlarged, otherwise than by agreement.[95]

(b) Compulsory retirement[96]

10–93 In professional firms it is now common to see partners being required to retire on or shortly after attaining a specified age, unless the operation of that provision is waived by agreement prior to the relevant retirement date. Indeed, in the case of medical and dental partnerships practising within the National Health Service, retirement from *practice* is now compulsory on age grounds.[97]

If a particular partner is to be exempted from such a requirement, or is to retire at a different age, this fact should obviously be recorded in the agreement.

---

[92] *Homfray v. Fothergill* (1866) L.R. 1 Eq. 567.
[93] *Glassington v. Thwaites* (1833) Coop., temp. Brough. 115.
[94] *Featherstonhaugh v. Turner* (1858) 25 Beav. 382.
[95] See *Holland v. King* (1848) 6 C.B. 727; *Brooke v. Garrod* (1857) 2 De G. & J. 62; *Lord Ranelagh v. Melton* (1864) 2 Dr. & Sm. 278; also *infra*, para. 10–127. And see as to the position when the recipient of the offer is mentally incapacitated, *Rowlands v. Evans* (1861) 30 Beav. 302.
[96] See the *Encyclopedia of Professional Partnerships*, Precedent 1, cl. 20.
[97] Health and Medicines Act 1988, s.8; National Health Service (General Medical Services) Regulations 1992 (S.I. 1992 No. 635), reg. 7(11); National Health Service (General Dental Services) Regulations 1992 (S.I. 1992 No. 661), reg. 9. See, further, the *Encyclopedia of Professional Partnerships*, Pts. 4, 5.

Provision should be made for the acquisition of the retiring partner's share, as in the case of voluntary retirement.[98]

Q. EXPULSION, ETC.[99]

In the absence of an express power in the agreement, no partner can **10–94** be expelled from, or otherwise forced to leave, a partnership.[1] It follows that, if one partner is so misconducting himself that the other partners are unable to carry on in partnership with him,[2] their only options may be to pay the recalcitrant partner off or to seek a dissolution from the court. Lord Lindley observed:

"In order, therefore, that an objectionable partner may be summarily got rid of, clauses are sometimes inserted providing for expulsion in certain events."

This is now something of an understatement: draconian though the power of expulsion is, it will be found in most well drawn agreements,[3] although its true value may only be appreciated by the partners when circumstances have arisen for its exercise. On occasion, such a power may be coupled with (or replaced by) a power of compulsory "retirement."[4]

(a) Powers of Expulsion

Grounds for expulsion

A traditional power of expulsion will set out a detailed list of **10–95** grounds on which the power will be exercisable, ranging from breach of the agreement and actual or impending bankruptcy[5] to mental or physical incapacity and conduct which is likely to have an adverse effect on the business or practice concerned.[6] Although it is usual for

---

[98] See *infra*, paras. 10–121 *et seq*.

[99] See the *Encyclopedia of Professional Partnerships*, Precedent 1, cll. 20, 21.

[1] Partnership Act 1890, s.25, *infra*, paras. 24–85 *et seq*.

[2] In such cases, the right to injunctive relief against the recalcitrant partner may be more theoretical than real: see *infra*, paras. 23–137, 24–72, 24–86.

[3] See, for example, *Walters v. Bingham* [1988] 1 F.T.L.R. 260, 268, *per* Browne-Wilkinson V.-C. See further, *supra*, para. 10–22.

[4] See *infra*, paras. 10–109 *et seq*.

[5] It is desirable to ensure that a partner can be expelled *before* he is made bankrupt, so that insolvency and/or an application for an interim order under the Insolvency Act 1986, s. 253 and/or the presentation of a bankruptcy (or insolvency) petition should normally be made a ground for expulsion. The inclusion of actual bankruptcy as a ground will, by implication, exclude the operation of the Partnership Act 1890, s.33(1), so far as it concerns bankruptcy. But see also *infra*, paras. 10–124, 10–125.

[6] This will be of particular importance in the case of a professional practice: see for example, *Goodman v. Sinclair*, *The Times*, January 24, 1951, *infra*, para. 10–96.

the last ground to refer to "conduct which would be a ground for dissolving the partnership under the Partnership Act 1890,"[7] in practice reliance will rarely be placed thereon.[8]

Insolvency: If a ground is framed by reference to a partner's "insolvency," the power will normally be exercisable before the initiation of insolvency proceedings,[9] as Lord Lindley explained:

"The word *insolvent*, unless controlled by the context, means unable to pay debts, in the ordinary acceptation of that phrase. A person may therefore be insolvent, although his assets, if all turned into money, might enable him to pay his debts in full;[10] and although he has not been adjudicated bankrupt or compounded with his creditors.[11] But a person is not deemed insolvent merely because he keeps renewing a bill which he cannot conveniently meet."[12]

Misconduct: Lord Lindley pointed out that:

"When a power of expulsion is given in the event of a partner omitting to do certain things, *e.g.* entering in the partnership books all monies he may receive on account of the partnership, the power will not, as a rule, be exercisable, unless the omission was a studied omission."[13]

However, this must be read subject to the precise terms of the agreement.

10–96   *Dishonesty, etc.*: Honesty, integrity and restraint are vital in a partner. Thus, in *Carmichael v. Evans*,[14] a member of a trading partnership was held to be guilty of a flagrant breach of his duties as a partner, having been convicted of travelling on the railway without a ticket with intent to avoid payment; again, in *Goodman v.*

---

[7] *Ibid.* s.35, *infra*, paras. 24–39 *et seq.*

[8] It is almost inconceivable that an expulsion could be founded on *ibid.* s.35(e) (partnership carried on at a loss) or (f) (the just and equitable ground). Note that reliance may only be placed on s.35(b) to (d) where the other partners are themselves blameless (which should in any event be the position if they are considering the exercise of a power of expulsion).

[9] See *infra*, paras. 27–44 *et seq.*

[10] See *Bayly v. Schofield* (1813) 1 M. & S. 338, 353, *per* Le Blanc J.

[11] See *Parker v. Gossage* (1835) 2 C.M. & R. 617; *Biddlecombe v. Bond* (1835) 4 A. & E. 332; also *London & Counties Assets Co. v. Brighton Grand Concert Hall and Picture Palace Ltd.* [1915] 2 K.B. 493 and the cases there cited.

[12] *Cutten v. Sanger* (1828) 2 Y. & J. 459; and see *Anon.* (1808) 1 Camp. 492.

[13] See *Smith v. Mules* (1852) 9 Hare. 556. Note, however, that, in this case, the power was exercisable only in the case of omissions made "knowingly and wilfully."

[14] [1904] 1 Ch. 486.

Sinclair,[15] a doctor was held to be guilty of flagrantly immoral behaviour by having an affair with a woman patient. It is clear that a physical assault by one partner on another will be regarded unsympathetically, even if it was provoked.[16]

Discretionary grounds: It is theoretically possible to frame a ground of expulsion which requires a degree of subjective judgment by the other partners, but this is not generally to be commended.[17]

Discrimination: The chosen grounds should not be discriminatory on the grounds of sex or race.[18]

Expulsion procedure

The agreement should provide the manner in which a partner can **10–97** be expelled. This will usually involve the service of an expulsion notice with the approval of all, or a specified majority, of the other partners.[19] It is prima facie undesirable to provide that the notice will specify the precise matters of complaint which have led to its service, although reference should in practice be made to the relevant ground(s) set out in the agreement.[20] It may, of course, be that the full extent of the expelled partner's misdeeds will only come to light *after* the expulsion; in such a case, it should be possible for the other partners to place reliance thereon in the event of the expulsion being challenged,[21] although much will depend on the precise terms of the power.[22]

---

[15] *The Times*, January 24, 1951. *Cf. Snow v. Milford* (1868) 16 W.R. 554 (which concerned a banking firm).

[16] *Greenaway v. Greenaway* (1940) 84 S.J. 43.

[17] The courts will, almost inevitably, scrutinise the ground relied on and may conclude that the partners are obliged to take a "reasonable" view of the expelled partner's conduct: see *Kerr v. Morris* [1987] Ch. 90, 111D, *per* Dillon L.J., although this part of his judgment was clearly *obiter*. But see *Wood v. Woad* (1874) L.R. 9 Ex. 190; *Russell v. Russell* (1880) 14 Ch.D. 471 (which concerned a power to dissolve).

[18] Sex Discrimination Act 1975, ss.11(4)(a), 82(1A) (as respectively amended and inserted by the Sex Discrimination Act 1986, ss.2(2), (3)); Race Relations Act 1976, s.10(1). In the latter case only, discrimination is permissible if the firm comprises less than six partners.

[19] Provided that all partners have concurred in (or are otherwise bound by) the decision to serve the notice, there is no need for them all to sign it, unless the agreement so requires. Some agreements provide that a preliminary "warning notice" should be served, thus giving the recipient an opportunity to mend his ways but, in the view of the current editor, such provisions are of questionable value, since the initial misconduct will usually be symptomatic of a serious underlying problem which can only be solved by expulsion. Other agreements require the power to be exercised within a fixed period after details of a partner's misconduct, etc., have come to the notice of the other partners; although this approach is attractive in terms of certainty, it may in practice prove to be unduly restrictive, *e.g.* where the partners would prefer to await the outcome of criminal or disciplinary proceedings before considering an expulsion.

[20] But see *Kerr v. Morris* [1987] Ch. 90, 111D, *per* Dillon L.J. It is submitted that this obiter view is not justified in law: see *Green v. Howell* [1910] 1 Ch. 493 and *infra*, paras. 10–102, 10–103.

[21] See *Boston Deep Sea Fishing and Ice Company v. Ansell* (1888) 39 Ch.D. 339, C.A. (an employment case).

[22] It might, in any event, be possible to serve a second expulsion notice in such a case.

If more than one partner is to be capable of being expelled at the same time, that fact should be clearly stated.[23]

It is becoming increasingly common to include a power to suspend a partner for a short period pending the decision to expel, in order to avoid unnecessary embarrassment, particularly where potentially criminal conduct is involved.[24] If this course is adopted, the suspended partner will normally continue to receive his full profit share and other benefits until such time as he is either fully reinstated or expelled.

Construction of expulsion clauses

10–98   Since a true power of expulsion is expropriatory in nature, it will always be construed strictly. Thus in *Re A Solicitor's Arbitration*,[25] a power which permitted "any partner" to be expelled by "the other partners" was held not to authorise a single partner to expel either or both of his co-partners. Moreover, in *Bond v. Hale*,[26] the Court of Appeal of New South Wales followed *Re A Solicitor's Arbitration* and held that, on a true construction of the power in question, three members of a five man firm could not expel the other two, even though grounds justifying an exercise of the power seemingly could be proved.[27]

In earlier editions of this work a distinction was sought to be drawn between the approach to construction in the case of firms comprising two partners and those comprising more than two partners, on the footing that, in the former case, the power is in truth a power to determine the partnership (albeit with different consequences than a normal dissolution), whereas in the latter it is a power of expulsion properly so called. Yet the fact remains that, if the sole continuing "partner" is entitled to acquire the partnership business following the expulsion, an exercise of the power is in commercial terms no different from the position where one partner is expelled from a multi-partner firm. The current editor accordingly considers this distinction to be of doubtful validity.

The courts will not, however, permit the strict rule of construction to be taken to extreme or absurd limits. Thus, in *Hitchman v. Crouch Butler Savage Associates*[28] a clause requiring a particular senior partner to sign all expulsion notices was construed in such a way as to avoid the need for him to sign his own expulsion notice.

---

[23] See *Re a Solicitors' Arbitration* [1962] 1 W.L.R. 353; *Bond v. Hale* (1969) 72 S.R. (N.S.W.) 201, noticed *infra*, para. 10–98.
[24] See the *Encyclopedia of Professional Partnerships*, Precedent 1, cl.21(1), proviso (i). See, as to the exercise of such a power, *McLory v. Post Office* [1992] I.C.R. 758 (albeit an employment case).
[25] [1962] 1 W.L.R. 353.
[26] (1969) 72 S.R. (N.S.W.) 201.
[27] *Ibid.* p.204F, *per* Wallace P.
[28] (1983) 127 S.J. 441.

Exercise of the power

A power of expulsion must not be exercised with an ulterior **10–99** motive, financial or otherwise. Lord Lindley put it in this way:

"The Court cannot control the exercise of a power to expel if it is exercised *bona fide*.[29] But all clauses conferring such a power are construed strictly, on account of the abuse which may be made of them, and of the hardship of expulsion[30]; and the Court will never allow a partner to be expelled if he can show that his co-partners, though justified by the wording of the expulsion clause, have, in fact, taken advantage of it for base and unworthy purposes of their own, and contrary to that truth and honour which every partner has a right to demand on the part of his co-partners."

Blisset v. Daniel[31] clearly illustrates this principle. There a majority **10–100** of partners were given a wide power of expulsion which did not require a reason to be given for its exercise nor any prior meeting of the partners to be convened. The power was exercised against one partner, Blisset, and the appropriate notice served on him. At the trial of the action it appeared that the other partners wished to get rid of Blisset, not because this would in any way benefit the firm but because he had objected to a proposal that the firm should appoint one of the other partners, Vaughan, and his son co-managers of the business.[32] Unknown to Blisset, Vaughan then delivered an ultimatum to the other partners, threatening to leave the partnership if Blisset remained, and thereby prevailed on them to sign the expulsion notice. However, before that notice was served on Blisset or any intimation of its existence given to him, the other partners induced him to sign certain accounts, with a view to acquiring his share at a favourable value following the expulsion. In these circumstances, the notice was declared void and Blisset was restored as a partner.

The editor of the 6th edition of this work expressed the view that the court would be unable to control the exercise of a power of expulsion which is exercisable "at the mere will and pleasure of one partner." However, since the authority which he cited concerned a power of dissolution in a two partner firm,[33] the proposition is highly questionable if it is taken as legitimising capricious expulsions.[34]

---

[29] *Russell v. Russell* (1880) 14 Ch.D. 471 (which was not a case of expulsion but of dissolution); also *Steuart v. Gladstone* (1878) 10 Ch.D. 626.

[30] The extent of such hardship will, of course, depend on the quantum of the expelled partner's financial entitlement and the manner in which it falls to be paid: see *infra*, paras. 10–121 *et seq.*

[31] (1853) 10 Hare 493. See also *Wood v. Woad* (1874) L.R. 9 Ex. 190; *Ebrahimi v. Westbourne Galleries* [1973] A.C. 360.

[32] Vaughan was already acting as sole manager.

[33] See *Russell v. Russell* (1880) 14 Ch.D. 471.

[34] Note the arguments canvassed in *Walters v. Bingham* [1988] 1 F.T.L.R. 260: see *infra*, paras. 10–118, 24–13. And see *infra*, para. 10–109.

Compliance with strict terms of expulsion clause

10–101   In his Supplement on the Partnership Act 1890, Lord Lindley explained that:

> "Powers of expulsion are '*strictissimi juris*,' and parties who seek to enforce them must exactly pursue all that is necessary in order to enable them to exercise this strong power."[35]

Thus, if the agreement requires all the other partners to concur in the expulsion, the power cannot normally be exercised if the concurrence of one or more partners has not been obtained.[36]

Opportunity for explanation

10–102   Where a power of expulsion is exercisable on certain specified grounds,[37] it is a vexed question whether, before it can be invoked against a partner, he must *invariably* be given an opportunity to explain his conduct. Lord Lindley originally observed:

> "... it is conceived that a power to expel for misconduct cannot safely be acted upon until the delinquent partner has had an opportunity of explaining his conduct."

This proposition was, somewhat surprisingly, supported by a reference to *Blisset v. Daniel*.[38] Yet, whilst it was held, on the facts of that case, that Vaughan should not have proceeded behind Blisset's back, it seems tolerably clear that, if there had been no breach of the duty of good faith, the result would have been otherwise.[39] In his Supplement on the Partnership Act 1890, Lord Lindley made the same point, if anything, more forcefully:

> "... the partner, whom his co-partners seek to expel, must have a full opportunity of explaining his conduct."[40]

However, in *Green v. Howell*,[41] which admittedly concerned a two partner firm, the Court of Appeal held that there is *no* general

---

[35] See *Clarke v. Hart* (1858) 6 H.L.C. 633, 650, *per* Lord Chelmsford. See also *Blisset v. Daniel* (1853) 10 Hare 493.

[36] See *Smith v. Mules* (1852) 9 Hare 556; *Steuart v. Gladstone* (1878) 10 Ch.D. 626; *Re A Solicitors' Arbitration* [1962] 1 W.L.R. 353; *Bond v. Hale* (1969) 72 S.R. (N.S.W.) 201. *Cf. Hitchman v. Crouch Butler Savage Associates* (1983) 127 S.J. 441. See further, *supra*, para. 10–98.

[37] See *supra*, para. 10–95.

[38] (1853) 10 Hare 493, *supra*, para. 10–100. Lord Lindley also referred to *Cooper v. Wandsworth Board of Works* (1863) 14 C.B.(N.S.) 180, but *not* to *Russell v. Russell* (1880) 14 Ch.D. 471.

[39] See (1853) 10 Hare 504, *per* Turner V.-C.; also the arguments advanced in *Kerr v. Morris* [1987] Ch. 90, 95.

[40] On this occasion, Lord Lindley referred to *Wood v. Woad* (1874) L.R. 9 Ex. 190; *Steuart v. Gladstone* (1878) 10 Ch.D. 626; *Labouchere v. Wharncliffe* (1879) 13 Ch.D. 346.

[41] [1910] 1 Ch. 495 (C.A.).

obligation to give a fair hearing, whilst in *Kerr v. Morris*[42] that court declined to express a final view. The courts in New Zealand originally appear to have followed the *Green v. Howell* line,[43] but more recently there appears to have been a move towards recognising a general right to a fair hearing in all cases.[44]

The position on the authorities thus appears to be somewhat **10–103** confused. It must, however, be borne in mind that, in situations of the type under consideration, any dispute as to whether a case for expulsion has arisen will in general be referred to the court or to an arbitrator, who will naturally afford each side a fair hearing. In those circumstances, it is, in the current editor's view, inappropriate to try to import into the law of partnership the principle *"audi alteram partem,"* as applied in trade union cases and the like.[45] On a true analysis, the position would seem to be as follows:

1. In general, and subject to the terms of the agreement, a partner need *not* be given an opportunity to explain his conduct before the expulsion notice is served;[46] *a fortiori* where all the partners entitled to exercise the power[47] independently form the view that grounds for an expulsion exist.[48]

2. Where one or more partners seek to persuade the others that grounds for expulsion exist, prudence dictates that the partner to be expelled should in all cases be given an opportunity to state his case, even if this is not always strictly required as a matter of law.[49]

---

[42] [1987] Ch. 90, 111, *per* Dillon L.J.

[43] *Wilkie v. Wilkie (No. 2)* (1900) 18 N.Z.L.R. 734. But note that, in this case, the court decided that an opportunity to explain in general had to be offered where no set grounds for an expulsion had to be established; *per contra*, where a prior warning had been given and ignored.

[44] *Jackson v. Moss* [1978] N.Z. Recent Law 20; *Re Northwestern Autoservices Ltd.* [1980] 2 N.Z.L.R. 302, 308–309, *per* Cooke J.; see also *Malborough Harbour Board v. Goulden* [1985] 2 N.Z.L.R. 378, 383, *per* Cooke J. This trend is discussed in Webb & Webb, *Principles of the Law of Partnership* (5th ed.), para. 54.

[45] See the arguments in *Kerr v. Morris* [1987] Ch. 90, 98, noticed by Dillon L.J. at *ibid.* p. 111. *Cf. McLory v. Post Office* [1992] I.C.R. 758 (an employment case). A similar view to that expressed in the text was advanced in an article by Bernard J. Davies in The Conveyancer and Property Lawyer (N.S.), Vol. 33, 1969, pp. 32–42.

[46] *Green v. Howell* [1910] 1 Ch. 495 (overruling, on this point, *Barnes v. Youngs* [1898] 1 Ch. 414).

[47] This may not be *all* the other partners, *e.g.* where the power is exercisable by a specified majority, as in *Blisset v. Daniel* (1853) 10 Hare 493, *supra*, para. 10–100; *Carmichael v. Evans* [1904] 1 Ch. 486.

[48] *Green v. Howell* [1910] 1 Ch. 495; also *Peyton v. Mindham* [1972] 1 W.L.R. 8, which concerned a power to dissolve.

[49] *Blisset v. Daniel* (1853) 10 Hare 493, *supra*, para. 10–100; *Wood v. Woad* (1874) L.R. 9 Ex. 190. In both cases there seems to have been collusion between the partners exercising the power. It is the current editor's view that the same principles do not apply where one partner draws another's conduct to the attention of his co-partners, merely with a view to their considering whether to exercise the power; similarly, perhaps, where such a partner *genuinely* seeks to argue that an expulsion is in the firm's best interests.

3. If, exceptionally, the partners serving the notice are themselves charged with the task of determining their *entitlement* to
exercise the power,[50] then an opportunity for explanation
should always be given.[51] Although there is no authority on
the point, it might perhaps be argued that a similar approach
should be adopted where the relevant ground(s) for expulsion
are framed in purely *subjective* terms.[52]

Nevertheless, it would in practice be most unusual for a partner to be
expelled without some intimation being given to him of his partners'
intentions and the grounds upon which they propose to rely.

Waiver of right to expel

10–104   Once partners have notice that a ground for expulsion exists, they
should not unduly delay their exercise of the power[53] or otherwise do
anything which might be construed as a waiver of their right to expel,
e.g. by admitting a new partner[54] or agreeing to a variation of the
agreement.

Effect of invalid expulsion notice

10–105   Lord Lindley explained that:

"A notice of expulsion under one clause cannot, if invalid, operate
as a notice of dissolution under some other clause."[55]

Such a notice will thus be ineffective for all purposes,[56] save as
evidence of a breakdown in the relationship between the partners,

---

[50] This presupposes that, under the agreement, the other partners (or a committee appointed for
the purpose) not only decide whether to serve an expulsion notice but also whether they are *entitled*
so to do: such a provision would be unusual.

[51] *Wood v. Woad* (1874) L.R. 9 Ex. 190; *Green v. Howell* [1910] 1 Ch. 493; *Peyton v. Mindham*
[1972] 1 W.L.R. 8 (which concerned a power to dissolve). *Cf. Blisset v. Daniel* (1853) 10 Hare 493.

[52] *e.g.* a power exercisable in the event of the other partners being "satisfied" that the expelled
partner's conduct is prejudicial to the interests of the partnership: see also, *supra*, para. 10–95.
Quaere, if the conduct is proved and the other partners have acted bone fide but, on any
reasonable analysis, misguidedly, could the court properly interfere? See also, in this context, the
approach adopted in *Wilkie v. Wilkie* (*No. 2*) (1900) 18 N.Z.L.R. 734.

[53] See Lord Lindley's statement of principle in relation to the exercise of powers to dissolve,
infra, para. 10–119.

[54] The admission of a new partner would in law constitute a new partnership and the current
editor submits that, quite apart from waiver, a partner could not be expelled on grounds relating to
his conduct in a *previous* partnership; much will, however, depend on the precise terms of the
power.

[55] Lord Lindley cited *Smith v. Mules* (1852) 9 Hare 556 and *Clarke v. Hart* (1858) 6 H.L.C. 633.
However, the current editor is of the view that the former decision is *not* authority for the
proposition in the text, since it turned on one partner's inability to exercise a power which, under
the terms of the agreement, was conferred on him and one of his co-partners.

[56] The recipient may, of course, choose to treat the notice as valid, but it is considered that he
could not later seek to argue that the partnership was thereby dissolved, otherwise than as regards
himself: *cf. Smith v. Mules*, *supra*. At most, he would be entitled to be paid the value of his share
at the date of his "expulsion": see *Sobell v. Boston* [1975] 1 W.L.R. 1587. If this is different from
his entitlement under the agreement as an expelled partner, questions of estoppel may also arise.

which may justify an application to the court for a dissolution under the Partnership Act 1890.[57]

Remedies for wrongful expulsion

It has been held that, since the service of an invalid notice of **10–106** expulsion does not affect the recipient's status as a partner, he cannot claim damages against his co-partners for wrongful expulsion.[58] However, the editors of the 7th edition of this work[59] pointed out that:

"... if a partner has been in fact wrongfully expelled and damnified, it is not easy to see why an action for damages should not lie."[60]

Although the current editor wholeheartedly agrees with this view, cases in which a recoverable loss can be proved are likely to be rare.[61]

Even if a remedy in damages is not available, the circumstances in which the notice was served, even if not its service *per se*, may provide grounds for the wronged partner either to serve a cross expulsion notice on his co-partner(s)[62] or, more usually, to seek a dissolution.[63]

Repudiation by wrongful expulsion

Although it might at first sight seem that the service of an invalid **10–107** notice *cannot* amount to a repudiatory breach of the partnership agreement,[64] the contrary appears to have been accepted by the court

---

[57] See *infra*, para. 10–106.

[58] *Wood v. Woad* (1874) L.R. 9 Ex. 190.

[59] Unlike the 6th edition, Lord Lindley was not involved in the preparation of this edition, which was published in 1905.

[60] The editors referred to *Catchpole v. Ambergate Ry. Co.* (1852) 1 E. & B. 111 (which did not concern a partnership) and to *Wood v. Woad* (1874) L.R. 9 Ex. 190, 199 (*per* Cleasby B.), 201 (*per* Pollock B.). And see also *infra*, para. 10–107. Note, however, that there will be no tortious remedy merely because the partners were acting *ultra vires* when they served the notice: see generally, *Abbott v. Sullivan* [1952] 1 K.B. 189. See also, as to claims for damages as between partners, *infra*, paras. 23–195 *et seq*.

[61] Such a loss might, perhaps, be provable if, by reason of his purported expulsion, the partner was not eligible to share in an incentive profit "pool": see *supra*, para. 10–67.

[62] In the case of a firm comprising three or more partners, this presupposes that the power is exercisable by one partner against *all* his co-partners: see *supra*, paras. 10–98, 10–99.

[63] See the Partnership Act 1890, s.35(d), (f), *infra*, paras. 24–66 *et seq.*, 24–75 *et seq*. But note that, in the case of the former ground, the partner seeking a dissolution must be blameless.

[64] See *Woodar Investment Development Ltd. v. Wimpey Construction U.K. Ltd.* [1980] 1 W.L.R. 277.

in *Fulwell v. Bragg*[65] and *Hitchman v. Crouch Butler Savage Associates*.[66] The current editor submits that, on a true analysis, the service of a notice in conformity with the terms of the power but on grounds which are ultimately held not to justify its exercise will not constitute a repudiatory breach, but that a notice which is defective on its face, *e.g.* because it is given by some but not all of the relevant partners,[67] may not be similarly regarded.

Expulsion and partnerships at will

10–108   Although it had long been regarded as settled law that a power of expulsion would not be carried over into a partnership at will constituted following the expiration of an initial fixed term,[68] it has already been seen that this proposition has recently been called into question.[69]

(b)   Powers of Compulsory Retirement, etc.[70]

10–109 As an alternative (or, more frequently, as an adjunct) to a traditional power of expulsion, some agreements now contain a power for a majority of partners to require one of their number to retire without the need to give or substantiate any grounds for its exercise. Needless to say, such a power is of an exceptional nature and will not be appropriate in all cases.

It should be noted that, in his Supplement on the Partnership Act 1890, Lord Lindley observed:

"It may be a question how far an express power to expel a partner without giving any reasons for such expulsion and without hearing him would be upheld by the Court."[71]

Yet, no such doubts were expressed in *Blisset v. Daniel*,[72] where the power was a forerunner of the modern provision.[73]

---

[65] (1983) 127 S.J. 171. Note, however, that this issue was not fully argued, as the plaintiff was merely seeking an interlocutory injunction compelling his former partners to circularise all the firm's clients. In the event, that application failed.

[66] (1983) 80 L.S. Gaz. 550. This aspect was not adverted to in the report of the decision of the Court of Appeal at (1983) 127 S.J. 441.

[67] See, as to the construction of expulsion clauses, *supra*, para. 10–98.

[68] *Clark v. Leach* (1863) 1 De G.J. & S. 409; *Neilson v. Mossend Iron Co.* (1886) 11 App.Cas. 298.

[69] *Walters v. Bingham* [1988] 1 F.T.L.R. 260, considered *supra*, paras. 10–21, 10–22.

[70] See the *Encyclopedia of Professional Partnerships*, Precedent 1, cl. 20.

[71] In a footnote reference, Lord Lindley referred to Pollock's *Digest of the Law of Partnership* (5th ed.), p. 76. It should be noted that a different view was espoused in later editions of that Digest: see the 15th ed. at p. 79.

[72] (1853) 10 Hare 493. See *supra*, para. 10–100.

[73] For a hybrid power, see *Kerr v. Morris* [1987] Ch. 90.

Since a power of this type is, in substance, a power of expulsion, similar principles will generally apply to its construction and exercise.[74]

Exercise of the power

The primary value of a power of compulsory retirement lies in the **10–110** fact that no overt ground or reason for its exercise need be relied on, thus substantially reducing the scope for the validity of that exercise to be challenged by the "retired" partner. In the opinion of the current editor, if the partners refuse to disclose their reasons, they cannot be forced to do so.[75] If, however, a reason is *volunteered*, it will almost inevitably be scrutinised by the court and its "reasonableness" may thereupon be called into question.[76]

As in the case of a power of expulsion, the power must be **10–111** exercised in perfect good faith and, thus, for the benefit of the partnership as a whole.[77] In a normal case, it would be wholly inappropriate to afford the partner on whom the notice is to be served an opportunity to meet any criticisms which are levelled against him, since this would run counter to the whole purpose of the provision;[78] whether such a partner would nevertheless be able to persuade the court that the other partners are, in effect, judges in their own cause and thus obliged to apply the rules of natural justice remains to be seen,[79] but the current editor ventures to suggest that this would involve serious and unwarranted inroads into partners' freedom of contract.[80] Be that as it may, consistently with the decision in *Blisset v. Daniel*,[81] different considerations will apply where one partner is endeavouring to cajole or persuade his co-partners to exercise such a power.

---

[74] See *supra*, paras. 10–98 *et seq*. Such clauses are subject to the same laws on discrimination as ordinary powers of expulsion: Sex Discrimination Act 1975, ss.11(4)(a), 82(1A) (as respectively amended and inserted by the Sex Discrimination Act 1986, ss.2(2), (3)); Race Relations Act 1976, s.10(1). In the latter case only, discrimination is permissible if the firm comprises less than six partners.

[75] See *Price v. Bouch* (1987) 53 P. & C.R. 257 (a case concerning restrictive covenants); also *Re Gresham Life Assurance Society* (1872) L.R. 8 Ch.App. 446; *Berry and Stewart v. Tottenham Hotspur Football & Athletic Co. Ltd.* [1935] Ch. 718; *Tett v. Phoenix Property and Investment Co. Ltd.* [1984] BCLC 599, 621, *per* Vinelott J.; and note *Wong v. Benn* [1992] C.L.Y. 528. But see *Kerr v. Morris* [1987] Ch. 90, 111, *per* Dillon L.J.

[76] See the (*obiter*) views expressed by Dillon L.J. in *Kerr v. Morris*, *supra*, at p. 111. Equally, the duty of good faith is not synonymous with a duty of reasonableness: *Imperial Group Pension Trust Ltd. v. Imperial Tobacco Ltd.* [1991] 1 W.L.R. 589, 597–598, *per* Browne-Wilkinson V.-C.

[77] *Blisset v. Daniel* (1853) 10 Hare 493. See *supra*, para. 10–100.

[78] See, generally, *Green v. Howell* [1910] 1 Ch. 495 and *supra*, paras. 10–102, 10–103. But note *Steuart v. Gladstone* (1879) 10 Ch.D. 626.

[79] See *supra*, para. 10–103.

[80] It appears that the New Zealand Courts take a different view: see *Wilkie v. Wilkie (No. 2)* (1900) 18 N.Z.L.R. 734; *Jackson v. Moss* [1978] N.Z. Recent Law 20; also *supra*, para. 10–102, n. 44.

[81] (1853) 10 Hare 493.

(c) Acquisition of Expelled/Retired Partner's Share

10–112 The agreement should always contain provision for the acquisition of the share of an expelled or compulsorily retired partner.[82] However, in some cases, the financial entitlement of an expelled partner may be less than that of any other outgoing partner.[83]

R. POWER TO DISSOLVE FIRM[84]

(a) General Power

10–113 A power for any partner to bring about a general dissolution by notice, which is of the essence of a partnership at will,[85] will rarely be encountered in a fixed term partnership, for obvious reasons.[86] Such a power may, nevertheless, sometimes have its place in a large partnership, where it is exercisable by a specified majority of partners, either generally or for a particular purpose, e.g. with a view to merger or incorporation.[87]

Subject to the precise terms of the agreement, the exercise of such a power will be governed by the same principles as apply to the dissolution of a partnership at will.[88] If the notice must expire on a certain date, *e.g.* at the end of an accounting period, a notice expiring on any other date will be invalid.[89]

Effect of invalid dissolution notice

10–114 If the recipients of an invalid dissolution notice choose to treat it as effective, the partnership will obviously be at an end, but it does not follow that any provisions of the agreement governing the position following the service of a valid notice will necessarily apply.[90]

Equally, if one partner serves a potentially invalid notice and is subsequently expelled by his co-partners pursuant to an express power in the agreement,[91] the expelling partners could not later seek

---

[82] See *infra*, para. 10–121 *et seq.*

[83] Thus, an expelled partner may not be entitled to a payment for goodwill: see *infra*, para. 10–128, n. 54. *Quaere* whether this is permissible in the case of expulsion on bankruptcy: see *infra*, paras. 10–124, 10–125. Compulsorily retired partners should not, in general, be treated in the same way, since such retirement does not necessarily connote any form of misconduct.

[84] See the *Encyclopedia of Professional Partnerships*, Precedent 1, cl. 23.

[85] See *supra*, paras. 9–01 *et seq.* and *infra*, paras. 24–10 *et seq.*

[86] See *infra*, paras. 24–02, 24–03, 25–01 *et seq.*

[87] In practice, the agreement may not contain an express power to dissolve as such, but will (more obliquely) record the fact that decisions involving the dissolution of the firm can be taken by a majority of partners.

[88] See *infra*, paras. 24–10 *et seq.*

[89] See *Watson v. Eales* (1857) 23 Beav. 294; also *Hunter v. Wylie*, 1993 G.W.D. 1–60; also reported (but less clearly on this point) at 1993 S.L.P. 1091. Equally, the court may not be prepared to adopt an unduly strict approach: see for example *Carradine Properties v. Aston* [1976] 1 W.L.R. 442 (which concerned a notice to quit).

[90] See *Smith v. Mules* (1852) 9 Hare 556 (which concerned an effective power to expel).

[91] See generally *supra*, paras. 10–95 *et seq.*

to contend either that his original notice was valid and effectual[92] or that it constituted a repudiatory breach of the agreement.[93]

(b) Power to Dissolve for Cause

It was formerly common for agreements, particularly in the case of **10–115** two partner firms, to include a power to dissolve on specified grounds as an *alternative* to a power of expulsion,[94] but this is now relatively unusual.[95] In practice, the inclusion of such a provision should only be considered where the continuation of the business will be impossible without the participation of all the original partners.[96]

Where the partners serving a "dissolution" notice are in fact entitled to acquire the recipient's share[97] or otherwise to prevent him from carrying on business in competition with them,[98] the power will be tantamount to a power of expulsion and should be construed accordingly.[99]

Grounds for dissolution

These will, in general, follow the same format as in a power of **10–116** expulsion, although purely subjective grounds are, perhaps, more susceptible of inclusion since there are no pejorative or expropriatory overtones.[1]

Dissolution procedure

This will usually involve the service of a written notice, which may **10–117** be expressed to take effect forthwith or to be of a certain minimum duration.[2] It is generally unnecessary to require the notice to specify

---

[92] Although it at first sight appears unlikely that the expelling partners would ever wish to adopt such an argument, one need only suppose the case where an outgoing partner is entitled to a notional goodwill payment which far exceeds his entitlement on a general dissolution (when the goodwill may be valueless).

[93] The expulsion would represent a clear affirmation of the contract. See also *supra*, para. 10–107.

[94] See for example, *Russell v. Russell* (1880) 14 Ch.D. 471; *Barnes v. Youngs* [1898] 1 Ch. 414; *Clifford v. Timms* [1908] A.C. 12; *Bellerby v. Heyworth* [1910] A.C. 377; *Tattersall v. Sladen* [1928] Ch. 318.

[95] But see *Peyton v. Mindham* [1973] 1 W.L.R. 8 (which was, however a quasi-expulsion case, since a restriction on competition was imposed on the recipient of the dissolution notice). Such powers are, perhaps, more common in corporate partnership agreements: see *infra*, para. 11–14. *Cf.* the observations of Browne-Wilkinson V.-C. in *Walters v. Bingham* [1988] 1 F.T.L.R. 260, 268, *supra*, para. 10–21.

[96] The partners must appreciate that such a power will effectively penalise all the partners for the misconduct of one.

[97] See for example, *Smith v. Mules* (1852) 9 Hare 556; *Steuart v. Gladstone* (1879) 10 Ch.D. 626; *Green v. Howell* [1910] 1 Ch. 495.

[98] See *Peyton v. Mindham* [1973] 1 W.L.R. 8.

[99] See *supra*, para. 10–98.

[1] See *Russell v. Russell* (1880) 14 Ch.D. 471.

[2] If the grounds include misconduct, it is usually desirable to ensure that a dissolution can be brought about as quickly as possible.

the actual complaint which has caused it to be served, although it should in practice contain a reference to the relevant ground set out in the agreement.[3]

Construction and exercise of powers to dissolve

10–118   Since a true power to dissolve is not of an expropriatory nature,[4] it should not be construed in the same strict manner as a power of expulsion; however, this does not mean that exact compliance with the procedure laid down in the agreement is unnecessary.[5]

Although *Russell v. Russell*[6] is sometimes cited as authority for the proposition that all powers of dissolution can be exercised capriciously, the actual decision turned on the particular nature of the power and on the fact that there were only two partners. It is submitted that, in cases of the type under consideration, the normal duty of good faith will apply so that a notice served for an improper purpose would not be upheld;[7] equally, it is difficult to see how the power could ever be truly exercised for the benefit of the partnership as a whole.

The current editor is of the view that there is, in general, no obligation to give the recipient of a dissolution notice an opportunity for explanation prior to its service.[8]

A valid notice, once given, cannot be withdrawn otherwise than with the consent of *all* the partners.[9] However, it might, perhaps, be superseded by a subsequent notice which specifies an earlier dissolution date.[10]

Waiver of right to dissolve

10–119   Lord Lindley observed that the power conferred by a clause of this type:

   "... may be waived by mutual consent; and even if not waived, advantage cannot be taken of it to dissolve the partnership on the ground of the commission of any forbidden act, after the lapse of

---

[3] See *supra*, para. 10–97.

[4] *i.e.* the partner upon whom the notice is served is entitled to precisely the same rights in the winding up as each of his co-partners.

[5] See, nevertheless, *supra*, para. 10–101.

[6] (1880) 14 Ch.D. 471. The power was exercisable by one of the two partners if "the business ... shall not be conducted or managed, or the results thereof shall not be to the satisfaction" of that partner.

[7] See *infra*, para. 24–13.

[8] (1880) *Green v. Howell* [1910] 1 Ch. 495; but see also, *supra*, paras. 10–102, 10–103.

[9] *Jones v. Lloyd* (1874) L.R. 18 Eq. 265. *Cf. Finch v. Oake* [1896] 1 Ch. 409; *Glossop v. Glossop* [1907] 2 Ch. 370.

[10] See *infra*, para. 24–16.

any considerable time since such act came to the knowledge of the partner seeking to avail himself of it."[11]

Invalid dissolution notice

The current editor considers that the position will, in principle, be **10–120** no different from that where there is a general power to dissolve,[12] although a right to damages might conceivably be available.[13]

S. Acquisition of Outgoing Partner's Share, etc.[14]

If it is intended that the partnership should continue notwithstanding **10–121** the death, bankruptcy,[15] retirement[16] or expulsion[17] of a partner, the agreement must contain provision for the continuing or surviving partners to acquire the outgoing partner's share. If the agreement is silent on the point, the outgoing partner (or his personal representatives) will be in a position to argue that the affairs of the partnership should be wound up, its assets sold and the proceeds applied in the manner specified in the Partnership Act 1890.[18] Although it might be possible to defeat such an argument, thus forcing the outgoing partner to accept the assessed value of his share,[19] this could not be guaranteed; moreover, an immediate obligation to pay out that assessed value might be financially ruinous to the remaining partners if, as will often be the case, goodwill and work in progress are valued as a high figure but no liquid funds or readily realisable assets are available.[20]

(a) Manner of Acquisition

There are, in essence, two ways in which continuing or surviving **10–122** partners can acquire an outgoing partner's share, *i.e.* pursuant to an

---

[11] Lord Lindley cited *Anderson v. Anderson* (1857) 25 Beav. 190 and went on to point out that this decision "must not be considered as an authority for the doctrine that the Court will not hold partners to their articles. The notice to dissolve in that case was given six months after the commission of the act complained of, and not on account of such act, but in consequence of other disputes." It is, however, doubtful whether the judgment of Sir John Romilly M.R. supports the proposition in the text.

[12] See *supra*, para. 10–114.

[13] See *supra*, para. 10–106.

[14] See the *Encyclopedia of Professional Partnerships*, Precedent 1, cl. 22, Precedent 2, Arts. 6.00 *et seq.*

[15] See *supra*, para. 10–33.

[16] See *supra*, paras. 10–33, 10–88 *et seq.*

[17] See *supra*, paras. 10–33, 10–95 *et seq.*

[18] See *infra*, paras. 19–10 *et seq.*, 19–28 *et seq.*, 23–179 *et seq.*, 25–39 *et seq.* It follows that the outgoing partner will be entitled to share in any increase in the capital value of the partnership assets prior to the date of sale: *Barclays Bank Trust Co. Ltd. v. Bluff* [1982] Ch. 172, approved in *Chandroutie v. Gajadhar* [1987] A.C. 147 (P.C.).

[19] See *Sobell v. Boston* [1985] 1 W.L.R. 1587. Note also that the court has jurisdiction to order one partner to sell his share to his co-partners (*Syers v. Syers* (1876) 1 App.Cas. 174), but this is rarely exercised. See further, *infra*, para. 23–182. The effect of the Partnership Act 1890, s.43 is, to say the least obscure: see *infra*, paras. 19–10 *et seq.*, 23–33, 26–04.

[20] If realisable assets are available, any capital gains could be rolled over into the acquisition of the outgoing partner's share: see *infra*, para. 35–07.

option or a so-called "automatic accruer." By the latter expression is
meant a provision which states that the share of an outgoing partner
will automatically vest in the remaining partners on the date that he
ceases to be a member of the partnership, whether by reason of his
death or otherwise.[21] In either case, the agreement will, of course,
establish the financial entitlement of the outgoing partner in respect
of his share, whether expressed in terms of an option price or the
sum payable on or in consideration of the accruer.

It will, perhaps, be self evident that an option will permit the
remaining partners to assess the viability of the partnership business,
having regard to the price which they must pay to the outgoing
partner, *before* deciding whether to acquire his share, whilst an
accruer will deprive them of that right. Regrettably, in some cases, as
where a high notional value has been placed on goodwill,[22] the effect
of an accruer can be financially devastating, particularly if more than
one partner chooses to retire at the same time;[23] on the other hand,
an inadvertent failure to exercise an option may be equally damaging
to the remaining partners' interests given that it will normally lead to
a general dissolution.[24]

10–123   It will be for consideration in each case whether to follow the
option or accruer route: in practice, the decision will often be
dictated by the nature of the partnership business[25] and the basis on
which the outgoing partner is to be paid out.[26]

The mere fact that one or more of the surviving partners are the
sole or only executors and trustees of a deceased partner's will does
not in any way preclude them from exercising their right to acquire
his share in the manner contemplated by the agreement.[27]

10–124   *Bankruptcy of partner*:   It was held in *Wilson v. Greenwood*[28] that
an option to acquire an outgoing partner's share in the event of his
bankruptcy, which was introduced by means of a deed entered into
some years after the commencement of the partnership but only a

---

[21] Note that, in drafting such a provision, care should be taken not to phrase it in terms of a
purchase of the share, so as to minimise (even if not to eliminate) the risk that it will be construed
as a "buy and sell agreement" for the purposes of inheritance tax: see *infra*, para. 36–20.
[22] See *infra*, paras. 10–131, 10–175 *et seq.*
[23] See also *supra*, para. 10–89.
[24] See *infra*, paras. 10–126, 10–221. It is, of course, open to the partners to negotiate terms to
avoid this result, but this will usually involve the outgoing partner seeking some form of financial
"sweetener."
[25] Most professional firms adopt automatic accruer provisions, although the current editor has
encountered a number of instances where this has caused severe financial hardship to the
continuing partners. Note, however, the possible inheritance tax implications: see *supra*,
para. 10–122, n. 21 and *infra* para. 36–20.
[26] See *infra*, paras. 10–128 *et seq.*
[27] *Vyse v. Foster* (1874) L.R. 7 H.L. 318; *Hordern v. Hordern* [1910] A.C. 465.
[28] (1818) 1 Swan. 471.

few months before one partner actually went bankrupt, was void as a fraud on the then bankruptcy laws.[29] This prompted Lord Lindley to write:

"*Wilson v. Greenwood* throws considerable doubt on the validity, in the event of bankruptcy, of an agreement that the share of a bankrupt partner shall be taken at a valuation by his co-partners."

However, this cautious view was seemingly not borne out by subsequent case law,[30] so that, in the 15th edition of this work, it was observed:

"Notwithstanding the case of *Wilson v. Greenwood* it would appear that a clause in the articles of partnership that the share of a bankrupt partner shall be taken at a valuation by his co-partners is valid if entered into bona fide."

The current editor believes that, under the current insolvency **10–125** legislation, the position is as follows:

1. A bona fide agreement providing for the acquisition of a bankrupt partner's share, whether pursuant to an option or an automatic accruer, will *per se* be valid provided that the continuing partners are required to pay the full value of the share.[31]

2. A bona fide agreement which provides for the acquisition of a bankrupt partner's share at *less* than its full value might conceivably be attacked as a preference[32] or, perhaps, as a general fraud on the insolvency laws,[33] but not as a transaction at an undervalue.[34]

---

[29] See also *Whitmore v. Mason* (1861) 2 J. & H. 204.

[30] See *Borland's Trustee v. Steel Bros. & Co. Ltd.* [1901] 1 Ch. 279 (a decision involving a company); *cf. Collins v. Barker* [1893] 1 Ch. 578.

[31] *Borland's Trustee v. Steel Bros. & Co. Ltd., supra.*

[32] Insolvency Act 1986, s.340. It would seem that prospective partners who are unrelated to each other will not fall to be treated as "associates," so that the agreement can only be treated as a preference if a partner is adjudicated bankrupt within six months, rather than two years: *ibid.* ss.341(1)(b), (c), 435(3). *Sed quaere.*

[33] This possibility was clearly contemplated by Stirling J. in *Borland's Trustee v. Steel Bros. & Co. Ltd.* [1901] 1 Ch. 279, 292. Although it might be thought questionable to what extent such an argument can be maintained in the face of the detailed restrictions on preferences, etc. contained in the Insolvency Act 1986, the availability of a separate common law remedy has been accepted in the case of a limited company in Scotland: see *Bank of Scotland, Petitioners*, 1988 S.L.T. 282 (O.H.)

[34] On the assumption that the agreement is bona fide and, thus, not tainted with any improper motive, each partner will, almost by definition, provide consideration of broadly equal value on entering into the partnership: see the Insolvency Act 1986, s.339(3)(c); also *ibid.* s.423(1)(c). Note that it is not enough to prove that a transaction is commercially sensible in order to escape it being treated as at an undervalue: *Arbuthnot Leasing International Ltd. v. Havelet Leasing Ltd. (No. 2)* [1990] BCC 636.

3. If the agreement cannot be attacked in the above ways, it will be binding on the bankrupt partner's trustee.[35]

4. Since the exercise of an option involves a disposition of the bankrupt partner's share, the consent of the court will seemingly be required if the date of exercise falls between the presentation of the bankruptcy petition and the date on which his estate vests in his trustee.[36] On the other hand, it is submitted that the operation of an automatic accruer will not, on a true analysis, involve any such disposition.[37]

The position will, in essence, be the same in the case of the insolvency of a corporate partner.[38]

(b) Option to Acquire Outgoing Partner's Share

Mechanics

10–126   An option to acquire a partnership share does not differ intrinsically from any other option, and will require the remaining partners to exercise their rights within a certain period prior to or following the date on which the outgoing partner ceases to be a member of the firm. In the case of expulsion or compulsory retirement, it is sometimes provided that the option must be exercised (if at all) in the expulsion or retirement notice, which is not unreasonable. For the avoidance of doubt, the agreement should also record the fact that, if the option is *not* exercised, the partnership will be placed in general dissolution.[39]

The agreement should in general require the option notice to be in writing for evidential purposes, even if this is not otherwise necessary.[40]

Perpetuity: Although the point is not entirely free from doubt, it is submitted that such an option will not be subject to a 21 year perpetuity period even where the partnership assets comprise land.[41]

---

[35] *Borland's Trustee v. Steel Bros. & Co. Ltd.* [1901] 1 Ch. 279.

[36] Insolvency Act 1986, s.284. See also *infra*, para. 27–37.

[37] See further *infra*, paras. 27–72, 35–19.

[38] See the Insolvency Act 1986, ss.127 (avoidance of dispositions), 238–240 (transactions at an undervalue and preferences), 423.

[39] See the *Encyclopedia of Professional Partnerships*, Precedent 1, cl. 24.

[40] The option notice need not be in writing even where the partnership assets include land, notwithstanding the requirements of the Law of Property (Miscellaneous Provisions) Act 1989, s.2 (*supra*, para. 7–02): see *Spiro v. Glencrown Properties Ltd.* [1991] Ch. 537. Equally, there is little to be said in favour of stipulating for an oral notice. Note that, unless it formed part of the original partnership terms (as to which see, *supra*, paras. 7–02 *et seq.*), the *grant* of the option would have to satisfy the s.2 requirements in so far as it relates to an interest in land.

[41] See *supra* n. 35 and see the Perpetuities and Accumulations Act 1964, s.9(2), which applies to an option to acquire "any interest in land." *Semble*, the interest of an outgoing partner is not such an interest: Partnership Act 1890, ss.22, 43; also *infra*, paras. 19–10 *et seq.*

Exercise

If the continuing or surviving partners' rights under the option are **10–127**
to be exercised within a given period, a purported exercise after the
expiration of that period will not be valid, unless the parties have
themselves agreed to its extension.[42] As Lord Lindley put it when
dealing with rights of pre-emption[43]:

"Courts will not extend the time on the ground that it was
accidentally allowed to slip by."[44]

The fact that the sole surviving partner was unable to serve the notice
in due time by reason of mental disorder will not affect the
position.[45]

If no time for the exercise of the option is specified in the
agreement, it must be exercised within a reasonable time.[46]

A notice required to be given to the personal representatives of a
deceased partner within a certain period after his death will be valid
if served on his executors before they have obtained a grant of
probate.[47]

(c) Financial Entitlement of Outgoing Partner

There are numerous bases on which the financial entitlement of an **10–128**
outgoing partner can be ascertained, but that entitlement will
normally be made up of the following components:

(*a*) his profit share up to the date he ceased to be a partner,
adjusted by reference to his drawings;[48]

---

[42] The period may be extended by express agreement (see *Hill v. Hill* [1947] Ch. 231) or by
conduct (see *Bruner v. Moore* [1904] 1 Ch. 305; *Morrell v. Studd and Millington* [1913] 2 Ch. 648).
However, it may be necessary for the agreement to be reduced to writing in order to satisfy the
requirements of the Law of Property (Miscellaneous Provisions) Act 1989, s.2: *Hill v. Hill, supra.*

[43] Such rights were once common but are not now encountered: see *supra*, paras. 10–91, 10–92.

[44] Lord Lindley cited *Holland v. King* (1848) 6 C.B. 727; *Brooke v. Garrod* (1857) 2 De G. & J.
62; *Lord Ranelagh v. Melton* (1864) 2 Dr. & Sm. 278. And see generally, *United Scientific Holdings
Ltd. v. Burnley Borough Council* [1978] A.C. 904, 928 (*per* Lord Diplock), 945 (*per* Lord Simon).

[45] See *Dibbins v. Dibbins* [1896] 2 Ch. 348; also *Rowlands v. Evans* (1861) 30 Beav. 302.

[46] See the decisions of the Australian courts in *Ballas v. Theophilos* (*No. 2*) (1957) 31 A.L.J.R.
917 and *Oliver v. Oliver* (1958) 32 A.L.J.R. 198. *Cf. Re Longlands Farm* [1968] 3 All E.R. 552.

[47] *Kelsey v. Kelsey* (1922) 91 L.J.Ch. 382. And note also *Biles v. Caesar* [1957] 1 W.L.R. 156.

[48] See generally, *supra*, paras. 10–65 *et seq*. It appears once to have been common for agreements
to provide for the payment of interest in lieu of a share of profits from the date of the last signed
annual accounts down to the date on which the outgoing partner left the partnership: see *Pettyt v.
Janeson* (1819) 6 Madd. 146 and other cases of that class, *infra*, paras. 10–136 *et seq*. This would
now be unusual: an outgoing partner should expect to receive either his *actual* profit entitlement up
to the relevant date or an apportioned part of his notional profit entitlement for the then current
accounting year (assuming that he does not leave at a year end).

(*b*) the balance on his capital account;[49]

(*c*) the balance on his current account;[50]

(*d*) his entitlement in respect of surplus assets.[51]

Subject to any adjustments in respect of sums due from the outgoing partner to the firm, *e.g.* in respect of overdrawings, there will usually be little question of his entitlement to components (*a*) to (*c*) and the real question will centre on component (*d*)).

It will also be for consideration whether his entitlement is to be computed by reference to the ordinary partnership accounts or to a special set of accounts prepared as at the date of his departure,[52] which may itself depend on whether that date coincides with the firm's normal accounting date[53] and whether all outgoing partners are to be treated in the same way.[54]

Outgoing partner's share of surplus assets

10–129   For this purpose, the surplus assets comprise those assets which do not appear in the firm's balance sheet, *e.g.* goodwill, and the amount by which the true value of those assets which *do* appear therein exceed their balance sheet value.[55] In some firms, the partners will at the outset decide that the surplus assets should benefit the partners for the time being, so that an outgoing partner will receive no payment on giving up his share of those assets,[56] but in others this will be wholly inappropriate.

There are, in fact, four basic approaches to this problem, which may, depending on the nature of the assets, be combined in a single agreement.

---

[49] See *supra*, paras. 10–47 *et seq.*

[50] This balance will represent profits undrawn in previous accounting periods: see *infra*, para. 17–07.

[51] See *infra*, paras. 10–129 *et seq.*

[52] See *infra*, paras. 10–133 *et seq.*

[53] See *supra*, paras. 10–61, 10–88. For obvious reasons, this will not usually be the case where a partner dies or is expelled.

[54] Thus, it is not uncommon to find that an expelled partner is treated less generously than, say, a retiring partner, *e.g.* by being deprived of any payment for goodwill. This will not, in general, be regarded as a penalty: see *C.R.A. Ltd. v. N.Z. Goldfields Investments* [1989] V.R. 873 (an analogous Australian decision concerning joint venturers). Care must, however, be taken to avoid any form of unlawful sexual or racial discrimination: see the Sex Discrimination Act 1975, ss.11(4)(a), 82(1A) (as respectively amended and inserted by the Sex Discrimination Act 1986, ss.2(2), (3)); Race Relations Act 1976, s.10(1). In the latter case only, discrimination is permissible if the firm comprises less than six partners. Note also the possible insolvency implications: see *supra*, paras. 10–124, 10–125.

[55] Surplus assets are, in this context, synonymous with capital profits: see *supra*, para. 10–66 and *infra*, para. 17–05. Note also that assets appearing in the firm's balance sheet may well appear at a written down value rather than their original acquisition cost.

[56] This is frequently the case in professional firms, at least so far as concerns goodwill and work in progress. Equally, in *Robertson v. Brent* [1972] N.Z.L.R. 406, it was held that work in progress does not exist as an asset on a partner's retirement from a solicitors' firm and cannot be treated as such in the absence of an *express* agreement. *Semble*, this cannot be correct.

(1) *Fixed Value*

Perhaps the simplest way of tackling the problem of surplus assets is **10–130** for the outgoing partner's entitlement to be determined by reference to a predetermined notional value,[57] but this is not to be commended since no account can be taken of the numerous variable factors which may affect the true value of those assets.

(2) *Profit Related Value*

Goodwill

The valuation of goodwill is extremely problematic[58] and is **10–131** frequently based on a multiple of the average net profits of the firm over a given period of between three and five years. There is no reason in principle why the calculation should not be based on a single year's net profit, but this is unlikely to produce a reliable figure.

Less common is a payment for goodwill which takes the form of an income provision funded out of the profits of the continuing firm since, quite apart from the tax implications,[59] this would place an undue burden on the continuing partners, both in terms of a reduction in their profit shares and an overall loss of flexibility.[60] Were this course, nevertheless, to be adopted, the agreement should establish whether the outgoing partner's entitlement is to abate in the event of the profits proving insufficient[61] and, if the outgoing partner's entitlement is computed by reference to the amount of those profits, it should specify how they are to be determined, *e.g.* what deductions may properly be made.[62]

Other assets

A profit based valuation or payment would be wholly inappropriate **10–132** in the case of assets other than goodwill, unless they are of such insignificant value that the partners are prepared to agree some notional addition to the average profit figure and/or multiplier or to the continuing profit share (as the case may be).

---

[57] See for example, *Essex v. Essex* (1855) 20 Beav. 442; *Wade v. Jenkins* (1860) 2 Giff. 509. See also *infra*, para. 10–177 n. 17.

[58] See further, *infra*, paras. 10–175 *et seq.*

[59] Thus, the payments would be taxable as income in the outgoing partner's hands, whilst the capital value of the right to those payments would also be subject to a charge to capital gains tax. See further, *infra*, paras. 34–93 *et seq.*, 35–24 *et seq.* (where the position is considered in relation to partnership annuities paid in consideration of goodwill).

[60] See *infra*, paras. 10–145 *et seq.*

[61] Equally, if an abatement is applied, it must be determined whether the outgoing partner is to be entitled to recover the shortfall in subsequent year(s).

[62] *e.g.* it might be provided that the continuing partners are to have a minimum "salary" entitlement before any payment is made to the outgoing partner: *Watson v. Haggitt* [1928] A.C. 127.

(3) *Book or Balance Sheet Value*

Reliance on last signed balance sheet

10–133   Agreements frequently provide for the entitlement of an outgoing
partner to be determined by reference to the last annual accounts
approved and signed by the partners prior to the date on which he
ceased to be a member of the firm. If the agreement establishes the
date to which and the basis on which such accounts are to be
prepared,[63] and the partners adhere to such terms, significant
problems are unlikely to arise, as Lord Lindley explained:

> "If ... the accounts have been regularly taken and signed, or
> regularly taken but not signed,[64] so that the shares of the partners
> appear from the accounts as intended, all parties must abide by the
> stipulation,[65] although difficulties may arise as to the true
> construction of the articles."[66]

10–134   The decision in *Coventry v. Barclay*[67] illustrates the latter point.
There the partners had, in preparing their accounts, habitually placed
a nominal value on its capital assets and carried part of their profits
to a reserve fund to meet contingent losses. Accounts were made up
on this basis shortly before the death of a partner and their contents
were duly approved (albeit not signed) by him. It was held that the
manner in which the partners had valued the capital assets was
consistent with the terms of the agreement, so that the deceased
partner's executors were bound thereby. On the other hand, whilst
the executors were not in a position to question the practice of taking
profits to the reserve fund, there was nothing in the agreement which
operated to deprive them of the deceased's share of any ultimate
balance remaining once the relevant losses had been met.

The position naturally becomes more complex where the partners
have not drawn up annual accounts on a regular basis or have drawn
them up otherwise than in accordance with the agreement.

10–135   *Accounts not drawn up*: If accounts are not drawn up as
contemplated by the agreement, the court will ensure that neither the
outgoing partner nor the continuing partners are unfairly prejudiced,
as Lord Lindley explained:

---

[63] See *supra*, paras. 10–61 *et seq.*
[64] See *Coventry v. Barclay* (1863) 3 De G.J. & S. 320; *Ex p. Barber* (1870) L.R. 5 Ch.App. 687.
[65] *Gainsborough v. Stork* (1740) Barn. 312; *King v. Chuck* (1853) 17 Beav. 325.
[66] *e.g.* see *Blisset v. Daniel* (1853) 10 Hare 493, where a provision that a share should be valued
"as it stood" on a certain date meant as it stood in the partnership books: *ibid.* p. 511. See also
Browning v. Browning (1862) 31 Beav. 316; *Ex p. Barber* (1870) L.R. 5 Ch.App. 687; *Steuart v.
Gladstone* (1878) 10 Ch.D. 626; *Ewing v. Ewing* (1882) 8 App.Cas. 822. *Cf. infra*, para. 25–39.
[67] (1863) 3 De G.J. & S. 320.

"But if, as frequently happens,[68] the accounts intended to be taken and signed have not been taken, or have been taken irregularly, so that the last-signed account is not so late a one as is contemplated by the articles, in such a case the account must be made up to the latest date at which it ought to have been made up, regard being had to the articles and the practice of the partners; and the share of the outgoing or deceased partner must be taken at its value, as the same appears by the account so taken."

Thus, in *Pettyt v. Janeson*,[69] the agreement provided that accounts **10–136** should be settled on March 25 in each year and that the entitlement of a deceased partner's estate should be determined by reference to the last account so settled. For an initial period, accounts were duly settled on March 25 but subsequently came to be settled on a very irregular basis. A partner died in February 1813 but the last account had been settled on November 5, 1811. The court accepted that the partners had agreed to change their accounting date but, in effect, ordered that an account should be settled as at November 5, 1812 (*i.e.* the accounting date prior to the deceased's death) and the executors' entitlement determined accordingly.[70]

The same principle was applied in *Simmons v. Leonard*,[71] where no accounts had ever been drawn up by the partners. However, in the particular circumstances, Wigram V.-C. treated the accounting date specified in the agreement as of little significance[72] and directed the account to be prepared not as at that date but as at the date of the partner's death.

Again, in *Lawes v. Lawes*[73] the agreement contained provision for the preparation of half-yearly accounts and for the share of a deceased partner to be taken at the value shown in the last such account. In fact, accounts were prepared on an annual basis. It was held, following a partner's death, that a half yearly account would have to be prepared and that his share could not be taken at the value shown in the last *annual* account.

In *Hunter v. Dowling*[74] the agreement provided for accounts to be **10–137** prepared on March 31 in each year but, in practice, this was usually

---

[68] Instances of firms failing to draw up accounts are, perhaps, now less frequent than in Lord Lindley's day, although it is by no means uncommon (despite pressure from the Inland Revenue).

[69] (1819) 6 Madd. 146.

[70] See the analysis of this decision in *Hunter v. Dowling* [1893] 3 Ch. 212, 216–217, *per* Bowen L.J.

[71] (1844) 3 Hare 581.

[72] The relevant clause of the agreement required accounts to be drawn up on a certain date in each year "or on such other day in any partnership year as should be most convenient, and agreed upon by all the partners."

[73] (1881) 9 Ch.D. 98.

[74] [1893] 1 Ch. 391, affirmed [1893] 3 Ch. 212. The defendant's argument that there was no time to prepare the March 1891 account before April 10 was rejected: but *cf.* [1893] 3 Ch. 214–215 (*per* Bowen L.J.) and *ibid.* 219–220 (*per* Kay L.J.). As to the subsequent proceedings, see [1895] 2 Ch. 223.

delayed until the end of April (although the March 31 accounting
date was adhered to). The accounts for the year ended March 31,
1890 were duly agreed and signed, but did not ascribe any value to
certain leasehold premises which had recently been acquired by the
firm, although other premises were valued. A partner died on April
10, 1891, before the accounts for the year ended March 31, 1891 had
been prepared. It was held that the deceased partner's share should
be determined by reference to those accounts when completed and
that the leaseholds omitted from the previous account should be
shown therein at their 1891 values.[75]

Lord Lindley remarked of the earlier decisions:

"These cases not only afford good illustrations of the rule that in
construing partnership articles regard must be had to the conduct
of the partners,[76] even where a circumstance has arisen of which
the partners had no previous experience,[77] but they also show that
this rule will not be applied unfairly ...".

10–138   *Accounts not reflecting terms agreed*: If the accounts have been
duly drawn up each year, but in a manner which was not
contemplated by the agreement, those accounts may not be definitive
when determining an outgoing partner's entitlement.

Thus, in *Cruickshank v. Sutherland*[78] the agreement provided that,
on April 30 in each year, a full and general account was to be made
of the partnership dealings for the preceding year, and of its
property, credits and liabilities, and that the share of a deceased
partner was to be determined by reference to the accounts prepared
up to April 30 next after the date of his death. One partner died.
Whilst the partnership was continuing, the accounts had, with his
approval, consistently shown its assets at book value. However, it was
clear that this did not accord with the requirements of the agreement
and, on that basis, it was held that the executors of the deceased
partner were not bound to accept the book values of the assets, but
were entitled to have them properly valued.

To the same effect is the Scottish case of *Noble v. Noble*[79] where,
from 1947 to 1963, the value of the partnership farm had been
entered in the balance sheet at £8,000. The Court of Session held
that, notwithstanding this practice, one partner was entitled to insist

---

[75] This emphasises the need for the agreement to establish whether the contents of the last signed
balance sheet are to be adjusted to take account of subsequent acquisitions or disposals of assets.
[76] See now the Partnership Act 1890, s.19, *supra*, paras. 10–10 *et seq.*
[77] See also *Jackson v. Sedgwick* (1818) 1 Swan. 460; *Coventry v. Barclay* (1863) 3 De G.J. & S.
320, *supra*, para. 10–134; *Ex p. Barber* (1870) L.R. 5 Ch.App. 687.
[78] (1922) 92 L.J.Ch. 136. The partnership had, in fact, only lasted from 1914 to 1917, and for two
years the deceased had been too ill to attend to the business. Note also *Wade v. Jenkins* (1860) 2
Giff. 509.
[79] 1965 S.L.T. 415 (Ct. of Sess.); also *Shaw v. Shaw*, 1968 S.L.T. (Notes) 94; *Clark v. Watson*,
1982 S.L.T. 450 (O.H.); *cf. Thom's Executrix v. Russel & Aitken*, 1983 S.L.T. 335 (O.H.).

on the farm being entered in the balance sheet at its real value, even though the partnership was continuing.

Special balance sheet to be drawn up

It will, perhaps, be apparent from the foregoing that, in cases **10–139** where the entitlement of an outgoing partner is to be determined by reference to a special set of accounts drawn up as at the date of his departure, all the assets should properly be included therein at full market value, unless the agreement provides otherwise.[80] The fact that goodwill and work in progress have been omitted from the firm's annual accounts will, of itself, be irrelevant.[81]

Where this is not the partners' intention, the agreement should clearly state the basis on which the accounts are to be prepared, even if this merely takes the form of a requirement that the partners should adhere to the same accounting principles and practices as are adopted when drawing up normal annual accounts.[82]

(4) Revaluation of Assets

Perhaps the most common (and, in many ways, the fairest) approach **10–140** is to revalue the partnership assets and to credit the outgoing partner with his full share of any increase over their book value, even though this will inevitably affect the financial burden on the remaining partners. The natural corollary is, of course, that the outgoing partner will bear a share of any *decrease* in the value of those assets.

Where this approach is adopted, the agreement should identify which assets are to be revalued,[83] the basis of valuation[84] and the manner in which it is to be carried out.[85] It is clear from the landmark decision in *Sudbrook Trading Estate Ltd. v. Eggleton*[86]

---

[80] See for example, *Clark v. Watson, supra.*

[81] Note, however, the decision in *Robertson v. Brent* [1972] N.Z.L.R. 406, where it was held that the work in progress of a solicitors' firm does not, in the absence of an express agreement, exist as an asset on a partner's retirement and therefore cannot be ascribed any value. The current editor considers that this decision cannot be correct in principle.

[82] Such a formula was adopted in *Smith v. Gale* [1974] 1 W.L.R. 9.

[83] See for example, *Hordern v. Hordern* [1910] A.C. 465. Particular attention should be directed to the treatment of goodwill (as in that case) and work in progress, which are notoriously contentious items. See further, as to the valuation of goodwill, *infra*, paras. 10–175 *et seq.* and, as to work in progress, *supra* para. 10–139, n. 81.

[84] Market value will usually be the most appropriate, although this may on occasion be discounted to take account of factors such as the costs of realisation, taxation, etc. The expression "just valuation" is not to be commended but is likely to be equated with market value: see *Hunter v. Dowling* [1893] 1 Ch. 391. As to the methods of valuing work in progress, see *infra*, para. 34–36, but see also para. 10–13a, n. 81.

[85] *i.e.* by a single valuer acting as an expert or an arbitrator, by two valuers (one representing each side) with or without an umpire, by arbitration, etc.

[86] [1983] A.C. 444. See also *Re Malpass* [1985] Ch. 42 (which concerned a testamentary option). The court will have no jurisdiction if the agreed machinery has not broken down: *Northern Regional Health Authority v. Crouch Construction Co. Ltd.* [1984] Q.B. 644. Note also *Miller v. Lakefield Estates Ltd.* [1989] 19 E.G. 67.

that, if no valuation machinery is specified or the chosen machinery breaks down, the court will normally itself supply the valuation unless, in the latter case, the particular machinery adopted can be regarded as an essential term of the agreement, *e.g.* valuation by a named individual.[87] Indeed, this was always the position in the case of partnership agreements, as Lord Lindley made clear:

"... where persons enter into partnership upon certain terms, one of which is, that on a dissolution one partner shall take the share of another at a valuation,[88] the Court will, on a dissolution under the articles, enforce such a stipulation, and if necessary itself ascertain the value of the share."[89]

10–141   A valuation of the assets carried out by an agreed expert valuer must, if honestly made, be accepted and cannot subsequently be attacked on the grounds that higher or lower valuations have been obtained elsewhere.[90] The remedy of a dissatisfied partner (or former partner) in such a case is solely against the valuer, assuming that negligence can be proved.[91]

A variation in the agreed valuation procedure may, where appropriate, be agreed to by a deceased partner's executors even before probate is obtained.[92]

---

[87] [1983] A.C. 483–484, *per* Lord Fraser.

[88] The expression "taking a share at a valuation" is commonly encountered in the older cases, but is not much used today. The transaction is, of course, the same as that currently under consideration.

[89] *Dinham v. Bradford* (1869) L.R. 5 Ch.App. 519; also *Smith v. Gale* [1974] 1 W.L.R. 9.

[90] See *Campbell v. Edwards* [1976] 1 W.L.R. 403; *Baber v. Kenwood Manufacturing Co. Ltd.* [1978] 1 Lloyd's Rep. 175; *Jones v. Sherwood Computer Services Plc* [1992] 1 W.L.R. 277; *Nikko Hotels (U.K.) Ltd. v. M.E.P.C. Plc* [1991] 28 E.G. 86. A valuation can clearly be upset if fraud or collusion is proved or if it is not made in accordance with the terms of the agreement, *e.g.* where the wrong property is valued: see, as to the latter possibility, *Jones v. Sherwood Computer Services Plc, supra.* Note that, in *Burgess v. Purchase & Sons (Farms) Ltd.* [1983] Ch. 216, Nourse J. took the view that a speaking valuation (*i.e.* a valuation supported by reasons or calculations) could be upset when it is made on a wholly erroneous basis, but the Court of Appeal has since refused to draw any distinction between speaking and non-speaking valuations: see *Jones v. Sherwood Computer Services Plc, supra*; also *Nikko Hotels (U.K.) Ltd. v. M.E.P.C. Plc. See* also, in this context, *Re Imperial Foods Ltd. Pension Scheme* [1986] 1 W.L.R. 717. Reference should also be made to the earlier cases: *Collier v. Mason* (1858) 25 Beav. 200; *Dean v. Prince* [1953] 1 Ch. 590 and [1954] 1 Ch. 409; *Frank H. Wright (Constructions) Ltd. v. Frodoor Ltd.* [1967] 1 W.L.R. 506; *Smith v. Gale* [1974] 1 W.L.R. 9. It will be for consideration whether the agreement should positively *require* a speaking valuation, although this is in practice somewhat rare. *Cf.* the Arbitration Act 1979, s.1(5), (6).

[91] *Sutcliffe v. Thackrah* [1974] A.C. 727; *Arenson v. Casson Beckman Rutley & Co.* [1977] A.C. 405. The effect of these cases would appear to be that a "mutual" valuer chosen by the parties may be held liable for negligence unless he is, on a true analysis, acting as an arbitrator, *i.e.* in a judicial or quasi-judicial capacity; however, even the immunity of an arbitrator cannot be assured: see *Arenson v. Casson Beckman Rutley & Co. supra*, pp. 431–432 (*per* Lord Kilbrandon), 440 (*per* Lord Salmon) and 442 (*per* Lord Fraser). As to determining the capacity in which a valuer is acting, see also *Palacath Ltd. v. Flanagan* [1985] 2 All E.R. 161; *North Eastern Co-operative Society Ltd. v. Newcastle upon Tyne City Council* (1987) 282 E.G. 1409.

[92] *Kelsey v. Kelsey* (1922) 91 L.J.Ch. 382; and see *Biles v. Caesar* [1957] 1 W.L.R. 156.

Failure to comply with agreed valuation procedure

The mere fact that the continuing or surviving partners have not **10–142** complied with the strict terms of the valuation procedure will not deprive them of their right to acquire the outgoing partner's share.[93]

(d) Payment of Outgoing Partner's Entitlement

The agreement should record the manner in which the outgoing **10–143** partner's entitlement is to be paid out. It is, in practice, not uncommon to find that part, if not the whole amount,[94] is made payable by instalments, thus easing the financial burden on the continuing partners.[95] In such a case, provision for interest on the outstanding balance and for such balance to become immediately due in the event of default is generally included.[96] If any retentions are to be made out of the amount due to the outgoing partner, *e.g.* in respect of taxation[97] or contingent liabilities,[98] this should be provided for since such a right will not normally be implied.

T. ANNUITIES TO OUTGOING PARTNERS, WIDOWS, ETC.[99]

Agreements sometimes provide for the payment of a fixed or profit **10–144** related annuity to an outgoing partner[1] or, if he is dead, to his widow and/or dependants. This device, which was once common, particularly in the professions, has now become something of a rarity, in large measure due to the popularity of the more tax efficient retirement annuity contract and its successor, the personal pension scheme.[2]

Although the Inland Revenue appear to regard most annuities as disguised goodwill payments, at least for the purposes of capital gains tax,[3] in reality this is not always the case.[4]

---

[93] *Hordern v. Hordern* [1910] A.C. 465.

[94] It would be unusual for payment of the outgoing partner's share of profits up to the date of his departure to be delayed much beyond the preparation and approval of the relevant accounts: see *supra*, para. 10–128, n. 48. On the other hand, capital and/or current account balances are more suitable for deferred payment.

[95] This may represent an alternative solution to the problem of multiple retirements: see *supra*, para. 10–89. Equally, it may be a way of penalising an expelled partner.

[96] The agreement should establish at what rate interest is to be paid (usually tied to the base rate of the partnership bankers) and from what date, *i.e.* the date of outgoing or some later date.

[97] It may be that sufficient provision has already been made annually out of profits: see *supra*, para. 10–73.

[98] It is not uncommon to encounter an agreement fixing an outgoing partner with liability for his own negligent or wrongful acts (to the extent that they are not covered by insurance) and requiring a sufficient retention to be made on that account.

[99] See the *Encyclopedia of Professional Partnerships*, Precedent 2, Art. 6.06.

[1] It will usually be considered appropriate to provide that an annuity will not be payable to an *expelled* partner.

[2] See the Income and Corporation Taxes Act 1988, ss.630 *et seq.*

[3] See *infra*, paras. 35–24 *et seq.*

[4] For an unusual example of an annuity conditional on the continuing partner enjoying continued occupation of certain premises, see *Holyland v. De Mendez* (1817) 3 Mer. 184.

Profit related annuities

10–145   It is clear that the receipt of a profit share in the form of an annuity will not, of itself, cause the recipient to be treated as a partner,[5] although an outgoing partner is more at risk than his widow or dependants.[6]

A true profit based annuity will only be payable if profits are actually realised by the continuing business; indeed, Lord Lindley illustrated this proposition with the following (now largely historical) example:

> "... if the surviving partner has an option to pay either an annuity or a share of the profits, and there should be no profits, he will not be bound to pay anything; for, *ex hypothesi*, it is competent for him to elect to pay out of the profits, and his right to make this election in no way depends on their amount."[7]

10–146   *Calculation of profits*:   The relevant profits for the purposes of the annuity will in large measure depend on the terms of the agreement which should identify not only those sources of income or expenditure which are to be left out of account, but also the extent to which the continuing partners can introduce changes, whether to the nature of the business or to the management structure of the firm, which may have an adverse effect on its profitability.[8] It does not follow that, because the partners have habitually been paid salaries as a first charge on profits,[9] those salaries should necessarily be deducted when computing the profits for the purposes of an annuity.[10] Equally, the recipient of the annuity cannot properly argue that the continuing partners are carrying on a new business, so that no account should be taken of the liabilities of the old firm.[11]

It is generally prudent to impose a maximum ceiling on the percentage of the continuing firm's profits which can be taken up by annuitants, since their aggregate entitlement may otherwise threaten the financial viability of the firm.

10–147   *Discontinuance of business*:   Since a discontinuance of the business would defeat the annuitant's rights, the continuing partners are subject to certain implied constraints whilst an annuity is payable, as Lord Lindley explained:

---

[5] See the Partnership Act 1890, s.2(3), *supra*, paras. 5–02, 5–32 *et seq.*
[6] See *ibid.* s.2(3)(c).
[7] *Ex p. Harper* (1857) 1 De G. & J. 180.
[8] Thus, if the firm acquires new premises and takes on additional staff, this will inevitably affect its profits, at least in the short term.
[9] See *supra*, para. 10–67.
[10] See *Watson v. Haggitt* [1928] A.C. 127.
[11] *Ex p. Harper* (1857) 1 De G. & J. 180.

"An agreement to pay an annuity out of profits for a certain period usually involves an obligation not wilfully to prevent the earning of profits during that period; if in such a case, therefore, the person who has to pay the annuity wilfully ceases to carry on business before the expiration of that period, he becomes liable to an action for damages."[12]

It is in this area that annuity provisions are at their most contentious. On the one hand, the continuing partners will wish to preserve their freedom to develop the business as they see fit, *e.g.* by mergers, hiving off, etc., without the need to consult the annuitants. On the other hand, the annuitants will be seeking some form of entrenched protection for their rights, along the following lines suggested by Lord Lindley:

". . . it is desirable that the partner continuing the business should covenant not only that he will carry on the business and pay the annuity,[13] but that he will not transfer the business, or take in any fresh partner, without procuring from the transferee or new partner a similar covenant on his part."[14]

It is prima facie impossible to legislate in advance for a merger **10–148** scenario, unless the annuitants' rights are to attach solely to the continuing partners' profit shares in the merged firm, and it is commercially undesirable for annuitants to be involved in potentially sensitive merger negotiations.

Enforcement of annuity provisions

It goes without saying that an outgoing partner will be entitled to **10–149** enforce his right to an annuity under the terms of the agreement, but his widow and/or dependants will be in a more difficult position. On the assumption that the annuitant was not a party to the original

---

[12] See *M'Intyre v. Belcher* (1863) 14 C.B.(N.S.) 654; *Telegraph Dispatch & Intelligence Co. v. McLean* (1873) L.R. 8 Ch.App. 658; and see, generally, *Turner v. Goldsmith* [1891] 1 Q.B. 544; *Ogdens Ltd. v. Nelson* [1905] A.C. 109; *Devonald v. Rosser* [1906] 2 K.B. 728; *Re R. S. Newman Ltd.* [1916] 2 Ch. 309; *Re Rubel Bronze & Metal Co. and Vos* [1918] 1 K.B. 315; *Collier v. Sunday Referee Publishing Co. Ltd.* [1940] 2 K.B. 647. *Cf. Rhodes v. Forwood* (1876) L.R. 1 App.Cas. 256; *Cowasjee Nanabhoy v. Lallbhoy Vullubhoy* (1876) L.R. 3 Ind.App. 200; *Re Railway and Electric Appliances Co.* (1888) 38 Ch.D. 597; *Hamlyn & Co. v. Wood & Co.* [1891] 2 Q.B. 488; *Turner v. Sawdon & Co.* [1901] 2 K.B. 653.

[13] It is in practice rare to see such an obligation framed as a covenant.

[14] It seems clear that a purchaser of the business, with or without notice of such a covenant, would not be bound by it unless the annuity constituted a charge thereon: see *Werderman v. Société Générale d'Electricité* (1881) 19 Ch.D. 246; *British Mutoscope Co. Ltd. v. Homer* [1901] 1 Ch. 671; *Dansk Rekylriffel Syndikat Aktieselskab v. Snell* [1908] 2 Ch. 127; also the criticism on these cases in *Barker v. Stickney* [1919] 1 K.B. 121 and *Bagot Pneumatic Tyre Co. v. Clipper Pneumatic Tyre Co.* [1902] 1 Ch. 146; and see *Law Debenture Trust Group v. Ural Caspian Oil Corp.* [1993] 1 W.L.R. 138.

agreement[15] and is not in a position to enforce the relevant term *qua* the deceased partner's personal representative,[16] it will be necessary to show either that there is a trust of the benefit of the annuity or that its payment is charged on the partnership assets. Neither course is straightforward.

10–150   *Trust of annuity*:   A trust of an annuity will not readily be inferred and must be clearly warranted by the terms of the agreement. Admittedly, the court had little hesitation in drawing the necessary inference in *Re Flavell*,[17] where the agreement, in essence, provided for the surviving partner to pay an annuity to his deceased co-partner's executors or administrators to be applied for the benefit of his widow,[18] but this was an exceptional case. In practice, the strict approach which found voice in *Re Schebsman*[19] will now be followed.

10–151   *Charge on partnership assets*:   If the annuity is charged on the partnership assets (or on the shares of the continuing partners) and it is clear that the annuitant is intended to have a direct right of enforcement, he may be able to rely on section 56(1) of the Law of Property Act 1925.[20] It was a failure to satisfy the latter condition that caused the annuities to be treated as unenforceable in *Re Miller's Agreement*.[21] As an alternative, the annuitant might seek to show that he is entitled to the benefit of the charge by virtue of an express assignment or the combined operation of the partnership agreement and the deceased's will.[22]

It follows that Lord Lindley may have been somewhat optimistic when remarking that:

"... after her husband's death [*the widow*] can enforce payment of the provision intended for her."[23]

---

[15] Although annuitants are, on occasion, made parties to a partnership agreement, this is not to be commended in the interests of long term flexibility.

[16] *Re Flavell* (1883) 25 Ch.D. 89, 99,*per* North J.; *Beswick v. Beswick* [1968] A.C. 58.

[17] (1833) 25 Ch.D. 89. See also *Page v. Cox* (1851) 10 Hare 163.

[18] The relevant clause was in fact redolent of the language of trusts, *viz.* "any yearly sum which may ... become payable to the executors or administrators of a deceased partner to be applied in such manner as such partner shall by deed or will direct for the benefit of his widow and children or child (if any) or any of them, and in default of such direction to be paid to such widow, if living, for her own benefit...".

[19] [1944] Ch. 83; also *Green v. Russell* [1959] 2 Q.B. 226.

[20] This subsection provides "A person may take an immediate or other interest in land or other property, or the benefit of any condition, right of entry, covenant or agreement over or respecting land or other property, although he may not be named as a party to the conveyance or other instrument." *Quaere* the extent of its application outside the sphere of real property: see *Beswick v. Beswick* [1968] A.C. 58; *Southern Water Authority v. Carey* [1985] 2 All E.R. 1077.

[21] [1947] Ch. 615.

[22] See *Att.-Gen v. Gosling* [1892] 1 Q.B. 545.

[23] Lord Lindley cited *Page v. Cox* (1851) 10 Hare 163 and *Re Flavell* (1883) 25 Ch.D. 89, *supra*, para. 10–150.

Taxation of annuities

The payment of annuities can give rise to a number of **10–152**
complications from the point of view of both income and capital
taxation: these are considered later in this work.[24]

U. GOODWILL AND RESTRICTIONS ON COMPETITION[25]

The goodwill of a firm will frequently be one of its most valuable **10–153**
assets, even though it may not feature as such in its annual accounts.
It is accordingly essential that the agreement deals with its ownership
and, where necessary, its protection in the event of one or more
partners leaving the firm.

(a) Meaning of goodwill

Given its intangible nature, it is difficult to produce a precise **10–154**
definition of goodwill,[26] as Lord Lindley explained:

"The term goodwill can hardly be said to have any precise
signification. It is generally used to denote the benefit arising from
connection and reputation; and its value is what can be got for the
chance of being able to keep that connection and improve it. Upon
the sale of an established business its goodwill may have a
marketable value, whether the business is that of a professional
man or of any other person.[27] But it is plain that goodwill has no
meaning except in connection with a continuing business[28]; it may
have no value except in connection with a particular house,[29] and

---

[24] See *infra*, paras. 34–92 *et seq.* (income tax), 35–24 *et seq.* (capital gains tax), 36–34 *et seq.*, 36–52, 36–59 (inheritance tax).

[25] See the *Encyclopedia of Professional Partnerships*, Precedent 1, cl. 22(2)(a), (l); also Precedent 8, cl. 26.

[26] See, generally, *Trego v. Hunt* [1896] A.C. 7, 16–18, *per* Lord Herschell; *Commissioners of Inland Revenue v. Muller & Co.'s Margarine Ltd.* [1901] A.C. 217; *Hill v. Fearis* [1905] 1 Ch. 466, 471, *per* Warrington J.; also *Whiteman Smith Motor Co. v. Chaplin* [1934] 2 K.B. 35; *Simpson v. Charrington & Co.* [1935] A.C. 325; *Clift v. Taylor* [1948] 2 K.B. 394 (all decisions under the Landlord and Tenant Act 1927); *Govt. of Malaysia v. Selangor Pilot Association* [1978] A.C. 337, 357–358, *per* Lord Salmon.

[27] See *Davidson v. Wayman* [1984] 2 N.Z.L.R. 115. Note that goodwill was formerly regarded as property for stamp duty purposes: see *Potter v. Commissioners of Inland Revenue* (1854) 10 Ex. 147; *Benjamin Brooke & Co. Ltd. v. Commissioners of Inland Revenue* [1896] 2 Q.B. 356; *West London Syndicate v. Commissioners of Inland Revenue* [1898] 2 Q.B. 507; *Eastern National Omnibus Co. Ltd. v. Commissioners of Inland Revenue* [1939] 1 K.B. 161; and see also *Commissioners of Inland Revenue v. Muller & Co.'s Margarine Ltd.* [1901] A.C. 217. Now goodwill is wholly outside the scope of stamp duty: see the Finance Act 1991, s.110. As to inheritance tax, see *infra*, paras. 36–05 *et seq.*, 36–27, 36–69.

[28] See *Kingston, Miller & Co. v. Thomas Kingston & Co.* [1912] 1 Ch. 575. See also *Robertson v. Quiddington* (1860) 28 Beav. 529 (which concerned a legacy of goodwill).

[29] This word, in the present context, merely denotes the partnership premises. However, in Scots cases it is used to describe a *partnership* as constituted from time to time.

may be so inseparably connected with it as to pass with it under a will or deed without being specially mentioned.[30] In such a case the goodwill increases the value of the house; but the value of the goodwill of any business to a purchaser depends, in some cases entirely, and in all very much, on the absence of competition on the part of those by whom the business has been previously carried on."

10–155   It is apparent from the above passage that the existence (in terms of marketability) of goodwill is dependent on a number of variable factors, including the nature of the business and the availability of identifiable premises.[31] However, it is possible to go further, particularly in the case of a trading concern, and to analyse goodwill into its component elements. In this connection, reference must inevitably be made to the following classic statement by Scrutton L.J. in *Whiteman Smith Motor Co. v. Chaplin*[32]:

"A division of the elements of goodwill was referred to during the argument and appears in Mr. Merlin's book[33] as 'cat, rat and dog' basis. The cat prefers the old home though the person who has kept the house leaves. The cat represents that part of the customers who continue to go to the old shop, though the old shopkeeper has gone; the probability of their custom may be regarded as an additional value given to the premises by the tenant's trading. The dog represents that part of the customers who follow the person rather than the place; these the tenant may take away with him if he does not go too far. There remains a class of customer who may neither follow the place nor the person, but drift away elsewhere. They are neither a benefit to the landlord nor the tenant, and have been called 'the rat' for no particular reason except to keep the epigram in the animal kingdom. I believe my brother Maugham has introduced the rabbit, but I will leave him to explain the position of the rabbit.[34] It is obvious that the division of customers, into 'cat, rat and dog'

---

[30] See *Chissum v. Dewes* (1828) 5 Russ. 29; *Pile v. Pile* (1876) 3 Ch.D. 36; *Ex p. Punnett* (1880) 16 Ch.D. 266; also *Cooper v. Metropolitan Board of Works* (1883) 25 Ch.D. 472, 479, *per* Cotton L.J. In *Blake v. Shaw* (1860) Johns. 732 and *Re Rhagg* [1938] Ch. 828, a bequest of goodwill carried the premises in which the business was carried on, but such a construction will not readily be adopted: see *Re Betts* [1949] 1 All E.R. 568. See also, as to the severance of goodwill and premises under the old stamp duty law, *West London Syndicate Ltd. v. Commissioners of Inland Revenue* [1898] 2 Q.B. 507. Now duty is only chargeable by reference to that part of the consideration which is apportioned to land, an interest in land or a licence to occupy land: Finance Act 1991, ss. 110, 111. And see *infra*, para. 38–02.
[31] See, for example, *Hill v. Fearis* [1905] 1 Ch. 466; also *infra*, para. 10–158, n. 47.
[32] [1934] 2 K.B. 35, 42. But see *ibid.* 49, *per* Maugham L.J.; also *Mullins v. Wessex Motors Ltd.* [1947] W.N. 316.
[33] *i.e.* Merlin on the Landlord and Tenant Act 1927.
[34] In fact, Maugham L.J. introduced both the rabbit and the mouse, the rabbit being the customers who come simply from propinquity to the premises, and the mouse being the somewhat strange result of a shrinking in the "cat"!

must vary enormously in different cases and different circumstances."

Firm name

An important element of a firm's goodwill may lie in its name.[35] **10–156**
Accordingly, the right to use that name may itself have a substantial
value, although it is doubtful whether it can be acquired independently of any other component of the goodwill.[36] Complications may,
however, arise where the name comprises the names of one or more
of the partners.[37]

Trade and service marks

The partnership trade or service marks may constitute yet another **10–157**
element of a firm's goodwill and, like any other asset, will fall to be
sold in the event of a dissolution.[38] Registered marks are assignable
or transmissible, with or without goodwill, for all or any of the goods
or services in respect of which they are registered.[39] Unregistered
marks may be assigned or transmitted in the same way, provided that
registered marks in respect of the same goods or services are assigned
or transmitted at the same time to the same person.[40]

The firm name may be registrable as a trade or service mark,[41] but
registration will not, of itself, prevent a partner from making bona
fide use of his own or any former partner's name.[42]

(b)   Ownership of Goodwill

Goodwill technically valueless

It will be seen hereafter that relatively few *implied* restrictions are **10–158**
imposed on a vendor of goodwill,[43] so that a valuable partnership

---

[35] See generally, as to existence of goodwill in a name, *Maxim's Ltd. v. Dye* [1977] 1 W.L.R.
1155; *My Kinda Bones Ltd. (T/A Chicago Rib Shack) v. Dr. Pepper's Stove Co. Ltd. (T/A Dr.
Pepper's Manhattan Rib Shack)* [1984] F.S.R. 289; *County Sound plc v. Ocean Sound plc* [1991]
F.S.R. 367.

[36] Although the propriety of such a transfer was clearly accepted in the Scottish case of *Barr v.
Lions*, 1956 S.L.T. 250, it seems unlikely that the point was fully argued: see further *supra*, para.
3–21.

[37] See *infra*, paras. 10–162, 10–163, 10–167 *et seq.*

[38] See *Hall v. Barrows* (1863) 4 De G.J. & S. 150; *Bury v. Bedford* (1864) 4 De G.J. & S. 352.

[39] Trade Marks Act 1938, s.22(1), (2) (as amended, in relation to service marks, by the Trade
Marks (Amendment) Act 1984, Sched. 1, para. 12(2), (3)). But see also *ibid.* s.22(4) (as
substituted, in relation to service marks, by the Trade Marks (Amendment) Act 1984, Sched. 1,
para. 12(5)) and *supra*, para. 3–20.

[40] *Ibid.* s.22(3) (as amended, in relation to service marks, by the Trade Marks (Amendment) Act
1984, Sched. 1, para. 12(4)).

[41] *Ibid.* ss.3, 9 (as amended, in relation to service marks, by the Trade Marks (Amendment) Act
1984, Sched. 1, paras. 1, 6). The name must be "represented in a special or particular manner":
ibid. s.9(1)(a); *Edgar Staines v. Victor La Rosa* [1953] 1 W.L.R. 474. See also *supra*, para. 3–19.

[42] *Ibid.* s.8 (as amended, in relation to service marks, by the Trade Marks (Amendment) Act
1984, Sched. 1, para. 5).

[43] See *infra*, paras. 10–168 *et seq.*

business may, in practical terms, be unsaleable and, thus, worthless to anyone but a former partner who wishes to acquire it.[44] Equally, goodwill may have no value independently of the partnership premises[45] or the firm name.[46]

Lord Lindley pointed out that:

"It is only so far as the goodwill has a saleable value, that it can be regarded as an asset of any partnership ..."[47]

However, the current editor submits that, as a statement of principle, this goes too far, since goodwill, even though unmarketable, clearly exists as an asset and is capable of protection.[48]

Goodwill as a partnership asset

10–159 It has already been seen that a well drawn agreement should establish whether or not goodwill is a partnership asset[49] and should, moreover, provide for the acquisition of an outgoing partner's share (including his share of goodwill) by the continuing partners.[50] Although this may not, in itself, afford adequate protection to the continuing partners, their position will inevitably be less secure if the agreement is silent on the latter point. This can best be illustrated by considering the consequences of:

(1) the dissolution of the partnership;
(2) the death of a partner;
(3) the retirement or expulsion of a partner.

In each case, it will be assumed that the goodwill is an asset of the firm.

---

[44] See *Davies v. Hodgson* (1858) 25 Beav. 177. *Cf. Davidson v. Wayman* [1984] 2 N.Z.L.R. 115.

[45] See for example, *Blake v. Shaw* (1860) Johns. 732; *Re Rhagg* [1938] Ch. 828.

[46] As an example of such a case, Lord Lindley referred to the goodwill of a newspaper, which "attaches to its name, and is scarcely, if at all, dependent on the place of publication."

[47] What Lord Lindley perhaps meant was that unsaleable goodwill must be ignored for accounting purposes: see *Wilson v. Williams* (1892) 29 L.R.Ir. 176, where the goodwill of a stockbroker's business was excluded from the accounts for this reason; *cf. Hill v. Fearis* [1905] 1 Ch. 466, where the goodwill of such a business was held to have a saleable value. Although it was once suggested that the goodwill of a solicitor's practice has no value (see *Arundell v. Bell* (1883) 52 L.J.Ch. 537), this is clearly not the present position: see *Sobell v. Boston* [1975] 1 W.L.R. 1587; *Bridge v. Deacons* [1984] A.C. 705; also *Burchell v. Wilde* [1900] 1 Ch. 551; *Fitch v. Dewes* [1921] 2 A.C. 158, 168, *per* Lord Cave. The goodwill of a medical partnership practising within the National Health Service (the sale of which is prohibited by the National Health Service Act 1977, s.54, Sched. 10), clearly exists as an asset of the firm: *Whitehill v. Bradford* [1952] Ch. 236; *Lyne-Pirkis v. Jones* [1969] 1 W.L.R. 1293; *Kerr v. Morris* [1987] Ch. 90. And see, generally, *Allied Dunbar (Frank Weisinger) Ltd. v. Weisinger* [1988] I.R.L.R. 60, 65, *per* Millett J.; also *Davidson v. Wayman* [1984] 2 N.Z.L.R. 115.

[48] See in particular, *Kerr v. Morris, supra.*

[49] See *supra*, para. 10–41; also *infra*, para. 18–18. It does not follow that, merely because goodwill is an asset of the firm, all the partners are interested therein: see *Stekel v. Ellice* [1973] 1 W.L.R. 191.

[50] See *supra*, paras. 10–121 *et seq.*

(1) *Dissolution of firm*

In the event of a *general* dissolution,[51] the goodwill must be sold, **10–160** unless the partners agree otherwise.[52] It follows that, whilst the winding-up is continuing, a partner will normally be prevented from attempting to appropriate the goodwill for himself, at least where it has a saleable value.[53] However, as Lord Lindley explained, the position on the older authorities is not entirely free from doubt:

"If ... the goodwill of the partnership business has any saleable value at all, it seems impossible to hold that on a dissolution of a partnership, whether by death or otherwise, any partner can continue the old business in the old name for his own benefit, unless there is some agreement to that effect, or at least to the effect that the assets are not to be sold. Such a right on his part is inconsistent with the right of the other partners to have the goodwill sold for the common benefit of all.[54] There are, however, authorities tending to show that, in the case of death, the surviving partners are entitled to continue to carry on business in the old name,[55] and to restrain the executors of the deceased partner from doing the like.[56] But if these cases are carefully examined, they will be found not to warrant so general a proposition."[57]

However, it must at the same time be appreciated that section 38 of the Partnership Act 1890 contemplates that the members of a

---

[51] See, as to the meaning of this expression, *infra*, para. 24–03.

[52] *Bradbury v. Dickens* (1859) 27 Beav. 53; *Pawsey v. Armstrong* (1881) 18 Ch.D. 698; *Re David and Matthews* [1899] 1 Ch. 378; *Hill v. Fearis* [1950] 1 Ch. 466. It is, of course, open to the partners not to insist on a sale. *Quaere* whether, if one partner gives his co-partners a power of attorney for the purposes of effecting the sale, this will authorise them to sell with the benefit of an *express* restriction on competition: see *Hawksley v. Outram* [1892] 3 Ch. 359. And, as to the treatment of the sale proceeds, note *McClelland v. Hyde* [1942] N.I. 1.

[53] See *Turner v. Major* (1862) 3 Giff. 442 (where there was an express agreement for the sale of goodwill). Lord Lindley commented "In *Lewis v. Langdon* (1835) 7 Sim. 421, 425, the V.-C. Shadwell seemed to think that a surviving partner was under no obligation to preserve the goodwill. But his opinion was probably influenced by *Hammond v. Douglas* (1800) 5 Ves.Jr. 539, which was not then overruled." See also *Re David and Matthews* [1899] 1 Ch. 378, 382, *per* Romer J.

[54] See *Hill v. Fearis* [1905] 1 Ch. 466.

[55] *Webster v. Webster* (1791) 3 Swan. 490; *Lewis v. Langdon* (1835) 7 Sim. 421; *Robertson v. Quiddington* (1860) 28 Beav. 529; *Banks v. Gibson* (1865) 34 Beav. 566.

[56] *Lewis v. Langdon* (1835) 7 Sim. 421.

[57] Lord Lindley analysed the cases thus: "In *Webster v. Webster* [*(1791) 3 Swan. 490*], the executors of a deceased partner sought to restrain the surviving partners from carrying on business in the name of the old firm; but the application was based upon the untenable ground that by so doing the surviving partners exposed the estate of the deceased partner to continued liability. No question of goodwill appears to have been in dispute. In *Lewis v. Langdon* [*(1835) 7 Sim. 421*], V.-C. Shadwell certainly intimated his opinion to be, that surviving partners had a right to continue to carry on business in the old name [*See, too, per* Lord Romilly in *Robertson v. Quiddington (1860) 28 Beav. 529, 536*]; but the real question there was, whether the executors of a deceased partner were entitled to continue the use of that name; and it was held that they were not, which is quite consistent with the absence of the same right on the part of the surviving partner. There seems, moreover, to have been some agreement not set out in the report [*See the last line in (1835) 7 Sim. 425*], which influenced the judge's decision; and at the time it was pronounced the doctrine that goodwill is, if saleable, a partnership asset, was not so well established as it is at present." See also *Re David and Matthews* [1899] 1 Ch. 378, 382–383, *per* Romer J.

dissolved firm will complete any unfinished business,[58] but not that they will take on any *new* work. Yet, it is self apparent that, if no new work can be taken on, the value of the firm's goodwill will be swiftly dissipated unless, exceptionally, a forced sale can be secured on or shortly following the dissolution date.[59] The tension between these two opposing principles is most apparent in the case of a professional practice, yet appears not to have received detailed attention from the courts, which can, perhaps, be attributed to the infrequency with which judicial assistance in the winding-up process is actually sought.[59a]

10–161   If one partner in fact manages to secure the benefit of the firm's goodwill for himself, he can be compelled to account for its value, but such value will naturally reflect the fact that he and the other partners would be entitled to set up business in competition with the notional purchaser.[60]

Where a partner purchases an interest in goodwill on his admission to the firm, his entitlement in the event of a dissolution will be as set out above; the price originally paid to acquire that interest will be irrelevant.[61]

The implied restrictions imposed following a sale of goodwill are considered in relation to the retirement and expulsion of a partner.[62]

Use of firm name following dissolution

10–162   If the goodwill is sold in the course of winding up the firm's affairs, the purchaser will be entitled to use the old firm name, even if it consists of the names of one or more of the former partners, but not in such a way as to expose them to an appreciable risk of continuing liability;[63] *per contra* if the name is expressly assigned to the purchaser without qualification.[64] If, on the other hand, the goodwill

---

[58] See *infra*, paras. 13–64 *et seq.*; also *infra*, para. 16–25.

[59] As to obtaining such an order, see *infra*, paras. 23–179 *et seq.*

[59a] Nevertheless, the current editor is aware of one instance in which the court declined to interfere to protect the goodwill of a solicitors' partnership which was about to be dissolved, on the basis that: (1) a forced sale of the goodwill would not, in the particular circumstances, have been practicable; (2) the former partners could not be forced to take on new work for the benefit of the dissolved firm, having regard to the provisions of the Partnership Act 1890, s.38; and (3) they could not be prevented from setting up new practices as from the dissolution date. Equally, there would on the facts have been no difficulty in debiting each of the former partners with the value of the goodwill appropriated in taking the accounts of the dissolved firm.

[60] *Smith v. Everett* (1859) 27 Beav. 446; *Mellersh v. Keen* (1860) 28 Beav. 453.

[61] See *Bond v. Milbourn* (1871) 20 W.R. 197, where an incoming partner failed in his attempt to obtain a return of the purchase price.

[62] See *infra*, paras. 10–168 *et seq.*

[63] *Thynne v. Shove* (1890) 45 Ch.D. 577; *Burchell v. Wilde* [1900] 1 Ch. 551; *Townsend v. Jarman* [1900] 2 Ch. 698. Note also *Banks v. Gibson* (1865) 34 Beav. 566 (an extreme case, which goes further than *Thynne v. Shove, supra*). In *Gray v. Smith* (1889) 43 Ch.D. 208, there was no agreement for the sale of goodwill; but note that the Court of Appeal authorised the sale of certain stock bearing the firm name: see *ibid.* p. 221.

[64] *Townsend v. Jarman* [1900] 2 Ch. 698; also *Levy v. Walker* (1879) 10 Ch.D. 436 (as explained in *Gray v. Smith* (1889) 43 Ch.D. 208).

has no saleable value, each partner will seemingly have an equal right to use the firm name, subject to two important qualifications. First, it is questionable whether that right can properly be exercised until the partnership affairs have been fully wound up.[65] Secondly, it may not, in general, be exercised by one of the former partners if this would involve holding out another as a partner in his *new* business.[66] Lord Lindley summarised the position in this way:

"... where [*a partner's*] name is part of the name of the firm, *e.g.* if his name is A B, and the name of the firm is A B & Co., so long as he lives he would, it is apprehended, in the absence of an agreement to the contrary, be entitled to restrain his late co–partners and their representatives from carrying on business under the old name, and so continually exposing him to risk ... The right of a late partner to prevent the continued use of his own name on the ground of exposing him to risk is a purely personal right, and does not devolve either on his executors or on his trustee in bankruptcy, for they would not be exposed to risk.[67] Their right, and indeed the right of any partner whose name does not appear in the name of the firm, to prevent the continuance of the use of the name of the firm, can only be maintained upon the ground that such right is involved in the more general right of having the partnership assets, including the goodwill, sold for the common benefit. And if upon a dissolution this right is waived, or if the terms of dissolution are such as to preclude its exercise, then each partner can not only carry on business in competition with the others, but each can represent himself as late of, or as successor to, the old firm: and each may use the old name without qualification[68]; at all events if he does not hold out the other partners as still in partnership with himself."[69]

Whether the use of the firm name does expose a former partner to **10–163** any appreciable risk of liability will involve a mixed question of law and fact.[70] However, it is apprehended that, if the name merely consists of a partner's surname with the addition of the words "and

---

[65] To commence such a business prior to the conclusion of the winding-up would involve a prima facie breach of the duty not to compete imposed by the Partnership Act 1890, s.30 (as seemingly applied by *ibid.* s.38) and, perhaps, a breach of the duty of good faith; see also *ibid.* s.29(2). However, no such difficulties appear to have been perceived by Romer J. in *Re David and Matthews* [1899] 1 Ch. 378, when considering the position of a surviving partner. And see *supra*, para. 10–160, n. 59a.

[66] See *Routh v. Webster* (1847) 10 Beav. 561; *Bullock v. Chapman* (1848) 2 De G. & Sm. 211; *Troughton v. Hunter* (1854) 18 Beav. 470. And see also *supra*, paras. 5–54 *et seq.*

[67] See the Partnership Act 1890, ss.14(2), 36(3); also *supra*, para. 5–64 and *infra*, paras. 13–54 *et seq.*

[68] See *Banks v. Gibson* (1865) 34 Beav. 566; *Burchell v. Wilde* [1900] 1 Ch. 551. And note *Glenny v. Smith* (1865) 2 Dr. & Sm. 476.

[69] See the cases cited *supra*, nn. 63, 64 and 66.

[70] See *supra*, para. 5–44. Note also the provisions of the Business Names Act 1985 *supra*, paras. 3–24 *et seq.*, 5–70.

Co." and he has not used that name otherwise than in connection with the firm, its continued use by his former partners will not expose him to risk.[71]

(2)   Death of a partner

10–164 Where death results in the dissolution of the partnership,[72] the position will generally be as described in the preceding paragraphs. There is no question of the goodwill accruing to the surviving partners beneficially, even though there is an old authority to that effect.[73] However, that is not to say that the surviving partners may not ultimately be in the same position *as if* they had acquired the goodwill by survivorship. Thus, their ability to carry on a competing business in the same locality[74] may, for all practical purposes, represent a sufficient deterrent to prospective purchasers to render the goodwill unsaleable[75] and, in those circumstances, the surviving partners might be in a position to carry on using the old firm name.[76] Lord Lindley observed:

"[The surviving partner] will therefore acquire all the benefit of the goodwill; but he does not acquire it by survivorship, as something belonging to him exclusively, and with which the executors of the deceased partner have no concern; for if he did, he might sell the goodwill for his own benefit whenever it had a saleable value, and this he cannot do.[77] When, therefore, it is said that on the death of one partner the goodwill of the firm survives to the other, what is meant is, that the survivor is entitled to the advantages incidental to his former connection with the firm, and that he is under no obligation, in order to render those advantages saleable, to retire from business himself."[78]

---

[71] *Burchell v. Wilde* [1900] 1 Ch. 551; *Townsend v. Jarman* [1900] 2 Ch. 698.

[72] Partnership Act 1890, s.33(1), *infra*, paras. 24–20, 24–21. See also *supra*, para. 10–33.

[73] *Hammond v. Douglas* (1800) 5 Ves.Jr. 539. This decision is wholly inconsistent with the later authorities: see *Wedderburn v. Wedderburn* (1856) 22 Beav. 84; *Smith v. Everett* (1859) 27 Beav. 446; *Mellersh v. Keen* (1860) 28 Beav. 453. And see, in particular, *Re David and Matthews* [1899] 1 Ch. 378, 382, *per* Romer J.

[74] See *Farr v. Pearce* (1818) 3 Madd. 74; *Davies v. Hodgson* (1858) 25 Beav. 177; *Trego v. Hunt* [1896] A.C. 7. The surviving partners may not, of course, use the old firm name: *Re David and Matthews* [1899] 1 Ch. 378; *Manley v. Sartori* [1927] 1 Ch. 157. Lord Lindley also referred to the possibility of them using the old place of business, but this must be dependent on whether the premises are in fact owned by them or by the firm. *Quaere*, are the rights of the surviving partners unrestricted whilst the winding up is continuing? See *supra*, para. 10–162, n. 65.

[75] Note that the sale particulars should refer to the rights of the surviving partners: see *Johnson v. Helleley* (1864) 34 Beav. 63; *Jennings v. Jennings* [1898] 1 Ch. 378, 389, *per* Stirling J.; *Re David and Matthews* [1899] 1 Ch. 378, 385, *per* Romer J.

[76] See *Hill v. Fearis* [1905] 1 Ch. 466.

[77] See *Wedderburn v. Wedderburn* (1856) 22 Beav. 84; *Smith v. Everett* (1859) 27 Beav. 446; *Mellersh v. Keen* (1860) 28 Beav. 458. But see *Farr v. Pearce* (1818) 3 Madd. 74; *Hammond v. Douglas* (1800) 5 Ves.Jr. 539. Lord Lindley commented that the latter case "cannot be regarded as now law"; see also *Re David and Matthews* [1899] 1 Ch. 378, 382, *per* Romer J.

[78] See *Farr v. Pearce* (1818) 3 Madd. 74; *Davies v. Hodgson* (1858) 25 Beav. 177; *Mellersh v. Keen* (1860) 28 Beav. 453.

If the personal representatives of the deceased partner do not seek **10–165** to force a sale of the partnership assets and are content to receive the value of his share as at the date of death,[79] a payment will only fall to be made in respect of goodwill if it has a marketable value.

It has already been seen that the personal representatives cannot restrain the surviving partners from continuing to use the old firm name on the grounds that it would expose the deceased partner's estate to continuing liability.[80]

(3)   *Retirement or expulsion of partner*

Although a partner's retirement or expulsion technically dissolves the **10–166** firm, it would seem that, if the agreement contains no provision specifically governing his entitlement in respect of goodwill[81] and the other assets of the partnership, the court would normally be reluctant to order anything but a payment out of the value of his share *as at the date he ceased to be a partner.*[82] To order a sale or a valuation as at some later date would be inconsistent with the concept of retirement or expulsion and would prima facie confer an unjustified "windfall" benefit on the outgoing partner.[83] This does not, however, mean that the outgoing partner is deprived of his right to the profits attributable to the use of his share of the goodwill, etc., up to the time that his entitlement is paid out.[84]

Continued use of outgoing partner's name

The agreement will normally provide, either expressly or by **10–167** necessary implication, for the continued use of the firm name following a retirement or expulsion, irrespective of the risk to the outgoing partner. Where, exceptionally, the agreement contains no

---

[79] *i.e.* relying on their strict rights under the Partnership Act 1890, s.43. The application of this section in the case of a *general* dissolution is, however, not without difficulty: see *infra*, paras. 19–09 *et seq.*, 23–33, 26–04.

[80] See *supra*, para. 10–162.

[81] The agreement may, of course, declare that goodwill should be treated as valueless, *e.g.* where the outgoing partner's entitlement is determined by reference to the firm's annual accounts, which ignore the existence of goodwill: see *supra*, paras. 10–133 *et seq.*

[82] *i.e.* his strict entitlement pursuant to the Partnership Act 1890, ss.43, 44. Lord Lindley observed that "when a partner retires not only from the firm, but from the business carried on by it, the continuing partners will acquire the benefit arising out of the goodwill for nothing, unless it has been agreed that they shall pay for it; for they retain possession of the old place of business, and they continue to carry on that business under the old name. This, in fact, secures the goodwill to them, and they cannot be compelled to pay separately for it, unless some agreement to that effect has been entered into." As a statement of principle, this cannot be right and, indeed, does not bear comparison with Lord Lindley's analysis of the position following the death of a partner: see *supra*, para. 10–62. It is only correct if (a) the goodwill has no value and (b) the continued use of the firm name would not expose the retired partner to the risk of continuing liability.

[83] See *Sobell v. Boston* [1975] 1 W.L.R. 1587, 1591, *per* Goff J. Although this case concerned the *retirement* of a partner, the current editor considers that the same principles will apply in the event of an expulsion. *Cf. Barclays Bank Trust Co. Ltd. v. Bluff* [1982] Ch. 172, *infra*, para. 25–27.

[84] Partnership Act 1890, s.42, *infra*, paras. 25–23 *et seq.*; *Manley v. Sartori* [1927] 1 Ch. 157.

such provision or, more commonly, where the retirement is the result of an *ad hoc* agreement, the retiring partner cannot necessarily be taken to have authorised his former partners to continue to use the old firm name, if by so doing they would expose him to the risk of liability on the basis of holding out;[85] *per contra*, if he seeks to be paid out the full value of his share in goodwill and attributes part of that value to the firm name.[86] The current editor submits that an expelled partner will, in the absence of any clear provision in the agreement, be in no different position.[87]

Implied restrictions on sale of goodwill by outgoing partner

10–168   If a partner retires and is paid out the value of his share, including his interest in the firm's goodwill,[88] but the agreement does not contain any express restriction on competition by outgoing partners, he, like any other vendor of goodwill, will be immediately entitled to set up a similar business in the same locality,[89] to advertise that fact[90] and to deal with any customer of the firm who chooses to do business with him.[91] What he may *not* do is (1) solicit such customers as long as they remain customers of the firm,[92] even if they have had dealings with him since the date of his retirement[93] and his right to carry on a

---

[85] See *Gray v. Smith* (1889) 43 Ch.D. 208, where an exception was made in the case of certain stock bearing the firm name: see *ibid*. p. 221, *per* Cotton L.J. See also, as to this decision, *Jennings v. Jennings* [1898] 1 Ch. 378, 384, 388–389, *per* Stirling J. And see *Churton v. Douglas* (1859) Johns. 174, 190, *per* Page Wood V.-C.

[86] See *supra*, para. 10–162. But *quaere* whether, if the outgoing partner merely receives his entitlement as a debt pursuant to the Partnership Act 1890, s.43, he can properly be regarded as a vendor of goodwill. The point will not arise if, as is usually the case, the agreement makes it clear that the partnership is not dissolved by the retirement of a partner (see *supra*, para. 10–33) and establishes the name under which it will carry on business (see *supra*, para. 10–34).

[87] Note, however, the approach adopted in *Dawson v. Beeson* (1882) 12 Ch.D. 504, *infra*, para. 10–172.

[88] For this purpose, it would not seem to matter whether any sum is actually paid in respect of the goodwill itself: see *Churton v. Douglas* (1859) Johns. 174, 186, *per* Page Wood V.-C.; *Trego v. Hunt* [1896] A.C. 7; also *Bridge v. Deacons* [1984] A.C. 705, 718. But see also *supra*, para. 10–167, n. 86.

[89] *Shackle v. Baker* (1808) 14 Ves.Jr. 468; *Cruttwell v. Lye* (1810) 17 Ves.Jr. 335; *Harrison v. Gardner* (1817) 2 Madd. 198; *Kennedy v. Lee* (1817) 3 Mer. 441; *Davies v. Hodgson* (1858) 25 Beav. 177; *Bradbury v. Dickens* (1859) 27 Beav. 53; *Mellersh v. Keen* (1859) 27 Beav. 236; *Smith v. Everett* (1859) 27 Beav. 446; *Churton v. Douglas* (1859) Johns. 174, *infra*, para. 10–169. Where goodwill is sold in the open market, the particulars should refer to this right: see *Johnson v. Helleley* (1864) 34 Beav. 63.

[90] *Hookham v. Pottage* (1872) L.R. 8 Ch.App. 91; *Labouchere v. Dawson* (1872) 13 Eq. 322; also *Cruttwell v. Lye* (1810) 17 Ves.Jr. 335.

[91] *Leggott v. Barrett* (1880) 15 Ch.D. 306; *Trego v. Hunt* [1896] A.C. 7.

[92] *Trego v. Hunt* [1896] A.C. 7 and the cases there cited; also *Jennings v. Jennings* [1898] 1 Ch. 378; *Re David and Matthews* [1899] 1 Ch. 378; *Gargan v. Ruttle* [1931] I.R. 152; and see *Davidson v. Wayman* [1984] 2 N.Z.L.R. 115. It appears that this restriction may not apply where the share of a bankrupt partner is sold by his trustee: see *Cruttwell v. Lye* (1810) 17 Ves.Jr. 335; *Walker v. Mottram* (1881) 19 Ch.D. 355; and note also *Farey v. Cooper* [1927] 2 K.B. 384; *Green & Sons v. Morris* [1914] 1 Ch. 562. The position of an expelled partner is less clear: see *infra*, para. 10–172. On the other hand, the restriction does apply in the case of the sale of a deceased partner's share by his personal representatives (*Boorne v. Wicker* [1927] 1 Ch. 667) and a sale pursuant to a court order in dissolution proceedings (*Johnson v. Helleley* (1864) 34 Beav. 63; *Jennings v. Jennings*, *supra*; *Re David and Matthews*, *supra*, p. 385, *per* Romer J.); see also *infra*, paras. 23–179 *et seq*.

[93] *Curl Bros. v. Webster* [1904] 1 Ch. 685.

competing business is expressly recognised by the agreement,[94] or (2) represent himself as continuing the firm's business.[95] It follows that he may not carry on business under the firm name or under a name which is so similar to the firm name as to lead members of the public to believe that it is the same business. Equally, if the firm name happens to be the same as his own, he cannot be restrained from carrying on business in that name, unless he seeks to make dishonest use of it.[96]

Thus, in *Churton v. Douglas*,[97] two of the plaintiffs and the **10–169** defendant, whose name was John Douglas, carried on a partnership business under the name "John Douglas & Co." The defendant retired and assigned his share, including his share of goodwill, to his co-partners and a new partner (the third plaintiff) who was admitted in his place. The plaintiffs thereafter continued to carry on the old business under a new name, but with the addition "late John Douglas & Co." The defendant entered into a new partnership with three employees of the old firm whom he had (on his own admission) enticed to join him: that partnership acquired premises next door to those occupied by the old firm and carried on an identical business under the name "John Douglas & Co." That name was prominently displayed outside the new premises and customers of the old firm were circularised in terms that would have lead them to suppose that the business of the old firm was being carried on by the defendant and his new partners. In proceedings brought by the plaintiffs against the defendant, his right to carry on business, either alone or in partnership with others, in direct competition with the business carried on by the plaintiffs was accepted,[98] but the court went on to hold that:

(i)   the plaintiffs alone had the right to carry on the business previously carried on by John Douglas & Co.;

(ii)   they alone had the right to represent themselves as the successors of that firm and the defendant had no such right;

(iii)   the defendant could not acquire such a right by taking other persons into partnership with him; and

(iv)   although his name was John Douglas, the defendant had no right, either alone or in partnership with others, to carry on the same kind of business in the same neighbourhood *under the name of "John Douglas & Co."*

---

[94] *Gillingham v. Beddow* [1900] 2 Ch. 242.

[95] *Churton v. Douglas* (1859) Johns. 174; *Hookham v. Pottage* (1872) L.R. 8 Ch.App. 91: *Mogford v. Courtenay* (1881) 45 L.T. 303.

[96] *Ibid.*; also *supra*, para. 3–18. And see *Vernon v. Hallam* (1886) 34 Ch.D. 748 (where there was a covenant not to carry on business under a particular name which happened to be that of the defendant); *Pomeroy Ltd. v. Scalé* (1907) 23 T.L.R. 170.

[97] (1859) Johns. 174.

[98] *Ibid.* p. 187, *per* Page Wood V.-C.

The defendant was accordingly restrained from carrying on such a business, either alone or in partnership, under that name or in any other manner which involved holding out that he was carrying on the business in continuation of, or in succession to, the business carried on by the old firm of John Douglas & Co.

10–170   *Express restriction invalid*:   If an *express* restriction on competition sought to be imposed on the outgoing partner is unenforceable as an unlawful restraint of trade,[99] there may be no scope for implying any restriction on solicitation, etc., at least to the extent that the two terms would be mutually inconsistent.[1]

10–171   *Post dissolution agreements*:   The position will be the same where one or more partners agree to sell their shares of goodwill to their former co-partners following a dissolution.[2]

10–172   *Expelled partners*:   Although there is authority for the proposition that an expelled partner will not be restrained from soliciting the customers of the firm,[3] the current editor submits that he will only enjoy such a freedom where the continuing partners are *not* obliged to purchase his share under the terms of the agreement.[4] Similarly, in the case of a partner compulsorily retired from the firm pursuant to an express power in the agreement.[5]

Other implied restrictions

10–173   Equally, even in the absence of an express restriction on competition, the partnership agreement or some subsequent agreement may justify an inference that an outgoing partner is not permitted to set up a competing business. Thus, where a power to retire was framed in terms of relinquishing involvement in a particular line of business carried on by the firm, it was held that a partner could not retire and still continue his involvement in that line

---

[99] See *infra*, paras. 10–181 *et seq*.

[1] See, for example, *Malden Timber v. McLeish*, 1992 S.L.T. 727 (O.H.). *Cf. Davey Offshore v. Emerald Field Contractors Ltd.* (1991) 55 B.L.R. 1.

[2] This, of course, presupposes that any goodwill exists following the dissolution: see *supra*, paras. 10–160 *et seq*.

[3] *Dawson v. Beeson* (1882) 22 Ch.D. 504. Although this decision was cited in *Trego v. Hunt* [1896] A.C. 7, it is not referred to in their Lordships' opinions.

[4] It is significant that in *Dawson v. Beeson, supra*, the expelled partner was to be paid out the amount of his capital as if he were dead (although it is not clear from the report whether this meant a mere return of capital contribution): see *ibid.* p. 511. It seems implicit in the judgment that, if he had not suffered financially as a result of the expulsion, the outcome would have been different. Where an outgoing partner's entire share is acquired by the continuing partners, it is immaterial that nothing is actually paid in respect of his share of goodwill: see *supra*, para. 10–168, n. 88. Equally, note the views expressed by the Court regarding the difference between voluntary and involuntary sales in *Walker v. Mottram* (1881) 19 Ch.D. 355.

[5] *i.e.* pursuant to the type of power considered *supra*, para. 10–109 *et seq*.

of business.[6] Similarly, where the amount to be paid to a retiring partner in respect of goodwill was left to be ascertained by arbitrators, who acted on the understanding that the retiring partner would not commence a new business in the same neighbourhood, the partner concerned was later restrained from carrying on business in that neighbourhood, even though the award was silent on the point.[7]

Court imposed restrictions

A more difficult question is whether a court or an arbitrator could, **10–174** when ordering the sale of the firm's goodwill, either to one or more of the partners or to a third party, impose more stringent restrictions on competition than those normally implied on such a sale. It is certainly right that the realisable value of goodwill would be much increased if such a jurisdiction were exercisable, but there is scant authority to support it. Certainly, such an order *appears* to have been made by the arbitrator in *Morley v. Newman*,[8] but the report of the decision is brief and it is difficult to discern any statement of principle therein. Although the Court of Appeal did, with some reservations, accept the existence of an analogous jurisdiction in *Crittenden v. Crittenden*,[9] this was pursuant to the wide powers conferred on the court by the Matrimonial Causes Act 1973. It thus remains to be seen whether this is an area in which judicial creativity is likely to be deployed.

(c) Valuation of Goodwill

It has already been seen that a well drawn agreement should provide **10–175** for the acquisition of an outgoing partner's share by the continuing or surviving partners.[10] Lord Lindley warned that:

"... too great care cannot be taken to express as clearly as possible what is intended to be done with respect to goodwill; and in order to avoid all ambiguity, the word goodwill itself should be made use of."

This still holds true as regards the *valuation* of goodwill, which would otherwise prima facie be comprehended within the expressions

---

[6] See *Cooper v. Watson* (1784) 3 Doug. 413, where a partnership agreement between two brewers provided that either partner might, on giving six months' notice to the other, "quit the trade and mystery of a brewer," and that the other would thereafter be at liberty to continue the trade on his own account. Such a provision might, of course, be regarded as an unlawful restraint of trade but this is a separate issue: see *infra*, paras. 10–181 *et seq.*

[7] *Harrison v. Gardner* (1817) 2 Madd. 198. The likelihood of competition will normally be taken into account in valuing the goodwill: see *Re David and Matthews* [1899] 1 Ch. 378 and *infra*, paras. 10–180 *et seq.*

[8] (1824) 5 D. &. R. 317.

[9] [1990] 2 F.S.R. 361.

[10] See *supra*, paras. 10–121 *et seq.*

"assets," "property," "effects," "stock"[11] or, perhaps, "premises"[12] of the partnership and paid for accordingly.

Goodwill treated as valueless

10–176 If goodwill is to be treated as valueless, this fact should be stated in the agreement.[13] The mere fact that goodwill has been written out of the partnership accounts or that it appears therein at a nominal value will, in itself, be irrelevant when determining the entitlement of an outgoing partner,[14] *unless* such entitlement is to be determined by reference to the contents of the last signed balance sheet which has, indeed, been prepared on that basis.[15]

Agreed basis for valuation

10–177 If goodwill is to be valued, the agreement should state on what basis and by whom the valuation is to be made.

Fixed value: Although the agreement could establish a fixed notional value for goodwill,[16] it would be dangerous to adopt anything other than a nominal figure, since its true value will fluctuate with the fortunes of the firm.[17]

Profit related value: The simplest method is essentially profit based and will usually involve applying an agreed number of years' purchase to the average profits of the firm over a set period, usually of between three and five years.[18] Equally, in some businesses, the

---

[11] See *Hall v. Barrows* (1863) 4 De G.J. & S. 150; *Page v. Ratcliffe* (1897) 75 L.T. 371; *Jennings v. Jennings* [1898] 1 Ch. 378; *Re David and Matthews* [1899] 1 Ch. 378; *Manley v. Sartori* [1927] 1 Ch. 157; *McClelland v. Hyde* [1942] N.I. 1. And see also *Salter v. Leas Hotel Co.* [1902] 1 Ch. 332. The decisions in *Kennedy v. Lee* (1817) 3 Mer. 452 and *Hall v. Hall* (1855) 20 Beav. 139 are no longer in point.

[12] See *Blake v. Shaw* (1860) Johns. 732; *Re Rhagg* [1938] Ch. 828. But *cf. Burfield v. Rouch* (1862) 31 Beav. 241; *Re Betts* [1949] W.N. 91. And see also *supra*, para. 10–154, n. 30.

[13] This is, however, strictly unnecessary in the case of a medical partnership practising within the National Health Service, since an outgoing partner could not in any event receive any consideration for his share of goodwill without committing an offence: see the National Health Service Act 1977, s.54, Sched. 10.

[14] See *Cruickshank v. Sutherland* (1922) 92 L.J. Ch. 136, *supra*, para. 10–138; also *Wade v. Jenkins* (1860) 2 Giff. 509.

[15] See *supra*, paras. 10–133 *et seq.*

[16] See, for example, *Wade v. Jenkins* (1860) 2 Giff. 509.

[17] If a substantive value were to be placed on goodwill at the outset, this could impose a severe (and possibly unsupportable) financial burden on the continuing or surviving partners in the event of an unexpected downturn in the profitability of the business. *A fortiori* if that sum was negotiated on the footing that outgoing partners would be restrained from competing with the partnership business but the chosen restriction proves to be wholly or partially invalid. Although the agreement might permit account to be taken of such imponderable factors by means of an adjustment to the fixed value, this is unlikely to produce a satisfactory result.

[18] This presupposes that the partnership has subsisted for that length of time. If it has not, eccentric results may be produced if account is taken of the profits of a predecessor firm or if the calculation is based on (say) a single year's profits (even assuming this to be permitted under the agreement). There is, perhaps, something to be said for adopting a fixed notional value for goodwill to cover the initial period.

same approach will be adopted but with the substitution of average gross receipts for profits.[19] In all such cases, the valuation exercise will be a simple one and can be carried out by the partnership accountants. However, the result may be arbitrary, particularly if the profits of the firm are subject to severe fluctuations.[20]

As an alternative, it is sometimes provided that a partner's interest **10–178** in goodwill should be valued by applying the relevant number of year's purchase to *his* average profit share over the designated period. Such a formula should be approached with caution if (*a*) the profit shares are variable[21] or (*b*) those shares do not accord with the partners' shares in surplus assets[22] since, in either case, the figure produced may bear no relation to the outgoing partner's interest in goodwill as at the date he ceases to be a member of the firm.

Market value: Some agreements require the market value of the **10–179** goodwill to be ascertained, although this is increasingly rare. There are, in fact, two recognised methods of valuing goodwill, *i.e.* "total capitalisation"[23] and "super profits,"[24] but these are appropriate only in the case of large firms and, even then, are not of universal application.[25] Moreover, account must always be taken of the particular circumstances of the firm and business under considera-tion.[26] Thus, if the partnership was originally constituted for a fixed term which has almost expired, the goodwill may have only a nominal value.[27] Again, if the continued existence of the goodwill is dependent on the active participation of a "key" partner, this will

---

[19] *e.g.* the goodwill of an accountancy practice is normally valued by reference to its gross annual recurring fees: see, for example, the evidence adduced in *Stekel v. Ellice* [1973] 1 W.L.R. 191, 195. Note, however, that there may, depending on the circumstances, be a dispute as to whether particular fees are recurring or non-recurring.

[20] *A fortiori* if the partnership is dissolved shortly after the death or retirement of a partner: see *Austen v. Boys* (1858) 2 De G. & J. 626.

[21] See, for example, *supra*, para. 10–67.

[22] See *supra*, paras. 10–66, 10–129.

[23] This basis requires the valuer to ascertain the average profits of the firm over a given period, to multiply that figure by the appropriate number of years' purchase and then to deduct the net value of the firm's tangible assets: see *Findlays' Trustees v. I.R.C.* (1938) 22 A.T.C. 437.

[24] This basis requires the valuer to estimate the average assumed yield attributable to the firm's tangible assets together with a sum representing a reasonable level of remuneration for the partners, and then to multiply this figure (the "super profit") by an appropriate number of years' purchase. Note that the expert witnesses in *Findlays' Trustees v. I.R.C.*, *supra*, did not consider this basis to be appropriate when valuing the goodwill of a partnership owning a newspaper.

[25] See, for example, *Page v. Ratcliffe* (1897) 75 L.T. 371 (where the goodwill of a brewery business fell to be valued); also *Findlays' Trustees v. I.R.C.*, *supra*, p. 440, *per* Lord Fraser. And see the Law Society's paper on Goodwill issued on July 16, 1981.

[26] Relevant factors will include the size of the firm, the location of its premises, profit trends, etc.

[27] *Austen v. Boys* (1858) 2 De G. & J. 626. This was an extreme case, where notice to retire was given two days before the expiration of a fixed term of seven years. This decision must, however, be approached with caution, since it does not follow that goodwill is necessarily unsaleable and, therefore, valueless in the event of a dissolution.

affect its value, as will the ability of outgoing partners to set up competing businesses.[28]

It follows that the valuation process involves a high degree of professional judgment on the part of the chosen valuer(s) and, if the partners opt for an "expert" valuation, they will normally be bound thereby.[29]

(d) Restrictions on Competition[30]

Need for express restriction

10–180   It has already been seen that an outgoing partner is subject to few implied restrictions on his ability to set up business in competition with his former partners, even where he has sold them his share of the firm's goodwill.[31] As Lord Lindley put it:

> "In the absence of any agreement upon the subject, a retiring partner is as much at liberty to set up for himself, in opposition to the firm he has quitted, as he would be if he had never belonged to it."

An expelled partner may, if anything, be in an even stronger position.[32]

It follows that effective protection from the possible depredations of an outgoing partner can only be secured if the agreement contains an *express* restriction on competition.[33]

Enforceability of restrictions

10–181   It has long been settled that the courts take a stricter and less favourable view of restrictions on competition as between employer and employee than of similar restrictions as between vendor and purchaser.[34] Partnership in the true sense does not create the relationship of employer and employee and may or may not involve

---

[28] See *supra*, paras. 10–166 *et seq.* This may be of particular relevance for the purposes of inheritance tax: see *infra*, paras. 36–27, 36–69.

[29] See *supra*, para. 10–141.

[30] See the *Encyclopedia of Professional Partnerships*, Precedent 1, cl. 22(2)(1).

[31] See *supra*, paras. 10–168 *et seq.*

[32] See *Dawson v. Beeson* (1882) 22 Ch.D. 504 and *supra*, para. 10–172.

[33] Note, however, that the existence of an express restriction will increase the value of the firm's goodwill for inheritance tax purposes: see *supra*, paras. 36–27, 36–69.

[34] See *Ronbar Enterprises v. Green* [1954] 1 W.L.R. 815 and the cases there cited. As to restraints of trade generally, see *Nordenfelt v. Maxim Nordenfelt Guns & Ammunition Co. Ltd.* [1894] A.C. 535; *Mason v. Provident Clothing & Supply Co. Ltd.* [1913] A.C. 724; *A.–G. of Australia v. Adelaide Steamship Co. Ltd.* [1913] A.C. 781; *Herbert Morris v. Saxelby* [1916] 1 A.C. 689; *Attwood v. Lamont* [1920] 3 K.B. 571; *Esso Petroleum Co. Ltd. v. Harper's Garage (Stourport) Ltd.* [1968] A.C. 269; *Greig v. Insole* [1978] 1 W.L.R. 302; *Bridge v. Deacons* [1984] A.C. 705. Note also the potential application of Art. 85 of the European Community Treaty, the Restrictive Trade Practices Act 1976 and the Competition Act 1980, *infra*, paras. 10–196 *et seq.*

the relationship of vendor and purchaser. It is, therefore, strictly *sui generis*. Although this was confirmed in *Bridge v. Deacons*,[35] the Privy Council emphasised that categorisation serves little purpose, since the true test of enforceability lies in the legitimate interests of the parties seeking to enforce the restraint.[36] Nevertheless, it is still true to say that an outgoing partner who disposes of his share in exchange for a payment will, at least to an extent, partake of the character of a vendor.[37] Equally, a so-called "salaried" partner,[38] who enjoys neither an interest in the partnership assets nor a right to participate in the management of the firm, may properly fall to be treated as an employee.[39]

Where a restraint has been entered into between partners who are on broadly equal terms at the inception of the partnership, this will represent a powerful argument in favour of enforceability.[40]

Test of reasonableness

In accordance with the general doctrine that restraint of trade is **10–182** against public policy, any restriction on a person's freedom to carry on his trade or profession is prima facie void, but may be valid if it is shown to be reasonable (1) in the interests of the parties, and (2) in the interests of the public.

(1) *Reasonableness in the Interests of the Parties*

The onus of proving that a particular restriction is reasonable in the **10–183** interests of the parties, and thus valid, is on the party seeking to enforce it.[41] Thus the burden will generally fall upon the continuing partners, although in certain circumstances an outgoing partner might himself seek to rely on the restriction, *e.g.* where there is some dependent obligation on the part of the continuing partners.[42]

---

[35] [1984] A.C. 705.

[36] *Ibid.* p. 714, endorsing the approach adopted by Lord Reid in *Esso Petroleum Co. Ltd. v. Harper's Garage (Stourport) Ltd.* [1968] A.C. 269, 301. The concept of proportionality has no place in this sphere: *Allied Dunbar (Frank Weisinger) Ltd. v. Weisinger* [1988] I.R.L.R. 60, 65, *per* Millett J.

[37] See *Re Jenkins' Deed of Partnership* [1948] W.N. 98 (which, however, was a case of a non-partner, who was a party to the partnership deed, seeking to enforce a restriction against a former partner); *Whitehill v. Bradford* [1952] Ch. 236; *Lyne-Pirkis v. Jones* [1969] 1 W.L.R. 1293; *Ronbar Enterprises v. Green* [1954] 1 W.L.R. 815.

[38] See, as to such partners, *supra*, paras. 5–65, 10–70.

[39] In considering the validity of covenants as between employer and employee, emphasis increasingly tends to be placed on their inequality of bargaining power: see *Schroeder Music Publishing Co. v. Macaulay* [1974] 1 W.L.R. 1308; *Clifford Davis Management Ltd. v. W.E.A. Records Ltd.* [1975] 1 W.L.R. 61. See also *Texaco Ltd. v. Mulberry Filling Station Ltd.* [1972] 1 W.L.R. 814.

[40] See *Lyne-Pirkis v. Jones* [1969] 1 W.L.R. 1293, 1301, *per* Edmund Davies L.J.; *Esso Petroleum Co. Ltd. v. Harper's Garage (Stourport) Ltd.* [1968] A.C. 269, 300, *per* Lord Reid. A fortiori, in the case of a solicitors' partnership: see *Bridge v. Deacons* [1984] A.C. 705, 716–717.

[41] See the cases cited *supra*, para. 10–181, n. 34.

[42] See, for example, *Wyatt v. Kreglinger & Furneau* [1933] 1 K.B. 793; *Macfarlane v. Kent* [1965] 1 W.L.R. 1019; *Bull v. Pitney-Bowes Ltd.* [1967] 1 W.L.R. 273.

Legitimate interest capable of protection

10–184   In order to show that the restriction is reasonable, the continuing
partners must above all else demonstrate that they have a legitimate
interest capable of being protected.[43] That interest will, inevitably, lie
in the firm's business and goodwill, a share of which will usually have
been acquired from the outgoing partner.[44] Whilst it is, within
reason, permissible to seek protection for any anticipated expansion
in the firm's business,[45] an attempt to impose a restriction in gross,
with a view to protecting a wholly different business in which the firm
has never been involved, will inevitably fail.[46]

   The fact that the firm's goodwill is inherently unsaleable in no way
affects the continuing partners' interest in its protection.[47]

10–185   In *Bridge v. Deacons*,[48] which concerned a solicitors' partnership,
the goodwill was of an unusually departmentalised nature. On that
basis, it was argued that the continuing partners were only entitled to
protection as regards the goodwill of the particular department in
which the outgoing partner had worked. This argument was rejected
by the Privy Council, who pointed out that the outgoing partner was,
prior to his retirement, interested in the totality of the firm's
goodwill.[49]

Restriction not excessive

10–186   On the assumption that the continuing partners have a legitimate
interest capable of protection, they must then go on to show that the
particular restriction is no more than adequate to protect that
interest, *i.e.* that it is not excessive as regards area,[50] duration,[51] or

---

[43] See in particular, *Bridge v. Deacons* [1984] A.C. 705, 714; also *Allied Dunbar (Frank Weisinger) Ltd. v. Weisinger* [1988] I.R.L.R. 60; *Office Angels Ltd. v. Rainer-Thomas* [1991] I.R.L.R. 214. And note *Prontaprint plc v. London Litho Ltd.* [1987] F.S.R. 315 (which concerned a franchising agreement).

[44] It does not matter whether or not the outgoing partner has received a cash consideration for his share of goodwill: *Bridge v. Deacons* [1984] A.C. 705, 718.

[45] *Lyne-Pirkis v. Jones* [1969] 1 W.L.R. 1293; also *Texaco v. Mulberry Filling Station* [1972] 1 W.L.R. 814. And see *Maxim's Ltd. v. Dye* [1977] 1 W.L.R. 1155; *My Kinda Bones Ltd. (T/A Chicago Rib Shack) v. Dr. Pepper's Stove Co. Ltd. (T/A Dr. Pepper's Manhattan Rib Shack)* [1984] F.S.R. 289.

[46] See *Horner v. Graves* (1831) 7 Bing. 735; *Townsend v. Jarman* [1900] 2 Ch. 698, 702–703, *per* Farwell J.; *Henry Leetham & Sons Ltd. v. Johnston-White* [1907] 1 Ch. 322; *Morris & Co. v. Ryle* [1910] 103 L.T. 545; *British Reinforced Concrete Co. Ltd. v. Schelff* [1921] 2 Ch. 563; *Vancouver Malt & Sake Brewing Co. Ltd. v. Vancouver Breweries Ltd.* [1934] A.C. 181; *Anscombe & Ringland v. Butchoff* (1984) 134 N.L.J. 37.

[47] This is clearly illustrated in the case of medical partnerships practising within the National Health Service: see *Whitehill v. Bradford* [1952] Ch. 236; *Macfarlane v. Kent* [1965] 1 W.L.R. 1019; *Anthony v. Rennie*, 1981 S.L.T. (Notes) 11; *Kerr v. Morris* [1987] Ch. 90.

[48] [1984] A.C. 705.

[49] *Ibid.* pp. 718–719.

[50] See *British Reinforced Concrete Co. Ltd. v. Schelff* [1921] 2 Ch. 563; *Butt v. Long* (1953) A.L.J. 576; *Ronbar Enterprises v. Green* [1954] 1 W.L.R. 815; *Scorer v. Seymour Jones* [1966] 1 W.L.R. 1419; *Lyne-Pirkis v. Jones* [1969] 1 W.L.R. 1293; *Marley Tile Co. Ltd. v. Johnson* [1982] I.R.L.R. 75; *Office Angels Ltd. v. Rainer-Thomas* [1991] I.R.L.R. 214. Distances are measured as the crow flies: see *Duignan v. Walker* (1859) Johns. 446; *Mouflet v. Cole* (1872) L.R. 8 Ex. 32.

[51] See *Fitch v. Dewes* [1921] 2 A.C. 158; *Re Jenkins' Deed of Partnership* [1948] W.N. 98; *Whitehill v. Bradford* [1952] Ch. 236; *Lyne-Pirkis v. Jones* [1969] 1 W.L.R. 1293. But see also *infra*, para. 10–187.

prohibited activities.[52] As a broad rule of thumb, it can be said that any restriction on competition by outgoing partners which is genuinely designed to protect the value of the firm's business and goodwill is likely to be upheld, provided that it is mutual[53] and does not exceed the geographical area and scope of the firm's business (allowing for any reasonable anticipated expansion)[54] or the duration of the partnership itself.[55] A *unilateral* restraint is likely to be treated less sympathetically.[56] The restriction may (and, indeed, frequently will) be taken for the benefit of both present and future partners.[57]

It will, as a general rule, be possible to justify a relatively wide restriction with a view to protecting trade secrets and confidential information, since they may be capable of use in more than one type of business.[58] Similarly, where the business is highly specialised and, thus, appeals only to a limited market.[59]

Although non-solicitation and non-dealing restrictions are, in **10–187** practice, more likely to be held upheld than area or "brass plate" restrictions,[60] the courts are by no means unsympathetic towards the latter, particularly in professional partnerships.[61]

---

[52] See *Nordenfelt v. Maxim Nordenfelt Guns & Ammunition Co.* [1894] A.C. 535; *Goldsoll v. Goldman* [1915] 1 Ch. 292; *Konski v. Peet* [1915] 1 Ch. 530; *British Reinforced Concrete Co. v. Schelff* [1921] 2 Ch. 563; *Routh v. Jones* [1947] 1 All E.R. 758; *Re Jenkins' Deed of Partnership* [1948] W.N. 98; *Ronbar Enterprises v. Green* [1954] 1 W.L.R. 815; *Lyne-Pirkis v. Jones* [1969] 1 W.L.R. 1293; *Peyton v. Mindham* [1972] 1 W.L.R. 8.

[53] *i.e.* it applies to all partners, irrespective of their age or seniority in the firm: see *Bridge v. Deacons* [1984] 705, 716.

[54] See *supra*, para. 10–184.

[55] See *Morris v. Colman* (1812) 18 Ves.Jr. 437; *Wilkinson v. Pettit* (1889) 7 N.Z.L.R. 342; *Ronbar Enterprises Ltd. v. Green* [1954] 1 W.L.R. 815.

[56] See *Hensman v. Traill, The Times*, October 22, 1980, which was an extreme case. This part of the decision was not overruled in *Kerr v. Morris* [1987] Ch. 90. But note that the Court of Appeal, without any apparent hesitation, enforced a unilateral restriction in *Clarke v. Newland* [1991] 1 All E.R. 397.

[57] *Hitchcock v. Coker* (1837) 6 A. & E. 438, cited with approval in *Eastes v. Russ* [1914] 1 Ch. 468, 482 (*per* Swinfen Eady L.J.) and *Fitch v. Dewes* [1921] 2 A.C. 158, 168–169 (*per* Viscount Cave).

[58] See generally *Hagg v. Darley* (1878) 38 L.T. 312; *Littlewoods Organisation Ltd. v. Harris* [1977] 1 W.L.R. 1472. As to what is confidential information, see *Thomas Marshall (Exporters) Ltd. v. Guinle* [1979] Ch. 227; *Faccenda Chicken Ltd. v. Fowler* [1987] Ch. 117 (both cases concerning employees). See also *supra*, para. 10–44.

[59] *e.g.* see *Nordenfelt v. Maxim Nordenfelt Guns & Ammunition Co. Ltd.* [1894] A.C. 535. Account must be taken of whether the business sought to be protected is conducted impersonally by, say, correspondence (which will merit a wide restraint) or is primarily dependent on personal contact (which will only warrant a more limited restraint). *Cf. Calvert, Hunt & Barden v. Elton* (1974) 233 E.G. 391 (where a three-year restraint on an employee of an estate agent was upheld) and *Marion White Ltd. v. Francis* [1972] 1 W.L.R. 1423 (where a 12-month restraint on an employee of a hairdresser was upheld). Note also *Office Angels Ltd. v. Rainer-Thomas* [1991] I.R.L.R. 214. Another relevant factor will be whether the clientele is of a casual or recurring character.

[60] *Baines v. Geary* (1887) 35 Ch.D. 154; *East Essex Farmers Ltd. v. Holder* (1926) 70 S.J. 1001; *Express Dairy Co. v. Jackson* (1929) 99 L.J.K.B. 181; *Gilford Motor Co. v. Horn* [1933] 1 Ch. 935; *Konski v. Peet* [1915] 1 Ch. 530; *Spafax (1965) Ltd. v. Dommett* (1972) 116 S.J. 711 (where a covenant not to solicit "customers" was held to be invalid as being too uncertain); *Marley Tile Co. Ltd. v. Johnson* [1982] I.R.L.R. 75. Note also *Office Angels Ltd. v. Rainer-Thomas* [1991] I.R.L.R. 214.

[61] See for example, *Lyne-Pirkis v. Jones* [1969] 1 W.L.R. 1293; also the observations on the inadequacy of restrictions of the former type in *Bridge v. Deacons* [1984] A.C. 705; *Allied Dunbar (Frank Weisinger) Ltd. v. Weisinger* [1988] I.R.L.R. 60.

Questions of *duration* have not been extensively considered by the courts; indeed, in *Bridge v. Deacons*,[62] the Privy Council observed that "there appears to be no reported case where a restriction which was otherwise reasonable has been held unreasonable solely because of its duration."[63] Although the House of Lords in *Fitch v. Dewes*[64] *did* uphold an area restriction as between a solicitor and his managing clerk which was unlimited in point of time, the current editor considers that exceptional circumstances would now be required to justify such an extreme approach. *Per contra*, in the case of restrictions on the solicitation of existing (as opposed to potential) customers or clients.[65]

It is, of course, for the partners to specify the precise terms of the restriction, since it is not possible to prevent competition "so far as the law allows."[66] Subject to any question of severance,[67] such terms are specified at the continuing partners' peril, *i.e.* the risk of invalidity falls solely on them. Moreover, the court will not be prepared to declare in advance what activities are likely to contravene the chosen restriction.[68]

10–188   In order to determine whether a particular restriction is reasonable, the court will first construe it according to its natural meaning, having regard to the object sought to be achieved[69] and to the factual matrix in which the agreement was prepared,[70] and only *then* apply the rule of reasonableness.[71] Opinion evidence of reasonableness is generally inadmissible since it involves a question of law and is, indeed, the primary issue to be decided by the court.[72] Evidence will, however,

---

[62] [1984] A.C. 705, 717.

[63] Note that in one unreported case (*Pandit v. Shah*, November 6, 1987), Whitford J. held that a 10 year restriction in the case of a doctors' partnership would be "impossible, in any circumstances, to support" at trial. However, consistently with the Privy Council's observation, the validity of the area restriction was also in doubt.

[64] [1921] 2 A.C. 158.

[65] *Cf. Konski v. Peet* [1915] 1 Ch. 530, where the restriction extended to *future* customers.

[66] *Davies v. Davies* (1887) 36 Ch.D. 359, where the covenant was held to be too uncertain to be enforced. Note also that the court will not be disposed to cut down the scope of an otherwise invalid restriction in order to render it valid: *J.A. Mont (U.K.) v. Mills* [1993] I.R.L.R. 172. And see, as to purporting to confer on the court to modify an invalid restriction, *Living Design (Home Improvments) Ltd. v. Davidson* [1994] I.R.L.R. 69.

[67] See *infra*, para. 10–193.

[68] *Mellstrom v. Garner* [1970] 1 W.L.R. 603.

[69] *Haynes v. Doman* [1899] 2 Ch. 13, 25, *per* Lindley M.R.; *Littlewoods Organisation Ltd. v. Harris* [1977] 1 W.L.R. 1472; *Clarke v. Newland* [1991] 1 All E.R. 397; *J.A. Mont (U.K.) v. Mills* [1993] I.R.L.R. 172. Note also *Office Angels Ltd. v. Rainer-Thomas* [1991 I.R.L.R. 214.

[70] See *supra*, para. 10–08.

[71] See *Moenich v. Fenestre* (1892) 67 L.T. 602; *Haynes v. Doman* [1899] 2 Ch. 13, 24–27, *per* Lindley M.R.; *Littlewoods Organisation Ltd. v. Harris* [1977] 1 W.L.R. 1472; *Clarke v. Newland* [1991] 1 All E.R. 397. The latter decision was a striking example of this approach, since the court was able to construe a restriction in a doctors' partnership agreement prohibiting practice in a certain area as confined to practice *as a general medical practitioner*, thus enabling the decisions in *Routh v. Jones* [1947] 1 All E.R. 758 and *Lyne-Pirkis v. Jones* [1969] 1 W.L.R. 1293 to be distinguished and the restriction upheld.

[72] *Haynes v. Doman, supra*; *Dowden & Pook Ltd. v. Pook* [1904] 1 K.B. 45; see also *Mason v. Provident Clothing and Supply Co. Ltd.* [1913] A.C. 724, 732–733, *per* Lord Haldane L.C.

be admissible as to the usual practice in any particular business;[73] if it is established that the restriction is an unusual one in that business, there is a greater likelihood of invalidity.[74]

Medical partnerships: There have, over the years, been a **10–189** relatively high proportion of decided cases relating to restrictions in medical partnerships[75] which, because of the unique characteristics of practice within the National Health Service, tend to be regarded as a separate sub-culture. However, in *Kerr v. Morris*,[76] the Court of Appeal in effect confirmed that normal principles apply, so that a special treatment of those cases is no longer appropriate in a work of this nature.[77]

(2)   Reasonableness in the Interests of the Public

Once the continuing partners have shown that the restriction is **10–190** reasonable in the interests of the parties, the burden of proving that the restriction is unreasonable in the interests of the public will fall on the outgoing partner. In such circumstances the burden of proof is extremely heavy,[78] and the current editor considers that the public interest alone would rarely invalidate a restriction, save, perhaps, where it affects the right of an outgoing partner to engage ex-employees of the firm.[79]

The apparent movement in the early 1980s towards striking down restrictions in professional partnerships on public policy grounds, merely because they deprive the client of his right to consult the adviser of his choice,[80] was summarily halted, first in the case of

---

[73] *Haynes v. Doman, supra*, at p. 20, *per* Lindley M.R.

[74] *Leng v. Andrews* [1909] 1 Ch. 763, 770, *per* Fletcher Moulton L.J.

[75] *Routh v. Jones* [1947] 1 All E.R. 758; *Jenkins v. Reid* [1948] 1 All E.R. 471; *Re Jenkins' Deed of Partnership* [1948] W.N. 98; *Whitehill v. Bradford* [1952] Ch. 236; *Macfarlane v. Kent* [1965] 1 W.L.R. 1019; *Lyne-Pirkis v. Jones* [1969] 1 W.L.R. 1293; *Peyton v. Mindham* [1972] 1 W.L.R. 8; *Hensman v. Traill, The Times*, October 22, 1980; *Anthony v. Rennie*, 1981 S.L.T. (Notes) 11; *Kerr v. Morris* [1987] Ch. 90; *Pandit v. Shah*, unreported, November 6, 1987, noticed *supra*, para. 10–187, n. 63; *Clarke v. Newland* [1991] 1 All E.R. 397, noticed *supra*, para. 10–188, n. 71. See also *Blakeley and Anderson v. de Lambert* [1959] N.Z.L.R. 356.

[76] [1987] Ch. 90.

[77] But see, further, the *Encyclopedia of Professional Partnerships*, Pt. 5.

[78] See *A.-G. Australia v. Adelaide Steamship Co. Ltd.* [1913] A.C. 781, 797, *per* Lord Parker.

[79] See *Kores Manufacturing Co. v. Kolok Manufacturing Co.* [1959] Ch. 108; *Esso Petroleum Co. Ltd. v. Harper's Garage (Stourport) Ltd.* [1968] A.C. 269, 300 (*per* Lord Reid), 319 (*per* Lord Hodson); *Hanover Insurance Brokers Ltd. v. Schapiro* [1994] I.R.L.R. 82. See also *Office Angels Ltd. v. Rainer-Thomas* [1991] I.R.L.R. 214, 219, *per* Slade L.J.

[80] See *Hensman v. Traill, The Times*, October 22, 1980 (doctors practising within the National Health Service); *Oswald Hickson Collier & Co. v. Carter-Ruck* [1984] A.C. 720, note (solicitors); *cf. Edwards v. Warboys* [1984] A.C. 724, note.

solicitors[81] and, subsequently, in the case of doctors practising within the National Health Service.[82]

Consideration

10–191 Lord Lindley wrote:

> "An agreement entered into when a partnership is formed, to the effect that a retiring partner[83] shall not carry on the business carried on by the firm, cannot be invalid for want of consideration."[84]

It has long been held unnecessary to enquire into the *adequacy* of the consideration,[85] but the Privy Council did just that in *Bridge v. Deacons*;[86] nevertheless, their Lordships appear not to have been much troubled thereby. However, when looking at the severability of a restriction,[87] the court will also have regard to the severability of the consideration given for it.[88]

Assignability

10–192 The benefit of a restriction will normally be incidental to the goodwill of the business and, thus, pass with an assignment of it.[89]

Severance

10–193 An excessive restriction will be void and unenforceable as to its entirety unless, as a matter of construction, any element which is confined within reasonable limits can be severed from the remainder. Such severance is only available if it is possible to apply the so-called

---

[81] *Bridge v. Deacons* [1984] A.C. 705, 719–720.

[82] *Kerr v. Morris* [1987] Ch. 90. The Court of Appeal also held that restrictions on competition are not invalidated by the National Health Service Act 1977, Sched. 10, para. 2(2)(a). See further the *Encyclopedia of Professional Partnerships*, Pt. 5.

[83] An expelled partner is, of course, in the same position.

[84] See *Austen v. Boys* (1858) 2 De G. & J. 626, 637, *per* Lord Cranworth. Note also *Clarkson v. Edge* (1863) 33 Beav. 227, where the consideration took the form of an agreement with a bankrupt to take his son into partnership and to employ the bankrupt. As to whether any consideration for accepting the imposition of a restriction would be taxable in the outgoing partner's hands, see *Kirby v. Thorn E.M.I. Plc* [1988] 1 W.L.R. 445.

[85] *Hitchcock v. Coker* (1837) 6 A. & E. 438.

[86] [1984] A.C. 705, 718.

[87] See *infra*, para. 10–193.

[88] See *Putsman v. Taylor* [1927] 1 K.B. 741; *Sadler v. Imperial Life Assurance Co. of Canada Ltd.* [1988] I.R.L.R. 388.

[89] *Jacoby v. Whitmore* (1883) 49 L.T. 335; *Showell v. Winkup* (1889) 60 L.T. 389; *Townsend v. Jarman* [1900] 2 Ch. 698; also *John Bros. Abergarw Brewery v. Holmes* [1900] 1 Ch. 188. For an example of a restriction of a personal nature (albeit too uncertain to be enforced), see *Davies v. Davies* (1887) 36 Ch.D. 359.

"blue pencil" test, *i.e.* can the offending part(s) be excised without altering the sense or requiring the amendment of what remains?[90] It follows that, in drafting a restriction, it is desirable to ensure that each element of the restriction in effect stands alone[91] and is, thus, readily severable. In the case of vendor and purchaser restrictions, the court will, in applying the blue pencil test, generally be prepared to excise parts of a restriction even if they are not of a merely trivial nature.[92]

Although agreements often seek to anticipate the possibility of severance by expressly declaring that each limb of the restriction is separate and distinct, this does not represent a substitute for careful drafting.[93]

Effect of dissolution

Subject to the precise terms of the agreement, a *general* dissolution **10–194** will effectively prevent any partner from seeking to enforce a restriction against his co-partners.[94]

Injunctive relief

A threatened breach of a valid restriction will normally be **10–195** restrained by injunction, unless the order would, in substance, involve the specific performance of a contract for personal services. Such relief will be granted on normal principles,[95] although it is in practice rare for proceedings to continue beyond the interlocutory stage.[96]

---

[90] See *T. Lucas & Co. v. Mitchell* [1974] Ch. 129; also *Goldsoll v. Goldman* [1915] 1 Ch. 292; *Putsman v. Taylor* [1927] 1 K.B. 637, affirmed at [1927] 1 K.B. 741 without considering the question of severance; *Macfarlane v. Kent* [1965] 1 W.L.R. 1019; *Scorer v. Seymour Jones* [1966] 1 W.L.R. 1419; *Sadler v. Imperial Life Assurance Co. of Canada Ltd.* [1988] I.R.L.R. 388; *Living Design (Home Improvements) Ltd. v. Davidson* [1994] I.R.L.R. 69.

[91] Thus, one element should not be dependent on another: see *Amoco Australia Pty. Ltd. v. Rocca Bros. Motor Engineering Co. Pty. Ltd.* [1975] A.C. 561; *Sadler v. Imperial Life Assurance Co. of Canada Ltd.*, *supra. Cf. Alec Lobb Ltd. v. Total Oil* [1985] 1 W.L.R. 173. As to clauses purporting to confer power on the court to modify a restriction, see *Living Design (Home Improvements) Ltd. v. Davidson* [1994] I.R.L.R. 69.

[92] See *Goldsoll v. Goldman* [1915] 1 Ch. 292.

[93] Note also the approach adopted by the court in *J.A. Mont (U.K.) Ltd. v. Mills* [1993] I.R.L.R. 172. *Cf. Hanover Insurance Brokers Ltd. Schapiro* [1994] I.R.L.R. 82, 87, *per* Nolan L.J.

[94] See, generally, *Brace v. Calder* [1895] 2 Q.B. 253; *cf. Peyton v. Mindham* [1972] 1 W.L.R. 8. *Per contra* in the case of enforcement against a partner who retired *prior* to the date of dissolution.

[95] See *Doherty v. Allman* (1878) 3 App.Cas. 709, 720, *per* Lord Cairns; *Snell's Principles of Equity* (29th ed.), pp. 645 *et seq.*; also *infra*, paras. 23–130 *et seq.*

[96] See as to the principles on which interlocutory injunctions are granted, *Fellowes & Son v. Fisher* [1976] Q.B. 122 (an employee case); *Kerr v. Morris* [1987] Ch. 90; *Prontaprint plc v. London Litho Ltd.* [1987] F.S.R. 315. The fact that customers have indicated that they do not wish to deal with the continuing partners will be an irrelevant consideration: see *John Michael Design v. Cooke* [1987] 2 All E.R. 232. And note also the decision in *Unigate Dairies Ltd. v. Bruce, The Times*, March 2, 1988.

An injunction may be obtained even though other provisions of the agreement are unenforceable, provided that the restriction sought to be enforced is not dependent on those provisions.[97]

It was formerly common to find agreements which provided for the payment of a fixed sum by way of liquidated damages on breach of a restriction,[98] thus in general forcing the continuing partners to decide between injunctive relief and the recovery of such damages.[99] However, provisions of this type are rarely encountered today.

Article 85 of the European Community Treaty

10–196   Article 85 of the European Community Treaty[1] renders null and void certain practices considered to be incompatible with the Common Market. The prohibited practices are summarised as:

"all agreements between undertakings, decisions by associations of undertakings and concerted practices, which may affect trade between Member States and which have as their object or effect the prevention, restriction or distortion of competition within the Common Market."[2]

10–197   The application of Article 85 to restrictions imposed for the protection of goodwill was considered in *Gottfried Reuter v. BASF A.G.*,[3] from which the following propositions may be drawn:

    (1) An outgoing partner would be regarded as an outgoing "undertaking" for the purposes of Article 85 and, thus, any restriction imposed on him which might interfere with trade

---

[97] As to interdependent provisions and conditions, see *Amoco Australia Pty. Ltd. v. Rocca Bros. Motor Engineering Co. Pty. Ltd.* [1975] A.C. 561; *Sadler v. Imperial Life Assurance Co. of Canada Ltd.* [1988] I.R.L.R. 388.

[98] See generally, as to the difference between penalties and liquidated damages, *Chitty on Contracts* (26th ed.), paras. 1829 *et seq.* A payment which is to be made on the occurrence of a specified event is *not* a penalty: see *Export Credits Guarantee Dept. v. Universal Oil Products Co.* [1983] 1 W.L.R. 399; *E.F.T. Commercial Ltd. v. Security Change Ltd. (No. 1)*, 1993 S.L.T. 128 (1st Div.), where both the English and Scots authorities are reviewed. See also *infra*, para. 10–243.

[99] *General Accident Assurance Corp. v. Noel* [1902] 1 K.B. 377. *Cf. Stiles v. Ecclestone* [1903] 1 K.B. 544, 546, *per* Lord Alverstone; *Imperial Tobacco Co. v. Parslay* [1936] 2 All E.R. 515; *Elsley v. Collins Insurance Agencies* (1978) 83 D.L.R.(3d) 1 (Can.Sup. Ct.). Note also that it may be possible to demonstrate that the liquidated damages were only intended to cover damage sustained *before* the grant of an injunction: see *Braid v. Lawes*, an unreported decision of a Divisional Court (Acton and Talbot JJ.) on May 18, 1933, affirming a decision of a former editor of this work sitting as a judge of the Exeter county court.

[1] See *infra*, paras. A5–01, A5–02.

[2] Art. 85(1), *infra*, para. A5–01. As to the territorial scope of Art. 85, see *Åhlström Osakeyhtiö v. E.C. Commission* [1988] 4 C.M.L.R. 901. *Quaere* whether the relationship of partnership can itself lead to a breach of Art. 85: see *supra*, para. 8–05. And see, generally, the Notice on Co-operation between National Courts and the Commission in applying Articles 85 and 86 of the European Community Treaty (1993) O.J. C39/6.

[3] [1976] 2 C.M.L.R. D.44 (76/743/EEC).

between Member States of the Common Market would prima facie be void under Article 85(2).[4]

(2) A restriction imposed on an outgoing partner will be regarded as infringing Article 85 if it affects goods and services which could be offered by that partner and which could be the subject of trade between Member States.[5]

(3) It is, however, permissible to impose a restriction on an outgoing partner if that is "necessary" to protect the goodwill or know-how acquired by the continuing partners, e.g. to prevent solicitation of customers.[6]

(4) The Commission's approach to potential infringements of Article 85 is broadly similar to that adopted by the English courts when applying the restraint of trade doctrine, i.e. in determining whether the restriction is wider than necessary to protect the value of the goodwill, account must be taken of the nature of the business carried on and of any know-how forming part of that business. It is permissible to protect reasonable developments of the business but, in normal circumstances, the restriction should not extend beyond the area and scope of the existing business.[7]

(5) Where a particular restriction is only partially invalid, severance will generally be possible.[8]

(6) The protection afforded by the restriction must be limited to a reasonable period, during which the continuing partners would be expected to have consolidated and safeguarded their position from competition by the outgoing partner.[9]

Even where a particular restriction does prima facie contravene **10–198** Article 85(1), it may be possible to obtain exemption for the agreement under Article 85(3),[10] on the basis that it "contributes to improving the production or distribution of goods or to promoting technical or economic progress, while allowing consumers a fair share of the resulting benefit," provided that it neither imposes on the undertakings concerned[11] restrictions which are not indispensable to

---

[4] *Ibid.* D.55, para. [35].

[5] *Ibid.* D.61, para. [71]. But there will be no such infringement where trade would be affected only to an insignificant extent: *Raygems v. Attias* (1978) 75 L.S. Gaz. 224.

[6] Note that an outgoing partner who disposes of his share in goodwill is, in any event, subject to certain implied obligations, including an obligation not to solicit: see *supra*, paras. 10–168 *et seq.*

[7] *Gottfried Reuter v. BASF A.G.*, *supra*, D.55–57, paras. [41]–[47]; and see generally *Technique Minière S.A. v. Maschinenbau Ulm GmbH* [1966] C.M.L.R. 357; *Consten S.A. and Grundig-Verkaufs GmbH v. EEC Commission* [1966] C.M.L.R. 418.

[8] See the cases referred to in the preceding footnote; also *Inntrepreneur Estalis (G.L.) Ltd. v. Boyes* [1993] 47 E.G. 140. And see an interesting article by Valentine Korah at (1984) 134 N.L.J. 134.

[9] See *Gottfried Reuter v. BASF A.G.*, *supra*, D.56, para. [43].

[10] See *infra*, para. A5–02.

[11] *i.e.* the outgoing partner: see *supra*, para. 10–198.

the achievement of the above objectives nor affords such undertakings the possibility of eliminating competition in respect of a substantial part of the products in question. However, a prerequisite to a claim to exemption under Article 85(3), when the validity of the restriction is called in question, is that notification of the agreement should have been made to the Commission in accordance with the Regulations.[12] Notification has to take place as quickly as possible since, in determining whether a particular agreement is exempt, the Commission must state the date from which its decision takes effect, and that date cannot precede the date of notification.[13]

10–199 In cases where it is thought likely that a particular restriction may infringe Article 85(1), application can be made to the Commission for negative clearance, *i.e.* the Commission is requested to certify that, according to the information received by it, there are no grounds for interference under Article 85(1).[14] However, even if such clearance is given, it will not bind the Commission if the validity of the restriction is subsequently called into question.[15]

The validity of a restriction may be challenged on the initiative of the Commission or at the request of a Member State or any natural or legal person with a legitimate interest.[16] Where an infringement of Article 85 has been found, the Commission can require the undertakings concerned to put an end to it.[17]

Restrictive Trade Practices Act 1976

10–200 It is submitted that there is limited scope for the application of the Restrictive Trade Practices Act 1976 in the case of restrictions sought to be imposed on an outgoing partner. The Act applies only where restrictions are accepted by at least two of the parties to the agreement[18] and, for this purpose, individuals carrying on business in partnership are treated as a single person.[19]

---

[12] Council Reg. 17, Art. 4, *infra*, paras. A5–06, A5–07. As to the effect of a partial notification, see *De Vereeniging Ter Bevordering Van De Belangen Des Boekhandels v. Eldi Records* B.V. [1980] 3 C.M.L.R. 719 (79/106/EEC).

[13] *Ibid.* Art. 6, *infra*, para. A5–09. The exemption must be for a specified period, and may be subject to conditions or obligations; it may also be renewed or revoked from time to time: see *ibid.* Art. 8, *infra*, para. A5–11, A5–12. A 15 year exemption was granted in one case: *Re the Volkswagen MAN Agreement* [1984] 1 C.M.L.R. 621.

[14] Council Reg. 17, Art. 2, *infra*, para. A5–04. See also the Practice Note on Comfort Letters at [1984] 1 C.M.L.R. 38.

[15] See *Bosch v. de Geus* [1962] C.M.L.R. 1.

[16] Council Reg. 17, Art. 3, para. 2, *infra*, para. A5–05.

[17] *Ibid.* Art. 3, para. 1. Note also *ibid.* para. 3.

[18] Restrictive Trade Practices Act 1976, ss.6(1), 11(1)(b).

[19] *Ibid.* s.43(2); *cf.* the position in Scotland: see *Donald Storrie Estate Agency Ltd. v. Adams,* 1989 S.L.T. 305 (O.H) The detailed application of this Act is outside the scope of the present work and the reader is referred to *Chitty on Contracts* (26th ed.), paras. 4353 *et seq.*

Competition Act 1980

Just as Article 85 of the European Community Treaty seeks to **10–201** prevent restrictions on competition within the Common Market, so the Competition Act 1980 seeks to control certain types of "anti-competitive practices" within the United Kingdom. A person[20] engages in an anti-competitive practice within the meaning of the Act where he:

"pursues a course of conduct which . . . has or is intended to have or is likely to have the effect of restricting, distorting or preventing competition in connection with the production, supply or acquisition of goods in the United Kingdom or any part of it or the supply or securing of services in the United Kingdom or any part of it."[21]

However, the Secretary of State has power to exclude from the application of the Act certain types of conduct, and in particular the conduct of any person by reference to the size of his business;[22] this power has, in fact, been exercised so as to exclude persons whose turnover in the United Kingdom does not exceed £5 million and who do not enjoy more than a one quarter share of the relevant market.[23]

Where it appears that a person has been or is pursuing a course of **10–202** conduct which may amount to an anti-competitive practice, the Director General of Fair Trading is entitled to carry out a preliminary investigation into the matter and must publish a report of the results.[24] If appropriate, the matter may then be referred to the Monopolies and Mergers Commission, whose report may ultimately lead to an order being made by the Secretary of State under section 10 of the Act prohibiting the anti-competitive practice concerned.[25] Obviously, the Act will have limited application in the case of most partnership agreements, simply by virtue of the £5 million turnover and market share thresholds, but the position of more substantial corporate[26] and other partnerships may require careful consideration.

---

[20] "Person" includes a partnership: Interpretation Act 1978, s.5, Sched. 1.
[21] Competition Act 1980, s.2(1). In the case of bodies corporate, account may be taken of the conduct of certain associated persons: *ibid.* s.2(1), (6).
[22] *Ibid.* s.2(3), (4).
[23] See the Anti-Competitive Practices (Exclusions) Order 1980 (S.I. 1980 No. 979), Art. 2(b), Sched. 2.
[24] Competition Act 1980, s.3. Following publication of the report, the Director must consider any representations made and undertakings offered to him by the person specified therein: *ibid.* s.4.
[25] As to the procedure to be adopted on and following the reference, see *ibid.* ss.5–9. Note also the powers of the Director under the Fair Trading Act 1973 to refer a "monopoly situation" (as defined in *ibid.* ss. 6, 7) or a "complex monopoly situation" (as defined in *ibid.* s.11(1)) to the Commission.
[26] See further, as to such partnerships, *infra*, paras. 11–02 *et seq.*

The Act will not, in general, apply concurrently with the Restrictive Trade Practices Act 1976.[27]

V. Provisions Consequential on the Death, Retirement or Expulsion of a Partner[28]

(a) Assignment of outgoing partner's share, etc.[29]

Assignment of share

10–203   Lord Lindley observed:

> "When a partner retires[30] or dies, and he or his executors[31] are paid what is due in respect of his share, it is customary for him or them formally to assign and release his interest in the partnership, and for the continuing or surviving partners to take upon themselves the payment of the outstanding debts of the firm, and to indemnify their late partner or his estate from all such debts."[32]

In practice, a formal assignment of an outgoing partner's share is unusual, even though there is now only limited scope for a charge to *ad valorem* stamp duty thereon.[33] As a result, modern agreements generally contain a standard "further assurance" obligation, so that an assignment can be called for if it should prove necessary. Such a provision will also facilitate the retirement of the outgoing partner from the trusteeship of any partnership assets which he may have undertaken.[34]

Assignment of debts

10–204   Although an express assignment of partnership debts will, if the requirements of section 136 of the Law of Property Act 1925 are satisfied, entitle the continuing partners to recover such debts without reference to the outgoing partner, this option is rarely adopted in practice.[35]

---

[27] Competition Act 1980, s.2(2).

[28] See the *Encyclopedia of Professional Partnerships*, Precedent 1, cl. 22(2)(f)–(k).

[29] See *ibid.* Precedent 1, cl. 22(2)(f), (k).

[30] An expelled partner will be in the same position.

[31] Similarly, in the case of an administrator.

[32] See *infra*, paras. 10–207 *et seq.*

[33] See *infra*, para. 10–206.

[34] Note that, if the outgoing partner is an original covenantor in respect of leasehold premises, he will normally remain liable on those covenants even *after* he has given up the trusteeship.

[35] This is largely because commercial considerations militate against giving express written notice of the assignment to all customers, etc. See also *infra*, para. 14–86. As to the effect on such an assignment of the bankruptcy of the assignor, see the Insolvency Act 1986, s.344.

Where the agreement obliges the continuing partners to get in the old firm's debts and requires such debts, when paid, to be taken into account in ascertaining the outgoing partner's entitlement, the continuing partners will be chargeable with the value of any debts that they, for whatever reason, choose not to get in.[36] Equally, an outgoing partner who, after assigning his interest in such debts, does anything to prejudice the continuing partners' rights, *e.g.* by releasing a creditor, will be guilty of a derogation from grant for which he can be held liable.[37]

Where a debt is owed by the outgoing partner to the firm and is intended to be recoverable by the continuing partners notwithstanding any financial settlement reached with him, this fact should be specifically mentioned.[38]

Assignment of share in partnership land

If the partnership assets consist of land, a written assignment of the **10–205** outgoing partner's interest therein will seemingly be required.[39]

Stamp duty

An assignment of an outgoing partner's share in consideration of a **10–206** payment from the continuing partners of what is due to him from the firm constitutes a sale for stamp duty purposes,[40] but *ad valorem* duty is now chargeable only in respect of an apportioned part of the consideration which represents the outgoing partner's interest in any land held by the firm.[41] However, even in such a case it does not necessarily follow that duty will be chargeable in all cases: in a passage which subsequently received judicial approval,[42] Lord Lindley pointed out that:

"... if the retiring partner, instead of assigning his interest, takes the amount due to him from the firm, gives a receipt for the money, and acknowledges that he has no more claims on his co-partners, they will practically obtain all they want; but such a transaction, even if carried out by deed, could hardly be held to

---

[36] *Lees v. Laforest* (1851) 14 Beav. 262.
[37] *Aulton v. Atkins* (1856) 18 C.B. 249. Such a situation is unlikely to arise if the requirements of the Law of Property Act 1925, s.136 are satisfied.
[38] *Ibid.* See also *infra*, para. 19–05.
[39] See *infra*, para. 19–76.
[40] *Christie v. Commissioners of Inland Revenue* (1866) L.R. 2 Ex. 46; *Phillips v. Commissioners of Inland Revenue* (1867) L.R. 2 Ex. 399; *Potter v. Commissioners of Inland Revenue* (1854) 10 Ex. 147. See also *supra*, para. 10–154, n. 27.
[41] Finance Act 1991, ss. 110, 111. See also *infra*, para. 38–02.
[42] See *Garnett v. I.R.C.* (1899) 81 L.T. 633, 637, *per* Darling J.

amount to a sale; and no *ad valorem* stamp, it is apprehended, would be payable."[43]

Where appropriate, the assignment should include a certificate of value, so as to gain the advantage of the nil rate of duty, which is now set at £60,000.[44]

(b) Indemnity to Outgoing Partner[45]

10–207 As already noticed,[46] it is usual for the continuing or surviving partners to indemnify the outgoing partner or his estate against the partnership debts and obligations,[47] although such an indemnity is, in practice, usually implied. Lord Lindley observed:

"... in the absence of any agreement to that effect, a retiring partner[48] or the executor of a deceased partner[49] has no right to an indemnity from the other partners, except so far as he may be entitled to have assets of the firm applied in payment of its debts, and to enforce contribution in case he has to pay more than his share of those debts.[50] But if all the assets of the firm are assigned to the continuing or the surviving partners, it is only fair that they should undertake to pay its debts: and if it appears that it was the intention of all parties that they should do so, effect will be given to such intention, although the undertaking on their part is not explicit in its terms."[51]

Consistently with this statement of principle, the Court of Appeal had no hesitation in recognising the existence of an implied right to indemnity in *Gray v. Smith*.[52] It is, of course, rare to encounter a

---

[43] See also *Fleetwood-Hesketh v. Commissioners of Inland Revenue* [1936] 1 K.B. 351. *Cf. Grey v. I.R.C.* [1960] A.C. 1. And note the decision in *Steer v. Crowley* (1863) 14 C.B.(N.S.) 337, which concerned a release by the executors of a deceased partner which did not state the consideration and only bore an ordinary deed stamp, but was nevertheless held to be a good document of title.

[44] See the Finance Act 1963, s.55(1)(a), as substituted by the Finance Act 1984, s.109(1) and amended by the Finance Act 1993, s.201(1)(a).

[45] See the *Encyclopedia of Professional Partnerships*, Precedent 1, cl. 22(2)(g).

[46] See *supra*, para. 10–203.

[47] Lord Lindley pointed out that the indemnity "is ordinarily given by a bond or covenant entered into by the continuing or surviving partners, in consideration of the assignment to them of all the share and interest of the retiring or deceased partner." This is now rarely done. However, if the agreement is executed under seal, the outgoing partner will be a specialty creditor of the continuing partners if he is called on to pay a partnership debt: *Musson v. May* (1814) 3 V. & B. 194.

[48] An expelled partner will be in the same position.

[49] Similarly, in the case of an administrator.

[50] See the Partnership Act 1890, s.39, *infra*, paras. 19–29 *et seq.*; also *infra*, paras. 20–04 *et seq.*

[51] See *Saltoun v. Houston* (1824) 1 Bing. 433; *Gray v. Smith* (1889) 43 Ch.D. 208, 220. See also, as to the position of a purchaser of a partnership share, *Dodson v. Downey* [1901] 2 Ch. 620; also *infra*, para. 19–67.

[52] (1889) 43 Ch.D. 208, 220, 221. See also the judgment of Kekewich J. at first instance: *ibid.* p. 213, 214.

case in which an outgoing partner does not, either expressly or by necessary implication, relinquish his share in the partnership assets.[53]

In its usual form the indemnity will not entitle the outgoing partner or his personal representatives to call on the continuing or surviving partners to pay the debts until a demand has been made for their payment.[54]

Debts, etc., excluded from ambit of indemnity

There will often be excluded from the terms of the express **10–208** indemnity:

(*a*) in the case of firms in existence prior to April 6, 1994, any income tax assessable on the partnership in respect of profits received by the outgoing partner;[55]
(*b*) any debt or liability attributable to the outgoing partner's own wrongful acts or omissions.[56]

However, this may be both unnecessary and inappropriate if sufficient retentions have been made on account of such matters pursuant to an express power in the agreement.[57]

Effect of indemnity

Whilst the outgoing partner remains directly liable for the **10–209** partnership debts and obligations,[58] such an indemnity places him in the position of surety *vis-à-vis* the continuing partners.[59] It follows that he may be discharged if a creditor, with notice of that arrangement, deals with the continuing partners in such a way as to prejudice the outgoing partner's rights against them.[60]

---

[53] *Ibid.*; see also *Sobell v. Boston* [1975] 1 W.L.R. 1587.

[54] *Bradford v. Gammon* [1925] Ch. 132.

[55] Otherwise, see *Stevens v. Britten* [1954] 1 W.L.R. 1340. In the case of firms formed on or after April 6, 1994, income tax is no longer assessed on the partners jointly. As from the tax year 1997/98 this treatment will be extended to all firms, whenever formed: see *infra*, paras. 34–1 *et seq.*

[56] See *infra*, para. 20–10. Note, however, that the usual form of exclusion goes beyond the type of case considered in that paragraph and applies to *all* wrongful acts, including "mere" negligence. What is more unusual is to find the exclusion also extended to the negligent acts and omissions of the continuing partners, although this is not unknown.

[57] See *supra*, paras. 10–73, 10–143.

[58] See *infra*, paras. 13–74 *et seq.*

[59] *Oakeley v. Pasheller* (1836) 4 Cl. & F. 207, *infra*, para. 13–99; *Rodgers v. Maw* (1846) 4 Dow. & L. 66. If the indemnity is given by deed, the outgoing partner will be specialty creditor in respect of any debt which he is called on to pay: *Musson v. May* (1814) 3 V. & B. 194.

[60] See *Oakeley v. Pasheller, supra*; *Overend, Gurney & Co. v. Oriental Financial Corpn.* (1874) L.R. 7 H.L. 348; *Rouse v. Bradford Banking Co.* [1894] A.C. 586; also *infra*, paras. 13–98 *et seq.* But see as to the position once a judgment has been obtained, *Re a Debtor (No. 14 of 1913)* [1913] 3 K.B. 11.

Equally, it would seem that, by taking such an indemnity, the outgoing partner will forfeit his partner's lien, as Lord Lindley explained:

"When a retiring partner[61] assigns his interest in the partnership assets, and obtains from the continuing partners a covenant of indemnity,[62] his lien on the partnership assets seems to be at an end."

Thus, in *Re Langmead's Trusts*,[63] the retiring partners were held to have no lien on the assets of the old firm, even though the assignment of their interest therein was expressed to be subject to the payment of their share of the partnership debts, and they were accordingly left to pursue their remedy on the covenant for indemnity given by the continuing partner, who was by then bankrupt.

(c) Gazette Notices, etc.[64]

10–210 Prior to the Partnership Act 1890, Lord Lindley wrote:

"When power is given to retire or dissolve the firm, or to expel a partner from it, power should also be given to any partner to sign, in the name of himself and co-partners, a notice of dissolution for insertion in the '*Gazette*.' "

Since this power is now given by the 1890 Act itself,[65] such a provision is now strictly unnecessary, although an express right to sign the *Gazette* notice on behalf of an unco-operative outgoing partners may prove valuable. Equally, a specific provision dealing with *Gazette* notices will be required if the outgoing partner's rights in this respect are to be in any way restricted.[66]

The agreement may also record the manner in which existing customers are to be notified, whether by circular letter or otherwise.[67]

---

[61] Or an expelled partner.

[62] As noted *supra*, para. 10–207, n. 47, a *covenant* of indemnity is, as such, no longer given.

[63] (1855) 7 De G.M. & G. 353. See also *Lingen v. Simpson* (1824) 1 Sim. & St. 600 and *infra*, para. 19–40.

[64] See the *Encyclopedia of Professional Partnerships*, Precedent 1, cl. 22(2)(h).

[65] s.37: see *infra*, para. 13–42.

[66] The continuing partners may, understandably, wish to retain control over the form of the advertisement, etc. However, so far as concerns the outgoing partner, he will continue to be exposed to risk until such time as the advertisement appears: see the Partnership Act 1890, s.36(1), (2), *infra*, paras. 13–42 *et seq.*

[67] See *ibid.* s.36(1) and *infra*, paras. 13–70 *et seq.* Note also that, in the case of a professional practice, there may be a rule of conduct which requires certain clients or classes of clients to be notified of a change in the firm: see, for example, the *Law Society's Guide to the Professional Conduct of Solicitors* (6th ed.), principle 3.13.

(d) Income Tax Elections[68]

In the case of a firm in existence prior to April 6, 1994, a well-drawn **10–211** agreement will invariably require an outgoing partner or his personal representatives to join in a notice of election under section 113(2) of the Income and Corporation Taxes Act 1988, with a view to avoiding a permanent discontinuance of the partnership business for income tax purposes.[69] Since such an election is revocable during the statutory two year period, some agreements also provide for the outgoing partner to sign a notice of revocation, so that the continuing partners will enjoy the maximum flexibility. In some cases, the continuing partners are given the right to sign the election (and revocation) on behalf of the outgoing partner, but this is relatively unusual. Where the firm comprises 50 or more partners, the Inland Revenue are, by concession, prepared to accept a "blanket" continuance election[70]: in such a case, it is prudent to insist on an incoming partner adding his name to the election as a condition of his entry into partnership, although this could equally well be provided for in the agreement.

The continuing partners, in their turn, will in general afford an **10–212** indemnity to the outgoing partner against any *additional* income tax which may become payable as a result of submitting the continuance election.[71] Since the rates of capital gains tax are now determined by reference to an individual's level of income,[72] it is for consideration whether the usual indemnity should also be extended to any additional capital gains tax liability thrown up by the election.[73]

As from the tax year 1997/98, there will be no need to submit a continuance election on any change in the firm, so that provisions of this type will gradually disappear; they are *already* unnecessary in the case of firms formed on or after April 6, 1994.[73a]

(e) Books and Papers[74]

It is usual to include in the agreement an express obligation on the **10–213** part of an outgoing partner to deliver up to the continuing partners all books and papers, etc., in his possession which relate to the partnership business, although a limited right of access may be

---

[68] See the *Encyclopedia of Professional Partnerships*, Precedent 1, cl. 22(2)(i).
[69] See, as to the tax consequences of a discontinuance in such a case, *infra*, paras. 34–45.
[70] See Extra Statutory Concession A80 "Blanket Partnership Continuation Elections", reproduced *infra*, para. A6–05.
[71] As to what this will involve, see *infra*, para. 34–49, n. 67.
[72] Finance Act 1988, s.98.
[73] *e.g.* if the effect of the election is to push the outgoing partner's capital gains into the higher rate band, is the additional 15 per cent tax to fall on him?
[73a] See *infra*, paras. 34–58, 34–59.
[74] See the *Encyclopedia of Professional Partnerships*, Precedent 1, cl. 22(2)(j).

afforded to the outgoing partner for, say, a period of 12 months after he ceases to be a member of the firm. This will normally reflect an attempt to balance the competing interests of the outgoing partner, who will be concerned to ensure that he has received his full financial entitlement, and the continuing partners, who will be concerned to ensure that the outgoing partner does not have access to confidential information regarding the affairs of the ongoing firm.

Clients' documents

10–214   It is also desirable, in the case of a firm which holds clients' documents in the course of its business, that the agreement addresses their disposition in the event of a change in the firm or a general dissolution.[75] However, subject to the availability of any lien, the partners obviously cannot thereby prejudice a client's right to his own papers.[76]

W.   ADMISSION OF NEW PARTNERS[77]

10–215 It is now by no means unusual, particularly in the professions, to encounter agreements which expressly provide for the admission of new partners, by requiring them either to execute a separate deed of accession or suchlike or to append their signatures to a special "signing schedule." In this way, the new partner will indicate his unequivocal acceptance of the existing partnership terms.[78] If he fails to do so, uncertainty will inevitably be created, as Lord Lindley explained:

> "When a person has been admitted into an existing firm, and no express agreement has been made as to his rights and liabilities, the inference is that as between themselves his position is the same as that of the other partners. If they are bound by existing articles he will be bound by the same articles, if his conduct justifies the conclusion that he has assented to them; and if any special agreement is made with him, it will be regarded as incorporated with any previous agreement between the other partners, although so far as the two agreements may be inconsistent, the latest will prevail.[79] If, indeed, the incoming partner has no knowledge of

---

[75] This avoids any doubt as to whether the custody of the papers passes with the goodwill: see *James v. James* (1889) 22 Q.B.D. 669, 675, note.

[76] *Ex p. Horsfall* (1827) 7 B. & C. 528; also *Casson Beckman & Partners v. Papi* [1991] BCLC 299. And see *supra*, para. 3–49.

[77] See the *Encyclopedia of Professional Partnerships*, Precedent 2, Art. 2.02, Precedent 9, cl. 21.

[78] See *ibid.* Precedent 2, Art. 2.02.00.

[79] See *Austen v. Boys* (1857) 24 Beav. 598 and, on appeal, (1858) 2 De G. & J. 626.

any prior agreement between the others, he cannot be bound thereby[80] for nothing that he can have done can be regarded, under these circumstances, as evidence of any assent thereto on his part; and it is upon such presumed assent that the rule in question is founded."[81]

In many instances, minor variations of the partnership agreement will be agreed at a partners' meeting and minuted accordingly, but it is rare to find such minutes being disclosed to an incoming partner; *a fortiori* in the case of variations by conduct.[82] In such circumstances, the presumption must be that the incoming partner is not bound thereby.

It has already been seen that a failure to agree terms with an incoming partner may even result in the creation of a partnership at will.[83]

The right to nominate a successor partner[84]

A provision entitling an outgoing partner or his executors to **10–216** nominate a successor to be admitted to the partnership in his place, which was once commonplace,[85] is now rarely, if ever, encountered in practice.[86] Nevertheless, it is useful to summarise the rules applicable to such provisions, as originally formulated by Lord Lindley.

Rule 1:

"... clauses of this kind, although they bind the surviving **10–217** partners[87] to let in the person nominated,[88] do not bind him to come in, but give him an option whether he will do so or not."[89]

---

[80] *Ibid.*

[81] *Cf.* the Partnership Act 1890, s.27, *supra*, paras. 10–16 *et seq.*

[82] See *supra*, para. 10–14.

[83] See *Firth v. Amslake* (1964) 108 S.J. 198, noticed *supra*, para. 9–12.

[84] See the *Encyclopedia of Professional Partnerships*, Precedent 9, cl. 21.

[85] Lord Lindley went as far as to say "It is a common provision in partnership articles that on the death of a partner his executors, or his son, or some other person, shall be entitled to take his place." In some cases, succession to the share was not even dependent on any form of nomination: see *Balmain v. Shore* (1804) 9 Ves.Jr. 500; *Ponton v. Dunn* (1830) 1 R. & M. 402.

[86] Note, however, that the current editor has explored the use of this device as a means of preserving the right to pay inheritance tax by instalments: see the *Encyclopedia of Professional Partnerships*, Pt. 6.

[87] Similarly, in the case of continuing partners, where the nomination is by a retiring partner.

[88] See *Byrne v. Reid* [1902] 2 Ch. 735; also *Wainwright v. Waterman* (1791) 1 Ves.Jr. 311, where a declaration was granted. *Cf. Milliken v. Milliken* (1845) 8 I.Eq.R. 16, where the nominee was held to be remediless. As to the position once the nominee has been admitted, see *infra*, para. 19–71. Subject to the terms of the agreement, a mere bequest of residue will not amount to a sufficient nomination: see *Beamish v. Beamish* (1869) 4 Eq. I.R. 120; *Thomson v. Thomson*, 1962 S.L.T. 109 (H.L.).

[89] *Pigott v. Bagley* (1825) McCle. & Yo. 569; *Madgwick v. Wimble* (1843) 6 Beav. 495; *Page v. Cox* (1851) 10 Hare 163; *Thomson v. Thomson*, *supra*, at p. 111, *per* Lord Reid. See also *Pearce v. Chamberlain* (1750) 2 Ves.Sen. 33.

If the nominee was not a party to the original agreement and is not the deceased partner's personal representative,[90] his right to enforce such a provision will seemingly be dependent on establishing the existence of an immediate trust in his favour,[91] as the widow was able to do in *Page v. Cox*.[92] Where, however, the nominee's right to be admitted is conditional on the consent of the continuing or surviving partners being obtained, no trust can exist if such consent is properly withheld.[93]

Even where the agreement clearly states that the nominee will join the firm, specific performance will not be ordered as against him, although the outgoing partner or his estate may be liable in damages.[94]

Rule 2:

10–218   "... before making up his mind [*the nominee*] is entitled to make himself acquainted with the state of the partnership affairs, although he is not entitled to have its accounts formally taken."[95]

It follows that the share of the outgoing partner may fall to be treated as a debt due to him or to his estate during the interim period.[96]

Rule 3:

10–219   "... if [*the nominee*] is desirous of coming in, he must comply strictly with the terms upon which alone he is entitled to do so."[97]

By so doing, he will, of course, indicate his acceptance of the partnership terms.[98]

---

[90] See *Beswick v. Beswick* [1968] A.C. 58.
[91] *Ehrmann v. Ehrmann* (1894) 72 L.T. 17. Note, however, that in *Byrne v. Reid* [1902] 2 Ch. 735, only Stirling L.J. referred to the existence of a trust: see *ibid.* pp. 744–745. This decision was distinguished in *Re Franklin and Swathling's Arbitration* [1929] 1 Ch. 238, although Maugham J. appears to have assumed that a trust was established: see *ibid.* p. 242. *Quaere* whether there is a residual class of cases in which *no* trust exists but an effective nomination confers all the rights of a partner on the nominee.
[92] (1851) 10 Hare 163. See also *Drimmie v. Davies* [1899] 1 I.R. 176; *Byrne v. Reid, supra; Re Franklin and Swathling's Arbitration, supra.* And see further, as to establishing the existence of a trust, *supra,* para. 10–150.
[93] *Re Franklin and Swathling's Arbitration, supra.* Note also *Ehrmann v. Ehrmann* (1894) 72 L.T. 17.
[94] See *Downs v. Collins* (1848) 6 Hare 418; also *Lisle v. Reeve* [1902] 1 Ch. 53 (affirmed *sub nom. Reeve v. Lisle* [1902] A.C. 461), where an inquiry as to damages was directed: see *ibid.* p. 70. The latter case concerned an option to become a partner, as to which see *supra,* paras. 2–13 *et seq. Cf. Byrne v. Reid* [1902] 2 Ch. 735, 745, *per* Stirling L.J.
[95] *Pigott v. Bagley* (1825) McCle. & Yo. 569.
[96] See the Partnership Act 1890, s.43; also *Thomson v. Thomson,* 1962 S.L.T. 109, 110–111, *per* Lord Reid.
[97] *Holland v. King* (1848) 6 C.B. 727; *Brooke v. Garrod* (1857) 3 K. & J. 608; also *Milliken v. Milliken* (1845) 8 I.Eq.R. 16. *Cf. Ex p. Marks* (1832) 1 D. & Ch. 499.
[98] See *supra,* para. 10–215.

Rule 4:

"... if [*the nominee*] declines to come in, and there is no **10–220** provision as to what is then to be done, the partnership must be dissolved and wound up in the usual way."[99]

X. WINDING-UP[1]

Agreements frequently make special provision for the winding up of **10–221** the partnership affairs in the event of a *general* dissolution, whether resulting from the continuing partners' failure to exercise an option to acquire an outgoing partner's share,[2] the exercise of an express power to dissolve[3] or even an order of the court (or an arbitrator).[4] Such a provision is, of course, strictly unnecessary if the partnership affairs are to be wound up in accordance with the provisions of the Partnership Act 1890,[5] although it may be useful to record the fact that each partner is to have liberty to purchase any partnership assets which fall to be sold.[6]

Division of assets in specie

Where it is intended that the partnership assets will be divided **10–222** between the partners *in specie*, this fact should be clearly stated. Lord Lindley explained:

"An agreement that on a dissolution the partnership property shall be fairly and equally divided, after payment of its debts, has been held to mean that the property shall be sold, and that the money produced by the sale shall be divided after the debts have been paid."[7]

Even if such a construction is avoided, it would seem that a court might still, in an appropriate case, order a sale.[8]

---

[99] *Kershaw v. Matthews* (1826) 2 Russ. 62; *Downs v. Collins* (1848) 6 Hare 418; *Madgwick v. Wimble* (1843) 6 Beav. 495.
[1] See the *Encyclopedia of Professional Partnerships*, Precedent 1, cl. 24.
[2] See *supra*, para. 10–126.
[3] See *supra*, paras. 10–113 *et seq.*
[4] See the Partnership Act 1890, s.35, *infra*, paras. 24–39 *et seq.*; see also *infra*, para. 10–232.
[5] See *ibid.* ss.37–39, 42, 44; also *infra*, paras. 25–21 *et seq.*
[6] Otherwise see *infra*, para. 23–186.
[7] *Rigden v. Pierce* (1822) 6 Madd. 353; *Cook v. Collingridge* (1822) Jac. 607.
[8] *Taylor v. Neate* (1888) 39 Ch.D. 538. However, it appears that the parties agreed to a sale in this case: see *ibid.* p. 542.

10–223   Some assets are obviously more susceptible of division than others. Goodwill, expressed in terms of client connection, is a case in point, as Lord Lindley observed in a passage written in relation to solicitors' partnerships, but which is equally applicable to firms carrying on business in other spheres:

"... as between the solicitors themselves, it is competent for them to agree that, if they dissolve partnership, the clients of the old firm, and all their deeds and papers, shall be divided amongst the partners, or belong solely to the partner who continues to carry on the business of the firm; and such an agreement will be enforced."[9]

However, where such an arrangement is implemented, a client or customer cannot be forced to deal with the partner to whom he is allocated[10] and, subject to any questions of lien, he may legitimately seek the delivery up of any papers, etc., which belong to him.[11] It will generally be desirable to prevent any partner attempting to frustrate such an arrangement by coupling it with a suitable *express* restriction on competition.[12]

Getting in debts

10–224   Lord Lindley observed:

"When a firm is dissolved, it is usual to appoint one of the partners, or some third person, to collect and get in the debts of the firm. But notwithstanding any such arrangement and notice thereof, a debtor to the firm will be discharged if he pays to any one of the partners.[13] Effect, however, will be given by the Court to an agreement of the nature in question, by appointing a receiver, and if necessary, granting an injunction."[14]

---

[9] *Whittaker v. Howe* (1841) 3 Beav. 383. But see *Davidson v. Napier* (1827) 1 Sim. 297. In the case of solicitors, it is considered that such an arrangement would not contravene the Solicitors' Practice Rules 1990, r. 1(b), provided that undue pressure is not applied in order to persuade the client to remain with the partner(s) in question. See also, in this context, the *Law Society's Guide to the Professional Conduct of Solicitors* (6th ed.), principle 3.13. As to the right of a solicitor to act against a former client of his firm, see *Cholmondeley v. Clinton* (1815) 19 Ves.Jr. 261; *Rakusen v. Ellis, Munday & Clarke* [1912] 1 Ch. 831; *David Lee & Co. (Lincoln) Ltd. v. Coward Chance* [1991] Ch. 229; *Re A Firm of Solicitors* [1992] Q.B. 959. As to the position in the absence of such an agreement, see *supra*, paras. 10–160 *et seq.*

[10] *Cook v. Rhodes* (1815) 19 Ves.Jr. 273, note.

[11] *Colegrave v. Manley* (1823) T. & R. 400; *Griffiths v. Griffiths* (1843) 2 Hare 587. See also *supra*, para. 3–49.

[12] See, as to the position in the absence of such a restriction, *supra*, paras. 10–168 *et seq.* And see generally, *supra*, paras. 10–180 *et seq.*

[13] See *infra*, para. 12–54.

[14] *Davis v. Amer* (1854) 3 Drew. 64.

In practice, an arrangement of this type is usually made on an *ad hoc* basis and will not be legislated for in the agreement itself.

A right to damages for breach of such an arrangement will, if the agreement establishing it is not under seal,[15] be dependent on showing that it is supported by consideration. This may in fact take the form of the other partners' acceptance that they will take no steps to collect in the debts.[16]

Gazette notices

It is, in general, unnecessary to include any specific provision **10–225** governing notification of the dissolution by means of a *Gazette* notice, since this is provided for in the Partnership Act 1890.[17]

Y.   ARBITRATION AND MEDIATION[18]

Arbitration

An arbitration clause will be found in the majority of modern **10–226** partnership agreements, even though it may not be of the "all disputes" variety,[19] and will, in general, be carried over when a partnership is continued beyond an initial fixed term.[20]

The conduct of arbitrations is governed by the Arbitration Acts 1950 to 1979,[21] and an agreement to refer disputes *otherwise* than in accordance with the provisions of those Acts will not be enforced by the courts.[22] Thus, the court cannot compel a party to appoint an arbitrator or itself make the appointment,[23] save in those cases where it has statutory authority so to do.[24]

---

[15] *Cf. Belcher v. Sikes* (1827) 6 B. & C. 185.

[16] See *Lewis v. Edwards* (1840) 7 M. & W. 300.

[17] *Ibid.* s.37, *infra*, paras. 13–42 *et seq.*

[18] See the *Encyclopedia of Professional Partnerships*, Precedent 1, cl. 26.

[19] Thus, it may deal only with accountancy or valuation matters, leaving questions of construction, etc., to be dealt with by the courts.

[20] *Gillett v. Thornton* (1875) L.R. 19 Eq. 599. See also *supra*, para. 10–19.

[21] See also, as to non-domestic arbitrations, the Arbitration Act 1975. At the time of writing, the enactment of a new Arbitration Act in place of the existing legislation has been proposed.

[22] *Street v. Rigby* (1802) 6 Ves.Jr. 818; *Agar v. Macklew* (1825) 2 Sim. & St. 418; *Re Smith & Service and Nelson & Sons* (1890) 25 Q.B.D. 545. *Sed quaere*: see *Sudbrook Trading Estate Ltd. v. Eggleton* [1983] A.C. 444; also *Booker Industries Pty. v. Wilson Parking (Q.L.D.) Pty.* [1983] 43 A.L.R. 68. An action will, however, lie where a party agrees to refer a dispute and then fails to do so: *Livingston v. Ralli* (1856) 5 E. & B. 132. See also, as to such actions, *Doleman & Sons v. Ossett Corporation* [1912] 3 K.B. 257, 267 *et seq., per* Fletcher Moulton L.J. Note, however, the decision in *Channel Tunnel Group Ltd. v. Balfour Beatty Construction Ltd.* [1993] A.C. 334 (H.L.).

[23] *Re Smith & Services and Nelson & Sons* (1890) 25 Q.B.D. 545; *Re Wilson & Sons and Eastern Counties Navigation & Transport Co.* [1892] 1 Q.B. 81; *National Enterprises Ltd v. Racal Communications Ltd.* [1975] Ch. 397 (but see now, the Arbitration Act 1950, s.10(2), as added by the Arbitration Act 1979, s.6(4)).

[24] Arbitration Act 1950, ss.8(3), 10 (as amended by the Arbitration Act 1979, s.6(3), (4)), 25; *Re Eyre and Corpn. of Leicester* [1892] 1 Q.B. 136. As to the exercise of the court's discretion when making an appointment, see *Re Bjornstad and Ouse Shipping Co.* [1924] 2 K.B. 673. And, as to the appointment of an umpire, see *Taylor v. Denny, Mott & Dickson* [1912] A.C. 666; *Gola Sports v. General Sportcraft Co.* [1982] Com.L.R. 51.

Arbitration agreement no defence

10–227   Lord Lindley wrote that an arbitration agreement:

> "... is one which (independently of the Common Law Procedure
> Act of 1854[25]) cannot be effectually set up as a defence to any
> action relative to a matter agreed to be referred[26]; unless, indeed,
> the reference has been ... made[27] a condition precedent to the
> right to sue."[28]

This is still the position under the Arbitration Acts 1950 to 1979.[29]

Even where the reference has been made a condition precedent, so
that no cause of action arises until after the award, a party to the
agreement may be precluded from setting up the absence of an award
as a defence, either by his conduct before the proceedings were
commenced[30] or by seeking to resist the claim on a ground which, in
effect, amounts to a repudiation of that agreement.[31] Moreover, the
court can itself abrogate the effect of such a condition when ordering
that a particular dispute is not to be referred.[32]

Assignee or mortgagee of a share not bound

10–228   The assignee or mortgagee of a partnership share is not bound by
an arbitration clause in the partnership agreement as regards his
statutory right to an account[33] save, perhaps, where the clause in
terms extends to persons claiming under a partner.[34]

---

[25] The forerunner of the Arbitration Act 1889 and, now, the Arbitration Act 1950.

[26] See *Doleman & Sons v. Ossett Corporation* [1912] 3 K.B. 257 and the cases there cited; also
Cooke v. Cooke (1867) L.R. 4 Eq. 77; *Dawson v. Fitzgerald* (1876) 1 Ex.D. 257; *Edwards v.
Aberayron Mutual Ship Insurance Soc.* (1876) 1 Q.B.D. 563. But see also *Russell on Arbitration*
(20th ed.), p. 64, n. 6.

[27] The word "expressly" originally appeared at this point, but this is no longer a requirement: see
Cipriani v. Burnett [1933] A.C. 83.

[28] See *Scott v. Avery* (1856) 5 H.L.C. 811; *Caledonian Ins. Co. v. Gilmour* [1893] A.C. 85;
Spurrier v. La Cloche [1902] A.C. 446; *Smith, Coney & Barrett v. Becker, Gray & Co.* [1916] 2 Ch.
86; *Woodall v. Pearl Ass. Co.* [1919] 1 K.B. 593; *Hallen v. Spaeth* [1923] A.C. 684. Lord Lindley
observed of the decision in *Halfhide v. Fenning* (1788) 2 Bro.C.C. 336: "[*This*] case is generally
regarded as overruled, but *quaere* whether it is not capable of being supported on the principle
recognised in *Scott v. Avery*. See the observations of Lord St. Leonards in *Dimsdale v. Robertson*
(1844) 2 Jo. & LaT. 91, and of V.-C. Wood in *Cooke v. Cooke* (1867) 4 Eq. 77."

[29] See generally, *The Padre Island* [1984] 2 Lloyd's Rep. 408 and *Russell on Arbitration* (20th
ed.), pp. 64–66, 199 *et seq.*

[30] *e.g.* by improperly interfering with the arbitrator in the discharge of his duties (*Hickman & Co.
v. Roberts* [1913] A.C. 229; *Eaglesham v. MacMaster* [1920] 2 K.B. 169) or by waiver (*Toronto
Railway v. National British and Irish Millers Ins. Co.* (1914) 111 L.T. 555).

[31] *Jureidini v. National British and Irish Millers Ins. Co. Ltd.* [1915] A.C. 499. *Cf. Stebbing v.
Liverpool & London Ins. Co.* [1917] 2 K.B. 433; *Woodall v. Pearl Ass. Co.* [1919] 1 K.B. 593;
Freshwater v. Western Australian Ass. Co. Ltd. [1933] 1 K.B. 515.

[32] Arbitration Act 1950, s.25(4); *W. Bruce v. J. Strong* [1951] 2 K.B. 447; *Getreide-Import-
Gesellschaft m.b.h. v. Contimar S.A. Compania Industrial Commercial y Maritima* [1953] 1 W.L.R.
793; *Kruger Townwear v. Northern Assurance Co.* [1953] 1 W.L.R. 1049.

[33] Partnership Act 1890, s.31(2). See further, *infra*, paras. 19–65, 19–66.

[34] *Bonnin v. Neame* [1910] 1 Ch. 732. See also *Shayler v. Woolf* [1946] Ch. 320.

Power of court to order stay of proceedings

The court has a wide power to order a stay of proceedings with a **10–229** view to the disputed matters being referred to arbitration, as originally contemplated by the parties to the agreement. That power is set out in section 4(1) of the Arbitration Act 1950, which provides as follows:

> "If any party to an arbitration agreement, or any person claiming through or under him, commences any legal proceedings in any court against any other party to the agreement, or any person claiming through or under him, in respect of any matter agreed to be referred, any party to those legal proceedings[35] may at any time after appearance,[36] and before delivering any pleadings or taking any other steps in the proceedings,[37] apply to that court to stay the proceedings, and that court or a judge thereof, if satisfied that there is no sufficient reason why the matter should not be referred in accordance with the agreement, and that the applicant was, at the time when the proceedings were commenced, and still remains, ready and willing to do all things necessary to the proper conduct of the arbitration, may make an order staying the proceedings."[38]

In addition to this statutory power, the court has an *inherent* power to stay proceedings brought in breach of an agreement to resolve disputes in a particular way, whether by arbitration or otherwise.[39]

A stay may be granted even where part of the relief sought in the **10–230** proceedings will fall outside the arbitrator's jurisdiction, *e.g.* an application for the appointment of a receiver; however, the court will normally either deal with that part of the claim or give liberty to apply.[40]

If the proceedings are not stayed, any award made after their commencement will be invalid, unless the parties have subsequently agreed to proceed with the arbitration.[41] Conversely, the power of an

---

[35] An additional party cannot be joined with a view to obtaining a stay: *Etri Fans Ltd. v. N.M.B. (U.K.) Ltd.* [1987] 1 W.L.R. 1110 (a decision under the Arbitration Act 1975, s.1).

[36] Now acknowledgment of service: see the Rules of the Supreme Court (Writ and Appearance) 1979 (S.I. 1979 No. 1716).

[37] In *Parker, Gaines & Co. v. Turpin* [1918] 1 K.B. 358, a defendant who had taken a step in the proceedings was refused a stay even though he did not know of the agreement to refer. And see generally, *Turner & Goudie v. McConnell* [1985] 1 W.L.R. 898, where the authorities are reviewed.

[38] See *W. Bruce v. J. Strong* [1951] 2 K.B. 447; *Olver v. Hillier* [1959] 1 W.L.R. 551; also, generally, *Russell on Arbitration* (20th ed.), pp. 163 *et seq.* As to the position in the case of a non-domestic arbitration agreement, see the Arbitration Act 1975, s.1 (replacing s.4(2) of the 1950 Act); also *Roussel-Uclaf v. G. D. Searle & Co. Ltd.* [1978] 1 Lloyd's Rep. 225; *Paczy v. Haendler & Natermann GmbH* [1979] F.S.R. 420.

[39] See *Channel Tunnel Group Ltd. v. Balfour Beatty Construction Ltd.* [1993] A.C. 334 (H.L.).

[40] See *Phoenix v. Pope* [1974] 1 W.L.R. 719, 727, *per* Goff J.; also the Arbitration Act 1950, s.12(6)(h).

[41] *Doleman & Sons v. Ossett Corpn.* [1912] 3 K.B. 257. However, the commencement of an action will extinguish the arbitration proceedings: *Lloyd v. Wright* [1983] Q.B. 1065.

arbitrator, once appointed, generally cannot be revoked otherwise than with the leave of the court.[42]

If arbitration proceedings prove abortive, the court will in any event entertain an action and decide the question in dispute.[43]

Exercise of court's discretion to order stay

10–231   The court must first determine whether the matters in dispute fall within the ambit of the arbitration agreement[44] and, if they do, it must then go on to consider the exercise of its discretion.[45] If some, but not all, of those matters are within the ambit of the agreement, a stay may be refused.[46]

Lord Lindley observed:

"Where ... there is a *bona fide* dispute within the meaning of an agreement to refer, and there is no satisfactory reason why such dispute should not be settled by arbitration, legal proceedings will be stayed[47]...".

The onus of showing such a reason naturally falls on the party seeking to avoid a stay.[48]

---

[42] Arbitration Act 1950, s.1. See also *ibid.* s.24(2).

[43] *Hamlyn & Co. v. Talisker Distillery* [1894] A.C. 202, 211, *per* Lord Watson; *Cameron v. Cuddy* [1914] A.C. 651. As to the conduct necessary to amount to a repudiation of an arbitration agreement, see *Bremer Vulkan Schiffbau und Maschinenfabrik v. South India Shipping Corporation Ltd.* [1981] A.C. 909; *Rederi Kommanditselskaabet Merc-Scandia IV v. Couniniotis S.A. (The "Merchanaut")* [1980] 2 Lloyd's Rep. 183. However, it would seem that an arbitration agreement can never be frustrated merely by reason of delay or inactivity, unless one party has acted to his detriment: see *Paal Wilson & Co. A/S v. Partenreederei Hannah Blumenhal* [1983] A.C. 854; also *André et Compagnie S.A. v. Marine Transocean Ltd.* [1981] Q.B. 694; *Allied Marine Transport Ltd. v. Vale Do Rio Doce Navegacao S.A.* [1985] 1 W.L.R. 925.

[44] See *Piercy v. Young* (1879) 14 Ch.D. 200; *Renshaw v. Queen Anne Residential Mansions and Hotel Co. Ltd.* [1897] 1 Q.B. 662; *Parry v. Liverpool Malt Co.* [1900] 1 Q.B. 339; *Olver v. Hillier* [1959] 1 W.L.R. 551; *Nova (Jersey) Knit Ltd. v. Kammgarn Spinnerei GmbH* [1977] 1 W.L.R. 713 (a case concerning the construction of an arbitration clause in a German partnership agreement). As to a claim for rectification and damages for misrepresentation, see *Ashville Investments Ltd. v. Elmer* [1989] Q.B. 488 and the cases there cited; also *cf. Fillite (Runcorn) Ltd. v. Aqua-Lift* (1989) 45 Build. L.R. 27 and *Ethiopian Oilseeds & Pulses Export Corp. v. Rio Del Mar Foods* [1990] 1 Lloyd's Rep 86.

[45] The Arbitration Act 1950, s.4(1) is not imperative: see *Finer v. Melgrave, The Times,* June 4, 1959. *Cf.* the Arbitration Act 1975, s.1.

[46] *Wheatley v. Westminster Brymbo Coal & Coke Co.* (1865) 2 Dr. & Sm. 347; *Turnock v. Sartoris* (1889) 43 Ch.D. 150; *Printing Machinery Co. v. Linotype Machinery Ltd.* [1912] 1 Ch. 567; *Finer v. Melgrave, The Times,* June 4, 1959. *Cf. Ives and Barker v. Willans* [1894] 2 Ch. 478. The court often allows the arbitration to proceed as to some matters only: *Bristol Corpn. v. John Aird & Co.* [1913] A.C. 241.

[47] See for example, *Russell v. Russell* (1880) 14 Ch.D. 471; also *Russell v. Pellegrini* (1856) 6 E. & B. 1020; *Hirsch v. Im Thurn* (1858) 4 C.B.(N.S.) 569; *Randegger v. Holmes* (1866) L.R. 1 C.P. 679; *Seligmann v. Le Boutillier* (1866) L.R. 1 C.P. 681; *Plews v. Baker* (1873) L.R. 16 Eq. 564; *Willesford v. Watson* (1873) L.R. 8 Ch.App. 473; *Law v. Garrett* (1878) 8 Ch.D. 26; *Kirchner & Co. v. Gruban* [1909] 1 Ch. 413. Elsewhere Lord Lindley remarked that "the Court will sometimes decline to interfere between partners who have agreed that their disputes should be referred to arbitration, and who have not attempted so to settle them," referring to *Waters v. Taylor* (1808) 15 Ves.Jr. 10. However, this would seem to add little to the statement of principle in the text.

[48] *Metropolitan Tunnel & Public Works Ltd. v. London Electric Ry. Co.* [1926] Ch. 371; *Heyman v. Darwins Ltd.* [1942] A.C. 356, 388, *per* Lord Wright; *Olver v. Hillier* [1959] 1 W.L.R. 551, 553, *per* Roxburgh J.

In practice, the court may be inclined to refuse a stay where a bona fide allegation of fraud,[49] dishonesty[50] or professional incompetence[51] is made against a partner who expresses the wish that the matter should be ventilated in court or where, in substance, the matter in dispute involves a pure question of law,[52] *e.g.* the validity of an expulsion notice.[53] Moreover, a stay will not be granted if the applicant's sole purpose is to delay[54] or obstruct[55] the resolution of the dispute.

Dissolution: Although there are a number of instances in which **10–232** the court has refused to stay on the ground that the matters in dispute involve the question whether a partnership has been or ought to be dissolved,[56] they do not establish any principle of general application. Provided that the arbitration clause is drawn in sufficiently wide terms, the court may, in the exercise of its discretion, order a stay and refer all questions, including that of dissolution, to the arbitrator.[57] If necessary, it will even appoint a

---

[49] The court will refuse a stay, almost as a matter of course, if the partner against whom fraud is alleged opposes it; if, on the other hand, the party *alleging* fraud seeks to oppose the application, he will have to put forward a convincing reason why that allegation should not be dealt with by the arbitrator: *Russell v. Russell* (1880) 14 Ch.D. 471; *Camilla Cotton Oil Co. v. Granadex S.A.* [1976] 2 Lloyds Rep. 10; *Cunningham-Reid v. Buchanan* [1988] 1 W.L.R. 678. *Cf. Wallis v. Hirsch* (1856) 1 C.B.(N.S.) 316; *Barnes v. Youngs* [1898] 1 Ch. 414. Note also the power of the court to revoke the arbitrator's authority where the dispute involves a question of fraud: Arbitration Act 1950, s.24(2), (3); also *Schaik v. Frederick C. Kane* (1936) 107 S.J. 273; *Ashville Investments Ltd. v. Elmer* [1989] Q.B. 488. *Cf.* the position under the Arbitration Act 1975, s.1: *Paczy v. Haendler & Natermann GmbH* [1979] F.S.R. 420.

[50] *Radford v. Hair* [1971] Ch. 758. But see the preceding footnote.

[51] *Turner v. Fenton* [1982] 1 W.L.R. 52. See also *Charles Osenton & Co. v. Johnston* [1942] A.C. 130; *Radford v. Hair, supra*; *Cunningham-Reid v. Buchanan* [1988] 1 W.L.R. 678.

[52] *Re Carlisle* (1890) 44 Ch.D. 200; *Metropolitan Tunnel & Public Works Ltd. v. London Electric Ry. Co.* [1926] Ch. 371; *Turner v. Fenton, supra* (all cases involving questions of construction). *Cf. Lyon v. Johnson* (1889) 40 Ch.D. 579; *Smith, Coney & Barrett v. Becker, Gray & Co.* [1916] 2 Ch. 86; *Rowe Bros. & Co. Ltd. v. Crossley Bros. Ltd.* (1913) 108 L.T. 11.

[53] See *Barnes v. Youngs* [1898] 1 Ch. 414.

[54] *Lury v. Pearson* (1857) 1 C.B.(N.S.) 639. Lord Lindley described this case as one where "there was really no question in dispute, and the defendant's only object was delay," but went on to comment "The true grounds of this decision appear to have been those stated above, but the report is obscure." *Cf. Hayter v. Nelson and Home Insurance Co.* [1990] 2 Lloyd's Rep. 265.

[55] *Corcoran v. Witt* (1871) L.R. 8 Ch.App. 476, note, explained in *Plews v. Baker* (1873) L.R. 16 Eq. 564, 571, *per* Bacon V.-C.

[56] *Cook v. Catchpole* (1864) 10 Jur.(N.S.) 1068; *Joplin v. Postlethwaite* (1889) 61 L.T.(N.S.) 629; *Turnell v. Sanderson* (1891) 64 L.T.(N.S.) 654 (disapproved by Goff J. in *Phoenix v. Pope* [1974] 1 W.L.R. 719); *Barnes v. Youngs* [1898] 1 Ch. 414; *Olver v. Hillier* [1959] 1 W.L.R. 551; note also the Scottish decision *Roxburgh v. Dinardo*, 1981 S.L.T. 291.

[57] *Plews v. Baker* (1873) L.R. 16 Eq. 564; *Russell v. Russell* (1880) 14 Ch.D. 471; *Walmsley v. White* (1892) 40 W.R. 675; *Belfield v. Bourne* [1894] 1 Ch. 521; *Vawdrey v. Simpson* [1896] 1 Ch. 166; *Barnes v. Youngs* [1898] 1 Ch. 414; *Machin v. Bennett* [1900] W.N. 146; *Phoenix v. Pope* [1974] 1 W.L.R. 719; also the South African case of *Ganas v. Naicker*, 1951 (1) S.A. 119; C.L.C. 7016. In *Hutchinson v. Whitfield* (1830) Hayes 78, where it was provided that the partnership could only be dissolved by deed, it was held that a reference by deed and a subsequent award under seal dissolving the partnership did bring about a dissolution, even though the reference did not mention dissolution. The decision is an extraordinary one and is unlikely to be of any general application. And see *Green v. Waring* (1764) 1 W.Blacks. 475. For the form of order, see *Machin v. Bennett, supra*.

receiver pending the reference.[58] Moreover, it would seem that, once the question of dissolution has been referred to the arbitrator, no application can subsequently be made to the court under section 35 of the Partnership Act 1890.[59]

Injunction to restrain arbitration

10–233   The court will, in an appropriate case, grant an injunction to restrain a party from referring a dispute to arbitration, but not merely on the grounds that the reference would be futile.[60]

Interlocutory orders

10–234   The High Court has the same power to grant interim injunctions or to order the appointment of a receiver in relation to an arbitration as it would have if the dispute were the subject of proceedings in that court.[61]

Powers of arbitrator

10–235   The extent of the arbitrator's powers will primarily depend on the terms of the arbitration clause.[62] Provided that it is in a wide form covering all disputes and differences between the partners, the arbitrator will in general be able to deal with the following matters (which are, for convenience, arranged in alphabetical order):

Accounts: The arbitrator can take an account as between the partners.[63]

Actions: The arbitrator can direct one partner to sue in the name of himself and his co-partners, subject to indemnifying them against costs.[64]

---

[58] *Pini v. Roncoroni* [1892] 1 Ch. 633.

[59] *Phoenix v. Pope* [1974] 1 W.L.R. 719, 727, *per* Goff J.

[60] *Farrar v. Cooper* (1890) 44 Ch.D. 323.

[61] Arbitration Act 1950, s.12(6)(h).

[62] There are, however, some limits on the powers and discretions which may be conferred on an arbitrator: see *Home and Overseas Insurance Co. Ltd. v. Mentor Insurance Co. (U.K.) Ltd.* [1990] 1 W.L.R. 153.

[63] See *Bonnin v. Neame* [1910] 1 Ch. 732 (where it was held that a mortgagee of a partner's share would not be bound by an account taken in the arbitration). See further *supra*, para. 10–228 and *infra*, para. 19–66.

[64] *Burton v. Wigley* (1835) 1 Bing.N.C. 665; also *Philips v. Knightley* (1731) 2 Str. 902; *Goddard v. Mansfield* (1850) 19 L.J.Q.B. 305.

Competition: In certain circumstances, the arbitrator may, in settling the terms on which a partnership is to be dissolved, direct that one partner should not carry on a business in competition with another who has taken over the former partnership business.[65] However, in the view of the current editor, the ambit of such a power, even if it is exercisable, will be confined within a very narrow compass.[66]

Conveyances: The arbitrator can order conveyances to be made.[67] **10–236**

Dissolution: It has already been seen that an arbitrator may be empowered to dissolve a partnership.[68]

Interlocutory orders: The arbitrator can (*inter alia*) order a partner to give discovery of documents, answer interrogatories[69] and allow the inspection of property which is the subject matter of the dispute.[70] If the order is not complied with, then the arbitrator or any party to the reference may apply to the High Court for an order permitting the arbitration to proceed in default of such compliance.[71]

Payments: The arbitrator can order one partner to pay or to give security for the payment of a certain sum to the other(s).[72] However, he may not direct one partner to pay money to himself (*i.e.* the arbitrator), in order that he may apply it in payment of certain specified debts.[73]

Premiums: An arbitrator may clearly award the return of a portion of any premium as one of the terms of a dissolution awarded by him.[74] It is submitted that such an award may also, in a proper case, be made where the dissolution *precedes* the arbitration.[75]

---

[65] *Morley v. Newman* (1824) 5 D. & R. 317. Note also *Burton v. Wigley* (1835) 1 Bing.N.C. 665, where the award permitted a partner to carry on the business, despite a contrary provision in the partnership agreement.

[66] See *supra*, para. 10–174.

[67] *Wood v. Wilson* (1835) 2 Cromp., M. & R. 241.

[68] See *supra*, para. 10–232.

[69] *Kursell v. Timber Operators Ltd.* [1923] 2 K.B. 202. Note that the court no longer has power to make such orders in relation to an arbitration, following the repeal of the Arbitration Act 1950, s.12(6)(b) by the Courts and Legal Services Act 1990, s.103.

[70] *The Vasso* [1983] 1 W.L.R. 838.

[71] Arbitration Act 1979, s.5.

[72] *Simmonds v. Swaine* (1809) 1 Taunt. 549.

[73] *Re Mackay* (1834) 2 A. & E. 356.

[74] *Bellfield v. Bourne* [1894] 1 Ch. 521. And see generally, as to the return of premiums, *infra*, paras. 25–05 *et seq.*

[75] But see *Tattersall v. Groote* (1800) 2 Bos. & Pul. 131, as explained in *Belfield v. Bourne*, *supra*. The editors of the 7th edition of this work observed that "... it is doubtful how far this decision would be followed at the present day."

10-237   *Releases*:   The arbitrator can direct the partners to execute mutual releases.[76]

Rights and duties of partners: The arbitrator can determine the existence of a custom affecting the rights and/or duties of the partners.[77]

Specific performance: The arbitrator can, in an appropriate case, order the specific performance of any contract, other than a contract relating to land or any interest in land.[78]

Winding up: The arbitrator can apportion the assets between the partners,[79] place a value on goodwill[80] and make other consequential orders.[81]

What an arbitrator seemingly *cannot* do is appoint a receiver to collect and get in the partnership assets and debts.[82] Nor, in general, can he determine any question on which the right to refer is itself dependant.[83]

A party to the reference who allows a question to be raised before the arbitrator without objection cannot subsequently dispute the arbitrator's authority to decide it.[84]

Limitation

10-238   The Limitation Act 1980 applies to arbitrations just as it applies to actions in the High Court.[85] For this purpose, any term in an arbitration clause which states that no cause of action is to accrue in respect of any matter agreed to be referred until an award is made will effectively be ignored.[86]

---

[76] See *Lingood v. Eade* (1747) 2 Atk. 501, 506 (where the arbitrator directed the form of the releases to be settled by a Chancery Master).

[77] *Produce Brokers Co. v. Olympia Oil Co.* [1916] 1 A.C. 314.

[78] Arbitration Act 1950, s.15.

[79] *Lingood v. Eade* (1747) 2 Atk. 501; *Wood v. Wilson* (1835) 2 Cromp., M. & R. 241; *Wilkinson v. Page* (1842) 1 Hare 276.

[80] *Re David and Matthews* [1899] 1 Ch. 378. See also *supra*, paras. 10-173, 10-174.

[81] See Competition, *supra*, para. 10-235.

[82] *Lingood v. Eade* (1747) 2 Atk. 501; *Re Mackay* (1834) 2 A. & E. 356; *Cook v. Catchpole* (1864) 10 Jur.(N.S.) 1068. But a receiver was appointed in *Routh v. Peach* (1795) 2 Anst. 519 and 3 Anst. 637. See also the obscure observation in Roxburgh J. in *Olver v. Hillier* [1959] 1 W.L.R. 551, 554.

[83] *Smith v. Martin* [1925] 1 K.B. 745. *Cf. Harbour Assurance Co. (U.K.) Ltd. v. Kansa General International Insurance Co. Ltd.* [1993] Q.B. 701 (C.A.), where the arbitration clause was held to be a collateral agreement which would survive the initial illegality of the main contract, thus permitting the arbitrators to decide the illegality issue. The decision would have been otherwise if the illegality of the main contract would also have impeached the arbitration clause. In cases of this type, much will naturally depend on the precise terms of the arbitration clause in question.

[84] *Macaura v. Northern Ass. Co. Ltd.* [1925] A.C. 619.

[85] Limitation Act 1980, s.34(1).

[86] *Ibid.* s.34(2).

Costs

Subject to the terms of the arbitration clause, the arbitrator will, **10–239** have a wide discretion in relation to the costs of the reference and award.[87] Although submissions on costs are normally made before the award is published,[88] the question of costs can be reserved for decision *after* the terms of the award are known.[89]

Interest on awards

Any sum directed to be paid by an award carries interest from the **10–240** date of the award at the same rate as a judgment debt.[90]

Appeals

An arbitration award cannot be set aside merely because it **10–241** discloses an error of fact or law on its face[91]; moreover, the parties to an arbitration may, by express agreement, entirely exclude their rights of appeal, even on questions of law.[92] Subject thereto, an appeal on a question of law can be brought either with the consent of all parties or with the leave of the court.[93] Appeals to the Court of Appeal are generally prohibited, save in exceptional cases.[94]

---

[87] Arbitration Act 1950, ss.18, 28 (read with Arbitration Act 1979, s.7); *Mansfield v. Robinson* [1928] 2 K.B. 353; *Smeaton Hanscomb & Co. v. Sassoon I. Setty, Son & Co. (No. 2)* [1953] 1 W.L.R. 1481; *Lewis v. Haverfordwest R.D.C.* [1953] 1 W.L.R. 1486. As to the effect of *ibid.* s.18(3), see *Windvale v. Darlington Insulation Co.*, *The Times*, December 22, 1983.

[88] *Harrison v. Thompson* [1989] 1 W.L.R. 1325.

[89] In *King v. Thomas McKena Ltd.* [1991] Q.B. 480, the failure of one party's counsel to request the arbitrator to defer consideration of costs was treated as a sufficient "procedural mishap" to warrant remission of the award on costs pursuant to the Arbitration Act 1950, s.22(1).

[90] Arbitration Act 1950, s.20. See as to the effect of this section, *Rocco Giuseppe & Figli v. Tradax Export S.A.* [1984] 1 W.L.R. 742. Note also that an arbitrator may award interest both on any sum which is the subject of the reference but paid before the award and on any sum actually awarded, such interest to run for such period ending not later than the date of payment or award (as the case may be) as he thinks fit: *ibid.* s.19A (as inserted by the Administration of Justice Act 1982, s.15, Sched. 1, Part IV). See also *Food Corp of India v. Marastro Compania Naviera S.A.* [1987] 1 W.L.R. 134; and *infra*, para. 20–39.

[91] Arbitration Act 1979, s.1(1).

[92] *Ibid.* ss.3, 4. The agreement excluding the right of appeal may, in appropriate circumstances, merely be incorporated by reference: *Arab African Energy Corp. Ltd. v. Olie Produkten Nederland B.V.* [1983] 2 Lloyd's Rep. 419.

[93] *Ibid.* s.1(3). Leave will only be granted if the determination of the question of law could substantially affect the rights of one or more of the parties to the arbitration agreement, and the discretion will be exercised sparingly: see *ibid.* s.1(4); *Pioneer Shipping Ltd. v. B.T.P. Tioxide Ltd.* [1982] A.C. 724; *Italmare Shipping Co. v. Ocean Tanker Co. Ltd.* [1982] 1 W.L.R. 158; *B.V.S. S.A. v. Kerman Shipping Co. S.A.* [1982] 1 W.L.R. 166; *Aden Refinery Co. Ltd. v. Ugland Management Co. Ltd.* [1987] Q.B. 650; *Ipswich Borough Council v. Fisons Ltd.* [1990] 1 Ch. 709. As to appeals on preliminary points of law, see *ibid.* s.2; also *Babanaft International Co. S.A. v. Avant Petroleum Inc.* [1982] 1 W.L.R. 871.

[94] *Ibid.* s.1(7); also *ibid.* ss.1(6A), 2(2A) (as added by the Supreme Court Act 1981, s.148(2), (3), Sched. 5). And see *Pioneer Shipping Ltd. v. B.T.P. Tioxide Ltd.*, *supra*; *Antaios Compania Naviera S.A. v. Salen Rederierna A.B.* [1985] A.C. 191; *Universal Petroleum Co. Ltd. v. Handels Und Transport GmbH* [1987] 1 W.L.R. 1178; *Ipswich Borough Council v. Fisons Ltd.* [1990] 1 Ch. 709.

Alternative Dispute Resolution[95]

10–242　　The introduction of so-called "alternative dispute resolution" techniques[96] has provided a realistic and, in the current editor's view, valuable alternative to the traditional arbitration route in the case of partnership disputes.[97] Although some agreements now provide for the parties to a dispute to attempt to resolve it by ADR *before* embarking on an arbitration, such clauses have not yet obtained general acceptance. In any event, even in the absence of such a clause, ADR can be set up on an *ad hoc* basis prior to or alongside a reference to arbitration.

Although the court could, in theory, order a stay of proceedings pending a reference to mediation under its inherent jurisdiction,[98] in practice such an order is unlikely to be made given the voluntary nature of the ADR process; *per contra* if the agreement provides for mediation and, in default of a successful outcome, arbitration.

Z. PENALTIES AND LIQUIDATED DAMAGES

10–243　　Lord Lindley wrote:

> "The last clause in a partnership deed is often one by which each partner binds himself to pay, either by way of penalty or by way of liquidated damages, a certain sum in case of the infringement by him of any agreement contained in the previous clauses."[99]

As already noted,[1] such clauses are now rarely, if ever, encountered. Since they do not involve any considerations peculiar to the law of partnership, they are not further considered in this work.[2]

---

[95] See the *Encyclopedia of Professional Partnerships*, Precedent 1, cl. 26 (second variation).

[96] *i.e.* conciliation, mediation and the "mini-trial" or "executive tribunal".

[97] The value of ADR in a partnership context was analysed by the current editor in an article entitled "Dispute, what dispute" at (1991) 135 S.J. 768.

[98] See *Channel Tunnel Group Ltd. v. Balfour Beatty Construction Ltd.* [1993] A.C. 334 (H.L.).

[99] Note that an agreement which provides for a payment to be made otherwise than on a breach of its provisions cannot amount to a penalty: see *Export Credits Guarantee Dept. v. Universal Oil Products Co.* [1983] 1 W.L.R. 399; *E.F.T. Commercial Ltd. v. Security Change Ltd. (No. 1)*, 1993 S.L.T. 129 (1st Div.), where the English and Scots authorities are reviewed.

[1] See *supra*, para. 10–195.

[2] It would, however, seem that the use of hypothetical situations to invalidate a liquidated damages clause as a penalty will be resisted in commercial contracts: see *Philips Hong Kong Ltd. v. Att.-Gen. of Hong Kong* (1993) 61 B.L.R. 41. And see generally, *Chitty on Contracts* (26th ed.), paras. 1829 *et seq.* And see *supra*, para. 10–195, n. 99.

CHAPTER 11

CORPORATE AND GROUP PARTNERSHIPS

ALTHOUGH not conceptually different from any other form of **11–01**
partnership, the corporate and the group partnership are two distinct
sub-species which are encountered in the commercial field.[1]

1. THE CORPORATE PARTNERSHIP

Nature and formation

The expression "corporate partnership" usually denotes a partner- **11–02**
ship all the members of which are companies, whether limited or
unlimited, but is occasionally used loosely to refer to any partnership
which has one or more corporate members. The existence of both
types of corporate partnership is clearly recognised by statute[2] and by
the courts.[3]

No special statutory provisions govern such partnerships and the **11–03**
Partnership Act 1890 will apply in the normal way, save to the extent
that its provisions are excluded by agreement.[4] The only limiting
factor may in practice be the terms of each prospective corporate
partner's memorandum and articles of association, even though the
ultra vires doctrine has now, for the most part, been swept away.[5] In
any event, the procedure for altering a company's memorandum and
articles has been greatly simplified.[6]

---

[1] Note that the incorporation of solicitors' practices is now permitted (see the Administration of
Justice Act 1985, s.9 and the Solicitors' Incorporated Practice Rules 1988). However, whilst the
Solicitors' Indemnity Rules 1994 expressly contemplate the creation of a corporate partnership
comprising one or more "recognised bodies" (*ibid.* r.12.19(b)), the take up rate for incorporation
appears to be almost non-existent. Similarly in the accountancy profession.

[2] See the Insolvent Partnerships Order 1986, Art. 8(2), Sched. 2, Part II, considered *infra*,
paras. 27–23 *et seq.*; Income and Corporation Taxes Act 1988, ss. 114–116, considered *infra*, paras.
34–80 *et seq.*; also the Partnerships and Unlimited Companies (Accounts) Regulations 1993, *infra*,
para. 11–16.

[3] See, for example, *Re Rudd & Son Ltd.* [1984] Ch. 237; *Pinkney v. Sandpiper Drilling Ltd.*
[1989] I.C.R. 389 (partnerships between companies); *Newstead v. Frost* [1980] 1 W.L.R. 135; *Scher
v. Policyholders Protection Board* [1994] 2 A.C. 57 (partnerships between companies and
individuals).

[4] Partnership Act 1890, s.19, *supra*, para. 10–10.

[5] See *supra*, para. 4–19.

[6] See the Companies Act 1985, ss.4–6, 9. *Ibid.* s.4 was substituted by the Companies Act 1989,
s.110(2).

Partnerships between "one man companies"

11–04   There is no reason why a valid partnership should not exist
between two companies owned and controlled by a single person,
since each will enjoy a distinct legal personality.[7] Indeed, the
formation of partnerships between members of the same group of
companies is by no means unusual. It should, therefore, in theory be
possible to constitute such a partnership on terms that, if a winding-
up petition is presented or order made against one corporate partner,
the partnership can be terminated, whereupon the insolvent partner's
share will automatically accrue to the continuing partner(s). The
current editor submits that such a provision would not be rendered
void by section 127 of the Insolvency Act 1986,[8] but that it would at
the very least be necessary to demonstrate its commercial justification
and the absence of any suspicion of that partner's insolvency at the
outset if an attack under other sections of the Act is to be resisted.[9]

Advantages

11–05   In its full form, the corporate partnership, as well as providing a
vehicle for two or more companies to pursue a particular business
objective,[10] can offer investors the twin attractions of flexibility and
limited liability, without the need to comply with the cumbrous
provisions of the Limited Partnerships Act 1907.[11] Equally, the ability
to "collapse" an unsuccessful corporate partner, with a view to
gaining the full benefit of its limited liability, will not always be
commercially acceptable to the directors and shareholders.[12]

---

[7] See *Salomon v. Salomon & Co.* [1897] A.C. 22; *Lee v. Lees Air Farming* [1961] A.C. 12; also
Woolfson v. Strathclyde Regional Council (1978) 38 P. & C.R. 521, and the cases cited therein.
Note also that the Companies Act 1985, s.24 has been amended by the Companies (Single Member
Private Limited Companies) Regulations 1992 (S.I. 1992 No. 1699), Sched. and, in the case of a
private company limited by shares or by guarantee, no longer imposes personal liability where the
company carried on business for more than six months with less than two members.

[8] See also *infra*, para. 27–72. But see *supra*, paras. 10–124, 10–125.

[9] See the Insolvency Act 1986, s.423, which entitles the court to set aside transactions intended
to defraud the company's creditors. Note that a commercial justification alone is not sufficient to
avoid the application of this section: *Arbuthnot Leasing International Ltd. v. Havelet Leasing Ltd.
(No. 2)* [1990] BCC 636; also *Chohan v. Saggar* [1992] BCC 306. See also *ibid.* s.238, under
which the court may set aside (*inter alia*) any transaction "on terms that provide for the company to
receive no consideration" (see *ibid.* s.238(4)(a)) or "for a consideration the value of which, in
money or money's worth, is significantly less that the value, in money or money's worth, of the
consideration provided by the company" (*ibid.* s.238(4)(b)) unless (i) the company entered into the
transaction in good faith and for the purposes of carrying on its business and (ii) there were at the
time reasonable grounds for believing that the transaction would benefit the company (see *ibid.*
s.238(5)). However, unlike the position under *ibid.* s.423, this power is only exercisable in respect
of transactions entered into within two years of the commencement of the winding up: *ibid.* s.240.

[10] In such a case, the possible application of Art. 85 of the European Community Treaty must
not be overlooked: see *supra*, para. 8–05.

[11] See *infra*, paras. 29–01 *et seq.*

[12] Note also the provisions of the Insolvency Act 1986, ss.213, 214 (fraudulent and wrongful
trading).

On the other hand, the corporate partnership in its restricted form, **11–06** *i.e.* a partnership comprising both companies and individuals, offers no special advantage (otherwise than in the field of taxation),[13] although it will permit some investors to participate in the venture indirectly, through the medium of a corporate partner. However, there is at least the potential for the formation of a limited partnership[14] in which the general partner[15] is a limited company, thus minimising the exposure which is normally attendant on that position.[16]

It should also be noted that either form of corporate partnership **11–07** also offers a means of circumventing the statutory restrictions governing the size of partnerships,[17] albeit at the cost of placing some or all of the prospective partners at one step removed from direct participation in the firm's affairs.[18] However, in practice, this is an option which is rarely pursued, save in the case of venture capital partnerships.

Contents of corporate partnership agreement

Relatively few alterations need to be made to a traditional **11–08** partnership agreement in order to accommodate the requirements of a corporate partnership.[19] It will naturally be essential to adapt any clause which refers to an event peculiar to an individual partner, *e.g.* death or incapacity,[20] but the draftsman's primary concern must be to legislate against the possibility of the corporate partner's actual or apprehended insolvency. This will, in particular, require him to identify the potential impact on the firm of:

(*a*) an administrative or other receiver being appointed in respect of the whole or any part of a corporate partner's assets;[21]

---

[13] *i.e.* by "sheltering" profits in the corporate partner's hands, thus avoiding the higher rate charge to income tax imposed on individual partners.

[14] See the Limited Partnerships Act 1907, s.4 and *infra*, paras. 29–02 *et seq.*

[15] *Ibid.* s.4(2): see *infra*, para. 29–03.

[16] Note, however, that the individual (limited) partners must not· control the management decisions taken by a general partner, unless they wish to risk forfeiture of their limited liability under *ibid.* s.6(1): see *infra*, paras. 31–02 *et seq.*

[17] See, as to ordinary partnerships, the Companies Act 1985, s.716 (as amended) and the various size regulations made or treated as made thereunder and, as to limited partnerships, the Limited Partnerships Act 1907, s.4(2) (as amended); the Companies Act 1985, s.717 (as amended) and the regulations made or treated as made thereunder. See further *supra*, paras. 4–28 *et seq.* and *infra*, para. 29–02.

[18] Save in the case of a limited partnership (as to which see *supra*, n. 16), there is no reason why some or all of those investors should not have a seat on the corporate partner's board.

[19] Various management structures are adopted: see for example, *Pinkney v. Sandpiper Drilling Ltd.* [1989] I.C.R. 389.

[20] But note that a corporate partner need not be *physically* capable of carrying on the firm's business: see *Newstead v. Frost* [1980] 1 W.L.R. 125, *supra*, para. 3–41.

[21] See, generally, the Insolvency Act 1986, ss.33 *et seq.* The expression "administrative receiver" is defined in *ibid.* s.29(2).

(b)   a corporate partner's directors making a proposal for a voluntary arrangement;[22]

(c)   an administration order being made against a corporate partner;[23]

(d)   the passing of a resolution for the voluntary winding up of an insolvent corporate partner;[24]

(e)   a winding-up petition being presented against a corporate partner, no concurrent petition being presented against the firm;[25] and

(f)   a winding-up order being made against a corporate partner.[26]

Each such event should, at the very least, be regarded as a potential ground either for expelling the corporate partner or for dissolving the partnership.

Expulsion

11–09   Consistently with the approach normally adopted in the case of individual partners,[27] the current editor suggests that most, if not all, of the foregoing events should give rise to a right to *expel* the relevant corporate partner. A power of expulsion is, after all, a remedy of last resort and need not be invoked by the other partners.

11–10   If the presentation of a winding-up petition is *not* made a ground for expulsion (or if the power is not, for whatever reason, exercised), there will inevitably be a degree of uncertainty for the firm during the period leading up to the hearing of the petition. If an order is made on the petition, the winding-up will be deemed to have commenced at the time when the petition was presented[28] and any disposition of the corporate partner's property thereafter will be void unless the court orders otherwise.[29] It follows that, in the interim period, the corporate partner is unlikely to be able to function as a fully active partner. The appointment of an interim liquidator[30] may exacerbate the difficulties. Whether the other partners will be prepared to countenance the potential disruption which this may cause must be open to doubt.

---

[22] *Ibid.* ss.1 *et seq.*

[23] *Ibid.* ss.8 *et seq.*

[24] *Ibid.* ss.84 *et seq.* As to the position where a *solvent* partner is voluntarily wound up, see *infra*, para. 11–12.

[25] As to the circumstances in which concurrent petitions may be presented against the firm and against two or more of the partners, see *infra*, paras. 27–23 *et seq.*

[26] See the Insolvency Act 1986, s.125.

[27] See *supra*, paras. 10–94 *et seq.*

[28] Insolvency Act 1986, s.129(2). Where, however, a winding up by the court supersedes a voluntary winding-up, the relevant date is that on which the original resolution was passed: see *ibid.* s.129(1).

[29] *Ibid.* s.127. See also *infra*, para. 27–16.

[30] *Ibid.* s.135(1), (2).

Even if a more benign approach is adopted, it will still prima facie **11–11** be desirable to ensure that expulsion is possible in the event that a winding-up order is actually made. If such a limited power is not included, the other partners may have to accept the continued presence of the insolvent partner until such time as it is finally dissolved on the completion of the winding up,[31] unless they apply to the court for an earlier dissolution of the partnership under the Partnership Act 1890.[32]

Similar considerations will in fact arise in the case of a voluntary **11–12** winding up, even where the corporate partner is *solvent*.[33] Cases of winding up with a view to reconstruction or amalgamation require special consideration: the other partners may well not be prepared to countenance the substitution of the reconstructed, etc., company for the company with which they originally entered into partnership.[34]

As already noted,[35] there would seem to be no reason why, in an **11–13** appropriate case, the share of an expelled corporate partner should not be expressed to accrue to the other partners without payment, although the grounds for expulsion should obviously be less extensive in such a case.

Alternative to expulsion: dissolution

If the continuation of the partnership business is dependent on the **11–14** involvement of a particular corporate partner, the expulsion of that partner in the event of its insolvency is unlikely to be an acceptable solution to the other partners. In such a case, a power to dissolve the partnership should be substituted.[36] Again, it will be matter for consideration whether the power should be exercisable on the presentation of a petition or merely on the making of a winding up order. However, in the case supposed, it is difficult to see how the partnership could effectively function until the latter date.[37]

---

[31] Unlike the position under some other statutes, *e.g.* the Law of Property Act 1925, s.205(1)(i), "bankruptcy" for the purposes of the Partnership Act 1890, s.33(1) does not include the winding-up of a company, so that a winding up order will not, of itself, work a dissolution; however, it is submitted that the actual dissolution of a company (see the Insolvency Act 1986, ss.202, 205) would do so: see further, *infra*, paras. 24–25 *et seq*.

[32] The existence of the winding-up order might justify an application on the "just and equitable" ground: see the Partnership Act 1890, s.35(f), *infra*, paras. 24–75 *et seq*.

[33] See the Insolvency Act 1986, s.87(1), which provides that "the company shall from the commencement of the winding up cease to carry on its business, except so far as may be required for its beneficial winding up." See also *ibid.* s.87(2).

[34] *i.e.* drawing an analogy with the Partnership Act 1890, s.24(7), *infra*, paras. 15–10, 19–56, 19–57.

[35] See *supra*, para. 11–04; see also *supra*, paras. 10–124, 10–125 and *infra*, 27–72.

[36] See *supra*, paras. 10–113 *et seq*.

[37] *A fortiori* once the petition has been advertised: see the Insolvency Rules 1986, r. 4.11.

Management structure of corporate partner

11–15   An individual partner will generally be admitted to a partnership on the strength of the personal qualities which he possesses; in the case of a corporate partner, those qualities may be possessed by its board of directors or by some other management team whose services it is able to offer to the firm. The other partners must decide whether, given the qualities of the relevant individuals, they should reserve the right to expel the corporate partner or to dissolve the partnership if, for whatever reason, those services can no longer be made available.[38]

A similar right may also, in appropriate cases, be reserved in the case of changes in the voting control of a corporate partner.

Annual accounts

11–16   The Partnerships and Unlimited Companies (Accounts) Regulations 1993[39] now require a qualifying corporate partnership[40] to prepare annual accounts, an annual report, and an auditor's report in the same way as any other registered company and each corporate partner must append those accounts to its own accounts for filing purposes.[41] The other requirements of the regulations are noted elsewhere in this work.[42]

Charge on partnership assets

11–17   It is submitted that a charge over the assets of a corporate partnership need not be registered under the Companies Act 1985,[43]

---

[38] The introduction of a new management team might, in such a case, be regarded as equivalent to the admission of a new partner: see the Partnership Act 1890, s.24(7), *infra*, paras. 15–10, 19–56, 19–57.

[39] (S.I. 1993 No. 1820). The regulations came into force on July 21, 1993, but do not apply in the case of a financial year commencing before December 23, 1994: *ibid.* reg. 12(1).

[40] *i.e.* a partnership governed by the laws of Great Britain all the members of which are (i) limited companies; (ii) unlimited companies or Scottish firms, each of whose members is a limited company; or (iii) comparable undertakings incorporated in or formed under the laws of another country: *ibid.* reg. 3(1), (4).

[41] *Ibid.* regs. 4(1), 5(1). As regards the contents of such accounts, *ibid.* Sched. makes certain modifications to the provisions of the Companies Act 1985, Pt. VII.

[42] See *infra*, para. 22–05.

[43] *Ibid.* ss. 395 *et seq. Per contra*, perhaps, if each partner were, for the purposes of these sections, regarded as entitled to a direct interest in each partnership asset (see, for example, *Burdett-Coutts v. I.R.C.* [1960] 1 W.L.R. 1027; *Gray v. I.R.C.* [1994] S.T.C. 360, 377) and the charged assets comprise land and/or a ship: *ibid.* s.396(1)(d), (h). *Cf.* the descriptions of the other registrable charges. Note in any event that *ibid.* s.395(1) only renders a charge void "so far as any security on the company's property or undertaking is conferred by the charge", so that, even if that subsection applies, the supposedly unregistered charge would, as regards the other partners, unquestionably be valid. As from a day to be appointed, the sections in question will be replaced by the Companies Act 1989, ss. 92 *et seq.* but it is considered that the position will, in essence, remain as set out in the text.

but a charge over a corporate partner's *share* would unquestionably require registration.

Insolvency

Where concurrent insolvency petitions are presented against the **11–18** firm and against two or more partners, one or both of whom are corporate partners, the Insolvency Act 1986 is specially adapted in its application to such corporate partner(s).[44]

Otherwise, insolvency proceedings against a corporate partner will follow the normal procedure laid down in the Act and the Insolvency Rules 1986.[45]

Taxation

The tax treatment of corporate partnerships is considered later in **11–19** this work.[46]

2. THE GROUP PARTNERSHIP

Nature and formation

Less common than the corporate partnership is the entity known as **11–20** the group partnership which, in essence, consists of a partnership between two or more partnerships. It may in many ways be likened to a series of sub-partnerships,[47] save that each member of a constituent firm will himself be a member of the group partnership.[48]

It follows from this distinctive feature that the statutory restrictions **11–21** on the formation of partnerships comprising more than twenty partners[49] severely limit the scope for the creation of a group partnership outside the professions.[50] Apart from the foregoing, no special statutory or other provisions govern the formation of such a partnership.

There is no reason why one or more members of a group partnership should not themselves be corporate partnerships.

---

[44] See the Insolvent Partnerships Order 1986, Art. 8(2), Sched. 2, Pt. II; see further *infra*, paras. 27–23 *et seq*.

[45] But note the effect of *ibid*. Art. 15(3), *infra*, paras. 27–48, 27–79.

[46] See *infra*, paras. 34–80 *et seq*.

[47] See *supra*, para. 5–75.

[48] This, in essence, seems to have been the arrangement in *Nixon v. Wood* (1987) 284 E.G. 1055.

[49] See the Companies Act 1985, ss.716(1). As to limited partnerships, see the Limited Partnerships Act 1907, s.4(2) (as amended).

[50] See the Companies Act 1985, s.716(2) (as amended) and the various size regulations made or treated as made thereunder *supra*, paras. 4–28 *et seq*. As to limited partnerships, see *ibid*. s.717 (as amended) and the regulations made or treated as made thereunder, *infra*, para. 29–02.

Advantages

11–22   The group partnership obviously provides a means whereby a number of separate partnerships carrying on business in a certain field of activity can pool their respective skills and resources, whilst retaining their individual identities and, to a greater or lesser extent, their autonomy.[51] In this way, small firms may be able to compete on more equal terms with their larger counterparts.

11–23   However, it must at the same time be appreciated that the partial integration which is the hallmark of the group partnership may itself present certain practical dangers: once common facilities are set up within the confines of the group, it may be difficult, if not impossible, for any of the constituent firms to withdraw in anything approaching a viable state; *a fortiori* if clients have developed an allegiance to the group, rather than to those firms.[52]

Firm name

11–24   Each constituent firm may either continue to function under its own name or under a single "flagship" name common to the group. In either case, the prior approval of the Secretary of State may be required under Business Names Act 1985.[53] It is considered that the Secretary of State would not object to approval being sought for a number of different names in respect of the same partnership; *sed quaere.*

Contents of group partnership agreement

Decision-making

11–25   The management structure of a group partnership will be critical to its survival. That structure will largely depend on the scope of the partnership business and the independence which is to be retained by each of the constituent firms. It must be remembered that, if the group partnership is to function as such, some decisions will require to be taken at group level and others at constituent firm level: the agreement must clearly state which decisions fall in each class.[54] Where the group partnership business will incorporate only some of the activities carried on by the constituent firms, the overall control exercised at group level will inevitably be reduced.

---

[51] Much will, of course, depend on the scope of the group partnership business and the terms of the agreement: see *infra*, paras. 11–25 *et seq.*

[52] This may occur notwithstanding the fact that each constituent firm retains the ownership of its own goodwill under the terms of the agreement.

[53] *Ibid.* ss.2, 3. See further,*supra*, paras. 3–24 *et seq.*

[54] As to the type of difficulties which can arise, see *Nixon v. Wood* (1987) 284 E.G. 1055.

However, the agreement should normally seek only to establish the **11–26** manner in which *group* level decisions will be taken, leaving other decisions to be taken in accordance with the established procedures in the constituent firms. There are a number of management structures which may be adopted for group level decisions, namely:

1. A majority vote of all the partners.[55] This is only likely to be workable if the group is relatively small.
2. A "block" vote system, treating each constituent firm as a single partner, with weighted voting where appropriate.
3. A management committee system. If, in fact, each constituent firm is represented on the committee, this may in practice not differ significantly from the previous alternative.

Consistently with the approach currently adopted by a number of the larger professional firms, a combination of the first and third options, with the procedure varying according to the nature of the decision to be taken, may in practice provide the most acceptable solution.

Property

The agreement must specify whether the property of the **11–27** constituent firms will remain in their ownership or will become assets of the group partnership.[56] If they are to be retained by the constituent firms but made available for the use of the group, the terms upon which such user is to be permitted should be expressly stated.[57]

The ownership of goodwill, whether as an asset of the group or of the constituent firms, should also be clearly stated.

Retirement and dissolution

Suitable provisions should normally be included in the agreement **11–28** dealing with:

(a) the automatic retirement or expulsion of any partner who ceases to be a member of a constituent firm;[58]

---

[55] This does not mean that all decisions must be decided by a simple majority, in the same way as "ordinary matters connected with the partnership business" under the Partnership Act 1890, s.24(8): see *infra*, para. 15–05. If necessary, different majorities may be required according to the nature of the decision required to be taken, following the example of the Companies Act 1985, s.378. If this approach is adopted, consideration should also be given to the quorum requirements at partners' meetings.
[56] Once, however, assets are held at group level, it may be more difficult for a constituent firm to disentangle itself with a view to regaining its independence: according to the circumstances, this may be seen as an advantage or a disadvantage.
[57] See, generally, *supra*, para. 10–38 and *infra*, paras. 18–31 *et seq.*
[58] It is obviously undesirable for there to be a "floating" partner who is a member of the group partnership but who is not also a member of one of the constituent firms.

(*b*) the voluntary retirement of a constituent firm;

(*c*) the expulsion of a constituent firm on set grounds, including insolvency[59] and failure to expel a member whose conduct might affect the reputation of the group;

(*d*) the dissolution of the group partnership and the distribution of its assets.

Insolvency

11–29   If a group partnership is insolvent, concurrent petitions may be presented against the group and against two or more of the constituent firms which will, for this purpose, be treated as corporate partners.[60] Insolvency proceedings against the group or against one or more of the constituent firms will proceed in the normal way.[61]

Taxation

11–30   There are no special provisions governing the taxation of group partnerships. However, it should be noted that a separate value added tax registration will be available to the group.[62]

---

[59] Note that insolvency proceedings may be commenced against some or all of the members of a constituent firm and/or against the constituent firm itself: see *infra*, paras. 27–23 *et seq*.

[60] Insolvent Partnerships Order 1986, Art. 12: see *infra*, para. 27–28. See also *ibid*. Art. 10(9), (10), *infra*, para. 27–85.

[61] See *infra*, paras. 27–09 *et seq*.

[62] See *Customs & Excise Commissioners v. Glassborow* [1975] Q.B. 465, *infra*, paras. 37–07 *et seq*.

Part Three

THE RIGHTS AND OBLIGATIONS OF
PARTNERS AS REGARDS THIRD PARTIES

CHAPTER 12

THE LIABILITY OF A PARTNER FOR THE ACTS OF HIS CO–PARTNERS

1. PARTNERS AS AGENTS

The general principle of agency as between partners

Writing prior to the Partnership Act 1890, Lord Lindley stated the **12–01** general principle in these terms:

"Every member of an ordinary partnership is its general agent for the transaction of its business in the ordinary way; and the firm is responsible for whatever is done by any of the partners when acting for the firm within the limits of the authority conferred by the nature of the business it carries on.[1] Whatever, as between the partners themselves, may be the limits set to each other's authority, every person not acquainted with those limits is entitled to assume that each partner is empowered to do for the firm whatever is necessary for the transaction of its business, in the way in which that business is ordinarily carried on by other people.[2] But no person is entitled to assume that any partner has a more extensive authority than that above described."

Partnership Act 1890, section 5

This principle was enacted by section 5 of the Partnership Act **12–02** 1890, which provides as follows:

"5. Every partner is an agent of the firm and his other partners for the purpose of the business of the partnership; and the acts of every partner who does any act for carrying on in the usual way business of the kind carried on by the firm of which he is a member bind the firm and his partners, unless the partner so acting has in fact no authority to act for the firm in the particular

---

[1] Lord Lindley observed in a footnote that "The case is different with mere part-ownerships, *Barton v. Williams* (1822) 5 B. & A. 395; *Helme v. Smith* (1831) 7 Bing. 709."

[2] See *Hawken v. Bourne* (1841) 8 M. & W. 703, 710, *per* Parke B.; *Baird's Case* (1870) L.R. 5 Ch.App. 725, 733, *per* James L.J.

matter, and the person with whom he is dealing either knows that he has no authority,[3] or does not know or believe him to be a partner."[4]

Analysis of the section

12–03   There are in fact two distinct but overlapping limbs in the section. The first, and most important, is contained in the opening words "Every partner is an agent of the firm and his other partners for the purpose of the business of the partnership": this governs the position both as between the partners themselves and as between them and third parties and may conveniently be styled the "general limb." The remainder of the section deals only with the rights of third parties and may therefore be styled the "third party limb."

12–04   Where a partner acts as agent of the firm within the scope of his *actual* authority, *i.e.* a case falling within the general limb, liability will attach to the firm irrespective of the provisions of the third party limb; this will be the usual case. However, it should not be imagined that the third party limb is thereby rendered otiose, since it is permissible for partners to agree that one or more of their number will have only limited, or possibly no, authority to bind the firm.[5] In such a case, the general limb would be effectively excluded, but liability would still be imposed by the third party limb unless the conditions set out at the end of the section are fulfilled.

Partners to whom the section does not apply

Partner by holding out

12–05   The section seems to presuppose the existence of a partnership in the true sense and will therefore not apply in a case of holding out;[6] this was so decided in *Hudgell Yeates & Co. v. Watson*.[7] Although the decision in *United Bank of Kuwait Ltd. v. Hammoud*[8] would appear to be an authority to the contrary, in that case the status of the salaried partner appears not to have been considered.

---

[3] See also Partnership Act 1890, s.8, *infra*, paras. 12–148 *et seq.*
[4] The concluding words of the section echo the judgments of Cockburn C.J. in *Nicholson v. Ricketts* (1860) 2 E. & E. 497, 524, and of Cleasby B. in *Holme v. Hammond* (1872) L.R. 7 Ex. 218, 233. See *infra*, para. 12–08, n. 12.
[5] See the Partnership Act 1890, s.8, *infra*, paras. 12–148 *et seq.*
[6] See, as to holding out, *ibid.* s.14, *supra*, paras. 5–43 *et seq.* Note that the section merely renders the person held out "liable as a partner"; it does not purport to make him a partner.
[7] [1978] Q.B. 451, 467B–F (*per* Waller L.J.) and, *semble*, 471B (*per* Megaw L.J.) *Cf.* the judgment of Bridge L.J. at *ibid.* 462H–463A.
[8] [1988] 1 W.L.R. 1051.

Dormant partner

In the case of a true dormant partner, *i.e.* an undisclosed partner[9] **12-06** who carries on business through his fellow partners, the section will apply in the normal way. However, a dormant partner who simply enjoys a share in the profits of a business carried on by others on their own account[10] cannot properly be regarded as a partner nor can the persons who carry on the business properly be treated as his agents, real or apparent; in such a case, no liability will attach to him either under the section or under the general law relating to undisclosed principals.

Partner not purporting to act on firm's behalf

The application of the section is also dependent on a partner **12-07** having acted, or purported to act, on the firm's behalf; if he at all times acted on his own behalf and this was recognised by the third party, the firm will not be bound.[11]

Practical effects of the section

The operation of section 5 of the Partnership Act 1890 may be **12-08** summarised in this way:

(1) An act done by a partner on behalf of the firm and within the scope of his *actual* authority will bind the firm, whether or not the act was done in carrying on the partnership business in the usual way.

(2) An act done by a partner on behalf of the firm in the course of carrying on the partnership business in the usual way will prima facie bind the firm, even if the partner acted without authority, unless the third party with whom he dealt knew of that lack of authority or did not know or believe him to be a partner.[12]

(3) An act done by a partner on behalf of the firm *otherwise* than in the course of carrying on the partnership business in the

---

[9] Note, in this context, the implications of the Business Names Act 1985: see *supra*, paras. 3–24 *et seq.*, 5–70.

[10] See the Partnership Act 1890, s.2(3), *supra*, paras. 5–02 *et seq.*

[11] *British Homes Assurance Corporation Ltd. v. Paterson* [1902] 2 Ch. 404.

[12] In the latter case, there is neither real nor apparent authority to bind the firm: see, generally, the cases cited *supra*, para. 12–02, n.4; also *Farquharson Bros. & Co. v. King & Co.* [1902] A.C. 325, 341, *per* Lord Lindley. *Watteau v. Fenwick* [1893] 1 Q.B. 346 and *Kinahan & Co. Ltd. v. Parry* [1910] 2 K.B. 389 (which was reversed on a question of fact: see [1911] 1 K.B. 459) are, however, inconsistent with this view; *sed quaere*: see 9 L.Q.R. 3, 111 (Sir Frederick Pollock); also *infra*, paras. 12–153 *et seq.*

usual way will prima facie not bind the firm, in the absence of express authority or subsequent ratification by the other partners.[13]

Usual course of business sets limit on authority

12-09   It is submitted that, just as was the position prior to the Partnership Act 1890,[14] the limit of a partner's *implied* authority to bind the firm is in all cases set by the usual course of the particular business carried on. However, it should be noted that, in earlier editions of this work, the same proposition was advanced more timidly, namely:

> "It will be observed that the extent of a partner's authority to bind the firm is related to things done in 'the usual way' of the 'business of the kind carried on,' where no actual authority or ratification can be proved. This probably means the same thing as saying that what is necessary to carry on the partnership business in the usual way is the test of a partner's implied authority to bind the firm. It is apprehended that the Act has not extended the power of a partner to bind the firm."[15]

12-10   It is the usual course of the business, not the nature of the particular partner's involvement therein which is generally material, hence Lord Lindley's footnote in these terms:

> "The fact that one partner ordinarily attends to one branch of the business does not prevent his binding the firm when acting out of his own department."[16]

Nature and ordinary course of business

12-11   Whether a given act will fall to be treated as done in the usual course of carrying on a particular business will naturally depend on the nature of that business and on the practices normally adopted by persons engaged in carrying on businesses of that type. Evidence will necessarily be admissible on both points and expert evidence on the latter may prove to be crucial,[17] given the diversity of business

---

[13] See *Dickinson v. Valpy* (1829) 10 B. & C. 128; *Crellin v. Brook* (1845) 14 M. & W. 11.

[14] See *supra*, para. 12-01.

[15] This quotation is taken from the 15th ed. (p. 287), but substantially the same view was expressed in the 6th ed. (1893) at p. 134. As appears from the preface to that edition, Lord Lindley did approve its content.

[16] *Morans v. Armstrong* (1840) Arm. M. & O. 25.

[17] See *United Bank of Kuwait Ltd. v. Hammoud* [1988] 1 W.L.R. 1051, *infra*, para. 12-12.

enterprises and the fact that what is normally done on a day to day basis in one type of business may be exceptional in another. It follows that general rules are difficult, if not impossible, to formulate, as Lord Lindley recognised:

"... no answer of any value can be given to the abstract question—Can one partner bind his firm by such and such an act? unless, having regard to what is usual in business, it can be predicated of the act in question either that it is one without which no business can be carried on, or that it is one which is not necessary for carrying on any business whatever. There are obviously very few acts of which any such assertions can be truly made. The great majority of acts, and practically all which give rise to doubt, are those which are usual in one business and not in another."[18]

Thus, whilst it is within the usual course of a solicitor's business to give undertakings[19] and to receive trust moneys as agent of the trustees,[20] it is not within such usual course for a partner to accept the office of trustee or, more obviously, to render his co-partners liable for the misapplication of trust property.[21]

Moreover, what is "usual" in a particular business will vary from **12–12** time to time[22] and, accordingly, the older authorities should be approached critically. This was emphasised in *United Bank of Kuwait Ltd. v. Hammoud*,[23] where Staughton L.J., having been referred to a number of "elderly cases" relating to the ordinary authority of a solicitor, observed:

"That material should today be treated with caution, in my judgment; the work that solicitors do can be expected to have

---

[18] Lord Lindley went on "Take, for example, negotiable instruments: it may be necessary for one member of a firm of bankers to draw, accept, or indorse a bill of exchange on behalf of the firm, and to require that each member should put his name to it would be ridiculous; but it by no means follows, nor is it in fact true, that it is usual for one of several solicitors to possess a similar power, for it is no part of the ordinary business of a solicitor to draw, accept, or indorse bills of exchange. The question, therefore, Can one partner bind the firm by accepting bills in its name? admits of no general answer; the nature of the business and the practice of those who carry it on (usage or custom of the trade) must be known before any answer can be given: see *Hogarth v. Latham* (1878) 3 Q.B.D. 643; *Taunton v. Royal Ins. Co.* (1864) 2 H. & M. 135." The current editor is of the opinion that it is now at the very least "usual" for a solicitor to draw cheques on behalf of the firm so that Lord Lindley's example is no longer accurate. See also *infra*, para. 12–51.

[19] *United Bank of Kuwait Ltd. v. Hammoud* [1988] 1 W.L.R. 1051.

[20] *Re Bell's Indenture* [1980] 1 W.L.R. 1217, *infra*, para. 12–118.

[21] *Ibid.*

[22] See for example, *Mann v. D'Arcy* [1968] 1 W.L.R. 893, where Megarry J. seems to have been swayed by considerations of commercial expediency without reference to evidence of what was "usual" in the particular business.

[23] [1988] 1 W.L.R. 1051, 1063F.

changed since 1888; it has changed in recent times and is changing now. So I prefer to have regard to the expert evidence of today in deciding what is the ordinary authority of a solicitor."

The opportunities for the diversification of a solicitors' practice presented by the Financial Services Act 1986 are a case in point.[24]

Commercial requirements of business

12–13   Commercial considerations will also be of relevance in this context. Thus, whilst one partner does not, in general, have implied authority to enter into partnership with a third party in order to carry on a business wholly different to that carried on by the main firm,[25] he may have such authority if the subsidiary partnership will, in effect, carry on the *same* business, *i.e.* where the arrangement represents a means of carrying on the main firm's business. This was the position in *Mann v. D'Arcy*.[26] However, it is doubtful whether the decision established any principle of more general application, given the exceptional circumstances, *i.e.* a subsidiary partnership formed for a single venture which at all times remained under the direct control of the main firm.

12–14   The current editor does not consider that the above argument could be deployed with a view to overriding the specific provisions of section 24(7) of the Partnership Act 1890, thus forcing an unwilling minority of partners to take on a new partner or partners, either for a particular venture or generally.[27]

Scope of business

12–15   What is usual in relation to a particular business may also depend on what can properly be regarded as within its scope. Thus, in *Lindern Trawler Managers v. W. H. J. Trawlers*,[28] a member of a firm formed for the purpose of promoting a trawler company was held to have ostensible (albeit not actual) authority to employ agents to manage a trawler. Similarly, in *Mercantile Credit Co. v. Garrod*,[29]

---

[24] See *infra*, para. 12–119.
[25] *Singleton v. Knight* (1888) 13 App.Cas. 788; *Hawksley v. Outram* [1892] 3 Ch. 359; also *Ex p. British Nation Life Assurance Association* (1878) 8 Ch.D. 679, 704. But see the review of these authorities by Megarry J. in *Mann v. D'Arcy* [1968] 1 W.L.R. 893.
[26] [1968] 1 W.L.R. 893.
[27] See the Partnership Act 1890, s.24(8), *infra*, paras. 15–05 *et seq*.
[28] (1949) 83 Ll.L.Rep. 131.
[29] [1962] 3 All E.R. 1103.

the scope of a garage business concerned mainly with letting lock-up garages and car repairs was treated as including the buying and selling of cars, even though this was expressly prohibited by the partnership agreement.[30]

The scope of a particular business will, of course, vary according to the circumstances.[31]

Authority in cases of urgency or necessity

Urgency or necessity does not alter the extent of a partner's **12–16** implied authority.[32] Thus, even if the firm's future or the safety of its assets depend on a partner doing a particular act, the firm will not be bound unless that act is done within the usual course of its business. Lord Lindley explained:

"Nor it seems will necessity itself be sufficient if it be an extraordinary necessity ... therefore, in a case where the nature of the business was one in which there was no necessity to borrow money to carry it on under ordinary circumstances and in the ordinary manner, the Court held the firm not liable for money borrowed by its agent under extraordinary circumstances, although money was absolutely requisite to save the property of the firm from ruin.[33] This case is an authority for saying that a power to do what is usual does not include a power to do what is unusual, however urgent[34]; and although in the case referred to the money was not borrowed by a partner, but by a person who was only an agent of the firm, the decision would, it is apprehended, have been the same if he had been a partner. For notwithstanding the fact that every partner is to a certain extent a principal as well as an agent, the liability of his co-partners for his acts can only be established on the ground of agency. As their agent he has no discretion except within the limits set by them to his authority, and the fact that he is himself, as one of the firm, a principal, does not warrant him in extending those limits, save on his own responsibility."[35]

---

[30] The plaintiff finance company, which had purchased a car from one of the partners, did not know of the restriction contained in the agreement and believed it was dealing with the partnership.

[31] See *Re Bell's Indenture* [1980] 1 W.L.R. 1217. Note also *Nixon v. Wood* (1987) 284 E.G. 1055.

[32] The current editor believes that the doctrine of agency of necessity will not apply, since it is confined to a number of recognised exceptional cases: see *Gwilliam v. Twist* [1895] 2 Q.B. 84, 87, *per* Lord Esher M.R.; *Jebara v. Ottoman Bank* [1927] 2 K.B. 254, 270; *Sachs v. Miklos* [1948] 2 K.B. 23, 35–36; *cf. Prager v. Blatspiel, Stamp & Heacock* [1924] 1 K.B. 566. And see generally, *Bowstead on Agency* (15th ed.), pp. 84 *et seq.*

[33] See *Hawtayne v. Bourne* (1841) 7 M. & W. 595; also *Ex p. Chippendale* (1854) 4 De G.M. & G. 19; *Simpson's Claim* (1887) 36 Ch.D. 532. See also *infra,* para. 12–47.

[34] And see *Cox v. Midland Counties Ry.* (1849) 3 Ex. 268; *Houghton v. Pilkington* [1912] 3 K.B. 308.

[35] See *Dickinson v. Valpy* (1829) 10 B. & C. 128; *Ricketts v. Bennett* (1847) 4 C.B. 686.

Admissions and representations

Partnership Act 1890, section 15

12-17   The Partnership Act 1890 contains the following section:

"15. An admission or representation made by any partner concerning the partnership affairs, and in the ordinary course of its business, is evidence against the firm."[36]

Although an admission may, in this way, be evidence against the firm,[37] it is not necessarily conclusive,[38] unless it gives rise to an estoppel.[39] Similarly, in the case of a representation.

Where the section does not apply

12-18   The section will only apply where the admission or representation is made in the "ordinary" course of the firm's business.[40] This will not only exclude the obvious case of admissions made in an action brought by or against the firm, *e.g.* in answers to interrogatories[41] or in pleadings,[42] but also representations as to a partner's authority to bind the firm.[43] As Lord Donaldson M.R. put it in *United Bank of Kuwait Ltd. v. Hammoud*[44]:

"... it is trite law that an agent cannot ordinarily confer ostensible authority on himself. He cannot pull himself up by his own shoe laces."

---

[36] This accords with the previous law: *Thwaites v. Richardson* (1790) Peake 23; *Grant v. Jackson* (1793) Peake 268; *Wood v. Braddick* (1808) 1 Taunt. 104; *Pritchard v. Draper* (1834) 2 Cl. & F. 379; *Nicholls v. Dowding* (1815) 1 Stark. 81; *Sangster v. Mazarredo* (1816) 1 Stark. 161; *Wright v. Court* (1825) 2 Car. & P. 232. As to representations, see *Rapp v. Latham* (1819) 2 B. & A. 795; *Blair v. Bromley* (1847) 2 Ph. 354. It should be noted that most out of court statements, whether written or oral, are now generally admissible in evidence, subject to compliance with the requirements of the Civil Evidence Acts 1968 and 1972.

[37] *Quaere* does the section apply in criminal cases?

[38] See *Newton v. Belcher* (1848) 12 Q.B. 921; *Newton v. Liddiard* (1848) 12 Q.B. 925; *Wickham v. Wickham* (1855) 2 K. & J. 478; *Hollis v. Burton* [1892] 3 Ch. 226; also *supra*, para. 7–30.

[39] See *Re Coasters Ltd.* [1911] 1 Ch. 86, where the estoppel was relied on by the firm.

[40] Note that the expression "usual" is not used in this section: *cf.* s.5, *supra*, para. 12–02. The current editor is of the opinion that the words "ordinary" and "usual" are to all intents and purposes synonymous.

[41] See *Dale v. Hamilton* (1846) 5 Hare 369; *Parker v. Morrell* (1848) 2 Ph. 453; also *Hollis v. Burton* [1892] 3 Ch. 226. Such an answer will be evidence against the other partners, notwithstanding the inapplicability of s.15, if they have an opportunity to contradict it but choose not to do so: *ibid.*

[42] *Hollis v. Burton* [1892] 3 Ch. 226.

[43] *Ex p. Agace* (1792) 2 Cox 312, *infra*, para. 12–102; *United Bank of Kuwait v. Hammoud* [1988] 1 W.L.R. 1051. See also *Armagas Ltd. v. Mundogas S.A.* [1986] A.C. 717 and the cases there cited.

[44] [1988] 1 W.L.R. 1051, 1066H.

The position is likely to be the same where a partner makes representations as to the nature and extent of the firm's business and, thus, only indirectly to his authority to bind the firm.[45]

An admission made by an *intending* partner does not fall within the **12–19** section since, by definition, he cannot have made it in the ordinary course of the firm's business.[46] The mere fact that he has become a partner when the admission is sought to be used against the firm is irrelevant.

Notice to partners

Lord Lindley summarised the application of the doctrine of notice **12–20** as between partners in this way:

"... as a general rule, notice to one partner of any matter relating to the business of the firm is notice to all the other members."[47]

Partnership Act 1890, section 16

This approach is now reflected in section 16 of the Partnership Act **12–21** 1890, which provides:

"16. Notice to any partner who habitually acts in the partnership business of any matter relating to partnership affairs operates as notice to the firm, except in the case of a fraud on the firm committed by or with the consent of that partner."

Effect of the section

The section has the following two consequences: **12–22**

(1) If a firm claims the benefit of a transaction entered into by a partner or is otherwise bound by his acts, it cannot use its own ignorance of what that partner knew to place itself in a more favourable position than could have been achieved by that partner if he had been acting on his own account.[48]

(2) When it is necessary to prove that a firm has notice of some fact, all that is required is to show that notice was given to

---

[45] *Ex p. Agace, supra.* See further *infra*, para. 12–103.
[46] *Tunley v. Evans* (1845) 2 Dow. & L. 747; *Catt v. Howard* (1820) 3 Stark. 3.
[47] *Porthouse v. Parker* (1807) 1 Camp. 82; *Alderson v. Pope* (1808) 1 Camp. 404; *Bignold v. Waterhouse* (1813) 1 M. & S. 255; also *Salomons v. Nissen* (1788) 2 T.R. 674.
[48] See, generally, *Collinson v. Lister* (1855) 7 De G.M. & G. 634; *Oppenheimer v. Frazer & Wyatt* [1907] 2 K.B. 50.

one of the partners who habitually acts in the partnership business.[49]

It should be emphasised that the firm does not have notice of everything done by each of its members, but only of those matters which relate to the partnership. Any other result would be absurd.[50]

Firms with a common partner

12-23   If two firms have a common partner, notice which is imputable to one firm is also imputable to the other, so long as it relates to the latter's business.[51] Where, however, a partner's knowledge relates to the affairs of a client or customer of one firm, that knowledge will not be imputed to the other firm.[52] This will be of particular relevance in the case of solicitors' firms who act for clients with opposing interests.[53]

Knowledge of solicitors

12-24   In addition to the case last supposed, it would seem that knowledge acquired by a partner in a firm of solicitors whilst transacting business on behalf of a client would not be imputed to the firm on a subsequent purchase of property by the firm itself.[54]

Constructive notice

12-25   The equitable doctrine of constructive notice[55] is not, as a general rule, imported into commercial transactions[56] and, accordingly, has no place in the law of partnership.[57]

---

[49] *Quaere*, must he be so acting when notice if given to him?

[50] This was the word used by Lord Lindley.

[51] See *Steele v. Stuart* (1866) L.R. 2 Eq. 84; also *Porthouse v. Parker* (1807) 1 Camp. 82; *Jacaud v. French* (1810) 12 East 317; *Powles v. Page* (1846) 3 C.B. 16; *Re Worcester Corn Exchange Co.* (1853) 3 De G.M. & G. 180.

[52] *Campbell v. McCreath*, 1975 S.L.T. (Notes) 5, distinguishing *Steele v. Stuart*, *supra*.

[53] *Semble*, it will only be in a rare case that a firm can act for both sides in a dispute: see *Rakusen v. Ellis, Munday & Clarke* [1912] 1 Ch. 831; *David Lee & Co. (Lincoln) Ltd. v. Coward Chance* [1991] Ch. 229; *Re A Firm of Solicitors* [1992] Q.B. 959.

[54] See the Law of Property Act 1925, s.199(1)(ii)(b). The same principle applies where the firm takes a lease or mortgage of property: *ibid.* s.205(1)(xxi).

[55] *i.e.* that a person is deemed to know what he might have discovered on inquiry.

[56] *Greer v. Downs Supply Co.* [1927] 2 K.B. 28; *Nelson v. Larholt* [1948] 1 K.B. 339; *Feuer Leather Corp. v. Frank Johnstone & Sons* [1981] Com.L.R. 251; also *Manchester Trust v. Furness* [1895] 2 Q.B. 539, 545, *per* Lindley L.J.; *Newsholme Bros. v. Road Transport and General Insurance Co.* [1929] 2 K.B. 356. Note that in *Re Montagu's Settlement* [1987] Ch. 264, 285, Megarry V.-C. doubted whether there is any general doctrine of imputed *knowledge* as opposed to imputed notice. See also *Agip (Africa) Ltd. v. Jackson* [1990] Ch. 265, 293, *per* Millett J., affirmed on this point *(sub silentio)* at [1991] Ch. 547; *Eagle Trust Plc. v. S.B.C. Securities Ltd.* [1993] 1 W.L.R. 484.

[57] See for example, *Lacey v. Hill* (1876) 4 Ch.D. 537, 547, *per* Jessel M.R.

Frauds

Lord Lindley stated that: **12–26**

"Where one member is acting beyond his powers, or is committing a fraud on his co-partners, or is the person whose duty it is to give his firm notice of what he himself has done, in all such cases notice on his part is not equivalent to notice to them."[58]

It is the view of the current editor that, as a statement of general principle, this must be approached with caution, since section 16 of the Partnership Act 1890 only excepts cases which amount to "a fraud on the firm committed by or with the consent of [*the partner who has notice of the matter in question*]." A partner who merely acts beyond his powers or who is otherwise in breach of a duty of disclosure will not *necessarily* be acting in fraud of his co-partners, even if fraud is construed in its widest sense.

An illustration of the fraud exception is to be found in *Bignold v.* **12–27**
Waterhouse.[59] There a partner in a firm of carriers had entered into an agreement to carry valuable parcels free of charge in fraud of his co-partners, so that they were not bound thereby. A particular parcel, which only the partner who had made the agreement knew to be valuable, was sent and lost. The other partners were held not to have had notice of the parcel's true nature and were not liable for its loss.

It should be noted that if, in a case of this class, an employee of the firm has notice of what the fraudulent partner is doing, such notice will not be imputed to the other partners.[60]

Breaches of trust

If one partner, who is a trustee, improperly employs trust money in **12–28**
the partnership business, his knowledge will not be imputed to the firm and the other partners will not, without more, be liable for the breach of trust.[61] Whether one partner's knowledge that money in the firm's hands belongs to a trust will be so imputed must be determined, according to the principles previously discussed,[62] by

---

[58] See the judgment of Jessel M.R. in *Williamson v. Barbour* (1877) 9 Ch.D. 529, 535 *et seq.*; also *Lacey v. Hill* (1876) 4 Ch.D. 537 (affirmed *sub nom. Read v. Bailey* (1877) 3 App.Cas. 94). See further *Re Hampshire Land Co.* [1896] 2 Ch. 743; *Houghton & Co. v. Nothard, Lowe & Wills Ltd.* [1928] A.C. 1, 14, 15 (*per* Viscount Dunedin), 19 (*per* Viscount Summer); *Newsholme Bros. v. Road Transport and General Insurance Co.* [1929] 2 K.B. 356.

[59] (1813) 1 M. & S. 255.

[60] See *Lacey v. Hill* (1876) 4 Ch.D. 537, affirmed *sub nom. Read v. Bailey* (1877) 3 App.Cas. 94; *Williamson v. Barbour* (1877) 9 Ch.D. 529, 536, *per* Jessell M.R.

[61] See the Partnership Act 1890, s.13, *infra*, paras. 12–134 *et seq.*; also *Ex p. Heaton* (1819) Buck 386.

[62] See *supra*, paras. 12–11 *et seq.*

reference to the nature of the partnership business and the purpose
for which the money was received by the firm.

12–29   Although a member of a firm of solicitors has implied authority to
receive trust money as agent for the trustees, he will not, as a general
rule, have authority to constitute himself a constructive trustee
thereof. If he does so, his co-partners will not be liable as
constructive trustees, if they have no knowledge of the circumstances
under which the constructive trust arose.[63]

The liability of a firm for breaches of trust committed by a partner
will be considered in greater detail later in this work.[64]

Incoming and outgoing partners

12–30   An incoming partner is not affected with notice of what occurred
before he joined the firm[65] and an outgoing partner is not in general
affected with notice of what has occurred since he left the firm,
provided that there is no continuing agency between him and the
remaining partners.[66] However, where notice of dishonour is given to
a continuing partner in respect of a partnership bill, that is,
exceptionally, treated as sufficient notice to the outgoing partner.[67]

Ratification

12–31   It is perhaps self evident that section 16 of the Partnership Act
1890 cannot be used to circumvent the provisions of section 5, *i.e.* so
as to show that the other partners have ratified an act which falls
outside the scope of a partner's implied authority. Lord Lindley,
writing prior to the Act, put it thus:

> "... if a partner exceeds his authority, and it is contended that the
> firm is bound by what he has done, on the ground that it has
> ratified his acts, evidence must be given to prove that at the time
> of the alleged ratification his co-partners knew of those acts. It
> would be absurd, if in such a case, knowledge by him was
> equivalent to knowledge by them."[68]

---

[63] *Mara v. Browne* [1896] 1 Ch. 199; *Re Bell's Indenture* [1980] 1 W.L.R. 1217: see *infra*, paras.
12–118, 12–141, 12–142. *Cf. Agip (Africa) Ltd. v. Jackson* [1991] Ch. 547 (C.A.). Constructive
notice of the breach is not *per se* sufficient to give rise to liability: see *Agip (Africa) Ltd. v. Jackson*
[1990] Ch. 265, 293, *per* Millett J. (affirmed on this point (*sub silentio*) by the Court of Appeal);
Eagle Trust Plc. v. S.B.C. Securities Ltd. [1993] 1 W.L.R. 484.

[64] See *infra*, paras. 12–133 *et seq.*

[65] See *Williamson v. Barbour* (1877) 9 Ch.D. 529, 535, *per* Jessel M.R.

[66] *Adams v. Bingley* (1836) 1 M. & W. 192. Note, however, the terms of the Partnership Act
1890, s.38, *infra*, paras. 13–64 *et seq.*

[67] *Goldfarb v. Bartlett and Kremer* [1920] 1 K.B. 639.

[68] See *Lacey v. Hill* (1876) 4 Ch.D. 537, affirmed *sub nom. Read v. Bailey* (1877) 3 App.Cas. 94;
Williamson v. Barbour (1877) 9 Ch.D. 529. See also *Marsh v. Joseph* [1897] 1 Ch. 213, 246;
Hambro v. Burnand [1903] 2 K.B. 399, 414, *per* Bigham J. (the actual decision being reversed at
[1904] 2 K.B. 10).

It should also, in this context, be noted that if one partner defrauds **12–32** another, *e.g.* by improperly withdrawing moneys from the partnership bank account and crediting the amount withdrawn to his own account at another bank, and his co-partner is minded to ratify his actions, the ratification must relate to the whole transaction: he cannot ratify only part, merely because that would best serve his interests.[69]

2. LIABILITY FOR ACTS WHICH ARE NOT IN THEMSELVES WRONGFUL

Although the difficulty of formulating general rules has already been **12–33** noted,[70] it is possible to demonstrate how the general principles embodied in the Partnership Act 1890 have been (and are, in the future, likely to be) applied in a number of practical contexts. For ease of reference, these are arranged in alphabetical order.

For present purposes, the incidence of torts and frauds is ignored.[71]

Accounts

An account rendered by one partner in respect of a partnership **12–34** transaction is equivalent to an account rendered by the firm and will bind it.[72]

The authority of a partner to settle an account in relation to a partnership debt is less clear and will be considered hereafter.[73]

Actions

A partner will in general have the implied authority of his co- **12–35** partners to bring or defend legal proceedings in their joint names or in the firm name, subject to indemnifying them against costs where he does so without their consent.[74] He may also enter, but not necessarily prosecute (otherwise than on his own behalf), an appeal against a joint assessment to income tax[74a] or value added tax.[75] What a partner seemingly cannot do is bring proceedings in his own name but on behalf of the firm[76] or, perhaps, bring proceedings in

---

[69] *Commercial Banking Co. of Sydney v. Mann* [1961] A.C. 1. But see also *Lipkin Gorman v. Karpnale Ltd.* [1989] 1 W.L.R. 1340, 1371, *per* Parker L.J. and [1991] 2 A.C. 548, 573, 584, *per* Lord Goff of Chievely.

[70] See *supra*, para. 12–11.

[71] See, as to liability for torts, frauds and breaches of trust, *infra*, paras. 12–88 *et seq.*

[72] *Fergusson v. Fyffe* (1841) 8 Cl. & F. 121. As to false accounts so rendered, see *infra*, para. 12–100.

[73] See *infra*, para. 12–58.

[74] See *infra*, paras. 14–69 *et seq.*

[74a] *Re Sutherland & Partners' Appeal* [1994] S.T.C. 387 (C.A.).

[75] See the *obiter* views of Glidewell J. in *Customs and Excise Commissioners v. Evans* [1982] S.T.C. 342, 349. *Quaere*, is it right that one partner can prosecute the appeal as Glidewell J. intimated? See *Re Sutherland & Partners Appeal, supra*.

[76] *Re Sutherland & Partners' Appeal* [1993] S.T.C. 399, 406, *per* Lindsay J. This issue was not addressed in the Court of Appeal.

the firm name where the other party knows that he is doing so against the opposition of his co-partners.[77]

The right of a partner to submit a dispute to *arbitration* is considered later in this chapter.[78]

Insolvency proceedings

12–36   Prior to the introduction of the new insolvency legislation,[79] the power of a partner to act for the firm was, by statute,[80] extended to bankruptcy proceedings, including the proof of debts and voting at creditors' meetings.[81] Moreover, it was held that, notwithstanding the general rule prohibiting a partner from binding his firm by deed,[82] one partner might execute a power of attorney authorising a third party to represent the firm in such proceedings.[83] Although the current legislation does not confer any express authority on partners in relation to insolvency proceedings, it would seem that the limits of their implied authority will be the same as in any other legal proceedings.[84]

Admissions

12–37   This subject has already been considered earlier in this chapter.[85]

Agents

12–38   It is submitted that a partner has implied authority to employ or to dispense with the services of an agent.[86]

Arbitration

12–39   Lord Lindley wrote:

"One partner cannot, without special authority, bind the firm by a submission to arbitration.[87] The power to refer disputes, even

---

[77] This point was ultimately left open by Lindsay J.: *ibid.* See also [1994] S.T.C. 387, 390, 392.
[78] See *infra*, para. 12–39.
[79] See now the Insolvency Act 1986, the Insolvency Rules 1986 (as amended) and the Insolvent Partnerships Order 1986, considered *infra*, paras. 27–01 *et seq.*
[80] Bankruptcy Act 1914, s.149; Bankruptcy Rules 1952, rr. 279 *et seq.*
[81] *Ex p. Mitchell* (1808) 14 Ves. Jr. 597.
[82] See Deeds, *infra*, para. 12–63.
[83] *Ex p. Mitchell* (1808) 14 Ves. Jr. 597; *Ex p. Hodgkinson* (1815) 19 Ves. Jr. 291, 298, *per* Lord Eldon.
[84] See the Insolvency Rules 1986, r. 7.51, which applies the normal High Court and county court practice to insolvency proceedings, albeit "with any necessary modifications". Note also *ibid.* rr. 8.1 *et seq.*, relating to proxies.
[85] See *supra*, paras. 12–17 *et seq.*
[86] See the cases cited *infra*, para. 12–67, in relation to employees.
[87] See *Antram v. Chace* (1812) 15 East 209; *Stead v. Salt* (1825) 3 Bing. 101; *Adams v. Bankart* (1835) 1 Cr. M. & R. 681; *Thomas v. Atherton* (1878) 10 Ch.D. 185, 190, *per* Bacon V.-C.

although they relate to dealings with the firm, cannot be said to be an act done for carrying on its business in the ordinary way."[88]

Thus, if, following a dissolution, one partner undertakes to get in the partnership debts and commences an action in the firm name in respect of one such debt, he cannot then agree to refer all matters in dispute in the action to an arbitrator.[89] The current editor is of the view that this is, in general, still the position. It should, however, be noted that a partner may properly enter into a contract in the usual way of business, *e.g.* for the supply of goods or services, under which all disputes are to be resolved by arbitration. In such a case, the firm will be bound. A distinction must thus be drawn between contractual and *ad hoc* references.

It goes almost without saying that the partner who actually agrees to the reference will be bound by the award[90] and the other partners may subsequently become bound by ratification.[91]

Bank accounts

Although it is considered that a partner will in general have **12–40** implied authority to open a bank account in the firm name, the same cannot be said of an account in his own name.[92]

Bills of exchange and promissory notes

Trading partnerships

Lord Lindley observed that: **12–41**

"Every member of an ordinary trading partnership[93] has implied power to bind the firm by drawing, accepting, or indorsing bills of exchange, or by making and indorsing promissory notes in its name and for the purposes of the firm."

Even prior to the Partnership Act 1890, this general proposition had to be read subject to the requirement that the member should be

---

[88] *Stead v. Salt* (1825) 3 Bing. 101; *Adams v. Bankart* (1835) 1 Cr. M. & R. 681; and see *Boyd v. Emmerson* (1834) 2 A. & E. 184.
[89] *Hatton v. Royle* (1858) 3 H. & N. 500.
[90] *Strangford v. Green* (1677) 2 Mod. 228.
[91] As in *Thomas v. Atherton* (1878) 10 Ch.D. 185.
[92] *Alliance Bank Ltd. v. Kearsley* (1871) L.R. 6 C.P. 433.
[93] There is no authoritative definition of the expression "trading partnership," although it has been said that its business must consist in buying and selling goods: see *Wheatley v. Smithers* [1906] 2 K.B. 321; *Higgins v. Beauchamp* [1914] 3 K.B. 1192.

acting in the ordinary course of business;[94] if it were otherwise, the firm would clearly not be bound.[95] This is still the position.

12-42 *Acceptances in blank.* A partner does not have implied power to accept bills in blank or to bind his co-partners, otherwise than jointly with himself. A bill accepted in blank by one partner in the firm name does not bind the firm, otherwise than in favour of a bona fide holder for value without notice of the manner of acceptance.[96]

Joint and several notes. A joint and several promissory note signed by one partner on behalf of himself and his co-partners, binds them jointly[97] but not severally.[98] The partner concerned is both jointly and severally liable.[99]

Two bills for same demand. If two partners, unknown to each other, give two bills in the firm name in payment of the same debt, the firm will be liable on both, provided that they are held by bona fide holders for value without notice of the mistake.[1]

Non-trading partnerships

12-43 Of such partnerships, Lord Lindley said this:

"With respect to partnerships which are not trading partnerships, the question whether one partner has any implied authority to bind his co-partners by putting the name of the firm to a negotiable instrument, depends upon the nature of the business of the partnership.[2] In the absence of evidence showing ... usage,[3] the power has been denied to one of several mining adventurers,[4] quarry workers,[5] farmers,[6] solicitors."[7]

---

[94] See *Pinckney v. Hall* (1696) 1 Salk. 126; *Smith v. Baily* (1727) 11 Mod. 401; *Sutton v. Gregory* (1797) 2 Peake 150; *Dickinson v. Valpy* (1829) 10 B. & C. 128; *Lewis v. Reilly* (1841) 1 Q.B. 349; *Stephens v. Reynolds* (1860) 5 H. & N. 513; *Re Riches* (1865) 4 De G.J. & S. 581. See also the Bills of Exchange Act 1882, s.23(2) and *Ringham v. Hackett, The Times*, February 9, 1980 and (1980) 124 S.J. 201.

[95] See *Simpson's Claim* (1887) 36 Ch.D. 532.

[96] *Hogarth v. Latham* (1878) 3 Q.B.D. 643.

[97] *Maclae v. Sutherland* (1854) 3 E. & B. 1.

[98] See *Perring v. Hone* (1826) 4 Bing. 28, 32, *per* Best C.J.

[99] *Elliot v. Davis* (1800) 2 Bos. & Pul. 338; *Gillow v. Lillie* (1835) 1 Bing.N.C. 695; *Maclae v. Sutherland* (1854) 3 E. & B. 1.

[1] *Davison v. Robertson* (1815) 3 Dow. 218.

[2] See *Dickinson v. Valpy* (1829) 10 B. & C. 128.

[3] Lord Lindley in fact referred to "necessity or usage" at this point, having previously rejected necessity as a ground for extending a partner's implied authority: see *supra*, para. 12–16. The reference thereto was deleted in subsequent editions.

[4] *Brown v. Byers* (1847) 16 M. & W. 252; *Dickinson v. Valpy* (1829) 10 B. & C. 128; *cf. Brown v. Kidger* (1858) 3 H. & N. 853.

[5] *Thicknesse v. Bromilow* (1832) 2 Cr. & J. 425.

[6] *Greenslade v. Dower* (1828) 7 B. & C. 635.

[7] *Hedley v. Bainbridge* (1842) 3 Q.B. 316; *Levy v. Pyne* (1842) Car. & M. 453; *Harman v. Johnson* (1853) 2 E. & B. 61. And see *supra*, para. 12–11, n. 18.

To this list were subsequently added auctioneers.[8] Save in relation to cheques,[9] this statement of principle would still seem to hold good.

Implied authority to endorse bill. If a partner in such a firm concurs in drawing, or authorises his partner to draw, a bill in the firm name, he thereby impliedly authorises its endorsement in the same name for the purpose for which it was drawn.[10]

Authority to transfer bill

Even though a partner may have no authority to use the firm name **12–44** so as to render his co-partners liable on a bill or note, he may nevertheless have sufficient authority to transfer the property in the firm's bills or notes.[11]

Bills not drawn in proper form

This subject will be considered later in this chapter.[12]

Promise to provide for bill

If one partner, in consideration of a person accepting a partnership bill, promises that the firm will put him in funds to meet it when it is due, the firm will be bound.[13]

Borrowing money

Trading partnerships

Lord Lindley was in no doubt as to the existence of the implied **12–45** authority of the members of a trading partnership to borrow money:

"One of the most important of the implied powers of a partner is that of borrowing money on the credit of the firm. The sudden

---

[8] *Wheatley v. Smithers* [1906] 2 K.B. 321. This decision was in fact reversed on the construction of the partnership deed and on the facts, the Court of Appeal declining to express any opinion on the point of law: [1907] 2 K.B. 684.

[9] See *infra*, para. 12–51.

[10] See *Lewis v. Reilly* (1841) 1 Q.B. 349; *Garland v. Jacomb* (1873) L.R. 8 Ex. 216. And see also *Ringham v. Hackett, The Times*, February 9, 1980 and (1980) 124 S.J. 201.

[11] See *Smith v. Johnson* (1897) 3 H. & N. 222; also *Heilbut v. Nevill* (1870) L.R. 5 C.P. 478 (where the property was held not to have passed).

[12] See *infra*, paras. 12–175 *et seq*.

[13] *Johnson v. Peck* (1821) 3 Stark. 66.

exigencies of commerce render it absolutely necessary that such power should exist in the members of a trading partnership, and accordingly in a comparatively early case this power was clearly recognised."[14]

This principle is clearly demonstrated by the unquestioned authority of partners to draw, accept or indorse bills of exchange[15] and to pledge partnership goods.[16]

12-46   It is, of course, still necessary to show that the money was borrowed in the usual way of the partnership business, if the firm is to be bound.[17] Thus if money is borrowed by a partner for the declared purpose of raising the whole or part of his capital contribution,[18] the borrowing will demonstrably be outside the scope of his implied authority. On the other hand, if money is actually required by the firm but can only be obtained on unusual terms, it is considered that acceptance of such terms will be within a partner's implied authority and the lender need not inquire whether such acceptance was justified.[19]

Non-trading partnerships

12-47   The implied power of a partner to borrow money will only exist where the firm's business is of such a kind that it cannot be carried on in the usual way without such a power.[20] In the case of a pure cash business[21] or a business where borrowing is not strictly necessary[22] the firm will not be bound unless some actual authority or ratification can be proved. It is the current editor's view that the older cases in this area are deserving of particularly critical consideration, given that a significant number, if not the majority, of businesses, both trading and non-trading, are now, to some extent, financed by borrowed money.

---

[14] See *Lane v. Williams* (1692) 2 Vern. 277, 292; *Rothwell v. Humphreys* (1795) 1 Esp. 406; *Ex p. Bonbonus* (1803) 8 Ves. Jr. 540; *Denton v. Rodie* (1813) 3 Camp. 493; *Loyd v. Freshfield* (1826) 2 Car. & P. 325; see also *Gordon v. Ellis* (1844) 7 Man. & G. 607; *De Ribeyre v. Barclay* (1857) 23 Beav. 125; *Brown v. Kidger* (1858) 3 H. & N. 853.

[15] See *supra*, para. 12–41.

[16] See *infra*, para. 12–77.

[17] Partnership Act 1890, s.5, *supra*, para. 12–02.

[18] *Greenslade v. Dower* (1828) 7 B. & C. 635; *Fisher v. Tayler* (1843) 2 Hare 218. See *infra*, para. 12–49.

[19] See *Montaignac v. Shitta* (1890) 15 App.Cas. 357, which concerned the general agent of a firm.

[20] See *supra*, paras. 12–09 *et seq*.

[21] Lord Lindley cited the case of mining on the cost-book principle as a "ready money" business: see *Hawtayne v. Bourne* (1841) 7 M. & W. 595; *Ricketts v. Bennett* (1847) 4 C.B. 686; *Burmester v. Norris* (1851) 6 Ex. 796.

[22] Lord Lindley cited a solicitor as the example in this case: *Plumer v. Gregory* (1874) L.R. 18 Eq. 621. A subsequent editor added the "cinematograph theatre proprietor" as a further example: *Higgins v. Beauchamp* [1914] 3 K.B. 1192.

Borrowing prohibited

It goes almost without saying that, where authority to borrow **12–48** would otherwise be implied, the firm will not be bound if borrowing is prohibited by the partnership agreement and the lender is aware of that fact.[23]

What amounts to borrowing on behalf of firm

Overdrawing a bank account. As is to be expected, this clearly **12–49** amounts to borrowing money.[24]

Increasing firm's capital. Care must be taken when considering loans taken out by a partner with the express purpose of increasing the firm's capital, since use of such an expression may be indicative of a confusion of terms. Lord Lindley explained the position in this way:

"A sole trader who borrows money for the purpose of his trade cannot with propriety be said to increase his capital; but if two or more persons are in partnership, and each borrows money on his own *separate* credit, and the money is then thrown into the common stock, the capital of the firm, as distinguished from the separate capitals of the persons composing it, may with propriety be said to be increased. But, in this case, the firm is not the borrower, nor is it debtor to the lender for the money borrowed. If a firm borrows money so as to be itself liable for it to the lender, the capital of the firm is no more increased than is the capital of an ordinary individual increased by his getting into debt. When, therefore, it is said that one partner has no implied power to borrow on the credit of the firm for the purpose of increasing its capital, what is meant is that one partner, as such, has no power to borrow, on the credit of himself and co-partners, money, which each was to obtain on his individual credit, and then to bring into the common stock.[25] Unless the expression means this, it means nothing."[26]

---

[23] Partnership Act 1890, ss.5, 8: see *supra*, para. 12–02 and *infra*, para. 12–148; *Re Worcester Corn Exchange Co.* (1853) 3 De G.M. & G. 180. See also the cases cited in the next note.

[24] *Looker v. Wrigley* (1882) 9 Q.B.D. 397; *Blackburn Building Society v. Cunliffe, Brooks & Co.* (1884) 9 App.Cas. 857; *Re Wrexham, Mold & Connah's Quay Ry. Co.* [1899] 1 Ch. 440; *Re Pyle Works (No. 2)* [1891] 1 Ch. 173. Lord Lindley observed that the contrary decisions in *Waterlow v. Sharp* (1869) L.R. 8 Eq. 501 and *Re Cefn Cilcen Mining Co.* (1868) L.R. 7 Eq. 88 must be considered as overruled.

[25] See *Greenslade v. Dower* (1828) 7 B. & C. 635; *Fisher v. Tayler* (1843) 2 Hare 218.

[26] See *Bryon v. Metropolitan Saloon Omnibus Co.* (1858) 3 De G. & J. 123.

It follows that a loan taken out for such a purpose cannot ordinarily bind the firm in the absence of subsequent ratification.

12–50   *Obtaining goods, etc., on credit*. The mere fact that a partner has implied authority to obtain goods or services on credit does not, of itself, authorise him to borrow money, since the two acts are quite different. Lord Lindley summarised the distinction in these terms:

> "The difference consists in this, that he who possesses power to borrow on the credit of another, has a much more extensive, and therefore more easily abused, trust reposed in him than one who is empowered only to pledge the credit of another for value received, when the pledge is given. A power, therefore, to incur debt, which is necessarily incidental to almost every partnership, by no means involves a power to borrow money."

This proposition is supported by a number of older cases concerning mines run on the cost-book principle,[27] and would still appear to be good law.[28]

See also *Mortgages and Pledges*, *infra*, paragraphs 12–75 *et seq*.

Firm enjoying benefit of improperly borrowed money

This subject will be considered later in this chapter.[29]

Cheques and transfers between accounts

12–51   A partner unquestionably has implied power to bind the firm by drawing a cheque in the firm name[30] and, seemingly, to stop payment on such a cheque.[31] There is, however, authority for the proposition that he may not properly draw a post-dated cheque.[32] There would seem to be no reason why a partner should not draw a cheque in his

---

[27] As to liability for supplies, see *Tredwen v. Bourne* (1840) 6 M. & W. 461; *Hawken v. Bourne* (1841) 8 M. & W. 703; as to borrowings, see *Hawtayne v. Bourne* (1841) 7 M. & W. 595; *Ricketts v. Bennett* (1847) 4 C.B. 686; *Brown v. Byers* (1847) 16 M. & W. 252; *Burmester v. Norris* (1851) 6 Ex. 796; also *Beldon v. Campbell* (1851) 6 Ex. 886.

[28] See also *Re Pyle Works (No. 2)* [1891] 1 Ch. 173, 185, *per* Stirling J.; *Jacobs v. Morris* [1901] 1 Ch. 261, 267–268 (*per* Farwell J.) and [1902] 1 Ch. 816, 828–829 (*per* Vaughan Williams L.J.).

[29] See *infra*, paras. 12–193 *et seq*.

[30] *Laws v. Rand* (1857) 3 C.B.(N.S.) 442; *Backhouse v. Charlton* (1878) 8 Ch.D. 444; also *Ringham v. Hackett, The Times*, February 9, 1980 and (1980) 124 S.J. 201. But see also, *supra*, para. 12–11, n. 18.

[31] Lord Lindley observed in a footnote at this point "Before the Judicature Acts, an action for dishonouring the cheque must have been brought in the names of all the partners, and in the case supposed such an action could not have been sustained ... It is conceived that the statement in the text is correct, notwithstanding the modern rules as to parties."

[32] See *Forster v. Mackreth* (1867) L.R. 2 Ex. 163. *Quaere* whether this will now always be the position.

own favour, *e.g.* in the case of drawings on account of his profit share, unless this is prohibited by the bank mandate or professional rules.[33]

There is also implied authority to transfer funds from one bank account to another.[34] Again, this would appear to include transfers from the firm's account to a partner's private account; *sed quaere.*[35]

Contracts

There can be little doubt that partners will have a general power to **12–52** bind the firm by contract, although the extent of the authority will inevitably depend on the nature of the business concerned.[36] In an appropriate case, this may include signing a contract satisfying the requirements of the Law of Property (Miscellaneous Provisions) Act 1989.[37]

A partner may also vary a contract entered into by all the partners in the ordinary course of business.[38]

Debts

Payment to one partner

A partner has implied authority to accept the payment of **12–53** partnership debts; hence the general rule that, if payment is received by any partner in respect of such a debt, the claims of all the partners are extinguished.[39]

The position is the same following a dissolution,[40] even where a **12–54** third party has been appointed to collect the debts and the debtor is

---

[33] Note that the Solicitors' Accounts Rules 1991, r.8(1)(a) prohibits certain withdrawals from a client account otherwise than by "a cheque drawn in favour of the solicitor." The latter expression is defined so as to include the firm: *ibid.* r.2(1). *Quaere,* does this authorise a partner to draw a client account cheque in his own favour rather than in favour of the firm? It is tentatively thought not.

[34] See *Backhouse v. Charlton* (1878) 8 Ch.D. 444.

[35] Note the terms of the Solicitors' Accounts Rules 1991, r. 8(1)(b). And see *supra,* n.33.

[36] See *Employees, Purchases* and *Sales, infra,* paras. 12–67, 12–81, 12–82, 12–84.

[37] *Ibid.* s.2(3). *Quaere* can the contract be signed by the partner as an undisclosed agent, and thereby bind the firm? It is thought that it may, as was the position under the Law of Property Act 1925, s.40: see *Davies v. Sweet* [1962] 2 Q.B. 300; *Basma v. Weeks* [1950] A.C. 441.

[38] *Leiden v. Lawrence* (1863) 2 N.R. 283.

[39] *Anon.,* 12 Mod. 446 (Case 777); see also *Powell v. Brodhurst* [1901] 2 Ch. 160. And see *Jacaud v. French* (1810) 12 East 198, where there were two firms with a common partner and a bill of exchange was given to one and indorsed by it to the other. Payment to the first firm was held to be an answer to an action brought on the bill by the second. Note that a partner who receives money as agent for the firm will not necessarily be regarded as doing so in a fiduciary capacity: see *supra,* para. 16–03.

[40] Partnership Act 1890, s.38, *infra,* para. 13–64; *Powell v. Brodhurst* [1901] 2 Ch. 160; and see *Duff v. East India Co.* (1808) 15 Ves. Jr. 198; *Brazier v. Hudson* (1836) 9 Sim. 1. The *obiter* observations to the contrary in *Gopala Chetty v. Vayaraghavachariar* [1922] 1 A.C. 488, 495 do not accord with the position under English law: see the Partnership Act 1890, s.38.

aware of that fact.[41] Where, however, a debt has been assigned to one of the partners and the debtor has notice of the assignment, he will only be discharged if he pays the assignee partner.[42]

12–55   *Debt not due to firm.* The above rule will not apply if the debt was owed not to the firm but to one of the partners. In such a case, payment must be made to that partner.[43] This may be of particular relevance where there is a partnership or other agreement to share the profits derived from the sale of certain goods. As Lord Lindley pointed out:

> "... if an owner of goods sells them the purchase-money must be paid to him or his agent; and payment to a person interested with him in the profits accruing from the sale will not do: for though the two may be liable as if they were partners by reason of their community of interest in the profits,[44] it does not therefore follow that he who is to share the profits is entitled to receive the proceeds of the sale of the goods themselves which belong exclusively to the other."[45]

If the court (exceptionally) orders payment to be made to one partner by name, that order must be complied with; payment to any other partner will not suffice.[46]

12–56   *Acceptance of bill of exchange.* A partner's implied authority to accept payment will normally extend to receipt of a bill of exchange by way of payment;[47] *per contra*, if the bill is drawn in the partner's own name and payable to his order, unless he had express authority to receive a bill in this form or the money is actually paid over to the firm.[48]

Releases and receipts

12–57   In the same way that he can accept payment, a partner may give a valid release[49] or receipt in respect of a partnership debt.[50] However,

---

[41] *Bristow v. Taylor* (1817) 2 Stark. 50; *Porter v. Taylor* (1817) 6 M. & S. 156; *King v. Smith* (1829) 4 Car. & P. 108.

[42] See *Duff v. East India Co.* (1808) 15 Ves. Jr. 198; also *Powell v. Brodhurst* [1901] 2 Ch. 160.

[43] Payment to the firm will not be sufficient unless the firm was authorised to receive the money: *Powell v. Brodhurst* [1901] 2 Ch. 160.

[44] This part of the passage (which was omitted in later editions) was, of course, written prior to the Partnership Act 1890: see now *ibid.* s.2(3) and *supra*, paras. 5–21 *et seq.*

[45] See *Smith v. Watson* (1824) 2 B. & C. 401.

[46] See *Showler v. Stoakes* (1844) 2 Dow. & L. 3.

[47] See *Tomlins v. Lawrence* (1830) 3 Moo. & Pay. 555.

[48] See *Hogarth v. Wherley* (1875) L.R. 10 C.P. 630.

[49] See *Hawkshaw v. Parkins* (1819) 2 Swan. 539; see also *Deeds* and *Releases, infra*, paras. 12–63, 12–83.

[50] *Henderson v. Wild* (1811) 2 Camp. 561.

a receipt is not conclusive so that, if the partner giving it was acting in fraud of his co-partners, they will not be bound by it;[51] similarly, if that partner colluded with the debtor in giving the release.[52]

Power to settle debts

A partner does not have authority to compromise a debt owing to **12–58** the firm, without receiving payment. Lord Lindley put it in this way:

"As a general proposition, an authority to receive payment of a debt does not include an authority to settle it in some other way[53]; and a partner has no implied authority to discharge a separate debt of his own by agreeing that it shall be set off against a debt due to his firm."[54]

Deeds of arrangement

It would seem that one partner has authority to assent to a deed of **12–59** arrangement executed by a debtor;[55] this represents an exception to the normal rule that a partner cannot bind the firm by deed.[56]

Transfer or assignment of debt

If a creditor of the firm transfers the debt due to him to a third **12–60** party, one partner may properly assent to the transfer.[57] Similarly, where the debt is assigned by the debtor, *e.g.* to his successor in business.[58]

It follows that one partner also has authority to assign a debt due to the firm.[59] Where two partners purport to assign the same debt, a question of priority as between the assignees will inevitably arise: this will be determined on the normal principles of notice.[60]

---

[51] *Henderson v. Wild* (1811) 2 Camp. 561; *Farrar v. Hutchinson* (1839) 9 A. & E. 641.

[52] *Aspinall v. London & N.W. Ry.* (1853) 11 Hare 325; see also *Releases, infra,* para. 12–83.

[53] See *Hogarth v. Wherley* (1875) L.R. 10 C.P. 630; *Pearson v. Scott* (1878) 9 Ch.D. 198; *Niemann v. Niemann* (1889) 43 Ch.D. 198; *cf. Weikersheim's Case* (1873) L.R. 8 Ch.App. 831. And see *Young v. White* (1844) 7 Beav. 506; *Underwood v. Nicholls* (1855) 17 C.B. 239.

[54] *Piercy v. Fynney* (1871) L.R. 12 Eq. 69. See also *Kendal v. Wood* (1870) L.R. 6 Ex. 243. *Cf. Wallace v. Kelsall* (1840) 7 M. & W. 264.

[55] See *Morans v. Armstrong* (1840) Arm. M. & O. 25; *Dudgeon v. O'Connell* (1849) 12 Ir.Eq. 566. And see generally, the Deeds of Arrangement Act 1914 (as amended) and *Muir Hunter on Personal Insolvency,* Pt. II.

[56] *Dudgeon v. O'Connell* (1849) 12 Ir.Eq. 566.

[57] *Lacy v. McNeile* (1824) 4 Dow. & Ry. 7.

[58] *Beale v. Caddick* (1857) 2 H. & N. 326. See also *Backhouse v. Charlton* (1878) 8 Ch.D. 444.

[59] *Ex p. Wright* [1906] 2 K.B. 209.

[60] *Marchant v. Morton, Down & Co.* [1901] 2 K.B. 829.

Promise to pay debt of firm

12–61 A promise by one partner to pay a debt owing by the firm undoubtedly binds the firm[61] and will prima facie constitute an acknowledgment of the debt for limitation purposes.[62]

Tender

12–62 Lord Lindley summarised the position in this way:

> "If a debt is owing to a firm, tender to one partner is tender to all; and if a debt is owing by a firm, tender by one partner is tender by all[63]; and if, after tender by a firm, the creditor demands the sum tendered, a refusal to pay made by the partner on whom the demand is made is a refusal by the firm."[64]

Deeds

12–63 The general rule is that a partner has no implied authority to bind his co-partners by deed, whether or not the partnership itself was originally constituted by deed.[65] However, an exception is made in the case of releases[66] and deeds of arrangement.[67]

A deed executed by one partner in the name and in the presence of his co-partners, is deemed to have been executed by them,[68] and represents a case of *express* authority.

Deed not necessary

12–64 If a deed is unnecessary for the validity of a particular transaction which is otherwise within the scope of a partner's implied authority, but he nevertheless executes a document in the form of a deed, the firm may still be bound by that transaction, even if not by the deed.[69] Thus, where a partner had executed such a deed in the name of his firm, purporting to assign a debt due to it, it was held that the deed

---

[61] *Anon. v. Layfield*, Holt K.B. 434; *Lacy v. McNeile* (1824) 4 Dow. & Ry. 7.

[62] Limitation Act 1980, ss.29(5), 30(2). See further, *infra*, paras. 13–137 *et seq.*

[63] *Douglas v. Patrick* (1790) 3 T.R. 683.

[64] *Peirse v. Bowles* (1816) 1 Stark. 323.

[65] *Harrison v. Jackson* (1797) 7 T.R. 207; *Steiglitz v. Egginton* (1815) Holt N.P. 141; *Marchant v. Morton, Down & Co.* [1901] 2 K.B. 829. As to the circumstances in which authority may be presumed, see *Steiglitz v. Egginton, supra*. Note that, even where there is *express* authority, the firm will only be bound if the deed is in proper form: see *infra*, paras. 12–171 *et seq.*

[66] See *Hawkshaw v. Parkins* (1819) 2 Swan. 539; also *Releases, infra*, para. 12–83.

[67] *Dudgeon v. O'Connell* (1849) 12 Ir.Eq. 566. See *supra*, para. 12–59. See also, as to a further (limited) exception, Actions, *supra*, para. 12–36.

[68] *Ball v. Dunsterville* (1791) 4 T.R. 313; *Burn v. Burn* (1798) 3 Ves. Jr. 573; *Orr v. Chase* (1812) 1 Mer. 729; *Brutton v. Burton* (1819) 1 Chitty 707. As to ratification, see *Tupper v. Foulkes* (1861) 9 C.B.(N.S.) 797.

[69] See further, as to the circumstances in which a firm will be bound by a deed executed by one partner, *infra*, paras. 12–171 *et seq.*

did not bind his co-partner but that there was nevertheless a good assignment of the debt, no deed being required.[70] The position may be the same where the inoperative deed is executed in pursuance of a contract, which is not required to be made by deed and therefore binds the firm.[71]

Executing partner bound

Although a deed may be inoperative against the other partners, the partner who executed it will generally be bound.[72]   **12–65**

Partnership Act 1890

The foregoing principles are unaffected by the Partnership Act 1890.[73]

Distress

Distress by partner

If the firm is a landlord of premises, any partner has authority to distrain, or to appoint a bailiff to distrain, for arrears of rent due to the firm.[74]   **12–66**

Distress against firm

In certain cases, the Law of Distress Amendment Act 1908 protects goods which are not the property of the immediate tenant against distress for rent. If the goods distrained on belong to a firm, the declaration required to obtain the protection of the Act may be made on behalf of the firm and signed by one partner.[75]

Employees

Lord Lindley observed: **12–67**

"One partner has implied authority to hire servants to perform the business of the partnership[76]; and the writer presumes that one

---

[70] *Marchant v. Morton, Down & Co.* [1901] 2 K.B. 829; see also *Ex p. Wright* [1906] 2 K.B. 209 (where one partner had forged the name of his co-partner).
[71] See *Davis v. Martin* [1894] 3 Ch. 181.
[72] *Elliot v. Davis* (1800) 2 Bos. & Pul. 338 (joint and several bond). See also *Bowker v. Burdekin* (1843) 11 M. & W. 128; *Cumberlege v. Lawson* (1857) 1 C.B.(N.S.) 709. Cf. *Latch v. Wedlake* (1840) 11 A. & E. 959; *Lascaridi v. Gurney* (1862) 9 Jur.(N.S.) 302.
[73] *Ibid.* s.6: see *infra*, paras. 12–161, 12–171 *et seq.*
[74] See *Robinson v. Hofman* (1828) 4 Bing. 562.
[75] *Ibid.* s.1; *Rogers, Eungblut & Co. v. Martin* [1911] 1 K.B. 19, explained in *Lawrence Chemical Co. Ltd. v. Rubinstein* [1982] 1 W.L.R. 284. Note, however, that the goods of a partner of the tenant are not protected: *ibid.* s.4(2)(a).
[76] *Beckham v. Drake* (1841) 9 M. & W. 79, affirmed (on this point) at (1843) 11 M. & W. 315.

partner has also implied authority to discharge them, although he cannot do so against the will of his co-partners."[77]

The current editor considers that Lord Lindley's reference to the will of the other partners (which is equally applicable to the engagement of employees) must be approached with a degree of caution. In the case which he cited, *Donaldson v. Williams*,[78] the plaintiff was an employee of two partners, Williams and Whyte, and resided in their jointly owned premises. His employment was terminated by Williams, who required him to vacate the premises, but Whyte authorised him to remain. Lord Lyndhurst held that such authority, given by one joint tenant, made the plaintiff's continued occupation of the premises lawful and observed "As the partners are jointly interested in the house, has not either of them a right to retain a servant in the house?" It would accordingly seem that this was, if anything, a case of re-engagement,[79] not a case where the original dismissal was invalid as being contrary to the wishes of the other partner.[80] In the result, there might be an endless succession of dismissals and re-engagements, so that it may properly be said that, at least in the case of a two partner firm, the *status quo ante* must ultimately prevail.[81]

Although the position may technically be the same in the case of a larger firm, the majority might properly restrict the partners' express authority to engage or dismiss staff with a view to resolving the position.[82]

Guarantees, etc.

12–68   A partner will not, in general, have power to give a guarantee binding on the firm. Lord Lindley summarised the position in these terms:

"How far one partner can bind the firm by a guarantee, obliging the firm to pay, if some other person does not, has been much disputed. The later cases, however, decide that unless it can be shown that the giving of guarantees is necessary for carrying on the business of the firm in the ordinary way, one of the members will be held to have no implied authority to bind the firm by them; for,

---

[77] *Donaldson v. Williams* (1833) 1 Cromp. & M. 345; also the unreported decision in *Williams v. Williams*, January 30, 1979 (1980 C.L.Y. p. 134). But see *Dixon on Partnership*, p. 139, where a contrary view is expressed. As to dismissal resulting from a change in the firm, see *supra*, para. 3–13.
[78] (1833) 1 Cromp. & M. 345.
[79] But re-engagement by whom, the firm or Whyte alone? The report is not clear on this point.
[80] Indeed, the headnote refers to the fact that Williams had "regularly given [*the plaintiff*] a week's notice to leave."
[81] See *infra*, para. 15–07.
[82] See *infra*, para. 15–06.

generally speaking, it is not usual for persons in business to make themselves answerable for the conduct of other people. The subject was much considered in *Brettel v. Williams*."[83]

The position under the Partnership Act 1890 is, of course, the same.[84]

A guarantee given without authority may become binding on the firm by ratification[85] or estoppel[86] and will, in any event, bind any partner who signs it.[87]

Statute of Frauds 1677

A guarantee signed by one partner in the name of the firm will be **12–69** sufficient for the purposes of the Statute of Frauds, section 4, provided that his authority can be proved.[88]

Promise to provide for bill

Such a promise, to which reference has already been made,[89] is not regarded in the same way as a guarantee.[90]

Representations as to credit

It has been held that a partner is not liable for a false and **12–70** fraudulent representation as to the character or solvency of another person, unless the representation is in writing and signed by that partner; accordingly, if he signs in the name of the firm, only he will be liable.[91] It is apprehended that this is still the position.[92]

---

[83] (1849) 4 Ex. 623. See also *Crawford v. Stirling* (1802) 4 Esp. 207; *Duncan v. Lowndes* (1813) 3 Camp. 478; *Hasleham v. Young* (1844) 5 Q.B. 833; *Simpson's Claim* (1887) 36 Ch.D. 532. Lord Lindley also pointed out that "The dictum of Lord Mansfield in *Hope v. Cust* (1774) 1 East 53, and the decision of Lord Eldon in *Ex p. Gardom* (1808) 15 Ves. Jr. 286, are opposed to these authorities, but cannot be relied on after the decision in *Brettel v. Williams*."

[84] *Ibid.* s.5, *supra*, para. 12–02.

[85] See *Sandilands v. Marsh* (1819) 2 B. & A. 673, where there was evidence of ratification by the firm of the contract of which the guarantee formed part.

[86] See for example, *Amalgamated Investment & Property Co. Ltd. (In Liquidation) v. Texas Commerce International Bank Ltd.* [1982] Q.B. 84 (parent company guaranteeing the indebtedness of subsidiary).

[87] *Ex p. Harding* (1879) 12 Ch.D. 557 (joint and several guarantee). Lord Lindley observed that this case and the case cited *supra*, n. 85 "cannot ... be considered as opposed to those in which it has been held that one partner has no implied power to bind the firm by guarantees in its name."

[88] See *Duncan v. Lowndes* (1813) 3 Camp. 478. This part of the Statute of Frauds, s.4, was unaffected by the provisions of the Law Reform (Enforcement of Contracts) Act 1954 (itself now repealed).

[89] See *supra*, para. 12–44.

[90] *Guild & Co. v. Conrad* [1894] 2 Q.B. 885.

[91] Statute of Frauds Amendment Act 1828, s.6; *Williams v. Mason* (1873) 28 L.T.(N.S.) 232; *Swift v. Jewsbury* (1874) L.R. 9 Q.B. 301; *Hirst v. West Riding Union Banking Co.* [1901] 2 K.B. 560. See also *infra*, para. 12–101.

[92] But see the Partnership Act 1890, ss.6, 10, *infra*, paras. 12–89, 12–161.

Insurance

12–71   A partner has implied authority to insure partnership property.[93]

Interest

12–72   An admission by one partner that a partnership debt bears interest at a given rate will prima facie bind the firm.[94]

See also *Debts*, *supra*, paragraphs 12–53 *et seq*.

Leases

12–73   Lord Lindley stated that:

> "One partner, as such, has no authority to contract on behalf of the firm for a lease of a house for partnership purposes."

This proposition was supported by reference to *Sharp v. Milligan*,[95] in which, as Lord Lindley noted, specific performance was decreed against the firm, the contract having been ratified by the other partners. However, the following *obiter* views of Sir John Romilly M.R. are instructive in this context:

> "I do not think it necessary to decide this point, but I am disposed to concur in the argument that where partners simply enter into an agreement to carry on a partnership of which the term is not fixed, one of those partners would not have authority, within the scope of the partnership contract, to take a lease for twenty-one years, and to bind the other partners."[96]

Accordingly, the current editor's view is that there is no *general* principle with regard to leases, such as Lord Lindley implied, but that in order to determine the extent of a partner's implied authority account must not only be taken of the nature of the business but also of the duration of the partnership.

---

[93] *Hooper v. Lusby* (1814) 4 Camp. 66; also *Armitage v. Winterbottom* (1840) 1 Man. & G. 130. As to notice of abandonment in the case of a marine insurance policy, see *Hunt v. Royal Exchange Assurance Co.* (1816) 5 M. & S. 47.

[94] See *Fergusson v. Fyffe* (1841) 8 Cl. & F. 121. See also *supra*, para. 12–61.

[95] (1856) 22 Beav. 606.

[96] *Ibid.* p. 609.

Notice to quit, etc.

Where a lease is granted by a number of partners jointly, a notice **12–74** to quit may be given by one on behalf of them all.[97]

In the case of a lease granted *to* partners, it would seem that a notice to quit given by one would only be valid in the case of a periodic tenancy.[98] If the lease is a partnership asset, the giving of such a notice might, as against the other partners (whether co-lessees or not), amount to a breach of trust.[99]

In certain circumstances, the concurrence of one partner in the service of a counter notice under section 26(1)(b) of the Agricultural Holdings Act 1986 may be dispensed with, if the operation of that Act would otherwise be frustrated. This was graphically demonstrated in *Featherstone v. Staples*,[1] where the partner withholding its concurrence was, in fact, a company controlled by the landlord which played no active part in the business.[2]

Mortgages and pledges

Mortgages of partnership land

Although, under the common law, a legal mortgage of partnership **12–75** land requires the concurrence of all the partners,[3] it is considered that two or more partners who hold such land on the statutory trusts[4] could create a valid mortgage without such concurrence.[5] However,

---

[97] *Doe d. Aslin v. Summersett* (1830) 1 B. & Ad. 135; also *Goodtitle v. Woodward* (1820) 3 B. & A. 689; *Doe v. Hulme* (1825) 2 Man. & Ry. 433; and see the review of the later authorities in *Featherstone v. Staples* [1986] 1 W.L.R. 861, 868 *et seq.* and *Hammersmith and Fulham London Borough Council v. Monk* [1992] A.C. 478.

[98] *Doe d. Aslin v. Summersett, supra*, as approved in *Hammersmith and Fulham London Borough Council v. Monk, supra; per contra*, in the case of a *contractual* break clause: *Hounslow London Borough Council v. Pilling* [1993] 1 W.L.R. 1242. A notice under the Law of Property Act 1925, s.146(1) should seemingly be served on each lessee partner: *Blewett v. Blewett* [1936] 2 All E.R. 188; *Wilson v. Hagon* (1958) 109 L.J. 204 (Cty.Ct.); *cf. Fairclough v. Berliner* [1931] 1 Ch. 60 (where the joint lessees were not partners). As to the service of notices under the Landlord and Tenant Act 1954, Pt. II, note the terms of *ibid.* s.41A (as added by the Law of Property Act 1969, s.9).

[99] See also the Law of Property Act 1925, s.26(3) (as substituted by the Law of Property (Amendment) Act 1926, Sched.) and the decision in *Sykes v. Land* (1984) 271 E.G. 1264.

[1] [1986] 1 W.L.R. 861; see also *Sykes v. Land* (1984) 271 E.G. 1264. *Cf. Dickson v. MacGregor*, 1992 S.L.T. 83 (Land Ct.).

[2] The decision did not ultimately turn on the provisions of the Partnership Act 1890, s.5 (see [1986] 1 W.L.R. 878), but on the principles enunciated in *Johnson v. Moreton* [1980] A.C. 37: see further *infra* para. 23–190.

[3] See Deeds, *supra*, para. 12–63. Note, however, that in *Juggeewundas Keeka Shah v. Ramdas Brjbooken Das* (1841) 2 Moo.Ind.App. 487, a mortgage by one partner was, in special circumstances, held to bind the firm.

[4] Law of Property Act 1925, ss.27(1), 34(2) and 35; and see *Re Fuller's Contract* [1933] Ch. 652.

[5] *Ibid.* s.28(1) (as amended by the Law of Property (Amendment) Act 1926, Sched.), applying the Settled Land Act 1925, s.71.

the creation of such a mortgage might, as against partners whose consent is not sought, constitute a breach of trust.[6]

12–76   On the footing that a member of an ordinary trading partnership has implied authority to borrow money on behalf of the firm,[7] it almost necessarily follows that he will also have power to pledge partnership property as security for such borrowing. It would therefore seem that, in such cases at least, a partner would have had power to create a valid equitable mortgage by deposit of the title deeds in respect of land held by the firm,[8] although it now seems clear that such a mortgage can no longer be created in the face of the requirements of section 2 of the Law of Property (Miscellaneous Provisions) Act 1989.[9]

Pledges of partnership chattels

12–77   The implied authority of partners to pledge chattels is clear and was stated by Lord Lindley in this way:

> "The implied authority of a partner who has power to borrow, to pledge the personal property of the firm for money borrowed, is beyond dispute[10]; and the power is not confined to cases in which there is a general partnership; for if several join in a purchase of goods to be sold for their common profit, a pledge of those goods by one of the persons interested is binding on them all.[11] The implied power to pledge, moreover, extends to pledges for antecedent debts."[12]

---

[6] See also *supra*, para. 12–74, n. 99.

[7] See *supra*, paras. 12–45, 12–46.

[8] Lord Lindley put it more tentatively: "The writer is not aware of any decision in which an equitable mortgage made by one partner by a deposit of deeds relating to partnership real estate, has been upheld, or the contrary; he can therefore only venture to submit, that such a mortgage ought to be held valid in all cases in which it is made by a partner having an implied power to borrow on the credit of the firm." He then referred, in a footnote, to the following cases: *Re Clough* (1885) 31 Ch.D. 324 (equitable mortgage by surviving partner for existing partnership debt held valid); *Ex p. Lloyd* (1834) 1 Mont. & Ayr. 494; *Re Patent File Co.* (1870) L.R. 6 Ch. 83; *Ex p. National Bank* (1872) L.R. 14 Eq. 507. See also, as to security for advances, *Re Bourne* [1906] 2 Ch. 427.

[9] *United Bank of Kuwait plc v. Sahib, The Times*, July 7, 1994. See also *Emmett on Title* (19th ed.), para. 25–116; *Snell's Equity* (29th ed.), p. 445. Cf. the preface to *Cousins, The Law of Mortgages*.

[10] See *Ex p. Bonbonus* (1803) 8 Ves. Jr. 540; *Gordon v. Ellis* (1844) 7 Man. & G. 607; *Brownrigg v. Rae* (1850) 5 Ex. 489; *Butchart v. Dresser* (1853) 4 De G.M. & G. 542; see also *Re Langmead's Trust* (1855) 20 Beav. 20, affirmed at 7 De G.M. & G. 353; *Ex p. Howden* (1842) 2 M.D. & D. 574.

[11] *Re Gellar* (1812) 1 Rose 297; *Tupper v. Haythorne* (1815) Gow 135; *Raba v. Ryland* (1819) Gow 133; *Reid v. Hollinshead* (1825) 4 B. & C. 867; but see *Barton v. Williams* (1822) 5 B. & A. 395, 405, *per* Best J. (where the goods pledged were not at the time partnership property). Lord Lindley pointed out that "In *Ex p. Copeland* (1833) 2 Mont. & Ayr. 177, it was questioned whether a pledge by one partner was valid if the pledgee had notice that the pledgor was not the only owner, but this it is conceived could only be material where the pledge is not made for ostensible partnership purposes."

[12] *Re Patent File Co.* (1870) L.R. 6 Ch.App. 83; *Re Clough* (1885) 31 Ch.D. 324; and see *Story on Partnership*, s.101.

Lord Lindley also considered the potential application of the then **12–78** Factors Acts[13] in this context, concluding:

"The writer is not aware of any authority upon this subject, but he conceives that those acts neither extend nor abridge the power in question. The Factors Acts do not apparently render valid any sale or pledge by one partner of partnership goods which is not valid independently of the acts upon the principles of the common law."

The current editor believes that Lord Lindley's observations are still pertinent in relation to the Factors Act 1889.

Redemption of pledge

It is the view of the current editor that, just as he may pledge the **12–79** firm's goods in the first instance, so one partner may redeem such a pledge.[14]

Mortgages and pledges to partners

It is clear that one partner will normally have implied authority to accept security for a debt due to the firm. This may even, exceptionally, include the acceptance of a security in the form of shares which are registered in the name of the firm, thus rendering all the partners liable as contributories.[15]

Partnerships

Although a partner will in general have no implied authority to **12–80** enter into a subsidiary partnership with a third party,[16] he may, in certain circumstances, have the requisite authority if the business to be carried on represents no more than an extension of the firm's existing business.[17]

---

[13] See now the Factors Act 1889. The present Act is wider in scope than its predecessors: see *ibid.* s.9 (as amended by the Consumer Credit Act 1974, Sched. 4), and the decisions thereunder; *Lee v. Butler* [1893] 2 Q.B. 318; *Shenstone & Co. v. Hilton* [1894] 2 Q.B. 452; *Payne v. Wilson* [1895] 2 Q.B. 537; *Helby v. Matthews* [1895] A.C. 471.

[14] Lord Lindley said, of redemption, "Any partner may, on behalf of the firm, redeem a pledge of the firm; but he alone is not the proper person to bring an action to recover the thing pledged." He then cited *Harper v. Godsell* (1870) L.R. 5 Q.B. 422, which was a case of an action in trover brought by an assignee of certain partners' shares in goods pledged to the defendant. In fact, the action was held not to be maintainable because the defendant had sold the pledged goods under an authority given by one of the other partners and scarcely seems to support Lord Lindley's proposition.

[15] *Weikersheim's Case* (1873) L.R. 8 Ch.App. 831; *cf. Niemann v. Niemann* (1889) 43 Ch.D. 198.

[16] *Singleton v. Knight* (1888) 13 App.Cas. 788; *Hawksley v. Outram* [1892] 3 Ch. 359; also *Ex p. British Nation Life Assurance Association* (1878) 8 Ch.D. 679, 704. These authorities were reviewed critically by Megarry J. in *Mann v. D'Arcy* [1968] 1 W.L.R. 893.

[17] *Mann v. D'Arcy* [1968] 1 W.L.R. 893: see further, *supra*, para. 12–13.

Payments

See *Debts*, *supra*, paragraphs 12–53 *et seq.*

Purchases

12–81   As might be expected, the implied authority of a partner to purchase goods on the firm's behalf is not open to question, even in the case of a non-trading partnership. Lord Lindley observed:

> "It has been long decided that every member of an ordinary trading partnership has implied power to purchase on the credit of the firm such goods as are or may be necessary for carrying on its business in the usual way.[18] This cannot be more strongly exemplified than by the case of *Bond v. Gibson*[19] ... The power of one partner to bind the firm by a purchase of goods on its credit is not confined to trading partnerships.[20] ... It is of no consequence what the partnership business may be, if the goods supplied are necessary for its transaction in the ordinary way."

In such cases, the firm's liability is dependent on a partner ordering the goods on its behalf in the usual way of business; it does not matter that the supplier did not know that he was a member of the firm, unless he appeared to be acting as a principal and not as an agent.[21] Equally, if a partner purchases goods which are to be introduced into the firm as his capital contribution, the firm will not be bound if that purpose was known to the supplier, in the absence of subsequent ratification.[22]

Return of goods sold on credit

12–82   If goods are sold to the firm on credit but the firm is unable to pay for them, one partner may properly return them to the supplier,[23] provided that this is not held to be a transaction defrauding the firm's creditors.[24]

---

[18] *Hyat v. Hare* (1696) Comb. 383.

[19] (1808) 1 Camp. 185. In that case, the partner had acquired goods on the credit of the firm and then pawned them for his own benefit; both partners were nevertheless held liable for the purchase price of the goods.

[20] In this context, Lord Lindley cited *Gardiner v. Childs* (1837) 8 Car. & P. 345; *cf. Wilson v. Whitehead* (1842) 10 M. & W. 503.

[21] *Ruppell v. Roberts* (1834) 4 Nev. & Man. 31; *Gardiner v. Childs* (1837) 8 Car. & P. 345; *City of London Gas Co. v. Nicholls* (1862) 2 Car. & P. 365. See also *infra*, paras. 12–163 *et seq.*

[22] See *supra*, para. 12–49 and *infra*, paras. 13–21 *et seq.*; also *Heap v. Dobson* (1863) 15 C.B.(N.S.) 460.

[23] *De Tastet v. Carroll* (1815) 1 Stark. 88.

[24] See the Insolvency Act 1986, ss.238, 239, 339, 340, 423.

Receipts

See *Debts*, *supra*, para. 12–57.

Releases, etc.

In this context, it is necessary to distinguish between a true release **12–83** and a mere covenant not to sue, since the former will in general bind the firm whilst the latter will not. Lord Lindley put it in this way:

"A covenant by one partner not to sue for a partnership debt does not amount to a release of that debt by the firm,[25] although a covenant by all the partners not to sue would be equivalent to a release,[26] and a release by one partner operates as a release by the firm."[27]

Thus, a bona fide release by one partner will not normally be set aside at the instance of the other partners,[28] unless there is evidence of fraud and collusion.[29]

Sales

Goods

A partner will, as a general rule, have implied authority to sell any **12–84** goods belonging to his firm.[30] This goes beyond mere sales of stock in trade and even, in one old case, was held to extend to a sale of the partnership books.[31] It is considered that the Factors Act 1889 does not apply to such sales.[32]

---

[25] *Walmesley v. Cooper* (1839) 11 A. & E. 216.

[26] *Deux v. Jefferies* (1594) Cro.Eliz. 352. It should be noted that a covenant not to sue will not be the equivalent of a release if given in favour of one joint debtor: see *Duck v. Mayeu* [1892] 2 Q.B. 511; *Re E. W. A.* [1901] 2 K.B. 642. See further, *infra*, para. 13–94.

[27] 2 Ro.Ab.Release, 410 D.; *Hawkshaw v. Parkins* (1819) 2 Swan. 539.

[28] *Arton v. Booth* (1820) 4 Moore 192; *Furnival v. Weston* (1822) 7 Moore 356; *Phillips v. Clagett* (1843) 11 M. & W. 84. See also *Jones v. Herbert* (1817) 7 Taunt. 421.

[29] See *Barker v. Richardson* (1827) 1 Y. & J. 362, where one partner had, following a dissolution, deliberately given a release to a partnership debtor as part of a scheme for discharging a private debt which he, in turn, owed to that debtor. The debtor knew it had been agreed that the other partner would get in the debts and clearly colluded in the fraud. See also *Phillips v. Clagett* (1843) 11 M. & W. 84; *Aspinall v. London and N.W. Ry.* (1853) 11 Hare 325.

[30] *Lambert's Case* (1690) Godb. 244. Lord Lindley then discoursed on what would be the position if the partners had become "mere" tenants in common of the partnership goods, referring to Litt. s.323; *Fox v. Hanbury* (1776) Cowp. 445; also *Buckley v. Barber* (1851) 6 Ex. 164, as to which see further *infra*, para. 18–64. However, since such a situation can only arise following a dissolution, in which case the authority of any partner to sell partnership goods is now clearly established by the Partnership Act 1890, s.38, *infra*, para. 13–64, the passage has not been retained. It is to be found in the 15th ed. of this work at p. 314.

[31] *Dore v. Wilkinson* (1817) 2 Stark. 287. The opinion of the current editor is that this decision was wholly exceptional and should not be regarded as a general authority in relation to partnership books.

[32] See *supra*, para. 12–78.

Land

12–85   Where land is held beneficially by a firm, the legal estate will inevitably be vested in not more than four partners as trustees for sale.[33] Those trustees, if they are more than two in number,[34] will be able to effect a sale without the concurrence of the other partners, even though this may involve the commission of a breach of trust.[35]

Ships

12–86   It appears that a partner will, in an appropriate case, have authority to charter a ship or to mortgage a ship belonging to the firm.[36]

Trusts

12–87   A partner in a firm of solicitors does not have authority in the ordinary course of his practice to accept office as a trustee of a trust or, indeed, to constitute himself as a constructive trustee.[37]

3. LIABILITY OF PARTNERS IN RESPECT OF TORTS AND FRAUDS

12–88 In his introduction to this subject, Lord Lindley said:

> "If it were necessary, in order that one person should be liable for the fraud or tort of another, that the former should have authorised the commission of such tort or fraud, it would be a comparatively easy matter to determine in any particular case whether a tort or fraud committed by an agent could or could not be imputed to his principal. But as a principal is liable, not only for the authorised acts of his agent, but also for such unauthorised acts as fall within the scope of the authority apparently conferred upon him, the question whether a tort or fraud committed by an agent is or is not imputable to his principal becomes one of considerable difficulty; for it is obvious that it does not follow from

---

[33] See Law of Property Act 1925, ss. 34(2), 35; and see *Re Fuller's Contract* [1933] Ch. 652 and *infra*, para. 18–60.

[34] *Ibid.* s.27(1).

[35] See *ibid.* ss.25, 26(3) (as amended by the Law of Property (Amendment) Act 1926, Sched.); also the decision in *Sykes v. Land* (1984) 271 E.G. 1264.

[36] See, as to charters, *Thomas v. Clarke* (1818) 2 Stark. 450 and, as to mortgages, *Ex p. Howden* (1842) 2 M.D. & D. 574.

[37] *Re Bell's Indenture* [1980] 1 W.L.R. 1217; also *Re Fryer* (1857) 3 K. & J. 317; *Mara v. Browne* [1896] 1 Ch. 199. See further, *infra*, paras. 12–118, 12–141, 12–142.

the circumstance that such tort or fraud was not authorised, that therefore the principal is not legally responsible for it."[38]

Partnership Act 1890, section 10

These principles are clearly reflected in section 10 of the **12–89** Partnership Act 1890, which provides:

"10. Where, by any wrongful act or omission of any partner acting in the ordinary course of the business of the firm, or with the authority of his co-partners, loss or injury is caused to any person not being a partner in the firm, or any penalty is incurred, the firm is liable therefor to the same extent as the partner so acting or omitting to act."[39]

Scope of the section

The section is only directed to establishing the secondary liability of **12–90** the firm, and the words "to the same extent" do not artificially restrict that liability. Thus, it does not follow that, merely because the partner who commits a wrongful act with the express or implied authority of his co-partners is not personally liable, such liability cannot, on normal principles, attach to some *other* partner.[40] In such a case, the liability of the firm will be determined by the extent of the latter partner's liability, not that of the former.[41] It should also be noted that the section has no application where one partner commits a wrongful act against another.[42]

Although the terminology used in the section is different to that **12–91** appearing in section 5,[43] the current editor takes the view that the test for identifying whether a partner was acting in the "ordinary course of the business of the firm" will be the same.[44] Indeed, Lord

---

[38] Lord Lindley then went on to explore the conditions which are required to be fulfilled before a principal will be held liable for the torts and frauds of his agent. The passage has not been retained, but is to be found in the 15th ed. of this work at pp. 315–318.

[39] As to the nature of the liability under this section see *ibid.* s.12, *infra*, para. 13–12.

[40] In *Meekins v. Henson* [1964] 1 Q.B. 472, one partner, with the authority of his co-partners, had defamed the plaintiff on a privileged occasion and without malice and was accordingly held not to have committed any tort. Malice was, however, proved against one of the other two partners and he alone was held liable to the plaintiff in damages. Winn J. held the Partnership Act 1890, s.10 to be irrelevant in this context.

[41] In *Meekins v. Henson*, *supra*, the action was brought against the three partners individually and no attempt was therefore made to argue in favour of the liability of the firm. Ironically, an argument framed by reference to the Partnership Act 1890, s.10 was advanced not by the plaintiff but by the partners themselves.

[42] See *Mair v. Wood*, 1948 S.C. 83, which concerned a Scots partnership enjoying separate legal personality. It is considered that the position is *a fortiori* in England, where the firm has no such personality.

[43] See *supra*, para. 12–02.

[44] See *supra*, paras. 12–09 *et seq.*

Lindley used the expression "carrying on the business in the usual way" in this context.

The practical operation of section 10 can best be illustrated by considering torts and frauds separately and by referring to a number of cases decided prior to the Partnership Act 1890.

(a) Torts

12–92 Examples of cases in which a firm had been held liable for torts committed by partners in the ordinary course of business are many and varied. They range from liability for the negligent driving of a coach,[45] failure to keep a mineshaft in a proper condition[46] and breach of the old revenue laws[47] to liability for negligent advice[48] or the negligent conduct of a claim by a partner in a firm of solicitors.[49]

12–93 It does not matter that the firm itself is incapable of committing the tortious act. Thus, where a partner, with the express authority of his co-partners or in the ordinary course of business, holds a particular office or appointment which the firm is ineligible to hold, the firm will be liable for his negligent acts and omissions in carrying out the duties attached to that position.[50]

Wilful torts

12–94 Lord Lindley observed:

> "As a rule ... the wilful tort of one partner is not imputable to the firm.[51] ... But a wilful tort committed by a partner in the course and for the purpose of transacting the business of the firm may make the firm responsible."[52]

Thus, if part of the normal business of a firm involves obtaining details of contracts entered into by its business competitors, albeit by legitimate means, the firm will be responsible if one partner obtains such information by the use of a bribe.[53]

---

[45] *Moreton v. Hardern* (1825) 4 B. & C. 223. As to ships, see *Steel v. Lester* (1878) 3 C.P.D. 121.
[46] *Mellors v. Shaw* (1861) 1 B. & S. 437; *Ashworth v. Stanwix* (1861) 3 E. & E. 701. See also *Duke of Brunswick v. Slowman* (1849) 8 C.B. 317.
[47] *R. v. Stranyforth* (1721) Bunb. 97; *Att.-Gen. v. Burges* (1726) Bunb. 223; *Att.-Gen. v. Weeks* (1726) Bunb. 223; *R. v. Manning* (1739) 2 Com. 616. See also *Att.-Gen. v. Siddon* (1830) 1 C. & J. 220.
[48] *Blyth v. Fladgate* [1891] 1 Ch. 337; *Midland Bank Trust Co. Ltd. v. Hett, Stubbs & Kemp* [1979] Ch. 384; and other cases of that class. See also *Sawyer v. Goodwin* (1867) 36 L.J.Ch. 578.
[49] *Welsh v. Knarston*, 1972 S.L.T. 96.
[50] *Kirkintilloch Equitable Co-Operative Society Ltd. v. Livingstone*, 1972 S.L.T. 154.
[51] Lord Lindley cited *Arbuckle v. Taylor* (1815) 3 Dow. 160 (malicious prosecution for theft of partnership property).
[52] See *Limpus v. London General Omnibus Co.* (1861) 1 H. & C. 526; also *Citizens' Life Assurance Co. v. Brown* [1904] A.C. 423.
[53] *Hamlyn v. John Houston & Co.* [1903] 1 K.B. 81; *Janvier v. Sweeney* [1919] 2 K.B. 316.

Right to indemnity

It would seem that, in cases where section 10 of the Partnership **12–95** Act 1890 applies, the innocent partners may be entitled to seek an indemnity from the partner who committed the tort, unless they expressly or impliedly authorised it.[54]

(b) Frauds and Fraudulent Representations

Section 10 of the Partnership Act 1890 introduced no change in the **12–96** law as regards the liability of the firm for frauds committed by its members, as is demonstrated by the following passage which, though written by Lord Lindley prior to the Act, clearly explains its operation in this context:

" . . . [a] firm is liable for frauds committed by one of its members whilst acting for the firm, and in transacting its business[55]; and the innocent partners cannot divest themselves of responsibility on the ground that they never authorised the commission of the fraud. On the other hand, the firm is not liable for the other frauds of its members, unless it has in fact sanctioned such frauds, or the transactions of which they form part."[56]

It should be noted that, as under the general law,[57] liability under the section is not dependent on showing that the firm has benefited from the fraud, although acceptance of such a benefit may justify an inference that the firm has adopted the fraud.[58]

Prior to the decision in *Hedley Byrne & Co. Ltd. v. Heller &* **12–97** *Partners Ltd.*[59] and the passing of the Misrepresentation Act 1967, there was in general no right to damages in respect of misrepresentations which were made otherwise than fraudulently.[60] Now damages are, in general, available for negligent mis-statements[61] and for

---

[54] See *infra*, para. 20–10.
[55] Of course, the formulation of the rule in s.10 now refers to the "ordinary course of the business," but this is not a change of substance.
[56] See further, *infra*, paras. 12–128 *et seq.*
[57] See *Lloyd v. Grace Smith & Co.* [1912] A.C. 716.
[58] See [1912] A.C. 716, 738, *per* Lord Macnaghten.
[59] [1964] A.C. 465.
[60] A fraudulent statement must, in essence, be false and either known to the maker to be false or made by him recklessly and without any belief as to its truth: see *Derry v. Peek* (1889) 14 App.Cas. 337; *Glasier v. Rolls* (1889) 42 Ch.D. 436; *Angus v. Clifford* [1891] 2 Ch. 449; *Low v. Bouverie* [1891] 3 Ch. 82; *Le Lievre v. Gould* [1893] 1 Q.B. 491. As to damages for breach of an implied warranty of authority, see *Collen v. Wright* (1857) 8 E. & B. 647; *Starkey v. Bank of England* [1903] A.C. 114; *Bowstead on Agency* (15th ed.), Art. 112, pp. 457 *et seq.* And see also, as to the position where there is a breach of a special or fiduciary duty arising from the relationship of the parties, *Nocton v. Lord Ashburton* [1914] A.C. 932 (solicitor and client).
[61] *Hedley Byrne & Co. Ltd. v. Heller & Partners Ltd.* [1964] A.C. 465; *Mutual Life and Citizens' Assurance Co. Ltd. v. Evatt* [1971] A.C. 793; *Esso Petroleum Ltd. v. Mardon* [1976] Q.B. 801. But see as to the possible limitations on such an action, *Argy Trading Development Co. Ltd. v. Lapid Developments Ltd.* [1977] 1 W.L.R. 444.

negligent and careless (but not wholly innocent) misrepresentations.[62] It is accordingly no longer as vital to distinguish, as Lord Lindley did, between those cases in which there is a right to damages and those in which there is some other remedy. Nevertheless, the distinction is useful as a means of illustrating the potential application of section 10 of the Partnership Act 1890.

Actions for damages

12–98   Whilst section 10 of the Partnership Act 1890 clearly establishes the liability of the firm for damages in respect of a fraud committed by a partner in the ordinary course of its business,[63] it is still necessary to prove an *actionable* fraud. Constructive fraud, *i.e.* a combination of a false statement made innocently by one partner and knowledge of the true facts on the part of another partner, is not sufficient[64]; moreover, it would seem that damages on the basis of innocent misrepresentation would not be recoverable in such a case.[65] Where, however, one partner, who knows the true facts, expressly authorises

---

[62] See the Misrepresentation Act 1967, s.2(1). To escape liability the person making the representation must prove that "he had reasonable grounds to believe and did believe up to the time the contract was made that the facts represented were true." See generally, as to this subsection, *Gosling v. Anderson* [1972] E.G.D. 709; *Watts v. Spence* [1976] Ch. 165; *Howard Marine and Dredging Co. Ltd. v. A. Ogden & Sons (Excavations) Ltd.* [1978] Q.B. 574; *Chesneau v. Interhome Ltd.* (1983) 134 N.L.J. 341 (C.A.); *Sharneyford Supplies Ltd. v. Edge* [1986] Ch. 128; *Cemp Properties (U.K.) Ltd. v. Dentsply Research & Development Corp.* [1991] 34 E.G. 62 (C.A.); *Royscot Trust Ltd. v. Rogerson* [1991] 2 Q.B. 297 (C.A.); also *Garden Neptune Shipping Ltd. v. Occidental Worldwide Investment Corp.* [1990] 1 Lloyd's Rep. 330. Although it has for some years been clear that the measure of damages under the subsection is tortious (indemnity for loss) rather than contractual (loss of expectation), the Court of Appeal in *Royscot Trust Ltd. v. Rogerson*, *supra*, decided that the true measure is that for *fraudulent* misrepresentation rather than mere negligence at common law, so that, where appropriate, unforeseen losses flowing from the fraud will be recoverable; see also *Cemp Properties (U.K.) Ltd. v. Dentsply Research & Development Corp., supra*. Somewhat confusingly, the subsection is often spoken of as having established liability for *innocent* misrepresentation (*e.g.* see *Howard Marine and Dredging Co. Ltd. v. A. Ogden & Sons (Excavations) Ltd., supra*, p. 592, *per* Denning M.R.), but in such cases the word "innocent" is used in a special sense. See also *infra*, para. 23–50. Note that *ibid.* s.3 does not apply to provisions which seek to restrict the ostensible authority of an agent: *Overbrooke Estates Ltd. v. Glencombe Properties Ltd.* [1974] 1 W.L.R. 1335 (a decision under s.3 in its original form, and not as substituted by the Unfair Contract Terms Act 1977, s.8(1)).

[63] In such a case, the firm will be liable to the same extent as the partner responsible for the fraud: see *supra*, para. 12–90. It should be noted that, whilst Lord Lindley, writing in the Supplement to the 5th ed. of this work, said of the section "... it removes the doubt as to whether a firm is or is not liable in an action of damages for the fraud of one of its members, if committed by him in the ordinary course of the business of the firm, by making the firm liable in every case in which the partner himself is liable", in subsequent editions the same view was expressed more tentatively, namely, that the section "seems clearly to make a firm liable..."

[64] See *Armstrong v. Strain* [1952] 1 K.B. 232, where an unsuccessful attempt was made to prove fraud by linking an innocent misrepresentation as to the state of a property made by an agent on behalf of the owner (but without his knowledge) with the owner's awareness of the true state of the property. And see also *supra*, para. 12–25.

[65] The Misrepresentation Act 1967, s.2(1) gives a remedy only where damages would have been recoverable if the misrepresentation had been made fraudulently, which for the above reasons they would not. *Quaere*, could the firm in any event rely on the reasonable belief of the partner who made the statement? Having regard to the terms of the Partnership Act 1890, s.10, the current editor tentatively submits that it could.

another partner, who has no such knowledge, to make a false statement,[66] or deliberately stands by in the knowledge, expectation or hope that he will make such a statement, that statement, although made innocently, would be treated as a fraudulent misrepresentation made by the firm.[67] Similarly, where the partner who makes the statement is reckless in not consulting his co-partners before doing so.[68]

Other remedies

Lord Lindley observed that: **12–99**

"... there is no doubt that a firm can be compelled to restore property, or refund money, obtained by it by the misrepresentation of one of its members. Nor in such a case is it necessary to prove that the misrepresentation was fraudulent as well as false."[69]

Thus, in *Rapp v. Latham*,[70] Parry, who was the active partner in a firm of wine and spirit merchants, had received a substantial sum of money from a customer to be applied in the purchase and sale of wine. He falsely and fraudulently represented that he was carrying out various transactions on the customer's behalf and accounted to him for the supposed proceeds. There was, however, a considerable sum unaccounted for, which Parry alleged had been invested in the purchase of wine. The customer sought to recover this amount against Parry and his partner, Latham. Notwithstanding an attempt by Latham to argue that he was not affected by Parry's fraud, on the basis that the fictitious purchases and sales were not made in the ordinary course of trade and were, therefore, not partnership transactions, it was held that Latham was liable to the customer. The decisions in *Lovell v. Hicks*[71] and *Blair v. Bromley*[72] are to the same effect.

---

[66] See *London County Freehold Properties Ltd. v. Berkeley Property Investment Co. Ltd.* [1936] 2 All E.R. 1039.

[67] See *Ludgater v. Love* (1881) 44 L.T. 694.

[68] See *Armstrong v. Strain* [1952] 1 K.B. 232, 244, *per* Singleton L.J. See also *supra*, n. 64.

[69] See *Arkwright v. Newbold* (1880) 17 Ch.D. 301; *Redgrave v. Hurd* (1881) 20 Ch.D. 1.

[70] (1819) 2 B. & A. 795.

[71] (1837) 2 Y. & C.Ex. 472.

[72] (1847) 2 Ph. 354. Lord Lindley pointed out that the case "was in fact decided by the Lord Chancellor [*Lord Cottenham*] expressly upon the ground that persons who, having a duty to perform, represent to those who are interested in the performance of it that it has been performed, make themselves responsible for all the consequences of non-performance; and as one partner may bind another as to any matter within the limits of their joint business, so he may by an act which, though not constituting a contract by itself, is on equitable principles considered as having all the consequences of one." See also, as to this case *infra*, para. 12–125. And see *Moore v. Knight* [1891] 1 Ch. 547.

False accounts rendered by partner

12–100   The cases cited in the previous paragraph would appear to demonstrate that a false and fraudulent account rendered by a partner, in the name of the firm and within the scope of its business, would have bound all the partners even prior to the Partnership Act 1890[73] and there is no reason to suppose that the current position is any different, having regard to the provisions of sections 10 and 15 of that Act.[74]

Cases where the firm is not liable

Statute of Frauds Amendment Act 1828, section 6

12–101   By section 6 of the Statute of Frauds Amendment Act 1828, a firm is not liable for a false and fraudulent representation as to the character or solvency of any person unless the representation is in writing and signed by all the partners.[75] It has been decided that the signature of one partner in the firm name will not bind any partner other than himself[76] and it is submitted that the same decision would still be reached today, notwithstanding the terms of section 10 of the Partnership Act 1890.[77]

It should be noted that the 1828 Act provides no defence in the case of a *negligent* misrepresentation as to character or solvency made by a partner in the ordinary course of the firm's business.[78]

Representations as to authority

12–102   Consistently with the views expressed earlier in this work,[79] Lord Lindley wrote:

"If a partner, acting apparently beyond the limits of his authority, untruly represents that he is acting with his co-partners' consent,

---

[73] Lord Lindley put it very tentatively: "Whether accounts, rendered by one partner in the name of the firm and showing that money is in the hands of the firm when in truth he has misapplied it, are to be treated as representations of the firm, is a question which has given rise to much discussion and upon which the cases are not uniform. But on the whole it is conceived that if the accounts relate to matters within the scope of the partnership business the firm is bound by them." He also referred to *Devaynes v. Noble, Baring's Case* (1816) 1 Mer. 611; *Marsh v. Keating* (1834) 2 Cl. & F. 250; *De Ribeyre v. Barclay* (1857) 23 Beav. 107, contrasting those decisions with *Hume v. Bolland* (1832) 1 Cromp. & M. 130 and *Sims v. Brutton* (1850) 5 Ex. 802, noticed *infra*, para. 12–116.

[74] See *supra*, paras. 12–17, 12–89.

[75] See as to the scope of the section, *Banbury v. Bank of Montreal* [1918] A.C. 626; also *Diamond v. Bank of London and Montreal Ltd.* [1979] Q.B. 333.

[76] See *Williams v. Mason* (1873) 28 L.T.(N.S.) 232; *Swift v. Jewsbury* (1874) L.R. 9 Q.B. 301; *Hirst v. West Riding Union Banking Co.* [1901] 2 K.B. 560.

[77] See *Keen v. Mear* [1920] 2 Ch. 574, a decision which turned on the application of the Partnership Act 1890, s.5 and the Statute of Frauds 1677, s.4 (it being held that the former section did not override the provisions of the latter).

[78] See *W. B. Anderson & Sons v. Rhodes (Liverpool)* [1967] 2 All E.R. 850; also *Banbury v. Bank of Montreal* [1918] A.C. 626.

[79] See *supra*, para. 12–18.

they are not bound by this representation, nor are they liable for what may be done on the faith of it."

He illustrated this proposition by reference to the decision in *Ex p. Agace*,[80] where one partner had given partnership bills in payment of a personal debt and represented to the creditor that his partner was agreeable to this being done. The other partner had done nothing to justify an inference that he consented to that arrangement or that he authorised the representation. On the bankruptcy of the firm, those bills were held not to be provable against the joint estate. Although the creditor was genuinely misled, he must be taken to have known that the partner who made the representation was not acting in the ordinary course of the firm's business and had thus exceeded the scope of his implied authority.[81]

Representations as to nature of business

It is submitted that the position is no different where the false **12–103** representation relates, not directly to the extent of the partner's authority, but to the nature of the partnership business and, thus, indirectly to the extent of that authority. Lord Lindley analysed the position in this way:

"A question of more difficulty arises when a partner alleges that the business of the firm is more extensive than it really is, or that it is different from what it is. But even in this case the firm would probably be held not liable[82] for such a misrepresentation. *Ex hypothesi* the representation is not referable to anything falling within the scope of the partnership business; and it would probably be contended in vain that each partner was impliedly authorised by his co-partners to answer questions as to what business they really carried on in partnership. If the person seeking to make the firm liable knew anything of the firm and of its business as ordinarily carried on, then *Ex p. Agace* is an authority to show that he could not succeed. If he knew nothing of the firm, he would be in the position of a person dealing with an agent whose authority is wholly unknown. Now an agent whose authority is wholly unknown cannot bind his principal by misrepresenting the authority conferred;[83] and it is difficult, therefore, to see upon

---

[80] (1792) 2 Cox 312.
[81] See also *Kendal v. Wood* (1870) L.R. 6 Ex. 243; *Mahony v. East Holyford Mining Co.* (1875) L.R. 7 H.L. 869, 879–880, *per* Kelly C.B; *United Bank of Kuwait v. Hammoud* [1988] 1 W.L.R. 1051, 1066, *supra*, para. 12–18. And see, generally, *Armagas Ltd. v. Mundogas S.A.* [1986] A.C. 717, where numerous authorities are reviewed in the context of employer and employee.
[82] In later editions, the words "can hardly be held liable" were substituted.
[83] See *United Bank of Kuwait v. Hammoud* [1988] 1 W.L.R. 1051; also *Armagas Ltd. v. Mundogas S.A.* [1986] A.C. 717 and the cases there cited.

what principle a partner could, in the case now supposed, bind the firm by misrepresenting his authority, or by misrepresenting the nature of the business of the firm which, as to strangers, determines that authority."[84]

Representations to incoming partner

12–104   It is doubtful whether a false or fraudulent representation designed to induce a person to become a partner could ever be given in the ordinary course of carrying on the firm's business,[85] although Lord Lindley put it more categorically:

> "It is not necessary, in order to carry on the business of a firm in the ordinary way, that any of the partners should have power to induce other persons to join the firm."

It follows that, in the absence of express authority or subsequent ratification by the other partners, such a representation will not be imputed to the firm. Ratification will, however, be inferred if the firm, with knowledge of the false or fraudulent nature of the representation, seeks to retain money or property introduced by the incoming partner; in such circumstances, the firm will clearly be liable for its return.[86]

4. LIABILITY OF PARTNERS FOR MISAPPLICATION OF MONEY AND PROPERTY

12–105 Although cases in this class are closely allied to those in the previous section, they are governed by a different section of the Partnership Act 1890 and, for that reason, are considered separately.

Lord Lindley's formulation

Lord Lindley explained the position prior to the Partnership Act 1890, in terms of four basic principles:

> "In order that a firm may be liable for the misapplication of money by one of its members, some obligation on the part of the firm to take care of the money must be shown. A receipt of the money by the firm prima facie imposes this obligation; but where

---

[84] Lord Lindley then put forward the following example, which is scarcely of relevance today: "A member of a banking firm could hardly bind it by underwriting a policy in the name of the firm, and by untruly representing that he and his partners were insurers as well as bankers."

[85] *Quaere*, might such an argument perhaps be sustainable in the case of an investment partnership?

[86] See the cases cited *supra*, para. 12–99.

there is no receipt by the firm, there is prima facie no obligation on its part with respect to the money in question. It becomes important, therefore, to determine accurately when money is to be considered as received by the firm. Upon this point the following observations suggest themselves:

1. The firm must be treated as receiving what any partner receives as its real or ostensible agent, *i.e.* in the course of transacting the business of the firm.
2. In a case of this sort it is immaterial whether the other partners know anything about the money or not; for *ex hypothesi*, it is in the custody of one who must be regarded as their agent.[87]
3. The firm cannot be treated as receiving what one partner receives otherwise than as its real or ostensible agent, unless the money actually comes into the possession or under the control of the other partners.[88]
4. Agency being excluded in such a case as the last, the money cannot be considered as in the possession or under the control of the innocent partners, unless they know that it is so, or unless they are culpably ignorant of the fact."[89]

Partnership Act 1890, section 11

The foregoing principles are all encapsulated in the Partnership Act 1890, which provides: **12–106**

"11. In the following cases; namely:
(*a*) Where one partner acting within the scope of his apparent authority receives the money or property of a third person and misapplies it; and
(*b*) Where a firm in the course of its business receives money or property of a third person, and the money or property so received is misapplied by one or more of the partners while it is in the custody of the firm;
the firm is liable to make good the loss."[90]

It will be apparent that the section seeks to impose liability in two distinct cases, *i.e.* where money or property has been received and misapplied by a partner (section 11(a)) and where money or property has been received by the firm and subsequently misapplied by a **12–107**

---

[87] See *infra*, paras. 12–109 *et seq.*
[88] See *infra*, paras. 12–120 *et seq.*
[89] See *infra*, paras. 12–113 *et seq*, 12–123. As to culpable ignorance, *cf. Marsh v. Keating* (1834) 2 Cl. & Fin. 289; *Sims v. Brutton* (1850) 5 Ex. 802; *Ex p. Greaves* (1856) 8 De G.M. & G. 291; *Cleather v. Twisden* (1884) 28 Ch.D. 340; *National Commercial Banking Corp. of Australia Ltd. v. Batty* (1986) 65 A.L.R. 385.
[90] As to the nature of the liability under this section, see *ibid.* s.12, *infra*, para. 13–12.

partner (section 11(b)). Both require an application of the same fundamental principle which underlies sections 5 and 10, *i.e.* the firm will only be liable where money is received within the scope of a partner's express or implied authority, the latter being determined by reference to the manner in which the partnership business is carried on in the usual or ordinary way.[91] However, as Lord Lindley pointed out, in all cases liability presupposes the receipt of money by or on behalf of the firm: if there is no receipt, there will be no liability.[92]

12–108   Given the relative dearth of decisions under section 11, the operation of the two limbs must in part be illustrated by reference to a number of pre-1890 authorities. These cases will be grouped according to result, *i.e.* those in which the firm was held liable and those in which it was not, each group being preceded by a general proposition or rule originally formulated by Lord Lindley.

Section 11(a): Receipt of money or property by partner

Group 1: Firm held liable

12–109   *Where one partner, acting within the scope of his authority, as evidenced by the business of the firm, obtains money and misapplies it, the firm is answerable for it.*[93]

In *Willett v. Chambers*,[94] a partner in a firm of solicitors and conveyancers received money from a client to invest on mortgage and misapplied it. A bill for the supposed transaction was rendered to the client in the firm name and was in fact paid to the other partner: it was therefore clearly a partnership transaction[95] and the other partner, whilst himself innocent of any wrongdoing, was held liable to the client for the return of the money.

12–110   A more unusual case was *Rhodes v. Moules*.[96] There R, again a partner in a firm of solicitors, was instructed by a client to arrange a loan secured by a mortgage on his freehold property. R duly arranged the loan, but informed the client that the mortgagees

---

[91] See *supra*, paras. 12–09 *et seq.* And see, in particular, *Re Bell's Indenture* [1980] 1 W.L.R. 1217, *infra*, para. 12–118.

[92] See *British Homes Assurance Corporation Ltd. v. Paterson* [1902] 2 Ch. 404, *infra*, para. 13–26.

[93] This was Lord Lindley's first rule.

[94] (1778) Cowp. 814. See also *Atkinson v. Mackreth* (1866) L.R. 2 Eq. 570; *St. Aubyn v. Smart* (1868) L.R. 3 Ch.App. 646; *Dundonald v. Masterman* (1869) L.R. 7 Eq. 515. *Cf. Bourdillon v. Roche* (1858) 27 L.J.Ch. 681; *Viney v. Chaplin* (1858) 2 De G. & J. 483; *Harman v. Johnson* (1853) 2 E. & B. 61; *Plumer v. Gregory* (1874) L.R. 18 Eq. 621; *Cleather v. Twisden* (1884) 28 Ch.D. 340: see further, *infra*, paras. 12–113 *et seq.* In *Mann v. Hulme* [1962] A.L.R. 75, the partner receiving the money gave his own promissory note as additional security, but this was held not to affect the firm's primary liability.

[95] Lord Mansfield relied upon the fact that the bill for the fictitious mortgage was made out in the name of the firm, and was paid to the innocent partner.

[96] [1895] 1 Ch. 236. *Cf. Cleather v. Twisden* (1884) 28 Ch.D. 340, *infra*, para. 12–115.

required collateral security, which was untrue. The client gave R some bearer share warrants to be used as such security, but these were misappropriated by R, who then absconded. The other partners did not know that the share warrants had been received and were innocent of any fraud. Significantly, R had on two previous occasions received the same share warrants from this client with a view to raising loans; moreover, the firm were in the habit of receiving and holding bearer bonds belonging to clients. In those circumstances, it was held that the share warrants were received in the course of a normal partnership transaction and that R's partners were liable for their value.

In *Brydges v. Branfill*,[97] a solicitor had connived at a fraud **12-111** committed by a client of his firm with a view to obtaining the payment out of certain funds in court. He received those funds under a power of attorney and handed them over to the client. The other partners knew nothing of the transaction, but were nevertheless held liable to make good the loss.

In each of the above cases, receipt by a partner was treated as **12-112** receipt by the firm, so that liability attached even though the other partners knew nothing of the transaction.[98] Where, however, money or property is received by a partner pursuant to a contract entered into by him *qua* individual and not *qua* partner, the firm will not be liable even if the contract was of a nature that would fall within the scope of the firm's business.[99]

Group 2: Firm not liable

If a partner in the course of some transaction unconnected with the **12-113** *business of the firm, or not within the scope of such business, obtains money and then misapplies it, the firm is not without more*[1] *liable to make good the loss.*[2]

In *Harman v. Johnson*,[3] a partner in a firm of solicitors was entrusted with money for the purpose of investing it on mortgage when a good opportunity arose, but misapplied it. His partner was not held liable

---

[97] (1842) 12 Sim. 369. See also *Todd v. Studholme* (1857) 3 K. & J. 324. *Cf. Marsh v. Joseph* [1897] 1 Ch. 213.

[98] See *St. Aubyn v. Smart* [1868] L.R. 3 Ch.App. 646. There was no such receipt in *Agip (Africa) Ltd. v. Jackson* [1991] Ch. 547.

[99] *British Homes Assurance Corporation v. Paterson* [1902] 2 Ch. 404, *infra*, para. 13–26; and see also *New Mining & Exploring Syndicate Ltd. v. Chalmers & Hunter*, 1912 S.C. 126.

[1] As to the effect of knowledge on the part of the other partners, see *Cleather v. Twisden* (1884) 28 Ch.D. 340, *infra*, para. 12–115. And see also the Partnership Act 1890, s.13, *infra*, para. 12–134.

[2] This was in fact Lord Lindley's third rule, being the corollary of the first. See also *infra*, para. 12–128.

[3] (1853) 2 E. & B. 61.

for the misapplication because there was no evidence to show that it was part of the business either of the particular firm or of solicitors in general to act as scriveners, *i.e.* to receive and hold money pending investment.[4] Consistently with the decision in *Willett v. Chambers*,[5] the court intimated that if it had been shown that the money was received with a view to investment on a specific mortgage, the co-partner would have been liable for its misapplication.

12–114 Similarly, in *Plumer v. Gregory*,[6] where the solicitor had borrowed money from a client without the knowledge of his co-partners, saying that the firm wanted to lend it to another client on mortgage. The other partners were held not to be liable, even though two of them had in fact previously borrowed money from that client.

12–115 In *Cleather v. Twisden*,[7] trustees had placed certain bearer bonds in the hands of a solicitor for safe custody but he misappropriated them. His partners, who did not know of the transaction, were held not to be responsible for the loss, since it was not part of their business to accept such securities for safe custody. The decision would, however, have been otherwise if it had been proved that those partners had known the bonds to be in the custody of their co-partner on behalf of the firm; in such circumstances, the bonds would have been treated as in their own custody.[8]

12–116 It would seem that the decision in *Sims v. Brutton*[9] also falls within this group, although the decision is an exceptional one and requires explanation. It again concerned a firm of solicitors comprising two partners, B and C. B received £500 from a client, S, to invest on a mortgage, and the money was duly invested. The mortgage deed was retained by the firm. The mortgage debt was ultimately repaid to C, who delivered up the deed to the mortgagor. Shortly thereafter, C re-lent part of the money to the mortgagor and the mortgage deed was returned to him as security. The new mortgage debt was then repaid and the deed again delivered up. C had no authority to receive payment of the original mortgage debt, to re-lend any part of it or to receive payment of the subsequent mortgage debt. Neither B nor S

---

[4] Note that a scrivenor would have been entitled, pending the investment of the money, to use it for his own purposes and to retain any profits made thereby. Such a person would now be required to comply with the strict provisions of the Financial Services Act 1986: see *infra*, para. 12–119. And see the Solicitors' Accounts Rules 1991, noticed *infra*, para. 12–137; also the *Encyclopedia of Professional Partnerships*, Pt. 8.

[5] (1778) Cowp. 814, *supra*, para. 12–109.

[6] (1874) L.R. 18 Eq. 621.

[7] (1884) 28 Ch.D. 340; also *National Commercial Banking Corp. of Australia Ltd. v. Batty* (1986) 65 A.L.R. 385. *Cf. Rhodes v. Moules* [1895] 1 Ch. 236, *supra*, para. 12–110. See in particular, *ibid.* pp. 244–245, *per* Lord Herschell.

[8] See *infra*, paras. 12–120 *et seq*.

[9] (1850) 5 Ex. 802. See also *Coomer v. Bromley* (1852) 5 De G. & Sm. 532, *infra*, para. 12–131.

knew anything about these transactions, although full details were contained in the partnership books. Moreover, S was at all times credited with the receipt of interest on the whole amount of the original payment, such interest being regularly paid to his agent. C having misapplied the original payment, B was held not to be liable to make it good. It was found that B and C had discharged their duty to S by laying out the money as directed and that they had no authority to receive it back. Therefore, whilst C may have treated the repayment of the original mortgage debt as a partnership transaction, in point of law it did not have that character and did not bind the firm. The entries in the partnership books were only evidence of knowledge on B's part and the case stated for the opinion of the court expressly declared that he had no knowledge of the true facts.

Lord Lindley observed: **12–117**

"... if, as appears to have been the case, the [*original payment*] when paid off was placed to the credit of the firm with its bankers, the decision is difficult to reconcile with *Stone v. Marsh*[10] and *Marsh v. Keating*."[11]

Furthermore, having regard to the representations made to the client by the regular payment of interest to him, it is also difficult to reconcile the decision with *Blair v. Bromley*[12] and other cases of that class.

Finally, in *Re Bell's Indenture*[13] a solicitor acting for the trustees of **12–118** a marriage settlement had actively assisted them to dissipate the entire trust fund, and thereby rendered himself liable to the beneficiaries as a constructive trustee. His partner had no knowledge of these activities, but moneys received and paid out in breach of trust clearly passed through the firm's client account. It was held that the other partner was not liable for the misapplication of the trust fund, since the moneys had not been received by the firm as trustees but by the partner concerned as a constructive trustee and he had no authority in the ordinary course of his practice either to constitute himself a constructive trustee or to accept office as a trustee of the trust.[14]

---

[10] (1827) 6 B. & C. 364, *infra*, para. 12–123.
[11] (1834) 2 Cl. & F. 250, *infra*, para. 12–123. Lord Lindley also pointed out that "The Statute of Limitations afforded a good defence to the action in *Sims v. Brutton*. The propriety of the decision in that respect is untouched by the observations in the text."
[12] (1847) 2 Ph. 354, *infra*, para. 12–125.
[13] [1980] 1 W.L.R. 1217, distinguishing *Blyth v. Fladgate* [1891] 1 Ch. 337. *Cf. Agip (Africa) Ltd. v. Jackson* [1991] Ch. 547.
[14] [1980] 1 W.L.R. 1230. And see *Mara v. Browne* [1894] 1 Ch. 199, *infra*, para. 12–141; *Re Fryer* (1857) 3 K. & J. 317.

Solicitors and the Financial Services Act 1986

12–119   All of the cases cited in the above groups concerned solicitors and
their ability to receive money and property in the normal course of
practice. As illustrations of instances in which section 11(a) of the
Partnership Act 1890 may apply, they are of considerable value.
However, they should not be taken as establishing principles of
general application as regards the implied authority of solicitors, for
two reasons. In the first place, as was recently emphasised by the
Court of Appeal in *United Bank of Kuwait Ltd. v. Hammoud*,[15] old
authorities are inherently unreliable, given that the scope of a
solicitor's implied authority is constantly changing.[16] Secondly, many
firms will now be authorised to conduct at least some forms of
investment business as defined by the Financial Services Act 1986,[17]
whether by virtue of holding a certificate issued by the Law Society
under the Solicitors' Investment Business Rules 1990,[18] membership
of one of the recognised self regulating organisations,[19] or direct
authorisation from the Securities and Investment Board.[20] Accordingly, it can no longer be said that a partner in a firm of solicitors
does not have implied authority to accept money for investment at
large; equally, the detailed requirements of the Act and Rules[21]
would seem to minimise, even if not entirely to eradicate, the
possibility of an unauthorised receipt of funds which does not come
to the attention of the other partners.

Section 11 (b): Money or property in custody of firm

Group 1: Firm held liable

12–120   *Where a firm in the course of its business*[22] *receives money
belonging to other people, and one of the partners misapplies that
money whilst it is in the custody of the firm, the firm must make it
good.*[23]

---

[15] [1988] 1 W.L.R. 1051, 1063F: see *supra*, para. 12–12.
[16] Of course, the authority may in some cases be derived from statute: *e.g.* see the Law of
Property Act 1925, s.69; *cf. Re Bellamy and Metropolitan Board of Works* (1883) 24 Ch.D. 387 (a
decision under the Conveyancing Act 1881, s.56).
[17] For the definition of investment business, see the Financial Services Act 1986, Sched. 1, Pt. II
(as amended). See further *supra*, paras. 8–33 *et seq.* and, generally, the *Encyclopedia of Financial
Services Law*, Pt. II.
[18] See further the Financial Services Act 1986, s.15; also *supra*, para. 8–36. And see the
Encyclopedia of Professional Partnerships, Pt. 8.
[19] See the Financial Services Act 1986, s.7 and *supra*, para. 8–35.
[20] See *ibid.* s.25 and *supra*, para. 8–34.
[21] It is not feasible, in a work of this nature, to investigate these requirements, which vary
according to the manner in which authorisation is obtained. Reference should accordingly be made
to the standard works on the subject, *e.g.* the *Encyclopedia of Financial Services Law.*
[22] See *supra*, para. 12–113, and Partnership Act 1890, s.13, *infra*, para. 12–134, as to the
importance of this qualification.
[23] This was in fact Lord Lindley's second rule.

Having formulated the above rule, Lord Lindley explained the principle which underlies the cases in this group, as follows:

"The principle ... is that the firm has, in the ordinary course of its business, obtained possession of the property of other people, and has then parted with it without their authority. Under such circumstances the firm is responsible[24]: and the fact that the property has been improperly procured and placed in the custody of the firm by one of the partners does not lessen the liability of the firm; for whether the firm is or is not liable for the original fraud by which the property got into his hands, it is responsible for the subsequent misapplication thereof by one of its members."

In *Devaynes v. Noble, Clayton's Case*,[25] the owner of some **12–121** exchequer bills had deposited them with a firm of bankers. The bills were sold by one of the partners without the owner's knowledge and the proceeds applied by the firm for its own benefit. It being clear that such proceeds had been received by the firm, all the partners were held liable to the owner of the bills, irrespective of whether they were privy to the sale.

In *Devaynes v. Noble, Baring's Case*,[26] certain stock belonging to **12–122** customers was, according to the firm's normal practice, held in the sole name of one of the partners. He improperly sold it and the proceeds were received by the firm which, in the accounts rendered to its customers, had falsely represented the stock as still standing in the name of that partner and had given credit for the dividends as if the stock was still so held. The firm was liable for the misapplication of the proceeds.

In the so-called *Fauntleroy Forgery* cases,[27] F, a partner in a firm **12–123** of bankers, M & Co., had forged powers of attorney for the sale of certain stock belonging to the firm's clients. The stock was sold by the firm's broker, who remitted the proceeds to its account with another banking firm, MS & Co. F later withdrew those proceeds, using a cheque drawn in the firm name, and misapplied them. M & Co. was held liable for the loss even though the other partners knew nothing of the fraud. Liability was imposed because the sale of the stock and receipt of the resultant proceeds fell within the scope of the

---

[24] See the Partnership Act 1890, s.11(b), *supra*, para. 12–106.

[25] (1816) 1 Mer. 572. See also *Rhodes v. Moules* [1895] 1 Ch. 236, *supra*, para. 12–110.

[26] (1816) 1 Mer. 611; see also *Warde's Case* (1816) 1 Mer. 624; *Vulliamy v. Noble* (1817) 3 Mer. 593.

[27] *Stone v. Marsh* (1827) 6 B. & C. 551; *Ex p. Bolland* (1828) 1 M. & A. 570; *Hume v. Bolland* (1832) 1 Cromp. & M. 130; *Keating v. Marsh* (1834) 1 M. & A. 582; *Marsh v. Keating* (1834) 2 Cl. & F. 250. Lord Lindley noted that *Hume v. Bolland* is "hardly consistent with *Stone v. Marsh, Marsh v. Keating*, or *Ex p. Bolland*."

firm's business and the transactions initiated by F were conducted in
the usual way of that business. F's fraudulent misappropriation of the
proceeds of sale was no defence once they had been received by the
firm; even though the other partners were not aware of such receipt,
if they had used ordinary diligence and not placed such implicit
confidence in their co-partners, they could have learned of it and,
thus, discovered their true source.[28]

12–124   In *Ex p. Biddulph*,[29] trust money in the hands of a firm of bankers
was drawn out and misapplied by one partner and all the partners
were held liable for the loss.
        Similarly, in *Sadler v. Lee*,[30] a partner in a firm of bankers sold
stock in the name of a customer, as he was authorised to do, and the
proceeds were credited to the firm. Those proceeds were subsequently misapplied by a partner and again the firm was held liable.

12–125   The decision in *Blair v. Bromley*[31] clearly illustrates the principle
under consideration. There a client of a firm of solicitors entrusted
certain money to one partner to be invested on mortgage; he was told
that the money had been so invested, but in fact the partner had
misapplied it. For many years the client was regularly paid interest by
that partner, and the fraud was not discovered until the latter went
bankrupt. The other partner, who knew nothing about the fraud, was
held liable to make good the money, which had originally been
credited to the firm's bank account. The representation that the
money had been duly invested was held to have been made in the
normal course of business and the other partner's attempts to avoid
liability, by showing that he had no control over the bank account
and was not involved in the financial side of the business, failed.

Partner becoming trustee: De Ribeyre v. Barclay

12–126   In cases where the firm has accepted custody of money or
property, it would not seem to matter if the partner responsible for
its subsequent misapplication has in the interim been appointed a
trustee thereof, provided that he continues to act *qua* partner. Thus,
in *De Ribeyre v. Barclay*[32] the defendants were in partnership as

---

[28] In *Stone v. Marsh* and *Ex p. Bolland, supra,* F's partners knew that the stock had been sold by
the broker, but did not know that the powers of attorney were forged. In *Marsh v. Keating, supra,*
they appear not to have known either of the sale or of the receipt of the proceeds. *Cf.* the cases
cited *supra,* paras. 12–113 *et seq.*and *infra,* paras. 12–128 *et seq.*
[29] (1849) 3 De G. & Sm. 587.
[30] (1843) 6 Beav. 324.
[31] (1847) 2 Ph. 354. See also *Eager v. Barnes* (1862) 31 Beav. 579; *Moore v. Knight* [1891] 1 Ch.
547. And see *supra,* paras. 12–96 *et seq.*
[32] (1857) 23 Beav. 107; *cf. Ex p. Eyre* (1842) 1 Ph. 227; *Coomer v. Bromley* (1852) 5 De G. &
Sm. 532; *Bishop v. The Countess of Jersey* (1854) 2 Drew. 143. See *infra,* paras. 12–129 *et seq.*

stockbrokers, and regularly received money from friends, etc., for investment. They also seem to have made a practice of retaining the investments so made on their customers' behalf. The plaintiff had some Portuguese bonds held by a partner in this way; when she married, the bonds were assigned to trustees, of whom the partner was one. The bonds remained in his custody as before, and were in fact deposited with the partnership bankers (seemingly along with a number of securities held on behalf of other customers). That partner later converted the bonds into other bonds, which were deposited with the partnership bankers as before. He at all times acted *qua* stockbroker in the ordinary course of the firm's business, periodically advising the plaintiff, in the name of the firm, of what had been done on her behalf. He later misapplied the bonds. It was held that the bonds were originally in the firm's custody and not in the custody of one partner *qua* trustee and that their assignment into the trust did not take them out of such custody. Accordingly, the firm was liable for the loss resulting from their unauthorised removal.

It should be noted that, in this case, the firm was also held liable **12–127** for the loss of other bonds and securities purchased on the plaintiff's behalf and left in its custody in the manner described above, as well as for money borrowed from her in the name of the firm, but from which the firm derived no benefit. The fact that the plaintiff had dealt only with one partner was held to be immaterial, since the business was transacted in the normal way and so appeared in the firm's books and accounts.

Group 2: Firm not liable

A fraud committed by a partner whilst acting on his own separate **12–128** *account is not imputable to the firm, although had he not been connected with the firm he might not have been in a position to commit the fraud.*[33]

This rule is, to an extent, little more than a re-statement of the rule which appears at paragraph 12–113; accordingly, reference should also be made to the cases cited in the succeeding paragraphs.

In *Ex p. Eyre*,[34] a customer deposited a box containing certain **12–129** securities with a firm of bankers and, subsequently, agreed to lend some of them to one of the partners, authorising him to withdraw them from the box but to replace them with others. That partner did so, but then secretly withdrew the substituted securities and

---

[33] This was Lord Lindley's fourth rule, being the corollary of rule stated at para. 12–120.
[34] (1842) 1 Ph. 227.

misapplied them. The firm was held not to be responsible for the loss, since it appeared that the firm as such did not have authority to open the box or to examine its contents: the removal of the securities was a tortious act committed by one partner, who had such authority but who was not acting on behalf of the firm but in an individual capacity and for his own purposes.[35]

12-130   In *Bishop v. The Countess of Jersey*,[36] a partner in a firm of bankers advised a customer to sell certain stock and informed her that a secured loan of £5,000 could be made on advantageous terms to his own son. The customer duly authorised the sale and the proceeds were credited to her account. She then drew a cheque for the £5,000 and handed it to the partner concerned. He misapplied it and then absconded, no proper security ever having been given. It appears that interest on the £5,000 was for some time credited to the customer's account at the bank, but by whom was not clear. The other partners only learned of the fraud subsequently and were held not to be liable for the customer's loss. The transaction had nothing to do with the firm's business and, as Lord Lindley observed "if [*the transaction*] had not taken place at the bank, there would have been no pretence for saying that the one partner was acting otherwise than in a separate affair of his own."

12-131   The decision in *Coomer v. Bromley*[37] is more difficult to account for, but would appear to rest on the same principle. There WB, a partner in a firm of solicitors, was a trustee of certain annuities, his co-trustees being three clients who were also life tenants under the trust. With a view to increasing the trust income, it was arranged that the annuities would be sold and the proceeds invested on a mortgage to be taken in WB's sole name. The sale was completed and the proceeds were paid into the firm's bank account. However, they were not in fact invested on mortgage as arranged, but apparently used as partnership money; WB nevertheless pretended that he had invested them and paid interest accordingly. With the clients' knowledge, a mortgage, under which WB was the sole mortgagee and with a value marginally less than the requisite amount, was later appropriated as security for the annuity proceeds, the excess being divided between the clients. This security was then realised by WB and the money misappropriated by him. Unlike the original sale proceeds, this money was not credited to the firm's bank account and the other partner, JB, knew nothing of its receipt or misapplication. In the

---

[35] It should be noted that the firm had, in a separate transaction, itself borrowed other securities in the box from the customer: see *ibid.* pp. 229, 236.

[36] (1854) 2 Drew. 143.

[37] (1852) 5 De G. & Sm. 532. See also *Sims v. Brutton* (1850) 5 Ex. 802, *supra*, para. 12–116. *Cf. St. Aubyn v. Smart* (1868) L.R. 3 Ch.App. 646.

circumstances, JB was held not to be responsible for the loss, since his duties were at an end once the moneys had, as originally contemplated, been invested on a mortgage in WB's sole name. The clients could not hold him liable for the loss of the mortgage money arising from WB's subsequent fraud.

Lord Lindley identified the distinguishing feature common to **12–132** *Bishop v. The Countess of Jersey* and *Coomer v. Bromley*, in these terms:

> "... it will be observed that although the money in question had at one time been in the custody of the firm, such was not the case when the money was misapplied. This circumstance distinguishes the cases last referred to from *De Ribeyre v. Barclay*[38] and other cases of that class ...".

This same feature is displayed in a later decision, *Tendring Hundred Waterworks Co. v. Jones*.[39] In that case, G, a partner in a firm of solicitors, held office as a company secretary in the course of the firm's business. The company purchased some property which, for its own convenience, was conveyed to G alone, without any declaration of trust. The firm acted on the transaction and settled the relevant conveyance. The conveyance was retained by G, who subsequently mortgaged the property to secure a personal debt. The company sought, unsuccessfully, to make G's partner liable for the loss: he had no knowledge of the transaction, save in so far as notice was imputed to him by reason of the firm having acted therein. So far as the firm was concerned, the transaction was completed and its duties were at an end when the executed conveyance was received by G, who was legally entitled to receive it; it was therefore not responsible for his subsequent acts. Significantly, it was neither a part of G's duties as company secretary nor within the scope of the firm's business for him to constitute himself a trustee for a client.[40]

5. LIABILITY OF PARTNERS FOR BREACHES OF TRUST

The liability of a firm for the improper employment of trust property **12–133** in the partnership business is based on similar principles to those considered in the previous section; indeed, Lord Lindley's fifth rule[41] was as follows:

---

[38] (1857) 23 Beav. 107, *supra*, para. 12–126.
[39] [1903] 2 Ch. 615. See also *Terrill v. Parker and Thomas* (1915) 32 T.L.R. 48.
[40] See [1903] 2 Ch. 621, 623, *per* Farwell J.; also *Re Bell's Indenture* [1980] 1 W.L.R. 1217, *supra*, para. 12–118.
[41] Lord Lindley's other rules, albeit not in their original order, are set out *supra*, paras. 12–109, 12–113, 12–120, 12–128.

"If a partner, being a trustee, improperly employs the money of his *cestui que trust* in the partnership business, or in payment of the partnership debts, this alone is not sufficient to entitle the *cestui que trust* to obtain repayment of his money from the firm."

Partnership Act 1890, section 13

12–134   The above rule is now incorporated in section 13 of the Partnership Act 1890, which provides:

"13. If a partner, being a trustee, improperly employs trust property in the business or on the account of the partnership, no other partner is liable for the trust property to the persons beneficially interested therein:
Provided as follows:
(1) This section shall not affect any liability incurred by any partner by reason of his having notice of a breach of trust[42]; and
(2) Nothing in this section shall prevent trust money from being followed and recovered from the firm if still in its possession or under its control."

Relevance of pre–1890 cases

12–135   Given the similarity between the opening words of the section and Lord Lindley's own formulation of the rule, it will be readily apparent that no change in the law was sought to be introduced thereby. Accordingly, the pre-1890 authorities are again of relevance.
     Thus, in *Ex p. Apsey*,[43] what would now be styled a trustee in bankruptcy[44] applied part of the bankrupt's estate towards his own firm's debts. On that firm's bankruptcy, the amount misapplied was held not to be provable against the joint estate. Similarly, in *Ex p. Heaton*,[45] where trust money had been misapplied by the trustees of a will, an inquiry was directed in order to determine whether the non-trustee partner knew that the money had been applied for partnership purposes.[46]

12–136   Since, in each of the above cases, the trust money came into the hands of the firm *otherwise* than in the ordinary course of its business, it is submitted that they cannot be regarded as inconsistent with the provisions of section 11 of the Partnership Act 1890[47] or, for

---

[42] See *supra*, para. 12–28.
[43] (1791) 3 Bro.C.C. 265. See also *Ex p. White* (1871) L.R. 6 Ch.App. 397.
[44] In fact, the partner concerned was one of two "assignees in bankruptcy."
[45] (1819) Buck 386.
[46] Lord Lindley considered that "*Ex p. Clowes* (1789) 2 Bro.C.C. 595 is not opposed to the case in the text, for there the joint and separate estates were consolidated."
[47] See *supra*, para. 12–106.

that matter, with *Marsh v. Keating*[48] and the other decisions which preceded the enactment of that section.[49] Lord Lindley explained the distinction in this way:

"... in [*Marsh v. Keating and the other cases*], the money came to the hands of the firm in the ordinary course of its business;[50] whilst in the cases now under consideration it is supposed to come otherwise. Liability must therefore attach to the firm, if at all, on wholly different principles, and the fact that the firm has had the benefit of the trust monies is not sufficient to render it responsible for them. To be liable, the firm must be implicated in the breach of trust, and this it cannot be unless all the partners either knew whence the money came, or knew that it did not belong to the partner making use of it. Knowledge on the part of one partner will not affect the others, for the fact to be known has nothing to do with the business of the firm;[51] and the case of *Ex p. Heaton* ... shows that in cases of this kind the liability as for a breach of trust does not extend to those who are ignorant of the matters before mentioned."

Application of section to solicitors and other professions

Solicitors are subject to stringent professional rules regarding the **12–137** receipt of clients' money, including trust money.[52] Thus, where one or more of the partners is a trustee and his firm receives money belonging to the trust, it must normally be paid either into a client account or into a special "controlled" trust account.[53] Withdrawals from such accounts may only be made for a number of specific purposes[54] and their operation will be scrutinised by an independent accountant each year.[55] Notwithstanding these safeguards, instances of the misapplication of money in such accounts do occur and, in such cases, section 13 of the Partnership Act 1890 will apply in the normal way.[56] The same observations are equally pertinent in the

---

[48] (1834) 2 Cl. & F. 250: see *supra*, para. 12–123.

[49] See *supra*, paras. 12–109 *et seq.*

[50] In a footnote at this point, Lord Lindley explained that, in *Marsh v. Keating*, the stock was sold in the ordinary course of the firm's business, albeit under a forged power of attorney: see *supra*, para. 12–123. Moreover, whilst F's partners did not know that the money had been received by the firm, their ignorance was considered culpable.

[51] See the Partnership Act 1890, s.16, *supra*, paras. 12–21 *et seq.*

[52] See the Solicitors Act 1974, ss.32–34 (as amended); the Solicitors Accounts Rules 1991; the Accountants' Reports Rules 1991. And see further, the *Encyclopedia of Professional Partnerships*, Pt. 8.

[53] Solicitors' Accounts Rules 1991, rr. 2(1) (definitions of "client's money" and "trust money"), 3, 9, 12, 18.

[54] *Ibid.* rr. 7, 8, 16, 17.

[55] See the Accountants' Reports Rules 1991.

[56] Note, however, the existence of the Compensation Fund, administered under the Solicitors Act 1974, s.36, which may be used to relieve hardship suffered by a defaulting solicitor's partner. It is doubted whether a grant would ever be made in a case where the Partnership Act 1890, s.13, proviso (1) applies, since this connotes a degree of complicity; *sed quaere.*

case of other professions or businesses which are subject to rules governing the treatment of clients' money.[57]

Where the section does not apply

12–138   The provisos to section 13 of the Partnership Act 1890[58] preserve the liability of the firm in those cases where all the partners have notice of the breach of trust or where a tracing remedy is available.

Proviso (1): Notice of breach of trust

12–139   This proviso ensures that section 13 does not relieve the firm of liability where all the partners are implicated in a breach of trust. Lord Lindley, writing prior to the Act, explained the position thus:

> "But if knowledge ... can be imputed to the other partners, if they know, or ought to be treated as knowing, that trust monies are being employed in the partnership business, they will be held bound to see that the trust to which the money is subject authorises the use made of it, and will be answerable for a breach of trust in case of its misapplication or loss."[59]

By way of qualification to the above passage, it should be noted that it is strictly immaterial whether the trust money has been applied in the partnership business or otherwise.[60]

However, the courts will not readily infer partners' knowledge of or implication in a breach of trust,[61] as demonstrated by three decisions concerning solicitors.

12–140   In *Brinsden v. Williams*,[62] a trustee wished to advance trust money on a mortgage, but the security was neither of a proper type nor of sufficient value. He instructed a partner in a firm of solicitors (who

---

[57] *e.g.* accountants, architects and surveyors. See also the Financial Services (Clients' Money) Regulations 1991. Note, however, that the revoked Financial Services (Clients' Money) Regulations 1987 continue to have effect as regards persons authorised to carry on investment business by the Chartered Association of Certified Accountants: Financial Services (Clients' Money) Regulations 1991, reg. 1.04(a). And see, generally, the *Encyclopedia of Professional Partnerships*.

[58] See *supra*, para. 12–134.

[59] See *Keble v. Thompson* (1790) 3 Bro.C.C. 112; *Smith v. Jameson* (1794) 5 T.R. 601; *Ex p. Watson* (1814) 2 V. & B. 414; *Ex p. Woodin* (1843) 3 M.D. & D. 399; *Ex p. Poulson* (1844) De Gex. 79. *Cf. Ex p. Burton* (1843) 3 M.D. & D. 364; *Ex p. Barnewall* (1855) 6 De G.M. & G. 795; *Ex p. Greaves* (1856) 8 De G.M. & G. 291.

[60] *Blyth v. Fladgate* [1891] 1 Ch. 337, 354, *per* Stirling J.

[61] Note, however, that "vicarious" liability was imposed on a partner in *Agip (Africa) Ltd. v. Jackson* [1991] Ch. 547, without reference to s.13. The report does not disclose what arguments were addressed to the Court on this issue, but it is perhaps significant that the defendants elected not to call any evidence. Note also, in this context, the decision of Vinelott J. in *Eagle Trust Plc. v. S.B.C. Securities Ltd.* [1993] 1 W.L.R. 484.

[62] [1894] 3 Ch. 185. See also *Rae v. Meek* (1889) 14 App.Cas. 558. *Cf. Blyth v. Fladgate* [1891] 1 Ch. 337.

also acted for the prospective mortgagors) to act for him. The partner knew that the transaction involved trust money but was not asked to advise the trustee on the propriety or sufficiency of the security. Accordingly, the trustee took personal responsibility for its acceptance. The title deeds of the property to be mortgaged were held by bankers as security for an overdraft; as arranged, the trustee gave a cheque for the mortgage advance to the partner concerned, who paid it into the firm's account and, the next day, drew a cheque for the advance in favour of the bankers, whereupon the title deeds were delivered up to him. The mortgage transaction was a breach of trust and a loss resulted. A beneficiary sought to make the partner (who was, by then, the sole surviving partner) liable for breach of trust but the court held that he was not implicated therein, having received the mortgage advance and paid it over to the bank as an agent of the trustee.

The facts in *Mara v. Browne*[63] were similar,[64] save that the partner **12–141** had paid the trust money into his own private account. The court held that the partner had not constituted himself a constructive trustee of the money and was not, therefore, liable for breach of trust but that, even if such liability had been established, this would not have been enough to render his co-partner, who knew nothing of the transaction, liable along with him. It was also observed that it is not within the scope of the implied authority of a partner in a firm of solicitors to constitute himself a constructive trustee and, thereby, to subject his partner to liability.

The decision in *Mara v. Browne* was applied in *Re Bell's* **12–142** *Indenture*,[65] where a partner in a firm of solicitors had rendered himself liable as a constructive trustee by actively assisting the trustees of a marriage settlement to dissipate the entire trust fund. It was held that the other partner, who did not know of the breach of trust, was not liable, even though trust moneys had clearly passed through the firm's client account. The basis for the decision was, again, that a solicitor has no authority in the ordinary course of practice either to constitute himself a constructive trustee or, indeed, to accept the office of trustee.[66]

---

[63] [1896] 1 Ch. 199. The firm might in fact have been liable for negligence in the performance of its duties as solicitor, but any such action was statute barred; see the cases cited in n. 62.

[64] In fact, there appears to have been some doubt whether the trustees, on whose instructions the partners acted, had been duly appointed, but they clearly had the trust money in their hands and were purporting to act as trustees.

[65] [1980] 1 W.L.R. 1217. And see *supra*, para. 12–118. *Cf. Agip (Africa) Ltd. v. Jackson* [1991] Ch. 547.

[66] [1980] 1 W.L.R. 1230H, *per* Vinelott J.; see also *Re Fryer* (1857) 3 K. & J. 317.

12–143   It has already been seen that section 16 of the Partnership Act 1890 does not generally apply in the case of a breach of trust.[67] However, particular note must be taken of the position following the death of a partner. Lord Lindley observed that

> "... if the surviving partners deal with his property, knowing that it belongs to his estate, knowledge of the trust on which the property is held will be imputed to them, and they may be thus involved in all the consequences of a breach of trust. But this doctrine can hardly extend to the case of incoming partners, who do nothing except leave matters as they find them when they enter the firm."[68]

The current editor's opinion is that, as a statement of general principle, this is no longer correct and that, if the deceased partner's personal representatives choose to leave his share outstanding in the surviving partners' hands, it can normally be assumed that they are acting within their powers;[69] *per contra*, if the surviving partners knew (or ought to have known) that a breach of trust was being committed.

12–144   As will be noted hereafter, where partners are implicated in a breach of trust, their liability will be joint and several.[70] However, such liability may seemingly not be enforced by third party proceedings instituted by a trustee who is being sued by his *cestuis que trust*.[71]

Proviso (2): Tracing remedy

12–145   The second proviso to section 13 confirms what should in any event be obvious, namely that, even if the firm is not implicated in the breach of trust, a *cestui que trust* should not be deprived of the right to trace his own money, if it is still in the firm's hands.[72] Lord Lindley explained the rationale behind this rule, which existed prior to the 1890 Act, as follows:

> "The true owner of money traced to the possession of another has a right to have it restored, not because it is a debt but because it is

---

[67] See *supra*, para. 12–28.
[68] See *Twyford v. Trail* (1834) 7 Sim. 92.
[69] See *infra*, para. 26–52.
[70] See *infra*, para. 13–13.
[71] *Wynne v. Tempest* [1897] 1 Ch. 110.
[72] See generally, as to the tracing remedy, *Snell's Equity* (29th ed.), pp. 297 *et seq.*; *Goff & Jones' The Law of Restitution* (4th ed.), Chap. 2. Also *Agip (Africa) Ltd. v. Jackson* [1991] Ch. 547.

his money. His right is incidental to his ownership; and whether the money is traced to the hands of a single individual or to the hands of a firm is wholly immaterial."

Secret profits where partner holds directorship

Although not strictly within the class of cases currently under **12–146** consideration, it should be noted that the firm will be liable to account for any profit which it may receive under a contract between a partner and a company of which he is a director, if the contract was made with the knowledge of the other partners and there was no full disclosure.[73]

6. LIABILITY OF PARTNERS FOR ACTS KNOWN TO BE UNAUTHORISED

It has already been seen that the extent of a partner's implied **12–147** authority is set by what is required to carry on the partnership business in the usual way.[74] It follows that a third party who knowingly deals with a partner[75] may in general assume that the firm will be bound by anything which that partner does within the scope of his implied authority but not by anything done outside that scope. However, the position will be different if the third party knows that wider or narrower limits have in fact been set on that partner's authority, as Lord Lindley explained[76]:

"So long as one partner does nothing beyond the scope of his apparent authority ... so long is the firm responsible for his conduct, although he may have acted beyond or in direct violation of the authority within which his co-partners may have attempted to confine him. Restrictions placed by the partners upon the powers which each shall exercise do not affect non-partners, who act bona fide and without notice of the restriction.[77]

But when it is sought to make the firm liable for some act not prima facie authorised by it, an actual authority by it must be

---

[73] *Imperial Mercantile Credit Association v. Coleman* (1871) L.R. 6 H.L. 189. And see also, generally, *Boardman v. Phipps* [1967] 2 A.C. 46; *Industrial Development Consultants Ltd. v. Cooley* [1972] 1 W.L.R. 443.

[74] See the Partnership Act 1890, s.5, *supra*, paras. 12–02 *et seq*.

[75] See the concluding words of *ibid.* s.5.

[76] This passage is composed of extracts from two separate paragraphs written by Lord Lindley, which were in fact transposed in the 5th ed. of this work. However, it is submitted that, presented in this manner, they more clearly state the relevant principles.

[77] See for example, *Morans v. Armstrong* (1840) Arm.M. & O. 25 (where the partnership business had been organised into separate departments and one partner had acted outside his department). In cases of this type, it is clearly not enough for one partner merely to tell his co-partners that he will not be bound by their acts: see *Gleadon v. Tinkler* (1817) Holt, N.P. 586. *Per contra*, if a third party has actual notice: see *infra*, paras. 12–153 *et seq*.

shown; and if this cannot be done, no case is made out against the firm, however ignorant the person seeking to charge it may have been of what was authorised and what was not. In the case now supposed the firm did not mislead him; and if he was misled by the representations of the partner with whom he dealt, his remedy is against that partner."[78]

Partnership Act 1890, sections 7 and 8

12–148   These principles are expressly recognised by two sections of the Partnership Act 1890, namely:

"7. Where one partner pledges the credit of the firm for a purpose apparently not connected with the firm's ordinary course of business, the firm is not bound, unless he is in fact specially authorised by the other partners; but this section does not affect any personal liability incurred by an individual partner.

8. If it has been agreed between the partners that any restriction shall be placed on the power of any one or more of them to bind the firm, no act done in contravention of the agreement is binding on the firm with respect to persons having notice of the agreement."

Apparent purpose of section 8

12–149   It appears that section 8 was intended to settle a doubtful question raised by *dicta* of Lord Ellenborough in *Gallway v. Mathew and Smithson*[79] and *Alderson v. Pope*,[80] to the effect that, if partners have agreed between themselves that none of them shall do a certain act, a third party with notice of that stipulation will be bound thereby, although Lord Lindley himself had already rejected such a proposition as "too wide."[81]

---

[78] See *supra*, paras. 12–96 *et seq*. And see, as to the circumstances in which an individual partner may be estopped from denying his authority, *Kendal v. Wood* (1870) L.R. 6 Ex. 243, 251 (*per* Blackburn J.), 253–254 (*per* Montague Smith J.).

[79] (1808) 10 East 264. Lord Ellenborough is reported to have said (at p. 266): "It is not essential to a partnership that one partner should have power to draw bills and notes in the partnership firm to charge the other: they may stipulate between themselves that it shall not be done: and if a third person, having notice of this, will take such a security from one of the partners, he shall not sue the others upon it in breach of such stipulation, nor in defiance of a notice previously given to him by one of them, that he will not be liable for any bill or note signed by the others."

[80] (1808) 1 Camp. 404n. Lord Ellenborough reportedly held that "where there was a stipulation between A, B and C, who appeared to the world as co-partners, that C should not participate in the profit and loss, and should not be liable as a partner, C was not liable as such to those who had notice of this stipulation."

[81] Lord Lindley explained, "A stranger dealing with a partner is entitled to hold the firm liable for whatever that partner may do on its behalf within certain limits. To deprive the stranger of this right, he ought to have distinct notice that the firm will not be answerable for the acts of one member, even within these limits. Now notice of an agreement between the members that one of them shall not do certain things is by no means necessarily equivalent to notice that the firm will not be answerable for them if he does. For there is nothing inconsistent in an agreement between the members of a firm that certain things shall not be done by one of them, and a readiness on the

—continued on next page

The current editor's view is that, in its terms, the section only **12–150** partially resolved this issue, since it is still technically unclear whether the third party must have notice that the partner is prohibited from doing a certain act *and thereby binding the firm* or whether mere notice of the prohibition is sufficient. It is, nevertheless, submitted that a restriction or prohibition on a partner's ability to do an act must necessarily carry with it the implication that he is not authorised to do that act and, thus, that the firm will not be bound if he exceeds his authority; *sed quaere.*[82]

Operation of section 8

It will be apparent from the terms of the section that questions of **12–151** notice will only arise where the firm is seeking to avoid liability in respect of an act which falls within the scope of a partner's implied authority but outside the scope of his actual authority; it is therefore not surprising to find that the authorities which illustrate the principles underlying the section[83] primarily concern frauds practised by one partner on the firm.

Cases where no notice

Lord Lindley observed that: **12–152**

"if one partner acts in fraud of his co-partners, still they will be bound, if he has not exceeded his apparent authority, and if the person dealing with him had no notice of the fraud."[84]

Thus, in *Bond v. Gibson*,[85] one partner purchased goods on the credit of the firm and immediately pawned them for his own benefit; the firm was nevertheless held liable to pay for the goods. Similarly, if a partner, who has implied authority to draw, accept or indorse bills of exchange in the firm name,[86] does so, but for a private

---

[81]—*continued from previous page*
part of all the members to be responsible to strangers for the acts of each other, as if no such an agreement had been entered into. It is immaterial to a stranger what stipulations partners may make amongst themselves, so long as they do not seek to restrict their responsibility as to him; and it is only when knowledge of an agreement between partners necessarily involves knowledge that they decline to be responsible for the acts of each other within the ordinary limits, that a stranger's rights against a firm may be prejudiced by what he may know of the private stipulations between its members." In this context, Lord Lindley referred to the decisions in *Brown v. Leonard* (1816) 2 *Chitty* 120, *supra*, para. 5–59; *Hawken v. Bourne* (1841) 8 M. & W. 703; *Greenwood's Case* (1854) 3 De G.M. & G. 459. See also *Pollock on Partnership* (15th ed.), pp. 40–41.
[82] It is interesting to note that, in his Supplement on the Partnership Act 1890, Lord Lindley wrote of s.8: "This section adopts the dicta of Lord Ellenborough in *Galway v. Mathew* and *Alderson v. Pope*, and is probably an extension of the law."
[83] In fact, all the relevant authorities pre-date the Partnership Act 1890.
[84] *Hambro v. Burnand* [1904] 2 K.B. 10; also *Bank of Bengal v. Fagan* (1849) 7 Moo.P.C. 61, 74; *Bryant, Powis, and Bryant Ltd. v. Quebec Bank* [1893] A.C. 170.
[85] (1808) 1 Camp. 185.
[86] See *supra*, paras. 12–41 *et seq.*

purpose of his own, still the firm will be liable on any such bill *vis-à-vis* a holder for value who does not have notice of the fraud.[87] It has already been seen that the position will be no different where a partner fraudulently misapplies money received by or in the custody of the firm in the ordinary course of its business.[88] In all of these cases, the fact that the *partners* have no notice of the fraud is wholly irrelevant.

Cases where express notice

12–153   The most effective method of invoking the protection of section 8 is, of course, to give express notice of any restriction on a partner's implied authority to bind the firm. Therefore, if one partner sends a circular to a supplier, instructing him not to supply goods to the firm without his written order, he will not be liable if the supplier chooses to ignore that instruction and supplies goods to his partner.[89] Equally, the extent of a partner's authority to accept bills of exchange in the firm name may, in an appropriate case, be publicly notified.[90]

12–154   In *Gallway v. Mathew and Smithson*[91] one partner, S, published an advertisement warning all persons not to give credit to his partner, M, on his, S's, account, and stating that he would not be liable for any bills or notes issued by M in the firm name. A third party, who had seen the advertisement, was nevertheless prevailed upon by M to accept a bill of exchange in respect of money required to pay partnership debts and to take a promissory note drawn by M in the firm name. M then discounted the bill and applied most (but not all) of the proceeds towards the firm's debts. It was held that the firm was not bound by the promissory note.

12–155   However, it should be noted that, notwithstanding the decisions in *Galway v. Mathew* and other cases, there is at least some doubt whether one partner can *unilaterally* restrict the implied authority of a co-partner, at least while the partnership continues.[92]

---

[87] *Ex p. Bushell* (1844) 3 M.D. & D. 615; *Ex p. Meyer* (1848) De Gex. 632. See also *Lane v. Williams* (1692) 2 Vern. 277; *Sutton v. Gregory* (1797) 2 Peake 150; *Swan v. Steele* (1806) 7 East 210; *Ridley v. Taylor* (1810) 13 East 175; *Sanderson v. Brooksbank* (1830) 4 Car. & P. 286; *Wintle v. Crowther* (1831) 1 C. & J. 316; *Thicknesse v. Bromilow* (1832) 2 C. & J. 425; *Lewis v. Reilly* (1841) 1 Q.B. 349. Note, in particular, the terms of the Bills of Exchange Act 1882, s.30(2) and, as to the meaning of "fraud" in that subsection, the decision in *Österreichische Landerbank v. S'Elite Ltd.* [1981] Q.B. 565. And see *Hogg v. Skeen* (1865) 18 C.B.(N.S.) 426.

[88] See *supra*, paras. 12–106 *et seq.*

[89] *Minnit v. Whinery* (1721) 5 Bro.P.C. 489; *Willis v. Dyson* (1816) 1 Stark. 164. See also *Vice v. Fleming* (1827) 1 Y. & J. 227; *Ex p. Holdsworth* (1841) 1 M.D. & D. 475.

[90] *Rooth v. Quin* (1819) 7 Price 193. Such notice will affect those who see or hear of it, save that an indorsee with notice may avail himself of the ignorance of his indorser.

[91] (1808) 10 East 264. See also *Ex p. Holdsworth* (1841) 1 M.D. & D. 475.

[92] See *infra*, paras. 13–33 *et seq.*

Cases where implied notice

In some cases, the circumstances of the transaction will be **12–156** sufficient to put a third party on notice that the partner with whom he is dealing is acting outside the scope of his implied authority, *i.e.* where the partner is clearly attempting to secure some purely personal benefit for himself. If this is the position, the firm will, on normal principles, be liable only if *express* authority can be proved. The decision in *Bignold v. Waterhouse*[93] would seem to fall within this class.

Three other obvious examples were cited by Lord Lindley, namely **12–157** where a partner:

(*a*) accepts a bill of exchange in the firm name for his own personal debts;[94]

(*b*) pledges partnership goods for such debts;[95] and

(*c*) otherwise uses partnership funds to pay such debts.[96]

All of these examples may be explained by reference to the following principle, as originally formulated by Lord Lindley:

"... a person who knows that a partner is using the name and assets of the firm for a private purpose of his own, knows that he is *prima facie* committing a fraud on his co-partners."[97]

Position of incoming partners

If, following the admission of a new partner, a bill of exchange is **12–158** drawn and accepted in the names of all the partners (both old and new) in settlement of a debt of the former firm, the new partner will not, by an extension of the same principle, be liable thereon. This was decided in *Shirreff v. Wilks*,[98] which Lord Lindley described as

---

[93] (1813) 1 M. & S. 255. See *supra*, para. 12–27.

[94] *Leverson v. Lane* (1862) 13 C.B.(N.S.) 278; *Re Riches* (1865) 4 De G.J. & S. 581. See also *Ellston v. Deacon* (1866) L.R. 2 C.P. 20. There are even older cases to the same effect: *Ex p. Agace* (1792) 2 Cox 312; *Arden v. Sharpe* (1797) 2 Esp. 524; *Wells v. Masterman* (1799) 2 Esp. 731; *Ex p. Bonbonus* (1803) 8 Ves. Jr. 540; *Green v. Deakin* (1818) 2 Stark. 347; *Frankland v. M'Gusty* (1830) 1 Knapp. 274; *Ex p. Thorpe* (1836) 3 M. & A. 716; *Ex p. Austen* (1840) 1 M.D. & D. 247; *Miller v. Douglas* (1840) 3 Ross L.C. 500. Lord Lindley also cited the following, more obscure, example: "And if a bill is drawn by one partner in the name of the firm in fraud of his co-partners, and is accepted by the drawee, and is afterwards indorsed by the drawer in the name of the firm, the acceptor may successfully deny the indorsement, although he cannot deny the drawing." See *Garland v. Jacomb* (1873) L.R. 8 Ex. 216.

[95] *Snaith v. Burridge* (1812) 4 Taunt. 684.

[96] *Kendal v. Wood* (1870) L.R. 6 Ex. 243; *Heilbut v. Nevill* (1870) L.R. 5 C.P. 478.

[97] In later editions, the wording was changed to "... a person who knows that a partner is using the credit of the firm for a private purpose of his own, knows that *he is using it for a purpose prima facie outside the limits of his authority*" (emphasis supplied).

[98] (1800) 1 East 48. There was no evidence to show that the incoming partner knew of the acceptance. Lord Lindley went on to observe that "Lord Kenyon went so far as to say that the transaction was fraudulent on the face of it; but that is going rather far, as it is not uncommon for

—*continued on page 362*

"clear law."[99] However, the position will be otherwise if the new partner has agreed to take on the liabilities of the existing firm.[1]

Position of outgoing partners

12–159   In addition to the more usual instances of restricted authority noticed in the preceding paragraphs, specific attention should also be drawn to the position of an outgoing partner, since the continuing partners' implied authority to bind him will continue for as long as he remains an apparent member of the firm.[2] Accordingly, due notice that he has ceased to be a partner must be given to all persons who have dealings with the firm, which effectively amounts to notice that the continuing partners' authority is, to this extent, now restricted.[3]

7. LIABILITY OF PARTNERS IN RESPECT OF CONTRACTS IN IMPROPER FORM

12–160   Before it can be said whether a contract made by a partner is binding on the firm, it must first be ascertained whether, in making the contract, that partner was purporting to act as the agent of the firm or as a principal in his own right, as Lord Lindley explained:

> "The general proposition that a partnership is bound by those acts of its agents which are within the scope of their authority[4] ... must be taken with the qualification that the agent whose acts are sought to be imputed to the firm, was acting in his character of agent, and not as a principal. If he did not act in his character of agent, but as a private individual on his own account, his acts cannot be imputed to the firm, and he alone is liable for them, even though the firm may have benefited by them."[5]

Partnership Act 1890, section 6

12–161   The same qualification is reflected in section 6 of the Partnership Act 1890, which provides:

> "6. An act or instrument relating to the business of the firm done or executed in the firm-name, or in any other manner showing an

---

[98]—*continued from page 361*
in-coming partners to agree to take upon themselves the existing liabilities of the firm. When such an agreement is entered into, the in-coming partner can hardly say he has been defrauded, if a bill in the name of the new firm is accepted for a debt of the old firm without any specific authority on his part."
[99] See also *Ex p. Goulding* (1829) 2 Gl. & J. 118; *Wilson v. Lewis* (1840) 2 Man. & G. 197.
[1] See *supra*, n. 98; also *supra*, para. 10–45.
[2] See the Partnership Act 1890, ss.36(1), 38. See further, *infra*, paras. 13–39 *et seq.*
[3] *Ibid.* s.36(2).
[4] See *supra*, paras. 12–01 *et seq.*
[5] See *British Homes Assurance Corporation Ltd. v. Paterson* [1902] 2 Ch. 404.

intention to bind the firm, by any person thereto authorised, whether a partner or not, is binding on the firm and all the partners.

Provided that this section shall not affect any general rule of law relating to the execution of deeds or negotiable instruments."[6]

Form of contract

Section 6 presupposes that it is apparent from the form of the **12–162** contract whether the partner is contracting as principal or agent, whereas in practice this will often be unclear. Given the terms of the proviso to the section, it is both necessary and convenient to consider this subject under three separate headings, namely:

(*a*) Written and oral contracts.
(*b*) Contracts under seal.
(*c*) Bills of exchange and promissory notes.

(a) Written and oral contracts

The general principle

The liability of the firm in the case of what Lord Lindley called **12–163** "ordinary contracts" is dependent on the application of normal agency principles, which may be summarised as follows:

1. If the agency is disclosed, liability under the contract will generally attach to the principal and not to the agent, even if the identity of the principal was not revealed.[7]
2. If the agency is undisclosed, liability under the contract will attach to the agent.[8]
3. If, in the latter case, the other contracting party discovers the existence of the undisclosed principal, he may hold him, as well as the agent, liable under the contract.[9]
4. In the case of an apparent agency, *i.e.* where the agent is in fact the principal, he will seemingly be liable under the contract once the true facts are known.[10]

Partner acting as a principal

Equally, if a partner enters into a contract in circumstances where **12–164** he is demonstrably acting on his own account, *i.e.* as a principal and

---

[6] For an example of the practical effects of the proviso, see *Littlejohn v. Mackay*, 1974 S.L.T. 82, Sh.Ct. (a Scottish case concerning holograph execution on behalf of a firm). And see also *Marchant v. Morton Down Co.* [1901] 2 K.B. 829, *infra*, para. 12–172.
[7] See *Bowstead on Agency* (15th ed.), Art. 75, pp. 281 *et seq.*; also Art. 104, pp. 424 *et seq.*
[8] See *ibid.* Arts. 105, 106, pp. 426 *et seq.*
[9] See *ibid.* Art. 79, pp. 312 *et seq.* And see, generally, *Siu Yin Kwan v. Eastern Insurance Co. Ltd.* [1994] 2 W.L.R. 370 (P.C.).
[10] See the discussion of this difficult question in *Bowstead on Agency* Art. 115, pp. 473 *et seq.*

not as agent of the firm, he alone will be liable,[11] even if the contract has some connection with the partnership business. Lord Lindley illustrated this (largely self evident) class of cases by the following two examples:

> "Thus, where persons work a coach in partnership, each having his own horses, and one of them orders fodder on his own account, he alone is liable for it.[12] So, in the ordinary case of an agreement between an author and a publisher, to the effect that the publisher shall pay for the paper, printing, and other expenses of publication, and that after reimbursing himself and deducting a commission, the profits shall be divided equally, the author is not liable for the paper or printing which may have been supplied and executed by the publisher."[13]

Written contracts

12–165   Having regard to the principles summarised in the preceding paragraphs, it is clear that, if one partner enters into a written contract, it cannot be determined whether the firm is bound simply by considering its terms, unless those terms expressly negative, or are otherwise inconsistent with, the status of the firm as contracting party.[14] Lord Lindley gave the following example:

> "... supposing a contract to be entered into by one partner in his own name only, still if in fact he was acting as the agent of the firm, his co-partners will be in the position of undisclosed principals; and they may therefore be liable to be sued on the contract, although no allusion is made to them in it."

12–166   This proposition is clearly supported by the decision in *Beckham v. Drake*.[15] In that case, there were three partners, A, B and C, but A's existence was undisclosed.[16] In the course of carrying on the firm's business, B and C entered into a written contract with a third party,

---

[11] See for example, *Ex p. Eyre* (1842) 1 Ph. 227, noticed *supra*, para. 12–129; *British Homes Assurance Corporation v. Paterson* [1902] 2 Ch. 404; also *Greer v. Downs Supply Co.* [1927] 2 K.B. 28 (which did not concern a partnership).

[12] *Barton v. Hanson* (1809) 2 Taunt. 49. Lord Lindley observed that "Mr. Collyer treats this as an exception depending on particular custom, but this view is not correct."

[13] See the Scottish case of *Venables v. Wood* (1839) 3 Ross L.C. on Com. Law, 529; *Wilson v. Whitehead* (1842) 10 M. & W. 503; and see *supra*, para. 5–30, n. 88. But note also the decision in *Gardiner v. Childs* (1837) 8 C. & P. 345.

[14] But see *Humble v. Hunter* (1848) 12 Q.B. 310; *O/Y Wasa S.S. Co. v. Newspaper Pulp and Wood Exports* (1949) 82 Ll.L.Rep. 936; *Formby Bros. v. Formby* (1910) 102 L.T. 116; *Drughorn Ltd. v. Rederiaktiebolaget Transatlantic* [1919] A.C. 203. These cases are considered in *Bowstead on Agency* (15th ed.), pp. 320, 321.

[15] (1843) 11 M. & W. 315.

[16] He was therefore what is commonly styled a "secret" or "dormant" partner: see *supra*, para. 12–06.

who later sued for breach of its terms. A neither signed nor was named in the contract and was not known to the third party to be a partner. Nevertheless, A, B and C were held jointly liable for the breach, since the contract was clearly entered into by the firm and A, like any other undisclosed principal, was liable to be sued as soon as his position was discovered.[17]

Form of contract

Two additional observations should be made in this context. First, **12–167** if the contract is required by statute to be in writing and signed by the party to be charged, then, notwithstanding the foregoing principles, only those partners who actually sign it will be bound;[18] *per contra*, if signature by an agent is permissible.[19]

Secondly, when construing a contract entered into by a partner, **12–168** care must be taken to identify whether he acted as agent for the firm and or as a principal, whether on his own account or for the benefit of the firm;[20] it is only in the former case that the firm will be rendered liable. This aspect is considered in greater detail later in this chapter.[21]

Oral contracts

Precisely the same principles apply in the case of an oral contract. **12–169** Thus, if one partner, whilst acting on the firm's behalf, places an order for goods and they are supplied to him, the firm will be liable to pay for them, even if no mention was made of the other partners[22] and they were unknown to the supplier.[23]

Position of dormant partners

It follows that a dormant partner cannot escape liability merely **12–170** because his existence was unknown when a contract was entered

---

[17] Lord Lindley cited the following additional example, which is of little current relevance: "So, if A in his own name only underwrites a policy of insurance, but the profit or loss arising from the transaction is to be divided between him and B, both A and B will be liable to the insured: *Brett v. Beckwith* (1856) 3 Jur.(N.S.) 31."

[18] See *Swift v. Jewsbury* (1874) L.R. 9 Q.B. 301.

[19] See, for example, the Law of Property (Miscellaneous Provisions) Act 1989, s.2(3). In cases of this class, the contract must be signed in the name or on behalf of the firm: see *Duncan v. Lowndes* (1813) 3 Camp. 478. In *Ex p. Harding* (1879) 12 Ch.D. 557, a letter of guarantee was framed in such a way as to bind both the firm *and* the actual signatories. *Cf. Keen v. Mear* [1920] 2 Ch. 574, where it was held that the Partnership Act 1890, s.5 did not override the (then) requirements of the Statute of Frauds, s.4. See also *Davies v. Sweet* [1962] 2 Q.B. 300.

[20] See, generally, *Paice v. Walker* (1870) L.R. 5 Ex. 173; *Southwell v. Bowditch* (1876) 1 C.P.D. 374; *Gadd v. Houghton* (1876) 1 Ex.D. 357; *Hough v. Manzanos* (1879) 4 Ex.D. 104; *H. O. Brandt & Co. v. H. N. Morris & Co. Ltd.* [1917] 2 K.B. 784.

[21] See *infra*, paras. 12–193 *et seq*.

[22] *Whitwell v. Perrin* (1858) 4 C.B.(N.S.) 412; *City of London Gas Light and Coke Co. v. Nicholls* (1862) 2 Car. & P. 365.

[23] *Robinson v. Wilkinson* (1817) 3 Price 538; *Ruppell v. Roberts* (1834) 4 Nev. & Man. 31; *Bottomley v. Nuttall* (1858) 5 C.B.(N.S.) 122. *Cf.* the position where the firm merely enjoys the benefit of a contract entered into by a partner, whilst acting beyond the scope both of his actual and of his implied authority: see *infra*, paras. 12–193 *et seq*.

into,[24] although the incidence of such partners is in any event much reduced by the requirements of the Business Names Act 1985.[25]

(b) Contracts under seal

The general rule

12–171   Reference has already been made to the fact that a partner will in general have no implied authority to bind his firm by deed.[26] However, even in a case where a partner has the *express* authority of his co-partners to enter into a deed on the firm's behalf, the form of the deed will ultimately determine whether or not the firm is bound. Somewhat surprisingly, Lord Lindley dealt with this important limitation in a terse way, as follows:

> "If a deed is executed by an agent in his own name, he and he only can sue or be sued thereon, although the deed may disclose the fact that he is acting for another.[27] Therefore, where a partner covenants that anything shall be done, he and he only is liable on the covenant, and the firm is not bound thereby to the covenantee.[28] A person who has to execute a deed as an agent, should take care that the deed and the covenants in it are expressed to be made not by him, but by the person intended to be bound. Thus, if A is the principal and B his agent, the deed and covenants should not be expressed to be made by B for A, but by A; and the execution in like manner should be expressed to be made by A by his agent B."[29]

12–172   This long standing rule is expressly preserved by the Partnership Act 1890[30] and was applied in *Marchant v. Morton Down Co.*[31] There, two partners, T. J. Woolls and J. Allen, carried on business under the name "T. J. Woolls & Co." Allen purported to execute an indenture made between "T. J. Woolls and J. Allen, trading in co-partnership as T. J. Woolls & Co. of the one part, and T. B. Marchant of the other part" by signing it "T. J. Woolls & Co., by J.

---

[24] *Beckham v. Drake* (1843) 11 M. & W. 315, *supra*, para. 12–166; see also *Court v. Berlin* [1897] 2 Q.B. 396.

[25] See *supra*, paras. 3–24 *et seq.*

[26] See *supra*, para. 12–63.

[27] *Appleton v. Binks* (1804) 5 East 148; *Pickering's Case* (1871) L.R. 6 Ch.App. 525; see also *infra*, n. 28 and *Bowstead on Agency* (15th ed.), Art. 80, pp. 325 *et seq.*

[28] *Hall v. Bainbridge* (1840) 1 Man. & G. 42. And note the decision in *John Brothers v. Holmes* [1900] 1 Ch. 188.

[29] *Combe's Case* (1613) 9 Co. 76b; *Wilks v. Back* (1802) 2 East 141.

[30] *Ibid.* s.6, proviso, *supra*, para. 12–161.

[31] [1901] 2 K.B. 829.

Allen, a partner in the said firm." Channell J. held that the indenture could not be treated as a deed made by Woolls, even though it was held to be binding on him on other grounds.[32]

The rule is not affected by the relaxations in the formalities for the execution of deeds introduced by the Law of Property (Miscellaneous Provisions) Act 1989.[33]

Exceptions to the general rule

It should, however, be noted that a deed may be validly executed **12-173** by and in the name of a partner who acts under a power of attorney given by his co-partners;[34] moreover, if a partner executes a deed as trustee for the firm, the firm may be entitled to sue on its provisions.[35]

All partners as parties to deed

The existence of this inflexible rule has, in recent years, caused **12-174** lessors of property to a tenant firm to insist that each partner is made a party to the lease, so as to ensure that he has a direct right to enforce the covenants against each of them.[36]

(c) Bills of Exchange and Promissory Notes

Bills of exchange and promissory notes are not governed by the same **12-175** rules as ordinary contracts not under seal.[37] The position was summarised by Lord Lindley in these terms:

"... subject to the qualification that the name of a firm is equivalent to the name of all the persons liable as partners in it,[38] no person whose name is not on a bill or note is liable to be sued upon it.[39] In order, therefore, that a bill or note may be binding on a firm, the name of the firm or the names of all its members must be upon it; and if the names of one or more of the partners only are upon it, the others will not be liable to be sued upon the

---

[32] *Ibid.* pp. 832, 833.

[33] s.1.

[34] Powers of Attorney Act 1971, s.1 (as amended by the Law of Property (Miscellaneous Provisions) Act 1989, Sched. 1, para. 6).

[35] *Harmer v. Armstrong* [1934] 1 Ch. 65. But note *Re Kay's Settlement* [1939] Ch. 329; *Re Cook's Settlement Trusts* [1965] Ch. 902.

[36] See further *infra*, para. 18–60.

[37] See *supra*, paras. 12–163 *et seq.*

[38] Bills of Exchange Act 1882, s.23(2); see further, *infra*, para. 12–176.

[39] *Ibid.* s.23; and see *Ducarry v. Gill* (1830) 4 C. & P. 121; *Lloyd v. Ashby* (1831) 2 C. & P. 138; *Eastwood v. Bain* (1858) 3 H. & N. 738.

instrument, whatever may be their liability as regards the consideration for which it may have been given."[40]

These rules are expressly preserved by the Partnership Act 1890.[41]

The decided cases in this area are numerous and may usefully be grouped as follows:

(1) Bills drawn, etc., in the firm name.
(2) Bills drawn, etc., in improper form.
(3) Promissory notes.

(1) Bills of Exchange Drawn, etc., in the Firm Name

12–176 As might be expected, a bill in the firm name will normally bind all the partners, as Lord Lindley explained:

"A bill drawn, indorsed or accepted in the name of the firm is considered as bearing the names of all the persons who actually or ostensibly compose the firm at the time its name is put to the bill; and consequently all those persons, including as well dormant partners[42] and *quasi-partners*,[43] may be sued upon the bill."[44]

Thus, where a cheque bearing the firm name is signed by a partner, his co-partner will be liable even though there is no connection on the face of the cheque between the firm name and the manuscript signature.[45]

12–177   The fact that the person drawing, indorsing or accepting the bill is not a true partner, but is merely held out as such,[46] is immaterial provided that he was acting within the scope of his implied authority.[47] However, it should be emphasised that such a person only has *apparent* authority to bind his co-partners, since section 5 of the Partnership Act 1890 is prima facie inapplicable in cases of holding out.[48]

---

[40] *Bottomley v. Nuttall* (1858) 5 C.B.(N.S.) 122; *Miles' Claim* (1874) L.R. 9 Ch.App. 635.

[41] *Ibid.* s.6, proviso, *supra*, para. 12–161.

[42] See *Swan v. Steele* (1806) 7 East 210; *Wintle v. Crowther* (1831) 1 C. & J. 316.

[43] See *Gurney v. Evans* (1858) 3 H. & N. 122. The expression "quasi-partner" is no longer in common usage; its modern equivalent is a partner by holding out or estoppel: see the Partnership Act 1890, s.14, *supra*, paras. 5–43 *et seq.* See also *supra*, para. 1–08.

[44] Bills of Exchange Act 1882, s.23(2).

[45] *Ringham v. Hackett*, *The Times*, February 9, 1980 and (1980) 124 S.J. 201; *Central Motors (Birmingham) v. P.A. & S.N.P. Wadsworth (Trading as Pensgain)*, May 28, 1982 (C.A.T. No. 231), [1983] C.L.Y., p. 80.

[46] Partnership Act 1890, s.14: see *supra*, paras. 5–43 *et seq.*

[47] *Edmonds v. Bushell* (1865) L.R. 1 Q.B. 97; also *Gurney v. Evans* (1858) 3 H. & N. 122. And see *Watteau v. Fenwick* [1893] 1 Q.B. 346; *Kinahan & Co. v. Parry* [1910] 2 K.B. 389 (reversed on a question of fact at [1911] 1 K.B. 459); and *supra*, para. 12–08, n. 12. Cf. *Odell v. Cormack* (1887) 19 Q.B.D. 223, where there was no holding out.

[48] See *Hudgell Yeates & Co. v. Watson* [1978] Q.B. 451, 467, *per* Waller L.J.

More difficult questions arise where a firm carries on business under the name of one of the partners or where two firms carry on business under the same name.

Business carried on in name of partner

In cases of this type, the normal rule is that the firm will be bound, **12–178** whether the bill is drawn, etc., by the partner in whose name the business is carried on or by one of his co-partners.[49] Indeed, in one case,[50] a firm was held liable under a bill accepted by one partner, B, in the name of his co-partner, A, even though it was addressed to A at a place where he carried on a wholly separate business.[51]

However, if it is possible to prove that a bill drawn, etc., by the **12–179** partner whose name the firm bears is in fact his own, and not the firm's, bill, the firm will not be liable, even to a bona fide holder for value. This was decided in *Yorkshire Banking Co. v. Beatson*,[52] where bills were accepted and indorsed by the partner in the course of a private transaction which was neither intended to bind the other (dormant) partner nor entered in the partnership books. Since the holders of the bills did not know of that other partner's existence, they could not be treated as having given credit to him merely because they gave credit to the partner whose name was on the bills.[53]

Similarly, where one partner accepts a bill drawn on him by a co- **12–180** partner, the firm will not be bound even if the partnership business is carried on in his name. Lord Lindley summarised the position in this way:

> "If A, B and C are partners, and A draws a bill of exchange on B, and he accepts the bill, A, B and C cannot be sued upon it; and this is so whether A, B and C have a business name or not; and even although the bill may have been used for the joint benefit of

---

[49] Lord Lindley quite naturally perceived the dangers solely in terms of bills drawn, etc., by the partner in whose name the business is carried on: "... persons may carry on business in partnership in the name of one of themselves, and if they do, they expose themselves to serious liability. Prima facie his acceptances will bind them, even although dishonestly given": see *Yorkshire Banking Co. v. Beatson* (1880) 5 C.P.D. 109, 123–124.

[50] *Stephens v. Reynolds* (1860) 5 H. & N. 513. The proceedings at *Nisi Prius* are reported at (1860) 1 Fost. & Fin. 739 and (1860) 2 Fost. & Fin. 147.

[51] It should be noted that the bill was drawn on Reynolds at Woolwich, not at Walworth, as stated in (1860) 1 Fost. & Fin. 740.

[52] (1880) 5 C.P.D. 109. See also *South Carolina Bank v. Case* (1828) 8 B. & C. 427; *Ex p. Law* (1839) 3 Deac. 541.

[53] Lord Lindley put it in this way: "The fact that the plaintiffs took the bill as the bill of the persons, whoever they were, who might be associated with the partner whose name was on the bill was held immaterial. The plaintiffs never knew of or gave credit to anyone else."

the three partners.[54] Even if it is agreed that the business of the three shall be carried on in the name of one of them, it will not follow that all bills accepted by him will bind all the three partners. The question remains, whose bill is it?"

12–181   This is clear from the decision commonly known as *Miles' Claim*,[55] where four separate firms, A & Co., B & Co., C & Co. and D & Co. became partners in a certain venture and carried on business under the name of D & Co.[56] They agreed that finance for the venture should be raised by means of bills drawn by any one of the individual firms on the others. A & Co. thereupon drew bills on B & Co., C & Co. and D & Co., which were duly accepted. It was held that none of these bills bound all four firms jointly. The bills drawn on B & Co. and C & Co. respectively were clearly not bills of the partnership venture, since they were neither drawn nor accepted in the firm name of D & Co. Although the remaining bills were drawn and accepted in the firm name, the court found that there was no evidence of any intention to bind all four firms, as opposed to the individual firm which carried on business under that name.

12–182   Lord Lindley then referred to the unreported decision in *Hall v. West*,[57] in which there were *dicta* to the same effect. This case is therefore of only limited value; nevertheless, since details of it were apparently taken from the shorthand writer's notes, the original passage has been retained in its entirety:

> "Again, in *Hall v. West*, three brothers of the name of Dawson carried on in partnership under the name of Dawson & Sons, the business of millers, farmers, coal and corn dealers, and bone crushers. The defendant was a dormant partner in the bone-crushing business only. Dawson & Sons overdrew their account with their bankers, who knew nothing of West, nor of his connection with the bone business. Having, however, discovered this, they sued him for the amount of the overdrawn account. He was held not liable; for in point of fact the balance due to the bankers was not in respect of any debt contracted by Dawson & Sons in connection with the bone-crushing business; it was not, therefore, as between the partners themselves a debt of the firm of which the defendant was a member; and there was no apparent as

---

[54] See *Nicholson v. Ricketts* (1860) 2 E. & E. 497; *Miles' Claim* (1874) L.R. 9 Ch.App. 635, *infra*, para. 12–181.

[55] *Re Adansonia Fibre Co.*, *Miles' Claim* (1874) L.R. 9 Ch.App. 635. This appears to have been an early example of a group partnership: see *supra*, paras. 11–20 *et seq*.

[56] It appears, significantly, that the name adopted for the partnership venture was not intended to be used publicly: see *ibid*. pp. 636, 647.

[57] The case went first to the Court of Exchequer and then to the Court of Exchequer Chamber in June 1875.

distinguished from real authority on which the bankers could rely as against West.

"In the same case bills were drawn by West on and accepted by Dawson & Sons. With one exception these bills were drawn for purposes unconnected with the bone business. On the facts stated (but which it is unnecessary here to detail) the court held that all these bills had in fact been paid: it became unnecessary, therefore, to consider whether West could have been sued as an acceptor. It was contended, on the authority of *Baker v. Charlton*,[58] that he was liable; but the Court of Exchequer[59] dissented from that case and expressed a clear opinion that West could not have been liable as an acceptor of the bills, with the exception of the one which had been given for the purposes of the bone business in which he was a partner. The Court of Exchequer Chamber expressed no opinion on this point, it being unnecessary to do so."

Two firms with same name

As Lord Lindley made clear, a factor of critical importance in this class of case will be whether the partner sought to be made liable is a member of one or both of the firms concerned: **12–183**

"If there are two firms with one name, a person who is a member of both firms is liable to be sued on all bills bearing that name, and binding on either firm. But if a member of only one of the two firms is sued on the bill, his liability will depend first on the authority of the person giving the bill to use the name of the firm of which the defendant is a member[60] and, secondly, on whether the name of that firm has in fact been used. If both these questions are answered in the affirmative, he will be liable, but not otherwise."[61]

In *Swan v. Steele*[62] such affirmative answers could clearly be given. There, two firms, one comprising A, B and C (the ABC Partnership) and the other comprising only B and C (the BC Partnership), carried on wholly separate businesses under the name "B & C." A was a dormant partner. A bill of exchange, payable to the order of the ABC Partnership, was received by that firm in respect of a debt due to it, but was indorsed over by B and C, in the name "B & C," for a **12–184**

---

[58] (1791) Peake 111 (a case where two firms carried on business under the same name). After a footnote reference to *Davison v. Robertson* (1815) 3 Dow. 218 and *McNair v. Fleming* (1812) 1 Mont. Part. 37, Lord Lindley observed "But *Baker v. Charlton* cannot now be relied on."

[59] Kelly C.B. and Amphlett B.

[60] See the Partnership Act 1890, s.5, *supra*, para. 12–02; also *supra*, paras. 12–41 *et seq*.

[61] *Cf. Baker v. Charlton* (1791) Peake 111, which is no longer good law: see *supra*, para. 12–182, n. 58.

[62] (1806) 7 East 210.

debt owed to a third party, X, by the BC Partnership. A was held liable on the bill, X being a bona fide holder for value, without notice of the fraud on A committed by his co-partners. It was clear that the bill was properly indorsed "B & C": the only real question was whether that indorsement referred to the ABC Partnership or the BC Partnership. Since the bill could only have been indorsed by the ABC Partnership, A's liability was inevitable; indeed, Lord Ellenborough held it to be too clear for argument.

12–185   The position is not affected by the Business Names Act 1985 since, even where the Act applies,[63] there is no restriction on the number of firms which can carry on business under the same name.[64] Certainly, the decision in *Swan v. Steele* would have been no different had there been equivalent provisions in force at the time.[65]

(2) *Bills Drawn, etc., in Improper Form*

12–186 Lord Lindley observed:

"In the absence of evidence to the contrary, a partner has no authority to use for partnership purposes any other name than the name of the firm[66]; and if he does, and there is any substantial variation which cannot be shown to be authorised by his co-partners, the firm will not be liable. If, however, there is no substantial variation, the firm will be bound."

Consistently with this principle, in *Faith v. Richmond*,[67] partners in a firm carrying on business under the name of "The Newcastle and Sunderland Wallsend Coal Company" were held not to be liable on a promissory note issued in the name of "the Newcastle Coal Company." Similarly, in *Kirk v. Blurton*,[68] where the business was

---

[63] The Act will not apply if each firm's name consists only of the surnames of its members, even if this results in two firms, who do not share identical partners, adopting the same name: *ibid.* s.1(a). See further, *supra*, para. 3–25.

[64] In certain circumstances, the approval of a firm name must be obtained from the Secretary of State: *ibid.* ss.2, 3; also the Company and Business Names Regulations 1981 (S.I. 1981 No. 1685), as amended by the Company and Business Names (Amendment) Regulations 1982 (S.I. 1982 No. 1653) and the Company and Business Names (Amendment) Regulations 1992 (S.I. 1992 No. 1196); also *supra*, para. 3–27. There would, in theory, appear to be no reason why such approval should not be given for the use of an identical name by two or more wholly separate firms; *sed quaere*.

[65] Since, even if the holder of the bill had seen both firms' notepaper, etc., (see *ibid.* s.4(1)(a)) and the statutory notices at their premises (see *ibid.* s.4(1)(b)), the indorsement on the bill would still have been ambiguous and the indorsing partners would still have been acting within the scope of their implied authority. See further, as to these requirements, *supra*, para. 3–32.

[66] *Kirk v. Blurton* (1841) 9 M. & W. 284; *Hambro v. Hull and London Fire Insurance Co.* (1858) 3 H. & N. 789.

[67] (1840) 11 A. & E. 339.

[68] (1841) 9 M. & W. 284. Lord Lindley observed "This case was decided on the right principle; but most persons will probably agree with Martin B., in thinking that the principle was not properly applied, and that it should have been left to the jury to say whether John Blurton and John Blurton & Co. did not in fact mean the same thing." See *Stephens v. Reynolds* (1860) 5 H. & N. 513, 517, *per* Martin B. See also *Odell v. Cormack* (1887) 19 Q.B.D. 223, 226, *per* Hawkins J.

carried on under the name of "John Blurton," one partner was held not to be liable on a bill of exchange drawn and indorsed by the other in the name of "John Blurton & Co."

However, the rule is not absolute: in *Norton v. Seymour*,[69] where **12–187** the firm name consisted of the partners' surnames, *i.e.* "Seymour and Ayres," both partners were held to be bound by a promissory note signed by one in the names "Thomas Seymour, Sarah Ayres." This signature obviously consisted of the partners' surnames, with the addition of their respective christian names; it is considered that the decision would have been otherwise if the wrong christian names had been used.

Acceptance in firm name

An acceptance in the firm name of a bill drawn on the firm in the wrong name will bind the firm.[70]

Habitual use of different name

However, notwithstanding the general principle described above, if **12–188** it can be proved that the name on the bill, though not the firm name, is a name which the firm habitually *uses*, the firm will be bound.[71] As Lord Lindley put it:

"... for whatever the name used may be, if it is that ordinarily employed by a partner whose business it is to attend to the bills and notes of the firm, the other partners will not be heard to say that such name is not the name of the firm for the purpose for which he has habitually used it."

Thus, where a firm carried on business under the name "Hapgood **12–189** & Co.," but the managing partner was in the habit of indorsing partnership bills in the name "Hapgood & Fowler" (which had formerly been the firm name), the indorsements were held to be binding on the firm, even though there was no proof that the other partners had authorised the use of that name.[72]

Such a situation is now, perhaps, less likely to arise, having regard to the requirements of the Business Names Act 1985, which the partners could not lightly ignore.[73]

---

[69] (1847) 3 C.B. 792.
[70] *Lloyd v. Ashby* (1831) 2 B. & Ad. 23.
[71] There was, of course, no such evidence in *Faith v. Richmond* (1840) 11 A. & E. 339 or *Kirk v. Blurton* (1841) 9 M. & W. 284, *supra*, para. 12–186.
[72] *Williamson v. Johnson* (1823) 1 B. & C. 146.
[73] See in particular, *ibid.* ss.4, 5 and, generally, *supra*, paras. 3–32 *et seq.*

Personal liability of persons using wrong name

12–190   Even if the firm is not bound, because its name (or a name which it habitually uses) does not appear on the bill, the partners who actually drew, etc., the bill in the wrong name will be treated as having adopted that name for the purposes of the bill and will, therefore, be personally liable thereon.[74]

On the same principle, where a firm draws and indorses blank bills in the firm name but, before they can be negotiated, one partner dies and the surviving partners change the firm name and then negotiate the bills, the new firm will be liable on the bills, even though its name does not appear thereon.[75]

Bill drawn, etc., in name of partner

12–191   A firm will not be liable on a bill drawn, etc., in the name of a partner,[76] unless it in fact carries on business under his name.[77] This will be the position even if the partner in whose name the bill is drawn accepts it on behalf of the firm, since the other partners will not be drawees.[78]

A bill drawn on a firm and accepted by one partner in the firm name and in his own name does not bind him separately if the firm is bound by his acceptance.[79] However, if he did not have authority to bind the firm, he will be liable on the bill. Thus, in *Owen v. Van Uster*,[80] Van Ulster was held to be personally liable on a bill drawn on "The Allty-Crib Mining Company," which had been accepted "per proc. The Allty-Crib Mining Company, W. T. Van Uster, London Manager."

(3) *Promissory Notes*

12–192   Lord Lindley formulated the following five rules[81] in relation to promissory notes, by reference to the decided cases:

---

[74] *Faith v. Richmond* (1840) 11 A. & E. 339; *Kirk v. Blurton* (1841) 9 M. & W. 284: see *supra*, para. 12–186. See also *Wilde v. Keep* (1833) 6 C. & P. 235; *Odell v. Cormack* (1887) 19 Q.B.D. 223, 226, *per* Hawkins J.

[75] *Usher v. Dauncey* (1814) 4 Camp. 97. And note also *Mitchell v. Lapage* (1816) Holt, N.P. 253; *cf. Boulton v. Jones* (1857) 2 H. & N. 564.

[76] *Williams v. Thomas* (1806) 6 Esp. 18; *Emly v. Lye* (1812) 15 East 7; *Ex p. Bolitho* (1817) Buck 100; *Lloyd v. Ashby* (1831) 2 C. & P. 138; . The cases of *Mason v. Rumsey* (1808) 1 Camp. 384 and *Jenkins v. Morris* (1847) 16 M. & W. 877, which decided that a firm might be bound by the acceptance of one partner in his own name of a bill drawn on the firm, are no longer good law: see the Bills of Exchange Act 1882, ss.17, 23.

[77] See *supra*, paras. 12–178 *et seq*.

[78] *Nicholls v. Diamond* (1853) 9 Ex. 154; *Mare v. Charles* (1856) 5 E. & B. 978.

[79] *Re Barnard* (1886) 32 Ch.D. 447; also *Malcolmson v. Malcolmson* (1851) L.R.Ir. 1 Ch.D. 228.

[80] (1850) 10 C.B. 318. Van Ulster was a partner in the Allty-Crib Mining Company and, therefore, both a drawee and an acceptor of the bill.

[81] The order in which the rules appear in the text is not that originally adopted by Lord Lindley. Moreover, his detailed illustrations of certain of the rules (involving the reproduction of various promissory notes culled from the decided cases) have not been retained.

(1) If a partner promises for himself and co-partner, this amounts to a promise by the firm.[82]

(2) If a partner promises for himself, and not for himself and co-partners, he only is liable on the note, though he may promise to pay a partnership debt.[83]

(3) If one partner promises in the name of the firm to pay that for which he and not the firm is liable, the promise binds him at all events.[84]

(4) If several partners sign a note in this form, "I promise to pay," all who sign the note are liable on it, jointly and severally.[85]

(5) One partner has no authority, as such, to bind himself and co-partners jointly and severally.[86] But if some members of a firm make a joint and *several* promissory note they will be personally liable, although they may have signed only on behalf of themselves and co-partners.[87]

8. LIABILITY OF PARTNERS IN RESPECT OF CONTRACTS BENEFITTING FIRM

When considering liability in respect of a contract entered into by a **12–193** partner *otherwise* than on behalf of the firm, it is wholly irrelevant that the firm may have received some direct or indirect benefit under or by virtue of the contract, as Lord Lindley explained in this passage:

"It is an erroneous but popular notion that if a firm obtains the benefit of a contract made with one of its partners, it must needs be bound by that contract. Now, although the circumstance that the firm obtains the benefit of a contract entered into by one of its members tends to show that he entered into the contract as the agent of the firm,[88] such circumstance is no more than evidence

---

[82] Bills of Exchange Act 1882, s.91; *Lane v. Williams* (1693) 2 Vern. 292; *Smith v. Baily* (1727) 11 Mod. 401; *Smith v. Jarves* (1727) 2 Ld. Ray. 1484. This was Lord Lindley's fifth rule. He specifically illustrated it by reference to *Galway v. Matthew and Smithson* (1808) 1 Camp. 403; *Ex p. Buckley* (1845) 14 M. & W. 469; *Ex p. Clarke* (1845) De Gex. 153 (the latter two decisions being contrary to the "older decision" in *Hall v. Smith* (1823) 1 B. & C. 407).

[83] *Siffkin v. Walker* (1809) 2 Camp. 308; *Murray v. Somerville* (1889) 2 Camp. 99n.; also *Ex p. Harris* (1816) 1 Madd. 583. This was Lord Lindley's first rule.

[84] *Shipton v. Thornton* (1838) 9 A. & E. 314; also *Hudson v. Robinson* (1816) 4 M. & S. 475. This was Lord Lindley's third rule.

[85] Bills of Exchange Act 1882, s.85; *Clerk v. Blackstock* (1816) Holt, N.P. 474; *March v. Ward* (1792) 1 Peake 177. This was Lord Lindley's second rule.

[86] *Maclae v. Sutherland* (1854) 3 E. & B. 1, which shows that a joint and several promissory note is valid as a joint note, even though it is not binding, as a several note, on any person who does not sign it.

[87] This was Lord Lindley's fourth rule. He specifically illustrated it by reference to *Healey v. Story* (1848) 3 Ex. 3; *Penkivil v. Connell* (1850) 5 Ex. 381; *Bottomley v. Fisher* (1862) 1 H. & C. 211.

[88] *Beckham v. Drake* (1841) 9 M. & W. 79, 100, *per* Rolfe B.

that this was the case, and the question upon which the liability or non-liability of the firm upon a contract depends is not—Has the firm obtained the benefit of the contract? but—Did the firm, by one of its partners or otherwise, enter into the contract?"[89]

Numerous cases have been decided on this principle, but Lord Lindley drew particular attention to *Emly v. Lye*[90] and *Bevan v. Lewis.*[91]

The most common cases in which the principle will fall to be applied are where partners borrow money or obtain the supply of goods or services.

Money borrowed by a partner

12–194   If a partner borrows money without the actual or implied authority of his co-partners,[92] he and not the firm will enter into the contract of loan and the nature of that contract will not be altered or affected by the manner in which he chooses to apply the money borrowed. Accordingly, the lender cannot seek repayment from the firm merely because the money has been applied for its benefit;[93] however, he may enjoy an equivalent right by way of an equitable form of subrogation.[94]

Goods supplied to a partner

12–195   The position will be no different where goods or services are supplied at the request of a partner who is acting either on his own account or (which amounts to the same thing) outside the scope of his actual or implied authority.[95] Thus, the firm does not enter into any contract nor does it incur any liability merely because its receives the benefit of the goods or services supplied.[96] However, again a right against the firm may arise by way of subrogation.

---

[89] *Ibid.* See also *Kingsbridge Flour Mill Co. v. The Plymouth Grinding Co.* (1848) 2 Ex. 718; *Ernest v. Nicholls* (1857) 6 H.L.Cas. 423. The position is analogous to that under the Partnership Act 1890, s.13: see *supra*, paras. 12–134 *et seq.* The corollary is also true, *i.e.* the fact that one partner has obtained the benefit of a contract does not conclusively prove that the firm is not liable thereunder: see *Ex p. Bonbonus* (1803) 8 Ves. Jr. 540.

[90] (1812) 15 East 7, where a partner had drawn bills in his own name, had them discounted and then applied the money for the benefit of the firm.

[91] (1827) 1 Sim. 376, where the partner had borrowed money and applied it for the firm's benefit. Interestingly, it appears that his partner had some knowledge of the borrowing.

[92] See *supra*, paras. 12–45 *et seq.*

[93] See *Smith v. Craven* (1831) 1 C. & J. 500; *Hawtayne v. Bourne* (1841) 7 M. & W. 595; *Fisher v. Tayler* (1843) 2 Hare 218; *Ricketts v. Bennett* (1847) 4 C.B. 686; *Burmester v. Norris* (1851) 6 Ex. 796; *Re Worcester Corn Exchange Co.* (1853) 3 De G.M. & G. 180.

[94] See *infra*, para. 12–196.

[95] See *supra*, para. 12–81.

[96] See in addition to the cases previously cited, *Ball v. Lanesborough* (1713) 5 Bro.P.C. 480; *Kilgour v. Finlyson* (1789) 1 H.Bl. 155, *Ex p. Wheatly* (1797) *Cooke's Bank. Law,* (8th ed.) 534; *Ex p. Peele* (1802) 6 Ves. Jr. 602, 604, *per* Lord Eldon; *Ex p. Hartop* (1806) 12 Ves. Jr. 349; *Gallway v. Mathew* (1808) 10 East 264; *Loyd v. Freshfield* (1826) 2 Car. & P. 325; *Kingsbridge Flour Mill Co. v. Plymouth Grinding Co.* (1848) 2 Ex. 718.

The creditor's right of subrogation

Where the firm is not liable on a contract entered into by a **12–196** partner, the other contracting party may not be entirely remediless, at least to the extent that the firm has been benefited thereby. Lord Lindley stated the equitable principle applied in such cases in these terms:

"Where, however, money borrowed by one partner in the name of the firm but without the authority of his co-partners has been applied in paying off debts of the firm, the lender is entitled in equity to repayment by the firm of the amount which he can show to have been so applied[97]: and the same rule extends to money *bona fide* borrowed and applied for any other legitimate purpose of the firm.[98] This doctrine is founded partly on the right of the lender to stand in equity in the place of those creditors of the firm whose claims have been paid off by his money; and partly on the right of the borrowing partner to be indemnified by the firm against liabilities *bona fide* incurred by him for the legitimate purpose of relieving the firm from its debts or of carrying on its business.[99] The equitable doctrine in question is limited in its application to cases falling under one or other of the principles above indicated."[1]

It is clear from the qualification at the end of the passage that a **12–197** right of subrogation will *not* arise in all cases. Thus, if money is borrowed by a partner and applied for the firm's benefit in a manner which does not increase or preserve its assets, that partner will not be entitled to reimbursement from his co-partners.[2] The lender can be in no better position.

---

[97] At this point a later editor added the words "even though he knew that the money was borrowed without authority": see *Reversion Fund and Insurance Co. v. Maison Cosway Ltd.* [1913] 1 K.B. 364; also the cases cited in the next note.

[98] See, in particular, *Ex p. Chippendale (The German Mining Co.'s Case)* (1854) 4 De G.M. & G. 19; *Re Cork and Youghal Ry.* (1866) L.R. 4 Ch.App. 748; *Blackburn Building Society v. Cunliffe, Brooks & Co.* (1884) 9 App.Cas. 857 and (1885) 29 Ch.D. 902; *Baroness Wenlock v. River Dee Co.* (1883) 36 Ch.D. 675n. and (1887) 19 Q.B.D. 155; *Bannatyne v. McIver* [1906] 1 K.B. 103. See also *Reid v. Rigby & Co.* [1894] 2 Q.B. 40; *cf. Wylie v. Carlyon* [1922] 1 Ch. 51.

[99] See *infra*, paras. 20–19 *et seq.*

[1] See in addition to the cases cited in n. 98, *Athenaeum Life Assurance Society v. Pooley* (1858) 3 De G. & J. 294; *Magdalena Steam Navigation Co.* (1860) Johns. 690; *Re National Permanent Benefit Building Society* (1870) L.R. 5 Ch.App. 309. And see also the general review of the doctrine of subrogation in *Orakpo v. Manson Investments Ltd.* [1978] A.C. 95.

[2] See *infra*, para. 20–21.

CHAPTER 13

THE NATURE AND DURATION OF A PARTNER'S LIABILITY TO THIRD PARTIES

1. NATURE AND EXTENT OF THE LIABILITY

13–01 IT has already been seen[1] that the liability of a firm for the acts of a partner will vary according to the nature of those acts. In cases where such liability is established, the nature of the acts in question will also determine whether that liability will be merely joint or both joint and several. For convenience, this subject will be considered under the same general classifications as were adopted in the previous Chapter.

A. LIABILITY FOR ACTS WHICH ARE NOT IN THEMSELVES WRONGFUL

13–02 This section is effectively confined to liability arising out of contract, of which Lord Lindley said:

"An agent who contracts for a known principal is not liable to be himself sued on the contract into which he has avowedly entered only as agent. Consequently, a partner who enters into a contract on behalf of his firm is not liable on that contract except as one of the firm: in other words, the contract is not binding on him separately, but only on him and his co-partners jointly.[2] One partner may render himself separately liable by holding himself out as the only member of the firm[3]; or by so framing the contract, as to bind himself separately from his co-partners as well as jointly with them[4]; but unless there are some special circumstances of this

---

[1] See *supra*, paras. 12–02 *et seq.*
[2] See *Ex p. Wilson* (1842) 3 M.D. & D. 57; *Ex p. Buckley* (1845) 14 M. & W. 469; *Re Clarke* (1845) De G. 153.
[3] *De Mautort v. Saunders* (1830) 1 B. & Ad. 398; *Bonfield v. Smith* (1844) 12 M. & W. 405.
[4] See *supra*, paras. 12–163 *et seq.*; also *Higgins v. Senior* (1841) 8 M. & W. 834; *Ex p. Wilson* (1842) 3 M.D. & D. 57; *Ex p. Harding* (1879) 12 Ch.D. 557. Note also that a contract framed in terms which leave it doubtful whether it is joint or joint and several will be construed as joint and several if it appears from the face of the contract that each partner has both a joint and a separate interest in its performance: see *Sorsbie v. Park* (1843) 12 M. & W. 146, 158, *per* Parke B; *Bradburne v. Botfield* (1845) 14 M. & W. 559; *Palmer v. Mallet* (1887) 36 Ch.D. 411. See also *infra*, para. 13–10.

sort, a contract which is binding on the firm is binding on all[5] the partners jointly and on none of them severally."[6]

Partnership Act 1890, section 9

This long established principle is incorporated directly into section **13–03** 9 of the Partnership Act 1890, which provides:

"9. Every partner in a firm is liable jointly with the other partners, and in Scotland severally also, for all debts and obligations[7] of the firm incurred while he is a partner; and after his death his estate is also severally liable in a due course of administration for such debts and obligations, so far as they remain unsatisfied, but subject in England or Ireland[8] to the prior payment of his separate debts."

Holding out

A person who is merely held out as a partner is liable "as a **13–04** partner"[9] and will therefore be jointly liable along with the actual partners. Indeed, it is the current editor's view that there will be such joint liability even if no partnership in fact exists.[10] Lord Lindley certainly considered this to be the position prior to the Partnership Act 1890:

"A creditor who alleges that A, B, and C are his debtors, can, it is apprehended, prove his case by showing that one of them contracted on behalf of all three and that the other two are estopped from denying his authority to do so. Cases in which persons have been held jointly liable on this principle are to be found in the books.[11] The case of *Scarf v. Jardine*,[12] which seems at first sight to throw some doubt on this doctrine, is really not opposed to it."[13]

---

[5] This will include a dormant partner: *Beckham v. Drake* (1843) 11 M. & W. 315; *Brett v. Beckwith* (1856) 3 Jur.(N.S.) 31; *Court v. Berlin* [1897] 2 Q.B. 396. See also *supra*, para. 12–06.

[6] In fact this was the position both at law and in equity: see *Kendall v. Hamilton* (1879) 4 App.Cas. 504.

[7] Given the terms of *ibid.* s.12, *infra*, para. 13–12, the debts and obligations referred to must arise by way of contract; see also *Friend v. Young* [1897] 2 Ch. 421; *Bagel v. Miller* [1903] 2 K.B. 212. But note the anomalous position of a firm's liability for breach of trust under *ibid.* s.13: see *infra*, para. 13–13.

[8] This should be construed as a reference to Northern Ireland: Irish Free State (Consequential Adaptation of Enactments) Order 1923 (S.R. & O. 1923 No. 405), Art. 2.

[9] Partnership Act 1890, s.14, *supra*, paras. 5–43 *et seq.*

[10] *Quaere* whether, in such a case, the apparent partners are partners "in a firm": see *ibid.* s.9. It is thought that the firm need not actually exist: see also the terms of *ibid.* s.14(1). Note also that *ibid.* s.5 apparently does not apply in the case of holding out: see *Hudgell Yeates & Co. v. Watson* [1978] Q.B. 451, 467, *per* Waller L.J. See also *infra*, para. 13–18, n. 50.

[11] *Waugh v. Carver* (1793) 1 H.Bl.235; see also *supra*, paras. 5–43 *et seq.*

[12] (1882) 7 App.Cas. 345.

[13] See further, as to this case, *supra*, para. 5–62.

He went on to explain that, in *Scarf v. Jardine*, the retired partner was at no time held out as a partner in the new firm.[14]

Judgment against one partner

13–05   It was formerly held that, because partners are only jointly liable, judgment against one partner in respect of a partnership debt would discharge the others,[15] but the bar on subsequent proceedings has now been completely removed by section 3 of the Civil Liability (Contribution) Act 1978.[16]

Liability of deceased partner's estate

13–06   The several liability attaching to a deceased partner's estate is of an exceptional nature and was recognised as such long before the Partnership Act 1890.[17] Indeed, judgment against one or more of the surviving partners would *never* have been a bar to subsequent proceedings against a deceased partner's estate.[18]

Discretion of creditor

13–07   The traditional view of the effect of section 9 has always been[19] that it creates concurrent rights against the surviving partners and

---

[14] Lord Lindley observed: "The importance of this case turns on the grounds on which it was held that J. [*the creditor*] could not have sued S. [*the retired partner*] jointly with the members of the new firm. The reason why he could not have done so was that J. did not in fact contract with the new firm upon the faith that S. was a member of it. If it had been proved that J. had so contracted he could, it is apprehended, have sued S. and the other members of the new firm, and have proved S. to have been a partner by estoppel." He referred in particular to the judgments of Lords Selborne and Blackburn at (1882) 7 App.Cas. 350, 357–358. See also *S. Kaprow & Co. v. MacLelland & Co.* [1948] 1 K.B. 618.

[15] *Kendall v. Hamilton* (1879) 4 App.Cas. 504; and see *infra*, paras. 13–134, 13–135. Note also *Wilson, Sons & Co. v. Balcarres Brook Steam Co.* [1893] 1 Q.B. 422.

[16] This section also extends to actions for damages, whether tortious, contractual or otherwise: see *ibid.* s.6(1). However, in the case of actions for damages, the plaintiff may be deprived of his costs in any action subsequent to that in which judgment was first given: *ibid.* s.4. See also *infra*, para. 20–16.

[17] Lord Lindley wrote: "It has often been said that in equity partnership debts are separate as well as joint; but this proposition is inaccurate and misleading. It is true that a creditor of a partnership can obtain payment of his debt out of the estate of a deceased partner; but the judgment which such a creditor obtains is quite different from that which a separate creditor is entitled to; and it is a mistake to say that the joint creditor of the firm is also in equity a separate creditor of the deceased partner. In Bankruptcy the joint debts of a firm are never treated as joint and several; and yet in Bankruptcy equitable as well as legal principles are always recognised." As to the form of the judgment to which Lord Lindley referred, see *Hills v. M'Rae* (1851) 9 Hare 297; *Re McRae* (1883) 25 Ch.D. 16; *Re Hodgson* (1885) 31 Ch.D. 177; *Re Barnard* (1886) 32 Ch.D. 447; *Moore v. Knight* [1891] 1 Ch. 547, 557; also *infra*, para. 26–19.

[18] *Jacomb v. Harwood* (1751) 2 Ves.Sen. 265; *Liverpool Borough Bank v. Walker* (1859) 4 De.G. & J. 24.

[19] Lord Lindley wrote of s.9, in his Supplement on the Partnership Act 1890: "In the event of the death of a partner, a creditor of the firm has concurrent remedies against the surviving partners and the estate of the deceased partner, and it is immaterial which remedy he pursues first. . .".

against the deceased partner's estate, so that a creditor may, if he wishes, proceed first against the estate, without the need to show that the surviving partners are insolvent or that the partnership assets are insufficient to meet the partnership debts.[20] Indeed, this view never appears to have been questioned, despite the qualification that the estate is liable "so far as [the debts] remain unsatisfied." It would therefore seem that these words must be construed merely as a reference to the fact of non–payment; sed quaere.[21]

The position will apparently be no different even where the **13–08** creditor has taken a joint bond or covenant by way of security for the debt.[22] This was clearly established in Bishop v. Church,[23] where two partners had borrowed £2,000, in respect of which they later gave a joint bond. One died and the other went bankrupt. The creditors sought payment out of the deceased partner's estate, which was held to be liable.[24] Similarly, in Beresford v. Browning,[25] four partners agreed that, on the death of any of them, the survivors should pay out his share in instalments. Although the agreement did not purport to bind the surviving partners jointly and severally, it was held that the estate of one of them was liable for the instalments due to a partner who had predeceased him.

Contrary to the position prior to the Partnership Act 1890,[26] the **13–09** doctrine applied in the above cases cannot now be applied so as to benefit joint creditors at the expense of a deceased partner's *separate* creditors. Section 9 is specific in its effect of postponing all partnership debts and obligations to the deceased's separate debts.

It is clear that, by first seeking payment from the deceased partner's estate, the creditor in no way prejudices his rights against the surviving partners.[27]

---

[20] *Wilkinson v. Henderson* (1833) 1 Myl. & K. 582. This is a rule of procedure: it was accordingly held to apply to an action against the executors of a partner in a Spanish firm, who had died in England and left property here, even though such an action would not have been allowed in Spain: see *Re Doetsch, Matheson v. Ludwig* [1896] 2 Ch. 836. See also *infra*, paras. 26–17 *et seq.* The necessary corollary is, of course, that the surviving partners (or their separate creditors) cannot force the partnership creditors to proceed first against the deceased partner's estate: *Ex p. Kendall* (1811) 17 Ves.Jr. 514.
[21] Note that a contrary view appears to be adopted by the editors of *Chitty on Contracts* (26th ed.), para. 1302.
[22] See, in addition to the other cases cited in this paragraph, *Lane v. Williams* (1692) 2 Vern. 292; *Primrose v. Bromley* (1739) 1 Atk. 90; *Darwent v. Walton* (1742) 2 Atk. 510; and see *Sleech's Case* (1816) 1 Mer. 539; *Devaynes v. Noble* (1839) 2 R. & M. 495; *Smith v. Smith* (1861) 3 Giff. 263. Cf. *Turner v. Turner* [1911] 1 Ch. 716.
[23] (1751) 2 Ves.Sen. It was also held that the bond ought to be treated as joint and several, so as to make the estate of the deceased partner liable for a specialty debt, and not merely a simple contract debt.
[24] See also *Simpson v. Vaughan* (1739) 2 Atk. 31; *Thomas v. Frazer* (1797) 3 Ves. Jr. 399; *Burn v. Burn* (1798) 3 Ves. Jr. 573; *Orr v. Chase* (1812) 1 Mer. 729, Appendix.
[25] (1875) 1 Ch.D. 30.
[26] See *Burn v. Burn* (1798) 3 Ves. Jr. 573.
[27] *Re Hodgson* (1885) 31 Ch.D. 177.

Cases where joint liability is express

13–10   Notwithstanding the terms of section 9, it must not be assumed that
a deceased partner's estate will be severally liable in all cases, since
the terms of the contract may expressly negative such liability, as
Lord Lindley explained:

> "If ... partners enter into a contract binding themselves jointly
> and not severally, and if such contract is not a mere security for
> the payment of a debt, or for the performance of a joint and
> several obligation, and if it has not been made joint in form by
> mistake, the effect of the contract will be in equity as in law to
> impose a joint obligation and no other."[28]

This was the basis for the decision in *Sumner v. Powell*,[29] where a
joint indemnity against partnership debts and liabilities was given to
the executors of a deceased partner by the surviving partners and by
a new partner. The new partner died and the executor sought to rely
on the indemnity as against his estate. It was held that the estate was
not liable, since the new partner's obligation existed solely by virtue
of the indemnity, which was clearly joint in form.

13–11   Similarly, in *Clarke v. Bickers*,[30] where two partners had taken a
lease of property and given the tenant's covenants jointly. One
partner having died, proceedings were commenced against his estate
for breach of the covenants, but it was held[31] that, the covenants
being joint, the estate was not liable.

This principle was carried to extreme lengths in *Wilmer v. Currey*,[32]
where, on the retirement of a partner, the continuing partners jointly
covenanted to pay and indemnify him against the partnership debts
and to pay him certain sums of money. One of the continuing
partners died and the retired partner sought to enforce the covenant
against his estate and against the surviving partner. It was held[33] that

---

[28] See, in addition to the cases cited in the text, *Rawstone v. Parr* (1827) 3 Russ. 424, 539;
Richardson v. Horton (1843) 6 Beav. 185; *Jones v. Beach* (1852) 2 De G.M. & G. 886; *Other v.
Iveson* (1855) 3 Drew. 177; and see, generally, as to construing a contract to be joint, several or
joint and several: *White v. Tyndall* (1888) 13 App.Cas. 263; *Tyser v. Shipowners' Syndicate (Reassured)* [1896] 1 Q.B. 135; *National Society for the Distribution of Electricity, etc. v. Gibbs* [1900] 2
Ch. 280; also *supra*, para. 13–02, n.4.
[29] (1816) 2 Mer. 30, affirmed at (1823) T. & R. 423.
[30] (1845) 14 Sim. 639. Now, by virtue of the Law of Property Act 1925, the lease would in any
event be held by the partners as joint tenants on trust for sale: see *infra*, para. 18–60. There is,
however, no reason why a landlord should not require joint and several covenants from the tenants
and, in practice, this is usually done.
[31] On demurrer.
[32] (1848) 2 De G. & Sm. 347.
[33] On demurrer.

the estate was not liable under the covenant, even though it was bound to contribute towards payment of the partnership debts. Lord Lindley observed that "It is ... difficult to reconcile this case with *Beresford v. Browning*."[34]

B. Liability in Respect of Torts, Frauds and Misapplication of Money and Property

Partnership Act 1890, section 12

The joint and several liability of partners for torts, frauds and the **13–12** misapplication of money and property received by or in the custody of the firm is clearly established by section 12 of the Partnership Act 1890, which provides:

"12. Every partner is liable jointly with his co-partners and also severally for everything for which the firm while he is a partner therein becomes liable under either of the two last preceding sections."[35]

This section introduced a partial alteration to the previous law.[36] Thus, it does not now matter whether a misapplication of money involves a breach of contract or a tort: the partners' liability will remain joint and several.[37] The current editor apprehends that the position will be the same in the case of a negligent misrepresentation which gives rise to a claim in damages under section 2(1) of the Misrepresentation Act 1967.[38]

C. Liability in Respect of Breach of Trust

It is clear that section 12 of the Partnership Act 1890[39] does not apply **13–13** to breaches of trust for which the firm is liable.[40] Since section 9 of the Act applies only to *contractual* debts and obligations,[41] liability

---

[34] (1875) 1 Ch.D. 30. The Court of Appeal, however, thought that they were distinguishable: *ibid.*

[35] See ss.10, 11, *supra*, paras. 12–89 *et seq.*, 12–106 *et seq.*

[36] See generally, as to torts and frauds, *Mitchell v. Tarbutt* (1794) 5 T.R. 649; *Ex p. Adamson* (1878) 8 Ch.D. 807; 1 Wms.Saund. 291 f and g; Com.Dig. Abatement, F.8. The old exception in the case of the wrongful use of land (see 1 Wms.Saund. 291 f and g) was not preserved.

[37] See the discussion in the 5th ed. of this work at pp. 198–200.

[38] See *supra*, para. 12–97 and, *infra*, para. 23–50.

[39] See *supra*, para. 13–12.

[40] Partnership Act 1890, s.13, *supra*, paras. 12–134 *et seq.*

[41] See *supra*, para. 13–03. Interestingly, the reference in that section to the "debts and obligations of the firm" is unqualified.

for breach of trust remains as it was prior to the Act, *i.e.* joint and several.[42]

D. EXTENT OF LIABILITY IN ALL CASES

13–14 A distinct feature of the law of partnership has always been the unlimited liability accepted by partners for the debts and obligations of the firm, as Lord Lindley explained:

> "By the common law of this country, every member of an ordinary partnership is liable to the utmost farthing of his property for the debts and engagements of the firm. The law, ignoring the firm as anything distinct from the persons composing it, treats the debts and engagements of the firm as the debts and engagements of the partners, and holds each partner liable for them accordingly. Moreover, if judgment is obtained against the firm for a debt owing by it, the judgment creditor is under no obligation to levy execution against the property of the firm before having recourse to the separate property of the partners; nor is he under any obligation to levy execution against all the partners rateably; but he may select any one or more of them and levy execution upon him or them until the judgment is satisfied, leaving all questions of contribution to be settled afterwards between the partners themselves."[43]

Attempts to limit liability

13–15 Attempts to avoid such unlimited liability by contract are unlikely to succeed, short of an express stipulation that a creditor of the firm is only entitled to payment out of the partnership assets, with no right of recourse against the partners personally. It need hardly be observed that such a term would rarely, if ever, be commercially acceptable.[44]

---

[42] *Blyth v. Fladgate* [1891] 1 Ch. 337, 353, *per* Stirling J. (a decision which in fact pre-dates the coming into force of Partnership Act 1890); see also *Re National Funds Assurance Co.* (1878) 10 Ch.D. 118; *Re Oxford Benefit Building Society* (1886) 35 Ch.D. 502; *Ex p. Shepherd* (1887) 19 Q.B.D. 84. And see the older cases: *Sleech's Case* (1816) 1 Mer. 539; *Clayton's Case* (1816) 1 Mer. 572; *Baring's Case* (1816) 1 Mer. 611; *Warde's Case* (1816) 1 Mer. 624; *Vulliamy v. Noble* (1817) 3 Mer. 593; *Wilson v. Moore* (1832) 1 Myl. & K. 126 and (1834) *ibid.* 337; *Brydges v. Branfill* (1842) 12 Sim. 369. *Cf. Parker v. McKenna* (1874) L.R. 10 Ch.App. 96; *Vyse v. Foster* (1874) L.R. 7 H.L. 318.

[43] See *Abbott v. Smith* (1760) 2 Wm.Blacks. 947, 949, *per* De Grey C.J.; also Com.Dig. Execution H. See further, as to execution against partners, *infra*, paras. 14–89 *et seq.*

[44] In fact, Lord Lindley himself observed that "in modern times [*such stipulations*] are practically confined to Insurance and other companies formed before the passing of the Companies Act 1862." *Quaere* whether such a provision would, in any event, be effective in the event of the firm being wound up as an unregistered company: see *infra*, paras. 27–08 *et seq.*, 27–57 *et seq.*, 27–82 *et seq.*

In practice, there are only two options which offer prospective **13–16** partners the benefits of limited liability. First, there is the limited partnership formed under the Limited Partnerships Act 1907;[45] however, this vehicle has proved unpopular in practice, due in large measure to the need to recruit at least one partner who is prepared to accept unlimited liability[46] and to the inability of the limited partners to participate in the management of the firm.[47] The second alternative is the corporate partnership,[48] which naturally precludes the prospective partner from *direct* participation in the venture and thus, to an extent, negates the essentially personal nature of the partnership relation.

2. DURATION OF LIABILITY

It has already been seen that a partner is regarded as the agent of the **13–17** firm for the purposes of carrying on its business in the usual or ordinary way.[49] This section addresses three distinct questions. First, when does a partner's agency (and, thus, his co-partners' liability for his acts) commence? Secondly, when and in what circumstances does such agency terminate? Finally, how can a partner rid himself of a liability once it has accrued?

A. COMMENCEMENT OF AGENCY

It is a largely self evident proposition that the agency of a partner **13–18** presupposes the existence of a partnership; indeed, it has been held that section 5 of the Partnership Act 1890 does not apply in a case of holding out.[50] Lord Lindley put it in these terms:

"The doctrine that each partner has implied authority to do whatever is necessary to carry on the partnership in the usual way, is based upon the ground that the ordinary business of a firm cannot be carried on either to the advantage of its members or with safety to the public unless such a doctrine is recognised. The existence of a partnership is, therefore, evidently presupposed; and although persons negotiating for a partnership, or about to become partners, *may* be the agents of each other before the partnership

---

[45] See *infra*, paras. 29–01 *et seq.*
[46] Limited Partnerships Act 1907, s.4(1). Note, however, that the general partner may be a limited company: see *supra*, para. 11–06 and *infra*, para. 29–06.
[47] *Ibid.* s.6(1), *infra*, paras. 31–02 *et seq.*
[48] See *supra*, paras. 11–02 *et seq.*
[49] See the Partnership Act 1890, s.5, *supra*, paras. 12–02 *et seq.*
[50] See *Hudgell Yeates & Co. v. Watson* [1978] Q.B. 451, 467, (*per* Waller L.J.) and, *semble*, 471B (*per* Megaw L.J.). *Cf.* the judgment of Bridge L.J. at *ibid.* 462H–463A.

commences, such agency, if relied on, must be established in the ordinary way, and is not to be inferred from the mere fact that the persons in question were engaged in the attainment of some common end, or that they have subsequently become partners."[51]

Intended partnership

13–19   It does not follow from the fact that prospective partners have agreed to enter into partnership with effect from a certain date, on terms to be embodied in a formal agreement to be executed on that date, that no partnership will come into existence if execution of the agreement is, in the event, deferred. In such a case, the only relevant question will be: when, as a matter of fact, did the partners begin to carry on business together? If they did so on the agreed date, then the partnership and, thus, the agency of each partner will be treated as commencing on that date.[52] Indeed, it may even be possible to prove an effective commencement of the partnership *prior* to the agreed date.

13–20   On the other hand, if the agreement is executed on the correct date, but the business is not in fact commenced for some time thereafter, there can be no implied agency in the interim period.[53] Equally, if in such a case the facts are equivocal or there is nothing to suggest that the partnership commenced at a later or earlier date, each partner's agency will be treated as commencing on the date of the agreement.[54]

Acts preparatory to partnership

13–21   Where a person agrees to do some preparatory act prior to entering into partnership, his prospective partners will obviously not be bound thereby. *A fortiori* if the act in question is the acquisition of an asset which is to be brought into the partnership by way of capital contribution or otherwise, as Lord Lindley explained:

"... if several persons agree to become partners, and contribute each a certain quantity of money or goods for the joint benefit of all, each one is solely responsible to those who may have supplied

---

[51] See the authorities cited *supra*, paras. 2–09 *et seq.*; also *Gabriel v. Evill* (1842) 9 M. & W. 297; *Edmundson v. Thompson* (1861) 2 F. & F. 564. Lord Lindley observed that "each of those cases in which the plaintiff failed is an authority for the proposition that so long as there is no partnership there is no implied authority similar to that which exists after a partnership is formed." And see *Keith Spicer v. Mansell* [1970] 1 W.L.R. 333.
[52] *Battley v. Lewis* (1840) 1 Man. & G. 155: see *supra*, para. 2–17. And see *Floydd v. Cheney* [1970] Ch. 602.
[53] In such a case, no partnership will exist during the interim period: see *supra*, para. 12–05.
[54] See *Williams v. Jones* (1826) 5 B. & C. 108.

him with the money or goods agreed to be contributed by him[55]; and the fact that the money or goods so supplied have been brought in by him as agreed will not render the firm liable."[56]

He then referred to *Wilson v. Whitehead*,[57] which was apparently decided on this principle. There, an author and a publisher, who had agreed with a printer to share the profits derived from the publication of a certain work, were held not to be liable for quantities of paper ordered by the printer.[58] However, it would seem that, even assuming the decision to have been correct,[59] it should more properly be regarded as a case of restricted authority.[60]

It must not be assumed that an act which appears to be merely **13–22** preparatory will always be regarded as such; this is illustrated by two cases which involved similar facts but strikingly different results. In the first, *Saville v. Robertson*,[61] several persons agreed to embark on a venture involving the shipment of certain goods. It was provided that each participant's share in the venture should be proportionate to the quantity of goods which he ordered and shipped and that no participant should be responsible for goods ordered or shipped by another. One ordered goods but did not pay for them and the supplier sought payment from the others on the basis that they were liable as his partners. The court held that the partnership did not commence until the goods were on board ship, that each partner was only to bring in his share of the cargo and that the other partners were not liable to the supplier of the goods which made up the defaulting partner's share.[62]

The venture in *Gouthwaite v. Duckworth*[63] was of a similar nature, **13–23** but two of the participants, Browne and Powell, were already in partnership together and were indebted to the third, Duckworth. It

---

[55] See *Greenslade v. Dower* (1828) 7 B. & C. 636; *Dickinson v. Valpy* (1829) 10 B. & C. 128; *Fisher v. Tayler* (1843) 2 Hare 218; also the cases in the next note.

[56] *Smith v. Craven* (1831) 1 C. & J. 500; *Heap v. Dobson* (1863) 15 C.B.(N.S.) 460.

[57] (1842) 10 M. & W. 503. See the observations of Wightman J. on this case in *Kilshaw v. Jukes* (1863) 3 B. & S. 847, 871.

[58] The case was likened to that of coach proprietors, as to which see *Barton v. Hanson* (1809) 2 Taunt. 49. And see *supra*, para. 12–164.

[59] The propriety of the decision was doubted by Wightman J. in *Kilshaw v. Jukes* (1863) 3 B. & S. 847, 871. Moreover, it is difficult to reconcile with *Gardiner v. Childs* (1837) 8 Car. & P. 345.

[60] Lord Lindley submitted that "upon principle *Wilson v. Whitehead* is perfectly correct; for the publisher had no real authority to buy the paper on the author's credit, and no authority so to do ought to be implied in favour of a person who knew nothing of the author or of any partnership or quasi-partnership existing between him and the publisher: see *Kilshaw v. Jukes* (1863) 3 B. & S. 847." And see now the concluding words of Partnership Act 1890, s.5, *supra*, para. 12–02.

[61] (1792) 4 T.R. 720. See also *Kilshaw v. Jukes* (1863) 3 B. & S. 847; *Hutton v. Bullock* (1874) L.R. 9 Q.B. 572.

[62] See also *supra*, para. 12–81.

[63] (1811) 12 East 421. *Kilshaw v. Jukes* (1863) 3 B. & S. 847 was a similar case, but the decision accorded with that in *Saville v. Robertson*, *supra*.

was agreed that the goods should be bought, paid for, and shipped by
Browne and Powell and the proceeds of sale remitted to Duckworth,
who would apply them in settlement of his debt, any remaining profit
(or loss) being shared between the three. In pursuance of this
agreement, Browne bought certain goods on credit, for which all
three partners were ultimately held liable, on the basis that, even
though it was never intended that Duckworth should pay for the
goods, the partnership commenced at and from the moment of their
purchase. Of this case, Lord Lindley said:

> "There is considerable difficulty in supporting this decision if
> rested on the ground of partnership and implied agency resulting
> therefrom; for it is not easy to see how any partnership existed
> prior to the purchase of the goods. But if rested on the ground of
> agency independently of partnership, there is not the same
> difficulty. For although the goods were to be paid for by Browne
> and Powell, that might be regarded as nothing more than a
> stipulation to take effect as between them and Duckworth; it did
> not necessarily exclude the inference that as Browne and Powell
> were to buy for the adventure, they were at liberty to procure the
> goods on the credit of all concerned."[64]

Incoming partners

13–24   It follows from the foregoing that the members of an existing firm
will not be liable for the acts of an incoming partner prior to the date
of his admission; the corollary is also true, *i.e.* that the incoming
partner will not be liable for their acts prior to that date. Lord
Lindley put it in this way:

> "... the firm is not distinguishable from the persons from time to
> time composing it; and when a new member is admitted he
> becomes one of the firm for the future, but not as from the past,
> and his present connection with the firm is no evidence that he
> ever expressly or impliedly authorised what may have been done
> prior to his admission.[65] It may perhaps be said that the entry of
> the new partner amounts to a ratification by him of what his now
> partners may have done before he joined them.[66] But it must be

---

[64] See the judgment of Gibbs J. in *Young v. Hunter* (1812) 4 Taunt. 582, 583. *Gouthwaite v.
Duckworth* was, in fact, followed and Lord Lindley's criticisms considered in *Karmali Abdullah
Allarakhia v. Vora Karimji Jiwanji* (1914) L.R. 42 Ind.App. 48.

[65] See, for example, *Ex p. Jackson* (1790) 1 Ves. Jr. 131; *Young v. Hunter* (1812) 4 Taunt. 582.
Lord Lindley also referred to *Beale v. Mouls* (1843) 10 Q.B. 976 and a number of other cases
demonstrating that the same principle applies as between the promoters of a company: see *Kerridge
v. Hesse* (1839) 9 Car. & P. 200; *Whitehead v. Barron* (1839) 2 Moo. & Rob. 248; *Bremner v.
Chamberlayne* (1848) 2 Car. & K. 569; *Newton v. Belcher* (1848) 12 Q.B. 921; *cf. Beech v. Eyre*
(1843) 5 Man. & G. 415.

[66] See *Horsley v. Bell* (1778) 1 Bro.C.C. 101n., *per* Gould J.

borne in mind that no person can be rendered liable for the act of another on the ground that he has ratified, confirmed, or adopted it, unless, at the time the act was done, it was done professedly on his behalf."[67]

To this might be appended the observation that the admission of an additional partner will, as a matter of law, constitute a new partnership[68] and it should therefore come as no surprise that special circumstances must be shown before that new firm will be treated as having taken over the debts and obligations of the old firm.

Partnership Act 1890, section 17(1)

This principle is expressly recognised by section 17 of the **13–25** Partnership Act 1890, which provides:

"17.—(1) A person who is admitted as a partner into an existing firm does not thereby become liable to the creditors of the firm for anything done before he became a partner."

Scope of section 17(1)

Because section 17(1) of the Partnership Act 1890 is expressed in **13–26** purely negative terms, it does not in itself render an incoming partner liable for debts contracted *after* he became a partner, and the extent of his liability will ultimately depend on the application of normal agency principles.[69] Thus, if a customer refuses to recognise the existence of the new firm and insists on dealing with a member of the old firm, the incoming partner will not in general incur any liability *vis-à-vis* that customer. This was the position in *British Homes Assurance Corporation Ltd. v. Paterson*.[70] There, the plaintiffs, who habitually employed the services of a solicitor, Atkinson (who practised under the name "Atkinson and Atkinson"), instructed him to act on their behalf in a mortgage transaction. Shortly after receiving these instructions, Atkinson took Paterson into partnership, informing the plaintiffs that he had done so and that the business would in future be carried on under the name "Atkinson and Paterson." The plaintiffs ignored this communication and continued to correspond with Atkinson under the old name. The plaintiffs then sent Atkinson a cheque, made payable to "Atkinson and Atkinson or

---

[67] *Wilson v. Tumman* (1843) 6 Man. & G. 236; *Keighley Maxsted & Co. v. Durant & Co.* [1901] A.C. 240.
[68] See *supra*, paras. 3–04 *et seq.*
[69] See *supra*, paras. 12–01 *et seq.*
[70] [1902] 2 Ch. 404.

order," to complete the mortgage transaction. Atkinson indorsed the cheque and signed the receipt in that name, the receipt then being sent to and accepted by the plaintiffs. Atkinson paid the cheque into his personal account, misapplied the proceeds and absconded. Paterson knew nothing of the transaction. It was held that the plaintiffs, by their conduct after receiving notice that Paterson had joined the firm, had elected to abide by the original contract with Atkinson alone and, therefore, declined to accept the joint liability of the two partners; they were, accordingly, bound by that election and could not thereafter pursue Paterson.[71]

New contract

13–27   Equally, the nature of the contractual arrangement with the existing firm may be such that the existence of a fresh contract entered into after the admission of the new partner can be inferred, thus rendering him liable on normal principles.[72] In *Dyke v. Brewer*,[73] the plaintiff had agreed to supply A with bricks at a price quoted per thousand. After supplies began, A took B into partnership. The plaintiff continued to supply bricks as before. A and B were both held liable to pay for the bricks supplied after the commencement of the partnership, at the rate originally quoted to A. The basis for the decision was that A had not ordered a specific number of bricks, so that each separate delivery and acceptance involved a new implied promise to pay on the terms previously agreed; had all the bricks delivered been ordered by A in the first instance, B would not have been liable.[74] Obviously, situations in which this principle can be invoked will be relatively rare.

Agreement to take on existing debts

13–28   It is, of course, open to an incoming partner voluntarily to take on liability for the firm's existing debts; indeed, the offer of partnership may be conditional on him so doing.[75] However, it does not follow from such an agreement that the incoming partner will be directly liable to creditors of the firm, as Lord Lindley explained:

"... if an incoming partner agrees with his co-partners that the debts of the old shall be taken by the new firm, this, although

---

[71] The court held also that the money had never come into the custody of the firm: see the Partnership Act 1890, s.11, *supra*, paras. 12–106 *et seq.*

[72] See *supra*, paras. 12–08 *et seq*. It should be noted that this is *not* a case of novation.

[73] (1849) 2 Car. & K. 828.

[74] *Helsby v. Mears* (1826) 5 B. & C. 504 was decided on the same basis: see *Beale v. Mouls* (1843) 10 Q.B. 976, 984, *per* Lord Denman.

[75] See generally, *supra*, para. 10–45.

valid and binding between the partners, is, as regards strangers, *res inter alios acta*, and does not confer upon them any right to fix the old debts on the new partner.[76] In order to render an incoming partner liable to the creditors of the old firm, there must be some agreement, express or tacit, to that effect entered into between him and the creditors, and founded on some sufficient considera- tion. If there be any such agreement, the incoming partner will be bound by it, but his liabilities in respect of the old debts will attach by virtue of the new agreement, and not by reason of his having become a partner."

It should be noted that an incoming partner who agrees to the debts of the existing firm being discharged out of profits received after the date of his admission may, *vis-à-vis* his co-partners, be accepting indirect liability for those debts, if his profit share is thereby reduced.

Evidence of agreement

An incoming partner's agreement to take on *direct* liability for the **13–29** existing debts of the firm will usually be a matter of inference.[77] Lord Lindley observed:

"The Courts, it has been said, lean in favour of such an agreement, and are ready to infer it from slight circumstances[78]; and they seem formerly to have inferred it whenever the incoming partner agreed with the other partners to treat such debts as those of the new firm.[79] But this certainly is not enough, for the agreement to be proved is an agreement with the creditor; and of such an agreement an agreement between the partners is of itself no evidence."[80]

The current editor doubts whether the courts would now be quite as ready to draw the necessary inference, although, as regards the incoming partner, the question is likely to be of only academic

---

[76] See *Vere v. Ashby* (1829) 10 B & C. 288, 298, *per* Parke J.; also *Ex p. Peele* (1802) 6 Ves. Jr. 602; *Ex p. Williams* (1817) Buck 13.

[77] In practice, the partners may not wish to draw attention to the change in the firm or, for that matter, to offer a creditor *additional* rights. Nevertheless, in the case of leases, landlords now sometimes require incoming partners to enter into express surety covenants: see *supra*, para. 12–174 and, *infra*, para. 18–60.

[78] *Ex p. Jackson* (1790) 1 Ves. Jr. 131; *Ex p. Peele* (1802) 6 Ves. Jr. 602. See also *Rolfe v. Flower* (1865) L.R. 1 P.C. 27.

[79] See *Cooke's Bankruptcy Law* (8th ed.), p. 534, citing *Ex p. Bingham* and *Ex p. Clowes* (1789) 2 Bro.C.C. 595.

[80] *Ex p. Peele* (1802) 6 Ves. Jr. 602; *Ex p. Parker* (1842) 2 M.D. & D. 511. See also *Ex p. Williams* (1817) Buck 13; *Ex p. Freeman* (1819) Buck 471; *Ex p. Fry* (1821) 1 Gl. & J. 96.

interest since the *quantum* of his potential liability will be unaffected.[81]

13-30   An example of the type of evidence required to establish such an agreement is to be found in *Ex p. Whitmore*.[82] In that case Warwick, having taken Clagett into partnership, duly informed persons with whom he had previously had business dealings in America of this fact, requesting them to make up their accounts and to transfer any balance due to or from him to the new firm. These instructions were subsequently repeated and confirmed by both Warwick and Clagett and acted on. A debt owing from Warwick was treated as a debt of the new firm and a bill of exchange was drawn on the firm for the amount of the debt. This bill was accepted but later dishonoured. On the bankruptcy of the firm, it was held that the debt had become the joint debt of Warwick and Clagett and that their joint liability had been accepted in substitution for the sole liability of Warwick.

Fraud on new partner

13-31   If the incoming partner has *not* agreed to undertake liability for the debts of the existing firm, but the other partners nevertheless settle such a debt by means of a bill of exchange drawn and accepted in his and their names, this will prima facie amount to a fraud on the incoming partner and he will not be liable on the bill.[83] On the same principle, it is considered that an incoming partner will not be bound if one of his co-partners states an account, admitting that such a debt is due from the new firm.[84]

The position in the case of an open running account maintained both before and after the date of the incoming partner's admission is more complex, as will been seen hereafter.[85]

B. Termination of Agency

13-32 It is a self evident proposition that each partner's express or implied authority to bind the firm will, on normal agency principles, continue until such time as it is revoked and notice of the revocation is given to any third party with whom he deals.[86] Of a partner's *implied* authority, Lord Lindley said:

---

[81] If the partnership is solvent, the incoming partner will be bound to contribute his due share of the liability, either by way of a reduction in his profit share or by way of contribution. If the other partners are insolvent, have absconded or are otherwise beyond the jurisdiction of the court, the creditor can in any event present a petition to wind up the firm, in which case the incoming partner, *qua* contributory, will be unable to evade the liability which he originally agreed to undertake. See further, *infra*, paras. 27–60 *et seq.*

[82] (1838) 3 Deac. 365. See also *Rolfe v. Flower* (1865) L.R. 1 P.C. 27.

[83] See *Shirreff v. Wilks* (1800) 1 East 48. See also *supra*, para. 12–158.

[84] See *French v. French* (1841) 2 Man. & G. 644; *Lemere v. Elliott* (1861) 6 H. & N. 656.

[85] See *infra*, paras. 13–81 *et seq.*

[86] See *supra*, paras. 12–147 *et seq.*

"The same reason which leads to the imputation of the power to act for the firm at all, demands that such power shall be imputed so long as it can be exercised and is not known to have been determined."[87]

It is the latter question, *i.e.* notice of the revocation of a partner's authority, that gives rise to difficulty in practice.

Express revocation

Implied authority

There is very little authority on the ability of a partner unilaterally **13–33** to revoke the authority of his co-partner whilst the partnership continues; the Partnership Act 1890 is itself silent on the point. Writing prior to that Act, Lord Lindley put forward the following view:

"The agency of each partner in an ordinary firm, and his consequent power to bind the firm, *i.e.* himself and his co-partners, may be determined by notice at any time during the continuance of the partnership[88]; for his power to act for the firm is not a right attaching to him as partner independently of the will of his co-partners, and although any stipulations amongst the partners themselves will not affect non-partners who have not notice of them, yet if any person has notice that one member of the firm is not authorised to act for it, that person cannot hold the firm liable for anything done in the teeth of such notice."[89]

On the other hand, in the 6th[90] and subsequent editions of this work, the following view was espoused:

"On general principles it would seem that unless he is in a position to dissolve the firm a notice that he will no longer be bound by their acts will be inoperative."[91]

---

[87] See *Lindern Trawler Managers. v. W. H. J. Trawlers* (1949) 83 Ll.L.Rep. 131. And see also *Scarf v. Jardine* (1882) 7 App.Cas. 345, *supra*, paras. 5–62, 13–04.

[88] Lord Lindley referred specifically to *Gallway v. Matthew* (1808) 10 East 264; *Willis v. Dyson* (1816) 1 Stark. 164; *Rooth v. Quin* (1819) 7 Price 193; *Vice v. Fleming* (1827) 1 Y. & J. 227. See also *Ex p. Holdsworth* (1841) 1 M.D. & D. 475.

[89] See *supra*, paras. 12–147 *et seq*. But note the precise terms of the Partnership Act 1890, s.8, *supra*, para. 12–148.

[90] Lord Lindley apparently approved the contents of this edition.

[91] A dissolution will not itself terminate the other partners' authority: see the Partnership Act 1890, s.38, *infra*, paras. 13–64 *et seq*.

13-34   Faced with these conflicting opinions, it is submitted that, in the absence of some contrary agreement, the true position as between the partners is as follows:

1. A revocation which purports to exclude one or more partners from their rightful participation in the management of the partnership business cannot be effective.[92]
2. Subject thereto, a majority of the partners may properly decide to introduce an express or implied limitation on the authority of each and every partner, if that can be justified as an ordinary matter connected with the partnership business.[93] This may take the form of a resolution that certain acts will, in the future, require the concurrence of two partners, *e.g.* cheque signing, or an alteration in the way in which the partnership business is carried on which incidentally alters the scope of each partner's implied authority.[94]
3. An attempt to place limitations on the implied authority of a single partner or group of partners would be unlikely to qualify as an ordinary matter and would, therefore, appear to be improper.[95]

13-35   A purported, but invalid, revocation of a partner's authority would not take effect as a notice of dissolution,[96] but might amount to an act of repudiation.[97] It would in any event prima facie give grounds for seeking an order dissolving the partnership.[98]

Of course, until such time as an *effective* revocation has been communicated to third parties, it can only have effect as between the partners *inter se*.[99]

Express authority

13-36   If express authority has been conferred on a partner under the terms of the partnership agreement, any attempt to revoke that authority would obviously involve varying those terms. On that basis, it is submitted that a purported revocation would only be valid if it is

---

[92] *Ibid.* ss.19, 24(5), 25: see *supra*, paras. 10–10 *et seq.* and *infra*, paras. 15–01 *et seq.*, 24–85. Note that there was a purported revocation of a partner's implied authority (limited to the service of a counter notice under the agricultural holdings legislation) in *Sykes v. Land* (1984) 271 E.G. 1264, but its effectiveness was not commented on by the court; a similar point was left open in *Re Sutherland & Partners' Appeal* [1993] S.T.C. 399 and was not commented on in the Court of Appeal at [1994] S.T.C. 387.
[93] See *ibid.* s.24(8), *infra*, paras. 15–05 *et seq.*
[94] *Ibid.* s.19, *supra*, paras. 10–10 *et seq.*
[95] But see *supra*, n. 92.
[96] See *infra*, para. 24–14.
[97] See *infra*, para. 24–04.
[98] Partnership Act 1890, s.35(d), (f): see *infra*, paras. 24–66 *et seq.*, 24–75.
[99] See *Gleadon v. Tinkler* (1817) Holt, N.P. 586; also, *supra*, para. 12–147.

expressly or impliedly accepted by the relevant partner[1] or if the agreement permits such a variation to be introduced against his wishes.[2] In any other circumstances, there would be a clear, and possibly repudiatory, breach of the agreement, as well as grounds for seeking a dissolution.[3]

On the other hand, if authority is only conferred on an *ad hoc* basis, it can *prima facie* be revoked at any time.[4]

Notice of purported revocation

If the express or implied authority of a partner is purportedly **13–37** revoked and a third party is notified of such revocation, he can thereafter safely deal with that partner only *qua* principal.[5] However, there would seem to be no reason why he should not hold the firm liable as an undisclosed principal[6] if the partner's authority did in fact continue; *sed quaere.*

It is submitted that the act of giving notice of a wrongful revocation might itself amount to a repudiatory breach of the partnership agreement[7] and could also found a claim for dissolution.[8]

Mental incapacity

If a partner becomes subject to a mental disorder but this is neither **13–38** apparent nor made known,[9] his power to bind the firm and his liability for the acts of his co-partners[10] will seemingly be unaffected.

Outgoing partners

It is obvious that when a person ceases to be a partner, he will no **13–39** longer be the agent of his co-partners nor they his agents, save for the purpose of winding up the firm's affairs (should that be required).[11] However, as regards third parties, effective termination of each partner's ostensible agency will normally depend on notice having been given of the change in or the dissolution of the firm (as the case may be). It is here that difficulties frequently arise.

---

[1] Partnership Act 1890, s.19, *supra*, para. 10–10.
[2] See *supra*, para. 10–11.
[3] See, as to repudiation, *infra*, para. 24–04 and, as to dissolution, the Partnership Act 1890, s.35(d), (f), *infra*, paras. 24–66 *et seq.*, 24–75.
[4] See *Tomlinson v. Broadsmith* [1896] 1 Q.B. 386 (managing partner).
[5] See *supra*, paras. 12–153 *et seq.*
[6] See *supra*, para. 12–163.
[7] See *infra*, para. 24–04.
[8] See the Partnership Act 1890, s.35(d), (f), *infra*, paras. 24–66 *et seq.*, 24–75.
[9] *Per contra* if Court of Protection proceedings have been initiated: *Re Walker* [1905] 1 Ch. 160; *Re Marshall* [1920] 1 Ch. 284; and see, generally, Heywood & Massey, *Court of Protection Practice* (12th ed.), p. 227.
[10] See *Imperial Loan Co. v. Stone* [1892] 1 Q.B. 599; also *Baxter v. The Earl of Portsmouth* (1826) 5 B. & C. 170; *Molton v. Camroux* (1849) 4 Ex. 17; *Drew v. Nunn* (1879) 4 Q.B.D. 661. And see *infra*, paras. 24–49 *et seq.*
[11] See the Partnership Act 1890, s.38, *infra*, paras. 13–64 *et seq.*

Position prior to the Partnership Act 1890

13–40   Lord Lindley summarised the position in these terms:

> "... when a dormant (*i.e.* non-apparent) partner retires, he need give no notice of his retirement in order to free himself from liability in respect of acts done after his retirement.[12] The reason is that, as he was never known to be a partner, no one can have relied on his connection with the firm, or truly allege that, when dealing with the firm, he continued to rely on the fact that the dormant partner was still connected therewith.
>
> But when an ostensible partner retires, or when a partnership between several known partners is dissolved, the case is very different; for then those who dealt with the firm before a change took place are entitled to assume that no change has occurred until they have notice to the contrary.[13] And even those who never had dealings with the firm, and who only knew of its existence by repute, are entitled to assume that it still exists until something is done to notify publicly that it exists no longer.[14] An old customer, however, is entitled to a more specific notice than a person who never dealt with the firm at all[15]; and in considering whether notice of dissolution or retirement is or is not sufficient, a distinction must be made according as the person sought to be affected by notice was or was not a customer of the old firm."

Position under the Partnership Act 1890

13–41   The Partnership Act 1890 embodies precisely the same principles. The relevant sections will be set out in full and then considered under three natural headings, namely (a) when such notice requires to be given and when it may be dispensed with; (b) the effect of such notice, once given; and (c) the form of such notice.

Partnership Act 1890, sections 36 and 37

13–42   The Partnership Act 1890 provides as follows:

> "36.—(1) Where a person deals with a firm after a change in its constitution he is entitled to treat all apparent members[16] of the

---

[12] See now the Partnership Act 1890, s.36(3), *infra*, para. 13–42.

[13] *Scarf v. Jardine* (1882) 7 App.Cas. 345, 349, *per* Lord Selborne. See now the Partnership Act 1890, s.36(1), *infra*, para. 13–42.

[14] *Parkin v. Carruthers* (1800) 3 Esp. 248. See now the Partnership Act 1890, s.36(1), *infra*, para. 13–42.

[15] *Graham v. Hope* (1792) Peake 208. See now the Partnership Act 1890, s.36(1), (2), *infra*, para. 13–42.

[16] In his Supplement on the Partnership Act 1890, Lord Lindley queried whether these words were intended to refer only to those partners whose names are included in the firm name, but

—*continued on next page*

old firm as still being members of the firm until he has notice of the change.

(2) An advertisement in the *London Gazette* as to a firm whose principal place of business is in England or Wales, in the *Edinburgh Gazette* as to a firm whose principal place of business is in Scotland, and in the *[Belfast]*[17] *Gazette* as to a firm whose principal place of business is in Ireland, shall be notice as to persons who had no dealings with the firm before the date of the dissolution or change so advertised.

(3) The estate of a partner who dies, or who becomes bankrupt, or of a partner who, not having been known to the person dealing with the firm to be a partner, retires from the firm, is not liable for partnership debts contracted after the date of the death, bankruptcy, or retirement[18] respectively.[19]

37. On the dissolution of a partnership or retirement[20] of a partner any partner may publicly notify the same, and may require the other partner or partners to concur for that purpose in all necessary or proper acts, if any, which cannot be done without his or their concurrence."

(a) Need for notice

Position in absence of notice

Section 36(1) of the Partnership Act 1890 merely applies the **13–43** normal rules of agency to an outgoing partner, *i.e.* the implied authority of his co-partners will continue until notice of its revocation is given.[21] Thus, if no notice is given, an outgoing partner may be liable on a promissory note given by his former partners after the date of his departure.[22]

Liability under the subsection is independent of (and strictly distinguishable from) that imposed in cases of pure holding out,[23]

---

[16]—*continued from previous page*
concluded that the question was of no practical importance, since persons who are otherwise known to be partners would, under the pre-existing law, have been liable in any event. And see *Tower Cabinet Co. Ltd. v. Ingram* [1949] 2 K.B. 397; *Bishop v. Tudor Estates* [1952] C.L.Y. 2493.

[17] A reference to the Belfast *Gazette* is substituted for the Dublin *Gazette* by virtue of the General Adaptation of Enactments (Northern Ireland) Order 1921 (S.R. & O. 1921 No. 1804), Art. 7(a).

[18] Of course, in the case of a partnership at will, the retirement of a partner may result in a dissolution: see the Partnership Act 1890, s.26(1), 32(c), *infra*, paras. 24–10 *et seq.*

[19] See *Court v. Berlin* [1897] 2 Q.B. 396, *infra*, para. 13–56.

[20] See *supra*, n. 18.

[21] See *Mulford v. Griffin* (1858) 1 F. & F. 145; *Faldo v. Griffin* (1858) 1 F. & F. 147. And see *supra*, paras. 5–54 *et seq.*, 12–30.

[22] See *Parkin v. Carruthers* (1800) 3 Esp. 248; *Brown v. Leonard* (1816) 2 Chitty 120; *Williams v. Keats* (1817) 2 Stark. 290; *Dolman v. Orchard* (1825) 2 C. & P. 104. See further, *supra*, paras. 5–58, 5–59.

[23] Partnership Act 1890, s.14, *supra*, paras. 5–43 *et seq.*

since a prospective plaintiff does not have to prove any form of reliance other than the fact that he dealt with the firm. His previous dealings with the firm (or lack of them) are prima facie irrelevant.

Partially dormant partner

13-44   A truly dormant partner will, by definition, not be an apparent member of the firm, so that section 36(1) will not apply to him.[24] If, however, his existence has been disclosed to any third party with whom the firm has had dealings, notice must be given to that third party if continuing liability is to be avoided.[25]

Expelled partner

13-45   Although sections 36 and 37 refer only to the "retirement" of a partner, it is submitted that they will equally apply where a partner is expelled under an express power in the agreement.[26]

Torts

13-46   Whilst section 36(1) will not in its terms apply,[27] an outgoing partner who fails to give notice of his retirement may also expose himself to the risk of liability in respect of torts committed by his co-partners.[28]

Unilateral power to notify retirement or dissolution

13-47   Each partner is given an express statutory power to give notice of the dissolution of the partnership or of the retirement (or expulsion)[29] of a partner.[30] However, that right may be excluded by agreement.[31] If, in the absence of any such agreement, a partner is prevented from exercising that right, his co-partners can be compelled to do whatever may be necessary to ensure that the requisite notice is given, *e.g.* to sign advertisements for publication in the *Gazette*.[32]

---

[24] See *infra*, paras. 13–54 *et seq*.

[25] See the Partnership Act 1890, s.36(3). This was also the position before the Act: see *Farrar v. Deflinne* (1844) 1 Car. & K. 580; also *Evans v. Drummond* (1801) 4 Esp. 89; *Carter v. Whalley* (1830) 1 B. & Ad. 11.

[26] But note that the Partnership Act 1890 does contain *one* reference to expulsion: see *ibid*. s.25, *infra*, para. 24–85. And see generally, as to powers of expulsion, *supra*, paras. 10–94 *et seq*.

[27] The section only applies in favour of a person who "deals with a firm"; and see also s.36(3).

[28] See *Stables v. Eley* (1825) 1 Car. & P. 614, where the true circumstances were proved but liability was based on holding out. However, it is doubtful whether this decision was correct: see *supra*, para. 5–68.

[29] See *supra*, para. 13–45.

[30] Partnership Act 1890, s.37, *supra*, para. 13–42.

[31] See *supra*, para. 10–210.

[32] *Troughton v. Hunter* (1854) 18 Beav. 470; *Hendry v. Turner* (1886) 32 Ch.D. 355.

Circumstances where no notice required

Section 36(3) of the Partnership Act 1890 provides for three **13-48** obvious exceptions to the general rule, in which freedom from continuing liability is not dependent on notice.

(1) *Death*

It is settled law that the authority of an agent is determined by the **13-49** death of his principal, so that, even before the Partnership Act 1890, Lord Lindley could write:

"Notice of death is not requisite to prevent liability from attaching to the estate of a deceased partner, in respect of what may be done by his co-partners after his decease."[33]

Authority given on behalf of firm

However, if a partner authorises a person to do an act, but the **13-50** authority in fact derives from the firm, it will be unaffected by that partner's death and any subsequent exercise will bind the surviving partners. Thus, in *Usher v. Dauncey*,[34] a partner drew and indorsed a number of bills of exchange in blank and gave them to a clerk to be completed and negotiated as and when required. The partner died and the firm name was altered. The clerk then completed and negotiated one of the bills. Lord Ellenborough held that the bill was binding on the surviving partners, on the footing that the clerk's authority derived from the firm and not from the deceased partner.

Contribution due from deceased partner

Even though a deceased partner's estate may not be *directly* liable **13-51** for the acts of the surviving partners after the date of death, it may nevertheless be liable to contribute towards debts and liabilities incurred after that date. This will, however, depend on the precise terms agreed.[35]

---

[33] See now the Partnership Act 1890, s.14(2), s.36(3), *supra*, paras. 5–43, 13–42; *Friend v. Young* [1897] 2 Ch. 421. Lord Lindley referred to *Webster v. Webster* (1791) 3 Swan. 490; *Devaynes v. Noble, Houlton's Case* (1816) 1 Mer. 616; *Johnes' Case* (1816) 1 Mer. 619; *Brice's Case* (1816) 1 Mer. 620. Also *Vulliamy v. Noble* (1817) 3 Mer. 593; *Brown v. Gordon* (1852) 16 Beav. 302, as to the position of surviving partners who are the executors of a deceased partner's will.

[34] (1814) 4 Camp. 97.

[35] See *Blakeley's Executor's Case* (1851) 3 Mac. & G. 726; *Hamer's Devisees' Case* (1852) 2 De G.M. & G. 366; *Baird's Case* (1870) L.R. 5 Ch. App. 725; also *McClean v. Kennard* (1874) L.R. 9 Ch. App. 356.

(2) *Insolvency*

13–52 Again, the effect of a partner's bankruptcy is just as it was prior to the Partnership Act 1890, as is clear from the following observation made by Lord Lindley:

> "If one partner only becomes bankrupt, his authority is at an end,[36] and his estate cannot be made liable for the subsequent acts of his solvent co-partners."[37]

Equally, if the solvent partners continue to hold the bankrupt partner out as a member of the firm, they will be liable for *his* acts.[38] If the partnership is dissolved by reason of the bankruptcy,[39] the solvent partners will, of course, have authority to wind up the firm's affairs.[40]

Insolvency of corporate partner

13–53 Since neither the presentation of a winding-up petition nor the making of a winding-up order against a corporate partner constitute "bankruptcy,"[41] section 36(3) of the 1890 Act will not apply.

Insolvency of firm

If, on the other hand, the firm is wound up as an unregistered company,[42] there will be no possibility of subsequent dealings with the firm, otherwise than through the liquidator, so that section 36 of the 1890 Act will be of no relevance.

(3) *Dormant Partner*

13–54 Section 36(3) of the Partnership Act 1890 exempts persons who are not known to be partners, *i.e.* truly dormant partners,[43] from the need to give notice of their retirement. Since such persons would not in any event be exposed to continuing liability under section 36(1),[44]

---

[36] See the Partnership Act 1890, ss.33(1), 38, proviso. But note that s.33(1) may be excluded by agreement: see *supra*, para. 10–33 and *infra*, para. 24–22.

[37] Partnership Act 1890, s.36(3), *supra*, para. 13–42.

[38] *Ibid.* s.38, proviso, *infra*, para. 13–64. As to the position before the Act, see *Lacy v. Woolcott* (1823) 2 Dow. & Ry. 458.

[39] *Ibid.* s.33(1) and, *infra*, paras. 24–22 *et seq.*

[40] *Ibid.* s.38, *infra*, para. 13–64. See also *infra*, paras. 27–67 *et seq.*

[41] *Cf.* the Law of Property Act 1925, s.205(1)(i). And see *infra*, paras. 24–25 *et seq.*

[42] See *infra*, paras. 27–57 *et seq.*

[43] As to the position of partners who are only *partially* dormant, see *supra*, para. 13–44.

[44] As dormant partners, they cannot be "apparent members" of the old firm. See, generally, *Elders Pastoral Ltd. v. Rutherford* noted at [1991] N.Z.L.J. 73 (a decision under the equivalent provision of the New Zealand Partnership Act 1908).

such an express exemption was scarcely required. The position was the same prior to the Act, as Lord Lindley explained:

"Another apparent but not real exception to the rule is that if a dormant partner (*i.e.* one not known to be a partner) retires, the authority of his late partners to bind him ceases on his retirement, although no notice of it be given.[45] But this is because he never was known to be a partner at all, and the reason for the general rule has therefore no application to his case."

Thus, in *Carter v. Whalley*,[46] Saunders was a partner in the "Plas **13–55** Madoc Colliery Co." but there was no evidence that his involvement in the business was known either to the plaintiff or to the public at large. Saunders retired but no notice was given of that fact. The firm later became indebted to the plaintiff. Saunders was held not to be liable for the debt, since the firm name did not indicate the identity of the partners and he was not known to be a partner, either to the plaintiff or generally, prior to his retirement. *Heath v. Sansom*[47] was a similar case.

The decision in *Court v. Berlin*[48] requires explanation as an **13–56** apparent (but not real) exception to this principle. There an active partner in a firm, which comprised himself and two dormant partners, retained a solicitor to conduct an action for the recovery of a partnership debt. The dormant partners retired while the proceedings were still pending, but were nevertheless held liable for the solicitor's costs incurred *after* the date of their retirement, even though the solicitor never knew of their existence. However, the true basis for the decision lay in the nature of the solicitor's retainer, which authorised him to conduct the action until its conclusion;[49] that retainer having been given whilst the dormant partners were still members of the firm, their liability continued on normal principles. Although the retainer could have been terminated by the dormant partners, that would have required notice to the solicitor, which was never given. Accordingly, there was no scope for the application of section 36(3).

---

[45] See the Partnership Act 1890, s.36(3).

[46] (1830) 1 B. & Ad. 11.

[47] (1831) 4 B. & Ad. 172. Note that, in this case, the firm name comprised the name of the active partner. See also *Evans v. Drummond* (1801) 4 Esp. 89. Lord Lindley pointed out in a footnote that "The case of the *Western Bank of Scotland v. Needell* (1859) 1 F. & F. 461, seems at first sight opposed to the authorities in the text, but it is conceived that in that case there must have been evidence to show that the defendant was known to the plaintiffs to have been a partner before he retired."

[48] [1897] 2 Q.B. 396.

[49] See *Elders Pastoral Ltd. v. Rutherford* noted at [1991] N.Z.L.J. 73. See generally, as to the duration of a solicitor's retainer, *Cordery on Solicitors* (8th ed.), pp. 71 *et seq.*

Technically dormant partner

13–57   It should be noted that the application of section 36(3) is not
confined merely to dormant partners in the true sense: it may equally
well apply in the case of a outgoing *active* partner, provided that the
conditions are fulfilled at the relevant time. Thus, in *Tower Cabinet
Co. v. Ingram,*[50] one partner, the defendant, retired, leaving the
other to carry on the business in the firm name. Thereafter, the
plaintiff company, which had not previously dealt with or had any
knowledge of the firm, received an order from it which, by mistake,
was written on its old notepaper and showed the defendant as a
partner. The defendant was held to be relieved of liability because, at
the date of his retirement, the requirements of section 36(3) were
satisfied.

Business Names Act 1985

13–58   Although the provisions of the Business Names Act 1985[51] have
reduced the scope for partners to maintain dormant status, section
36(3) of the Partnership Act 1890 will still apply in cases where such
provisions are not, for whatever reason, complied with. Thus, there
are no truly effective safeguards against mistakes of the type
exemplified in *Tower Cabinet Co. v. Ingram.*[52]

(b)   Effect of notice

The general principle

13–59   The effect of giving notice either of the dissolution of a firm or of
the retirement of a partner[53] was summarised by Lord Lindley prior
to the Partnership Act 1890 in this way:

"Subject to two exceptions, . . . notice of dissolution of a firm or of
the retirement of a partner duly given, determines the power
previously possessed by each partner to bind the others. Hence,
after the dissolution of a firm or the retirement of a member and
notification of the fact, no member of the previously existing firm
is, by virtue of his connection therewith, liable for goods supplied
to any of his partners subsequently to the notification[54]; nor is he

---

[50] [1949] 2 K.B. 397.
[51] *Ibid.* s.4: see *supra,* para. 3–32.
[52] [1949] 2 K.B. 397. See *supra,* para. 13–57.
[53] This will include cases of expulsion: see *supra,* para. 13–45.
[54] *Minnit v. Whinery* (1721) 5 Bro.P.C. 489.

liable on bills or notes subsequently drawn, accepted, or indorsed by any of them in the name of the late firm[55]; even although they may have been dated before the dissolution[56]; or have been given for a debt previously owing from the firm[57] by the partner expressly authorised to get in and discharge its debts."[58]

Although Lord Lindley only referred specifically to two exceptions to the general principle, he in fact went on to consider three, namely (1) bills or notes binding on outgoing partners in special cases; (2) continued holding out; and (3) continuing authority for the purposes of winding up the affairs of a dissolved firm. Each of these exceptions will now be considered in turn.

Exceptional cases in which liability continues

(4) Bills of Exchange and Promissory Notes—Special Cases

All of the cases in this supposed class had distinct features which **13–60** justified a departure from the normal rule. Thus, in Burton v. Issitt,[59] the continuing partner had authority to use the name of the retired partner in any proceedings for the recovery of partnership property; this authority was held to extend to giving a promissory note for the sum of sixpence payable to the defendant under what was known as the Lord's Act.[60] Similarly, in Smith v. Winter,[61] the continuing partner had express permission to use the former partner's name and his liability on a bill of exchange given in the old firm name after the date of his retirement was not seriously in doubt.

A more perplexing decision was that in Lewis v. Reilly.[62] There **13–61** two partners, A and B, had previously drawn a bill of exchange payable to their own order. They then dissolved their partnership and A indorsed the bill to the plaintiff in the firm name. Although the plaintiff appears to have known of the dissolution, it was held that this was immaterial and that he was entitled to recover on the bill against both of the former partners. Lord Lindley observed:

"The precise ground of this decision does not distinctly appear. The Court seems to have proceeded on the supposition that an

---

[55] Ex p. Central Bank of London [1892] 2 Q.B. 633; also Abel v. Sutton (1800) 3 Esp. 108; Paterson v. Zachariah (1815) 1 Stark. 71; Spenceley v. Greenwood (1858) 1 F. & F. 297.
[56] Wrightson v. Pullan (1816) 1 Stark.
[57] Kilgour v. Finlyson (1789) 1 H.Bl. 155; Dolman v. Orchard (1825) 2 Car. & P. 104.
[58] Kilgour v. Finlyson, supra. But see also infra, para. 13–61.
[59] (1821) 5 B. & A. 267.
[60] The Debtors Imprisonment Act 1758.
[61] (1838) 4 M. & W. 454.
[62] (1841) 1 Q.B. 349.

indorsement by one of several payees in the name of all is sufficient; but the writer has been unable to find any previous authority for such a doctrine, save where the indorsers are partners, which in the case in question they were not, as the plaintiff was found by the jury to have known. The case is certainly anomalous and requires reconsideration."[63]

It is the opinion of the current editor that, *Lewis v. Reilly* apart, this class (if, indeed, such an appellation is justified) represents little more than examples of liability imposed by reason of express authority or holding out.

(5)   *Continued Holding Out*

13–62 If, notwithstanding notification of his retirement,[64] an outgoing partner permits himself to be represented as a continuing member of the firm, he will, on normal principles, be liable to any third party who gives credit to the firm in reliance on that representation.[65] Whether merely authorising his former partners to continue using the old firm name will have that result has already been considered earlier in this work.[66]

(6)   *Continuing Authority for Purposes of Winding Up*

13–63 Prior to the Partnership Act 1890, the extent of each partner's authority to bind his co-partners following a dissolution was in doubt, although Lord Lindley submitted that the true position was as follows:

"... notwithstanding dissolution, a partner has implied authority to bind the firm so far as may be necessary to settle and liquidate existing demands, and to complete transactions begun, but unfinished, at the time of the dissolution."[67]

---

[63] See *Abel v. Sutton* (1800) 3 Esp. 108. Lord Lindley added in a footnote "The cases go further than is suggested in *Garland v. Jacomb* (1873) L.R. 8 Ex. 216, for the notice of dissolution is what creates the difficulty."

[64] Or expulsion: see *supra*, para. 13–45.

[65] Partnership Act 1890, s.14, *supra*, paras. 5–43 *et seq*. And see *Brown v. Leonard* (1816) 2 Chitty 120; also *Bishop v. Tudor Estates* [1952] C.L.Y. 2493.

[66] See *supra*, paras. 5–54 *et seq*., 10–163. Note also the implications of the Business Names Act 1985, *supra*, paras. 5–70, 5–71.

[67] See *Lyon v. Haynes* (1843) 5 Man. & G. 541; also *Smith v. Winter* (1838) 4 M. & W. 454, 462, *per* Parke B. For cases supporting the less restrictive view, see *Ex p. Williams* (1805) 11 Ves. Jr. 3; *Crawshay v. Collins* (1808) 15 Ves. Jr. 218 and (1826) 2 Russ. 325; *Peacock v. Peacock* (1809) 16 Ves. Jr. 49; *Wilson v. Greenwood* (1818) 1 Swan. 471; *Crawshay v. Maule* (1818) 1 Swan. 495; *Butchart v. Dresser* (1853) 4 De G.M. & G. 542. But note that Lord Eldon's observations were all *obiter*, since in none of the cases did any question concerning the authority of a partner following a dissolution strictly arise for decision.

Partnership Act 1890, section 38

Lord Lindley's summary presaged the content of section 38 of the **13–64**
Partnership Act 1890, which provides as follows:

"38. After the dissolution of a partnership the authority of each
partner to bind the firm, and the other rights and obligations of
the partners continue notwithstanding the dissolution so far as may
be necessary to wind up the affairs of the partnership, and to
complete transactions begun but unfinished at the time of the
dissolution, but not otherwise.

Provided that the firm is in no case bound by the acts of a
partner who has become bankrupt; but this proviso does not affect
the liability of any person who has after the bankruptcy
represented himself or knowingly suffered himself to be represented as a partner of the bankrupt."[68]

Duty of partners under section

The scope and practical consequences of section 38 were **13–65**
considered by the House of Lords in *I.R.C. v. Graham's Trustees*,[69]
where Lord Reid observed:

"What is meant by transactions begun but unfinished when the
partnership was dissolved? If the common law had been clearly
settled before 1890, I would interpret this section in light of the
earlier law. But it appears that there was then little authority on
this matter. So this section should if possible be construed so as to
reach a reasonable result. It was argued that 'transactions' meant
bargains. But that would deprive this provision of all content, for it
is clear that surviving partners have no right to bind the assets of
the dissolved firm by making new bargains and contracts. Their
right and duty is to wind up its affairs. In my view this must mean
that the surviving partners have the right and duty to complete all
unfinished operations necessary to fulfil contracts of the firm which
were still in force when the firm was dissolved.

Otherwise the position would be intolerable. Suppose the firm
was employed to build a bridge and the bridge was half finished
when the firm was dissolved. The surviving partners must be
bound to finish the work, for otherwise they could hold the
employer to ransom by refusing to proceed unless he made a new
contract more favourable to them, and conversely the employer
could refuse to allow the work to proceed unless the surviving

---

[68] See, as to this proviso, *supra*, para. 13–52.
[69] 1971 S.L.T. 46.

partners made a new contract more favourable to him. That could not be right."[70]

Naturally, whilst attending to unfinished business, the partners must show a proper degree of care and skill if they are to avoid liability in negligence to third parties; such claims will naturally be unaffected by the dissolution.[71]

It has already been seen that the apparent inability of the partners to take on new business (otherwise than at their own individual risk) appears to conflict with their obligation to preserve the goodwill of the firm pending its realisation.[72]

Scope of a partner's implied authority

13–66   Notwithstanding Lord Reid's strictures about the state of the law prior to the Partnership Act 1890,[73] the current editor's view is that a partner will clearly have authority to do any of the following acts in the course of winding up the firm's affairs:

Bills and notes: A partner may draw, accept or indorse a bill of exchange of promissory note in settlement of (or as security for) partnership debts.[74] Moreover, notice of dishonour may be given to a single partner.[75]

Contracts: A partner may complete a current contract, whether involving the supply of goods or services.[76]

Debts: A partner may pay a debt owing by or receive payment of a debt owing to the firm.[77]

Deposits: A partner may withdraw money deposited with the firm's bankers.[78]

---

[70] *Ibid.* p.48; see also *Hillerns and Fowler v. Murray* (1932) 17 T.C. 77; *Welsh v. Knarston*, 1972 S.L.T. 96, 97, *per* Lord Stott.

[71] See *Welsh v. Knarston*, *supra*.

[72] See *supra*, para. 10–160 and *infra*, para. 16–25.

[73] See *supra*, para. 13–65.

[74] *Ex p. Robinson* (1833) 3 D. & C. 376. But note the decision in *Re McGae* (1816) 19 Ves. Jr. 606, as to the position where bills are accepted and notes issued in the name of a firm after the bankruptcy of one or more partners; see also *Jombart v. Woolett* (1837) 2 Myl. & Cr. 389.

[75] *Goldfarb v. Bartlett and Kremer* [1920] 1 K.B. 639. *Quaere* can a partner waive notice of dishonour? See *ibid.* p. 650, *per* McCardle J.

[76] *I.R.C. v. Graham's Trustees*, 1971 S.L.T. 46, 48, *supra*, para. 13–65; also *Hillerns and Fowler v. Murray* (1932) 17 T.C. 77; *Welsh v. Knarston*, 1972 S.L.T. 96.

[77] See *supra*, para. 12–54.

[78] *Dickson v. National Bank of Scotland*, 1917 S.C. (H.L.) 50. In this case, the money was deposited by one of the firm's clients, on terms that it could be withdrawn by the firm. Note that the receipt and withdrawal of clients' money in other circumstances may now, in the case of certain professions and businesses, be governed by strict accounts rules: see *supra*, para. 12–137.

Partnership assets: A partner may sell the partnership assets;[79] he may also pledge them for the purpose of (i) completing a transaction already commenced;[80] (ii) securing a debt already incurred;[81] or (iii) securing an overdraft on the firm's bank account. Thus, in *Re Bourne*[82] the survivor of two partners was held to have created a valid mortgage by deposit in respect of certain partnership land as security for the overdraft on the firm's bank account, that account having been overdrawn at the date of dissolution.[83]

The anomalous decision in Ault v. Goodrich

Finally, brief reference should be made to the curious decision in **13–67** *Ault v. Goodrich*.[84] In that case, Wilcox the elder (W1) and Wilcox the younger (W2), who carried on the business of timber merchants in partnership, agreed with the plaintiff and another party to engage in a joint speculation involving the purchase and sale of certain trees. W2 was seemingly engaged to manage this venture but, before it was completed, the partnership between W1 and W2 was dissolved. W2 then appears to have misapplied certain money derived from the venture. Sir John Leach M.R. considered that W1 was clearly responsible for the actions of W2 whilst their partnership was continuing and went on to hold that, in the absence of any evidence of a new agreement between the parties to the venture following the dissolution of W1 and W2's partnership, the other parties should be treated as having continued to rely on the joint responsibility of W1 and W2 for the actions of W2. On that basis, W1 was declared to be responsible for the conduct of W2 after the date of dissolution.

Lord Lindley explained the unsatisfactory nature of this decision in **13–68** this way:

"Upon this case it may be observed: first, that the facts are not satisfactorily stated; and, secondly, that the judgment leads to the

---

[79] See *Fox v. Hanbury* (1776) Cowp. 445; *Smith v. Stokes* (1801) 1 East 363; *Smith v. Oriell* (1801) 1 East 368; *Harvey v. Crickett* (1816) 5 M. & S. 336; *Morgan v. Marquis* (1853) 9 Ex. 145; *Fraser v. Kershaw* (1856) 2 K. & J. 496; *Lewis v. White* (1863) 2 N.R. 81. But see also, *infra*, paras. 18–62 *et seq.*

[80] *Butchart v. Dresser* (1853) 4 De G.M. & G. 542.

[81] *Re Clough* (1885) 31 Ch.D. 324.

[82] [1906] 2 Ch. 427. See also *supra*, paras. 12–75, 12–76.

[83] In fact, the executors also made an unsuccessful attempt to invoke the rule in *Clayton's Case* in order to show that the original overdraft at the date of dissolution had been paid off before the title deeds were deposited. Note, however, that the creation of an equitable mortgage by the deposit of title deeds is no longer possible, having regard to the requirements of the Law of Property (Miscellaneous Provisions) Act 1989, s.2: *United Bank Kuwait plc v. Sahib*, *The Times*, July 7, 1994.

[84] (1828) 4 Russ. 430.

inference that the responsibility of Wilcox the elder for the conduct of Wilcox the younger did not turn upon the circumstance that they were partners,[85] but upon the circumstance that they were jointly entrusted with the management of the tree speculation. In this view of the case it was obviously immaterial whether the Wilcoxes had dissolved partnership or not."

The current editor submits that, consistently with Lord Lindley's views, the decision could equally well be explained as a case of the completion of unfinished business following the dissolution.

Restrictions on implied authority

13–69   Any restrictions placed upon the implied authority of a partner following a dissolution will, on normal principles, bind a third party with notice.[86]

(c) Form of notice

13–70   It has already been seen that no notice is required in the case of a truly dormant partner,[87] so that the precise form in which notice is to be given to actual and potential customers of the firm will only be of concern to an *apparent* partner. As was the position prior to the Partnership Act 1890,[88] a general notice will normally be given by advertisement but, in the case of persons with whom the firm has previously had dealings, a more specific notice will also be required.

Notice by advertisement

13–71   Since section 36(2) of the Partnership Act 1890 introduced no change in the law and since the only authorities pre-date that Act, it is convenient to set out Lord Lindley's summary of the law in full:

"Public notice given by advertisement in the *Gazette* is sufficient, not only against all who can be shown to have seen it, but also as against all who had no dealings with the old firm, whether they

---

[85] Yet at *ibid.* pp. 432–433, Sir John Leach M.R. observed that "Prima facie it must be intended, that, the partnership being interested in one third of this joint speculation, all sales and all receipts of money by Wilcox the younger, during the continuance of the partnership, were partnership transactions."

[86] See the Partnership Act 1890, s.8, *supra*, paras. 12–148 *et seq. Quaere* to what extent such a restriction may properly be imposed: see *supra*, paras. 13–33 *et seq.*

[87] See *supra*, paras. 13–54 *et seq.*

[88] See *supra*, para. 13–40.

saw it or not.[89] But an advertisement in any other paper is no evidence against anyone who cannot be shown to have seen it.[90] If, however, it can be shown that he was in the habit of taking the paper,[91] that is evidence ... of his having seen not only the particular paper containing the advertisement, but also the advertisement itself[92]; and if the [*court is satisfied*][93] that he saw the advertisement, that will be sufficient, although no advertisement was inserted in the *Gazette*.[94] An advertisement, moreover, is not indispensable; its place may be supplied by something else. Thus a change in the name of a firm painted on its counting-house, accompanied by a removal of the business of the old firm (for the purpose of winding up), and coupled with announcements of the change by circulars sent to the old customers, was held to be sufficient without any advertisement as against a person who had not been an old customer, and who was not proved to have had any distinct notice."[95]

It follows that a *Gazette* notice is a desirable precaution in all cases; indeed, most partnership agreements contain a specific provision relating thereto.[96]

Notice to existing customers

As regards the firm's existing customers, a *Gazette* notice or other **13–72** public advertisement will, in Lord Lindley's words, be "of little or no value."[97] If, however, *actual* notice can be proved, that will be sufficient.

No particular form of notice to existing customers is prescribed by the Partnership Act 1890[98] nor was it required under the pre-existing law. It will obviously be sufficient to prove that the customer saw an advertisement, whether in the *Gazette* or elsewhere; proof that he took a certain paper is some evidence that he saw an advertisement placed in it.[99] A change in the firm name and general publicity may

---

[89] *Godfrey v. Turnbull* (1795) 1 Esp. 371; *Godfrey v. Macaulay* (1795) Peake 290n.; *Newsome v. Coles* (1811) 2 Camp. 617; *Wrightson v. Pullan* (1816) 1 Stark. 375. See now the Partnership Act 1890, s.36(2), *supra*, para. 13–42.

[90] *Boydell v. Drummond* (1808) 2 Camp. 157; *Leeson v. Holt* (1816) 1 Stark. 186.

[91] It is not enough to show that the paper is available in the relevant neighbourhood: *Norwich and Lowestoft Co. v. Theobald* (1828) M. & M. 153.

[92] See *Jenkins v. Blizard* (1816) 1 Stark. 418 (where, however, the plaintiff succeeded before the jury); *Rowley v. Horne* (1825) 3 Bing. 2.

[93] The original words were "the jury are satisfied".

[94] *Rooth v. Quin* (1819) 7 Price 193.

[95] *M'Iver v. Humble* (1812) 16 East 169; but see also *Gorham v. Thompson* (1791) Peake 60.

[96] See *supra*, para. 10–210. See also the Partnership Act 1890, s.37, *supra*, para. 13–42.

[97] See *Graham v. Hope* (1792) Peake 208.

[98] See the Partnership Act 1890, s.36(1), *supra*, para. 13–42.

[99] See *supra*, para. 13–71, n. 92.

be sufficient, depending on the circumstances.[1] Thus where, following a change in a firm of bankers, the new firm name appeared on the face of its cheques, that was held to be sufficient notice to those customers who had used such cheques.[2]

Business Names Act 1985

13-73   The Business Names Act 1985 will in practice often ensure that notice of a change in the firm is given to its customers. Thus, if the firm name does not itself disclose the names of the present partners[3] their names must appear on all documents issued by the firm, as well as in a notice prominently displayed in any partnership premises to which customers have access.[4]

C.   TERMINATION OF ACCRUED LIABILITY

13-74   Writing prior to the Partnership Act 1890, Lord Lindley observed:

"When once it can be shown that liability has attached to any partner, the onus of proving that such liability has ceased is upon that partner or those representing him."[5]

Consistently with this principle, where partners take a lease of premises, they will normally remain liable on the covenants in that lease notwithstanding the dissolution of their partnership.[6]

Partnership Act 1890, section 17(2)

13-75   The same principle is reflected in section 17(2) of the Partnership Act 1890, which provides as follows:

"17.—(2) A partner who retires[7] from a firm does not thereby cease to be liable for partnership debts or obligations incurred before his retirement."

---

[1] See, for example, *Hart v. Alexander* (1837) 2 M. & W. 484.
[2] *Barfoot v. Goodall* (1811) 3 Camp. 147.
[3] *Ibid.* s.1. See further, *supra*, para. 3–25.
[4] *Ibid.* s.4(1). See *supra*, para. 3–32.
[5] See *Vulliamy v. Noble* (1817) 3 Mer. 593, 619; also *Wood v. Braddick* (1808) 1 Taunt. 104; *Blundell v. Winsor* (1837) 8 Sim. 613.
[6] See *Hoby v. Roebuck* (1816) 7 Taunt. 157; *Graham v. Whichelo* (1832) 1 C. & M. 188. Note also *Court v. Berlin* [1897] 2 Q.B. 396, *supra*, para. 13–56.
[7] This subsection will also apply in the case of an expulsion: see *supra*, para. 13–45.

It is accordingly necessary to identify the circumstances in which an outgoing partner *will* cease to be liable for accrued debts and liabilities.

Events terminating accrued liability

Following Lord Lindley's own classification, there are four classes **13–76** of event which are capable of affecting a partner's accrued liability to a creditor of the firm, namely:

(*a*) Events over which neither he nor the creditor has any effective control, *i.e.* the partner's death or insolvency. These will be considered later in this work.[8]

(*b*) Dealings and transactions between the partner and the creditor. Since this does not raise any question peculiar to the law of partnership, it does not justify further consideration in this work.

(*c*) Dealings and transactions between the creditor and the *other* partners.[9]

(*d*) Limitation.

The remainder of this chapter is devoted to the third and fourth classes.

(a)   Dealings and transactions terminating accrued liability

General principles applicable to joint obligations

It has already been seen that the liability imposed on partners for **13–77** the debts and obligations of the firm may, according to the circumstances, be either joint or joint and several.[10] Once its precise nature has been established, the termination of a partner's liability will be governed by the same principles as apply in the case of any other joint/joint and several obligation. Although Lord Lindley summarised these principles in general terms,[11] they can more usefully be reformulated in terms of partnership, as follows:

(i)   Performance by one partner of a joint (or joint and several) obligation will discharge the other partners.[12]

---

[8] See, as regards the position following the death of a partner, *infra*, paras. 26–13 *et seq*. As to insolvency, see *infra*, paras. 27–44 *et seq*.

[9] See the Partnership Act 1890, s.17(3), *infra*, paras. 13–103 *et seq*.

[10] See *supra*, paras. 13–02 *et seq*.

[11] This summary is to be found, in its original form, in the 15th ed. of this work at pp. 393, 394.

[12] See *infra*, para. 13–78.

(ii)   Anything which extinguishes the joint (or joint and several) obligation of one partner will also discharge the other partners.[13]

(iii)   Anything which merely prevents one partner being sued on a joint (or joint and several) obligation will not necessarily discharge the other partners.[14]

(iv)   If partners agree, as between themselves, that one of their number will only be surety for the performance of a joint (or joint and several) obligation, any person who, with notice of that agreement, seeks to enforce the obligation must not do anything to prejudice that partner's rights against his co-partners; if he does so without that partner's consent, the latter will be discharged.[15]

The practical application of these principles in the case of outgoing partners can most usefully be illustrated under three heads namely (1) payment and appropriation of payments; (2) release and discharge; and (3) substitution of debtors and securities.

(1)   *Payment and appropriation of payments*

Payment of partnership debt by one partner

13–78   Whether payment of a partnership debt made by one partner will discharge his co-partners from liability in respect of that debt will depend on his intentions and on the derivation of the funds so applied, as Lord Lindley made clear:

"Payment of a partnership debt by any one partner discharges all the others, if the object of the partner paying was to extinguish the whole debt, or if he made the payment out of the partnership funds.[16] But if a firm is unable to pay a debt, and one partner out of his moneys pays it, but in such a way as to show an intention to keep the debt alive against the firm for his own benefit, this

---

[13] See *infra*, paras. 13–94 *et seq*. And see, generally, *Jenkins v. Jenkins* [1928] 2 K.B. 501; *Re E. W. A.* [1901] 2 K.B. 642; *Deanplan Ltd. v. Mahmoud* [1993] Ch. 151 and the cases there cited; also *Cheetham v. Ward* (1797) 1 Bos. & Pul. 630; *Ex p. Slater* (1801) 6 Ves. Jr. 146; *Ballam v. Price* (1818) 2 Moo. 235; *Cocks v. Nash* (1832) 9 Bing. 341; *Nicholson v. Revill* (1836) 4 A. & E. 675; *Wallace v. Kelsall* (1840) 7 M. & W. 264.

[14] See *infra*, para. 13–94. And see, generally, *Duck v. Mayeu* [1892] 2 Q.B. 511; *Re E. W. A.*, *supra*; *Deanplan Ltd. v. Mahmoud, supra*; also *Lacy v. Kinnaston* (1701) 1 Ld.Ray. 688; *Dean v. Newhall* (1799) 8 T.R. 168; *Walmesley v. Cooper* (1839) 11 A. & E. 216. And note *Watters v. Smith* (1831) 2 B. & Ad. 889.

[15] See *infra*, para. 13–98.

[16] See *Watters v. Smith* (1831) 2 B. & Ad. 889; *Beaumont v. Greathead* (1846) 2 C.B. 494; *Thorne v. Smith* (1851) 10 C.B. 659.

payment by him will be no answer to an action brought against the firm by the creditor suing on behalf of the partner who made the payment."[17]

Position where partner and firm have common creditor

If a partner and his firm are both indebted to the same creditor, **13–79** any payment made by that partner out of partnership funds must be applied towards the partnership debt, even though not specifically paid on that account.[18]

Payment by new firm

Similar principles will be applied following a change in a firm, if **13–80** the new firm pays the debts of the old, as Lord Lindley explained:

". . . a payment by the new firm expressly or impliedly on behalf of the old firm, of the debts contracted by the old firm, will extinguish its debts as between that firm and its creditor.[19] But if there are circumstances showing that the money was paid, not on behalf of the old firm, and in discharge of its liability, but as the consideration for a transfer to the new firm of the creditor's right against the old firm, the right of the creditor to sue the old firm will not be extinguished, but can still be exercised for the benefit of the new firm."[20]

Appropriation of payments: the rule in *Clayton's Case*

The general principle governing the appropriation of payments will **13–81** be well known and may be summarised as follows: if a debtor owes several debts to the same creditor, he is entitled to appropriate any payment to the debt of his choice; but if he does not exercise that right, either expressly or by implication, at the time of making the payment, it will become exercisable by the creditor, who may even appropriate the payment to a debt the recovery of which is barred by

---

[17] *M'Intyre v. Miller* (1845) 13 M. & W. 725.
[18] *Thompson v. Brown* (1827) Moo. & M. 40. See also *Nottidge v. Prichard* (1834) 2 Cl. & F. 379.
[19] Lord Lindley had earlier referred, in support of a proposition framed in more general terms, to Co.Litt. 207a; also *Jones v. Broadhurst* (1850) 9 C.B. 193; *Belshaw v. Bush* (1851) 11 C.B. 191; *Kemp v. Balls* (1854) 10 Ex. 607; *Lucas v. Wilkinson* (1856) 1 H. & N. 420. See also *Hirachand Punamchand v. Temple* [1911] 2 K.B. 330.
[20] See *M'Intyre v. Miller* (1845) 13 M. & W. 725; *Lucas v. Wilkinson* (1856) 1 H. & N. 420.

the Limitation Act 1980.[21] Further consideration of this principle is outside the scope of the present work.

13–82   However, the rule in *Clayton's Case*,[22] which may displace the normal right of appropriation, is of particular importance in the present context. Lord Lindley stated the rule as follows:

> "... where there is one single open current account between two parties, every payment which cannot be shown to have been made in discharge of some particular item, is imputed to the earliest item standing to the debit of the payer at the time of payment."

It will perhaps be self evident that the operation of this rule may, in an appropriate case, result in the discharge of an outgoing partner, whether active[23] or dormant,[24] or of the estate of a deceased partner.[25]

Application of the rule in Clayton's Case

13–83   In his consideration of the rule in *Clayton's Case*, Lord Lindley formulated a number of general propositions by way of illustration of its scope. Those propositions are retained in their original form.

Proposition 1:

13–84   "The rule ... applies to all accounts of the nature of one entire debit and credit account[26] without reference to any question of partnership, and is available not only by a firm against an old creditor, but also against a firm for the benefit of its debtors."

Thus, if a person guarantees a debt owing to a firm by a third party and the debt, being an item in a single running account between the third party and the firm, is liquidated by the operation of the rule, the guaranteed debt will be extinguished and the guarantor

---

[21] Lord Lindley formulated eight general rules regarding the appropriation of payments, with copious references to the older authorities, but these are not reproduced in the present edition. They will, however, be found in the 15th ed. of this work at pp. 395 *et seq*. And see, generally, *Chitty on Contracts* (26th ed.), paras. 1533 *et seq*.; *Halsbury's Laws of England* (4th ed.), Vol. 9, paras. 505 *et seq*.

[22] (1816) 1 Mer. 572. See generally, as to this rule, *Ex p. Randleson* (1833) 2 D. & Ch. 534; *Copland v. Toulmin* (1840) 7 Cl. & F. 349; *Brown v. Adams* (1869) L.R. 4 Ch. App. 764; *Laing v. Campbell* (1865) 36 Beav. 3; *Re Yeovil Glove Co.* [1965] Ch. 148; *Re James R. Rutherford & Sons* [1964] 1 W.L.R. 1211.

[23] *Hooper v. Keay* (1875) 1 Q.B.D. 178.

[24] *Newmarch v. Clay* (1811) 14 East 239; *Brooke v. Enderby* (1820) 2 Brod. & B. 70.

[25] As in *Clayton's Case* (1816) 1 Mer. 572.

[26] *e.g.* current accounts for the supply of goods which have been treated as one account: see *Hooper v. Keay* (1875) 1 Q.B.D. 178; *Albemarle Supply Co. Ltd. v. Hind & Co.* [1928] 1 K.B. 307. See also the cases cited *infra*, para. 13–85, n. 29.

discharged, even though there may at all times have been an overall balance due from the third party to the firm.[27] *Per contra* if the guaranteed debt is not wholly extinguished.[28]

Proposition 2:

"The rule ... applies only to an entire unbroken account,[29] and to **13–85** items in that account.[30] It has no application to cases where one person is indebted to another in respect of several matters, each of which forms the subject of a distinct account."[31]

Accordingly, where there are such distinct accounts and the debtor does not himself make the appropriation, the creditor can apply the payment to whichever account he sees fit.[32]

This is of particular relevance following a change in a firm, since a **13–86** creditor of the old firm is not bound to agree that his debt should be carried over to a fresh account with the new firm; if he prefers to keep the two accounts separate and distinct, general payments made by the new firm will not *necessarily* liquidate the debt owed by the old firm. Thus, in *Simson v. Ingham*,[33] where a bank to whom two partners were indebted had, following the death of one, sent in two separate accounts of receipts and payments, one relating to the period prior to the death and the other to the subsequent period, it was held that the rule in *Clayton's Case* did not apply, even though in the bank's own books the original account had been continued.

The same principle is applicable in the case of a debt owed *to* a **13–87** firm, as demonstrated by the decision in *Jones v. Maund*.[34] There being no evidence in that case that the debt had been made an item in the account between the debtor and the new firm,[35] it was held

---

[27] See *Kinnaird v. Webster* (1878) 10 Ch.D. 139; also *Bodenham v. Purchas* (1818) 2 B. & A. 39; *Field v. Carr* (1828) 5 Bing. 13; *Pemberton v. Oakes* (1827) 4 Russ. 154; *Toulmin v. Copland* (1836) 3 Y. & C.Ex. 625; *Copland v. Toulmin* (1840) 7 Cl. & F. 349; *Bank of Scotland v. Christie* (1841) 8 Cl. & F. 214; *Re Medewe's Trust* (1859) 26 Beav. 588. *Cf. Ex p. Whitworth* (1841) 2 M.D. & D. 164; *City Discount Co. v. Maclean* (1874) L.R. 9 C.P. 692.

[28] *Re Sherry* (1884) 25 Ch.D. 692; also *Williams v. Rawlinson* (1825) 3 Bing. 71; *Bradford Old Bank v. Sutcliffe* [1918] 2 K.B. 833, where there were two separate accounts, only one of which had been satisfied. The latter decision was applied by Buckley J. in *Re E. J. Morel (1934)* [1962] Ch. 21.

[29] *Cory Brothers & Co. v. Owners of The Mecca* [1897] A.C. 286; also *Re Sherry* (1884) 25 Ch.D. 692, 702; *A.M.K.M.K. v. Chettiar* [1955] A.C. 230. See also *supra*, para. 13–84, n. 26.

[30] See *Smith v. Betty* [1903] 2 K.B. 317, 323, *per* Stirling L.J.

[31] See *Bradford Old Bank v. Sutcliffe* [1918] 2 K.B. 833, *supra*, n. 28.

[32] *i.e.* in accordance with the general principle summarised *supra*, para. 13–81.

[33] (1823) 2 B. & C. 65.

[34] (1839) 3 Y. & C.Ex. 347.

[35] In fact there was no identity between the partners in the new firm and those in the old; however, it is considered that the decision would have been the same even if this had not been the case.

that he could not insist on payments made by him generally to the
new firm being applied to a balance due from him in respect of that
debt.[36]

It should, however, be noted in this connection that one partner
will normally have implied authority to assent to the transfer of a
debt owed by or to the firm from one account to another.[37]

Proposition 3:

13–88   "... the rule applies even as between persons who do not know
that they are being affected by it, and who, if they did, might take
care to exclude its operation."[38]

It follows that a deceased or outgoing partner may be discharged
by the operation of the rule, even if the creditor does not know that
there has been a change in the firm. The fact that the creditor might,
if he had known of the change, have refused to deal with the new
firm unless the old and new accounts were kept distinct, is strictly
irrelevant if he has dealt with both firms on the footing that there is
only one continuous account.[39]

Proposition 4:

13–89   "... a debtor, after making general payments in respect of one
entire account, is not at liberty to have those payments applied in
liquidation of the subsequent rather than of the earlier items."[40]

This proposition is of particular relevance to an incoming partner.
It has already been seen that he will not normally be liable for debts
contracted prior to the date of his admission;[41] yet if he permits those
debts to form a single running account with other debts incurred *since*

---

[36] This case was decided on demurrer. It was reportedly held that the balance due to the old firm
could not be considered as liquidated, unless it could be shown that it had, with the consent of one
of the partners of that firm (who had, in fact, assigned her share to one of the partners of the new
firm), been made an item in the account between the debtor and the new firm. Lord Lindley
observed in a footnote: "But *quaere* what [*that partner*] had to do with it, she having assigned all
her interest in the debt to the new firm? Did she not thereby authorise the new firm to deal with
the debt as it liked? See *Pemberton v. Oakes* (1827) 4 Russ. 154."
[37] *Beale v. Caddick* (1857) 2 H. & N. 326. See further, *supra*, para. 12–60.
[38] *Newmarch v. Clay* (1811) 14 East 239; *Brooke v. Enderby* (1820) 2 Brod. & B. 70; *Scott v.
Beale* (1859) 6 Jur.(N.S.) 559; *Merriman v. Ward* (1860) 1 J. & H. 371. Note, however, that the rule
may, in certain circumstances, be held not to apply where it would be impractical or where injustice
would be caused: *Barlow Clowes International v. Vaughan* [1992] 4 All E.R. 22 (C.A.). See also *Re
Registered Securities* [1991] 1 N.Z.L.R. 545.
[39] *Ibid.*
[40] *Beale v. Caddick* (1857) 2 H. & N. 326.
[41] Partnership Act 1890, s.17(1): see *supra*, paras. 13–25 *et seq.*

that date, general payments made by the new firm in respect of that account will be applied first in the liquidation of the old debts and may accordingly leave a balance due in respect of new debts, for which the incoming partner is clearly liable.[42]

However, such a result can only be achieved with the express or **13–90** implied consent of the incoming partner: a creditor of the old firm who continues to deal with the new firm has no inherent right to appropriate a payment made by a new partner to a debt owing by his co-partners, nor to run two otherwise distinct accounts together in order to bring the rule into play.[43]

Proposition 5:

"The rule ... is ... based on the presumed intention of the **13–91** parties.[44] It is not, as is sometimes represented, a rule of law obtaining independently of their will; and consequently, if it can be shown that some other appropriation was intended, the rule ceases to be applicable."

There is, in fact, no inconsistency between this and proposition 3. In cases where the parties are not aware that the rule is applicable, there is obviously no scope for an express or implied agreement to exclude or modify its operation; accordingly, their *presumed* intention will not be displaced. Where, on the other hand, some other intention can be inferred from the parties' conduct, *e.g.* to appropriate a payment to a later rather than an earlier item in the account, the rule will not apply.[45] Among the circumstances which may give rise to such an inference are the usual course of business between the parties[46] and the source of the funds applied in making

---

[42] See *Beale v. Caddick* (1857) 2 H. & N. 326; also *Scott v. Beale* (1859) 6 Jur.(n.s.) 559. Of the latter decision, Lord Lindley observed "This case is badly reported, but it is tolerably plain that the incoming partner was held liable to pay, not the debt due to the plaintiff when the partnership commenced, but the balance of monies due to him on his whole account, and which balance consisted of monies received by the defendants after the partnership between them was created."

[43] *Burland v. Nash* (1861) 2 F. & F. 687. In a footnote, Lord Lindley queried "whether the evidence did not warrant the inference that the two accounts had been run into one with the consent of the defendant."

[44] *Re Hodgson's Trusts* [1919] 2 Ch. 189, 195–196, *per* Peterson J.; *Barlow Clowes International v. Vaughan* [1992] 4 All E.R. 22 (C.A.); *Re Registered Securities* [1991] 1 N.Z.L.R. 545; also *Wilson v. Hurst* (1833) 4 B. & Ad. 760, 767, *per* Denman C.J.; *Re Hallett's Estate* (1880) 13 Ch.D. 696; *Cory Brothers & Co. v. Owners of The Mecca* [1897] A.C. 286; *Deeley v. Lloyds Bank* [1912] A.C. 756. In *Copland v. Toulmin* (1840) 7 Cl. & F. 349, there was evidence of an agreement for a different appropriation, but it was not regarded as sufficient to exclude the rule.

[45] For a recent example of a case in which the rule was held to be inconsistent with the presumed intention of the parties, see *Barlow Clowes International v. Vaughan, supra*; and see also *Re Registered Securities, supra*.

[46] *Lysaght v. Walker* (1831) 5 Bli.(n.s.) 1; *Taylor v. Kymer* (1832) 3 B. & Ad. 320.

the relevant payment.[47] In *Wickham v. Wickham*,[48] the rule was held to be displaced as between two firms by representations made to a third party[49] by a partner common to both firms that the relevant debts were still owing.

Proposition 6:

13–92   "... the rule ... cannot be applied as against a person who is a creditor in respect of a fraud committed on him of which he is ignorant."

This is founded on the same principle as the previous proposition and was, in fact, determined in *Clayton's Case*[50] itself, where the liability of a firm in respect of the fraudulent sale of certain exchequer bills was held not to be extinguished by payments which the surviving partners had subsequently made.[51]

Similarly, if one partner fraudulently overdraws his account with the firm and keeps paying money in and drawing money out, so that his fraudulent overdrawing is never discovered, it will not be treated as having been made good so long as there is a balance due from him.[52]

Partner and firm sharing common debtor/creditor

13–93   The position where a partner makes a payment out of partnership funds to a person who is both his own and the firm's creditor has already been noticed.[53] Greater difficulties are encountered in the converse situation, *i.e.* where a debtor who owes money both to a partner and to the firm makes a payment to that partner without specifying to which debt the payment is to be applied. Lord Lindley observed

"Pothier[54] says that good faith requires that the partner receiving the money, should apply it proportionately to both demands. The writer is not aware of any decision on this subject, but he

---

[47] *Stoveld v. Eade* (1827) 4 Bing. 154; *Thompson v. Brown* (1827) Moo. & M. 40. For examples of other relevant circumstances, see *Newmarch v. Clay* (1811) 14 East 240 (nature of security); *City Discount Co. v. Maclean* (1874) L.R. 9 C.P. 692 (earlier item secured and intended to be kept separate); also, generally, *Hancock v. Smith* (1889) 41 Ch.D. 456; *Cory Brothers & Co. v. Owners of The Mecca* [1897] A.C. 286; *Re Hodgson's Trusts* [1919] 2 Ch. 189; and the cases cited *supra*, n. 45. *Cf. Henniker v. Wigg* (1843) 4 Q.B. 792 and *Re Boys* (1870) L.R. 10 Eq. 467.

[48] (1855) 2 K. & J. 478; *Merriman v. Ward* (1860) 1 J. & H. 371; see also *Firestone Tyre & Rubber Co. Ltd. v. Evans* [1977] S.T.C. 104.

[49] The third party was in fact the plaintiff, for whom one of the firms acted as agent in the supply of goods to the other.

[50] (1816) 1 Mer. 572–580.

[51] See further, as to frauds committed by a partner, *supra*, paras. 12–88 *et seq.*

[52] *Lacey v. Hill* (1876) 4 Ch.D. 537, affirmed *sub nom. Read v. Bailey* at (1877) 3 App.Cas. 94.

[53] See *supra*, para. 13–79.

[54] Pothier, *Société*, s. 121.

apprehends that, as between the partner and the debtor, the payment might be applied to either debt at the option of the partner, whilst, as between the partner and his co-partners, good faith would require that the payment should be applied wholly to the partnership debt."[55]

The position is no clearer now, but the opinion of the current editor is that Lord Lindley's view is the correct one.

(2) Release and discharge

Releases and covenants not to sue

A creditor may discharge a partner from a partnership debt or **13–94** obligation by means of a release or a covenant not to sue, with differing consequences for the other partners, as Lord Lindley explained:

"A release of one partner from a partnership debt discharges all the others[56]; for where several persons are bound jointly, or jointly and severally, a release of one is a release of them all.[57] But in this respect a covenant not to sue differs from a release; for, although where there is only one debtor and one creditor, a covenant by the latter never to sue the former is equivalent to a release, it has been decided on several occasions that a covenant not to sue does not operate as a release of a debt owing to or by other persons besides those who are parties to the covenant."[58]

The position will be no different in the case of a tortious liability.[59]

True nature of a purported release

It should not, however, be assumed that a purported release will **13–95** *necessarily* discharge the other partners: if, on a true construction,[60] it

---

[55] See *Thompson v. Brown* (1827) Moo. & M. 40; *Nottidge v. Prichard* (1834) 2 Cl. & F. 379.

[56] *Bower v. Swadlin* (1738) 1 Atk. 294; *Cheetham v. Ward* (1797) 1 Bos. & Pul. 630; *Ex p. Slater* (1801) 6 Ves. Jr. 146; *Cocks v. Nash* (1832) 9 Bing. 341.

[57] The authorities for this proposition were recently reviewed in *Deanplan Ltd. v. Mahmoud* [1993] Ch. 151. See also, generally, Co.Lit. 232a; *Kiffin v. Evans* (1694) 4 Mod. 379; *Lacy v. Kinnaston* (1701) 1 Ld.Ray 688; *Jenkins v. Jenkins* [1928] 2 K.B. 501. The same rule applies to judgment debts: *Re E.W.A.* [1901] 2 K.B. 642.

[58] *Clayton v. Kynaston* (1699) 2 Salk. 573; *Lacy v. Kinnaston* (1701) 1 Ld.Ray 688; *Dean v. Newhall* (1799) 8 T.R. 168; *Hutton v. Eyre* (1815) 6 Taunt. 289; *Walmesley v. Cooper* (1839) 11 A. & E. 216; *Commercial Bank of Tasmania v. Jones* [1893] A.C. 313, 316, *per* Lord Morris; *Deanplan Ltd. v. Mahmoud* [1993] Ch. 151, 170B, *per* Judge Paul Baker Q.C. See also *Price v. Barker* (1855) 4 E. & B. 760.

[59] *Duck v. Mayeu* [1892] 2 Q.B. 511; *Gardiner v. Moore* [1969] 1 Q.B. 55.

[60] Note that the true purpose and scope of a release may be apparent from its recitals and, thus, require a restrictive interpretation to be placed on its operative clauses: see, generally, *Payler v. Homersham* (1815) 4 M. & S. 423; *Lampon v. Corke* (1822) 5 B. & A. 606; *Simons v. Johnson* (1832) 3 B. & Ad. 175; *Lindo v. Lindo* (1839) 1 Beav. 496; *Boyes v. Bluck* (1853) 13 C.B. 652.

does not preclude a subsequent action against all the partners, including the partner to whom it is given, it will not in fact operate as a release and the continuing liability of the other partners will be unaffected.[61]

13–96   Thus, in *Solly v. Forbes*,[62] two partners, A and B, were indebted to a third party, C. B paid a certain sum to C, in consideration of which he was released from all further demands in respect of the debt. However, under the terms of the release, C expressly reserved all his rights not only against A but also against A and B jointly, so that he could obtain repayment either from the partnership or from A. As might be anticipated, that release was held not to be a bar to C's subsequent proceedings against A and B. *Hartley v. Manton*[63] was decided on the same principle.

Receipt in full

13–97   Similarly, a receipt given to one partner in satisfaction of all demands against him will discharge his co-partners unless its operation is qualified, either by its terms or by the surrounding circumstances.[64]

Outgoing partner entitled to indemnity against debts, etc.

13–98   Continuing or surviving partners who, either expressly or impliedly,[65] agree to indemnify an outgoing partner (or the estate of a deceased partner) against the accrued debts and liabilities of the firm thereby constitute themselves as principal debtors and the outgoing partner (or his estate) as surety for the payment of those debts and liabilities.[66] Where a creditor of the firm has notice of such an agreement and subsequently deals with the remaining partners in a way which will or may prejudice the outgoing partner's rights *qua* surety, *e.g.* by giving additional time to pay, this will on normal

---

[61] *Gardiner v. Moore* [1969] 1 Q.B. 55.
[62] (1820) 2 Brod. & B. 38. See also *Thompson v. Lack* (1846) 3 C.B. 540; *Price v. Barker* (1855) 4 E. & B. 760; *Willis v. De Castro* (1858) 4 C.B.(N.S.) 216; *Bateson v. Gosling* (1871) L.R. 7 C.P. 9; *Duck v. Mayeu* [1892] 2 Q.B. 511; *Re E.W.A.* [1901] 2 K.B. 642.
[63] (1843) 5 Q.B. 247.
[64] *Ex p. Good* (1877) 5 Ch.D. 46; *Re E.W.A.* [1901] 2 K.B. 642; *Deanplan Ltd. v. Mahmoud* [1993] Ch. 151.
[65] See further, *supra*, para. 10–207.
[66] *Oakeley v. Pasheller* (1836) 10 Bli.(N.S.) 548; *Rodgers v. Maw* (1846) 4 Dow. & L. 66; also *Overend, Gurney & Co. v. Oriental Financial Corporation* (1874) L.R. 7 H.L. 348; *Rouse v. Bradford Banking Co.* [1894] A.C. 586; *Goldfarb v. Bartlett & Kremer* [1920] 1 K.B. 639. And see *supra*, para. 10–209.

principles[67] discharge the outgoing partner, unless the creditor expressly reserved his rights or the outgoing partner consented. The fact that the creditor neither knew of nor consented to the agreement prior to its conclusion is immaterial.

This is clearly demonstrated by the decision in *Oakeley v.* **13–99** *Pasheller*.[68] There two partners, A and B, had given a number of joint and several bonds to the plaintiff. A died. B carried on the partnership business for a time and then took in C as a partner. B and C agreed to indemnify A's executors against the debts of the old firm, including the liability under the bonds, and the plaintiff seemingly had notice of this agreement.[69] The new firm accordingly adopted the debt due under the bonds and paid the plaintiff interest thereon. It appears that the plaintiff later agreed with B and C to defer payment under the bonds for three years, but A's executors were not informed of this arrangement. It was held that, by so doing, the plaintiff had discharged A's executors from liability.[70]

It should, however, be noted that the giving of time will not **13–100** discharge the outgoing partner once judgment has been obtained both against him and the remaining partners.[71]

(3) *Substitution of debtors and securities*

An outgoing partner may be discharged from liability in respect of an **13–101** accrued debt or obligation if the creditor acquires new and different rights against other persons *in place* of that liability. This may either occur with the creditor's agreement[72] or by operation of the doctrine of merger.

---

[67] See, generally, *Chitty on Contracts* (26th ed.), paras. 5052 *et seq.*; and see also the general statement of the law in *Bank of India v. Trans Continental Commodity Merchants Ltd.* [1982] 1 Lloyd's Rep. 506.

[68] (1836) 10 Bli.(N.S.) 548 and 4 Cl. & F. 207. This decision was followed in *Wilson v. Lloyd* (1873) L.R. 16 Eq. 60, even though no new partners had been admitted. However, Lord Lindley observed that "*Wilson v. Lloyd* cannot be relied upon"; see also *Simpson v. Henning* (1875) L.R. 10 Q.B. 406, 413, *per* Amphlett B. Although *Oakeley v. Pasheller* was distinguished in *Swire v. Redman* (1876) 1 Q.B.D. 536, its authority was reaffirmed in *Rouse v. Bradford Banking Co.* [1894] 2 Ch. 32 and, on appeal, [1894] A.C. 586.

[69] See (1836) 4 Cl. & F. 212. The marginal note seems to be misleading: but see also *ibid.* p. 211. This point is not mentioned in the report at 10 Bli.(N.S.) 548.

[70] It appears that the plaintiff had subsequently taken an assignment of some policies from B and C by way of collateral security for payment of sums due under the bonds, at that point expressly reserving his rights against A's estate. However, by this time, the estate had already been released from liability, for the reasons mentioned in the text. Lord Lindley originally observed of this case "The true *ratio decidendi*, however, was that the plaintiff had accepted B and C as his sole debtors." This view was shared by Kekewich J. (see *Rouse v. Bradford Banking Co.* [1894] 2 Ch. 32, 45–46), but Lord Lindley later resiled therefrom (see *ibid.* pp. 57 *et seq.*).

[71] *Jenkins v. Robertson* (1854) 2 Drew. 351; *Re A Debtor* [1913] 3 K.B. 11.

[72] Lord Lindley observed that this is "[s]ometimes called novation but nothing is really gained by using this word." However, the word is commonly used: see, for example, *Re Head* [1893] 3 Ch. 426; *Head v. Head (No. 2)* [1894] 2 Ch. 236.

(A) SUBSTITUTION BY AGREEMENT

General principle

13–102   It is perhaps self evident that a creditor's rights will not normally be prejudiced by an agreement transferring an accrued liability from one partner to another unless the creditor is made a party to the agreement or assents to its operation. Otherwise the agreement will, as regards him, be strictly *res inter alios acta*.[73] Lord Lindley illustrated this proposition by the following example:

> "... let it be supposed that a firm of three members, A, B, and C, is indebted to D; that A retires, and B and C either alone, or together with a new partner, E, take upon themselves the liabilities of the old firm. D's right to obtain payment from A, B and C is not affected by the above arrangement, and A does not cease to be liable to him for the debt in question.[74] But if, after A's retirement, D accepts as his sole debtors B and C, or B, C, and E (if E enters the firm), then A's liability will have ceased, and D must look for payment to B and C, or to B, C and E, as the case may be."

Partnership Act 1890, section 17(3)

13–103   This approach is directly reflected in the Partnership Act 1890, which provides:

> "17.—(3) A retiring partner may be discharged from any existing liabilities, by an agreement to that effect between himself and the members of the firm as newly constituted and the creditors, and this agreement may be either express or inferred as a fact from the course of dealing between the creditors and the firm as newly constituted."

Lord Lindley's rules on substitution

13–104   Before turning to the numerous authorities on this topic, it may be convenient to set out nine rules, which were originally formulated by Lord Lindley prior to the Partnership Act 1890 but which still retain current relevance.[75]

---

[73] But note that such an agreement may result in an outgoing partner becoming a surety for the continuing partners' obligations and thereby indirectly prejudice the creditor's rights once he has notice of the agreement: see *supra*, para. 13–98.

[74] *Smith v. Jameson* (1794) 5 T.R. 601; *Dickenson v. Lockyer* (1798) 4 Ves. Jr. 36; *Cummins v. Cummins* (1845) 8 I. Eq. R. 723; *Rodgers v. Maw* (1846) 4 Dow. & L. 66. But see also the previous footnote.

[75] In fact, the rules set out in the text represent a combination of (1) three rules set out in the 5th ed. of this work at p. 241, (2) three propositions incorporated in Lord Lindley's discussion of the decided cases and (3) six propositions set out in his review of the effect of those cases at *ibid.* pp. 253, 254. The latter were also in fact reproduced in his commentary on the Partnership Act 1890, s.17(3) (Supplement, p. 45).

General rules

Rule 1: "There is no *a priori* presumption to the effect that the **13–105** creditors of a firm do, on the retirement of a partner, enter into any agreement to discharge him from liability."[76]

Rule 2: "An express agreement by the creditor to discharge a retired partner, and to look only to a continuing partner, is not [*necessarily*][77] inoperative for want of consideration...."[78]

Introduction of new partners

Rule 3: "The introduction of a new partner has no effect on the **13–106** liability of a retired partner, unless the liability of the former is substituted for that of the latter, which cannot be the case unless the creditor can, as of right, hold the new partner liable for the old debt."[79]

Rule 4: "The inference that a retired partner has been discharged is greatly facilitated by the circumstance that a new partner has joined the firm and become liable to the creditor in respect of the debt in question.[80] But this is not necessarily conclusive; for there may be circumstances showing that such was not the intention of the parties."[81]

Adoption of new firm as debtor

Rule 5: "An adoption by the creditor of the new firm as his **13–107** debtor does not by any means necessarily deprive him of his rights against the old firm....[82] And it will certainly not do so if, by

---

[76] Such an agreement must be proved: see *Benson v. Hadfield* (1844) 4 Hare 32.

[77] The current editor believes it is appropriate to include this additional word since Lord Lindley's general formulation of the rule (see the 5th ed. of this work at p. 241) was in these terms: "An agreement by a creditor of several persons, liable to him jointly, to discharge one or more of them, and look only to the others, is not necessarily invalid for want of consideration." The version in the text has been retained, since it was stated in terms of partnership and was, moreover, reproduced by Lord Lindley in his Supplement on the Partnership Act 1890: see *supra*, n. 75.

[78] *Lyth v. Ault* (1852) 7 Ex. 669; *Smith v. Patrick* [1901] A.C. 282. *Cf.* the earlier decisions to the contrary: see *infra*, paras. 13–111 *et seq.*

[79] *Gough v. Davies* (1817) 4 Price 200; *Blew v. Wyatt* (1832) 5 Car. & P. 397; *Kirwan v. Kirwan* (1836) 2 C. & M. 617: see *infra*, para. 13–117.

[80] See, as to the acceptance of liability for existing debts by an incoming partner, *supra*, paras. 13–28 *et seq.*

[81] See *Thompson v. Percival* (1834) 5 B. & Ad. 925, *infra*, para. 13–112; *Hart v. Alexander* (1837) 2 M. & W. 484, *infra*, para. 13–122; also *Keay v. Fenwick* (1876) 1 C.P.D. 745. And see *infra*, paras. 13–117 *et seq.*

[82] Lord Lindley noted that the rule was the same at law and in equity. As to the position at law, he referred to *David v. Ellice* (1826) 5 B. & C. 196; *Thompson v. Percival* (1834) 5 B. & Ad. 925; also *Heath v. Percival* (1720) 1 P.W. 682; *Gough v. Davies* (1817) 4 Price 200; *Blew v. Wyatt* (1832) 5 C. & P. 397; *Kirwan v. Kirwan* (1836) 2 C. & M. 617. As to the position in equity, see *Oakford v. European and American Steam Shipping Co.* (1863) 1 Hem. & M. 182; also *Sleech's Case* (1816) 1 Mer. 539; *Clayton's Case* (1816) 1 Mer. 572; *Palmer's Case* (1816) 1 Mer. 623; *Braithwaite v. Britain* (1836) 1 Keen 206; *Winter v. Innes* (1838) 4 M. & C. 101; *Re Head* [1893] 3 Ch. 426; *Rouse v. Bradford Banking Co.* [1894] A.C. 586. And see *Matthews v. Ruggles Brise* [1911] 1 Ch. 194.

expressly reserving his rights against the old firm, he shows that by adopting the new firm he did not intend to discharge the old firm."[83]

Rule 6: "... by adopting a new firm as his debtor, a creditor cannot be regarded as having intentionally discharged a person who was a member of the old firm, but was not known to the creditor so to be."[84]

13–108   *Rule 7*: "... the fact that a creditor has taken from a continuing partner a new security for a debt due from him and a retired partner jointly is strong evidence of an intention to look only to the continuing partner for payment."[85]

Rule 8: "... a creditor who assents to a transfer of his debt from an old firm to a new firm, and goes on dealing with the latter for many years, making no demand for payment against the old firm, may not unfairly be inferred to have discharged the old firm[86] ... [*although*] the leaning of the Court is strongly in favour of the creditor."[87]

13–109   *Rule 9*: "In whatever way a creditor may have dealt with the surviving partners, he cannot be held to have adopted them as his sole debtors, in respect of a demand arising out of a fraudulent transaction, of which he has been constantly kept in ignorance."[88]

One additional point should be noted in this context. It has already been seen that a release of one partner will release all his co-partners.[89] It follows that if a creditor discharges an outgoing partner but does not acquire any new rights against the continuing or new partners, he is likely to be remediless.[90] However, the position may be otherwise where the outgoing partner was, to the creditor's knowledge, merely a surety for the continuing partners' obligations.[91]

---

[83] *Jacomb v. Harwood* (1751) 2 Ves.Sen. 265; *Bedford v. Deakin* (1818) 2 B. & A. 210.
[84] *Robinson v. Wilkinson* (1817) 3 Price 538.
[85] *Evans v. Drummond* (1801) 4 Esp. 89; *Reed v. White* (1804) 5 Esp. 122. *Cf. Re Head* [1893] 3 Ch. 426 and *Head v. Head (No. 2)* [1894] 2 Ch. 236.
[86] Lord Lindley pointed out that, in such a case, the court will consider all the circumstances and infer a discharge if "upon the whole, justice to all parties so requires": see *Ex p. Executors of James Douglas* [1930] 1 Ch. 342, 350, *per* Luxmoore J.; also *Ex p. Kendall* (1811) 17 Ves. Jr. 514; *Oakeley v. Pasheller* (1836) 10 Bli.(N.S.) 548; *Brown v. Gordon* (1852) 16 Beav. 302; *Wilson v. Lloyd* (1873) L.R. 16 Eq. 60.
[87] This view was based on the relative paucity of cases in which a discharge had been inferred, as compared to the number of cases in which it had not.
[88] See *Clayton's Case* (1816) 1 Mer. 572: see further, *supra*, para. 13–92.
[89] See *supra*, para. 13–94.
[90] On this basis, Lord Lindley observed "One test, therefore, by which to determine whether a retired partner has been discharged is to see whether the creditor has obtained a new right to demand payment; for if he has not, no discharge can possibly be made out by any evidence which fails to establish an extinguishment of the creditor's demand altogether."
[91] See *supra*, para. 13–98.

The decided cases

Virtually all the cases which illustrate Lord Lindley's rules pre-date **13–110** the Partnership Act 1890 and may conveniently be grouped under the following headings:

Group 1: Cases in which the outgoing partner was not discharged and either:

(a) no new partner was introduced; or
(b) one or more new partners were introduced.

Group 2: Cases in which the outgoing partner was discharged.

Group 3: Analogous cases concerning the discharge of the estate of a deceased partner.

GROUP 1(a): *Outgoing partner not discharged; no new partner introduced*

Agreement to look only to continuing partners for payment[92]

The most extreme cases in this group are *Lodge v. Dicas*[93] and **13–111** *David v. Ellice*.[94] Both involved a similar set of facts, *i.e.* one partner retiring and the other(s) continuing the business and agreeing to pay the debts of the old firm. The plaintiff creditor in each case appears to have known of the arrangement and to have assented to the transfer of his debt to the books of the new firm; moreover, there was strong evidence indicating that he had agreed to discharge the retired partner and to look only to the other(s) for payment. In both cases, the retired partner was nevertheless held not to have been discharged, the court relying on the fact that no additional person had become liable to the plaintiff as evidence that the supposed agreement was not supported by consideration.[95]

On the other hand, this approach was not followed in *Thompson v.* **13–112** *Percival*,[96] where the facts were almost identical, save that the creditor, C, having applied to the remaining partner, A, for payment and been informed that he ought thereafter to look to A alone, had drawn a bill of exchange on A, which he subsequently accepted. This

---

[92] See Rules 1, 2 and 5, *supra*, paras. 13–105, 13–107.
[93] (1820) 3 B. & A. 611.
[94] (1826) 5 B. & C. 196.
[95] See also *Thomas v. Shillibeer* (1836) 1 M. & W. 124.
[96] (1834) 5 B. & Ad. 925.

bill was dishonoured and proceedings were commenced against A and the retired partner, B. The jury gave a verdict in C's favour, whereupon A and B moved for a nonsuit on the grounds that B had been discharged. Although the court did not finally decide the point, it ordered a new trial, holding that there was a question of fact for the jury whether C had agreed to accept A as his sole debtor and to take the bill accepted by him in satisfaction of A and B's joint debt. It was clearly recognised that such an agreement, if proved, would have discharged B, on the basis of accord and satisfaction.[97]

13–113   Lord Lindley explained the true legal position as follows:

> "[*Lodge v. Dicas*[98] *and David v. Ellice*[99]] have been much criticised[1] and they certainly went too far: for the proposition that a creditor of a firm cannot, for want of consideration, abandon his right against a retiring partner, and retain it against the others, unless they give some fresh security, has been shown to be erroneous, and is now exploded[2]. . .
>
> It is not unusual to represent [*both cases*] as altogether overruled by *Thompson v. Percival*[3] and other cases. This, however, is not quite correct. The three cases together establish (1) that a creditor who treats the continuing partners as his debtors, does not necessarily abandon his right to resort to a retired partner for payment; (2) that whether he does or does not is a mixed question of law and fact . . . and (3) that [*a decision*][4] will not be disturbed by the court upon the grounds acted on in *Lodge v. Dicas* and *David v. Ellice*."

Treating continuing partners as debtors[5]

13–114   As noted in the preceding paragraphs, if a creditor merely treats the continuing partners as his debtors, this will not in itself be enough to discharge an outgoing partner. In addition to the cases cited therein, the old case of *Heath v. Percival*[6] clearly illustrates this

---

[97] Retired partners were held to be discharged on this basis in *Evans v. Drummond* (1801) 4 Esp. 89 and *Reed v. White* (1804) 5 Esp. 122: see *infra*, para. 13–121.

[98] (1820) 3 B. & A. 611.

[99] (1826) 5 B. & C. 196.

[1] See *Thompson v. Percival* (1834) 5 B. & Ad. 925, 933, *per* Denman C.J.; *Kirwan v. Kirwan* (1834) 2 C. & M. 617, 624; *Hart v. Alexander* (1837) 2 M. & W. 484, 493, *per* Parke B.

[2] See *Lyth v. Ault* (1852) 7 Ex. 669 and Rule 2, *supra*, para. 13–105. Lord Lindley in fact went on "and there can be little doubt that if similar cases were to arise again, and the jury found for the defendant, the verdict would not be disturbed."

[3] (1834) 5 B. & Ad. 925.

[4] The original reference was to the verdict of a jury.

[5] See Rules 1 and 5, *supra*, paras. 13–105, 13–107.

[6] (1720) 1 P.Wms. 682. See also *Harris v. Farwell* (1846) 15 Beav. 31, *infra*, para. 13–127; *Rouse v. Bradford Banking Co.* [1894] A.C. 586; *Smith v. Patrick* [1901] A.C. 282.

principle. There two partners, A and B, were liable to the plaintiff under a bond, in respect of which interest was payable at the rate of 5 per cent. The partnership was dissolved and one partner, A, agreed to carry on the business and to take over the partnership debts. Creditors were publicly notified that they should either seek immediate payment of their debts or in future look for payment from A alone. The plaintiff called in the money due to him but, instead of being paid off, he kept the bond and was paid interest at an increased rate. It was held that he did not thereby discharge the retired partner, B, from his liability under the bond.

New security taken from continuing partners[7]

An outgoing partner will not necessarily be discharged even if the **13–115** continuing partners give the creditor a new security for his debt. In *Bedford v. Deakin*,[8] three partners were indebted to the plaintiff on certain bills of exchange. The partnership was dissolved and it was agreed that one of the partners, A, should pay the plaintiff. The plaintiff was so informed and accepted three promissory notes from A for the amount of the debt; however, he expressly reserved his right to look to all three partners for payment and retained the bills already in his possession. Two of the notes were renewed several times, but the third was not. The plaintiff successfully sued all three partners on the original bills, never having discharged any of them, either intentionally or otherwise.[9]

Dormant partners[10]

The position is in many ways *a fortiori* in the case of a dormant **13–116** partner, since the creditor, being unaware of his existence, cannot intentionally discharge him. Lord Lindley gave the following simple example:

".... if A and B are partners, and the two become indebted to a creditor who knows only of A, and then B, the dormant partner, retires, no dealings between the creditor and A will discharge B from his liability to be sued when discovered, unless those dealings extinguished the original debt not only as against B, but also as against A."

---

[7] See Rule 7, *supra*, para. 13–108.

[8] (1818) 2 B. & A. 210. See also *Swire v. Redman* (1876) 1 Q.B.D. 536 (but note the observations of the Court of Appeal in *Rouse v. Bradford Banking Co.* [1894] 2 Ch. 32, 59–60, 69 *et seq.*). And see *Featherstone v. Hunt* (1822) 1 B. & C. 113; *Spenceley v. Greenwood* (1858) 1 F. & F. 297. Cf. *Evans v. Drummond* (1801) 4 Esp. 89, *infra*, para. 13–121.

[9] See also *Re Head* [1893] 3 Ch. 426; cf. *Head v. Head (No. 2)* [1894] 2 Ch. 236, *infra*, para. 13–126.

[10] See Rule 6, *supra*, para. 13–107.

This was clearly decided in *Robinson v. Wilkinson*.[11]

GROUP 1(b): *Outgoing partner not discharged; one or more partners introduced*

Effect of introducing new partner[12]

13–117   If an outgoing partner is to be discharged following the admission of a new partner, it is not sufficient merely to show that the new firm has adopted an old debt pursuant to some express or implied agreement between the partners.[13] Thus, in *Kirwan v. Kirwan*,[14] three partners, C, M and N, were indebted to the plaintiff. On C's retirement, M and N continued in partnership together and agreed to discharge the debts of the old firm. M then retired and N took in a new partner. The plaintiff's account was, on each change, transferred to the books of the new firm; interest was paid and accounts rendered to him as before. The plaintiff, having been informed of the dissolution of the old firm, had apparently stated in a letter written to C that he was aware he had no further claim on him. It was nevertheless held that C, M and N remained liable, as there was nothing to show that the liability of either new firm had been substituted for that of the old; moreover, the plaintiff's letter to C did not amount to an agreement to discharge him.

13–118   In *Gough v. Davies*,[15] which concerned a banking partnership, it is not entirely clear whether the plaintiff had assented to the transfer of his debt to the books of the new firm;[16] nevertheless he continued to deposit money with that firm, which paid him interest on both the old debt and the new deposits, as if they formed a single debt. It was again held that this did not prove an agreement by the plaintiff to discharge the retired partner, who was consequently held liable for the old debt. *Blew v. Wyatt*[17] was a similar case, save that the creditor was at all times an employee of the firm and thus had first hand knowledge of the changes in its membership.

---

[11] (1817) 3 Price 538.

[12] See Rules 3 and 4, *supra*, para. 13–106; also *supra*, paras. 13–24 *et seq*.

[13] Lord Lindley pointed out that "... even if the new firm adopts the old debt and pays interest on it, this is *prima facie* only in pursuance of some agreement between the partners themselves: and a creditor who does no more than allow the partners to carry out that agreement does not debar himself of his right to look for payment to those originally indebted to him." See *supra*, para. 13–28.

[14] (1836) 2 C. & M. 617.

[15] (1817) 4 Price 200.

[16] Lord Lindley stated that he did so assent, but this does not appear to be borne out by the judgments of Graham B. (*ibid.* p. 212) or Wood B. (*ibid.* p. 214).

[17] (1832) 5 Car. & P. 397.

Lord Lindley observed: **13–119**

"Whether in these cases ... the creditor could have sued the new firm, may perhaps be open to doubt.[18] If he could not, it would be absurd to contend that the liability of the new firm was substituted for that of the old; whilst if he could, the evidence was not sufficient to show an intention on his part to deprive himself of the security afforded by the undoubted liability of the original firm before any change in it took place. It by no means follows that a creditor who assents to an arrangement by which a new person becomes liable to him consents to abandon his hold on another person clearly liable to him already; and unless a substitution of liability can be established, the old liability remains."[19]

GROUP 2: *Outgoing partner discharged*

In each of the cases in this group, the court (or a jury) concluded **13–120** that the creditor had, either expressly or by implication, treated the members of the new firm as his sole debtors, thereby discharging the outgoing partner.[20]

No new partner introduced[21]

An obvious example of such a case is *Thompson v. Percival*,[22] the **13–121** facts of which have already been outlined.

In *Evans v. Drummond*,[23] two partners, A and B, gave a bill of exchange to the creditor in respect of certain goods which he had supplied to them. A retired and B continued the business. The bill fell due but was not paid; it was renewed by another bill given by B. The creditor took this bill knowing of the change in the firm. It was held that, by so doing, the creditor had relied on the sole liability of B, and had thereby discharged A. *Reed v. White*[24] is a decision to the same effect.

---

[18] See *Kirwan v. Kirwan* (1836) 2 C. & M. 617, 628, *per* Bolland B.; also *Daniel v. Cross* (1796) 3 Ves. Jr. 277; *Fergusson v. Fyffe* (1841) 8 Cl. & F. 121.

[19] See *Harris v. Farwell* (1846) 15 Beav. 31, *infra*, para. 13–127; *Rouse v. Bradford Banking Co.* [1894] 2 Ch. 32, 54, *per* Lindley L.J. (the decision being affirmed at [1894] A.C. 586); *Matthews v. Ruggles Brise* [1911] 1 Ch. 194.

[20] Lord Lindley commented (by way of footnote) "[*Sir Frederick*] Pollock says truly that there is nothing to prevent a firm from stipulating with any creditor that he shall look only to the members of the firm for the time being": see *Pollock on the Law of Partnership* (15th ed., 1952), p. 61. Also *Hort's Case* and *Grain's Case* (1875) 1 Ch.D. 307.

[21] See Rules 1, 2, 5 *et seq.*, *supra*, paras. 13–105, 13–107 *et seq.*

[22] (1834) 5 B. & Ad. 925; see *supra*, para. 13–112.

[23] (1801) 4 Esp. 89. *Cf. Bedford v. Deakin* (1818) 2 B. & A. 210, *supra*, para. 13–115. Note, however, the possible implications of renewing a bill where an outgoing partner is, to the knowledge of the creditor, merely a surety for the continuing partners: see *Goldfarb v. Bartlett and Kremer* [1920] 1 K.B. 639 and *supra*, para. 13–98.

[24] (1804) 5 Esp. 122.

One or more new partners introduced[25]

13–122   *Hart v. Alexander*[26] demonstrates the relative ease with which the discharge of an outgoing partner may be inferred from a creditor's acceptance of direct rights against a new partner. In that case, the plaintiff had opened an account with a firm of bankers. The defendant retired from the firm some years later, when a new partner was introduced; his retirement was duly advertised and there was evidence to show that the plaintiff was aware of it. The new firm thereafter rendered accounts to the plaintiff and paid him interest, at rates which varied from time to time. After a number of other changes in the membership of the new firm, it was bankrupted and the plaintiff proceeded to prove his debt against the joint estate. He then sued the defendant. Lord Abinger's summing up to the jury was in forceful terms[27] and the verdict was given to the defendant. The plaintiff sought a new trial on the ground that there was no evidence to show that the plaintiff had agreed to discharge the defendant from his liability, but this application was refused. A majority of the court[28] considered that there was abundant evidence to show that the plaintiff knew of the defendant's retirement.

Ex p. Whitmore[29] was a similar case.

Estoppel

13–123   In certain circumstances, a creditor may so conduct himself that he will be estopped from proceeding against an outgoing partner. However, such cases will be rare, as Lord Lindley explained:

> "A settlement by partners of their accounts on the footing that one of them only is liable to a creditor will not affect him[30] unless he has been guilty of some fraud, or has done some act or made some

---

[25] See Rule 4, *supra*, para. 13–106.

[26] (1837) 2 M. & W. 484. See also *Oakeley v. Pasheller* (1836) 10 Bli.(N.S.) 548, *supra*, para. 13–99; *Wilson v. Lloyd* (1873) L.R. 16 Eq. 60 (this decision is unsatisfactory: see *supra*, para. 13–99, n. 68). *Cf. Re Commercial Bank Corporation of India and the East* (1869) 16 W.R. 958 and *Ex p. Gibson* (1869) L.R. 4 Ch.App. 662.

[27] (1837) 7 C. & P. 746. The summing up reportedly contained the following passage: "I take the law to be this: Where a debtor who is a partner in a firm, leaves that firm, and any person trading with the firm has notice of it, and he goes on dealing with the firm and making fresh contracts, that discharges the retiring partner, though no new partner comes in. So it is if the creditor draws for part of his balance, and sends in more goods; so, if the creditor strikes a fresh balance with the new partners for a different rate of interest; so, if a new partner comes in, and the creditor accept an account in which the new partner is made liable for the balance—that discharges the old firm, as both firms cannot be liable at once for the same debt. This is the law as laid down in several cases, in which indeed, there is some contradiction: however, I believe that what I have stated is the result of them.": see *ibid.* p. 754. However, Lord Lindley observed that "the learned judge was scarcely warranted by those cases in going so far as he did."

[28] Lord Abinger C.B. and Parke B (Bolland B. dissenting).

[29] (1838) 3 Deac. 365, *supra*, para. 13–30. See also *Rolfe v. Flower* (1865) L.R. 1 P.C. 27.

[30] So far as the creditor is concerned, such a settlement will normally be *res inter alios acta*.

statement in order to induce the partners, or one of them, to settle their accounts on the faith that one of them is no longer liable."[31]

GROUP 3: *Discharge of estate of deceased partner*

The principles illustrated in the previous paragraphs are also **13–124** applicable following the death of a partner.[32]

No new partner introduced[33]

If a creditor of a firm, knowing that one partner has died, **13–125** continues to deal with the surviving partners, he will not lose his rights against the deceased partner's estate, unless there is evidence of his intention to abandon those rights.[34] Such an intention will not, without more, be inferred from an attempt to obtain payment from the surviving partners, *e.g.* by suing them to judgment[35] or proving against the joint estate of the new firm in the event of its insolvency.[36]

Thus, in *Re Head*[37] a customer of a banking partnership, knowing **13–126** of the death of one of the partners, had accepted a fresh deposit note from the surviving partner for the balance of a debt due from the firm. The deceased partner's estate was held not to have been discharged thereby. On the other hand, in *Head v. Head (No. 2)*[38] the customer, who wished to withdraw the balance on his current account, was persuaded by the surviving partner to transfer that balance to an interest bearing deposit account and accepted a deposit note for that balance. By so doing he was held to have discharged the estate of the deceased partner.

---

[31] See *Davison v. Donaldson* (1882) 9 Q.B.D. 623; also *Featherstone v. Hunt* (1822) 1 B. & C. 113 (a case of alleged fraud). And see *The Huntsman* [1894] P. 214, 219, *per* Gorell Barnes J.

[32] Noting the similarities between the position of a retired partner and the estate of the deceased partner, Lord Lindley observed: "The parallel between the two would be complete were it not that before the Judicature Acts the estate of a partner who died in the lifetime of his co-partners was liable for the joint debts of the firm in equity only; and there might have been circumstances to induce a Court of equity to hold that estate discharged, although the same circumstances would not, in the case of a retiring partner, have operated as a discharge at law, and *vice versa*." He then referred to *Ex p. Kendall* (1811) 17 Ves. Jr. 514 and *Jacomb v. Harwood* (1751) 2 Ves.Sen. 265. The position is now, of course, governed by the Partnership Act 1890, s.9, *supra*, paras. 13–03 *et seq.*

[33] Note Rules 1, 5 *et seq.*, *supra*, paras. 13–105, 13–107 *et seq.*

[34] *Winter v. Innes* (1838) 4 M. & Cr. 101; also *Devaynes v. Noble, Sleech's Case* (1816) 1 Mer. 539; *Clayton's Case* (1816) 1 Mer. 579; *Palmer's Case* (1816) 1 Mer. 623; *Braithwaite v. Britain* (1836) 1 Keen 206. These were cases decided in equity: see *supra*, para. 13–124, n. 32. See also *supra*, paras. 13–111 *et seq.*

[35] *Jacomb v. Harwood* (1751) 2 Ves. Sen. 265. See also *supra*, para. 13–06 and *infra*, para. 13–135.

[36] *Sleech's Case* (1816) 1 Mer. 570; *Harris v. Farwell* (1846) 15 Beav. 31, *infra*, para. 13–127. See also *Rouse v. Bradford Banking Co.* [1894] 2 Ch. 32 (affirmed at [1894] A.C. 586). *Cf. Brown v. Gordon* (1852) 16 Beav. 302, *infra*, para. 13–129; *Bilborough v. Holmes* (1876) 5 Ch.D. 255, *infra*, para. 13–127, n. 42; *Ex p. Executors of James Douglas* [1930] 1 Ch. 342, 350, *per* Luxmoore J.

[37] [1893] 3 Ch. 426.

[38] [1894] 2 Ch. 236.

It is perhaps self evident that a creditor will not be prejudiced by any dealings with the surviving partner which are induced by fraud.[39]

One or more new partners introduced[40]

13–127   Again, a creditor of the old firm who, following the admission of a new partner, continues to deal with the new firm and is paid interest by that firm as if the debt was its own, will not thereby deprive himself of his rights against the estate of a deceased member of the old firm.[41]

Thus, in *Harris v. Farwell*,[42] the three partners of a banking firm were indebted to a customer on a deposit note. One partner died and his son was admitted to the partnership. The new firm paid interest on the note for some time and then became bankrupt. The plaintiff proved for the amount of his debt and received a dividend out of the new firm's joint estate. By so doing, he was held not to have precluded himself from subsequently proceeding against the deceased partner's estate.

Where creditor allows estate to be administered

13–128   However, once he has learned of a partner's death, a creditor should prudently take steps to obtain payment out of his estate: if he fails to do so and allows the administration to proceed on the footing that there is no liability, his rights may be prejudiced, as Lord Lindley explained:

> "... if, after the death of a partner, a creditor of the old firm knows of the death, and ... lies by and allows [*the*] estate to be administered as if he had no claim upon it, and if he continues to deal with the surviving partners as if they and they alone were his debtors, in that case the creditor will not be allowed to resort to the assets of the deceased."[43]

13–129   This doctrine is illustrated by *Brown v. Gordon*.[44] There the plaintiff had deposited money with a banking partnership comprising three partners, A, B and C. D subsequently became a partner. A

---

[39] As in *Plumer v. Gregory* (1874) L.R. 18 Eq. 621.
[40] Note Rules 3 and 4, *supra*, para. 13–106.
[41] *Daniel v. Cross* (1796) 3 Ves. Jr. 277.
[42] (1851) 15 Beav. 31. The report does not indicate when the customer first learned of the change in the firm. *Cf. Bilborough v. Holmes* (1876) 5 Ch.D. 255, which was a somewhat similar case. There the deceased partner's estate was again held to be discharged, although the proof was for money lent (or deemed to have been lent) to the new firm.
[43] *Oakeley v. Pasheller* (1836) 10 Bli.(N.S.) 548: see *supra*, para. 13–99 and, in particular, nn. 68, 70.
[44] (1852) 16 Beav. 302; *Bilborough v. Holmes* (1876) 5 Ch.D. 255 is a somewhat similar case: see *supra*, para. 13–128, n. 42.

died, having made a will containing a trust for the payment of his debts. E (who was A's son and the executor and residuary beneficiary under his will) was admitted as a partner. B and C then died. Each successive firm paid interest to the plaintiff on his debt. D and E were eventually made bankrupt and the plaintiff proved for the amount of his debt. He then sought payment out of A's estate, but it was held that, by neglecting to make any claim against that estate for some 16 years and by treating the successive firms as his debtors, he had discharged the estate from liability; accordingly, he could not be regarded as a creditor of the deceased, so as to benefit under the express trust for the payment of his debts.

(B) MERGER AND JUDGMENT RECOVERED

Merger of securities

Reference must also be made in this context to the doctrine of **13–130** merger, which may operate to discharge a partnership debt or obligation where a creditor obtains a security of a *higher* nature than that which he previously possessed,[45] provided that he does not accept it as a collateral security.[46]

Nature of obligation

The application of the doctrine to joint and joint and several **13–131** obligations is not entirely clear. Lord Lindley wrote:

"... there is no mean authority for saying that if two parties are jointly indebted by simple contract, and one of them gives his bond for payment of the debt, the joint debt is at an end[47]; but there are more recent decisions to the contrary,[48] and the question cannot be considered as yet settled."

Although subsequent editors have expressed the view that the "more recent decisions will probably prevail,"[49] it is submitted in the

---

[45] *Higgen's Case* (1605) 6 Co. 44b; *Owen v. Homan* (1851) 3 Mac. & G. 378; *Price v. Moulton* (1851) 10 C.B. 561; *Kidd v. Boone* (1871) 40 L.J. Ch. 531; *Ex p. Oriental Financial Corporation* (1876) 4 Ch.D. 33.
[46] *Twopenny v. Young* (1824) 3 B. & C. 208; *Ex p. Hughes* (1872) 4 Ch.D. 34, note; *Barclays Bank v. Beck* [1952] 2 Q.B. 47.
[47] *Owen v. Homan* (1851) 3 Mac. & G. 378; *Ex p. Hernaman* (1848) 12 Jur. 642 (*quaere* was this not a case of satisfaction rather than merger?).
[48] *Ansell v. Baker* (1850) 15 Q.B. 20; *Sharpe v. Gibbs* (1864) 16 C.B.(N.S.) 527.
[49] This change in fact dates from the 6th ed., in the preparation of which Lord Lindley was involved.

latest edition of *Chitty on Contracts*[50] that, in the case supposed, there will be a merger in the case of a joint debt but not in the case of a joint and several debt. On that basis, a security given by continuing partners in respect of a debt of the old firm will be capable of discharging an outgoing partner; *per contra*, perhaps, if the security is given by the continuing partners and other persons subsequently admitted to the partnership.[51]

Security for future advances

13–132   The operation of the doctrine is dependent on the existence of a present debt: it cannot apply where security is given in respect of a present *and* future debt, *e.g.* the fluctuating balance due on a running account.[52]

Nature of security

13–133   To effect a merger, the security must clearly be of a higher nature that the existing security. A bill of exchange or promissory note does not enjoy such a character, as Lord Lindley recognised:

> "If a person solely indebted enters into partnership with another, and the two give a joint note or bill for the debt of the first, and the note or bill is not paid, the creditor is not precluded from demanding payment from his original debtor,[53] unless it can be shown that the bill or note was taken in satisfaction of the original demand.[54] So, if two partners are indebted on the partnership account, and one of them gives a bill or note for the debt, and that bill or note is dishonoured, the creditor who took it will not be precluded from having recourse to both partners for payment,[55] unless it can be shown that he intended to substitute the liability of the one for the joint liability of the two."[56]

---

[50] 26th ed., para. 1741.

[51] Surely, in such a case the security will not be co-extensive with the existing security, since it will be made between different parties: see, for example, *Bell v. Banks* (1841) 3 Man. & G. 258. But see *Ex p. Hernaman* (1848) 12 Jur. 642, *supra*, n. 47.

[52] *Holmes v. Bell* (1840) 3 Man. & G. 213; *Barclays Bank v. Beck* [1952] 2 Q.B. 47.

[53] *Ex p. Seddon* (1788) 2 Cox. 49; *Ex p. Lobb* (1802) 7 Ves. Jr. 592; *Ex p. Hay* (1808) 15 Ves. Jr. 4; *Ex p. Kedie* (1832) 2 D. & C. 321; *Ex p. Meinertzhagen* (1838) 3 Deac. 101.

[54] *Ex p. Kirby* (1819) Buck 511; *Ex p. Whitmore* (1838) 3 Deac. 365; *Ex p. Jackson* (1841) 2 M.D. & D. 146.

[55] *Ex p. Hodgkinson* (1815) 19 Ves.Jr. 291; *Whitwell v. Perrin* (1858) 4 C.B.(N.S.) 412; *Bottomley v. Nuttall* (1858) 5 C.B.(N.S.) 122; *Keay v. Fenwick* (1876) 1 C.P.D. 745. See also *Bedford v. Deakin* (1818) 2 B. & A. 210, *supra*, para. 13–115; *Ex p. Raleigh* (1838) 3 M. & A. 670.

[56] See, for example, *Evans v. Drummond* (1801) 4 Esp. 89, *supra*, para. 13–121; *Reed v. White* (1804) 4 Esp. 122. *Cf.* the cases in the previous note.

Judgment recovered

Joint obligations

Although judgment recovered does technically effect a merger,[57] a **13–134** judgment against one partner in respect of a partnership debt or obligation will not be a bar to a subsequent action against other partners who are jointly liable with him.[58]

Joint and several obligations

As in the case of joint liability, judgment recovered against a **13–135** partner in respect of a joint and several partnership debt or obligation will not prevent a subsequent action against other partners jointly liable with him;[59] nor will it affect the *several* liability of any partner,[60] unless the judgment is satisfied.[61] It follows that judgment against the surviving partners of a firm will not discharge the estate of a deceased partner.[62]

Proof against insolvent partner's estate

It should be noted that proof against an insolvent partner's estate[63] **13–136** will not prevent a partnership creditor from subsequently proceeding against the solvent partners for the balance of the debt.[64]

(C) LIMITATION

A consideration of the general law governing the limitation of actions **13–137** is obviously outside the scope of the present work.[65] What is, however, of importance is to identify the extent to which an

---

[57] *Ex p. Oriental Financial Corporation* (1876) 4 Ch.D. 33; *Kendall v. Hamilton* (1879) 4 App. Cas. 504. See also *supra*, para. 13–05.

[58] Civil Liability (Contribution) Act 1978, s.3; see also *infra*, para. 20–16. For a summary of the law prior to that Act, see the 15th ed. of this work at pp. 422, 423.

[59] *Ibid.* If, however, judgment is obtained against all the partners jointly, their several liability will be extinguished, by operation of the principle *nemo debet bis vexari pro una et eadem causa* (it is a rule of law that man shall not be twice vexed for one and the same cause).

[60] *Ex p. Christie* (1832) Mont. & Bl. 352; *Lechmere v. Fletcher* (1833) 1 C. & M. 623, 635, *per* Bayley B.; *Re Davison* (1884) 13 Q.B.D. 50; *Blyth v. Fladgate* [1891] 1 Ch. 337, 353, *per* Stirling J. See also *Ansell v. Baker* (1850) 15 Q.B. 20.

[61] *Higgen's Case* (1605) 6 Co.44b; *Lechmere v. Fletcher* (1833) 1 C. & M. 623; *Field v. Robins* (1838) 8 A. & E. 90; *King v. Hoare* (1844) 13 M. & W. 494; also *Drake v. Mitchell* (1803) 3 East 251.

[62] Partnership Act 1890, s.9, *supra*, paras. 13–03 *et seq.*; *Jacomb v. Harwood* (1751) 2 Ves.Sen. 265; *Rawlins v. Wickham* (1858) 3 De G. & J. 304; *Liverpool Borough Bank v. Walker* (1859) 4 De G. & J. 24.

[63] See generally, *infra*, paras. 27–82 *et seq.*

[64] *Whitwell v. Perrin* (1858) 4 C.B.(N.S.) 412; *Bottomley v. Nuttall* (1858) 5 C.B.(N.S.) 122; *Keay v. Fenwick* (1876) 1 C.P.D. 745.

[65] See, generally, *McGee, Limitation Periods; Preston and Newsom's Limitation of Actions* (4th ed.).

acknowledgment or part payment[66] may be made by a single partner and, thus, extend the limitation period against the firm.

Continuing partnership

13-138   It is submitted that both an acknowledgment and a part payment made by a partner within the scope of his express or implied authority[67] will bind his co-partners, since it will be given by him in his capacity as agent of the firm.[68] If, however, in giving an acknowledgment, the partner has exceeded such authority, his co-partners will not be affected thereby;[69] *per contra* in the case of a part payment.[70]

Dissolved partnership

13-139   The position will be the same following the dissolution of a partnership, since each partner's authority will continue for the purposes of winding up its affairs.[71]

Notwithstanding the views expressed in previous editions of this work,[72] the current editor considers that neither an outgoing partner nor the estate of a deceased partner can escape the consequences of an acknowledgment or part payment given by the continuing or surviving partners, save only in the case of an acknowledgment given without authority. The fact that a deceased partner's estate is only *severally* liable for the debts and obligations of the firm is immaterial.[73]

---

[66] Limitation Act 1980, ss.29–31.

[67] See generally, *supra*, para. 12–02 *et seq.*

[68] Partnership Act 1890, s.5; Limitation Act 1980, s.30(2).

[69] Limitation Act 1980, s.31(6).

[70] *Ibid.* s.31(7). See also, under the old law, *Watson v. Woodman* (1875) L.R. 20 Eq. 721; *Goodwin v. Parton* (1880) 42 L.T. 568.

[71] Partnership Act 1890, s.38, *supra*, paras. 13–64 *et seq.*

[72] See the 15th ed. of this work at p. 427 and the decisions in *Watson v. Woodman* (1875) L.R 20 Eq. 721 (retired partner) and *Thompson v. Waithman* (1856) 3 Drew. 628 (executors of deceased partner). *Cf. Re Tucker* [1894] 3 Ch. 429 (where the retirement was not advertised).

[73] See the Partnership Act 1890, s.9, *supra*, para. 13–03; and see, in particular, the terms of the Limitation Act 1980, s.31(7).

CHAPTER 14

ACTIONS BY AND AGAINST PARTNERS

CIVIL actions brought by partners against a third party or vice versa **14–01**
are governed by the same rules of procedure as other actions, save
that the partners may sue or be sued in the firm name.[1] However,
this procedural nicety should not be permitted to obscure the
importance of identifying the *correct* parties to such an action,
particularly where the composition of the firm has not remained
static. This aspect will be considered in the first section of this
chapter. Subsequent sections are devoted to the authority of a
partner to act for the firm in legal proceedings, set off and the
execution of money and other judgments obtained against partners.

As regards criminal proceedings, the existence of a partnership is
of little significance,[2] save perhaps in the case of a prosecution under
certain provisions of the Trade Descriptions Act 1968.[3]

1. PARTIES TO ACTIONS AND RELATED MATTERS

In earlier editions of this work there were set out, by way of **14–02**
introduction to this section, a number of general propositions
regarding the joinder and misjoinder of parties, based on Lord
Lindley's original formulation, but these have not been retained in
the present edition.[4]

A. ACTIONS IN FIRM NAME

The general rule

Proceedings[5] by or against two or more partners who carry on **14–03**
business within the jurisdiction may be commenced in the name
under which they carried on business when the cause of action

---

[1] R.S.C. Ord. 81, r. 1, *infra*, para. A2–09; C.C.R. Ord. 5, r. 9(1). See further, *infra*, paras.
14–03 *et seq.*

[2] See *R. v. Bonner* [1970] 1 W.L.R. 838 (theft of partnership property); *Garrett v. Hooper* [1973]
Crim.L.R. 61; *Bennett v. Richardson* [1980] R.T.R. 358 (both road traffic cases).

[3] See *Clode v. Barnes* [1974] 1 W.L.R. 544, where *ibid.* s.1(1) was held to create an offence of
strict liability; *cf. Parsons v. Barnes* [1973] Crim.L.R. 537, where the Divisional Court declined to
lay down a general proposition that one partner will *necessarily* be responsible for the acts of his co-
partner in relation to an offence under *ibid.* s.14(1).

[4] The propositions are to be found in the 15th ed. of this work, at pp. 430 *et seq.*

[5] Including proceedings by way of originating summons: see R.S.C. Ord. 81, r. 8, *infra*, para.
A2–16.

accrued.[6] However, as Lord Lindley observed in relation to a forerunner of the modern rule[7]:

".... the firm's name, when used in any action, is merely a convenient method of expressing the names of those who constituted the firm when the cause of action accrued. The rule does not incorporate the firm[8]; so that if A is a creditor of a firm, B, C and D, and D retires and E takes his place and the name of the firm continues unchanged, A cannot maintain an action against B, C and E in the name of the firm, unless B, C and E have become or are content to be treated as his debtors.[9] In the case supposed, an action against the firm would mean an action against B, C and D, *i.e.* A's real debtors."

Thus, the composition of the firm at the date the proceedings are *issued* will normally be irrelevant.

It should be noted that this is a mere rule of procedure, which will neither affect the rights of the parties nor give rise to any new or independent cause of action.[10]

Carrying on business within the jurisdiction

14–04   The firm name may only be used where the partners were carrying on business within the jurisdiction when the cause of action accrued.[11] It would not seem to matter that the business has since ceased to be carried on or that the partnership has been dissolved.[12]

---

[6] *Ibid.* r. 1, *infra*, para. A2–09; C.C.R. Ord. 5, r. 9(1).

[7] *i.e.* the (then) R.S.C. Ord. xvi, r. 9.

[8] Lord Lindley referred at this point to the judgment of James L.J. in *Ex p. Blain* (1879) 12 Ch.D. 522, which scarcely seems in point. See, as to the derivation of this rule, *Bullock v. Caird* (1875) L.R. 10 Q.B. 276.

[9] See further, as to agreements to take on existing debts, *supra*, paras. 13–28 *et seq.* and *infra*, paras. 14–48 *et seq.*

[10] *Meyer & Co. v. Faber (No. 2)* [1923] 2 Ch. 421, 441, *per* Warrington L.J.; *Mephistopheles Debt Colection Service v. Lotay, The Times*, May 17, 1994.

[11] R.S.C. Ord. 81, r. 1 *infra*, para. A2–09; C.C.R. Ord. 5, r. 9(1). As to what will amount to carrying on business within the jurisdiction, see *Baillie v. Goodwin* (1886) 33 Ch.D. 604; *Grant v. Anderson & Co.* [1892] 1 Q.B. 108; *Singleton v. Roberts & Co.* (1894) 70 L.T. 687; *The Lalandia* [1933] P. 56; *Okura v. Forsbacka Jernverks Aktiebolag* [1914] 1 K.B. 715; *Thames and Mersey Marine Insurance Co. v. Societa di Navigazione a Vapore del Lloyd Austriaco* (1914) 111 L.T. 97; *Adams v. Cape Industries Plc* [1990] Ch. 433; and see also *Re Brauch* [1978] Ch. 316 (a decision under the former Bankruptcy Act 1914, s.4).

[12] See *Re Wenham* [1900] 2 Q.B. 698. Note also the decision in *Willmott v. Berry Brothers* (1982) 126 S.J. 209 (writ served in accordance with R.S.C. Ord. 81 held valid even though the partnership business had by then been transferred to a company). *Cf.* the decision of the Sheriff's Court in *D. Forbes Smith & Johnston v. Kaye*, 1975 S.L.T. 33, in relation to the Sheriff Courts (Scotland) Act 1907, Sched. 1, r. 11, which provides that "any individual or individuals, or any corporation or association carrying on business under a firm or trading or descriptive name, may sue or be sued in such name without the addition of the name or names of such individual or individuals or any of them, or of any member or official of such corporation or association ...". It should, of course, be remembered that, in Scotland, the firm has separate legal personality: see the Partnership Act 1890, s.4(2).

Provided that this test is satisfied, the nationality, domicile or residence of the partners will be immaterial.[13]

Where, on the other hand, the partners cannot be shown to be **14-05** carrying on business within the jurisdiction at the relevant time, the proceedings must be issued in their individual names,[14] unless it can be proved that the firm has separate legal personality under the law by which it was constituted.[15]

It is, perhaps, questionable whether the members of a dissolved **14-06** partnership can still be said to be carrying on business when they are merely engaged in winding up its affairs.[16] Since much is likely to turn on the precise stage reached in the winding up, prudence would seem to dictate that proceedings in respect of any cause of action accruing *after* the date of dissolution should, where possible, not be commenced in the firm name.[17]

Use of firm name in specific instances

Apparent partnership

Proceedings in a supposed firm name may properly be commenced **14-07** by or against the members of an apparent partnership.[18] If it transpires that a true partnership does not exist, the court will ensure that the action proceeds against the correct parties.[19]

Two firms with common partner

Proceedings between two firms with a common partner may be **14-08** brought in their respective names, even though, by so doing, that partner will technically be constituted both a plaintiff and a defendant.[20]

---

[13] See *Hobbs v. Australian Press Association* [1933] 1 K.B. 1; *Worcester City and County Banking Co. v. Firbank, Pauling & Co.* [1894] 1 Q.B. 784. Although this proposition was doubted in *Grant v. Anderson & Co.* [1892] 1 Q.B. 108, the effect of the then R.S.C. Ord. 48A, r. 8 (see now, Ord. 81, r. 5) appears to have been overlooked.

[14] *Indigo Co. v. Ogilvy* [1891] 2 Ch. 31; *Western National Bank of the City of New York v. Perez Triana & Co.* [1891] 1 Q.B. 304; *Dobson v. Festi Rasini & Co.* [1891] 2 Q.B. 92; *Von Hellfeld v. Rechnitzer and Mayer Frères & Co.* [1914] 1 Ch. 748.

[15] *Ibid.* A Scots partnership is, of course, a case in point: see the Partnership Act 1890, s.4(2). And see also *Dreyfus v. I.R.C.* (1929) 14 T.C. 560.

[16] See the Partnership Act 1890, s.38, *supra*, paras. 13–64 *et seq.*

[17] See *D. Forbes Smith & Johnston v. Kaye*, 1975 S.L.T. 33, noticed *supra*, para. 14–04, n. 12.

[18] R.S.C. Ord. 81, r. 1 applies in the case of "two or more persons *claiming* to be entitled, or *alleged* to be liable, as partners. . ." (emphasis supplied). C.C.R. Ord. 5, r. 9(1) is in similar terms.

[19] *Noble Lowndes and Partners (a firm) v. Hadfields Ltd.* [1939] Ch. 569. And see generally, R.S.C. Ord. 15, r. 6 (as amended); C.C.R. Ord. 5, r. 4.

[20] Although the present Rules do not expressly provide for this eventuality, it is clear that the old practice continues to apply: see R.S.C. Ord. 81, r. 6(1)(b), *infra*, para. A2–14; C.C.R. Ord. 25, r. 10(1)(b).

Change in firm

14-09   The use of the firm name following a change in the firm is permissible,[21] even though little, if any, advantage will be derived therefrom, *i.e.* it will still be necessary to identify the persons who were partners when the cause of action accrued so that service can be effected on them.[22]

Dissolved partnership

14-10   There can be no objection to proceedings being commenced against a dissolved partnership in the firm name,[23] save perhaps where the cause of action accrued after the date of dissolution.[24] However, it will again be necessary to serve the proceedings on each of the former partners;[25] *per contra*, if the plaintiff was unaware of the dissolution.

Disclosure of partners' names

14-11   Where proceedings are commenced by or against a firm in the firm name, the plaintiff or defendant (as the case may be) may require the production of a written statement setting out the full names and addresses of those partners who were members of the firm when the cause of action accrued.[26] The contents of this statement will thereafter identify the true parties to the proceedings.[27]

14-12   Although the court may direct such a statement to be verified by affidavit, there is no jurisdiction to order cross-examination of the deponent or the trial of an issue with a view to determining whether the persons named therein were in fact partners at the relevant date.[28]

Service on firm in the High Court

14-13   Where proceedings are commenced against partners in the firm name, service on them may be effected in one of three ways, namely:

(*a*) by effecting service on one or more of the partners;[29]

---

[21] *Re Wenham* [1900] 2 Q.B. 698.
[22] See R.S.C. Ord. 81, r. 3(3), *infra*, para. A2–11; C.C.R. Ord. 7, r. 13(2). See also *infra*, paras. 14–21, 14–92.
[23] *Re Wenham* [1900] 2 Q.B. 698.
[24] See *supra*, para. 14–06.
[25] See R.S.C. Ord. 81, r. 3(3), *infra*, para. A2–11; C.C.R. Ord. 7, r. 13(2). See also *infra*, paras. 14–17, 14–21, 14–92.
[26] R.S.C. Ord. 81, r. 2(1), (3), *infra*, para. A2–10; C.C.R. Ord. 5, r. 9(2), (3).
[27] R.S.C. Ord. 81, r. 2(2), *infra*, para. A2–10; C.C.R. Ord. 5, r. 9(4).
[28] *Abrahams & Co. v. Dunlop Pneumatic Tyre Co.* [1905] 1 K.B. 46.
[29] In this case, service may be effected pursuant to R.S.C. Ord. 10, r. 1(2) or C.C.R. Ord. 7, r. 1(1) (as the case may be), but strict compliance with those provisions is essential. Thus, personal service cannot be effected under R.S.C. Ord. 10, r. 1(2)(B) by posting the writ through the *firm's*
—continued on next page

(b) by effecting service on any person who, at the time, has control or management of that part of the firm's business which is carried on at its principal place of business within the jurisdiction;[30] or

(c) by sending a copy of the proceedings to the firm by ordinary first class post at that place.[31]

If service is effected in manner (a) or (b), the recipient must be notified whether he is being served as a partner or as a person having control or management of the partnership business, or both.[32] However, failure to do so would not seem to invalidate the service.[33]

Where a copy of the proceedings is to be served in manner (c) but **14–14** is sent to the wrong address, the service will nevertheless be treated as effective if the copy in fact comes into the hands of a partner at the correct address.[34]

It is equally clear that, if a partner (or the firm) agrees to accept service in some other way, e.g. service on an employee authorised for the purpose, this will be good service.[35]

Provided that service is successfully effected in one of the above ways, it will not matter that some or all of the partners are outside the jurisdiction.[36] However, it may not be possible to levy execution on such partners in respect of a judgment obtained against the firm.[37]

Substituted service

An order for substituted service may be made where attempts to **14–15** serve the proceedings on a partner and on any person having management or control of the partnership business have been unsuccessful.[38]

---

[29]—continued from previous page
letter box: *Marsden v. Kingswell* [1992] 2 All E.R. 239. The absence of express or implied authority to accept service is irrelevant. And see *Kenneth Allison Ltd. v. A.E. Limehouse & Co.* [1992] A.C. 105, 113E (*per* Lord Bridge), 124C (*per* Lord Goff).

[30] Personal service is required. Note the exceptional decision in *Willmott v. Berry Brothers* (1982) 126 S.J. 209, where the writ was held to have been validly served on the person having control of the former partnership business (which was, unknown to the plaintiff, then being carried on by a limited company) notwithstanding the fact that he had never been an employee of the firm. And see also *Meyer v. Louis Dreyfus et Cie* [1940] 4 All E.R. 157.

[31] R.S.C. Ord. 81, r. 3(1), *infra*, para. A2–11. If anything *other* than ordinary first-class post is used and actual receipt cannot be proved, it will obviously not be possible to place reliance on this limb. See also, as to service by post, *ibid.* r. 3(2). Similar (but not identical) provisions apply in the county court: C.C.R. Ord. 7, r. 13.

[32] R.S.C. Ord. 81, r. 3(4), *infra*, para. A2–11. There is no equivalent provision in the County Court Rules.

[33] It is expressly provided that, if the notice is not given, the recipient of the proceedings will be deemed to have been served as a partner: *ibid.*

[34] *Austin Rover Group Ltd. v. Crouch Butler Savage Associates* [1986] 1 W.L.R. 1102.

[35] *Kenneth Allison Ltd. v. A.E. Limehouse & Co.* [1992] A.C. 105 (service on the senior partner's personal assistant).

[36] R.S.C. Ord. 81, r. 3(1), *infra*, para. A2–11; C.C.R. Ord. 7, r. 13(1). And see *Shepherd v. Hirsch, Pritchard & Co.* (1890) 45 Ch.D. 231; *Lysaght Ltd. v. Clark & Co.* [1891] 1 Q.B. 553; *Meyer v. Louis Dreyfus et Cie* [1940] 4 All E.R. 157.

[37] See R.S.C. Ord. 81, r. 5(3), *infra*, para. A2–13; C.C.R. Ord. 25, r. 9(2). See further, *infra*, para. 14–21.

[38] See R.S.C. Ord. 65, r. 4; C.C.R. Ord. 7, r. 8. But see also *Worcester City and County Banking Co. v. Firbank, Pauling & Co.* [1894] 1 Q.B. 784, 788, *per* Lord Esher M.R.

Service out of jurisdiction

14–16   Where it is required,[39] leave to effect service of the proceedings on a partner who is outside the jurisdiction must be obtained in the normal way;[40] substituted service on a person within the jurisdiction will not be permitted.[41] Service effected with such leave will be good service on the firm.[42] Where, however, there is some special reason for effecting service on a partner outside the jurisdiction, *e.g.* with a view to executing any judgment in the proceedings against him,[43] the proceedings should either be commenced both against him *and* the firm or against all the partners in their individual names "trading as . . ."; leave to serve such proceedings on that partner should then be obtained.[44]

Dissolved firm

14–17   Where the plaintiff *knows* that the firm has been dissolved, he must serve the proceedings on all partners within the jurisdiction.[45]

Acknowledgment of service in the High Court

14–18   The service of proceedings commenced against a firm in the firm name must be acknowledged by the partners in their own names and not in the firm name, even though the proceedings will continue in that name.[46] Any person served as a partner may acknowledge service subject to a denial that he was a partner at the relevant time (or at all).[47] Such an acknowledgment will stand as an acknowledgment by the firm[48] until such time as it is set aside on the application of the plaintiff[49] or the alleged partner.[50] If such an application is not made, the issue may be raised in the alleged partner's defence.[51]

---

[39] See R.S.C. Ord. 11, r. 1(1), (2) (as amended); C.C.R. Ord. 8, r. 2(1), (2). See also, R.S.C. Ord. 81, r. 5(3)(c), *infra*, para. A2–13; C.C.R. Ord. 25, r. 9(2)(b).

[40] See R.S.C. Ord. 11, rr. 1, 4 (as amended by *ibid.*); C.C.R. Ord. 8, rr. 2, 6.

[41] *Worcester City and County Banking Co. v. Firbank, Pauling & Co.* [1894] 1 Q.B. 784.

[42] *Hobbs v. Australian Press Association* [1933] 1 K.B. 1. In that case, the plaintiff did not know that the firm was carrying on business within the jurisdiction.

[43] See R.S.C. Ord. 81, r. 5(3), *infra*, para. A2–13; C.C.R. Ord. 25, r. 9(2). See also *infra*, para. 14–21.

[44] *West of England Steamship Owners' Protection and Indemnity Association v. John Holman & Sons* [1957] 1 W.L.R. 1164.

[45] R.S.C. Ord. 81, r. 3(3), *infra*, para. A2–11; C.C.R. Ord. 7, r. 13(2). See also *Shepherd v. Hirsch, Pritchard & Co.* (1890) 45 Ch.D. 231; *Wigram v. Cox, Sons, Buckley & Co.* [1894] 1 Q.B. 793.

[46] R.S.C. Ord. 81, r. 4(1), *infra*, para. A2–12; see also *Ellis v. Wadeson* [1899] 1 Q.B. 714. And see, as to the form of the acknowledgment, the Supreme Court Practice 1995, para. 81/4/1–2.

[47] *Ibid.* Ord. 81, r. 4(2), *infra*, para. A2–12.

[48] *Ibid.*

[49] *Ibid.* Ord. 81, r. 4(3)(a), (4), *infra*, para. A2–12.

[50] *Ibid.* Ord. 81, r. 4(3)(b), (4), *infra*, para. A2–12.

[51] *Ibid.* The alleged partner may, by his defence, deny either or both (i) his liability as a partner and (ii) the liability of the firm.

If the proceedings are served on a person who has the control or management of the partnership business, he may only acknowledge service if he is in fact a partner.[52]

Judgment

Where proceedings are commenced against a firm in the firm **14–19** name, judgment must normally be entered against the firm in that name.[53] Where, however, it appears that one of the partners is a minor, judgment should be entered against the firm "other than" the minor partner.[54]

It follows that, if one partner fails to acknowledge service, **14–20** judgment cannot be entered against him separately for failure to give notice of intention to defend;[55] on the same principle, if one partner *does* acknowledge service, judgment cannot be entered against the firm.[56]

Persons against whom judgment may not be executed

A judgment against a firm cannot, without leave,[57] be executed **14–21** against any person who has not (i) acknowledged service as a partner; (ii) been served as a partner and failed to acknowledge service; (iii) pleaded that he was a partner; or (iv) been held to be a partner.[58] There is, moreover, an absolute bar on execution against any partner who was out of the jurisdiction when the proceedings were issued, unless he acknowledged service as a partner or was served as a partner within or (if leave was obtained)[59] outside the jurisdiction.[60] Accordingly, a plaintiff who has obtained judgment against a firm, not realising that it comprises foreign partners or that its composition has changed since his cause of action accrued, may find that, at best, its effective enforcement requires the initiation of further proceedings.[61]

---

[52] *Ibid.* Ord. 81, r. 4(5), *infra*, para. A2–12.
[53] *Jackson v. Litchfield* (1882) 8 Q.B.D. 474. *Cf. Munster v. Cox* (1885) 10 App.Cas. 680.
[54] *Lovell & Christmas v. Beauchamp* [1894] A.C. 607.
[55] *Jackson v. Litchfield* (1882) 8 Q.B.D. 478. The position will be the same in the county court where a default judgment is obtained under C.C.R. Ord. 9, r.6 or where judgment is obtained on the defendant's non-appearance under *ibid.* Ord. 17, r.7 or 8.
[56] *Adam v. Townend* (1884) 14 Q.B.D. 103. See also *Alden v. Beckley & Co.* (1890) 25 Q.B.D. 543.
[57] R.S.C. Ord. 81, r. 5(4), *infra*, para. A2–13.
[58] *Ibid.* Ord. 81, r. 5(2), *infra*, para. A2–13. As to the equivalent provisions in the county court, see C.C.R. Ord. 25, r. 9(1), (3).
[59] See *supra*, para. 14–16. *Quaere* what is the position if leave to serve out the jurisdiction was not required? See R.S.C. Ord. 11, r. 1(2); C.C.R. Ord. 8, r. 2(2).
[60] R.S.C. Ord. 81, r. 5(3), *infra*, para. A2–13; C.C.R. Ord. 25, r. 9(2).
[61] See *Munster v. Cox* (1885) 10 App.Cas. 680. And see also *infra*, paras. 14–90 *et seq.*

B.   PARTIES WHERE FIRM UNCHANGED

(1)   Actions by the firm

14-22 Since a claim can no longer be defeated by the misjoinder or non-joinder of parties,[62] it is not as important as it once was to identify the proper parties to an action brought by a firm; *a fortiori* where the proceedings are commenced in the firm name.[63] Nevertheless, Lord Lindley correctly observed:

> "... mistakes create delay and expense ... and if all the members of a firm sue when one only ought to do so, or one only sues when all ought to do so, and the defendant can show that he is thereby prejudiced, he can apply to have the improper parties struck out or the proper parties joined, as the case may be."[64]

Actions in Contract

14-23 Just as the liability of a firm depends on the precise nature and form of any contract entered into by a partner on its behalf,[65] so does identification of the correct parties to an action by the firm in respect of such a contract. It is, accordingly, necessary to distinguish between:

(*a*)   Written and oral contracts.[66]
(*b*)   Contracts under seal.[67]
(*c*)   Bills of exchange and promissory notes.[68]

(a)   Written and oral contracts

Rights of firm as principal

14-24 If a partner, acting within the scope of his express or implied authority,[69] enters into a written or oral contract with a third party, the firm will, as principal, be entitled to sue on that contract, whether or not its existence was disclosed to the third party.[70] As Lord Lindley put it:

---

[62] R.S.C. Ord. 15, rr. 4(2), 6(1); C.C.R. Ord. 5, r. 4. And see *Noble Lowndes and Partners (a firm) v. Hadfields Ltd.* [1939] Ch. 569, noticed *supra,* para. 14–07.
[63] See R.S.C. Ord. 81, r. 1, *infra,* para. A2–09, considered *supra,* paras. 14–03 *et seq.*; C.C.R. Ord. 5, r. 9(1). And note, in particular, R.S.C. Ord. 81, r. 2; C.C.R. Ord. 5, r. 9(2), (3): see *supra,* para. 14–11.
[64] R.S.C. Ord. 15, r. 6(2); C.C.R. Ord. 15, r. 1(1).
[65] See *supra,* paras. 12–160 *et seq.*
[66] See further, *supra,* paras. 12–163 *et seq.*
[67] See further, *supra,* paras. 12–171 *et seq.*
[68] See further, *supra,* paras. 12–175 *et seq.*
[69] Partnership Act 1890, s. 5, *supra,* paras. 12–02 *et seq.*
[70] See *supra,* para. 12–163.

"... it happens every day that a firm sues on a contract entered into on its behalf by one of its members, and it is not by any means necessary that the person dealing with him should have been aware that the one partner was acting on behalf of himself and other people. The question is, With whom was the contract made in point of law? And the true answer to this question does not by any means entirely depend on the answer to be given to the more simple question, With whom was the contract made in point of fact?"

Thus in *Garrett v. Handley*[71] all the members of a firm were held **14–25** to be entitled to sue on a written guarantee given to one of them, there being evidence to show that it was intended to benefit the firm. Similarly, where one partner in a firm of bankers had made a loan out of partnership funds, it was held that an action for the recovery of that loan was properly brought by all the partners, even though the borrower had not sought a loan from the firm.[72] Numerous other examples can be imagined.[73]

All partners should join as parties

Where a firm sues as principal, *all* the partners should normally be **14–26** made parties to the proceedings, even though a failure to join one or more of them will not itself be fatal.[74]

Dormant and apparent partners

A dormant partner may be joined as a party,[75] but this is strictly **14–27** optional, as Lord Lindley pointed out:

"... a dormant partner never *need* be joined as a co-plaintiff in an action on a contract entered into with the firm or with one of its members."[76]

---

[71] (1825) 4 B. & C. 664; and see, as to the previous proceedings (where an action by the one partner failed), (1824) 3 B. & C. 462. See also *Hopkinson v. Smith* (1822) 1 Bing. 13, as to an action by an attorney not retained by the defendant.

[72] *Alexander v. Barker* (1831) 2 C. & J. 133. *Cf. Sims v. Britain* (1832) 4 B. & Ad. 375; *Sims v. Bond* (1833) 5 B. & Ad. 389.

[73] *e.g.* the supply of goods and services: see *Townsend v. Neale* (1809) 2 Camp. 189; *Skinner v. Stocks* (1821) 4 B. & A. 437; *Arden v. Tucker* (1832) 4 B. & Ad. 815. See also *Cooke v. Seeley* (1848) 2 Ex. 746, where a bank account maintained in a partner's name was held to be a partnership account, thus entitling all the partners to sue the bank for dishonouring a cheque drawn by that partner for partnership purposes.

[74] R.S.C. Ord. 15, r. 4(2); *Cabell v. Vaughan* (1669) 1 Wms.Saund. 291k. *Cf.* C.C.R. Ord. 5, r. 2.

[75] *Cothay v. Fennell* (1830) 10 B. & C. 671; also *Robson v. Drummond* (1831) 2 B. & Ad. 303, 307, *per* Littledale J. This proposition was originally doubted: see *Mawman v. Gillett* (1809) 2 Taunt. 235; *Lloyd v. Archbowle* (1810) 2 Taunt. 324.

[76] *Leveck v. Shafto* (1796) 2 Esp. 468.

Similarly, the joinder of a person who is merely held out as a partner is not essential.[77]

Rights of contracting partner

14–28   In certain circumstances, it may be either unnecessary or inappropriate for the firm to commence proceedings, as Lord Lindley explained:

> "One partner may sue alone on a written contract made with himself if it does not appear from the contract itself that he was acting as agent of the firm[78]; and one partner ought to sue alone on a contract entered into with himself, if such contract is in fact made with him as a principal, and not on behalf of himself and others."

Thus, if a number of partners make loans out of their respective personal funds, each ought to sue individually for repayment of his loan, even if it was made pursuant to some arrangement between the partners.[79] Similarly, if one partner is the holder of an office or appointment, he alone ought to sue for payment in respect of work done in that capacity.[80]

A partner who sues on a contract made in his own name but for the benefit of the firm may recover liquidated or unliquidated damages on the firm's behalf.[81]

Partner as apparent principal

14–29   Where a contract is entered into by a partner who represents himself as a principal but is in fact acting on the firm's behalf, he alone should sue on it since it was ostensibly entered into on his own account.[82]

---

[77] *Kell v. Nainby* (1829) 10 B. & C. 20. See also *Cox v. Hubbard* (1847) 4 C.B. 317; *Spurr v. Cass* (1870) L.R. 5 Q.B. 656. Lord Lindley used the expression "nominal" partners in this context. See generally, as to holding out, the Partnership Act 1890, s.14, *supra*, paras. 5–43 *et seq.*

[78] See *Skinner v. Stocks* (1821) 4 B. & A. 437; *Cothay v. Fennell* (1830) 10 B. & C. 671. See also *Agacio v. Forbes* (1861) 14 Moo.P.C. 160, where the Privy Council held that one partner might sue on a written agreement made by him alone, even though the agreement related to the partnership business and was entered into for its benefit, and the consideration was a release of a debt due to the firm.

[79] *Thacker v. Shepherd* (1773) 2 Chitty 652; *Brand v. Boulcott* (1802) 3 Bos. & Pul. 253.

[80] *Brandon v. Hubbard* (1820) 2 Brod. & B. 11. See further, as to the status of an office or appointment held by a partner, *supra*, para. 10–43 and *infra*, paras. 18–19, 18–20.

[81] *Roberts v. Ward*, unreported, February 8, 1985 (C.A.T. No. 71); [1985] C.L.Y. p. 137.

[82] *Lucas v. De la Cour* (1813) 1 M. & S. 249.

(b) Contracts under seal

The old rule was strict in the case of a contract under seal, *i.e.* that **14–30** only the parties to that contract might sue on it.[83] Lord Lindley summarised the position in this way:

> "... if such a contract was entered into with one partner only, he alone could sue upon it; ... if it was entered into with more than one partner, all those with whom it was expressly entered into must sue upon it, and no others could, whatever their interest in its performance might be."[84]

Although this rule no longer applies, the court will still be concerned to ensure that the correct parties are joined.[85]

It follows that, whilst it is proper to join a person who is merely held out as a partner if he was a party to the contract,[86] in practice such joinder will rarely be essential.

Covenant with firm

Lord Lindley summarised the position in these terms: **14–31**

> "It is apprehended that a covenant entered into with A, B & Co. may be sued upon by the persons who, when the covenant was made, constituted that firm."[87]

Recovery of partnership moneys

If one partner enters into a contract under seal and, pursuant **14–32** thereto, a payment is made out of partnership funds, that partner may sue for the return of the money if it ultimately transpires that the contract was invalidated by some fraud.[88]

(c) Bills of exchange and promissory notes

Unless the only or last indorsement is in blank, the proper parties to **14–33** an action on a bill or note are those named in it as drawers, payees, or indorsees, as the case may be.[89] The fact that they are partners or

---

[83] The law relating to such contracts is unaffected by the Partnership Act 1890: see *ibid.* s.6, *supra*, paras. 12–161, 12–171 *et seq.*

[84] See *Cabell v. Vaughan* (1669) 1 Wms.Saund. 291; *Scott v. Godwin* (1797) 1 Bos. & Pul. 67; *Vernon v. Jefferys* (1740) 2 Str. 1146; *Metcalf v. Rycroft* (1817) 6 M. & S. 75.

[85] See R.S.C. Ord. 15, r. 6; C.C.R. Ords. 5, r. 4 and 15, r. 1(1). And see *supra*, para. 14–22.

[86] *Guidon v. Robson* (1809) 2 Camp. 302 (a case of a bill of exchange).

[87] See generally, *supra*, paras. 3–06 *et seq.*

[88] *Lefevre v. Boyle* (1832) 3 B. & Ad. 877.

[89] See *Pease v. Hirst* (1829) 10 B. & C. 122; also *Guidon v. Robson* (1809) 2 Camp. 302. But see now R.S.C. Ord. 15, r. 6; C.C.R. Ord. 5, r. 4.

that the bill or note relates to partnership matters is strictly irrelevant: thus, if a debtor of the firm makes his promissory note payable to one partner, that partner should himself sue on the note.[90] If, on the other hand, the only or last indorsement is in blank, any person holding the bill or note may sue on it.[91]

If the name of a person who is merely held out as a partner appears on the bill or note, he may be joined as a party to the proceedings,[92] although failure to join him is unlikely to be fatal.[93]

Bills in firm name

14–34   Lord Lindley observed:

> "If a bill is drawn by or in favour of a firm in its commercial name, the persons who composed the firm when the bill was drawn ought to be the plaintiffs."[94]

Those partners may normally sue in the firm name.[95]

Bills accepted for honour

14–35   If one partner in his own name accepts a bill drawn on a third party for honour and, with his co-partners' consent, pays that bill when it falls due out of partnership funds, he should sue the drawee for indemnity.[96]

ACTIONS IN TORT

14–36 In the cases of tortious claims, the general rule, as formulated by Lord Lindley, is that:

> "... where a joint damage accrues to several persons from a tort, they ought all to join in an action founded upon it[97]; whilst on the other hand several persons ought not to join in an action *ex delicto*, unless they can show a joint damage."[98]

---

[90] *Bawden v. Howell* (1841) 3 Man. & G. 638.
[91] See the Bills of Exchange Act 1882, ss.8(3), 89. And see the old cases: *Ord v. Portal* (1812) 3 Camp. 239; *Attwood v. Rattenbury* (1822) 6 Moore 579; *Lowe v. Copestake* (1828) 3 Car. & P. 300.
[92] *Guidon v. Robson* (1809) 2 Camp. 302. But *cf.* the Bills of Exchange Act 1882, s.23(2).
[93] See R.S.C. Ord. 15, r. 6(1); C.C.R. Ord. 5, r. 4; also *supra*, para. 14–22.
[94] At this point, Lord Lindley cited *McBirney v. Harran* (1843) 5 I.L.R. 428 and *Phelps v. Lyle* (1839) 10 A. & E. 113; yet the former case, if anything, appears to be contrary to the proposition in the text, whilst the latter hardly seems relevant. A later editor added a reference to the Bills of Exchange Act 1882, s.23(2), which deals with the *liability* of a firm.
[95] See R.S.C. Ord. 81, r. 1, *infra*, para. A2–09; C.C.R. Ord. 5, r. 9(1). And see *supra*, paras. 14–03 *et seq.*
[96] *Driver v. Burton* (1852) 17 Q.B. 989.
[97] See *Cabell v. Vaughan* (1669) 1 Wms.Saund. 291m; *Addison v. Overend* (1796) 6 T.R. 766; *Sedgworth v. Overend* (1797) 7 T.R. 279.
[98] 2 Wms.Saund. 116a.

Thus, if a firm is libelled, all the partners may maintain an action for damages;[99] and if the libel directly affects one partner and, through him, the firm, two independent causes of action will arise, one in favour of the libelled partner and the other in favour of him and his co-partners.[1] Where, however, the firm suffers no damage, only the libelled partner should sue.[2]

Wrongful interference with goods

An action for wrongful interference[3] with goods belonging to the **14–37** firm should be brought in the firm name or (which obviously amounts to the same thing) by all the partners; however, one partner may seemingly be authorised to sue on the firm's behalf.[4] If he does not have such authority, he will prima facie only be entitled to recover damages in respect of *his* interest in the goods.[5] This will not prevent one of his co-partners bringing a subsequent action, unless this would involve "double liability."[6]

Fraud and collusion between partner and third party

If one partner and a third party collude together with a view to **14–38** perpetrating a fraud on the firm, the innocent partners may clearly maintain an action against the third party. Thus, where one partner was, to the knowledge of the firm's bankers, in the habit of drawing bills in the firm name for his own private purposes and the bankers colluded with him, keeping the true facts from the other partners and paying the bills when they fell due out of funds standing to the firm's credit, it was held that the other partners could bring an action against the bankers.[7] In such cases, the fraudulent partner will normally be joined as a defendant, if he refuses to be a co-plaintiff.[8]

---

[99] See *Cook v. Batchellor* (1802) 3 Bos. & Pul. 150; *Forster v. Lawson* (1826) 3 Bing. 452; *Williams v. Beaumont* (1833) 10 Bing. 260; *Le Fanu v. Malcolmson* (1848) 1 H.L.C. 637; *Metropolitan Saloon Omnibus Co. v. Hawkins* (1859) 4 H. & N. 87; and see generally, *South Hetton Coal Co. v. North-Eastern News Association* [1894] 1 Q.B. 133.

[1] The two actions can now be combined: see Ord. 15, r. 4(1); *Thomas v. Moore* [1918] 1 K.B. 555. And see as to the damage recoverable in each action, *Forster v. Lawson* (1826) 3 Bing. 452; *Haythorn v. Lawson* (1827) 3 Car. & P. 196; *Harrison v. Bevington* (1838) 8 Car. & P. 708.

[2] *Solomons v. Medex* (1816) 1 Stark. 191; also *Pullman v. Hill & Co.* [1891] 1 Q.B. 524. It is immaterial that the libel affects him in his business capacity: see *Harrison v. Bevington* (1838) 8 Car. & P. 708; *Robinson v. Marchant* (1845) 7 Q.B. 918.

[3] See the Torts (Interference with Goods) Act 1977, s.1.

[4] See R.S.C. Ord. 15, r. 10A (as added by R.S.C. (Amendment No. 3) 1978 (S.I. 1978 No. 579), r. 7 and amended by R.S.C. (Writ and Appearance) 1979 (S.I. 1979 No. 1716), Sched.); C.C.R. Ord. 15, r. 4.

[5] See the Torts (Interference with Goods) Act 1977, ss.5, 7; also *Addison v. Overend* (1796) 6 T.R. 766; *Bleadon v. Hancock* (1829) 4 Car. & P. 152.

[6] *Ibid.* s.5(4); see also *Sedgworth v. Overend* (1797) 7 T.R. 279.

[7] *Longman v. Pole* (1828) Moo. & M. 223.

[8] R.S.C. Ord. 15, r. 4(2); *Johnson v. Stephens & Carter Ltd. and Golding* [1923] 2 K.B. 857. See also *Williamson v. Barbour* (1877) 9 Ch.D. 529, 536, *per* Jessel M.R. The position is no different in the county court.

ACTIONS IN RESPECT OF LAND

14-39 Where a firm seeks possession of land, the action should be brought in the names of those partners (or other persons)[9] in whom the legal estate is vested.[10] However, Lord Lindley went on to point out:

> "[*if*] one partner only has made a lease of the partnership property, then, as his title cannot be disputed by the lessee, notice to quit may be given and ejectment maintained by the lessor alone; and if he alone has the legal estate, the circumstances that rent has been paid to the firm, and receipts for it have been given by all the partners, will not affect his right to give the notice and bring the action in his own name."[11]

(2) Actions against the firm

14-40 When considering actions against a firm, it should be remembered that not only is the misjoinder or non-joinder of parties no longer fatal,[12] but the recovery of judgment against one partner in respect of any debt or damage is no longer a bar to subsequent proceedings against another partner jointly liable with him.[13] Nevertheless, it will still be desirable to ensure that the correct parties are joined so as to avoid unnecessary argument[14] and, more importantly, adverse consequences in costs.[15]

ACTIONS IN CONTRACT

The general rule

14-41 The circumstances in which partners may become bound in contract, and thus liable to be sued by a third party, have been considered in some detail in the preceding chapters. It follows that, if the firm is liable on a contract, all the partners ought normally to be

---

[9] *e.g.* one or more former partners or the estate of a deceased partner.

[10] In this connection, Lord Lindley referred to *Chitty on Pleading* (7th ed., 1844), Vol. 1, p. 74.

[11] See *Doe v. Baker* (1818) 8 Taunt. 241.

[12] R.S.C. Ord. 15, r. 6(1); C.C.R. Ord. 5, r. 4.

[13] Civil Liability (Contribution) Act 1978, s.3. See further *supra*, para. 13–05 and *infra*, para. 20–16.

[14] *i.e.* under R.S.C. Ord. 15, r. 6(2) or C.C.R. Ord. 15, r. 1(1). See, for example, *Pilley v. Robinson* (1887) 20 Q.B.D. 155; *Wilson, Sons & Co. Ltd. v. Balcarres Brook Steamship Co. Ltd.* [1893] 1 Q.B. 422; *Robinson v. Geisel* [1894] 2 Q.B. 685; *Norbury, Natzio & Co. v. Griffiths* [1918] 2 K.B. 369.

[15] Civil Liability (Contribution) Act 1978, s.4.

sued jointly;[16] if, on the other hand, a contract entered into by a partner does *not* bind the firm,[17] that partner alone should be sued.[18] Where, as will usually be the case, the liability of the firm is in doubt, prudence dictates that all the partners should in the first instance be joined and the claim formulated in the alternative, so that judgment can be obtained against the correct parties at trial.[19] If one of the original contracting partners is dead, his personal representatives may (and, in some cases, should) be joined along with the surviving partners.[20]

Where all the partners are joined, failure to serve one partner will not prevent the action from proceeding against the others.[21]

Dormant partners

Since a dormant partner will be liable in the same way as any other **14–42** partner,[22] he ought normally to be joined as a party to any action brought on a contract which binds the firm.[23] However, it may be that the other partners will not themselves be able to apply to have the dormant partner joined as a party, as Lord Lindley explained:

"... a person who holds himself out to another, as the only person with whom that other is dealing, cannot be allowed afterwards to say that such other was also dealing with somebody else."[24]

This rule will prima facie apply whenever a partner enters into a written contract without making it clear that he is acting on behalf of the firm.[25]

---

[16] This is no longer mandatory: see *supra*, para. 14–40. See also *Cabell v. Vaughan* (1669) 1 Wms.Saund. 291b, note; *Byers v. Dobey* (1789) 1 H.Blacks. 236; *Bonfield v. Smith* (1844) 12 M. & W. 405; *Robinson v. Geisel* [1894] 2 Q.B. 685. And note the Carriers Act 1830, ss.5, 6.

[17] See, generally, *supra*, paras. 12–01 *et seq.*

[18] If the partner contracted as a principal, he can be sued on the contract; if he contracted as an agent, he can be sued for damages for breach of an implied warranty of authority: see *Lewis v. Nicholson* (1852) 18 Q.B. 503; *Collen v. Wright* (1857) 8 E. & B. 647. See also *Hudson v. Robinson* (1816) 4 M. & S. 475, as to the recovery of money paid under a contract which does not bind the firm.

[19] R.S.C. Ord. 15, r. 4(1); C.C.R. Ord. 5, r. 2; *Honduras Ry. v. Tucker* (1877) 2 Ex.D. 301; *Bullock v. L.G.O. Co.* [1907] 1 K.B. 264.

[20] See *infra*, para. 26–22.

[21] *Robinson v. Geisel* [1894] 2 Q.B. 685.

[22] *Robinson v. Wilkinson* (1817) 3 Price 538; *Beckham v. Drake* (1843) 11 M. & W. 315, *supra*, para. 12–166; *Court v. Berlin* [1897] 2 Q.B. 396, *supra*, para. 13–56. And see also *supra*, paras. 12–170, 13–54 *et seq.*

[23] See *Bonfield v. Smith* (1844) 12 M. & W. 405; also *Dubois v. Lubert* (1814) 5 Taunt. 609 (but see the next note). If a person is sued as a dormant partner, his membership of the firm must be proved if liability is to be established: see *Hall v. Bainbridge* (1840) 8 Dow. 583.

[24] See *Stansfield v. Levy* (1820) 3 Stark 8; *De Mautort v. Saunders* (1830) 1 B. & Ad. 398. Whether a defendant has held himself out in such way is, for the most part, a question of fact: *cf.* the cases in the preceding note. See also *Colson v. Selby* (1796) 1 Esp. 452; *Baldney v. Ritchie* (1816) 1 Stark. 338; *Mullett v. Hook* (1827) Moo. & M. 88. Lord Lindley observed that the contrary decision in *Dubois v. Ludert* (1814) 5 Taunt. 609 "cannot, it is conceived, be supported."

[25] See *Higgins v. Senior* (1841) 8 M. & W. 834.

No distinction now requires to be drawn between actions in respect of joint and joint and several contracts.[26]

Partners out of the jurisdiction

14-43   A partner who is out of the jurisdiction need not be joined.[27] If, however, he is to be made a party, leave to serve the proceedings on him may be required,[28] unless the proceedings are issued in the firm name.[29]

Minor partners

14-44   Since a minor partner will not be bound by any contract entered into by or on behalf of the firm, he ought not be joined;[30] however, there is nothing improper in issuing proceedings in the firm name.[31]

ACTIONS IN TORT

14-45 It has already been seen that partners are jointly and severally liable for torts committed by a partner in the ordinary course of carrying on the firm's business,[32] so that proceedings may properly be issued against any one or more of them.[33] It seems that, under the old law, if some of the partners were sued, they could not insist on the others being joined,[34] even where the tort was committed by an employee,[35]

---

[26] *Cf.* the former R.S.C. Ord. 15, r. 4(3) (revoked by R.S.C. (Amendment No. 2) 1979 (S.I. 1979 No. 402), r. 15). And see as to the old law, *Cabell v. Vaughan* (1669) 1 Wms.Saund. 291g, note.

[27] See *Wilson, Sons & Co. Ltd. v. Balcarres Brook Steamship Co. Ltd.* [1893] 1 Q.B. 422. But *cf. West of England Steamship Owners' Protection and Indemnity Association v. John Holman & Sons* [1957] 1 W.L.R. 1164, *supra*, para. 14–16.

[28] See R.S.C. Ord. 11, r. 1(1), (2); C.C.R. Ord. 8, r. 2(1), (2).

[29] See *supra*, para. 14–04.

[30] See 1 Wms.Saund. 207a; *Chandler v. Danks* (1800) 3 Esp. 76; *Jaffray v. Frebain* (1803) 5 Esp. 47; *Burgess v. Merrill* (1812) 4 Taunt. 468. *Cf.* the views expressed in *Ex p. Henderson* (1798) 4 Ves.Jr. 164; *Gibbs v. Merrill* (1810) 3 Taunt. 307.

[31] See *Harris v. Beauchamp Bros.* [1893] 2 Q.B. 534; *Lovell & Christmas v. Beauchamp* [1894] A.C. 607; also *supra*, para. 14–19. *Quaere* whether, if the plaintiff knows of the minor partner's existence, he should issue the proceedings against the firm "other than" the minor partner.

[32] See the Partnership Act 1890, ss.10, 12, *supra*, paras. 12–89 *et seq.*, 13–12.

[33] This will prima facie extend to tortious claims in respect of land held by the firm and to actions for the recovery of penalties imposed by statute. This represented a change in the law: see as to claims relating to land, 1 Wms.Saund. 298f and g; *Mitchell v. Tarbutt* (1794) 5 T.R. 649; and, as to penalties, *Bristow v. James* (1797) 7 T.R. 257.

[34] *Sutton v. Clarke* (1815) 6 Taunt. 29.

[35] *Mitchell v. Tarbutt* (1794) 5 T.R. 649; *Ansell v. Waterhouse* (1817) 6 M. & S. 385.

but it is by no means certain that the court would still adopt this approach.

(3) Equitable remedies

Lord Lindley dealt with equitable remedies as a separate subject, **14–46** observing that:

> "As a general rule an action in the Chancery Division by or against an ordinary partnership will be defective for want of parties, unless all the partners are before the Court."[36]

Since, however, the same rules as to parties now apply to all Divisions of the High Court,[37] no such general rule now exists. Nevertheless, since the court might, in the exercise of its discretion, have regard to the older cases, the following passage from Lord Lindley's original text has been retained:

> "All the members of a firm ought to be parties to an action for a general account[38]; and in an action for payment of a partnership debt out of the assets of a deceased partner the surviving partners ought to be parties.[39] But if the ground of action is fraud it is not necessary to join a partner not implicated in it and not sought to be made liable."[40]

Actions for account against agents

Where the services of an agent are employed by one partner in the **14–47** course of carrying on the partnership business, the firm may, on normal principles, sue the agent for an account even though he did not know of its existence.[41] *Per contra* if the partner concerned was himself acting as a principal or if the agent was induced by the other partners to *believe* that he was so acting.[42] Equally, in such a case, the agent prima facie cannot insist on the other partners being joined as parties to the action.[43]

---

[36] There were exceptions to this rule: see *Cowslad v. Cely* (1698) Pr. Ch. 83; *Darwent v. Walton* (1742) 2 Atk. 510; also *Orr v. Chase* (1812) 1 Mer. 729.
[37] See R.S.C. Ord. 15, rr. 4, 6. See also *supra*, para. 14–22. The position is the same in the county court: C.C.R. Ord. 5, rr. 2, 4.
[38] *Coppard v. Allen* (1864) 2 De G.J. & S. 173.
[39] *Hills v. M'Rae* (1851) 9 Hare 297; *Re Hodgson* (1885) 31 Ch.D. 177. See also *infra*, para. 26–17.
[40] See *Atkinson v. Mackreth* (1866) L.R. 2 Eq. 570; *Plumer v. Gregory* (1874) L.R. 18 Eq. 621.
[41] See *Killock v. Greg* (1828) 4 Russ. 285; *Anon.* (1653) Godb. 90.
[42] See *Killock v. Greg, supra*; *Maxwell v. Greig* (1828) 1 Coop. P.C. 491.
[43] *Benson v. Hadfield* (1844) 4 Hare 32; see also *Aspinall v. The London and North-Western Ry.* (1853) 11 Hare 325.

A surviving partner may clearly sue an agent of the firm for an account, since he alone has authority to wind up the firm's affairs.[44]

C. PARTIES WHERE CHANGE IN FIRM HAS OCCURRED

Incoming and outgoing partners

14–48   It has already been seen that, as a general rule, an outgoing partner will not be freed from liability in respect of the debts and obligations of the firm incurred prior to the date on which he ceased to be a partner, but that his liability for *future* debts and obligations will cease once his retirement (or expulsion) has been duly notified.[45] Similarly, an incoming partner will not normally undertake liability for debts and obligations incurred prior to the date of his admission to the firm.[46] Although an application of these principles may (and, indeed, frequently will) determine who should properly be made a party to an action by or against a firm following a change in its composition, further guidance is to be found in a number of propositions originally formulated by Lord Lindley.[47] These propositions must, however, be read subject to the overriding rule that proceedings cannot be defeated by the misjoinder or non-joinder of parties.[48]

14–49   *Proposition 1: Joinder of outgoing partners*

"... a retired partner[49] ought to join as a plaintiff, and be joined as a defendant, in every action to which, had he not retired, he would have been a necessary party.[50] This rule holds good even where a contract is entered into before, and the breach of it occurs after the retirement of a partner."[51]

It is, however, prima facie neither necessary nor appropriate to join an outgoing partner as a co-plaintiff if he has no beneficial

---

[44] Partnership Act 1890, s.38, *supra*, paras. 13–64 *et seq.*; and see *Dixon v. Hammond* (1819) 2 B. & A. 310; *Philips v. Philips* (1828) 3 Hare 281; also *Haig v. Gray* (1850) 3 De G. & Sm. 741.
[45] See the Partnership Act 1890, ss.17(2), (3), 36, *supra*, paras. 13–42 *et seq.*
[46] *Ibid.* s.17(1), *supra*, paras. 13–25 *et seq.* See also *supra*, para. 10–45.
[47] These propositions, which do not appear in their original order, are drawn from various statements which appeared in the 5th ed. of this work at pp. 284–287.
[48] See R.S.C. Ord. 15, r. 6; C.C.R. Ord. 5, r. 4; see also *supra*, para. 14–22.
[49] An expelled partner will be in precisely the same position.
[50] Lord Lindley did, however, refer to the fact that, in *Atkinson v. Laing* (1822) Dowl. & Ry.N.P. 16, "it was held at Nisi Prius that where two partners sold goods, and they afterwards dissolved partnership, an action for the price of those goods was sustainable by the one partner who continued to carry on the business of the late firm; but the propriety of this decision is more than questionable."
[51] See *Dobbin v. Foster* (1844) 1 Car. & K. 323.

interest in the outcome of the proceedings and the defendant has no claim against him.[52]

Proposition 2: Joinder of incoming partners   **14–50**

"... an incoming partner can neither sue nor be sued in respect of a liability of the old firm, unless there is some agreement express or implied between himself and the person suing him or being sued by him."[53]

Proposition 3: Incoming partner undertaking debts, etc.   **14–51**

"... if an incoming partner has agreed with his co-partners to take upon himself the debts and liabilities of the old firm,[54] they can require him to be made a defendant for their own partial indemnity."

What is contemplated here is, in practice, the joinder of the incoming partner pursuant to a third party notice.[55]

Proposition 4: Incoming partner with interest in action   **14–52**

"... a new partner may, it is apprehended, always be joined in an action to recover a debt or enforce a demand in which he has an interest,[56] provided his joinder does not prejudice the rights of the defendants."[57]

Proposition 5: Express assignment of debts   **14–53**

"... if on the introduction of a new partner or the retirement of an old partner the debts due to the old firm are ... assigned to the new firm, the new firm can sue in respect of them, either in its mercantile name or in the names of its members."

---

[52] See *William Brandt's Sons & Co. v. Dunlop Rubber Co. Ltd.* [1905] A.C. 454, 462, where Lord Macnaghten considered the position of the trustees in bankruptcy of the members of a bankrupt firm who were the assignors of the debt sought to be recovered by the plaintiffs. Lord Lindley's original proposition was more tentative: "Whether, however, it is now necessary to joint as a plaintiff a retired partner against whom the defendant has no claim, and who has no beneficial interest in what is sought to be recovered admits of some doubt."
[53] See *Wilsford v. Wood* (1794) 1 Esp. 182; *Ord v. Portal* (1812) 3 Camp. 239, note; *Young v. Hunter* (1812) 4 Taunt. 582; *Waters v. Paynter* (1826) Chitty on Bills (10th ed.), p. 406, note 5; *Vere v. Ashby* (1829) 10 B. & C. 288. And see *supra*, paras. 13–24 *et seq.*
[54] See *supra*, paras. 10–45, 13–28 *et seq.*
[55] R.S.C. Ord. 16, r. 1; C.C.R. Ord. 12, r. 1.
[56] Such an interest may be acquired by means of an equitable assignment of the debt or other chose in action: see *Holt v. Heatherfield Trust* [1942] 2 K.B. 1.
[57] R.S.C. Ord. 15, r. 6; C.C.R. Ord. 5, r. 4, Ord. 15, r. 1(1)

The rights of the new firm are dependent on an express assignment of the debts pursuant to section 136 of the Law of Property Act 1925,[58] but such assignments are, in practice, rare.

14–54   *Proposition 6: Contract made by agent in ignorance of change*

"[*If*] one partner retires, and a new partner comes in, and an agent of the firm, in ignorance of the change which has occurred, enters into a contract on behalf of the firm ... the members of the new firm may sue on the contract, unless the defendant is prejudiced by their so doing.[59] The liability of the retired partner on such a contract will, however, cease if the creditor sues the new firm and recovers judgment against it."[60]

14–55   *Proposition 7: Bills of exchange and promissory notes*

"As regards negotiable instruments, ... any persons who can agree to sue jointly upon them may do so, provided the instrument is in such a state as to pass by delivery; therefore, if a bill or note, indorsed in blank, is given to a firm consisting of certain individuals, who afterwards take in a new partner, they and he, or some or one of them, may sue on that bill or note."[61]

14–56   *Proposition 8: Fresh contract*

"A new firm may sue or be sued in respect of a fresh contract entered into by or with it to pay a debt owing to or by an old firm."

Thus, if a debtor of the old firm contracts a further debt with the new firm and then settles an account with the latter in respect of the debts due to it and to the old firm, the new firm may sue on an account stated for the entire amount due.[62]

14–57   *Proposition 9: Where firm cannot sue*

"Although a change in a firm, whether by the introduction of a new partner or the retirement of an old one, cannot, except as already mentioned, confer upon the partners any new right of action against strangers, or *vice versa*, as regards what may have occurred before the change took place, it may, nevertheless,

---

[58] This section replaced the Judicature Act 1873, s.25(6).
[59] *Mitchell v. Lapage* (1816) Holt, N.P. 253; but see also *Boulton v. Jones* (1857) 2 H. & N. 564.
[60] See *Scarf v. Jardine* (1882) 7 App. Cas. 345, *supra*, paras. 5–62, 13–04.
[61] See *Ord v. Portal* (1812) 3 Camp. 239; also *supra*, para. 14–33.
[62] *Moor v. Hill* (1795) Peake Add. Cases 10.

operate so as to discharge a person from a contract previously entered into by him."

The potential consequences of a change in the firm as regards contracts of a personal nature and sureties have already been noticed earlier in this work.[63]

Deceased partners

The personal representatives of a deceased partner may be joined **14-58** as co-plaintiffs or co-defendants with the surviving partners,[64] although this would be inappropriate where the obligation sought to be enforced by or against the firm is solely of a joint nature.[65] Nevertheless, it is considered that the surviving partners will usually be the only *necessary* parties to proceedings brought by the firm.[66]

Bankrupt or insolvent partners

A bankrupt partner need not be joined as a party to any **14-59** proceedings brought by or against the firm,[67] and the position would seem to be the same in the case of an insolvent corporate partner.[68] However, in an appropriate case, the trustee in bankruptcy or liquidator should, perhaps, be joined as a co-plaintiff.[69] If a bankrupt partner is joined as a co-defendant with the solvent partners, the court may order a stay as against him;[70] in contrast, proceedings may only be commenced against an insolvent corporate partner with the leave of the court.[71]

---

[63] See *supra*, paras. 3–36 *et seq.*, 3–43 *et seq.*

[64] R.S.C. Ord. 15, r. 4; C.C.R. Ord. 5, r. 2.

[65] This will be relatively rare: see the Partnership Act 1890, ss.9, 12; also *supra*, paras. 13–06 *et seq.*

[66] See *Chandroutie v. Gajadhar* [1987] A.C. 147; as to the position in Scotland, see *Nicoll v. Reid*, 1877 S.C. 137. And see, as to the devolution of the title to debts and other partnership assets, *infra*, paras. 18–62 *et seq.*; also, generally, the following cases decided prior to the Judicature Acts: *Martin v. Crompe* (1698) 1 Ld. Ray. 340; *Richards v. Heather* (1817) 1 B. & A. 29; *Dixon v. Hammond* (1819) 2 B. & A. 310; *Calder v. Rutherford* (1822) 3 Brod. & B. 302; *Philips v. Philips* (1828) 3 Hare 281; *Haig v. Gray* (1850) 3 De G. & Sm. 741.

[67] Insolvency Act 1986, s.345(4). A similar provision was contained in the Bankruptcy Act 1914, s.118, as to which see *Josselson v. Borst* [1938] 1 K.B. 723, 736, *per* Greer L.J.; and see *Hawkins v. Ramsbottom* (1814) 6 Taunt. 179.

[68] See generally, the Insolvency Act 1986, ss.126(1), 128(1), 130(2). No provision corresponding to *ibid.* s.345(4) applies to insolvent companies. See also the Insolvent Partnerships Order 1986, Art. 15(3).

[69] See, for example, the views expressed in *Williams and Muir Hunter on Bankruptcy* (19th ed.), p. 471. If the success of the action is dependent on impeaching an act of the bankrupt or insolvent partner and this can only be done by the trustee or liquidator, the latter will be a *necessary* party: see *Heibut v. Nevill* (1870) L.R. 5 C.P. 478, *infra*, para. 14–64. There is no provision in the Insolvency Act 1986 equivalent to that contained in the Bankruptcy Act 1914, s.117, which enabled the court to authorise the trustee to commence proceedings on the firm's behalf.

[70] Insolvency Act 1986, s.285(1). And see *Ex p. Mills* (1871) L.R. 6 Ch. App. 594; also the notes to *ibid.* s.285 in *Muir Hunter on Personal Insolvency*.

[71] *Ibid.* s.130(2).

Once a firm has been ordered to be wound up as an unregistered company,[72] no action may be commenced against it or against any partner, solvent or insolvent, without the leave of the court.[73]

D. CONDUCT OF ONE PARTNER AFFECTING FIRM'S RIGHTS

Actions by firm: disability affecting one partner

14–60   The general principle that a disability affecting one partner will also affect the firm has already been noticed,[74] and it is nowhere more pertinent than in the present context. Summarising the apparent effect of the decided cases, Lord Lindley observed:

> "... the conduct of one partner affords a defence to an action by him and his co-partners, or by them without him, where they are bound by his act, either by adopting and seeking the benefit of it,[75] or upon the ground that it is on ordinary principles of agency the act of the firm; and binding upon him and his co-partners accordingly."[76]

14–61   Thus, it has repeatedly been held that if a solicitor accepts the office of trustee but has no power under the trust instrument to charge for his services, that disability will prevent his firm from recovering any profit costs for acting as solicitors to the trust.[77] Similarly, if a partner committed some fraud when entering into a contract on behalf of the firm[78] or is involved in some illegal act in the course of a partnership transaction,[79] he and his co-partners may be unable to sue because, as Lord Lindley put it, "their innocence does not purge his guilt." A civil proceedings order[80] against one partner will necessarily prevent the firm from instituting proceedings without the leave of the court.[80a]

---

[72] See *infra*, paras. 27–08 *et seq.*
[73] Insolvency Act 1986, s.227. And see *infra*, paras. 27–20, 27–41.
[74] See *supra*, paras. 3–41 *et seq.* And see also *Salomons v. Nissen* (1788) 2 T.R. 674.
[75] As in *Ex p. Bell* (1813) 1 M. & S. 751, *infra*, para. 14–63; *Broughton v. Broughton* (1854) 5 De G.M. & G. 160.
[76] Lord Lindley then went on to point out that "... the cases at law which go further than this cannot, it is submitted, be now relied upon."
[77] See *Collins v. Carey* (1839) 2 Beav. 128; *Christophers v. White* (1847) 10 Beav. 523; *Broughton v. Broughton* (1854) 5 De G.M. & G. 160; *Matthison v. Clarke* (1854) 3 Drew. 3; also *Re Boyle* [1947] I.R. 61. An exception is made in the case of litigation: see *Craddock v. Piper* (1850) 1 Mac. & G. 664; *Re Corsellis* (1883) 34 Ch.D. 675; and see *Re Doody* [1893] 1 Ch. 129, 141–142, *per* Lindley L.J. The worst effects of such disability may be avoided by suitable arrangements between the solicitor trustee and the other partners: see *Clack v. Carlon* (1861) 30 L.J. Ch. 639; *Re Gates* [1933] 1 Ch. 913.
[78] See *Kilby v. Wilson* (1825) Ry. & M. 178.
[79] See *Biggs v. Lawrence* (1789) 3 T.R. 454.
[80] See, as to such orders, the Supreme Court Act 1981, s.42 (as amended by the Prosecution of Offences Act 1985, s.24.
[80a] *Mephistopheles Debt Collection Service v. Lotay, The Times*, May 17, 1994. The partner in question was a *limited* partner.

The same principle will prevent a partner, who has drawn a bill of **14–62** exchange in his own name and secured its acceptance by a third party subject to conditions, from seeking to avoid those conditions merely by indorsing the bill to his firm.[81] His partners will be in no better position even if they alone sue on the bill.[82]

Death of partner affected by disability

It is, perhaps, self evident that a disability which affects one **14–63** partner and, through him, the firm may persist even after the date of his death.[83] Thus, in *Ex p. Bell*,[84] where one partner had loaned partnership money to a third party for an illegal purpose and then died, the surviving partners were not able to recover that loan from the third party.

Insolvency of partner affected by disability

In the same way, the trustee in bankruptcy or liquidator of an **14–64** insolvent partner or firm will in general be in no better position than the partners,[85] unless he can set aside the transaction entered into by the insolvent partner which gives rise to the disability.[86] Thus, in *Heilbut v. Nevill*,[87] which was decided under the old bankruptcy laws, a solvent partner and the assignees of a bankrupt partner were able to maintain an action on a bill of exchange belonging to the firm, which the bankrupt partner had indorsed to his own creditor in circumstances which constituted a fraudulent preference.

Frauds on firm and other exceptional cases

Although the position was formerly otherwise,[88] the principle under **14–65** consideration does not apply in cases where one partner has, with the connivance of the defendant, committed a fraud on the firm.[89]

---

[81] *Sparrow v. Chisman* (1829) 9 B. & C. 241; see also *Richmond v. Heapy* (1816) 1 Stark. 202.
[82] *Astley v. Johnson* (1860) 5 H. & N. 137.
[83] Although the disability will persist as to *past* transactions, it may be removed for the future, *e.g.* where, in the example given *supra*, para. 14–61, the solicitor trustee dies.
[84] (1813) 1 M. & S. 751. See also *Brandon v. Scott* (1857) 7 E. & B. 234; *cf. Innes v. Stephenson* (1831) 1 Moo. & Rob. 147.
[85] See *Jones v. Yates* (1829) 9 B. & C. 532.
[86] See the Insolvency Act 1986, ss.238, 239 (winding up), 339, 340 (bankruptcy), 423. See also *supra*, paras. 10–124, 10–125 and *infra*, para. 27–103.
[87] (1870) L.R. 5 C.P. 478.
[88] As to the position at law, see *Jones v. Yates* (1829) 9 B. & C. 532; *Wallace v. Kelsall* (1840) 7 M. & W. 264; *Gordon v. Ellis* (1844) 7 Man. & G. 607; *Brownrigg v. Rae* (1850) 5 Ex. 489; *Brandon v. Scott* (1857) 7 E. & B. 234. The position was otherwise in equity: see *Midland Ry. v. Taylor* (1862) 8 H.L.C. 751; *Piercy v. Fynney* (1871) L.R. 12 Eq. 69. Lord Lindley apprehended that "the cases at law above referred to can no longer be relied upon; the Judicature Acts having removed the technical difficulties which led to their decision."
[89] See further, as to such cases, *supra*, paras. 12–26, 12–27.

14–66 Moreover, if a partner colludes with a partnership debtor and gives him a receipt for his debt, even though it remains unpaid, the firm may bring proceedings to recover the debt,[90] since a receipt does not preclude the person giving it from demonstrating that the money has not in fact been received[91] nor does it discharge the debt.

14–67 Similarly, if a partner covenants not to sue for a partnership debt he may join with his co-partners in an action brought to recover that debt.[92] Again a right of set-off which might be raised against one partner cannot be raised against him and his co-partners.[93] As Lord Lindley explained:

> "In each of these cases there is only a right of cross-action[94] against the one partner; and although such right might be relied on as a defence to an action by him alone, it is held not to affect the firm to which he belongs."

Actions against firm

14–68 If all the partners are sued in respect of a joint debt or obligation and each puts in a separate defence, any ground of defence pleaded and established by one partner which is fatal to the plaintiff's entire claim will benefit both him and his co-partners.[95]

2. AUTHORITY OF PARTNERS IN LEGAL PROCEEDINGS

Actions by firm

14–69 Any partner may, without the consent of his co-partners, commence proceedings in his and their names or (which amounts to the same thing) in the firm name.[96] However, if his co-partners'

---

[90] *Henderson v. Wilde* (1811) 2 Camp. 561; *Farrar v. Hutchinson* (1839) 9 A. & E. 641.
[91] *Skaife v. Jackson* (1824) 5 Dow. & Ry. 290.
[92] See *Walmesley v. Cooper* (1839) 11 A. & E. 216.
[93] See *infra*, paras. 14–78 *et seq.*
[94] Or counterclaim: see R.S.C. Ord. 15, r. 2; C.C.R. Ord. 9, r. 2.
[95] *Pirie v. Richardson* [1927] 1 K.B. 448.
[96] *Whitehead v. Hughes* (1834) 2 C. & M. 318; *Tomlinson v. Broadsmith* [1896] 1 Q.B. 386; *Seal v. Kingston* [1908] 2 K.B. 579; see also *Harwood v. Edwards* (1739) Gow on Partnership p. 65, note; *Court v. Berlin* [1897] 2 Q.B. 396. *Quaere*, does the Partnership Act 1890, s.24(8) enable a majority of partners to prevent an action being brought? It has been so held in Scotland: see *Hutcheon & Partners v. Hutcheon*, 1979 S.L.T. (Sh. Ct.) 62. This point was often left open in *Re Sutherland & Partners' Appeal* [1994] S.T.C. 387, 392. Note also *Mephistopheles, Debt Collection Service v. Lotay, The Times*, May 17, 1994

consent is not forthcoming, such a partner must normally[97] offer them an indemnity against costs.[98] Where, on the other hand, a partner purports to commence proceedings in his own name and against the express wishes of his co-partners, it would seem that the proceedings cannot be treated as brought of their behalf.[99]

If an interlocutory order is made *against* the partners, the partner who initiated the proceedings may seemingly enforce that order against his co-partners if their non-compliance will prejudice the firm's claim.[1]

Stay of proceedings, etc.

Lord Lindley observed: **14–70**

"... if it is competent for one partner to sue for the firm, it is as competent to any other partner to stay proceedings, or to put an end to the action altogether by means of a release; and, although the Court will not allow this to be done by collusion with the defendant, for the purpose of defrauding the other partners of their rights,[2] a release will be effectual where there is no fraud in the case."

Thus, in *Harwood v. Edwards*,[3] one partner, without the knowledge or consent of his co-partners, brought an action in their joint names for the recovery of a debt due to the firm. The other partners later agreed with the defendant that proceedings should be stayed and this agreement was held to be binding on all the partners, even though the partner who had commenced the action disputed its validity and could point to a provision in the partnership agreement which prohibited any partner from giving a release without the consent of the others.

---

[97] Such an offer need not be made in certain circumstances, *e.g.* where the partner refusing his consent is acting in collusion with the defendant: *Johnson v. Stephens & Carter Ltd.* [1923] 2 K.B. 857.

[98] *Whitehead v. Hughes* (1834) 2 C. & M. 318; *Tomlinson v. Broadsmith* [1896] 1 Q.B. 386; *Seal v. Kingston* [1908] 2 K.B. 579. See also *Cullen v. Knowles and Birks* [1898] 2 Q.B. 380 *Re Sutherland & Partners' Appeal* [1994] S.T.C. 387, 391.

[99] *Re Sutherland & Partners' Appeal* [1993] S.T.C. 399; this point was not addressed in the Court of Appeal: see [1994]. What would have been the position if the proceedings had been brought in the firm name or the names of all the partners was left open by Lindsay J.: [1993] S.T.C. 406f. But see, on this point, *Harwood v. Edwards* (1739) Gow on Partnership, p. 65, note, noticed *infra*, para. 14–70. See also *supra*, para. 12–35. The position is *a fortiori* in Scotland, where the firm has separate legal personality: see *Arif v. Levy & McRae*, 1992 G.W.D. 3–156.

[1] *Seal v. Kingston* [1908] 2 K.B. 579 (where the partnership had been dissolved).

[2] See *supra*, paras. 14–65 *et seq.*

[3] (1739) Gow on Partnership, p. 65, note.

Reference to arbitration

14–71   On the other hand, once proceedings have been commenced, one partner may not consent to all matters in dispute being referred to arbitration.[4]

Actions against firm

14–72   A managing partner has implied authority to instruct a solicitor to defend proceedings brought against the firm and to acknowledge service on behalf of all the partners.[5] If there is no managing partner, it is considered that any partner will have the same authority, but he must offer his co-partners an indemnity against costs should they not consent to him defending the proceedings.[6]

Service

14–73   It has already been seen that proceedings commenced in the firm name may be served on any partner or on any person authorised by a partner to accept service on the firm's behalf.[7] This procedure does not apply where the proceedings are commenced in the names of the individual partners nor, obviously, where they do not concern partnership matters.[8]

Lord Lindley pointed out that:

"... even in proceedings relating to partnership matters, although service on one partner is sometimes held equivalent to service on all, this is not the case where the service is relied on as the foundation of process of contempt, or of any proceedings of a penal nature."[9]

This would still seem to be the position.[10]

---

[4] *Hatton v. Royle* (1858) 3 H. & N. 500. And also *supra*, para. 12–39.

[5] *Tomlinson v. Broadsmith* [1896] 1 Q.B. 386. In such a case, the solicitor must keep the managing partner informed as to the progress of the action, but need not report to all the partners.

[6] *Ibid.* And see R.S.C. Ord. 81, r. 4(2), *infra*, para. A2–12 and the following decisions under the old appearance procedure: *Harrison v. Jackson* (1797) 7 T.R. 207; *Morley v. Strombom* (1802) 3 Bos. & Pul. 254; *Goldsmith v. Levy* (1812) 4 Taunt. 299; *Goodman v. De Beauvoir* (1848) 12 Jur. 989 and 1037.

[7] See *supra*, para. 14–13.

[8] See *Petty v. Smith* (1828) 2 Y. & J. 111; *Fairlie v. Quin* (1839) Smythe 189.

[9] See *Young v. Goodson* (1826) 2 Russ. 255; also *Moulston v. Wire* (1843) 1 Dow. & L. 527; *Re Holiday* (1841) 9 Dow. 1020. The following additional cases were referred to by Lord Lindley in this context: *Carrington v. Cantillon* (1722) Bunb. 107; *Coles v. Gurney* (1815) 1 Madd. 187; *Grant v. Prosser* (1824) Sm. & Bat. 95; *Carter v. Southall* (1831) 3 M. & W. 128; *Figgins v. Ward* (1834) 2 C. & M. 242; *Murray v. Moore* (1835) 1 Jo. 129; *Doe d. Overton v. Roe* (1841) 9 Dow. 1039; *Nolan v. Fitzgerald* (1851) 2 I.C.L.R. 79; *Kitchen v. Wilson* (1858) 4 C.B.(N.S.) 483; *Leese v. Martin* (1871) L.R. 13 Eq. 77.

[10] See R.S.C. Ord. 46, r. 5(2) (sequestration); Ord. 52, rr. 3(3), 4(2) (committal); also C.C.R. Ord. 29, r. 1(2).

Death of partner

If the proceedings against a firm have been commenced in the firm **14–74** name and one partner dies after service has been acknowledged, the surviving partners must put in a defence in the firm name.[11]

Consenting to judgment

One partner seemingly has no authority to bind the firm by **14–75** consenting to a judgment against it.[12]

Costs

If costs are ordered to be paid to one partner, payment to another **14–76** partner is not sufficient.[13]

Payment out of court

Before money can be paid out of court to a partner, the **14–77** Accountant General may require to be satisfied as to his identity and entitlement.[14] Such a partner may thus be required to demonstrate his authority to receive the payment out.[15]

3.   SET-OFF

Lord Lindley's rules on set-off

Where proceedings are brought against a defendant in respect of a **14–78** money claim, he may pursue a monetary cross claim against the plaintiff by means of a set-off[16] or counterclaim.[17] Although the right

---

[11] *Ellis v. Wadeson* [1899] 1 Q.B. 714.

[12] *Hambidge v. De La Crouée* (1846) 3 C.B. 742; also *Munster v. Cox* (1885) 10 App.Cas. 680. And see *Rathbone v. Drakeford* (1830) 4 M. & P. 57.

[13] *Showler v. Stoakes* (1844) 2 Dow. & L. 3.

[14] Court Funds Rules 1987, r. 40(4).

[15] See generally, as to the authority of a partner to receive payments on behalf of the firm, *supra*, paras. 12–53 *et seq.*

[16] R.S.C. Ord. 18, r. 17; see also C.C.R. Ord. 9, r. 2. The scope and availability of equitable set off has been explored in the following cases: *Aries Tanker Corp. v. Total Transport Ltd.* [1977] 1 W.L.R. 185 (set-off against freight not allowed); *Federal Commerce & Navigation Co. Ltd. v. Molena Alpha Inc.* [1978] Q.B. 927 (set-off against hire under a charterparty allowed, although this question was left open by the House of Lords on appeal: see [1979] A.C. 757); *British Anzani (Felixstowe) Ltd. v. International Marine Management (U.K.) Ltd.* [1980] Q.B. 137 (set-off against rent under lease allowed); *Sim v. Rotherham Metropolitan Borough Council* [1987] Ch. 216 (set-off against salary due under a contract of employment allowed); *Colonial Bank v. European Grain and Shipping Ltd.* [1989] A.C. 1056 (set-off against freight not allowed); see also, generally, *Dole Dried Fruit and Nut Co. v. Trustin Kerwood Ltd.* [1990] 2 Lloyd's Rep. 309; *Insituform (Ireland) Ltd. v. Insituform Group Ltd., The Times*, November 27, 1990. And note R.S.C. Ord. 77, r. 6; C.C.R. Ord. 42, r. 9 (set-off against Crown not permitted). A right of set-off may be excluded by agreement: *Hong Kong and Shanghai Banking Corp v. Kloeckner & Co. A.G.* [1990] 2 Q.B. 514. However, such a term may, in an appropriate case, fail to satisfy the test of reasonableness under the Unfair Contract Terms Act 1977, s.13: *Stewart Gill Ltd. v. Horatio Myer & Co. Ltd.* [1992] 2 All E.R. 257. Any such term will in any event be ineffective on the insolvency of one of the parties: see *infra*, para. 27–81.

[17] R.S.C. Ord. 15, r. 2; C.C.R. Ord. 9, r. 2. And note that a counterclaim may be struck out or ordered to be tried separately if it cannot conveniently be disposed of in the same action: R.S.C. Ord. 15, r. 5(2).

to raise a set-off is more extensive that it once was, it is still governed by the principles originally developed by the courts of equity which, so far as concerns partnerships, were encapsulated by Lord Lindley in four rules,[18] *viz.*:

Rule 1:
"Joint debts owing to and by the same persons in the same right can be set off."

Rule 2:
"Separate debts owing to and by the same person in the same right can also be set off."

Rule 3:
"Debts not owing to and by the same persons in the same rights cannot be set off."

14–79   It is this third rule which prevents a debt owed to or by a sole surviving partner on his own account from being set off against a debt owed by or to the former firm.[19] Where, however, the debt owed by the surviving partner is, in substance, a partnership debt, a set-off may be permitted.[20]

On the same basis, a partnership creditor may not, when seeking payment out of a deceased partner's estate, set off a debt which he owes to that estate on his own account, at least where this would place him in competition with the deceased's separate creditors.[21]

Rule 4:
"Except under special circumstances, a debt due to or from several persons jointly cannot be set off against a debt due from or to one of such persons separately."[22]

---

[18] In Lord Lindley's original formulation, the words "both at law and in equity" appeared at the end of Rules 1–3; the same point was also made in relation to Rule 4, albeit in a separate sentence.
[19] *Cf.* the position at law: *Golding v. Vaughan* (1782) 2 Chitty 436; *Slipper v. Stidstone* (1794) 5 T.R. 493; *French v. Andrade* (1796) 6 T.R. 582.
[20] *Smith v. Parkes* (1852) 16 Beav. 115. See also *Government of Newfoundland v. Newfoundland Ry.* (1888) 13 App.Cas. 199.
[21] *Addis v. Knight* (1817) 2 Mer. 117. Lord Lindley explained the rationale behind this application of the rule as follows: "... the creditor must pay [*the debt due from himself to the deceased*] in full, and then, as regards the debt in respect of which he sues, rank as any other creditor of the firm against the assets of the deceased. It is obvious that if in such a case the two debts were set against each other, the separate creditors of the deceased would be paying a joint creditor of the firm, unless the assets of the deceased were sufficient to pay both classes of creditors in full." *Quaere*, would a set-off not be allowed if there were such a sufficiency: see also the Partnership Act 1890, s.9, which establishes the *several* liability of a deceased partner for the debts and obligations of the firm. And see *supra*, paras. 13–06 *et seq.*
[22] See *Bowyear v. Pawson* (1881) 6 Q.B.D. 540; *Re Pennington and Owen* [1925] Ch. 825; also the Supreme Court Act 1981, s.49(2). And see *Kinnerley v. Hossack* (1809) 2 Taunt. 170; *Vulliamy v. Noble* (1817) 3 Mer. 593; *Jebsen v. East and West India Dock Co.* (1875) L.R. 10 C.P. 300. Lord Lindley pointed out that, in *Manchester, Sheffield, and Lincolnshire Ry. v. Brooks* (1877) 2 Ex.D. 243, a defendant was permitted to plead a separate debt by way of set-off in an action on a joint debt but concluded "This can hardly have been right." Indeed, equity did not permit such a set-off even in a case of fraud: see *Middleton v. Pollock* (1875) L.R. 20 Eq. 515.

It follows that a debt owed by a firm may not be set off against a **14–80** debt owed to a partner in his personal capacity or vice versa,[23] because to allow a set-off in either case would, in Lord Lindley's words, "enable a creditor to obtain payment of what is due to him from persons in no way indebted to him."[24]

Single partner dealt with

The fourth rule applies even where the third party has only had **14–81** dealings with a single partner, so long as he was acting on the firm's behalf. Thus, in *Gordon v. Ellis*,[25] three partners, A, B and C, sued the defendant to recover money received by him in respect of goods sold on the firm's behalf. The defendant in effect sought to plead that A had employed him to sell the goods as if they were A's own, that they had accordingly been sold as A's goods and that A was indebted to him in an amount greater than that sought to be recovered in the action. It was admitted that, if B and C had, by their conduct, induced the defendant to believe that A was the sole owner of the goods and to deal with him on that basis, the defendant would have had a good defence but, since that was not alleged, a set-off was not permissible.[26]

Where, however, the debt apparently owed by the partner is in fact **14–82** shown to be a partnership debt, a set-off will be allowed. In this connection, Lord Lindley referred to the earlier proceedings in *Gordon v. Ellis*,[27] observing:

"... the defendant ... was held entitled to set off a debt due to him for an advance made by him to one of the partners on account of those goods. The court thought that although the money was advanced to one partner only, the defendant had a right to treat it as an advance to the firm made on that partner's requisition, whilst acting within the scope of his apparent authority as agent of the

---

[23] *MacGillivray v. Simson* (1826) 2 Car. & P. 320; *Boswell v. Smith* (1833) 6 Car. & P. 60; *France v. White* (1839) 8 Scott 257; *Gordon v. Ellis* (1844) 2 C.B. 821; *Arnold v. Bainbrigge* (1853) 9 Ex. 153.

[24] *Powell v. Brodhurst* [1901] 2 Ch. 160, 165, *per* Farwell J.

[25] (1844) 2 C.B. 821.

[26] Lord Lindley pointed out that, in this case, "an attempt was made to extend the principle on which Lord Kenyon decided *Stracey v. Deey* [*(1789) 7 T.R. 261, note*], to all cases in which one partner only transacts the business of the firm, and becomes himself indebted to the person with whom he deals." See, as to the latter decision, *infra*, para. 14–85. And see *Bonfield v. Smith* (1844) 12 M. & W. 405; also *Baring v. Corrie* (1818) 2 B. & A. 137; *Ramazotti v. Bowring* (1859) 7 C.B.(N.S.) 851.

[27] (1844) 7 Man. & G. 607.

firm. In point of fact, the defendant, instead of waiting until he had sold the goods, and then handing over the money produced by their sale, made a payment on account; and he sought nothing more than to have the amount so prepaid deducted from the sum for which he sold the goods."

It should, however, be observed that no plea of set-off had been raised at this stage.[28]

Bank accounts

14-83   The fourth rule is also applied, by analogy, where a firm shares the same bankers as one or more of the partners. Thus, any sum due from the firm on the partnership account may not be set off against sums due to those partners on their personal accounts.[29]

Although set-off *is* available as between two current accounts maintained by a firm, it will not be permitted as between a current account and a loan account, unless the firm consents.[30] The position will naturally be the same as between accounts maintained by a single partner.

Exceptions to rule 4

14-84   The general rule which precludes a debt due to a firm being set off against a debt owing by a partner, and vice versa, is subject to the following exceptions:

Agreement: It is almost too obvious to require comment that effect will be given to any express or implied agreement authorising a set-off, and that such an agreement may be inferred from the conduct of the parties.[31]

---

[28] See *ibid.* p. 620, *per* Tindal C.J.

[29] See *Watts v. Christie* (1849) 11 Beav. 546; *Cavendish v. Geaves* (1857) 24 Beav. 163. Lord Lindley stated the principle in these terms: "In strict analogy to the above rule, it has been decided in equity that if the members of a firm have separate private accounts with the bankers of the firm, and a balance is due to the bankers from the firm on the partnership account, the bankers have no lien for such balance on what may be due from themselves to the members of the firm on their respective separate accounts; and that the debt due to the bankers from the partners jointly cannot be set off against the debts due from the bankers to the partners separately." *Per contra*, perhaps, if the partners hold their personal accounts as nominees for the firm: see *Ex p. Morier* (1879) 12 Ch.D. 491; *Re Hett, Maylor & Co. Ltd.* (1894) 10 T.L.R. 412; *Bhogal v. Punjab National Bank* [1988] 2 All E.R. 296; *Uttamchandani v. Central Bank of India* (1989) 139 N.L.J. 222.

[30] *Bradford Old Bank Ltd. v. Sutcliffe* [1918] 2 K.B. 833, 844, *per* Scrutton L.J., approved in *National Westminster Bank Ltd. v. Halesowen Presswork & Assemblies Ltd.* [1972] A.C. 785, 819, *per* Lord Kilbrandon.

[31] See *Downam v. Matthews* (1721) Pr. Ch. 580; *Kinnerley v. Hossack* (1809) 2 Taunt. 170; *Vulliamy v. Noble* (1817) 3 Mer. 593; *Cheetham v. Crook* (1825) McCle. & Y. 307. Equally, a right of set-off may be excluded by agreement: *Hong Kong and Shanghai Banking Corp. v. Kloeckner & Co. A.G.* [1990] 2 Q.B. 514. But see also *supra*, para. 14-78, n. 16.

However, if one partner agrees that a personal debt which he owes to a third party will be set off against a debt owed by that third party to the firm, he will prima facie be acting in fraud of his co-partners; Lord Lindley pointed out that:

"... a set-off founded on such an agreement cannot, it is apprehended, be maintained in the absence of special circumstances, rendering such an agreement binding on the other parties."[32]

Joint and several obligation: If a debt is owed by partners jointly and severally, it may be set off against a separate debt due to one of them alone.[33]

Dormant partners, etc.: Where one partner has been permitted to **14–85** act as if he were a principal, and not merely the agent of his firm, a set-off of what are technically joint and separate debts may be allowed. Thus, whilst dormant partners may clearly be joined as co-plaintiffs in an action on a contract entered into on the firm's behalf,[34] Lord Lindley observed that:

"... dormant partners cannot, by coming forward and suing on such contracts, deprive the defendant of any right of set-off of which he might have availed himself if the non-dormant partners only had been plaintiffs."

This principle was established in *Stracey v. Deey*.[35] There the defendant had dealt with the one active member of the firm, R, who in fact appeared to be the only person concerned in the business, and had become indebted in respect of certain goods supplied by him. At the same time, the defendant had incurred expenditure on R's behalf, assuming that a set off would take place. The plaintiffs (R and his two dormant partners) contended that a set-off should not be permitted but this argument was rejected by Lord Kenyon, who effectively held that the defendant should be able to take advantage of all the defences which would have been available to him if the

---

[32] *Nottidge v. Pritchard* (1834) 2 Cl. & F. 379; *Piercy v. Fynney* (1871) L.R. 12 Eq. 69; see also *supra*, paras. 14–65 *et seq*. Lord Lindley noted that "*Wallace v. Kelsall* (1840) 7 M. & W. 264, is the other way, but is to be explained by the old technical rules of pleading, which are now abolished."

[33] See *Owen v. Wilkinson* (1858) 5 C.B.(N.S.) 526.

[34] See *supra*, para. 14–27.

[35] (1789) 7 T.R. 361, note. See also *Teed v. Elworthy* (1811) 14 East 213; *De Mautort v. Saunders* (1830) 1 B. & Ad. 398. *Cf. Gordon v. Ellis* (1844) 2 C.B. 821, *supra*, para. 14–81, where the court refused to extend the *Stracey v. Deey* principle.

action had been brought by R alone.[36] Of course, the position would
have been otherwise if R had not led the defendant to believe that he
alone was being dealt with.[37]

Change in firm: express assignments of debts

14-86   It is, perhaps, obvious that there may be difficulties raising a set-off
defence following a change in a firm, *e.g.* where a debt owing to the
old firm is sought to be set off against a debt incurred by the new
firm.[38] In such a case, the set-off can, however, usually be preserved
by the members of the new firm taking an express assignment of the
debt owed to the old firm and giving the debtor notice thereof.[39]

Attempts to avoid set-off

14-87   It is no longer possible to prevent a defence of set-off being raised
by a firm merely by suing one of the partners: in such a case, the
defendant may, if necessary, require his co-partners to be joined as
parties,[40] unless they are out of the jurisdiction.[41]

Other devices designed to achieve such a procedural advantage are
also likely to be unsuccessful. Thus, a firm which holds a promissory
note made by a third party cannot indorse it over to one of the
partners with a view to him suing on it and thereby depriving that
third party of a right of set-off which he would otherwise have
enjoyed against the firm.[42] A similar attitude would, in the current
editor's view, be adopted if the firm were to assign a debt to a
partner for that purpose.

---

[36] See *George v. Clagett* (1797) 7 T.R. 359; *Borries v. Imperial Ottoman Bank* (1873) L.R. 9 C.P.
38; *Cooke v. Eshelby* (1887) 12 App.Cas. 271.
[37] Commenting on the decision in *Gordon v. Ellis* (1844) 2 C.B. 821, *supra*, para. 14–81, Lord
Lindley observed "... it was held, and rightly, that a person liable to be sued by a firm cannot set
off a debt due from one only of its members, on the ground that he only was dealt with by the
defendant, unless it can be shown that the other members of the firm induced the defendant by
their conduct to treat their co-partner as the only partner with whom the defendant had to do"
(sic). See *Bonfield v. Smith* (1844) 12 M. & W. 405; also *Baring v. Corrie* (1818) 2 B. & A. 137;
Ramazotti v. Bowring (1859) 7 C.B.(N.S.) 851.
[38] See Rule 3, *supra*, para. 14–78; also *supra*, paras. 14–48 *et seq.*
[39] Law of Property Act 1925, s.136. See, in particular, *Cavendish v. Geaves* (1857) 24 Beav. 163
(from the judgment in which Lord Lindley quoted extensively); also *Bennett v. White* [1910] 2 K.B.
643. Note that the assignee takes subject to all equities having priority over his rights: *ibid.*
s.136(1). See, in this context, *Jeffrys v. Agra and Masterman's Bank* (1866) L.R. 2 Eq. 674; *Watson
v. Mid Wales Ry.* (1867) L.R. 2 C.P. 593; *Young v. Kitchin* (1878) 3 Ex.D. 127; *Government of
Newfoundland v. Newfoundland Ry.* (1888) 13 App.Cas. 199; *Christie v. Taunton, Delmard, Lane
& Co.* [1893] 2 Ch. 175; *Stoddard v. Union Trust Ltd.* [1912] 1 K.B. 181; *Re Pinto Leite and
Nephews* [1929] 1 Ch. 221. Notice of the assignment must be clear and distinct to prevent a set-off:
see, generally, *Lloyd v. Banks* (1868) L.R. 3 Ch.App. 488, 490, *per* Lord Cairns; *Bence v.
Shearman* [1898] 2 Ch. 582, 587, *per* Chitty L.J.; also *W. F. Harrison & Co. v. Burke* [1956] 1
W.L.R. 419.
[40] R.S.C. Ord. 15, rr. 6(2)(b); C.C.R. Ord. 15, r. 1(1). And see *Stackwood v. Dunn* (1842) 2
Q.B. 823; *Bonfield v. Smith* (1844) 12 M. & W. 405; *Pilley v. Robinson* (1887) 20 Q.B.D. 155; also
Norbury, Natzio & Co. v. Griffiths [1918] 2 K.B. 369.
[41] *Wilson, Sons & Co. Ltd. v. Balcarres Brook Steam Co. Ltd.* [1893] 1 Q.B. 422.
[42] See *Puller v. Roe* (1793) 1 Peake N.P. 260.

Insolvency

Set-off in the case of bankruptcy or insolvency is considered later **14–88** in this work.[43]

4. EXECUTION AGAINST PARTNERS

(a) Judgment in firm name

Execution without leave

A judgment obtained against a firm[44] may be freely enforced **14–89** against any partnership property within the jurisdiction and against any partner who (i) acknowledged service of the proceedings as a partner; (ii) though served as a partner, failed to acknowledge service; (iii) pleaded that he was a partner; or (iv) was held to be a partner.[45] It follows that the judgment creditor does not need to levy execution against the partnership property before proceeding against such partners' separate estates.

The judgment debt may obviously found an insolvency petition against the firm.[46]

Execution with leave, etc.

Subject to the exceptions noted in subsequent paragraphs, **14–90** execution can only issue against the separate estate of any other partner with the leave of the court.[47] If, on the hearing of the judgment creditor's application for leave, a dispute as to liability arises, e.g. in a case of alleged holding out,[48] the court can direct a trial of that issue.[49]

The above procedure is, however, optional: the judgment creditor may, if he wishes, bring a separate action against the alleged partner founded on the judgment in the previous action and, in due course, execute any judgment obtained therein.[50]

---

[43] See infra, paras. 27–74 et seq.

[44] See supra, paras. 14–19, 14–20.

[45] R.S.C. Ord. 81, r. 5(2), infra, para. A2–13. See also supra, para. 14–21. As to the equivalent provision in the county court, see C.C.R. Ord. 25, r. 9(1).

[46] Re a Debtor (No. 72 of 1982) [1984] 1 W.L.R. 1143 (a decision under the Bankruptcy Act 1914). See generally, as to petitions against a firm, infra, paras. 27–09 et seq.

[47] R.S.C. Ord. 81, r. 5(4), infra, para. A2–13; C.C.R. Ord. 25, r. 9(3). See also Davis v. Morris (1883) 10 Q.B.D. 436.

[48] See, generally, the Partnership Act 1890, s.14, supra, paras. 5–43 et seq.

[49] R.S.C. Ord. 81, r. 5(5), infra, para. A2–13; C.C.R. Ord. 25, r. 9(4); Davis v. Hyman & Co. [1903] 1 K.B. 854. But see also infra, para. 14–92.

[50] Clark v. Cullen (1882) 9 Q.B.D. 355.

Two firms with common partner

14-91   Leave to issue execution is required where judgment has been obtained by one firm against another, if both firms share one or more members in common.[51] On the application for leave, the court may (*inter alia*) order any necessary accounts and inquiries.

No execution allowed

14-92   *Minor partner*: Although execution may obviously not issue against a minor partner, where a judgment has been obtained against the firm other than the minor, execution may seemingly issue against the partnership property without leave.[52]

Outgoing partner: It appears that leave to execute a judgment against a former partner will not be given nor the issue of his liability ordered to be tried, if the plaintiff knew, prior to issuing the proceedings, that he had left the firm and did not effect service on him.[53]

Partner out of the jurisdiction: A judgment may not be executed against a partner who was out of the jurisdiction when the proceedings were issued, unless he acknowledged service as a partner or was served with the proceedings as a partner within or, with leave,[54] outside the jurisdiction.[55]

Receiver already appointed

14-93   Where the court has already appointed a receiver in respect of the partnership assets,[56] leave to issue execution must be obtained in that action. In an appropriate case, the receiver will be directed to pay the judgment creditor out of moneys coming into his hands[57] or the judgment creditor will be given a charge on such moneys for his debt and costs.[58]

---

[51] R.S.C. Ord. 81, r. 6(1), *infra*, para. A2–14; C.C.R. Ord. 25, r. 10.
[52] *Lovell & Christmas v. Beauchamp* [1894] A.C. 607; also *Harris v. Beauchamp Bros.* [1893] 2 Q.B. 534.
[53] *Wigram v. Cox, Sons, Buckley & Co.* [1894] 1 Q.B. 793.
[54] See *supra*, para. 14–16.
[55] R.S.C. Ord. 81, r. 5(3), *infra*, para. A2–13. As to the position in the county court, see C.C.R. Ord. 25, r. 9(2).
[56] See *infra*, paras. 23–149 *et seq.*
[57] *Mitchell v. Weise* [1892] W.N. 139.
[58] *Kewney v. Attrill* (1886) 34 Ch.D. 345. Such a charging order gives the judgment creditor priority over the general body of creditors in the application of the partnership assets: *Newport v. Pougher* [1937] 1 Ch. 214. *Quaere*, would such an order be set aside as a transaction at an undervalue (within the meaning of the Insolvency Act 1986, ss. 239, 339) on the application of the trustee in bankruptcy or liquidator of an insolvent partner? It is tentatively thought not: see *Re Gershon & Levy* [1915] 2 K.B. 527 (a decision under the Bankruptcy Act 1914, s.45).

Amending judgment with a view to execution

If proceedings have been commenced against a firm in the firm **14–94** name but have at all times been treated as brought against an individual defendant trading under that name, the court will not, once judgment by consent has been obtained in the latter form and execution levied against the defendant, amend that judgment into a judgment against the firm, with a view to enabling the plaintiff to issue execution against someone whom he has since discovered to be a partner.[59]

Garnishee proceedings

Garnishee proceedings[60] may be issued without leave against a firm **14–95** carrying on business within the jurisdiction, even if one or more of the partners are resident outside the jurisdiction.[61] However, an order to show cause must be served either on a partner within the jurisdiction or on some other person who has control or management of the partnership business.[62]

(b) Manner of execution

Where a judgment has been obtained against two or more partners **14–96** jointly, a writ of execution should be issued against all of those partners,[63] even though it may be levied on any one or more of them.[64] Lord Lindley pointed out:

"The consequence of this is that the sheriff may execute a writ issued against several partners jointly, either on their joint property, *or* on the separate property of any one or more of them, *or* both on their joint and on their respective separate properties[65] ... Of course, if the judgment creditor has had execution and satisfaction against one of the partners, he cannot afterwards go against any of the others[66]; but ... the sheriff is not bound to levy on the goods of the firm before having recourse to the separate

---

[59] *Munster v. Cox* (1885) 10 App.Cas. 680.

[60] R.S.C. Ord. 49, r. 1; C.C.R. Ord. 30, r. 1.

[61] R.S.C. Ord. 81, r. 7(1), *infra*, para. A2–15; C.C.R. Ord. 30, r. 14(1).

[62] R.S.C. Ord. 81, r. 7(2); C.C.R. Ord. 30, r. 14(2).

[63] See *Penoyer v. Brace* (1698) 1 Lord Ray. 244; *Clarke v. Clement* (1796) 6 T.R. 526; 2 Wms.Saund. 72, 1; Bac.Ab.Exec.G. 1.

[64] See *Abbot v. Smith* (1760) Wm.Blacks 974, 949, *per* De Gray C.J.; also *Herries v. Jamieson* (1794) 5 T.R. 553, 556, *per* Lord Kenyon.

[65] Lord Lindley went on "and so long as there is, within the sheriff's bailiwick, any property of the partners, or any of them, a return of *nulla bona* is improper: see *Jones v. Clayton* (1815) 4 M. & S. 349." See as to the present procedure in the High Court, R.S.C. Ord. 46, r. 9. There are, of course, certain restrictions on execution against a partner's separate estate where judgment has been obtained in the firm name: see *supra*, paras. 14–90 *et seq.*

[66] See Com.Dig. Execution, H.

properties of its members, and ... they cannot require the sheriff to execute the writ in one way rather than another."[67]

A similar rule applies to garnishee proceedings.[68]

Insolvency

14-97   The inhibitions on the right of a judgment creditor to issue execution against an insolvent firm or partner will be noticed later in this work.[69]

(c)   Execution in respect of separate debts

Execution against partnership share

14-98   The manner in which a partner's share can be made liable for his separate debts will be examined in a subsequent chapter.[70]

Interpleader by sheriff

14-99   Since execution may not be levied against partnership property in respect of a partner's separate debts,[71] if the sheriff seizes goods under a judgment against one partner but the other partners claim that they are partnership property, the sheriff should either withdraw, if he is satisfied that their claim is valid, or interplead.[72] If a partner of the judgment debtor claims that the goods are his own property but, on the trial of the interpleader issue, it appears that they are in fact partnership property, that partner will be entitled to succeed, unless this would result in injustice to the execution creditor, *e.g.* if he has been misled.[73]

(d)   Order for possession of land

14-100 An order for possession is normally obtained against the persons in whom the legal estate is vested.[74] The order is enforced in the High Court by means of a writ of possession,[75] which may not be issued without the leave of the court unless the order was made in a

---

[67] This must, of course be read subject to the provisions of R.S.C. Ord. 81, r. 5, *infra*, paras. A2-13.

[68] *Miller v. Mynn* (1859) 1 E. & E. 1075. See generally, R.S.C. Ord. 49, r. 1; C.C.R. Ord. 30, r. 1.

[69] See *infra*, paras. 27-20, 27-41.

[70] See the Partnership Act 1890, s.23, *infra*, paras. 19-43 *et seq*.

[71] *Ibid.* s.23(1).

[72] *Peake v. Carter* [1916] 1 K.B. 652.

[73] *Peake v. Carter, supra*; *cf. Flude Ltd. v. Goldberg* [1916] 1 K.B. 662, note.

[74] See *supra*, para. 14-39.

[75] R.S.C. Ord. 45, r. 3(1)(a).

mortgage action.[76] Leave to issue will not be granted unless it can be shown that every person in actual possession of the whole or any part of the land has received such notice of the proceedings as appears to the court sufficient to enable him to apply for any relief to which he may be entitled and, if the operation of the judgment or order is suspended under the Landlord and Tenant Act 1954,[77] that the applicant has not received notice in writing from the tenant that he desires certain provisions of that Act[78] to have effect.[79] In the county court, an order for the recovery of land or for the delivery of possession is enforced by a warrant of possession,[80] which may be issued at any time after the order for possession is made or, if later, the date on which the defendant is ordered to give possession.[81]

Once a writ of possession has been obtained, the plaintiff goes on **14–101** the premises with the sheriff so as to identify the property in respect of which the order has been made. Thereafter the sheriff is obliged to deliver complete and vacant possession of those premises to the plaintiff and the writ is not fully executed until all persons and goods have been removed therefrom. Thus, where an order for possession is made in respect of partnership premises, the sheriff is entitled to remove all partners and partnership property which he finds there.[82] On the other hand, in executing a warrant of possession issued in the county court, the bailiff is only required to remove *persons* from the premises, and not any goods or chattels.[83]

In either case, it would seem that any person on the premises can be evicted, irrespective of whether he was made a party to the proceedings.[84]

---

[76] *Ibid.* Ord. 45, r. 3(2).
[77] See the Landlord and Tenant Act 1954, s.16(2), which affords relief to long leaseholders in respect of the performance of certain covenants.
[78] *Ibid.* s.16(2)(a), (b).
[79] R.S.C. Ord. 45, r. 3(3).
[80] C.C.R. Ord. 26, r. 17.
[81] See also *ibid.* Ord. 24, r. 6(1).
[82] See *Upton & Wells Case* (1589) 1 Leo. 145.
[83] County Courts Act 1984, s.111(1).
[84] See *Re Wykeham Terrace* [1971] Ch. 204; *McPhail v. Persons, Names Unknown* [1973] Ch. 447; *R. v. Wandsworth County Court* [1975] 1 W.L.R. 1314.

Part Four

THE RIGHTS AND OBLIGATIONS OF
PARTNERS BETWEEN THEMSELVES

CHAPTER 15

MANAGEMENT AND DECISION-MAKING

Management of firm

It is inherent in the contract of partnership that each partner will **15–01** be permitted and, indeed, have the right to participate in the management and administration of the firm. Lord Lindley put it thus:

"In partnerships, the good faith of the partners is pledged mutually to each other that the business shall be conducted with their actual personal interposition, so that each may see that the other is carrying it on for their mutual advantage."[1]

That right is enshrined in the Partnership Act 1890, section 24(5), which provides:

"Every partner may take part in the management of the partnership business"

although this takes effect subject to any express or implied agreement between the partners.[2]

So fundamental is this right that, if one of two partners mortgages **15–02** his share to the other, the latter cannot, during the continuance of the partnership, exercise his rights as mortgagee with a view to excluding his co-partner from the management of the firm.[3] Indeed, Lord Lindley went so far as to remark that:

"... speaking generally ... nothing is considered as so loudly calling for the interference of the Court between partners, as the improper exclusion of one of them by the others from taking part in the management of the partnership business."[4]

---

[1] See *Peacock v. Peacock* (1809) 16 Ves.Jr. 49, 51, *per* Lord Eldon.
[2] See the opening words of *ibid.* s.24. As to the position before the Act, see *Rowe v. Wood* (1795) 2 J. & W. 558; also *Lloyd v. Loaring* (1802) 6 Ves. Jr. 773.
[3] *Rowe v. Wood* (1795) 2 J. & W. 553; see also the Partnership Act 1890, s.31, considered *infra*, paras. 19–59 *et seq.*
[4] See, in addition to the cases cited above, *Goodman v. Whitcomb* (1820) 1 J. & W. 589; *Marshall v. Colman* (1820) 2 J. & W. 266.

Exclusion from management by agreement

15–03   Notwithstanding the general rule, partners may, of course, agree that the right to manage the whole or some part of the firm's affairs is to be conferred on one or more of their number to the exclusion of the others.[5] Such agreements are now common as many large firms move towards a more corporate style of management at the cost of what may conveniently be styled "partner power," and may confer on the designated partner(s) the right to take all or merely a certain class of management decisions without reference to the general body of partners. Although Lord Lindley observed that "it is not competent for those who have agreed to take no part in the management, to transact the partnership business without the consent of all the other partners", the current editor submits that this confuses the management function with the conduct of the partnership business[6]: the extent of each partner's actual authority will inevitably depend on the terms of the agreement. Even where that authority is limited in the manner described by Lord Lindley, the partners who are excluded from the management may still retain *apparent* authority to bind the firm *vis-à-vis* third parties,[7] unless those third parties have actual notice of the true position.[8]

15–04   It should, however, be noted that any term purporting to exclude a partner from taking part in the management of the partnership business might in theory be unenforceable as against a particular partner if it constitutes unlawful racial or sexual discrimination.[9]

Disputes between partners

15–05   Questions frequently arise as to the manner in which decisions affecting the partnership are to be taken in the absence of unanimous agreement between the partners. It might be supposed that the majority of partners can always prevail over the minority, but that is only true within strictly defined limits. The starting point when considering such a question will inevitably be the partnership agreement itself. If it contains an express provision dealing with decision making, as will often be the case, then the prescribed procedure must be followed.[10] If the agreement is silent on the point,

---

[5] See *supra*, para. 10–87.

[6] This distinction is clearly drawn by the Limited Partnerships Act 1907, s.6(1).

[7] Partnership Act 1890, s.5, *supra*, paras. 12–02 *et seq.*

[8] *Ibid.* s.8, *supra*, para. 12–148.

[9] Sex Discrimination Act 1975, ss. 11(1) (as amended by the Sex Discrimination Act 1986, s. 1(3)), 77(2); Race Relations Act 1976, ss. 10(1), 72(2). See further, *supra*, paras. 8–08, 8–09.

[10] See generally, *supra*, paras. 10–82 *et seq.* Note *Clements v. Norris* (1878) 8 Ch.D. 129, which might be regarded as a case of this class; see also *infra*, paras. 15–07, 16–19, 23–135.

then it is necessary to identify the precise subject matter of the decision, since the Partnership Act 1890 distinguishes between those differences which relate to "ordinary matters" and those which relate to other matters, in the following way:

"24.—(8) Any difference arising as to ordinary matters connected with the partnership business may be decided by a majority of the partners, but no change may be made in the nature of the partnership business without the consent of all existing partners."[11]

This subsection was largely declaratory of the existing law.[12]

Disputes on ordinary matters

If it is sought to argue that a particular decision relates to **15–06** "ordinary matters connected with the partnership business" and thus can properly be taken by a majority but the court is not prepared to take judicial notice of the usual practice in the relevant trade or profession, evidence of that practice must be adduced, since a question of fact is seemingly involved. It is the connection with the business which is emphasised in section 24(8), rather than what is required to carry on the business "in the usual way,"[13] although the current editor submits that any decision which satisfies the latter test must also necessarily satisfy the "connection" test. In *Highley v. Walker*,[14] the decision whether a partner's son should be brought in to learn the business was held to fall within this category. It is submitted that most decisions involving the manner in which the business is to be conducted on a day to day basis, including the enlargement of a partner's authority to bind the firm,[15] the engagement and dismissal of staff, the choice of the firm's bankers and accountants and the renewal of a lease of partnership premises

---

[11] *Cf. ibid.* s.19, *supra*, para. 10–10.

[12] Lord Lindley's summary of the pre-1890 law in relation to differences "which relate to matters incidental to carrying on the legitimate business of a partnership" was as follows: "If ... in a case of this description, unprovided for by previous agreement, the partners are unequally divided, the minority must, the author apprehends, give way to the majority. ... The only alternative is to hold that if the partners disagree, even as to trifling matters of detail, the minority can forbid all change, and perhaps bring the business of the firm to a dead-lock, for which the only remedy is a dissolution. At the same time the author is not aware of any clear and distinct authority in support of the proposition that even in such matters a dissentient partner must give way to his co-partners." See *Robinson v. Thompson* (1687) 1 Vern. 465; *Const v. Harris* (1824) T. & R. 496; *Gregory v. Patchett* (1864) 33 Beav. 595; also *Morgan's Case* (1849) 1 Mac. & G. 225. *Cf. Beveridge v. Beveridge* (1872) L.R. 2 Sc.App. 183; *Clements v. Norris* (1878) 8 Ch.D. 129.

[13] See the Partnership Act 1890, s.5, considered *supra*, paras. 12–02 *et seq.*

[14] (1910) 26 T.L.R. 685.

[15] *Per contra* in the case of a restriction sought to be imposed on only one partner, if that would be inconsistent with his right to participate in the management of the business: see the Partnership Act 1890, ss.19, 24(5), 25. See also *supra*, paras. 13–33, 13–34.

should normally be regarded in the same way;[16] *sed quaere*, in the case of bringing or defending actions.[17]

Power of the majority

15–07   Although the Act clearly empowers a numerical majority of the partners to take decisions on ordinary matters, notwithstanding the other partners' objections,[18] it is of no assistance where the partners are equally divided. In such circumstances, the general rule is in favour of maintaining the *status quo ante*, as Lord Lindley explained:

> "With respect to [*this*] class of differences, regard must be had to the state of things actually existing; for, as a rule, if the partners are equally divided, those who forbid a change must have their way: *in re communi potior est conditio prohibentis.*"[19]

On this basis, one of two partners cannot unilaterally insist on engaging or dismissing an employee[20] or renewing an expired lease of the partnership premises with a view to the firm continuing to carry on business there.[21]

Rights of the minority

15–08   If a majority of partners is to outvote a minority, the former must ensure that they act with complete good faith and, in particular, that the views of the latter are fully canvassed, since it is a fundamental right of every partner to be heard and to have his views duly considered before any decision is taken. Lord Eldon stated the law thus:

---

[16] In *Donaldson v. Williams* (1833) Cr. & M. 345 and *Clements v. Norris* (1878) 8 Ch.D. 129, the partners were *equally* divided. See further, as to these decisions, *supra*, para. 12–67 and *infra*, paras 16–19, 23–135.

[17] In Scotland it has been held that a majority of partners can prevent an action being brought against their wishes: *Hutcheon & Partners v. Hutcheon*, 1979 S.L.T. (Sh. Ct.) 62. This decision appears to be out of line with the English authorities: see *supra*, paras. 12–35, 14–69. The point was argued, but not decided, in *Re Sutherland & Partners' Appeal* [1994] S.T.C. 387.

[18] Partnership Act 1890, s.24(8). This was probably the law even before the Act, but the point was not settled: see *supra*, para. 15–05, n.12.

[19] The original footnote to this passage read: "But see as to the employment of a ship, *Abbott on Shipping*, p. 82, ed. 9 and p. 58 ed. 12; and as to completing contracts already entered into, *Butchart v. Dresser* (1853) 4 De G.M. & G. 545." See also *supra*, para. 10–84.

[20] *Donaldson v. Williams* (1833) 1 Cr. & M. 345. However, this decision does not go as far as is commonly supposed: see *supra*, para. 12–67.

[21] *Clements v. Norris* (1878) 8 Ch. D. 129. But note that the terms of the partnership had not expired and that a specific clause in the agreement governed decisions as to the premises from which the business was to be carried on. *Quaere* would the trust for sale which would now be implied have affected the decision? It is thought not: see *Harris v. Black* (1983) 46 P. & C.R. 366, where one trustee beneficiary sought (unsuccessfully) to compel another, who was his ex-partner, to renew a lease; and see *infra*, paras. 16–15 *et seq*. As to the extent of a partner's implied authority to take a lease of premises, see *supra*, para. 12–73.

"... I call that the act of all, which is the act of the majority, provided all are consulted, and the majority are acting *bona fide*, meeting, not for the purpose of negativing, what any one may have to offer, but for the purpose of negativing, what, when they are met together, they may, after due consideration, think proper to negative: For a majority of partners to say; We do not care what one partner may say, we, being the majority, will do what we please, is, I apprehend, what this Court will not allow."[22]

Majorities at meetings

It is perhaps self-evident that if a majority of partners are **15–09** empowered to take decisions at a quorate partners' meeting, that power may only be exercised at a duly convened meeting at which the requisite number of partners is present. Although it may be correct that all the partners have been requested to attend and that, even if they had attended, the result would have been the same, failure to adhere to the agreed procedure will clearly invalidate any decision taken at an inquorate meeting.[23]

Disputes on other matters

So far as concerns decisions which do *not* relate to ordinary matters **15–10** connected with the partnership business, it has long been settled law that, in the words of Lord Lindley,

"no majority, however large, can lawfully engage the partnership in such matters against the will of even one dissentient partner. Each partner is entitled to say to the others, 'I became a partner in a concern formed for a definite purpose, and upon terms which were agreed upon by all of us, and you have no right, without my consent, to engage me in any other concern, nor to hold me to any other terms, nor to get rid of me, if I decline to assent to a variation in the agreement by which you are bound to me and I to you.' Nor is it at all material that the new business is extremely profitable."[24]

---

[22] *Const v. Harris* (1824) T. & R 496, 525 (as applied in *Abbatt v. Treasury Solicitor & Others* [1969] 1 W.L.R. 1575); see also Lord Eldon's observations in the course of argument, at *ibid.* p.518; *G.W. Ry. v. Rushout* (1852) 5 De G. & Sm. 310; *Blisset v. Daniel* (1853) 10 Hare 493; *Wall v. London and Northern Assets Corp.* [1898] 2 Ch. 469.

[23] See *Ex p. Morrison* (1847) De Gex 539; *Howbeach Coal Co. v. Teague* (1860) 5 H. & N. 151; *Re London and Southern Counties Freehold Land Co.* (1885) 31 Ch.D. 223; *Young v. Ladies' Imperial Club Ltd.* [1920] 2 K.B. 523; *Knowles v. Zoological Society of London* [1959] 1 W.L.R. 823.

[24] *Att.-Gen. v. Great Northern Ry.* (1860) 1 Dr. & Sm. 154.

This principle, which is embodied in section 24(8) of the Partnership Act 1890 itself,[25] will, in the absence of some other agreement, apply to all firms, large and small, and scarcely requires specific authority, although Lord Lindley particularly commended the reader to two decisions of Lord Eldon.[26] The position will be precisely the same where the decision concerns the admission of a new partner,[27] the expulsion of an existing partner[28] or, indeed, the dissolution of the firm itself.[29]

---

[25] See *supra*, para. 15–05.

[26] *Natusch v. Irving* (1824) Gow on Partnership (3rd. ed.), p. 398 and the 5th ed. of this work at p. 316; *Const v. Harris* (1824) T. & R. 496. See also *Hole v. Garnsey* [1930] A.C. 472, 494, *per* Lord Atkin; *Abbatt v. Treasury Solicitor & Others* [1969] 1 W.L.R. 1575. The following cases also illustrate the principle: *Fennings v. Grenville* (1808) 1 Taunt. 241; *Davies v. Hawkins* (1815) 3 M. & S. 488; *Glassington v. Thwaites* (1823) 1 Sim. & St. 124; *Re Phoenix Life Insurance Co.* (1862) 2 J. & H. 441; *Auld v. Glasgow Working Men's Society* (1887) 12 App.Cas. 197; *The Hereward* [1895] p. 284. Note also *Nixon v. Wood* (1987) 284 E.G. 1055.

[27] Partnership Act 1890, s.24(7).

[28] A majority of partners cannot expel a partner otherwise than pursuant to an express power (*ibid.* s. 25, *infra*, para. 24–35) and such a power will be strictly construed: See *Re A Solicitor's Arbitration* [1962] 1 W.L.R. 353; also *supra*, paras. 10–98 *et seq.* Equally, a majority has no power to sell the shares of a dissentient minority: see *Chapple v. Cadell* (1822) Jac. 537.

[29] See, for example, the Partnership Act 1890, s.33(2), considered *infra*, para. 24–29.

CHAPTER 16

THE DUTY OF GOOD FAITH

1. THE NATURE OF THE DUTY

The general duty

Perhaps the most fundamental obligation which the law imposes on **16–01** a partner is the duty to display complete good faith towards his co-partners in all partnership dealings and transactions. Lord Lindley summarised that duty in the following terms:

"The utmost good faith is due from every member of a partnership towards every other member[1]; and if any dispute arise between partners touching any transaction by which one seeks to benefit himself at the expense of the firm, he will be required to show, not only that he has the law on his side, but that his conduct will bear to be tried by the highest standard of honour."[2]

Thus, if one partner enters into an agreement with another, at a time when he possesses relevant information regarding the state of the partnership accounts which is not known to that other partner and which he fails to disclose, the agreement will not be allowed to stand.[3] However, if the innocent partner subsequently learns that material facts have been concealed from him by his co-partner, but deliberately elects to stand by the agreement without insisting on full disclosure, the existence of the duty of good faith will not prevent his co-partner from relying on that election and treating the agreement as binding.[4]

This general obligation is to a large extent reflected in the terms of **16–02** the Partnership Act 1890, s.28 which provides as follows:

"28. Partners are bound to render true accounts and full information of all things affecting the partnership to any partner or his legal representatives."

---

[1] This principle may be traced back to Roman law, where it was stated thus "*In societatis contractibus fides exuberet*": Cod. iv, tit. 37, 1, 3.

[2] See *Blisset v. Daniel* (1853) 10 Hare 493. The application of the principle will not always be straightforward: *cf. Cassels v. Stewart* (1881) 6 App.Cas. 64 and *Trimble v. Goldberg* [1906] A.C. 494, noticed *infra*, para. 16–33.

[3] See *Maddeford v. Austwick* (1826) 1 Sim. 89; *Law v. Law* [1905] 1 Ch. 140.

[4] *Law v. Law, supra*. But see generally, as to the requirements for a valid election, *Peyman v. Lanjani* [1985] Ch. 457.

Needless to say, it is of particular importance that good faith should be shown where one partner is attempting to get rid of another or to buy out his interest in the firm[5] and, indeed, where a majority of partners are proposing to outvote a minority on some issue affecting the firm.[6] Moreover, whilst the point is not entirely free from doubt, the current editor takes the view that a partner must display good faith when he seeks to dissolve the firm by notice, whether pursuant to an express power in the agreement or the provisions of the Partnership Act 1890.[7]

The nature of the duty

16-03   It hardly needs to be stated that the duty of good faith is of general application[8] and arises out of the fiduciary relationship which exists between partners, as Vice-Chancellor Bacon made clear in *Helmore v. Smith*[9]:

> "If fiduciary relation means anything I cannot conceive a stronger case of fiduciary relation than that which exists between partners. Their mutual confidence is the life blood of the concern. It is because they trust one another that they are partners in the first instance; it is because they continue to trust each other that the business goes on."

However, whilst there is a fiduciary relationship between partners, it does not follow that a partner who, as the agent of the firm,[10] receives partnership money from a third party will necessarily be treated as acting in a fiduciary capacity.[11]

16-04   The duty is a reciprocal one: thus, if one partner chooses to repudiate the contract of partnership and refuses to perform his duty towards his co-partners, he cannot complain if they adopt a similar

---

[5] See *Chandler v. Dorsett* (1679) Finch 431; *Maddeford v. Austwick* (1826) 1 Sim. 89; *Blisset v. Daniel* (1853) 10 Hare 493; *Perens v. Johnson* (1857) 3 Sm. & G. 419; *Law v. Law* [1905] 1 Ch. 140; also *Ferguson v. Mackay*, 1985 S.L.T. (O.H.) 94. And see the South African case of *Purdon v. Muller* 1961 (2) S.A. 211 and the Canadian case of *Hogar Estates Ltd. In Trust v. Shebron Holdings Ltd.* (1979) 23 O.R. (2d) 543. As to withholding information, see *McLure v. Ripley* (1850) 2 Mac. & G. 274.

[6] See *supra*, para. 15–08.

[7] See *infra*, para. 24–13.

[8] See, for example, *Moser v. Cotton* (1990) 140 N.L.J. 1313, where a partner in a firm of solicitors sought (unsuccessfully) to argue that his duty to his partners was overridden by a solicitor/client relationship between himself and the firm which was created *after* the date of his retirement. Although the duty of good faith could, in theory, be excluded by agreement (*ibid.*), it is hard to imagine circumstances where this would be appropriate.

[9] (1886) 35 Ch.D. 436, 444; see also *Cassels v. Stewart* (1881) 6 App.Cas. 64, 79, *per* Lord Blackburn; *Roxburgh Dinardo & Partners' Judicial Factor v. Dinardo*, 1993 S.L.T. 16 (2nd Div.); *Hogar Estates Ltd. In Trust v. Shebron Holdings Ltd.* (1979) 23 O.R. (2d.) 543.

[10] See *supra*, paras. 12–53 *et seq.*

[11] See *Piddocke v. Burt* [1894] 1 Ch. 343 (a decision under the Debtors Act 1869, s.4(3)). *Cf.* the observation of Lord Blackburn in *Cassels v. Stewart*, *supra*.

attitude towards him.[12] As observed by Lord Eldon in *Const v. Harris*[13]:

"A partner who complains that the other partners do not do their duty towards him, must be ready at all times and offer himself to do his duty towards them."

Accordingly, if a partner, faced with his co-partner's breach of duty, chooses to commit a breach of his own, by way of retaliation or otherwise, he may find that he has substantially prejudiced his position.[14] There are, however, limits to this principle: partners obviously cannot complain of a co-partner's failure to perform his duties towards them if they have previously sought to deny that he was a partner and rejected his right to participate in the firm's affairs.[15]

Although a breach of the duty will give rise to a claim for damages **16–05** in an appropriate case,[16] there may be difficulties where the breach involves a mere non-disclosure.[17]

Inchoate and dissolved partnerships

The duty of good faith exists not only as between persons who are **16–06** actually in partnership together, but also as between persons who are merely negotiating their entry into partnership.[18] Thus, if an intending partner receives a bonus or commission when acquiring property for the use of the firm, he must account for it once the firm has come into existence.[19] Equally, the duty will continue to be owed

---

[12] See *McLure v. Ripley* (1850) 2 Mac. & G 274; *Reilly v. Walsh* (1848) 11 I.Eq. R. 22. *Quaere*: could the partners invoke this principle if one of their number *deliberately* neglects the affairs of the partnership? See *supra*, para. 10–75.

[13] (1824) T. & R. 496, 524. See also *Abbatt v. Treasury Solicitor* [1969] 1 W.L.R. 1575.

[14] Although such a scenario may seem fanciful, the current editor's experience is that "tit-for-tat" breaches are by no means uncommon.

[15] See *Dale v. Hamilton* (1847) 2 Ph. 266. A partner who finds himself in such a situation should not, however, delay in asserting his rights: see further, *infra*, paras. 23–17 *et seq*.

[16] *Trimble v. Goldberg* [1906] A.C. 494, 500; also *Ferguson v. Mackay*, 1985 S.L.T. (O.H.) 94. And see *Sanders v. Parry* [1967] 1 W.L.R. 753 (duty owed by employee); *Downsview Nominees Ltd. v. First City Corporation Ltd.* [1993] A.C. 295 (duty owed by mortgagee/receiver); *Imperial Group Pension Trust Ltd. v. Imperial Tobacco Ltd.* [1991] 1 W.L.R. 589, 597, *per* Browne-Wilkinson V.-C. (a pension fund case). Note, however, that claims for damages as between partners are not without difficulty: see *infra*, paras. 23–195 *et seq*.

[17] In *Uphoff v. International Energy Trading*, The Times, February 4, 1989, it was held that no claim for damages lay as between co-venturers, even though the duty of disclosure was of a fiduciary nature. The position is *a fortiori* where the duty is not fiduciary: see *Banque Keyser Ullman SA v. Skandia Life (U.K.) Insurance Co. Ltd.* [1990] 1 Q.B. 665; *Bank of Nova Scotia v. Hellenic Mutual War Risks Assoc. (Bermuda) Ltd.* [1990] 1 Q.B. 818 (both decisions relating to insurance contracts).

[18] See *Hichens v. Congreve* (1828) 1 Russ. & M. 150. Also *New Brunswick Ry. v. Muggeridge* (1860) 1 Dr. & Sm. 363; *Central Ry. of Venezuela v. Kisch* (1867) L.R. 2 H.L. 99.

[19] *Fawcett v. Whitehouse* (1829) 1 Russ. & M. 132. *Quaere*: would the other intending partners have any rights if, in the event, the firm never came into existence? The answer will depend on the circumstances, *e.g.* the derivation of the funds applied in acquiring the property or the misuse of confidential information. A breach of duty in relation to the latter was established in *LAC Minerals Ltd. v. International Corona Resources Ltd.* [1990] F.S.R. 441 (Supreme Court of Canada).

by an outgoing partner[20] and will also apply as between the partners of a dissolved firm, until such time as its affairs are finally wound up and settled.[21]

The duty of honesty

16–07   In addition to the general duty of good faith, a partner owes his co-partners a duty to be honest in his dealings with third parties. This duty will apply to all transactions, whether or not they are of a partnership nature.[22]

2. THE OBLIGATION OF PARTNERS NOT TO BENEFIT THEMSELVES AT THE EXPENSE OF THEIR CO-PARTNERS

16–08 Although this obligation is, for present purposes, formulated separately from the general duty of good faith, it in truth represents no more than a particular branch of that duty. Lord Lindley explained it thus:

> "Good faith requires that a partner shall not obtain a private advantage at the expense of the firm. He is bound in all transactions affecting the partnership, to do his best for the common body, and to share with his co-partners any benefit which he may have been able to obtain from other people, and in which the firm is in honour and conscience entitled to participate; *Semper enim non id quod privatim interest unius ex sociis servari solet, sed quod societati expedit.*"[23]

The passage from the Digest which Lord Lindley quoted may be translated as follows: "The invariable practice being not to have regard to the private interest of one of the partners but to the advantage of the firm."[24]

Accountability of partners for private profits

16–09   In accordance with this principle, it was established by numerous decisions prior to the Partnership Act 1890, that one partner was not at liberty to make a profit at the expense of his co-partners without their full knowledge and consent, whether that profit was made

---

[20] See *Moser v. Cotton* (1990) 140 N.L.J. 1313, noticed *supra*, para. 16–03, n.8.
[21] Partnership Act 1890, ss.29(2) (*infra*, para. 16–09), 38 (*supra*, para. 13–64). And see *Clegg v. Fishwick* (1849) 1 Mac. & G. 294; *Lees v. Laforest* (1851) 14 Beav. 250; *Perens v. Johnson* (1857) 3 Sm. & G. 419; *Clements v. Hall* (1858) 2 De G. & J. 173.
[22] See *Carmichael v. Evans* [1904] 1 Ch. 486; and see *supra*, para. 10–96.
[23] Dig. xvii, tit. 2, pro socio, 1. 65, para. 5.
[24] Trans. by C.H. Munro, 1902.

directly or indirectly, *e.g.* by appropriating some benefit to himself which he ought to have acquired, if at all, on behalf of all the partners.[25] The obligation established by those decisions was placed on a statutory footing in the Partnership Act 1890:

"29.—(1) Every partner must account to the firm for any benefit derived by him without the consent of the other partners from any transaction concerning the partnership, or from any use by him of the partnership property name[26] or business connexion.

(2) This section applies also to transactions undertaken after a partnership has been dissolved by the death of a partner, and before the affairs thereof have been completely wound up, either by any surviving partner or by the representatives of the deceased partner.

30. If a partner, without the consent of the other partners, carries on any business of the same nature as and competing with that of the firm, he must account for and pay over to the firm all profits made by him in that business."

Although all questions of accountability must now be determined by reference to the above sections, the pre-1890 cases still afford a valuable illustration of the principles on which the sections were based and will frequently indicate the way in which they are likely to be applied by the courts.

Sale by or to the firm

A partner may not make a secret profit in the course of buying **16–10** property from, or selling property to, his own firm.[27] Thus, in *Bentley v. Craven*,[28] a partner, who had been employed to purchase sugar on the firm's behalf, unbeknown to his co-partners supplied the firm with sugar which he had previously purchased on his own account at a favourable price and for which he charged the firm full market value. He was held accountable to the firm for the profit so realised.

---

[25] This passage, in an earlier formulation, was cited with approval in *Thompson's Trustees v. Heaton* [1974] 1 W.L.R. 605.

[26] Even apart from this section, a partner might be liable to account for profits made whilst representing himself as an agent of the firm, when he in fact has no express authority: see *English v. Dedham Vale Properties Ltd.* [1978] 1 W.L.R. 93.

[27] See in addition to the cases cited in the text, *Gordon v. Holland* (1913) 108 L.T. 385, where a partner improperly sold partnership property to a purchaser for value without notice and subsequently repurchased it for his own benefit; also the Canadian case of *Denison v. Fawcett* (1958) 12 D.L.R. (2d) 537, where a partner secretly procured a third party to buy the partnership business, ostensibly as a principal but in fact as his agent.

[28] (1853) 18 Beav. 75. See also *Kuhlirz v. Lambert* (1913) 108 L.T. 560.

16–11   Similarly in *Dunne v. English*,[29] the plaintiff and the defendant had
agreed to buy a mine for £50,000, with a view to reselling it at a
profit. It was ultimately arranged that the defendant would sell the
mine to a third party for £60,000 and that the plaintiff and the
defendant would divide the resulting profit of £10,000.[30] In fact the
defendant sold the mine for a sum far in excess of £60,000 to a
company in which he himself had a substantial interest. The plaintiff
was held entitled to one-half of the actual profit made on the resale.

Full disclosure

16–12   If the duty to account is to be avoided in such a case, it is essential
that the partner concerned makes full disclosure of his interest to his
co-partners. However, nothing short of such full disclosure will
suffice. It appears that, in *Dunne v. English*, the plaintiff knew that
the defendant had some interest in the purchase beyond his share of
the known profit of £10,000 but he did not know what that interest
was and the real position was concealed from him. It was held that
the defendant, being the plaintiff's partner and expressly entrusted
with the conduct of the sale, was bound to make full disclosure of the
true facts; having failed to do so, he could not exclude the plaintiff
from his due share of the profits realised on the sale.[31]

Authority to sell at a fixed price

16–13   *Dunne v. English* is also authority for the (largely self-evident)
proposition that, if one partner authorises another to sell partnership
property at a certain price, he does not thereby deprive himself of his
right to a full share of the sale proceeds if a higher price is in fact
realised.[32]

Other benefits due to the firm

16–14   The same principles apply where a partner attempts to secure a
personal benefit for himself which should, consistently with his duties
to his co-partners, only be obtained for the benefit the firm as a
whole.[33]

---

[29] (1874) 18 Eq. 524.
[30] It was in fact part of the arrangement ultimately agreed that the defendant would acquire the
mine so as to be able to sell it on to the third party without involving the plaintiff.
[31] See also *Imperial Mercantile Credit Association v. Coleman* (1871) L.R. 6 H.L. 189, and the
cases cited *infra*, para. 16–14, n. 34.
[32] See also *Parker v. McKenna* (1874) 10 Ch.App. 96; *De Bussche v. Alt* (1878) 8 Ch.D. 286 and,
in particular, *ibid.* p. 317, as to the illegality of a custom authorising such a practice.
[33] Lord Lindley remarked in a footnote that the decision in *Parker v. Hills* (1861) 7 Jur. (N.S.)
833 "is not opposed to these cases, for there the money was paid for a lease which was held to
belong to one partner only."

Thus, in *Carter v. Horne*[34] the plaintiff and the defendant agreed to purchase an estate subject to certain incumbrances, which fell to be discharged out of the purchase price. Some of the incumbrancers were, for personal reasons, prepared to allow the defendant to enjoy the benefit of a reduction in certain sums due in respect of interest and otherwise. However, in proceedings brought against him by the plaintiff for an account of rents and profits, the defendant was held liable to account for these reductions, since the purchase had been made for their joint benefit and on the basis of mutual trust.

Leases: renewal

It is settled law that, in Lord Lindley's own words,   **16–15**

"... if one partner obtains in his own name, either during the partnership or before its assets have been sold,[35] a renewal of a lease of the partnership property, he will not be allowed to treat this renewed lease as his own and as one in which his co-partners have no interest."

This principle was established by Sir William Grant in *Featherstonhaugh v. Fenwick*,[36] where two partners had obtained a renewal of the lease of the partnership premises in their own names and immediately dissolved the partnership. They sought to exclude the plaintiff (their co-partner) from all interest in the new lease but, in taking the accounts of the partnership, it was held that the lease was an asset of the firm.

Clegg v. Fishwick[37] was a similar case. There the plaintiff, who was **16–16** the administratrix of a partner in a coal-mine, commenced proceedings against the surviving partners some years after the date of death, by which she sought an account and a dissolution, and a declaration that a renewed lease, which had been obtained by the

---

[34] (1728) Eq.Ab. 7. See also *Morison v. Thompson* (1874) L.R. 9 Q.B. 480; *De Bussche v. Alt* (1878) 8 Ch.D. 286; *Powell and Thomas v. Evan Jones & Co.* [1905] 1 K.B. 11; *Nitedals Taendstikfabrik v. Bruster* [1906] 2 Ch. 408, as to the right of a principal to profits made by his agent or sub-agent. In earlier editions of this work, this footnote contained extensive references to decided cases establishing the extent of a principal's right to recover commissions, bribes, etc., from his agent; however, given the wide nature of the duty to account which the law imposes on partners, such references have not been retained. The full footnote is to be found in the 15th ed., at p. 485, n. 26.

[35] *i.e.* following a dissolution.

[36] (1810) 17 Ves.Jr. 298. See also *Keech v. Sandford* (1726) Sel.Cas. Ch. 61; *Re Biss* [1903] 2 Ch. 40, 56 (*per* Collins M.R.), 60, 62 (*per* Romer L.J.); *Griffith v. Owen* [1907] 1 Ch. 195; *Re Knowles' Will Trusts* [1948] 1 All E.R. 866 (where a trustee had renewed a lease of trust property in his own name); *Chelsea Estates Investment Trust Co. v. Marche* [1955] Ch. 328 (where a mortgagee of a lease had renewed the mortgaged lease under an option contained therein); *Gordon v. Gonda* [1955] 1 W.L.R. 885 (tracing partnership asset into other property following a dissolution); *Chan (Kak Loui) v. Zacharia* (1984) 154 C.L.R. 178.

[37] (1849) 1 Mac. & G. 294. See also *Clements v. Hall* (1858) 2 De G. & J. 173.

defendants, was held in trust for the benefit of the former firm. Two defences were set up: first, it was said that the former firm had come to an end at the same time as the old lease and the plaintiff could not therefore claim any interest in the new lease. Secondly, it was said that, before the proceedings were commenced, the plaintiff had assigned the deceased's partnership share to his children, so that she, at least, had no right to institute proceedings in respect thereof. On the first defence, it was held that the old lease was the "foundation" for the new lease and that, where parties are jointly interested in a lease, some of them cannot take the benefit of a renewal to the exclusion of the others; on the second, it was held that what had been assigned by the plaintiff was the deceased's share, which had never been ascertained, and that the assignment constituted her as a trustee of the share for the assignees but did not to deprive her of her right to call for the partnership property to be realised.

16–17   In cases of this type, the other partners cannot restrain the landlord from granting the new lease to their co-partner: their remedy is rather to treat the lessee as holding the lease for the benefit of the firm.[38]

Open renewal

16–18   In both *Featherstonhaugh v. Fenwick* and *Clegg v. Fishwick*, the lease was renewed in a clandestine way, but this is by no means an essential ingredient. This is illustrated by the decision in *Clegg v. Edmondson*[39] where a partnership at will was dissolved by the managing partners, who gave notice to the other partners of their intention to renew the old lease for their own benefit. They in fact did so, despite those other partners' objections, and evidence was adduced to the effect that the landlord would have opposed the grant of a renewed lease to anyone other than the managing partners.[40] It was nevertheless held that the managing partners could not acquire the benefit of the renewed lease for their own exclusive benefit.[41] A similar decision was reached by the Privy Council in *Robert Watte Pathirana v. Ariya Pathirana*,[42] when considering the renewal of certain petrol supply agreements by one of two partners for his own benefit.

---

[38] *Alder v. Fouracre* (1818) 3 Swans. 489. Where the lease is the sole property of one partner, see *Burdon v. Barkus* (1862) 4 De G.F. & J. 42; *Bevan v. Webb* [1905] 1 Ch. 620, 631, *per* Warrington J; also *infra*, para. 18–15. And see *Re Thomson* [1930] 1 Ch. 203, 210, (*per* Clauson J.), where one of three executors took a new lease for his own benefit.

[39] (1856) 8 De G.M. & G. 787. See also *Re Biss* [1903] 2 Ch. 40, 61, 62, *per* Romer L.J.

[40] See *Fitzgibbon v. Scanlan* (1813) 1 Dow. 269.

[41] However, the other partners were in fact denied any relief by reason of laches and delay: see further, *infra*, paras. 23–22 *et seq.*

[42] [1967] 1 A.C. 233. See further, *infra* para. 16–24.

Right to reject renewed lease

Although one partner cannot exclude his co-partners from the **16–19** benefit of the renewed lease, he cannot force them to treat it as acquired on behalf of the firm, unless he acted with their authority or they have otherwise bound themselves to accept such treatment.[43]

Laches

It goes almost without saying that a claim of the above type must **16–20** be brought promptly, if a successful plea of laches is to be avoided.[44]

Leases: purchase of reversion

A partner who purchases the reversion to the firm's lease may **16–21** enjoy a more secure position, since the purchase may be entirely independent of any interest in the lease.[45] Thus, in *Bevan v. Webb*,[46] a partner who had purchased such a reversion out of his own moneys was held to be entitled to retain it, there being no evidence that the purchase had been obtained by virtue of his interest in the lease and the lease not being renewable by custom or by contract.[47] On the other hand, in *Thompson's Trustee v. Heaton*,[48] where a lease remained as an undistributed asset after the dissolution of a firm, it was held that each of the former partners was precluded from acquiring the reversion for his own benefit without giving the other the opportunity of coming in on the acquisition. As a result, the partner who had acquired the reversion was under a fiduciary duty to account to the other for the benefit derived therefrom.

Use of partnership property

The principle which precludes a partner from retaining benefits **16–22** which he ought properly to share with his co-partners is equally applicable where those benefits result from the use of partnership property, as is made clear in the Partnership Act 1890 itself.[49] Thus,

---

[43] *Clements v. Norris* (1878) 8 Ch.D. 129. But see also *supra*, paras. 15–05, 15–07.

[44] *Clegg v. Edmondson* (1856) 8 De G.M. & G. 787; *Re Jarvis* [1958] 1 W.L.R. 815; see also, generally, *infra*, paras. 23–17 *et seq.*

[45] See *Griffith v. Owen* [1907] 1 Ch. 195.

[46] [1905] 1 Ch. 620.

[47] See as to such leases, *Phillips v. Phillips* (1884) 29 Ch.D. 673; *Griffith v. Owen* [1907] 1 Ch. 195, 204–205, *per* Parker J. In view of the provisions of the Landlord and Tenant Act 1954, Part II (as amended), these cases may now be of more general application.

[48] [1974] 1 W.L.R. 605. See also *Wix v. Bennet* (1971) 30 C.L.R. 80; *Brenner v. Rose* [1973] 1 W.L.R. 443; and see generally, *Boardman v. Phipps* [1967] 2 A.C. 46. For the position as between husband and wife, see *Protheroe v. Protheroe* [1968] 1 W.L.R. 519.

[49] s.29, *supra*, para. 16–09.

in *Burton v. Wookey*,[50] the plaintiff and the defendant (who was a shopkeeper) were partners as dealers in *lapis calaminaris*. The defendant lived near the mines and purchased the ore from the miners, paying them not in money but in goods from his shop. In his account with the plaintiff, the defendant treated the ore as having been purchased for an amount equal to the *sale* price of those goods; the plaintiff contended that, as between himself and the defendant, the purchase price should be treated as the *cost* price of the goods, and that the defendant should account to the firm for the profit on the transaction. That argument was upheld, the court holding that it was the defendant's duty to buy the ore at the lowest possible price and to charge the firm with no more than the cost price of the goods given in exchange therefor.

16–23   Similarly, in *Gardner v. McCutcheon*,[51] the defendant, who was both the master and a part owner of a ship, was held liable to account for profits which he had obtained by trading on his own account whilst the ship was employed for the joint benefit of himself and his co-owners, the plaintiffs. Although he contended that the profits were made solely by the employment of his own private funds and that, by custom, masters of ships were allowed to trade for their own benefit, the court declined to recognise such a custom and held the profits to have been made by the use of jointly owned property.

Post-dissolution profits

16–24   If a partner continues in business following the dissolution of his firm and makes use of the firm's assets or a business connection derived therefrom, he will be accountable to his former partners for any profits which he may make thereby. Thus, in *Robert Watte Pathirana v. Ariya Pathirana*,[52] the plaintiff and the defendant were partners in a petrol service station business in Ceylon. A dispute arose and the defendant gave notice terminating the partnership; before that notice had expired, he obtained the renewal of certain petrol supply agreements in his sole name and, after the determination of the partnership, carried on trading from the same premises in his own name. The Privy Council held that he was accountable to the plaintiff for a share of the profits attributable to those new petrol supply agreements.

---

[50] (1882) 6 Madd. 367.
[51] (1842) 4 Beav. 534. See also *Benson v. Heathorn* (1842) 1 Y. & C. Ch. 326; *Shallcross v. Oldham* (1862) 2 J. & H. 609; *Miller v. Mackay* (1865) 31 Beav. 77; *Williamson v. Hine* [1891] 1 Ch. 390. *Cf. Miller v. Mackay* (1865) 34 Beav. 295; also *Moffat v. Farquharson* (1788) 2 Bro.C.C. 338 (but see the note on this case in Belt's edition of Brown's Reports). And see *infra*, para. 18–16.
[52] [1967] 1 A.C. 233.

It should be noted that, following a dissolution, each partner's **16–25** authority to bind the firm only continues "as far as may be necessary to wind up the affairs of the partnership, and to complete transactions begun but unfinished at the time of the dissolution, *but not otherwise*"[53] (emphasis supplied). Accordingly, a partner who exploits the firm's business connection in order to take on *new* business for his own benefit will normally be accountable for any profits realised, even though such business could not properly have been transacted by the firm without the agreement of all the other partners.[54]

Information gained as a partner

If a partner comes into possession of information in the course of **16–26** carrying on the partnership business or otherwise as a result of his connection with the firm, and uses it to secure some personal benefit from a transaction which is within the scope of the partnership business, he will be accountable therefor.[55] However, no such duty to account will in general arise if the transaction does not involve competition with the partnership business and falls outside its scope, as illustrated by the decision in *Aas v. Benham*.[56] There the defendant, a partner in a firm of shipbrokers, used information which he had acquired in transacting the firm's business when setting up a shipbuilding company, for which he received both remuneration and a salaried directorship. His co-partners sought an account of both remuneration and salary, but failed because the company's business was held to be entirely beyond the scope of the firm's business. Nevertheless, an injunction was granted to restrain the defendant from making use of the firm name for his own purposes.

Similarly, in *Re Coffey's Registered Design*,[57] it was held that a **16–27** partner in a firm trading in home brewing materials, who had himself developed a design for a container for brewing beer, was beneficially entitled to the design and innocent of any breach of the duty of good faith owed to his co-partners, since the firm was involved solely in the

---

[53] Partnership Act 1890, s.38. See further, *supra*, paras. 10–160, 13–63 *et seq.*

[54] Conceptually this must be correct, because the partner in the example has, in effect, appropriated part of the firm's goodwill (*i.e.* customer connection) for his own benefit. See also, *infra*, para. 16–28. And note the decision in *Castle v. Castle* [1951] G.L.R. 541.

[55] See *Regal (Hastings) Ltd. v. Gulliver* [1942] 1 All E.R. 378; *Boardman v. Phipps* [1967] 2 A.C. 46; *Industrial Development Consultants Ltd. v. Cooley* [1972] 1 W.L.R. 443. As to the assessment of damages, see *Seager v. Copydex (No. 2)* [1969] 1 W.L.R. 809.

[56] [1891] 2 Ch. 244, explaining *Dean v. Macdowell* (1878) 8 Ch.D. 345. *Aas v. Benham* was considered by the House of Lords in *Boardman v. Phipps*, *supra*. And see, generally, *Faccenda Chicken Ltd. v. Fowler* [1987] Ch. 117 (an employment case) and the cases cited therein. When applying decisions of this class to partners, it must be remembered that they are, at one and the same time, both principals *and* agents: see *Trego v. Hunt* [1895] 1 Ch. 462, 467 (*per* Stirling J.) and [1896] A.C. 7, 26 (*per* Lord Davey).

[57] [1982] F.S.R. 227. In fact, the firm had been incorporated prior to registration of the design, and the company (unsuccessfully) claimed rectification of the register.

business of buying and selling products manufactured by others, and not in manufacturing such products itself.

Other benefits derived from connection with the firm

16–28   However, notwithstanding the exception noted in the preceding paragraphs, there may be circumstances in which a duty to account will arise even in respect of a transaction unconnected with the partnership business, as Lord Lindley explained:

> "A partner ... is not allowed in transacting the partnership affairs, to carry on for his own sole benefit any separate trade or business which, were it not for his connection with the partnership, he would not have been in a position to carry on. Bound to do his best for the firm, he is not at liberty to labour for himself to their detriment; and if his connection with the firm enables him to acquire gain, he cannot appropriate that gain to himself on the pretence that it arose from a separate transaction with which the firm had nothing to do."

The operation of this principle has already been seen when considering the renewal of leases[58] and the use of partnership property,[59] and is further illustrated by the decisions in *Russell v. Austwick* and *Lock v. Lynham*.[60]

Russell v. Austwick[61]

16–29   In this case, several persons agreed to carry on business as carriers between London and Falmouth, on terms that they would each carry on such business along the route between the towns assigned to them and that no partnership would exist between them. In pursuance of this business, Austwick, who appears to have been the London agent of the carriers, entered into a contract for the carriage of a new silver coinage to towns on the road between London and Falmouth. Shortly afterwards, he entered into a second contract for the carriage of such coinage to towns in Middlesex and the adjoining counties, none of which lay on the London to Falmouth route and many of which were only accessible by cross-country roads, thus involving increased risks. As a result, the mint authorities agreed to increase all payments for

---

[58] See *supra*, paras. 16–15 *et seq.*
[59] See *supra*, para. 16–25.
[60] See also the following New Zealand authorities: *Gibson v. Tyree* (1901) 18 N.Z.L.R. 701; *Gibson v. Tyree (No. 2)* (1901) 20 N.Z.L.R. 278.
[61] (1826) 1 Sim. 52. This decision demonstrates that the same principles apply whenever there is an agreement to share profits, whether or not a partnership is created. See also *Clegg v. Clegg* (1861) 3 Giff. 322. *Cf. Trimble v. Goldberg* [1906] A.C. 494, noticed *infra*, para. 16–33. And see, generally, the Partnership Act 1890, s.29, *supra*, para. 16–09.

the carriage of the coinage, so that the consideration payable under the first contract was increased by a sizeable amount. No dispute arose in relation thereto, but Austwick, on behalf of himself and Maddeford (another party to the original agreement), sought to retain the benefit of the second contract, on the basis that it had nothing to do with the London to Falmouth business. However, the court held that he was accountable for the profits made thereunder, seemingly accepting the plaintiff's argument that the second contract represented a continuation of the first and resulted from the confidence reposed in Austwick by the mint authorities resulting from his participation therein.

Lock v. Lynham[62]

Here the plaintiff and the defendant had agreed to share the profits **16–30** and losses arising from contracts entered into by the defendant for the supply of foodstuffs to the armed forces in Ireland. Whilst this agreement was operating, the defendant secretly agreed to share the profits and losses arising from similar contracts entered into by third parties. The plaintiff claimed a share of such profits, but the defendant contended that he was entitled to retain them for his own exclusive benefit. The Lord Chancellor observed that, even though the partners were not under any obligation to refrain from entering into another partnership of the same kind, it never could have been in their contemplation that one of them could, in his own name or in that of a third party, enter into contracts prejudicial to the other's interests.[63] An inquiry was accordingly directed with a view to ascertaining whether, whilst the partnership was subsisting, the defendant had either alone or jointly with some other person or persons entered into, or been beneficially interested in, any other contract or dealing of the like nature to those in which the plaintiff and the defendant were engaged as partners.

One partner competing with firm

A partner must not, without the consent of his co-partners, carry **16–31** on any business in competition with the firm; if he does so, he will be accountable for any profits he may realise, even if he has acted in an entirely open manner.[64] Where, however, the business is not carried

---

[62] (1854) 4 Ir.Ch.R. 188. *Cf. Miller v. Mackay* (1865) 34 Beav. 295; and see *Somerville v. Mackay* (1810) 16 Ves.Jr. 382.

[63] See the Partnership Act 1890, s.30, *supra*, para. 16–09.

[64] *Ibid.*; and see *Glassington v. Thwaites* (1823) 1 Sim. & St. 124; *England v. Curling* (1844) 8 Beav. 129 (in which there was more than mere business rivalry). See also *Re Thomson* [1930] 1 Ch. 203, 210 *et seq.*, *per* Clauson J. (an executor competing with his testator's business). Reference may also usefully be made to the following New Zealand authorities: *Gibson v. Tyree* (1901) 18 N.Z.L.R. 701; *Gibson v. Tyree (No. 2)* (1901) 20 N.Z.L.R. 278.

on in competition with the firm and has no connection with its business, no duty to account will arise, even if the partner concerned has agreed not to carry on any other business whilst he remains a member of the firm.[65] For this reason, it may in some cases be appropriate to include an express duty to account for profits derived from non-competing businesses in the partnership agreement.[66]

Exceptional cases: purchase of co-partner's share, etc.

16–32   One notable exception to the principles discussed in the preceding paragraphs is recognised in the freedom of one partner, in the absence of any contrary provision in the agreement, to acquire another's partnership share for his own benefit, without informing the other partners or giving them an opportunity to join in such acquisition.[67]

16–33   An analogous principle was applied in *Trimble v. Goldberg*,[68] where three partners had purchased certain building plots and shares in a company with a view to re-sale. Most, if not all, of the company's assets consisted of other building plots in the same locality as those purchased. Two of the partners bought such other plots from the company without the knowledge of the third. The latter's claim to share in the benefit of this purchase was rejected, since it was not within the scope of the partnership business, nor made in competition with it, nor forbidden by the partnership agreement. It was further held that, even if the purchase had been forbidden by the agreement, it did not necessarily follow that the third partner could claim a share of the profits made by his co-partners.[69]

---

[65] *Aas v. Benham* [1891] 2 Ch. 244, *supra*, para. 16–26; *Dean v. Macdowell* (1878) 8 Ch.D. 345. In the former case the defendant was not bound to give his whole time to the partnership business; in the latter he was so bound, and damages for breach of covenant might, perhaps, have been obtained, even though the covenant probably could not have been enforced by injunction. And see, as to claims in damages, *supra*, para. 16–05; also *Grimston v. Cuningham* [1894] 1 Q.B. 125; *Davis v. Foreman* [1894] 3 Ch. 655; *Kirchner & Co. v. Gruban* [1909] 1 Ch. 413. But see *Hill v. C. A. Parsons & Co. Ltd.* [1972] Ch. 305.

[66] See also *supra*, para 10–78.

[67] *Cassels v. Stewart* (1881) 6 App.Cas. 64. In this case, the partnership agreement did not forbid such a purchase and it was not part of the firm's business to buy the shares of its members.

[68] [1906] A.C. 494.

[69] *Ibid.* p. 500.

CHAPTER 17

PARTNERSHIP CAPITAL

The nature of capital

Lord Lindley defined partnership capital in these terms: **17–01**

"By the capital of a partnership is meant the aggregate of the sums contributed by its members for the purpose of commencing or carrying on the partnership business, and intended to be risked by them in that business. The capital of a partnership is not therefore the same as its property: the capital is a sum fixed by the agreement of the partners; whilst the actual assets of the firm vary from day to day, and include everything belonging to the firm and having any money value ... The amount of each partner's capital ought ... always to be accurately stated, in order to avoid disputes on a final adjustment of account; and this is more important where the capitals of the partners are unequal, for if there is no evidence as to the amounts contributed by them, the shares of the whole assets will be treated as equal."[1]

Distinction between capital and assets

As Lord Lindley pointed out there is a fundamental distinction **17–02** between a firm's capital on the one hand and its assets (sometimes confusingly called its capital assets) on the other. That distinction is critical to an understanding of the true nature of capital and is, moreover, frequently overlooked by partners and their advisers. It has already been pointed out that a partner's capital should be expressed in cash terms, whether the contribution from which it was derived took the form of cash or a specific asset, *e.g.* land or goodwill.[2] Although a value must be placed upon any asset so contributed, there is in principle no reason why partners should not agree, as between themselves, to ascribe a notional value thereto, whether higher or lower than the true value.[3] Once a partner has brought in the asset and been credited with its agreed "capital" value in the firm's books, the asset as such will cease to be his property and will thereafter belong to the firm. Equally, that partner's capital will be unaffected by fluctuations in the value of the asset, which will

---

[1] See the Partnership Act 1890, s.24(1) and *infra*, paras. 17–08, 17–09, 19–18 *et seq.*
[2] See *supra*, para. 10–48.
[3] Note, however, that the adoption of an artificially low value may have inheritance tax implications, depending on the partners' respective capital profit shares: see *infra*, para. 36–24.

represent capital profits or losses potentially divisible between the partners in their capital profit/loss sharing ratios.[4] It is, of course, at any time open to the partners to revalue the asset and to credit any increase in value to their capital accounts, thus increasing the firm's capital, or to debit any reduction in value against to those accounts, thus writing off part of its capital.

17-03　　Provided that the foregoing procedure is strictly adhered to, there should be no difficulty in identifying the amount of the firm's capital and the size of each partner's interest therein. Where, however, an attempt is made to treat the underlying assets of the firm as its capital, such identification will become impossible, in the absence of a full scale valuation of all the partnership assets. This (*inter alia*) means that the partners cannot agree any sensible basis either for the payment of interest on capital[5] or for the acquisition of an outgoing partner's share following his retirement, expulsion, etc.,[6] without incurring the costs attendant on such a valuation, which must in any event be carried out in the certain knowledge that, once completed, it will be virtually obsolete. Equally, such an approach causes less difficulty in the case of a full scale dissolution, since a realisation of the partnership assets is inevitable, thus enabling each partner's capital entitlement (in the form of his due share of the proceeds of sale) to be readily identified.

17-04　　A further variation on the above theme is occasionally encountered: this involves each partner who contributes capital in the form of an asset being treated as entitled to that asset.[7] In such a case, it is doubtful whether there is any contribution of capital by such a partner; rather he is merely permitting his firm to have the use of the asset for so long as he remains a partner.

Distinction between capital and capital profits

17-05　　The failure properly to distinguish between a firm's capital and its assets can also lead to confusion with regard to the partners' ownership of capital profits, particularly following the admission of a new partner. If (as will usually be the case) the assets appear in the partnership accounts at their written down book value, there will be a hidden fund of capital profits, commonly referred to as an "asset surplus," which is not reflected in the partners' capital accounts. That

---

[4] *Robinson v. Ashton* (1875) L.R. 20 Eq. 25; *McClelland v. Hyde* [1942] N.I. 1, 7, *per* Andrews L.C.J. *Cf. Sykes v. Land* (1984) 271 E.G. 1265 (which turned on the construction of the agreement).

[5] See *supra*, para. 10–55 and *infra*, para. 17–13.

[6] See *supra*, paras. 10–128 *et seq*. But see *Sykes v. Land* (1984) 271 E.G. 1265.

[7] This was, in substance, the position in *Faulks v. Faulks* [1992] E.G. 82, *para* 18–21.

fund when realised, *e.g.* on a dissolution, will be shared between the partners in their normal profit sharing ratios, in the absence of some contrary agreement.[8] An incoming partner will be just as much entitled to a share of that fund as an existing partner, even though it may have been made clear to him when he joined the firm that he would be required to contribute a sum of capital and that he would not be interested in the old firm's "capital," *i.e.* the aggregate of the existing partners' contributions.[9] To avoid such a result it would either be necessary to revalue the assets and credit the existing partners' capital accounts with the increase in value,[10] or to provide that all capital profits up to the date of admission will belong to the existing partners.[11] Although an attempt to treat the underlying assets as the firm's capital might avoid this difficulty, such an approach is wrong in principle and, moreover, may create as many problems as its solves.[12]

Distinction between capital and advances

When ascertaining the amount due to a partner from the firm, **17–06** there are, of course, numerous items to be taken into account and it will only be the net balance which is ultimately due. If the partner concerned owes money to the firm, he will not be entitled to the return of his full capital contribution. Equally, the firm may owe him sums in addition to his capital entitlement, *e.g.* in respect of advances to the firm by way of loan, which were not intended to be wholly risked in the business, or in respect of undrawn profits. It is always necessary to distinguish between such sums and a partner's capital. As Lord Lindley observed:

"The distinction between a partner's capital and what is due to him for advances by way of loan to the firm is frequently very material: *e.g.* with reference to interest[13]; with reference to clauses in partnership articles fixing the amount of capital to be advanced and risked, and prohibiting the withdrawal of capital; and above all with reference to priority of payment in the event of dissolution and a deficiency of assets."[14]

Joint capital and current accounts—the accounting heresy

Particular difficulty in identifying a partner's capital will often be **17–07** encountered in the case of firms which adopt the increasingly

---

[8] See the Partnership Act 1890, ss.24(1), 44; *Robinson v. Ashton* (1875) L.R. 20 Eq. 25. See also *supra*, para. 10–66 and *infra*, para. 25–42.

[9] This may, of course, have inheritance tax implications: see *infra*, paras. 36–24 *et seq.*

[10] But note the capital gains tax consequences which may flow from such a revaluation: see *infra*, para. 35–17.

[11] See *supra*, para. 10–66 and *infra*, paras. 36–24, 36–47.

[12] See *supra*, para. 17–03.

[13] See the Partnership Act 1890, s.24(3), (4) and *infra*, paras. 17–13, 20–28, 20–29.

[14] *Ibid.* s.44. See further, *infra*, paras. 25–39 *et seq.*

common accounting practice of maintaining a single account for each partner (almost invariably styled a "capital" account) to which is credited his undrawn profits and against which he is permitted to draw at will in subsequent years. In such circumstances, it may be almost impossible to ascertain whether the partners have intended to capitalise those undrawn profits or to treat them as what is often loosely styled "circulating capital,"[15] even though the latter will usually represent the correct analysis in law.[16] It is for this reason that separate capital and current accounts should be maintained in the firm's books, so that transfers from current to capital account (or vice versa) are only effected when the partners have positively decided to increase (or decrease) the firm's "fixed capital."[17]

Shares of capital

17–08　　The Partnership Act 1890, section 24 provides as follows:

"24. The interests of partners in the partnership property and their rights and duties in relation to the partnership shall be determined, subject to any agreement express or implied between the partners by the following rules;
(1) All the partners are entitled to share equally in the capital and profits of the business, and must contribute equally towards the losses whether of capital or otherwise sustained by the firm."[18]

In his Supplement on the 1890 Act Lord Lindley said of the subsection:

"If it be proved that the partners contributed the capital of the partnership in unequal shares it is presumed that, in the absence of an agreement to the contrary, on a final settlement of accounts, the capital of the business remaining after the payment of outside debts and liabilities, and of what is due to each partner for advances, will, subject to all proper deductions, be divided amongst the partners in the proportions in which they contributed it and not equally."[19]

---

[15] This expression will often be encountered in practice together with the expression "fixed capital," *i.e.* capital properly so called. Whilst in strict partnership law both expressions are misnomers, they represent a useful shorthand method of distinguishing between two types of funding which may at any one time be available to a firm.

[16] See generally, as to the capitalisation of undrawn profits, *Re Bridgewater Navigation Co.* [1891] 2 Ch. 317, 327, *per* Lindley L.J.

[17] For the desirability of this, see *Smith v. Gale* [1974] 1 W.L.R. 9.

[18] The subsection must also be read in the light of *ibid.* s.44(b), which deals with the distribution of the proceeds of partnership property on dissolution: see *infra*, paras. 25–40 *et seq.* As to losses, see *infra*, paras. 20–04 *et seq.*

[19] See also *infra*, para. 19–21.

In earlier editions of this work, Lord Lindley's original interpreta- **17–09** tion was sought to be justified in this way:

"Despite the ambiguous reference in subsection (1) to 'capital,' it is conceived that the opening words of the section which refer to 'partnership property' make it clear that 'capital' in this context means such property—though generally this is not so."[20]

Although this approach has its attractions, it is difficult to see how the second reference to "capital" in section 24(1) can be to anything other than capital properly so called, since it would be a misuse of language to speak of partners contributing towards losses of partnership property.[21] Moreover, despite the opening words of the section, it is clear beyond argument that when the expression "capital" is used in sections 24(3) and (4),[22] it cannot refer to partnership property. On that footing, the current editor submits that "capital" should be given its normal meaning throughout the section so that, if the partners contribute capital in unequal proportions but do not agree to share it in those proportions, they will each be entitled to an equal share of the firm's capital.

Equally, an agreement displacing the provisions of section 24(1) need not be express and may well be implied from the circumstances, *e.g.* where the capital contributions precisely reflect the partners' agreed (unequal) profit sharing ratios.[23]

Increase, reduction and return of capital

It is a fundamental principle of partnership law that, in the absence **17–10** of some contrary agreement, the capital of a firm cannot be increased or reduced without the consent of all the partners.[24] Thus, where the original capital has been exhausted, the partners cannot be compelled to replace it; indeed, if the business can no longer be carried on profitably, a dissolution may be ordered at the instance of any one of the partners.[25] Similarly, if the firm is offered a lucrative deal which

---

[20] The original footnote stated "The distinction is clearly made by s.44 of the Partnership Act 1890." This is so: *cf.* the references to "capital" in para. (a) and sub-para. 2 of para. (b) and the reference to "the assets of the firm" at the beginning of para. (b).

[21] In view of the contents of the previous footnote, it should be noted that *ibid.* s.44(a) and (b) both refer to "losses ... of capital" *not* of partnership property.

[22] See *infra*, paras. 17–13, 20–27 *et seq.*

[23] However, it might, in such a case, be argued that there is no necessary correlation between the partners' capital contributions and their profit shares: see further, *infra*, para. 19–22.

[24] See *Heslin v. Hay* (1884) 15 L.R. Ir. 431, where an attempt was made to violate this principle; see also *Bouche v. Sproule* (1887) 12 App.Cas. 385, 405, *per* Lord Bramwell; *Re Bridgewater Navigation Co.* [1891] 2 Ch. 317, 327, *per* Lindley L.J.; *McClelland v. Hyde* [1942] N.Ir. 1, 6, *per* Andrews L.C.J. For an example of a case (not involving a partnership) in which damages were awarded for breach of an agreement not to withdraw capital from a business, see *Teacher v. Calder* [1899] A.C. 451, 467. *Quaere* would such a claim lie against a partner? See, as to such claims, *infra*, paras. 23–195 *et seq.*

[25] See *infra*, para. 24–73.

can only be taken up if additional capital is raised,[26] no partner can be forced to make a contribution against his will, whatever may be the consequences for the firm.

17–11   The corollary of the foregoing is, of course, that a partner who agrees to contribute a sum of capital is not only bound to bring that sum into the firm but he will be prevented from withdrawing any part of it for so long as he remains a partner. Whether he will be entitled to the return of his capital once he has ceased to be a partner will depend on the terms of the agreement[27] and/or the proper application of section 44 of the Partnership Act 1890[28] and the rule in *Garner v. Murray*.[29]

Borrowing money to fund capital contribution

17–12   It has already been seen[30] that if the firm borrows money, there cannot properly be said to have been an increase in its capital; *per contra* if individual partners borrow money on their own account and bring it into the firm *qua* capital. Equally, whilst the members of a trading partnership will normally have implied authority to borrow money on behalf of the firm, that authority will not extend to loans taken out in order to fund their capital contributions.[31]

Interest on capital

17–13   Section 24(4) of the Partnership Act 1890 is quite explicit:

"(4) A partner is not entitled, before the ascertainment of profits,[32] to interest on the capital subscribed by him."

This accorded with the previous law.[33]

Accordingly, in those cases in which partners are to be entitled to interest on their respective capitals, *e.g.* where their contributions are disproportionate, it is essential that this is expressly provided for in the agreement.[34]

---

[26] Such instances are becoming increasingly rare, with many firms now relying more on bank financing than partners' capital.

[27] See *supra*, paras. 10–128 *et seq.*

[28] See *infra*, para. 25–40.

[29] [1904] 1 Ch. 57. See further, *infra*, paras. 25–45 *et seq.*

[30] See *supra*, para. 12–49.

[31] See *supra*, paras. 12–45, 12–46, 13–21.

[32] These somewhat enigmatic words do not, by inference, suggest that interest on capital is normally payable *after* the ascertainment of profits. Note, however, that where such interest is payable, it is treated as an allocation of profits for income tax purposes: see *supra*, para. 10–55 and *infra*, para. 34–30.

[33] See *infra*, para. 20–28.

[34] See *supra*, para. 10–55.

CHAPTER 18

PARTNERSHIP PROPERTY

18–01 IN earlier editions of this work, this chapter was, somewhat **18–01** inelegantly, entitled "Joint and separate property," thereby reflecting the fundamental distinction between the joint estate of the firm and the respective separate estates of the partners, which is still of such importance in the event of the insolvency of the firm or of any one or more of the partners.[1] However, since the Partnership Act 1890 itself contains a section headed "Partnership property,"[2] that is surely the more appropriate title, even though the expression "separate property" will still, for convenience, be used to denote property belonging to a partner.

Lord Lindley's definition

Lord Lindley defined partnership property in this way: **18–02**

"The expressions partnership property, partnership stock, partnership assets, joint stock, and joint estate,[3] are used indiscriminately to denote everything to which the firm, or in other words *all* the partners composing it, can be considered to be entitled as such. The qualification *as such* is important; for persons may be entitled jointly or in common to property, and the same persons may be partners, and yet that property may not be partnership property; *e.g.* if several persons are partners in trade, and land is devised or a legacy is bequeathed to them jointly or in common, it will not necessarily become partnership property and form part of the common stock in which they are interested as partners."[4]

In fact, with the development of the so-called "salaried" partner, Lord Lindley's pure definition must now be qualified to take account of those cases in which assets are treated as partnership property even though one or more partners have no beneficial interest therein.[5] Although it might once have been argued that such assets

---

[1] See *infra*, paras. 27–82 *et seq.*

[2] *Ibid.* s.20, *infra*, para. 18–03.

[3] Lord Lindley observed in a footnote that "The expression joint estate sometimes has a wider signification, including all property which, on the bankruptcy of the firm, is distributable amongst its creditors." However, this comment was framed by reference to the (then) doctrine of reputed ownership, which has not been preserved under the Insolvency Act 1986: see *infra*, para. 27–100.

[4] *Morris v. Barrett* (1829) 3 Y. & J. 384; see also *Ex p. Fife Banking Co.* (1843) 6 Ir.Eq. 197 and, on appeal, *sub nom. Re Littles* (1847) 10 Ir.Eq. 275.

[5] In such cases, those partners who are interested in the assets are frequently styled "equity" partners.

cannot truly constitute partnership property, the current editor submits that any theoretical definition must ultimately give way to the clear intention and agreement of the parties[6] and the relevant assets be treated accordingly.

Importance of agreement

18–03   As intimated in the previous paragraph, it is up to the partners to agree between themselves what assets are to be treated as partnership property.[7] In the absence of an express agreement, the relevant factors will generally be (1) the circumstances of the acquisition, with particular reference to the source from which it was financed, (2) the purpose of the acquisition, and (3) the manner in which the asset has subsequently been dealt with. The importance of these factors, which are illustrated in many of the earlier cases, is firmly established by sections 20 and 21 of the Partnership Act 1890, which provide as follows:

> "20.—(1) All property and rights and interests in property originally brought into the partnership stock or acquired, whether by purchase or otherwise, on account of the firm, or for the purposes and in the course of the partnership business, are called in this Act partnership property, and must be held and applied by the partners exclusively for the purposes of the partnership and in accordance with the partnership agreement.
>
>   (2) Provided that the legal estate or interest in any land, or in Scotland the title to and interest in any heritable estate, which belongs to the partnership shall devolve according to the nature and tenure thereof, and the general rules of law thereto applicable, but in trust, so far as necessary, for the persons beneficially interested in the land under this section.[8]
>
>   (3) Where co-owners of an estate or interest in any land, or in Scotland of any heritable estate, not being itself partnership property, are partners as to profits made by the use of that land or estate, and purchase other land or estate out of the profits to be used in like manner, the land or estate so purchased belongs to them, in the absence of an agreement to the contrary, not as partners, but as co-owners for the same respective estates and interests as are held by them in the land or estate first mentioned at the date of the purchase.

---

[6] See the Partnership Act 1890, s.19, *supra*, paras. 10–10 *et seq.*

[7] Note, however, the potential application of the Law of Property (Miscellaneous Provisions) Act 1989, s.2: see *supra*, paras. 7–02 *et seq.*

[8] See, as to the effect of this proviso, *infra*, para. 18–62. And see also *Re Fuller's Contract* [1933] Ch. 652.

21. Unless the contrary intention appears, property bought with money belonging to the firm is deemed to have been bought on account of the firm."

Although these statutory rules will assist in determining what is and **18–04** what is not partnership property when the intentions of the partners are not readily apparent, they cannot be applied in the face of a contrary agreement, whether express or implied.[9] Moreover, the status of a particular asset, once determined in accordance with the statutory rules, may subsequently be altered by agreement of the partners, so that what was partnership property may be converted in to the separate property of one or more of the partners or vice versa.

It follows from the foregoing that any attempt to analyse what is **18–05** and what is not partnership property requires a consideration of three separate (albeit inter-related) topics, *viz.*:

1. partnership property;
2. separate property;
3. agreements transferring assets from one class to the other.

Attention will then be drawn to a number of points relating to the *legal* title to partnership property.

1. PARTNERSHIP PROPERTY

Lord Lindley posited the following general rule: **18–06**

"Whatever at the commencement of a partnership is thrown into the common stock, and whatever has from time to time during the continuance of the partnership been added thereto or obtained by means thereof, whether directly, by purchase or circuitously by employment in trade, belongs to the firm, unless the contrary can be shown."[10]

This is in fact the principle which is incorporated in section 20(1) of the Partnership Act 1890.

It has already been seen that, where the terms of the partnership expressly or by necessary implication require one or more partners to introduce land as an asset of the firm, there is seemingly no need to comply with the requirements of section 2 of the Law of Property (Miscellaneous Provisions) Act 1989.[11]

---

[9] Partnership Act 1890, s.19, *supra*, para. 10–10.
[10] See *Crawshay v. Collins* (1826) 15 Ves.Jr. 218; *Nerot v. Burnand* (1827) 4 Russ. 247, affirmed at (1828) 2 Bli. (N.S.) 215; *Bone v. Pollard* (1857) 24 Beav. 283. As to outlays of partnership money on the separate property of a partner, see *infra*, paras. 20–25, 20–26.
[11] See *supra*, paras. 7–02 *et seq.*

Property paid for by the firm

18-07   Lord Lindley said of such acquisitions:

> "The mere fact that the property in question was purchased by one
> partner in his own name is immaterial, if it was paid for out of the
> partnership monies; for in such a case he will be deemed to hold
> the property in trust for the firm, unless he can show that he holds
> it for himself alone.[12] Upon this principle it has been held that
> land purchased in the name of one partner, but paid for by the
> firm, is the property of the firm, although there may be no
> declaration or memorandum in writing disclosing the trust, and
> signed by the partner to whom the land has been conveyed.[13] So,
> if shares in a company are bought with partnership money, they
> will be partnership property, although they may be standing in the
> books of the company in the name of one partner only, and
> although it may be contrary to the company's deed of settlement[14]
> for more than one person to hold shares in it."[15]

This principle is given statutory force by the Partnership Act 1890.[16]

Property apparently paid for by firm

18-08   The statutory presumption that assets purchased with partnership
money constitute partnership property may, of course, be rebutted.
Thus, if it can be shown that what appeared to be the firm's money
was in fact lent by the firm to one of the partners and thus became
his money prior to the acquisition, no trust in favour of the firm will
arise.[17]

Land purchased by co-owners out of profits

18-09   Where co-owners of land[18] are partners in the profits produced by
its use but the land itself is not a partnership asset,[19] the general rule
will not apply where *additional* land is purchased out of such profits.

---

[12] See *per* Lord Eldon in *Smith v. Smith* (1880) 5 Ves.Jr. 189, 193; also *Robley v. Brooke* (1833) 7 Bli. (N.S.) 90; *Morris v. Barrett* (1829) 3 Y. & J. 384. And see *Helmore v. Smith* (1887) 35 Ch.D. 436.

[13] *Forster v. Hale* (1800) 5 Ves.Jr. 308; *cf.* Law of Property Act 1925, s.53. If, however, the payment made by the firm is insignificant, *e.g.* the payment of a small amount of stamp duty, a trust in favour of the partnership would not necessarily arise: see *Hodson v. Cashmore* (1972) 226 E.G. 1203 (where, on the facts, a trust was established).

[14] Now the articles of association.

[15] *Ex p. Connell* (1838) 3 Deac. 201; *Ex p. Hinds* (1850) 3 De G. & Sm. 613. Lord Lindley then went on to consider a difficulty formerly presented, in the case of ships, by the ship registration Acts, but concluded that this difficulty would no longer arise: see generally, the 15th ed. of this work at p. 499.

[16] *Ibid.* ss.20(1), 21, *supra*, para. 18-03.

[17] See *Smith v. Smith* (1880) 5 Ves.Jr. 189; also *Ex p. Emly* (1811) 1 Rose 61; *Walton v. Butler* (1861) 29 Beav. 428.

[18] This will include any interest in land.

[19] See further, *infra*, para. 18-24.

The statutory presumption in such a case is that the co-owners intended to acquire and hold the additional land in the same way as the original land.[20] In earlier editions of this work the operation of the presumption was illustrated (*inter alia*) by reference to the decision in *Davis v. Davis*;[21] however, no land was in fact acquired by the partners in that case.

The earlier decision in *Phillips v. Phillips*,[22] which was cited by **18–10** Lord Lindley in this context, is something of an enigma. There, certain public houses had been devised to two persons who carried on a brewery business in partnership; it was (conventionally) held that those public houses were not assets of the firm, even though they were used for the purposes of its business. Moreover, it appears that certain mortgage debts secured on public houses were also bequeathed to the two partners and they later purchased the equities of redemption out of partnership funds: it was held that the equities followed the mortgage debts and thus again did not become partnership property. However, it was also held that other public houses, which had been purchased out of partnership funds and used for the purposes of its business, *did* belong to the firm.[23]

Rebutting the statutory presumption

The statutory presumption may be rebutted. An example of such **18–11** case, decided long before the Partnership Act 1890, is *Morris v. Barrett*,[24] where land had been devised to two persons as joint tenants and farmed by them for many years. Profits derived from the farming enterprise were paid into a joint fund to which they each had access, but no account was ever taken. Further land was purchased in the name of one partner out of the joint fund and farmed with the original land. It was held that, although the original land was not partnership property, the further land was.

---

[20] Partnership Act 1890, s.20(3), *supra*, para. 18–03; see also *Steward v. Blakeway* (1869) L.R. 4 Ch.App. 603.

[21] [1894] 1 Ch. 393: see *infra*, para. 18–12.

[22] Details of this case are derived from a passage in *Bisset on Partnership* (1847), p. 50, which was based on the notes of one of the counsel appearing in the case. The report at (1832) 1 M. & K. 649 does not refer to the property devised. Lord Lindley observed: "Mr. Bisset considers the decision as an authority on the point of conversion. But if, as he represents, the court came to the conclusion that the devised property was not in fact partnership property, the question of conversion would not have arisen. Compare *Waterer v. Waterer* (1873) L.R. 15 Eq. 402."

[23] See (1832) 1 M. & K. 649, 663. Lord Lindley considered that these public houses were "partnership property to all intents and purposes"; yet surely the decision of Sir John Leach M.R. is clear upon the point.

[24] (1829) 3 Y. & J. 384; also *Christie v. Christie* [1917] 1 I.R. 17. And see *infra*, paras. 18–27, 18–28.

Scope of the statutory presumption

18–12   The statutory presumption is confined to the *purchase* of land and strictly does not apply to the improvement of land or to the acquisition of chattels and other assets. However, the court may, in certain circumstances, be prepared to apply the presumption by analogy, as in *Davis v. Davis*.[25] There a testator had devised his residuary estate, comprising his business, the freehold premises on which it was carried on, and some adjoining freehold premises, to his two sons as tenants in common. The sons carried on the business without any express agreement. On one occasion they mortgaged the adjoining premises and used the money raised to extend their workshops onto those premises; on another, they mortgaged the business premises and used the money in the business, mainly in the purchase of new plant and machinery. The premises on which the business was carried on were not particularly suitable for that purpose. It was held that the sons were partners in the business, but that none of the premises constituted partnership property. North J. recognised that, because no land was acquired, section 20(3) of the Partnership Act 1890 was strictly inapplicable, but observed that "the same law applies."[26]

It would also seem that the presumption may not apply where part of the original land is held by the co-owners as joint tenants and part as tenants in common.[27]

Circumstances of acquisition

18–13   In order to determine whether an asset acquired by a partner has in truth been acquired "on account of the firm, or for the purposes and in the course of its business,"[28] all the surrounding circumstances must inevitably be taken into account.[29] Thus, where a partner had applied for the grant of a new tenancy under Part II of the Landlord and Tenant Act 1954 in respect of premises at which the firm carried on its business and it could be shown that all the partners (including the applicant) regarded the application as having been made by and for the benefit of the firm, just as had happened on a previous occasion, it was held that the tenancy, when acquired, was a partnership asset and that, on the death of the tenant partner, it vested in his personal representatives on trust for the benefit of the surviving partners.[30]

---

[25] [1894] 1 Ch. 393. *Cf. Jackson v. Jackson* (1804) 9 Ves.Jr. 591; *Waterer v. Waterer* (1873) 15 Eq. 402: see further, *infra*, paras. 18–27, 18–28.
[26] [1894] 1 Ch. 405.
[27] *Christie v. Christie* [1917] 1 I.R. 17, 36, *per* O'Connor M.R.
[28] Partnership Act 1890, s.20(1), *supra*, para. 18–03.
[29] See, for example, *Harwood v. Harwood* [1991] 2 F.L.R. 274.
[30] See *Hodson v. Cashmore* (1972) 226 E.G. 1203.

Property used by the firm

More difficult questions arise when an asset paid for by a partner **18–14** has been used by the firm and treated as its property. There is no presumption that it remains the property of the partner concerned, simply because he paid for it; in fact, the presumption is the reverse, *i.e.* that he has brought the asset in question "into the common stock."[31] In such a case, the crucial question is always: was the asset both used *and treated* as partnership property? Mere use in itself is usually insufficient to bring about a change in the status of such an asset.[32] This principle has, in particular, been applied in the case of goodwill[33] and a lease of premises from which a firm carried on business.[34]

Secret and other benefits obtained by a partner

It has been already seen that property acquired by a partner in **18–15** breach of the duty of good faith which he owes to his co-partners will be treated as acquired for the benefit of all the partners and must be accounted for to the firm;[35] it is, however, questionable whether such property constitutes a partnership asset in the acquiring partner's hands on acquisition[36] or only when accounted for to the firm.[37] Precisely the same rule applies to property acquired by a continuing or surviving partner in breach of the duty owed to a former partner

---

[31] See *Ex p. Hare* (1835) 1 Deac. 16, 25, *per* Sir J. Cross; also the Partnership Act 1890, s.20(1) *supra*, para. 18–03. And see, in this context, the unusual decision in *Faulks v. Faulks* [1992] 15 E.G. 82, noticed *infra*, para. 18–21.

[32] Note, however, that the partners may acquire limited *rights* in respect of such an asset: see *supra*, para. 10–38 and *infra*, para. 18–33. As to the position where the asset is improved by expenditure financed by the firm or by one or more of the non-owning partners, see *infra*, para. 18–37 *et seq.*

[33] *Miles v. Clarke* [1953] 1 W.L.R. 537: see *infra*, para. 18–35.

[34] *Gian Singh v. Devraj Nahar* [1965] 1 W.L.R. 412; *Eardley v. Broad, The Times*, April 28, 1970 and (1970) 215 E.G. 823, *infra*, para. 18–32. See also *Barton v. Morris* [1985] 1 W.L.R. 1257 (where both partners were in any event co-owners).

[35] See *supra*, paras. 16–08 *et seq.*

[36] Lord Lindley put it thus: "Whatever property has been so acquired, will be treated as obtained for the benefit of all the partners, and as being part of the assets of the firm." If it is such an asset, the acquiring partner will be bound to deliver it up to the liquidator in the event of the firm being wound up as an unregistered company: Insolvent Partnerships Order 1986, Art. 3(b); see also *infra*, para. 27–65. Moreover, no period of limitation will normally apply as regards such an asset, at least while the partnership continues: see *infra*, paras. 23–31 *et seq.* As to the position where a partner holds an asset on trust for the firm, see *infra*, para. 23–41.

[37] In earlier editions of this work, it was submitted that such property only becomes a partnership asset *when recovered* and that, until then, the relationship is arguably that of debtor and creditor. Reference was made to the decision in *Gordon v. Scott* (1858) 12 Moo. P.C. 1 (which concerned a partnership, but which does not otherwise appear to support the proposition) and to the following non-partnership cases: *Lister & Co. v. Stubbs* (1890) 45 Ch.D. 1; *Re Thorpe* [1891] 2 Ch. 360; *Archer's Case* [1892] 1 Ch. 322; *Powell and Thomas v. Evan Jones & Co.* [1905] 1 K.B. 11. Now, of course, *Lister & Co. v. Stubbs* has been disapproved by the Privy Council in *Att.-Gen. for Hong Kong v. Reid* [1994] 1 A.C. 324, which would seem to suggest that Lord Lindley's view (see *supra*, n. 36) was correct. In any event, it should be noted that the other partners' interest in the property may be defeated by laches so that, even if it *does* constitute a partnership asset from the outset, that status is by no means absolute: see *supra*, para. 16–20 and *infra*, paras. 23–17 *et seq.*

or to the representatives of a deceased partner, so long as he or they retain an interest in the partnership assets.[38]

18-16   The position will be otherwise if there is no breach of duty and the benefit is unconnected with the partnership or, though connected, is conferred on the partner *personally*. Thus, if one partner holds a lease of property to which the firm is entitled only so long as the partnership continues[39] and that lease is sold or renewed following a dissolution, the proceeds of sale or the renewed lease (as the case may be) will belong not to the firm but to the partner in whom the lease is, by reason of such dissolution, exclusively vested.[40] Similarly, in the case of compensation payable to two out of three partners following the capture of their ship during a time of war, where the third partner, as an alien enemy, was expressly excluded from sharing therein.[41]

Property acquired after dissolution

18-17   Assets acquired by a partner whilst the affairs of a dissolved firm are still in the course of being wound up will not necessarily be regarded as partnership property, even though that partner has continued to carry on the firm's business without the consent of his former partners. In any such case, it will prima facie be necessary for the court to order an inquiry, with a view to identifying those assets which were, or which can properly be said to represent,[42] partnership property as at the date of dissolution and those which have subsequently been acquired by the partner concerned out of his own moneys. This is demonstrated by the decision in *Nerot v. Burnand*.[43] There Lord Chancellor Lyndhurst affirmed an order for the sale of a freehold hotel property (which was, on the facts, held to be partnership property), but declined to uphold an order requiring a sale of all the stock-in-trade and other effects on the premises at the

---

[38] See, as to outgoing partners, the decision in *Robert Watte Pathirana v. Ariya Pathirana* [1967] 1 A.C. 233, noticed *supra*, para. 16–24; as to deceased partners, see the Partnership Act 1890, s.29(2), *supra*, para. 16–09.

[39] See *Rye v. Rye* [1962] A.C. 496; *Gian Singh & Co. v. Devraj Nahar* [1965] 1 W.L.R. 412; *Eardley v. Broad, The Times*, April 28, 1970 and (1970) 215 E.G. 823; *Faulks v. Faulks* [1992] 15 E.G. 82.

[40] See *Burdon v. Barkus* (1861) 3 Giff. 412, affirmed at (1862) 4 De G.F. & J. 42; *Bevan v. Webb* [1905] 1 Ch. 620, 631, *per* Warrington J. See also *supra*, paras. 16–15 *et seq*.

[41] *Campbell v. Mullett* (1819) 2 Swan. 551. In that case, the captured ship was a partnership asset. See also *Thompson v. Ryan* (1817) 2 Swan. 565n.; *Moffat v. Farquharson* (1788) 2 Bro.C.C. 338; *Burnand v. Rodocanachi* (1882) 7 App.Cas. 333.

[42] *Quaere* whether, where a partner sells partnership property and reinvests the proceeds in the purchase of other property, he can properly claim the latter as his own. It is tentatively thought not, but see the decisions referred in the next two footnotes. However, the current editor doubts whether this argument could be sustained where a partner has used both his own and partnership money to acquire an asset.

[43] (1827) 4 Russ. 247, affirmed at (1828) 2 Bli. (N.S.) 215; see also *Payne v. Hornby* (1858) 25 Beav. 280.

time of the order appealed from, without inquiring whether they did in fact belong to the partnership at the dissolution date.[44]

Goodwill

In so far as the goodwill of a firm has a pecuniary value, it is **18–18** capable of constituting and, in most cases, will constitute partnership property. This will be so even if, as in the case of National Health Service goodwill,[45] such pecuniary value is incapable of being realised. Where a firm establishes a new business and thereby generates its own goodwill, such goodwill will almost inevitably constitute partnership property.[46] Whilst the position may be the same where a partnership is formed in order to carry on an *existing* business,[47] there is no such inevitability about the result: in such a case it will be necessary to consider all the circumstances, including the conduct of the partners and, where relevant, the anticipated duration of the partnership.[48]

Offices and appointments

Offices and appointments held by partners frequently give rise to **18–19** difficulty. Although it may be wrong to speak of a particular office or appointment as a partnership asset, especially if, as will often be the case, it is not in the disposition of the firm, nevertheless it may properly be regarded as held *on behalf of* the firm, which in practical terms amounts to the same thing. Thus, in *Collins v. Jackson*,[49] various appointments were held by a partner in a firm of solicitors[50] and the question arose whether the fees, etc., derived therefrom belonged to the partnership. No written agreement covered the point, but there was a memorandum relating to a number of other appointments retained by the father of one of the partners when he retired from practice. In the circumstances, it was held that all the

---

[44] See also *Ex p. Morley* (1873) L.R. 8 Ch.App. 1026, where a surviving partner had continued the business and sold the stock-in-trade: it was held that the new stock-in-trade formed part of his separate estate; *Sobell v. Boston* [1975] 1 W.L.R. 1587. Cf. *Robert Watte Pathirana v. Ariya Pathirana* [1967] 1 A.C. 233, *supra*, para. 16–24.

[45] See the National Health Service Act 1977, s.54, Sched. 10 and the decisions in *Whitehill v. Bradford* [1952] Ch. 236; *Macfarlane v. Kent* [1965] 1 W.L.R. 1019; *Anthony v. Rennie* 1981, S.L.T (Notes) 11; *Hensman v. Traill, The Times*, October 22, 1980; *Kerr v. Morris* [1987] Ch. 90. See also *infra*, para. 23–189.

[46] See *Steuart v. Gladstone* (1879) 10 Ch.D. 626; *Hunter v. Dowling* [1895] 2 Ch. 223; *Jennings v. Jennings* [1898] 1 Ch. 378. See also *supra*, paras. 10–41, 10–153 *et seq.*

[47] This will also include any case where a new firm is constituted by the admission of one or more additional partners to an *existing* firm.

[48] See *Miles v. Clarke* [1953] 1 W.L.R. 537, *infra*, para. 18–35; *Stekel v. Ellice* [1973] 1 W.L.R. 191.

[49] (1862) 31 Beav. 645.

[50] The particular positions held were: clerk to poor law guardians, superintendent registrar of births, marriages and deaths, treasurer of a turnpike trust, steward of a manor, treasurer of a charity, and receiver of tithes.

appointments in question were to be treated as held on behalf of both partners, and not for the exclusive benefit of the holder.[51]

18–20   There will be less doubt if the fees, etc., derived from the office or appointment are paid to the firm rather than to the office holder: in such a case, the office in question will be treated as held for the benefit of the firm and any duties associated therewith performed in the course of its business, notwithstanding the fact that the firm, as such, could not hold such an office.[52]

The tax treatment of fees received by partners in respect of offices and appointments held on behalf of the firm will be noticed later in this work.[53]

Milk quota

18–21   Milk quota is deserving of particular mention in this context as an asset which is *per se* incapable of existing as a partnership asset independently of the land to which it relates. This was decided in *Faulks v. Faulks*,[54] where two brothers, John and Harry Faulks, were farming certain land in partnership. The agreement provided that the tenancy of that land, which was held by John Faulks and in respect of which quota was allocated to the firm, should only be held on trust for the firm during the continuance of the partnership. Harry Faulks died and the partnership was duly determined. It was held that the firm's equitable interest in the tenancy ceased on Harry's death and that the quota thereupon passed to John. As a result, the value of the quota fell to be ignored when calculating the price to be paid for Harry's share under the terms of an option contained in the agreement.

2. SEPARATE PROPERTY

18–22 It was noted at the outset that this and the previous section are inter-related: accordingly, certain rules for identifying what constitutes the separate property of the individual partners have already been noticed in that section. Any agreement between the partners is, of course, paramount[55] but in most cases where which the status of a particular asset is in dispute there will be little tangible evidence of such an agreement, as illustrated by the various cases referred to in subsequent paragraphs.

---

[51] See also *Smith v. Mules* (1852) 9 Hare 556; *Ambler v. Bolton* (1871) L.R. 14 Eq. 427; *Casson Beckman & Partners v. Papi* [1991] BCLC 299, 310f–h, *per* Balcombe L.J. See also *infra*, para. 23–188, as to the position on a dissolution.
[52] See *Kirkintilloch Equitable Co-operative Society Ltd. v. Livingstone*, 1972 S.L.T. 154; *Casson Beckman & Partners v. Papi* [1991] BCLC 299 (which concerned the office of liquidator held by a *salaried* partner); note, in particular, the nature of the expert evidence given in the latter case: see *ibid.* p. 302b–d.
[53] See *infra*, paras. 34–33, 37–15, 37–16.
[54] [1992] 15 E.G. 82. But see also, as to the implications of this decision, an article at (1992) 126 S.J. 824. And note *R. v. M.A.F.F.*, *ex p. Bostock*, *The Times*, May 11, 1994 (European Court of Justice).
[55] See *supra*, para. 18–03.

Property producing partnership profits

The mere fact that there is a partnership in the profits produced by **18–23** a certain asset does not, in itself, indicate that the asset is partnership property. Numerous cases on one or other side of the line may be imagined, but Lord Lindley cited the following examples:

> "To take an old example, coach-proprietors who horse a coach and divide the profits, may each make use of horses which belong to himself alone and not to the firm of proprietors.[56] So, where a merchant employs a broker to buy goods for him and to sell them again on his account, although it may be agreed that the profits are to be divided, the goods themselves, and the money arising from their sale, are the property of the merchant, and not the joint property of himself and the broker[57]; and it not infrequently happens that dormant partners have no interest in anything except the profits accruing to the firm to which they belong."[58]

A more recent illustration is perhaps to be found in the case of a landowner and a builder who agree to develop and sell land and to share the resulting profit.[59]

Co-owners sharing profits

The position may be less clear in those cases where co-owners **18–24** become partners in respect of the profits produced by their jointly owned property,[60] in view of the complete identity between the partners and the co-owners. However, the current editor submits that the same general principle applies, *i.e.* the mere fact that profits and expenses are shared is not, of itself, sufficient to change the status of an asset. Lord Lindley recognised this:

> "Suppose, for example, that two or more joint tenants, or tenants in common of a farm or a mine, work their common property together as partners, contributing to the expenses and sharing all profits and losses equally, there will certainly be a partnership; and yet, unless there is something more in the case, it seems that the land will not be partnership property, but will belong to the partners as co-owners, just as if they were not partners at all."[61]

---

[56] As in *Barton v. Hanson* (1809) 2 Taunt. 49; *Fromont v. Coupland* (1824) 2 Bing. 170.
[57] *Meyer v. Sharpe* (1813) 5 Taunt. 74; *Smith v. Watson* (1824) 2 B. & C. 401; *Burnell v. Hunt* (1841) 5 Jur. 650.
[58] See *Ex p. Hamper* (1811) 17 Ves.Jr. 403; *Ex p. Chuck* (1831) Mont. 373.
[59] This seems to be implicit in the decision in *Walker West Developments Ltd. v. F.J. Emmett Ltd.* (1979) 252 E.G. 1171.
[60] See further, as to such cases, *supra*, paras. 5–08 *et seq.*
[61] See *Crawshay v. Maule* (1818) 1 Swan. 495; *Roberts v. Eberhardt* (1853) Kay 148; also *Williams v. Williams* (1867) L.R. 2 Ch.App. 294.

18–25 This would also seem to be an incidental effect of section 2(1) of the Partnership Act 1890, which provides:

"Joint tenancy, tenancy in common, joint property, common property or part ownership does not of itself create a partnership as to anything so held or owned, whether the tenants or owners do or do not share any profits made by the use thereof."[62]

A case cited by Lord Lindley as falling within this class was *Brown v. Oakshot*[63] where, in essence, two sons used certain land, the reversion to which had been devised to them jointly by their father, in carrying on his brewing business in partnership. In an *obiter* part of the decision, it was held that the reversion continued to belong to the sons as joint tenants and not as tenants in common (in which capacity they would necessarily have held the reversion if it had become partnership property).[64]

The "accessory" principle

18–26 Land may nevertheless, in certain circumstances, fall to be treated as partnership property where it is acquired solely for the purposes of the partnership business and there is some indication of the co-owners' intention to treat it as partnership property, or, as it was put in earlier editions of this work,

"the land is merely accessory to the trade and is treated as part of the common stock."[65]

Land devised to co-owners for purposes of trade

18–27 The "accessory" principle is well illustrated by and, in fact, originates from a number of cases involving the devise of a business and land to be used for the purpose of carrying it on. In *Jackson v. Jackson*[66] a testator had, in effect, devised his business and land to his two sons jointly, with a view to them carrying on that business after his death.[67] They did so as partners. Lord Eldon held that the land had become partnership property, so that the joint tenancy was severed.[68] There was some evidence to show that the sons regarded

---

[62] The principal purpose of this subsection is, of course, to avoid any prima facie implication of partnership as between co-owners: see *supra*, paras. 5–03 *et seq.*
[63] (1857) 24 Beav. 254; see also *Morris v. Barrett* (1829) 3 Y & J. 384, *supra*, para. 18–11; *Phillips v. Phillips* (1832) 1 M. & K. 649, *supra*, para. 18–10.
[64] See *infra*, para. 19–14.
[65] See *Steward v. Blakeway* (1869) L.R. 4 Ch.App. 603.
[66] (1804) 9 Ves.Jr. 591. *Cf.* the cases cited *supra*, para. 18–25, n. 63.
[67] Details of the devise are set out at (1802) 7 Ves.Jr. 535.
[68] See further, as to implied severance, *infra*, para. 19–14.

the land as partnership property; moreover, as Lord Lindley pointed out:

"... there was also this peculiarity, that a trading business was left to them, and that the land was accessory to that trade; so that it was very difficult, as observed by the Lord Chancellor, to sever the profits from the land and to hold the devisees to be partners as to the former, but not as to the latter."

A similar case was *Crawshay v. Maule*,[69] where certain mines were devised for the express purpose of being worked by the beneficiaries in partnership. The mines were worked in that way and were accordingly held to be partnership property.

In *Waterer v. Waterer*,[70] a nurseryman who carried on business with **18-28** his sons, although not in partnership, left his residuary estate, including the goodwill of his business and the nursery ground, to his sons as tenants in common. After his death, the sons carried on the business in partnership and completed the purchase of additional land which the father had previously contracted to buy for the purposes of the business, paying for it out of moneys in the estate. One son then died and the others bought out his share, partly with money raised by a mortgage of the nursery ground and again partly out of moneys in the estate. On the death of one of the surviving sons, it was held that all the land, including the nursery ground, had become partnership property.

Land acquired for purposes of trade

As is demonstrated by the case last cited, the "accessory" principle **18-29** may also be applied in the case of land acquired for the purposes of a trade *otherwise* than pursuant to a devise. Lord Lindley stated the position in this way:

"By a slight extension of the same principle, if several persons take a lease of a colliery, in order to work the colliery as partners, and they do so work it, the lease will be partnership property.[71] So, if co-owners of land form a partnership, and the land is merely accessory to their trade, and is treated as part of the common stock of the firm, the land will be partnership property."[72]

---

[69] (1818) 1 Swan. 495.
[70] (1873) L.R. 15 Eq. 402. See also *Davies v. Games* (1879) 12 Ch.D. 813.
[71] *Faraday v. Wightwick* (1829) 1 R. & M. 45. See also *Bentley v. Bates* (1840) 4 Y. & C. Ex. 182.
[72] *Essex v. Essex* (1855) 20 Beav. 442. *Cf. Steward v. Blakeway* (1869) L.R. 4 Ch.App. 603. See also *Rye v. Rye* [1962] A.C. 496; *Barton v. Morris* [1985] 1 W.L.R. 1257. If the beneficial interests in the land do not change when it becomes partnership property, no question can arise as to the need for a written disposition under the Law of Property Act 1925, s.53(1)(c). See also, *infra*, para. 18-43.

To this statement should be added one important qualification, namely that there must be no indication that what is treated as forming part of the common stock is an interest in the land *less* than the co-owners' full interest.

As will be seen hereafter,[73] if the land is acquired by one partner, to the exclusion of the others, the position will be very different, in the absence of evidence indicating that partner's intention to treat the land as partnership property.[74]

Land purchased by co-owners out of profits

18–30   It has already been seen that, if the land is not partnership property but profits derived from its use are applied in purchasing additional land, there is a statutory presumption that such additional land does *not* constitute partnership property.[75]

Property used for partnership purposes

18–31   Lord Lindley observed that:

"... it by no means follows that property used by all the partners for partnership purposes is partnership property. For example, the house and land in and upon which the partnership business is carried on often belongs to one of the partners only, either subject to a lease to the firm, or without any lease at all."[76]

Land

18–32   It has already been seen that, in some cases, land may belong to *all* the partners, but solely in the capacity of co-owners.[77] Indeed, the land may even be owned in shares different to those in which the co-owners share profits or, indeed, surplus assets within the firm.[78] The mere fact that the land forms the substratum of the partnership

---

[73] See *infra*, paras. 18–31 *et seq.*

[74] Merely showing the land as an asset in the partnership balance sheet may not, in itself, be enough: see *Barton v. Morris* [1985] 1 W.L.R. 1257. See further, *infra*, para. 18–56.

[75] Partnership Act 1890, s.20(3), *supra*, paras. 18–03, 18–09.

[76] This passage was quoted with approval by Lord Pearce and applied by the Privy Council in *Gian Singh & Co. v. Devraj Nahar* [1965] 1 W.L.R. 412; see also *Eardley v. Broad, The Times,* April 28, 1970 and (1970) 215 E.G. 823, *infra*, para. 18–32; *Harrison-Broadley v. Smith* [1964] 1 W.L.R. 456; *Harvey v. Harvey* [1970] 120 C.L.R. 529; *Barton v. Morris* [1985] 1 W.L.R. 1257. See further, as to the rights which may be implied in favour of the firm, in a case where land is held not to have become partnership property, *supra*, para. 10–38 and, *infra*, para. 18–33.

[77] See *supra*, paras. 18–24, 18–25.

[78] As in *Rye v. Rye* [1962] A.C. 496. See also *Brown v. Oakshot* (1857) 24 Beav. 254, *supra*, para. 18–25. See further, as to the significance of the partners' asset surplus sharing ratios, *supra*, para. 17–05 and *infra*, paras. 19–04 *et seq.*

business and that the firm is debited with the outgoings is not, of itself, sufficient to make it partnership property. This is clearly demonstrated by *Eardley v. Broad*,[79] where the deed governing a farming partnership between a father and son stated that the partnership "capital" was to consist of the stock, machinery and other "assets" of the farming business carried on by the father at certain premises, but did not specifically refer to the lease of those premises. Nield J. held that, even though the rent had been paid by the firm and the premises were indispensable to its business, there was no ground for inferring an assignment of the lease to the firm.

If the land itself does not become partnership property, it would **18–33** seem that no tenancy in favour of the firm can, as a matter of law, be inferred.[80] However, each partner will normally be regarded as entitled to a non-exclusive licence to enter the land for the purposes of carrying on the partnership business,[81] although that licence will be a personal right and will not as such belong to the firm.[82]

Assets other than land

Cases in which assets other than land, *e.g.* office furniture and **18–34** equipment, are used by the firm but remain the separate property of a partner, are occasionally encountered. Thus, in *Ex p. Owen*,[83] Bowers carried on business as a grocer, provision dealer, and wine merchant and had certain stock in trade and household furniture at his business premises. He took in two partners, who were entitled to share in profits but who neither contributed capital nor paid a premium. No formal agreement was entered into. Bowers purchased new stock in the name of the firm and for the purposes of its business, but paid for it out of his own moneys. The firm then went bankrupt and questions arose as to the ownership of both the stock and the furniture. It was held, on the available evidence, that there was an express or implied agreement that all the stock should belong to the firm, but that Bowers would be credited with the value of any

---

[79] *The Times*, April 28, 1970 and (1970) 215 E.G. 823. See also *Gian Singh & Co. v. Devraj Nahar* [1965] 1 W.L.R. 412; *Re John's Assignment Trusts* [1970] 1 W.L.R. 955; *Barton v. Morris* [1985] 1 W.L.R. 1257. And note also *Parker v. Hills* (1861) 7 Jur.(N.S.) 833 (lease of saltworks).
[80] *Rye v. Rye* [1962] A.C. 496. It is submitted that *Pocock v. Carter* [1912] 1 Ch. 663 (where a tenancy was inferred) is no longer good law. It is equally impermissible to infer an exclusive licence under the Agricultural Holdings Act 1986, s.2: *Harrison-Broadley v. Smith* [1964] 1 W.L.R. 456; *cf. Harrison v. Wing* [1988] 29 E.G. 101, 103, where a contrary view appears to be expressed. However, it seems that the point may not have been fully argued, since their Lordships made no reference to the decision in *Harrison-Broadley v. Smith*. See also *Bahamas International Trust Co. Ltd. v. Threadgold* [1974] 1 W.L.R. 1514.
[81] *Harrison-Broadley v. Smith*, *supra*. See further *supra*, para. 10–38.
[82] Note, however, that each partner's licence will only subsist as long as he remains a member of the firm. And see *infra*, para. 25–03.
[83] (1851) 4 De G. & Sm. 351. See also *Pilling v. Pilling* (1887) 3 De G.J. & S. 162.

items which belonged to him or for which he had paid. However, there were no grounds for making a similar inference in the case of the furniture, which was held to have remained in the ownership of Bowers alone and thus formed part of his separate estate.

18–35   A similar case was *Miles v. Clarke*.[84] There the plaintiff and the defendant carried on a photography business as partners at will. The plaintiff, who was well-known in the field, brought his goodwill into the partnership; the leasehold premises, furniture and studio equipment belonged to the defendant. Both partners contributed to the stock in trade. They had originally intended to enter into a formal partnership agreement under which all such property would be brought into the partnership but no terms, other than as to the sharing of profits, were ever finally agreed. On the dissolution of the partnership, it was held that no terms ought to be implied except those required to give business efficacy to the arrangement; accordingly, only the consumable items of stock in trade actually used in the business were to be regarded as partnership assets.

It appears from these cases that, as a general rule, stock in trade is more likely to be treated as partnership property than other chattels used in the business.[85]

Capital contribution in form of assets

18–36   It should, perhaps, be noted in this context that, once a partner has brought an asset into the firm by way of capital contribution, it will become partnership property and he will cease to enjoy any beneficial interest therein which is qualitatively different to that of his co-partners.[86]

Outlays and improvements

18–37   Difficult questions may arise where there is an outlay of partnership money on an asset belonging to one of the partners or, conversely, an outlay of a partner's own money on an asset belonging to the firm. In either case, it must be determined whether such an outlay will confer any rights in respect of the asset benefited. Of the

---

[84] [1953] 1 W.L.R. 537.
[85] See, in addition to the cases previously cited, *Ex p. Smith* (1818) 3 Madd. 63; *Ex p. Hare* (1835) 1 Deac. 16; *Ex p. Murton* (1840) 1 M.D. & D. 252.
[86] Partnership Act 1890, s.20(1), *supra*, para. 18–03. See also *supra*, para. 17–02 and *infra*, paras. 19–04 *et seq*. Naturally, any increase in the value of the asset will also constitute partnership property and, when realised, be distributable to the partners as a capital profit: see *Robinson v. Ashton* (1875) 20 Eq. 25; also *supra*, paras. 17–02 *et seq*.

possibility that it might give rise to a charge over the asset, Lord Lindley observed:

"The agreement of the partners, if it can be ascertained, determines the rights in such cases. But where, as often happens, it is extremely difficult, if not impossible, to ascertain what was agreed, the only guide is that afforded by the burden of proof. It is for those claiming an allowance in respect of the outlay to establish their claim.[87] On the other hand, an intention to make a present of a permanent improvement is not to be presumed."

He then referred to the somewhat perplexing decision known as the *Bank of England Case*.[88] There two partners had used partnership money to purchase a property known as the Trotsworth Estate, which was conveyed to them in undivided moieties. A Trotsworth Estate account was opened in the partnership books and debited with the purchase price and all other sums expended on the Estate and credited with the rent received from a tenant and other receipts derived from the Estate. Having regained possession of certain parts of the Estate from the tenant, each partner built a dwelling house thereon. At least one partner[89] used partnership money for this purpose, debiting the amount drawn to his private account in the partnership books. Although there was apparently an understanding that the Estate would be divided between the partners, they were bankrupted before the arrangements could be finalised. In the circumstances, it was held that both the Estate and the dwelling houses were partnership property. Yet, if it is right that the construction of one of the houses was financed by a partner out of his own resources, it is somewhat surprising that his separate estate was not given any allowance in respect of that expenditure.

The same theme was developed further (and in many ways more **18–38** forcibly) when Lord Lindley considered the subject of outlays and advances: he expressed the view that, in the case of an outlay of partnership money on an asset belonging to one partner, justice would require the improved value to be treated as a partnership asset.[90] The general principle was recently endorsed (albeit in an *obiter* part of his judgment) by Chadwick J. in *Faulks v. Faulks*.[91]

---

[87] A later editor added a footnote reference to *Pawsey v. Armstrong* (1881) 18 Ch.D. 698 at this point. But note also the decision in *Harvey v. Harvey* (1970) 120 C.L.R. 529.

[88] (1861) 3 De G.F. & J. 645.

[89] Lord Lindley stated that both partners used partnership money, which was the assumption made by Turner L.J. at (1861) 3 De G.F. & J. 657; however, in the statement of the facts at *ibid.* p. 648, it is clearly stated that one partner, Laurence, drew "upon an account which he kept with his own private bankers." The headnote is equivocal.

[90] See *infra*, para. 20–25. Note also that, in certain circumstances, a wife may be able to claim an interest in her husband's business as a result of her contributions to its success: see *Nixon v. Nixon* [1969] 1 W.L.R. 1676; also *supra*, para. 4–18.

[91] [1992] 15 E.G. 82, 95.

Purpose of outlay

18–39 The purpose of the outlay will in all cases be highly material and may go a long way towards discharging the burden of proof.[92]

Need for an inquiry

18–40 Where the court is satisfied that the outlay justifies some form of charge or allowance, an inquiry will be directed in order to ascertain the precise amount thereof.[93]

Proprietary estoppel

18–41 When Lord Lindley considered this subject, the so-called doctrine of "proprietary estoppel"[94] was in its relative infancy. That doctrine, in its developed state, might now operate in a case where a partner is induced to make an outlay of his own money on a partnership asset or to authorise an outlay of partnership money on an asset belonging to one of his co-partners. However, the current editor submits that, in the latter case, no substantive proprietary interest could be conferred on the firm as such, since the partner who owns the improved asset cannot raise an estoppel against himself.

Offices and appointments

18–42 The questions which can arise where offices and appointments are held by members of a firm have already been noted.[95]

3. ASSETS TRANSFERRED INTO OR OUT OF PARTNERSHIP

18–43 Whilst all the partners remain solvent,[96] they may at any time agree, both as between themselves and as against their creditors, either to remove assets from or to introduce assets into the common pool of partnership property. Lord Lindley wrote of such agreements:

"It is competent for partners by agreement amongst themselves to convert that which was partnership property into the separate

---

[92] See *Miles v. Clarke* [1953] 1 W.L.R. 537, where Harman J. directed an inquiry whether any, and if so what, sum should be allowed to the partnership in respect of an outlay on the leasehold property of one of the partners, having regard to the terms of the partnership and the purpose for which the outlay was made. In this respect, the headnote at [1953] 1 W.L.R. 537 is inaccurate. Note also *Harwood v. Harwood* [1991] 2 F.S.R. 274.

[93] See *Burdon v. Barkus* (1862) 4 De G.F. & J. 42, *infra*, para. 20–26; *Pawsey v. Armstrong* (1881) 18 Ch.D. 698 (buildings erected on the separate property of a partner but paid for by firm); *Miles v. Clark, supra.*

[94] See generally, *Dillwyn v. Llewellyn* (1862) 4 De G.F. & J. 517; *Inwards v. Baker* [1965] 2 Q.B. 29; *Hopgood v. Brown* [1955] 1 W.L.R. 213; *Crabb v. Arun District Council* [1976] Ch. 179; and see generally *Snell's Equity* (29th ed.) pp. 573 *et seq.*

[95] See *supra*, paras. 18–19, 18–20.

[96] But see *supra*, paras. 10–124, 10–125 and *infra*, paras. 27–102 *et seq.*

property of an individual, or vice versa.[97] And the nature of the property may be thus altered by any agreement to that effect; for neither a deed nor even a writing is absolutely necessary[98]; but so long as the agreement is dependent on an unperformed condition, so long will the ownership of the property remain unchanged."[99]

To this must, of course, be added one important qualification, to which Lord Lindley briefly referred in a footnote,[1] namely that a written disposition will normally be necessary in order to effect a transfer of an interest in land.[2] Where, however, no such interest is transferred, *e.g.* where co-owners, who are partners only as to the profits produced by their jointly owned land,[3] agree to treat the land as a partnership asset, there being no change in the quantum of their beneficial interests, writing will be unnecessary.[4]

Agreement binding on creditors

The general rule is that, in the absence of fraud, the joint creditors **18–44** of the firm and the separate creditors of each partner have no right to prevent the implementation of a bona fide agreement converting partnership property into the separate property of one or more of the partners or vice versa, even though they may be prejudiced thereby. Lord Lindley's formulation of the rule was as follows:

"... as the ordinary creditors of an individual have no lien on his property, and cannot prevent him from disposing of it as he pleases, so the ordinary creditors of a firm have no lien on the property of the firm so as to be able to prevent it from parting with that property to whomsoever it chooses. Accordingly it has frequently been held, that agreements come to between partners converting the property of the firm into the separate estate of one or more of its members, and *vice versa*, are, unless fraudulent, binding not only as between the partners themselves, but also on

---

[97] *Ex p. Ruffin* (1801) 6 Ves.Jr. 119; *Ex p. Fell* (1805) 10 Ves.Jr. 348; *Ex p. Williams* (1805) 11 Ves.Jr. 3; *Ex p. Rowlandson* (1811) 1 Rose 416.

[98] Lord Lindley referred at this point to *Pilling v. Pilling* (1887) 3 De G.J. & Sm. 162; *Ex p. Williams* (1805) 11 Ves.Jr. 3; *Ex p. Clarkson* (1834) 4 D. & Ch. 56, 67, *per* Sir G. Rose; *Ex p. Owen* (1851) 4 De G. & Sm. 351; he then observed "None of these cases, however, turned on the effect of an unwritten agreement relating to land." See now the Partnership Act 1890, s.19, *supra*, para. 10–10.

[99] *Ex p. Wheeler* (1817) Buck. 25; *Ex p. Cooper* (1840) 1 M.D. & D. 358; *Hawkins v. Hawkins* (1858) 4 Jur.(N.S.) 1044. See further, *infra*, para. 18–46.

[1] See *supra*, n. 98.

[2] Law of Property Act 1925, s.53(1)(a), (c); also the Law of Property (Miscellaneous Provisions) Act 1989, s.2. However, no writing will be necessary in the case of an implied or constructive trust: Law of Property Act 1925, s.53(2). See further, *infra*, para. 19–76. *Cf.* the position when a partnership is created: see *supra*, paras. 7–02 *et seq.*

[3] See *supra*, paras. 5–08 *et seq.*, 18–24, 18–25.

[4] The point was not even argued in *Barton v. Morris* [1985] 1 W.L.R. 1257, *infra*, para. 18–56.

their joint and on their respective several creditors; and that, in
the event of bankruptcy, the trustees must give effect to such
agreements."[5]

There are in fact two further conditions implicit in the foregoing,
which assume particular importance where insolvency orders are
made against the firm or against one or more partners[6]: these are that
the agreement must not remain executory and that, in any case where
partnership property is converted into the separate property of a
partner, it must not remain subject to the liens of the other partners.

Fraudulent agreements

18–45   It is a self evident proposition that an agreement tainted by fraud
will not be capable of altering the status or ownership of an asset.
However, Lord Lindley took care to point out that a distinction must
sometimes be drawn between a fraud practised by one partner on his
co-partners and a fraud practised by all the partners on their
creditors:

> "... an agreement which can be successfully impeached for fraud
> will not affect the property to which it may relate[7]; and it must not
> be forgotten, that in the event of bankruptcy, the trustee, as
> representing the creditors, may be able to impeach as fraudulent
> against them, agreements by which the bankrupt himself would
> have been bound.[8] In a case where both the partnership and the
> individual partners were insolvent, an agreement by one of them
> transferring his interest to the others, and thereby converting what
> was joint estate into the separate estate of the transferee, was held
> invalid; for, although no fraud may have been intended, the
> necessary effect of the arrangement was to delay and defeat the
> joint creditors.[9] The firm became bankrupt shortly after the
> assignment was made."

The current editor submits that this still represents the position under
the Insolvency Act 1986, although it should be noted that such an

---

[5] See *Re Jane* (1914) 110 L.T. 556; also *Ex p. Peake* (1816) 1 Madd. 346; *Campbell v. Mullett* (1819) 2 Swan. 551; *Ex p. Clarkson* (1834) 4 D. & Ch. 56. And see the cases cited in subsequent paragraphs.

[6] See, as to the circumstances in which such orders can be made against a firm and/or against one or more of the partners, *infra*, paras. 27–08 *et seq*.

[7] *Ex p. Rowlandson* (1813) 1 Rose 416.

[8] See *Anderson v. Maltby* (1793) 2 Ves.Jr. 244; *Ex p. Rowlandson* (1813) 1 Rose 416; *Billiter v. Young* (1856) 6 E. & B. 1, 40, *per* Jervis C.J.; *Re Kemptner* (1869) L.R. 8 Eq. 286.

[9] *Ex p. Walker* (1862) 4 De G.F. & J. 509; *Ex p. Mayou* (1865) De G.J. & S. 664; see also *Luff v. Horner* (1862) 3 Fos. & Fin. 480. *Cf. Pearce v. Bulteel* [1916] 2 Ch. 544, where there was no intention to defeat the creditors: *ibid.* p. 555.

agreement might now equally well be impeached by the liquidator of the insolvent firm.[10] Moreover, the court will, within certain limits, have power to set aside such an agreement if it is unsupported by consideration or is otherwise at an undervalue, if it is intended to prefer one set of creditors over another or otherwise represents a fraud on the insolvency laws.[11]

Executory agreements

An agreement of the type under consideration will only be effective **18–46** if it is executed, not if it still remains executory.[12] Although this may, in some cases, be difficult to determine and reference should always be made to the precise terms agreed, an agreement will, as a general rule, be treated as executory if the transfer of the relevant asset into or out of the partnership can properly be regarded as dependent on the completion of some further act.[13] Thus, in *Ex p. Wheeler*,[14] a retiring partner had agreed to assign partnership property to the continuing partner on terms that the latter would make certain payments to or for his benefit, with the continuing partner's father acting as a surety therefor. On the bankruptcy of the continuing partner, the agreement was held to be executory because his father, who was not a party to the agreement (but who was, apparently, a witness to it), had declined to stand as surety. On the other hand, in *Ex p. Clarkson*,[15] the retiring partner had, in consideration of the assignment, agreed to accept a certain sum of money, partly in cash and partly in bills; that sum was duly paid, but the bills were subsequently dishonoured. It was, nevertheless, held that the assignment was effective.[16]

Although not strictly within this class of case, reference should **18–47** perhaps be made to the special position of tenancies protected by the Landlord and Tenant Act 1954, Part II or by the Agricultural Holdings Act 1986, since agreements to contract out of the protection

---

[10] See generally, *infra*, paras. 27–102 *et seq.*

[11] See *supra*, paras. 10–124, 10–125 and *infra*, para. 27–103.

[12] But note that, in the case of an insolvency, the court may have power to set aside even an *executed* agreement: see *infra*, para. 27–103.

[13] It would seem that, if nothing remains to be done to make the agreement operative, it does not matter that it has not been entirely completed: see *Pearce v. Bulteel* [1916] 2 Ch. 544, 556, *per* Neville J.; see also *Re Jane* (1914) 110 L.T. 556; *Re Fox* (1915) 49 I.L.T. 224; *Re Owen* [1949] W.N. 201; *Re Rose* [1952] Ch. 499; *Re Wale* [1956] 1 W.L.R. 1346.

[14] (1817) Buck 25. See also *Ex p. Wood* (1879) 10 Ch.D. 554; *Ex p. Cooper* (1840) 1 M.D. & D. 358; and see the *Bank of England case* (1861) 3 De G.F. & J. 645, noticed *supra*, para. 18–37. *Cf. Ex p. Gibson* (1834) 2 Mont. & Ayr. 4; *Ex p. Sprague* (1853) 4 De G.M. & G. 866; *Hawkins v. Hawkins* (1858) 4 Jur.(N.S.) 1044.

[15] (1834) 4 D. & Ch. 56.

[16] *Cf. Ex p. Cooper* (1840) 1 M.D. & D. 358 and *Ex p. Gurney* (1842) 2 M.D. & D. 541; *Re Kemptner* (1869) L.R. 8 Eq. 286.

of either Act are in general void and unenforceable.[17] It follows that, in a case where the firm holds such a tenancy from one or more of the partners, any agreement which provides for its surrender or assignment to those partners[18] cannot affect the status of the tenancy as a partnership asset,[19] unless the surrender or assignment is actually completed.[20]

Property still subject to liens of other partners

18–48   Even if the partners have agreed that, in the event of a dissolution, the continuing or surviving partners will be entitled to all the firm's assets, such assets will still technically constitute partnership property, at least for insolvency purposes, as long as they remain subject to the liens of the outgoing partners.[21] Accordingly, such an agreement will only be effective if it is inconsistent with the continued existence of those liens[22] or they are otherwise lost or discharged.[23]

Agreements where intention clear

18–49   An express agreement is often encountered in cases where there has been a change in the firm or where one or more partners are carrying on a trade distinct from that carried on by the firm.

Change in firm

18–50   Although most partnership agreements now provide that, in the event of a partner's death, retirement or expulsion, the other partners will, as against him, become entitled to all the partnership assets,[24] similar terms are often negotiated on an *ad hoc* basis, prior to or following a dissolution.[25] Equally, partners occasionally agree to a division of the partnership assets *in specie*, with a view to carrying on a number of separate businesses, *e.g.* following an unsuccessful

---

[17] As to business tenancies, see *Joseph v. Joseph* [1967] Ch. 78; also the Landlord and Tenant Act 1954, s.38 (as amended by the Law of Property Act 1969, s.5). As to agricultural tenancies, see *Johnson v. Moreton* [1980] A.C. 37; *Featherstone v. Staples* [1986] 1 W.L.R. 861; also *Gisborne v. Burton* [1989] Q.B. 390; but *cf. Elsden v. Pick* [1980] 1 W.L.R. 898 (tenant agreeing to accept short notice to quit); *Dickson v. MacGregor*, 1992 S.L.T. (Land Ct.) 83 (landlord attempting unsuccessfully to argue that his own scheme to evade security of tenure was void and unenforceable).

[18] See *Re Hennessey's Agreement* [1975] Ch. 60.

[19] *Quaere*, would the position be the same if the landlord partners were not parties to the agreement? It is tentatively thought not, provided that the agreement is bona fide.

[20] See as to business tenancies, the Landlord and Tenant Act 1954, s.24(2) and *Joseph v. Joseph* [1967] Ch. 78. There is no equivalent provision in the Agricultural Holdings Act 1986.

[21] As to partners' liens, see the Partnership Act 1890, s.39 and *infra*, paras. 19–28 *et seq.*

[22] See *Ex p. Morley* (1873) L.R. 8 Ch.App. 1026; *Ex p. Dear* (1876) 1 Ch.D. 514; *Ex p. Butcher* (1880) 13 Ch.D. 465. *Cf. Re Simpson* (1874) L.R. Ch.App. 572.

[23] See *infra*, para. 19–40.

[24] See *supra*, paras. 10–121 *et seq.*

[25] The terms agreed will normally be incorporated in a formal retirement or dissolution deed, although this is not strictly necessary: see *Ex p. Williams* (1805) 11 Ves.Jr. 3, *infra*, para. 18–52.

merger. In each of these cases, assets which were partnership property will, on a true analysis, become the separate property of one or more of the partners, even though, as between the acquiring partners, the assets may become the property of a new firm. Conversely, where a new partnership is formed, which includes the case of a new partner admitted to an existing firm[26] and the merger of two or more existing firms, assets which were the separate property of one or more of the partners[27] may become the property of the new, enlarged or merged firm.

Lord Lindley observed: **18–51**

"All such agreements, if bona fide, and not fraudulent against creditors, are valid, and have the effect of altering the equitable ownership in the property affected by them."[28]

This proposition was clearly established in *Ex p. Ruffin*,[29] which Lord Lindley described as "the leading case on this subject." There, two partners agreed to dissolve their partnership, one retiring from the business and the other taking an assignment of the former firm's buildings, premises, stock-in-trade, debts and effects. The partner who continued the business was then bankrupted and some of the former firm's debts remained unpaid. It was argued that the partnership assets which had been assigned to the bankrupt partner should be applied towards meeting those debts, but it was held that such assets no longer constituted the joint property of the two former partners, but had been converted into the separate property of the bankrupt partner.

The position in *Ex p. Williams*[30] was similar, save that there was **18–52** neither a written agreement nor an assignment of the relevant assets. However, it was possible to show that the partner who continued the business was intended to take over all the stock and effects of the former firm and, on that basis, they were held to have become his separate property.

---

[26] As a matter of law, the admission of a new partner will technically result in the dissolution of the old firm and the creation of a new firm, whether or not such admission is contemplated by the partnership agreement: see *supra*, paras. 3–01 *et seq.*

[27] Of course, in the case of an existing firm, the assets will, as between such partners, constitute partnership property.

[28] This will certainly be so in the case of land (subject to the requirements of the Law of Property Act 1925), since the partner's respective interests will subsist behind a trust for sale; however, in the case of chattels, the agreement may well also be effective to transfer the *legal* title. See further, *infra*, paras. 18–60 *et seq.*, 19–76.

[29] (1801) 6 Ves.Jr. 119. See also *Ex p. Fell* (1805) 10 Ves.Jr. 348; *Ex p. Peake* (1816) 1 Madd. 346; *Ex p. Clarkson* (1834) 4 D. & Ch. 56; *Ex p. Gurney* (1842) 2 M.D. & D. 541; *Ex p. Sprague* (1853) 4 De G.M. & G. 866; *Ex p. Walker* (1862) 4 De G.F. & J. 509; *Re Jane* (1914) 110 L.T. 556.

[30] (1805) 11 Ves.Jr. 3. *Cf. Ex p. Cooper* (1840) 1 M.D. & D. 358.

18–53 The authority of these cases is unquestioned, as Lord Lindley explained:

> "These decisions have always been regarded as settling the law upon the subject of conversion of partnership property, and have been constantly followed. They were not, it will be observed, decided with reference to the doctrine of reputed ownership,[31] but with reference only to the real agreement come to between the partners. They apply as much to cases of a change of interest on death as on retirement."[32]

The decision in *Ex p. Owen*[33] demonstrates that the same principles are applicable in the converse situation, *i.e.* on the formation of a partnership.[34]

Distinct trades

18–54 If one or more of the partners, in the normal course of carrying on a business which is separate and distinct from that carried on by the firm, acquire assets from or dispose of assets to the firm, such transactions will be binding on their respective joint and separate creditors. Lord Lindley stated the principle thus:

> "When a firm and one of its members carry on distinct trades, property passing in the ordinary way of business from the partner to the firm ceases to be his and becomes the property of the partnership, and vice versa, just as if he were a stranger to the firm. This was settled in the great case of *Bolton v. Puller*."[35]

18–55 In *Bolton v. Puller* the entitlement to certain bills of exchange was in issue as between two insolvent banking firms, in circumstances where all the members of one firm were also members of the other. In the course of his judgment, Lord Chief Justice Eyre said:

---

[31] It should be noted that this doctrine has not been preserved under the Insolvency Act 1986 and now has no place in insolvency law. As to the position under the Bankruptcy Act 1914, see *ibid*. s.38(c) and the 15th ed. of this work at pp. 844 *et seq*.

[32] See *Re Simpson* (1874) L.R. 9 Ch.App. 572; *cf. Ex p. Morley* (1873) L.R. 8 Ch.App. 1026; *Ex p. Butcher* (1880) 13 Ch.D. 465, affirming (1879) 12 Ch.D. 917. All three cases turned on the construction of the partnership agreement and (in the second and third cases only) the wills of the deceased partners; in both of those cases the combined effect of the agreement and the will prevented a conversion.

[33] (1851) 4 De G. & Sm. 351, *supra*, para. 18–34.

[34] See also *Ex p. Barrow* (1815) 2 Rose 255. In *Belcher v. Sikes* (1828) 8 B. & C. 185, certain contracts, which constituted the separate property of one partner, were (unusually) converted into partnership property by a deed of dissolution. And see *Gian Singh & Co. v. Devraj Nahar* [1965] 1 W.L.R. 412.

[35] (1796) 1 Bos. & Pul. 539.

"There can be no doubt, that, as between themselves, a partnership may have transactions with an individual partner, or with two or more of the partners having their separate estate engaged in some joint concern in which the general partnership is not interested; and that they may by their acts convert the joint property of the general partnership into the separate property of an individual partner, or into the joint property of two or more partners or *è converso*. And their transactions in this respect will, generally speaking, bind third persons, and third persons may take advantage of them in the same manner as if the partnership were transacting business with strangers; for instance, suppose the general partnership to have sold a bale of goods to the particular partnership, a creditor of the particular partnership might take those goods in execution for the separate debt of that particular partnership. In some respects therefore an individual partner, or a particular partnership consisting of two or more of those persons, who are partners in some larger partnership, may be considered as third persons in transactions, in which the general partnership may happen to be engaged with their correspondent."[36]

Agreements where intention unclear

Difficult questions may arise where an *implied* agreement to **18–56** transfer an asset into or out of the partnership is sought to be proved merely by reference to the partners' conduct. Thus, in *Barton v. Morris*,[37] two partners had purchased a farmhouse/guest house which was conveyed to them as beneficial joint tenants. One of the partners, Miss Barton, who had contributed the greater part of the purchase price, prepared partnership accounts which showed the property as a partnership asset for tax purposes. She later died and her administratrix sought to argue that the joint tenancy had been severed when the property became a partnership asset.[38] Nicholls J. rejected that argument, holding that the mere inclusion of the property in the accounts was not in itself sufficient evidence of an agreement or course of dealing which would alter the status of the property. However, it is submitted that the circumstances were exceptional[39] and the decision should not be regarded as establishing

---

[36] *Ibid.* pp. 546, 547. Lord Chief Justice Eyre then continued: "On the other hand it will be difficult, if not impossible, for individual partners, or for particular partnerships composed of individual partners, to shake off privity in all transactions of the general partnership, or to avoid all the consequences of privity. Each partner is a party, as well as privy, to the transactions of the general partnership, though the general partnership is not party to the separate transactions of the individual partners."

[37] [1985] 1 W.L.R. 1257. Note also *Helm v. Facey* (1981) 131 N.L.J. 291.

[38] See *infra*, para. 19–14.

[39] Thus, Miss Barton appears to have been motivated to include the property in the accounts "for the sake of completeness" and by a desire to disclose everything to the Inland Revenue: see [1985] 1 W.L.R. 1260D.

a general principle that the implications of including an asset in the partnership balance sheet can, in this context, be effectively ignored.

18–57 On the other hand, the *exclusion* of an asset from the balance sheet is more equivocal: it is in practice common to find that certain assets, such as goodwill and rack rent tenancies, are omitted from the partnership balance sheet, even though no partner would seek to question their status as partnership property. The position may, however, be otherwise if an asset is deliberately excluded from the balance sheet.[39a]

Leases and covenants against assignment

18–58 If the agreement alters the status and, where relevant, quantum of the partners' beneficial interests in a leasehold property but does not affect the *legal* title thereto,[40] there may be no breach of a covenant against assignment or parting with possession contained in the lease, until such time as a formal assignment is completed;[41] *per contra*, perhaps, where there is a covenant against parting with or sharing the *occupation* of the demised premises.[42]

Milk quota

18–59 It has already been seen that milk quota cannot exist as an asset independently of the land to which it relates.[43] It follows that if, as in *Faulks v. Faulks*,[44] the agreement provides that a particular tenancy is to be held as a partnership asset but will automatically revert to a named partner in the event of a dissolution or other change in the firm, any quota enjoyed in relation to that land will cease to be a partnership asset at the same time as the tenancy. Whether any allowance will be given for the value of the "lost" quota in taking accounts between the partners will depend on the precise circumstances.[45]

[39a] Note, in this context, *Robertson v. Brent* [1972] N.Z.L.R. 406.

[40] The Law of Property Act 1925, s.52(1) requires any assignment of a lease to be made by deed, even where the lease was originally granted by parol pursuant to *ibid.* s.54(2): *Crago v. Julian* [1992] 1 W.L.R. 372. However, such a deed may not be necessary where the lease is already vested in the partners concerned *qua* trustees for the firm.

[41] See *Corporation of Bristol v. Westcott* (1879) 12 Ch.D. 461; *Harrison v. Povey* (1956) 168 E.G. 613; *Gian Singh & Co. v. Devraj Nahar* [1965] 1 W.L.R. 412; also *Pincott v. Moorstons Ltd.* (1937) 156 L.T. 139; *Gentle v. Faulkner* [1900] 2 Q.B. 267. *Cf. Varley v. Coppard* (1872) L.R. 7 C.P. 505; *Langton v. Henson* (1905) 92 L.T. 805. And see also *Corporation of Bristol v. Westcott, supra,* p. 465, *per* Jessel M.R. Each case will naturally depend on the precise terms of the covenant under consideration.

[42] This, of course, presupposes that the relevant partners have taken up exclusive occupation. Even then, could there properly be said to be an impermissible *sharing* of occupation in such a case? Much will depend on the nature of the covenant, which might well be framed in terms of occupation by the firm.

[43] See *supra*, para. 18–21.

[44] [1992] 15 E.G. 82.

[45] See *ibid.* p. 95, *per* Chadwick J.

4. LEGAL TITLE TO PARTNERSHIP PROPERTY

Land

Land held by a firm can be vested in no more than four partners;[46] **18–60** accordingly in any case in which the firm comprises five or more partners, the legal estate in partnership land will inevitably be held by some of the partners on trust for themselves and their fellow partners, according to their respective beneficial interests.[47] Where a lease is to be granted to a firm comprising more than four partners, as a matter of strict conveyancing practice only the trustee partners need be made parties thereto. It should, however, be noted that some landlords are now in fact insisting that all the partners be joined, either as contractual tenants[48] or, more usually, as sureties for the trustee partners' obligations. In this way the landlord secures direct rights of action against all the partners, albeit that complications inevitably arise when an additional partner joins the firm or when a partner retires.[49]

Enforcing trust for sale of land

Notwithstanding the fact that all land held for the benefit of a **18–61** partnership will be subject to a trust for sale,[50] it is submitted that no partner can in general insist on a sale pursuant thereto as long as the partnership continues.[51] However, it would seem that the trustee partners, if they are more than two in number,[52] may properly sell the land without the concurrence of the other partners, even if by so doing they commit a breach of trust.[53]

---

[46] Trustee Act 1925, s.34(2); Law of Property Act 1925, s.34(2).

[47] See *infra*, paras. 19–02 *et seq*.

[48] Although the Trustee Act 1925, s.34(2) and the Law of Property Act 1925, s.34(2) restrict the number of trustees to four, they do not appear to affect the *contractual* liability of the parties to the relevant disposition.

[49] Thus, new surety covenants will have to be taken from an incoming partner and (ideally) a release given to an outgoing partner. However, the landlord may insist that an outgoing partner's release is conditional on his place being taken by a new partner. Ironically, arrangements of the type considered in the text may provide incidental benefits for the firm, by ensuring that all partners are treated alike; otherwise, the partners whose names are on the lease may find themselves at a disadvantage when compared to their colleagues who have not undertaken direct liability to the landlord and who can, by the simple expedient of retiring from the firm, even free themselves from any liability to indemnify the former in respect of rent, etc. due under the lease.

[50] Law of Property Act 1925, s.34; *Re Fuller's Contract* [1933] Ch. 652.

[51] In such a case, surely the trustee partners' acceptance of the land as partnership property carries with it the general implication that, whilst the partnership is continuing, they will postpone sale under the powers conferred upon them by the Law of Property Act 1925, s.25(1) or by an equivalent express power: see *Re Buchanan-Wollaston's Conveyance* [1939] Ch. 738. See also *ibid.* s.26(3) (as substituted by the Law of Property (Amendment) Act 1926) and the Partnership Act 1890, s.24(8), *supra*, para. 15–05. *Cf. Re John's Assignment Trusts* [1970] 1 W.L.R. 955.

[52] Law of Property Act 1925, s. 27(1).

[53] See *ibid.* s.26(3) (as substituted by the Law of Property (Amendment) Act 1926) and the decision in *Sykes v. Land* (1984) 271 E.G. 1264. See also *supra*, n. 51.

Devolution of title

18–62   Devolution of the legal estate in land will in all cases be governed
by the normal law affecting real property;[54] thus, on the death of a
partner, any land vested in him and his co-partners will devolve on
the latter in their capacity as surviving trustees for sale, express or
statutory.[55] Those partners will accordingly be entitled to charge or
sell the land for the purpose of paying partnership debts or otherwise
winding up its affairs.[56] As regards the *beneficial* entitlement of the
deceased partner in respect of the land (if any),[57] the surviving
partners on whom the legal estate devolves are naturally bound to
account to his estate therefor.[58]

If an insolvency order is made against one of the partners in whom
the land is vested,[59] it is doubtful whether the trustee or liquidator
will become a joint tenant with the solvent partners, although the
better view is that he will not.[60]

Choses in action

18–63   On the death of a partner, the right to recover a debt owed to the
firm will devolve on the surviving partners,[61] although the debt must
be brought into account in determining the entitlement of the

---

[54] Partnership Act 1890, s.20(2), *supra*, para. 18–03.

[55] *Jefferys v. Small* (1683) 1 Vern. 217; *Elliot v. Brown* (1791) 3 Swan. 489n.; *Wray v. Wray* [1905] 2 Ch. 349; *Green v. Whitehead* [1930] 1 Ch. 38; *Re Fuller's Contract* [1933] Ch. 652.

[56] See the Partnership Act 1890, s.38, *supra*, paras. 13–64 *et seq.* And see (as to charges) *Re Clough* (1885) 31 Ch.D. 324, *Re Bourne* [1906] 2 Ch. 427 and (as to sales) *West of England and South Wales Bank v. Murch* (1883) 23 Ch.D. 138 (which all naturally preceded the imposition of the statutory trust for sale under the Law of Property Act 1925).

[57] See *infra*, paras. 19–02 *et seq.*

[58] Partnership Act 1890, s.20(2), *supra*, para. 18–03; see also *Jefferys v. Small* (1683) 1 Vern. 217; *Lake v. Gibson* (1729) 1 Eq.Ca.Abr. 290; *Lake v. Craddock* (1732) 3 P.W. 158; *Elliot v. Brown* (1791) 3 Swan. 489n; *Lyster v. Dolland* (1792) 1 Ves.Jr. 435; *Jackson v. Jackson* (1804) 9 Ves.Jr. 591. See also *Re Ryan* (1868) L.R.Ir. 3 Eq. 222, where the title of persons claiming under a deceased partner prevailed against a mortgagee of the surviving partner. Note that the mortgage was taken to secure a separate debt of the surviving partner and the mortgagee had notice of the equitable interest; as to part of the property there was no such notice and the mortgagee's title prevailed. The position will, of course, be otherwise if the land was not partnership property: see *Morris v. Barrett* (1829) 3 Y. & J. 384; *Reilly v. Walsh* (1848) 11 Ir.Eq. 22 (lease acquired for the purposes of a partnership which was never formed).

[59] See, as to the circumstances in which such an order may be made against a partner, *infra*, paras. 27–23 *et seq.*

[60] See *infra*, para. 27–70.

[61] This was the position at law prior to the Judicature Acts: see *Kemp v. Andrews* (1691) Carth. 170; *Martin v. Crompe* (1698) 1 Ld. Raymd. 340; *Dixon v. Hammond* (1819) 2 B. & A. 310; *Knox v. Gye* (1872) L.R. 5 H.L. 656; *McLean v. Kennard* (1874) L.R. 9 Ch.App. 336; also *Slipper v. Stidstone* (1794) 5 T.R. 493; *French v. Andrade* (1796) 6 T.R. 582. Lord Lindley observed "There is indeed an old case in which an action of *assumpsit* for a partnership debt was held to be properly brought by the executors of a deceased partner and the surviving partners jointly: *Hall v. Huffam*, alias *Hall v. Rougham* (1677) 2 Lev. 188 and 228, and 3 Keble 798; but this case is in direct opposition to those last cited, and is contrary to what was clearly settled before the Judicature Acts." As to receipts by the surviving partners, see *Brazier v. Hudson* (1836) 9 Sim. 1; *Philips v. Philips* (1828) 3 Hare 281.

deceased partner's estate.[62] The position will be the same in the case of any other chose in action belonging to the firm.

Chattels

Although it was formerly held otherwise,[63] it is clear that the **18–64** surviving partners may give a good title to chattels owned by the firm, without the co-operation of the personal representative(s) of a deceased partner.[64] Nevertheless, it is seemingly arguable that, in strict law, the legal title devolves to the surviving partners *and* such personal representative(s).[65]

Goodwill

On the death of a partner, legal (but not beneficial) title to the **18–65** firm's goodwill vests in the surviving partners.[66]

Partnership property held by trustees

Any actual or theoretical doubt as to the devolution of the legal **18–66** title to partnership property may be avoided if the partners expressly declare that all partnership assets will be held by two or more of them[67] as joint tenants upon trust for the partners as partnership property. There will clearly be survivorship as between such trustees, so that the surviving partners will always be in a position to make title to all such assets. However, such a course is rarely, if ever, adopted.

---

[62] See *infra*, paras. 19–04 *et seq*.

[63] *Buckley v. Barber* (1851) 6 Ex. 164; also *R. v. Collector of Customs* (1813) 2 M. & S. 223; *Fox v. Hanbury* (1776) Cowp. 445. Note that *Buckley v. Barber* (which Lord Lindley described as "perplexing") was disapproved by James L.J. (sitting for Wickens V.-C.) in *Taylor v. Taylor*, March 7, 1873.

[64] Partnership Act 1890, s.38, *supra*, paras. 13–64 *et seq*. See also *Chandroutie v. Gajadhar* [1987] A.C. 147.

[65] See for example, Williams, *Law of Personal Property* (18th ed., 1926), p. 521 (seemingly endorsing *Buckley v. Barber, supra*); *Crossley Vaines on Personal Property* (11th ed., 1973), p. 56; *Halsbury's Laws of England* (4th ed.), Vol. 35, para. 1146. Note, however, that the Privy Council appears to have taken a different view in *Chandroutie v. Gajadhar* [1987] A.C. 147, 153. In earlier editions of this work, it was submitted that "the principle underlying *Buckley v. Barber* (if it exists) is of great importance in relation to other matters, *e.g.* s.43 of the Partnership Act 1890." The point sought to be made is obscure: why should such a question arise in relation to a chattel, but not in relation to land? Arguably s.43 imposes a limited form of survivorship in these cases.

[66] See *supra*, para. 10–164.

[67] In the case of land, there must, of course, be no more than four trustees: Trustee Act 1925, s.34(2); Law of Property Act 1925, s.34(2).

CHAPTER 19

PARTNERSHIP SHARES

1. THE NATURE OF A PARTNERSHIP SHARE

Precise definition impossible

19–01   Although it is convenient to refer to a partner's interest in the firm as his "share," that expression is notoriously difficult to define, not least because its meaning differs according to the context in which it is used. In common parlance, a share is usually seen merely in terms of an interest in the profits of a business and of a capital or "equity" stake therein; indeed, this may well be the partners' own perception. However, in legal terms, such an approach is too simplistic, since the constituent elements which go to make up a share are not only infinitely variable but subject to alteration during the continuance of the partnership and thereafter. Thus, whilst the "share" of an outgoing partner may quite properly be viewed solely in financial terms,[1] reference to the "share" of a *continuing* partner must include the totality of the rights which he enjoys under the partnership agreement and under the general law.[2] It follows that no single meaningful definition is possible and, if the expression is used without regard to the context, confusion and potential disputes are inevitable.

Proprietary nature of a share

19–02   It has already been seen that partnership is a relationship which results from a contract.[3] Although generalisation is dangerous in this (as in any other) area, it might be said that one feature which distinguishes a partnership from an ordinary contract is that, in addition to creating contractual rights and obligations between the partners, it will usually (but by no means necessarily)[4] confer on each partner certain proprietary rights in respect of the partnership assets.[5] Certainly, it is difficult to imagine a partnership which involves no

---

[1] See for example, the Partnership Act 1890, s.43, considered *infra*, paras. 23–33, 26–04. And see *infra*, para. 19–11.

[2] As a result, a share is often conveniently referred to as a "bundle of rights": see, for example, *infra*, para. 35–19.

[3] See *supra*, para. 2–07.

[4] Note, however, that one of the primary attributes of a so-called "salaried partner" may be the absence of any interest in partnership property: see *Stekel v. Ellice* [1973] 1 W.L.R. 191 and, generally, *supra*, paras. 5–65, 10–70, 18–02.

[5] But see, in this context, *Gray v. I.R.C.* [1994] S.T.C. 360, 377 c-e. With the proliferation of contractual arrangements (other than partnership) which involve the creation of proprietary rights, this feature is in any event less distinctive than it once was.

proprietary rights whatsoever, even though the only partnership property may be of an intangible nature, *e.g.* goodwill, or of negligible value.

Although it is clear that, in the absence of some other agreement, **19–03** all the members of an ordinary partnership have identical and equal interests in its assets,[6] an analysis of the precise legal and beneficial nature of those interests may be more difficult.[7] Nevertheless, it follows from the foregoing that, without the concurrence of all the partners, no partner is entitled to claim any particular item of partnership property as his own,[8] either during the continuance of the partnership or following its dissolution.[9]

The classic definition

Lord Lindley observed: **19–04**

"What is meant by the *share* of a partner is his proportion of the partnership assets after they have been all realised and converted into money, and all the debts and liabilities have been paid and discharged.[10] This it is, and this only, which on the death of a partner passes to his representatives, or to a legatee of his share[11]; which under the old law was considered as *bona notabilia*[12]; which on his bankruptcy passes to his trustee[13] . . .".

---

[6] This results from the combined effect of the Partnership Act 1890, ss.24(1), 44(b)(4), provided that each partner has contributed (or is treated as having contributed) an identical sum of capital: see further *supra*, paras. 17–08, 17–09 and *infra*, paras. 19–19 *et seq.* As to what assets may properly be treated as belonging to the firm, see *supra*, paras. 18–01 *et seq.*

[7] See for example, *Brown v. Oakshot* (1857) 24 Beav. 254; *Re Fuller's Contract* [1933] Ch. 652; *Green v. Whitehead* [1930] 1 Ch. 38. See further *supra*, paras. 18–60 *et seq.* and, *infra*, paras. 19–04 *et seq.* Note also that a partner's beneficial share has been described as an equitable interest and not a "mere" equity: see *Canny Gabriel Castle Jackson Advertising Pty. Ltd. v. Volume Sales (Finance) Pty. Ltd.* (1974) 131 C.L.R. 321.

[8] *Lingen v. Simpson* (1824) 1 Sim. & St. 600; *Cockle v. Whiting* (1829) Tam. 55. See also the cases cited in the next two notes and *infra*, para. 19–08, n. 24.

[9] *Gopala Chetty v. Vijayaraghavachariar* [1922] 1 A.C. 488. *Cf.* the terms of the agreement in *Faulks v. Faulks* [1992] E.G. 82, noticed *supra*, para. 18–21.

[10] See *Rodriguez v. Speyer Bros.* [1919] A.C. 59, 68, *per* Finlay L.C.; *Re Ritson* [1899] 1 Ch. 128; *Burdett-Coutts v. I.R.C.* [1960] 1 W.L.R. 1027; *Livingstone v. Commissioner of Stamp Duties* [1961] A.L.R. 534; *Dimov v. Dimov* [1971] W.A.R. 113; *Re Ward* [1985] 2 N.Z.L.R. 352. Lord Lindley in fact referred to the following pre-1890 cases: *Croft v. Pyke* (1733) 3 P.W. 180; *West v. Skip* (1749) 1 Ves.Sen. 239; *Doddington v. Hallet* (1750) 1 Ves.Sen. 497; *Taylor v. Fields* (1799) 4 Ves.Jr. 396; *Crawshay v. Collins* (1808) 15 Ves.Jr. 218; *Featherstonhaugh v. Fenwick* (1810) 17 Ves.Jr. 298; *Darby v. Darby* (1856) 3 Drew. 495; see also *Richardson v. Bank of England* (1838) 4 Myl. & Cr. 165. Note the decisions in *Re Rhagg* [1938] Ch. 828; *Re Betts* [1949] W.N. 91; *Re White* [1958] Ch. 762. And see *supra*, paras. 10–128 *et seq.*

[11] *Re Ritson* [1899] 1 Ch. 128. And see *Farquar v. Hadden* (1871) L.R. 7 Ch.App. 1, noticed *infra*, paras. 19–05, n. 18, 26–65; *Re Holland* [1907] 2 Ch. 88; see also *Re Rhagg, Re Betts* and *Re White*, *supra*. The situs of a share for tax and other purposes will in general be determined by reference to the firm's principal place of business: *Re Ewing* (1881) 6 P.D. 19; *Laidlay v. Lord Advocate* (1890) 15 App.Cas. 468; *Beaver v. Master in Equity of Supreme Court of Victoria* [1895] A.C. 251; *Commissioners of Stamp Duties v. Salting* [1907] A.C. 449. See also *infra*, paras. 36–63 *et seq.*

[12] *Ekins v. Brown* (1854) 1 Spinks, Ecc. & Adm.Rep. 400; *Att.-Gen. v. Higgins* (1857) 2 H. & N. 339.

[13] See *infra*, para. 27–71; also *Smith v. Stokes* (1801) 1 East 363.

19–05   Although it would be more accurate to speak of a partner's
entitlement to a proportion of the *net proceeds of sale* of the assets,
the correctness of the statement of principle embodied in the above
passage cannot seriously be questioned, reflecting as it does the
proper application of sections 39 and 44 of the Partnership Act
1890.[14] Accordingly, a partner's entitlement will reflect not only his
capital and current account balances[15] and the size of his capital
profit (or asset surplus) share,[16] but also any amounts which he may
owe to the firm, *e.g.* in respect of overdrawings.[17] It is submitted that
any attempt to demonstrate that a particular element of a partner's
share, *e.g.* his entitlement to capital, has an existence independent of
the remainder must, in the absence of an express agreement, fail.[18]
Moreover, to speak of a share in financial terms *otherwise* than by
reference to a partner's net entitlement (whether calculated in the
above way or in some other manner prescribed by the partnership
agreement) is both misleading and legally incorrect.

19–06   Nevertheless, it is considered that Lord Lindley's definition is, as
such, incomplete and that a full understanding of the nature of a
share (viewed solely in terms of the financial and proprietary
entitlement which it confers upon its owner) is only possible if that
entitlement is analysed at three stages in the life of a firm, namely (1)
whilst the partnership is continuing; (2) on a general dissolution and
(3) on the death, retirement or expulsion of a partner.

The nature of a share—an analysis

(1) *Continuing partnership*

19–07   Whilst the partnership continues, each partner interested in the
capital and assets of the firm[19] will unquestionably be entitled to a
beneficial interest in respect of those assets and *may* also hold the
legal title thereto, either alone or in conjunction with one or more of

---

[14] See *infra*, paras. 19–29 *et seq.*, 25–40 *et seq.*

[15] See generally, as to the need to distinguish between such balances, *supra*, para. 17–07 and
infra, paras. 22–02, 22–03.

[16] See *supra*, paras. 10–65, 17–05 and *infra*, para. 19–20.

[17] *Richardson v. Bank of England* (1838) 4 Myl. & Cr. 165; *Rodriguez v. Speyer Bros.* [1919]
A.C. 59, 68; *Dewan v. Hiranandani* (unreported), February 23, 1989. See also *Aulton v. Atkins*
(1856) 18 C.B. 249; *Meyer & Co. v. Faber (No. 2)* [1923] 2 Ch. 421; *Brown v. Rivlin*, unreported,
February 1, 1983 (C.A.T. No. 56), [1984] C.L.Y., p. 138; also *Re Ward* [1985] 2 N.Z.L.R. 352.

[18] Such an attempt was made (unsuccessfully) in *Dewan v. Hiranandani*, *supra*, albeit that the
decision ultimately turned on the construction of a deed of retirement. See also *Green v. Hertzog*
[1954] 1 W.L.R. 1309. Note that a bequest by a testator of his share in particular partnership assets
may be valid as between the beneficiaries under his will, so that, if the partnership is solvent, the
legatee will take free from liability to contribute to the partnership debts: *Re Holland* [1907] 2 Ch.
88. *Per contra*, if the partnership is insolvent: *Farquhar v. Hadden* (1871) L.R. 7 Ch.App. 1. See
also, as to the latter cases, *infra*, para. 26–61.

[19] There may, of course, be partners who do not enjoy such an interest: see *supra*, para. 18–02.

the other partners. If the legal title is vested in *all* the partners, it might be described as an incident of each partner's share, even if not part of the share itself;[20] if, on the other hand, title is vested in only some of the partners,[21] they will hold the relevant assets as trustees for the firm and the title therefore cannot properly be regarded even as an incident of their shares.

So far as concerns each partner's *beneficial* interest in the **19–08** partnership assets, its precise nature will to an extent depend on the contents of the agreement, which may, for example, direct that, as between the partners, no account is to be taken of goodwill, thus purportedly negativing their interests therein,[22] or declare that an outgoing partner is only to be entitled to the return of his capital. Nevertheless, it is submitted that, irrespective of the terms of the agreement, each partner's share will display two characteristics which may be regarded as constants. First, each partner's beneficial interest, expressed in terms of its realisability, is in the nature of a *future* interest taking effect in possession on (and not before) the determination of the partnership, whether brought about by his departure or by a general dissolution. This limitation on his entitlement may be explained by reference to the fact that, as long as the partnership continues,[23] each partner is entitled to require the partnership assets to be applied for partnership purposes and no partner is entitled to use or enjoy his share of those assets to the exclusion of his co-partners.[24] Secondly, when the partnership is determined and the partner's beneficial interest in the partnership assets notionally falls into possession, it will take effect subject to the right of the other partners to have those assets applied towards payment of the firm's debts and liabilities and any surplus divided between the partners in the manner prescribed by the Partnership Act 1890.[25] This will normally entail a sale of such property.[26] Thus, in the absence of any agreement to the contrary,[27] the share of a

---

[20] See for example, *Re Bourne* [1906] 2 Ch. 427, 432, 433, *per* Romer L.J.

[21] *e.g.* where land is vested in four of the partners pursuant to the Trustee Act 1925, s.34(2) or the Law of Property Act 1925, s.34(2).

[22] This does not, of course, mean that the goodwill ceases to be an asset of the firm, merely that, in the events contemplated by the agreement, its value is to be ignored. The position will, however, be different on a general dissolution: see further, *supra*, para. 10–139 and *infra*, para. 25–39.

[23] For this purpose a partnership must be regarded as continuing notwithstanding the death, retirement or expulsion of a partner, unless that event causes a general dissolution: see further, *supra*, para. 10–33.

[24] See *Lingen v. Simpson* (1824) 1 Sim. & St. 600; *Cockle v. Whiting* (1829) Tam. 55; *Marshall v. Maclure* (1885) 10 App.Cas. 325; *Gray v. I.R.C.* [1994] S.T.C. 360, 377 also *Re Bainbridge* (1878) 8 Ch.D. 218 (where a mortgage of a partnership share in chattels was held not to be subject to the Bills of Sale Acts).

[25] See *ibid.* ss.39, 44, *infra*, paras. 19–29 *et seq.*, 25–40 *et seq.*

[26] See *infra*, paras. 23–179 *et seq.*

[27] It is, of course, possible for the partnership agreement to provide that, subject to payment of the firm's debts and liabilities, its assets will be distributed between the partners *in specie*: see *supra*, paras. 10–222, 10–223.

partner will represent (and should always be stated in terms of) his proportionate share in the net proceeds of sale of the partnership assets, after all the firm's debts and liabilities have been paid or provided for.[28]

The foregoing analysis appears to have been accepted by the Privy Council in *Hadlee v. Commissioner of Inland Revenue*.[29]

(2) *General dissolution*

19–09   In the event of a general dissolution,[30] each partner will again be entitled to insist on the partnership assets being applied towards payment of the firm's debts and liabilities and a division of any surplus proceeds.[31] Until such time as those assets are either sold or divided *in specie*,[32] it is submitted that each partner's share will have the same proprietary character as it had prior to the dissolution.[33] Nevertheless, in terms of value, the share must still be expressed as a net entitlement since, in the absence of some specific agreement between the partners, it cannot properly be viewed in any other light.[34]

(3) *Death, retirement or expulsion of a partner*

19–10   If any of the above events cause a general dissolution, the position will be as described in the preceding paragraph.[35] Where, however, it is expressly or impliedly agreed that the partnership will continue notwithstanding the change in the firm,[36] the precise nature and value of the deceased or outgoing partner's share will depend on the terms of the partnership agreement.

---

[28] See *supra*, paras. 19–04, 19–05.

[29] [1993] A.C. 524, 532G. In this case, a partner in a firm of accountants sought (unsuccessfully) to argue that, by assigning part of his share to trustees for his wife and child, he had divested himself of liability for income tax under the relevant New Zealand legislation in respect of the income profits attributable to that part. See also *infra*, para. 19–67.

[30] Such a dissolution may be brought about in any of the ways discussed *infra*, paras. 24–04 *et seq.*

[31] Partnership Act 1890, ss.39, 44, *infra*, paras. 19–29 *et seq.*, 25–40 *et seq.* And see *Re Ward* [1985] 2 N.Z.L.R. 352.

[32] Such a division must be made with the agreement of the partners or, conceivably, by an order of the court or an arbitrator.

[33] See *supra*, para. 19–08. Note also, in this context, the partners' continuing obligations *inter se* pursuant to the Partnership Act 1890, s.38: see *supra*, paras. 13–64 *et seq.*

[34] This is quite apart from the provisions of *ibid.* s.43, which is strictly inapplicable in the case of a general dissolution: see *infra*, paras. 23–33, 26–04. Note that the potential application of that section was not considered by the court in *Barclays Bank Trust Co. Ltd. v. Bluff* [1982] Ch. 172, *infra*, para. 25–27.

[35] In the case of a partnership at will, the death or bankruptcy of a partner will cause such a dissolution: Partnership Act 1890, s.33(1). See further, *infra*, paras. 24–20 *et seq.*

[36] See *supra*, para. 10–33 and *infra*, para. 23–180.

If, as will usually be the case, the agreement establishes the **19–11** manner in which the deceased or outgoing partner's financial entitlement in respect of his share is to be ascertained and paid[37] and provides for the devolution of the legal title to any partnership assets which may be vested in him,[38] his share may properly be regarded as a pure debt with effect from the date on which he ceased to be a partner.[39] It is only where such terms are omitted that difficulties may arise.

In the absence of any *express* provision in the agreement, the **19–12** entitlement of the deceased or outgoing partner in respect of his share will, in the normal way, strictly be represented by his proportionate share in the net proceeds remaining after all the partnership assets have been sold and the partnership debts and liabilities paid and discharged.[40] However, where there is an implied recognition on the part of the outgoing partner that the other partners will continue the business, those other partners will be treated as entitled to acquire his share at a valuation and the court will direct the necessary accounts and inquiries for that purpose.[41] If, on the other hand, there is no such implied recognition but the other partners wish to carry on the business and are prepared to pay the outgoing partner the market value of his share, the court may, in its discretion, refuse to order a sale of the partnership assets and order an inquiry as to the market value of the share and the payment of that value by the continuing partners.[42] However, the latter discretion is exercised sparingly and, as a general rule, only when the outgoing partner's share is of modest size or when, as in the case of a professional firm, a sale of all its assets, including goodwill, is regarded as impracticable.[43]

In any case in which a share falls to be valued in the above way, it **19–13** will be important to determine the date on which such value is to be taken. Where there is an implied agreement for the acquisition of the deceased or outgoing partner's share, the relevant date will be the

---

[37] See *supra*, para. 10–121.

[38] See *supra*, paras. 10–203 *et seq.*

[39] In such a case, it is submitted that the Partnership Act 1890, s.43 will apply: see *infra*, paras. 23–33, 26–04. Note, however, that the agreement could in theory provide that the share will be retained by the outgoing partner *in specie* until its value has been ascertained. In such a case, the operation of s. 43 will be deferred.

[40] See *supra*, para. 19–04.

[41] See *Sobell v. Boston* [1975] 1 W.L.R. 1587. Although the report is wholly inadequate, it would seem that *Small v. Cohen, The Times*, September 7, 1992, was also a case of this class.

[42] *Syers v. Syers* (1876) 1 App.Cas. 174. And see *Rivett v. Rivett* (1966) 200 E.G. 858. See also *infra*, para. 23–182.

[43] In the current editor's experience, compelling evidence of such impracticability would have to be adduced before the Court could be persuaded to deprive the "outgoing" partner of his right to test the value of the assets by means of a sale in the open market. Even then, acceptance of the argument could not be assured.

date on which he ceased to be a partner;[44] where, however, a valuation is directed by the court in the exercise of its discretion, the relevant date will be the date on which the share is actually valued.[45] Although it might, in the former case, be thought that the outgoing partner can only be "compensated" for any delay in the payment of his financial entitlement by a claim under section 42 of the Partnership Act 1890 to interest at 5 per cent. or, at his (or his estate's) option, the share of profits attributable to the use of his share,[46] the current editor considers that a claim to interest at more realistic rates could properly be formulated under the Supreme Court Act 1981.[47] What such a partner cannot on any footing claim is a share of any *capital* profits attributable to increases in the value of the partnership assets since the date on which he ceased to be a partner.[48] On the other hand, in the latter case, the outgoing partner will in effect be entitled to share in any capital profits accruing prior to the date of valuation but otherwise must necessarily be limited to his rights under section 42 of the 1890 Act.[49]

The doctrine of non-survivorship between partners

19–14   It has long been recognised that partnership is not a species of joint tenancy and that, in the absence of some contrary agreement,[50] there is no survivorship as between partners, at least so far as concerns their *beneficial* interests in the partnership assets. Lord Lindley put it thus:

> "It is an old and well-established maxim, that *Jus accrescendi inter mercatores locum non habet*.[51] This is a common law, and not only an equitable maxim; but whilst its application in equity was subject to few, if any, exceptions,[52] it was not at law so universally

---

[44] Partnership Act 1890, s.43; *Sobell v. Boston* [1975] 1 W.L.R. 1587.

[45] See *Syers v. Syers* (1876) 1 App.Cas. 174.

[46] See further, as to the nature of the entitlement under the section, *infra*, paras. 25–23 *et seq*.

[47] Supreme Court Act 1981, s.35A; similarly in the county court: County Courts Act 1984, s.69. See further *infra*, para. 20–39. So far as the current editor is aware, there is no reported case in which payment of interest has been awarded under the 1981 Act in such circumstances. Moreover, it must be recognised that the claim in *Sobell v. Boston, supra*, was, in the orthodox manner, formulated under s.42 of the 1890 Act.

[48] Consistently with the earlier decisions (and with the provisions of the Partnership Act 1890, s.43), it is considered that the decision in *Barclays Bank Trust Co. Ltd. v. Bluff* [1982] Ch. 172 is confined to cases where there is a *general* dissolution.

[49] It could, of course, be argued that the Partnership Act 1890, s.43 in any event applies in such a case so as to ground a claim under the 1981 Act, but this would be difficult to sustain: see *infra*, para. 23–33.

[50] *e.g.* for the automatic accruer of an outgoing partner's share without payment: see *infra*, paras. 35–19, 36–29. But see also *supra*, para. 10–125.

[51] Co. Lit. 182a.

[52] In *Nelson v. Bealby* (1862) 4 De G.F. & J. 321, a partnership agreement between A and B provided that, on A's death, his executors should receive one-half of the assets from B, but did not specify what was to happen on B's death. It was, nevertheless, held that B's executors were entitled to one-half of the assets from A.

applicable as the generality of its terms might lead one to suppose."

He then concluded:

"Before quitting the present subject, it may be observed that the doctrine of non-survivorship amongst partners is not confined to merchants nor even to traders, but extends to partners generally."[53]

The devolution of the *legal* title to land and other assets owned by a firm was considered in the previous chapter.[54]

Conversion of shares in partnership land

Writing prior to the Partnership Act 1890, Lord Lindley said: **19–15**

"From the principle that a share of a partner is nothing more than his proportion of the partnership assets after they have been turned into money and applied in liquidation of the partnership debts, it necessarily follows that, in equity, a share in a partnership, whether its property consists of land or not, must, as between the real and personal representatives of a deceased partner, be deemed to be his personal and not real estate, unless indeed such conversion is inconsistent with the agreement between the parties."[55]

Although there were conflicting authorities on this point, those **19–16** favouring Lord Lindley's view were preponderant.[56] Any remaining doubt there may have been was entirely removed by section 22 of the Partnership Act 1890, which provides:

---

[53] See *Buckley v. Barber* (1851) 6 Ex. 164; also *Aunand v. Honiwood* (1682) 2 Ch.Ca. 129; *Jefferys v. Small* (1683) 1 Vern. 217; *Lake v. Gibson* (1729) 1 Eq.Ca.Abr. 290; *Lake v. Craddock* (1732) 3 P.W. 158. *Cf. Barton v. Morris* [1985] 1 W.L.R. 1257, 1262, *per* Nicholls J.

[54] See *supra*, paras. 18–60 *et seq.*

[55] See *Steward v. Blakeway* (1869) L.R. 4 Ch.App. 603; *Re Wilson* [1893] 2 Ch. 340; also *Re Kent County Gas, Light and Coke Co. Ltd.* [1909] 2 Ch. 195.

[56] In favour of Lord Lindley's view were *Ripley v. Waterworth* (1802) 7 Ves.Jr. 425; *Townshend v. Devaynes* (1808) 1 Mont.Part., note 2, Appx., p. 96; and see also 11 Sim. 498n.; *Phillips v. Phillips* (1832) 1 M. & K. 649, noticed *supra*, para. 18–10; *Broom v. Broom* (1834) 3 M. & K. 443; *Morris v. Kearsley* (1836) 2 Y. & C.Ex. 139; *Houghton v. Houghton* (1841) 11 Sim. 491; *Essex v. Essex* (1855) 20 Beav. 442; *Darby v. Darby* (1856) 3 Drew. 495; *Holroyd v. Holroyd* (1859) 7 W.R. 426; *Waterer v. Waterer* (1873) 15 Eq. 402, noticed *supra*, para. 18–28; *Murtagh v. Costello* (1881) 7 L.R.Ir. 428. Opposing authorities were *Thornton v. Dixon* (1791) 3 Bro.C.C. 199; *Bell v. Phyn* (1802) 7 Ves.Jr. 453; *Randall v. Randall* (1835) 7 Sim. 271; *Cookson v. Cookson* (1837) 8 Sim. 529.

"22. Where land or any heritable interest therein has become partnership property, it shall, unless the contrary intention appears, be treated as between the partners (including the representatives of a deceased partner), and also as between the heirs of a deceased partner and his executors or administrators, as personal or moveable and not real or heritable estate."

19–17 The above provision was later supplemented by sections 34 and 36 of the Law of Property Act 1925, which in all cases ensure that, in the absence of an express trust for sale, partnership land vested in one or more partners is held on the statutory trusts for sale, so that all beneficial interests therein are converted into personal property.[57] Unlike section 22 of the 1890 Act,[58] the former sections are mandatory and cannot be excluded by agreement.

However, notwithstanding the imposition of the statutory trusts for sale and the provisions of section 22 of the Partnership Act 1890, the court may in exceptional circumstances be prepared to treat a partner's share in land as identified with the land itself.[59]

2. THE SIZE OF EACH PARTNER'S SHARE

19–18 The size of each partner's share, expressed in terms of his interest in the partnership assets, is primarily dependent on the terms agreed by the partners.[60] It is only in the absence of such terms that it is necessary to resort to the provisions of section 24(1) of the Partnership Act 1890.

The normal rule: equality

19–19 Lord Lindley, writing before the Partnership Act 1890, said:

"In the event of a dispute between the partners as to the amount of their shares, such dispute, if it does not turn on the construction of written documents, must be decided like any other pure question of fact[61]; and if there is no evidence from which any

---

[57] Such trusts will usually be imposed by *ibid.* s.34: see *Re Fuller's Contract* [1933] Ch. 652.

[58] See the following pre-1890 Act cases: *Steward v. Blakeway* (1869) L.R. 4 Ch.App. 603; *Re Wilson* [1893] 2 Ch. 340. *Cf. Davis v. Davis* [1894] 1 Ch. 393, noticed *supra*, para. 18–12.

[59] See for example, the decision in *Burdett-Coutts v. I.R.C.* [1960] 1 W.L.R. 1027 (estate duty); *Gray v. I.R.C.* [1994] S.T.C. 360, 377 (inheritance tax); also *Cooper v. Critchley* [1955] Ch. 431 and the authorities cited therein.

[60] See *supra*, paras. 10–65 *et seq.*

[61] *Binford v. Dommett* (1799) 4 Ves.Jr. 756; *Peacock v. Peacock* (1809) 16 Ves.Jr. 49; *McGregor v. Bainbrigge* (1848) 7 Hare 164.

satisfactory conclusion as to what was agreed can be drawn,[62] the shares of all the partners will be adjudged equal."[63]

This still remains true, as is made clear by section 24 of the Partnership Act 1890, which provides that:

"24. The interests of partners in partnership property and their rights and duties in relation to the partnership shall be determined, subject to any agreement express or implied between the partners by the following rules:
(1) All the partners are entitled to share equally in the capital and profits of the business, and must contribute equally towards the losses whether of capital or otherwise sustained by the firm."

The potential application of the above section to the fixed capital **19–20** of a firm has already been noticed.[64] Whatever view is taken as to the effect of the section in that context, it is beyond argument that the rule of equality will, in the absence of any other agreement, always be applied when determining the partners' shares in capital profits or asset surpluses, *i.e.* the amount by which the market value of the partnership assets exceeds their acquisition or book value.[65]

Even where it is clear that capital has been contributed *and is* **19–21** *thereafter to be owned* in unequal proportions, the rule of equality will still apply in the case of a loss of that capital, as Lord Lindley explained:

"When it is said that the shares of partners are prima facie equal, although their capitals are unequal, what is meant is that losses of capital like other losses must be shared equally; but it is not meant that, on a final settlement of accounts, capitals contributed unequally are to be treated as one aggregate fund which ought to be divided between the partners in equal shares."

As previously observed,[66] the proposition contained in the latter part of the above passage must be approached with a degree of caution.

---

[62] *Copland v. Toulmin* (1840) 7 Cl. & F. 349; *Stewart v. Forbes* (1849) 1 Mac. & G. 137; *Webster v. Bray* (1849) 7 Hare 159.

[63] *Robinson v. Anderson* (1855) 20 Beav. 98 and, on appeal, (1855) 7 De G.M. & G. 239 (noticed *infra*, para. 19–26); also *Peacock v. Peacock* (1809) 16 Ves.Jr. 49; *Farrar v. Beswick* (1836) 1 Moo. & Rob. 527; *Webster v. Bray* (1849) 7 Hare 159.

[64] See *supra*, paras. 17–08, 17–09. As to losses, see *infra*, paras. 19–21, 20–05 *et seq.*

[65] See *supra*, para. 17–05. This may be of critical importance for the purposes of any charge to capital gains or inheritance tax: see *infra*, paras. 35–05, 36–24 *et seq.*, 36–47.

[66] See *supra*, para. 17–09.

Justification for the rule

19–22   Lord Lindley explained the basis for the pre-1890 Act rule of equality in the following terms:

> "This rule no doubt occasionally leads to apparent injustice; but it is not easy to lay down any other rule which, under the circumstances supposed, could be fairly applied. It is sometimes suggested that the shares of partners ought to be proportionate to their contributions; but without in any way denying this, it may be asked, how is the value of each partner's contribution to be measured? Certainly not merely by the capital he may have brought into the firm. His skill, his connection, his command of the confidence and respect of others, must all be taken into account; and if it is impossible to set a money value on each partner's contribution in this respect, it is impossible to determine in the manner suggested the shares of the partners in the partnership. Nor is it unreasonable to infer, in the absence of all evidence to the contrary, that the partners themselves have agreed to consider their contributions as of equal value, although they may have brought in unequal sums of money, or be themselves unequal as regards skill, connection, or character. Whether, therefore, partners have contributed money equally or unequally, whether they are or are not on a par as regards skill, connection, or character, whether they have or have not laboured equally for the benefit of the firm, their shares will be considered as equal, unless some agreement to the contrary can be shown to have been entered into."[67]

Evidence of an agreement displacing the rule

19–23   An agreement displacing the normal rule of equality may be inferred from a course of conduct or from the contents of the partnership books.[68] Thus, if the proceeds of the sale of a particular partnership asset have been shared between the partners in proportion to their capital contributions, this will represent strong evidence in favour of an inference that all capital profits are to be shared in those proportions. This may be so, even though the partners have shared income profits equally or in some other way.[69]

---

[67] See the cases cited in the footnotes to para. 19–19, *supra*. Lord Lindley pointed out that the decisions in *Peacock v. Peacock* (1809) 2 Camp. 45 and *Sharpe v. Cummings* (1844) 2 Dow. & L. 504 cannot be supported.

[68] As in *Stewart v. Forbes* (1849) 1 Mac. & G. 137.

[69] But see *infra*, para. 19–25.

Once unequal sharing ratios have been adopted, the partners will **19–24** not be presumed to have abandoned those ratios merely because one or more of their number have retired from the firm. As Lord Lindley said "in the absence of evidence to the contrary, the inference is that the shares of the retiring members have been taken by the continuing parties in the proportions in which these last were originally interested in the concern."[70] Where, however, a new partner has been admitted to the firm, such an inference will be more difficult to draw.

Relation between income and capital profit shares

If the partners agree to share income profits in unequal shares, the **19–25** inference must be, in the absence of evidence indicating a contrary intent, that they will share capital profits, and thus be interested in the partnership assets, in the same proportions. Any other approach would result in absurdity, *i.e.* an application of the presumption of equality under section 24(1) whilst the partnership continues, but its rejection in the event of a dissolution, when the agreed (unequal) profit sharing ratios are applied by virtue of section 44 of the Partnership Act 1890.[71]

Application of the rule to single adventure

The fact that the partnership has been formed in order to carry out **19–26** a single business transaction or venture in itself provides no justification for departing from the normal rule of equality. This is illustrated by the decision in *Robinson v. Anderson*,[72] where two solicitors, who were not in partnership together, were jointly retained to defend certain actions. In the absence of any satisfactory evidence as to the proportions in which they were to divide their remuneration, the rule of equality was applied, even though the amount of work they had done was not equal and they had received separate payments therefor. Sir John Romilly M.R.,[73] after stressing the importance of the burden of proof in such cases, said:

"Now I should entertain no doubt, even if I had not been confirmed by the two cases of *Webster v. Bray*[74] and *McGregor v.*

---

[70] *Robley v. Brooke* (1833) 7 Bli.(N.S.) 90; and see *Copland v. Toulmin* (1840) 7 Cl. & F. 349. A similar observation was made in Lord Lindley's commentary on s.24(1) in his Supplement on the Partnership Act 1890.

[71] *Ibid.* paragraph 4: see *infra*, paras. 25–40 *et seq.* This argument would also ignore the true nature of a partner's interest in the partnership assets, as discussed *supra*, paras. 19–02 *et seq.*

[72] (1855) 20 Beav. 98 and, on appeal, (1855) 7 De G.M. & G. 239. See also *Hanslip v. Kitton* (1862) 8 Jur.(N.S.) 835.

[73] See (1853) 20 Beav. 102.

[74] (1848) 7 Hare 159.

Bainbrigge,[75] that where two solicitors undertake a matter of business on behalf of a client, the same rule would follow in that, as in any other undertaking where two persons carry on a business jointly on behalf of themselves, or as agents of other persons. It is, in point of fact, a limited partnership[76] for a particular sort of business. Assuming nothing to have been said as to the manner in which the profits were to be divided, it appears to me to follow as a necessary consequence of law that they are to be divided equally between them. ... It was the duty of the party who intended that this should not be a partnership transaction, and that he should be paid for the amount of business which he did, without participating in that of the other, so to express himself."

Position where a firm enters into partnership

19–27   Where a firm (AB) comprising two partners (A and B) enters into partnership with a third party (C), the question arises whether, in applying the rule of equality, the partnership should be treated as having two partners (*i.e.* the firm AB and the third party C) or three (*i.e.* A, B and C). The answer must depend on the capacity in which A and B entered into the partnership venture: if they purported to do so as a firm, *e.g.* in the name AB, they will prima facie be treated as a single partner and the size of their joint share determined accordingly; if they contracted as individuals, they will each be treated as partners and their joint entitlement correspondingly increased.[77] Such difficulties will obviously be avoided if the profit shares are clearly specified in the agreement.[78]

3. THE PARTNER'S LIEN AND ITS CONSEQUENCES

19–28   Reference has already been made to the right of a partner to insist on the partnership property being applied in payment of the partnership debts and any surplus divided between the partners according to their respective entitlements.[79] It is this right which is conventionally styled "the partner's lien," even though that expression will not be found in

---

[75] (1848) 7 Hare 164, note.

[76] This expression referred to the restricted nature of the venture; at the time of the judgment, the concept of limited partnership (as it is now formulated under the Limited Partnerships Act 1907) had been under consideration but had not been introduced into English law: see *infra*, paras. 28–03 *et seq.*

[77] See *Warner v. Smith* (1863) 1 De G.J. & S. 337, where, in the circumstances supposed, the profits were held to be divisible into two and not three parts.

[78] As in *Mann v. D'Arcy* [1968] 1 W.L.R. 893, where the agreement was for an equal division of profits between the firm and the individual.

[79] See *supra*, paras. 19–08 *et seq.*

the Partnership Act 1890 itself. Prior to that Act, Lord Lindley defined the lien thus:

"In order to discharge himself from the liabilities to which a person may be subject as partner, every partner has a right to have the property of the partnership applied in payment of the debts and liabilities of the firm. And in order to secure a proper division of the surplus assets, he has a right to have whatever may be due to the firm from his co-partners, as members thereof, deducted from what would otherwise be payable to them in respect of their shares in the partnership. In other words, each partner may be said to have an equitable lien on the partnership property for the purpose of having it applied in discharge of the debts of the firm; and to have a similar lien on the surplus assets for the purpose of having them applied in payment of what may be due to the partners respectively, after deducting what may be due from them, as partners, to the firm."[80]

Partnership Act 1890, section 39

Lord Lindley was at pains to point out that, irrespective of the title **19–29** which it may be given, the foregoing right normally has little practical application prior to the dissolution of a partnership, when its affairs fall to be wound up or the share of a partner ascertained. This is now expressly recognised by section 39 of the Partnership Act 1890, which provides as follows:

"39. On the dissolution of partnership every partner is entitled, as against the other partners in the firm, and all persons claiming through them in respect of their interests as partners, to have the property of the partnership applied in payment of the debts and liabilities of the firm, and to have the surplus assets after such payment applied in payment of what may be due to the partners respectively after deducting what may be due from them as partners to the firm; and for that purpose any partner or his representatives may on the termination of the partnership apply to the court to wind up the business and affairs of the firm."

---

[80] *Skipp v. Harwood* (1747) 2 Swan. 586; *West v. Skip* (1749) 1 Ves.Sen. 239; *Doddington v. Hallet* (1750) 1 Ves.Sen. 497, 498–499, *per* Hardwicke L.C.; *Ex p. Ruffin* (1801) 6 Ves.Jr. 119; *Ex p. Williams* (1805) 11 Ves.Jr. 3; *Holderness v. Shackels* (1828) 8 B. & C. 612. Lord Lindley pointed out that "*Smith v. De Silva* (1776) Cowp. 469 can hardly be reconciled with the other cases, but see upon it the observations of Lord Tenterden in *Holderness v. Shackels* (1828) 8 B. & C. 618." See also *Re Ward* [1985] 2 N.Z.L.R. 352, 354. As to the right of a minority of partners to insist on the payment of a partnership debt out of the partnership assets, see the observations of Turner V.-C. in *Stevens v. The South Devon Ry.* (1851) 9 Hare 313, 326. A member of a firm is normally entitled to pay any of its debts and to charge that sum to the firm; see *infra*, paras. 20–04 *et seq.*

19–30   It is submitted that the above section does no more than give statutory recognition to the partner's lien on dissolution and does not purport to exclude its operation at other times. Thus, the possibility of its enforcement could conceivably arise during the continuance of the partnership, *e.g.* if a partner in whom is vested the legal title to a partnership asset were to dispose of it to a third party who had notice of its status. In such a case, the existence of the lien could well be material in the event of the third party's insolvency.[81]

Property subject to the lien

19–31   Whilst the partnership continues, the lien attaches to *every* item of partnership property, including stock-in-trade. Of the latter, Lord Lindley pointed out that the lien "is not ... lost by the substitution of new stock in trade for old," thus recognising that, to this extent at least, the lien has a "floating" character, *i.e.* it attaches to the stock for the time being.[82] This aspect of the lien will be considered in greater detail hereafter.[83]

The corollary of the foregoing is, naturally, that the lien does not attach to anything other than partnership property. Thus, if there is in truth no such property because the partnership is confined to the profits produced by property belonging to one or more of the partners, there will be nothing to which the lien can attach.[84]

Position on dissolution

19–32   On a dissolution, the lien will only be exercisable in respect of the partnership property at that time and will not extend to assets acquired subsequently, unless they can properly be said to be partnership assets.[85] It follows that, if surviving or continuing partners

---

[81] In the case of a purchaser acquiring the legal estate in partnership land (other than trading stock), it would appear that enforcement would depend on the prior registration of the lien as a general equitable charge under the Land Charges Act 1972 (in the case of unregistered land) or as a minor interest (in the case of registered land); but note also the decision in *London & Cheshire Insurance Co. Ltd. v. Laplagrene Property Co.* [1971] Ch. 499.

[82] See *Skipp v. Harwood* (1747) 2 Swan. 586; *West v. Skip* (1749) 1 Ves.Sen. 239; *Stocken v. Dawson* (1845) 9 Beav. 239, affirmed (1848) 17 L.J.Ch. 282. *Cf.* the cases cited *infra*, para. 19–32, n. 86.

[83] See *infra*, paras. 19–35 *et seq.*

[84] See *Stekel v. Ellice* [1973] 1 W.L.R. 191. Lord Lindley also cited the following example, which is of more limited relevance: "Moreover, if two persons engage in a joint adventure, each consigning goods for sale upon the terms that each is to have the produce of his own goods, neither of them will have a lien on the goods of the other, nor on the produce of such goods, although each may have raised the money to pay for his own goods by a bill drawn on himself by the other, and ultimately dishonoured": *Ex p. Gemmel* (1843) 3 M.D. & D. 198. It is clear from the report that no partnership existed between the consignors.

[85] *Quaere*, could the lien attach to an asset acquired after the date of dissolution which in effect *represents* a partnership asset, *e.g.* where a particular asset is sold and the proceeds reinvested in some other asset? A similar issue is canvassed, *supra*, para. 18–17, n. 42.

carry on the business and, in the course of so doing, acquire property, it will prima facie be free of the lien. Lord Lindley observed that "in this respect the lien in question differs from the lien of a mortgagee on a varying stock-in-trade assigned to him as a security for his loan."[86] Subject to the foregoing, on the death or insolvency of a partner, his lien continues in favour of his personal representatives or trustee, and does not terminate until his share has either been ascertained and paid by the other partners[87] or, seemingly, extinguished by effluxion of time under the Limitation Act 1980.[88]

Enforceability of lien against persons claiming through partner

The Partnership Act 1890[89] confirms that the lien may not only be **19–33** enforced as between the partners, but also as against persons claiming through them, *e.g.* personal representatives, trustees in bankruptcy, liquidators, assignees and execution creditors.[90]

In *Re Ritson*[91] one of two partners charged his own land as security **19–34** for a debt owed by his firm to its bankers. He died, having devised the land to his son and the residue of his property, including his partnership share, to all his children.[92] The partnership assets were sufficient to pay all the partnership debts, including the secured debt. It was argued on behalf of the children (other than the son) that the testator's share of that debt should be borne by the land charged with its payment but they were ultimately unsuccessful. The court held that (1) the share bequeathed to the children was only the testator's share in the surplus partnership assets remaining after payment of *all* the partnership debts, including the secured debt, (2) as the assets were sufficient to pay all the debts, Locke King's Act[93] did not apply and (3) the surviving partner being entitled to insist on the partnership assets being applied in payment of its debts, the devisee

---

[86] *Payne v. Hornby* (1858) 25 Beav. 280. See also *Nerot v. Burnand* (1827) 4 Russ. 247, affirmed (1828) 2 Bli.(N.S.) 215, *supra*, para. 18–17; *Ex p. Morley* (1873) L.R. 8 Ch.App. 1026. *Cf.* the cases cited *supra*, para. 19–31, n. 82.

[87] See *Stocken v. Dawson* (1845) 9 Beav. 239, affirmed (1848) 17 L.J.Ch. 282; also *Re Fox* (1915) 49 Ir.L.T. 224 and the cases cited *supra*, para. 19–31, n. 82.

[88] It is submitted that, where the Partnership Act 1890, s.43 applies, a partner's lien will normally become statute-barred, along with his entitlement under that section, six years after the date on which he ceases to be a partner: see *infra*, paras. 19–41, 23–33 *et seq.*

[89] See the opening words of *ibid.* s.39, *supra*, para. 19–29.

[90] See *West v. Skip* (1749) 1 Ves.Sen. 239 and the other cases cited *supra*, para. 19–31, n. 82.

[91] [1899] 1 Ch. 128.

[92] The testator had in fact given his wife a prior life interest both in the land and the residue, but this is not material.

[93] See now the Administration of Estates Act 1925, s.35, which substantially re-enacted the Real Estate Charges Acts. Note also *Re Turner* [1938] Ch. 593 (bequest of shares in a company subject to a lien).

of the land should have the same right as against the testator's executors and children.

Enforceability of lien against purchasers

19–35   In relation to purchasers of partnership property, a distinction must, on the one hand, be drawn between trading stock and fixed assets and, on the other, between a continuing and a dissolved partnership.

Trading stock: Brief reference has already been made to the operation of the lien as regards trading stock.[94] It has long been recognised that trading stock disposed of in the normal course of business ceases to be subject to the lien;[95] to hold otherwise would effectively prevent any sale of that stock without the consent of all the partners and make the transaction of business impossible. The position will be the same where the disposal merely *appears* to be effected in the normal course of business, but the purchaser is unaware of the irregularity. On the other hand, a purchaser of a partner's share inevitably acquires his interest in the partnership assets subject to the liens of the other partners, even as regards trading stock.[96]

19–36   *Fixed Assets*:   It is, however, considered that the same arguments cannot *necessarily* be applied to the fixed assets of a firm, at least while the partnership is continuing. In such a case, a purchaser with notice of the asset's true status would prima facie be bound by a partner's lien, unless the partner(s) purporting to effect the sale are clothed with the necessary authority.[97]

19–37   *Sales following dissolution*:   Be that as it may, once the partnership has been dissolved, a partner's authority to sell the partnership assets (whether trading stock or fixed assets) will derive from the Partnership Act 1890[98] and any sale pursuant thereto will clearly be free from the other partners' liens.[99]

---

[94] See *supra*, para. 19–31.

[95] See *Re Langmead's Trusts* (1855) 20 Beav. 20, affirmed at 7 De G.M. & G. 353. Interestingly, Lord Lindley referred only to a sale of chattels at this point, having earlier referred to trading stock.

[96] *Cavander v. Bulteel* (1873) L.R. 9 Ch.App. 79.

[97] See generally, the Partnership Act 1890, s.5 and *supra*, paras. 12–01 *et seq.*

[98] *Ibid.* s.38: see *supra*, paras. 13–64 *et seq.*

[99] *Re Langmead's Trusts* (1855) 20 Beav. 20, affirmed at 7 De G.M. & G. 353; *Re Bourne* [1906] 2 Ch. 427.

Limits of lien

Ordinary debts, etc., due from partner to firm

The partner's lien is exercisable only in respect of sums due as **19–38** between the firm and a partner *in that capacity*. It therefore clearly applies in the case of a partner who has failed to introduce his agreed capital contribution[1] or who has borrowed money from the firm;[2] however, any attempt to extend that application to non-partnership debts owed by one partner to another will fail, as Lord Lindley explained:

"The lien of partners on the partnership property extends ... to whatever is due to or from the firm by or to the members thereof, as such. It does not, however, extend to debts incurred between a partner and the other members of the firm, otherwise than in their character of members. It has therefore been held that where a partner borrowed money (not partnership money) from his co-partners for some private purpose of his own, and then became bankrupt, his assignees were entitled to his share in the partnership, ascertained without taking into account the sum due from him to his co-partners in respect of this loan; and that the solvent partners were driven to prove against his estate in order to obtain payment of the money lent."[3]

Illegality

No lien will exist if the partnership is illegal.[4] Its members have no **19–39** lien upon the common property, or upon each other's shares therein, otherwise than by virtue of some agreement which is not tainted by the illegality.

Loss of lien

Once partnership property is converted into the separate property **19–40** of a partner, the other partners' liens thereover will inevitably be lost. Thus, if the partners agree, following a dissolution, that the partnership assets will be divided between them *in specie* and that

---

[1] *Re Ward* [1985] 2 N.Z.L.R. 352.
[2] See *Meliorucchi v. Royal Exchange Assurance Co.* (1728) 1 Eq.Ca.Abr. 8; *Croft v. Pyke* (1733) 3 P.W. 180.
[3] See *Croft v. Pyke* (1733) 3 P.W. 180; *Ryall v. Rowles* (1749) 1 Ves.Sen. 348. Lord Lindley questioned whether *Smith v. De Silva* (1776) Cowp. 469 was perhaps decided on this principle, as suggested by Lord Tenterden in *Holderness v. Shackels* (1828) 8 B. & C. 618. See also *Re Ward* [1985] 2 N.Z.L.R. 352, 354.
[4] See *Ewing v. Osbaldiston* (1837) 2 Myl. & Cr. 53. *Per contra* if the lien can be substantiated under some agreement which is not tainted by the illegality.

some other provision will be made for the partnership debts, once that agreement has been implemented and the assets divided, each partner's lien will have been forfeited, even though the debts are not ultimately paid in the manner contemplated. In such a case, there will be no direct right of recourse to the former partnership assets in order to meet those debts.[5]

Alternatively, a partner's lien may be lost if he impliedly abandons it in favour of some other security, *e.g.* by taking a specific charge over certain assets.[6]

Limitation

19–41   The right of an outgoing partner or the estate of a deceased partner in respect of his share is, by virtue of section 43 of the Partnership Act 1890, stated to be a debt accruing at the date of dissolution or death,[7] although it must, in the current editor's view, be open to question whether this section applies in the case of a *general* dissolution.[8] Where the section does apply, the outgoing/deceased partner's entitlement will prima facie become statute-barred after six years;[9] it would seem unlikely that a lien in support of that debt would survive its extinguishment.

Insolvency

19–42   If a partnership is wound up as an unregistered company,[10] whether or not concurrent petitions are presented against two or more of the partners,[11] the solvent partners' liens will not be enforceable against the liquidator; however, this is largely irrelevant, since the partnership property will in any event be applied towards

---

[5] *Lingen v. Simpson* (1824) 1 Sim. & St. 600; and see the judgment of Turner L.J. in *Re Langmead's Trusts* (1855) 7 De G.M. & G. 353, 360 *et seq.* Lord Lindley also cited the following example, on the authority of *Holroyd v. Griffiths* (1856) 3 Drew. 428: "... if two partners consign goods for sale, and direct the consignee to carry the proceeds of the sale equally to their separate accounts without any reserve, and this is done, neither partner has any lien on the share of the other in those proceeds; although it would have been otherwise if they had remained part of the common property of the two." In *Holderness v. Shackels* (1828) 8 B. & C. 612, the lien was not lost because the transfer to each partner was expressed to be subject thereto.

[6] See *Burston Finance Ltd. v. Speirway* [1974] 1 W.L.R. 1648 (a case concerning the loss of an unpaid vendor's lien).

[7] See *infra*, para. 23–33; also *supra*, para. 19–11.

[8] See *infra*, paras. 23–33, 26–04.

[9] It is not clear whether the debt under s.43 is a sum recoverable by statute (to which the Limitation Act 1980, s.9 would apply) or a simple contract debt (to which *ibid.* s.5 would apply) but, in either case, the limitation period is the same. As to the limitation period where an account is sought, see *infra*, para. 23–35.

[10] See *infra*, paras. 27–08 *et seq.*

[11] See *infra*, paras. 27–23 *et seq.*

payment of the partnership debts and any surplus returned to the partners according to their respective entitlements.[12]

4. EXECUTION AGAINST SHARE FOR PARTNER'S SEPARATE DEBTS

The Partnership Act 1890 introduced a new procedure whereby a **19–43** judgment obtained against a partner could be executed against his share rather than, as under the previous law,[13] against the property of the partnership itself. That procedure is set out in section 23 of the Act which provides as follows:

"23.—(1) [...][14] a writ of execution[15] shall not issue against any partnership property except on a judgment against the firm.

(2) The High Court, or a judge thereof, [...][16] or a county court, may, on the application by summons of any judgment creditor of a partner, make an order charging that partner's interest in the partnership property and profits with payment of the amount of the judgment debt and interest thereon, and may by the same or a subsequent order appoint a receiver of that partner's share of profits (whether already declared or accruing), and of any other money which may be coming to him in respect of the partnership, and direct all accounts and inquiries, and give all other orders and directions which might have been directed or given if the charge had been made in favour of the judgment creditor by the partner, or which the circumstances of the case may require.

(3) The other partner or partners shall be at liberty at any time to redeem the interest charged, or in case of a sale being directed, to purchase the same.

(4) This section shall apply in the case of a cost-book company as if the company were a partnership within the meaning of this Act.

(5) This section shall not apply to Scotland."

It should be noted that charging orders under this section are distinct from charging orders made under the Charging Orders Act 1979.

---

[12] See *infra*, paras. 27–82 *et seq*.

[13] See generally, as to the difficulties under the old procedure, the 5th ed. of this work at pp. 356 *et seq*. and the 4th ed. (Vol. 1) at pp. 687 *et seq*.

[14] The words "After the commencement of this Act," which appeared at this point, were repealed by the Statute Law Revision Act 1908.

[15] See R.S.C. Ord. 46, r. 1.

[16] The words omitted were repealed by the Courts Act 1971, Sched. 11, Pt. II.

Foreign firms

19–44 It is clear that the section applies to a foreign firm with a branch office in England.[17]

R.S.C. Order 81, r. 10

19–45 The procedure for obtaining an order under the section, both in the High Court and county court,[18] is now governed by Order 81, r. 10, of the Rules of the Supreme Court, which provides as follows:

"10.—(1) Every application to the Court by a judgment creditor of a partner for an order under section 23 of the Partnership Act 1890 (which authorises the High Court or a judge thereof to make certain orders on the application of a judgment creditor of a partner, including an order charging the partner's interest in the partnership property), and every application to the Court by a partner of the judgment debtor made in consequence of the first-mentioned application must be made by summons.

(2) A master or the Admiralty Registrar or a district registrar[19] may exercise the powers conferred on a judge by the said section 23.

(3) Every summons issued by a judgment creditor under this rule, and every order made on such a summons, must be served on the judgment debtor and on such of his partners as are within the jurisdiction or, if the partnership is a cost book company, on the judgment debtor and the purser of the company.

(4) Every summons issued by a partner of a judgment debtor under this rule, and every order made on such a summons, must be served—

(a) on the judgment creditor, and

(b) on the judgment debtor, and

(c) on such of the other partners of the judgment debtor as do not join in the application and are within the jurisdiction or, if the partnership is a cost book company, on the purser of the company.

(5) A summons or order served in accordance with this rule on the purser of a cost book company or, in the case of a partnership not being such a company, on some only of the partners thereof, shall be deemed to have been served on that company or on all the partners of that partnership, as the case may be."

---

[17] *Brown, Janson & Co. v. A. Hutchinson & Co.* [1895] 1 Q.B. 737.

[18] R.S.C. Ord. 81, r. 10 will apply in the county court by virtue of the County Courts Act 1984, s.76.

[19] This expression must now be construed as a reference to a district judge by virtue of the Courts and Legal Services Act 1990, s.74(3).

It is pointed out in the Supreme Court Practice[20] that a summons under the above rule will usually also seek the appointment of a named receiver,[21] although it is apprehended that such applications are, in practice, comparatively rare.

Mentally disordered and deceased partners

A charging order may be obtained in respect of the share of a **19–46** partner suffering from a mental disorder,[22] but seemingly not in respect of a share held by the executors of a deceased judgment debtor.[23]

Rights of creditor under charging order

Although a charging order under section 23 of the Partnership Act **19–47** 1890 will charge the whole of the debtor's share, it will not give the judgment creditor any rights more extensive than those enjoyed by the debtor (*qua* partner) when the order was obtained.[24] Thus, the judgment creditor will have no priority over an assignee of the share, where the assignment was effected between the date of judgment and the date of the order.[25] Equally, it would seem that the partners (including the debtor) will subsequently be free to implement an arrangement detrimental to the judgment creditor's interests, *e.g.* reducing the profits distributable in the normal profit sharing ratios by paying preferential "salaries"[26] to partners, provided that they can demonstrate that the arrangement is bona fide and introduced pursuant to a specific provision in the partnership agreement or otherwise pursuant to their normal management powers.[27]

---

[20] Supreme Court Practice 1995, para. 81/10/2.

[21] Such an application can be made irrespective of the size of the judgment debt: *Summers v. Simpson*, May 1, 1902 (Bucknell J., unreported).

[22] *Re Sir F. Seager Hunt* [1900] 2 Ch. 54, note; also *Horne v. Pountain* (1889) 23 Q.B.D. 264; *Re Leavesley* [1891] 2 Ch. 1 (cases decided under the Judgments Act 1838).

[23] See *Stewart v. Rhodes* [1900] 1 Ch. 386 (also a decision under the Judgments Act 1838), and the observations therein on *Haly v. Barry* (1868) L.R. 3 Ch.App. 452 and *Finney v. Hinde* (1899) 4 Q.B.D. 102. See also *supra*, paras. 19–10 *et seq.*, as to the nature of a partnership share on the death of a partner.

[24] *Gill v. Continental Gas Co.* (1872) L.R. 7 Ex. 332; *Re Onslow's Trusts* (1875) L.R. 20 Eq. 677; *Cooper v. Griffin* [1892] 1 Q.B. 740; *Howard v. Sadler* [1893] 1 Q.B. 1; *Sutton v. English and Colonial Produce Co.* [1902] 2 Ch. 502 (cases decided under Judgments Act 1838).

[25] *Brearcliff v. Dorrington* (1850) 4 De G. & Sm. 122; *Scott v. Lord Hastings* (1858) 4 K. & J. 633 (again, cases decided under the Judgments Act 1838).

[26] See, as to such salaries, *supra*, para. 10–67 and *infra*, para. 20–41.

[27] See *Watts v. Driscoll* [1901] 1 Ch. 294 (and particularly at p. 311, *per* Vaughan Williams L.J., citing *Kelly v. Hutton* (1868) L.R. 3 Ch.App. 703); *Re Garwood* [1903] 1 Ch. 236; and see also an article entitled "Partnership: Equitable Execution" by Mr. H. E. Markson in (1981) 125 S.J. 109. Both of the above cases were, of course, decided under the Partnership Act 1890, s.31 (see further *infra*, para. 19–64), but it is thought that the same principles apply. Of course, if the partners can be shown to have acted mala fide or fraudulently, any arrangement of the type supposed will be ineffective as regards the judgment creditor.

If the debtor seeks to dispose of his share before a charging order can be obtained, an *ex parte* interlocutory injunction may be obtained pending the hearing of the application under the section.[28]

Accounts and inquiries

19–48   Consistently with the foregoing, a charging order gives the judgment creditor no greater rights than would be enjoyed by a mortgagee or assignee of a share,[29] so that he will normally have no right to insist on an account of the partnership dealings being taken whilst the partnership subsists. However, the court might direct such an account in special circumstances, *e.g.* with a view to a dissolution.[30]

Sale or foreclosure

19–49   A judgment creditor who has obtained a charging order will be entitled to an order for the sale of the debtor's share[31] and, seemingly, to an order for foreclosure against him.[32] Either of such orders may be obtained without commencing a separate action.[33] The rights and duties of the other partners in the event that a sale is ordered will be considered hereafter.[34]

Insolvency of judgment debtor

19–50   A charging order made under section 23 of the Partnership Act 1890 was not regarded as a completed execution for the purposes of section 40 of the Bankruptcy Act 1914;[35] it is apprehended that a similar approach will now be adopted in relation to sections 183[36] and

---

[28] Such an injunction bears a marked resemblance to the *Mareva* injunction and might properly be regarded as one of its precursors. See further *infra*, para. 23–147.

[29] Partnership Act 1890, s.31: see *infra*, paras. 19–59 *et seq.*

[30] See *Brown, Janson & Co. v. A. Hutchinson & Co.* [1895] 1 Q.B. 737.

[31] Partnership Act 1890, s.23(3), *supra*, para. 19–43.

[32] See the following cases decided under the Judgments Act 1838, s.13: *Ford v. Wastell* (1847) 6 Hare 229 and 2 Ph. 591; *Jones v. Bailey* (1853) 17 Beav. 582; *Messer v. Boyle* (1856) 21 Beav. 559; *Beckett v. Buckley* (1874) L.R. 17 Eq. 435. See also *Redmayne v. Forster* (1866) L.R. 2 Eq. 467 and the comments of Lord Cozens-Hardy M.R. on *D'Auvergne v. Cooper* [1899] W.N. 256 in *Hosack v. Robins* [1917] 1 Ch. 332, 336. *Cf. Footner v. Sturgis* (1852) 5 De G. & Sm. 736. And see generally, as to when foreclosure is an appropriate remedy, *Re Owen* [1894] 3 Ch. 220; *Harrold v. Plenty* [1901] 2 Ch. 314. See also *infra*, para. 19–51.

[33] See R.S.C. Ord. 81, r. 10, *supra*, para. 19–45. *Cf. Legott v. Western* (1884) 12 Q.B.D. 287.

[34] See *infra*, paras. 19–51, 19–52.

[35] In *Re Hutchinson* (1885) 16 Q.B.D. 515, it was held that a charging order did not amount to "execution" for the purposes of what was later to become s.40; see also *Re O'Shea's Settlement* [1895] 1 Ch. 325; *Wild v. Southwood* [1897] 1 Q.B. 317. However, those decisions could seemingly not stand in the face of *Re Overseas Aviation Engineering (G.B.) Ltd.* [1963] Ch. 24 (subsequently overruled by the Charging Orders Act 1979, s.4) and *Roberts Petroleum Ltd. v. Bernard Kennedy Ltd.* [1983] 2 A.C. 192.

[36] This section will apply in the case of a winding up order against a corporate partner: see *infra*, paras. 27–26 *et seq.*, 27–44 *et seq.*

346[37] of the Insolvency Act 1986. Accordingly, if the debtor is adjudged bankrupt (or wound up) after the order has been obtained, the judgment creditor will lose his rights thereunder. Moreover, it would appear that if the other partners have paid a sum of money into court with a view to redeeming or purchasing the debtor's share,[38] his trustee (or liquidator) will be entitled to that sum, unless the money has been paid out to the creditor before the adjudication or winding-up order; similarly if the purchase or redemption moneys have been paid directly to the judgment creditor prior to that date.[39]

Rights and duties of judgment debtor's partners

The partners of a judgment debtor against whom a charging order **19–51** has been obtained may at any time redeem his share.[40] It would, however, seem that this right will be exercisable only whilst the charge subsists, so that its existence would not preclude a foreclosure or entitle a partner to reopen a foreclosure once it had become absolute.

If a sale of the debtor's share is ordered on the application of the **19–52** judgment creditor, the other partners are entitled to purchase it.[41] However, in so doing they must act with absolute fairness. If they do anything to conceal the true value of the share, thus enabling themselves to purchase it at less than its market value, the sale will be overturned. Such a case was *Perens v. Johnson*,[42] where the partners in a colliery had by various underhand means concealed the fact that a valuable seam of coal would soon be uncovered. The seam was in fact reached with a single day's work after the partners had purchased the debtor's share at auction. The sale was subsequently set aside at the instance of the debtor, on the basis of his partners' breach of good faith.[43]

---

[37] This section will apply in the case of a bankruptcy order against an individual partner: see *infra*, paras. 27–29 *et seq.*, 27–44 *et seq.*

[38] Partnership Act 1890, s.23(3), *supra*, para. 19–43.

[39] See, under the old law, *Wild v. Southwood* [1897] 1 Q.B. 317. In the case of a bankrupt partner, either payment would arguably amount to a sum paid to avoid the execution, within the meaning of the Insolvency Act 1986, s.346(1); *sed quaere*. The same words do not appear in *ibid.* s.183(1). *Semble* such a purchase or redemption would not involve a disposition by a bankrupt partner for the purposes of *ibid.* s.284. The position may be otherwise in the case of an insolvent corporate partner: *ibid.* s.127. *Cf.* the position in the case of a payment in under R.S.C. Ord. 22: *W. A. Sherratt Ltd. v. John Bromley (Church Stretton) Ltd.* [1985] Q.B. 1038.

[40] Partnership Act 1890, s.23(3), *supra*, para. 19–43.

[41] *Ibid.*

[42] (1857) 3 Sm. & G. 419. See also *Smith v. Harrison* (1857) 26 L.J. Ch. 412; *Helmore v. Smith* (1887) 35 Ch.D. 436. It should, however, be noted that the partners might already have properly agreed some amendment to the partnership terms which adversely affect the value of the debtor's share: see *supra*, para. 19–47. If their motives cannot be impugned (*e.g.* by showing that the amendment was introduced with a view to depressing the sale price), there would seem to be no basis on which the sale could be attacked.

[43] See further, as to the duty of good faith, *supra*, paras. 16–01 *et seq.*

Management decisions

19–53   The right of all the partners (including the judgment debtor) to agree bona fide changes in the partnership terms, even if they may have the effect of devaluing the share in respect of which the charging order was obtained, has already been noticed.[44]

Share purchased with partnership moneys

19–54   If the other partners buy the judgment debtor's share with partnership moneys, it will be partnership property and they cannot claim it as exclusively theirs.[45]

Right to dissolve

19–55   If a judgment creditor obtains a charging order on a partner's share, this will entitle the other partners, if they so wish, to dissolve the partnership.[46]

5.   THE TRANSFER OF A SHARE

19–56   A hallmark of the partnership relation has always been its essentially *personal* character, as Lord Lindley recognised in this passage:

> "When persons enter into a contract of partnership, their intention ordinarily is that a partnership shall exist between themselves and themselves alone. The mutual confidence reposed by each in the other is one of the main elements in the contract, and it is obvious that persons may be willing enough to trust each other, and yet be unwilling to place the same trust in any one else. Hence it is one of the fundamental principles of partnership law that no person can be introduced as a partner without the consent of all those who for the time being are members of the firm. If, therefore, a partner dies, his executors or devisees have no right to insist on being admitted into partnership with the surviving partners, unless some agreement to that effect has been entered into by them.[47]
> Still less can a partner by assigning his share entitle his assignee to take his place in the partnership against the will of the other members.[48] The assignment, however, is by no means inoperative; on the contrary, it involves several important consequences, more

---

[44] See *supra*, para. 19–47.
[45] See *Helmore v. Smith* (1887) 35 Ch.D. 436.
[46] Partnership Act 1890, s.33(2): see *infra*, paras. 24–29 *et seq.*
[47] *Pearce v. Chamberlain* (1750) 2 Ves.Sen. 33; *Tatam v. Williams* (1844) 3 Hare 347; *Gillespie v. Hamilton* (1818) 3 Madd. 251; *Crawshay v. Maule* (1818) 1 Swan. 495; *Bray v. Fromont* (1821) 6 Madd. 5. See also *supra*, paras. 10–216 *et seq.*
[48] See *Jefferys v. Smith* (1827) 3 Russ. 158.

especially as regards the dissolution of the firm and the right of the assignee to an account."[49]

The fundamental principle to which Lord Lindley referred is **19–57** naturally recognised in the Partnership Act 1890,[50] which also contains an express provision governing the rights of an assignee of a partnership share.[51] However, as will be seen hereafter,[52] the assignment of a partner's share does not now, of itself, give the other partners grounds to dissolve the firm.

Partner's right to transfer share

The ability of a partner to transfer his share to a third party (or to **19–58** one of his co-partners), though expressly recognised by the Partnership Act 1890, does not derive therefrom: a share is no different from any other asset and may, subject to the terms of the partnership agreement,[53] be transferred in any manner authorised by law.[54]

It follows that, whatever may be the scope of section 31 of the 1890 Act,[55] a transfer of part of a share will be valid and effectual.[56]

Partnership Act 1890, section 31

The rights of the assignee of a share are set out in section 31 of the **19–59** Partnership Act 1890, which is in the following terms:

"31.—(1) An assignment by any partner of his share in the partnership, either absolute or by way of mortgage or redeemable charge, does not, as against the other partners, entitle the assignee, during the continuance of the partnership, to interfere in the management or administration of the partnership business or affairs, or to require any accounts of the partnership transactions, or to inspect the partnership books, but entitles the assignee only to receive the share of profits to which the assigning partner would

---

[49] Lord Lindley's footnote at this point read: "In *Marshall v. Maclure* (1885) 10 App.Cas. 325, a surrender of a partner's share in property mortgaged was held, under special circumstances, to include the firm's share." In fact, the firm's share appears to have been held by the partner concerned as trustee; he sought (unsuccessfully) to argue that the "share" surrendered was limited to the proportionate part of the firm's share to which he was entitled *qua* partner.

[50] *Ibid.* s.24(7); see also *supra*, para. 15–10. As to the position in a limited partnership, see *infra*, paras. 31–15 *et seq.*

[51] *Ibid.* s.31, *infra*, para. 19–59.

[52] See *infra*, para. 24–77.

[53] See *supra*, paras. 10–216 *et seq.* and *infra*, para. 19–70.

[54] Note that the Bills of Sale Acts 1878 and 1882 do not apply to the assignment of a partner's share: *Re Bainbridge* (1878) 8 Ch.D. 218 (a decision under the Bills of Sale Act 1854).

[55] See *infra*, paras. 19–60, 19–61.

[56] For a recent example of such a transfer, see *Hadlee v. Commissioner of Inland Revenue* [1993] A.C. 442 (P.C.).

otherwise be entitled, and the assignee must accept the account of profits agreed to by the partners.

(2) In case of a dissolution of the partnership, whether as respects all the partners or as respects the assigning partner, the assignee is entitled to receive the share of the partnership assets to which the assigning partner is entitled as between himself and the other partners, and for the purpose of ascertaining that share, to an account as from the date of the dissolution."

Scope of section

19–60 There is at least some doubt as to whether the section applies in the case of an assignment of a share in a *dissolved* partnership, particularly given the terms of subsection (2). However, in *Public Trustee v. Elder*,[57] Sargant L.J expressed the *obiter* view that, even if the section does not apply, its provisions should be applied to such an assignment by analogy.[58]

19–61 The section is also framed in terms of an assignment of an entire share and, thus, arguably has no application where only part of a share is assigned.[59] However, since the section precludes an assignee from interfering in management, etc. and from demanding the taking of an account whilst the partnership continues, and since an assignee of part can have no greater rights than an assignee of the whole, the point may well be largely academic.[60]

Position as between the assignee and the other partners

19–62 Section 31 settled the doubts which had arisen prior to the Act,[61] as to whether an assignee of a share had a right to an account *vis-à-vis* the other partners, by emphatically rejecting the existence of any such right, otherwise than following a dissolution. In other respects, the section did not alter the law, as is demonstrated by the following passage written by Lord Lindley prior to the 1890 Act:

"... if a partner does assign or mortgage his share, he thereby confers upon the assignee or mortgagee a right to payment of

---

[57] [1926] Ch. 776.

[58] [1926] Ch. 790. See also *ibid.* p. 785, *per* Lord Hanworth M.R. Warrington L.J. appears to have had no doubts: see *ibid.* p. 786. Although the contrary appears not to have been argued, the Court of Appeal in *Harwood v. Harwood* [1991] 2 F.L.R. 274 treated s.31(2) as *authorising* the assignment of a share following a dissolution.

[59] *Quaere*, can the application of the section in such a case not be justified on the principle that "*omne majus continet in se minus*" (the greater includes the less)?

[60] In such a case, the section might again be applied by analogy: see, *supra*, para. 19–60, n. 58.

[61] See the decisions in favour of such a right (*Glyn v. Hood* (1859) 1 Giff. 328, affirmed at (1859) 1 De G.F. & J. 334; *Kelly v. Hutton* (1868) L.R. 3 Ch.App. 703; *Whetham v. Davey* (1885) 30 Ch.D. 574) and against (*Brown v. De Tastet* (1819) Jac. 284).

what, upon the taking the accounts of the partnership, may be due to the assignor or mortgagor.[62] But the assignee or mortgagee acquires no other right than this[63]; and he takes subject to the rights of the other partners; and will be affected by equities arising between the assignor and his co-partners subsequently to the assignment.[64] Even if the assignee gives notice of the assignment, he cannot (if the partnership is for a term) acquire a right to the assignor's share as it stands at the time of the assignment or notice, discharged from subsequently arising claims of the other partners."[65]

The 1890 Act clearly establishes that, whilst the partnership **19–63** continues, an assignee of a partner's share cannot, as against the other partners, interfere in the management or administration of the partnership, require the taking of accounts or inspect the partnership books and that he is, moreover, bound to accept an account of profits agreed[66] by the partners. However, once the partnership has been dissolved,[67] the assignee will be entitled to insist on an account being taken in order to ascertain the amount due to him in respect of the assigned share.

Arrangements affecting the assignee's rights

Subject to the point made in the next paragraph, the partners **19–64** (including the assignor) will, so long as their actions are bona fide, be free to manage the partnership in any way they see fit, even if this prejudices the position of the assignee. Thus, where partners had, following a mortgage of one partner's share, implemented a bona fide arrangement under which partners were to receive "salaries" in consideration of additional services undertaken, it was held that the payment of such salaries formed part of the management and administration of the partnership business and bound the mortgagee, even though he thereby suffered a financial detriment.[68] The current

---

[62] *Glyn v. Hood* (1859) 1 Giff. 328, affirmed at (1859) 1 De G.F. & J. 334; *Whetham v. Davey* (1885) 30 Ch.D. 574. See also *Cassels v. Stewart* (1881) 6 App.Cas. 64.

[63] *Smith v. Parkes* (1852) 16 Beav. 115.

[64] See *Lindsay v. Gibbs* (1856) 3 De G. & J. 690; *Guion v. Trask* (1860) 1 De G.F. & J. 373, 379, *per* Turner L.J.; *Cavander v. Bulteel* (1873) L.R. 9 Ch.App. 78. See also *Morris v. Livie* (1842) 1 Y. & C.C. 380; *Bergmann v. McMillan* (1881) 17 Ch.D. 423; *Re Knapman* (1881) 18 Ch.D. 300.

[65] See *Redmayne v. Forster* (1866) L.R. 2 Eq. 467; *Kelly v. Hutton* (1868) L.R. 3 Ch.App. 703; *Cavander v. Bulteel* (1873) L.R. 9 Ch.App. 78; *Bergmann v. McMillan* (1881) 17 Ch.D. 423.

[66] It is implicit that such agreement must be bona fide: see *infra*, para. 19–64.

[67] The dissolution may be either general or limited, *e.g.* a technical dissolution resulting from the death, retirement or expulsion of the assignor partner: Partnership Act 1890, s.31(2), *supra*, para. 19–59. But see also *infra*, para. 19–65.

[68] *Re Garwood's Trusts* [1903] 1 Ch. 236. No attempt was made to analyse whether the "salaries" concerned should more properly be treated as an allocation of profit: see further, *infra*, paras. 20–41, 34–30. See also an article entitled "Partnership: Equitable Execution" by Mr. H. E. Markson in (1981) 125 S.J. 109.

editor is of the opinion that the position would be the same in the case of a bona fide arrangement which does *not* fall under the "management and administration" umbrella, provided that it is introduced pursuant to a specific provision in the partnership agreement and not on a purely *ad hoc* basis.[69]

Account following a dissolution

19–65   The assignee's right to an account following a dissolution is a statutory right which exists independently of the partnership agreement and it is questionable to what extent (if at all) it may be affected or excluded thereby.[70] It is clear that, once the partners have notice of the assignment, they cannot agree to adopt new terms which will adversely affect that right.[71] What is, perhaps, more doubtful is whether they could extend the duration of a fixed term partnership,[72] thereby deferring the exercise of the assignee's right to an account. It is tentatively submitted that they could not.[73]

19–66   If the partnership agreement contains an arbitration clause limited to differences arising between the partners, their executors or administrators, the assignee cannot be forced to have the account taken by an arbitrator and will, moreover, not be bound by any account taken in an arbitration to which he was not made a party; however, the position may be otherwise if the arbitration clause is also applicable to persons claiming through or under the partners.[74]

Position as between the assignor and the assignee

19–67   Although the assignee does not become a partner in place of the assignor, he effectively stands in his shoes and is accordingly bound to indemnify the assignor against any liability for the partnership debts.[75] In this way, the assignee will be indirectly liable for the

---

[69] See *Watts v. Driscoll* [1901] 1 Ch. 294, 311, *per* Vaughan Williams L.J., citing *Kelly v. Hutton* (1868) L.R. 3 Ch.App. 703.

[70] It is submitted that if the agreement clearly establishes the financial entitlement of the assignor partner in respect of his share, *e.g.* by reference to his capital and current account balances, there will be little or no scope for the taking of an account. In such a case, notwithstanding the assignee's statutory right, it seems likely that a court would refuse to order an account. Equally, an attempt to exclude the assignee's right by a specific provision would seem to be ineffective.

[71] *Watts v. Driscoll* [1901] 1 Ch. 294.

[72] See the Partnership Act 1890, s.27.

[73] This was an issue raised by Lord Lindley in his Supplement on the Partnership Act 1890, although he did not go so far as to express a view thereon.

[74] *Bonnin v. Neame* [1910] 1 Ch. 732. See also *Shayler v. Woolf* [1946] Ch. 320 and the provisions of the Arbitration Act 1950, s.4, *supra*, para. 10–229.

[75] *Dodson v. Downey* [1901] 2 Ch. 620. See in particular the judgment of Farwell J. at p. 623. Note, however, that previous editors of this work have questioned whether the headnote is supported by the facts or the judgment. The current editor does not share these doubts.

assignor's share of any losses.[76] It is, however, doubtful whether the assignor could properly seek an indemnity in respect of liabilities attributable to his own wrongful acts whilst conducting the partnership business.[77]

As was made clear in *Hadlee v. Commissioner of Inland Revenue*,[78] when a partner assigns his share to a third party, he is not normally to be taken thereby to have disposed of an income producing asset. The assignee's right to the assignor's profit share may in reality be attributable not to the share itself but to the assignor continuing to fulfil his obligations under the agreement.[79]

Charge by deed

If one partner charges his share in favour of another by deed, the **19–68** latter will, as against the former, prima facie be entitled either to sell the share or to appoint a receiver under the powers conferred by the Law of Property Act 1925.[80]

Insolvency of assignor

The bankruptcy of a partner will normally dissolve the partner- **19–69** ship,[81] thus entitling the assignee to exercise his rights under section 31(2) of the Partnership Act 1890.[82]

In one exceptional case decided under the old bankruptcy law, it was held that the trustee in bankruptcy of a partner in a firm of dentists, who had previously mortgaged his share, was entitled to the profits which that partner derived from the practice carried on after the commencement of the bankruptcy, even though the mortgagees had previously obtained the appointment of a receiver in an action to enforce their security.[83] However, it should be noted that the decision appears to have turned on the nature of the "new" arrangement

---

[76] There is no *direct* liability for losses: the Partnership Act 1890, s.31(1) refers only to the receipt of a share of profits.

[77] In such a case, the assignor partner's claim might, in appropriate case, be defeated by the principle "*ex turpi causa non oritur actio.*"

[78] [1993] A.C. 524 (P.C.). In this case, which concerned a professional firm, the partner concerned had assigned part of his share to a trust for his wife and child and sought (unsuccessfully) to argue that, under the relevant New Zealand income tax legislation, he thereby ceased to be liable for tax on an equivalent part of his profit share.

[79] See [1993] A.C. 533D. *Quaere*, would this analysis hold up in the case of an investment partnership where profits are *not* dependent on the partners' efforts?

[80] See *ibid.* ss.101, 205(xvi), (xx). The definition of "property" would seem to be wide enough to cover a share in a partnership; but see *Blaker v. Herts and Essex Waterworks Co.* (1889) 41 Ch.D. 399 (a decision under the Conveyancing Act 1881).

[81] Partnership Act 1890, s.33(1): see *infra*, paras. 24–20, 24–22 *et seq.*

[82] See *supra*, para. 19–59.

[83] *Ex p. Collins* [1894] 1 Q.B. 425; also *Re Collins* [1925] Ch. 556.

under which the practice was continued, which was not subject to the mortgage.

Transfer allowed by agreement

19–70   A partnership agreement may, exceptionally, give a partner the right to transfer his share to a third party and, thereby, to constitute that third party a partner in his place.[84] Lord Lindley observed:

> "If partners choose to agree that any of them shall be at liberty to introduce any other person into the partnership, there is no reason why they should not; nor why, having so agreed, they should not be bound by the agreement.[85] Persons who enter into such an agreement consent prospectively and once for all to admit into partnership any person who is willing to take advantage of their agreement, and to observe those stipulations, if any, which may be made conditions of his admission. Such an agreement as this is the basis of every partnership, the shares in which are transferable from one person to the other. Those who form such partnerships, and those who join them after they are formed, assent to become partners with anyone who is willing to comply with certain conditions."[86]

19–71   It follows that if, having entered into such an agreement, the other partners refuse to admit the new partner or to complete the consequential steps required to confer the rights of a partner on him, he may be in a position to seek relief from the court in the same way as any other partner,[87] whether in the form of specific performance,[88] an injunction,[89] an account[90] or even an order for the dissolution of the partnership. However, he will only be entitled to such relief if he has himself complied with any conditions which must be satisfied by him under the terms of the agreement.[91]

---

[84] See *supra*, paras. 10–216 *et seq.*
[85] *Lovegrove v. Nelson* (1834) 3 M. & K. 1.
[86] See *Fox v. Clifton* (1832) 9 Bing. 120. Lord Lindley also cited the following passage taken from the judgment Lord Brougham L.C. in *Lovegrove v. Nelson* (1834) 3 M. & K. 1 (at p. 20): "To make a person a partner with two others their consent must clearly be had, but there is no particular mode or time required for giving that consent; and if three enter into partnership by a contract which provides that on one retiring, one of the remaining two, or even a fourth person who is no partner at all, shall name the successor to take the share of the one retiring, it is clear that this would be a valid contract which the court must perform, and that the new partner would come in as entirely by the consent of the other two as if they had adopted him by name."
[87] See *supra*, para. 10–217.
[88] See *infra*, paras. 23–43 *et seq.*
[89] See *infra*, paras. 23–130 *et seq.*
[90] See *infra*, paras. 23–70 *et seq.*
[91] *Byrne v. Reid* [1902] 2 Ch. 735; also *Ehrmann v. Ehrmann* (1894) 72 L.T. 17. And see *supra*, para. 10–217.

Transfer to a man of straw

A partner under such an agreement might seek to free himself **19–72** from continuing liability by transferring his share to a man of straw or to a company which is subsequently wound up.[92] This possibility was recognised by Lord Lindley, who observed:

"Where a partner has an unconditional right to transfer his share, he may transfer it to a pauper, and thus get rid of all liability as between himself and his co-partners in respect of transactions subsequent to the transfer and notice thereof given to them.[93] But even in this case the transfer alone does not render the transferee a member of the partnership, and liable as between himself and the other members to any of the debts of the firm. In order to render him a partner with the other members, they must acknowledge him to be a partner, or permit him to act as such."[94]

Such a course should be adopted with circumspection, since the other partners might seek to argue that the transfer amounts to a breach of the transferor partner's express or implied duty of good faith or, perhaps, of some other provision of the agreement.[95]

Effect of transfer on firm and firm name

A transfer of a share which constitutes the transferee a partner in **19–73** the place of the transferor will, on normal principles, result in a dissolution of the old firm and the creation of a new firm.[96] It may also result in continued use of the firm name requiring approval to be sought from the Secretary of State under the Business Names Act 1985.[97]

Mining partnerships

Lord Lindley observed: **19–74**

"An apparent exception to the rule that a share in a partnership cannot be transferred without the consent of all the partners exists

---

[92] *i.e.* an approach similar to that adopted in the 1950's with a view to getting rid of onerous leases: see *Morelle v. Waterworth* [1955] 1 Q.B. 1; *Morelle v. Wakeling* [1955] 2 Q.B. 379; *Att.-Gen. v. Parsons* [1956] A.C. 421.

[93] The assumption underlying this sentence is, of course, that the transfer of the share is capable of constituting the transferee as a partner: *cf.* the Partnership Act 1890, s.24(7). See also *supra*, para. 10–91.

[94] *Jefferys v. Smith* (1827) 3 Russ. 158.

[95] As to whether a breach of the implied duty of good faith would sound in damages, see *supra*, para. 16–05 and *infra*, paras. 23–195 *et seq.*

[96] See *supra*, paras. 3–01 *et seq.*

[97] *Ibid.* s.2, and *supra*, para. 3–27.

in the case of mining partnerships.[98] Mines are a peculiar species of property, and are in some respects governed by the doctrines of real property law, and in others by the doctrines which regulate trading concerns. Regarding them as real property, and their owners as joint tenants or tenants in common, each partner is held to be at liberty to dispose of his interest in the land without consulting his co-owners[99]; and a transfer of this interest confers upon the transferee all the rights of a part-owner, including a right to an account against the other owners.[1] But even here, if the persons originally interested in the mine are not only part-owners but also partners, a transferee of the share of one of them, although he would become a part-owner with the others, would not become a partner with them in the proper sense of the word, unless by agreement, express or tacit."[2]

19-75   It is perhaps questionable to what extent mining partnerships can be as treated as strictly *sui generis* since the Partnership Act 1890[3] but, in any event, it would seem that, on a true analysis, the position in relation to such partnerships does not differ significantly from that discussed in the preceding paragraphs.

Form of transfer

19-76   It has already been seen that a share in a continuing partnership will comprise a beneficial interest in each of the partnership assets.[4] It follows that a transfer of a share will involve a transfer of those beneficial interests and must be in a form appropriate to the asset concerned. Thus, if the assets consist of chattels and legal (as opposed to equitable) choses in action, in respect of which there is no prescribed form of transfer, the transfer may be effected informally by word of mouth,[5] even though this may be undesirable from an evidential standpoint. Where, however, such assets include land[6] or an equitable interest[7] in land or personalty,[8] section 53(1)(a) or (c) of

---

[98] Lord Lindley appears to have had in mind a transfer which would confer on the assignee all the rights of a partner, thus regarding mining partnerships as within the class "Transfer allowed by agreement."

[99] Of course, the interests of a co-owner must now subsist behind a trust for sale: Law of Property Act 1925, ss.34 *et seq.* A legal joint tenancy in land cannot be severed: *ibid.* s.36(2).

[1] See *Bentley v. Bates* (1840) 4 Y. & C.Ex. 182; *Redmayne v. Foster* (1866) L.R. 2 Eq. 467.

[2] As in *Crawshay v. Maule* (1818) 1 Swan. 495; *Jefferys v. Smith* (1827) 3 Russ. 158. Lord Lindley added that the same principles apply in the case of transfers of shares in ships.

[3] See *ibid.* s.46.

[4] See *supra*, paras. 19–02 *et seq.*

[5] See *Brandt's Sons and Co. v. Dunlop Rubber Co. Ltd.* [1905] A.C. 454. Note that, for a *legal* assignment of a *legal* chose in action, writing is required by virtue of the Law of Property Act 1925, s.136.

[6] The beneficial interest of a partner in land held as a partnership asset will in all cases consist of an equitable interest under a trust for sale: see *Re Fuller's Contract* [1933] Ch. 652.

[7] See the Law of Property Act 1925, ss.1(8), 205(1)(x).

[8] See *Grey v. I.R.C.* [1960] A.C. 1; *Oughtred v. I.R.C.* [1960] A.C. 206.

the Law of Property Act 1925[9] will require a written transfer to be signed by or on behalf of the assigning partner. This is considered to be the position notwithstanding the terms of section 22 of the Partnership Act 1890 and irrespective of whether the share is transferred to a third party or to one or more of the other partners. Equally, where the partnership assets comprise land or an interest in land, a contract for the transfer of a partner's share therein must now invariably be reduced to writing and otherwise satisfy the strict requirements of section 2 of the Law of Property (Miscellaneous Provisions) Act 1989.[10]

Since a transfer of a share does not normally affect the assigning **19–77** partner's continued membership of the firm,[11] there will be no impact on the *legal* title to any partnership assets which may be vested in him on trust for the firm. The position may, however, be different where the transfer is linked to the partner's retirement from the firm, when it may be necessary, *as a wholly separate matter*, to ensure that he also gives up his trusteeship and vests the relevant assets in one or more of the continuing partners.[12]

---

[9] *Quaere* whether a partner's interest in land held as a partnership asset constitutes an interest in land for the purposes of *ibid.* s.53(1)(a) or an equitable interest for the purposes of *ibid.* s.53(1)(c): see, generally, *Stevens v. Hutchinson* [1953] Ch. 299; *Cooper v. Critchley* [1955] Ch. 431; *Irani Finance Ltd. v. Singh* [1971] Ch. 59. However, given the similarity between the two paragraphs, the distinction may be of little importance in practice.

[10] *Ibid.* s.2(6) provides that " 'interest in land' means any estate, interest or charge in or over land or in or over the proceeds of sale of land." This is clearly apt to include a share in land held by a partnership. Note, however, that this section has only a limited application to agreements for the *creation* of a partnership: see *supra*, paras. 7–02 *et seq.*

[11] See *supra*, paras. 10–91, 19–67.

[12] This will usually be secured pursuant to the so called "further assurance" obligation: see *supra*, para. 10–203.

CHAPTER 20

THE FINANCIAL RIGHTS AND DUTIES OF A PARTNER

20–01 In taking partnership accounts it is necessary to differentiate between those expenses and losses which, as between the partners, are chargeable to the firm and those which are properly chargeable to one or more of the partners on an individual basis. Once the expenses and losses of the former class have been identified, it must be determined in what shares they are to be borne by the partners. This chapter is devoted to a consideration of these and other related issues which must be addressed when ascertaining a partner's financial rights and duties *vis-à-vis* his co-partners.

The fundamental principles

20–02 Writing prior to the Act, Lord Lindley observed that the following principles form the basis for this branch of partnership law:

"... it must always be borne in mind that every member of an ordinary firm is, to a certain extent, both a principal and an agent. He is liable as a principal to the debts and engagements of the firm, and in respect of them he is entitled to contribution from his co-partners; for they have no right to throw on him alone the burden of obligations which, *ex hypothesi*, are theirs as much as his.[1] Again, each member as an agent of the firm is entitled to be indemnified by the firm against losses and expenses bona fide incurred by him for the benefit of the firm, whilst pursuing the authority conferred upon him by the agreement entered into between himself and his co-partners.[2] On the other hand, a partner has no right to charge the firm with losses or expenses incurred by his own negligence or want of skill, or in disregard of the authority reposed in him."[3]

Partnership Act 1890, section 24

20–03 The above principles are clearly reflected in section 24 of the Partnership Act 1890 which, so far as material, provides as follows:

"24. The interests of partners in the partnership property and their rights and duties in relation to the partnership shall be determined,

---

[1] See *Lefroy v. Gore* (1844) 1 Jo. La T. 571; *Spottiswoode's Case* (1855) 6 De G.M. & G. 345; *Robinson's Case* (1856) 6 De G.M. & G. 572.

[2] See further, as to such agency, *supra*, paras. 12–01 *et seq.*

[3] *Bury v. Allen* (1845) 1 Colly. 589; *Thomas v. Atherton* (1878) 10 Ch.D. 185. See further *infra*, paras. 20–10, 20–11.

subject to any agreement express or implied between the partners, by the following rules:

(1) All the partners are entitled to share equally in the capital and profits of the business, and must contribute equally towards the losses whether of capital or otherwise sustained by the firm.

(2) The firm must indemnify every partner in respect of payments made and personal liabilities incurred by him
    (a) In the ordinary and proper conduct of the business of the firm; or
    (b) In or about anything necessarily done for the preservation of the business or property of the firm.

(3) A partner making, for the purpose of the partnership, any actual payment or advance beyond the amount of capital which he has agreed to subscribe, is entitled to interest at the rate of five per cent. per annum from the date of the payment or advance.

(4) A partner is not entitled, before the ascertainment of profits, to interest on the capital subscribed by him.

. . .

(6) No partner shall be entitled to remuneration for acting in the partnership business."

The practical application of these statutory rules can best be illustrated by considering the rights and duties of partners with respect to (1) debts, liabilities and losses; (2) outlays and advances; (3) interest; and (4) remuneration for services rendered to the firm.[4]

1. DEBTS, LIABILITIES AND LOSSES

General obligation of partners to contribute to losses

Section 24(1) and (2) of the Partnership Act 1890 clearly **20–04** establishes the rule that, in the absence of some other agreement, losses are to be borne by all the members of a firm in equal shares, thereby giving statutory recognition to principles which had long been recognised as fundamental to the law of partnership. Lord Lindley summarised the previous law in these terms:

---

[4] In earlier editions of this work, there appeared at this point an analysis of the general right of agents and trustees to a contribution or indemnity, both before and after the Judicature Acts. Save to the extent that points of principle of direct relevance to the law of partnership are concerned, the relevant passage has not been retained. For reference purposes, the original passage appeared in the 15th ed. at pp. 546 *et seq.*

"The general principle ... that partners must contribute rateably to their shares towards the losses and debts of the firm, is not open to question. Their obligation to contribute is not necessarily founded upon, although it may be modified and even excluded altogether by, agreement.[5] For example, where there is no agreement to the contrary, it is clear that if execution for a partnership debt contracted by all the partners, or by some of them when acting within the limits of their authority, is levied on any one partner, who is compelled to pay the whole debt, he is entitled to contribution from his co-partners.[6] So, if one partner enters into a contract on behalf of the firm, but in such a manner as to render himself alone liable to be sued, he is entitled to be indemnified by the firm, provided he has not, as between himself and his co-partners, exceeded his authority in entering into the contract[7]; and if, in such a case, he with their knowledge and consent defend an action brought against him, he is entitled to be indemnified by the firm against the damages, costs, and expenses which he may be compelled to pay."[8]

Sharing of losses: the general presumption

20–05   It is self evident from the terms of section 24(1) that, in the absence of any agreement to the contrary, each partner is entitled to an equal share of the firm's profits and must bear an equal share of the firm's losses.[9] However, where profits are divisible in some other proportions, the normal inference is that losses are to be divided in

---

[5] At this point Lord Lindley cross referred to an earlier passage, in which he had observed: "Whether a person who has suffered loss is entitled to be indemnified wholly or partly by others is a question which cannot be decided in the negative merely upon the ground that no agreement for contribution or indemnity has been entered into. An agreement may undoubtedly give rise to a right to indemnity or contribution; but the absence of an agreement giving rise to such a right, is by no means fatal to its existence. The general principle which prescribes equality of burden and of benefit, is amply sufficient to create a right of contribution in many cases in which it is impossible to found it upon any genuine contract, express or tacit. The common feature of such cases is, that one person has sustained some loss which would have fallen upon others as well as upon himself, but which has been averted from them at his expense ... In all these cases a right of contribution arises; not by virtue of any contract, but because the safety of some cannot justly be purchased at the expense of others; and all must therefore contribute to the loss sustained... But although a right to contribution may exist where there is no contract upon which it can be founded, it cannot exist if excluded by agreement; and it is so excluded whenever those who would otherwise be contributories have entered into any contract, express or tacit, amongst themselves, which is inconsistent with a right on the part of one to demand contribution from the others. This is too obvious to require comment, but it must be borne in mind as qualifying the common saying, that the right to contribution is independent of agreement." See generally, *Gillan v. Morrison* (1847) 1 De G. & S. 421; *Re Worcester Corn Exchange Co.* (1853) 3 De G.M. & G. 180; also *Mowatt and Elliott's Case* (1853) 3 De G.M. & G. 254; *Carew's Case* (1855) 7 De G.M. & G. 43. But note the terms of the Civil Liability (Contribution) Act 1978, s.7(3)(b); *quaere*, can the right to contribution under that Act be excluded by an *implied* as opposed to an express agreement?

[6] *Evans v. Yeatherd* (1824) 2 Bing. 132; *McOwen v. Hunter* (1838) 1 Dr. & Wal. 347; *Robinson's Executor's Case* (1856) 6 De G.M. & G. 572. See also *Lefroy v. Gore* (1844) 1 Jo. & La T. 571.

[7] *Gleadow v. Hull Glass Co.* (1849) 13 Jur. 1020; *Sedgwick's Case* (1856) 2 Jur. (N.S.) 949.

[8] *Browne v. Gibbins* (1725) 5 Bro P.C. 491; *Croxton's Case* (1852) 5 De G. & Sm. 432.

[9] Partnership Act 1890, s.24(1), *supra*, para. 20–03. See also *supra*, paras. 19–18 *et seq.*; and *Walker West Developments Ltd. v. F.J. Emmett Ltd.* (1979) 252 E.G. 1171.

those proportions, unless there is some express or implied agreement which requires them to be divided in some other way.[10] Accordingly, where one partner is compelled to pay more than his share of a partnership debt or incurs a personal liability in the course of carrying on the firm's business, he will in general be entitled to a contribution from his co-partners to the extent necessary to reflect those express or implied loss-sharing ratios.[11]

Presumption rebutted by evidence

However, the mere fact that a person is liable to third parties as a **20-06** partner does not necessarily render him liable, as between himself and his co-partners, to bear a share of the firm's losses: his co-partners may have agreed to indemnify him against such losses, in which case they cannot require him to contribute thereto.[12] This will frequently be the case with a so-called "salaried partner," who is liable on the basis of holding out[13] but whose entitlement to a fixed or variable "salary" (frequently expressed to be payable irrespective of the firm's profitability) is prima facie inconsistent with any liability to contribute towards losses *vis-à-vis* the other partners.[14] Accordingly, if such a partner is forced to meet a partnership debt or liability, he may be entitled to a *full* indemnity from his co-partners.

One partner unable to contribute his due share

As was the position in equity prior to the Judicature Acts, if one **20-07** partner is unable to contribute his due share of a loss, *e.g.* by reason of insolvency, the other partners must, in the absence of some other agreement, make good the defaulting partner's share in the relevant proportions.[15] Thus, in *Wadeson v. Richardson*,[16] one of four

---

[10] See *Re Albion Life Assurance Society* (1880) 16 Ch.D. 83, where this rule was recognised, but was held not to apply to policy-holders participating in profits. The inference referred to in the text is also supported by the terms of the Partnership Act 1890, s.44(a), *infra*, para. 25–40. See also *supra*, para. 10–69.

[11] Partnership Act 1890, s.24(2), *supra*, para. 20–03; *Wright v. Hunter* (1801) 5 Ves.Jr. 792. See also *Lefroy v. Gore* (1844) 1 Jo. & La T. 571; *Robinson's Executor's Case* (1856) 6 De G.M. & G. 572; *Hamilton v. Smith* (1859) 7 W.R. 173, as to promoters of companies.

[12] See *Geddes v. Wallace* (1820) 2 Bli. 270; also *Gillan v. Morrison* (1847) 1 De G. & Sm. 421; *Re Worcester Corn Exchange Co.* (1853) 3 De G.M. & G. 180; *Mowatt and Elliott's Case* (1853) 3 De G.M. & G. 254; *Carew's Case* (1855) 7 De G.M. & G. 43.

[13] Partnership Act 1890, s.14; see *supra*, paras. 5–43 *et seq.*

[14] See *Marsh v. Stacey* (1963) 107 S.J. 512; *Stekel v. Ellice* [1973] 1 W.L.R. 191; also the cases cited in n. 12 *supra*. The salaried partner's right to remuneration is prima facie inconsistent with such remuneration being of a negative amount; however, if there are no profits, such a partner may (but need not necessarily) forego his salary. See further, *supra*, para. 10–70.

[15] Lord Lindley illustrated the general proposition thus: "if A, B, C, and D are liable to a debt, A can compel B and C to contribute one-third each, if D can contribute nothing; and this, as between A, B, and C, is evidently only fair and just: *Dering v. Winchelsea* (1787) 1 Cox 318; *Hole v. Harrison* (1673) 1 Ch.Ca. 246; *Peter v. Rich* (1629) 1 Rep. Ch. 34." See also *Lowe v. Dixon* (1886) 16 Q.B.D. 455. Cf. the position at law: *Cowell v. Edwards* (1800) 2 Bos. & Pul. 268; *Batard v. Hawes* (1853) 2 E. &. B. 287. As to agreements negativing the equitable rule, see *McKewan's Case* (1877) 6 Ch.D. 447. Note also the terms of the Civil Liability (Contribution) Act 1978, *infra*, para. 20–16. And see, as to the manner in which losses of capital will be shared when one or more of the partners are insolvent, *infra*, paras. 25–45 *et seq.* As to the position where an insolvent firm is wound up as an unregistered company, see *infra*, paras. 27–60 *et seq.*

[16] (1812) 1 V. & B. 103.

partners assigned property to trustees upon trust *inter alia* to pay his proportion or share of all such debts as were or should be owing by him and the other three partners. On the subsequent bankruptcy of all four partners, it was held that the trustees were bound to pay not merely the share and proportion of the firm's debts which, as between the assignor and his co-partners, he was bound to contribute to the funds of the firm, but the share and proportion which, as between him and the firm's creditors, was required to ensure that those creditors received payment in full. The creditors were therefore entitled to come in under the deed for any balance which could not be recovered out of partnership funds or from the estates of the other partners.

20–08   The position will be the same where a loss is properly chargeable against only one partner, if he personally is unable to meet the liability.[17]

Losses for which one partner is primarily responsible

20–09   It is often (wrongly) supposed that a loss for which one partner is primarily responsible ought properly to be shared by his co-partners, but there in no justification for a departure from the normal principle in such a case *provided that* the relevant partner was himself acting properly. As Lord Lindley explained:

> "Even if a loss sustained by a firm is imputable to the conduct of one partner more than to that of another, still, if the former acted bona fide with a view to the benefit of the firm, and without any culpable negligence,[18] the loss must be borne equally by all."[19]

Thus, where A had represented to his co-partner B that a holding of shares in a certain company entailed only limited liability and B had thereupon, at A's request, authorised him to take shares on account of the firm, it was held that, as between A and B, B could not throw the loss on A alone when it transpired that the liability of the shareholders was not limited and A and B were both made contributories.[20] Similarly in *Cragg v. Ford*,[21] where the partnership

---

[17] See *Oldaker v. Lavender* (1833) 6 Sim. 239; *Cruikshank v. McVicar* (1844) 8 Beav. 106, 118, *per* Lord Langdale M.R. See further, as to such cases, *infra*, para. 20–10 *et seq.*

[18] *i.e. vis-à-vis* his co-partners. See *infra*, para. 20–10, n. 26.

[19] Notwithstanding what Lord Lindley said in this passage, losses are not necessarily shared equally: see *supra*, paras. 20–04, 20–05.

[20] *Ex p. Letts and Steer* (1857) 26 L.J.Ch. 455. See also *Lingard v. Bromley* (1812) 1 V. & B. 114.

[21] (1842) 1 Y. & C.Ch. 280.

between the plaintiff and the defendant had been dissolved and the winding-up of its affairs had devolved on the defendant, who had formerly acted as managing partner. Part of the partnership assets consisted of bales of cotton, and the plaintiff requested their immediate sale. The defendant, however, delayed the sale, as a result of which a much lower price was achieved. The plaintiff contended that the loss sustained by the postponement of the sale ought to be borne by the defendant alone, but the court held that the plaintiff could himself have sold the cotton, if he had so chosen, and that the defendant had acted bona fide and in the exercise of his discretion in delaying the sale. As a result, the loss fell to be borne by both of the former partners.

Cases of the above type must, however, be distinguished from those in which the loss arises out of a breach of the duty which one partner owes to his co-partners: these are considered in the following paragraphs.

Exceptions to the normal rights of contribution

Losses attributable to one partner's misconduct or negligence

Prior to the Partnership Act 1890, if a partner was guilty of a **20–10** breach of his duty to the firm and loss resulted therefrom, he was in effect required to bear the entirety of that loss. As Knight Bruce V.-C. observed in *Bury v. Allen*[22]:

"... it is, I apprehend, plain, that one of two partners may have a demand against the other for compensation, substantially in the nature of liquidated damages, enforceable in equity, and in equity only. Suppose the case of an act of fraud, or culpable negligence, or wilful default, by a partner during the partnership, to the damage of its property or interests, in breach of his duty to the partnership: whether at law compellable, or not compellable, he is certainly in equity compellable to compensate or indemnify the partnership in this respect."[23]

It is apprehended that the Partnership Act 1890 did not alter the law in this respect and that reliance may still be placed on the earlier cases, although it is not entirely clear *what* degree of misconduct or negligence is required to invoke this principle. The current editor takes the view that, consistently the Vice-chancellor's observations, something more than "mere" negligence must normally be shown,

---

[22] (1845) 1 Colly. 589, 604.
[23] See also *Thomas v. Atherton* (1878) 10 Ch.D. 185 (a case of gross negligence on the part of the managing partner of a mine).

i.e. gross negligence or recklessness in the course of carrying on the partnership business.[24] Thus, where a claim is made for payment of a debt allegedly (but not in fact) due from a firm and one partner chooses to pay it, he will not be permitted to charge such payment to the account of the firm.[25] Equally, it is difficult to see why the principle should not also be invoked in cases where a partner incurs a liability to a third party as a result of an act or omission which is negligent not as regards a third party but as regards his co-partners.[26]

In more obvious cases the position is not in doubt. So, where a partner has done an act which, though imputable to the firm on normal agency principles, is in fact a fraud on his co-partners, the latter will clearly be entitled, as between themselves and such partner (but *not* as between themselves and a third party), to throw any resultant losses onto him alone.[27] Again where one partner, without the authority of his co-partners, wilfully commits an illegal act, he will be required to indemnify them against the consequences.[28]

20–11   However, this principle will not apply if the relevant partner's conduct has been ratified by his co-partners and the loss accepted by them as a partnership loss which is to be shared by them all. However, in order to establish such ratification, the other partners must be shown to have *knowingly* allowed a loss properly chargeable to the account of one partner to be charged to the account of the firm and thus to have assumed liability therefor. This is clearly illustrated by the decision in *Cragg v. Ford*,[29] where the defendant had engaged in adventures not authorised by the partnership agreement. The plaintiff (his partner) protested but did not at the time object to the fact that losses attributable to those adventures were charged against the firm in the partnership books nor, indeed, did he insist that they should be borne by the defendant alone. However, when the partnership was later dissolved and its accounts taken, the plaintiff refused to allow the losses in question to be

---

[24] See *Thomas v. Atherton, supra.* But note that in *McIlreath v. Margetson* (1785) 4 Doug. 278, 279, Lord Mansfield merely observed that the defendant had been "guilty of negligence."

[25] *Re Webb* (1818) 8 Taunt. 443; also *McIlreath v. Margetson, supra,* where a payment was made bona fide and on the faith of false and fraudulent representations. *Quaere,* would the same rule apply if a partner paid a time-barred debt of the firm? See *Stahlschmidt v. Lett* (1853) 1 Sm. & G. 415.

[26] See, in particular, the reference to the plaintiff's "want of reasonable care" in *Thomas v. Atherton* (1878) 10 Ch.D. 185, 202. There appears to be a degree of confusion in this area as between the duty which a partner (and the firm) owes to third parties and the duties which partners owe each other. Equally, where a partner breaches an express or implied obligation to his co-partners, an independent right to damages may arise: see *infra,* paras. 23–195 *et seq.* And note the decision in *Gallagher v. Schulz* (1988) 2 N.Z.B.L.C. 103, 196 (where one partner with particular skills had encouraged the other to leave the organisation of a development project to him, with financially disastrous results).

[27] See *Robertson v. Southgate* (1848) 6 Hare 536.

[28] See *Campbell v. Campbell* (1839) 7 Cl. & F. 166. And see *infra,* paras. 20–13, 20–14.

[29] (1842) 1 Y. & C.Ch. 280; but see, as to losses arising from illegal acts, the observations of Lord Eldon on *Watts v. Brooks* (1798) 3 Ves.Jr. 612, in *Aubert v. Maze* (1801) 2 Bos. & Pul. 371; also *infra,* paras. 20–13, 20–14.

charged against the firm. The court held that, under the circumstances, the Master had not acted incorrectly in charging the losses against the firm and the plaintiff's objections were overruled.

As might be expected, questions of the above type will usually be raised in the course of taking accounts between the partners.[30]

Partnership induced by fraud or misrepresentation

Where a person is induced to join a partnership by the fraud or **20–12** misrepresentation of one or more of the other partners, he is entitled to rescind the partnership contract and, as between himself and his co-partners, to throw all losses upon the guilty partner(s).[31]

Illegal partnerships

It has already been pointed out that one member of an illegal **20–13** partnership cannot maintain an action for a contribution against another;[32] however, the mere fact that an illegal act has been committed will not of itself constitute a defence to such an action, unless the illegality taints the partnership itself.[33] As Lord Lindley pointed out,

"... there is no authority for saying that if one of the members of a firm sustains a loss owing to some illegal act not attributable to him, but nevertheless imputable to the firm, such loss must be borne entirely by him, and that he is not entitled to contribution in respect thereof from the other partners."[34]

Equally, if the illegal act was committed by the partner seeking a contribution and he knew or ought to have known of its illegality, his claim must necessarily fail, leaving him alone to face the consequences of that act.[35]

---

[30] See *Bury v. Allen* (1845) 1 Colly. 589, 604, *per* Knight Bruce V.-C. As to the circumstances in which accounts will be ordered between partners, see *infra*, paras. 23–71 *et seq.*

[31] See the Partnership Act 1890, s.41, *infra*, paras. 23–52 *et seq.*; also *Pillans v. Harkness* (1713) Colles P.C. 442; *Rawlins v. Wickham* (1858) 1 Giff. 355 and, on appeal, 3 De G. & J. 304; *Adam v. Newbigging* (1888) 13 App.Cas. 308. And see *Carew's Case* (1855) 7 De G.M. & G. 43.

[32] See *supra*, paras. 8–52 *et seq.*

[33] See *supra*, paras. 8–60 *et seq.*

[34] See (at law) *Adamson v. Jarvis* (1827) 4 Bing. 66; *Betts v. Gibbins* (1834) 2 A. & E. 57; and (in equity) *Lingard v. Bromley* (1812) 1 V. & B. 114; *Baynard v. Woolley* (1855) 20 Beav. 583; *Ashurst v. Mason* (1875) 20 Eq. 225; *Ramskill v. Edwards* (1885) 31 Ch.D. 100; *Jackson v. Dickinson* [1903] 1 Ch. 947, in which the principle of *Ashurst v. Mason* was explained and applied to the case of a breach of trust and contribution between trustees. As to criminal acts, see *R. Leslie Ltd. v. Reliable Advertising, etc. Agency* [1915] 1 K.B. 652; also *Weld Blundell v. Stephens* [1919] 1 K.B. 520, 529, 539, *per* Scrutton L.J. *Quaere*, can the decision in *Campbell v. Campbell* (1839) 7 Cl. & F. 166 be reconciled with the former decision, where it was not cited? See also *Wooley v. Batte* (1826) 2 Car. & P. 417; *Pearson v. Skelton* (1836) 1 M. & W. 504; *Thomas v. Atherton* (1878) 10 Ch.D. 185.

[35] See *Adamson v. Jarvis* (1827) 4 Bing. 66; *Betts v. Gibbins* (1834) 2 A. & E. 57; *Thomas v. Atherton* (1878) 10 Ch.D. 185. See also *Burrows v. Rhodes* [1899] 1 Q.B. 816; *Haseldine v. Hosken* [1933] 1 K.B. 822.

20–14   The more difficult case is where an unlawful act has been knowingly committed by all the partners, so that they all are *in pari delicto*. Although there is a dictum of Lord Cottenham which might be cited in support of the proposition that, in such a case, each partner must bear any loss which he may happen to sustain without any contribution from his co-partners,[36] there is, in Lord Lindley's words,

> "a decision which goes far to show that the loss ought to be apportioned between all the partners,[37] unless the illegal act in question is a pure tort,[38] or a direct violation of some statute, or unless the contract of partnership is itself void on the ground of illegality."

Breach of trust

20–15   On the basis of the above principle, Lord Lindley apprehended that, in the case of a breach of trust committed by all the members of a firm, if one partner were to make good the breach out of his own moneys, he would be allowed, in taking the partnership accounts, to charge his co-partners, rateably with himself, with the amount so paid.[39]

Civil Liability (Contribution) Act 1978

20–16   This Act places the right to contribution in respect of damages, both as between partners or other wrongdoers, on a clear statutory footing.[40]

Having established that judgment recovered against any person liable in respect of damage suffered as a result of a tort, breach of contract, breach of trust or otherwise is no longer a bar to an action against another person jointly liable in respect of the same damage,[41] the Act provides that any person liable or bona fide compromising a claim in respect of such damage[42] may recover a contribution from

---

[36] See *Att.-Gen. v. Wilson* (1840) Cr. & Ph. 1, 28, *per* Lord Cottenham L.C.

[37] See *Baynard v. Woolley* (1855) 20 Beav. 583. But see also *Thomas v. Atherton* (1878) 10 Ch. D. 185.

[38] This exception must now be read subject to the wide provisions of the Civil Liability (Contribution) Act 1978: see *infra*, para. 20–16. And note also the decision in *K. v. P.* [1993] Ch. 140.

[39] See *Ashurst v. Mason* (1875) 20 Eq. 225; *Jackson v. Dickinson* [1903] 1 Ch. 947; also *Baynard v. Woolley* (1855) 20 Beav. 583. And see the Civil Liability (Contribution) Act 1978, ss.1, 2, 6(1), noticed *infra*.

[40] See *K. v. P.* [1993] Ch. 140.

[41] Civil Liability (Contribution) Act 1978, ss.3, 6(1). The former section also applies to debts. However, in the case of an action for damages (but not debt), a successful plaintiff may be deprived of his costs in any action other than that in which judgment is first given: *ibid.* s.4.

[42] See *ibid.* s.1(4).

any person liable in respect of the same damage, *whether jointly with him or otherwise.*[43] A contribution may be obtained notwithstanding that the person claiming it, or the person from whom it is claimed, has subsequently ceased to be liable in respect of such damage, unless (in the latter case) he has ceased to be liable by reason of a limitation defence[44] and, moreover, cannot be defeated by a defence of *ex turpi causa non oritur actio.*[45] The amount of the contribution is in the court's discretion, regard being had to responsibility for the damage.[46] The court also has power to exempt any person from liability to make a contribution, or to direct that the contribution to be recovered from any person will amount to a complete indemnity.[47]

The Act does not affect any express or implied contractual or other **20–17** right to indemnity, but it would seem that the statutory right to *contribution* may only be excluded by means of an express contractual provision.[48]

The right to contribution will be lost two years after the date on which it accrued, *i.e.* the date of any judgment or arbitration award or, where some form of compensation payment is to be made, the earliest date on which its amount is agreed.[49]

Time for claiming contribution or indemnity

As was the position in equity prior to the passing of the Judicature **20–18** Acts, any person entitled to a contribution or indemnity from another can, even in the absence of any special agreement, enforce his right before sustaining an actual loss,[50] provided that a loss is imminent.[51] Thus, where continuing partners have agreed to indemnify an outgoing partner or the estate of a deceased partner against partnership liabilities, the creditor must have made a demand for payment before the right to indemnity can be pursued.[52] Similarly, where partners are individually liable to be sued on a bond or promissory note, which as between them and their co-partners is to

---

[43] *Ibid.* s.1(1).

[44] *Ibid.* s.1(2), (3). Judgment given in any action brought by the person suffering the damage is conclusive evidence in the contribution proceedings as to any issue determined thereby in favour of the person from whom contribution is sought: *ibid.* s.1(5).

[45] See *K. v. P.* [1993] Ch. 140. Note, however, that Ferris J. contemplated that, in cases affected by illegality, the court *might* set the contribution at zero: *ibid.* p. 149B.

[46] Civil Liability (Contribution) Act 1978, s.2(1). And see the preceding note.

[47] *Ibid.* s.2(2). See also *Semtex v. Gladstone* [1954] 1 W.L.R. 945; *Lister v. Romford Ice and Cold Storage Co.* [1957] A.C. 555 (decisions under the former Law Reform (Married Women and Tortfeasors) Act 1935).

[48] *Ibid.* s.7(3). The Act does not, however, render enforceable any agreement for indemnity or contribution which would not be enforceable apart from the Act: *ibid.*

[49] Limitation Act 1980, s.10.

[50] See *Lacey v. Hill* (1874) L.R. 18 Eq. 182; *Hobbs v. Wayet* (1887) 36 Ch.D. 256; *Ex p. Governors of St. Thomas's Hospital* [1911] 2 K.B. 705.

[51] *Ibid.*; *Hughes-Hallett v. Indian Mammoth Gold Mines Co.* (1882) 22 Ch.D. 561.

[52] *Bradford v. Gammon* [1925] 1 Ch. 132.

be regarded as the bond or note of the firm, they are entitled to call for contribution before it is actually paid.[53] Nevertheless, such a claim as between partners may (and, indeed, usually will) entail the taking of an account.[54]

2. OUTLAYS AND ADVANCES

Outlays and advances made by one partner

20–19   Even before that right was expressly recognised by the Partnership Act 1890,[55] a partner was entitled to charge the partnership with sums bona fide expended by him in conducting its business.[56] This was made clear by Lord Hardwicke in *West v. Skip*,[57] when he observed that:

> "when an account is to be taken, each [*partner*] is intitled to be allowed against the other everything he has advanced or brought in as a partnership transaction, and to charge the other in the account with what that other has not brought in, or has taken out more than he ought; and nothing is to be considered as his share, but his proportion of the residue on balance of the account."[58]

20–20   On this principle, a partner is clearly entitled to charge the firm with any sums he may have been compelled to pay in respect of its debts[59] or in respect of an obligation which he has personally incurred at the request of the firm,[60] or indeed where he sacrifices a debt due to himself in order to enable the firm to recover its own debt.[61]

Authorised but useless outlays

20–21   It need hardly be pointed out that moneys laid out by a partner for the benefit of the firm with the consent of his co-partners must be

---

[53] See, for example, *Norwich Yarn Co.'s Case* (1850) 22 Beav. 143. Lord Lindley appended the following comment: "the money borrowed by the directors in that case was secured by their own notes, but these notes had not been actually paid when the call on the shareholders was made. This does not appear very clearly from the report referred to, but the writer was informed by persons conversant with the case that the above statement is correct."

[54] See further, as to the taking of partnership accounts, *infra*, paras. 23–70 *et seq.*

[55] *Ibid.* s.24(2), *supra*, para. 20–03.

[56] See *Burden v. Burden* (1813) 1 V. & B. 172, where a surviving partner (who was also an executor) was allowed to charge expenses actually incurred, but not an allowance for his time and trouble. *Cf. Hutcheson v. Smith* (1842) 5 I.Eq.R. 117. See also *infra*, paras. 20–40 *et seq.* And note *Ex p. Chippendale* (1854) 4 De G.M. & G. 19; *Ex p. Sedgwick* (1856) 2 Jur. (N.S.) 949 (both of which concerned mining companies).

[57] (1749) 1 Ves.Sen. 239, 241.

[58] See also *supra*, paras. 19–04 *et seq.*

[59] *Prole v. Masterman* (1855) 21 Beav. 61. As to the position where a partner negligently pays a debt claimed but not due, see *Re Webb* (1818) 8 Taunt. 443; *McIlreath v. Margetson* (1785) 4 Doug. 278, noticed *supra*, para. 20–10, n. 25.

[60] *Gleadow v. Hull Glass Co.* (1849) 13 Jur. 1020; *Croxton's Case* (1852) 5 De G. & Sm. 432; *Sedgwick's Case* (1856) 2 Jur. (N.S.) 949.

[61] *Lefroy v. Gore* (1844) 1 Jo. & La T. 571, where one partner released a witness whose evidence was essential to the firm.

made good by the firm, however useless such outlay may have been. Thus, if a partner personally finances the purchase by his firm of a particular patent, the purchase price will be chargeable to the firm, even if the patent proves wholly worthless.[62] On the other hand, if such an outlay is not authorised in advance, it cannot be charged to the firm unless it is subsequently ratified by the other partners or the firm's assets have been increased or preserved thereby.[63]

Unauthorised but useful outlays

An outlay made by a partner, which is otherwise proper and even **20–22** necessary for the conduct of the partnership business, cannot be charged to the firm, if that would be inconsistent with (or, more obviously, a breach of) the partnership agreement. In *Thornton v. Proctor*,[64] the plaintiff and the defendant were in partnership as wine-merchants and the plaintiff, who had for some time been primarily responsible for running the business, had spent considerable sums entertaining customers, which was found to be a necessary incident of the trade. In keeping the accounts of the partnership, which he had done for several years, the plaintiff neither made any charge for such entertainment nor sought any allowance therefor. He nevertheless subsequently contended that an entertainment allowance of £50 a year ought to be made in taking the accounts of the partnership and proved this to be a reasonable sum. However, it was demonstrated that, in such cases, a specific provision authorising the payment of such an allowance would usually be included in the partnership agreement, whereas the agreement under consideration contained no such provision, but merely a general stipulation that all losses and expenses should be borne by the partners equally. It was accordingly held that the plaintiff was not entitled to the allowance claimed; although he might have treated the sums laid out as a direct partnership expense, he was precluded from doing so by omitting them from the annual accounts.

Particulars of outlays

A partner may not charge the firm with moneys allegedly laid out **20–23** by him for its benefit if he declines to give particulars thereof. Thus, he cannot charge for expenditure incurred in securing or rewarding the services of third parties, the nature of which he refuses to

---

[62] *Gleadow v. Hull Glass Co.* (1849) 13 Jur. 1020.
[63] The latter qualification is rendered necessary by *Ex p. Chippendale* (1854) 4 De G M. & G. 19. See further *supra*, paras. 12–193 *et seq.*
[64] (1792) 1 Anst. 94. See also *East India Co. v. Blake* (1673) Finch 117; *Hutcheson v. Smith* (1842) 5 I.Eq.R. 117.

disclose,[65] nor for general expenses.[66] Moreover, he obviously cannot charge the firm with travelling expenses, unless they were bona fide and properly incurred by him when travelling on partnership business.[67]

Transactions between partners

20–24   Where a partner pays for a valuation required in connection with a transaction between himself and his co-partners which is subsequently set aside on the application of those other partners, they cannot be charged with any part of the valuation costs.[68]

Outlays by the firm on a partner's own property

20–25   Where a firm expends money for the benefit of a partner, the outlay will in general amount to a loan by the firm in his favour and must be treated as such in taking the partnership accounts. However, more difficult cases inevitably arise, such as where a firm expends money on property which is owned by one of the partners but used by the firm for the purposes of its business. In the absence of a specific agreement or circumstances giving rise to a "proprietary estoppel,"[69] Lord Lindley took the view that

> "... justice seems to require that in taking the partnership accounts the owner of the property in question should not be allowed exclusively to gain the benefit of the outlay, but that the improved value of his property should be treated as a partnership asset, and be shared between him and his co-partners accordingly."[70]

20–26   Thus, in *Burdon v. Barkus*,[71] a managing partner had, with the knowledge of his co-partner, expended partnership moneys in sinking a pit on the latter's land for partnership purposes. The managing partner had erroneously supposed that the partnership was for a term of years, but it was suddenly and unexpectedly dissolved and the pit thereby became the sole property of the landowning partner. An inquiry was directed as to whether any allowances should be made in respect of the outlay in sinking the pit. A similar inquiry was directed

---

[65] See *York and North Midland Ry. v. Hudson* (1845) 16 Beav. 485.
[66] *East India Co. v. Blake* (1673) Finch 117.
[67] *Stainton v. The Carron Co.* (1857) 24 Beav. 346.
[68] *Stocken v. Dawson* (1843) 6 Beav. 375.
[69] See *supra*, para. 18–41.
[70] See *supra*, paras. 18–37 *et seq*. But note the decision in *Harvey v. Harvey* (1970) 120 C.L.R. 529; also *Harwood v. Harwood* [1991] 2 F.L.R. 274.
[71] (1862) 4 De G. F. & J. 42.

in *Pawsey v. Armstrong*,[72] in respect of buildings erected by a firm on the property of one of the partners.

3. INTEREST

Interest not generally payable

As a matter of general law, a loan does not bear interest in the 20–27 absence of some contrary custom or agreement.[73] Mercantile custom has, however, long recognised the commercial realities which justify a demand for interest in cases where it would not otherwise have been payable.[74] Furthermore, the court has a wide statutory power to award interest in any proceedings brought for the recovery of a debt.[75]

It is accordingly necessary, when applying what appears to be a general rule *against* the allowance of interest in the taking of partnership accounts,[76] to have regard not only to any express agreement between the partners, but also to the firm's accounting practices and (where relevant) to the customs of the trade which it seeks to carry on.

Interest on capital

The Partnership Act 1890[77] confirms the pre-existing rule that 20–28 partners are not, in the absence of some contrary agreement, entitled to interest on their respective capital contributions; however, an agreement for the payment of interest may be inferred if the partners have themselves been in the habit of charging such interest in their accounts.[78] The rule applies even where one partner has brought in his agreed sum of capital but his co-partner has not[79] and as against a person remunerated for his services by a share of profits.[80]

---

[72] (1881) 18 Ch.D. 698. See also *Miles v. Clarke* [1953] 1 W.L.R. 537; *Faulks v. Faulks* [1992] 15 E.G. 82, 95, *per* Chadwick J.; *cf. the Bank of England Case* (1861) 3 De G.F. & J. 645; and see *supra*, para. 18–37.

[73] This rule prevailed both at common law and in equity and was doubtless attributable to the old laws against usury. See (for the position at law) *Calton v. Bragg* (1812) 15 East 223; *Gwyn v. Godby* (1812) 4 Taunt. 346; *Higgins v. Sargent* (1823) 2 B. & C. 349; *Shaw v. Picton* (1825) 4 B. & C. 723; *Page v. Newman* (1829) 9 B. & C. 378; and (in equity) *Tew v. Earl of Winterton* (1792) 1 Ves.Jr. 451; *Creuze v. Hunter* (1793) 2 Ves.Jr. 157; *Booth v. Leycester* (1838) 3 Myl. & Cr. 459.

[74] See *Ex p. Chippendale* (1854) 4 De G.M. & G. 19.

[75] Supreme Court Act 1981, s.35A; County Courts Act 1984, s.69: see *infra*, para. 20–39.

[76] Although Lord Lindley recognised the existence of this general rule, he had previously observed "The principles on which, in taking partnership accounts, interest is allowed or disallowed, do not appear to be well settled. The state of the authorities is, in fact, not such as to justify the deduction from them of any general principle upon this important subject."

[77] *Ibid.* s.24(3): see *supra*, para. 20–03. And see *supra*, para. 17–13, n. 32.

[78] See *Millar v. Craig* (1843) 6 Beav. 433; *Cooke v. Benbow* (1865) 3 De G.J. & S. 1 (where interest was allowed); also *Pim v. Harris* (1876) Ir.Rep. 10 Eq. 442, where the decision was based on the terms of the contract.

[79] *Hill v. King* (1863) 3 De G.J. & Sm. 418.

[80] *Rishton v. Grissell* (1870) L.R. 10 Eq. 393, where the capital had been borrowed at interest.

20-29   The mere fact that interest is payable on capital does not necessarily mean that such interest is also payable on undrawn profits,[81] unless they can be treated as an advance.[82]

Position following a general dissolution

20-30   It scarcely needs to be stated that, if interest on capital is not payable whilst the partnership is continuing, it will not be payable following a general dissolution.[83] Indeed, where interest on capital *is* payable under an agreement, the partners' continuing entitlement thereto will automatically cease in the event of a dissolution, unless there is an express provision to the contrary.[84]

20-31   However, in either case the partners may still retain a residual entitlement in lieu of any right to interest. As will be seen hereafter, on a general dissolution the assets of the partnership will normally be converted into cash and the fund thereby produced applied in the manner set out in section 44 of the Partnership Act 1890.[85] If, after the payment of the firm's debts and liabilities and the repayment of any advances, that fund is more than sufficient to repay the partners' capital contributions,[86] each such contribution will carry its proportionate share of the income of the fund, which must be accounted for *before* the ultimate residue (if any) is divided between the partners.[87]

Interest on advances

20-32   Where a partner advances money to the firm over and above his capital contribution, the advance is, as might be expected, treated not as an increase in his capital but as a loan on which interest ought to be paid,[88] and this is expressly recognised in the Partnership Act 1890.[89] Accordingly, provided that the advance was made for

---

[81] *Dinham v. Bradford* (1869) L.R. 5 Ch.App. 519. See also *Rishton v. Grissell* (1870) 10 Eq. 393, as to interest on arrears of a share of profits. *Quaere* whether such undrawn profits are to be treated as advances attracting interest under the Partnership Act 1890, s.24(3): see *infra*, para. 20-33. In many firms, undrawn profits are indiscriminately credited to the partners' capital accounts, and it may be extremely difficult to ascertain their true status: see *supra*, para. 17-07.
[82] See the Partnership Act 1890, s.24(3) and *infra*, para. 20-32.
[83] But see *ibid.* s.42, *infra*, paras. 25-21 *et seq.*
[84] *Barfield v. Loughborough* (1872) L.R. 8 Ch.App. 1; *Watney v. Wells* (1861) L.R. 2 Ch.App. 250; Lord Lindley observed that the contrary decision in *Pilling v. Pilling* (1887) 3 De G.J. & S. 162 is, on this point, "practically overruled." As to the calculation of interest where the capital is payable by instalments with interest, see *Ewing v. Ewing* (1882) 8 App.Cas. 822.
[85] See *infra*, paras. 23-179 *et seq.*, 25-39 *et seq.*
[86] Partnership Act 1890, s.44(b), paras. 1-3.
[87] *Watney v. Wells* (1861) L.R. 2 Ch.App. 250. *Quaere*, could this principle be extended to a case where the partners' capital contributions are, in effect, represented by an income producing asset of the former firm which has not yet been realised? But see *Barfield v. Loughborough* (1872) L.R. 8 Ch.App. 1, 3, 4, *per* Lord Selborne L.C.
[88] See *Ex p. Chippendale* (1854) 4 De G.M. & G. 19; also *Omychund v. Barker* (1744) Collyer on Partnership (2nd ed.), 231, note; *Denton v. Rodie* (1813) 3 Camp. 493. *Per contra, Stevens v. Cook* (1859) 5 Jur.(N.S.) 1415.
[89] *Ibid.* s.24(3): see *supra*, para. 20-03.

partnership purposes, simple interest will be payable thereon at the rate of 5 per cent.[90] However, an agreement to pay a different rate may be inferred if interest at that rate has been charged and allowed in the books of the firm[91] or, perhaps, where it is payable by the custom of the particular trade.[92]

Interest on overdrawings and balances in hand

Of the converse situation, *i.e.* a partner owing money to the firm, **20–33** Lord Lindley observed:

"Inasmuch as what is fair for one partner is so for another, and the firm when debtor is charged with interest, it seems to follow that if one partner is indebted to the firm either in respect of money borrowed, or in respect of balances in his hands, he ought to be charged with interest on the amount so owing, even though on the balance of the whole account, a sum might be due to him.[93] Except, however, where there has been a fraudulent retention,[94] or an improper application[95] of money of the firm, it is not the practice of the Court to charge a partner with interest on money of the firm in his hands[96]; for example, under ordinary circumstances a partner is not charged with interest on sums drawn out by him or advanced to him."[97]

Although Lord Lindley cited the decision in *Rhodes v. Rhodes*[98] in this context, the current editor submits it is not directly in point. There A and B were partners; A died and his son and executor, C, succeeded him in partnership with B. B then retired in favour of his own son, D. At the time of his retirement, a considerable sum was

---

[90] *Ibid.* And see, as to the position prior to the Act, *Ex p. Bignold* (1856) 22 Beav. 143; *Troup's Case* (1860) 29 Beav. 353. See also *Hart v. Clarke* (1854) 6 De G.M. & G. 232, 254, *per* Turner L.J. (affirmed *sub nom. Clarke v. Hart* (1858) 6 H.L.C. 633).

[91] As in *Re Magdalena Steam Navigation Co.* (1860) Johns. 690, where interest at 6 per cent was allowed.

[92] As to compound interest in the case of bankers, see *National Bank of Greece S.A. v. Pinios Shipping Co. No. 1* [1990] 1 A.C. 637, where the authorities are reviewed. *Sed quaere*, would such a custom necessarily justify the implication of an agreement for the payment of interest at such a rate, in the face of the statutory rate under the Act? Note also the exceptional decision in *Roxburgh Dinardo & Partners' Judicial Factor v. Dinardo*, 1993 S.L.T. 16 (2nd Div.), noticed *infra*, para. 20–36.

[93] See *Beecher v. Guilburn* (1726) Moseley 3.

[94] As in *Hutcheson v. Smith* (1842) 5 I.Eq.R. 117, where, however, the partner retaining the money was also a receiver appointed by the court.

[95] As in *Evans v. Coventry* (1857) 8 De G.M. & G. 835; see also *Daniels v. Angus* [1947] N.Z.L.R. 329.

[96] See *Webster v. Bray* (1849) 7 Hare 159, where interest on balances in the hands of the defendants was sought but not obtained. See also *Stevens v. Cook* (1859) 5 Jur.(n.s.) 1415; *Turner v. Burkinshaw* (1867) L.R. 2 Ch.App. 488.

[97] *Meymott v. Meymott* (1862) 31 Beav. 445; *Cooke v. Benbow* (1865) 3 De G.J. & S. 1; *Barfield v. Loughborough* (1872) L.R. 8 Ch.App. 1, 7, *per* Lord Selborne L.C.

[98] (1860) 6 Jur.(n.s.) 600. See also *Barfield v. Loughborough* (1872) L.R. 8 Ch.App. 1, 7, *per* Lord Selborne.

due to B from A's estate in respect of moneys drawn out by A. This sum was treated as a debt of the new firm of C and D, and was not paid. B died and his executors claimed interest but only from the date of B's retirement: the claim was rejected on the ground that there was no agreement for the payment of interest and that such a claim was in any event inconsistent with the course of dealing between the partners themselves. It should be noted that, in a case of this type, interest might now be awarded by the court under its statutory jurisdiction.[99]

Interest on benefits obtained by one partner

20–34   Where one partner successfully claims to share a benefit obtained by his co-partner, he must, as the price of obtaining such relief, give credit for all expenditure bona fide incurred in obtaining that benefit together with interest on his (the claimant's) due share thereof at the rate of 5 per cent.[1] On the other hand, where a partner has, in breach of the duty of good faith, obtained money for which he is bound to account to the firm, he will be charged with interest thereon at the rate of 4 per cent,[2] unless the court were prepared to award interest at a higher rate.[3]

Interest following a dissolution

20–35   Where a partnership has been dissolved by the death of one partner and the surviving partner keeps the accounts in such a way that the balances due to himself and to the deceased partner's estate cannot be ascertained for a considerable time, neither the surviving partner nor his representatives can claim interest on the sum ultimately found due to him or his estate.[4]

20–36   This may be contrasted with the exceptional decision in *Roxburgh Dinardo & Partners' Judicial Factor v. Dinardo*,[5] where a Scottish firm had been dissolved and a judicial factor (X) had *de facto* distributed its assets between the partners in such a way that one

---

[99] Supreme Court Act 1981 s.35A; County Courts Act 1984, s.69: see *infra*, para. 20–39.

[1] See *Hart v. Clarke* (1854) 6 De G.M. & G. 232, 254, *per* Turner L.J. The order was subsequently affirmed at (1858) 6 H.L.C. 633. See also *Perens v. Johnson* (1857) 3 Sm. & G. 419.

[2] See *Fawcett v. Whitehouse* (1829) 1 Russ. & M. 132.

[3] See *Wallersteiner v. Moir* (*No. 2*) [1975] Q.B. 373 (compound interest at 1 per cent. above bank base rate/minimum lending rate with yearly rests awarded where a party had improperly profited from a fiduciary position); *O'Sullivan v. Management Agency and Music Ltd.* [1985] Q.B. 428; *Westdeutsche Landesbank Girozentrale v. Islington London Borough Council, The Times,* December 30, 1993. In *Roxburgh Dinardo & Partners' Judicial Factor v. Dinardo*, 1993 S.L.T. 16 (2nd Div.) (noticed *infra*, para. 20–36), compound interest at an unspecified rate was awarded as between partners, albeit in unusual circumstances. The older cases should be approached with caution: *e.g.* interest at only 3 per cent. was awarded in *Re Olympia Ltd.* [1898] 2 Ch. 153 and *Barclay v. Andrews* [1899] 1 Ch. 674; *cf.* the remarks of Lord Macnaghten in *Gluckstein v. Barnes* [1900] A.C. 240, 255.

[4] *Boddam v. Ryley* (1787) 4 Bro.P.C. 561. But see also *supra*, para. 20–33.

[5] 1993, S.L.T. 16 (2nd Div.).

partner (A) took the net assets whilst the other (B) took the net liabilities.[6] When X sought the court's approval for a scheme of division of those assets, he sought to charge A with compound interest in respect of the assets in his hands. The court held that such interest was, on the facts, properly chargeable, since B had had to finance the liabilities which he had taken over on overdraft, in respect of which compound interest was obviously payable. It was also held that compound interest could in any event be charged against A on the grounds that he was accountable for the assets in his hands as a result of his fiduciary relationship with B.

A partner may also be entitled to interest at the rate of 5 per cent. **20–37** pursuant to section 42 of the Partnership Act 1890 where, following a dissolution, the remaining partners continue to carry on the business without any settlement of accounts as regards him.[7]

Alien enemy

It is apprehended that any entitlement which a partner may have to **20–38** interest will not cease if he becomes an alien enemy,[8] so that interest will continue to accrue during the relevant hostilities even though it cannot be recovered until they are concluded.[9]

Interest awarded by the court

The High Court[10] and the county court[11] have power to order the **20–39** inclusion, in the judgment given in any proceedings for the recovery of a debt or damages, of simple interest at such rate as they think fit, or as rules of court may provide, on all or part of the debt or damages for all or any part of the period between the date when the cause of action arose and the date of judgment.[12] Such interest is payable without deduction of tax.[13] It is perhaps, questionable to

---

[6] It appears that such a distribution was not agreed by A and B.

[7] *Quaere*, does this section apply on a *general* dissolution? See, *infra*, paras. 25–23 *et seq.*

[8] See, as to the meaning of this expression, *supra*, para. 4–04.

[9] *Hugh Stevenson & Sons v. Aktiengesellschaft für Cartonnagen Industrie* [1918] A.C. 239, 245, *per* Finlay L.C.

[10] Supreme Court Act 1981, s.35A (as inserted by the Administration of Justice Act 1982, s.15, Sched. 1). This power superseded the provisions of the Law Reform (Miscellaneous Provisions) Act 1934, s.3. Note also that an arbitrator may now award interest: s.19A of the Arbitration Act 1950 (as inserted by *ibid.*).

[11] County Courts Act 1984, s.69.

[12] Where a sum is paid before judgment, interest may be ordered down to the date of payment: Supreme Court Act 1981, s.35A(1)(a); County Courts Act 1984, s.69(1)(a); but see *Wadsworth v. Lydall* [1981] 1 W.L.R. 598; *President of India v. La Pintada Compania* [1985] A.C. 104, as to the position where a debt is paid late, but prior to the commencement of proceedings. Where interest already runs on a debt, no interest may be ordered under either section: s.35A(4) of the 1981 Act and s.69(4) of the 1984 Act.

[13] The only cases in which tax may now be deducted at source from interest payments are those set out in the Income and Corporation Taxes Act 1988, s.349 (as amended); interest of the kind considered in the text does not fall within these provisions.

what extent the statutory power has altered the rights of partners to interest as between themselves: certainly, where a balance can be shown to be due to a partner following the taking of a partnership account, there is in principle no reason why the court should not order the payment of interest under its statutory power.[14] What is more difficult is the question whether such an order can be made in a case to which section 42 of the Partnership Act 1890 would otherwise apply.[15] Although both the Supreme Court Act 1981 and the County Courts Act 1984 provide that interest shall not be awarded in respect of a period "during which, for whatever reason, interest on the debt already runs",[16] a claim for interest under section 42 of the 1890 Act is at the *option* of the outgoing partner. The current editor tentatively submits that the jurisdictions are co-extensive, so that a claim for interest can properly be formulated under the 1981 or 1984 Act (as appropriate) at a rate greater than 5 per cent.[17]

4.   REMUNERATION FOR SERVICES RENDERED TO FIRM

The general rule

20–40   Writing prior to the Partnership Act 1890, Lord Lindley stated the general rule as follows:

> "Under ordinary circumstances the contract of partnership excludes any implied contract for payment for services rendered for the firm by any of its members.[18] Consequently, under ordinary circumstances and in the absence of an agreement to that effect, one partner cannot charge his co-partners with any sum for compensation, whether in the shape of salary, commission, or otherwise, on account of his own trouble in conducting the partnership business."

This rule was given statutory force by section 24(6) of the Partnership Act 1890.[19]

---

[14] Although a partner was awarded interest (pursuant to the Law Reform (Miscellaneous Provisions) Act 1934) in respect of sums due under a dissolution agreement in *Wadsworth v. Lydall* [1981] C.L.Y. 2015 (this point not being referred to in the report at [1981] 1 W.L.R. 598), his entitlement thereto could not have been seriously questioned even by reference to the older cases.
[15] See *infra*, paras. 25–23 *et seq.*
[16] Supreme Court Act 1981, s.35A(4); County Courts Act 1984, s.69(4).
[17] See also *Sobell v. Boston* [1975] 1 W.L.R. 1587. In the current editor's experience, claims for interest under the Supreme Court Act 1981 or the County Courts Act 1984 are now routinely pleaded in such cases. Obviously if a share of profits is sought, the claim *must* be formulated under the 1890 Act. See also *infra*, para. 25–38.
[18] *Holmes v. Higgins* (1822) 1 B. & C. 74. *Cf. Thompson v. Williamson* (1831) 7 Bli.(N.S.) 432, *per* Lord Wynford.
[19] See *supra*, para. 20–03.

On this basis it was held that, in taking the accounts of three **20-41**
successive firms, comprising (1) A and B, (2) A, B and C, and (3) B
and C, the latter firm was not entitled to charge a commission for
collecting the debts due to the two preceding firms.[20] Similarly, a
partner employed to buy or sell goods for his firm was not permitted
to charge commission for so doing.[21]

It is clear that a managing partner has no greater right to
remuneration than any other partner.[22]

Where (exceptionally) it is agreed that a partner *will* be
remunerated in respect of services provided to the firm in his capacity
as a partner, any remuneration paid to him will not be deductible by
the firm for income tax purposes.[23]

Exceptions to the general rule

Wilful inattention to business

The general rule will be applied no matter how unequal the effort **20-42**
which each partner may put into promoting the success and
prosperity of the firm.[24] Where, however, the partnership agreement
imposes an express (or, perhaps, an implied) obligation on the
partners to attend to the firm's affairs,[25] the position may be
different, as Lord Lindley pointed out:

"... where, as is usually the case, it is the duty of each partner to
attend to the partnership business, and one partner in breach of his
duty wilfully leaves the others to carry on the partnership business
unaided, they are, it would seem, entitled to compensation for
their services."

Thus, in *Airey v. Borham*[26] two partners had agreed to devote their
whole time to the partnership business but later quarrelled, with the

---

[20] *Whittle v. McFarlane* (1830) 1 Knapp 311.

[21] See *Bentley v. Craven* (1853) 18 Beav. 75.

[22] *Hutcheson v. Smith* (1842) 5 I.Eq.R. 117. And see *Thornton v. Proctor* (1792) 1 Anst. 94,
noticed *supra*, para. 20–22; also *East India Co. v. Blake* (1673) Finch 117.

[23] *MacKinlay v. Arthur Young McClelland Moores & Co.* [1990] 2 A.C. 239, 249A–C; also
Heastie v. Veitch & Co. (1934) 18 T.C. 305; *Watson and Everitt v. Blunden* (1933) 18 T.C. 402. See
also, *infra*, para. 34–30.

[24] Lord Lindley put it thus: "Even where the amount of the services rendered by the partners is
exceedingly unequal, still, if there is no agreement that their services shall be remunerated, no
charge in respect of them can be allowed in taking the partnership accounts. In such a case the
remuneration to be paid to either for personal labour exceeding that contributed by the other, is
considered as left to the honour of the other; and where that principle is wanting, a court of justice
cannot supply it." See *Webster v. Bray* (1849) 7 Hare 159, 179, *per* Wigram V.-C. In that case an
allowance was given to the defendant, pursuant to an offer made by the plaintiff. In a similar case,
Robinson v. Anderson (1855) 20 Beav. 98, no such offer was made so that the court could not
award any allowance.

[25] See *supra*, paras. 10–75 *et seq.*

[26] (1861) 29 Beav. 620.

result that one of them was left to carry the business on alone. The partnership was ultimately dissolved and an inquiry was directed in order to ascertain what allowance ought to be made to him for so doing. It is the opinion of the current editor that such a claim is still maintainable in an appropriate case.

Services rendered after dissolution

20–43   Before the Partnership Act 1890, the general rule was not applied in the case of services rendered by a partner in carrying on the firm's business following a dissolution. On that basis, a surviving partner who had carried on the business to its ultimate benefit was held to be entitled to remuneration for his trouble in so doing,[27] unless no profits were realised[28] or there was some special reason for denying his entitlement.[29] Both Lord Lindley and the editor of the 6th edition of this work apprehended that, in this respect, the Act had not altered the law, a view which proved to be amply justified when it was subsequently held that a partner appointed as a receiver and manager without remuneration in a dissolution action was entitled to wages for work done by him which proved beneficial to the business, even though such work formed no part of his duties as receiver and manager.[30]

20–44   In the same way, where a claim for a share of profits is made by a former partner under section 42 of the Partnership Act 1890,[31] an allowance is normally made to the partners who have carried on the business by way of remuneration for their services.[32]

---

[27] *Brown v. De Tastet* (1819) Jac. 284; *Crawshay v. Collins* (1826) 2 Russ. 325; *Featherstonhaugh v. Turner* (1858) 25 Beav. 382; *Page v. Ratcliffe* (1897) 75 L.T.(N.S.) 371. See also *Mellersh v. Keen* (1859) 27 Beav. 236, where one partner became of unsound mind and the business was continued by the others. *Cf. Tibbits v. Phillips* (1853) 10 Hare 355, where there was a *contractual* right to a salary which, on a true construction of the argument, ceased on the dissolution.
[28] *Re Aldridge* [1894] 2 Ch. 97.
[29] *e.g.* where he is the personal representative of the deceased partner: see *Burden v. Burden* (1813) 1 V. & B. 170; *Stocken v. Dawson* (1843) 6 Beav. 371. *Cf. Forster v. Ridley* (1864) 4 De G.J. & S. 452.
[30] *Harris v. Sleep* [1897] 2 Ch. 80. See also *Meyer & Co. v. Faber (No. 2)* [1923] 2 Ch. 421, 450–451, *per* Younger L.J.
[31] See *infra*, paras. 25–23 *et seq.*
[32] See *infra*, para. 25–28.

CHAPTER 21

ASCERTAINMENT AND DIVISION OF PROFITS

DESPITE the apparently strict terms of the statutory definition,[1] the **21–01** ultimate object of a normal partnership will be the realisation *and division* of profits.[2] Thus, Lord Lindley justifiably observed that:

"... the right of every partner to a share of the profits made by the firm to which he belongs is too obvious to require comment."

However, with the increasing popularity of so-called "salaried" partnership, such a generalisation must be approached with a degree of caution, even though a partner who receives remuneration rather than a share of profits may well not, as a matter of law, fall to be treated as a partner properly so called.[3]

What is divisible as profit

It has already been seen that profit is the excess of receipts over **21–02** expenses[4]: in winding up a partnership, nothing is properly divisible as profits which does not answer this description.[5] However, such a counsel of perfection is in practice modified in the case of a continuing firm, so as to facilitate the annual division of profits. Thus, a distinction is usually drawn between ordinary and extraordinary receipts and expenses: ordinary expenses will be treated as defrayed out of the normal trading income of the firm and extraordinary expenses out of capital or borrowings. Accordingly, the divisible profits in a given year will in general be ascertained merely by comparing ordinary receipts with ordinary expenses. As Lord Lindley pointed out:

"... unless some such principle as this were had recourse to, there could be no division of profits, even of the most flourishing business, whilst any of its debts were unpaid, and any of its capital sunk."

When asked, partners' views may genuinely differ as to whether a particular expense ought to be treated as ordinary or extraordinary;

---

[1] Partnership Act 1890, s.1(1): see *supra*, para. 2–01.

[2] See *supra*, para. 2–06.

[3] See *supra*, paras. 2–06, 5–65, 10–70.

[4] See *supra*, paras. 2–05, 5–15; also *Re Spanish Prospecting Co. Ltd.* [1911] 1 Ch. 92. As to profits for the purposes of income tax, see *infra*, paras. 34–23 *et seq.*

[5] Profits may be of an income or capital nature: see *supra*, paras. 10–66, 17–05.

in such a case, unless the agreement provides otherwise, the wishes of the majority will prevail.[6]

21-03   There is, in general, no obligation to replace lost capital prior to the division of profits,[7] although this may be provided for in the agreement.[8]

Method of accounting

21-04   There appears to be some authority for the proposition that, under ordinary circumstances and in the absence of any agreement to the contrary, moneys earned ought to be treated as profits of the year in which they are *received* and not as profits of the year in which they are earned.[9] However, this does not accord with the requirements of the Inland Revenue, who are only rarely prepared to accept accounts prepared on a "cash" as opposed to an "earnings" basis.[10] Indeed, the general (but by no means the universal) practice is also to include in a firm's annual profit and loss account an estimated sum in respect of work in progress, *i.e.* the value of work actually done which has neither been billed nor paid.[11]

21-05   Nevertheless, although it remains true that, for the purposes of income tax, profits must be ascertained according to the correct principles of commercial accountancy,[12] there is a general and

---

[6] See *Gregory v. Patchett* (1864) 33 Beav. 595; *Re Bridgewater Navigation Co.* [1891] 1 Ch. 155; *Re National Bank of Wales Ltd.* [1899] 2 Ch. 629, affirmed *sub nom. Dovey v. Cory* [1901] A.C. 477.

[7] Lord Lindley put it thus: "... if the current receipts exceed the current expenses, the writer apprehends that the difference can be divided as profit, although the capital may be spent and not represented by saleable assets." See, as to the construction of clauses relating to the payment of dividends out of profits, *Davison v. Gillies* (1879) 16 Ch.D. 347n.; *Dent v. London Tramways Co.* (1880) 16 Ch.D. 344; *Birch v. Cropper* (1889) 14 App. Cas. 525; *Re Bridgewater Navigation Co.* [1891] 1 Ch. 155 (varied at [1891] 2 Ch. 317); *Fisher v. Black and White Publishing Co.* [1901] 1 Ch. 174; *Bagot Pneumatic Tyre Co. v. Clipper Pneumatic Tyre Co.* [1902] 1 Ch. 146, 158, 159 *per* Romer L.J. As to paying dividends after a loss of capital, see *Flitcroft's case* (1855) 21 Ch.D. 519; *Bloxam v. Metropolitan Ry.* (1868) L.R. 3 Ch. App. 337; *Lee v. Neuchatel Asphalte Co.* (1886) 41 Ch.D. 1; *Bolton v. Natal Land, etc., Co.* [1892] 2 Ch. 124; *Lubbock v. British Bank of South America* [1892] 2 Ch. 198; *Verner v. General & Commercial Investment Trust* [1894] 2 Ch. 239; *Dovey v. Cory* [1901] A.C. 477, and the other cases referred to in *Buckley on the Companies Acts* (14th ed.), pp. 1031 *et seq.*

[8] See *supra*, para. 10–61.

[9] See *Hall & Co. v. Inland Revenue Commissioners* [1921] 3 K.B. 152; *Elson v. Prices Tailors Ltd.* [1963] 1 W.L.R. 287; also *Maclaren v. Stainton* (1852) 3 De G.F. & J. 202, 214, *per* Turner L.J.; *Badham v. Williams* (1902) 86 L.T.(N.S.) 191. *Cf. Browne v. Collins* (1871) 12 Eq. 586.

[10] See further, *infra*, para. 34–34.

[11] In some cases, the Revenue are now insisting that firms show work in progress in their accounts. As to the valuation of work in progress for tax purposes, see *infra*, paras. 34–34 *et seq.* Note also that, in New Zealand, it has been held that a retiring partner's share of the work in progress of a solicitors' firm is not an asset and therefore has no value: *Robertson v. Brent* [1972] N.Z.L.R. 406. The current editor doubts the correctness of this decision.

[12] *Odeon Associated Theatres Ltd. v. Jones* [1971] 1 W.L.R. 442; also *Symons v. Weeks* [1983] S.T.C. 195. But see *Ostime v. Duple Motor Bodies* [1961] 1 W.L.R. 739; *Gallagher v. Jones* [1993] S.T.C. 199.

overriding principle that neither profit nor loss may be anticipated.[13] Thus in *Willingale v. International Commercial Bank Ltd.*,[14] it was held that the taxpayer bank was not chargeable to tax upon any annual increase in the value of discounted bills of exchange as the maturity date approached (even though such increase was included in the bank's accounts upon normal accountancy principles) but should only be chargeable when the bills were disposed of or reached maturity and any profit was actually realised. The position would, however, have been different if the bills of exchange had been stock-in-trade.[15]

Similarly, in *Symons v. Weeks*,[16] Warner J. held that progress payments received by a firm of architects under standard R.I.B.A. long-term contracts did not need to be brought into account when computing the firm's profits for tax purposes, at least until the contracts were sufficiently far advanced that the profit thereon could be ascertained with some degree of certainty.

It follows from the foregoing cases that, although firms will **21–06** frequently use the accounts prepared for the purposes of submission to the Inland Revenue for all internal purposes, including the division of profit, they are not obliged so to do and may, as between themselves, choose to treat as a divisible profit some source of income which is not taxable at the time of receipt or, indeed, at all.

Time and manner of division

The partnership agreement will in general prescribe: **21–07**

(*a*) the ratios in which the profits are to be shared between the partners, which may involve the payment of preferential "salaries," interest on capital and the like;

(*b*) the time or times at which division is to take place.[17]

However, once a division of the profits has taken place, each partner will not necessarily be entitled to withdraw his share: under the terms of the agreement, a set or variable proportion may be taken to a taxation or other reserve.[18] Only, where there is no express or

---

[13] See *B.S.C. Footwear Ltd. v. Ridgway* [1972] A.C. 544, 552, *per* Lord Reid; *Beauchamp v. Woolworth plc* [1990] 1 A.C. 478, 489, *per* Lord Templeman; *R. v. I.R.C., ex p. S.G. Warburg & Co. Ltd.* [1994] S.T.C. 518.

[14] [1978] A.C. 834.

[15] *Per* Sir John Pennycuick in the Court of Appeal, reported at [1977] Ch. 78, 99.

[16] [1983] S.T.C. 195. And note in particular the expert evidence given by Mr. E.E. Ray: see *ibid.* pp. 215–221.

[17] See generally, *supra*, paras. 10–65 *et seq.* And see, as to the income tax treatment of payments made to partners out of profits, *infra*, paras. 34–29, 34–30.

[18] See *supra*, para. 10–73.

implied agreement between the partners will the rules contained in the Partnership Act 1890 apply.[19]

The agreement will also normally provide a framework authorising each partner to draw sums on account of his anticipated share of profits as it accrues.[20] In the absence of such a provision, no partner will be entitled to anything until the profit is ascertained and divided at the year end.

Power of the majority

21–08   Lord Lindley observed that:

"With respect to the times of division and quantum to be divided at any given time, it is conceived that the majority must govern the minority where no agreement upon the subject has been come to[21]; for these are matters of purely internal regulation, and with respect to such matters a dissentient minority have only one alternative, *viz.*, either to give way to the majority, or, if in a position so to do, to dissolve the partnership."

The current editor ventures to suggest that, as a statement of general principle, this goes too far, since what is an "ordinary" matter connected with the partnership business will inevitably vary from firm to firm.[22]

Exclusion from share of profits

21–09   Just as partners have no inherent right to expel one of their number or to forfeit his share,[23] they cannot properly exclude him from the enjoyment of his share of profits.[24] If they attempt to do so, they can be compelled to restore the excluded partner to his rightful share and to account to him accordingly.[25]

---

[19] Partnership Act 1890, s.24(1): see *supra*, para. 19–19. As to the mode of ascertaining profits where a third party is entitled to a share thereof, see *Geddes v. Wallace* (1820) 2 Bli. 270; *Rishton v. Grissell* (1870) L.R. 10 Eq. 393.

[20] See *supra*, para. 10–72.

[21] See the Partnership Act 1890, s.24(8), *supra*, para. 15–05. Lord Lindley also referred to the following cases in this context: *Stevens v. South Devon Railway Co.* (1851) 9 Hare 313; *Corry v. Londonderry and Eniskillen Railway Co.* (1860) 29 Beav. 263, as to declaring dividends before paying debts; *Browne v. Monmouthshire Railway and Canal Co.* (1851) 13 Beav. 32, as to paying dividends before works are finished.

[22] See *supra*, para. 15–06.

[23] Partnership Act 1890, s.25; see also *infra*, paras. 24–85 *et seq.*

[24] *Adley v. Whitstable Co.* (1815) 19 Ves.Jr. 304; *Griffith v. Paget* (1877) 5 Ch.D. 894.

[25] *Ibid.* See also *infra*, paras. 23–82 *et seq.*, 23–133.

CHAPTER 22

PARTNERSHIP ACCOUNTS

By partnership accounts are meant, for present purposes, those **22–01**
accounts maintained within a firm in order to show the financial
standing of each partner *vis-à-vis* the firm and his co-partners and, by
inference, the financial standing of the firm *vis-à-vis* third parties.[1]
Partnership accounts as taken by the court are considered elsewhere
in this work.[2]

1. MANNER IN WHICH ACCOUNTS SHOULD BE KEPT

Capital and current accounts

It has already been observed[3] that, in keeping partnership **22–02**
accounts, it is desirable that a capital account and a current or
"drawings" account be opened for each partner in the books of the
firm. This will enable the capital of the firm to be kept separate from
any temporary retentions of undrawn profits, thus minimising the
risks of confusion. Nevertheless, the maintenance of combined
capital/current accounts is commonplace.

A partner's capital and current accounts will show his personal
position as regards the firm. The value of any cash or property
brought into the firm by way of capital contribution will be credited
to his capital account and the value of any such cash or property
which is subsequently withdrawn will be debited thereto.

On the other hand, when a partnership profit or loss is divided, **22–03**
each partner's share thereof will normally be credited or debited to
his current account, as will any drawings which he may have made in
anticipation of such share. A share of profits attributable to the sale
or revaluation of a partnership asset will be similarly treated, unless
the partners have agreed to take such profits to capital account, thus
increasing the firm's fixed capital.[4] Balances may be transferred

---

[1] The contents of these internal accounts will ultimately be reflected in the balance sheet, which
inevitably shows the firm's overall financial standing.

[2] See *infra*, paras. 23–121 *et seq*.

[3] See *supra*, para. 17–07.

[4] See, as to the possible tax consequences attendant on a revaluation of assets, *infra*, para.
35–17.

between the partners' capital and current accounts in order to accommodate changes in the firm's capital structure, *e.g.* funding a new partner's capital contribution pursuant to a "lockstep" or other system or, indeed, restoring an existing partner's capital contribution to the agreed level following a proper or improper reduction therein.

Where a combined capital and current account is maintained, the operation is that much simpler, since all debits and credits will appear in a single account.

Other internal accounts

22–04   In addition to capital and current accounts, other accounts may also be maintained within the firm. Thus, where a retention is made out of each partner's profit share year by year on account of income tax, it may be taken to a special tax reserve account.[5] Equally, capital profits "realised" on a revaluation of assets may, instead of being credited to the partners' current accounts, be taken to a special revaluation reserve, against which no drawings may be made.[6] In fact, the number of different types of account is limited only by the imagination of the partners and the need to preserve a manageable accounting structure within the firm.

Partners treated as debtors or creditors of firm

22–05   The result of the above treatment is effectively to constitute each partner as a creditor of the firm, to the extent that there is a net credit balance on his accounts, or as a debtor of the firm, to the extent that there is a net debit balance thereon. On the ultimate payment of any balance due to or from him, his account with the firm will be closed and settled.

However, that analysis is by no means perfect, as was made clear by Lord Cottenham,[7] when he observed:

"... though these terms 'debtor' and 'creditor' are so used, and sufficiently explain what is meant by the use of them, nothing can be more inconsistent with the known law of partnership, than to consider the situation of either party as in any degree resembling the situation of those whose appellation has been so borrowed. The supposed creditor has no means of compelling payment of his debt; and the supposed debtor is liable to no proceedings either at

---

[5] See *supra*, para. 10–73.
[6] But see, as to the treatment of such a reserve for the purposes of capital gains tax, *infra*, para. 35–06.
[7] *Richardson v. Bank of England* (1838) 4 Myl. & Cr. 165, 171–172.

law or in equity—assuming always that no separate security has been taken or given. The supposed creditor's debt is due from the firm of which he is partner; and the supposed debtor owes the money to himself in common with his partners."[8]

Ultimate adjustment of accounts

The final adjustment of the accounts as between the partners **22–06** following a dissolution inevitably gives rise to questions of difficulty and is considered later in this work.[9]

Annual accounts

There is no general statutory requirement that firms must produce **22–07** annual accounts[10] in a certain form (or at all), although this will normally be the subject of an express provision in the agreement;[11] moreover, the production of such accounts will inevitably be required for the purposes of production to the Inland Revenue.

Corporate partnerships: In the case of a qualifying corporate **22–08** partnership,[12] it is now provided by the Partnerships and Unlimited Companies (Accounts) Regulations 1993[13] that annual accounts and an annual report, together with an auditors' report, should be prepared just as if the firm were a company formed and registered under the Companies Act 1985.[14] Each corporate partner is required to append a copy of those accounts to its own annual accounts prior to their delivery to the Registrar of Companies[15] and must, in effect, supply the names of the partners to any person who requests them.[16] Where the firm's head office is situate in Great Britain and each of the partners is an undertaking comparable to a limited company incorporated outside the United Kingdom or an unlimited company or partnership incorporated or formed outside the United Kingdom

---

[8] See also *Lee v. Neuchatel Asphalte Co.* (1889) 41 Ch.D. 1, 23, *per* Lindley L.J.; *Green v. Hertzog* [1954] 1 W.L.R. 1309. And see *supra*, para. 19–05.

[9] Partnership Act 1890, s.44: see *infra*, paras. 25–40 *et seq.*

[10] *i.e.* a balance sheet and profit and loss account.

[11] See *supra*, paras. 10–61, 10–133 *et seq.*

[12] *i.e.* a partnership governed by the laws of Great Britain all the members of which are (i) limited companies; (ii) unlimited companies or Scottish firms, each of whose members is a limited company; or (iii) comparable undertakings incorporated in or formed under the laws of another country.

[13] (S.I. 1993 No. 1820). The Regulations came into force on July 21, 1993, but do not apply in the case of a financial year commencing before December 23, 1994: *ibid.* reg. 12(1).

[14] *Ibid.* regs. 3(1), (4), 4(1). As regards the contents of such accounts, *ibid.* Sched. makes certain modifications to the provisions of the Companies Act 1985, Pt. VII. Changes in the firm are, in general, ignored: *ibid.* reg. 3(3). See also, as to the penalties for non-compliance: *ibid.* reg. 8(1), (2).

[15] *Ibid.* reg. 5(1). See also *ibid.* reg. 8(3), as to the penalty for non-compliance.

[16] *Ibid.* reg. 5(2). And see the preceding note.

all the members of which are undertakings comparable to a limited company so incorporated (but not in any member state of the EC), those accounts must in general be held available for inspection by any person at that office.[17] These provisions do not, however, apply where the partnership is dealt with on a consolidated basis in group accounts prepared by a member of the partnership or its parent undertaking, provided that certain conditions are satisfied.[18]

2. THE PARTNERS' RIGHTS AND OBLIGATIONS

The primary duty

22–09   Lord Lindley pointed out that:

> "it is one of the clearest rights of every partner to have accurate accounts kept of all money transactions relating to the business of the partnership, and to have free access to all its books and accounts."[19]

These rights are, of course, expressly recognised by the Partnership Act 1890 which provides:

> "24.—(9) The partnership books are to be kept at the place of business of the partnership (or the principal place, if there is more than one), and every partner may, when he thinks fit, have access to and inspect and copy any of them.[20]
> 28. Partners are bound to render true accounts and full information of all things affecting the partnership to any partner or his legal representatives."[21]

---

[17] *Ibid.* reg. 6(1), (3)(a). This requirement does not apply where the relevant undertaking is, if comparable to a limited company, incorporated in a member state of the EC or, if comparable to an unlimited company or partnership, incorporated in or formed under the laws of such a state and comprising partners which are undertakings comparable to limited companies so incorporated, provided that the firm's accounts are appended to the accounts of any such partner and duly published under the laws of that state: *ibid.* reg. 6(2). The penalties for non-compliance are set out in *ibid.* reg. 8(3).

[18] *Ibid.* reg. 7. As to the meaning of the expression "dealt with on a consolidated basis", see *ibid.* reg. 2(1).

[19] See *per* Lord Eldon in *Rowe v. Wood* (1822) 2 Jac. & W. 553, 558–559 and *Goodman v. Whitcomb* (1820) 1 Jac. & W. 589, 593; also *Trego v. Hunt* [1896] A.C. 7, 26, *per* Lord Davey.

[20] This is subject to any agreement between the partners: see the words at the beginning of s.24, *supra*, para. 20–03; and see *supra*, paras. 10–59 *et seq.* For the position prior to the Act, see (as to custody of books) *Charlton v. Poulter* (1753) 19 Ves.Jr. 148, note; *Taylor v. Davis* (1842) 3 Beav. 388, note; *Greatrex v. Greatrex* (1847) 1 De G. & Sm. 692; and (as to the right to inspect and copy) *Stuart v. Lord Bute* (1841) 11 Sim. 442 and (1842) 12 Sim. 460; *Taylor v. Rundell* (1843) 1 Ph. 222. This right was not enforceable at law even in an action by one partner against another: *Ward v. Apprice* (1704) 6 Mod. 264.

[21] Although the expression "legal representatives" is not defined, it will prima facie extend to a partner's trustee in bankruptcy or liquidator: see *Wilson v. Greenwood* (1818) 1 Swan. 471.

Duty of continuing or surviving partners

It is the duty of continuing or surviving partners to keep the **22–10** accounts of the firm in such a way as to show the financial position when the composition of the firm changed.[22]

Presumptions where books not kept or destroyed

If no books of account whatsoever are kept, or if such books as are **22–11** kept are unintelligible or are destroyed or otherwise wrongfully withheld, on an account being directed by the court all necessary presumptions will be made against those partners responsible for the non-production of proper accounts.[23] However, where all the partners are *in pari delicto*, this rule cannot be applied.

The right of inspection

A partner cannot deprive his co-partners of their right of inspection **22–12** by keeping records in a private book containing other material which is said to be of no concern to them.[24] However, it would seem that a partner could in theory bind himself not to investigate the partnership books or accounts and to accept balance sheets prepared by his co-partners.[25]

An assignee or mortgagee of a partner's share has no right of inspection whilst the partnership is continuing.[26]

Inspection by agent

A partner is in general entitled to examine the firm's books and **22–13** accounts through the medium of an agent appointed for the purpose, provided that the agent is a person to whom no reasonable objection can be taken by the other partners.[27] However, this right, unlike the right to personal inspection, is not absolute: it may be denied if the court is satisfied that the assistance of an agent is not reasonably

---

[22] See *Ex p. Toulmin* (1815) 1 Mer. 598, note; *Toulmin v. Copland* (1836) 3 Y. & C.Ex. 625.

[23] See *Walmsley v. Walmsley* (1846) 3 Jo. & La T. 556; *Gray v. Haig* (1855) 20 Beav. 219; also *Armorie v. Delamirie* (1722) 1 Str. 505. And see, as to the loss of a right to interest, *Boddam v. Ryley* (1787) 4 Bro.P.C. 561, noticed *supra*, para. 20–35.

[24] See *Freeman v. Fairlie* (1812) 3 Mer. 43; *Toulmin v. Copland* (1836) 3 Y. & C.Ex. 625.

[25] See *Turner v. Bayley* (1864) 4 De G.J. & S. 332. This case involved a profit sharing arrangement falling short of true partnership.

[26] Partnership Act 1890, s.31: see *supra*, paras. 19–59 *et seq.*

[27] *Bevan v. Webb* [1901] 2 Ch. 59; also *Dadswell v. Jacobs* (1887) 34 Ch.D. 278. And see *Re Credit Co.* (1879) 11 Ch.D. 256; *Nelson v. Anglo-American Land Mortgage Agency Co.* [1897] 1 Ch. 130 (decisions as to the right of inspection of a company's register under the Companies Act 1862, s.43); also *Mutter v. East & Midlands Ry.* (1888) 38 Ch.D. 92. See, as to the remedy for enforcing these rights and the irrelevance of the applicant's motive in seeking so to do, *Davies v. Gas Light & Coke Co.* [1909] 1 Ch. 248, 708.

required or that the inspection is sought for an improper purpose.[28] It is, perhaps, self evident that, having obtained information as a result of such an inspection, neither the partner nor his agent is entitled to make use of it for such an improper purpose;[29] indeed, an agent may be required to give an undertaking to this effect.[30]

Removal of books for inspection

22–14   Whilst the Partnership Act 1890 secures the right of each partner to have access to and to inspect and copy the partnership books, it does not entitle any partner to remove those books from the place where they are kept unless the other partners are agreeable. This may give rise to difficulty in practice, where, for example, a partner wishes to obtain a photographic or other reproduction of the books or to have them scrutinised by his financial advisers, neither of which can conveniently be done on the partnership premises. As a result, it may be desirable for the agreement expressly to authorise temporary removal, provided that free access to the books by the other partners is not inhibited.[31] Such a provision may be particularly valuable in the case of a non-active or dormant partner who is not kept fully informed as to the day to day running of the partnership business.

---

[28] See *Duché v. Duché* (1920) 149 L.T. 300; *Dodd v. Amalgamated Marine Workers' Union* [1924] 1 Ch. 116; *cf. Davies v. Gas Light and Coke Co.* [1909] 1 Ch. 248, 708.
[29] *Bevan v. Webb* [1901] 2 Ch. 59. See also *infra*, para. 23–99.
[30] *Bevan v. Webb*, *supra*. See also *Norey v. Keep* [1909] 1 Ch. 561; *Dodd v. Amalgamated Marine Workers' Union* [1924] 1 Ch. 116 (decisions under the Trade Union Act 1871).
[31] See the *Encyclopaedia of Professional Partnerships*, Precedent 1, cl. 9(3).

CHAPTER 23

ACTIONS BETWEEN PARTNERS

1. INTRODUCTION

Effect of Judicature Acts

Prior to the Judicature Acts, proceedings could not be brought as **23-01** between a firm and one or more of its members.[1] At the heart of this rule lay the fundamental objection, which still persists,[2] to any party to proceedings being at the same time both a plaintiff and a defendant. Moreover, because the old action for an account had become obsolete, it was also a rule that no action at law could be maintained by one partner against another if it in any way involved taking a partnership account.[3]

In their strict application, these rules were effectively swept away by the Judicature Acts, causing Lord Lindley to observe:

"... there appears to be no reason why an action should not now be maintained for the recovery of a debt due from one partner to the firm[4]; nor why, if two firms have a common partner, an action should not be maintainable by one firm against another."[5]

In the former respect, Lord Lindley perhaps went too far, since a **23-02** debt owed by a partner to his firm (*i.e.* to himself and his co-partners) cannot normally be recovered *otherwise* than by means of a partnership account.[6] Elsewhere, he went on to explain:

---

[1] Lord Lindley explained that, as a consequence, "All proceedings, ... which had for their object the enforcement of the mutual rights and obligations of partners, had to be taken by some or one of the members of a firm individually against some others or other of them also individually. The consequences of this rule were important, for it followed from it—

1. That no action at law could be brought by one partner against another for the recovery of money or property payable to the firm as distinguished from the partner suing;

2. That no suit in equity was maintainable by one partner against another in respect of a matter in which the firm was interested, without bringing all the members thereof before the court."

The pre-Judicature Act law was summarised in greater detail in the 11th ed. of this work, at pp. 665–672. And see also *infra*, para. 23–196.

[2] See *Ellis v. Kerr* [1910] 1 Ch. 529; *Meyer & Co. v. Faber (No. 2)* [1923] 2 Ch. 421. But see also, *supra*, para. 14–08.

[3] See the summary of the pre-Judicature Act law in the 11th ed. of this work, at pp. 665–672.

[4] The footnote at this point read "*Piercy v. Fynney* (1871) L.R. 12 Eq. 69; *Taylor v. Midland Rail. Co.* (1860) 28 Beav. 287 and (1862) 8 H.L.C. 751, show that suits in equity would lie in these cases in aid of legal rights. See also *Luke v. South Kensington Hotel Co.* (1879) 11 Ch.D. 121; *Williamson v. Barbour* (1877) 9 Ch.D. 536, *per* Jessel M.R." Reference might also, perhaps, be made to *Palmer v. Mallet* (1887) 36 Ch.D.

[5] See *supra*, para. 14–08.

[6] See *Meyer & Co. v. Faber (No. 2)* [1923] 2 Ch. 421, although the headnote of this case is framed in misleadingly wide terms; *Green v. Hertzog* [1954] 1 W.L.R. 1309. See also *supra*, paras. 19–04 *et seq.*

"... the fact that an account has to be taken in order to ascertain what is due from one party to another is no longer any reason why an action by one against the other should fail; at most, such a circumstance may render it expedient to transfer the action from one division of the High Court to another at some stage of the action."[7]

This is still the position under the Supreme Court Act 1981.[8]

Actions in firm name

23-03   It has already been seen that proceedings may be commenced by or against a firm in the firm name, but that this is merely a rule of procedure which does not affect the rights of the parties or give rise to any new or independent cause of action.[9] The use of the firm name is permissible in the case of an action between partners or between two firms with a common partner,[10] but will, in the former case, amount to no more than a compendious expression denoting the partners other than the plaintiff or defendant (as the case may be).[11]

2. PARTIES

The general rule

23-04   In those, relatively rare, cases in which the proceedings do *not* involve the taking of a partnership account or some other form of relief which materially affects all the partners, *e.g.* an injunction or the appointment of a receiver, the choice of parties will be determined on normal principles.[12] Otherwise, all the partners should in general be joined, as Lord Lindley explained:

"... it has been a long standing rule in Chancery that where the number of partners is not great they must all be parties to a suit

---

[7] Notwithstanding the terms of the Supreme Court Act 1981, Sched. 1, para. 1(f) (which assigns to the Chancery Division all causes and matters relating to the taking of partnership accounts), the mere fact that a claim will involve the taking of an account may, in practice, not be regarded as a sufficient ground for seeking a transfer to that Division. *Sed quaere*: see the observations of Harman J. in *Apac Rowena Ltd. v. Norpol Packaging Ltd.* [1991] 4 All E.R. 516, 518.

[8] See *ibid.* s.49. This Act repealed and replaced the Supreme Court of Judicature (Consolidation) Act 1925.

[9] See *supra*, para. 14-03.

[10] This would seem to be a necessary implication of R.S.C. Ord. 81, r. 6(1), *infra*, para. A2-14 and C.C.R. Ord. 25, r. 10(1).

[11] *Meyer & Co. v. Faber (No. 2)* [1923] 2 Ch. 421, 435 (*per* Sterndale M.R.), 441 (*per* Warrington L.J.). Younger L.J. left the point open: see *ibid.* p. 450. The headnote of this case is misleading.

[12] See *supra*, paras. 14-22 *et seq.*

for an account if within the jurisdiction of the court[13]; and subject to the question how far the firm can be treated as representing them all,[14] this rule is still in force."

However, the failure to join one or more of the partners will not, in such circumstances, be fatal.[15]

Sub-partners, assignees, etc.

It is perhaps self evident that, where an account is sought as **23-05** between a third party and a partner which does not, as such, concern the partnership, the other partners are neither necessary nor proper parties. Lord Lindley cited the following example:

"If ... a partner has agreed to share his profits with a stranger, and the latter seeks an account of those profits, he should bring his action against that one partner alone, and not make the others parties."[16]

The same rule applies in the case of an account sought by an assignee of a partner's share whilst the partnership is continuing, but not following a dissolution.[17]

Although it was in one case held that all the partners ought to be joined as parties to a foreclosure action brought by an equitable mortgagee of a share in a mine,[18] it is doubtful whether this would now, as a general rule, be necessary.[19]

Action for account against surviving partners

Where surviving partners, who are also the personal representatives **23-06** of a deceased partner, render themselves liable to account for profits made by the wrongful employment of his share in the partnership business,[20] it is unclear whether the other partners will also be *necessary* parties to the proceedings. Lord Lindley observed:

---

[13] See *Hills v. Nash* (1845) 1 Ph. 594. *Cf. Weymouth v. Boyer* (1792) 1 Ves.Jr. 416; *Smith v. Snow* (1818) 3 Madd. 10.

[14] See *infra*, paras. 23–08, 23–09, 23–12.

[15] R.S.C. Ord. 15, r. 6(1); C.C.R. Ord. 5, r. 4. And see *supra*, para. 14–22.

[16] *Raymond's case*, cited in *Ex p. Barrow* (1815) 2 Rose 252, 255, *per* Lord Eldon; *Brown v. De Tastet* (1819) Jac. 284; *Bray v. Fromont* (1821) 6 Madd. 5. See also *Killock v. Greg* (1828) 4 Russ. 285.

[17] See the Partnership Act 1890, s.31, *supra*, paras. 19–59, 19–63, 19–65; also *Public Trustee v. Elder* [1926] Ch. 776.

[18] *Redmayne v. Forster* (1866) L.R. 2 Eq. 467.

[19] See the Partnership Act 1890, s.31(1). In *Redmayne v. Forster, supra*, the other partners had pre-emption rights over the mortgagee partner's share and, to that extent, they were necessary parties as persons interested in the equity of redemption; *cf. Re Corporate Equitable Society* [1940] Ch. 654.

[20] See *infra*, paras. 25–35 *et seq.*, 26–49 *et seq.*

"The rule appears to be that they are necessary parties if the account sought is an account of all the profits made by the use of the capital of the deceased; but not if the account is confined to so much of those profits as the executors have themselves received."[21]

Relief other than account

23–07   A party who would not otherwise be a proper party to an action for an account as between partners may be joined if some other form of relief, *e.g.* an injunction, is sought against him in the same proceedings.[22]

Representative proceedings

23–08   The stringent statutory restrictions on the size of partnerships have for some years been relaxed in the case of certain professions,[23] but further significant relaxations, extending into the trading sphere, seem unlikely.[24] Nevertheless, where proceedings between members of a large firm[25] are contemplated, it may be convenient to join representative plaintiffs and/or defendants.[26] The use of this device was well established in Lord Lindley's day, as the following passage makes clear:

"It was held in *Wallworth v. Holt*,[27] that where partners are too numerous to be brought before the Court, and they are divisible into classes, and all the individuals in one class have a common interest, a suit instituted by a few individuals of that class on behalf of themselves and all the other individuals of the same class against the other members of the company is sustainable. Since this decision, there have been many suits by some shareholders on behalf of themselves and others, praying for very general accounts (but studiously avoiding a prayer for a dissolution),[28] and such

---

[21] *Simpson v. Chapman* (1853) 4 De G.M. & G. 154; *Vyse v. Foster* (1874) L.R. 7 H.L. 318. *Cf. Macdonald v. Richardson* (1858) 1 Giff. 81.

[22] See, for example, *Vulliamy v. Noble* (1817) 3 Mer. 593; *Bevan v. Lewis* (1827) 1 Sim. 376.

[23] See *supra*, paras. 4–28 *et seq.*

[24] See *supra*, paras. 4–28, n. 5.

[25] As to what will be regarded as a large firm, see *Re Braybrook* [1916] W.N. 74.

[26] See, generally, R.S.C. Ord. 15, r. 12; C.C.R. Ord. 5, r. 5; and *Irish Shipping Ltd. v. Commercial Union Assurance Co. Plc* [1991] 2 Q.B. 206, where numerous authorities are reviewed. And see, as to actions brought by representative plaintiffs on behalf of a firm, *Chancey v. May* (1722) Pr. Ch. 592; *Hichens v. Congreve* (1828) 4 Russ. 562; *Attwood v. Small* (1838) 6 Cl. & F. 232; *Taylor v. Salmon* (1838) 4 Myl. & Cr. 134; *Beck v. Kantorowicz* (1857) 3 K. & J. 230.

[27] (1841) 4 Myl. & Cr. 619. See also *Cockburn v. Thompson* (1809) 16 Ves.Jr. 321.

[28] As to the position where a dissolution is sought, see *infra*, para. 23–12.

suits have been successful whenever the interest of the absent partners has been the same as that of the plaintiffs on the record."[29]

Whether representative proceedings will be appropriate in any **23–09** given case will naturally depend on the nature of the relief sought. Thus, where an account is required, a decision on representation can only be made once the interest of each partner has been identified: if each partner's interest is distinct from and in conflict with that of *all* his co-partners, then representative proceedings will be inappropriate and, in accordance with the normal rule, all the partners must be joined, however numerous they may be.[30] Where, on the other hand, no such conflict arises and two or more partners share the same interest,[31] it will be sufficient if one partner is joined to represent each distinct interest.[32] Representative proceedings may be particularly useful where one or more partners are outside the jurisdiction.[33]

A partner can, where appropriate, be appointed to represent the interests of himself and his co-partners against his will.[34]

Whilst a judgment or order will bind all partners represented in the proceedings, it cannot be enforced against a partner who was not made a party without the leave of the court.[35]

Dissolution and winding-up

All the partners should normally be joined as parties to a **23–10** dissolution action.[36] This long standing rule was originally of an

---

[29] See *Apperley v. Page* (1847) 1 Ph. 779; also *Wilson v. Stanhope* (1846) 2 Colly. 629; *Harvey v. Collett* (1846) 15 Sim. 332; *Cooper v. Webb* (1847) 15 Sim. 454; *Richardson v. Hastings* (1847) 7 Beav. 323; *Sibson v. Edgeworth* (1848) 2 De G. & Sm. 73; *Clements v. Bowes* (1852) 17 Sim. 167 and (1853) 1 Drew 684; *Butt v. Monteaux* (1854) 1 K. & J. 98; *Sheppard v. Oxenford* (1855) 1 K. & J. 491; *Cramer v. Bird* (1868) L.R. 6 Eq. 143. *Cf. Williams v. Salmond* (1855) 2 K. & J. 463. The position in mutual assurance societies and friendly societies is analogous: see *Pare v. Clegg* (1861) 29 Beav. 589; *Bromley v. Williams* (1863) 32 Beav. 177; *Harvey v. Beckwith* (1864) 2 Hem. & M. 429.

[30] See *Van Sandau v. Moore* (1826) 1 Russ. 441; *McMahon v. Upton* (1829) 2 Sim. 473; *Seddon v. Connell* (1840) 10 Sim. 58; *Abraham v. Hannay* (1843) 13 Sim. 581; *Sibley v. Minton* (1857) 27 L.J.Ch. 53.

[31] As to the meaning of the expression "the same interest" in R.S.C. Ord. 15, r. 12(1) and C.C.R. Ord. 5, r. 5(1), see *Prudential Assurance Co. Ltd. v. Newman Industries Ltd.* [1981] Ch. 229; *Roche v. Sherrington* [1982] 1 W.L.R. 599; also *Irish Shipping Ltd. v. Commercial Union Assurance Co. Plc* [1991] 2 Q.B. 206, where numerous authorities were reviewed by the Court of Appeal.

[32] *Cf. Harrison v. Brown* (1852) 5 De.G. & Sm. 728.

[33] See *Irish Shipping Ltd. v. Commercial Union Assurance Co. Plc* [1991] 2 Q.B. 206. *Cf. Public Trustee v. Elder* [1926] Ch. 776.

[34] See R.S.C. Ord. 15, r. 12(2); C.C.R. Ord. 5, r. 5(2)(b); *Wood v. McCarthy* [1893] 1 Q.B. 775.

[35] R.S.C. Ord. 15. r. 12(3); C.C.R. Ord. 5, r. 5(5).

[36] *Ireton v. Lewes* (1673) Finch 96; *Moffat v. Farquharson* (1788) 2 Bro.C.C. 338; *Long v. Yonge* (1830) 2 Sim. 369; *Evans v. Stokes* (1836) 1 Keen 24; *Wheeler v. Van Wart* (1838) 9 Sim. 193; *Deeks v. Stanhope* (1844) 14 Sim. 57; *Richardson v. Hastings* (1844) 7 Beav. 301; *Harvey v. Bignold* (1845) 8 Beav. 343.

absolute nature[37] and, in Lord Lindley's words, its justification lay in the fact that:

"... the affairs of a partnership cannot be finally wound up and settled without deciding all questions arising between all the partners, which cannot be done in the absence of any one of them."[38]

On the same principle, the personal representatives of a deceased partner should also be joined as parties, if they will be interested in the accounts taken in winding up the firm's affairs.[39] However, it is unnecessary to join any person who, though nominated as a partner, is not legally in a position to assert his rights as such.[40]

Action for account by assignee

23–11   It has already been seen that an assignee of a partnership share has a statutory right to an account following a dissolution.[41] If that right is exercised, *all* the partners, including the assignor, must be joined as parties to the proceedings, since the assignment does not affect their rights and obligations *inter se*.[42] Indeed, it would seem that the assignor will be regarded as a necessary party even if he is out of the jurisdiction: the assignee's personal undertaking to pay whatever may be found due to the other partners will not, in such a case, be sufficient.[43]

Representative proceedings

23–12   Although the use of representative parties in dissolution actions was once effectively proscribed,[44] the current editor submits that this approach is no longer warranted and that the considerations applicable to such actions are, in principle, no different to any

---

[37] Lord Lindley observed "This rule is supposed to admit of no exception, and it has, though with expressions of regret, been held to apply to unincorporated companies as well as to ordinary partnerships." See, in addition to the cases cited in the last note, *Van Sandau v. Moore* (1826) 1 Russ. 441; *Davis v. Fisk*, cited in *Small v. Attwood* (1832) Younge 407, 425; *Seddon v. Connell* (1840) 10 Sim. 58; *Abraham v. Hannay* (1843) 13 Sim. 581.

[38] See *Richardson v. Hastings* (1847) 7 Beav. 301.

[39] See *Cox v. Stephens* (1863) 9 Jur.(N.S.) 1144; also *Baboo Janokey Doss v. Bindabun Doss* (1843) 3 Moo.Ind.App. 175. As to the position where there is no personal representative, see *Cawthorn v. Chalie* (1824) 2 Sim. & St. 127 and *infra*, para. 26–10.

[40] *Ehrmann v. Ehrmann* (1894) 72 L.T. 17. Cf. *Page v. Cox* (1851) 10 Hare 163. See also *supra*, para. 10–217.

[41] Partnership Act 1890, s.31(2), *supra*, paras. 19–59, 19–65.

[42] See *supra*, para. 19–62.

[43] *Public Trustee v. Elder* [1926] Ch. 776.

[44] See the cases cited *supra*, para. 23–10, nn. 36, 37.

other.[45] Lord Lindley put it more tentatively, but in a statement of principle which cannot realistically be bettered:

"... it may be permitted to doubt whether it can be considered as a rule admitting of no exception whatsoever, that to every action for a dissolution, all the partners must individually be parties. All that can on principle be requisite, is that every conflicting interest shall be substantially represented by some person before the court. If, which is possible, the interest of each partner conflicts with that of all the others, then all must undoubtedly be parties. But if the partners are numerous,[46] and it can be shown that they are divisible into classes, and that all the individuals in each class have a common interest, then although the interest in each class conflicts with that of every other class, there seems to be no reason why, if each class is represented by one or two of the individuals composing it, a decree for a dissolution should not be made.[47] There is not, however, so far as the writer is aware, any case in which a decree for a dissolution has actually been made in the absence of any of the partners."[48]

3. CASES IN WHICH THE COURT WILL NOT INTERFERE BETWEEN PARTNERS

Courts of equity would, in general, decline to grant relief to a partner **23–13** in proceedings brought against his co-partners in three distinct cases, namely:

(1) where a dissolution was not sought;
(2) where a matter of internal regulation was involved; or
(3) where the partner concerned was guilty of laches.

This is still technically the position in all Divisions of the High Court, where the relief sought by a partner is of an equitable nature,[49]

---

[45] See, generally, the pragmatic approach adopted by the Court of Appeal in *Irish Shipping Ltd. v. Commercial Union Assurance Co. Plc* [1991] 2 Q.B. 206; also *Bank of America National Trust & Savings Assoc. v. Taylor* [1992] 1 Lloyd's Rep. 484.

[46] Five partners are not "numerous": *Re Braybrook* [1916] W.N. 74.

[47] See *Richardson v. Larpent* (1843) 2 Y. & C.Ch. 514; also the observations of Lord Cottenham in *Wallworth v. Holt* (1841) 4 Myl. & Cr. 619, 637 *et seq.* As to the decision in *Cockburn v. Thompson* (1809) 16 Ves.Jnr. 321, Lord Lindley referred to the observations of Shadwell V.-C. in *Long v. Yonge* (1830) 2 Sim. 369, 380, and cautioned the reader to "observe that the real object was to make the defendants account for the money they had received, and that the question as to want of parties was not raised with reference to that part of the prayer of the bill which sought a dissolution."

[48] Note that an order has been made in a representative action for the winding-up of an unregistered friendly society: *Re Lead Company's Workmen's Fund Society* [1904] 2 Ch. 196.

[49] *i.e.* specific performance, rescission, accounts, a receiver or an injunction. These subjects are considered in successive sections of this chapter. See, generally, the Supreme Court Act 1981, s.49.

although, as will be seen hereafter, the first rule is no longer applied with its original strictness.

23–14 *Rule 1: The court will not interfere otherwise than with a view to dissolution.*

The courts of equity normally displayed a marked reluctance to interfere as between partners otherwise than with a view to dissolving the firm or, if it had already been dissolved, winding up its affairs. Accordingly, instances in which an account or injunctive relief was refused solely on the ground that a dissolution was not sought can be found in the older reported cases. It is not surprising that this rule, which Lord Lindley described as "at no time perhaps very inflexible," was gradually relaxed. Yet, while the courts more readily granted relief as between the members of a continuing partnership, traces of the original strict rule remained,[50] as Lord Lindley explained:

"... one of the first points for consideration, even now, when one partner sues another for equitable relief, is, can relief be had without dissolving the partnership? Undoubtedly it may, much more certainly than formerly, but not always when perhaps it ought.[51] ... [It] may be stated as a general proposition, that courts will not, if they can avoid it, allow a partner to derive advantage from his own misconduct by compelling his co-partner to submit either to continued wrong, or to a dissolution[52]; and that rather than permit an improper advantage to be taken of a rule designed to operate for the benefit of all parties, the court will interfere ... where formerly it would have declined to do so. At the same time courts will not take the management of a going concern into their own hands, and, if they cannot usefully interfere in any other manner, they will not interfere at all unless for the purpose of winding up the partnership."

Although the courts are now likely to adopt a more flexible and constructive approach than in Lord Lindley's day, it is submitted that the general proposition formulated in the above passage still, in essence, holds good.

---

[50] This is particularly evident in the decisions relating to the specific performance of partnership agreements and to the appointment of receivers and managers: see *infra*, paras. 23–43 *et seq.*, 23–149 *et seq.*

[51] See *infra*, paras. 23–66 *et seq.*

[52] See *Fairthorne v. Weston* (1844) 3 Hare. 392; also *infra*, paras. 23–82, 23–137, 24–72.

Rule 2: The court will not interfere in matters of internal regulation.   **23–15**

Trivial disputes

The court will inevitably take a view of any matters of complaint raised by one partner against another and, if they are of an essentially trivial nature, will usually decline to give relief. Lord Lindley summarised the position in these terms:

"A court of justice will not interfere between partners merely because they do not agree. It is no part of the duty of the Court to settle all partnership squabbles: it expects from every partner a certain amount of forbearance and good feeling towards his co-partner; and it does not regard mere passing improprieties, arising from infirmities of temper, as sufficient to warrant a decree for dissolution, or an order for an injunction, or a receiver."[53]

Interference with managing partner

If partners have agreed to entrust the management of the firm to a **23–16** particular partner, the court will not readily deprive him of his responsibilities, by the appointment of a receiver or otherwise, unless he can clearly be shown to have acted improperly.[54]

Rule 3: The court will not interfere at the instance of partner guilty of **23–17** *laches.*

A partner may, on normal principles, be precluded from obtaining equitable relief by reason of laches. Laches is, of course, quite independent of the Limitation Act 1980,[55] and presupposes not only the passage of time, but also the existence of circumstances which render it inequitable to afford a plaintiff the relief which he seeks.[56]

Where, however, a partner has himself acted in an underhand fashion, the court may be unwilling to give credence to any plea of laches which he may seek to raise against his co-partners.[57]

---

[53] See *Lawson v. Morgan* (1815) 1 Price 303; *Cofton v. Horner* (1818) 5 Price 537; *Marshall v. Colman* (1820) 2 J. & W. 266; *Smith v. Jeyes* (1841) 4 Beav. 503; *Warder v. Stilwell* (1856) 3 Jur.(N.S.) 9; *Anderson v. Anderson* (1857) 25 Beav. 190. See also *infra*, paras. 24–67, 24–68.

[54] See *Waters v. Taylor* (1808) 15 Ves.Jr. 10; *Lawson v. Morgan* (1851) 1 Price 303. *Cf.* the position following a dissolution: *Tibbits v. Phillips* (1853) 10 Hare 355.

[55] See, as to limitation as between partners, *infra*, paras. 23–31 *et seq.*

[56] Laches may preclude relief, even though actual assent or conscious acquiescence on the part of the plaintiff is not proved: see *Lindsay Petroleum Co. v. Hurd* (1874) L.R. 5 P.C. 221; *Erlanger v. New Sombrero Phosphate Co.* (1878) 3 App.Cas. 1218, 1230 (*per* Lord Penzance), 1279 (*per* Lord Blackburn). However, mere delay is not sufficient: *Ridgway v. Newstead* (1861) 3 D.F. & J. 474; *Blake v. Gale* (1886) 32 Ch.D. 571; *Re Eustace* [1912] 1 Ch. 561. And see also, as to acquiescence, *Evans v. Smallcombe* (1868) L.R. 3 H.L. 256; *De Bussche v. Alt* (1878) 8 Ch.D. 286.

[57] *Blundon v. Storm* (1971) 20 D.L.R. (3d) 413, noticed *infra*, para. 23–21.

Action for account precluded by laches

23–18   It has long been recognised that proceedings for an account may be defeated by laches.[58] Moreover, the court will not, in the absence of fraud, re-open an erroneous account which has been rendered and thereafter acquiesced in, even if it has not been finally settled.[59]

The same principle is applied in taking accounts as between partners, so that if one partner has improperly sought to charge an item to the firm and this has been acquiesced in by his co-partners or, conversely, if he has knowingly omitted to charge a legitimate item to the firm, the court may, in the absence of fraud, infer that this was done by agreement and is not open to challenge on the grounds of mistake.[60]

Agreements for partnership and laches

23–19   Questions of laches frequently arise where a person has agreed to enter into partnership but has, in effect, hung back in order to see whether participation in the venture is worthwhile. Lord Lindley explained:

> "The doctrine of laches is of great importance where persons have agreed to become partners, and one of them has unfairly left the other to do all the work, and then, there being a profit, comes forward and claims a share of it. In such cases as these, the plaintiff's conduct lays him open to the remark that nothing would have been heard of him had the joint adventure ended in loss instead of gain; and a court will not aid those who can be shown to have remained quiet in the hope of being able to evade responsibility in case of loss, but of being able to claim a share of gain in case of ultimate success."[61]

23–20   Thus, in *Cowell v. Watts*[62] the plaintiff and the defendant agreed to acquire and improve certain leasehold land with a view to subletting it for building purposes. However, the lease was taken in the sole name of the defendant, who declined to enter into a written

---

[58] *Sherman v. Sherman* (1692) 2 Vern. 276; *Sturt v. Mellish* (1743) 2 Atk. 610. For a recent reaffirmation of this principle, see *John v. James* [1991] F.S.R. 397.

[59] *Scott v. Milne* (1843) 7 Jur. 709. See also *Stupart v. Arrowsmith* (1856) 3 Sm. & G. 176; *Williams v. Page* (1858) 24 Beav. 654.

[60] *Thornton v. Proctor* (1792) 1 Anst. 94, noticed *supra*, para. 20–22.

[61] *Cf. Clarke v. Hart* (1858) 6 H.L.C. 633, *infra*, para. 23–27.

[62] (1850) 2 H. & Tw. 224.

agreement recording the terms of the venture. He thereafter treated the land as his own, mortgaging it and applying the funds raised in erecting buildings, and even removing the plaintiff's cattle which were grazing there. The plaintiff, though aware of the defendant's activities, did nothing for some 18 months. He then called on the defendant to perform the original agreement and, when the defendant refused, sought specific performance. That claim was dismissed, on the ground that the plaintiff had, by his conduct, induced the defendant to believe that he had abandoned the venture and that the defendant was solely entitled to the land.

On the other hand, a plea of laches failed in *Blundon v. Storm*,[63] **23–21** because the partner who sought to raise it had himself acted in an unscrupulous manner. Here, a partnership had been formed to search for sunken treasure "for an indefinite period of time ... [or until] all parties agree in writing that the purposes of the partnership have been completed ... ." One partner served a notice purporting to terminate the partnership, which under Canadian law was of no legal effect, and at the same time informed the other partners of his intention to continue the search on his own account. The other partners took no further part in the search and made no objection until 14 months later, after treasure had been found. It was held by the Canadian Supreme Court (reversing the decision of the Nova Scotia Supreme Court) that, as the partner who had purported to terminate the partnership had, before serving the notice, secretly obtained a renewal of his licence under the Treasure Trove Act and the approval of the Receiver of Wrecks, the other partners were in no way barred from relief by a plea of laches or acquiescence, notwithstanding their delay.

Mining partnerships and other speculative ventures

A plea of laches is most likely to succeed where the partnership **23–22** business is of a highly speculative nature.[64] Lord Lindley took mining partnerships as the most obvious example, observing that:

"Mining operations are so extremely doubtful as to their ultimate success that it is of the highest importance that those engaged in them should know on whom they can confidently rely for aid."

---

[63] (1971) 20 D.L.R. (3d) 413.
[64] See, for example, *Blundon v. Storm* (1971) 20 D.L.R. (3d) 413, *supra*, para. 23–21 (where, however, the plea did not succeed).

A significant factor in cases of this type will usually be the expenditure required to carry on the mining or other operations. Thus, in *Senhouse v. Christian*,[65] the defendant, one of five joint lessees of a colliery, had obtained a renewal of the lease in his own name. The other lessees, though aware of all the facts, did nothing for four years, during which time the defendant worked the colliery single handed and at great expense.[66] Lord Rosslyn dismissed their claim to the benefit of the renewed lease. This decision was subsequently cited with approval by Lord Eldon in *Norway v. Rowe*.[67]

A laches defence may still succeed even where the mining or other operation is self financing, as demonstrated by the decision in *Clegg v. Edmondson*,[68] where the facts were otherwise broadly similar to those in *Senhouse v. Christian*.

Evidence of abandonment, etc.

23-23   In order to sustain a plea of laches, it is not necessary to provide positive evidence that the plaintiff has abandoned his rights.[69] Indeed, in *Clegg v. Edmondson*,[70] the plaintiffs had repeatedly insisted on their right to participate in the profits obtained by the defendants under the renewed lease, but this was held, on the facts, not to be sufficient to preserve that right.[71] However, this case should not be taken as establishing a principle of general application, as Lord Lindley explained:

"It cannot be laid down as universally true that protests are useless. They exclude inferences which, in their absence, might fairly be drawn from the conduct of the party protesting, and are conclusive to show that no abandonment of right was intended."[72]

---

[65] (1795), reported in a note to *Hart v. Clarke* (1854) 19 Beav. 349, 356. See also *Norway v. Rowe* (1812) 19 Ves.Jr. 144, 157.

[66] This fact does not appear from the brief report at (1854) 19 Beav. 356.

[67] (1812) 19 Ves.Jr. 144. Lord Lindley commented "There were more grounds than one for this decision, but the case is always regarded as an authority in support of the doctrine acted on by Lord Rosslyn in *Senhouse v. Christian*."

[68] (1856) 8 De G.M. & G. 787.

[69] See, for example, *Davis v. Johnston* (1831) 4 Sim. 539; *Reilly v. Walsh* (1848) 11 I.Eq.R. 22 (speculative development of leasehold land). Lord Lindley also cited the decision in *Jekyl v. Gilbert*, which appeared in McNaghten's *Select Cases in Chancery*, p. 29. There, in his own words, "two artificers agreed to do work for their joint benefit; after the work was done, the person for whom it was done refused to pay; the defendant requested the plaintiff to join in legal proceedings to compel payment, but the plaintiff declined. Thereupon the defendant brought an action for payment of the work done by him, and obtained a verdict. The plaintiff then claimed half the amount recovered, but the Court held that he was not entitled to any share of it."

[70] (1856) 8 De G.M. & G. 787.

[71] See the apparently wide statement of principle formulated by Turner L.J. at *ibid.* p. 810.

[72] See *Clarke v. Hart* (1858) 6 H.L.C. 633, *infra*, para. 23-27. Cf. *Blundon v. Storm* (1971) 20 D.L.R. (3d) 413, *supra*, para. 23-21.

It goes almost without saying that, whilst mere protests may be insufficient, a plea of laches will be defeated if there is positive evidence of the defendant continuing to recognise the plaintiff's rights.[73]

Where abandonment can be proved, it may in practice be **23–24** unnecessary to rely on laches. Lord Lindley observed:

"... if a partner formally withdraws from an adventure when its prospects are bad [*he will*] be unable to claim a share of the profits resulting from it if it ultimately proves to be profitable[74]; such cases, however, are not so much cases of laches as of estoppel or agreements to release."

It would seem that *Prendergast v. Turton*,[75] falls within this class, although it has often been cited as a simple case of laches.[76] There the partnership capital was exhausted and the plaintiff partners refused to contribute additional funds. The other partners did, however, provide such funds and, several years later, succeeded in running the mine at a profit. Only then did the plaintiffs seek to assert their interest in the concern, but their claim was rejected.

Similarly, in *Rule v. Jewell*,[77] where a member of a cost-book **23–25** mining company, which was seriously in debt, had his shares forfeited for non-payment of calls. After five years he disputed the validity of the forfeiture and claimed to be reinstated as a partner. That claim was duly rejected on the basis of estoppel and, if necessary, abandonment.[78]

In *Palmer v. Moore*,[79] a joint lessee of a gold mine had given written notice to his co-lessees that he was unable to contribute to the joint expenses and that they could do as they liked with the lease; this was held to be an abandonment of his beneficial interest therein, which was accepted by one of his co-lessees subsequently working the mine at his own expense.

---

[73] See *Penny v. Pickwick* (1852) 16 Beav. 246; also *Clements v. Hall* (1858) 2 De G. & J. 173, *infra*, para. 23–29.

[74] *Maclure v. Ripley* (1850) 2 Mac. & G. 274. *Cf. Blundon v. Storm* (1971) 20 D.L.R. (3d) 413, *supra*, para. 23–21.

[75] (1841) 1 Y. & C.Ch. 98 and, on appeal, (1843) 13 L.J.Ch. 268.

[76] Indeed, Lord Lindley treated it in this way. But see *Clarke v. Hart* (1858) 6 H.L.C. 633, 657–659, *per* Lord Chelmsford; *Rule v. Jewell* (1880) 18 Ch.D. 660, 666, *per* Kay J.; *Garden Gully United Quartz Mining Co. v. McLister* (1875) 1 App.Cas. 39, 57.

[77] (1880) 18 Ch.D. 660. *Cf. Clarke v. Hart* (1858) 6 H.L.C. 633, *infra*, para. 23–27.

[78] (1880) 18 Ch.D. 667–668, *per* Kay J. Although the Statute of Limitations was pleaded, it was held not to be a defence, even though the action was commenced more than six years after the purported forfeiture: see *ibid.* p. 662. *Quaere* is this correct? See *infra*, para. 23–34.

[79] [1900] A.C. 293.

Exceptional cases: *Clarke v. Hart* and *Clements v. Hall*

23-26   Leaving aside the decision in *Lake v. Craddock*,[80] which turned on another point,[81] there are two notable cases which appear to be inconsistent with the principles described in the preceding paragraphs, *i.e. Clarke v. Hart* and *Clements v. Hall*.

Clarke v. Hart[82]

23-27   In this case, A, B and C were shareholders in a mining company run on the cost-book principle and lessees of the mine worked by the company. Finance was required for mining operations but C failed to provide his due proportion when called on so to do. C was on more than one occasion warned by A and B that, if this failure continued, they would forfeit his shares in the company (even though they did not, in fact, have power to do so under the agreement). Ultimately, A and B did purport to forfeit C's shares. C, who had at all times denied that there was any such right and who had also suggested other methods of raising the necessary finance, gave A and B notice that, if the mining operation proved successful, he would expect his share of the profits and, if necessary, take legal proceedings to enforce his claim. Some 18 months passed and C then asserted his claim. A and B rejected it and proceedings were commenced. The House of Lords held that the purported notice of forfeiture did not cause a dissolution[83] and that, in the particular circumstances, C could not be held to have indicated an intention to abandon his interest in the concern.

23-28   Lord Lindley explained the rationale underlying this decision as follows:

"The ground of the decision ... and that which distinguishes it from *Senhouse v. Christian*[84] and other cases alluded to above,[85] is this, *viz.* that the plaintiff in *Hart v. Clarke*[86] had, as one of the

---

[80] (1732) 3 P.W. 158. This case concerned an action for an account brought by one partner against his co-partners, one of whom had long ceased to take any part in the partnership affairs.

[81] Lord Lindley observed that "this case, in truth, only decided that if one of several partners chooses to claim the benefit of partnership dealings, after having for some time ceased to take any part in the affairs of the partnership, he must contribute his share of the outlays made by the other partners, with interest. It was not decided ... that a partner could, on the above terms, claim the benefit of what had been done by the others; and although the decree gave a partner who had long abandoned the concern the option of either claiming a share on proper terms or of being excluded altogether, the other partners do not appear to have raised any objection to this option being given."

[82] (1858) 6 H.L.C. 633, affirming *Hart v. Clarke* (1854) 6 De G.M. & G. 232. See also *Garden Gully United Quartz Mining Co. v. McLister* (1875) 1 App.Cas. 39. *Cf. Rule v. Jewell* (1881) 18 Ch.D. 660, *supra*, para. 23–25.

[83] See further, *infra*, para. 24–14.

[84] (1795), reported in a note to *Hart v. Clarke* (1854) 19 Beav. 349, 356.

[85] See *supra*, para. 23–22.

[86] Lord Lindley used the title of the action at first instance.

lessees of the mine, a legal interest therein, which nothing had displaced. The Court, therefore, was in this position: it was compelled either to make a decree in favour of the plaintiff, or to declare him a trustee of his share in the mine for the defendants; and there not being sufficient grounds for justifying the latter alternative, the former was necessarily adopted.[87] Upon no other ground can the case, it is submitted, be distinguished from *Clegg v. Edmondson*[88] and the other cases alluded to above; for, although reliance was placed, in the judgment in *Hart v. Clarke*, on the distinct notice given by the plaintiff that he did not acquiesce in the defendant's conduct, and should insist on his rights, it was decided in *Clegg v. Edmondson* that a protest did not enlarge the time within which redress must be sought in a court of equity."[89]

Equally, it would seem that the House of Lords may have treated *Clarke v. Hart* more as a case of potential abandonment[90] than laches, unlike the position in *Clegg v. Edmondson*.

Clements v. Hall[91]

The facts of this case were most unusual. A and B were lessees of **23–29** a mine which they worked as partners. The lease expired but A and B continued in possession as tenants from year to year, working the mine as before. In 1847 A died, leaving a will in which he appointed C as his executor and bequeathed an interest in the mine to D. B thereafter treated the mine as his own and, despite constant pressure from C, refused to render any accounts. In 1850 B, without C's knowledge, negotiated a new lease from the landlord, but on more onerous terms than before. Prior to the grant of the new lease, B had merely kept the mining operation "ticking over" so that no profits were produced; now he began to work the mine in earnest and at a profit. In 1851 D commenced an action against B and C in order to establish his interest in the mine. C admitted D's title, but B put in no defence, because the action was stayed pending security for costs being given. In the event, D did not proceed further with the action. B died in 1853 and C became his personal representative. In 1854 the plaintiff, who was the assignee of D's interest in the mine, sought to have that interest secured for his own benefit.[92] C, who had (as A's executor) admitted D's right, now (as B's personal representative)

---

[87] See *Rule v. Jewell* (1881) 18 Ch.D. 660; *Palmer v. Moore* [1900] A.C. 293, *supra*, para. 23–25.
[88] (1856) 8 De G.M. & G. 787.
[89] But see *supra*, para. 23–23.
[90] See (1858) 6 H.L.C. 633, 655–660 (*per* Lord Chelmsford), 670 (*per* Lord Wensleydale); *cf. ibid.* pp. 662 (*per* Lord Brougham), 666 (*per* Lord Cranworth).
[91] (1858) 2 De G. & J. 173. See also (1857) 24 Beav. 333.
[92] In fact, procedurally, this claim was raised by the plaintiff in a bill supplemental to the bill originally filed by D.

opposed the plaintiff's claim. Although the decision was not unanimous, it was held (1) that on A's death, his interest in the mine did not determine; (2) that his estate was entitled to share the benefit of the renewed lease; (3) that C, as A's executor, was not precluded in 1853 from asserting this right against B, since B had kept C in ignorance of the real state of the concern; and (4) that there had been no laches on the part of the plaintiff or D, through whom he claimed, because there had, since 1851, been proceedings on foot to secure their interest.[93]

Lord Lindley's final summary

23–30   The exceptional nature of the decisions in *Clarke v. Hart*[94] and *Clements v. Hall*[95] will be self evident and they do not in fact call into question the general principles which may be drawn from the other cases, as Lord Lindley confirmed:

"... it is submitted that the doctrine laid down and acted upon in *Norway v. Rowe*,[96] *Senhouse v. Christian*,[97] *Prendergast v. Turton*,[98] *Clegg v. Edmondson*,[99] and *Rule v. Jewell*[1] may still be safely relied on in all cases except those in which the court can be driven, as it was in *Hart v. Clarke*,[2] to the alternative of holding either that the plaintiff is entitled to relief, or that he has abandoned and lost his former *legal* status."[3]

4. LIMITATION AS BETWEEN PARTNERS

Application of the Limitation Act 1980

23–31   It appears that time will only run under the Limitation Act 1980 once the partnership has terminated. Lord Lindley stated the general principle thus:

"So long ... as a partnership is subsisting, and each partner is exercising his rights and enjoying his own property, the statute of

---

[93] *Semble* the position would have been different if D's action had been struck out for want of prosecution.
[94] (1858) 6 H.L.C. 633.
[95] (1858) 2 De G. & J. 173.
[96] (1812) 19 Ves.Jr. 144.
[97] (1795), reported in a note to *Hart v. Clarke* (1854) 19 Beav. 349, 356. See *supra*, para. 23–22.
[98] (1841) 1 Y. & C.Ch. 98 and, on appeal, (1843) 13 L.J.Ch. 268. See *supra*, para. 23–24.
[99] (1856) 8 De G.M. & G. 787.
[1] (1881) 18 Ch.D. 660, *supra*, para. 23–25.
[2] Again, Lord Lindley used the title of the case at first instance.
[3] See also *Garden Gully United Quartz Mining Co. v. McLister* (1875) 1 App.Cas. 39; *Palmer v. Moore* [1900] A.C. 293, *supra*, para. 23–25. In *Beningfield v. Baxter* (1886) 12 App.Cas. 167, the defendant was an executor.

limitations has, it is conceived, no application at all[4]; but as soon as a partnership is dissolved, or there is any exclusion of one partner by the others, the case is very different, and the statute begins to run."[5]

Continuing partnership

It follows that a claim for an account by one or more partners **23–32** against the other or others will, seemingly, never become time barred whilst the partnership is continuing.[6] The position will be the same as between continuing or surviving partners if, notwithstanding a dissolution, they carry on the old firm's business without any break in or settlement of its accounts. Thus, in *Betjemann v. Betjemann*[7] A, B and C carried on business as partners from 1856 to 1886; following A's death in 1886, B and C continued the business until 1893, when B died. C obtained an order for accounts to be taken as against B's executors with effect from 1856, on the footing that the accounts of the original firm had been carried on into the new firm without interruption or settlement.

There is authority for the proposition that time will not run where there has been a purported (but ineffective) forfeiture of a partner's share by his co-partners, but this is obviously dependent on showing that the partnership still continues.[8] Of course, defences other than limitation may be available to the forfeiting partners in such a case.[9]

Dissolved partnership

That a limitation defence will be effective as between the **23–33** continuing or surviving partners on the one hand and the outgoing partner or his estate on the other was clearly decided in *Knox v. Gye*.[10] This proposition might at first sight appear to be reinforced by the terms of section 43 of the Partnership Act 1890, which provides:

---

[4] *Miller v. Miller* (1869) L.R. 8 Eq. 499. But see *infra*, para. 23–33, n. 10.

[5] *Noyes v. Crawley* (1878) 10 Ch.D. 31; also *Barton v. North Staffs Ry.* (1887) 38 Ch.D. 458; *The Pongola* (1895) 73 L.T. 512.

[6] This would seem to be the position even in respect of secret profits made by a partner, for which he is bound to account to the firm under the Partnership Act 1890, s.29 (*supra*, paras. 16–09 *et seq.*): *The Pongola, supra. Sed quaere.*

[7] [1895] 2 Ch. 474. See also *The Pongola, supra.*

[8] See *Rule v. Jewell* (1881) 18 Ch.D. 660, 662, *per* Kay J.

[9] See *Rule v. Jewell, supra*; also *supra*, para. 23–25.

[10] (1872) L.R. 5 H.L. 656. In a footnote, Lord Lindley observed "*Miller v. Miller* (1869) L.R. 8 Eq. 499, is hardly consistent with this, unless it be upon the ground that there was no dissolution, or that there was a trust deed excluding the statute." See *Noyes v. Crawley* (1878) 10 Ch.D. 31, 37, *per* Malins V.-C. And see *Gopala Chetty v. Vayaraghavachariar* [1922] 1 A.C. 488. It should be noted that, prior to 1876, equitable suits for an account were not caught by any Statutes of Limitation and, whilst the Court of Chancery frequently applied them by analogy if pleaded (see *Knox v. Gye, supra*, at p. 674), it even more frequently ignored them. See also *infra*, n. 12.

"43. Subject to any agreement between the partners, the amount due from surviving or continuing partners to an outgoing partner or the representatives of a deceased partner in respect of the outgoing or deceased partner's share is a debt accruing at the date of the dissolution or death."

It is, however, difficult to see how this section can apply in the case of a *general* dissolution: if the outgoing/deceased partner's share is indeed converted into a debt, it is of a most unusual nature, since it is clear that he or his estate is entitled to a full share of any increase in the value of the partnership assets accruing in the period between the date of dissolution and the date of realisation[11] and, conversely, must bear a full share of any diminution in value during that period. Interestingly, in the commentary on the above section in his Supplement on the Partnership Act 1890, Lord Lindley observed, as regards the position under *Scots* law:

"This section proceeds on the footing that there is no winding up, but that by contract, the value of the deceased or retiring partner's share is to be ascertained and paid out. Accordingly, the date, unless otherwise stipulated, at which the value falls to be ascertained will be the date of dissolution. The amount thus becomes a debt bearing interest from that date."

Why the same point was not made in relation to English law is by no means clear, and the current editor remains of the view that the above analysis should be treated as of general application.

23–34   Where section 43 *does* apply, the debt will become time barred six years after the date of dissolution[12] or death on normal principles.[13] Where, however, the partnership was originally constituted by deed, the sum due to the outgoing partner thereunder will be recoverable as a specialty, to which a 12 year limitation period will apply.[14]

23–35   In practice, claims between the members of a dissolved firm will normally be framed as actions for an account, in respect of which the relevant limitation period is that applicable to the claim on which the duty to account is based.[15] Accordingly, an account will not normally

---

[11] See *Barclays Bank Trust Co. Ltd. v. Bluff* [1982] Ch. 172; *Chandroutie v. Gajadhar* [1987] A.C. 147. See also *infra*, paras. 25–27, 26–04.

[12] Time will, of course, only start running as from the *actual* date of dissolution, rather than from some earlier deemed dissolution date adopted by the parties: see *Coull v. Maclean*, 1991 G.W.D. 21–1249.

[13] It is, however, unclear whether this will be by virtue of the Limitation Act 1980, s.5 (simple contract debt) or s.9 (sum recoverable by statute). The point is, in any event, largely academic.

[14] *Ibid.* s.8(1).

[15] *Ibid.* s.23.

be ordered in respect of the dealings and transactions of a partnership which has been dissolved more than six years before the proceedings were issued,[16] unless the original agreement was under seal.[17]

Right to an account

Nevertheless, a number of factors may affect an outgoing or other **23–36** partner's right to an account and these are, for convenience, arranged in alphabetical order:

Acknowledgment: An acknowledgment will only result in the accrual of a fresh cause of action for limitation purposes if it is in writing and signed by the person making it.[18] In one old case, where no account had been taken for six years, it was held that a signed acknowledgment of a liability to account in respect of matters more than six years old was sufficient to justify an account being ordered in respect of those matters, even though the acknowledgment did not contain an admission that any debt was actually due.[19] The current editor considers that a similar approach might now be adopted under the Limitation Act 1980.[20]

Agreed accounts: If the partners have agreed that the firm's **23–37** annual accounts, once approved, should not be re-opened,[21] that agreement will normally be given effect to, unless fraud,[22] misrepresentation or serious errors can be proved.[23]

Assets received after accounts settled: If, after the affairs of the **23–38** partnership have been wound up and its accounts settled, an asset is received by one of the former partners which was *not* included in those accounts, time will only start to run as regards the other

---

[16] See *Noyes v. Crawley* (1878) 10 Ch.D. 31. *Cf. Betjemann v. Betjemann* [1895] 2 Ch. 474, *supra*, para. 23–32.

[17] Limitation Act 1980, ss.8(1), 23.

[18] *Ibid.* ss.29(5), 30(1). Note that a signed balance sheet can constitute an acknowledgment for the purposes of the subsection: see *Re Compania De Electricidad, etc.* [1980] Ch. 146, applying *Jones v. Bellgrove Properties Ltd.* [1949] 2 K.B. 700; *cf. Re Overmark Smith Warden Ltd.* [1982] 1 W.L.R. 1195.

[19] See *Prance v. Sympson* (1854) Kay 678, where one partner had written "You and I must go into it and settle the account." See also *Skeet v. Lindsay* (1877) 2 Ex.D. 314; *Banner v. Berridge* (1881) 18 Ch.D. 254; *Friend v. Young* [1897] 2 Ch. 421; *Kamouh v. Associated Electrical Industries International Ltd.* [1980] Q.B. 199. *Cf. Mitchell's Claim* (1871) L.R. 6 Ch.App. 822. Note that the pre-1940 cases contain references to the need for an express or implied promise to pay, but this requirement has no place in the modern law. Moreover, the decided cases provide only limited guidance in this area: see *Spencer v. Hemmerdale* [1922] 2 A.C. 507, 519, *per* Lord Sumner.

[20] On the basis that an acknowledgement of a right to an account must relate to the claim which is the basis for the duty to account under the Limitation Act 1980, s.23. Note, however, the terms of *ibid.* s.29(5)(a); and see also *Re Flynn (No. 2)* [1969] 2 Ch. 403, 412, *per* Buckley J.

[21] See *supra*, para. 10–62.

[22] See the Limitation Act 1980, s.32(1)(a).

[23] See *infra*, paras. 23–107 *et seq.*

partners' entitlement in respect of that asset with effect from the date of its receipt: the fact that those other partners have lost their general right to an account will, in such circumstances, be irrelevant.[24] *Per contra*, if the dissolution accounts have not been settled and the right to a general account is time barred.[25]

23-39 *Fraud and concealment:* Time will not run in the case of a partner's fraud or concealment, unless the other partners could with reasonable diligence have discovered the true position.[26] As a general rule, partners will be regarded as having shown reasonable diligence even where they have had ample means of discovering the concealment or fraud, but have not in fact done so nor had their suspicions aroused.[27] In such cases, the court will demonstrate a willingness to interfere many years after the event, as demonstrated by *Betjemann v. Betjemann*[28] and *Stainton v. The Carron Co.*,[29] where accounts were directed over a 25 year period.

23-40 *Part payment:* A part payment will result in the accrual of a fresh cause of action, but only if it is made in respect of the relevant debt or liquidated pecuniary claim by the partner or his agent.[30] In *Whitley v. Lowe*,[31] a payment was made by a receiver to the personal representatives of a deceased partner, A, with the approval of the surviving partner and the personal representatives of the other deceased partner, B. Although it was estimated that B's estate was then indebted to A's estate, the payment was held not to have been made in recognition of that indebtedness, so that time continued to run.[32]

23-41 *Trusts and fiduciary relationships:* It has been held that there is limited scope for a limitation defence in the case of a claim for an account based on a fiduciary relationship,[33] although the current editor doubts whether this decision affects the authority of *Knox v.*

---

[24] *Gopala Chetty v. Vayaraghavachariar* [1922] 1 A.C. 488, 494 *et seq.*
[25] *Ibid.* p. 496.
[26] Limitation Act 1980, s.32(1). The deliberate commission of a breach of duty in circumstances in which it is unlikely to be discovered for some time amounts to deliberate concealment for this purpose: *ibid.* s.32(2).
[27] See *Rawlins v. Wickham* (1858) 3 De G. & J. 304; *Betjemann v. Betjemann* [1895] 2 Ch. 474.
[28] [1895] 2 Ch. 474. See *supra*, para. 23–32.
[29] (1857) 24 Beav. 346. See also *Wedderburn v. Wedderburn* (1838) 4 Myl. & Cr. 41; *Allfrey v. Allfrey* (1849) 1 Mac. & G. 87. And see *infra*, para. 26–44.
[30] Limitation Act 1980, s.29(5).
[31] (1858) 2 De. G. & J. 704.
[32] Sir John Romilly M.R. in fact based his decision on the fact that the receiver could not have been acting as the agent of B's personal representatives: see (1858) 25 Beav. 421, 431. This aspect was not highlighted in the Court of Appeal.
[33] See *Att.-Gen. v. Cocke* [1988] Ch. 414, 421, *per* Harman J. See also *Pearse v. Green* (1819) 1 J. & W. 135; *Re Landi* [1939] Ch. 828; *Tito v. Waddell (No. 2)* [1977] Ch. 106, 250–251, *per* Megarry V.-C. *Cf. John v. James* [1991] F.S.R. 397, 439, *per* Nicholls J.

Gye.[34] Be that as it may, where freehold or leasehold land is held for the benefit of a firm on an express or implied trust for sale,[35] it must follow that an outgoing partner's rights will not be prejudiced as long as he retains an interest under that trust.[36] In addition, no limitation period will apply where the claim against the trustees involves fraud or a fraudulent breach of trust.[37]

Arbitrations

The Limitation Act 1980 applies to arbitrations in the same way as **23–42** it applies to proceedings in the High Court.[38]

5. ACTIONS FOR SPECIFIC PERFORMANCE

Agreements for partnership: the general rule

It has long been an established rule that the court will not order **23–43** the specific performance of an agreement for partnership. Lord Lindley explained the basis for this rule as follows:

"If two persons have agreed to enter into partnership, and one of them refuses to abide by the agreement, the remedy for the other is an action for damages, and not, excepting in the cases to be presently noticed, for specific performance. To compel an unwilling person to become a partner with another would not be conducive to the welfare of the latter, any more than to compel a man to marry a woman he did not like would be for the benefit of the lady. Moreover, to decree specific performance of an agreement for a partnership at will would be nugatory, inasmuch as it might be dissolved the moment after the decree was made; and to decree specific performance of an agreement for a partnership for a term of years would involve the court in the superintendence of the partnership throughout the whole continuance of the term.[39] As a rule, therefore, courts will not decree

---

[34] (1872) L.R. 5 H.L. 656: see *supra*, para. 23–33. Yet, partnership clearly *does* involve a fiduciary relationship: see *supra*, para. 16–03.

[35] See *Re Fuller's Contract* [1933] Ch. 652. Also *supra*, paras 18–60 *et seq.*, 19–15 *et seq.*

[36] *Quaere*, could this principle be extended to *any* case involving an asset held by a former partner in respect of which he is bound to account to the firm, *e.g.* under the Partnership Act 1890, s.29? It is tentatively thought not: see *supra*, para. 23–32, n. 6.

[37] Limitation Act 1980, s.21(1). Note also *ibid.* s.21(2).

[38] *Ibid.* s.34.

[39] *Quaere* to what extent this particular objection to a decree of specific performance still holds good. See *Shiloh Spinners Ltd. v. Harding* [1973] A.C. 691, 724, *per* Lord Wilberforce; *Tito v. Waddell (No. 2)* [1977] Ch. 106, 321–323, *per* Megarry V.-C.; *Gravesham Borough Council v. British Railways Board* [1978] Ch. 379, 404, *per* Slade J.

specific performance of an agreement for a partnership.[40] Nor will specific performance be decreed of an agreement to become a partner and bring in a certain amount of capital, or in default to lend a sum of money to the plaintiff."[41]

This is still the position.[42]

Exceptions to the general rule

23-44   There are two recognised exceptions to the general rule, although these are, on a true analysis, more apparent than real.

(1) *Execution of formal agreement*

Whilst the court will not be prepared to force a person into partnership against his will, once he has become a partner, it will readily order him to execute a formal agreement setting out the terms of the partnership, if that was what the parties intended. In such a case, it does not matter that the execution of the agreement will, in effect, alter the partners' rights. Lord Lindley put it in this way:

"... if the parties have agreed to execute some formal instrument which would have the effect of conferring rights which do not exist so long as the agreement is not carried out, in such a case, and for the purpose of putting the parties into the position agreed upon, the execution of that formal instrument may be decreed, although the partnership thereby formed might be immediately dissolved.[43] The principle upon which the Court proceeds in a case of this description, is the same as that which induces it to decree execution of a lease under seal, notwithstanding the term for which the lease was to continue has already expired."[44]

Such an order was made in *England v. Curling*,[45] after the partners had carried on business for some 12 years under what were, in effect,

---

[40] *Hercy v. Birch* (1804) 9 Ves.Jr. 357; *Downs v. Collins* (1848) 6 Hare 418; *Sheffield Gas Consumers' Co. v. Harrison* (1853) 17 Beav. 294; *Scott v. Rayment* (1868) L.R. 7 Eq. 112. Note also *Vivers v. Tuck* (1863) 1 Moo.(N.S.) 516 (an exceptional case, in which the plaintiff had drawn up the agreement but the defendant did not understand its contents).

[41] *Sichel v. Mosenthal* (1862) 30 Beav. 371.

[42] One of the more "recent" reaffirmations of this principle is to be found in *Byrne v. Reid* [1902] 2 Ch. 735, 743, *per* Stirling L.J.; also *Blundon v. Storm* (1971) 20 D.L.R. (3d) 413, 421. And see *Fry on Specific Performance* (6th ed.), pp. 699–700; *Snell's Equity* (29th ed.) p. 593. *Cf.* the observations of Megarry J. in *C.H. Giles & Co. v. Morris* [1972] 1 W.L.R. 307, regarding the enforcement of contracts involving the performance of personal services; also *supra*, n. 39.

[43] *Buxton v. Lister* (1746) 3 Atk. 385; and see *Crawshay v. Maule* (1813) 1 Swanst. 495, 513, note; *Stocker v. Wedderburn* (1857) 3 K. & J. 403.

[44] See *Wilkinson v. Torkington* (1837) 2 Y. & C.Ex. 726.

[45] (1844) 8 Beav. 129. See further, as to this case, *Sichel v. Mosenthal* (1862) 30 Beav. 371, 376, *per* Lord Romilly.

initialled heads of agreement and after one partner (the defendant) had purported to given a notice of dissolution.[46] The value of such an order was also clearly recognised in *Byrne v. Reid*,[47] where one partner had nominated his son to take over a part of his share pursuant to an express power in the agreement but, despite his acceptance of the nomination, the other partner had refused to recognise the son as a partner.

(2) *Account following dissolution*

The court may also, in effect, order the specific performance of an **23–45** agreement for partnership where two or more persons have agreed to share the profits derived from a particular venture and one seeks the payment of his share after the venture has come to an end. Lord Lindley observed:

"Although the decree giving him the relief he asks may be prefaced by a declaration that the agreement relied upon ought to be specifically performed, this has not the effect of creating a partnership to be carried on by the litigants, but merely serves as a foundation for the decree for an account, which is the substantial part of what is sought and given."

Cases of this type will almost inevitably involve an outright denial of partnership by the defendant(s), as in *Dale v. Hamilton*[48] and *Webster v. Bray*.[49]

Other instances where specific performance granted

A partner may, in an appropriate case, seek an order for specific **23–46** performance or, more usually, an injunction to compel his co-partners to adhere to the terms of their agreement whilst the partnership is continuing. The principles on which the court will act in such cases is considered later in this chapter.[50]

---

[46] The following was the minute of the decree: "The Court doth declare that the agreement for a co-partnership dated, etc., is a binding agreement between the parties thereto, and ought to be specifically performed and carried into execution, and doth order and decree the same accordingly. Refer it to the Master to inquire whether any and what variations have been made in the said agreement, by and with the assent of the several parties thereto since the date thereof. Let the Master settle and approve of a proper deed of co-partnership between the said parties in pursuance of the said agreement, having regard to any variations which he may find to have been made in the said agreement as hereinbefore directed, and let the parties execute it. Continue the injunction against the defendant Curling. Liberty to apply." For the form of the injunction see (1844) 8 Beav. 130.

[47] [1902] 2 Ch. 735. See also *supra*, paras. 10–217, 19–71.

[48] (1846) 5 Hare 369 and (1847) 2 Ph. 266. See further, *supra*, paras. 7–08 *et seq*.

[49] (1849) 7 Hare 159. See also *Robinson v. Anderson* (1855) 20 Beav. 98 and 7 De G.M. & G. 239.

[50] See *infra*, paras. 23–130 *et seq*.

The enforcement of obligations arising on and following the dissolution of a partnership does not give rise to any questions peculiar to the law of partnership and is not further considered in this work. However, it should be noted that the courts have, by way of specific performance or injunction, enforced (*inter alia*) the following agreements, which are for convenience arranged in alphabetical order:

23-47 *Annuities:* Agreements to pay an annuity to an outgoing partner or his widow.[51]

Books: Agreements as to the custody of partnership books and the provision of copies thereof.[52]

Getting in debts: Agreements that a particular person will get in the partnership debts.[53]

Outgoing partner's share: Agreements that the value of an outgoing or deceased partner's share will be ascertained and/or acquired in a certain way.[54]

Retirement: Agreements by one partner to retire from a firm and to assign his share to his co-partners.[55]

6. ACTIONS FOR FRAUD AND MISREPRESENTATION

23-48 When considering the remedies available to a partner who has been induced to enter into partnership by fraud or misrepresentation, it is necessary to identify whether the fraud or misrepresentation has been perpetrated by one of the other partners or by a third party. As Lord

---

[51] *Aubin v. Holt* (1855) 2 K. & J. 66; *Re Flavell* (1833) 25 Ch.D. 89. *Cf. Bonville v. Bonville* (1860) 6 Jur. (N.S.) 414, where the terms of the agreement were unclear. See also *supra*, paras. 10–149 *et seq.*

[52] *Lingen v. Simpson* (1824) 1 Sim. & St. 600; also *Whittaker v. Howe* (1841) 3 Beav. 383. And see, generally, *supra*, paras. 10–60, 22–07 *et seq.*

[53] See *Davis v. Amer* (1854) 3 Drew. 64; *Turner v. Major* (1862) 3 Giff. 442. See also *supra*, para. 10–224.

[54] *Morris v. Kearsley* (1836) 3 Y. & C.Ex. 139; *King v. Chuck* (1853) 17 Beav. 325; *Gibson v. Goldsmid* (1854) 5 De G.M. & G. 757; *Essex v. Essex* (1855) 20 Beav. 442; *Featherstonhaugh v. Turner* (1858) 25 Beav. 382; *Homfray v. Fothergill* (1866) L.R. 1 Eq. 567; *Daw v. Herring* [1892] 1 Ch. 284. *Cf. Downs v. Collins* (1848) 6 Hare 418, where enforcement would have been tantamount to specific performance of a contract for a partnership; also *Cooper v. Hood* (1858) 7 W.R. 83, where the agreement was too vague. And see, generally, *supra*, paras. 10–121 *et seq.*

[55] *Gray v. Smith* (1889) 43 Ch.D. 208.

Lindley explained, in a passage dealing solely with the consequences of fraud:

> "Speaking generally and subject to certain qualifications ... if the fraud complained of has been committed by the other partner, the person defrauded has the option of affirming or of rescinding the contract into which he has been induced to enter; and whether he affirms it or disaffirms it he is entitled to damages for any loss which he may have sustained by reason of the fraud.[56] But if the fraud has been committed by some third person and is not in point of law imputable to the other partner, then the person defrauded has no such option; he cannot rescind the contract: he can only sue those who defrauded him for damages."

The position is, in essence, the same in the case of a negligent or careless (but not wholly innocent) misrepresentation, although damages are not in any event recoverable under the Misrepresentation Act 1967 against a non-contracting party.[57]

This section is, of course, concerned solely with claims as between partners and not as between one partner and a third party.

A. Damages

Fraud

On the assumption that a partner has in fact been induced to enter **23–49** into partnership by a false and fraudulent representation made by one of his co-partners,[58] an action in damages will clearly lie in respect of any loss which he may thereby suffer.[59]

---

[56] *Archer v. Brown* [1985] Q.B. 401; also *Attwood v. Small* (1838) 6 Cl. & F. 232; *Cruikshank v. McVicar* (1844) 8 Beav. 106; *Pulsford v. Richards* (1853) 17 Beav. 87; *Redgrave v. Hurd* (1881) 20 Ch.D. 1. And see *Beck v. Kantorowicz* (1857) 3 K. & J. 230, and cases of that class. As to the measure of damages, see *Doyle v. Olby (Ironmongers) Ltd.* [1969] 2 Q.B. 158; *Archer v. Brown*, *supra*.

[57] See *ibid.* s.2(1), (2). See also *supra*, para. 12–97. Note, however, that damages for negligent mis-statement can be obtained against a third party: see *Hedley Byrne & Co. Ltd. v. Heller & Partners* [1964] A.C. 465; *Mutual Life and Citizens' Assurance Co. Ltd. v. Evatt* [1971] A.C. 793; *Esso Petroleum Ltd. v. Mardon* [1976] Q.B. 801. As to the limitations on such a claim, see *Argy Trading Development Co. Ltd. v. Lapid Developments Ltd.* [1977] 1 W.L.R. 444, 459 *et seq.*, *per* Croom-Johnson J.

[58] Lord Lindley summarised the requirements which must be satisfied to sustain an allegation of fraud under the headings (1) Untruth necessary; (2) Untruth must be material and have been relied upon; and (3) Whether untruth must have been known at the time. This passage has not been retained in the present edition as it raises no considerations peculiar to the law of partnership. The reader is referred to the treatment of this subject in *Chitty on Contracts* (26th ed.), paras. 431 *et seq.*

[59] See *Derry v. Peek* (1889) 14 App.Cas. 337; *Doyle v. Olby (Ironmongers) Ltd.* [1969] 2 Q.B. 158; *Archer v. Brown* [1985] Q.B. 401. Cf. *Redgrave v. Hurd* (1881) 20 Ch.D. 1.

Misrepresentation

23–50   Prior to the Misrepresentation Act 1967, damages could in certain circumstances be recovered by a person induced to enter into a contract as a result of a negligent misrepresentation[60] but not, in general, if the misrepresentation was innocent.[61] That Act, in effect, extended the right to damages to *any* case in which a negligent misrepresentation is made by one contracting party to another, provided that damages would have been recoverable if the misrepresentation been made fraudulently.[62] To avoid liability, the party making the misrepresentation must prove that he had reasonable grounds to believe and *did* believe up to the time the contract was made that the facts represented were true. Thus, mere belief in the truth of a representation is not, in itself, sufficient.[63] Where damages are recoverable, they are assessed according to the tortious measure, but on the basis of fraud rather than negligence.[64]

The 1967 Act also empowered the court, in any case where it would be equitable to do so, to award damages in lieu of rescission where a person has been induced to enter into a contract as a result of a negligent *or a wholly innocent* misrepresentation.[65] It is not yet clear whether the tortious or contractual measure of damages applies in such a case.[66]

B. Rescission

Agreements for partnership

23–51   A fraudulent, negligent or innocent misrepresentation made by one prospective partner to another which induces the latter to enter into partnership will give rise to a right of rescission, on normal principles.[67] However, rescission of a partnership contract has long

---

[60] See *Hedley Byrne & Co. Ltd. v. Heller & Partners Ltd.* [1964] A.C. 465; also the cases cited *supra*, para. 23–48, n. 57. And see, generally, *Chitty on Contracts* (26th ed.), paras. 445 *et seq.*

[61] *Heilbut, Symonds & Co. v. Buckleton* [1913] A.C. 30; *Gilchester Properties Ltd. v. Gomm* [1948] W.N. 71.

[62] Misrepresentation Act 1967, s.2(1). See, generally, *Gosling v. Anderson* [1972] E.G.D. 701; *Watts v. Spence* [1976] Ch. 165; *Howard Marine and Dredging Co. Ltd. v. A. Ogden & Sons (Excavations) Ltd.* [1978] Q.B. 574; *Chesnau v. Interhome Ltd.* (1983) 134 N.L.J. 341; *Sharneyford Supplies Ltd. v. Edge* [1986] Ch. 128; *Naughton v. O'Callaghan* [1990] 3 All E.R. 191; *Cemp Properties (U.K.) Ltd. v. Dentsply Research & Development Corp.* [1991] 34 E.G. 62; *Royscot Trust Ltd. v. Rogerson* [1991] 2 Q.B. 297; also *Garden Neptune Shipping Ltd. v. Occidental Worldwide Investment Corp.* [1990] 1 Lloyd's Rep. 330. Note that the expression "innocent" misrepresentation is used in these cases in a special sense: the 1967 Act did *not* introduce a general right of action in the case of all forms of innocent misrepresentation.

[63] See *Howard Marine and Dredging Co. Ltd. v. A. Ogden & Sons (Excavations) Ltd.*, *supra*.

[64] See *Royscot Trust Ltd. v. Rogerson* [1991] 2 Q.B. 297 (C.A.) and the other cases cited *supra*, n. 62.

[65] Misrepresentation Act 1967, s.2(2).

[66] See *Chitty on Contracts* (26th ed.), para. 456.

[67] See *Adam v. Newbigging* (1888) 13 App.Cas. 308; *Redgrave v. Hurd* (1881) 20 Ch.D. 1; and, generally, *Chitty on Contracts* (26th ed.), paras. 458 *et seq.* Note also *Museprime Properties Ltd. v. Adhill Properties Ltd.* [1990] 61 P. & C.R. 111.

been attended by a number of specific and well recognised consequences, as Lord Lindley made clear, when writing prior to the Partnership Act 1890:

"Where a person is induced by the false representations of others to become a partner with them, the Court will rescind the contract of partnership at his instance; and will compel them to repay him whatever he may have paid them, with interest, and to indemnify him against all the debts and liabilities of the partnership, and if the defendants have been guilty of fraud[68] against all claims and demands to which he may have become subject by reason of his having entered into partnership with them, he on the other hand accounting to them for what he may have received since his entry into the concern."[69]

This was the position even where the partner to whom the misrepresentation was made had the means of ascertaining the true facts but did not do so.[70]

Partnership Act 1890, section 41

The same principles are, for the most part, reflected in section 41 **23–52** of the Partnership Act 1890, which provides as follows:

"41. Where a partnership contract is rescinded on the ground of the fraud or misrepresentation of one of the parties thereto, the party entitled to rescind is, without prejudice to any other right, entitled—

(a) to a lien on, or right of retention of, the surplus of the partnership assets, after satisfying the partnership liabilities, for any sum of money paid by him for the purchase of a share in the partnership and for any capital contributed by him, and is

(b) to stand in the place of the creditors of the firm for any payments made by him in respect of the partnership liabilities, and

---

[68] The words "if the defendants have been guilty of fraud" were, in the current editor's view inappropriately, omitted in later editions. *Cf.* the Partnership Act 1890, s.41(c), *infra*, and the judgments of the Court of Appeal in *Newbigging v. Adam* (1886) 34 Ch.D. 582.

[69] See *Pillans v. Harkness* (1713) Colles. P.C. 442; *Ex p. Broome* (1811) 1 Rose 69; *Hamil v. Stokes* (1817) 4 Price 161; *Stainbank v. Fernley* (1839) 9 Sim. 556; *Rawlins v. Wickham* (1858) 1 Giff. 355 and, on appeal, 3 De G. & J. 304; *Jauncey v. Knowles* (1859) 8 W.R. 69; *Senanayake v. Cheng* [1966] A.C. 63. *Clifford v. Brooke* (1806) 13 Ves.Jr. 131 was not a case of this class.

[70] *Rawlins v. Wickham, supra.*

(c)   to be indemnified by the person guilty of the fraud or making the representation against all the debts and liabilities of the firm."[71]

An express indemnity against the partnership debts and obligations is, of course, required because rescission in no way affects a partner's accrued liability to third parties.[72]

Additional rights preserved by the Act

23–53   It will be noted that the rights conferred by the section are expressed to be "without prejudice to any other right," thus obviously preserving any right to damages which may exist.[73] Indeed, that right may prove more valuable than the statutory indemnity.[74] However, it would seem that certain other rights, which were established prior to the Act, have also been preserved. Thus, the partner concerned may, in addition to an order for the repayment of the purchase price originally paid for his share and any capital contributed, be entitled to interest on those sums[75] and to a lien on the surplus assets both for such interest and for the costs of the action.[76] Furthermore, he may also be entitled to interest on all payments made by him in respect of partnership debts and liabilities, although he must give credit with interest for any share of profits received whilst he remained a partner.[77]

Dissolution agreements, etc.

23–54   Although not governed by a specific statutory provision in the same way as agreements for partnership, questions of rescission also arise in relation to agreements reached in and about the *termination* of a partnership.

---

[71] This paragraph accords with the views expressed regarding the extent of the indemnity in the case of a contract induced by misrepresentation in *Newbigging v. Adam* (1886) 34 Ch.D. 582. This point was, in fact, left open by the House of Lords in *Adam v. Newbigging* (1888) 13 App.Cas. 308.

[72] See *Ex p. Broome* (1811) 1 Rose 69; *Jefferys v. Smith* (1827) 3 Russ 158; *Macbride v. Lindsay* (1852) 9 Hare 574. Also *Howard v. Shaw* (1846) 9 I.L.R. 335; *Henderson v. Royal British Bank* (1857) 7 E. & B. 356; *Daniell v. Royal British Bank* (1857) 1 H. & N. 681; *Powis v. Harding* (1857) 1 C.B. (N.S.) 533; *Reese River Mining Co. v. Smith* (1869) L.R. 4 H.L. 64, 70, *per* Lord Cairns.

[73] See *supra*, paras. 23–49, 23–50. And see *Archer v. Brown* [1985] Q.B. 401.

[74] See the judgments in *Newbigging v. Adam* (1886) 34 Ch.D. 582.

[75] *Adam v. Newbigging* (1888) 13 App.Cas. 308, affirming *Newbigging v. Adam, supra*. In this case the plaintiff had withdrawn part of his capital and the defendants were held jointly and severally liable for the balance with interest at 4 per cent. See also *Pillans v. Harkness* (1713) Colles, P.C. 442; *Rawlins v. Wickham* (1858) 1 Giff. 355 and, on appeal, 3 De G. & J. 304.

[76] *Mycock v. Beatson* (1879) 13 Ch.D. 384. Interest was allowed at 5 per cent.

[77] *Rawlins v. Wickham, supra*.

No rescission for bad bargain

It is, perhaps, self evident that the rescission of a dissolution agreement cannot be obtained merely because it turns out to be disadvantageous to one or more of the partners. As Lord Lindley explained:

"Supposing every member of a firm to be *sui juris*, any one may retire upon any terms to which he and his co-partners may choose to assent; and if there is no fraud, misrepresentation, or concealment on either side, all will be bound by any agreement into which he and they may enter, although it may ultimately turn out that a bad bargain has been made."

Thus, in *Knight v. Marjoribanks*,[78] a partner unsuccessfully sought to set aside an agreement, under which he had, in effect, sold his share in the firm to his co-partners in exchange for a modest payment and the release of his indebtedness to the firm, on the grounds of fraud, collusion and inadequacy of consideration. The partnership venture was at the time unprofitable and his partners had stated that a sum in excess of £5,000 was due from him. He never sought to question this statement or to examine the partnership books in order to establish its accuracy, nor did he seek independent advice before concluding the agreement, even though he was then in a financially distressed state. In the absence of any evidence that his co-partners had practised a fraud or otherwise taken unfair advantage of his financial position, the agreement was held to be binding on him.[79]

Blay v. Pollard and Morris[80] was a somewhat similar case, although **23–55** rescission was not actually sought. There, two partners, P and M, orally agreed to dissolve their partnership on terms that M should take over all the liabilities of the firm incurred after a certain date. Subsequently a written agreement was drawn up by P's father, who was a solicitor, under which M was required to indemnify P against all rent due *before* that date. The agreement was handed to M, who looked through it and signed it, but said he did not understand it. The landlord then brought an action against P and M for such rent. P sought to rely on the indemnity as against M, who in turn argued that he had signed the agreement in the belief that it embodied the terms of the previous oral agreement and that it was drawn up under a

---

[78] (1848) 11 Beav. 322 and, on appeal, 2 Mac. & G. 10.
[79] See also *Ex p. Peake* (1816) 1 Madd. 346; *Ramsbottom v. Parker* (1821) 6 Madd. 5; *Cockle v. Whiting* (1829) Taml. 55; *McLure v. Ripley* (1850) 2 Mac. & G. 274.
[80] [1930] 1 K.B. 628. See also *Saunders v. Anglia Building Society* [1971] A.C. 1004.

mutual mistake of fact. In the absence of any allegation of fraud or misrepresentation, it was held that M was bound by the agreement, since he knew its nature when he signed it and there was no evidence of mutual mistake.

In cases of this type, the dissolution agreement will not only bind the partners but also their respective personal representatives, trustees in bankruptcy or liquidators,[81] save to the extent that it can be set aside under the insolvency legislation or the general law.[82]

Agreements based on false accounts

23-56   A dissolution agreement may, and often will, be rescinded if there has been fraud or misrepresentation with regard to the state of the partnership accounts, as Lord Lindley explained:

"Notwithstanding the inability of a retiring partner, and of those claiming under him, to avoid an agreement fairly come to between him and his co-partners,[83] the good faith and open dealing which one partner has a right to expect from another never require to be more scrupulously observed than when one of them is retiring upon terms agreed to upon the strength of representations as to the state of the partnership accounts; and an agreement entered into on a dissolution will be set aside if it can be shown to have been based upon error[84] or to have been tainted by fraud, whether in the shape of positive misrepresentation or of concealment of the truth."

In *Chandler v. Dorsett*,[85] the plaintiff and the defendant had dissolved their partnership and the defendant drew up an account in a form which made it appear that a balance was due to him from the plaintiff. The plaintiff gave the defendant a promissory note for this sum, but later discovered mistakes in the account and commenced proceedings for a fresh account to be taken. The defendant's plea of account stated[86] was not upheld and a new account was ordered.

---

[81] *Ex p. Peake* (1816) 1 Madd. 346; *Ramsbottom v. Parker* (1821) 6 Madd. 5; *Luckie v. Forsyth* (1846) 3 Jo. & LaT. 388.

[82] See *supra*, paras. 10–124, 10–125 and *infra*, paras. 27–16, 27–37, 27–102, 27–103. And see the following decisions under the old bankruptcy laws: *Anderson v. Maltby* (1793) 2 Ves.Jr. 244, 254, *per* Lord Loughborough; *Billiter v. Young* (1856) 6 E. & B. 1, 40, *per* Jervis C.J.; *Warden v. Jones* (1857) 23 Beav. 497; *Heilbut v. Nevill* (1870) L.R. 5 C.P. 478.

[83] See *supra*, para. 23–54.

[84] This expression seemingly comprehends any non-fraudulent misrepresentation, as well as a mutual mistake of fact.

[85] (1679) Finch 431. See also *Maddeford v. Austwick* (1826) 1 Sim. 89; *Spittal v. Smith* (1829) Taml. 45; *Law v. Law* [1905] 1 Ch. 140.

[86] Or, more properly, a settled account: see *infra*, para. 23–106.

Accounts agreed prior to expulsion

On the same basis, where a partner is induced to sign accounts in **23–57** ignorance of his impending expulsion, he will not subsequently be bound by those accounts if they affect the nature or quantum of his entitlement as an outgoing partner.[87]

Agreements made with personal representatives of deceased partner

Special considerations apply where an agreement is reached **23–58** between the surviving partners and the personal representatives of a deceased partner.

(a)   Where Personal Representatives are not Partners

In the simple case, where the personal representatives are not themselves partners, it is clear that any agreement that the deceased's share will be ascertained in a certain way or taken at a certain value cannot be impeached, unless there has been fraud or collusion between them and the surviving partners.[88] Naturally, if such fraud or collusion can be proved, the agreement will be set aside at the instance of any person interested in the deceased partner's estate.[89]

However, it should be noted that, even if the agreement is binding, the personal representatives may still be liable for any loss suffered by the estate, as Lord Lindley pointed out in the following passage:

"... even although there be no fraud or collusion, still if the executor[90] has obtained less than the true value of the deceased's share in the partnership estate, the executor may be liable as for a *devastavit*, although the surviving partner may be protected against all demands. But if, in a case of difficulty, the executor has acted

---

[87] See *Blisset v. Daniel* (1853) 10 Hare 493. The expulsion was, of course, held to be wrongful in this case: see further, *supra*, para. 10–100.

[88] See the Trustee Act 1925, s.15. At this point, Lord Lindley explained that "although it has been said that the creditors, or other persons interested in the estate of the deceased, may impeach such an agreement by instituting proceedings against the surviving partners and the executors of the deceased, [*See Bowsher v. Watkins (1830) 1 R. & M. 277; Gedge v. Traill (1823) 1 R. & M. 281*] still agreements of the kind in question cannot be successfully impeached, unless there has been some fraud or collusion between them and the executors." He then quoted from the judgment of Lord Langdale in *Davies v. Davies* (1837) 2 Keen 534, 539. See also *Chambers v. Howell* (1847) 11 Beav. 6; *Stainton v. The Carron Co.* (1853) 18 Beav. 146; *Smith v. Everett* (1859) 27 Beav. 446.

[89] See *Cook v. Collingridge* (1823) Jac. 607; *Rice v. Gordon* (1848) 11 Beav. 265; also *Beningfield v. Baxter* (1886) 12 App.Cas. 167. Lord Lindley added in a somewhat elliptical footnote at this point: "Less than fraud or collusion will justify an action against an executor of a deceased partner and the surviving partners, *Travis v. Milne* (1851) 9 Hare 141, but will not, it is apprehended, invalidate arrangements into which they may have entered for payment of the share of the deceased." *Quaere*, is this correct? If the agreement amounts to a breach of trust in which the surviving partners are implicated, it seems unlikely that it would be upheld by the court. And see also, as to bringing actions against surviving partners, *infra*, para. 26–52.

[90] An administrator will be in the same position.

with a bona fide view to do his best for the estate he represents, the Court will not be willing to make him account for what, without his wilful default, he might have received from the surviving partners."[91]

(b) Where Personal Representatives are Partners

23–59 Where the personal representatives are also surviving partners, there will be such a conflict of interest and duty that, in Lord Lindley's words, it will be "almost impossible for [*them*] to enter into any arrangement with respect to the share of the deceased in the partnership estate which those interested in that share may not afterwards succeed in setting aside."[92] This is a principle of general application,[93] although in the decided cases some other ground for setting aside the arrangement has usually been found.

Thus, in *Wedderburn v. Wedderburn*,[94] where an account of a deceased partner's estate was directed 30 years after the date of his death, despite a number of changes in the firm and the execution of partial releases by the beneficiaries, it appears that the releases were executed in ignorance of the true state of the partnership accounts. In *Stocken v. Dawson*,[95] the surviving partner was one of the deceased's executors and purported to purchase his share at a valuation pursuant to an express power in the will. It appears that the valuation was not a proper one and the sale was set aside seven years later on the application of the deceased's son.

Acquisition of share pursuant to partnership agreement

23–60   These difficulties will not, however, arise where surviving partners who are also the deceased partner's personal representatives acquire his share pursuant to an express term of the partnership agreement.[96] In such a case, it will not be possible to impugn the acquisition, unless any impropriety on the part of those partners can be proved.[97] If the agreement requires the deceased partner's share to be valued, but some error is made in the valuation, this will not, in general, affect the surviving partner's right to acquire the share, although the error will, in an appropriate case, be corrected by the court.[98]

---

[91] See *Rowley v. Adams* (1844) 7 Beav. 395 and (1849) 2 H.L.C. 725. And note also the Trustee Act 1925, s.61.

[92] See *Cook v. Collingridge* (1822) Jac. 607.

[93] See *ibid.* at p. 621, *per* Lord Eldon.

[94] (1838) 2 Myl. & Cr. 41. See also *infra*, para. 26–44. *Millar v. Craig* (1843) 6 Beav. 433 was a somewhat similar case, although no question was raised as against the partners who were not executors.

[95] (1848) 17 L.J.Ch. 282. Note also *Rice v. Gordon* (1848) 11 Beav. 265.

[96] See generally, as to such provisions, *supra*, paras. 10–121 *et seq.*

[97] As in *Stocken v. Dawson*, *supra*, para. 23–59.

[98] *Vyse v. Foster* (1874) L.R. 7 H.L. 318; *Hordern v. Hordern* [1910] A.C. 465.

Equally, an honest and fair valuation prepared substantially in accordance with the terms of the agreement, which has stood unimpeached for many years, will not be upset save, perhaps, where it is clearly proved to be erroneous.[99] It has already been seen that a valuation carried out by an agreed expert valuer cannot normally be challenged.[1]

Position where one executor is not a partner

If at least one of the deceased partner's executors is not himself a **23–61** member of the firm, he will have power to settle any claim which the other executor(s) may have against the estate.[2] This will obviously facilitate any arrangement in relation to the deceased's share.

Right of retainer out of assets

It should be noted that, despite the conflict of interest previously **23–62** referred to, a surviving partner who was the executor of his deceased co-partner was formerly entitled to retain out of the estate any sum found to be due from the deceased to the firm or to himself on taking the partnership accounts,[3] but this right was later abolished.[3a]

Loss of right to rescind

Where a right to rescind exists, it can, on normal principles, be lost **23–63** (1) by laches or affirmation or (2) if *restitutio in integrum* is impossible. Moreover, in the case of an innocent or negligent misrepresentation, the court may, if it considers it equitable to do so, refuse to rescind the contract and award damages in lieu.[4]

Laches and affirmation

A partner entitled to rescind a contract for fraud or misrepresenta- **23–64** tion will lose that right if he does not repudiate the contract within a reasonable time after discovering the true facts;[5] *a fortiori*, if he then

---

[99] *Hordern v. Hordern, supra,* at pp. 475–476.
[1] See *supra,* para. 10–141.
[2] *Re Houghton* [1904] 1 Ch. 622. *Semble* an administrator has the same power.
[3] *Morris v. Morris* (1874) L.R. 10 Ch.App. 68. In this case, the accounts were still unsettled.
[3a] Administration of Estates Act 1971, s.10(1).
[4] Misrepresentation Act 1967, s.2(2). See also *supra,* para. 23–50.
[5] See, generally, *Clough v. L. & N.W. Ry.* (1871) L.R. 7 Ex. 26, 35, *per* Mellor J. Note, however, that it is not enough to prove that the partner seeking rescission has for some time had the *means* to discover the true facts: *Rawlins v. Wickham* (1858) 3 De. G. & J. 304; *Betjemann v. Betjemann* [1895] 2 Ch. 474. And see, for examples of cases in which the contract was repudiated too late, *Ashley's case* (1870) L.R. 9 Eq. 263; *Scholey v. Central Ry. of Venezuela* (1868) L.R. 9 Eq. 266, note. Cf. *Campbell v. Fleming* (1834) 1 A. & E. 40; *Macneill's case* (1868) L.R. 10 Eq. 503. See also *supra,* paras. 23–17 *et seq.*

affirms the contract or otherwise does anything which is inconsistent with his right to rescind.[6]

Thus, in *Law v. Law*,[7] a partner sold his share to his co-partner and later discovered that material information had been withheld from him. Notwithstanding his belief that further material facts had been concealed, he agreed to a modification of the terms on which the share had been sold without insisting on a full disclosure. It was held that he could not, on discovering the full extent of the concealment, repudiate the sale.

Restitution impossible

23–65   A partner who seeks rescission must, in general, be in a position to ensure that *restitutio in integrum* is possible, unless his inability to do so can be attributed to the partner(s) responsible for the fraud or misrepresentation.[8] The fact that the share acquired has become worthless will not prevent rescission,[9] but the incorporation of the partnership will.[10]

7. RELIEF COMMONLY SOUGHT BETWEEN PARTNERS

23–66 In this section there will be considered those forms of relief most commonly sought between partners, namely:

A.   Accounts, inquiries and discovery.
B.   Injunctions.
C.   Receivers.
D.   Orders for the sale of partnership property.
E.   Declarations and ancillary relief.

As will be seen hereafter, cases in which such relief is sought whilst the partnership is continuing are comparatively rare, but nevertheless require special consideration, given the traditional reluctance of the courts to interfere between partners otherwise than with a view to

---

[6] See *Senanayake v. Cheng* [1966] A.C. 63; also *Ex p. Briggs* (1866) L.R. 1 Eq. 483; *Sharpley v. Louth and East Coast Ry.* (1876) 2 Ch.D. 663; *Abram Steamship Co. v. Westville Shipping Co.* [1923] A.C. 773, 779 (per Lord Dunedin), 787 *et seq.* (per Lord Atkinson). And see *Chitty on Contracts* (26th ed.), para. 474.

[7] [1905] 1 Ch. 140.

[8] See *Urquhart v. McPherson* (1878) 3 App.Cas. 831, which concerned a deed of dissolution and release. Also *Maturin v. Tredinnick* (1863) 2 N.R. 514 and (1864) 4 N.R. 15; *Laing v. Campbell* (1865) 36 Beav. 3; *Phosphate Sewage Co. v. Hartmont* (1876) 5 Ch.D. 394; *Erlanger v. New Sombrero Phosphate Co.* (1878) 3 App.Cas. 1218; *Lagunas Nitrate Co. v. Lagunas Syndicate* [1899] 2 Ch. 392; *Armstrong v. Jackson* [1917] 2 K.B. 822, 828 *et seq.*, per McCardie J; *Abram Steamship Co. v. Westville Shipping Co.* [1923] A.C. 773.

[9] *Adam v. Newbigging* (1888) 13 App.Cas. 308.

[10] *Clarke v. Dickson* (1858) E.B. & E. 148.

dissolution.[11] It follows that, in the case of a dissolution action, such relief will tend to be more routinely awarded.

Jurisdiction in partnership actions

A dissolution action should, in general, be commenced in the **23–67** Chancery Division of the High Court or, if the value of the partnership assets does not exceed £30,000, in the relevant county court.[12] However, in the case of a husband and wife partnership, if the dissolution coincides with the breakdown of the marriage, it may be that any proceedings should be commenced in the Family Division rather than in the Chancery Division.[13]

Proceedings for an account as between partners should also be brought in the Chancery Division,[14] unless they fall within the jurisdiction of the county court.[15]

In an appropriate case, proceedings commenced in the Chancery Division may be transferred to another Division or to the county court, just as proceedings commenced in the county court may be transferred to the High Court.[16]

Dissolution actions

In practice, the majority of proceedings between partners will **23–68** involve the dissolution of their firm, so that it is desirable to outline the nature of a dissolution action as a prelude to what follows.

Form and content of proceedings

A dissolution action in the High Court will normally be commenced by writ, although an originating summons may be used if there is unlikely to be any real dispute of fact.[17] Similarly, in the county court, the plaint procedure is most commonly used.

If the partnership is still subsisting when the proceedings are commenced, the relief sought will invariably comprise an order for dissolution of the partnership, an order that its affairs be wound up

---

[11] See *supra*, para. 23–14.

[12] See *infra*, paras. 24–44 *et seq.*

[13] See *Williams v. Williams* [1976] Ch. 278; also *Bothe v. Amos* [1976] Fam. 46; *Bernard v. Josephs* [1982] Ch. 391. *Cf. Matz v. Matz* (1984) 14 Fam.Law 178.

[14] See the Supreme Court Act 1981, s.61(1), Sched. 1, para. 1(1)(f). Note, in this context, the strict approach adopted by Harman J. in *Apac Rowena Ltd. v. Norpol Packaging Ltd.* [1991] 4 All E.R. 516, 518.

[15] *e.g.* where the accounts fall to be taken in winding up the affairs of the partnership: see the County Courts Act 1984, s.23(f). Otherwise, it would seem necessary to establish a claim, upon which the right to an account is based, within the county court jurisdiction: see *ibid.* ss.15, 65(1)(b); C.C.R. Ord. 6, r. 2, Ord. 19, Pt. II.

[16] See *infra*, para. 24–46.

[17] In practice, the originating summons procedure is rarely resorted to.

and all necessary consequential accounts directions and inquiries. Where necessary, there may be added a claim for the appointment of a receiver/manager[18] and an injunction to restrain the defendants from dealing with the partnership assets.[19] In the case of a partnership at will, the service of the writ will itself work a dissolution.[20]

If, on the other hand, the partnership has already been dissolved before the commencement of proceedings, the plaintiff should claim a declaration to that effect in lieu of an order for dissolution.[21]

There is no objection to proceedings in which rescission of the partnership contract and dissolution are sought as alternative remedies.[22]

If neither the existence of the partnership nor the plaintiff's right to dissolve is contested, it will usually be appropriate to seek a consent order either on motion or by summons.[23]

The grounds on which a dissolution order may be made if the action is defended are outlined later in this work.[24]

Insolvent partnerships

23–69   The procedure for winding up an insolvent partnership as an unregistered company, with or without concurrent petitions being presented against two or more of the partners, is also considered later in this work.[25]

A. Accounts, Inquiries and Discovery

23–70   This subject can most conveniently be considered under three headings, namely:

(*a*)   The right to an account, inquiries and discovery.
(*b*)   The defences to an action for an account, inquiries and discovery.
(*c*)   The order for a partnership account.

---

[18] It should not be assumed that the appointment of a receiver will always be appropriate: see *infra*, para. 23–149.

[19] Lord Lindley also referred to the need for an injunction to restrain the partners from issuing bills of exchange or promissory notes in the name of the firm, but such an order is, in practice, rarely sought.

[20] See *infra*, para. 24–19. And see *Master v. Kirton* (1796) 3 Ves.Jr. 74.

[21] The precise date on which the partnership was dissolved will, of course, depend on the circumstances: see generally, *infra*, paras. 24–07 *et seq.*

[22] *Bagot v. Easton* (1877) 7 Ch.D. 1.

[23] See *Thorp v. Holdsworth* (1876) 3 Ch.D. 637, where the terms of the partnership were in dispute.

[24] See *infra*, paras. 24–48 *et seq.*

[25] See *infra*, paras. 27–08 *et seq.* And see also, as to the winding-up of banking partnerships and insurance companies, *infra*, paras. 24–42, 24–43.

(a) The right to an account, inquiries and discovery

(1) *Accounts and inquiries*

Lord Lindley wrote: **23–71**

"The right of every partner to have an account from his co-
partners of their dealings and transactions is too obvious to require
comment."

That right is now enshrined in the Partnership Act 1890.[26] It follows
that an action for an account will in almost all cases be maintainable
by a partner,[27] even where he has himself destroyed some of the
firm's books of account, made false entries in the accounts, and
otherwise misconducted himself in relation to the partnership
business.[28]

Account normally required between partners

It is a well recognised rule that, whenever money allegedly **23–72**
belonging or owing to the firm in respect of a partnership transaction
is sought to be recovered from a partner, an action for an account is
required,[29] unless an account has already been taken between the
partners or, exceptionally, taking an account would serve no useful
purpose.[30] In such an action, it will, of course, be open to the
defendant partner to show that the money is his or even that a larger
sum is due to him.

Other persons entitled to an account

Assignee/mortgagee of share: An assignee or mortgagee of a **23–73**
partnership share will, so long as the partnership continues, have no
right to seek an account of partnership transactions.[31] However, once
the partnership has been dissolved, he will be entitled to an account

---

[26] See *ibid.* s.28. And see *supra*, paras. 16–01 *et seq.*
[27] Lord Lindley pointed out that "an action for an account may be maintained by partners
although the partnership accounts are not complicated [*Cruikshank v. McVicar (1844) 8 Beav. 106;
also Frietas v. Dos Santos (1827) 1 Y. & J. 574*]; and although an action for damages may be
sustainable [*Wright v. Hunter (1801) 5 Ves.Jr. 792; Blain v. Agar (1826) 1 Sim. 37 and (1828) 2
Sim. 289; also Townsend v. Ash (1745) 3 Atk. 336*]; and although the defendant may have stolen or
embezzled the money of the firm [*Roope v. D'Avigdor (1883) 10 Q.B.D. 412*]." In the latter case,
no prosecution had been brought against the partner concerned. It is immaterial that the defendant
and the books and documents relied on are abroad: *International Corporation v. Besser
Manufacturing Co.* [1950] 1 K.B. 488.
[28] *Ram Singh v. Ram Chand* (1923) L.R. 51 Ind.App. 154.
[29] *Meyer & Co. v. Faber (No. 2)* [1923] 2 Ch. 421, 439, *per* Warrington L.J.; *Gopala Chetty v.
Vayaraghavachariar* [1922] 1 A.C. 488; *Green v. Hertzog* [1954] 1 W.L.R. 1309.
[30] See *Brown v. Rivlin*, unreported, February 1, 1983 (C.A.T. No. 56); [1984] C.L.Y., p.138.
[31] Partnership Act 1890, s.31(1), *supra*, paras. 19–59 *et seq.* And see also, as to the rights of a
creditor who has obtained a charging order over a partner's share, *ibid.* s.23, *supra*, paras. 19–43 *et
seq.*

as from the date of dissolution.[32] Where, unusually, a partner has an express right to assign his share and thereby to constitute the assignee as a partner in his place,[33] the assignee *will* be entitled to an account from the other partners.[34]

23–74   *Creditors, legatees, etc. of deceased partner:*   Although a partnership creditor can, in effect, seek an account of a deceased partner's share as against his personal representatives and the surviving partners, with a view to obtaining payment out of the estate,[35] the deceased's separate creditors, legatees and next-of-kin do not enjoy an equivalent right. Their only remedy lies against the personal representatives, unless the latter have colluded with the surviving partners or are otherwise unable or unwilling to seek an account from them.[36]

23–75   *Employee:*   An employee who is remunerated by means of a share of profits, *e.g.* a salaried "partner,"[37] has a right to an account.[38]

Personal representatives: An account may be sought by or against the personal representatives of a deceased partner.[39]

Sub-partner: A sub-partner will have no right to an account against the head partnership or any member of it, other than the person with whom he is in partnership.[40]

Trustee in bankruptcy/liquidator: An account may be sought by or against the trustee or liquidator of an insolvent partner.[41]

Scope of account

23–76   The scope of the account will naturally vary according to the subject matter of the dispute. Lord Lindley explained:

"The account which a partner may seek to have taken, may be either a general account of the dealings and transactions of the

---

[32] *Ibid.* s.31(2); and see *supra*, para. 19–65.

[33] See *supra*, paras. 19–70 *et seq.*; also, *supra*, paras. 10–216 *et seq.*

[34] See *Fawcett v. Whitehouse* (1829) 1 R. & M. 132, 148, *per* Lord Lyndhurst L.C.; *Redmayne v. Forster* (1866) L.R. 2 Eq. 467.

[35] *Wilkinson v. Henderson* (1833) 1 M. & K. 582. See also *infra*, paras. 26–39 *et seq.*

[36] See *infra*, paras. 26–41, 26–42.

[37] See further, as to the status of such "partners," *supra*, para. 5–65.

[38] See *Harrington v. Churchward* (1860) 6 Jur.(N.S.) 576; *Turner v. Bayley* (1864) 4 De G.J. & S. 332; *Rishton v. Grissell* (1870) L.R. 10 Eq. 393. Although Lord Lindley expressed an unqualified view in favour of such an employee's right to an account, the terms of Bovill's Act left some room for doubt; no such doubt persists under the Partnership Act 1890, s.2(3)(b), *supra*, para. 5–02. *Semble*, there will be no right to an account if the salaried partner's entitlement is to a fixed sum payable out of profits.

[39] *Heyne v. Middlemore* (1665) 1 Rep. Ch. 138; *Hackwell v. Eustman* (1616) Cro.Jac. 410; *Beaumont v. Grover* (1701) 1 Eq.Ab. 8, pl. 7; *Addis v. Knight* (1817) 2 Mer. 117.

[40] *Raymond's case*, cited in *Ex p. Barrow* (1815) 2 Rose 252, 255; *Brown v. De Tastet* (1819) Jac. 284; *Bray v. Fromont* (1821) 6 Madd. 5. See also *Killock v. Greg* (1828) 4 Russ. 285.

[41] See *Addis v. Knight* (1817) 2 Mer. 117; *Wilson v. Greenwood* (1818) 1 Swan. 471.

firm, with a view to a winding up of the partnership; or a more limited account, directed to some particular transaction as to which a dispute has arisen."

The court will, in general, deal with every claim and cross-claim which must be investigated in order to adjust and finally settle the account,[42] although any dispute which does not affect the account will naturally be excluded.

Several partnerships

The account sought may relate to the dealings of a number of firms **23–77** which have carried on the same business in succession,[43] but is likely to be objectionable if it relates to the dealings of two or more co-existing firms.[44]

Summary order for accounts and inquiries

Where a partnership action is commenced by a writ indorsed with a **23–78** claim for an account and not only is the existence of the partnership admitted, but there is either nothing in dispute between the parties except the accounts or the defendant is unable to satisfy the court that there is some other preliminary question to be tried, a summary order for accounts and inquiries can be obtained at any time after the defendant has acknowledged service or after the time limited for such acknowledgment has expired.[45] A similar order may be obtained on a counterclaim.[46] The application is made by summons and will generally be supported by affidavit evidence setting out the history of the dispute.[47] When making such an order, the court will usually give directions as to the manner in which the account is to be taken or the inquiry made.[48]

Such an order may be obtained even in a case in which fraud is alleged.[49]

---

[42] See, for example, *Green v. Hertzog* [1954] 1 W.L.R. 1309. This was also the position in the old Court of Chancery: see *Bury v. Allen* (1845) 1 Colly. 589; *Mackenna v. Parkes* (1866) 36 L.J.Ch. 366. *Cf. Great Western Insurance Co. v. Cunliffe* (1879) 9 Ch.D. 525.

[43] See *Jefferys v. Smith* (1827) 3 Russ. 158.

[44] See *Rheam v. Smith* (1848) 2 Ph. 726.

[45] R.S.C. Ord. 43, r. 1, *infra*, para. A2–01; and see *Turquand v. Wilson* (1875) 1 Ch.D. 85. An order under this rule may also be obtained where the writ is indorsed with a claim which necessarily involves taking an account, *e.g.* an order for the dissolution of a partnership and the winding up of its affairs. Somewhat surprisingly, there is no reference to inquiries in r. 1, but they can clearly be ordered under *ibid.* r. 2, *infra*, para. A2–02. See also *ibid.* r. 3(1), *infra*, para. A2–03. Ord. 43 also applies in the county court: see C.C.R. Ord. 13, r. 7(1)(h); see also *ibid.* Ord. 23, r. 2(1), (3).

[46] R.S.C. Ord. 43, r. 1(1A), *infra*, para. A2–01.

[47] See *ibid.* r. 1(2).

[48] *Ibid.* r. 3, *infra*, para. A2–03.

[49] See *Newton Chemical Ltd. v. Arsenis* [1989] 1 W.L.R. 1297, 1303, *per* Nicholls L.J. Stocker and O'Connor L.JJ. concurred with this view: see *ibid.* p. 1307.

Account without a dissolution

23–79   Although it was formerly considered that an account could only be taken between partners with a view to a dissolution,[50] it has long been recognised that a strict application of this rule would lead to injustice.[51] Lord Lindley observed:

> "The old rule ... that a decree for an account between partners will not be made save with a view to the final determination of all questions and cross-claims between them, and to a dissolution of the partnership, must be regarded as considerably relaxed, although it is still applicable where there is no sufficient reason for departing from it."

23–80   He then went on to summarise the three classes of case in which an action for an account *without* a dissolution is most commonly encountered, although these should, in the current editor's view, more properly be divided into four classes, *viz.*:

1. Where one partner seeks to withhold some private profits in which his co-partners are interested.
2. Where the partnership is for a fixed term and one partner has sought to exclude or expel his co-partner or otherwise to drive him into a dissolution.
3. Where the existence of the partnership is denied.[52]
4. Where, exceptionally, the partnership venture has failed and the partners are too numerous to be made parties to the action, but a limited account will do justice between them.

Class 1: Partner withholding private profits

23–81   Of this class, Lord Lindley wrote:

> "Where one partner has obtained a secret benefit, from which he seeks to exclude his co-partners, but to which they are entitled, they can obtain their share of such benefit by an action for an account, and such action is sustainable, although no dissolution is sought."

---

[50] *Forman v. Homfray* (1813) 2 V. & B. 329; *Loscombe v. Russell* (1830) 4 Sim. 8; *Knebell v. White* (1836) 2 Y. & C.Ex. 15.

[51] Lord Lindley explained "... it has been felt that more injustice frequently arose from the refusal of the Court to do less than complete justice, than could have arisen from interfering to no greater extent than was desired by the suitor aggrieved." See *supra*, para. 23–14. See, generally, *Prole v. Masterman* (1855) 21 Beav. 61 (a decision concerning the promoters of a company); also *Wright v. Hunter* (1801) 5 Ves.Jr. 792; *cf. Munnings v. Bury* (1829) Tam. 147. And see the following cases relating to mutual insurance societies: *Taylor v. Dean* (1856) 22 Beav. 429; *Hutchinson v. Wright* (1858) 25 Beav. 444; *Bromley v. Williams* (1863) 32 Beav. 177.

[52] Lord Lindley in fact treated this head as part of Class 2.

The principles on which a partner will be held liable to account to his co-partners for private profits made at their expense have already been noticed[53] and it is sufficient in the present context to note that there are four decided cases, all of which pre-date the Partnership Act 1890, in which an account was directed, even though the plaintiff did not seek to have the partnership dissolved or its affairs wound up.[54] In most of the other cases, it is unclear whether or not a general winding up was sought.[55]

Where the agreement under which a benefit will be obtained by a partner has not been performed by the other contracting party, his co-partners will, in general, have no *locus standi* as against that party to restrain further performance.[56] In such a case, they should proceed against the partner concerned and claim the benefit of the agreement from him.[57]

Class 2: Exclusion, etc.

The general proposition that an account will be ordered without a **23–82** dissolution where a fixed term partnership is continuing and one partner seeks improperly to exclude or expel his co-partner or to drive him into a dissolution was originally laid down by Sir John Leach V.-C. in *Harrison v. Armitage*.[58] Lord Lindley cited *Chapple v. Cadell*[59] in this context, but the facts there were wholly exceptional and scarcely afford a convincing example. The decision in *Fairthorne v. Weston*[60] is more in point. This case concerned a fixed term solicitors' partnership, in which the defendant was trying to force the plaintiff into a dissolution by conducting himself in such a way that no business could be carried on. However, instead of seeking a dissolution, the plaintiff commenced proceedings for an account and for the appointment of a receiver. The defendant's objection to this tactic failed.

Richards v. Davies[61] appears to be a more extreme case. There a fixed term partnership had been entered into but the defendants would not account to the plaintiff in respect of the partnership

---

[53] See *supra*, paras. 16–08 *et seq.*

[54] *Hichens v. Congreve* (1828) 1 R. & M. 150; *Fawcett v. Whitehouse* (1829) 1 R. & M. 132; *The Society of Practical Knowledge v. Abbott* (1840) 2 Beav. 559; *Beck v. Kantorowicz* (1857) 3 K. & J. 230.

[55] A dissolution was, in fact, sought in *Clegg v. Fishwick* (1849) 1 Mac. & G. 294. In *Aas v. Benham* [1891] 2 Ch. 244 and *Dean v. MacDowell* (1878) 8 Ch.D. 345 (where the partnership had expired) an account was in any event refused on the merits.

[56] *Per contra*, in the case of a bribe: see, generally, *Bowstead on Agency* (15th ed.), art. 50.

[57] *Cf. Powell and Thomas v. Evan Jones & Co.* [1905] 1 K.B. 11; and see *Alder v. Fouracre* (1818) 3 Swan. 489, where an injunction was granted restraining the executors of a deceased partner, who had, prior to his death, agreed to take a lease of premises to be used for partnership purposes, from disposing of the lease when granted, except for the benefit of the partnership.

[58] (1819) 4 Madd. 143.

[59] (1822) Jac. 537.

[60] (1844) 3 Hare 387.

[61] (1831) 2 R. & M. 347.

dealings and transactions. Although an account of those dealings and transactions was ordered by Sir John Leach (by then the Master of the Rolls), on the grounds that the plaintiff would otherwise be remediless, it would seem that an effective case of exclusion may have been made out.[62]

The fact that new proceedings will be required as and when further profits are received is, seemingly, an irrelevant consideration.[63]

Expulsion

23-83   Lord Lindley expressed the view that:

"... if a partner is wrongfully expelled, and he is restored to his status as partner by the judgment of the Court, an account will be directed, but the partnership will not necessarily be dissolved."[64]

The current editor would, however, observe that a failed expulsion will *usually* result in a dissolution.[65]

Mining partnerships

23-84   Although Lord Lindley also referred to the position in the case of mining partnerships in this context,[66] he concluded that:

"... as each co-owner of a mine can sell his share[67] without the consent of the other owners, there is no occasion for him to ask for a dissolution, and the case of a mine is therefore, perhaps, not an apt illustration of the doctrine in question."

Class 3: Existence of partnership denied

23-85   Although he did not treat this class as in any way distinct from the previous class, Lord Lindley observed:

"... where a person seeks to establish a partnership with another who denies the plaintiff's title to be considered a partner, if the

---

[62] Such an allegation was made: see the statement of facts at *ibid.* p. 347.
[63] See *Richards v. Davies, supra,* at pp. 351–352. *Cf. Forman v. Homfray* (1813) 2 V. & B. 329, *per* Lord Eldon; *Loscombe v. Russell* (1830) 4 Sim. 8, *per* Shadwell V.-C.; *Knebell v. White* (1836) 2 Y. & C.Ex. 15, *per* Baron Alderson.
[64] See *Blisset v. Daniel* (1853) 10 Hare 493, where a dissolution was sought but not, in the event, ordered. Lord Lindley regarded the underlying principle as similar to that which applies in a case where the existence of a partnership is denied: see *infra,* para. 23–85.
[65] See *supra,* para. 10–106 and *infra,* para. 24–04.
[66] See *Bentley v. Bates* (1840) 4 Y. & C.Ex. 182; also *Redmayne v. Forster* (1866) L.R. 2 Eq. 467.
[67] *Quaere,* in any event, whether this is still the position: see *supra,* paras. 19–74, 19–75.

former is successful upon the main point in dispute, an account of the past dealings and transactions will be decreed, although the plaintiff does not seek for a dissolution of the partnership which he has proved to exist."[68]

Class 4: Failure of large concern

Lord Lindley formulated the following general proposition, by **23-86** reference to the celebrated judgment of Lord Cottenham in *Wallworth v. Holt*[69]:

"Where the partnership has proved a failure, and the partners are too numerous to be made parties to the action, and a limited account will result in justice to them all, such an account will be directed, although a dissolution is not asked for."

In *Wallworth v. Holt*, certain shareholders of an insolvent joint-stock banking company, acting on behalf of themselves and others, sought an account against the officers of the company and a number of other shareholders who had not paid up their calls, for the sole purpose of having the assets of the company applied in payment of its debts. An objection to the proceedings by way of demurrer was overruled.

Although Lord Lindley doubted whether the result would have **23-87** been the same if an account had been sought in order to obtain a division of profits,[70] subsequent decisions had demonstrated that proceedings seeking a division of surplus assets might be maintained even where a dissolution was not expressly claimed.[71] In the light of these and other cases,[72] he then went on to express the following view:

"... it is conceived that the doctrine established in *Wallworth v. Holt* may be considered as extending not only to cases where an account is sought for the purpose of having joint assets applied in

---

[68] *Knowles v. Haughton* (1805) 11 Ves.Jr. 168, as reported in Collyer on Partnership, p. 198, note. The defendant did not, however, resist the account after the question of partnership was decided against him. See also the judgment of Stirling L.J. in *Byrne v. Reid* [1902] 2 Ch. 735, 741 *et seq.*

[69] (1841) 4 Myl. & Cr. 619.

[70] Either on the basis that a dissolution ought to have been sought or that all the shareholders were not parties to the proceedings: see *Richardson v. Hastings* (1844) 7 Beav. 301, 323 and (1847) 11 Beav. 17; *Deeks v. Stanhope* (1844) 14 Sim. 57.

[71] See *Wilson v. Stanhope* (1846) 2 Colly. 629; *Apperly v. Page* (1847) 1 Ph. 779; *Cooper v. Webb* (1847) 15 Sim. 454; *Clements v. Bowes* (1852) 17 Sim. 167; also *Sheppard v. Oxenford* (1855) 1 K. & J. 491, 493, where all forms of relief normally associated with a dissolution were sought, but not dissolution itself.

[72] See, in particular, *Apperly v. Page, supra*; *Clements v. Bowes, supra*.

discharge of the joint liabilities, but also to cases where an account is sought for the additional purpose of obtaining a division of the surplus assets and profits amongst the persons entitled thereto. If this be so, the last remnant of the doctrine that, in partnership cases, there can be no account without a dissolution, must be considered as swept away, at least as regards partnerships the members of which are too numerous to be made parties to the action."

Of course, the scope for partnerships comprising more than twenty partners is currently restricted to certain professions,[73] and a more general relaxation seems unlikely.[74]

The possible use of representative proceedings in cases of this class should not be forgotten.[75]

Payment into court[76]

Payment in pending trial

23–88   The general rule is clear and was stated by Lord Lindley in the following terms:

"... a partner having partnership monies in his hands, cannot be made to pay those monies into court before trial, if he insists that, on taking the accounts, a balance will be found due to him."[77]

Nevertheless, it would seem that, where proceedings for an account are pending and the defendant admits that he has or has had money in his hands which belongs to the firm and, in the latter case, he also admits, or it otherwise plainly appears,[78] that he ought still to have that money,[79] a payment in may be ordered.[80] *A fortiori* if it appears from that partner's own statements that the money came into his

---

[73] See *supra*, paras. 4–28 *et seq*.

[74] See *supra*, para. 4–28, n. 5.

[75] See *supra*, paras. 23–08, 23–09, 23–12.

[76] The payments into court under consideration in the following paragraphs should not be confused with voluntary payments in pursuant to R.S.C. Ord. 22 or C.C.R. Ord. 11. Those orders do *not* apply to an action for an account: see *Nichols v. Evens* (1883) 22 Ch.D. 611.

[77] *Richardson v. Bank of England* (1838) 4 Myl. & Cr. 165. *Cf. Birley v. Kennedy* (1865) 6 N.R. 395, where a partner who admitted that he had drawn more out of the partnership than he ought to have done was ordered to pay the excess into court.

[78] See, generally, *Freeman v. Cox* (1878) 8 Ch.D. 148; *Dunn v. Campbell* (1879) 27 Ch.D. 254, note; *Hampden v. Wallis* (1884) 27 Ch.D. 251; *Porrett v. White* (1885) 31 Ch.D. 52; *Wanklyn v. Wilson* (1887) 35 Ch.D. 180; *Re Benson* [1899] 1 Ch. 39.

[79] See the cases cited in the previous note; also *Neville v. Matthewman* [1894] 3 Ch. 345; *Crompton and Evans' Union Bank v. Burton* [1895] 2 Ch. 711.

[80] In *White v. Barton* (1854) 18 Beav. 192, an admission by one partner that he and his co-partner (who was not a party) had money in their hands was held to be sufficient. *Cf.* the cases cited *infra*, para. 23–89, n. 87.

hands improperly[81] or in breach of the duty of good faith which he owes to his co-partners.[82]

However, a partner will not, in general, be compelled to pay any partnership moneys into court unless the other partners are also prepared to do likewise.[83]

Debt owed to firm: A partner will not be ordered to pay in any **23–89** sum in respect of a debt owed to the firm, where the amount is not admitted and cannot be readily ascertained.[84] Where, however, the amount of the debt is ascertained and the partner concerned does not insist that an overall balance is due to him from the firm, he may be ordered to make a payment in.[85]

Admissions: A verbal admission is sufficient for these purposes,[86] but a payment in will not be ordered on the strength of an admission made by another partner.[87] An inadvertent admission may be withdrawn with the leave of the court.[88]

Debtors Act 1869: An order for the payment of partnership **23–90** moneys into court cannot be enforced by attachment or committal under the Debtors Act 1869 since, for this purpose at least, a partner does not act in a fiduciary capacity.[89]

Partnership debts unpaid: If the partnership debts are unpaid and the defendant is liable to be sued for them, the order directing payment in should give him liberty to apply for a payment out of the amount of any such debts which he may be compelled or pressed to pay.[90]

Mareva injunction: Where, for any of the reasons discussed above, the court is unable to compel a partner to pay money into court, it may be possible to obtain a *Mareva* injunction to prevent dissipation of his assets pending the trial of the action.[91]

---

[81] *Jervis v. White* (1802) 6 Ves.Jr. 737; *Costeker v. Horrox* (1839) 3 Y. & C.Ex. 530.

[82] *Foster v. Donald* (1820) 1 J. & W. 252. See also *Hichens v. Congreve* (1828) 1 R. & M. 150, note; *Gaskell v. Chambers* (1858) 26 Beav. 360; *cf. Hagell v. Currie* (1867) L.R. 2 Ch.App. 449.

[83] *Foster v. Donald, supra.*

[84] See *Mills v. Hanson* (1802) 8 Ves.Jr. 68; *Wanklyn v. Wilson* (1887) 35 Ch.D. 180.

[85] *Toulmin v. Copland* (1836) 3 Y. & C.Ex. 625, affirmed at (1840) 7 Cl. & F. 349; *Costeker v. Horrox* (1839) 3 Y. & C.Ex. 530. See also *Domville v. Solly* (1826) 2 Russ. 372, where an order was made even though the defendants insisted that the plaintiff was entitled to nothing.

[86] *Re Beeny* [1894] 1 Ch. 499.

[87] *Hollis v. Burton* [1892] 3 Ch. 226; also *Boschetti v. Power* (1844) 8 Beav. 98. *Cf. White v. Barton* (1854) 18 Beav. 192, *supra*, para. 23–88, n. 80.

[88] *Hollis v. Burton, supra.*

[89] *Ibid.* s.4, para. 3; *Piddocke v. Burt* [1894] 1 Ch. 343. See also *supra*, para. 16–03.

[90] *Toulmin v. Copland* (1836) 3 Y. & C.Ex. 625, 643 *et seq. Cf. Toulmin v. Copeland* (1819) 6 Price 405.

[91] See *infra*, para. 23–147.

Payment in after trial

23–91   After trial, the court will order a partner to pay into court any sum which is plainly due from him, even though there may be no certificate to that effect.[92]

Interim payments

23–92   A partner who has obtained both an order for an account against his co-partner[93] *and* an order for the payment of any sum found due to him on taking that account may now apply for an interim payment as opposed to an order for a payment into court.[94] However, cases in which a balance can clearly be shown to be due to one partner without a full account being taken are, in practice, likely to be rare.

(2) *Discovery etc.*

Right to discovery

23–93   Lord Lindley observed:

> "The right of every partner to a discovery from his co-partner of all matters relating to the partnership dealings and transactions is as incontestable as his right to an account; and such right, like the right to an account, devolves upon and is enforceable against a partner's legal personal representatives and trustees in bankruptcy."

This right, which is enshrined in the Partnership Act 1890,[95] is separate and distinct from any right to discovery under the Rules of the Supreme Court.[96]

If a partner chooses to keep his own personal records in the same book as the partnership records, he will normally be compelled to produce the entire book, unless the former can be physically severed from the latter.[97] Moreover, a former partner in a firm of solicitors

---

[92] *Creak v. Capell* (1821) 6 Madd. 114; *London Syndicate v. Lord* (1878) 8 Ch.D. 84.

[93] *e.g.* under R.S.C. Ord. 43: see *supra*, para. 23–78.

[94] See R.S.C. Ord. 29, rr.10, 12(a). These rules also apply in the county court: C.C.R. Ord. 13, r.12(1), (2).

[95] Partnership Act 1890, ss.24(9), 28. See *supra*, paras. 22–09 *et seq.*

[96] See R.S.C. Ord. 24; also C.C.R. Ord. 14. But see *Bevan v. Webb* [1901] 2 Ch. 59, 76, *per* Collins L.J.

[97] See *Pickering v. Pickering* (1883) 25 Ch.D. 247. *Cf. Mansell v. Feeney* (1861) 2 J. & H. 313, *infra*, para. 23–109. See also *supra*, para. 22–12.

cannot refuse to produce his ledger, if it is relevant, on the ground of professional privilege.[98]

Disputed partnership

The extent to which discovery can be obtained from a person who **23-94** denies the existence of an alleged partnership will be considered later in this work.[99]

Anton Piller order

There is no reason why, in an appropriate case, an *Anton Piller* **23-95** order[1] should not be obtained with a view to protecting any documents which, even though not the subject matter of the proceedings, will constitute vital evidence therein, *e.g.* the sole copy of the partnership agreement or books of account.[2] However, this jurisdiction is exercised sparingly, and a strong prima facie case would have to be made out.[3]

Interrogatories

Where potentially oppressive interrogatories are administered in an **23-96** action for an account,[4] the obligation of the interrogated partner will, in Lord Lindley's words, be as follows:

"... all that he is bound to do is to furnish the interrogator with every means of information possessed or obtainable by himself, leaving the interrogator to make what he can of the materials thus furnished to him. The party interrogated is not bound to digest accounts, nor to set out voluminous accounts existing already in another shape which he offers to produce."

Thus, in *Christian v. Taylor*,[5] where an account was sought by the executor of one deceased partner against the executors of another deceased partner, it was held that the defendants were under no

---

[98] *Brown v. Perkins* (1843) 2 Hare 540; *Lewthwaite v. Stimson* (1966) 110 S.J. 188.
[99] See *infra*, paras. 23–103 *et seq.*
[1] See *Anton Piller K.G. v. Manufacturing Processes Ltd.* [1976] Ch. 55.
[2] See *Yousif v. Salama* [1980] 1 W.L.R. 1540; *Emanuel v. Emanuel* [1982] 1 W.L.R. 669; *Distributori Automatici Italia SpA v. Holford General Trading Co. Ltd.* [1985] 1 W.L.R. 1066.
[3] See further, *Lock International Plc v. Beswick* [1989] 1 W.L.R. 1268, 1281, where Hoffman J. emphasised that there must be proportionality between the perceived threat and the remedy granted. As to the duty of an applicant for such an order to make the fullest possible disclosure to the court, see *Columbia Picture Industries Inc. v. Robinson* [1987] Ch. 38 and the cases there cited. As to the manner in which such an order is to be executed, see *Universal Thermosensors Ltd. v. Hibben* [1992] 1 W.L.R. 840.
[4] This, of course presupposes that such interrogatories are allowed: see R.S.C. Ord. 26, r. 1(3); C.C.R. Ord. 14, r. 11.
[5] (1841) 11 Sim. 401.

obligation to go through the books in their possession in order to supply the plaintiff with the information requested: all that they were required to do was to refer to those books in such a way as to entitle the plaintiff to have them produced for his inspection.[6]

Where, on the other hand, the interrogatories are of a specific nature, it will not be sufficient merely to refer to the partnership books, etc., in general terms and to say that, save as appears therein, no answer can be given. The partner interrogated must go further, and point out where the particular information required by each interrogatory is to be found.[7] This may entail making inquiries and obtaining documents of which he is entitled to possession.[8]

Production and inspection of documents

Books belonging to defendant and another

23–97   It is a general rule that a person cannot be compelled to produce books which belong both to himself and to other persons who are not parties to the action.[9] Thus, where the existence of a partnership is disputed, it may not be possible to compel the production of any books unless all the alleged partners are joined.[10] However, there are limits to this rule, as Lord Lindley made clear:

"... the doctrine[11] ... does not apply to cases in which the absent parties interested in the books are in fact represented by the defendants on the record, and have no interest in conflict with

---

[6] See also *Seeley v. Boehm* (1817) 2 Madd. 176; *White v. Barker* (1852) 5 De G. & Sm. 746; *Lockett v. Lockett* (1869) L.R. 4 Ch.App. 336.

[7] *Drake v. Symes* (1859) Johns. 647, 651 *per* Page Wood V.-C.; also *Telford v. Ruskin* (1860) 1 Dr. & Sm. 148.

[8] See *Taylor v. Rundell (No. 1)* (1841) Cr. & Ph. 104; *Stuart v. Lord Bute* (1841) 11 Sim. 442 and (1842) 12 Sim. 460; *Earl of Glengall v. Frazer* (1842) 2 Hare 99; *Taylor v. Rundell (No. 2)* (1843) 1 Ph. 222; *Att.-Gen. v. Rees* (1849) 12 Beav. 50; *Bolckow v. Fisher* (1882) 10 Q.B.D. 161; *Alliott v. Smith* [1895] 2 Ch. 111. *Cf. Martineau v. Cox* (1837) 2 Y. & C.Ex. 638, where a partner in a firm carrying on business in another country was held not to be bound to set out a list of documents in the possession of the partners abroad. As to setting out a list of the firm' debtors, see *Telford v. Ruskin* (1860) 1 Dr. & Sm. 148. *Cf.* the observation of Page Wood V.-C. in *Drake v. Symes* (1859) Johns. 647, 651.

[9] *Stuart v. Lord Bute* (1841) 11 Sim. 442 and (1842) 12 Sim. 460; *Reid v. Langlois* (1849) 1 Mac. & G. 627; *Burbidge v. Robinson* (1850) 2 Mac. & G. 244; *Penney v. Goode* (1853) 1 Drew. 474; *Hadley v. McDougall* (1872) L.R. 7 Ch.App. 312. *Cf. Vyse v. Foster* (1872) L.R. 13 Eq. 602. See also *supra*, para. 7–22. In such cases, the interest of the absent parties must be stated: *Bovill v. Cowan* (1870) L.R. 5 Ch.App. 495. But note the powers of the court under R.S.C. Ord. 24, rr. 12, 13(1), Ord. 29, r. 2, and Ord. 38, r. 13; C.C.R. Ord. 14, r. 7. And see *Re Smith* [1891] 1 Ch. 323. As to interrogatories directed to the contents of such documents, see *Rattenberry v. Monro* [1910] W.N. 245.

[10] *Murray v. Walter* (1839) Cr. & Ph. 114. It is not, however, permissible to join a party solely with a view to obtain inspection of a document: *Douihech v. Findlay* [1990] 1 W.L.R. 269; also *Unilever v. Chefaro, The Times*, March 29, 1993. Equally, a *subpoena duces tecum* may be appropriate where a third party is in possession of a document the production of which is required for the purposes of deciding an issue in the proceedings: see *Macmillan Inc. v. Bishopsgate Investment Trust Plc* [1993] 1 W.L.R. 837.

[11] *i.e.* the doctrine laid down in *Murray v. Walter, supra*.

theirs[12]; nor, it is said, to an action by a *cestui que trust* against a trustee who is charged with trading with trust monies in partnership with other persons not before the Court."[13]

Agreement precluding inspection

If one partner agrees to accept his co-partner's computation of the **23-98** partnership profits and, moreover, agrees not to examine or investigate the partnership books and accounts, the court will not order the production of those books and accounts until his right to an account has been established and, even then, may still decline to do so.[14]

Inspection by agent

Where a partner obtains an order for the production and inspection **23-99** of documents, he may, if he wishes, have them inspected by his solicitors or some other agent,[15] but not by an agent to whom his co-partners reasonably object.[16]

Information obtained on such an inspection may not be made public[17] and an injunction will, if necessary, be granted to restrain its communication to third parties.[18]

Books in constant use

Production of partnership books which are in constant use will **23-100** normally be ordered to take place at the firm's premises unless a verified copy will suffice:[19] a special reason must be shown before they will be ordered to be deposited in court.[20]

---

[12] *Glyn v. Caulfield* (1851) 3 Mac. & G. 463.

[13] See *Vyse v. Foster* (1872) L.R. 13 Eq. 602; also *Freeman v. Fairlie* (1812) 3 Mer. 24, 43, *per* Lord Eldon.

[14] *Turner v. Bayley* (1864) 4 De G.J. & S. 332. See also, as to such agreements, *supra*, para. 22–12; and generally, *supra*, paras. 10–59 *et seq.*

[15] *Williams v. Prince of Wales' Life, etc., Co.* (1857) 23 Beav. 338; *Bevan v. Webb* [1901] 2 Ch. 59; *McIvor v. Southern Health and Social Services Board* [1978] 1 W.L.R. 757. As to production to an accountant or other expert appointed for the purpose, see *Bonnardet v. Taylor* (1861) 1 J. & H. 383; *Swansea Co. v. Budd* (1866) L.R. 2 Eq. 274; *Lindsay v. Gladstone* (1869) L.R. 9 Eq. 132. And see *supra*, para. 22–13.

[16] *Draper v. Manchester & Sheffield Ry.* (1861) 7 Jur.(N.S.) 86; *Dadswell v. Jacobs* (1887) 34 Ch.D. 278; *Bevan v. Webb, supra; Davies v. Eli Lilly & Co.* [1987] 1 W.L.R. 428. And see *supra*, para. 22–13.

[17] *Per contra*, perhaps, where the order is obtained pursuant to a partner's statutory rights under the Partnership Act 1890, ss.24(9), 28. But see also *supra*, para. 22–13.

[18] *Williams v. Prince of Wales' Life, etc., Co.* (1857) 23 Beav. 338; *Distillers Co. (Biochemicals) Ltd. v. Times Newspapers Ltd.* [1975] Q.B. 613; *Riddick v. Thames Board Mills Ltd.* [1977] Q.B. 881; *Church of Scientology of California v. Department of Health and Social Security* [1979] 1 W.L.R. 723; *I.T.C. Film Distributors Ltd. v. Video Exchange Ltd.* [1982] Ch. 431. But note *Crest Homes Plc v. Marks* [1987] A.C. 929; *Levi Strauss & Co. v. Barclays Trading Corp. Inc.* [1993] F.S.R. 179.

[19] See R.S.C. Ord. 24, r. 14. This rule also applies in the county court.

[20] *Mertens v. Haigh* (1860) Johns. 735.

Arbitrations

23–101   The High Court no longer has power to order discovery of documents and interrogatories in connection with an arbitration;[21] it follows that only the arbitrator himself can make such orders.[22]

(b) Defences to an action for an account

23–102   A number of defences to an action for an account have already been considered earlier in this work, *i.e.* illegality,[23] fraud,[24] laches[25] and limitation.[26] It has also been seen that the non-joinder of any necessary parties is no longer fatal.[27]

There are, however, a number of additional defences which merit attention, namely:

    (i)   Denial of partnership.
   (ii)   Settled account.
  (iii)   Arbitration award.
  (iv)   Accord and satisfaction.
   (v)   Waiver.
  (vi)   Release.

(i) *Denial of alleged partnership*

23–103   It is self evident that an action for an account of the dealings and transactions of an alleged partnership may be met by a denial that any such partnership exists.[28] Such a defence may have certain implications so far as concerns discovery and interrogatories, as Lord Lindley explained:

> "This defence if relied upon as a reason for not answering interrogatories or making a discovery of documents, must be accompanied by statements on oath denying those allegations which, if true, would establish the partnership, and denying the

---

[21] The Arbitration Act 1950, s.12(6)(b), which formerly conferred such a power, was repealed by the Courts and Legal Services Act 1990, s.103.

[22] See *supra*, para. 10–236.

[23] See *supra*, paras. 8–52 *et seq.*

[24] See *supra*, paras. 23–48 *et seq.*

[25] See *supra*, paras. 23–17 *et seq.*

[26] See *supra*, paras. 23–31 *et seq.*

[27] See *supra*, para. 23–04.

[28] Notwithstanding the obviousness of the proposition in the text, Lord Lindley referred to *Drew v. Drew* (1813) 2 V. & B. 159; *Hare v. London and North-Western Ry.* (1860) John. 722. Note, however, that the position was more complicated prior to the Judicature Acts: see the 15th ed. of this work at p. 635.

possession of documents relevant to the question of partnership or no partnership."[29]

In *Mansell v. Feeney*,[30] it was held that the plaintiff was entitled to **23–104** inspect all documents admitted by the defendant to be in his possession which were relevant to the dispute, even though the defendant denied the alleged partnership and, moreover, denied that those documents tended to prove its existence. The defendant was, however, permitted to seal up parts of certain books which he swore had no bearing on the issues in the action.[31] On the same principle, the plaintiff in *Kennedy v. Dodson*,[32] who was seeking to establish the existence of a partnership in the acquisition of certain land, was not permitted to administer interrogatories directed towards proving that the defendant and he had been partners in various other purchases, both before and after the acquisition in question.

In practice, unnecessary disputes as to discovery, etc., can be **23–105** avoided by having the existence of the partnership determined as a preliminary issue.[33] If that course is adopted, then in Lord Lindley's words,

"Whilst on the one hand [*the defendant*] must give all such discovery as bears upon the question of partnership or no partnership, he will not be compelled to set out accounts or produce documents which he swears throw no light on that question and can only be material after it has been decided in favour of the plaintiff."[34]

(ii) *Settled account*

Nature of settled account

An account which has been agreed between the partners,[35] **23–106** conventionally referred to as a "settled account" or, more inaccurately, as an "account stated,"[36] naturally constitutes a good

---

[29] *Sanders v. King* (1821) 6 Madd. 61; *Harris v. Harris* (1844) 3 Hare 450; *Mansell v. Feeney* (1861) 2 J. & H. 313.

[30] (1861) 2 J. & H. 313. See also *Saull v. Browne* (1874) L.R. 9 Ch.App. 364. *Cf. Pickering v. Pickering* (1883) 25 Ch.D. 247, *supra*, para. 23–93.

[31] See the hearing reported at (1861) 9 W.R. 610.

[32] [1895] 1 Ch. 334.

[33] See R.S.C. Ord. 33, r. 3; C.C.R. Ord. 17, r. 1.

[34] See *Re Leigh* (1876) 6 Ch.D. 256; *Parker v. Wells* (1881) 18 Ch.D. 477; *Whyte v. Ahrens* (1884) 26 Ch.D. 717.

[35] If the account has not been settled as between all the partners, it will be *res inter alios acta* as regards those partners who are not bound by it: see *Carmichael v. Carmichael* (1846) 2 Ph. 101. An account settled by a majority of partners might, in certain circumstances, bind the minority: see *Robinson v. Thompson* (1687) 1 Vern. 465; *Kent v. Jackson* (1852) 2 De G.M. & G. 49; *Stupart v. Arrowsmith* (1856) 3 Sm. & G. 176 (non-partnership cases). Much will, of course, depend on the terms of the agreement.

[36] A true "account stated" is wholly distinct from a settled account and, in fact, gives rise to a cause of action: see *Chitty on Contracts* (26th ed.), paras. 2152 *et seq.*

defence to an action seeking a further account of any transactions or dealings covered thereby.[37] Lord Lindley summarised the requirements for a settled account as follows:

"No precise form is necessary to constitute a stated and settled account; but an account stated,[38] unless it be in writing, is no defence to an action for a further account. It is not, however, necessary that the account should be signed by the parties, if it can be shown to have been acquiesced in by them[39]; and an account may be stated and settled, although a few doubtful items are omitted."[40]

However, merely *rendering* an account is clearly not sufficient to deprive the plaintiff of his right to have the same account taken under the direction of the court:[41] he must be shown both to have received and acquiesced in the account.[42] Moreover, such acquiescence must relate not only to the principles on which the account was prepared, but also to the items included in it.[43]

Settled accounts not normally reopened

23–107   In taking accounts under an ordinary judgment, a settled account will not be disturbed in the absence of a specific direction to that effect.[44] Such a direction may, however, be obtained if fraud, misrepresentation or errors can be proved.

Fraud and misrepresentation

23–108   If any part of a settled account is affected by fraud[45] or misrepresentation,[46] a new account will be directed, even after a considerable lapse of time.

---

[37] *Taylor v. Shaw* (1824) 2 Sim. & St. 12; *Endo v. Caleham* (1831) Younge 306.
[38] This is strictly a misuse of the term: see *supra*, n. 36.
[39] See *Morris v. Harrison* (1701) Colles 157; *Willes v. Jernegan* (1741) 2 Atk. 252; *Hunter v. Belcher* (1864) 2 De G.J. & S. 194. A verbal account and a receipt in full is not equivalent to a settled account: *Walker v. Consett* (1801) Forest 157.
[40] *Sim v. Sim* (1861) 11 I.Ch.R. 310.
[41] See *Clements v. Bowes* (1853) 1 Drew. 684, 692, *per* Kindersley V.-C.
[42] *Irvine v. Young* (1823) 1 Sim. & St. 333.
[43] See *Clancarty v. Latouche* (1810) 1 Ball & Beatty 420; *Mosse v. Salt* (1863) 32 Beav. 269. *Cf. Hunter v. Belcher* (1864) 2 De. G.J. & S. 194.
[44] See *Newen v. Wetten* (1862) 31 Beav. 315; *Holgate v. Shutt* (1884) 27 Ch.D. 111 and 28 Ch.D. 111. But see also *Milford v. Milford* (1868) McCle. & Yo. 150. Note that this rule will only apply where the account is mutual.
[45] *Vernon v. Vawdry* (1740) 2 Atk. 119; *Wharton v. May* (1799) 5 Ves.Jr. 26, 68, *per* Lord Loughborough; *Beaumont v. Boultbee* (1800) 5 Ves.Jr. 484a and (1802) 7 Ves.Jr. 599; *Clarke v. Tipping* (1846) 9 Beav. 284; *Allfrey v. Allfrey* (1849) 1 Mac. & G. 87; *Coleman v. Mellersh* (1850) 2 Mac. & G. 309; *Stainton v. The Carron Co.* (1857) 24 Beav. 346; *Williamson v. Barbour* (1877) 9 Ch.D. 529; *Gething v. Keighley* (1878) 9 Ch.D. 547.
[46] See *supra*, para. 23–56.

Errors

Where errors affect the whole of a settled account, a new account **23–109** will be directed,[47] unless the account has stood unimpeached for many years. Lord Lindley explained:

> "... if no fraud be proved, an account which has been long settled will not be reopened *in toto*; the utmost which the Court will then do will be to give leave to surcharge and falsify[48]; and there are cases in which, in consequence of lapse of time, the Court will do no more than itself rectify particular items, instead of giving leave to surcharge or falsify generally."[49]

In any other case, leave to surcharge and falsify will be the only available remedy.[50] An item omitted by mutual mistake will normally be put right.[51] However, the mere fact that items are treated in an improper way, or are improperly omitted, is not in itself sufficient to induce the court to reopen a settled account; if the partners knew about those items and no fraud or undue influence can be proved, it will be inferred that they were dealt with in an agreed manner.[52]

In order to impeach a settled account, any errors must be positively identified and proved;[53] similarly, where the account is settled on an "errors excepted" basis.[54]

If leave to surcharge and falsify is obtained, errors both of fact and law can be corrected.[55] All parties to the action will normally be given such leave.[56]

Settled account accompanied by release

If, following the death, retirement or expulsion of a partner, an **23–110** account is settled between the surviving or continuing partners and the outgoing partner or his personal representatives and mutual releases are given, that account can only be impeached once the relevant release has been set aside.[57] The circumstances in which rescission may be obtained have already been considered earlier in this chapter.[58]

---

[47] *Williamson v. Barbour* (1877) 9 Ch.D. 529; *Gething v. Keighley* (1878) 9 Ch.D. 547.

[48] See *Brownell v. Brownell* (1786) 2 Bro.C.C. 61; *Millar v. Craig* (1843) 6 Beav. 433; *Gething v. Keighley*, *supra*. Cf. *Williamson v. Barbour*, *supra*.

[49] See *Twogood v. Swanston* (1801) 6 Ves.Jr. 485; *Maund v. Allies* (1840) 5 Jur. 860.

[50] *Vernon v. Vawdry* (1740) 2 Atk. 119; *Pit v. Cholmondeley* (1754) 2 Ves.Sen. 565; *Gething v. Keighley* (1878) 9 Ch.D. 547; *Holgate v. Shutt* (1884) 27 Ch.D. 111 and 28 Ch.D. 111.

[51] *Pritt v. Clay* (1843) 6 Beav. 503.

[52] See *Maund v. Allies* (1840) 5 Jur. 860; *Laing v. Campbell* (1865) 36 Beav. 3 (where bad debts were treated as good). And see *supra*, paras. 10–63, 23–18.

[53] *Dawson v. Dawson* (1737) 1 Atk. 1; *Taylor v. Haylin* (1788) 2 Bro.C.C. 309; *Kinsman v. Barker* (1808) 14 Ves.Jr. 579; *Parkinson v. Hanbury* (1867) L.R. 2 H.L. 1.

[54] *Johnston v. Curtis* (1791) 2 Bro.C.C. 311, note.

[55] *Roberts v. Kuffin* (1741) 2 Atk. 112; also *Daniell v. Sinclair* (1881) 6 App.Cas. 181.

[56] See 1 Madd.Ch.Pr., 3rd ed., 144, where it is said to have been so held by Leach V.-C. in *Anon.*, March 6, 1821.

[57] See *Millar v. Craig* (1843) 6 Beav. 433; *Fowler v. Wyatt* (1857) 24 Beav. 232; *Parker v. Bloxham* (1855) 20 Beav. 295.

[58] See *supra*, para. 23–56.

(iii) *Arbitration award*

23–111 It is a good defence to an action for an account that the matters in dispute between the partners have previously been settled by arbitration, provided that the award is binding on the plaintiff.[59] However, a mere agreement to refer such matters to arbitration is not sufficient,[60] although a stay of the action may be obtained in such a case.[61]

Where the award relates to matters other than those which are the subject matter of the action, it will obviously not represent a ground of defence.[62] Lord Lindley gave the following example:

"... an award on a reference of all matters in difference is no defence to an action for an account of moneys received after the making of the award, and not dealt with by it, owing to a mistake on the part of the arbitrator."[63]

23–112   Thus, in *Spencer v. Spencer*[64] all matters in dispute between the partners on a dissolution had been referred to arbitration and the arbitrator's award directed one partner to get in the outstanding debts, which were estimated at a certain amount. The award was acted on, but it appeared that the debts, when collected, exceeded the estimate put on them by the arbitrator. A partner claimed a share of that excess and an account was duly ordered, it being evident that the award was founded on a mistake.

(iv) *Accord and satisfaction*

23–113 Payment, as such, is not a defence to an action for an account, since the purpose of the action is to ascertain how much is or was payable. However, where a sum of money is paid by one partner to another and is accepted in lieu of all demands, that will amount to an accord and satisfaction, which *is* a good defence.[65]

Although the agreement representing the accord must be certain, it is not, in general, necessary to show that it has been performed in

---

[59] *Tittenson v. Peat* (1747) 3 Atk. 529; *Routh v. Peach* (1795) 2 Anst. 519 and 3 Anst. 637. See also *supra*, para. 10–228.

[60] *Michell v. Harris* (1793) 4 Bro.C.C. 312; *Thompson v. Charnock* (1799) 8 T.R. 139. See also *supra*, para. 10–227.

[61] See *supra*, para. 10–229 *et seq.*

[62] As in *Farrington v. Chute* (1682) 1 Vern. 72.

[63] Note, however, the arbitrator's power to correct clerical errors in the award: Arbitration Act 1950, s.17.

[64] (1827) 2 Y. & J. 249. An analogous principle was applied in *Teacher v. Calder* [1899] A.C. 451, where an accountant was required to certify the profits of a particular business, but did so without knowing that his certificate was intended to bind a person interested in such profits. In the circumstances, his certificates were held not to be binding.

[65] See, generally, *Chitty on Contracts* (26th ed.), paras. 1581 *et seq.* Lord Lindley's footnote at this point read "Bac.Ab.Accompt.E.; Vin.Ab.Account N.; *Brown v. Perkins* (1842) 1 Hare 564. But see Com.Dig.Accompt.E. 6, pl. 8."

order to show satisfaction. The satisfaction lies in the consideration which makes the agreement operative and may take the form of executory promise.[66]

(v) *Waiver*

Lord Lindley observed: **23–114**

"... if an agreement to waive all accounts is entered into, and is founded on a sufficient consideration,[67] and is free of all taint of fraud or undue influence, the parties to it will be precluded from suing each other in respect of the accounts so agreed to be waived."[68]

(vi) *Release*

A release is obviously a good defence to an action for an account,[69] **23–115** unless it was executed on the faith that certain accounts were correct which are later shown to be erroneous. In such a case, the release will be set aside and an fresh account ordered,[70] unless the parties clearly intended to abide by those accounts, irrespective of their content. A release can also be set aside on the grounds of fraud or misrepresentation.[71]

An effectual release must be by deed; if it is not, it will be regarded as a settled account.[72]

(c) Judgments for a partnership account

Form of judgment

Lord Lindley stated that a judgment for a partnership account **23–116** would, in its simplest form, be as follows:

"Let an account be taken of all partnership dealings and transactions between the plaintiff and the defendant as co-partners from —. And let what upon taking the said account shall be

---

[66] See *British Russian Gazette and Trade Outlook Ltd. v. Associated Newspapers Ltd.* [1933] 2 K.B. 616, 643 *et seq.*, *per* Scrutton L.J. Also *Chitty on Contracts* (26th ed.), para. 1584. Previously the view of the courts was otherwise: see *Brown v. Perkins* (1842) 1 Hare 564.

[67] Such an agreement might, alternatively, be supported by a promissory estoppel.

[68] Lord Lindley referred, in this context, to the decision in *Sewell v. Bridge* (1749) 1 Ves.Sen. 297. This, however, would seem to be more a case of a settled account; *sed quaere*.

[69] See, generally, *Chitty on Contracts* (26th ed.), paras. 1573 *et seq.* Lord Lindley referred to Mitford, *Pleas* (5th ed.), p. 304 and the decision in *Brooks v. Sutton* (1868) L.R. 5 Eq. 361.

[70] See, for example, *Phelps v. Sproule* (1833) 1 M. & K. 231; *Wedderburn v. Wedderburn* (1838) 4 Myl. & Cr. 41; *Millar v. Craig* (1843) 6 Beav. 433; *Pritt v. Clay* (1843) 6 Beav. 503. See also *supra*, paras. 23–106 *et seq.*

[71] See *supra*, paras. 23–54 *et seq.*

[72] See *Chitty on Contracts* (26th ed.), para. 1573. Lord Lindley referred to Mitford, *Pleas* (5th ed.), p. 307. As to agreements to waive accounts, see *supra*, para. 23–114.

certified to be due from either of the said parties to the other of them, be paid by the party from whom to the party to whom the same shall be certified to be due. Liberty to apply."[73]

This is, in essence, the form of order which is still in use, although the consequential order for payment is commonly omitted.[74] When giving judgment, the court may, in addition, give directions as to the manner in which the account is to be taken in chambers[75]; alternatively it may leave such directions to the Master.

Costs

Initial order

23-117 Although a different practice was once adopted,[76] it has long been an established rule that all the costs of dissolution proceedings should be paid out of the partnership assets, unless there is a good reason for making some other order.[77] Where, however, such proceedings are, in reality, commenced in order to obtain an adjudication on some disputed claim between the partners, the unsuccessful litigant will normally be ordered to pay the costs up to the date of trial.[78]

Where an account is sought without a dissolution,[79] the costs are likely to follow the event, in the usual way.

---

[73] This form was derived from *Seton on Decrees* (4th ed.), p. 1197. A number of the older decided cases may usefully be referred to for the form of order adopted; for convenience, these are arranged alphabetically, according to the circumstances in which the account was sought (all references being to the relevant page of the report at which the order is to be found): (i) application of surplus assets (*Binney v. Mutrie* (1886) 12 App.Cas. 165; *Beningfield v. Baxter* (1886) 12 App.Cas. 181); (ii) executors trading with deceased partner's assets (*Travis v. Milne* (1851) 9 Hare 157); (iii) fraudulent representations (*Pillans v. Harkness* (1713) Colles, P.C. 448; *Rawlins v. Wickham* (1858) 1 Giff. 362); (iv) mortgagee of a partner's share (*Whetham v. Davey* (1885) 30 Ch.D. 580); (v) post-dissolution profits (*Crawshay v. Collins* (1808) 15 Ves.Jr. 230; (1826) 2 Russ. 347; *Manley v. Sartori* [1927] 1 Ch. 166); (vi) property acquired by one partner (*Fereday v. Wightwick* (1829) Tam. 262); (vii) release set aside and accounts reopened (*Millar v. Craig* (1843) 6 Beav. 442); (viii) sale, receiver and account (*Wilson v. Greenwood* (1818) 1 Swan. 483); (ix) sale of share set aside (*Cook v. Collingridge* (1822) Jac. 624 and, more fully, at 27 Beav. 456, note); (x) specific performance of agreement for partnership (*England v. Curling* (1844) 8 Beav. 140); (xi) successor firm (*Wedderburn v. Wedderburn* (1836) 2 Keen 752); (xii) wrongful expulsion (*Blisset v. Daniel* (1853) 10 Hare 538).

[74] See *Heward's Chancery Orders*, p. 62; also *Atkin's Court Forms* (2nd ed.), Vol. 30 (1990 Issue), pp. 118 *et seq.* However, an order for payment will be essential if the plaintiff is minded to apply for an interim payment under R.S.C. Ord. 29, rr.10, 12(a).

[75] R.S.C. Ord. 43. r. 3, *infra*, para. A2–03; Ord. 44, r. 3(a). These rules seemingly apply in the county court: C.C.R. Ord. 13, r. 7(1)(h), Ord. 23, r. 2(1), (3). See also the County Courts Act 1984, s.65(1)(b); C.C.R. Ord. 19, Pt. II.

[76] See *Hawkins v. Parsons* (1862) 8 Jur.(N.S.) 452; *Parsons v. Hayward* (1862) 4 De G.F. & J. 474.

[77] *Hamer v. Giles* (1879) 11 Ch.D. 942.

[78] *Warner v. Smith* (1863) 9 Jur.(N.S.) 169; *Hamer v. Giles, supra*; also *Norton v. Russell* (1875) L.R. 19 Eq. 343 (where a surviving partner refused to account to the executor of his deceased co-partner).

[79] See *supra*, paras. 23–79 *et seq.*

An order for costs cannot be avoided by the defendant making a payment into court.[80]

Taking the account

The costs of taking any accounts, etc., which may be directed are, **23–118** as a general rule, paid out of the partnership assets, and, if necessary, by a contribution between the partners.[81]

Priority of costs

Costs payable out of the partnership assets rank after the **23–119** partnership debts and liabilities, including any sums due to the partners in respect of advances and the like.[82] Moreover, a partner will only be permitted to take his costs out of the partnership assets if he has made good any sums due from him to the firm, either by means of an actual payment or by an appropriate adjustment in the account. Thus, in *Ross v. White*,[83] where the plaintiff and defendant were equal partners, it appeared that £649 was due to the plaintiff in respect of an advance to the firm and that the defendant had withdrawn £601 more capital than the plaintiff. The funds in court being insufficient to defray these two sums as well as the costs of the action, it was held that the rights of the partners ought first to be adjusted by paying to the plaintiff the sums of £649 and £601 out of such funds, with the balance being applied towards payment of the costs of the action. The remainder of the costs fell to be borne by the partners in equal shares. This approach naturally accords with the requirements of the Partnership Act 1890.[84]

Solicitor's lien and charge for costs

If, after obtaining an order for dissolution and the appointment of **23–120** a receiver, the plaintiff changes his solicitors, his former solicitors are not entitled to assert their lien for costs by retaining papers which have come into their hands in the course of the action, but must deliver them up to the new solicitors in return for the usual undertaking to preserve the lien.[85] This limitation on their rights is imposed in order to avoid embarrassment to the other partners and to the partnership creditors.

---

[80] R.S.C. Ord. 22 and C.C.R. Ord. 11 do not apply to an action for an account: *Nichols v. Evens* (1883) 22 Ch.D. 611.

[81] *Austin v. Jackson* (1878) 11 Ch.D. 942, note; *Hamer v. Giles* (1879) 11 Ch.D. 942; *Potter v. Jackson* (1880) 13 Ch.D. 845; *Butcher v. Pooler* (1883) 24 Ch.D. 273.

[82] *Austin v. Jackson, supra; Hamer v. Giles, supra; Potter v. Jackson, supra.*

[83] [1894] 3 Ch. 326.

[84] *Ibid.* s.44, *infra*, paras. 25–40 *et seq.*

[85] *Dessau v. Peters, Rushton & Co.* [1922] 1 Ch. 1.

If a partner's solicitor obtains a charge over the partnership assets for his taxed costs,[86] that charge may take priority over the rights of the partnership creditors,[87] even where the latter have previously obtained orders, in the usual form,[88] giving them a charge for their respective debts and costs on any moneys in the receiver's hands.[89] However, since the power is discretionary, where assets are "recovered" by one partner from his co-partners, the charge will only extend to that partner's interest in such assets and will, thus, be subject to the prior claims of the partnership creditors.[90]

Taking the account

23–121   Lord Lindley summarised the method of taking a partnership account under a judgment in the usual form as follows:

" (1) Ascertain how the firm stands as regards non-partners.

(2) Ascertain what each partner is entitled to charge in account with his co-partners; remembering, in the words of Lord Hardwicke, that 'each is entitled to be allowed as against the other, everything he has advanced or brought in as a partnership transaction, and to charge the other in the account with what that other has not brought in, or has taken out more than he ought.'[91]

(3) Apportion between the partners all profits to be divided or losses to be made good; and ascertain what, if anything, each partner must pay to the others, in order that all cross-claims may be settled."

23–122   This still holds true. It is accordingly necessary, when taking a partnership account, to identify and distinguish between:

(*a*)   partnership property and the separate property of the partners;[92]

(*b*)   joints debts and separate debts;[93]

---

[86] See the Solicitors Act 1974, s.73. As to the operation of this section, see *Harris v. Yarm* [1960] Ch. 256 (a decision under the equivalent provision in the Solicitors Act 1957); *Fairfold Properties Ltd. v. Exmouth Docks Co. Ltd. (No. 2)* [1993] Ch. 196.

[87] *Jackson v. Smith* (1884) 53 L.J.Ch. 972; *Ridd v. Thorne* [1902] 2 Ch. 344; *Newport v. Pougher* [1937] Ch. 214.

[88] *Kewney v. Attrill* (1886) 34 Ch.D. 345. See further, *supra*, para. 14–93.

[89] *Ridd v. Thorne* [1902] 2 Ch. 344.

[90] *Wimbourne v. Fine* [1952] Ch. 869. In this case, the solicitor's charge did, however, rank in priority to a mortgage of the partner's interest in the assets.

[91] *West v. Skip* (1749) 1 Ves.Sen. 239, 242. Note that the rule in *Clayton's case*, relating to the appropriation of payments (*supra*, paras. 13–82 *et seq.*), applies as between partners: see *Toulmin v. Copland* (1840) 7 Cl. & F. 349. Lord Lindley also observed, by way of footnote, that "It is said a partner is not to be charged as such with what he might have received, without his wilful default, *Rowe v. Wood* (1795) 2 J. & W. 553, but *quaere* whether a surviving partner could not be made so to account, as he alone can get in the assets of the firm. See, also, *Bury v. Allen* (1845) 1 Colly. 589." See further, *infra*, paras. 26–38 *et seq.*

[92] See *supra*, paras. 18–01 *et seq.*

[93] See *supra*, paras. 12–01 *et seq.*

(c) those profits and losses which are to be credited or debited to all the partners and those which are only to be credited or debited to one or more of them to the exclusion of the others.[94]

Obviously, much will depend on the terms of the original partnership agreement[95] and the subsequent conduct of the partners.[96]

Just allowances

Just allowances will be made in taking the account even where the **22–123** judgment is silent on the point.[97] Lord Lindley pointed out that:

"... when a partnership account is ordered, it is not usual for the Court to determine beforehand what are, and what are not, just allowances. That is determined on taking the account; and, if necessary, the order will direct the [*Master*][98] to state the facts and reasons upon which he shall adjudge any allowances to be just allowances."[99]

In order to identify what allowances ought to be made, regard must be had to the terms of the partnership agreement and the principles noticed earlier in this work.[1]

Period to which account will relate

Commencement: A general account of partnership dealings and **23–124** transactions will normally be taken as from the date on which the partnership commenced, unless some account has been settled between the partners in the meantime.[2] Since a settled account will not normally be reopened,[3] the general account will, in such a case, be taken as from the date of the last settled account.[4]

---

[94] See *supra*, paras. 10–65 *et seq.*, 16–08 *et seq.* (profits), 20–04 *et seq.* (losses).

[95] See *supra*, paras. 10–62 *et seq.*, 10–133 *et seq.* But see also *Watney v. Wells* (1867) L.R. 2 Ch.App. 250.

[96] See *supra*, paras. 10–10 *et seq.*, 10–135 *et seq.*

[97] See R.S.C. Ord. 43, r. 6, *infra*, para. A2–06. This rule seemingly applies in the county court: C.C.R. Ord. 13, r. 7(1)(h), Ord. 23, r. 2(1), (3); also the County Courts Act 1984, s.38(1).

[98] In the original passage, the words "chief clerk" appeared at this point.

[99] See *Brown v. De Tastet* (1819) Jac. 284; *Cook v. Collingridge* (1823) Jac. 607; *Crawshay v. Collins* (1826) 2 Russ. 325; *Wedderburn v. Wedderburn* (1836) 2 Keen 753.

[1] See *supra*, paras. 20–42 *et seq.*

[2] *Beak v. Beak* (1675) Finch 190; *Cook v. Collingridge* (1822) Jac. 607, 624. An incoming partner has no right to profits made before he became a partner, unless there is an agreement to that effect: *Gordon v. Rutherford* (1823) T. & R. 373. See, as to laches and limitation, *supra*, paras. 23–17 *et seq.*, 23–31 *et seq.*

[3] See *supra*, paras. 23–106 *et seq.*

[4] This used to be expressly provided for by inserting the following words in the order: "And in case it shall appear that any account has been settled and agreed upon between the parties up to any given time, the same is not to be disturbed." However, this is not necessary: see *Newen v. Wetten* (1862) 31 Beav. 315; *Holgate v. Shutt* (1884) 27 Ch.D. 111 and 28 Ch.D. 111; *cf. Milford v. Milford* (1868) McCle. & Yo. 150. See, nevertheless, as to the current recommended form, *Atkin's Court Forms* (2nd ed.), Vol. 30 (1990 issue), pp. 118, 119. *Cf. Heward's Chancery Orders*, p. 62.

Notwithstanding the normal rule, account *may* also be taken of the partners' dealings whilst the partnership was being set up, as Lord Lindley made clear:

"Where the partners have had dealings together preparatory to the commencement of their partnership, these dealings cannot be excluded from consideration in taking the partnership accounts."[5]

23–125   *Termination:*   Although it might be thought that a general account of partnership dealings and transactions should not extend beyond the date of dissolution,[6] it cannot be assumed that such dealings and transactions will automatically come to a halt on that date.[7] Indeed, the Partnership Act 1890 provides that each partners' authority to bind to firm will continue for the purposes of winding up the partnership affairs.[8] Thus, in practice, the account will be taken up to the conclusion of the winding up, as Lord Lindley explained:

"... some time or other must elapse between the dissolution and the final winding up of the affairs of the concern, and such time cannot in fairness to anyone be excluded from consideration.[9] ... [A]n account of partnership dealings and transactions, although in one sense it stops at the date at which the partnership is dissolved, must still be kept open for the purpose of debiting and crediting the proper parties with the monies payable by or to them in respect of fresh transactions incidental to the winding up, as well as in respect of old transactions engaged in prior to the dissolution."[10]

Where a deceased or outgoing partner's share is retained in the partnership business in circumstances which attract the application of section 42(1) of the Partnership Act 1890,[11] any account of profits will, of course, extend from the date of death, retirement, etc., until the share is actually paid out.

---

[5] See *Cruikshank v. McVicar* (1844) 8 Beav. 106, 116, *per* Lord Langdale.

[6] See *Beak v. Beak* (1675) Finch 191 (dissolution by death); *Jones v. Noy* (1833) 2 M. & K. 125 (dissolution on grounds of mental disorder).

[7] See *infra*, paras. 24–01 *et seq.*, 25–01.

[8] *Ibid.* s.38. See *supra*, paras. 13–64 *et seq.*

[9] See *Crawshay v. Collins* (1826) 2 Russ. 325, 345, *per* Lord Eldon; *Hale v. Hale* (1841) 4 Beav. 369, 375, *per* Lord Lansdale.

[10] See *Willett v. Blanford* (1842) 1 Hare 253, 270, *per* Wigram V.-C. However, the rights of the partners may be different after the date of dissolution: see *Watney v. Wells* (1867) L.R. 2 Ch.App. 250, noticed *supra*, para. 20–31; also *Booth v. Parks* (1828) 1 Moll. 465. And see *supra*, paras. 10–63, 10–138.

[11] See *infra*, paras. 25–23 *et seq.*

Evidence on which accounts are taken

Where any item is challenged in the course of taking the account,[12] **23–126**
it will ultimately have to be vouched if the parties cannot agree it.
For this purpose, the contents of the partnership books will be of
considerable importance. Lord Lindley pointed out that the partnership books:

"... being accessible to all the partners,[13] and being kept more or
less under the surveillance of them all, are *prima facie* evidence
against each of them, and, therefore, also, for any of them against
the others.[14] But entries made by one partner without the
knowledge of the other do not prejudice the latter as between
himself and his co-partners[15] ...".

In *Morehouse v. Newton*,[16] a surviving partner drew up an account
which he furnished to the executors of his late partner. It was held
that the account was admissible against the surviving partner, but that
the executors were not bound, merely because they had used it
against him, to accept the accuracy of its contents.

If any books, etc., have been lost, so that the account cannot be
vouched in the normal way, special directions can be obtained from
the court as to the manner in which the accounts are to be taken and
vouched.[17]

Production of books, etc.: It was formerly the practice that a **23–127**
judgment for an account would direct all parties to produce on oath
all books and papers in their custody relating to the taking of the
accounts, but this is no longer generally the case.[18] Nevertheless,
production of such books and papers will inevitably be required by
way of discovery.[19]

It has already been seen that a partner who chooses to keep
partnership records in a private book of his own will be compelled to

---

[12] See R.S.C. Ord. 43, r. 5, *infra*, para. A2–05. This rule seemingly applies in the county court:
C.C.R. Ord. 13, r. 7(1)(h), Ord. 23, r. 2(1), (3).

[13] But see *supra*, para. 22–12.

[14] See *Lodge v. Prichard* (1853) 3 De G.M. & G. 906; *Gething v. Keighley* (1878) 9 Ch.D. 551;
also *Smith v. Duke of Chandos* (1740) Barnard.Ch. 412 and (1741) 2 Atk. 158. But see *Stewart's
Case* (1866) L.R. 1 Ch.App. 574, 587, *per* Turner L.J.

[15] *Hutcheson v. Smith* (1842) 5 I.Eq. R. 117.

[16] (1849) 3 De G. & Sm. 307. See also *Reeve v. Whitmore* (1865) 2 Dr. & Sm. 446.

[17] R.S.C. Ord. 43, r. 3, *infra*, para. A2–03. This rule seemingly applies in the county court:
C.C.R. Ord. 13, r. 7(1)(h), Ord. 23, r. 2(1), (3). Note, as to the old practice, *Adley v. Whitstable
Co.* (1810) 17 Ves.Jr. 315; *Turner v. Corney* (1841) 5 Beav. 515; *Millar v. Craig* (1843) 6 Beav.
444; *Rowley v. Adams* (1844) 7 Beav. 391; *Lodge v. Prichard* (1853) 3 De G. M. & G. 906;
Stainton v. The Carron Co. (1857) 24 Beav. 346; *Ewart v. Williams* (1855) 7 De G.M. & G. 68.
And see, as to the provisions of the Bankers' Books Evidence Act 1879 (as amended), *Phipson on
Evidence* (14th ed.), paras. 31–49 *et seq.*

[18] See *Heward's Chancery Orders*, p. 62. *Cf. Atkin's Court Forms* (2nd ed.), Vol. 30 (1990 issue),
pp. 118, 119.

[19] See *supra*, paras. 23–93 *et seq.*

produce it and that professional privilege cannot be used to avoid such production.[20] The same obviously goes for any new books opened following a dissolution, if they relate to the subject matter of the account.[21] Where, however, the relevant books belong to the partner and a third party, the latter may be entitled to object to their production if he is not joined as a party to the proceedings.[22]

If a partner has destroyed any books or accounts in his possession or otherwise improperly refuses to produce them, all necessary presumptions will be made against him when the account is taken.[23] This may even involve estimating the profits of the firm.[24]

23–128   *Accountants employed by court:* The court has power to employ professional accountants to assist it in taking the accounts and may act on their report.[25]

Official referee

23–129   The court may, in an appropriate case, refer the taking of the accounts to an official referee, with or without assessors.[26]

B. Injunctions

Distinction between injunction and receiver

23–130   Where one or more partners are intent on ignoring the terms of the partnership agreement or otherwise acting in breach of the implied duty of good faith which they owe to their co-partners,[27] the court will, in an appropriate case, intervene either by granting an injunction against the miscreant partner(s) or by appointing a receiver or a receiver and manager.[28] These two remedies are very different in their effect, not least because the appointment of a receiver will affect all the partners, both plaintiffs and defendants alike.[29] Lord Lindley summarised the position as follows:

---

[20] See *supra*, paras. 22–12, 23–93; also *supra*, paras. 23–103 *et seq.* Of the partner who has intermingled partnership records with his own, Lord Lindley commented "... he should have kept his private accounts elsewhere, if he did not want them to be seen."

[21] *Hue v. Richards* (1839) 2 Beav. 305.

[22] See *supra*, para. 23–97.

[23] See *supra*, para. 22–11.

[24] *Walmsley v. Walmsley* (1846) 3 Jo. & LaT. 556; see also *Gray v. Haig* (1855) 20 Beav. 219.

[25] See R.S.C. Ord. 32, r. 16; also Ord. 40. The same power would seem to be available in the county court: County Courts Act 1984, s.39. See, generally, *Re London, Birmingham & Bucks Ry.* (1855) 6 W.R. 141; *Hill v. King* (1863) 1 N.R. 341; *Meymott v. Meymott (No. 2)* (1864) 33 Beav. 590.

[26] R.S.C. Ord. 36, r. 1; County Courts Act 1984, s.65(1)(b); C.C.R. Ord. 19, Pt. II. And see *Sarandis v. Wigham-Richardson & Co.* (1950) 84 Ll.L.R. 188.

[27] See *supra*, paras. 16–01 *et seq.*

[28] In practice, the court may grant an injunction as well as a receiver, in Lord Lindley's words "to mark its sense of the impropriety of the conduct of those it specially restrains." See *Evans v. Coventry* (1854) 3 Drew. 75, 82, *per* Kindersley V.-C. See further, as to receivers, *infra*, paras. 23–149 *et seq.*

[29] See *Dixon v. Dixon* [1904] 1 Ch. 164 and, *infra*, para. 23–149.

"These two modes of interference require to be considered separately; for they are not had recourse to indiscriminately. The appointment of a receiver, it is true, always operates as an injunction, for the Court will not suffer its officer to be interfered with by anyone[30]; but it by no means follows that because the Court will not take the affairs of a partnership into its own hands, it will not restrain some one or more of the partners from doing what may be complained of."[31]

Injunction without a dissolution

It has already been seen that courts were once reluctant to **23–131** interfere between partners, save with a view to dissolution.[32] However, as Lord Lindley explained:

"Whatever doubt there may formerly have been upon the subject, it is clear that an injunction will not be refused simply because no dissolution of partnership is sought."[33]

Degree of misconduct required

Even though the court is prepared to grant injunctive relief as **23–132** between partners, it will not do so lightly. In a passage which was echoed in his consideration of the grounds on which a court will dissolve a partnership,[34] Lord Lindley observed:

"Mere squabbles and improprieties, arising from infirmities of temper, are not considered sufficient ground for an injunction[35]; but if one partner excludes his co-partner from his rightful interference in the management of the partnership affairs, or if he persists in acting in violation of the partnership articles on any point of importance, or so grossly misconducts himself as to render it impossible for the business to be carried on in a proper manner, the court will interfere for the protection of the other partners.[36]

---

[30] See *Helmore v. Smith (No. 2)* (1887) 35 Ch.D. 449. As to restraining interference with a receiver, see *infra*, para. 23–177.

[31] See *Hall v. Hall* (1850) 12 Beav. 414; but see also, as to the injunctions that were granted, *ibid.* (1850) 3 Mac. & G. 79, 84, *per* Truro L.C. And see *Tate v. Charlesworth* (1962) 106 S.J. 368 (where partnership principles were applied by analogy).

[32] See *supra*, para. 23–14; also *Hall v. Hall* (1850) 3 Mac. & G. 79.

[33] This is, if anything, underlined by the terms of the Supreme Court Act 1981, s.37(1)–(3) and its predecessors. See also the County Courts Act 1984, s.38.

[34] See *infra*, para. 24–67; also *infra*, para. 24–69.

[35] See *Lawson v. Morgan* (1815) 1 Price 303; *Cofton v. Horner* (1818) 5 Price 537; *Marshall v. Colman* (1820) 2 J. & W. 266; *Smith v. Jeyes* (1841) 4 Beav. 503; *Warder v. Stilwell* (1856) 3 Jur.(N.S.) 9.

[36] See generally, *infra*, paras. 24–72, 24–86. And note the decision in *Anderson v. Wallace* (1835) 2 Moll. 540.

Where, however, the partner complained of has by agreement been constituted the active managing partner, the court will not interfere unless a strong case be made out against him[37]; nor will the Court restrain a partner from acting as such, merely because if he is known so to do, the confidence placed in the firm by the public will be shaken."[38]

By way of illustration, an injunction has been granted in the following circumstances, which are, for convenience, arranged in alphabetical order:

23-133 *Exclusion:* Where a partner, who had recovered from a temporary mental disorder, was excluded from the management of the partnership affairs, he was granted an injunction restraining the other partners from seeking to prevent him transacting the business of the partnership.[39] In another case,[40] an excluded partner was granted an injunction restraining the defendant from applying any of the moneys and effects of the partnership otherwise than in the ordinary course of business, and from obstructing or interfering with the plaintiff in the exercise or enjoyment of his rights under the partnership agreement. A similar attitude will be adopted where any partner seeks to exclude his co-partners from possession of any partnership chattels[41] or land, even if he is the sole trustee thereof.[42]

23-134 *Purported retirement:* Where a partner in a fixed term partnership purported to retire and entered into a new partnership with third parties, which assumed the name of the old firm, opened letters addressed to it, and circulated notices of its dissolution, an injunction

---

[37] See *Waters v. Taylor* (1808) 15 Ves.Jr. 10; *Lawson v. Morgan* (1815) 1 Price 303; *Automatic Self-Cleaning Filter Syndicate Co. Ltd. v. Cuninghame* [1906] 2 Ch. 34, 44, *per* Cozens Hardy L.J. See also *Walker v. Hirsch* (1884) 27 Ch.D. 460.

[38] *Anon.* (1856) 2 K. & J. 441.

[39] *Ibid.*

[40] *Hall v. Hall* (1855) 20 Beav. 139; but see also *ibid.* (1850) 3 Mac. & G. 79, 84, *per* Truro L.C. And see *Blisset v. Daniel* (1853) 10 Hare 493; *Carmichael v. Evans* [1904] 1 Ch. 486 (where an injunction was refused on the merits); *Barnes v. Youngs* [1898] 1 Ch. 414.

[41] Lord Lindley wrote "Partners are tenants in common or joint tenants of the goods and chattels belonging to the firm; but one partner has no right to take possession of them and to exclude his co-partners from them; and he can, it is apprehended, be restrained from doing so." See also *supra,* para. 19–03.

[42] Lord Lindley observed "The equitable as well as the legal ownership must be considered; no partner can eject or expel his co-partners from land in which he may have the legal estate, but of which he is a trustee for the firm; nor can he maintain an action against his co-partners for coming on such land. On the other hand, they can restrain him from excluding them therefrom. [*See Peaceable v. Read (1801) 1 East 568; Doe v. Horn (1838) 3 M. & W. 333*] Whether the relation of trustee and *cestuis que trustent* exists depends upon whether the property is partnership property or not, upon whether the partnership is dissolved or not, and upon whether, if dissolved, the property is a partnership asset in which all the partners are still interested." See also *Hawkins v. Hawkins* (1858) 4 Jur.(N.S.) 1044. Note also that the excluded partners might, perhaps, seek the payment of an occupation rent if there has in truth been an ouster: *Dennis v. McDonald* [1982] Fam. 63. However, it is doubtful whether such a rent could be recovered otherwise than by an action for an account: see *supra,* para. 23–72.

was granted restraining the "retired" partner from carrying on any business otherwise than with his original partners and from publishing or circulating any notice of the old firm's dissolution, before the expiration of the fixed term. Moreover, his new partners were restrained from carrying on business with him, or otherwise, in the name of the old firm, from receiving or opening letters addressed to it, and from interfering with its property.[43]

Unauthorised business: Where the lease of a particular branch **23–135** office had expired and the plaintiff was unwilling to concur in taking a new lease, the defendant was restrained from carrying on the partnership business at that office against the plaintiff's wishes.[44]

Use of firm name: An injunction has been granted restraining a **23–136** partner from using the firm name in a business carried on by him on his own account.[45]

Misconduct with a view to dissolution

It is clear that the courts will, where appropriate, interfere by way **23–137** of injunction with a view to preventing one partner from misconducting himself in such a way that his co-partners are forced either to condone his misconduct or agree to a dissolution.[46]

Attempts to frustrate the decision making process

On the same basis, it may be that injunctive relief could be **23–138** obtained against a partner who seeks to obstruct a particular course of action which will benefit the partnership at no detriment to himself, if his actions involve a deliberate breach of the duty of good faith, *e.g.* where he is attempting to secure an alteration to the partnership agreement in his own favour as the price of his co-operation.[47] However, the current editor considers that such an order would only be entertained by the court in exceptional circumstances.[48]

---

[43] *England v. Curling* (1844) 8 Beav. 129. See also *Warder v. Stilwell* (1856) 3 Jur.(N.S.) 9; *Tate v. Charlesworth* (1962) 106 S.J. 368.

[44] *Clements v. Norris* (1878) 8 Ch.D. 129. See also *Nixon v. Wood* (1987) 284 E.G. 1055, where an interlocutory injunction was in fact refused, following an application of the principles enunciated in *American Cyanamid Co. v. Ethicon Ltd.* [1975] A.C. 396.

[45] *Aas v. Benham* [1891] 2 Ch. 244.

[46] See *supra*, paras. 23–14, 23–82 and *infra*, paras. 24–72, 24–86.

[47] For an analogous case involving consent to the amendment of a pension scheme, see *Imperial Group Pension Trust Ltd. v. Imperial Tobacco Ltd.* [1991] 1 W.L.R. 589. There, however, injunctive relief was not sought.

[48] *e.g.* where a *Mareva* injunction would be justified: see *infra*, para. 23–147.

Injunction where partnership is at will

23–139   Although the view was advanced, in some earlier cases,[49] that it is more difficult for the court to interfere by way of injunctive relief in the case of a partnership at will, on the grounds that the court's order can be rendered nugatory by the simple expedient of giving notice of dissolution,[50] such caution was not in truth justified. As Lord Lindley put it, if the partnership is dissolved,

> "... an injunction will not necessarily be futile, inasmuch as so long as it continues in force, the defendant is rendered powerless for evil,[51] and a notice by him to dissolve the partnership cannot, *per se*, operate as a dissolution of the injunction."

Surprisingly, there appear to be no direct authorities on this point: Lord Lindley referred to the decisions in *Glassington v. Thwaites*,[52] *Morris v. Colman*[53] and *Homfray v. Fothergill*,[54] but conceded that, according to the reports, none of them actually involved a partnership at will.[55]

However, in *Floydd v. Cheney*,[56] where an interlocutory injunction restraining the defendant, who was an assistant in the plaintiff's architectural practice, from making improper use of certain papers, Megarry J. held that there was no evidence of a partnership at will as the defendant contended, but that the same relief would have been ordered even if the existence of such a partnership had been proved.[57]

It should also be noted in this context that a notice of dissolution served with the sole purpose of evading the effects of the injunction might be held mala fide and, thus, invalid.[58]

Injunction in dissolution actions

23–140   There has never been any doubt that the court will, in appropriate circumstances, grant injunctive relief where dissolution proceedings are pending or, in the case of a dissolved partnership, where it is sought, in Lord Lindley's words, "to restrain one of the partners

---

[49] See *Peacock v. Peacock* (1809) 16 Ves.Jr. 49; *Miles v. Thomas* (1839) 9 Sim. 606.
[50] See generally, *infra*, paras. 24–10 *et seq*. And note the implications of the decision in *Walters v. Bingham* [1988] 1 F.T.L.R. 260: see *infra*, para. 24–13.
[51] *i.e.* he cannot damage or otherwise act against the interests of the partnership.
[52] (1823) 1 Sim. & St. 124.
[53] (1812) 18 Ves.Jr. 437.
[54] (1866) L.R. 1 Eq. 567.
[55] Lord Lindley observed "It does not appear from the reports of these cases whether the partnerships were partnerships at will or not; but supposing them to have been merely partnerships at will, it is clear that the injunctions were far from valueless."
[56] [1970] Ch. 602.
[57] *Ibid.* p. 608. This part of the judgment is clearly *obiter*.
[58] See *infra*, para. 24–13.

from doing any act which will impede the winding up of the concern."[59] Examples in the reports are numerous, and may be classified as follows:

Assets: A partner will be restrained from disposing of or getting **23–141** in the partnership assets if he is likely to misapply them.[60] Moreover, the personal representatives of a deceased partner will be restrained from making any improper use of partnership property, if the legal estate happens to devolve on them.[61]

Bills of exchange: A partner will be restrained from drawing, accepting or indorsing bills of exchange in the firm name otherwise than for partnership purposes.[62]

Books: A partner will be restrained from withholding the **23–142** partnership books.[63]

Business: A partner will be restrained from carrying on the partnership business for any purpose other than winding up[64] or from improperly interfering with, obstructing or otherwise damaging such business.[65] Such an order can, if necessary, be made against a partner suffering from a mental disorder.[66]

Debts: A partner will, in an appropriate case, be restrained from **23–143** getting in debts owing to the firm[67] and any debtor who, with knowledge of the order, makes a payment to that partner will not be discharged from liability to the firm.[68]

---

[59] A person who merely shares the profits of the business will normally have no such right: see *Walker v. Hirsch* (1884) 27 Ch.D. 460.

[60] *Hartz v. Schrader* (1803) 8 Ves.Jr. 317 (surviving partner); *O'Brien v. Cooke* (1871) I.R. 5 Eq. 51 (where the plaintiff was allowed to get in the debts, on indemnifying the defendant against costs, etc.). See also *Garrett v. Moore* (1891), Seton (6th ed.), p. 696, where an interlocutory injunction was granted to restrain a partner from drawing out partnership moneys which he had paid into his private account. The case was not, however, referred to in the 7th edition of Seton.

[61] *Alder v. Fouracre* (1818) 3 Swan. 489.

[62] *Williams v. Bingley* (1692) 2 Vern. 278, note, and Coll.Prt. (2nd. ed.) 233; *Jervis v. White* (1802) 6 Ves.Jr. 738; *Hood v. Aston* (1826) 1 Russ. 412.

[63] *Charlton v. Poulter* (1753) 19 Ves.Jr. 148, note; *Taylor v. Davis* (1842) 3 Beav. 388, note; *Greatrex v. Greatrex* (1847) 1 De G. & Sm. 692.

[64] See *De Tastet v. Bordenave* (1822) Jac. 516 (where, on the evidence, an injunction was refused). The report is, however, less than clear on the point. See also the Partnership Act 1890, s.38, considered *supra*, paras. 13–64 *et seq.*

[65] *Charlton v. Poulter* (1753) 19 Ves.Jr. 148, note; *Smith v. Jeyes* (1841) 4 Beav. 503; also *Hermann Loog v. Bean* (1884) 26 Ch.D. 306, (an agency case which is, by analogy, applicable to partnerships). Note that in *Marshall v. Watson* (1858) 25 Beav. 501, an injunction to restrain a partner from publishing the accounts of the firm was, under special circumstances, refused.

[66] *J. v. S.* [1894] 3 Ch. 72.

[67] *Read v. Bowers* (1793) 4 Bro.C.C. 441.

[68] *Eastern Trust Co. v. McKenzie, Mann & Co. Ltd.* [1915] A.C. 750.

Dissolution agreements: The court will naturally grant relief in order to restrain any breach of the partnership agreement or any other agreement governing the dissolution. Thus, it will readily enforce an express[69] or implied[70] restriction on competition or a term relating to the collection of debts[71] or the treatment of trade secrets.[72]

23–144   *Goodwill:* A partner will be restrained from damaging the value of the goodwill if it ought to be sold for the benefit of all the partners,[73] or if it belongs solely to his co-partners.[74] However, a surviving partner will not be restrained from continuing to carry on business in the name of himself and his deceased co-partner, unless this would involve a breach of the partnership agreement or the goodwill ought to be sold.[75]

Representatives of deceased or insolvent partner: The personal representatives of a deceased partner or the trustee in bankruptcy or liquidator of an insolvent partner will be restrained from interfering in the business, at the instance of the surviving partners.[76] Equally, a surviving partner will, where necessary, be restrained from improperly ejecting such personal representatives, etc.[77]

Misconduct by partner seeking injunction

23–145   It is self evident that injunctive relief cannot, in general, be obtained by a partner who is himself in breach of any obligation owed to his co-partners, whether arising by agreement or pursuant to the provisions of the Partnership Act 1890. As Lord Lindley put it:

"... a partner who seeks an injunction against his co-partner must himself be able and willing to perform his own part of any agreement which he seeks to restrain his co-partner from

---

[69] See *supra*, paras. 10–180 *et seq.*

[70] *Churton v. Douglas* (1859) Johns. 174; *Hookham v. Pottage* (1872) L.R. 8 Ch.App. 91. See further, *supra*, paras. 10–168 *et seq.*

[71] *Davis v. Amer* (1854) 3 Drew. 64. See also *supra*, para. 10–224.

[72] *Morison v. Moat* (1851) 9 Hare 241. See also *supra*, para. 10–44.

[73] *Bradbury v. Dickens* (1859) 27 Beav. 53; *Turner v. Major* (1862) 3 Giff. 442; *Dixon v. Dixon* [1904] 1 Ch. 161; also *Davis v. Smaggasgale* (1890), Seton (7th ed.), pp. 680, 681; *Re David and Matthews* [1899] 1 Ch. 378.

[74] *Trego v. Hunt* [1896] A.C. 7; *Boorne v. Wicker* [1927] 1 Ch. 667; *Gargan v. Ruttle* [1931] I.R. 152.

[75] See *supra*, paras. 10–159 *et seq.*, 10–180 *et seq.*

[76] See *Allen v. Kilbre* (1819) 4 Madd. 464; *Davidson v. Napier* (1827) 1 Sim. 297; *Ex p. Finch* (1832) 1 D. & Ch. 174; *Freeland v. Stansfeld* (1854) 2 Sm. & G. 479; *Fraser v. Kershaw* (1856) 2 K. & J. 496. *Cf.* the position where all the partners are dead: *Philips v. Atkinson* (1787) 2 Bro.C.C. 272.

[77] *Hawkins v. Hawkins* (1858) 4 Jur.(N.S.) 1044. Note also *Elliot v. Brown* (1791) 3 Swan. 489, note.

breaking[78]; and the plaintiff's own misconduct may be a complete bar to his application, however wrong the defendant's conduct may have been.[79] As stated by Lord Eldon in *Const v. Harris*,[80] a partner who complains that his co-partners do not do their duty to him must be ready at all times, and offer to do his duty to them."

This principle does, however, have limits.[81]

Injunction to restrain holding out

The liability undertaken by a person who is held out as a partner **23–146** has already been noticed.[82] Unauthorised holding out will, not unnaturally, be restrained by the court.[83]

Mareva injunction

The so-called *Mareva* injunction[84] was developed in order to **23–147** prevent defendants seeking to frustrate judgments by removing from the jurisdiction of the court, or otherwise dissipating, money or assets in their hands.[85] There are no reported cases in which such an injunction has been sought or obtained as between partners,[86] which may, perhaps, be explained by reference to the difficulty faced by prospective plaintiffs when seeking to satisfy the court that they are likely to recover judgment "for a certain or approximate sum"[87] or, indeed, any sum, until such time as a general account has been taken.[88] This the court might not be prepared to do on an

---

[78] *Smith v. Fromont* (1818) 2 Swan. 330.
[79] See *Littlewood v. Caldwell* (1822) 11 Price 97, where an injunction was refused because the plaintiff had taken away the partnership books.
[80] (1824) T. & R. 496, 526.
[81] See *supra*, para. 16–04.
[82] See *supra*, paras. 5–43 *et seq.*
[83] See *Dixon v. Holden* (1869) L.R. 7 Eq. 488; *Thynne v. Shove* (1890) 45 Ch.D. 577; *Gray v. Smith* (1889) 43 Ch.D. 208. See also *supra*, paras. 10–162, 10–163.
[84] The injunction takes its name from the order made in *Mareva Compania Naviera S.A. v. International Bulk Carriers S.A.* [1975] 2 Lloyd's Rep. 509. See now the Supreme Court Act 1981, s.37(1), (3). Note that such an injunction can be sought in aid of execution: *Orwell Steel (Erection and Fabrication) Ltd. v. Asphalt and Tarmac (U.K.) Ltd.* [1984] 1 W.L.R. 1097; *Babanaft International Co. S.A. v. Bassatne* [1990] Ch. 13. Moreover, despite doubts expressed (*inter alia*) in the latter case, it is now recognised that a world-wide injunction can be granted where appropriate: see *Derby & Co. Ltd. v. Weldon* [1990] Ch. 48; *Derby & Co. Ltd. v. Weldon (Nos. 3 and 4)* [1990] Ch. 65.
[85] See, as to the type of assets which may be made subject to a *Mareva* injunction, *Darashah v. U.F.A.C. (U.K.) Ltd.*, *The Times*, March 30, 1982 (goodwill); *C.B.S. United Kingdom Limited v. Lambert* [1983] Ch. 37.
[86] In *Investment and Pensions Advisory Service Ltd. v. Gray* [1990] BCLC 38 a *Mareva* injunction was obtained by an insolvent *firm* (acting by the official receiver) against a member of that firm.
[87] These are the words used by Kerr L.J. in *Z Ltd. v. A-Z and AA-LL* [1982] Q.B. 558, 585. But note also the doubts, expressed by Lord Denning M.R. in *Darashah v. U.F.A.C. (U.K.) Ltd.*, *supra*.
[88] As to the need for a general account to be taken before the respective entitlements of the partners can be ascertained, see *supra*, para. 23–72.

interlocutory hearing.[89] To have any prospect of obtaining an injunction in such a case, the current editor submits that, at the very least, clear evidence that some money is likely to be due to the plaintiffs on the taking of the account would be required.[90] On the other hand, where a general account has already been taken, and a balance found due from the defendant to his co-partners, no such difficulties will arise.

Although it would, in theory, be possible for a court to grant a *Mareva*-type injunction preventing a partner from voting against a particular resolution on the ground that he is actuated by an ulterior and improper motive, it would seemingly be necessary to demonstrate that his withholding of consent would have such catastrophic effects for the firm that it is akin to a wilful dissipation of assets.[91] Cases of this type will obviously be extremely rare.

The court will not grant a *Mareva* injunction if, by so doing, it would interfere with the business rights of third parties.[92] It is accordingly desirable to ensure that all the partners are before the court, either as plaintiffs or defendants.

Arbitrations

23–148   The court has the same powers of granting interim injunctions where a dispute has been referred to arbitration as it has in relation to proceedings in court.[93]

C. RECEIVERS[94]

Purpose and desirability of appointing receiver and manager

23–149   Lord Lindley summarised the position in these terms:

"The object of having a receiver appointed by the Court is to place the partnership assets under the protection of the Court, and to

---

[89] Note, however, the circumstances in which a court may order a partner to pay partnership monies into court: see *supra*, paras. 23–88 *et seq.* Moreover, the court undoubtedly has jurisdiction to order an interim payment in an appropriate case: see *supra*, para. 23–92. If anything, the court should be *more* inclined to grant *Mareva* relief than either of these remedies. There must, of course, be a cause of action in support of which *Mareva* relief is sought: *Zucker v. Tyndall Holdings Plc* [1992] 1 W.L.R. 1127.

[90] See, *e.g.*, *Wanklyn v. Wilson* (1887) 35 Ch.D. 180 (where a payment into court was sought). The fact that an account must be taken is not, *per se*, a reason for the court refusing to make an order: see, *e.g.*, *Ali & Fahd Shobokshi Group Ltd. v. Moneim* [1989] 1 W.L.R. 710, 714, *per* Mervyn Davies J. (although a continuation of the injunction was refused in this case on the grounds of non-disclosure).

[91] See *Standard Chartered Bank v. Walker* [1992] 1 W.L.R. 561, where the injunction was granted against a shareholder in a company.

[92] *Galaxia Maritime S.A. v. Mineralimportexport* [1982] 1 W.L.R. 539. Note also the obligations which may be imposed upon the plaintiff in respect of expenses incurred by third parties when a *Mareva* injunction is granted: see *Z Ltd. v. A-Z and AA-LL* [1982] Q.B. 558.

[93] Arbitration Act 1950, s.12(6)(h).

[94] See generally, as to the High Court's jurisdiction to appoint a receiver, the Supreme Court Act 1981, s.37(1).

prevent everybody, except the officer of the court, from in any way intermeddling with them. The object of having a manager is to have the partnership business carried on under the direction of the Court[95]; a receiver, unless he is also appointed manager, has no power to carry on the business."

In practice, claims for the appointment of a receiver or receiver and manager tend to be included in partnership actions as a matter of course, with scant regard to the suitability of that form of relief or the consequences for the partners, either in terms of disruption or expense.[96] It is essential to appreciate that the appointment of a receiver operates in a very different way from an injunction, in that it affects the rights of *all* the partners[97] and will be granted according to different principles. As Lord Lindley put it:

"It ... does not follow that because the Court will grant an injunction it will also appoint a receiver; nor that because it refuses to appoint a receiver it will also decline to interfere by injunction."[98]

In the current editor's view, the appointment of a receiver (or a receiver and manager) should normally be regarded as a remedy of last resort.

Nature of partnership business

In all cases in which the appointment of a receiver (or receiver and **23–150** manager) is sought, the court will have regard to the nature of the business carried on and the probable effects which such an appointment would have on the reputation of the firm and the partners. This will be of particular relevance in the case of a professional practice.[99]

Size of partnership

The other relevant factor when considering the appointment of a **23–151** receiver (or receiver and manager) will be the size of the firm. In essence, the larger the firm, the more reluctant the court will be to interfere otherwise than by way of injunctive relief, particularly

---

[95] Note that the manager's powers may be limited: see *Taylor v. Neate* (1888) 39 Ch.D. 538. And see, generally, as to the appointment of managers, *Gardner v. London, Chatham and Dover Ry.* (1867) L.R. 2 Ch.App. 201; *Re Manchester and Milford Ry.* (1881) 14 Ch.D. 645, 653, *per* Jessell M.R.; *Re Newdigate Colliery* [1912] 1 Ch. 468.

[96] See, as to the remuneration of a receiver, *infra*, para. 23–173.

[97] *Dixon v. Dixon* [1904] 1 Ch. 161; see also *supra*, para. 23–130.

[98] See *Read v. Bowers* (1793) 4 Bro.C.C. 441; *Hartz v. Schrader* (1803) 8 Ves.Jr. 317; *Hall v. Hall* (1850) 3 Mac. & G. 79.

[99] See *Floydd v. Cheney* [1970] Ch. 602, 610, *per* Megarry J.; *Sobell v. Boston* [1975] 1 W.L.R. 1587, 1593, *per* Goff J.

where complaints are levelled at the conduct of some but not all of the other partners. Lord Lindley explained why:

"In those cases in which special grounds for the appointment of a receiver must be shown,[1] it follows that in a firm of several members there is more difficulty in obtaining a receiver than in a firm of two. For the appointment of a receiver, operating in fact as an injunction against all the members, there must be some ground for excluding all who oppose the application. If the object is to exclude some or one only from intermeddling, the appropriate remedy is rather by an injunction than by a receiver."[2]

Receiver and manager without a dissolution

23–152 The general reluctance of the courts to interfere between partners otherwise than with a view to dissolution has already been noticed,[3] and is nowhere more apparent than in the present context. Indeed, Lord Lindley wrote:

"Courts of justice are by no means anxious to take upon themselves the management of a partnership business, and they will, it is said, never do so, save with a view to a dissolution or final winding up of the affairs of the concern."

This rule still appears to hold good in the case of applications for the appointment of a receiver *and manager*, since there is no reported instance in which such an appointment has been made in the case of an ongoing partnership. Indeed, in such cases as have come before the courts, relief has always been refused.[4] However, it would seem that if the relief sought is confined to the appointment of a receiver *simpliciter*, the rule will not apply, as Lord Lindley explained:

"If the appointment of a receiver does not involve the appointment of a manager, *Const v. Harris*[5] is a clear authority to show that a

---

[1] Lord Lindley in effect used the phrase "special grounds" to denote those cases in which a receiver is not appointed as a matter of course: see *infra*, paras. 23–156, 23–157.

[2] See *Hall v. Hall* (1850) 3 Mac. & G. 79.

[3] See *supra*, para. 23–14.

[4] *Hall v. Hall*, *supra*; *Roberts v. Eberhart* (1853) Kay 148. See also *Oliver v. Hamilton* (1794) 2 Anstr. 453; *Waters v. Taylor* (1808) 15 Ves.Jr. 10; *Harrison v. Armitage* (1819) 4 Madd. 143; *Goodman v. Whitcomb* (1820) 1 Jac. & W. 589; *Smith v. Jeyes* (1841) 4 Beav. 503; *Rowlands v. Evans* (1862) 30 Beav. 302. Lord Lindley noted that, in *Morris v. Colman* (1812) 18 Ves.Jr. 438, "there was a reference for the appointment of a manager"; however, whilst a perusal of the report demonstrates that such relief was sought, it does not appear to have been granted.

[5] (1824) T. & R. 496.

receiver may be obtained in an action not seeking a dissolution of the partnership; the later cases are not opposed to this."

It is considered that the wide discretions conferred on the courts by the Supreme Court Act 1981[6] and its predecessors[7] are unlikely to have materially altered the position.

Receiver and manager in dissolution action

Where an action is brought seeking the dissolution of a partnership **23–153** and/or the winding up of its affairs, a receiver and, in particular, a receiver and manager will more readily be appointed.

Dissolution not sought in terms

It goes without saying that the court will not refuse relief on the **23–154** ground that no dissolution is sought, if it can be demonstrated that the purpose of the action is to wind up the firm's affairs and the appointment of a receiver and manager is sought to that end.[8]

Right to a receiver

The considerations which apply where the appointment of a **23–155** receiver (or receiver and manager) is sought by one partner against his co-partners differ from those which apply where such appointment is sought by or against the representatives of a deceased or bankrupt partner.

(a) As between partners

Lord Lindley wrote: **23–156**

"Where one partner seeks to have a receiver appointed against his co-partners, the first thing to ascertain is, whether the partnership between them is still subsisting, or has already been dissolved; for if it is still subsisting no receiver will be appointed unless some

---

[6] *Ibid.* s.37. And see the County Courts Act 1984, s.38.

[7] See the Supreme Court of Judicature Act 1873, s.25(8); the Supreme Court of Judicature (Consolidation) Act 1925, s.45.

[8] *Shepherd v. Oxenford* (1855) 1 K. & J. 491. In this case, various forms of relief normally associated with dissolution were sought, but not dissolution itself. See also *Evans v. Coventry* (1854) 5 De G.M. & G. 911. Of this case, Lord Lindley commented "It does not appear very distinctly what the manager, as distinguished from the receiver, was expected to do."

special grounds for the appointment can be shown,[9] or unless it is plain that an order for a dissolution will be made[10]; whilst if the partnership is already dissolved, the Court usually appoints a receiver, almost as a matter of course."[11]

Consistently with the views which he had previously expressed,[12] the current editor takes the view that Lord Lindley's strictures concerning the position whilst the partnership is subsisting apply only where the appointment of a receiver *and manager* is sought. Moreover, whilst the court may be prepared to appoint a receiver "almost as a matter of course" in the case of a general dissolution,[13] the position will be otherwise where one partner has retired by mutual agreement, on the understanding that the other partners can continue to carry on the business without him: in such a case, relief by way of a receiver will almost inevitably be refused.[14] *A fortiori* if a partner retires or is expelled pursuant to an express provision of the partnership agreement.

A receiver (or receiver and manager) may be appointed even though all other matters in dispute between the partners are referred to arbitration.[15]

(b) As between partners and non-partners

23-157 The outcome of any application for the appointment of a receiver and manager in this type of case will, for the most part, depend on whether the person principally[16] sought to be excluded from interference in the business is a partner. If he is, special grounds

---

[9] See *supra*, para. 23–151 and *infra*, paras. 23–158 *et seq.*

[10] *Goodman v. Whitcomb* (1820) 1 Jac. & W. 589.

[11] See *Goodman v. Whitcomb, supra*; *Tibbits v. Phillips* (1853) 10 Hare 355; *Thomson v. Anderson* (1870) L.R. 9 Eq. 533; *Sargant v. Read* (1876) 1 Ch.D. 600; *Taylor v. Neate* (1888) 39 Ch.D. 538; *Pini v. Roncoroni* [1892] 1 Ch. 633; *Tottey v. Kemp* (1970) 215 E.G. 1021; *Sobell v. Boston* [1975] 1 W.L.R. 1587, 1591, *per* Goff J.; *Re a Company (No. 00596 of 1986)* [1987] BCLC 133 (where partnership principles were applied by analogy in the case of a company constituting a "quasi-partnership"). *Cf. Harding v. Glover* (1810) 18 Ves.Jr. 281, where Lord Eldon disavowed any principle that a dissolution is, in itself, a sufficient ground for appointing a receiver. Lord Lindley also, somewhat elliptically, added at this point in the text "In the case supposed, the common property has to be applied in paying the partnership debts, and has to be divided amongst the partners; and each partner has as much right as the others to wind up the partnership affairs. Their position is, therefore, essentially different from that of mere co-owners, between whom courts decline to interfere by appointing a receiver, except under special circumstances." The effect of appointing a receiver and manager is, of course, to *deprive* all the partners of their right to wind up the partnership affairs.

[12] See *supra*, para. 23–152.

[13] See, as to the meaning of this expression, *infra*, para. 24–03.

[14] See *Sobell v. Boston* [1975] 1 W.L.R. 1587, 1591, *per* Goff J. See also *Tottey v. Kemp* (1970) 215 E.G. 1021, where one partner has exercised a contractual option to acquire the other's share following the dissolution.

[15] *Pini v. Roncoroni* [1892] 1 Ch. 633; also *Phoenix v. Pope* [1974] 1 W.L.R. 719.

[16] A successful application will, of course, exclude both plaintiff and defendant from interfering in the business.

justifying the court's interference must be made out.[17] Lord Lindley explained the underlying rationale as follows:

"... whilst the Court is reluctant to exclude a partner from the management of the partnership affairs, it will readily interfere to prevent other persons from intermeddling therewith. The reason given for this is, that each partner is at the outset trusted by his co-partners, and has confidence reposed by them in him; and until it can be shown that he ought not to be allowed to take part any longer in the management of the partnership affairs, the court will not interfere with him. But this reasoning has no application to persons who acquire an interest in the partnership assets by events over which the partners have no control, *e.g.* the death or bankruptcy of one of the members of the firm."

It follows that a receiver will be appointed, in Lord Lindley's words, "as a matter of course" where all the partners are dead and an action is pending between their representatives[18]; similarly, where the appointment is sought by a partner against a deceased partner's personal representatives or the trustee in bankruptcy or liquidator of an insolvent partner.[19]

The assignee or mortgagee of a partnership share will, if anything, be in an even weaker position.[20]

Grounds for appointment of receiver and manager

Reference has previously been made to those circumstances in **23–158** which special grounds for the appointment of a receiver (or a receiver and manager) must be shown.[21] In practice, there are four recognised grounds, namely:

(1) Breach of a dissolution agreement under which the partners have given up their personal right to wind up the firm's affairs.

---

[17] *Collins v. Young* (1853) 1 Macq. 385; see also *Harding v. Glover* (1810) 18 Ves.Jr. 281; *Lawson v. Morgan* (1815) 1 Price 303; *Kennedy v. Lee* (1817) 3 Mer. 441; *Kershaw v. Matthews* (1826) 2 Russ. 62; *Horrell v. Witts* (1866) L.R. 1 P. & D. 103. And see, as to showing special grounds, *supra*, para. 23–151 and *infra*, paras. 23–158 *et seq.*

[18] *Philips v. Atkinson* (1787) 2 Bro.C.C. 272.

[19] *Freeland v. Stansfeld* (1854) 2 Sm. & G. 479.

[20] See *Fraser v. Kershaw* (1856) 2 K. & J. 496, where the assignees of a bankrupt partner (*i.e.* what would now be the trustee in bankruptcy) obtained the appointment of a receiver against a creditor of the solvent partner, who (under the then law) had taken an assignment of his share from the sheriff, following execution under a *fi. fa.* And see *Candler v. Candler* (1821) Jac. 225. See further, as to the rights of an assignee or mortgagee of a partnership share, *supra*, paras. 19–56 *et seq.*

[21] See *supra*, paras. 23–151, 23–156, 23–157.

(2) Misconduct plus jeopardy to the partnership assets.
(3) Fraud.
(4) Wrongful exclusion.

(1) *Breach of dissolution agreement*

23–159 A receiver will be appointed, even at the instance of the representatives of a deceased or insolvent partner,[22] where one or more partners act in breach of the terms of an agreement under which, in Lord Lindley's words,

> "... the partners have divested themselves more or less of their right to wind up the affairs of the concern."

Thus, in *Davis v. Amer*,[23] the plaintiff and the defendant, on dissolving their partnership, agreed to appoint a third party to get in the firm's assets. They also agreed not to interfere with the third party while he was so engaged. The agreement was partially implemented, prior to the death of one of the partners. Thereafter, disputes arose between that partner's executors and the surviving partner, whereupon the latter proceeded to get in the partnership debts, contrary to the terms of the agreement. The court appointed a receiver at the instance of the executors, but declined to grant an injunction on the ground that no sufficient impropriety had been shown to warrant such an order being made.[24]

It need hardly be said that agreements of this type are rarely encountered in practice.[25]

(2) *Misconduct plus jeopardy to assets*

23–160 Lord Lindley described this ground as where:

> "... by misconduct, the right of personal intervention has been forfeited, and the partnership assets are in danger of being lost ..."

and then went on to elaborate:

---

[22] See *supra*, para. 23–157.
[23] (1854) 3 Drew. 64. See also *Turner v. Major* (1862) 3 Giff. 442 (where an injunction was held to be sufficient).
[24] See *Evans v. Coventry* (1854) 3 Drew. 75, 82, *per* Kindersley V.-C. See also *supra*, para. 23–130, n. 28.
[25] It will usually be one of the partners who is appointed to get in the debts, etc.: see *supra*, para. 10–224.

"If the partnership is not yet dissolved,[26] there must be something more than a partnership squabble; the due winding up of the affairs of the concern must be endangered to induce the Court to appoint a receiver of its assets; and non-co-operation of one partner, whereby the whole responsibility of management is thrown on his co-partner, is not sufficient."[27]

The position will be *a fortiori* where the appointment of a receiver and manager is sought.

Degree of misconduct required

The degree of misconduct necessary to induce a court to interfere **23–161** between partners by way of injunction has already been noticed,[28] and the principles applicable in the case of the appointment of a receiver (or receiver and manager) are broadly the same, *i.e.* it must, in essence be demonstrated that the misconduct is of such a nature that the partner concerned can no longer be trusted. By way of illustration, the following forms of misconduct, which are, for ease of reference, arranged alphabetically, have been held sufficient[29]:

Misappropriation of assets: Where a partner in control of **23–162** partnership assets has already made off with some of them,[30] or where partnership property is abroad and a partner has absconded, as Lord Lindley put it, "in order to do what he likes with it there."[31]

Collusion with debtors: Where one partner has colluded with the partnership debtors and permitted them to delay payment of their debts.[32]

Improper use of partnership assets: Where a partner is carrying on a business on his own account using partnership property,[33] or where a surviving partner insists on carrying on the partnership business, utilising the share of his deceased partner.[34]

---

[26] Where the partnership has already been dissolved, a receiver is appointed almost as a matter of course: see *supra*, para. 23–156.

[27] See *Rowe v. Wood* (1795) 2 J. & W. 553; *Roberts v. Eberhardt* (1853) Kay 148.

[28] See *supra*, paras. 23–132 *et seq.*

[29] And see, generally, *Smith v. Jeyes* (1841) 4 Beav. 503.

[30] *Evans v. Coventry* (1854) 5 De G.M. & G. 911.

[31] *Sheppard v. Oxenford* (1855) 1 K. & J. 491. Note that there was no evidence of impropriety in this case, other than the clandestine manner in which the partner had left the country.

[32] *Estwick v. Conningsby* (1682) 1 Vern. 118.

[33] *Harding v. Glover* (1810) 18 Ves.Jr. 281.

[34] *Madgwick v. Wimble* (1843) 6 Beav. 495. Note also, in this context, the provisions of the Partnership Act 1890, s.42(1), *infra*, paras. 25–23 *et seq.*

Mismanagement: Where a partner is guilty of such mismanagement as to endanger the whole concern.[35]

Jeopardy to assets

23–163   Misconduct alone is never sufficient: it is also necessary to demonstrate that the safety of the partnership assets is in jeopardy. In some cases, the danger will be obvious from the very nature of the misconduct, whilst, in others, positive evidence will have to be adduced.

(3) *Fraud*

23–164 Although fraud was not, in earlier editions of this work, treated as a separate ground for the appointment of a receiver,[36] it does not partake of the same characteristics as the other grounds, as Lord Lindley made clear in the following passage:

> "... the reluctance of the Court in appointing a receiver against a partner, being based on the confidence originally reposed in him, ... disappears if it can be shown that such confidence was originally misplaced. Therefore, where a defendant, by false and fraudulent representations, induced the plaintiff to enter into partnership with him, and the plaintiff soon afterwards filed a bill, praying that the partnership might be declared void, and for a receiver, the Court on motion ordered that a receiver should be appointed."[37]

(4) *Exclusion*

23–165   Lord Lindley observed:

> "... even although there be no misconduct jeopardising the partnership assets, the Court will appoint a receiver if the defendant wrongfully excludes his co-partner from the management of the partnership affairs.[38] This doctrine is acted on where the

---

[35] See *De Tastet v. Bordieu* (1805), cited in a note in 2 Bro.C.C. 272. The expression used in the report is "mutual" mismanagement, but its import is not explained. But see also *Const v. Harris* (1824) T. & R. 496.

[36] Lord Lindley appears to have treated this ground as an offshoot of "misconduct plus jeopardy to assets," even though jeopardy seemingly need not be shown.

[37] See *Ex p. Broome* (1811) 1 Rose 69.

[38] See the judgment of Long Innes J. in *Tate v. Barry* (1928) 28 S.R. (N.S.W.) 380, 387, with which Megarry J. concurred in *Floydd v. Cheney* [1970] Ch. 602, 610. And see *Wilson v. Greenwood* (1818) 1 Swan. 481; *Goodman v. Whitcomb* (1820) 1 J. & W. 589.

defendant unsuccessfully contends that the plaintiff is not a partner,[39] or that he has no interest in the partnership assets."[40]

Interlocutory application where partnership disputed

Where the existence of the partnership is disputed and the **23–166** appointment of a receiver (or receiver and manager) is sought in interlocutory proceedings, the court will, in an appropriate case, have jurisdiction to make the order sought, but will be reluctant to do so if such an order would inflict irreparable injury on the defendant (who might, of course, succeed at trial) or adequate protection can be otherwise afforded to the plaintiff.[41] The court is likely to be especially sensitive to the potential implications of the publicity attendant on appointing a receiver in the case of a professional practice.[42]

Illegal partnerships

It has already been seen that illegality will, in general, constitute a **23–167** defence to an action concerning the affairs of an illegal partnership.[43] On that footing, Lord Lindley went so far as to say:

"If the illegality is established, the Court cannot, it is conceived, interfere."

Where, however, a receiver is sought in interlocutory proceedings before the illegal nature of the partnership has been proved, the court may be prepared to intervene, unless it is satisfied that, such is the obvious nature of the illegality, no relief will ultimately be awarded. Indeed, Lord Lindley pointed out that:

"... the character of the defence will go far to remove any scruples the Court might otherwise have in interfering."

Thus, in *Hale v. Hale*,[44] a receiver and manager was appointed in the case of a brewing business claimed by the defendant to be illegal, notwithstanding the fact that the plaintiff was only a dormant partner and that no complaint was made as regards the manner in which the defendant had managed the business.

---

[39] *Peacock v. Peacock* (1809) 16 Ves.Jr. 49; *Blakeney v. Dufaur* (1851) 15 Beav. 40.

[40] See *Wilson v. Greenwood* (1818) 1 Swan. 471, where the plaintiffs were the assignees (*i.e.* what would now be the trustee in bankruptcy) of a bankrupt partner; *Clegg v. Fishwick* (1849) 1 Mac. & G. 294, where the plaintiff was a deceased partner's administratrix.

[41] *Peacock v. Peacock* (1809) 16 Ves.Jr. 49; *Chapman v. Beach* (1820) 1 J. & W. 594; *Fairburn v. Pearson* (1850) 2 Mac. & G. 144; *Hardy v. Hardy* (1917) 62 S.J. 142.

[42] See *Floydd v. Cheney* [1970] Ch. 602; *Sobell v. Boston* [1975] 1 W.L.R. 1587. And see *supra*, para. 23–150.

[43] See *supra*, paras. 8–52 *et seq.*

[44] (1841) 4 Beav. 369. See also *Sheppard v. Oxenford* (1855) 1 K. & J. 491.

Partnerships comprising alien enemies

23–168   There are a number of cases, dating from the 1914–18 War, in which an application was made for the appointment of a receiver in respect of a firm comprising alien enemies,[45] but such questions are usually covered by specific wartime legislation.[46]

Mining partnerships

23–169   Prior to the Partnership Act 1890, mining partnerships constituted a distinct sub-species, governed by different rules to those applicable to ordinary trading partnerships, but it is questionable to what extent such treatment is now justified.[47] Nevertheless, it is clear that the appointment of a receiver (or receiver and manager) of a mining partnership will be governed by normal principles.[48] There are, admittedly, two cases in which a receiver was refused following the exclusion of a partner,[49] but in each the facts were exceptional.[50]

Defendant may apply for receiver

23–170   A defendant may seek the appointment of a receiver (or receiver and manager) by summons or motion in the plaintiff's action or by way of counterclaim.[51] Where, however, the defendant denies the existence of the partnership, a suitable counterclaim *must* be filed, since the application will not arise out of the plaintiff's cause of action.[52] Equally, if the plaintiff's action is not based on the existence

---

[45] A receiver was appointed in *Rombach v. Rombach* [1914] W.N. 423; *Armitage v. Borgmann* (1914) 84 L.J.Ch. 784; *Re Bechstein* (1914) 58 S.J. 863; *Kupfer v. Kupfer* [1915] W.N. 397. However, such an appointment was refused in *Maxwell v. Grunhut* (1914) 31 T.L.R. 79; *Re Gaudig and Blum* (1915) 31 T.L.R. 153. See, further, the 9th ed. of this work, at pp. 655–656.

[46] No equivalent cases were reported in respect of the 1939–45 War, doubtless because the position was governed by the Trading with the Enemy Acts. See generally, as to alien enemies and the effects of war, *supra*, paras. 4–04 *et seq.*

[47] See *supra*, paras. 5–14, 19–74, 23–84.

[48] See, as to the position whilst the partnership is continuing, *Roberts v. Eberhardt* (1853) Kay 148; *Rowlands v. Evans* (1861) 30 Beav. 302 and, as to the appointment of a receiver and manager with a view to a dissolution or winding up, *Clegg v. Fishwick* (1849) 1 Mac. & G. 294; *Sheppard v. Oxenford* (1855) 1 K. & J. 491 (where, however, a dissolution was not sought). And see, as to cases in which the partners cannot agree on the proper method of working the mine until a sale can be arranged, *Jefferys v. Smith* (1820) 1 J. & W. 298; *Lees v. Jones* (1857) 3 Jur.(N.S.) 954.

[49] *Rowe v. Wood* (1795) 2 J. & W. 553; *Norway v. Rowe* (1812) 19 Ves.Jr. 144.

[50] Lord Lindley explained "... *Rowe v. Wood* ... was a peculiar case, for the partner complained of was not only a partner, but also a mortgagee in possession, and his mortgage debt was still unsatisfied. Again, in *Norway v. Rowe*, although the plaintiff was excluded, a receiver was refused on the ground of his laches, he having been excluded for some time, and having taken no steps to assert his rights until the mine proved profitable."

[51] See R.S.C. Ord. 15, r. 2; Ord. 30, r. 1; C.C.R. Ord. 9, r.2(1)(d); Ord. 32, r. 1. And see *Sargant v. Read* (1876) 1 Ch.D. 600. *Cf.* the position prior to the Judicature Acts: *Robinson v. Hadley* (1849) 11 Beav. 614.

[52] *Hardy v. Hardy* (1917) 62 S.J. 142; also *Carter v. Fey* [1894] 2 Ch. 541; *Collison v. Warren* [1901] 1 Ch. 812. And see also, as to cases of disputed partnership, *supra*, paras. 23–103 *et seq.*

of a partnership, separate proceedings for the appointment of a receiver may well be required.[53]

Identity and remuneration of receiver

Where the application is made by motion in the High Court, the **23–171** usual practice is now to seek the appointment of a named receiver (or receiver and manager), although it was once common to adjourn the actual appointment back to the Master. This can still be done[54] and may, in practice, provide a useful stimulus to the partners to agree terms in the interim. In such cases, leave may be given to each partner to propose himself as receiver.[55]

Partner appointed as receiver

In an appropriate case one of the partners may be appointed **23–172** receiver (or receiver and manager), as Lord Lindley explained:

"If the Court, on being applied to for the appointment of a receiver, thinks that a proper case for such appointment is made, and the partner actually carrying on the business has not been guilty of such misconduct as to have rendered it unsafe to trust him, the Court generally appoints him receiver and manager without salary.[56] It is usual, however, to require him to give security duly to manage the partnership affairs, and to account for money received by him.[57] ... A partner who is appointed receiver becomes the officer of the court, and must act and be respected accordingly."

Although the above passage appears to be framed in terms of a single partner carrying on the partnership business, the court's discretion will also be exercisable where there are two or more partners competing for appointment; however, in such a case, care will obviously be taken to ensure that no partner thereby obtains an unfair advantage.[58]

Where the receiver is not a partner, he may be given liberty to employ a partner as manager, thus securing a degree of continuity in the partnership business.

---

[53] See *Floydd v. Cheney* [1970] Ch. 602.
[54] See *Heward's Chancery Practice* (2nd ed.), p.102; also *Heward's Chancery Orders*, p. 259.
[55] See *Sargant v. Read* (1876) 1 Ch.D. 600.
[56] See *Wilson v. Greenwood* (1818) 1 Swan. 471; *Blakeney v. Dufaur* (1851) 15 Beav. 40; *Collins v. Barker* [1893] 1 Ch. 578; *Harris v. Sleep* [1897] 2 Ch. 80. It is, however, no longer the general practice to deprive a partner of remuneration for acting as receiver: see *infra*, para. 23–173.
[57] See *Collins v. Barker*, *supra*; also the form of order in *Heward's Chancery Orders*, at p. 257.
[58] See *Sargant v. Read* (1876) 1 Ch.D. 600.

Remuneration, etc.

23–173   A receiver (or receiver and manager) is normally remunerated on the basis of a *quantum meruit*, even where he is a partner.[59] Where a partner is appointed without salary,[60] he may, nevertheless, be allowed remuneration for services performed beyond the scope of his duties, if they prove beneficial.[61]

A partner's remuneration and receivership costs will be payable out of any funds in his hands *qua* receiver,[61a] even if he owes money to the firm and is unable to discharge that indebtedness.[62]

Order appointing receiver

23–174   Lord Lindley wrote:

"The order appointing a receiver usually directs the partners to deliver up to him all the effects of the partnership, and all securities in their hands, for the outstanding personal estate, together with all books and papers relating thereto. The receiver is directed to get in the debts of the firm, and he is, if necessary, empowered to bring actions with the approbation of the judge; he is directed to pay the partnership debts, and to pass his accounts and to pay balances in his hands into court."[63]

This is still, in essence, the form of order used today.[64] However, an order for the delivery up of the partnership books, etc., will not be made if that would either be unnecessary or unduly inconvenient.[65]

Powers of receiver

23–175   The court cannot confer power on a receiver to do anything which a partner would not have authority to do, whether pursuant to the terms of the partnership agreement or, where relevant, under the general law.[66]

---

[59] *Davy v. Scarth* [1906] 1 Ch. 55.
[60] This was formerly a common practice: see *supra*, para. 23–172, n. 56.
[61] *Harris v. Sleep* [1897] 2 Ch. 80. See also *supra*, para. 20–43.
[61a] The receiver's right to remuneration cannot be made to rank before a prior charge on the partnership assets: *Chandhri v. Palta* [1992] BCC 787.
[62] *Davy v. Scarth* [1906] 1 Ch. 55.
[63] See the forms of order in *Wilson v. Greenwood* (1818) 1 Swan. 471, 484; *Whitley v. Lowe* (1858) 4 Jur.(N.S.) 815 (where the application was not opposed: see *ibid.* p. 197); *Taylor v. Neate* (1888) 39 Ch.D. 538; *Collins v. Barker* [1893] 1 Ch. 578; also Seton (7th ed.), p. 728.
[64] See *Heward's Chancery Orders*, pp. 257 *et seq.*
[65] See *Dacie v. John* (1824) McCle. 206.
[66] *Niemann v. Niemann* (1889) 43 Ch.D. 198, 201–202, *per* Cotton L.J. This passage is framed solely by reference to the partnership contract, but the current editor takes the view that the same considerations apply to any act authorised by the Partnership Act 1890, save to the extent that its provisions are excluded by the agreement. Note also *Murray v. King* [1986] F.S.R. 116, a decision of the Federal Court of Australia.

Conversely, the court will not restrict the activities of a receiver *after* he has ceased to hold that position. Thus, a person who has acted as receiver and manager of a partnership business up to the time of its sale will not be restrained from soliciting orders from or doing business with the customers of the firm on his own account after he has ceased so to act;[67] *per contra* if he is one of the partners.[68]

Liability of receiver

A receiver appointed by the court is neither the agent of the **23–176** parties to the action nor of the party on whose application he was appointed.[69] Thus, he is prima facie personally liable on all contracts entered into *qua* receiver,[70] unless such liability is excluded by express or implied agreement.[71] He is, however, entitled to be indemnified out of the partnership assets in his hands in priority to the claims of the creditors of the business,[72] but he does not enjoy a similar right to indemnity from the partners, even if he was appointed with their consent.[73] To the extent that the receiver is entitled to be indemnified out of the partnership assets, any creditors to whom he is personally liable will enjoy subrogated rights against those assets.[74]

Interference with receiver

A receiver is an officer of the court and, accordingly, any **23–177** interference with him, or with property under his control,[75] constitutes a contempt of court[76] and will, if necessary, be restrained by injunction.[77] It has already been seen that a judgment creditor

---

[67] *Re Irish* (1880) 40 Ch.D. 49.

[68] See *supra*, paras. 10–160 *et seq.*

[69] *Burt, Boulton and Hayward v. Bull* [1895] 1 Q.B. 276; *Re Flowers* [1897] 1 Q.B. 14; *Re Glasdir Copper Mines Ltd.* [1906] 1 Ch. 365; *Boehm v. Goodall* [1911] 1 Ch. 155; *Moss S.S. Co. v. Whinney* [1912] A.C. 254; *Evans v. Clayhope Properties Ltd.* [1988] 1 W.L.R. 358.

[70] *Burt, Boulton and Hayward v. Bull*, *supra*.

[71] *Re Boynton Ltd.* [1910] 1 Ch. 519. See also *Burt, Boulton and Hayward v. Bull*, *supra*; *Moss S.S. Co. v. Whinney* [1912] A.C. 254.

[72] *Batten v. Wedgwood Coal Co.* (1884) 28 Ch.D. 317; *Strapp v. Bull, Sons & Co.* [1895] 2 Ch. 1; *Re Glasdir Copper Mines* [1906] 1 Ch. 365; *Re British Power Traction and Lighting Co. Ltd.* [1906] 1 Ch. 497 and [1907] 1 Ch. 528; *Re Boynton Ltd.* [1910] 1 Ch. 519. *Cf.* the position of a *secured* creditor: *Choudhri v. Palta* [1992] BCC 787. As to the costs of actions brought against the receiver, see *Walters v. Woodbridge* (1878) 7 Ch.D. 504; *Re Dunn, Brinklow v. Singleton* [1904] 1 Ch. 648.

[73] *Boehm v. Goodall* [1911] 1 Ch. 155; *Evans v. Clayhope Properties Ltd.* [1988] 1 W.L.R. 358; also *Choudhri v. Palta*, *supra*. *Quaere* whether an order for costs can be made covering the receiver's remuneration and expenses after final judgment in the action: *ibid.*

[74] *Re British Power Traction and Lighting Co. Ltd.* [1910] 2 Ch. 470. *Cf. Re Boynton Ltd.* [1910] 1 Ch. 519.

[75] As to the position where the property is out of the jurisdiction, see *Re Maudslay Sons and Field* [1900] 1 Ch. 602.

[76] See *Lane v. Sterne* (1862) 3 Giff. 629; *Helmore v. Smith (No. 2)* (1887) 35 Ch.D. 449; *Re Bechstein (No. 2)* (1914) 58 S.J. 864; *Dixon v. Dixon* [1904] 1 Ch. 161. *Cf.* the position before the receiver's appointment has been perfected: see *Defries v. Creed* (1865) 6 N.R. 17.

[77] *Dixon v. Dixon*, *supra*.

who wishes to levy execution against property in the receiver's hands should apply to the court in the action in which he was appointed, thus enabling that court to make a suitable order, whether for payment of the judgment debt or otherwise.[78]

Arbitrations

23–178 The court has the same powers of appointing a receiver where a dispute has been referred to arbitration as it has in relation to proceedings in court.[79]

D. ORDERS FOR THE SALE OF PARTNERSHIP PROPERTY

The normal rule

23–179 It has already been seen that, in the event of a general dissolution,[80] each partner[81] is normally entitled to insist that all the partnership property is sold,[82] even if the firm's debts and liabilities could be discharged without such a sale.[83] Indeed, Lord Lindley observed:

> "This mode of ascertaining the value of the partnership effects is adopted by the Courts, unless some other course can be followed consistently with the agreement between the partners. And even where the partners have provided that their shares shall be ascertained in some other way, still, if owing to any circumstances their agreement in this respect cannot be carried out, or if their agreement does not extend to the event which has in fact arisen, realisation of the property by a sale is the only alternative which a Court can adopt."[84]

---

[78] See *supra*, para. 14–93.

[79] Arbitration Act 1950, s.12(6)(h). And note, in this context, *Young v. Buckett* (1882) 51 L.J. Ch. 504.

[80] As to the meaning of this expression, see *infra*, para. 24–03.

[81] But not a person who is merely remunerated by a share of profits: see *Walker v. Hirsch* (1884) 27 Ch.D. 460; *Stekel v. Ellice* [1973] 1 W.L.R. 191. Lord Lindley observed "*Pawsey v. Armstrong* (1881) 18 Ch.D. 698, went too far. See [*Walker v. Hirsch*]."

[82] See *supra*, paras. 19–04 *et seq.* And see *Rowlands v. Evans* (1861) 30 Beav. 302; *Burdon v. Barkus* (1862) 4 De G.F. & J. 42; *Hugh Stevenson & Sons v. Aktiengesellschaft für Cartonnagen Industrie* [1917] 1 K.B. 842, affirmed [1918] A.C. 239; also *Crawshay v. Collins* (1808) 15 Ves.Jr. 218, 227, *per* Lord Eldon; *Featherstonhaugh v. Fenwick* (1810) 17 Ves.Jr. 298; *Crawshay v. Maule* (1818) 1 Swan. 495; *Hale v. Hale* (1841) 4 Beav. 369, 375, *per* Lord Langdale. *Cf.* the position where a partnership business is transferred to a company: *Re A Company (No. 002567 of 1982)* [1983] 1 W.L.R. 927. As to unsaleable assets, etc., see *infra*, paras. 23–188 *et seq.*

[83] See *Wild v. Milne* (1859) 26 Beav. 504.

[84] But see *Syers v. Syers* (1876) 1 App.Cas. 174, *infra*, para. 23–182; also *Taylor v. Neate* (1888) 39 Ch.D. 538, where the parties appear to have agreed to a sale: see *ibid.* p. 542.

Thus, in *Cook v. Collingridge*,[85] where the partners had agreed that, on the expiration of their partnership, the stock-in-trade would be divided between them, it was held that, since a physical division of the stock was impossible, it would have to be sold and the proceeds divided. A sale will, similarly, be directed where continuing partners have an option to acquire an outgoing partner's share[86] but fail to exercise it,[87] or where any other provision for such acquisition cannot, for whatever reason, be implemented.[88]

Agreements excluding the normal rule

It goes without saying that a sale will not normally be ordered **23–180** where that would be inconsistent with the terms or spirit of the agreement between the partners.[89] Thus, where a partner agrees to retire from the partnership and thereby recognises the continuing partners' right to continue the business, he will normally be taken to have forgone his right to insist on a sale.[90]

The court's discretion

The effective presumption in favour of a sale is not, however, **23–181** absolute, as Lord Lindley explained:

"The rule as to selling partnership property is merely adopted in order that justice may be done to all parties, when no other course has been or can be agreed upon. It is not an arbitrary rule, inflexibly applied in all cases whether it is necessary or not; and although, if one partner or his representatives insist on a sale, the Court may not be able to refuse to enforce that right,[91] still the Court is always inclined to accede to any other mode of settlement which may be fair and just between the partners."

Thus, in one case,[92] the court declined to order a sale where the business had been carried on by one of the partners for some years after the date of dissolution.

---

[85] (1822) Jac. 607. See also *Rigden v. Pierce* (1822) 6 Madd. 353.

[86] See generally, as to such options, *supra*, paras. 10–122 *et seq.*

[87] See *Kershaw v. Matthews* (1826) 2 Russ. 62; *Madgwick v. Wimble* (1843) 6 Beav. 495; *Downs v. Collins* (1848) 6 Hare 418. The agreement may itself specify what is to happen in the event of the option not being exercised: see *supra*, para. 10–221.

[88] See, for example, *Wilson v. Greenwood* (1818) 1 Swan. 471.

[89] See the cases noticed *supra*, paras. 10–133 *et seq.*

[90] *Sobell v. Boston* [1975] 1 W.L.R. 1587, 1591, *per* Goff J.; also *Bothe v. Amos* [1976] Fam. 46. *Small v. Cohen, The Times*, September 7, 1992 appears to be a case of this class. And see *supra*, para. 19–12.

[91] *Wild v. Milne* (1859) 26 Beav. 504; *Rowlands v. Evans* (1861) 30 Beav. 302.

[92] *Latchan v. Martin* (1984) 134 N.L.J. 745. The report is, however, very brief and gives little indication of the true basis for the decision.

Syers v. Syers orders

23–182   In the exercise of its discretion, the court may order one partner to sell his share to his co-partners. Such an order was made in the important case of *Syers v. Syers*,[93] where partners together entitled to a seven-eighths interest in a firm carrying on the business of running a music hall and tavern were authorised to buy in the remaining one-eighth interest held by their co-partner. As was made clear by the House of Lords, the court will, in such cases, have regard both to the nature of the business and to the size of the interest sought to be acquired.[94] Where the partner concerned is entitled to a substantial stake in the firm or, perhaps, where the business is of a readily saleable nature, a *Syers v. Syers* order is, in practice, unlikely to be obtained.

An order of the type under discussion may also be made in other exceptional cases, *e.g.* where one partner is a minor[95] and a sale of his share to his co-partners would demonstrably be for his benefit. However, the other partners cannot be forced to purchase such a partner's share, as Lord Lindley pointed out:

"... although it may[96] be for the benefit of an infant[97] ... partner that his share should be sold, yet if the other partners insist on the sale of the whole property they are entitled to such a sale."[98]

Land

23–183   Under the Law of Property Act 1925 the court may authorise the partition of land held on trust for sale, notwithstanding the opposition of any person beneficially interested therein.[99] Whilst the discretion conferred by the Act is obviously of a wide nature, it is submitted that, save in exceptional circumstances, it would not justify the court

---

[93] (1876) 1 App.Cas. 174. Of this case, Lord Lindley commented "The agreement between the partners was probably not intended to create a partnership but a loan; and *quaere* whether the discretion alluded to exists in all cases. But why should it not? Its exercise would often be most beneficial." See also *Taylor v. Neate* (1888) 39 Ch.D. 538.

[94] See (1876) 1 App.Cas. 174, 183 (*per* Lord Cairns), 191 (*per* Lord Hatherley). See also *supra*, para. 19–12.

[95] See *Crawshay v. Maule* (1818) 1 Swan. 495, 530. Here the minors were, in fact, beneficially interested in the share of a deceased partner. In the case of a mentally disordered partner, the decision to accept the other partners' offer to purchase his share ought properly to be referred to the Court of Protection. See, as to the position under the old lunacy laws, *Leaf v. Coles* (1851) 1 De G.M. & G. 171; *Prentice v. Prentice* (1853) 10 Hare (App.) 22.

[96] Unaccountably, Appendix II to Lord Lindley's Supplement on the Partnership Act 1890 introduced the word "not" at this point. Surely, the distinction between a sale of the infant partner's share and the sale of all the partnership assets is the correct one? If the other partners insist on the latter, there will, as such, be no sale of the infant's share.

[97] The words "or lunatic" formerly appeared at this point.

[98] See *Rowlands v. Evans* (1861) 30 Beav. 302; also *Burdon v. Barkus* (1862) 4 De G.F. & J. 42.

[99] Law of Property Act 1925, ss.28(3) (as amended), 30.

overriding the normal right of a partner or his representatives to insist on a sale of any land which is proved to be an asset of the partnership.[1]

It goes almost without saying that a trust for sale of land owned by or acquired for the use of a firm will not normally be enforced whilst the partnership is continuing.[2]

Chattels

The Law of Property Act 1925 also authorises the court to direct **23–184** the division of any chattels held in undivided shares.[3] However, it is again submitted that a court will rarely be justified in exercising its discretion to make such an order.

Manner of sale

The court has a discretion as to the manner in which any sale of **23–185** the partnership assets will be conducted. As Lord Lindley observed:

"The sale to which each partner has a right is a sale to the highest bidder.[4] But with a view to doing as little injustice as possible, when the Court orders a sale, it will, if necessary, direct an inquiry as to the proper mode of selling[5]; and whether it will be for the benefit of all parties that there should be an immediate sale, or that the concern should be carried on for the purpose only of winding up its affairs: and if the latter is the case, the Court will give any of the parties liberty to propose himself as manager until a sale."[6]

Thus, in *Rowlands v. Evans*,[7] partnership property was ordered to be sold as a going concern by a disinterested third party, each partner

---

[1] See *supra*, para. 23–179. See further, as to proving that land is an asset of a firm, *supra*, paras. 7–02 *et seq.* and 18–01 *et seq.*

[2] See *Re John's Assignment Trusts* [1970] 1 W.L.R. 955 where, following the parties' divorce, Goff J. ordered the sale of the matrimonial home, at which they had carried on a business in partnership. *Cf. Bothe v. Amos* [1976] Fam. 46. See also *supra*, para. 18–61.

[3] Law of Property Act 1925, s.188. And see, as to the nature of a partner's interest in partnership chattels, *Re Fuller's Contract* [1933] Ch. 652, 656, *per* Luxmoore J.

[4] See *Burdon v. Barkus* (1862) 4 De G.F. & J. 42 and the other cases cited *supra*, para. 23–179, n. 82.

[5] See *Wilson v. Greenwood* (1818) 1 Swan. 471, 484; *Cook v. Collingridge* (1822) Jac. 607. And see *Syers v. Syers* (1876) 1 App.Cas. 174, where an inquiry was directed as to the value of the plaintiff's share.

[6] *Waters v. Taylor* (1813) 2 V. & B. 299; *Crawshay v. Maule* (1818) 1 Swan. 495, 529, *per* Lord Eldon; *Wild v. Milne* (1859) 26 Beav. 504. As to the position where a sale is delayed and the partnership assets increase in value in the meantime, see *Barclays Bank Trust Co. Ltd. v. Bluff* [1982] Ch. 172, noticed *infra*, para. 25–27.

[7] (1861) 30 Beav. 302.

being given liberty to bid, and an interim receiver and manager was appointed.[8]

Conduct of sale and leave to bid

23–186   Conduct of the sale is normally given to the plaintiff. However, since the court is, in Lord Lindley's words, "extremely reluctant" to give liberty to bid to the party who has the conduct of a sale, if the plaintiff wishes to bid it will usually be necessary to entrust such conduct to a third party.[9] Other interested parties, other than a receiver,[10] are unlikely to have any difficulty in obtaining liberty to bid.[11]

Where the court has given the conduct of a sale to any person, it will not allow him to be interfered with.[12]

Goodwill

23–187   Lord Lindley wrote:

"In selling the goodwill of a going concern, the book debts and business ought to be sold in one lot, and the purchaser ought to be informed, if the facts be so, that the sellers are entitled to carry on business in competition with him."[13]

Unsaleable but valuable assets

23–188   Complications inevitably arise where the firm owns assets which, although valuable to the partners, have no *realisable* value. In Lord Lindley's day, the only assets giving rise to difficulty were offices and appointments held by partners on behalf of the firm,[14] in relation to which he observed:

"If one of the partners holds an appointment which is not saleable, but the profits of which are by agreement to be accounted for by him to the partnership, the partner holding the appointment will be debited with its value; for that is the only mode in which, upon

---

[8] See also *Pawsey v. Armstrong* (1881) 18 Ch.D. 698; *Taylor v. Neate* (1888) 39 Ch.D. 538.
[9] As in *Rowlands v. Evans, supra.*
[10] A receiver requires special sanction from the court before he may purchase any asset of which he is receiver: *Nugent v. Nugent* [1908] 1 Ch. 546.
[11] See Seton (7th ed.), p. 330. Note that the partnership agreement may itself provide for such liberty: see *supra*, para. 10–221.
[12] *Dean v. Wilson* (1878) 10 Ch.D. 136.
[13] See *Johnson v. Helleley* (1864) 34 Beav. 63 and 2 De G.J. & S. 446; *Jennings v. Jennings* [1898] 1 Ch. 378; *Re David and Matthews* [1899] 1 Ch. 378, 385, *per* Romer J. See further, as to the respective rights of a vendor and purchaser of goodwill, *supra*, paras. 10–160 *et seq.*
[14] See generally, *supra*, paras. 18–19, 18–20.

a dissolution, such a source of gain can be dealt with.[15] The same principle applies to other unsaleable but valuable assets, to which one partner has no exclusive right."[16]

There are two specific areas in which the application of this apparently straightforward principle gives rise to acute problems.[17]

National Health Service goodwill

The goodwill of a medical practice carried on within the National **23–189** Health Service unquestionably has a value, but any direct or indirect attempt to realise that value will involve an offence under the National Health Service Act 1977.[18] It follows that it would not be permissible to debit a partner with the value of the goodwill in the way that Lord Lindley suggested. Yet, because the goodwill effectively lies in each partner's list of patients, if the court were to do nothing and merely to leave each partner with his individual list, great injustice might be caused if, as will often be the case, each partner's list size does not correspond with his interest in the partnership assets, including goodwill. In those circumstances, the current editor submits that the court *must* intervene and, so far as possible, reallocate the patients so as to achieve a fair division of the goodwill.[19] This process will obviously be assisted if the co-operation of the relevant Family Health Services Authority can be secured.

Although such an approach might seem controversial, in that it runs contrary to the supposed right of patients to consult the doctor of their choice,[20] a close analysis of the National Health Service legislation demonstrates that there is, in reality, no such general

---

[15] See *Smith v. Mules* (1852) 9 Hare 556; *Ambler v. Bolton* (1871) L.R. 14 Eq. 427. See also *supra*, para. 10–43.

[16] *Ibid.* And see *Lees. v. Jones* (1857) 3 Jur.(N.S.) 954.

[17] Another asset which might be thought to give rise to difficulty is milk quota, but it has recently been held that such quota cannot exist independently of the land to which it relates: see *Faulks v. Faulks* [1992] 15 E.G. 82, noticed *supra*, para. 18–21. It follows that if, as in that case, the land in question ceases to be a partnership asset, the firm cannot lay claim either to the quota or, in the absence of an express agreement or some other exceptional circumstances (as to which, see *ibid.* at p. 95, *per* Chadwick J.), to any part of its assumed value; *a fortiori* if the land was never a partnership asset. Note also that, in New Zealand, it has been held that work in progress does not exist as an asset on the retirement of a partner from a firm of solicitors (see *Robertson v. Brent* [1972] N.Z.L.R. 406), but the current editor does not consider the decision to be correct in principle.

[18] *Ibid.* s.54, Sched. 10. And see, generally, as to the application of these provisions to partnership agreements, *Kerr v. Morris* [1987] Ch. 90; also the *Encyclopedia of Professional Partnerships*, Pt. 5.

[19] The National Health Service (General Medical Services) Regulations 1992 (S.I. 1992 No. 635) contain a mechanism whereby patients can be removed from a particular doctor's list: *ibid.* Sched. 2, paras. 9, 9A (as added by the National Health Service (General Medical Services) Amendment Regulations 1994 (S.I. 1994 No. 633), reg. 8(4)). Such removal would give rise to a likelihood, *but no guarantee*, that the patients would apply for acceptance on the lists of other members/former members of the same practice: see *ibid.* reg. 20, Sched. 2, para. 6.

[20] Proponents of this view principally rely on the National Health Service Act 1977, s.29(2)(b).

right.[21] If the position were otherwise, all restrictions on competition would be unenforceable on public policy grounds, which is obviously not the case.[22] Nevertheless, it should be recognised that, if the suggested approach is to work effectively, the court must also impose some restriction on a former partner's ability to accept patients back onto his list immediately following their removal therefrom[23] and, moreover, there is an inevitable risk that disgruntled patients will move to another practice and thus be lost to *all* the former partners. At its heart, the issue comes down to a choice between the lesser of two potential evils: perpetuating an inequitable allocation of patients as between the partners or forcing patients to be treated by another doctor.[24] The current editor submits that the court should not lightly abdicate its responsibility to hold an even balance between the partners in a case of this type.

Needless to say, it might be preferable if this problem were catered for in the partnership agreement.

Unassignable tenancies

23-190   Unassignable tenancies[25] may have a significant, albeit hypothetical, value to the partners whilst the partnership is continuing, but little, if any, real market value.[26] To attempt to bring that hypothetical value into account would be unrealistic and would, moreover, distort the dissolution accounts. It is accordingly suggested that, unless an agreed value can be placed on the tenancy, a surrender should be negotiated with the landlord and any sums received on the surrender brought into account.[27] The position will, of course, be different if the tenancy is assignable or if the landlord is prepared to consent to an *ad hoc* assignment.

Where the landlord is one of the partners, he will usually have been concerned to ensure that the partnership agreement contains a

---

[21] See the National Health Service (General Medical Services) Regulations 1992, regs. 6(2), 21(1), Sched. 2, paras. 9–11. See also *Kerr v. Morris* [1987] Ch. 90, 106C-F (*per* Dillon L.J.), 113C-E (*per* Lloyd L.J.), 116C-D (*per* Nicholls L.J.).

[22] See *Kerr v. Morris, supra.*

[23] *i.e.* an analogous approach to that adopted by the arbitrator in *Morley v. Newman* (1824) 5 D. & R. 317: see *supra*, paras. 10–174, 10–235.

[24] Of course, the reality is that patients will not always be treated by the partner on whose list their names appear; indeed, some may go out of their way to be treated by another partner.

[25] *e.g.* tenancies protected by the Agricultural Holdings Act 1986. Although such tenancies are not inherently unassignable, they will usually contain a specific covenant against assignment, either at the insistence of the landlord or on the terms of the tenancy being referred to arbitration pursuant to *ibid.* s.6. In the latter case, the covenant will not be absolute but will prohibit assignment, etc., without the written consent of the landlord: *ibid.* Sched. 1, para. 9. The landlord does, however, have an unfettered right to withhold his consent, since the Landlord and Tenant Act 1927, s.19, is inapplicable to agricultural tenancies: see *ibid.* s.19(4) (as amended).

[26] The Revenue have been known to argue that, for tax purposes, an unassignable, rack-rent tenancy has a substantial value: see, for example, *Baird's Executors v. I.R.C.* 1991 S.L.T. 9 (Lands Tr.). It is submitted that this approach is incorrect and should be resisted. See further *infra*, para. 36–71.

[27] See *Re Martin Coulter Enterprises Ltd.* [1988] BCLC 12 (concerning a company winding up).

specific provision dealing with the tenancy in the event of a dissolution.[28]

Pending contracts

It has already been seen that it is, in general, the duty of the **23–191** partners to complete all unfinished contracts as at the dissolution date.[29] Consistently therewith, Lord Lindley wrote:

"... if the object of the partnership is to carry out a certain contract which is unfinished when the partnership is dissolved, the Court will not necessarily order the benefit of it to be sold; nor order the share of a partner in it at the time of dissolution to be ascertained by valuation; but will leave the partners to complete the contract, and will postpone the ultimate account until its completion."[30]

Interim order for sale

An interlocutory order for the sale of any asset or, if appropriate, **23–192** of the entire business can be obtained, although a strong case would need to be made out. As Lord Lindley explained:

"Although it is not usual for the Court to direct a sale before the trial of the action, still, if circumstances require it, an order for a sale will be made on motion,[31] even although the partnership has not been previously dissolved."[32]

---

[28] It would, however, appear to be impossible to provide that an agricultural tenancy *must* be surrendered in the event of a dissolution: see the decision of the House of Lords in *Johnson v. Moreton* [1980] A.C. 37; *cf. Elsden v. Pick* [1980] 1 W.L.R. 898. However, the same result may, in practice, be achieved by providing either that the tenancy shall belong solely to the landlord partner on a dissolution (*i.e.* the converse of the situation in *Sykes v. Land* (1984) 271 E.G. 1264; see also *Faulks v. Faulks* [1992] 15 E.G. 82) or, perhaps, that no partner shall be entitled to claim or to acquire the tenancy beneficially. With the latter provision, there would, at least theoretically, be no real alternative to a surrender, but *quaere* would the court strike such a provision down on the *Johnson v. Moreton* principle? Irrespective of any such provision, it would seem that the non-landlord partners could prima facie serve a valid counter notice under the Agricultural Holdings Act 1986: see *Featherstone v. Staples* [1986] 1 W.L.R. 861; *cf. Dickson v. MacGregor*, 1992 S.L.T. (Land Ct.) 83. Moreover, if decisions relating to the dissolution are permitted to be taken on a majority basis, the non-landlord partners might conceivably agree that one of their number should have the benefit of the tenancy in exchange for a cash consideration and that the partners should all continue to hold the tenancy as trustees for him, in return for a suitable indemnity. However, to authorise such an unusual arrangement (which, surprisingly, would not constitute a breach of a covenant against assignment contained in the lease: see *Pincott v. Moorstons Ltd.* (1936) 156 L.T. 139; *Gentle v. Faulkner* [1900] 2 Q.B. 267), an exceptionally wide discretion would have to be made available under the agreement. Milk quota will follow the land (freehold or leasehold) to which it relates: see *supra*, para. 23–188, n. 17.

[29] Partnership Act 1890, s.38, *supra*, paras. 13–64 *et seq.*

[30] See *McClean v. Kennard* (1874) L.R. 9 Ch.App. 336. See also *infra*, para. 26–03.

[31] See generally, to the propriety of proceeding by motion for an order which, in substance, amounts to all the relief sought, *Heywood v. B.D.C. Properties Ltd.* [1963] 1 W.L.R. 975.

[32] See *per* Lord Eldon in *Wilson v. Greenwood* (1818) 1 Swan. 471, 483; *Crawshay v. Maule* (1818) 1 Swan. 495, 506, 523 *et seq.* And see also *Bailey v. Ford* (1843) 13 Sim. 495; *Hargreaves v. Hall* (1871) L.R. 11 Eq. 415 (the order made on July 22, 1869).

E. Declarations and Ancillary Relief

23–193 The court will, in an appropriate case, grant declaratory relief as to the rights and duties of a partner under a partnership or dissolution agreement, or, in the view of the current editor, under the general law.[33] Thus, in *Smith v. Gale*,[34] it was declared that an auditor's certificate, on which the entitlement of a retiring partner was to be based, was founded on an erroneous interpretation of the dissolution agreement and was, therefore, not binding on that partner. However, what the court will not do is to grant a declaration "in the air," *i.e.* where there is only a theoretical dispute between the partners, of the "what if . . ." variety.[35]

The court will also be prepared, where necessary, to give directions (whether by way of final or interlocutory relief) in an action between partners, *e.g.* as to the manner in which clients should be circularised following the purported expulsion of a partner.[36]

8. ACTIONS FOR DAMAGES

Agreements for partnership

23–194 There is no doubt that an action for damages may be maintained for breach of an agreement for partnership, whether involving a person's admission to an existing firm or the establishment of a wholly new business venture. Lord Lindley explained:

"If a person agrees to become a partner, and he breaks his agreement, an action for damages will lie against him; and any premium he may have agreed to pay may be recovered[37]; and it is no defence that the defendant has discovered that the plaintiff is a person with whom a partnership is undesirable.[38] So, if a member of a firm agrees to introduce a stranger, an action lies at the suit of the stranger against the partner for a breach of this agreement, although it may have been made without the knowledge of the

---

[33] See R.S.C. Ord. 15, r.16. *Per contra* in the county court, unless the declaration sought is ancillary to a claim within the court's jurisdiction (*De Vries v. Smallridge* [1928] 1 K.B. 482) or jurisdiction is expressly conferred by statute. As regards declarations relating to land, see the County Courts Act 1984, s.21 (as amended) and C.C.R. Ord. 6, rr.3, 4. *Ibid.* s.22 was repealed by the Courts and Legal Services Act 1990, Sched. 20.

[34] [1974] 1 W.L.R. 9. The main part of this decision must be read subject to the later authorities: see *supra*, para. 10–141, n. 90.

[35] *Mellstrom v. Garner* [1970] 1 W.L.R. 603.

[36] See *Fulwell v. Bragg* (1983) 127 S.J. 171 (interlocutory proceedings relating to a firm of solicitors).

[37] *Walker v. Harris* (1793) 1 Anst. 245; *Gale v. Leckie* (1817) 2 Stark. 107. In *Figes v. Cutler* (1822) 3 Stark. 139, it was held that an action for breach of an agreement for partnership could not be sustained without proof of the terms of such partnership; and note *Morrow v. Saunders* (1819) 1 Brod. & B. 318. *Cf. M'Neill v. Reid* (1832) 9 Bing. 68. See also, as to premiums, *infra*, paras. 25–06 *et seq.*

[38] *Andrewes v. Garstin* (1861) 10 C.B.(N.S.) 444.

other members of the firm, and they may decline to recognise it."[39]

Similarly, if a partner agrees with his co-partners that his executors will become partners in the event of his death but the executors refuse to do so, the surviving partners will have a right of action in damages for the breach of that agreement.[40]

The right to damages as between partners

The extent to which one partner can recover damages for breach of **23–195** the partnership agreement from his co-partners is, in many ways, one of the most difficult and unresolved areas of partnership law. Lord Lindley's analysis of the position was of such an unspecific nature that little real guidance is to be found therein, but it is appropriate to set the passage out in full, as a prelude to the current editor's own conclusion:

"The three following rules may be taken as guides:
1. An action for damages may be maintained by one partner against another in all those cases in which such an action might have been maintained before the Judicature Acts; provided the action would not have been restrained by a court of equity.
2. Any action which would have been so restrained cannot be supported.
3. An action may be maintained by one partner against another for any money demand which before the Judicature Acts could have been made the subject of a suit for an account.[41]
Practically, the important questions which will arise under the new procedure[42] are reduced to the following:
1. When can an action be maintained between partners without taking a general account of all the partnership dealings and transactions?
2. When will such an account be ordered without a dissolution of the firm?
The second of these questions has been already considered.[43] The first, which has already been alluded to,[44] can only be answered generally by saying that each case must depend upon its own circumstances, and upon whether justice can really be done

---

[39] *M'Neill v. Reid* (1832) 9 Bing. 68.
[40] See *Downs v. Collins* (1848) 6 Hare 418 and, in particular, the decree at *ibid.* p. 441. See also *supra*, para. 10–217.
[41] A transfer to the Chancery Division will sometimes be necessary: see *supra*, para. 23–67.
[42] *i.e.* the post Judicature Acts procedure.
[43] See *supra*, paras. 23–79 *et seq.*
[44] See *supra*, para. 23–72.

without taking such an account.[45] But there appears to be no reason why an action should not be brought to have some disputed item in an account settled, and why a declaratory judgment should not be pronounced settling that dispute without going further, unless it should become necessary to do so."[46]

Pre-Judicature Act law

23-196   It seems clear that, prior to the Judicature Acts, a breach of the express terms of a partnership agreement would have sounded in damages: in a summary of the earlier law which was eliminated in more recent editions of this work, Lord Lindley wrote:

"An action for damages for the breach of an express agreement entered into by one partner with another would lie, if the damages when recovered would have belonged to the plaintiff alone. Thus where a partner retired, and he covenanted with his co-partners not to carry on business within certain limits, or they covenanted to indemnify him against the debts of the firm, actions for damages occasioned by breaches of these covenants would clearly lie.[47] So, if a partnership was entered into for a definite time, and one partner was turned out by his co-partners before that time had expired, he could sue them for this breach by them of their agreement, and recover damages for the injury he had sustained[48]; so an action might be maintained for not rendering accounts and dividing profits[49]; for a penalty stipulated to be paid in case of a breach of agreement[50]; for rent covenanted to be paid[51]; for not

---

[45] In this context Lord Lindley cross-referred to the old cases where an action at law was brought "in respect of a matter which, though relating to the partnership business, was separate and distinct from all other matters in question between the partners." The cases may be classified as follows: (a) action on agreement to take partnership property at a valuation: *Jackson v. Stopherd* (1834) 2 Cromp. & M. 361; (b) action after final balance struck between partners: *Wells v. Wells* (1669) 1 Vent. 40; *Moravia v. Levy* (1786) 2 T.R. 483, note; *Foster v. Allanson* (1788) 2 T.R. 479; *Preston v. Strutton* (1792) 1 Anst. 50; *Rackstraw v. Imber* (1816) Holt 368; *Henley v. Soper* (1828) 8 B. & C. 16; *Brierly v. Cripps* (1836) 7 C. & P. 709; *Wray v. Milestone* (1839) 5 M. & W. 21; *Morley v. Baker* (1862) 3 Fost. & Fin. 146; *cf. Fromont v. Coupland* (1824) 2 Bing. 170; (c) action on bill or note given by partner personally: *Preston v. Strutton, supra; Neale v. Turton* (1827) 4 Bing. 151; *Heywood v. Watson* (1828) 4 Bing. 496; *Fox v. Frith* (1842) 10 M. & W. 131; *Graves v. Cook* (1856) 2 Jur.(N.S.) 475; *Beecham v. Smith* (1858) E.B. & E. 442; (d) action for rent against partners holding as trustees for firm: *Bedford v. Brutton* (1834) 1 Bing.(N.S.) 399; (e) action in respect of money which ought to be divided without reference to other matters: *Graham v. Robertson* (1788) 2 T.R. 282; (f) action in respect of money placed in one partner's hands by another for a particular purpose: *Wright v. Hunter* (1800) 1 East 20; (g) action for money overpaid by purchaser of share: *Townsend v. Crowdy* (1860) 8 C.B.(N.S.) 477; (h) action on express and independent indemnity: *Coffee v. Brian* (1825) 3 Bing. 54; (i) action for contribution in respect of a particular loss: *Sedgwick v. Daniel* (1857) 2 H. & N. 319; *cf. Sadler v. Nixon* (1834) 5 B. & Ad. 936.
[46] See *supra*, para. 23-193.
[47] *White v. Ansdell* (1836) T. & G. 785; *Leighton v. Wales* (1838) 3 M. & W. 545. See also *Haddon v. Ayers* (1858) 1 E. & E. 118; *Barker v. Allan* (1859) 5 H. & N. 61.
[48] See *Greenham v. Gray* (1855) 4 I.C.L.R. 501.
[49] *Owston v. Ogle* (1811) 13 East 538; also *Stavers v. Curling* (1836) 3 Bing.(N.C.) 355.
[50] *Radenhurst v. Bates* (1826) 3 Bing. 463.
[51] *Bedford v. Brutton* (1834) 1 Bing.(N.C.) 399.

indemnifying the plaintiff against a debt[52]; for not putting the plaintiff in funds to enable him to defray expenses as agreed."[53]

To the above list might also be added the right of a partner to compensation in the nature of damages in respect of a loss resulting from the misconduct or culpable negligence of his co-partner.[54]

The modern law

There is clear authority for the largely self evident proposition that **23–197** a partnership agreement is a contract like any other, so that the normal remedies for breach are available.[55] The current editor submits that there can be no realistic doubt that one partner is entitled to recover damages against another for breach of such an agreement.[56] In fact, the only question is, as Lord Lindley pointed out, whether, in order to establish a right to such damages, a partnership account *must* first be taken: on the basis of the pre-Judicature Act cases,[57] it is submitted that it need not.[58] Equally, a breach serious enough to warrant one partner seeking damages against his co-partners will almost inevitably lead to a dissolution, thus enabling that claim to be pursued in taking the final accounts between the partners.

9. EXECUTION BETWEEN PARTNERS

Where a partner sues or is sued by his own firm in the firm name, **23–198** any judgment or order made in the proceedings may only be enforced with the leave of the court.[59] Similarly in the case of proceedings between two firms with a partner in common.[60] In each case, when giving leave, the court may direct the taking of accounts and inquiries.[61]

In any other case, execution will take its normal course.

---

[52] *Want v. Reece* (1822) 1 Bing. 18.
[53] *Brown v. Tapscott* (1840) 6 M. & W. 119.
[54] See *supra*, para. 20–10.
[55] *Hitchman v. Crouch Butler Savage Associates* (1983) 80 L.S. Gaz. 554. And see *supra*, para. 10–106.
[56] See *Trimble v. Goldberg* [1906] A.C. 494, 500; also *supra*, para. 16–05. Note that damages are clearly recoverable in New Zealand: see *Gallagher v. Schulz* (1988) 2 N.Z.B.L.C. 103, 196.
[57] See *supra*, para. 23–196, nn. 47 *et seq.*
[58] *Per contra* in the case of a loss suffered by *the firm* as opposed to one or more individual partners. And note also the decision in *Brown v. Rivlin*, unreported, February 1, 1983 (C.A.T. No. 56); [1984] C.L.Y., p. 138, noticed *supra*, para. 23–72.
[59] R.S.C. Ord. 81, r. 6(1)(a), *infra*, para. A2–14. The application should be made by summons before the Master. The equivalent rule in the county court is C.C.R. Ord. 25, r. 10(1)(a).
[60] R.S.C. Ord. 81, r. 6(1)(b), *infra*, para. A2–14; C.C.R. Ord. 25, r. 10(1)(b). Both firms must sue and/or be sued in the firm name.
[61] R.S.C. Ord. 81, r. 6(2), *infra*, para. A2–14; C.C.R. Ord. 25, r. 10(2). See generally, as to taking accounts between partners, *supra*, paras. 23–70 *et seq.*

Part Five

DISSOLUTION AND WINDING-UP

CHAPTER 24

DISSOLUTION AND ITS CAUSES

1. INTRODUCTION

Meaning of dissolution

WHAT is meant by the "dissolution" of a partnership is often **24–01** misunderstood, not only because that word is used in two distinct senses but also because it has a very different meaning when applied to a company.[1] In the case of a partnership, it invariably refers to the moment of time when the ongoing nature of the partnership relation terminates, even though the partners may continue to be associated together in a new partnership or merely for the purposes of winding up the firm's affairs.[2] Indeed, the outward appearance of a partnership immediately prior to and immediately following a dissolution will frequently be unchanged. For a company, on the other hand, dissolution marks not the commencement of the winding up but its conclusion, *i.e.* the moment of extinction.[3]

Distinction between technical and general dissolution

It does not necessarily follow from the fact that a partnership has **24–02** been dissolved that its affairs will fall to be wound up in the manner prescribed by the Partnership Act 1890.[4] It has already been seen that, as a matter of law, a change in the composition of a partnership results in a dissolution of the existing firm and the creation of a new firm;[5] in such a case, the new firm will usually take on the assets and liabilities of the old, without any break in the continuity of the business.[6] This is often referred to as a "technical" dissolution and is usually, but not always,[7] the result of agreement.

---

[1] The words "dissolved" and "dissolution" are not defined by the Partnership Act 1890.
[2] Ibid s.38, *supra*, paras. 13–64 *et seq.*
[3] Insolvency Act 1986, ss.202(5), 205(2). See also *infra*, para. 24–27.
[4] *Ibid.* ss.39, 44: see further, *supra*, paras. 19–08 *et seq.*, 19–29 *et seq.*, 23–179 *et seq.* and *infra*, paras. 25–39 *et seq.*
[5] See *supra*, paras. 3–01 *et seq.* And see, in particular, *Jardine-Paterson v. Fraser*, 1974 S.L.T. 93, 97 *per* Lord Maxwell (albeit a decision relating to Scots partnership with a separate legal identity); also *Hadlee v. Commissioner of Inland Revenue* [1989] 2 N.Z.L.R. 447, 455, *per* Eichelbaum J. This aspect was not pursued on appeal: see [1993] A.C. 524.
[6] Note, however, that a creditor of the old firm is unlikely to acquire rights against the new firm, even where the liabilities are taken over: see *supra*, paras. 13–24 *et seq.* See also *supra*, para. 10–45.
[7] See, for example, *Hudgell Yeates & Co. v. Watson* [1978] Q.B. 451, where the partnership was dissolved under the Partnership Act 1890, s.34. See *infra*, para. 24–37.

24-03   In contrast, the expression "general" dissolution is used to denote
a dissolution involving a full scale winding-up, which may well have
been brought about at the instance of one partner, against the wishes
of the others. When a firm is referred to as "in dissolution," this
usually indicates that a general dissolution has taken place, but that
the winding up of its affairs is still continuing. Once the winding-up is
complete and the accounts finally settled as between the partners,[8]
there will be nothing left which could properly be referred to as a
partnership, whether in dissolution or otherwise.

This and subsequent chapters are primarily concerned with
dissolution in the second sense.

Causes of dissolution

24-04   The general dissolution of a partnership may be brought about in a
number of ways, which can be classified into the following groups:

1. By mutual agreement of the partners. Thus, whatever
    duration may have been agreed at the outset, the partners
    can, if they so wish, bring the partnership to an end at an
    earlier date.[9] However, in the absence of some enabling
    power in the agreement,[10] no one partner or group of
    partners can unilaterally bring about such a dissolution:
    unanimity is an effective prerequisite.
2. By the exercise of an express power to dissolve reserved by
    the agreement.[11]
3. By rescission for fraud or misrepresentation.[12]
4. By repudiation. Doubts were expressed in some earlier
    editions of this work with regard to the potential application
    of the doctrine of repudiation to partnerships. However, these
    doubts were emphatically rejected in *Hitchman v. Crouch
    Butler Savage Associates*,[13] where Harman J. held the doctrine
    to apply to partnership agreements in the same way as it
    applies to other forms of contract. It is, accordingly, open to
    the innocent partners faced with a repudiatory breach of the

---

[8] See *supra*, paras. 23–70 *et seq.* and *infra*, paras. 25–39 *et seq.*

[9] If authority were required for this self evident proposition, reference should be made to the
Partnership Act 1890, s.19, *supra*, para. 10–10. See also *infra*, para. 24–79.

[10] *e.g.* a power for a majority of partners to take *any* decision in relation to the partnership's
affairs, including the decision to dissolve. See *supra*, paras. 10–82 *et seq. Cf.* the position under the
Partnership Act 1890, s.24(8), *supra*, paras. 15–05 *et seq.*

[11] See *supra*, paras. 10–113 *et seq.*

[12] See *supra*, paras. 23–51 *et seq.*

[13] (1983) 80 L.S.Gaz. 550 (an appeal was subsequently allowed on other grounds: see (1983) 127
S.J. 441 and *supra*, para. 10–98); also *Fulwell v. Bragg* (1983) 127 S.J. 171. Note that it has now, in
the same way, been confirmed that a lease can be repudiated: see *Hussein v. Mehlman* [1992] 32
E.G. 59.

partnership terms either to affirm the agreement or to treat the partnership as at an end.[14]

5. By the service of notice or the occurrence of some other determining event prescribed by the Partnership Act 1890.[15] It should, however, be appreciated that the relevant provisions of the Act can, for the most part, be excluded by agreement.[16]

6. By order of a court of competent jurisdiction or, where relevant, by an arbitration award.[17]

Subsequent sections of this chapter principally concentrate on dissolutions brought about in the fifth and sixth ways.

Doctrine of frustration apparently excluded

Although the question never appears to have been considered by the courts,[18] the current editor submits that the normal doctrine of frustration cannot be applied to partnership agreements. This view is advanced on the basis that a number of potentially frustrating events are specifically catered for by the Partnership Act 1890,[19] so that, by necessary implication, the application of the doctrine to those and other events must be excluded.[20] **24–05**

Retirement and expulsion

The retirement and expulsion of partners will normally be regulated by the partnership agreement[21] and will not involve anything other than a technical dissolution.[22] However, more serious **24–06**

---

[14] See, generally, as to repudiation, *Chitty on Contracts* (26th ed.), paras. 1701 *et seq. Quaere*, is the service of an invalid expulsion notice a repudiatory act? See further, *supra*, para. 10–107.

[15] *Ibid.* ss.26(1), 32–34, *infra*, paras. 24–07 *et seq.*

[16] Partnership Act 1890, s.19, *supra*, para. 10–10; see also *infra*, paras. 24–07, 24–11, 24–21. It is, however, impossible to exclude *ibid.* s.34, even though the practical effects of that section may be avoided: see *infra*, paras. 24–36, 24–37.

[17] Partnership Act 1890, s.35, *infra*, paras. 24–39 *et seq.* As to the power of an arbitrator to order a dissolution, see *supra*, para. 10–232.

[18] However, in *Hitchman v. Crouch Butler Savage Associates* (1983) 80 L.S.Gaz. 550, 555, Harman J. reportedly held that "the doctrine of repudiation *and other contractual provisions* applied to a partnership ... in the same way as it did to all other contracts" (emphasis supplied), thus providing some (strictly inferential) support for an argument that the frustration doctrine does apply. This aspect was not raised on the appeal: see (1983) 127 S.J. 441.

[19] See *ibid.* ss.33(1), 34, 35(b); see also the Mental Health Act 1983, s.96(1)(g). *Cf.* the Partnership Act 1890, s.40 and the Law Reform (Frustrated Contracts) Act 1943, s.1.

[20] See also The Conveyancer and Property Lawyer (N.S.), Vol. 11, p. 43. *Cf. F.C. Shepherd & Co. Ltd. v. Jerrom* [1987] Q.B. 301, 328–329, *per* Mustill L.J. An analogy might formerly have been drawn with leases (see, for example, *Total Oil Great Britain v. Thompson Garages (Biggin Hill)* [1972] 1 Q.B. 318), but it has now been held by the House of Lords that a lease can, in principle, be frustrated: see *National Carriers Ltd. v. Panalpina (Northern) Ltd.* [1981] A.C. 675.

[21] See *supra*, paras. 10–88 *et seq.*, 10–94 *et seq.*

[22] See *supra*, para. 24–02.

dissolution-related questions will on occasion arise: these are considered in the last two sections of this chapter.

2. DISSOLUTION OTHERWISE THAN BY THE COURT

A. EXPIRATION OF TERM, ETC.

24-07 If a partnership is entered into for a fixed term,[23] it must necessarily be dissolved once that term has expired, unless the partners agree to extend its duration. Similarly, if a partnership is formed solely with a view to carrying out a particular transaction, it will be dissolved once the transaction is complete,[24] again subject to any contrary agreement. These somewhat obvious propositions are clearly established by section 32(a) and (b) of the Partnership Act 1890, which provides:

> "32. Subject to any agreement between the partners, a partnership is dissolved—
>
> (*a*) If entered into for a fixed term, by the expiration of that term:
>
> (*b*) If entered into for a single adventure or undertaking, by the termination of that adventure or undertaking".

Continuation after fixed term: the statutory presumptions

24-08 If, however, the partnership is continued *after* the expiration of the fixed term, then, in the absence of any evidence as to its intended further duration, it will be regarded as a partnership at will and, thus, determinable at any time on notice.[25] Such a consequence was only avoided in *Walters v. Bingham*[26] because the partners had agreed to be bound by the terms of a draft agreement "pending the adoption of a new deed."

If the partners, or those of them who were actively involved in the firm's business, continue that business after the expiration of the term without attempting to wind up its affairs, a continuation of the partnership will be presumed.[27]

Continuation after transaction complete

24-09 No statutory presumption applies where a partnership formed to carry out a particular transaction is continued beyond the completion

---

[23] See generally, *supra*, para. 10–33.

[24] See *Lindern Trawler Managers v. W.H.J. Trawlers* (1949) 83 Ll.L.R. 131; also *J. & J. Cunningham v. Lucas* [1957] 1 Lloyd's Rep. 416; *Mann v. D'Arcy* [1968] 1 W.L.R. 893.

[25] Partnership Act 1890, s.27(1): see *supra*, paras. 10–16 *et seq*. The position was the same prior to the Act: see *Neilson v. Mossend Iron Co.* (1886) 11 App.Cas. 298; also *Featherstonhaugh v. Fenwick* (1810) 17 Ves.Jr. 298; *Booth v. Parks* (1828) 1 Moll. 465.

[26] [1988] 1 F.T.L.R. 260.

[27] Partnership Act 1890, s.27(2).

of that transaction.[28] However, the current editor submits that, in practice, the same presumptions as are made in the case of fixed term partnerships will be applied by analogy.[29]

B. NOTICE

Partnership Act 1890, sections 26(1) and 32

The Partnership Act 1890 contains two separate provisions dealing **24–10** with the termination of partnerships by notice. Under the rubric, "Retirement from partnership at will," section 26(1) provides:

"(1) Where no fixed term has been agreed upon for the duration of a partnership, any partner may determine the partnership at any time on giving notice of his intention so to do to all the other partners."

Section 32 then provides as follows:

"32. Subject to any agreement between the partners, a partnership is dissolved—

. . .

(c) If entered into for an undefined time, by any partner giving notice to the other or others of his intention to dissolve the partnership.
In the last-mentioned case the partnership is dissolved as from the date mentioned in the notice as the date of dissolution, or, if no date is so mentioned, as from the date of the communication of the notice."

The difference in wording between these two sections is discussed in an earlier part of this work.[30]

Exclusion of right to dissolve

Notwithstanding that difference in wording, it is clear that the right **24–11** to dissolve may be excluded by an express or implied agreement.[31] In such a case, the partnership will neither be "at will" nor for an

---

[28] Unaccountably, *ibid.* s.27(1) applies only to "a partnership entered into for a fixed term."

[29] However, where the partnership is continued for the purposes of carrying out a second transaction identical to the first, there may be an almost irresistible implication that the partners intend the partnership to subsist until the completion of that second transaction. See also *supra,* para. 9–09.

[30] See *supra,* para. 9–01.

[31] See *Moss v. Elphick* [1910] 1 K.B. 465 (this decision being affirmed at [1910] 1 K.B. 846); *Abbott v. Abbott* [1936] 3 All E.R. 823; *Walters v. Bingham* [1988] 1 F.T.L.R. 260. And see *supra,* paras. 9–01 *et seq.*

undefined time.[32] This accords with the position prior to the Partnership Act 1890.[33]

When notice will dissolve

24-12   In the case of a true partnership at will, notice of dissolution may be given by any partner at any time.[34] It is a commonly held misconception that a "reasonable" period of notice is required but, in fact, the notice can be instantaneous.[35]

A dissolution notice may be served even though one of the recipient partners is suffering from a mental disorder.[36]

Fraud and mala fides

24-13   Although there is no duty on a partner to act reasonably in deciding whether to serve a dissolution notice,[37] a notice served with fraudulent intent[38] or, in the current editor's view, mala fide and for an improper purpose[39] will not be upheld. Indeed, Lord Lindley, writing prior to the Partnership Act 1890, observed:

"... it is apprehended that the court can restrain an immediate dissolution and sale of the partnership property, if it appears that irreparable mischief will ensue from such a proceeding."[40]

---

[32] The usual implication, if a partnership cannot be determined otherwise than by agreement, is that it will subsist during the joint lives of the partners: see *supra*, para. 9–03. See also *Walters v. Bingham* [1988] 1 F.T.L.R. 260, 266–267, *per* Browne-Wilkinson V.-C.

[33] See *Heath v. Sansom* (1831) 4 B. & Ad. 172, 175, *per* Parke J.; *Frost v. Moulton* (1856) 21 Beav. 596; *Syers v. Syers* (1876) 1 App.Cas. 174. See also *supra*, para. 9–02.

[34] See *Firth v. Amslake* (1964) 108 S.J. 198; also *Connell v. Slack* (1909) 28 N.Z.L.R. 560, 561, *per* Edwards J. As to the position prior to the Act (which was the same), see *Peacock v. Peacock* (1809) 16 Ves.Jr. 49; *Featherstonhaugh v. Fenwick* (1810) 17 Ves.Jr. 298; *Crawshay v. Maule* (1818) 1 Swan. 495, 508, *per* Lord Eldon; *Ex p. Nokes* (1801) cited 1 Mont.Part. 108, note.

[35] The contrary argument was taken without success several times prior to the Partnership Act 1890: see the cases cited in the previous footnote. Note, however, that the notice can only have effect once communicated to all the partners: see *infra*, para. 24–14.

[36] *Mellersh v. Keen* (1859) 27 Beav. 236.

[37] *Russell v. Russell* (1880) 14 Ch.D. 471.

[38] *Walters v. Bingham* [1988] 1 F.T.L.R. 260, applying *Lazarus Estates Ltd. v. Beasley* [1956] 1 Q.B. 702. This part of the decision was, however, strictly *obiter*.

[39] *Neilson v. Mossend Iron Co.* (1886) 11 App.Cas. 298, 309, *per* Lord Watson; *Daw v. Herring* [1892] 1 Ch. 284, 291, *per* Stirling J.; *Peyton v. Mindham* [1972] 1 W.L.R. 8. The point was left open in *Walters v. Bingham* [1988] 1 F.T.L.R. 260, on the basis that the law may be different in England than in Scotland, although it is not clear from the report what authorities were cited to Browne-Wilkinson V.-C. It should be noted that Lord Lindley was at pains to point out that *Neilson v. Mossend Iron Co.*, *supra*, was a Scottish case (even though this did not later deter Stirling J.). He then went on, "By the civil law a dissolution made *mala fide*, and at an unreasonable time, is not allowed": see Pothier, *Partnership*, 150. Note also, in this context, *Hunter v. Wylie*, 1993 S.L.T. 1091 (O.H.), where it was held that two partners, who were in material breach of the partnership terms by withdrawing capital without their co-partners' consent, were not entitled to serve a notice of dissolution under an *express* power in the agreement. In the current editor's view, this case cannot properly be regarded as having established a principle of general application.

[40] See *Chavany v. Van Sommer* (1771) 3 Woodd.Lect. 416 and 1 Swan. 512n. Lord Lindley also referred to *Blisset v. Daniel* (1853) 10 Hare 493 (which was a case of compulsory retirement).

Even if the notice cannot be attacked on the grounds of fraud or mala fides, it does not follow that the partner giving it can necessarily retain any personal benefit he may secure as a result of the dissolution.[41]

No damages are recoverable where a wrongful act, *e.g.* the exclusion of a partner, causes the dissolution of a partnership at will.[42]

Form of notice

A dissolution notice must be clear and unambiguous[43] but it is not **24–14** necessary that the partner giving it appreciates its legal effect.[44] It follows that a proposal to dissolve on terms which are not accepted will not be effective;[45] neither will a notice that a partner's share has been forfeited, since that is indicative of an intention to dissolve only as regards that partner.[46] References to "retirement" or "resignation" should, for the same reason, be avoided.[47] The notice may take effect immediately[48] or on a future date,[49] but will only be effective once it has been communicated to all the partners.[50]

If a dissolution action is commenced by a partner, the writ will be treated as an immediate notice to dissolve.[51]

Whether written notice required

Section 26(2) of the Partnership Act 1890 provides: **24–15**

"(2) Where the partnership has originally been constituted by deed, a notice in writing, signed by the partner giving it, shall be sufficient for this purpose."

---

[41] See, for example, *Clegg v. Edmondson* (1856) 8 De G.M. & G. 787; also *supra*, paras. 16–08 *et seq.* As to the return of premiums, see *infra*, paras. 25–06 *et seq.*

[42] *Connell v. Slack* (1909) 28 N.Z.L.R. 560.

[43] But see *Syers v. Syers* (1876) 1 App.Cas. 174, 183, *per* Lord Cairns; *Walters v. Bingham* [1988] 1 F.T.L.R. 260, 267, *per* Browne-Wilkinson V.-C. As to the problems which can arise where an ambiguous notice is given, see *Toogood v. Farrell* [1988] 2 E.G.L.R. 233 (which concerned a notice of *retirement* given pursuant to a contractual provision).

[44] *Toogood v. Farrell, supra.*

[45] *Hall v. Hall* (1855) 20 Beav. 139.

[46] See *Clarke v. Hart* (1858) 6 H.L.C. 633.

[47] See, for example, *Sobell v. Boston* [1975] 1 W.L.R. 1587. But note that the Partnership Act 1890, s.26 is headed "Retirement from partnership at will," even though there is no reference to retirement in the body of the section.

[48] See *supra*, para. 24–12.

[49] *Mellersh v. Keen* (1859) 27 Beav. 236.

[50] Partnership Act 1890, ss.26(1), 32; *Walters v. Bingham* [1988] 1 F.T.L.R. 260; also *Van Sandau v. Moore* (1826) 1 Russ. 441; *Wheeler v. Van Wart* (1838) 9 Sim. 193; *Parsons v. Hayward* (1862) 4 De G.F. & G. 474.

[51] *Unsworth v. Jordan* [1896] W.N. 2(5).

Surprisingly, no similar qualification is attached to section 32(c).[52] Nevertheless, it would seem that, since the former subsection establishes that a notice in writing is merely *sufficient*, not necessary, to work a dissolution, an oral notice will be effective in all cases, even where the partnership was originally constituted by deed.[53] This accords with the law prior to the Act.[54] However, since a written notice will usually be desirable for evidential purposes, it is perhaps sensible to heed the admonition which has appeared in all editions of this work since the Act:

"... it would be imprudent not to give a notice in accordance with this provision, in cases to which it applies."[55]

On the same principle, it should perhaps be ensured that the partner signs the notice personally; where, however the partnership was not constituted by deed, no such precautions are necessary and it is, indeed, not unusual to find notices being given in the course of inter-solicitor correspondence.

Withdrawal of notice

24-16   A dissolution notice, once given, cannot be withdrawn without the consent of all the partners.[56]

However, it would seem that a *prospective* notice may, at any time up to the moment of its expiration, be superseded by the occurrence of an event which dissolves the partnership at an earlier date.[57] It is the current editor's view that such an event may be the service of a subsequent dissolution notice, requiring an immediate dissolution; *sed quaere*.[58]

---

[52] See *supra*, para. 24–10.

[53] See, for example, *Walters v. Bingham* [1988] 1 F.T.L.R. 260, 267, *per* Browne-Wilkinson V.-C. (albeit that this part of the decision was *obiter* and it is not clear to what extent the point was argued). *Quaere*, is s.32(c) merely declaratory of the effects of a notice under section 26(1)? This has, so far as the current editor is aware, never been argued. Alternatively, should effect be given to section 26 in preference to s.32(c), on the grounds that the former section contains a qualification? See *Moss v. Elphick* [1910] 1 K.B. 465, 468, *per* Pickford J. Although interesting, the point is largely academic given the terms of s.26(2).

[54] Lord Lindley put it thus: "It has never been determined that a partnership constituted by deed can only be dissolved either by deed or by operation of law; and it is apprehended that no deed is requisite." He then referred to *Doe v. Miles* (1816) 1 Stark 181 and 4 Camp. 373. Note also *Hutchinson v. Whitfield* (1830) Hayes 78.

[55] As to the problems which may arise when reliance is placed on an oral notice, see *Toogood v. Farrell* [1988] 2 E.G.L.R. 233.

[56] *Jones v. Lloyd* (1874) L.R. 18 Eq. 265; also *Finch v. Oake* [1896] 1 Ch. 409; *Glossop v. Glossop* [1907] 2 Ch. 370; *Toogood v. Farrell*, *supra*; and see *supra*, para. 10–90.

[57] *McLeod v. Dowling* (1927) 43 T.L.R. 655 (dissolution resulting from the death of a partner).

[58] Account must, however, be taken of (a) the provisions of the partnership agreement (if any); (b) any potential estoppel; and (c) the (somewhat ambitious) argument that the other partners' acceptance of the first notice impliedly converts the partnership into a partnership for a fixed term (*i.e.* until the date specified in the notice) which cannot be determined by any one partner prior to that date.

Express dissolution clauses

The considerations applicable to the exercise of an *express* power **24–17** to dissolve a partnership for a fixed term[59] will be no different, subject to the precise terms of the agreement.[60]

Dissolution inferred although no notice

Lord Lindley observed that   **24–18**

"A dissolution of a partnership at will may be inferred from circumstances, *e.g.* a quarrel, although no notice to dissolve may have been given."[61]

This is still the position.[62]

Date of dissolution

The partnership will be dissolved as soon as the notice is **24–19** communicated to *all* the partners or, if that is later, on the date specified in the notice.[63] However, it has already been seen that a prospective notice may be superseded by a subsequent determining event, *e.g.* the death of a partner.[64]

If the notice takes the form of a writ in a dissolution action, the partnership will be dissolved on the date of its service.[65]

C. DEATH AND BANKRUPTCY, ETC.

Partnership Act 1890, section 33(1)

This subsection provides as follows: **24–20**

"33.—(1) Subject to any agreement between the partners, every partnership is dissolved as regards all the partners by the death or bankruptcy of any partner."

---

[59] See *supra*, paras. 10–113 *et seq.*

[60] Thus, it would seem that, if there are sufficient grounds (and the other partners' motives cannot be impugned), a partner who has served a prospective dissolution notice might, at least in theory, be expelled before his notice has expired.

[61] *Pearce v. Lindsay* (1860) 3 De G.J. & S. 139.

[62] See *Bothe v. Amos* [1976] Fam. 46 (husband and wife partnership). The contrary appears to have been assumed in *Millar v. Strathclyde Regional Council*, 1988 S.L.T. 9 (Lands Tribunal): see also *infra*, para. 24–38.

[63] Partnership Act 1890, s.32, *supra*, para. 24–10. And see also *Robertson v. Lockie* (1846) 15 Sim. 285; *Bagshaw v. Parker* (1847) 10 Beav. 532; *Mellersh v. Keen* (1859) 27 Beav. 236; *Jones v. Lloyd* (1874) L.R. 18 Eq. 265.

[64] See *supra*, para. 24–16.

[65] *Unsworth v. Jordan* [1896] W.N. 2(5); see also *Kirby v. Carr* (1838) 3 Y. & C.Ex. 184; *Shepherd v. Allen* (1864) 33 Beav. 577. And note *Phillips v. Melville* [1921] N.Z.L.R. 571, noticed *infra*, para. 24–78.

1. Death

24–21   The inclusion of the death of a partner as an event which will, in the absence of some contrary agreement,[66] dissolve the firm[67] accorded with the law prior to the Partnership Act 1890.[68] Lord Lindley explained this rule as:

> "... obviously reasonable, for by the death of one of the members it is no longer possible to adhere to the original contract, the essence of which is (in the case supposed), that all the parties to it shall be alive."

It is important to note that this rule is applied strictly: the mere fact that the partnership was originally entered into for a fixed term which has not expired will not, of itself, be sufficient to prevent a dissolution caused by the untimely death of a partner.[69]

The position is even the same in Scotland, where a firm is accorded separate legal personality.[70]

Date of dissolution

It hardly needs to be observed that the partnership will be dissolved as from the date of the partner's death.[71]

2. Bankruptcy

24–22   As was the position prior to the Partnership Act 1890,[72] the bankruptcy of an individual partner will clearly dissolve the firm, unless the partners have agreed otherwise.[73] Although mining partnerships were once treated as an apparent exception to the general rule,[74] this is no longer permissible under the Act.

Foreign bankruptcy

24–23   It is not clear whether the equivalent of a bankruptcy order made against a partner in a foreign country will cause a dissolution.

---

[66] See, as to such agreements, *supra*, para. 10–33.

[67] See *McLeod v. Dowling* (1927) 43 T.L.R. 655; *I.R.C. v. Graham's Trustees*, 1971 S.L.T. 46; *Jardine-Paterson v. Fraser*, 1974 S.L.T. 93.

[68] See *Pearce v. Chamberlain* (1750) 2 Ves.Sen. 33; *Vulliamy v. Noble* (1817) 3 Mer. 593; *Gillespie v. Hamilton* (1818) 3 Madd. 251; *Crawshay v. Maule* (1818) 1 Swan. 495; *Crosbie v. Guion* (1857) 23 Beav. 518.

[69] *Crawford v. Hamilton* (1818) 3 Madd. 251; *Downs v. Collins* (1848) 6 Hare 418; *Lancaster v. Allsup* (1887) 57 L.T. (N.S.) 53.

[70] *Jardine-Paterson v. Fraser*, 1974 S.L.T. 93 (Ct. of Session).

[71] Partnership Act 1890, s.33(1), *supra*, para. 24–20.

[72] See *Fox v. Hanbury* (1776) Cowp. 445; also *Hague v. Rolleston* (1768) 4 Burr. 2175; *Ex p. Smith* (1800) 5 Ves.Jr. 295; *Crawshay v. Collins* (1808) 15 Ves.Jr. 218, 228, *per* Lord Eldon.

[73] Partnership Act 1890, s.33(1), *supra*, para. 24–20; *Re Ward* [1985] N.Z.L.R. 352. As to the circumstances in which a partner can be made the subject of a bankruptcy order, see *infra*, paras. 27–44 *et seq*. *Cf.* the position of a corporate partner, *infra*, paras. 24–25 *et seq*. The current editor considers that an express power to expel a bankrupt partner will be sufficient evidence of an agreement to exclude s.33(1): see *supra*, para. 10–95, n.5.

[74] *Ex p. Broadbent* (1834) 1 Mont. & Ayr. 635; *Bentley v. Bates* (1840) 4 Y. & C.Ex. 182.

Although there are no reported decisions on the point, the current editor tentatively submits that it will, provided that the partner is domiciled in that country or, if he is not, that he submits to the jurisdiction of its court. In any other case, it is doubtful whether an English court would recognise the title of the creditors' representative appointed under the relevant foreign law[75] and he might therefore be unable to lay claim to the bankrupt partner's share. In such circumstances, it is prima facie unlikely that the partnership would be treated as dissolved.

Date of dissolution

The Partnership Act 1890 does not state when the partnership is to **24–24** be treated as dissolved but, under the current insolvency legislation, the dissolution will clearly date from the making of the bankruptcy order.[76]

Where, however, the partnership is ordered to be wound up as an unregistered company, whether on a concurrent petition or otherwise,[77] the date of dissolution may precede any bankruptcy order made against an individual partner.[78]

3. Winding-up and dissolution of corporate partner

Winding-up order

An order for the winding-up of a corporate partner is the nearest **24–25** equivalent to the bankruptcy of an individual.[79] On the other hand, a resolution for a *voluntary* winding-up may be passed for many reasons other than insolvency.[80] Given that the relationship between partners will inevitably be of a less personal nature where a corporate partner is involved,[81] it is submitted that neither an order nor a resolution to wind up such a partner would *per se* dissolve the firm, although there is, admittedly, no authority on the point.

---

[75] See, generally, *Dicey & Morris on the Conflict of Laws* (12th ed.), pp. 1172 *et seq.* and *Re Blithman* (1866) L.R. 2 Eq. 23; *Ex p. André Châle* (1890) 24 Q.B.D. 640; *Re Hayward* [1897] 1 Ch. 905; *cf. Emanuel v. Symon* [1908] 1 K.B. 302. But see also *Re Davidson's Settlement Trusts* (1873) L.R. 15 Eq. 383; *Re Lawson's Trusts* [1896] 1 Ch. 175; *Re Anderson* [1911] 1 K.B. 896 (although the reasoning in this case is open to criticism). And note the provisions of the Civil Jurisdiction and Judgments Act 1982, ss.2, 18(3)(c), and Sched. 1, Title 1, Art. 1(2) (as substituted by the Civil Jurisdiction and Judgments Act 1982 (Amendment) Order 1990 (S.I. 1990 No. 2591), Sched. 1).

[76] Insolvency Act 1986, s.278(a). *Cf.* the position under the Bankruptcy Act 1914, s.37(1), (2).

[77] See *infra*, paras. 27–08 *et seq.*

[78] Where there are concurrent petitions, the petition against the firm will be heard first: Insolvency Act 1986, s.124(7) (as substituted by the Insolvent Partnerships Order 1986, Sched. 2, Part I, para. 2). See further, *infra*, paras. 27–38, 27–39.

[79] *Cf.* the Law of Property Act 1925, s.205(1)(i).

[80] See the Insolvency Act 1986, s.84.

[81] But see *supra*, para. 11–15.

24-26   Nevertheless, given that the ability of a corporate partner to function effectively would be severely impaired by the presentation of a winding up petition,[82] the current editor is of the opinion that there would in that event be grounds for an application to the court for a dissolution on the just and equitable ground.[83] In practice, this option is more theoretical than real, since it is doubtful whether the application could be brought on for hearing *before* the petition. This underlines the desirability of including a specific provision in the agreement to cater for such an eventuality.[84]

Where concurrent petitions are presented against the firm and against two or more partners,[85] the petition against the firm will be heard and determined first,[86] so that it may not in any event be necessary to enquire into the effect of a subsequent winding up order made against a corporate partner.

Dissolution

24-27   The dissolution of a corporate partner by the law of the country of its incorporation terminates its existence and is equivalent to the death of an individual.[87] On that footing, it is considered that such an event will, in the absence of an agreement to the contrary,[88] dissolve the firm. *A fortiori* where there are only two partners. Even if this conclusion were wrong, there would clearly be grounds for the court to order a dissolution.[89]

Foreign corporate partner

24-28   Although a winding up order made in accordance with the law of a company's place of incorporation will normally be recognised under English law,[90] a corporate partner might, exceptionally, be regarded as *dissolved* in one country but not in another.[91] The attitude of the

---

[82] See *supra*, para. 11–10.

[83] See *infra*, paras. 24–75 *et seq.*

[84] See *supra*, paras. 11–08 *et seq.*

[85] See *infra*, paras. 27–23 *et seq.*

[86] Insolvency Act 1986, s.124(7) (as substituted by the Insolvent Partnerships Order 1986, Sched. 2, Part I, para. 2). See further, *infra*, paras. 27–38, 27–39.

[87] See *Salton v. New Beeston Cycle Co.* [1900] 1 Ch. 43. As to when a company will be dissolved, see the Insolvency Act 1986, ss.201(2), 205(2).

[88] *Quaere* whether a provision that the "death" of a partner shall not dissolve the partnership, would amount to such an agreement.

[89] Partnership Act 1890, s.35(b), (f), *infra*, paras. 24–55 *et seq.*, 24–75 *et seq.*

[90] See, generally, *Dicey & Morris on the Conflict of Laws* (12th ed.), pp. 1137 *et seq.* Note the Civil Jurisdiction and Judgments Act 1982, ss.2, 18(3)(c), Sched. 1, Title 1, Art. 1(2), (as substituted by the Civil Jurisdiction and Judgments Act 1982 (Amendment) Order 1990 (S.I. 1990 No. 2591), Sched. 1), Sched. 4, Art. 16(2), Sched. 5, para. 1 (as amended by the Insolvency Act 1986, Sched. 14).

[91] See *Russian Commercial and Industrial Bank v. Comptoir D'Escompte de Mulhouse* [1923] 2 K.B. 630; *Banque Internationale de Commerce de Petrograd v. Goukassow* [1923] 2 K.B. 682. Note, however, that both decisions were reversed on the facts: see [1925] A.C. 112 and 150. See also *Lazard Bros. & Co. v. Midland Bank Ltd.* [1933] A.C. 289; *Re Russian Commercial and Industrial Bank* [1955] Ch. 148.

English courts will obviously determine whether or not the continued existence of the partnership is affected.

D. CHARGING ORDER ON A PARTNER'S SHARE

Partnership Act 1890, section 33(2)

This subsection provides as follows: **24–29**

"33.—(2) A partnership may, at the option of the other partners, be dissolved[92] if any partner suffers his share of the partnership property to be charged under this Act for his separate debt."

The circumstances in which a charging order may be obtained in respect of a partner's share have already been noted.[93]

Nature of the option

It is not entirely clear whether each of the other partners has an **24–30** independent option to dissolve the partnership, as Lord Lindley explained in his Supplement on the Act:

"As a general rule, if several persons have an election the first election made by any one of them would seem to determine the election for all,[94] but this rule can hardly apply to the case referred to in this section. The majority would not, it is conceived, have the power to dissolve the partnership against the wishes of the minority.[95] The meaning apparently is either that all the other partners must be unanimous, or that a separate option is given to each of the other partners, so that any one of them can dissolve the partnership, whether the others have or have not expressed their intention of not doing so."

The current editor considers that the former view is correct and **24–31** that, notwithstanding the provisions of the Interpretation Act 1978,[96] the reference to "the other partners" should not be construed as "the other partners or any of them."[97] The position is, of course, wholly different under sections 26(1) and 32(c),[98] where the right to dissolve

---

[92] It should be noted that the word "dissolved" is not followed by the words "as regards all the partners", as in s.33(1), *supra*, para. 24–20. However, this omission is not thought to be significant. As Lord Lindley pointed out, the additional words do not appear in ss.26, 32, 34 or 35 either.

[93] Partnership Act 1890, s.23, *supra*, paras. 19–43 *et seq.*

[94] Co.Litt. 145a.

[95] This would not on any footing constitute an ordinary matter connected with the partnership business: see the Partnership Act 1890, s.24(8), *supra*, paras. 15–05 *et seq.*

[96] s.6(c).

[97] It would obviously not be sufficient merely to construe the reference as "the other partners or partner."

[98] See *supra*, para. 24–10.

the firm is clearly expressed to be exercisable by a single partner. Accordingly, the other partners must be unanimous in their decision to exercise the option.[99]

Exercise of option

24–32   The Act gives no guidance as to when and how the option is to be exercised. However, Lord Lindley observed:

> "Any unequivocal act done to the knowledge of the partner whose share is charged will be an exercise of the option which cannot be withdrawn.[1] The option must be exercised within a reasonable time."[2]

Date of dissolution

24–33   Although the Act does not state when the partnership is to be dissolved, it would seem beyond argument that the relevant date will be that on which the option is exercised. As already noted, an effective exercise presupposes knowledge on the part of every partner.

E. ILLEGALITY

24–34 Prior to the Partnership Act 1890, Lord Lindley wrote:

> "... if, by any change in the law, it becomes illegal to carry on a business, every partnership formed before the making [of] the law for the purpose of carrying on that business, must be taken to have been dissolved by the law in question. So if, the law remaining unchanged, some event happens which renders it illegal for the members of a firm to continue to carry on their business in partnership, such event dissolves the firm. For example, if a partnership exists between two persons residing and carrying on trade in different countries, and war between those countries is proclaimed, a stop is thereby put to further intercourse between the partners, and the partnership subsisting between them is consequently dissolved."[3]

---

[99] See *Re a Solicitor's Arbitration* [1962] 1 W.L.R. 353; *Bond v. Hale* (1969) 72 S.R. (N.S.W.) 201; and see *supra*, para. 10–98.

[1] Lord Lindley treated this as a case of election, referring to *Scarf v. Jardine* (1882) 7 App.Cas. 345, 361, *per* Lord Blackburn; *Clough v. L.N.W. Ry.* (1871) L.R. 7 Ex. 26, 34, *per* Mellor J. And see *Jones v. Carter* (1846) 15 M. & W. 718, cited therein.

[2] *Scarf v. Jardine* (1882) 7 App.Cas. 345, 360, *per* Lord Blackburn. Lord Lindley also referred to *Anderson v. Anderson* (1857) 25 Beav. 190, which scarcely seems to support the proposition. And see *Re Longlands Farm* [1968] 3 All E.R. 552.

[3] See generally, *supra*, paras. 4–05, 8–14. *Feldt v. Chamberlain* (1914) 58 S.J. 788 is not good law.

Partnership Act 1890, section 34

This principle is now clearly embodied in section 34 of the **24-35** Partnership Act 1890, which provides:

"34. A partnership is in every case dissolved by the happening of any event which makes it unlawful for the business of the firm to be carried on, or for the members of the firm to carry it on in partnership."

Scope of section

The section refers to *the* business of the firm and thus does not **24-36** appear to contemplate the possibility of more than one business being carried on. The current editor's view is that if only one of the businesses is illegal, there will be no dissolution.[4] *Per contra*, if the illegality of the one business taints the others or if the legal business(es) will not remain viable independently of the illegal business.

The application of the section is not dependent on the partners' knowledge of the illegality: indeed, a partnership may be treated as dissolved even though the partners carry on in business just as if nothing had happened.[5] The duration of the illegality will also be irrelevant.[6]

It is clear from the inclusion of the words "in every case" that the section cannot be excluded by agreement.

Illegality caused by one partner

In *Hudgell Yeates & Co. v. Watson*[7] a partner in a firm of solicitors **24-37** accidentally failed to renew his practising certificate, thus rendering himself unqualified.[8] Since a partnership between a solicitor and an unqualified person was, as the law then stood, prohibited by statute,[9] the partnership became illegal and was automatically dissolved. In the

---

[4] *Quaere* whether this will still be the case where the firm's *main* business is illegal. Clearly this will be a matter of degree.

[5] *Hudgell Yeates & Co. v. Watson* [1978] Q.B. 451: see *infra*, para. 24–37. And see also *supra*, para. 8–43.

[6] *Ibid. Cf. Denny, Mott and Dickson Ltd. v. James B. Fraser & Co. Ltd.* [1944] A.C. 265.

[7] [1978] Q.B. 451.

[8] Such a failure will no longer *per se* have this effect: see the Solicitors Act 1974, s.14(5), (6) (as substituted by the Courts and Legal Services Act 1990, s.86).

[9] Solicitors Act 1974, s.39 (repealed by the Courts and Legal Services Act 1990, ss.66(1), 125(7), Sched. 20). Note, however, that *ibid.* ss.20, 21 (as amended) remain in force. See further, *supra*, para. 8–42. See also the *Encyclopedia of Professional Partnerships*, Pt. 8.

same way, a partnership between dentists would clearly be dissolved if one partner should cease to be registered.[10]

In cases of this type, it may be possible to avoid the worst effects of a dissolution by including a suitable provision in the agreement, *e.g.* to the effect that the unqualified partner should be deemed to have retired from the partnership on the date of dissolution.[11]

F. CESSATION OF BUSINESS

24-38   A temporary cessation of the partnership business will not cause a dissolution.[12] However, the current editor is of the view that, if the partners agree a *permanent* cessation of all forms of business, this must take effect as an agreement to dissolve since, in the absence of a business, no partnership can exist within the meaning of the Partnership Act 1890.[13]

3. DISSOLUTION BY THE COURT

A. STATUTES UNDER WHICH A PARTNERSHIP MAY BE DISSOLVED

Partnership Act 1890, section 35

24-39   Section 35 of the Partnership Act contains the five grounds on which a court may order the dissolution of a partnership. It provides as follows:

> "35. On application by a partner the Court may decree a dissolution of the partnership in any of the following cases:
> (*a*) [...][14]
> (*b*) When a partner, other than the partner suing, becomes in any other way permanently incapable of performing his part of the partnership contract:
> (*c*) When a partner, other than the partner suing, has been guilty of such conduct as, in the opinion of the court, regard being had to the nature of the business, is calculated to prejudicially affect the carrying on of the business:

---

[10] Dentists Act 1984, ss.40, 41; *Hill v. Clifford* [1907] 2 Ch. 236, 247 (*per* Cozens Hardy M.R.), 255 (*per* Sir John Gorrell Barnes P.), affirmed on other grounds *sub nom. Clifford v. Timms* [1908] A.C. 12. See also the *Encyclopedia of Professional Partnerships*, Pt. 4.

[11] See further the *Encyclopedia of Professional Partnerships*, Precedent 7, cl. 3(3), Precedent 11, cl. 3(3).

[12] See *Millar v. Strathclyde Regional Council*, 1988 S.L.T. 9 (Lands Tribunal). However, the assumption made by the Lands Tribunal that a notice to dissolve is required in all cases is not correct: see *supra*, para. 24–18. Note also that in Scotland the firm has separate legal personality: Partnership Act 1890, s.4(2).

[13] *Ibid.* s.1: see *supra*, paras. 2–01 *et seq. Cf. Millar v. Strathclyde Regional Council, supra.* Note also the Insolvency Act 1986, s.221(5)(a), *infra*, para. 27–09.

[14] This para. was repealed by the Mental Health Act 1959, Sched. 8.

(*d*) When a partner, other than the partner suing, wilfully or persistently commits a breach of the partnership agreement, or otherwise so conducts himself in matters relating to the partnership business that it is not reasonably practicable for the other partner or partners to carry on the business in partnership with him:

(*e*) When the business of the partnership can only be carried on at a loss:

(*f*) Whenever in any case circumstances have arisen which, in the opinion of the court, render it just and equitable that the partnership be dissolved."

Mental Health Act 1983, sections 95 and 96

Sections 95 and 96 of the Mental Health Act 1983 contain the **24–40** following powers which are exercisable in relation to a partnership of which a patient[15] is a member:

"95.—(1) The judge[16] may, with respect to the property and affairs of a patient do or secure the doing of all such things as appear necessary or expedient—

. . .

(*d*) . . . for administering the patient's affairs.

(2) In the exercise of the powers conferred by this section regard shall be had first of all to the requirements of the patient, and the rules of law which restricted the enforcement by a creditor of rights against property under the control of the judge in lunacy shall apply to property under the control of the judge; but subject to the foregoing provisions of this subsection the judge shall, in administering a patient's affairs, have regard to the interests of creditors and also to the desirability of making provision for obligations of the patient notwithstanding that they may not be legally enforceable.

96.—(1) Without prejudice to the generality of section 95 above, the judge shall have power to make such orders and give such directions and authorities as he thinks fit for the purposes of that section, and in particular may for those purposes make orders or give directions or authorities for—

. . .

(*g*) the dissolution of a partnership of which the patient is a member."[17]

---

[15] This expression is defined in *ibid.* 94(2) and, in essence, means a person who, by reason of mental disorder, is incapable of managing and administering his property and affairs.

[16] As to who can exercise the powers of "the judge," see *ibid.* s.94(1) (as amended by the Public Trustee and Administration of Funds Act 1986, s.2(2)). And see *infra*, para. 24–49.

[17] See further *infra*, para. 24–50.

Insolvency Act 1986

24-41 Any insolvent partnership may now be wound up as an unregistered company, irrespective of its size.[18] The petition against the firm may be accompanied by concurrent petitions against two or more of the partners, whether individuals or companies.[19] In the latter case, the only grounds for the petition are that the firm is unable to pay its debts;[20] otherwise a winding up order may also be sought on the ground that the firm has already been dissolved or ceased to carry on business[21] or on the "just and equitable" ground.[22]

Banking partnerships

24-42 A partnership which is or was an authorised institution under the Banking Act 1987[23] may be wound up as an unregistered company on a petition presented by the Bank of England either on the ground that it is unable to pay its debts or on the "just and equitable" ground.[24]

Insurance companies

24-43 A partnership which carries on insurance business within the United Kingdom[25] may be wound up under the Insolvency Act 1986 and, in certain circumstances, the petition may be presented by ten or more policy holders, provided that the leave of the court is first obtained.[26]

B. JURISDICTION TO DISSOLVE A PARTNERSHIP

High Court—Chancery Division

24-44 By the Supreme Court Act 1981,[27] all causes and matters for the dissolution of partnerships, or the taking of partnership and other accounts, are assigned to the Chancery Division of the High Court. If

---

[18] See the Insolvent Partnerships Order 1986, Art. 7, *infra*, paras. 27–08 *et seq*. *Cf.* the position under the Companies Act 1985, ss.665 *et seq*. (now repealed).

[19] Insolvent Partnerships Order 1986, Art. 8, *infra*, paras. 27–23 *et seq*.

[20] Insolvency Act 1986, s.221(5) (as substituted by the Insolvent Partnerships Order 1986, Art. 8(1)(c)): see *infra*, para. 27–24, 27–25.

[21] *Ibid.* s.221(5)(a), (b): see further *infra*, paras. 27–09 *et seq*.

[22] *Ibid.* s.221(5)(c): see *infra*, paras. 24–75, 27–11.

[23] See, as to authorisation, the Banking Act 1987, ss.8 *et seq*. And see *supra*, paras. 8–18 *et seq*.

[24] *Ibid.* s.92(1), (2). See, generally, *Re Goodwin Squires Securities Ltd.*, *The Times*, March 22, 1983 (a decision under the Banking Act 1979, s.18(1)(a)).

[25] See the Insurance Companies Act 1982, ss.15(1), 96(1). Note, however, the terms of *ibid.* s.15(1A), as added by the Insurance Companies (Third Insurance Directives) Regulations 1994 (S.I. 1994 No. 1696), reg. 13.

[26] *Ibid.* s.53 (as amended by the Insolvency Act 1986, Sched. 14). Leave is not required in the case of a petition presented by a creditor in the ordinary way: *Re A Company (No. 0010382 of 1992)*, [1993] BCLC 597.

[27] s.61(1), Sched. 1, para. 1(f). But note the powers of the Lord Chancellor under the Courts and Legal Services Act 1990, s.1.

the proceedings are commenced in another Division, a transfer to the Chancery Division *may* be ordered, but this is by no means obligatory.[28] Equally, in the case of a husband and wife partnership, it may on occasion be appropriate to transfer dissolution proceedings out of the Chancery Division, if matrimonial proceedings are pending in the Family Division; such an order was, however, refused in *Matz v. Matz*.[29]

County court

By the County Courts Act 1984,[30] the county court is given all the **24-45** jurisdiction of the High Court to hear and determine proceedings for the dissolution or winding up of any partnership[31] where the value of the partnership assets does not exceed £30,000. Accordingly, the court's jurisdiction may ultimately depend on which assets can properly be regarded as partnership property.[32] Nevertheless, such jurisdiction may be extended by agreement in writing between the parties or their legal representatives.[33]

Transfer of proceedings between High Court and county court

If proceedings are commenced in the county court which are in fact **24-46** outside its jurisdiction, they will either be struck out or transferred to the High Court,[34] unless the parties agree to extend the county court's jurisdiction.[35] Such a transfer may also be ordered in other appropriate cases,[36] *e.g.* where some important question of law or fact is likely to arise. The order may be made by the court of its own motion or on the application of any party to the proceedings.[37]

Proceedings commenced in the High Court may be transferred to the county court if the High Court is satisfied that the value of the

---

[28] Supreme Court Act 1981, ss.61(6), 65; see also the Practice Direction (High Court: Divisions) [1973] 1 W.L.R. 627, as applied in *Midland Bank Ltd. v. Stamps* [1978] 1 W.L.R. 635. Note in this context, *Bothe v. Amos* [1976] Fam. 46; and see generally, *Andrews v. Andrews* [1958] P. 217; *Re Andrews (Infants)* [1958] Ch. 665; *Re A.-H. (Infants)* [1963] Ch. 232; *Williams v. Williams* [1976] Ch. 278; *Re Holliday* [1981] Ch. 405. *Cf. Apac Rowena Ltd. v. Norpol Packaging Ltd.* [1991] 4 All E.R. 516.

[29] (1984) 14 Fam.Law. 178. *Cf. Williams v. Williams, supra.*

[30] s.23(f); County Courts Jurisdiction Order 1981 (S.I. 1981 No. 1123).

[31] Including a partnership the existence of which is disputed: *ibid.* This had, in any event, been decided in *R. v. Lailey* [1932] 1 K.B. 568.

[32] See *supra*, paras. 18–02 *et seq.*

[33] County Courts Act 1984, s.24 (as amended by the Courts and Legal Services Act 1990, Sched. 18).

[34] *Ibid.* s.42(1), (7) (as substituted by the Courts and Legal Services Act 1990, s.2(3)).

[35] *Ibid.* s.24 (as amended by the Courts and Legal Services Act 1990, Sched. 18).

[36] *Ibid.* s.42(2) (as substituted by the Courts and Legal Services Act 1990, s.2(3)); also the High Court and County Courts Jurisdiction Order 1991 (S.I. 1991 No. 724), Art. 7(5); Practice Direction (County Courts: Transfer of Actions) [1991] 1 W.L.R. 643. As to a transfer by order of the High Court, see *ibid.* s.41 (as amended by the Courts and Legal Services Act 1990, s.2(2)).

[37] *Ibid.* s.42(3) (as substituted by the Courts and Legal Services Act 1990, s.2(3)).

partnership assets does not exceed the sum of £30,000[38] or such a transfer is otherwise appropriate,[39] *e.g.* if the parties consent or the court considers that *no* important question of law or fact is likely to arise. Again, the requisite order may be made by the court of its own motion or on the application of any party.[40]

Court of Protection

The Court of Protection has jurisdiction to dissolve a partnership of which a patient is a member.[41]

Foreign court

24-47   An order for the dissolution of a partnership made by a foreign court will not normally be recognised under English law unless that court had jurisdiction over the defendant(s) according to the rules of private international law. Jurisdiction will not be established merely by showing that the partnership was entered into in the country concerned or that its assets included land situated there.[42] However, in the case of a decree made by a court of one of the Contracting States[43] under the 1968 Convention on jurisdiction and the enforcement of judgments[44] in respect of a partnership formed in or having its central control or management in that State,[45] enforcement in the United Kingdom will now be governed by the complex provisions of the Civil Jurisdiction and Judgments Act 1982.[46]

Arbitrator

An arbitrator may be given jurisdiction to order the dissolution of a partnership.[47]

---

[38] *Ibid.* s.40(1), (8) (as substituted by the Courts and Legal Services Act 1990, s.2(1)). As to the exercise of the discretion conferred on the High Court, see *Restick v. Crickmore* [1994] 1 W.L.R. 421 (C.A.).

[39] *Ibid.* s.40(2) (as substituted by the Courts and Legal Services Act 1990, s.2(1)). And see *supra*, n. 36.

[40] *Ibid.* s.40(3) (as substituted by the Courts and Legal Services Act 1990, s.2(1)).

[41] Mental Health Act 1983, s.96(1)(g), *supra*, para. 24-40. See further, *infra*, paras. 24-49 *et seq.*

[42] *Emanuel v. Symon* [1908] 1 K.B. 302; *cf. Blohn v. Desser* [1962] 2 Q.B. 116. See further, as to these cases, *Dicey & Morris on the Conflict of Laws* (12th ed.), p. 484. And see also the Foreign Judgments (Reciprocal Enforcement) Act 1933 and the Administration of Justice Act 1956, s.51.

[43] *i.e.* Belgium, Germany, France, Italy, Luxembourg, the Netherlands, Denmark, Ireland, the U.K., the Hellenic Republic, Spain and Portugal: Civil Jurisdiction and Judgments Act 1982, s.1(3) (as substituted by the Civil Jurisdiction and Judgments Act 1982 (Amendment) Order 1990 (S.I. 1990 No. 2591), Art. 6 and amended by the Civil Jurisdiction and Judgments Act 1991, s.2(5)).

[44] The full text of the Convention is set out in its amended form in *ibid.* Sched. 1 (as substituted by the Civil Jurisdiction and Judgments Act 1982 (Amendment) Order 1990 (S.I. 1990 No. 2591), Sched. 1).

[45] *Ibid.* s.43 (as amended by the Civil Jurisdiction and Judgments Act 1991, Sched. 2, para. 18), Sched. 1, Title II, Art. 16(2) (as substituted by the Civil Jurisdiction and Judgments Act 1982 (Amendment) Order 1990, Sched. 1), Sched. 4, Arts. 5A, 16(2).

[46] As to judgments obtained without notice to the defendant, note the decision in *E.M.I. Record Ltd. v. Modern Music Karl-Ulrich Walterbach G.m.b.H.* [1992] 1 Q.B. 115.

[47] See *supra*, para. 10-232.

C. GROUNDS FOR DISSOLUTION

Overriding discretion of court

In his Supplement on the Partnership Act 1890, Lord Lindley **24–48** stressed the discretionary nature of the court's power to order a dissolution under the Act:

"The Court has a wide discretion given to it, and though in exercising that discretion it will no doubt follow the principle of previous decisions, it must not be forgotten that the Court has a discretion and will not be bound to dissolve a partnership *ex debito justitiae* in any of the cases mentioned in [*section 35 of the Act*]."

The same comment is equally applicable to the power conferred on the Court of Protection under the Mental Health Act 1983.

(a) Mental Disorder

Effect of Mental Health Acts 1959 and 1983

Prior to the Mental Health Act 1959, the Chancery Division of the **24–49** High Court had concurrent jurisdiction with the Judge in Lunacy to order the dissolution of a partnership where one or more of its members became of unsound mind.[48] However, the 1959 Act removed that jurisdiction from the Chancery Division, and the sole jurisdiction in such cases is now, by the Mental Health Act 1983,[49] conferred exclusively on the "judge," which expression in fact includes all the Chancery judges as "nominated judges."[50]

Under section 96(1)(g) of the 1983 Act[51] the judge has power to make orders or give directions or authorities for the dissolution of any partnership of which a "patient" is a member.[52] A "patient" is, for this purpose, a person as to whom the judge is satisfied, after considering medical evidence, that he is incapable, by reason of mental disorder, of managing and administering his property and affairs.[53]

---

[48] Partnership Act 1890, s.35(a); Lunacy Act 1890, s.119. It may be noted that the concurrent jurisdiction was somewhat theoretical, since in practice all the Chancery judges were also the Judges in Lunacy.

[49] s.94(1) (as amended by the Public Trustee and Administration of Funds Act 1986, s.2(2)).

[50] *Ibid.* ss.93(1), 94(1) (as amended).

[51] See *supra*, para. 24–40.

[52] It is pointed out in Heywood & Massey, *Court of Protection Practice* (12th ed.), p. 228, n.24, that the normal practice is to authorise the patient's receiver to take the necessary formal steps to dissolve the partnership. This, of course, presupposes the existence of a partnership at will or the inclusion of an express power to dissolve in the agreement. For present purposes it is, of course assumed that there is *no* such power.

[53] Mental Health Act 1983, s.94(2).

Exercise of discretion

24–50   In exercising the power to order a dissolution, the judge must first consider all the patient's requirements; the interests of his creditors are of secondary importance.[54] Moreover, it appears that, in practice, a dissolution will only be ordered where a receiver has already been appointed for the patient[55] and there are no disputes under the partnership agreement, whether as to accounts or otherwise.[56] If those conditions are not satisfied, an order will have to be sought under section 35 of the Partnership Act 1890.[57]

Relevance of old law

24–51   It is doubtful whether the principles adopted by the Chancery Court prior to the Mental Health Act 1959 are of any continuing relevance under the 1983 Act.[58] It may, however, be noted that, under the old lunacy laws, a dissolution would be ordered both for the protection of the lunatic[59] and to relieve his co-partners from the difficult position in which they were placed.[60] In one case,[61] the court ordered a dissolution on the application of one partner, even though the incapacitated partner's representatives had made a cross application for the appointment of a manager, on the ground that the affairs of the partnership could be carried on to the advantage of all parties, notwithstanding such incapacity.[62] Equally, the other partners did not have to apply for a dissolution: if they preferred to wait and see whether the incapacity was temporary or permanent, the partnership would continue.[63]

In the absence of any authority, the current editor submits that a broadly similar approach is likely to be adopted under the present law, subject to the primary obligation of the judge to have regard to the patient's requirements.[64]

---

[54] *Ibid.* s.95(2).

[55] As to the court's power to appoint a receiver, see *ibid.* s.99.

[56] Heywood & Massey, *Court of Protection Practice* (12th ed.), p. 228.

[57] *i.e.* on the ground of the patient's permanent incapacity (*ibid.* s.35(b)) or on the "just and equitable" ground (*ibid.* s.35(f)). See *infra*, paras. 24–55, 24–75.

[58] It is perhaps significant that no reference is made to the old cases in Heywood & Massey, *Court of Protection Practice* (12th ed.), pp. 228, 229.

[59] *Jones v. Lloyd* (1874) L.R. 18 Eq. 265.

[60] See *Wrexham v. Hudleston* (1734) 1 Swan. 514, note; *Sayer v. Bennet* (1784) 1 Cox 107; *Jones v. Noy* (1833) 2 M. & K. 125; *Sadler v. Lee* (1843) 6 Beav. 324; *Leaf v. Coles* (1851) 1 De G.M. & G. 171; *Anon.* (1856) 2 K. & J. 441; also *Waters v. Taylor* (1813) 2 V. & B. 299, 303, *per* Lord Eldon.

[61] *Rowlands v. Evans* (1861) 30 Beav. 302.

[62] The partnership property was ordered to be sold as a going concern, with liberty to all parties to bid, and a receiver and manager was appointed pending sale.

[63] *Jones v. Noy* (1833) 2 M. & K. 125.

[64] Mental Health Act 1983, s.95(2), *supra*, para. 24–40.

Dormant partner

If the patient is in fact a dormant partner, his incapacity is unlikely **24–52** to have any appreciable effect on his status within the firm.[65] In those circumstances, it is thought that a dissolution will not normally be ordered, unless the judge considers it to be in the patient's interests to realise his share and/or to be freed from any continuing liability for the firm's debts and obligations.

Date of dissolution

It is submitted that, as under the old law, if the judge orders a **24–53** dissolution, he will declare the partnership dissolved as from the date judgment is delivered and not from some earlier date.[66] If, however, the order merely authorises the patient's receiver to take some formal step to terminate the partnership, the dissolution will inevitably occur on a subsequent date.

Costs

When the court dissolves a partnership on the ground of a partner's **24–54** mental disorder, it will direct the costs to be paid out of the partnership assets.[67]

(b) Permanent Incapacity[68]

Mental incapacity

Prior to the Partnership Act 1890, a dissolution could be ordered **24–55** where a partner was of unsound mind, on the grounds that he had become permanently incapable of performing his duties as a partner. Thus, in *Jones v. Noy*,[69] Sir John Leach M.R. observed:

"It is clear upon principle that the complete incapacity of a party to an agreement to perform that which was a condition of the

---

[65] See *supra*, para. 13–38.

[66] *Besch v. Frolich* (1842) 1 Ph. 172. See also *Sander v. Sander* (1845) 2 Coll. 276; *Jones v. Welch* (1855) 1 K. & J. 765 (although it is not clear from the reports whether these cases involved partnerships at will). Of course, the dissolution may have occurred at some earlier date, *e.g.* by the service of notice under the partnership agreement or under the Partnership Act 1890, s.26(1) and/or 32(c): see *Robertson v. Lockie* (1846) 15 Sim. 285; *Bagshaw v. Parker* (1847) 10 Beav. 532; *Mellersh v. Keen* (1859) 27 Beav. 236; also *supra*, paras. 10–113, 24–19. Lord Lindley observed "It was probably on the ground that a partnership at will is determinable on notice, that in *Kirby v. Carr* (1838) 3 Y. & C.Ex. 184 the dissolution was decreed as from the filing of the bill, no previous notice having been given." See also *Shepherd v. Allen* (1864) 33 Beav. 577 and *infra*, para. 24–78.

[67] *Jones v. Welch* (1855) 1 K. & J. 765.

[68] Partnership Act 1890, s.35(b), *supra*, para. 24–39.

[69] (1833) 2 M. & K. 125, 129–130.

agreement is a ground for determining the contract. The insanity of a partner is a ground for the dissolution of the partnership, because it is immediate incapacity; but it may not in the result prove to be a ground of dissolution, for the partner may recover from his malady."

This is still the position, in those cases in which the Court of Protection declines to order a dissolution.[70]

Other forms of incapacity

24–56   Although mental incapacity is the most obvious illustration of this ground, it is clear that any other form of incapacity will suffice, provided that it appears to the court to be permanent at the date of trial. In the case of a physical incapacity, medical evidence will almost invariably be required. In *Whitwell v. Arthur*[71] one of two partners was unable to perform his duties as a partner following an attack of paralysis but the medical evidence showed that his health was improving and a probability that the incapacity was only of a temporary nature. On that basis a dissolution was refused. Although this would seem to militate in favour of an early application to the court, unseemly haste would be counter-productive; the current editor suggests that, save in the clearest of cases, time should normally be allowed for the relevant condition to stabilise.

Partial incapacity

24–57   A dissolution can only be obtained if the partner is "incapable of performing his part of the partnership contract."[72] Whilst this will not generally be in doubt in the case of *total* mental or physical incapacity, the position may be less clear where a partner is only able to perform some, but not all, of his duties. It is, nevertheless, submitted that a partial incapacity of this type should suffice, subject to an application of the normal *de minimis* principle.[73]

On the other hand, it is not enough to prove an overall reduction in a partner's capacity, which merely causes him to perform his duties in a way that his co-partners consider unsatisfactory.[74]

---

[70] See *supra*, para. 24–50.

[71] (1865) 35 Beav. 140.

[72] See Partnership Act 1890, s.35(b), *supra*, para. 24–39.

[73] Although there is no authority for the view put forward in the text, any other result would hold the partners to a bargain different from the one that they originally made; *cf. Peyton v. Mindham* [1972] 1 W.L.R. 8. However, in practice the point is largely academic, given that a dissolution could be sought on the "just and equitable" ground: see the Partnership Act 1890, s.35(f), *supra*, para. 24–39 and *infra*, para. 24–75.

[74] *Sadler v. Lee* (1843) 6 Beav. 324.

Who may seek dissolution

The incapacitated partner may not himself apply for a dissolution **24–58** on this ground, so that any proceedings must be brought by one or more of his co-partners.[75]

(c) Conduct Injurious to the Partnership Business[76]

In deciding whether a partner's conduct is "calculated to prejudicially **24–59** affect the carrying on of the [*partnership*] business," the court is required to form an essentially subjective view,[77] having regard to the precise nature of the business concerned. This, coupled with the absence of any reported cases, makes the formulation of general propositions somewhat difficult.

Criminal conduct

The current editor submits that the commission of a criminal act of **24–60** a violent or dishonest nature would prima facie have an adverse effect on any type of business, given the risk of prosecution and its attendant publicity. Thus it was held, prior to the Partnership Act 1890, that a partnership should stand dissolved where one partner had rendered himself liable to prosecution by committing a fraudulent breach of trust.[78] On the other hand, the commission of a minor road traffic offence would clearly be ignored.

Immoral behaviour

The effect of sexual promiscuity and other forms of immoral **24–61** conduct will vary according to the nature of the business carried on. Although it will be of little concern in the case of a trading partnership,[79] the same cannot be said of partnerships in the medical and allied professions, where the integrity of the practitioner/patient relationship is paramount.[80] In one old case, which was not fully reported but mentioned in argument before Page Wood V.-C., a partnership between *accoucheurs* (male midwives) appears to have

---

[75] Partnership Act 1890, s.35(b), *supra*, para. 24–39.

[76] *Ibid.* s.35(c), *supra*, para. 24–39.

[77] This is emphasised by the words "in the opinion of the court": see also *supra*, para. 24–48.

[78] *Essel v. Hayward* (1860) 30 Beav. 158 (where, in fact, a notice to dissolve had been given, even though the partnership was not at will). See also *Carmichael v. Evans* [1904] 1 Ch. 486, noticed *supra*, para. 10–96.

[79] See *Snow v. Milford* (1868) 16 W.R. 554, which concerned a banking firm.

[80] See the General Medical Council's booklet "Professional Conduct and Fitness to Practise" (December 1993), paras. 68 *et seq.*, reproduced in the *Encyclopedia of Professional Partnerships*, Pt. 5; also the General Dental Council's Notice for the Guidance of Dentists on Professional Conduct and Fitness to Practise (May 1993), paras. 16 *et seq.*, reproduced in *ibid.* Pt. 4.

been dissolved on the ground of one partner's immoral conduct.[81] An affair between a doctor and his (or her) patient would unquestionably have an adverse effect on the partnership practice, since it would involve professional misconduct.[82] On the other hand, it is submitted that sexual conduct *outside* the practice would have to be of a well publicised or exaggerated nature before a dissolution could be obtained.

Professional misconduct

24-62   In the case of a professional firm, anything which amounts to professional misconduct must *ipso facto* be capable of having a prejudicial effect on the partnership business.[83]

Conduct unconnected with the business

24-63   It will already be apparent that the conduct complained of need not, as such, be connected with the partnership business, provided that it is capable of injuring it.[84]

Guilt and intent

24-64   It must be shown that the partner is "guilty" of the conduct complained of: this obviously does not connote criminal guilt, but rather an element of intent, as Lord Lindley explained in his Supplement on the Partnership Act 1890:

> "This expression implies voluntary action, and an attempt by one partner to commit suicide while suffering from temporary insanity[85] would not justify a dissolution under this clause, even if such conduct would otherwise be within it."[86]

A more difficult question is whether the use of the word "calculated" implies the existence of a positive *intention* to injure the

---

[81] *Anon.* (1856) 2 K. & J. 441, 446. The Vice-Chancellor reportedly observed "In such a case, immoral conduct would materially affect the particular business of the firm." However, in his Supplement on the Partnership Act 1890, Lord Lindley questioned whether the Vice-Chancellor would have granted a dissolution on this ground, referring to *ibid.* pp.452, 453.

[82] See *Goodman v. Sinclair, The Times*, January 24, 1951, where Vaisey J. held the partner to be guilty of flagrantly immoral conduct, thus entitling his co-partner to dissolve under an express power in the agreement.

[83] See for example, *Clifford v. Timms* [1908] A.C. 12; also *supra*, para. 24-37.

[84] *Pearce v. Foster* (1886) 17 Q.B.D. 536 (a case concerning an employee speculating in "differences" on the Stock Exchange). See also *Carmichael v. Evans* [1904] 1 Ch. 486, noticed *supra*, para. 10-96.

[85] *Anon* (1856) 2 K. & J. 441; see also *supra*, para. 24-61, n. 81.

[86] See also *Anderson v. Kydd*, 1991 G.W.D. 11-670.

business or merely a likelihood of injury. The current editor submits that the latter interpretation is to be preferred.[87]

Who may seek dissolution

A partner seeking a dissolution on this ground must be innocent of **24–65** any misconduct of the type discussed above.[88]

(d) Breach of Agreement and Destruction of Mutual Confidence[89]

This ground in fact comprises two wholly separate limbs, *i.e.*: **24–66**

(i) a wilful or persistent breach of the partnership agreement; and
(ii) conduct in relation to the partnership business which makes the continuation of that business impracticable.[90]

In his Supplement on the Partnership Act 1890, Lord Lindley noted that this accorded with the previous law, although it is submitted that the two limbs were then less distinct.[91]

Reluctance of court to interfere

Writing prior to the 1890 Act, Lord Lindley explained that the **24–67** court will not readily become embroiled in trivial differences between partners:

"... it is not considered to be the duty of the Court to enter into partnership squabbles, and it will not dissolve a partnership on the

---

[87] Such an interpretation has been adopted in a number of statutory contexts: see, for example, *North Cheshire & Manchester Brewery Co. Ltd. v. Manchester Brewery Co. Ltd.* [1899] A.C. 83, 86, *per* Lord Halsbury L.C.; *British Vacuum Cleaner Co. Ltd. v. New Vacuum Cleaner Co. Ltd.* [1907] 2 Ch. 313, 320, *per* Parker J. (both decisions under the Companies Act 1862, s.20); *R. v. Davison* [1972] 1 W.L.R. 1540 (a decision under the House to House Collections Act 1939, s.5); *Turner v. Shearer* [1973] 1 W.L.R. 1387 (a decision under the Police Act 1964, s.52). *Cf. Re Registered Trade-Marks of Bass, Ratcliffe & Gretton Ltd.* [1902] 2 Ch. 579; *Re Maeder's Trade Mark Application* [1916] 1 Ch. 304 (a decision under the Trade Marks Act 1905, ss.11, 19). See also *Stroud's Judicial Dictionary* (5th ed.), Vol. 1, p. 342; *Words and Phrases Legally Defined* (3rd ed.), Vol. 1, pp. 211, 212. Alternatively, the word might be construed in such a way as to require merely an element of wilfulness or recklessness, *i.e.* a realisation or conscious disregard of the potential injury to the business.
[88] Partnership Act, s.35(c), *supra*, para. 24–39.
[89] *Ibid.* s.35(d), *supra*, para. 24–39.
[90] It is considered that, on a true construction of *ibid.* s.35(d), it is not necessary to show a practical impossibility of continuing the business under limb (a), although this view is, for example, advanced in *Miller's Partnership*, p. 467 (dealing with Scots law).
[91] See *Charlton v. Poulter* (1753) 19 Ves.Jr. 148, note; *Waters v. Taylor* (1813) 2 V. & B. 299; *Marshall v. Colman* (1820) 2 J. & W. 266; *Smith v. Jeyes* (1841) 4 Beav. 503; *Harrison v. Tennant* (1856) 21 Beav. 482, *infra*, para. 24–70. Note, however, that the test under limb (b) is whether it is "reasonably practicable" for the other partners to carry on the business with the partner whose conduct is in question, whereas Lord Lindley referred to the partners' mutual confidence being "utterly" destroyed: see *infra*, para. 24–67, n. 93.

ground of the ill-temper or misconduct of one or more of the partners, unless the others are in effect excluded from the concern[92]; or unless the misconduct is of such a nature as ... to destroy[93] the mutual confidence which must subsist between partners if they are to continue to carry on their business together."[94]

24-68   Although the discretion conferred on the court is now arguably wider than when Lord Lindley wrote the above passage,[95] the general reluctance to which he referred is still likely to persist, so that partners should be wary of over-exaggerating the consequences of a minor difference of opinion or breach of the agreement.[96] Equally, little sympathy is likely to be extended to a partner who is intent on flouting the terms of the agreement, even in relatively unimportant respects.

Nature and degree of misconduct

24-69   Lord Lindley, again writing prior to the Partnership Act 1890, pointed out that, where a dissolution is sought on the grounds of a partner's misconduct,

"... it would seem that the misconduct must be such as to affect the business, not merely by shaking its credit in the eyes of the world, but by rendering it impossible for the partners to conduct their business together according to the agreement into which they have entered."[97]

The current editor considers that this passage may have become accidentally misplaced between the 5th and 6th editions of this work, since it is clearly more apposite to the previous ground.[98] Lord Lindley cannot properly be taken to have suggested that the court's discretion is limited to those cases in which a partner's conduct adversely affects the public image of the firm, thus penalising

---

[92] See *Goodman v. Whitcomb* (1820) 1 Jac. & W. 589; *Marshall v. Colman* (1820) 2 Jac. & W. 266; *Wray v. Hutchinson* (1834) 2 M. & K. 235; *Roberts v. Eberhardt* (1853) Kay 148. See also *Re Davis and Collett Ltd.* [1935] Ch. 693; *Re Lundie Brothers* [1965] 1 W.L.R. 1051.

[93] The original text in fact read "utterly to destroy"; however, the word "utterly" was expunged in the 6th ed. of this work.

[94] See *Smith v. Jeyes* (1841) 4 Beav. 503; *Harrison v. Tennant* (1856) 21 Beav. 482, *infra*, para. 24–70. The remainder of this passage is reproduced *infra*, at the beginning of para. 24–69.

[95] See *supra*, para. 24–66, n. 91.

[96] See *Goodman v. Whitcomb* (1820) 1 Jac. & W. 589, 592, *per* Lord Eldon; *Loscombe v. Russell* (1830) 4 Sim. 8, 11, *per* Shadwell V.-C.; *Anderson v. Anderson* (1857) 25 Beav. 190.

[97] See *Anon.* (1856) 2 K. & J. 441: noticed *supra*, para. 24–61.

[98] See *supra*, paras. 24–59 *et seq.*

partners for their ability to mask internal strife from the public gaze. Indeed, he himself went on to observe:

"It is not necessary, in order to induce the court to interfere, to show personal rudeness on the part of one partner to the other, or even any gross misconduct as a partner. All that is necessary is to satisfy the court that it is impossible for the partners to place that confidence in each other which each has a right to expect, and that such impossibility has not been caused by the person seeking to take advantage of it."[99]

A clear (but somewhat unusual) example of the type of misconduct **24–70** required is to be found in *Harrison v. Tennant*.[1] There A, B and C carried on practice as solicitors in partnership, in succession to the practice formerly carried on by A and B. Proceedings were commenced against A and B in respect of the conduct of that former practice and involved allegations of gross misconduct and fraud against A. Against B and C's express wishes, A placed himself on the record instead of the firm and put in his own defence to the proceedings without consulting them.[1a] B and C accordingly sought a dissolution, which A attempted to resist, arguing that he was not guilty of any misconduct towards his co-partners in relation to the partnership business nor of any breach of the partnership agreement. However, a dissolution was ordered, on the grounds that:

(1) mutual confidence had, not unreasonably, ceased;
(2) the business could no longer be carried on in the way the partners had originally contemplated; and
(3) although there had not as yet been any open conflict between the partners, continuation of the partnership would make this inevitable, to the detriment of them all.

What is in essence required is conduct which leads to a serious and **24–71** irretrievable breakdown in the relationship between the partners. A physical assault by one partner on another, even if provoked, would undoubtedly justify a dissolution,[2] as would a groundless accusation

---

[99] See *Re Yenidje Tobacco Co. Ltd.* [1916] 2 Ch. 426, 430, where this passage was cited with approval by Cozens-Hardy M.R. See also *Re Davis and Collett Ltd.* [1935] Ch. 693; *Ebrahimi v. Westbourne Galleries Ltd.* [1973] A.C. 360; and note *Jesner v. Jarrad Properties Ltd.*, *The Times*, October 26, 1992; 1992 G.W.D. 31–1797.

[1] (1856) 21 Beav. 482.

[1a] As to the extent of a partner's implied authority to defend actions brought against the firm, see *supra*, paras. 12–35, 14–72.

[2] See *Greenaway v. Greenaway* (1940) 84 S.J. 43, which in fact concerned an expulsion under an express power.

of fraud,[3] use of partnership money for private purposes[4] or failure to account to the firm for sums received on its behalf.[5] Conduct which disrupts the running of the partnership business may be sufficient, *e.g.* a refusal to attend meetings with the other partners.[6] Moreover, even a relatively trifling argument precipitated by one partner may cause such hostility to develop between the partners that a continuation of the partnership is no longer possible; indeed, Lord Lindley specifically referred to the following as possible grounds for a dissolution[7]:

"... continued quarrelling, and such a state of animosity as precludes all reasonable hope of reconciliation and friendly co-operation ...".

It is the current editor's view that the service of an invalid expulsion or dissolution notice under an express power in the agreement may, in itself, give the recipient partner(s) grounds to seek a dissolution under this head, provided that their own behaviour has not invited the service of that notice.[7a]

Misconduct with a view to dissolution

24–72   Lord Lindley pointed out that:

"... the Court will never permit a partner, by misconducting himself and rendering it impossible for his partners to act in harmony with him, to obtain a dissolution on the ground of the impossibility so created by himself."[8]

This is still, in theory, the position.[9] However, if injunctive or other relief cannot, for whatever reason, be obtained,[10] the other partners may in practice have no option other than to apply for a dissolution, even though this is precisely what the miscreant partner had

---

[3] *Leary v. Shout* (1864) 33 Beav. 582; *Re Yenidje Tobacco Co. Ltd.* [1916] 2 Ch. 426, 431, *per* Cozens-Hardy M.R.

[4] See *Smith v. Jeyes* (1841) 4 Beav. 502.

[5] *Cheeseman v. Price* (1865) 35 Beav. 142.

[6] *De Berenger v. Hammel* (1829) 7 Jar.Byth, 3rd ed., 83.

[7] *Baxter v. West* (1858) 1 Dr. & Sm. 173; *Watney v. Wells* (1861) 30 Beav. 56; *Pease v. Hewitt* (1862) 31 Beav. 22; *Leary v. Shout* (1864) 33 Beav. 582.

[7a] Where the recipients' behaviour *has* invited expulsion, a dissolution could still, in theory, be sought under the Partnership Act 1980, s.35(f), *infra.* paras. 24–75 *et seq.*

[8] See *Harrison v. Tennant* (1856) 21 Beav. 482, 493–494, *per* Sir John Romilly M.R.; *Fairthorne v. Weston* (1844) 3 Hare 387.

[9] See the Partnership Act 1890, s.35(d), *supra*, para. 24–39.

[10] See *supra*, paras. 23–130 *et seq.*

intended; the court clearly cannot authorise that partner's expulsion in the absence of an express power in the agreement.[11]

Who may seek dissolution

It follows from the previous paragraph that only the innocent partners may apply for a dissolution on this ground.[12]

(e) Partnership Business Carried on at a Loss[13]

Partnership being "the relation which subsists between persons **24–73** carrying on a business in common with a view of profit,"[14] the expectation of profit must be implied in every partnership.[15] It is thus a natural consequence that the court may dissolve a partnership where that expectation no longer exists and the business can only be carried on at a loss.[16]

It was on this basis that a dissolution was ordered in *Jennings v. Baddeley*,[17] where the partnership capital had been exhausted and the business could only have continued to make a profit if the partners contributed further funds, which some of them were unable or unwilling to do. Lord Lindley observed of this case:

"Under such circumstances as these it is unimportant whether the concern is already embarrassed or not. After everything has been done which was agreed to be done, and certain loss is the only result of going on, any partner is entitled to have the concern dissolved . . .".

The same theme was developed by Farwell J. in *Handyside v. Campbell*,[18] where he expressed the view that a dissolution on this ground would only be ordered where it could be proved that there was a practical *impossibility* of profit; such an impossibility would not be inferred where the losses could be attributed to special circumstances, rather than to an inherent defect in the business itself.

---

[11] See *infra*, paras. 24–84 *et seq*. Note, however, the jurisdiction of the court to make a *Syers v. Syers* order: see *supra*, para. 23–182.

[12] Partnership Act 1890, s.35(d), *supra*, para. 24–39.

[13] *Ibid*. s.35(e), *supra*, para. 24–39.

[14] *Ibid*. s.1, *supra*, paras. 2–01 *et seq*.

[15] See *Jennings v. Baddeley* (1856) 3 K. & J. 78, 83, *per* Page Wood V.-C.

[16] This was well established prior to the Partnership Act 1890: *Baring v. Dix* (1786) 1 Cox 213; *Bailey v. Ford* (1843) 13 Sim. 495; *Jennings v. Baddeley*, *supra*. See also *Re Suburban Hotel Co.* (1867) 2 Ch.App. 732, 744–745, *per* Laing L.J.; *Wilson v. Church* (1879) 13 Ch.D. 1, 65, *per* Cotton L.J. As to the position where there is *no* business to be carried on (whether at a loss or otherwise), see *supra*, para. 24–38.

[17] (1856) 3 K. & J. 78, which concerned a mining partnership.

[18] [1901] 17 T.L.R. 623, 624. See also *Janson v. McMullen* [1922] N.Z.L.R. 677. *Cf. Wilson v. Church* (1879) 13 Ch.D. 1, 65, where Cotton L.J. referred to the court's willingness to order a dissolution where "the purposes of the partnership cannot be carried into effect with any *reasonable prospect* of profit" (emphasis supplied). And note *Re A Company, ex p. Burr* [1992] BCLC 724 (a decision under the Companies Act 1985, s.459).

Insolvency

24-74   A dissolution on this ground is not dependent on proof of actual insolvency; indeed, the partners would risk disqualification orders by carrying on the business knowing it to be insolvent.[19] If a partner is not himself in a position to present a winding-up petition against the firm,[20] the court may, in a clear case, be prepared to intervene on motion, as Lord Lindley explained:

> "If ... the firm is already insolvent and becomes more and more so every day, the court will interfere on motion, and appoint a person to sell the business and wind up the affairs of the partnership, although it is not usual to grant such relief until the hearing of the cause."[21]

(f)   The Just and Equitable Ground[22]

24-75 This represents the final "catch all" ground on which a court may order a dissolution. It will not be construed *ejusdem generis* with the grounds which precede it in section 35 of the Partnership Act 1890,[23] nor will the court tie itself down to any rigid rules governing its application.[24] Nevertheless, it is apprehended that, as was the position prior to the Act,[25] an order is likely to be made if, for whatever reason, the objects for which the partnership was formed can no longer be attained, either at all or in the manner originally contemplated by the partners, and a dissolution cannot be obtained on one of the other grounds.[26] In the exercise of its discretion, the

---

[19] Insolvency Act 1986, s.214; Company Directors Disqualification Act 1986, s.10, as applied by the Insolvent Partnerships Order 1986, Art. 6. See further, *infra*, para. 27–64.

[20] See *infra*, paras. 27–14, 27–32.

[21] *Bailey v. Ford* (1843) 13 Sim. 495; and see *Heywood v. B.D.C. Properties* [1963] 1 W.L.R. 975.

[22] Partnership Act, s.35(f), *supra*, para. 24–39.

[23] See *Re Yenidje Tobacco Co.* [1916] 2 Ch. 426, 432 (*per* Cozens-Hardy M.R.), 435 (*per* Warrington L.J.); also *Re Amalgamated Syndicate* [1897] 2 Ch. 600; *Loch v. John Blackwood Ltd.* [1924] A.C. 783.

[24] See *Re Yenidje Tobacco Co.*, *supra*; *Ebrahimi v. Westbourne Galleries Ltd.* [1973] A.C. 360 and the cases there cited. Note, however, that in *Harrison v. Povey* (1956) 168 E.G. 613 the Court of Appeal expressed the view that, in order to justify a dissolution on this ground, a breach "going to the root of the agreement" would have to be shown by the plaintiff. *Semble*, the court will not permit a partner to justify a dissolution by reference to extraneous considerations which will only be of benefit to himself, *e.g.* where a property-owning partner wishes to dissolve his firm in order to recover vacant possession: see *J.E. Cade & Son Ltd.* [1991] BCC 360.

[25] See generally, *Harrison v. Tennant* (1856) 21 Beav. 482; *Baring v. Dix* (1786) 1 Cox 213. See also *supra*, para. 24–70.

[26] This is a new formulation of principle. Writing in his Supplement on the Partnership Act 1890, Lord Lindley put it in this way: "Any case ... in which it is no longer reasonably practicable to carry out the partnership contract according to its terms will, it is apprehended, be within this section." In later editions (including the 15th), this was expanded to read "... any case in which it is no longer reasonably practicable to attain the object with a view to which the partnership was entered into or to carry out the partnership contract according to its terms will, it is apprehended, be within this section."

court will inevitably take the provisions of the partnership agreement into account, but will obviously not be bound thereby.[27]

Although there is no bar on a partner who is guilty of misconduct **24-76** applying for a dissolution on this ground,[28] an order is unlikely to be made in his favour.[29] However, in practice, the very fact that such an application is made, and the other partners' response to it, may lead, directly or indirectly, to an irresistible inference that mutual trust and confidence has been destroyed.[30] This element of circularity may render the outcome of an apparently straightforward dissolution action less than certain.

Once an application has been made by one partner, the court may be reluctant to entertain another partner's application for a stay, with a view to the question being referred to arbitration.[31]

Assignment of share

Although Lord Lindley was much vexed by the question whether **24-77** the assignment of a partner's share would work a dissolution,[32] the current editor submits that, since the Partnership Act 1890 itself recognises the validity of such an assignment[33] and does not specify it as a ground of dissolution,[34] the point is now virtually unarguable. Indeed, Buckley J. clearly did not countenance such a possibility in *Re Garwood's Trusts*.[35] Admittedly, an assignment might justify the other partners seeking a dissolution on this or some other ground[36] but, unless it involved a deliberate breach of the agreement,[37] exceptional circumstances would need to be shown before the court would be prepared to make an order. On any footing, the assignee could not himself make the application.[38]

It will, however, be recalled that if a charging order is made on a partner's share, the other partners will normally have the *option* to dissolve the partnership without involving the court.[39]

---

[27] *Re American Pioneer Leather Co. Ltd.* [1918] 1 Ch. 556 (a company case).

[28] *Cf.* the Partnership Act 1890, s.35(b)–(d), *supra*, para. 24–39.

[29] See *Harrison v. Tennant* (1856) 21 Beav. 482, 493–494, *per* Sir John Romilly M.R.; *cf. Fairthorne v. Weston* (1844) 3 Hare 387. And see *supra*, para. 24–72.

[30] See *supra*, paras. 24–66 *et seq.*

[31] See *Olver v. Hillier* [1959] 1 W.L.R. 551. And see *supra*, para. 10–232.

[32] For a summary of Lord Lindley's views, see the 15th ed. of this work at pp. 707, 708.

[33] *Ibid.* s.31: see *supra*, paras. 19–59 *et seq.*

[34] *Ibid.* s.35, *supra*, para. 24–39; see also *ibid.* s.33(2), *supra*, para. 24–29.

[35] [1903] 1 Ch. 236, 239. See also *Campbell v. Campbell* (1893) 6 R. 137 (which concerned the construction of an express clause in the agreement). But note the terms of the Partnership Act 1890, s.46; see *Sturgeon v. Salmon* (1906) 22 T.L.R. 584; *Emanuel v. Symon* [1907] 1 K.B. 235, 241–242, *per* Channell J. (the actual decision being reversed at [1908] 1 K.B. 302).

[36] *e.g.* under the Partnership Act 1890, s.35(c) or (d), *supra*, paras. 24–59 *et seq.*, 24–66 *et seq.* See also *Pollock on Partnership* (15th ed.), p. 77.

[37] *Ibid.* s.35(d).

[38] *Ibid.* ss.31, 35.

[39] *Ibid.* s.33(2), *supra*, para. 24–29.

D. DATE OF DISSOLUTION

24–78 Section 35 of the Partnership Act 1890 does not specify the date on which the partnership will stand dissolved; accordingly the old law still applies, as Lord Lindley noted in his Supplement on the Act:

> "The rule ... was, and still is,[40] that where the order of the Court is necessary for the dissolution of the partnership, the dissolution will, in the absence of special reasons, date from the judgment."[41]

The position where a partnership is dissolved by the Court of Protection has already been noted.[42]

The court can, of course, declare a partnership dissolved with effect from a date earlier than the date of judgment where the dissolution resulted from the service of a notice[43] or the occurrence of some other determining event specified in the Act or in the agreement.[44] Although there is one New Zealand authority which *appears* to be authority for the proposition that the court can order a dissolution retrospectively,[45] the partnership was at will and was clearly dissolved by the service of the writ.[46] If the decision went any further than merely recognising this, it was, in the current editor's view, *per incuriam.*[47]

4. THE RIGHT TO RETIRE

Lord Lindley's rules on retirement

24–79   Writing prior to the Partnership Act 1890, Lord Lindley formulated the following three rules, which still accurately summarise the position under the Act:

1. "... it is competent for a partner to retire with the consent of his co-partners at any time and upon any terms."
2. "... it is competent for him to retire without their consent by dissolving the firm, if he is in a position to dissolve it."
3. "... it is not competent for a partner to retire from a partnership which he cannot dissolve, and from which his co-partners are not willing that he should retire."

---

[40] See *ibid.* s.46.

[41] *Lyon v. Tweddell* (1881) 17 Ch.D. 529; *Besch v. Frolich* (1842) 1 Ph. 172; but see *Essell v. Hayward* (1860) 30 Beav. 158 (which can, however, no longer be regarded as good law as regards the date of dissolution).

[42] See *supra*, para. 24–53.

[43] See *supra*, paras. 10–113 *et seq.*, 24–10 *et seq.* And see *supra*, para. 24–53, n. 66.

[44] See generally *supra*, paras. 24–07 *et seq.*

[45] *Phillips v. Melville* [1921] N.Z.L.R. 571.

[46] *Ibid.* pp. 573, 574, *per* Cooper J.

[47] Cooper J. purported to follow the decision in *Unsworth v. Jordan* [1896] W.N. 2(5), which was clearly a case involving a partnership at will.

To rule 1 must be added the obvious rider that such consent may be granted prospectively, by the inclusion of an express right to retire in the partnership agreement.[48]

Position where no power to retire

Partnership at will

It follows that if a partner decides to retire from a partnership at **24–80** will, his departure will cause a *general* dissolution of the firm,[49] unless by the act of retiring he can be taken to have forfeited his right to force a sale of the partnership assets, etc. in exchange for a right to be paid out the market value of his share as at the date of his "retirement."[50]

Partnership for a term

On the other hand, if the partnership is for a fixed term, a partner **24–81** who has no right to retire[51] will be effectively "locked into" the firm and, if his co-partners are unwilling to negotiate terms for his departure, his only legitimate option may be to seek a dissolution from the court under section 35 of the Partnership Act 1890.[52] The consequences of any partner actively seeking grounds to dissolve are too obvious to require comment.[53]

If the frustrated partner chooses to ignore his legal obligations and merely walks out of the partnership, the other partners will have a number of courses open to them, *i.e.* they may:

(a) treat the recalcitrant partner's actions as a repudiatory breach of the agreement, which they accept;[54]

(b) apply for a dissolution of the partnership;[55]

(c) seek injunctive relief;[56]

(d) continue to treat the recalcitrant partner as a member of the firm,[57] but force him to account for any profits he may make

---

[48] See *supra*, paras. 10–88 *et seq.*

[49] See, as to the meaning of this expression, *supra*, para. 24–03.

[50] See *Sobell v. Boston* [1975] 1 W.L.R. 1587. See also *supra*, paras. 19–12, 23–180.

[51] The position may be no different where the right to retire is restricted, *e.g.* by reference to age or period of notice: see also *supra*, paras. 10–88, 10–89, 10–93.

[52] This will, of course, result in a general dissolution: see, as to the implications for the other partners, the Partnership Act 1890, ss.39, 44; and see further *supra*, paras. 19–08 *et seq.*, 19–28 *et seq.*, 23–179 *et seq.* and *infra*, paras. 25–39 *et seq. Cf. Sobell v. Boston* [1975] 1 W.L.R. 1587.

[53] But see *supra*, paras. 23–137, 24–72 and *infra*, para. 24–86.

[54] See *Hitchman v. Crouch Butler Savage Associates* (1983) 80 L.S.Gaz. 550; also *supra*, para. 24–04.

[55] *i.e.* under the Partnership Act 1890, s.35(c), (d) and/or (f): see *supra*, paras. 24–59 *et seq.*, 24–75.

[56] See *England v. Curling* (1844) 8 Beav. 129 and *supra*, paras. 23–44, 23–130 *et seq.*

[57] It follows that he will still be entitled to his profit share; but see *Airey v. Borham* (1861) 29 Beav. 620, *supra*, para. 20–42.

elsewhere[58] and/or seek damages for breach of the partnership agreement;[59] or

(e)   attempt to negotiate terms.

24-82   Since courses (a) and (b) will merely achieve the freedom which the recalcitrant partner seeks and, at the same time, penalise the innocent partners, a combination of courses (c) and (d) should, in practice, be used as a prelude to a negotiated settlement. Theoretical remedies are of no real avail once a partner has determined to leave and the sooner that this is recognised by the other partners the better.

Although an express power of expulsion might be seen as the answer in cases of this sort,[60] particularly if its exercise will permit the other partners to acquire the recalcitrant partner's share on favourable terms, the firm will still be deprived of his services earlier than any partner had originally contemplated and, moreover, in circumstances which may even threaten the continued viability of its business.

Retirement from insolvent firm

24-83   Lord Lindley observed:

"... a partner desirous of retiring from an insolvent firm, is at perfect liberty to sell his interest in it for any sum the continuing partners think proper to give him; and a sale by him to them cannot be set aside or impeached as a fraud upon the creditors of the firm unless there be clear evidence *aliunde* of such fraud.[61] At the same time, the present share of a partner in an insolvent firm[62] is obviously less than nothing, whatever may be the amount of the capital brought in by him. Consequently a partner who retires from an insolvent firm, and withdraws from it a sum of money which he is pleased to call his share, is defrauding the creditors of the firm; and such a transaction cannot stand and may be impeached by the trustee in bankruptcy of the continuing firm."[63]

---

[58] See *supra*, paras. 16–08 *et seq.*

[59] See *supra*, paras. 23–195 *et seq.*

[60] See *supra*, paras. 10–94 *et seq.* and *infra*, paras. 24–84 *et seq.*

[61] See *Ex p. Birch* (1801) 2 Ves.Jr. 260, note; *Ex p. Peake* (1816) 1 Madd. 346; *Parker v. Ramsbottom* (1824) 3 B. & C. 257; *Ex p. Carpenter* (1826) Mont. & MacA. 1.

[62] Lord Lindley, referring to the definition of an insolvent firm in *Ex p. Carpenter* (1826) Mont. & MacA. 1, 5, *per* Sir John Leach M.R., stated that "An insolvent firm is one in which the joint assets are less than the joint liabilities. Such a firm is insolvent whatever the wealth of the individual partners composing it may be."

[63] See *Anderson v. Maltby* (1793) 2 Ves.Jr. 244; *Re Kemptner* (1869) L.R. 8 Eq. 286. It is immaterial that the agreement was binding as between the partners: *ibid.*; see also *Billiter v. Young* (1856) 6 E. & B. 1, 40, *per* Jervis C.J.

The current editor considers that the position will be no different under the new insolvency legislation, subject to the time limits within which transactions at an undervalue may be set aside;[64] since, however, the retired partner will in any event be liable as a contributory if the firm is wound up as an unregistered company,[65] the point is only likely to become critical if he is also insolvent, so that his own separate creditors are, in this respect, in direct competition with the joint creditors.[66]

Similar considerations will arise if a retiring partner relinquishes his share at an undervalue and *subsequently* becomes insolvent.[67]

5. THE RIGHT TO EXPEL

The general principle

Prior to the Partnership Act 1890, Lord Lindley wrote: **24–84**

"In the absence of an express agreement to that effect, there is no right on the part of the members of a partnership to expel any other member. Nor, in the absence of express agreement, can any of the members of an ordinary partnership forfeit the share of any other member, or compel him to quit the firm on taking what is due to him. As there is no method, except a dissolution, by which a partner can retire against the will of his co-partners, so there is no method except a dissolution by which one partner can be got rid of against his own will."[68]

Partnership Act 1890, section 25

This basic level of security is preserved by the Partnership Act **24–85** 1890, which provides as follows:

"25. No majority of partners can expel any partner unless a power to do so has been conferred by express agreement between the partners."

---

[64] See the Insolvency Act 1986, ss.238 *et seq.*, 339 *et seq.* and *infra*, para. 27–103. See also *ibid.* s.423. *Quaere* whether such a transaction could be set aside as a fraud on the insolvency laws: see further, *supra*, paras. 10–124, 10–125.

[65] See *infra*, paras. 27–60 *et seq.*

[66] See *infra*, paras. 27–108 *et seq.* As to the circumstances in which insolvency orders may be made against the firm and against one or more partners, see *infra*, paras. 27–08 *et seq.*, 27–23 *et seq.*

[67] See the Insolvency Act 1986, ss. 238 *et seq.*, 339 *et seq.*, 423. See also *supra*, paras. 10–124, 10–125 and *infra*, paras. 27–71, 27–72.

[68] See *Clarke v. Hart* (1858) 6 H.L.C. 633; also *Crawshay v. Collins* (1808) 15 Ves.Jr. 218, 226, *per* Lord Eldon; *Featherstonhaugh v. Fenwick* (1810) 17 Ves.Jr. 298.

Alternative remedies

24–86   It has already been seen that where a partner, by his own conduct, seeks to force his co-partners into a dissolution, the court will readily interfere with injunctive or other relief, but clearly cannot authorise an expulsion in the absence of a specific power in the agreement.[69]

Express powers of expulsion

24–87   A power of expulsion is now, as a matter of routine, included in most well drawn agreements.[70] The exercise of such a power has already been considered earlier in this work.[71]

Expulsion and partnerships at will

24–88   Although a contrary view was voiced by Browne-Wilkinson V-C. in *Walters v. Bingham*,[72] the current editor submits that a power of expulsion is *not* consistent with the existence of a partnership at will; accordingly, in the absence of an express agreement, it is by no means certain that such a power will survive the expiration of a fixed term partnership.[73]

---

[69] See *Fairthorne v. Weston* (1844) 3 Hare 387 and *supra*, paras. 23–137, 24–72.
[70] See *supra*, paras. 10–94 *et seq.* See further, as to drafting such a power, the *Encyclopedia of Professional Partnerships*, Precedent 1, cl. 21.
[71] See *supra*, paras. 10–99 *et seq.*
[72] [1988] 1 F.T.L.R. 260, 268–269.
[73] Partnership Act 1890, s.27; *Clark v. Leach* (1863) 32 Beav. 14; *Campbell v. Campbell* (1893) 6 R. 137. See further, *supra*, paras. 10–21 *et seq.*

CHAPTER 25

WINDING UP THE PARTNERSHIP AFFAIRS

1. CONSEQUENCES OF DISSOLUTION

Effect on business

It has already been seen that, when a partnership is dissolved, each **25–01**
partner's authority will continue for the purposes of winding up its
affairs.[1] Where the dissolution is not of a purely technical nature,[2]
the business will enter an unsatisfactory "limbo" state, in which the
partners are obliged to complete any work then in progress but
strictly ought not to take on any new work, save (perhaps) where that
is required to facilitate a sale of the business as a going concern.[3]

Employees

It has been decided that a general dissolution will terminate the **25–02**
contracts of employment of all the firm's employees, thus inevitably
leading to claims for redundancy payments.[4] However, the current
editor submits that those contracts should not properly be regarded as
terminated until the conclusion of the winding-up, since the
partnership in effect continues for that purpose.[5] On the other hand,
a *technical* dissolution brought about by the death, retirement or
expulsion of a partner is unlikely to have the same effect, provided
that the partnership continues in existence.[6]

---

[1] Partnership Act 1890, s.38, *supra*, paras. 13–64 *et seq.*

[2] See *supra*, paras. 24–02, 24–03.

[3] See *supra*, paras. 10–160, 13–65, 16–25.

[4] *Tunstall v. Condon* [1980] I.C.R. 786; see also *Briggs v. Oates* [1990] I.C.R. 473. Much will, of course, depend on the terms of each contract of employment: see *Brace v. Calder* [1895] 2 Q.B. 253, *supra*, para. 3–39; *Philips v. Alhambra Palace Co.* [1901] 1 Q.B. 59. *Quaere* whether, if the business is sold or transferred as a going concern following the dissolution, the employees' rights will be preserved by the Transfer of Undertakings (Protection of Employment) Regulations 1981 (S.I. 1981 No. 1794). It is doubted whether *ibid.* reg. 5 will apply, since the contracts will already have been terminated on dissolution and would not "otherwise have been terminated by the transfer": *ibid.* reg. 5(1); and see *Secretary of State for Employment v. Spence* [1987] Q.B. 179, where the authorities are reviewed.

[5] Partnership Act 1890, s.38, *supra*, paras. 13–64 *et seq.*; also *infra*, para. 25–54. But see *Tunstall v. Condon*, *supra*, at pp. 793, 794, *per* Talbot J. *Semble*, the Tribunal was not asked to consider the effect of s.38.

[6] See *supra*, para. 3–13.

Occupation of premises

25-03   If, whilst the partnership was continuing, one partner permitted his co-partners to use and occupy premises on a non-exclusive licence basis,[7] the current editor is of the view that he will be unable to terminate those licences immediately following the dissolution, if by so doing he would prevent an orderly winding up of the partnership affairs.[8]

Agricultural floating charges

25-04   It should also be noted that an agricultural floating charge on partnership property under the provisions of the Agricultural Credits Act 1928 will crystallise into a fixed charge on a dissolution.[9]

25-05   Having noticed these incidental points, the remainder of this chapter is devoted to a consideration of the following topics:

1. The return of premiums.
2. The treatment of post-dissolution profits.
3. The distribution of assets.

At the very end of the chapter appears a brief recapitulation of the general principles applicable in winding up the partnership affairs, which are considered in greater detail elsewhere in this work.

2. THE RETURN OF PREMIUMS

Nature of premium

25-06   Prior to the Partnership Act 1890, Lord Lindley wrote:

"It frequently happens, when one person is admitted into partnership with another already established in business, that it is agreed that the incoming partner shall pay the other a premium, *i.e.* a sum of money for his own private benefit ... The consideration for the premium is not only the creation of a partnership between the person who takes, and him who parts with, the money, but also the continuance of that partnership ...".

The premium is thus, in its true sense, the price of entry into partnership: it does *not* represent the purchase price for a share of

---

[7] See *Harrison-Broadley v. Smith* [1964] 1 W.L.R. 456; and see *supra*, paras. 10–38, 18–33.
[8] See *Harrison-Broadley v. Smith, supra*, p. 465, *per* Harman L.J.; also *I.R.C. v. Graham's Trustees*, 1971 S.L.T. 46, 48, *per* Lord Reid. *Cf. Doe v. Bluck* (1838) 8 C. & P. 464; *Benham v. Gray* (1847) 5 C.B. 138.
[9] ss.5, 7(1)(a)(iii).

goodwill or any other asset nor a contribution towards the capital of the firm.[10] In those circumstances, it will come as no surprise that the popularity of the premium has over the years seen a drastic decline, to such an extent that it is now rare to encounter a case in which an incoming partner is asked to make such a payment.

Nevertheless, where an incoming partner *has* paid a premium in the expectation that the partnership will endure for a certain period, the question inevitably arises whether he is entitled to the return of the whole or any part of that sum if the partnership is determined prematurely.

A. Partnership Induced by Fraud

Even before the Partnership Act 1890, there was no doubt that a **25–07** return of premium could be obtained in cases of fraud. Lord Lindley explained the rights of the incoming partner in these terms:

"If a person has been deluded into becoming a partner by false and fraudulent representations, and has paid a premium, he may take one of two courses; *viz.* either abide by the contract and claim compensation for the loss occasioned by the fraud, which he may do in taking the partnership accounts; or he may disaffirm the contract, and thereby entitle himself to a return of the whole of the money he has paid."[11]

This is still the position: it was only those cases which were *not* tainted by fraud where the authorities prior to the 1890 Act were, in Lord Lindley's own words, "not easy to reconcile" and, thus, merited legislative attention.

If the fraudulent partner is insolvent, the incoming partner may prove against his estate for the amount of the premium in competition with his separate creditors.[12]

B. Partnership at Will

Just as it did not seek to regulate the return of premiums in cases of **25–08** fraud, the Partnership Act 1890 did not deal with the position following the dissolution of a partnership at will,[13] so that the law

---

[10] See *Re Bruges and Gow* [1926] N.Z.L.R. 893.

[11] See further, as to rescission for fraud, *supra*, paras. 23–51 *et seq.* And see *infra*, para. 25–12.

[12] *Ex p. Turquand* (1841) 2 M.D. & D. 339; also *Bury v. Allen* (1845) 1 Colly. 589. The decision in *Ex p. Broome* (1811) 1 Rose 69 appears to be to the contrary: but see the footnote in *Bury v. Allen, supra,* p. 598; also the observations of Knight Bruce V.-C. at *ibid.* p. 607.

[13] The Partnership Act 1890, s.40 applies only to partnerships for a fixed term: see *infra*, para. 25–09.

seemingly remains in the same state as when Lord Lindley wrote the following passage:

"Where a partnership is entered into for no specified time, and there is no agreement for a return or an apportionment of the premium in the event of an unexpected determination of the partnership, no part of the premium is returnable on the happening of such event. A case of fraud must be dealt with on its own demerits; and a person taking another into partnership for no definite time cannot, as soon as he has received the premium, dissolve the partnership and retain what has been paid as the consideration for it.[14] But laying aside fraud, and supposing there to be nothing except a partnership created for no specified time and determined soon after its creation, it is difficult to hold that it was in fact entered into for a longer time, and that the person who came in, paying a premium, has not got all for which he stipulated."[15]

C. PARTNERSHIP FOR A FIXED TERM

Partnership Act 1890, section 40

25–09   In an attempt to settle the uncertainties raised by the decided cases,[16] section 40 of the Partnership Act 1890 provided as follows:

"40. Where one partner has paid a premium[17] to another on entering into a partnership for a fixed term, and the partnership is dissolved before the expiration of that term otherwise than by the death of a partner, the court may order the repayment of the premium, or of such part thereof as it thinks just, having regard to the terms of the partnership contract and to the length of time during which the partnership has continued; unless

(a)   the dissolution is, in the judgment of the Court, wholly or chiefly due to the misconduct of the partner who paid the premium, or

(b)   the partnership has been dissolved by an agreement containing no provision for a return of any part of the premium."

---

[14] *Featherstonhaugh v. Turner* (1858) 25 Beav. 382. See also *Hamil v. Stokes* (1817) 4 Price 161; *Burdon v. Barkus* (1862) 4 De G.F. & J. 42, 52, *per* Turner L.J.
[15] See *Tattersall v. Groote* (1800) 2 Bos. & Pul. 131, 134, *per* Lord Eldon.
[16] In his Supplement on the Partnership Act 1890, Lord Lindley pointed out that "This section, according to a statement in the memorandum to the original bill, is intended to adopt the law laid down in the case of *Atwood v. Maude* (1868) L.R. 3 Ch.App. 369."
[17] There is no definition of this word in the Act.

Save in the event of a dissolution brought about by the death of a partner and in the cases specifically mentioned in paragraphs (a) and (b), the section confers an unfettered discretion on the court, which will, perhaps, be guided in the exercise of that discretion by the pre-1890 authorities.

Importance of agreement

It is largely self evident that, if the partners originally agreed terms **25–10** for the return (or non-return) of the premium in the event of a dissolution, effect will, in the absence of fraud,[18] normally be given thereto;[19] *a fortiori*, if an agreement was entered into at the time of the dissolution.[20] Writing prior to the Partnership Act 1890, Lord Lindley explained that if a dissolution agreement

"... is silent with respect to the premium, the inference is that the parties did not intend to deal with it, nor to vary their rights to it under the original agreement for its payment."

This inference has now been given statutory force. It is, however, questionable whether a partner will be regarded as having entered into such an agreement merely by consenting to a dissolution sought by his co-partners.[21]

Cause of dissolution

Where there is no such agreement, the exercise of the court's **25–11** discretion is likely to depend on the manner in which the dissolution was brought about.

(1) *Death*[22]

Prior to the Partnership Act 1890, a return of premium could not normally be obtained where the partnership was dissolved by the death of a partner since, in Lord Lindley's own words,

"Death is a contingency which all persons entering into partnership know may unexpectedly put an end to it."

---

[18] See *supra*, para. 25–07.

[19] *Handyside v. Campbell* [1901] 17 T.L.R. 623, 624, *per* Farwell J. Note also that the Partnership Act 1890, s.40 expressly directs the court to have regard to the terms of the partnership contract, when determining the quantum of the premium to be returned.

[20] *Ibid.* s.40(b); see also, prior to the Act, *Lee v. Page* (1861) 30 L.J.Ch. 857.

[21] See *Bury v. Allen* (1845) 1 Colly. 589; *Astle v. Wright* (1856) 23 Beav. 77; *Wilson v. Johnstone* (1873) L.R. 16 Eq. 606.

[22] See the Partnership Act 1890, s.33(1), *supra*, paras. 24–20, 24–21.

This exception is now embodied in the section 40 of the 1890 Act.[23]

25–12 Nevertheless, a return of premium may still conceivably be obtained if fraud can be proved. Lord Lindley cited the following example:

> "... if a person knows himself to be in a dangerous state of health, and conceals that fact, and induces another to enter into partnership with him, and to pay him a premium, and shortly afterwards dies, the fraud so practised will entitle the partner paying the premium to a return of part of it; and, if so, he can obtain such return in an action for a partnership account: he need not rescind the contract *in toto*."[24]

Whether a court would readily override the *express* provisions of the 1890 Act in such a case remains open to doubt.[25]

(2) Insolvency of firm or partner[26]

25–13 Lord Lindley apprehended that the insolvency of a firm would not justify a court ordering the repayment of any part of a premium, again on the basis that this is

> "a contingency which every one may fairly be taken as contemplating."[27]

The position is, if anything, *a fortiori* where a firm is wound up as an unregistered company under the new insolvency legislation.[28]

On the other hand, where the recipient of the premium was, unknown to the incoming partner, already in financial difficulties when the partnership commenced, a dissolution caused by his subsequent bankruptcy was, prior to the 1890 Act, treated as a sufficient ground for ordering a partial repayment;[29] *per contra*, if the incoming partner was aware of such difficulties before paying the premium.[30] There appears to be no reported case dealing with the position where the bankruptcy of the recipient was not anticipated, but the current editor tentatively submits that such an event should

---

[23] See *supra*, para. 25–09. And see, as to the position prior to the Act, *Whincup v. Hughes* (1871) L.R. 6 C.P. 78; *Ferns v. Carr* (1885) 28 Ch.D. 409.
[24] *Mackenna v. Parkes* (1867) 36 L.J.Ch. 366. See also *supra*, para. 25–07.
[25] Lord Lindley did, however, cite this as a continuing exception in his Supplement on the Partnership Act 1890: *ibid.* p. 105.
[26] See the Partnership Act 1890, s.33(1), *supra*, paras. 24–20, 24–22 *et seq.* and *infra*, paras. 27–08 *et seq.*
[27] See *Akhurst v. Jackson* (1818) 1 Swan. 85.
[28] See generally, *infra*, paras. 27–08 *et seq.*
[29] *Freeland v. Stansfeld* (1854) 2 Sm. & G. 479.
[30] *Akhurst v. Jackson* (1818) 1 Swan. 85.

be regarded no differently from death or the insolvency of the firm, *i.e.* as a normal contingency.

If the dissolution is brought about by the bankruptcy of the partner **25–14** who *paid* the premium, an order for repayment will be unlikely, save (perhaps) where the petition was presented by the recipient partner.[31]

It has already been noticed that the insolvency of a corporate partner will not, of itself, bring about a dissolution,[32] so that no question of a return of premium will arise.

(3) Disagreements and misconduct[33]

Prior to the Partnership Act 1890, Lord Lindley wrote: **25–15**

"Disagreements between the partners resulting in a dissolution have given rise to much difficulty. The tendency ... is to apportion the premium in these cases not only where neither partner is to blame[34]; but *a fortiori* where the partner receiving the premium has so misconducted himself as to give the partner paying it a right to have the partnership dissolved[35]; and it matters not that the latter may himself not be altogether free from blame[36]; nor is the rule altered by the fact that the partners have consented to dissolve since the institution of legal proceedings."[37]

It would seem likely that the court would now adopt a similar approach, although a return of premium cannot in any event be ordered where the court takes the view that dissolution was caused "wholly or chiefly" by the misconduct of the partner who paid it.[38] The existence of such misconduct will normally presuppose a dissolution obtained on the application of some other partner,[39] who might in fact be the recipient of the premium.[40]

---

[31] See *Hamil v. Stokes* (1817) 4 Price 161. Lord Lindley took care to observe that, in this case, "the contract of partnership was not rescinded on the ground of fraud."

[32] See *supra*, para. 24–25.

[33] See the Partnership Act 1890, s.35(c), (d) and (f), *supra*, paras. 24–39, 24–59 *et seq.*, 24–66 *et seq.*, 24–75 *et seq.*

[34] *Atwood v. Maude* (1868) L.R. 3 Ch.App. 369. And see *supra*, para. 25–09, n. 16.

[35] *Bullock v. Crockett* (1862) 3 Giff. 507. See also *Rooke v. Nisbet* (1881) 50 L.J.Ch. 588.

[36] See *Atwood v. Maude* (1868) L.R. 3 Ch.App. 369; also *Astle v. Wright* (1856) 23 Beav. 77; *Pease v. Hewitt* (1862) 31 Beav. 22. Cf. *Airey v. Borham* (1861) 29 Beav. 620.

[37] *Bury v. Allen* (1845) 1 Colly. 589; *Astle v. Wright* (1856) 23 Beav. 77; *Wilson v. Johnstone* (1873) L.R. 16 Eq. 606. Cf. *Lee v. Page* (1861) 30 L.J.Ch. 857.

[38] Partnership Act 1890, s.40(a), *supra*, para. 25–09. And see, as to the position prior to the Act, *Airey v. Borham* (1861) 29 Beav. 620; *Atwood v. Maude* (1868) L.R. 3 Ch.App. 369; *Wilson v. Johnstone* (1873) L.R. 16 Eq. 606; *Bluck v. Capstick* (1879) 12 Ch.D. 863.

[39] Alternatively, the dissolution might be brought about pursuant to an express power in the agreement: see further, *supra*, paras. 10–113 *et seq.*

[40] A dissolution cannot be obtained under the Partnership Act 1890, s.35(c) or (d) (or, perhaps, (f)) at the instance of a partner guilty of misconduct: see *supra*, paras. 24–39, 24–59 *et seq.*, 24–69 *et seq.*, 24–75 *et seq.*

Equally, a dissolution brought about by the misconduct of a partner will not relieve him of the liability to pay a premium which is due but unpaid.[41]

(4) *Mental disorder*

25–16 Where a partnership is dissolved on the grounds of a partner's mental disorder,[42] the judge could certainly order a return of premium pursuant to the wide powers conferred on him by the Mental Health Act 1983.[43] However, it is submitted that, where such a question is likely to arise, the judge might well decline to order a dissolution, with a view to proceedings being brought under the 1890 Act.[44]

(5) *Illegality*[45]

25–17 Although a return of premium could theoretically be ordered where a partnership is dissolved by reason of illegality, the current editor considers that, in general, the court would not be prepared to intervene;[46] much will, however, depend on the precise circumstances.[47] It is in any event clear that an action to enforce the *payment* of a premium in such a case will not succeed.[48]

D. Amount of Premium Returnable

25–18 It has already been seen that a wide discretion is conferred on the court under section 40 of the Partnership Act 1890.[49] Nevertheless, it is considered that the following observations made by Lord Lindley prior to the Act are still pertinent:

"There is no definite rule for deciding in any particular case the amount which ought to be returned. The time for which the partnership was entered into, and the time for which it has in fact lasted, are the most important matters to be considered; but other circumstances must often been taken into account in order to decide what is fair between the parties.[50] At the same time, the

---

[41] *Akhurst v. Jackson* (1818) 1 Swan. 85; *Bluck v. Capstick* (1879) Ch.D. 863.
[42] See *supra*, paras. 24–49 *et seq.*
[43] *Ibid.* ss.95, 96, *supra*, para. 24–40.
[44] See *supra*, para. 24–50.
[45] Partnership Act 1890, s.34, *supra*, paras. 24–35 *et seq.*
[46] See *supra*, paras. 8–52 *et seq.*
[47] A previous editor suggested that relevant factors might include the foreseeability of the event making the business illegal: *quaere*, can this be correct?
[48] *Williams v. Jones* (1826) 5 B. & C. 108. See also *supra*, para. 8–49.
[49] See *supra*, para. 25–09.
[50] See *Lyon v. Tweddell* (1881) 17 Ch.D. 529.

rule generally adopted is to apportion the premium with reference to the agreed and actual duration of the partnership."[51]

In his Supplement on the Act, Lord Lindley qualified his view as **25–19** follows:

"In the exercise of [*the Court's*] discretion attention must be paid to the terms of the partnership contract, and to the length of time during which the partnership has continued, and it would seem ... that the Court is not to take other matters into consideration; if this be so the discretion of the Court will be more limited than has hitherto been the case."

Yet, if the court is to take all the circumstances into account when determining whether or not to order a return of premium,[52] it is somewhat surprising if those circumstances must be ignored when it comes to consider the quantum of any repayment.[53] Consistently therewith, in one New Zealand case[54] where the recipient of the premium had lost the agencies which the partnership had been formed to work, the court ordered a dissolution of the partnership and the return of the *whole* premium.[55]

An exercise of the court's discretion will not normally be overturned on appeal.[56]

Time for application

Where dissolution proceedings have been brought by a partner, an **25–20** application for a return of premium should be made at the hearing in those proceedings: an inquiry on such an issue will not normally be ordered at a later date.[57]

Arbitration

An arbitrator may order a return of premium if power to dissolve the firm is conferred on him by the partnership agreement.[58]

---

[51] See *Bury v. Allen* (1845) 1 Colly. 589; *Astle v. Wright* (1856) 23 Beav. 77; *Pease v. Hewitt* (1862) 31 Beav. 22; *Atwood v. Maude* (1868) L.R. 3 Ch.App. 369; *Wilson v. Johnstone* (1873) L.R. 16 Eq. 606. *Cf. Hamil v. Stokes* (1817) 4 Price 161; *Freeland v. Stansfeld* (1854) 1 Sm. & G. 479; *Bullock v. Crockett* (1862) 3 Giff. 507.

[52] See *supra*, paras. 25–11 *et seq.*

[53] *Quaere* whether, even though the court must take into account the factors mentioned in the section, it retains a residual discretion as to other factors.

[54] *Janson v. McMullen* [1922] N.Z.L.R. 677.

[55] *Ibid.* pp. 681, 682, *per* Sim A.C.J.

[56] *Lyon v. Tweddell* (1881) 17 Ch.D. 529.

[57] *Edmunds v. Robinson* (1885) 29 Ch.D. 170.

[58] *Belfield v. Bourne* [1894] 1 Ch. 521, explaining *Tattersall v. Groote* (1800) 2 Bos. & Pul. 131. And see, as to the powers of an arbitrator, *supra*, paras. 10–232, 10–235 *et seq.*

3. THE TREATMENT OF POST-DISSOLUTION PROFITS

25–21 It has already been seen that an account of partnership dealings and transactions must be kept open following the date of dissolution,[59] since each partner's authority continues for the purposes of winding up the firm's affairs.[60] Where all the partners are actively involved in the winding-up, profits realised following the dissolution will be shared in the normal profit sharing ratios, unless some special allowance is given to a particular partner by the court.[61]

Different considerations will, however, arise where the winding up is delayed and, in the interim, the business is carried on by one or more of the former partners to the exclusion of the others or where the entitlement of a deceased or outgoing partner in respect of his share is not satisfied on the due date.[62]

As an introduction to the law as it stood prior to the Partnership Act 1890, Lord Lindley analysed the circumstances in which a person who has employed another person's property in his trade may be rendered liable to account for any profits made thereby. This analysis has not been retained.[63]

Position prior to the Partnership Act 1890

25–22 The right of a former partner to an account of profits where the business was carried on following a dissolution was well settled prior to the Partnership Act 1890. Thus, after citing the more important cases, which established the nature of that right following a dissolution brought about by the death[64] or bankruptcy[65] of a partner, Lord Lindley went on:

"The rule established in these cases has been applied in a variety of instances; *e.g.* where a managing partner had continued the business after the period fixed for the dissolution and winding up

---

[59] See *supra*, para. 23–125.
[60] Partnership Act 1890, s.38, *supra*, paras. 13–64 *et seq*.
[61] See *supra*, para. 20–43.
[62] Equally, in such a case it *may* be possible to seek interest under the Supreme Court Act 1981, s.35A: see *supra*, para. 20–39 and *infra*, para. 25–38.
[63] The relevant passage is to be found in 15th edition of this work, at pp. 719–723.
[64] *Crawshay v. Collins* (1808) 15 Ves.Jr. 218; (1820) 1 J. & W. 267; (1826) 2 Russ. 325. Lord Eldon later pointed out that the decision reported at 15 Ves.Jr. 218 did not go as far was commonly supposed: see *Brown v. De Tastet* (1821) Jac. 284, 297; *Cook v. Collingridge* (1822) Jac. 607, 622; *Crawshay v. Collins* (1826) 2 Russ. 325, 330.
[65] *Yates v. Finn* (1880) 13 Ch.D. 839; see also *Brown v. De Tastet* (1821) Jac. 284 (the decision in which was apparently affirmed by the House of Lords, although the plaintiff later abandoned his claim, having found it impossible to implement the decree: see *Docker v. Somes* (1834) 2 M. & K. 655, 658). And see *Booth v. Parkes* (1829) Beatty 444; *Featherstonhaugh v. Turner* (1858) 25 Beav. 382; *Smith v. Everett* (1859) 27 Beav. 446.

of the partnership[66]; where a partner had become lunatic and the firm had been dissolved, but the business had been continued by the other partners, and they had not paid out the capital of the lunatic partner[67]; where partners had agreed to dissolve and to have the partnership property wound up, and its assets got in and converted by a third person, and one of the partners nevertheless carried on the business in the meantime for his own benefit[68]; where a mining partnership had been dissolved, but one of the partners had obtained a renewed lease of the mine, and had continued to work it for his own benefit."[69]

Partnership Act 1890, section 42

The treatment of post-dissolution profits is now governed by **25–23** section 42 of the Partnership Act 1890, which provides as follows:

"42.—(1) Where any member of a firm has died or otherwise ceased to be a partner, and the surviving or continuing partners carry on the business of the firm with its capital or assets without any final settlement of accounts as between the firm and the outgoing partner or his estate, then, in the absence of any agreement to the contrary, the outgoing partner or his estate is entitled at the option of himself or his representatives to such share of the profits[70] made since the dissolution as the Court may find to be attributable to the use of his share of the partnership assets,[71] or to interest at the rate of five per cent. per annum[72] on the amount of his share of the partnership assets.

(2) Provided that where by the partnership contract an option is given to surviving or continuing partners to purchase the interest of a deceased or outgoing partner, and the option is duly exercised, the estate of the deceased partner, or the outgoing partner or his estate, as the case may be, is not entitled to any further or other share of profits; but if any partner assuming to act in exercise of the option does not in all material respects comply with the terms thereof, he is liable to account under the foregoing provisions of this section."

---

[66] *Parsons v. Hayward* (1862) 4 De G.F. & J. 474.

[67] *Mellersh v. Keen* (1859) 27 Beav. 236.

[68] *Turner v. Major* (1862) 3 Giff. 442.

[69] *Featherstonhaugh v. Fenwick* (1810) 17 Ves.Jr. 298. See also *Clements v. Hall* (1858) 2 De.G. & J. 173.

[70] See, as to the meaning of "profits," *Barclays Bank Trust Co. Ltd. v. Bluff* [1982] Ch. 172, *infra*, para. 25–27.

[71] Including goodwill: *Manley v. Sartori* [1927] 1 Ch. 157.

[72] This rate has remained unchanged, despite judicial prompting: see *Sobell v. Boston* [1975] 1 W.L.R. 1587, 1593, *per* Goff J.; also the Law Commission Report "Law of Contract: Report on Interest," Part VI, para. 245, reproduced at (1978) 122 S.J. 468. And see *infra*, para. 25–26.

Nature of the option under section 42(1)

25–24   Although the partner whose entitlement has not been paid out
theoretically has an option to take a share of profits or interest at five
per cent. in all cases, that option will in fact be exercisable only
where the continuing partners can be shown to have derived profits
from the use of his share. This is not as straightforward a question as
it might seem, as Lord Lindley explained prior to the Act, when
considering the rights of the executors of a deceased partner[73]:

> "It is very easy to say [*the share of profits to which the executors
> are entitled*] can be calculated by the rule of three—as the whole
> capital is to the whole profits, so is the late partner's share in the
> capital to his share of the profits—but this assumes that the profits
> in question have been made by capital only. Profits, and very large
> profits, may be made by skill, and an extensive connection, with
> little or no capital; and even if there be capital, the profits may be
> attributable less to it than to other matters, and it may be
> impossible to determine with any precision the extent to which the
> capital has contributed to the realisation of the profits obtained.[74]
> Special inquiries on this subject, therefore, are almost always
> necessary,[75] and if it can be shown that, having regard to the
> nature of the business or other circumstances, the profits which
> have been made cannot be justly attributed to the use of the
> capital or assets of the late partner, his prima facie right to share
> such profits will be effectually rebutted."

25–25   In *Willet v. Blanford*,[76] Wigram V.-C., concluding that it was not
possible to lay down any general rules in this area, observed that,

> "... the nature of the trade, the manner of carrying it on, the
> capital employed, the state of the account between the partnership
> and the deceased partner at the time of his death, and the conduct
> of the parties after his death, may materially affect the rights of
> the parties."[77]

Thus, in *Wedderburn v. Wedderburn*,[78] it was demonstrated that
the greater part of the profits realised by successive firms following a

---

[73] This passage in fact *preceded* Lord Lindley's consideration of the treatment of post-dissolution
profits *stricto sensu*.
[74] See *Featherstonhaugh v. Turner* (1858) 25 Beav. 382, *infra*, para. 25–25, n. 79; also *Page v.
Ratcliffe* (1897) 75 L.T. 371.
[75] See, for example, *Manley v. Sartori* [1927] 1 Ch. 157.
[76] (1842) 1 Hare 253.
[77] Lord Lindley added that "This conclusion of the Vice-Chancellor was entirely in accordance
with previous decisions" and referred, in particular, to Lord Eldon's observations on *Crawshay v.
Collins* (1808) 15 Ves.Jr. 218 in *Brown v. De Tastet* (1821) Jac. 284, 297; *Cook v. Collingridge*
(1822) Jac. 607, 622; *Crawshay v. Collins* (1826) 2 Russ. 325, 330.
[78] (1856) 22 Beav. 84; as to the original order, see (1836) 2 Keen 722; (1838) 4 Myl. & Cr. 41.

partner's death were attributable not to the surplus assets of the original firm, in which he had an interest, but to the goodwill and business connection of that firm, in which he had *no* interest,[79] and to the reputation, skill and ability of the partners in each successive firm. On that basis, the deceased partner's estate was held not to be entitled to a share of such profits.[80] *Simpson v. Chapman*[81] was a somewhat similar case, although there it was shown that the deceased partner had no capital in the firm (in the ordinary sense of that word)[82] and, moreover, it appears merely to have been *assumed* that the goodwill belonged to the surviving partners.[83]

Problems associated with the option under section 42(1)

As is apparent from the preceding paragraphs, in many cases the **25–26** right to opt for a share of profits may be more theoretical than real. To this must be added the practical difficulties associated with an exercise of that right, as expressed by Lord Lindley in the following passage written prior to the Act:

"... owing to the extreme difficulty of taking an account of subsequent profits, so far as they are attributable only to one particular source, the tendency of the courts ... appears to be rather in favour of not exercising than of exercising the power alluded to, except in cases of gross fraud or breach of trust."

He then observed in a footnote:

"Judgments for an account of profits after dissolution are fearfully oppressive; and the writer is not aware of any instance in which such a judgment has been worked out and has resulted beneficially to the person in whose favour it was made."[84]

It was these practical difficulties which prompted Lord Lindley, in his Supplement on the Partnership Act 1890, to express regret that

---

[79] This was the result of an express provision in the agreement. *Cf. Featherstonhaugh v. Turner* (1858) 25 Beav. 382, where an inquiry was directed with a view to ascertaining whether any and, if so, what profits made since the date of death were attributable to persons who had become customers by reason of the deceased partner having been a member of the firm; also *Manley v. Sartori* [1927] 1 Ch. 157. And see *Gordon v. Gonda* [1955] 1 W.L.R. 885; *Robert Watte Pathirana v. Ariya Pathirana* [1967] 1 A.C. 233 (P.C.).

[80] In fact, Sir John Romilly M.R. appears to have accepted the entitlement of the estate to a share of profits derived from *other* sources, but he effectively held that this would be covered by interest on the value of the deceased's share: see (1856) 22 Beav. 84, 121.

[81] (1853) 4 De G.M. & G. 154. Lord Lindley noted that "This case is the more important as the non-liability to account for subsequent profits was decided on the hearing of the cause."

[82] Although, at the time of the partner's death, the firm's assets exceeded its liabilities, one of those assets was in fact a debt due from the deceased partner; if no account had been taken of that debt, the firm would have been insolvent.

[83] Such an assumption will rarely be justified: see *supra*, para. 10–164.

[84] Unaccountably, this comment was relegated to a footnote. And see also *Hugh Stevenson and Sons v. Aktiengesellschaft fur Cartonnagen-Industrie* [1917] 1 K.B. 842, 849, *per* Swinfen Eady L.J.

the court was not empowered to award interest at a rate greater than 5 per cent. An increase in that rate has been suggested in recent years,[85] although fluctuations in interest rates tend to alter the perspective from time to time.

Capital profits

25–27   Section 42(1) of the Partnership Act 1890 has no application where the profits realised by the continuing or surviving partners are of a *capital* nature. This was established in *Barclays Bank Trust Co. Ltd. v. Bluff.*[86] There a father and son carried on a farming business in partnership. The father died, thus dissolving the firm. There was a substantial delay in winding up the partnership affairs, during which time the son continued to carry on the business and the value of the farm appreciated considerably. It was held that the father's executor was entitled, at its election, to interest at the rate of 5 per cent. on the father's share of the partnership assets or to a share of the profits accruing in the ordinary course of carrying on the business since the date of death, *i.e.* profits arising from the use of the farm land and buildings, but that those profits did not include any capital profits which might be realised on a sale of the land and buildings, to a share of which the father's estate was entitled quite apart from the provisions of section 42.[87]

It should, however, be noted that the position might have been different if the land and buildings had been trading stock.[88]

Remuneration for services

25–28   Prior to the Partnership Act 1890, Lord Lindley pointed out that

"... in taking an account of subsequent profits, the partner by whose exertions they have been made is usually allowed

---

[85] See *Sobell v. Boston* [1975] 1 W.L.R. 1587, 1593, *per* Goff J.; also the Law Commission Report "Law of Contract: Report on Interest," Part VI, para. 245, reproduced at (1978) 122 S.J. 468. But see also *infra*, para. 25–38.

[86] [1982] Ch. 172, where the unsatisfactory Irish decision of *Meagher v. Meagher* [1961] I.R. 96 was distinguished. The facts in *Meagher v. Meagher* were similar to those in *Barclays Bank Trust Co. Ltd. v. Bluff*, save that the premises in question were part of the trading stock of the firm and had been sold prior to the action. The Supreme Court of Eire held that (1) the value of the deceased partner's share at the date of dissolution should be based on the actual proceeds of sale with such deductions as the facts might justify; (2) the increased value of the assets should be treated as profits; and (3) any interest payable under the Partnership Act 1890, s.42(1) should be calculated on the value of the deceased partner's share as at the date of his death. However, the difficulties inherent in the decision were avoided when it came to the point of ascertaining the value of the deceased partner's share, since the court made no attempt to separate the capital and profit elements therein.

[87] See also *Chandroutie v. Gajadhar* [1987] A.C. 147 (P.C.). *Cf.* the position of a retired partner: see *Sobell v. Boston* [1975] 1 W.L.R. 1587.

[88] See [1982] Ch. 172, 183, *per* H.E. Francis Q.C. (sitting as a deputy judge of the Chancery Division).

compensation for his trouble,[89] unless he is, in the proper sense of the word, a trustee, and guilty of a breach of trust, when no such compensation is allowed."[90]

Such an allowance is still afforded where an order is made under section 42.[91]

Election to take interest in lieu of profits

If a claim to a share of profits is not sustainable[92] or the outgoing **25-29** partner or his estate so elects, simple interest will be payable at the rate of 5 per cent., a rate which has remained unchanged over the years.[93]

An election for the payment of interest will not, of itself, deprive the outgoing partner or his estate of his rightful share of any increase in the value of the partnership assets (save, perhaps, for stock in trade) between the date of dissolution and the date of sale. This was clearly established in *Barclays Bank Trust Co. Ltd. v. Bluff*.[94]

Personal representatives unable to sue

Although the rights conferred by section 42(1) of the Partnership **25-30** Act 1890 ought properly to be enforced by the deceased partner's personal representatives, if this is not, for whatever, reason possible, the persons interested in his estate may do so.[95]

Alien enemy

Where a partnership is dissolved by the outbreak of war,[96] any **25-31** partner who is treated as an alien enemy will not be deprived of his rights under section 42(1) of the Partnership Act 1890, but will not be in a position to enforce those rights until the hostilities are over.[97]

Exclusion of right to profits

It is clear that the right of election under section 42(1) of the **25-32** Partnership Act 1890 may be excluded by the partnership agree-

---

[89] *Brown v. De Tastet* (1819) Jac. 284; *Yates v. Finn* (1880) 13 Ch.D. 839. See also *Cook v. Collingridge* (1822) Jac. 623; *Featherstonhaugh v. Turner* (1858) 25 Beav. 382; *Mellersh v. Keen* (1859) 27 Beav. 236.

[90] *Burden v. Burden* (1813) 1 Ves. & Bea. 170; *Stocken v. Dawson* (1843) 6 Beav. 371 and (1848) 17 L.J.Ch. 282. But see *Cook v. Collingridge* (1822) Jac. 607, 622–623, *per* Lord Eldon.

[91] See the Partnership Act 1890, s.46; *Page v. Ratcliffe* (1897) 75 L.T. 371; *Manley v. Sartori* [1927] 1 Ch. 157. See also *Castle v. Castle* [1951] G.L.R. 541.

[92] See *supra*, paras. 25–24, 25–25.

[93] It has been suggested that the rate should be increased: see *supra*, para. 25–26, n. 85.

[94] [1982] Ch. 172. See further, *supra*, para. 25–27.

[95] See *Travis v. Milne* (1851) 9 Hare 141; *Beningfield v. Baxter* (1887) 12 App.Cas. 167, 178–179. And see *infra*, paras. 26–41, 26–42.

[96] See *supra*, paras. 4–04 *et seq.*

[97] *Hugh Stevenson & Sons Ltd. v. Aktiengesellschaft fur Cartonnagen-Industrie* [1918] A.C. 239; *Gordon v. Gonda* [1955] 1 W.L.R. 885.

ment.[98] Moreover, it is also provided that the right to a share of profits is not available where the continuing or surviving partners have an option to acquire the outgoing or deceased partner's share, provided that the option is duly exercised *and* its terms subsequently adhered to. In his Supplement on the Act, Lord Lindley explained that this rule

"... is in accordance with the statement of the law by Lord Cairns in *Vyse v. Foster*.[99] [*Subsection (2)*] deals with the case of an option to purchase, as in *Willett v. Blanford*,[1] and not with an executed contract to purchase, which was the case in *Vyse v. Foster*. In the latter case the continuing partners will not in the absence of fraud be liable to account for profits, unless by neglecting to fulfil some condition, or not complying with some stipulation of the essence of the contract, or otherwise, they repudiate or give the representatives of the deceased partner[2] a right to rescind the contract."

25-33   In *Vyse v. Foster*,[3] the agreement provided that, on the death of a partner, the value of his share should be ascertained and paid, with interest, by instalments over a two year period. One partner died leaving three executors, one of whom was a surviving partner. The deceased's share was ascertained but, instead of being paid out as contemplated by the agreement, was retained in the business, which was carried on for many years, first by one and then by two of the executors, with other persons. Interest was paid on the deceased's share and all the beneficiaries interested in his estate, except the plaintiff (who was minor), acquiesced in this arrangement. The plaintiff, having attained the vesting age specified in the will, demanded payment of her share of the estate and the profits made by its employment in the business. She was offered the principal sum due to her, together with compound interest at the rate of 5 per cent., but no share of profits. She commenced proceedings solely against the executors, seeking an account of the profits and succeeded

---

[98] The subsection contains the words "in the absence of any agreement to the contrary": see *supra*, para. 25-23.

[99] (1874) L.R. 7 H.L. 318, 329.

[1] (1842) 1 Hare 253.

[2] An outgoing partner will, of course, be in the same position.

[3] (1872) L.R. 8 Ch.App. 309, affirmed (1874) L.R. 7 H.L. 318. Lord Lindley pointed out that "The decision in this case is extremely important, as it decided, 1, that the clause in the partnership articles was binding both on the executors of the deceased partner and on the surviving partners, although one of them was also an executor; 2, that the amount due to the estate of the deceased was in effect a loan to the survivors, and its non-payment at the time and in manner prescribed by the articles of partnership did not entitle the plaintiff to any profits, but only to interest; 3, that even if the plaintiff's claim to profits could have been sustained, the executor who was not a partner would not have been liable for such profits; and 4, that the executors who were partners would not have been liable for more profits than they respectively themselves received." Note also the subsequent proceedings reported at (1875) L.R. 10 Ch.App. 236.

at first instance, but the decision was overturned on appeal. Whilst recognising that there had been a technical breach of trust, the Court of Appeal held that the executors had at all times acted with perfect fairness and were not bound to account for any profits received by them. This decision was affirmed by the House of Lords, who went on to analyse the distinction between a contract and an option to purchase a deceased partner's share.[4]

It follows that any provision for the automatic accruer of an outgoing partner's share[5] will necessarily exclude his rights under section 42(1).

Option to purchase

It would seem that the right to a share of profits or interest may be **25–34** exercisable in respect of the period between the date of dissolution and the date on which the option is exercised, although much will depend on the precise terms of the agreement. Whilst section 42(2) also appears to preserve the outgoing partner's right to *interest* even where there is an option which is duly exercised,[6] the current editor considers that this right will normally be excluded by necessary implication.[7]

Position where surviving partners are also personal representatives

Where the executors or trustees of the deceased partner's will or **25–35** the administrators of his estate[8] are surviving partners or are admitted to the partnership after the date of his death, it would seem that the rights of the legatees or next-of-kin are strictly analogous to those which exist under section 42 of the Partnership Act 1890. Writing prior to the Act, Lord Lindley summarised these rights as follows:

"The right of the *cestui que trust* against his trustee in these cases is to an account of profits made by him by the use of the trust property, or at the option of the *cestui que trust* to simple interest at £5 per cent.[9]; or in special cases to compound interest."[10]

---

[4] (1874) L.R. 7 H.L. 334–335 (*per* Lord Cairns), 337–339 (*per* Lord Hatherley); see also *Hordern v. Hordern* [1910] A.C. 465.

[5] See *supra*, para. 10–122.

[6] The subsection is quite specific: "the outgoing partner or his estate ... is not entitled to any further or other share of profits": see *supra*, para. 25–23.

[7] *e.g.* an option which provides for the outgoing partner's share to be paid by instalments without interest would clearly be a contrary agreement excluding the operation of *ibid.* subs. (1).

[8] Lord Lindley dealt with this subject primarily in terms of executors and trustees but the administrators of a deceased intestate partner will, of course, be in no different position.

[9] *Heathcote v. Hulme* (1819) 1 Jac. & W. 122.

[10] *Jones v. Foxall* (1852) 15 Beav. 388; *Williams v. Powell* (1852) 15 Beav. 461; *Vyse v. Foster* (1874) L.R. 7 H.L. 318, 346, *per* Lord Selborne. Note also, in this context, *Roxburgh Dinardo & Partners' Judicial Factor v. Dinardo*, 1993 S.L.T. 16 (2nd Div.).

In his Supplement on the Act, he added:

> "If the partners are also trustees and bound to accumulate, compound interest may be charged against them, but the liability is a liability *qua* trustee and not *qua* partner and is therefore beyond the scope of this section."

Save in cases of this type, it is largely academic whether the proceedings against such partners are framed under section 42(1) or otherwise.

Extent of liability to account

25–36   In cases of this type, the personal representatives are not liable to account for any profits other than those which they have actually received. Although originally subject to some doubt,[11] this was decided in *Vyse v. Foster*.[12] It follows that, if they are not the only surviving partners, all such partners should be joined as parties to the proceedings.[13] However, the effective joinder of partners admitted *after* the date of death will be dependent on establishing that they are implicated in the breach of trust, as in *Flockton v. Bunning*.[14] The following account of this case was prepared by Lord Lindley from the shorthand writer's notes[15]:

> "... a partner died, leaving his wife his executrix, and having directed her to get in his estate and invest it for the benefit of herself and children. She wound up the partnership in which her husband was engaged, but continued to carry on the business with his capital, in partnership with other persons, who knew that in so doing she and they were committing a breach of trust.[16] A bill was filed by some of the children against her and her co-partners, seeking to make them jointly and severally liable for the trust estate employed in the business, and for the profits made by its use; and a decree to that effect was made and was affirmed on an appeal by the wife's partners. This case was decided on the principle that the wife's partners were clearly implicated in the breach of trust committed by her, and were jointly and severally responsible with her for the trust estate and all the profits made thereby. The widow's capital was trust property; there was no loan

---

[11] See *Palmer v. Mitchell* (1809) 2 M. & K. 672, note; *Docker v. Somes* (1834) 2 M. & K. 655; *Macdonald v. Richardson* (1858) 1 Giff. 81; *Townend v. Townend* (1859) 1 Giff. 201.

[12] (1874) L.R. 7 H.L. 318, 333–334, *per* Lord Cairns.

[13] The claim against the non-executor/trustee partners will, of course, be brought under the Partnership Act 1890, s.42(1).

[14] (1868) L.R. 8 Ch.App. 323, note.

[15] Lord Lindley was, in fact, counsel for the appellants and his account of the case differs marginally from that in the report.

[16] In fact, she agreed to indemnify them against the consequences.

as in *Stroud v. Gwyer*,[17] but the widow's capital became part of the capital of the firm; and she and her co-partners wrongfully traded with it.[18] Both L.J. Wood and L.J. Selwyn agreed that a mere loan, although in breach of trust, would not involve liability to account for profits, but that trust property which was traded with by a trustee in partnership with others could not be regarded as a loan."[19]

Cook v. Collingridge[20] is a more extreme case. There the executors **25–37** of a deceased partner sold his share to the surviving partners, who included one of the executors; those partners then proceeded to resell the share to another of the executors. A legatee succeeded in getting the sale set aside and the surviving partners were ordered to account for profits made since the date of death, even though the proceeds from the sale of the share were not retained in the business.

Interest under the Supreme Court Act 1981

It has already been seen[21] that it is doubtful to what extent section **25–38** 43 of the Partnership Act 1890 will apply in the case of a *general* dissolution. Whilst it is clear that section 42 is of more general application, the current editor considers that, in a case falling within section 43, the outgoing partner may be able to claim interest under section 35A of the Supreme Court 1981[22] *in lieu* of his entitlement under section 42; *sed quaere*.[23]

4. DISTRIBUTION OF ASSETS AND ADJUSTMENT OF ACCOUNTS

Importance of agreement

Before the winding-up of the partnership affairs can be concluded, **25–39** it is necessary to complete the partnership accounts by incorporating any final adjustments which may be required to reflect the respective rights, entitlements and obligations of each partner.[24] At this point it will be necessary to pay close attention to the terms of the

---

[17] (1860) 28 Beav. 130.
[18] *Cf. Vyse v. Foster* (1874) L.R. 7 H.L. 318, *supra*, para. 25–33.
[19] See also *Travis v. Milne* (1851) 9 Hare 141, where no account of profits was sought: see *ibid.* pp. 147–148.
[20] (1822) Jac. 607; see also the decree in (1825) 27 Beav. 456. *Stocken v. Dawson* (1848) 17 L.J.Ch. 282 was a somewhat similar case.
[21] See *supra*, paras. 19–41, 23–33; also *infra*, para. 26–04.
[22] Similarly in the case of the County Courts Act 1984, s.69.
[23] See *supra*, paras. 19–13, 20–39.
[24] It goes without saying that account must be taken of any sums due *from* a partner to the firm: see *supra*, paras. 19–28 *et seq.*

partnership agreement,[25] as well as to the partners' subsequent conduct, even though this is not always decisive. As Lord Lindley explained prior to the Partnership Act 1890:

"... an express agreement with reference to the taking of accounts may be, and frequently is, only applicable to the case of a continuing partnership, and may not be intended to be observed on a final dissolution of the firm, or even on the retirement of one of its members.[26] A similar observation applies to the mode in which the partners themselves have been in the habit of keeping their accounts: that which has been done for the purpose of sharing annual profits or losses is by no means necessarily a precedent to be followed when a partnership account has to be finally closed."[27]

Partnership Act 1890, section 44

25–40   Subject to any contrary agreement, the rules which govern the final settlement of a partnership account on dissolution are contained in section 44 of the Partnership Act 1890, which provides as follows:

"44. In settling accounts between the partners after a dissolution of partnership, the following rules shall, subject to any agreement, be observed:
   (a)   Losses, including losses and deficiencies of capital,[28] shall be paid first out of profits, next out of capital, and lastly, if necessary, by the partners individually in the proportion in which they were entitled to share profits:
   (b)   The assets of the firm including the sums, if any, contributed by the partners to make up losses or deficiencies of capital, shall be applied in the following manner and order:
         1.   In paying the debts and liabilities of the firm to persons who are not partners therein:

---

[25] In *Faulks v. Faulks* [1992] 15 E.G. 82, the agreement provided for a tenancy of certain land (which enjoyed the benefit of a milk quota) to revert to the ownership of a particular partner in the event of a dissolution. It was held that because milk quota cannot exist independently of the land to which it relates, the quota could not be treated as a partnership asset and its value fell to be ignored on the dissolution. See further *supra*, para. 18–21. See also *Robertson v. Brent* [1972] N.Z.L.R. 406, noticed *supra*, para. 23–188, n. 17.

[26] See *supra*, paras. 10–63, 10–133 *et seq.*; also *Watson v. Haggitt* [1928] A.C. 127; and note *Re London India Rubber Co.* (1868) L.R. 5 Eq. 519; *Re Bridgewater Navigation Co.* [1891] 2 Ch. 317, varied *sub. nom. Birch v. Cropper* (1889) 14 App.Cas. 525. *Cf. Re Barber* (1870) L.R. 5 Ch.App. 687.

[27] *e.g.* goodwill rarely, if ever, features in a firm's annual accounts but may, nevertheless, be one of its most valuable assets: see *Wade v. Jenkins* (1860) 2 Giff. 509; *Steuart v. Gladstone* (1878) 10 Ch.D. 626, 659, *per* Jessel M.R. See also *supra*, paras. 10–63, 10–138. Where an asset has been realised, regard must naturally be had to its actual rather than its book value: *Re Bridgewater Navigation Co.* [1891] 2 Ch. 317, 329, *per* Lindley L.J.

[28] There can be no such deficiency caused by a partner's own failure to contribute capital: *Re Ward* [1985] 2 N.Z.L.R. 352, 355.

2. In paying to each partner rateably what is due from the firm to him for advances as distinguished from capital[29]:

3. In paying to each partner rateably what is due from the firm to him in respect of capital:

4. The ultimate residue, if any, shall be divided among the partners in the proportion in which profits are divisible."[30]

Although it is traditionally said that only debts and advances have priority over the costs of dissolution proceedings,[31] it would seem that each partner's capital entitlement should also be taken into account before determining how any excess costs are to be borne.[32]

Application of the section

Section 44(b) requires the partners to proceed through each of the **25–41** four stages in turn, and to identify whether there is a deficiency of assets at any of the first three stages. If there is, that deficiency must be treated as a loss and borne by the partners as such. Writing prior to the Partnership Act 1890, Lord Lindley explained the process in this way:

"If the assets are not sufficient to pay the debts and liabilities to non-partners, the partners must treat the difference as a loss and make it up by contributions *inter se*. If the assets are more than sufficient to pay the debts and liabilities of the partnership to non-partners, but are not sufficient to repay the partners their respective advances, the amount of unpaid advances ought, it is conceived, to be treated as a loss, to be met like other losses. In such a case the advances ought to be treated as a debt of the firm, but payable to one of the partners instead of to a stranger.[33] If, after paying all the debts and liabilities of the firm and the advances of the partners, there is still a surplus, but not sufficient to pay each partner his capital, the balances of capitals remaining unpaid must be treated as so many losses to be met like other losses."[34]

---

[29] It follows that a partner will have no independent cause of action to recover an advance: *Green v. Hertzog* [1954] 1 W.L.R. 1309.

[30] In his Supplement on the Partnership Act 1890, Lord Lindley rightly pointed out that the section follows "almost word for word" the statement of the law set out in the 5th ed. of this work at p. 402. See further, as to the position prior to the Act, *Crawshay v. Collins* (1826) 2 Russ. 325; *Richardson v. Bank of England* (1838) 4 Myl. & Cr. 165; *Binney v. Mutrie* (1886) 12 App.Cas. 160

[31] See *Austin v. Jackson* (1879) 11 Ch.D. 942, note; *Potter v. Jackson* (1880) 13 Ch.D. 845.

[32] *Ross v. White* [1894] 3 Ch. 326. See also *supra*, para. 23–119.

[33] See *Wood v. Scoles* (1866) L.R. 1 Ch.App. 369.

[34] See now the Partnership Act 1890, s.24(1), *supra*, paras. 20–03 *et seq. Cf. Binney v. Mutrie* (1886) 12 App.Cas. 160. As to costs, see *supra*, paras. 23–119, 25–40.

If there is an insufficiency at stage 1, the overall loss borne by the partners will be that amount together with any sums which would otherwise be payable to them at stages 2 and 3 (which, by definition, cannot be returned to them); if the insufficiency occurs at stage 2, the loss will comprise that amount together with any sum otherwise payable at stage 3. In either of these cases, a global calculation of each partner's share of the loss may be possible.[35]

Division of ultimate residue

25-42   If there is an ultimate residue to be divided between the partners at stage 4, the relevant profit shares will be those applied to residual or capital profits.[36] Any form of preferential profit share which is only applicable to profits of an *income* nature, *e.g.* so-called "salaries," "bonus shares" or "incentive profit shares," must be left out of account.[37] In the case of a graduated profit sharing system, whether by reference to a partner's holding of "points" or his position on a "lockstep" system, the relevant profit sharing proportions will in general be those which applied at the date of dissolution.[38]

Of course, it may be that a partner, though entitled to a share of the firm's income profits, is excluded from participating in the division of capital profits.[39] The existence of such a partner will naturally be ignored for present purposes.[40]

Equality of loss and inequality of capital

25-43   Where the partners have contributed (and thereafter own)[41] capital in unequal proportions but share profits and losses equally, any loss of capital must in general be shared *equally*, in the same way as any other loss.[42] Accordingly, any surplus assets remaining after payment

---

[35] Thus, suppose that partners A and B share profits and losses equally. A has made an advance of £1,000 and a capital contribution of £2,000, whilst B has made an advance of £2,000 and a capital contribution of £2,000. The surplus assets remaining after stage 1 are merely £1,500, so that £1,500 of the advances and the entirety of the capital has been lost. Technically, the £1,500 will at stage 2 be divided rateably between A and B, A receiving £500 and B £1,000. The lost balance of £1,500 will be shared equally between them, so that A must in fact refund £250 of the £500 notionally received. The lost capital will not require an adjustment. The same result could be achieved by taking the overall loss of £5,500, of which A and B each bear £2,750. B is thus entitled to the return of his advance and capital contribution (£2,000 + £2,000) less his share of the loss (£2,750) = £1,250. He should thus be paid that sum out of the available surplus, the remainder being paid to A. See also *infra*, para. 25–43.

[36] See *supra*, paras. 10–66, 17–05.

[37] See *supra*, paras. 10–67, 10–68.

[38] But see *supra*, para. 10–69.

[39] *e.g.* in the case of a salaried partner: see *supra*, para. 18–02.

[40] In *Stekel v. Ellice* [1973] 1 W.L.R. 191, 202, Megarry J. expressed doubts whether such a partner could properly seek an order for the winding up of the firm's affairs.

[41] See *supra*, paras. 17–08, 17–09.

[42] Partnership Act 1890, s.24(1), *supra*, paras. 20–03 *et seq. Cf. Binney v. Mutrie* (1886) 12 App.Cas. 160.

of the debts and advances must be distributed between the partners in such a way as to achieve that equality.[43] Thus, if partner A has contributed capital of £10,000 and partner B £5,000, but the surplus is only £10,000, the loss of £5,000 must be shared equally, so that A will receive £7,500 and B £2,500. If equality cannot be achieved in this way, then the necessary contributions must be made as between the partners.[44] Thus if, in the previous example, the surplus is only £3,000, in order to ensure that the loss of £12,000 is shared equally A must receive the entire surplus of £3,000, together with a contribution from B of a further £1,000. Although at first sight surprising, this result is, in fact, entirely logical, once it is appreciated that the benefit of the lost capital must have accrued to the partners in their profit sharing ratios, since it will either have been applied in the acquisition of additional assets[45] or in reducing the trading losses. The same principles will, of course, be applied where the partners share profits and losses otherwise than in equal proportions.

If, however, the partners' true intention is that, once the debts **25–44** have been paid, any surplus assets will be divided between them in their normal profit sharing ratios or in proportion to their original capital contributions or in some other manner, effect must be given to that agreement; in such a case, those partners with the largest capital contributions will bear the majority of the loss.[46]

The rule in *Garner v. Murray*

The position is more complex where one of the partners is **25–45** insolvent and thus unable to contribute his share of the lost capital. In *Garner v. Murray*[47] Joyce J. held that section 44 of the Partnership Act 1890 does not compel the solvent partners to make up any shortfall resulting from that inability, so that a deficiency in the capital available for distribution is inevitable. Since such capital as is available must be distributed rateably, the deficiency will ultimately be borne by the partners *pro rata* to their capital contributions and not equally. This is, with deceptive simplicity, styled "the rule in *Garner v. Murray*."

---

[43] See *Ex p. Maude* (1867) L.R. 6 Ch.App. 51; *Re Weymouth Steam Packet Co.* [1891] 1 Ch. 66; *Re Wakefield Rolling Stock Co.* [1892] 3 Ch. 165.

[44] *Binney v. Mutrie* (1886) 12 App.Cas. 160; also *Nowell v. Nowell* (1869) L.R. 7 Eq. 538. And see *Re Anglesea Colliery Co.* (1866) L.R. 1 Ch.App. 555; *Re Crookhaven Mining Co.* (1866) L.R. 3 Eq. 69.

[45] Those additional assets (or their proceeds) will prima facie have been applied in liquidation of debts owed to third parties.

[46] See *Wood v. Scoles* (1866) L.R. 1 Ch.App. 369; also *Re Holyford Mining Co.* (1869) I.R. 3 Eq. 208; *Re Eclipse Gold Mining Co.* (1874) L.R. 17 Eq. 490; *Binney v. Mutrie* (1886) 12 App.Cas. 160.

[47] [1904] 1 Ch. 57.

25–46   Thus, suppose that partner A has contributed capital of £10,000, partner B, £5,000 and partner C, £1,000, but that profits and losses are shared equally. C is insolvent and the surplus remaining after discharging the debts and advances is £10,000, *i.e.* a loss of £6,000. A, B and C each bear £2,000 of that loss, but C is unable to contribute his share. Accordingly, the total assets available for distribution consist of the surplus (£10,000) and the notional contributions of lost capital from A and B (£4,000), *i.e.* £14,000. That amount is shared rateably between A and B in the proportions 2:1 (reflecting the size of their original capital contributions),[48] *i.e.* A notionally receives £9,333 and B, £4,666. However, there must be deducted from each partner's entitlement his share of the loss, so that A ultimately receives £7,333 and B, £2,666.[49]

25–47   Where the insolvent partner's capital account is already overdrawn before the loss of capital is deducted,[50] there appear to be two schools of thought as to the correct method of proceeding. Either that deficit is ignored when applying the rule or the deficit is itself treated as a loss *which must be shared between all the partners*. It has been submitted that the latter represents the true effect of the decision in *Garner v. Murray*,[51] but this cannot be elicited from the terms of the judgment reportedly delivered by Joyce J.[52]

The application of the rule would seem to presuppose that the insolvent partner's capital account is overdrawn either at the date of dissolution or when his share of the lost capital is debited thereto.[53]

25–48   It was submitted in earlier editions of this work that the rule works logically, since the insolvent partner must already have received his share of the lost capital in one of the ways previously described[54] or by making excessive (and presumably unauthorised) drawings on his

---

[48] If, in fact, any partner has withdrawn a part of his original contribution, regard will be had to the partners' respective capital entitlements as at the date of dissolution (as in *Garner v. Murray* itself).

[49] This appears to be the conventional method of calculation and reflects the requirements of the words "including the sums, if any, contributed by the partners to make up losses or deficiencies of capital" in the Partnership Act 1890, s.44(b), *supra*, para. 25–40. However, precisely the same result is in fact achieved if the partners' respective shares of the loss are deducted from their capital entitlements and the deficiency attributable to C's failure to contribute his share (*i.e.* £1,000 – £2,000, a net deficiency of £1,000) is shared between A and B pro rata to their original contributions.

[50] This was in fact the position in *Garner v. Murray*.

[51] This view appears to be based on the actual terms of the order made by Joyce J., although this is not set out in the reports; *quaere* is it borne out by the statement of the facts at [1904] 52 W.R. 208? The whole question appears to have been subject to detailed analysis in Australia: the current editor expresses his gratitude to Professor K. A. Houghton for drawing his attention to various articles in the journal Abacus. See in particular, Vol. 17, No. 1, p. 41 and Vol. 18, No. 1, p. 91. Also Higgins & Fletcher, *The Law of Partnership in Australia and New Zealand* (5th ed.), pp. 254 *et seq.*

[52] But see the terms of the Partnership Act 1890, s.44(a), *supra*, para. 25–40.

[53] If there were a positive balance *after* debiting the insolvent partner's share of the loss, there would in fact be no shortfall.

[54] See *supra*, para. 25–43.

capital account, so that there is no justification for requiring the solvent partners to restore sums which they have not received prior to the return of their capital. However, in the current editor's view, this somewhat over-simplifies the position, particularly if it is right that the deficit on the insolvent partner's capital account must itself be treated as a loss.

Entitlement where capital repaid in full

Where realisation of the surplus assets has produced a fund which **25-49** is more than sufficient to repay all the partners' capital contributions, each such contribution may carry a proportionate share of the income of that fund, so that only the balance will be divided between them in their profit sharing ratios.[55]

Need for court order

There is no reason why the affairs of a partnership should not be **25-50** wound up by the partners or their representatives without the intervention of the court,[56] save where disputes arise.[57]

Adjustments pursuant to court order

If the surplus assets are distributed amongst the partners pursuant **25-51** to a court order which is later reversed, any partner who has received more than his true entitlement will be ordered to repay the excess.[58]

5. SUMMARY OF WINDING-UP PRINCIPLES

Various consequences of a partnership dissolution which impinge **25-52** directly on the winding up of its affairs have been considered in this work and may, for convenience, be summarised in the following general principles:

A. PRINCIPLES WHICH APPLY AS REGARDS CREDITORS

(1) A dissolution, whether general or technical,[59] will not, of **25-53** itself, discharge any partner from a debt or liability incurred prior to the dissolution.[60]

---

[55] See *supra*, para. 20–31.

[56] See *Lyon v. Haynes* (1843) 5 Man. & G. 505.

[57] See the Partnership Act 1890, s.39, *supra*, paras. 19–29 *et seq.* Lord Lindley, referring to the (then exclusive) jurisdiction of the Chancery Division, observed that, in the event of any dispute, "it is under [*that Division's*] superintendence only that the assets of the partnership can be properly sold and applied, that the partnership accounts can be satisfactorily taken, and that contribution can be enforced."

[58] *Re Birkbeck Permanent Building Society* [1915] 1 Ch. 91.

[59] See *supra*, paras. 24–02, 24–03.

[60] See *supra*, paras. 13–74 *et seq.*

(2) In order to secure a discharge from such a debt or liability a partner must, in general, show that the creditor has (a) been paid or otherwise satisfied; (b) released or discharged him; or (c) accepted a substitute debtor or security.[61]

(3) Notwithstanding the dissolution, the partners will be obliged to attend to any unfinished business and, in the course of so doing, must exercise a proper degree of care and skill.[62]

(4) Save in a few exceptional cases,[63] a partner will remain liable for the *future* acts of his former co-partners until such time as the dissolution is duly notified.[64]

(5) Notice of dissolution will, in general, be given by advertisement, but this is unlikely to be sufficient in the case of existing customers.[65]

(6) Even after the dissolution has been notified, a partner may be liable for the acts of his former co-partners in winding up the partnership affairs.[66]

(7) Furthermore, a partner will remain liable for the acts of his former co-partners if he allows them to hold him out as a continuing partner.[67]

B. Principles Which Apply as Between the Partners

25–54   (1) Each partner is entitled to have the partnership property applied in liquidation of the partnership debts, and to have any surplus assets divided.[68]

(2) Each partner is, in general, entitled to force a sale of all partnership assets which are capable of being sold and to have the value of any unsaleable asset brought into account by the partner who retains it.[69]

(3) As a corollary of (2), save in special circumstances, no partner can insist on taking the share of any other partner at a valuation or to insist on a division of the partnership assets in specie.[70]

(4) No partner can retain the exclusive right to any increase in the value of the partnership assets between dissolution and sale,[71]

---

[61] See *supra*, paras. 13–77 *et seq.*
[62] See *supra*, paras. 13–63 *et seq. Quaere* to what extent (if at all) they can take on *new* business: see *supra*, paras. 10–160, 16–25.
[63] See *supra*, paras. 13–48 *et seq.*
[64] See *supra*, paras. 13–40 *et seq.*
[65] See *supra*, paras. 13–70 *et seq.*
[66] See *supra*, paras. 13–63 *et seq.*
[67] See *supra*, para. 13–62.
[68] See *supra*, paras. 19–28 *et seq.*
[69] See *supra*, paras. 10–121, 10–160, 19–04 *et seq.*, 23–179 *et seq.*
[70] See *supra*, paras. 10–121, 19–10 *et seq.*, 23–180 *et seq.*
[71] See *supra*, para. 25–27.

but more difficult questions may arise in relation to trading profits realised during that period.[72]

(5) Both the authority of each partner and the duties which he owes to the other partners continue whilst the partnership affairs are being wound up.[73] As Lord Lindley put it:

"For the purposes of winding up, the partnership is deemed to continue; the good faith and honourable conduct due from every partner to his co-partners during the continuance of the partnership being equally due so long as its affairs remain unsettled[74]; and that which was partnership property before, continuing to be so for the purpose of dissolution, as the rights of the partners require."[75]

Account must, however, be taken of any agreement between the partners.[76]

(6) Each partner can insist that no further business is transacted or acts done, otherwise than with a view to the winding-up.[77]

(7) In the absence of some contrary agreement, the right to wind up the partnership affairs does not fall on any particular partner to the exclusion of the others. If any dispute arises, the winding-up should proceed under the supervision of the court.[78]

(8) The right to wind up the partnership affairs is, however, personal to the partners, so that the representatives of a deceased, insolvent or mentally disordered partner will not normally be permitted to interfere.[79]

(9) A return of premium may be ordered if the partnership was dissolved prior to the expiration of a fixed term.[80]

(10) If, on settling the final account, the partnership assets are insufficient to pay the partnership debts, or to repay the sums due to each partner in respect of advances or capital, the

---

[72] See *supra*, paras. 25–21 *et seq*.

[73] See *supra*, paras. 13–63 *et seq*.

[74] See *supra*, paras. 16–09 *et seq*.

[75] See *Ex p. Williams* (1805) 11 Ves.Jr. 3; *Crawshay v. Collins* (1826) 2 Russ. 325, 342–343, *per* Lord Eldon; *Nerot v. Burnand* (1827) 4 Russ. 247, affirmed at (1828) 2 Bli. (N.S.) 215; *Payne v. Hornby* (1858) 25 Beav. 280; also *Ex p. Trueman* (1832) 1 D. & Ch. 464. This passage was cited with approval in *Thompson's Trustee v. Heaton* [1974] 1 W.L.R. 605, 613, *per* Pennycuick V.-C.

[76] See, for example, *Souhrada v. Bank of New South Wales* [1976] 2 Lloyd's Rep. 444.

[77] See *Ex p. Williams* (1805) 11 Ves. Jr. 3; *Wilson v. Greenwood* (1818) 1 Swan. 471; *Crawshay v. Maule* (1818) 1 Swan. 495; also *supra*, paras. 13–59 *et seq*. *Quaere*, what is the position where new business must be taken on to preserve the goodwill of the firm pending its realisation? See *supra*, paras. 10–160, 16–25.

[78] See *supra*, paras. 23–66 *et seq*. Thus, the court will, where necessary, appoint a receiver, direct the sale of assets and the payment of debts and liabilities and restrain a partner from interfering with the conduct of the winding-up.

[79] See *supra*, para. 23–144.

[80] See *supra*, paras. 25–09 *et seq*. As to cases of fraud, see *supra*, para. 25–07.

deficiency must, subject to any contrary agreement, be made good by the partners in their profit sharing ratios.[81]

(11) Although interest on capital is not normally payable following a dissolution,[82] a partner's capital contribution may carry any income attributable thereto.[83]

(12) Unless that right is excluded by agreement, each partner is entitled to give notice of the dissolution[84] and, where appropriate, to prevent his former co-partners from continuing to hold him out as a partner by using the old firm name.[85]

(13) Once the winding up is complete, each partner will, in general, be entitled to start up a business of the same nature as that carried on by the dissolved firm, either alone or in partnership with others.[86]

---

[81] See *supra*, paras. 25–40 *et seq.*

[82] See *supra*, para. 20–30.

[83] See *supra*, paras. 20–31, 25–49.

[84] See *supra*, paras. 13–39 *et seq.*

[85] Lord Lindley described each partner's right in these terms: "It seems that he has also a right to restrain [*the other partners*] from carrying on business under the old name, if such name is or includes his own; for even if their continued use of the old name, with his knowledge, is not of itself sufficient to render him liable, by virtue of the doctrine of holding out, such use undoubtedly exposes him to the risk of having actions brought against him as if he still belonged to the firm, and in the case supposed his co-partners have no right to expose him to that risk." See *supra*, paras. 5–54 *et seq.*, 10–162, 10–163, 23–146. The position will, of course, be different where the other partners have acquired the right to use the old firm name, by purchase or otherwise.

[86] See *supra*, paras. 10–162, 10–168 *et seq.* Lord Lindley put it thus: "... each partner has a right to commence a new business in the old line, and in the old neighbourhood; either alone, or in partnership with other people."

CHAPTER 26

DEATH OF A PARTNER

IT is convenient to analyse the consequences of a partner's death in **26–01** terms of the respective rights and, where relevant, duties of the three groups of persons actually or potentially affected thereby, namely:

1. The surviving partners and the personal representatives of the deceased partner.
2. The creditors of the partnership.
3. The separate creditors and legatees, etc., of the deceased partner.

Each group will be considered in turn.

1. THE SURVIVING PARTNERS AND PERSONAL REPRESENTATIVES OF THE DECEASED PARTNER

Dissolution and winding-up

It has already been seen that, subject to any contrary agreement, **26–02** the death of a partner dissolves the partnership as regards *all* the partners.[1] Although the doctrine of survivorship will not in general apply to any part of the deceased partner's beneficial share,[2] the conduct of the winding-up is vested exclusively in the surviving partners.[3] It follows that the rights of the personal representatives are limited, as Lord Lindley explained:

"Unless all the partners have agreed to the contrary, when one of them dies, his executors have no right to become partners with the surviving partners[4]; nor to interfere with the partnership business[5]; but the executors of the deceased represent him for all purposes of account, and, unless restrained by special agreement, they have the power, by bringing an action, to have the affairs of the partnership

---

[1] Partnership Act 1890, s.33(1), *supra*, paras. 24–20, 24–21.
[2] See *supra*, para. 19–14; also *supra*, para. 10–164. As to the devolution of *title* to the partnership assets, see *supra*, paras. 18–60 *et seq*.
[3] Partnership Act 1890, s.38, *supra*, paras. 13–64 *et seq*.
[4] *Pearce v. Chamberlain* (1750) 2 Ves.Sen. 33. See also *McClean v. Kennard* (1874) 9 L.R. Ch.App. 336.
[5] See *supra*, para. 23–144.

wound up in a manner which is generally ruinous to the other partners."[6]

26–03   The reference to the "ruinous" effects of a winding-up reflects the fact that a deceased partner's share will normally be ascertained and paid out by means of a sale of all the partnership assets, whether or not pursuant to a court order, since the surviving partners have no inherent right to acquire that share at a valuation.[7] Equally, the surviving partners will be obliged to complete any business left unfinished at the date of dissolution,[8] so that the court may defer a forced sale of those assets and the ultimate adjustment of accounts as between the partners until a particular subsisting contract has been fully performed.[9]

Deceased partner's share as a debt

26–04   Section 43 of the Partnership Act 1890 provides that the amount due to the personal representatives of a deceased partner in respect of his share is a debt accruing at the date of death.[10] Although the application of this section is not open to doubt where it is recognised, either expressly or by implication, that the partnership will continue notwithstanding a partner's death,[11] the position is less clear where the death brings about a *general* dissolution. If the share is indeed converted into a debt on such a dissolution, it is a debt of a most unusual nature, since the estate is clearly entitled to a full share of any increase in the value of the partnership assets accruing in the period between the date of death and the date of realisation[12] and, conversely, must bear a full share of any diminution in value during that period.[13] For this reason, the current editor shares Lord Lindley's view[14] that the section was not intended to apply in such a case.[15]

---

[6] Partnership Act 1890, s.39, *supra*, paras. 19–29 *et seq.*
[7] See *supra*, paras. 19–04 *et seq.*, 23–179 *et seq.*
[8] See *supra*, paras. 13–64, 13–65.
[9] *McClean v. Kennard* (1874) 9 Ch.App. 336. See also *supra*, para. 23–191.
[10] See *supra*, para. 23–33. And see also the Partnership Act 1890, s.39, *supra*, paras. 19–29 *et seq.*
[11] See *supra*, paras. 10–33, 19–11, 19–12, 23–33.
[12] See *Barclays Bank Trust Co. Ltd. v. Bluff* [1982] Ch. 172; *Chandroutie v. Gajadhar* [1987] A.C. 147. And see also *supra*, para. 25–27.
[13] There does not appear to be any decision to this effect but it is in the natural corollary of the decision in *Barclays Bank Trust Co. Ltd. v. Bluff*, *supra*. This presupposes that the loss cannot be attributed to the misconduct of the surviving partners: see *supra*, paras. 20–10, 20–11.
[14] See *supra*, para. 23–33. Unaccountably, this view was only expressed in relation to the position under *Scots* law. See also *supra*, para. 19–41.
[15] Equally, it is undeniable that the Partnership Act 1890, s.42 will apply in the case of a general dissolution: see *supra*, paras. 25–23 *et seq.* and *infra*, para. 26–08. One of the options under this section is a claim for interest "on the amount of [*the deceased's*] share of the partnership assets." This presumably refers to his share of the assets as at the date of dissolution, so that s.43 *may* apply for this limited purpose.

Sale of share and arrangements to avoid general dissolution

Because of the potential implications for the surviving partners, the **26–05** personal representatives of a deceased partner will often wish to explore ways in which a general dissolution and winding up can be avoided.

There is, in general, no bar on the personal representatives selling the deceased's share to the surviving partners, unless one of those representatives is also a member of the firm.[16] If such a sale cannot, for whatever reason, be arranged, the only option may be to leave the deceased's share in the business. This course is not without risk, even if the consent of the beneficiaries is obtained,[17] since the representatives might inadvertently become (or be held out as) partners[18] and thereby incur personal liability for the continuing firm's debts and obligations, notwithstanding their trustee status.[19] Lord Lindley summarised the difficulty which executors[20] face in these terms:

"The position of the executors of a deceased partner is, in fact, often one of considerable hardship and difficulty; if they insist on an immediate winding up of the firm, they may ruin those whom the deceased may have been most anxious to benefit; whilst if for their advantage the partnership is allowed to go on, the executors may run the risk of being ruined themselves."[21]

Accordingly, the representatives may in practice have no choice *but* to force a sale of all the assets and a winding-up of the partnership affairs in the normal way.

Position where surviving partner is appointed executor

Needless to say, the foregoing difficulties are exacerbated rather **26–06** than resolved where one of the surviving partners has been appointed an executor of the deceased partner's will, as Lord Lindley explained:

"... his own personal interest as a surviving partner is brought into direct conflict with his duty as an executor. Everything therefore

---

[16] See *supra*, paras. 23–59 *et seq.* and *infra*, paras. 26–06, 26–44.

[17] The representatives will not necessarily have power to adopt this course: see *infra*, paras. 26–29, 26–30.

[18] See the Partnership Act 1890, ss.2(3), 14, *supra*, paras. 5–21 *et seq.*, 5–43 *et seq.* As to the position prior to the Act, see *Holme v. Hammond* (1872) L.R. 7 Ex. 218 (where the personal representatives were not liable); *cf. Ex p. Garland* (1804) 10 Ves.Jr. 110; *Wightman v. Townroe* (1813) 1 M. & S. 412; *Ex p. Holdsworth* (1841) 1 M.D. & D. 475.

[19] A trustee partner's liability is normally no different from that of any other partner: see *Muir v. City of Glasgow Bank* (1879) 4 App.Cas. 337.

[20] Administrators are in no different position.

[21] See *infra*, paras. 26–26 *et seq.*, 26–49 *et seq.*

which he does is liable to question and misconstruction on the part of the persons beneficially entitled to the estate of the deceased; and he is practically much more fettered in the discharge of his duties, and in the exercise of his rights, than if he did not have to act in the double character imposed upon him."[22]

Debts paid to and by surviving partners

26–07 The surviving partners are clearly the proper persons to get in and pay the partnership debts.[23] It is, perhaps, self evident that any sums got in will reduce the debts owed to the former firm, whilst any sums paid out will reduce the debts owed by it,[24] but this may have important consequences as between the surviving partners and the personal representatives of the deceased partner. Thus, the representatives will, on the one hand, be entitled to treat payments received by the surviving partners from a debtor of the former firm as made in respect of a debt owed to it,[25] whilst the surviving partners will, on the other hand, be entitled to reimbursement out of the deceased partner's estate if they pay his share of the debts owed by the former firm.[26]

Post-dissolution profits

26–08 It has already been seen that, if the surviving partners have carried on the partnership business without any final settlement of accounts as between them and the personal representatives of the deceased partner, the latter are entitled, at their option, to the share of profits attributable to the use of the deceased's share of the partnership assets or to interest thereon at the rate of 5 per cent.[27] However, in such a case, the surviving partners will normally be made an allowance out of the profits in recognition of their efforts, unless they are also the deceased's personal representatives.[28]

Actions by surviving partners against deceased's estate

26–09 Surviving partners may commence proceedings against the estate of a deceased partner in two distinct capacities,[29] as identified by Lord Lindley in the following passage:

---

[22] See, generally, *Hutton v. Rosseter* (1855) 7 De G.M. & G. 12; *Wright v. Morgan* [1926] A.C. 788, 796–798.

[23] See *supra*, paras. 13–63 *et seq.*, 18–63.

[24] In book-keeping terms, the payment of debts owed to the former firm will result in a debit entry in the list of its debtors, and the payment of debts owed by it will result in a credit entry in the list of its creditors.

[25] *Lees v. Laforest* (1851) 14 Beav. 250.

[26] *Musson v. May* (1814) 3 V. & B. 194.

[27] Partnership Act 1890, s.42(1), *supra*, paras. 25–23 *et seq.* Note also *ibid.* s.29, *supra*, paras. 16–09, 16–24. As to the possibility of seeking interest under the Supreme Court Act 1981, s.35A, see *supra*, paras. 20–39, 25–38.

[28] See *supra*, 25–28.

[29] Proceedings may obviously be framed in the alternative, where appropriate: see R.S.C. Ord. 15, r. 4; C.C.R. Ord. 5, r. 2.

"A surviving partner, if a creditor of the deceased, may sue either in that character for a common administration judgment, or, in the character of a partner, for a judgment for a partnership account and for payment of what is due on that account; and if assets are not admitted, then for a judgment for the administration of the estate of the deceased."

The surviving partners will, of course, be creditors of the estate for **26–10** any sums found due to them on taking the partnership accounts and may seek an administration order in that capacity.[30]

The deceased partner's personal representatives must be joined as parties to any action for an account brought by one or more of the surviving partners[31] and, in such a case, it is permissible to commence proceedings against the estate where no grant of probate or letters of administration has been obtained.[32] However, an application must then be made either to have someone appointed to represent the estate or to have the deceased partner's personal representatives (if any) joined as parties, together with an order to carry the proceedings on against him/them.[33]

Rights of representatives where administration order made

Where an administration order is made in respect of a deceased **26–11** partner's estate, his personal representatives will, in general, be free from all forms of personal liability. Lord Lindley summarised the rights of a deceased partner's executors in these terms:

"... his executors, if they act properly, are personally protected from all consequences, and no action can be sustained against them in respect of what they so do.[34] If there are liabilities which will have to be met, the Court will order part of the assets to be set aside to meet them when they arise.[35] But if the liabilities are remote and contingent, and may possibly never arise at all, the utmost that the executors can obtain in the shape of indemnity, in

---

[30] See *Addis v. Knight* (1817) 2 Mer. 117; *Robinson v. Alexander* (1834) 2 Cl. & F. 717.

[31] Lord Lindley noted that "If there is no ... representative, but the assets of the deceased or of the partnership are in danger, and the object of the plaintiff is to have them protected, he should confine his claim for relief accordingly, and not seek for an account: *Rawlings v. Lambert* (1860) 1 J. & H. 458." *Semble*, it would not be fatal if the relief claimed were *not* so confined: see R.S.C. Ord. 15, r. 6(1); C.C.R. Ord. 5, r. 4.

[32] R.S.C. Ord. 15, r. 6A(1), (3); Supreme Court Act 1981, s.87(2). And see *Re Amirteymour* [1979] 1 W.L.R. 63. As to the equivalent rule in the county court, see C.C.R. Ord. 5, r. 8(1), (3).

[33] R.S.C. Ord. 15, r.6A(4)(a); C.C.R. Ord. 5, r.8(4)(a). Note also R.S.C. Ord. 15, r.15; C.C.R. Ord. 5, r.7. Formerly, a limited grant could have been obtained by a nominee of the surviving partners for the purposes of the proceedings (*Cawthorn v. Chalie* (1824) 2 Sim. & St. 127), but this is no longer necessary.

[34] *Waller v. Barrett* (1857) 24 Beav. 413.

[35] *Fletcher v. Stevenson* (1844) 3 Hare 360; *Brewer v. Pocock* (1857) 23 Beav. 310.

addition to that afforded by the orders of the Court itself, is a covenant from the testator's legatees or next of kin."[36]

Surviving partners' right to carry on similar business

26–12   Unless the goodwill of the former firm has been or is to be sold in the course of winding up its affairs,[37] the surviving partners will seemingly be free to start up a "new" business under the old firm name.[38]

2. THE CREDITORS OF THE PARTNERSHIP

26–13 The rights of partnership creditors against the estate of a deceased partner will vary according to whether their debts were incurred before or after the date of his death.

A. DEBTS INCURRED PRIOR TO A PARTNER'S DEATH

General rules affecting liability of estate

26–14   Numerous decided cases illustrating the consequences of a partner's death on his liability to existing partnership creditors are noticed elsewhere in this work. It is accordingly sufficient, in the present context, to formulate a number of general rules and, where necessary, to classify the authorities by reference thereto.

26–15   *Rule 1*:   The estate of a deceased partner will, in general, remain liable not only for all partnership debts and obligations incurred prior to the date of his death[39] but also for any tort,[40] fraud or breach of trust committed prior to that date which can be imputed to the firm.[41]

The authorities may be classified as follows:

Group A: Ordinary case (liability unaffected).

---

[36] See *Dean v. Allen* (1855) 20 Beav. 1; *Waller v. Barrett* (1857) 24 Beav. 413; *Addams v. Ferick* (1859) 26 Beav. 384; *Bennett v. Lytton* (1860) 2 J. & H. 155; also *Re Nixon* [1904] 1 Ch. 638 and the cases there cited.

[37] See *supra*, paras. 10–160 *et seq.*

[38] See *Hill v. Fearis* [1905] 1 Ch. 466; also *supra*, para. 10–162.

[39] See generally, *supra*, paras. 13–06 *et seq.* Lord Lindley also referred readers to the "celebrated judgment in *Devaynes v. Noble* (1839) 1 Mer. 529."

[40] Note that, with the sole exception of defamation, tortious claims by or against a partner are unaffected by his death: Law Reform (Miscellaneous Provisions) Act 1934, s.1(1) (as amended); Law Reform (Miscellaneous Provisions) Act 1970, s.5.

[41] See *supra*, paras. 13–12, 13–13.

Sub-group (i): contracts.[42]

Sub-group (ii): torts, frauds and breaches of trust.[43]

Group B: Exceptional case (liability extinguished).[44]

Rule 2: The liability of the estate will be unaffected by any arrangement between the personal representatives and the surviving partners.[45]

Rule 3: The liability of the estate will be unaffected by any **26–16** subsequent dealings between the creditors and the surviving partners,[46] unless it can be established either that the creditors have lost or abandoned their rights against the estate[47] or that the debts have been paid or discharged.[48]

Rule 4: Although the estate may be discharged by the expiration of the relevant limitation period, it will, in general, be bound by an acknowledgement or part payment given by the surviving partners.[49]

---

[42] See *Lane v. Williams* (1692) 2 Vern. 292; *Clavering v. Westley* (1735) 3 P.W. 402; *Simpson v. Vaughan* (1739) 2 Atk. 31; *Darwent v. Walton* (1742) 2 Atk. 510; *Jacomb v. Harwood* (1751) 2 Ves.Sen. 265; *Bishop v. Church* (1751) 2 Ves.Sen. 371 (*supra*, para. 13–08); *Thomas v. Frazer* (1797) 3 Ves.Jr. 399; *Burn v. Burn* (1798) 3 Ves.Jr. 573; *Orr v. Chase* (1812) 1 Mer. 729; *Devaynes v. Noble* (1816) 1 Mer. 529 and (1831) 2 R. & M. 495; *Cheetham v. Crook* (1825) McCle. & Yo. 307; *Wilkinson v. Henderson* (1833) 1 M. & K. 583; *Thorpe v. Jackson* (1837) 2 Y. & C.Ex. 553; *Harris v. Farwell* (1846) 13 Beav. 403; *Hills v. Mc'Rae* (1851) 9 Hare 297; *Brett v. Beckwith* (1856) 3 Jur. (N.S.) 31 (*infra*, para. 26–20); *Beresford v. Browning* (1875) L.R. 20 Eq. 564 (*supra*, para. 13–08).

[43] See *Clayton's case* (1816) 1 Mer. 576 (*supra*, paras. 12–121, 13–82); *Warde's case* (1816) 1 Mer. 624; *Vulliamy v. Noble* (1817) 3 Mer. 619; *Sadler v. Lee* (1843) 6 Beav. 324 (*supra*, para. 12–124); *Blair v. Bromley* (1847) 2 Ph. 354 (*supra*, paras. 12–125); *Sawyer v. Goodwin* (1867) 36 L.J.Ch. 578 (negligence); *New Sombrero Phosphate Co. v. Erlanger* (1877) 5 Ch.D. 73 (fraud); *Blyth v. Fladgate* [1891] 1 Ch. 337; *Smith v. Blyth* [1891] 1 Ch. 337, 366, *per* Stirling J. (negligence); *Moore v. Knight* [1891] 1 Ch. 547.

[44] See *Sumner v. Powell* (1823) Tur. & Rus. 423 (*supra*, para. 13–10); *Clarke v. Bickers* (1845) 14 Sim. 639 (*supra*, para. 13–11); *Wilmer v. Currey* (1848) 2 De G. & Sm. 347 (*supra*, para. 13–11); *Hill's case* (1875) L.R. 20 Eq. 585 (joint holders of shares).

[45] See *supra*, paras. 13–102 *et seq.*

[46] See *Jacomb v. Harwood* (1751) 2 Ves.Sen. 265; *Daniel v. Cross* (1796) 3 Ves.Jr. 277; *Sleech's case* (1816) 1 Mer. 539; *Clayton's case* (1816) 1 Mer. 572 (*supra*, paras. 12–121, 13–82); *Palmer's case* (1816) 1 Mer. 623; *Braithwaite v. Britain* (1836) 1 Keen 206; *Winter v. Innes* (1838) 4 Myl. & Cr. 101 (which Lord Lindley described as "very important"); *Harris v. Farwell* (1851) 15 Beav. 31 (*supra*, para. 13–127); *Re Hodgson* (1885) 31 Ch.D. 177; *Re Head* [1893] 3 Ch. 426 (*supra*, para. 13–126); *cf. Head v. Head (No. 2)* [1894] 2 Ch. 236. And see *supra*, paras. 13–102 *et seq.*

[47] See (i) as to the effect of general dealings, *Brown v. Gordon* (1852) 16 Beav. 302 (*supra*, para. 13–129); also *Wilson v. Lloyd* (1873) L.R. 16 Eq. 60 (which is, however, unreliable: see *supra*, para. 13–99, n. 68); (ii) as to the effect of opening a new account, *Head v. Head (No. 2)* [1894] 2 Ch. 236 *supra*, para. 13–126; *cf. Re Head* [1893] 3 Ch. 426; and (iii) as to the position where the deceased partner has become a surety for the surviving partner's obligations, *Oakeley v. Pasheller* (1836) 10 Bli. (N.S.) 548 and 4 Cl. & F. 207 (*supra*, para. 13–99).

[48] See *Clayton's case* (1816) 1 Mer. 572 (*supra*, paras. 12–121, 13–82); *Merriman v. Ward* (1860) 1 J. & H. 371, of which Lord Lindley commented "This case is important as showing that where a debt of a deceased partner has been discharged by the application of the rule in *Clayton's case*, it is not competent for his executors to revive such a debt against his estate."

[49] See *supra*, para. 13–139.

Rule 5:   The estate will not be liable for any income tax assessed
on the firm after the date of death.[50]

Creditor's right to proceed first against the estate

26–17   Prior to the Partnership Act 1890, Lord Lindley wrote:

"... whatever doubt there may formerly have been upon the
subject,[51] it has been long settled that a creditor of the firm can
proceed against the estate of a deceased partner, without first
having recourse to the surviving partners, and without reference to
the state of the accounts between them and the deceased.[52] But it
is necessary to make the surviving partners parties to the action,
for they are interested in the issues raised between him and the
executors."[53]

This is still the position,[54] although a creditor's failure to join the
surviving partners as parties to the action would not, in itself, be
fatal.[55] In practice, a single action brought against the surviving
partners and the deceased partner's personal representatives is
generally to be preferred.[56]

Creditor's rights postponed to separate debts

26–18   A partnership creditor who seeks payment out of a deceased
partner's estate will not rank equally with his separate creditors: this
is clearly established by the Partnership Act 1890.[57] The creditor's
rights are circumscribed in such a case, as Lord Lindley explained:

"The right of the creditor ... is to have the separate estate of the
deceased ascertained and applied in payment of his separate debts

---

[50] See *Harrison v. Willis Bros.* [1966] Ch. 619. Note that, in the case of firms formed on or after
April 6, 1994, tax will no longer be assessed on the partners jointly, but firms in existence prior to
that date will continue to be subject to the existing regime until the fiscal year 1997/98: see the
Finance Act 1994, s.204, amending the provision of the Income and Corporation Taxes Act 1988,
s.111. See also *infra*, paras. 34–19 *et seq.*

[51] *Cf. Braithwaite v. Britain* (1836) 1 Keen 206; *Winter v. Innes* (1838) 4 Myl. & Cr. 101; *Way v.
Bassett* (1845) 5 Hare 55; *Brown v. Gordon* (1852) 16 Beav. 302.

[52] *Wilkinson v. Henderson* (1833) 1 M. & K. 582; *Thorpe v. Jackson* (1837) 2 Y. & C.Ex. 553;
Devaynes v. Noble (1839) 2 R. & M. 495; *Re McRae* (1883) 25 Ch.D. 16; *Re Hodgson* (1885) 31
Ch.D. 177. Equally, the surviving partners cannot insist on the creditors proceeding first against the
deceased partner's estate: *Ex p. Kendall* (1811) 17 Ves.Jr. 514.

[53] See, in addition to the cases in the last note, *Stephenson v. Chiswell* (1797) 3 Ves.Jr. 566;
Sleech's Case (1816) 1 Mer. 539; *Rice v. Gordon* (1848) 11 Beav. 265; *Hills v. M'Rae* (1851) 9 Hare
297.

[54] See *supra*, paras. 13–07 *et seq.*

[55] R.S.C. Ord. 15, r. 6(1); C.C.R. Ord. 5, r. 4. See also *supra*, para. 14–58.

[56] See *infra*, para. 26–22.

[57] *Ibid.* s.9, *supra*, para. 13–03. And see also, as to the effect of this section, *supra*, para. 13–07.

and liabilities, and to have the surplus applied in payment of his joint liabilities."[58]

The corollary is, of course, that the separate creditors have no rights against the deceased's share in the firm until all the partnership debts have been paid.[59]

The same basic rule applies in the administration of an insolvent estate.[60]

Form of administration order

If there is, in fact, sufficient to meet the demands of all the **26-19** deceased's creditors, both joint and separate, the estate can be administered as a single fund and the creditors paid out *pari passu*.[61] However, since the solvency of the estate cannot be assured, a partnership creditor will not, unless he is also a separate creditor of the deceased, be entitled to the usual form of administration order, but to an order designed to ensure the proper distribution of the estate between the two potentially competing classes of creditors.[62] It appears that such an order should be sought by writ rather than by originating summons.[63]

If an administration action is already proceeding, a partnership creditor will be able to obtain the requisite order without bringing an action of his own.[64]

---

[58] *Hills v. M'Rae* (1851) 9 Hare 297; *Re McRae* (1883) 25 Ch.D. 16; *Re Hodgson* (1885) 31 Ch.D. 177; *Re Barnard* (1886) 32 Ch.D. 447; *Smith v. Blyth* [1891] 1 Ch. 337, 367, *per* Stirling J.; *Moore v. Knight* [1891] 1 Ch. 547; also *Kendall v. Hamilton* (1879) 4 App.Cas. 504. *Cf. Burn v. Burn* (1798) 3 Ves.Jr. 573, where a joint and several bond had been given by the partners.

[59] See *Hills v. M'Rae, supra*; *Ridgway v. Clare* (1854) 19 Beav. 111; *Moore v. Knight* [1891] 1 Ch. 547; *Re Ritson* [1899] 1 Ch. 128.

[60] See *infra*, paras. 26–23, 26–24.

[61] See *Ridgway v. Clare* (1854) 19 Beav. 111, where there were four separate actions relating to the estates of two deceased partners.

[62] See *Hills v. M'Rae* (1851) 9 Hare 297, as followed in *Re Hodgson* (1885) 31 Ch.D. 177; *Smith v. Blyth* [1891] 1 Ch. 337; *Moore v. Knight* [1891] 1 Ch. 547. See also *Harris v. Farwell* (1846) 13 Beav. 403; *Rice v. Gordon* (1848) 11 Beav. 265. Lord Lindley summarised the substance of the judgment given as follows: "1. It is declared that all persons who are creditors of the deceased, are entitled to the benefit of the judgment. 2. It is declared that the surplus of the estate of the deceased, after satisfying his funeral and testamentary expenses and separate debts, was liable at the time of his death to the joint debts of the firm, but without prejudice to the liability of the surviving partner, as between himself and the estate of the deceased. 3. An account is directed to be taken of the funeral and testamentary expenses and separate debts of the deceased, and of the debts of the firm. If the surviving partner is not a party to the action, liberty is given him to attend in the prosecution of this last inquiry. 4. An account is directed to be taken of the *personal* estate of the deceased. 5. It is ordered that his *personal* estate be applied, in the first instance, in the payment of his separate debts and funeral expenses, in a due course of administration, and then in payment of the debts of the firm. 6. *And if the personal estate of the deceased is insufficient for the purposes of the action, inquiries are ordered to be made for the purpose of ascertaining the real estate to which the deceased was entitled.*" Those parts of the judgment which appear in italics do not accord with the order in which assets are now applied under the Administration of Estates Act 1925, Sched. 1, Pt. II. As to the normal form of administration order, see *Heward's Chancery Orders*, p. 66. But see also *infra*, para. 26–22, n. 72.

[63] See *Re Barnard* (1886) 32 Ch.D. 447. *Sed quaere.*

[64] *Gray v. Chiswell* (1803) 9 Ves.Jr. 118; *Cowell v. Sikes* (1827) 2 Russ. 191. See also *Re McRae* (1883) 25 Ch.D.

Accounts, inquiries, etc.

26–20   Although it is correct to say that a partnership creditor is not
directly concerned with the state of the accounts as between the
partners,[65] it is clear from the decision in *Brett v. Beckwith*[66] that this
will not always be the case. There a firm comprised two partners, A
and B. A was bankrupt and B had died. A creditor of the firm
commenced proceedings against B's executors and A's assignees[67]
seeking *inter alia* administration of B's estate and the taking of
accounts as between A and B. The court held that he was entitled to
have the estate fully administered and, for that purpose, to have such
accounts taken in order to determine what was comprised in the joint
estate.

26–21   The court will order any inquiry which appears necessary,[68] *e.g.*
with a view to ascertaining whether the partnership creditors have
continued to deal with the surviving partners and, thereby, released
the deceased's estate from liability.[69]

Although directions could, in an appropriate case, be made for the
joint and separate estates to be kept distinct, this is not usually
done.[70]

Parties to actions

26–22   The creditor can issue one set of proceedings against the surviving
partners and the personal representatives of the deceased partner or
he may proceed against them separately.[71] If he adopts the former
course, priority will still be accorded to the deceased's separate
creditors, so that in practice he may have to look for payment solely
to the surviving partners.[72] It has already been seen that the surviving
partners will in any event be necessary parties if accounts are to be
taken pursuant to the administration order in respect of the estate.[73]

---

[65] See *supra*, para. 26–17.

[66] (1856) 3 Jur.(N.S.) 31.

[67] The forerunners of the trustee in bankruptcy.

[68] See, for example, *Barber v. Mackrell* (1879) 12 Ch.D. 534, where one partner had fraudulently
withdrawn money from the firm.

[69] *Devaynes v. Noble* (1839) 1 Mer. 530.

[70] See *Paynter v. Houston* (1817) 3 Mer. 297; *Woolley v. Gordon* (1829) Tam. 11; *Rice v. Gordon*
(1848) 11 Beav. 271; *Ridgway v. Clare* (1854) 19 Beav. 111.

[71] Judgment against the surviving partners was not a bar to proceedings against the estate of a
deceased partner (and *vice versa*) even prior to the Civil Liability (Contribution) Act 1978: see
supra, para. 13–06. Note also that the feasibility of a single set of proceedings prior to the
Judicature Acts appears to have been sufficiently uncertain to have required specific comment: for
a summary of the position, see the 15th ed. of this work at p. 752.

[72] The order made against the estate will be in the form considered *supra*, para. 26–19, unless, in
Lord Lindley's words "assets are admitted." This would seem to indicate that, in a clear case, a
money judgment might be ordered; *sed quaere*.

[73] See *supra*, para. 26–17.

If more than one partner is dead, the creditor may seek an administration order against each estate in the same proceedings.[74]

Insolvent estate

A basic principle of the old bankruptcy laws, and of the current **26–23** insolvency legislation, is that partnership debts are primarily payable out of the joint estate and the separate debts of each partner are primarily payable out of his separate estate.[75] That rule is seemingly applied in the administration of an insolvent estate.[76] Thus, the separate creditors will have priority as regards the deceased partner's separate estate,[77] even where all the other partners are insolvent.[78] However, it would seem that the partnership creditors could, in certain circumstances, rank equally with the separate creditors.[79]

Similarly, a surviving partner will not be permitted to prove against **26–24** the separate estate of his deceased co-partner if, by so doing, he would compete with his own creditors, *i.e.* the partnership creditors.[80] If, however, the separate estate is insufficient to pay the separate creditors, there will be no surplus for the payment of the partnership creditors and the surviving partner will be permitted to prove.[81]

A creditor who holds a security on any part of the deceased's partner's estate may realise his security and prove for the balance of his debt or give up his security and prove for the whole debt.[82]

Administration in bankruptcy

Provided that no proceedings for the administration of the estate **26–25** have been commenced, a creditor or the personal representatives of the deceased partner may petition for an insolvency administration order, with a view to the estate being administered under a modified

---

[74] See *Brown v. Douglas* (1840) 11 Sim. 283; *Brown v. Weatherby* (1841) 12 Sim. 6.

[75] See *infra*, paras. 27–82 *et seq.* Note, however, that some inroads into this principle seem likely to be made in the proposed new Insolvent Partnerships Order.

[76] This would seem to be the effect of the Administration of Insolvent Estates of Deceased Persons Order 1986 (S.I. 1986 No. 1999), Art. 4, although the position is not entirely clear in cases where the Insolvent Partnerships Order 1986 (S.I. 1986 No. 2142), Arts. 9, 10 do not apply: see *infra*, para. 27–87. As to when an estate is insolvent, see the Insolvency Act 1986, s.421(4); also the following pre-Act decisions: *Re Leng* [1895] 1 Ch. 652; *Re Whitaker* [1904] 1 Ch. 299; *Re Pink* [1927] 1 Ch. 237.

[77] See *Croft v. Pyke* (1733) 3 P.W. 180; *Gray v. Chiswell* (1803) 9 Ves.Jr. 118; *Addis v. Knight* (1817) 2 Mer. 117; *Lodge v. Prichard* (1863) 1 De G.J. & S. 610; *Whittingstall v. Grover* (1886) 10 W.R. 53.

[78] *Lodge v. Prichard, supra; Whittingstall v. Grover, supra.*

[79] See the exceptions considered *infra*, paras. 27–132 *et seq.* Lord Lindley appeared to consider that the only exception which clearly applied was that where "there is not and never was, since the death of the deceased, any joint estate whatever, and no solvent partner": see *Cowell v. Sikes* (1827) 2 Russ 191; *Lodge v. Prichard* (1853) 1 De G.J. & Sm. 610; also *infra*, para. 27–133. *Quaere*, why should the other exceptions not apply?

[80] *Lacey v. Hill* (1872) 8 Ch.App. 441; (1876) 4 Ch.D. 537. See also *infra*, para. 27–142.

[81] *Ex p. Head* [1894] 1 Q.B. 638; *Ex p. Topping* (1865) 4 De G.J. & S. 551. See also the other exceptions considered *infra*, paras. 27–143 *et seq.*

[82] See *infra*, para. 27–113.

version of the Insolvency Act 1986.[83] Where such proceedings are already on foot, the court may, if satisfied that the estate is insolvent, transfer them to the relevant bankruptcy court.[84] It is presumed that, if insolvency petitions are subsequently presented against one or more of the surviving partners, the proceedings can be consolidated, although there appears to be no provision authorising this in the Act or the rules made thereunder.[85]

Although the Act, as modified, does not state that the deceased's separate creditors have priority over the partnership creditors, as under the general law,[86] the current editor submits that this rule will still continue to apply.[87]

B. DEBTS INCURRED AFTER A PARTNER'S DEATH

The general rule: estate not directly liable

26–26   The general rule was summarised by Lord Lindley in these terms:

> "... it may be taken as a general proposition that the estate of a deceased partner is not liable to third parties for what may be done after his decease by the surviving partners[88]; and on that ground it has been held that they cannot be restrained at the suit of the executors of the deceased from continuing to carry on the business of the late firm in the old name."[89]

The rationale behind this rule seemingly lies in the limited control which the deceased partner's personal representatives are entitled to exercise over the conduct of the surviving partners.[90] However, whilst third parties may have no direct rights against it, the estate may be liable, *vis-à-vis* the surviving partners, to bear a share of any debts or liabilities properly incurred in winding up the partnership affairs.[91]

---

[83] Insolvency Act 1986, ss.264, 271(2), 272 (as amended and/or substituted by the Administration of Insolvent Estates of Deceased Persons Order 1986 (S.I. 1986 No. 1999), Sched. 1, Pt. II, paras. 1, 5, 6). Insolvency is defined in *ibid.* s.421(4); see also *supra*, para. 26–23, n. 76.

[84] *Ibid.* s.271(3) (as substituted by the Administration of Insolvent Estates of Deceased Persons Order 1986, Sched. 1, Pt. II, para. 5). And see *Morley v. White* (1872) L.R. 8 Ch.App. 214; *Ex p. Gordon* (1873) L.R. 8 Ch.App. 555; *Hulme v. Rowbotham* [1907] W.N. 162 and 189.

[85] See the terms of the Insolvency Rules 1986 (S.I. 1986 No. 1925), r. 6.236 and the Insolvent Partnerships Order 1986 (S.I. 1986 No. 2142), art. 14(2), (3). Consolidation was possible under the old bankruptcy laws: see *Re C. Greaves* [1904] 2 K.B. 493.

[86] See *supra*, para. 26–18.

[87] There is a similar lacuna under the Insolvent Partnerships Order 1986: see *infra*, para. 27–87.

[88] See *Bagel v. Miller* [1903] 2 K.B. 212.

[89] *Webster v. Webster* (1791) 3 Swan. 490, note. The words "on that ground" are significant, since the court will, in general, intervene with a view to protecting the firm's goodwill pending sale: see *supra*, paras. 10–160 *et seq.*

[90] See *Devaynes v. Noble, Houlton's case, Johnes's case,* and *Brice's case* (1816) 1 Mer. 529, 616 *et seq.*; and, in particular, pp. 622–623, *per* Sir William Grant M.R. See also *Vulliamy v. Noble* (1817) 3 Mer. 593 and *supra*, para. 26–02.

[91] See *supra*, paras. 13–63 *et seq.*

Liability of personal representatives

If the deceased partner's personal representatives are admitted as **26–27** partners they will obviously incur personal liability for the debts and obligations of the new firm, on normal principles.[92] However, as Lord Lindley observed:

> "... the acts of an executor, to whatever extent they may render him personally liable, do not impose liability on the assets of the deceased, unless those acts have been properly performed by the executor in the execution of his duty as executor."

An administrator is, essentially, in the same position.

Liability of estate for acts of personal representatives

In order to determine whether the estate is liable for the acts of the **26–28** personal representatives, regard must be had to the nature of those acts and to the terms of the deceased partner's will or, if he died intestate, the provisions of the Administration of Estates Act 1925.[93]

Authority of personal representatives to carry on business, etc.

Lord Lindley wrote: **26–29**

> "Executors, unless authorised by their testator so to do, ought not to leave his assets outstanding in the trade or business in which he was engaged when he died. It has been laid down as a rule without exception, that to authorise executors to carry on a trade, or to permit it to be carried on with the property of a testator held by them in trust, there ought to be the most distinct and positive authority, and direction given by the testator for that purpose."[94]

Thus, a bequest of a partnership share to one partner for life, and then to another, does not, without more, warrant the trustees of his will leaving the share unconverted.[95] Again a trust to sell a business

---

[92] See *Wightman v. Townroe* (1813) 1 M. & S. 412; *Labouchere v. Tupper* (1857) 11 Moo. P.C. 198; *Ex p. Garland* (1804) 10 Ves.Jr. 110; *Ex p. Holdsworth* (1841) 1 M.D. & D. 475. But personal representatives will not necessarily render themselves liable as partners merely by sharing profits with the surviving partners: see the Partnership Act 1890, s.2(3), *supra*, paras. 5–02, 5–20 *et seq.* and, prior to the Act, *Holme v. Hammond* (1872) L.R. 7 Ex. 218. See also, as to the liability of personal representatives on bills of exchange or promissory notes accepted or indorsed in the course of carrying on the deceased's business, *Liverpool Borough Bank v. Walker* (1859) 4 De G &. J. 24; *Lucas v. Williams* (1862) 3 Giff. 150.

[93] See, in particular, the power to postpone sale under *ibid.* s.33(1).

[94] *Kirkman v. Booth* (1848) 11 Beav. 273; and see *Williams, Mortimer and Sunnucks on Executors, Administrators and Probate* (17th ed.), pp. 722 *et seq.* An express power conferred on executors may not be available to an administrator: *Lambert v. Rendle* (1863) 3 New Rep. 247.

[95] See *Kirkman v. Booth, supra*; *Skirving v. Williams* (1857) 24 Beav. 275; *Re Chancellor* (1884) 26 Ch.D. 42.

may not be equivalent to a trust to carry it on until sale,[96] but a power to *postpone* sale will normally authorise the executors to carry the business on during any period of postponement,[97] but not indefinitely.[98]

26–30   A general direction to carry on a business in which the testator was engaged at the time of his death has been held not to authorise the employment of any *additional* assets therein.[99] Moreover, a testator does not, merely by authorising his share to be left in the partnership business, necessarily contemplate that his executors or trustees should do anything more than leave it outstanding by way of loan.[1]

It should be noted that, even where this is not directly or indirectly authorised by the will, a personal representative will usually be entitled to carry on the deceased's business for a short period, purely with a view to realisation.[2]

Acts which impose liability on estate

26–31   There are certain acts which, if done by a personal representative, automatically impose liability on the estate.[3] Lord Lindley pointed out that,

"... if a partner appoints a co-partner his executor, and dies, and the executor continues to carry on the business, it is possible that some of his acts, attributed to him not as a partner but as executor, may render the assets of the deceased liable for what may have occurred since his death.[4] But this is quite an exceptional case."[5]

Assets actually employed in business

26–32   If any part of the deceased partner's estate is properly employed in carrying on the partnership business, it will obviously be available to meet partnership debts incurred since the date of death and cannot be proved for in the event of the firm's insolvency. However, such proof will be allowed to the extent that assets are employed in the

---

[96] *Strickland v. Symons* (1884) 26 Ch.D. 245; *Re Rooke* [1953] Ch. 716.
[97] *Re Crowther* [1895] 2 Ch. 56. But *cf. Re Rooke, supra; Re Berry* [1962] Ch. 97.
[98] *Re Smith* [1896] 1 Ch. 171; *Re Berry, supra.*
[99] See *McNeillie v. Acton* (1853) 4 De G.M. & G. 744; *Re Cameron* (1884) 26 Ch.D. 19.
[1] See *Travis v. Milne* (1851) 9 Hare 141.
[2] *Marshall v. Broadhurst* (1831) 1 C. & J. 403; *Garrett v. Noble* (1834) 6 Sim. 504; also *Dowse v. Gorton* [1891] A.C. 190, 199, *per* Lord Herschell. And see *Williams, Mortimer and Sunnucks on Executors, Administrators and Probate* (17th ed.), p. 723.
[3] See *Williams, Mortimer and Sunnucks on Executors, Administrators and Probate* (17th ed.), pp. 725 *et seq.*
[4] See *Vulliamy v. Noble* (1817) 3 Mer. 593.
[5] See *Farhall v. Farhall* (1871) L.R. 7 Ch.App. 123; *Owen v. Delamere* (1872) L.R. 15 Eq. 134; *Re Johnson* (1880) 15 Ch.D. 548; *Strickland v. Symons* (1884) 26 Ch.D. 245; *Re Evans* (1887) 34 Ch.D. 597.

business *without* authority. This is demonstrated by the decision in *Ex p. Garland*.[6]

Right to indemnity

If the deceased partner's personal representatives carry on the **26–33** partnership business pursuant to a direction in his will or the statutory power to postpone sale,[7] or with a view to realisation, or otherwise with the consent of the beneficiaries, they will be entitled to an indemnity out of the estate for any personal liability thereby incurred.[8] It is, however, clear that the liability of the estate will not, in general, exceed the amount (if any) expressly authorised by the deceased to be employed in the business.[9]

It does not follow from the existence of this right to indemnity that **26–34** the personal representatives' trade creditors can necessarily stand in their place with a view to seeking payment out of the estate,[10] as Lord Lindley explained:

"Prima facie, a creditor must look for payment to his legal debtor, and the fact that the latter is entitled to be indemnified by some one else, or out of some estate, does not confer any additional right on the creditor. To avail the creditor something more is necessary, namely the existence of a trust fund expressly devoted to carrying on the business in respect of which the debt to the creditor has been contracted."[11]

In cases of the latter type, the trade creditors are, ironically, placed **26–35** in a better position than the creditors of an ordinary partnership, since they have a right of recourse both against the personal representatives and against the estate.[12] However, the normal priority

---

[6] (1804) 10 Ves.Jr. 110. See also *Ex p. Richardson* (1818) Buck. 202; *Thompson v. Andrews* (1832) 1 M. & K. 116; *Cutbush v. Cutbush* (1839) 1 Beav. 184; *Ex p. Butterfield* (1847) De G. 570; *Scott v. Izon* (1865) 34 Beav. 434; and see *Hall v. Fennell* (1875) Ir.Rep. 9 Eq. 615. *Cf. Ex p. Edmonds* (1862) 4 De G.F. & J. 488. See also, *infra*, para. 27–117.

[7] Administration of Estates Act 1925, s.33 and *supra*, para. 26–29. See also, in the case of land, the Law of Property Act 1925, s.25.

[8] *Ex p. Garland* (1804) 10 Ves.Jr. 110; *Labouchere v. Tupper* (1857) 11 Moo. P.C. 198; *Re Johnson* (1880) 15 Ch.D. 548; *Dowse v. Gorton* [1891] A.C. 190; *Re Bracey* [1936] Ch. 690. The indemnity will be available even in respect of a tortious liability: *Benett v. Wyndham* (1862) 4 De G.F. & J. 259; *Re Raybould* [1900] 1 Ch. 199.

[9] *Cutbush v. Cutbush* (1839) 1 Beav. 184; *McNeillie v. Acton* (1853) 4 De G.M. & G. 744; *Owen v. Delamere* (1872) L.R. 15 Eq. 134; *Re Johnson* (1880) 15 Ch.D. 548; *Strickland v. Symons* (1884) 26 Ch.D. 245. Lord Kenyon's decision in *Hankey v. Hammock* (1786) Buck. 210 was formerly thought to justify the view that the liability extended to *all* the assets of the estate.

[10] A creditor of a personal representative is not a creditor of the deceased: see *Re Kitson* [1911] 2 K.B. 109.

[11] See *Strickland v. Symons* (1884) 26 Ch.D. 245; *Re Evans* (1887) 34 Ch.D. 597.

[12] As Lord Lindley put it, "the creditors have not only the personal security of the executors and trustees who carry on the business, but also a right to stand in their place to the extent to which they are entitled to indemnity out of the assets of the deceased." See generally *Re Johnson* (1880) 15 Ch.D. 548.

accorded to the deceased's creditors[13] will not be affected unless those creditors have in fact consented to the business being carried on for their benefit.[14]

26–36   Any default by the personal representative must, in general, be made good before his creditors can obtain anything out of the relevant fund.[15] Where there are two or more personal representatives, each will enjoy a separate right to indemnity, so that one will not be prejudiced by the default of the other.[16]

3.   THE SEPARATE CREDITORS, LEGATEES, ETC., OF THE DECEASED

26–37   The consequences of a partner's death as regards his separate creditors and the persons interested in his estate are, for the most part, entirely straightforward; complications only arise when the deceased's share is continued in the business or, on occasion, where that share is specifically bequeathed.

A.   THE GENERAL RULE

26–38   As might be expected, a deceased partner's separate creditors and the persons beneficially interested in his estate will, as a general rule, only have a right of recourse against his personal representatives. Lord Lindley summarised the position in the following way:

"Under ordinary circumstances, the separate creditors, legatees, and next-of-kin of a deceased partner, must look for payment of what is due to them out of his assets to his legal personal representative, and to him alone.[17] The executors[18] are, under ordinary circumstances, the only persons who have a right to call

---

[13] Lord Lindley's formulation of this general principle was in these terms: "The liability of the estate of a deceased partner to persons who become creditors after his decease, is subject to its liability to those who were his creditors at his decease."

[14] *Dowse v. Gorton* [1891] A.C. 190; *Re Oxley* [1914] 1 Ch. 604. It is not enough to show that the deceased's creditors knew that the business was being carried on and took no steps to prevent it: *Re Oxley, supra.* The decisions to the contrary in *Re Brooke* [1894] 2 Ch. 600 and in the Irish case, *Re Hodges* [1899] 1 I.R. 480, cannot be relied on.

[15] *Re Johnson* (1880) 15 Ch.D. 548 (where the previous authorities were reviewed by Jessel M.R.); *Dowse v. Gorton, supra.* See also *Re British Power Electric Traction Co. Ltd.* [1910] 2 Ch. 470.

[16] *Re Frith* [1902] 1 Ch. 342. As to the position in the event of the personal representative's insolvency, see *Jennings v. Mather* [1902] 1 K.B. 1. Cf. *St. Thomas's Hospital v. Richardson* [1910] 1 K.B. 271; *Ex p. Governors of St. Thomas's Hospital* [1911] 2 K.B. 705.

[17] *Langley v. Earl of Oxford* (1748) 2 Amb. 795; *Alsager v. Rowley* (1802) 6 Ves.Jr. 748; *Seeley v. Boehm* (1817) 2 Madd. 176, 180, *per* Sir Thomas Plumer V.-C.; *Davies v. Davies* (1837) 2 Keen 534; *Travis v. Milne* (1851) 9 Hare 141; *Saunders v. Druce* (1855) 3 Drew. 140. As to the position where there is no personal representative, see *supra*, para. 26–10; also *Maclean v. Dawson* (1859) 5 Jur. (N.S.) 1091.

[18] Similarly in the case of an administrator.

upon the surviving partners for an account; and of this right they do not divest themselves by a sale and assignment of the share of the deceased; for the effect of such sale and assignment is only to make the executors trustees for the purchaser."[19]

Account ordered against personal representatives

However, this does not mean that an account in respect of the **26–39** deceased partner's share cannot be taken in proceedings brought against the personal representatives: in Lord Lindley's words, it is "the common course" to direct an inquiry as to the sum due to the estate in respect of that share.[20] Whilst the point is not entirely free from doubt, it even appears that such an inquiry ought to be pursued under a normal administration order, as Lord Lindley explained:

"It seems that, under an ordinary judgment for the administration of the estate of a deceased partner, the partnership accounts will not be gone into, unless the Court specially directs some inquiry to be made with reference to the share of the deceased. But it is difficult to see how any account of his personal estate can be taken without such an inquiry; and it has been decided more than once, that if the surviving partners seek to obtain payment of a balance from the estate of the deceased on the partnership accounts, these accounts must be taken, although no special direction as to them may be contained in the judgment."[21]

Be that as it may, it is clear that the surviving partners cannot be ordered to pay any sum found due to the estate on completion of the inquiry: to obtain such payment, third party or other proceedings by the personal representatives will be required.[22]

Account on footing of wilful default

Subject to any provision contained in the deceased partner's will, **26–40** his personal representatives will have power at their discretion to postpone the conversion of his estate without being liable for any consequential losses.[23] It follows that, unless they have effectively

---

[19] *Clegg v. Fishwick* (1849) 1 Mac & G. 294; *Stainton v. The Carron Company* (1853) 18 Beav. 146.
[20] As in *Macdonald v. Richardson* (1858) 1 Giff. 81. See also *Pointon v. Pointon* (1871) L.R. 12 Eq. 547, where the only surviving partner was an executor and trustee.
[21] See *Paynter v. Houston* (1817) 3 Mer. 297; *Woolley v. Gordon* (1829) Tam. 11; *Baker v. Martin* (1832) 5 Sim. 380.
[22] Despite doubts expressed in earlier editions of this work, there would, in principle, seem to be no reason why the requisite order should not be obtained in third party proceedings: see R.S.C. Ord. 16, rr. 1(1)(b), 8(1)(b); C.C.R. Ord. 12, rr. 1(1)(b), 5(1).
[23] Administration of Estates Act 1925, ss.33(1), (7), 39(1)(ii); Law of Property Act 1925, ss.25, 26(3) (as substituted by the Law of Property (Amendment) Act 1926, Sched.). As to the application of s.33 of the former Act, see *Public Trustee v. Trollope* [1927] 1 Ch. 596, 604, *per* Tomlin J.; *Re Sullivan* [1930] 1 Ch. 84; *Re McKee* [1931] 2 Ch. 145; *Re Thornber* [1937] Ch. 29; *Re Plowman* [1943] Ch. 269.

ignored the terms of the will or they are otherwise in breach of their overriding duty to administer the estate for the benefit of the persons interested therein, only in exceptional circumstances will the personal representatives be liable to account for sums which they have not actually received during any period of postponement.[24]

Account ordered against surviving partners

26–41   The general rule which precludes a deceased partner's separate creditors and legatees, etc., from proceeding against the surviving partners is not absolute, although the extent of the exceptions is not clearly defined. Lord Lindley analysed the position in this way:

"... there are cases to be met with, which apparently warrant the inference that surviving partners may always be sued along with the executor or administrator of the deceased.[25] But the authority of these cases has ... been called in question, and the better opinion now is that some special circumstances are necessary to justify such a course."[26]

26–42   The "special circumstances" which have been held sufficient for this purpose have all involved a degree of actual or potential impropriety on the part of the personal representatives. Thus, proceedings against the personal representatives and the surviving partners will be permissible where they are in collusion,[27] where the personal representatives have refused to seek an account from the surviving partners,[28] where the personal representatives have, by their dealings, precluded themselves from seeking such an account,[29] where the personal representatives are themselves partners[30] or, in Lord Lindley's words, generally

"... where the relation between the executors[31] and the surviving partners is such as to present a substantial impediment to the prosecution, by the executors, of the rights of the persons

---

[24] As to charging the executor of a deceased partner with wilful default, see *Ward v. Ward* (1843) 2 H.L.C. 777; *Kirkman v. Booth* (1848) 11 Beav. 273; *Rowley v. Adams* (1849) 2 H.L.C. 726; *Grayburn v. Clarkson* (1868) L.R. 3 Ch.App. 605; *Sculthorpe v. Tipper* (1871) L.R. 13 Eq. 232.

[25] See *Newland v. Champion* (1748) 1 Ves.Sen. 106; *Bowsher v. Watkins* (1830) 1 R. & M. 277.

[26] See *Davies v. Davies* (1837) 2 Keen 534; *Law v. Law* (1847) 11 Jur. 463; *Travis v. Milne* (1851) 9 Hare 141; *Stainton v. The Carron Co.* (1853) 18 Beav. 146; *Yeatman v. Yeatman* (1877) 7 Ch.D. 210.

[27] *Doran v. Simpson* (1799) 4 Ves.Jr. 651; *Alsager v. Rowley* (1802) 6 Ves.Jr. 748; *Gedge v. Traill* (1823) 1 R. & M. 281, note.

[28] *Burroughs v. Elton* (1805) 11 Ves.Jr. 29; but cf. *Yeatman v. Yeatman* (1877) 7 Ch.D. 210, where a mere refusal was held *not* to be sufficient.

[29] *Braithwaite v. Britain* (1836) 1 Keen 206; *Law v. Law* (1847) 11 Jur. 463.

[30] *Cropper v. Knapman* (1836) 2 Y. & C. Ex. 338; *Travis v. Milne* (1851) 9 Hare 141; *Beningfield v. Baxter* (1886) 12 App.Cas. 167. And see, as to the position where the deceased's assets are continued in the business, *infra*, paras. 26–49 *et seq.*

[31] Or administrators.

interested in the estate of the deceased, against the surviving partners ...".[32]

Account settled between personal representatives and surviving partners

A bona fide account settled between the personal representatives **26–43** and the surviving partners, provided that they are not the same persons, will bind the deceased partner's separate creditors and all persons interested in his estate.[33]

Surviving partners as personal representatives

It is self evident that no such account can be settled when the **26–44** personal representatives are also surviving partners; indeed, as Lord Lindley pointed out:

"if the executors are themselves the surviving partners, or some of them, it becomes exceedingly difficult to make any arrangement which will be binding on the persons interested in the estate of the deceased; for even if any arrangement is assented to by such persons, it will be liable to be successfully disputed, on any of those numerous grounds which are held to invalidate arrangements between trustees and their *cestuis que trustent*, and by which trustees do, or may, obtain a benefit at the expense of the trust estate."

A graphic and, in many ways, extreme demonstration of this principle is to be found in *Wedderburn v. Wedderburn*,[34] where an account was directed, on the application of the persons beneficially interested in a deceased partner's estate, 30 years after the date of his death, notwithstanding subsequent changes in the firm and partial releases given to the executors by the beneficiaries.[35]

Costs

The costs of an administration action brought by a deceased **26–45** partner's separate creditor are paid in priority to the claims of his joint creditors.[36]

---

[32] *Travis v. Milne* (1851) 9 Hare 141.
[33] *Davies v. Davies* (1837) 2 Keen 534; *Smith v. Everett* (1859) 27 Beav. 446. And see the Trustee Act 1925, s.15; also *Re Houghton* [1904] 1 Ch. 622 (a decision under a predecessor section); *Re Hoyle* [1947] I.R. 61.
[34] (1836) 2 Keen 722 and (1838) 4 Myl. & Cr. 41. See further, as to this case, *supra*, para. 25–25.
[35] See *Beningfield v. Baxter* (1886) 12 App.Cas. 167 and the other cases cited *supra*, paras. 25–35 *et seq*.
[36] *Re McRea* (1883) 32 Ch.D. 613.

B. DECEASED PARTNER'S SHARE LEFT IN BUSINESS

26–46 It has already been seen that, subject to the terms of the deceased partner's will[37] and to their right to postpone the realisation of his estate with a view to sale, the personal representatives ought not properly to leave his share outstanding in the partnership business, whether or not they are themselves members of the firm.[38] If they nevertheless do so, it is necessary to ascertain the extent of their and the surviving partners' liability to account for any profits made by the employment of the share.

Loan of deceased's share

26–47   In the most simple case, *i.e.* where the personal representatives lend the deceased's share to the surviving partners at interest pursuant to an express power in his will, the surviving partners will obviously be bound to pay such interest, but will not otherwise be accountable for any profits made by the use of the share.[39] This will be the position even where the surviving partners do not pay off the loan on the due date.[40] At the same time, the personal representatives will not be liable for any loss resulting from the exercise of such a power, provided that they scrupulously adhere to its terms.[41]

26–48   It is apprehended that the separate creditors and legatees, etc. will enjoy no greater rights where the loan is made in breach of trust, save where the surviving partners are implicated therein.[42]

It goes without saying that, subject to the terms of the will, the position will be otherwise where the personal representatives are also surviving partners.

Share employed in business by personal representative

26–49   It has already been seen that where a personal representative who is also a surviving partner continues to employ the deceased partner's share in the partnership business, he will normally be liable to

---

[37] It is, for present purposes, assumed that there are no provisions in the partnership agreement which would entitle the continuing partners to retain the deceased's share in the business.

[38] See *supra*, paras. 26–29, 26–30. *Semble*, the court could authorise trustees (but not personal representatives as such) to adopt such a course, pursuant to the Trustee Act 1925, s.57 or the Variation of Trusts Act 1958, s.1. And see, generally, *Trustees of the British Museum v. Att.-G.* [1984] 1 W.L.R. 418.

[39] *Parker v. Bloxham* (1855) 20 Beav. 295; *Vyse v. Foster* (1872) L.R. 8 Ch. App. 309, affirmed at (1874) L.R. 7 H.L. 318. In the latter case, one of the executors was a surviving partner: see further, *supra*, para. 25–33.

[40] *Vyse v. Foster, supra.*

[41] *Paddon v. Richardson* (1855) 7 De G.M. & G. 563. See also, as to the construction of such powers, *supra*, para. 3–09. If the personal representatives are, during the continuance of the loan, authorised to examine the accounts of the firm with a view to satisfying themselves as to its solvency, the costs of so doing will be payable out of the capital of the estate: *Re Bennett* [1896] 1 Ch. 778.

[42] See *Stroud v. Gwyer* (1860) 28 Beav. 130; *Flockton v. Bunning* (1868) L.R. 8 Ch.App. 323, note. See also *supra*, para. 25–36.

account for the value of the share together with interest at the rate of 5 per cent. or, at the option of the persons beneficially interested in the estate, any profits received by the personal representative which are attributable to the use of the share.[43] This obligation seemingly co-exists with the statutory obligation under section 42 of the Partnership Act 1890, since it derives from a simple breach of trust, as Lord Lindley explained prior to that Act:

"... the obligation of the executor[44] ... to account is founded on a breach of trust committed by him, for which he is liable, at all events to the extent to which he has benefited by it, whether other persons are also liable or not; and being founded on a breach of trust, an action in respect of it may be sustained against the executor alone, though he may only be one of several, by whom the profits have been made."[45]

It is, perhaps, self evident that the potentially onerous nature of **26–50** the obligation imposed on the personal representative in such a case is no justification for depriving the separate creditors and legatees, etc., of their right to opt for profits in lieu of interest. Lord Lindley put it thus:

"... such persons are not deprived of this option by the circumstance that it will be difficult and expensive to ascertain what part of the profits has arisen from the employment of the assets of the deceased; for whatever difficulty may exist is attributable to the conduct of the executor himself, and cannot therefore be effectually urged by him as a reason why no account of profits should be taken."[46]

Where the option is exercised, it will usually be desirable to join **26–51** the other surviving partners, so as to ensure that any profits attributable to the use of the deceased's share can be recovered, even though they have not been received by the personal representative.[47]

Compound interest will be awarded in certain cases,[48] but a mixed claim which is comprised of part interest and part profits will not be permitted, unless there has been an intermediate settlement of account[49] or other special circumstances.[50]

---

[43] See *supra*, paras. 25–35 *et seq.*
[44] The position of an administrator is no different.
[45] See also *supra*, para. 25–35.
[46] *Docker v. Somes* (1834) 2 M. & K. 655; *Townend v. Townend* (1859) 1 Giff. 201; *Flockton v. Bunning* (1868) L.R. 8 Ch.App. 323, noticed *supra*, para. 25–36.
[47] See *supra*, para. 25–36. Note, however, the problems associated with such claims: see *supra*, para. 25–26.
[48] See *Jones v. Foxall* (1852) 15 Beav. 388; *Williams v. Powell* (1852) 15 Beav. 461; *Vyse v. Foster* (1874) L.R. 7 H.L. 318, 346, *per* Lord Selborne. See also *supra*, para. 25–35. And note the exceptional decision in *Roxburgh Dinardo & Partners' Judicial Factor v. Dinardo*, 1993 S.L.T. 16 (2nd Div.).
[49] *Heathcote v. Hulme* (1819) 1 J. & W. 122.
[50] As in *Townend v. Townend* (1859) 1 Giff. 201.

Liability of surviving partners who are not personal representatives

26–52   The extent of the liability attaching to the surviving partners who
are *not* the deceased partner's personal representatives is less clear.
Their obligation under section 42 of the Partnership Act 1890 is, of
course, well defined.[51] However, writing prior to that Act, Lord
Lindley expressed the following view:

> "Upon the principle that everyone concerned in a breach of trust
> with notice of the trust is answerable for such breach, it follows
> that if a partner dies, and his surviving partners allow his assets to
> remain in their business, with the knowledge that to suffer them so
> to remain is a breach of trust on the part of the executors, the
> surviving partners will themselves be responsible to the separate
> creditors, legatees, or next-of-kin of the deceased, for any loss
> which may be thereby sustained."[52]

The current editor is, however, of the opinion that, as long as they
are not also the deceased partner's personal representatives, the
surviving partners will, in general, be entitled to assume that his
share has been properly left in the business unless they either know,
or ought to know, that a breach of trust is being committed. The
burden of proof will, in such cases, lie on the persons who seek to
hold the surviving partners liable.[53]

Personal representative becoming partner

26–53   Where a personal representative is admitted to the partnership by
the surviving partners, the question arises whether any share of
profits received by him *qua* partner belongs to him personally or to
the estate which he represents. The answer will inevitably depend on
the circumstances, as Lord Lindley made clear:

> "If he became a partner in his representative character, or, as in
> *Cook v. Collingridge*,[54] under circumstances entitling the legatees
> to treat him still as their trustee, he must account for any profits
> which he may have obtained as a partner. On the other hand, if,
> as in *Simpson v. Chapman*,[55] he became a partner not in his

---

[51] See *supra*, paras. 25–23 *et seq. Quare*, can interest alternatively be claimed under the Supreme
Court Act 1981, s.35A? See *supra*, paras. 20–39, 25–38.
[52] See *Wilson v. Moore* (1834) 1 M. & K. 337; *Booth v. Booth* (1838) 1 Beav. 125; *Travis v.
Milne* (1851) 9 Hare 141. *Cf. Ex p. Barnewall* (1855) 6 De G.M. & G. 795. And see also *supra*,
para. 12–143.
[53] See, for example, the approach adopted prior to 1926 in the case of sales of leasehold
property: *Re Whistler* (1887) 35 Ch.D. 561; *Venn and Furze's Contract* [1894] 2 Ch. 101; *Verrell's
Contract* [1903] 1 Ch. 65. And see also *supra*, para. 12–143.
[54] (1822) Jac. 607. See *supra*, para. 25–37.
[55] (1853) 4 De G.M. & G. 154. And see *supra*, para. 25–25.

representative character, nor under such circumstances as those above mentioned, the profits accruing to him as a partner will be his own, and not form part of the assets for which he must account as executor."

The decided cases

Those cases in which an account of profits has been sought **26–54** following the death of a partner, to which reference has been made elsewhere in this work,[56] may conveniently be classified as follows:

Group 1:   Account of profits decreed

  A.   Personal representatives against surviving partners.[57]
  B.   Legatees against personal representatives who were not partners.[58]
  C.   Legatees against personal representatives who were, or who became, partners.[59]

Group 2:   Account of profits refused

  A.   Personal representatives against surviving partners.[60]
  B.   Legatees against personal representatives who were, or who became, partners.[61]

C.   SPECIFIC BEQUESTS OF PARTNERSHIP SHARES

A partner will normally have complete freedom to dispose of his **26–55** partnership share by will,[62] even though, as noticed hereafter, the

---

[56] See *supra*, paras. 25–24 *et seq.*

[57] *Brown v. De Tastet* (1819) Jac. 284; *Booth v. Parks* (1829) Beatty 444; *Featherstonhaugh v. Turner* (1858) 25 Beav. 382; *Smith v. Everett* (1859) 27 Beav. 446; *Yates v. Finn* (1880) 13 Ch.D. 839; *Manley v. Sartori* [1927] 1 Ch. 157; *Robert Watte Pathirana v. Ariya Pathirana* [1967] A.C. 233; *Barclays Bank Trust Co. Ltd. v. Bluff* [1982] Ch. 172 (where it was held that the executor had not yet elected between interest and profits and there was a declaration accordingly: see *supra*, para. 25–27); *Chandroutie v. Gajadhar* [1987] A.C. 147 (P.C.).

[58] *Palmer v. Mitchell* (1809) 2 M. & K. 672, note; *Heathcote v. Hulme* (1819) 1 J. & W. 122; *Docker v. Somes* (1834) 2 M. & K. 654.

[59] *Cook v. Collingridge* (1822) Jac. 607 (*supra*, para. 25–37); *Wedderburn v. Wedderburn* (1836) 2 Keen 722, (1838) 4 Myl. & Cr. 41 and (1856) 22 Beav. 84 (*supra*, paras. 25–25, 26–44); *Willett v. Blandford* (1842) 1 Hare 253; *Stocken v. Dawson* (1843) 6 Beav. 371 and (1848) 17 L.J. Ch. 282; *Macdonald v. Richardson* (1858) 1 Giff. 81; *Townend v. Townend* (1859) Giff. 201; *Flockton v. Bunning* (1868) L.R. 8 Ch.App. 323, note (*supra*, para. 25–36).

[60] *Knox v. Gye* (1872) L.R. 5 H.L. 656, *supra*, para. 23–33. In this case, the claim was statute barred.

[61] *Simpson v. Chapman* (1853) 4 De G.M. & G. 154 (*supra*, para. 25–25); *Vyse v. Foster* (1872) L.R. 8 Ch.App. 309 and (1874) L.R. 7 H.L. 318 (*supra*, para. 25–33). See also *Wedderburn v. Wedderburn*, *supra*; *Willett v. Blandford*, *supra*; *Hordern v. Hordern* [1910] A.C. 465; *Re Mulholland's Will Trusts* [1949] W.N. 103.

[62] For a case in which this was held to be the position notwithstanding the inclusion in the agreement of what at first sight appeared to be a power of appointment in respect of the share: see *Ponton v. Dunn* (1830) 1 R. &. M. 402.

subject matter of the bequest will, in practice, normally be
represented by his financial entitlement under the agreement[63] or the
Partnership Act 1890.[64]

Construction of particular bequests

26–56   The normal form of bequest will be of "all that the share and
interest of the testator in the capital, assets and profits of the
partnership." However, where a more limited form of words is used,
questions of construction will inevitably arise.[65]

Bequest of capital

26–57   A bequest of a partner's capital has been held to include what was
due to him in respect of advances.[66] Although it is probable that such
a bequest would also include undrawn profits credited to the
deceased partner's capital account, which are withdrawable at will
and do not form part of the firm's fixed capital,[67] such a construction
could not be guaranteed.

Bequest of goodwill

26–58   In *Robertson v. Quiddington*[68] it was held that a legatee of a
deceased partner's share of goodwill could not sue the surviving
partner for a sale of the goodwill and payment out of his share, even
though an assent had been made in his favour by the deceased's
executors. However, Lord Lindley commented:

> "This case was somewhat peculiar as in truth the surviving partner
> was entitled to everything which gave a saleable value to the
> goodwill."[69]

Bequest of net profits

26–59   A bequest of a partner's share of the net profits in his partnership
business will entitle the legatee to the share of such profits receivable
by his executors whilst the partnership business is being carried on,
but will not entitle him to any interest in the partnership assets.[70]

---

[63] See generally, *supra*, paras. 10–128 *et seq*.
[64] See *ibid*. s.44, *supra*, paras. 25–40 *et seq*. But see also, *supra*, paras. 19–10 *et seq*.
[65] See, generally, *Re Rhagg* [1938] Ch. 828 and the cases there cited.
[66] *Bevan v. Att.-Gen.* (1863) 4 Giff. 361. And see *Terry v. Terry* (1863) 33 Beav. 232. Note the
decision in *Robertson v. Brent* [1972] N.Z.L.R. 406 (which concerned the position on a partner's
retirement and is, in any event, of doubtful authority on the work in progress issue: see *supra*,
para. 23–188, n. 17).
[67] See further, as to the practice of dealing with profits in this way, *supra*, para. 17–07.
[68] (1860) 28 Beav. 529.
[69] See further *supra*, para. 10–164.
[70] *Re Lawes-Wittewronge* [1915] 1 Ch. 408.

Bequest of specific partnership asset or a share therein

Given the nature of a partnership share,[71] it is obviously not **26–60** competent for one partner, *vis-à-vis* his co-partners, to dispose of a particular partnership asset by will,[72] although such a bequest may, if coupled with legacies in favour of the surviving partners, put the latter to their election whether to allow the asset to go to the legatee or to compensate him out of their own legacies.[73]

It does not, however, follow that such a bequest will be ineffective **26–61** as between the beneficiaries claiming under the deceased partner's will: effect will, so far as possible, be given to a bequest of his share in the particular asset and, for this purpose, the partnership debts will be treated as primarily payable out of the other partnership assets.[74] If the partnership is insolvent, the legatee will, of course, receive nothing: in such a case, the solvency of the partners (including the deceased partner) is immaterial.[75]

Ademption

A specific bequest of a partnership share will be adeemed if the **26–62** testator, after making his will, leaves the firm and is paid out the value of that share. However, there will be no ademption so long as he remains a partner, even if the size or nature of his share is altered after the date of the will.[76] Indeed, such a bequest may even carry the entire business where the testator has acquired his co-partners' shares prior to the date of his death.[77]

Legacy to partner indebted to testator

A legatee is not entitled to receive any payment out of the **26–63** testator's estate until he has discharged any debts which he owes to that estate.[78] This principle does not, however, apply where the debt is due, not from the legatee personally, but only from a partnership of which he is a member.[79]

---

[71] See generally, *supra*, paras. 19–01 *et seq.*

[72] But see *supra*, para. 17–04. It is, of course, permissible for a partner to retain the right to all capital profits attributable to a particular asset, thus effectively preserving its value in his estate. See *infra*, para. 35–05, n. 11.

[73] See generally, as to the doctrine of election, *Re Dicey* [1957] Ch. 145; *Re Gordon's Will Trusts* [1978] Ch. 145, and the cases there cited.

[74] *Re Holland* [1907] 2 Ch. 88. Note also the concession made in *Re Rhagg* [1938] Ch. 828.

[75] *Farquhar v. Hadden* (1871) L.R. 7 Ch.App. 1.

[76] *Backwell v. Child* (1755) Amb. 260; *Ellis v. Walker* (1756) Amb. 309; also *Re Rhagg* [1938] Ch. 828. Cf. *Re Quibell's Will Trusts* [1956] 3 All E.R. 679. And see, as to the position where a legatee of a share is admitted to the partnership during the testator's lifetime, *Lacon v. Lacon* [1891] 2 Ch. 482.

[77] *Re Russell* (1882) 19 Ch.D. 432.

[78] See *Cherry v. Boultbee* (1839) 3 Keen 319, affirmed at 4 My. & Cr. 442. See also *Williams, Mortimer and Sunnucks on Executors, Administrators and Probate* (17th ed.), pp. 648 *et seq.*

[79] *Turner v. Turner* [1911] 1 Ch. 716, explaining and distinguishing *Smith v. Smith* (1861) 3 Giff. 263. See also *Re Pennington and Owen Ltd.* [1925] Ch. 825.

Nomination of successor partner

26–64   It need hardly be observed that a specific bequest of a partnership share will not entitle the beneficiary to become a partner, unless there is an agreement to that effect which is binding on the surviving partners. In those (increasingly rare) cases where a partner is entitled to nominate a successor by will,[80] a mere bequest of residue is unlikely to be treated as a sufficient nomination.[81]

Effect of bequest

26–65   A specific bequest of a partnership share confers only limited rights on the legatee, as Lord Lindley explained:

> "The right of the legatee is simply to be paid the amount due to the testator at the time of his death in respect of his share[82]; and also, under the circumstances and subject to the qualifications already noticed,[83] to receive a proportion of the profits made since the testator's death. However, as between the legatee and the executor, the legatee is entitled to have the share kept in the business, if he so wishes, subject only to the superior right of the executor to sell the testator's estate for the payment of debts."[84]

The current editor does, however, consider that the beneficiary cannot force the executor to leave the share in the business if he will thereby risk incurring personal liability as a partner.[85]

Settled share

26–66   Where the testator has settled his share on life interest trusts, the question arises whether it must be converted into money and the proceeds invested pursuant to the rule in *Howe v. Lord Dartmouth*.[86] Since a share constitutes personal property,[87] the application of the

---

[80] See *supra*, paras. 10–216 *et seq.*
[81] See *Beamish v. Beamish* (1869) I.R. 4 Eq. 120.
[82] *Re Ritson* [1899] 1 Ch. 128, noticed, *supra*, para. 19–34; also *Farquhar v. Hadden* (1871) L.R. 7 Ch.App. 1 (where the bequest was of the deceased's share of a partnership lease). As to what is comprised in the share, see *supra*, paras. 19–01 *et seq.*; also *Re Rhagg* [1938] Ch. 828; *Re White* [1958] Ch. 762. It should not, however, be assumed that the value of the share must be ascertained as at the date of death in all cases, notwithstanding the terms of the Partnership Act 1890, s.43: see *supra*, paras. 19–11, 19–12, 23–33, 26–04.
[83] See *supra*, paras. 26–46 *et seq.*
[84] See *Fryer v. Ward* (1862) 31 Beav. 602, where the legatees were entitled to elect whether or not to take over the business.
[85] See *supra*, paras. 26–05, 26–27.
[86] (1802) 7 Ves.Jr. 137a; also *Dimes v. Scott* (1828) 4 Russ. 195.
[87] See, in particular, the Partnership Act 1890, s.22, *supra*, para. 19–16.

rule will depend on the terms of the will.[88] Clear language is required if the life tenant is to be entitled to have the share kept unconverted[89]: neither an express power to postpone sale nor a provision directing the executors to treat any "dividends rents interest or moneys of the nature of income" as income will suffice.[90]

On the other hand, in the case of an intestacy, the deceased **26–67** partner's personal representatives can distribute the income derived from the share as if the rule in *Howe v. Lord Dartmouth* did not exist.[91]

It should be noted that trading losses attributable to the share must not be thrown on capital so as to benefit a life tenant at the expense of the remaindermen.[92]

Legatee's or life tenant's right to profits

The legatee's or life tenant's entitlement in respect of profits may **26–68** not, on normal principles, extend to profits declared prior to the testator's death[93] nor to profits which, though declared after his death, were earned and ought to have been declared before the death.[94] If so, the testator's share of such profits will prima facie form part of his general estate.[95]

Where a legatee is, under the terms of the will, entitled to receive **26–69** profits earned and declared *before* the testator's death, *e.g.* where the legacy is expressed to include the testator's share of all moneys standing to the credit of the partnership bank account at the time of his death and those moneys include such profits, the legatee may be entitled to receive such share without any deduction on account of basic or higher rate income tax assessable by reference thereto.[96]

---

[88] See *Re Trollope* [1927] 1 Ch. 596.

[89] See *Re Chancellor* (1884) 26 Ch.D. 42; *Re Crowther* [1895] 2 Ch. 56.

[90] *Re Berry* [1962] Ch. 97; see also *Re Robbins* [1941] Ch. 434.

[91] *Re Trollope* [1927] 1 Ch. 596, 604, *per* Tomlin J.; *Re Fisher* [1943] Ch. 377; Administration of Estates Act 1925, ss.33(5), (7), 49 (as amended).

[92] See *Upton v. Brown* (1884) 26 Ch.D. 588; *cf. Gow v. Forster* (1884) 26 Ch.D. 672. As to the apportionment of profits and losses between the life tenant and the remainderman where the share ought to be realised, see *Re Earl of Chesterfield's Trusts* (1883) 24 Ch.D. 643; *Re Godden* [1893] 1 Ch. 292; *Re Hengler* [1893] 1 Ch. 586; *Re Elford* [1910] 1 Ch. 814; *Re Parry* [1947] Ch. 23; *Re Berry* [1962] Ch. 97. Note also, as to the position where the purchase price of the share is payable by instalments, *Re Hollebone* [1919] 2 Ch. 93.

[93] *Ibbotson v. Elam* (1865) L.R. 1 Eq. 188; *Browne v. Collins* (1871) L.R. 12 Eq. 586. See also *Jacques v. Chambers* (1846) 2 Colly. 435; *Wright v. Warren* (1851) 4 De G. & Sm. 367. Note, however, that if declared, but undrawn, profits have been treated as a form of circulating capital (see *supra*, para. 17–07), they may properly fall to be regarded as part of the *corpus* of the share.

[94] *Browne v. Collins* (1871) L.R. 12 Eq. 586. Cf. *Ibbotson v. Elam, supra.*

[95] *Browne v. Collins, supra.*

[96] See *Re Betts* [1949] W.N. 91; *Re White* [1958] Ch. 762. *Per contra*, perhaps, if there is a right of retention in respect of such tax under the agreement: see *supra*, para. 10–73.

Apportionment of profits

26–70   Partnership profits are not within the Apportionment Act 1870.[97]

---

[97] *Jones v. Ogle* (1872) L.R. 8 Ch.App. 192; *Re Cox's Trusts* (1878) 9 Ch.D. 159. As to the position prior to the Act, see *Johnston v. Moore* (1858) 27 L.J.Ch. 453; *Ibbotson v. Elam* (1865) L.R. 1 Eq. 188; *Browne v. Collins* (1871) L.R. 12 Eq. 586.

CHAPTER 27

INSOLVENCY*

1. INTRODUCTION

THE law of bankruptcy, which had evolved through successive **27-01**
Bankruptcy Acts,[1] was completely reformulated by the Insolvency
Act 1985, which swept away most of the previous legislation,
including the Bankruptcy Acts 1914 and 1926.[2] However, before the
majority of the provisions contained in the 1985 Act came into force,
they were themselves repealed and replaced by the consolidating
Insolvency Act 1986.[3] The present insolvency legislation is now
principally contained in the latter Act and the Insolvency Rules 1986
(as amended),[4] although the regime governing insolvent partners and
partnerships is contained in the Insolvent Partnerships Order 1986.[5]
This Order seeks to adapt the provisions of the 1986 Act piecemeal in
order to accommodate the procedures applicable on the winding-up
of an insolvent firm, whether in conjunction with or independently of
the insolvency of one or more of the partners. The product of this
approach is an indigestible patchwork of provisions, several of which
are palpably ill-suited to their task.

In earlier editions of this work, the present chapter contained a **27-02**
detailed account of the law of bankruptcy as it affected partners and
partnerships, much of which will now be of interest only in the case
of bankruptcy petitions presented under the law in force immediately
prior to December 29, 1986 or bankruptcy proceedings pending on
that date,[6] which for this purpose includes cases where a bankruptcy
notice was *served* on a firm or partner on or before that date.[7]
Readers interested in such material are referred to those earlier

---

* At the time of writing, the Insolvent Partnerships Order 1994 (S.I. 1994 No. 2421) had not
been made. The main text of the Order is reproduced at Appendix 7.
[1] Bankruptcy Act 1883; Bankruptcy Act 1890; Bankruptcy and Deeds of Arrangement Act 1913,
Pt. 1; Bankruptcy Act 1914; Bankruptcy (Amendment) Act 1926.
[2] Insolvency Act 1985, s.235(3), Sched. 10.
[3] Insolvency Act 1986, s.438, Sched. 12.
[4] (S.I. 1986 No. 1925); Insolvency (Amendment) Rules 1987 (S.I. 1987 No. 1919); Insolvency
(Amendment) Rules 1989 (S.I. 1989 No. 397); Insolvency (Amendment) Rules 1991 (S.I. 1991 No,
495); Insolvency (Amendment) Rules 1993 (S.I. 1993 No. 294).
[5] (S.I. 1986 No. 2142). At the time of writing, it seems likely that this Order will be replaced in
near future, although the precise nature of the new provisions is not yet known.
[6] Insolvent Partnerships Order 1986, art. 15(1). *Cf.* the Insolvency Act 1986, s.437, Sched. 11,
para. 10.
[7] Insolvent Partnerships Order 1986, art. 15(2). *Quaere* whether, in a case where the bankruptcy
notice was served prior to December 29, 1986 but the adjudication was made on a petition
presented *after* that date, the transitional provisions contained in the Insolvency Act 1986, Sched.
11, paras. 13 (discharge) and 14 (trustee in bankruptcy) will apply. The current editor tentatively
submits that they will. *Cf. ibid.* para. 15.

editions.[8] Equally, the rules governing the administration of what are conveniently styled the "joint" estate (*i.e.* the partnership property) and the partners' "separate" estates (*i.e.* their own property) has been preserved under the new legislation, so that a consideration thereof still remains essential.[9]

27–03   Given the scope of this work, a detailed review of general insolvency law would be inappropriate and readers are referred to the standard works in relation thereto.[10] What this chapter will, however, attempt to do is to identify those areas which give rise to questions peculiar to partners and partnerships under the current legislation.

The statutory approach to insolvent partners and partnerships

27–04   Under the Bankruptcy Act 1914, the same regime applied both to insolvent partners and to insolvent partnerships, save in the case of a firm with eight or more partners, which could formerly be wound up under the Companies Acts as an unregistered company.[11] In its application to all insolvent partnerships,[12] irrespective of size, the new legislation, as applied by the Insolvent Partnerships Order 1986, endeavours to assimilate firms into the general framework of corporate insolvency.

27–05   In essence, there are now four ways in which the insolvency legislation may be applied to a partnership, namely:

(*a*)   where the firm itself is wound up as an unregistered company;[13]

(*b*)   where the firm is wound up as an unregistered company, but with concurrent petitions being presented against two or more of the partners;[14]

(*c*)   where all the individual partners present a joint debtor's petition against themselves, but the firm itself is *not* wound up as an unregistered company;[15] and

---

[8] See the 15th ed. of this work at pp. 774 *et seq.*

[9] See *infra*, paras. 27–82 *et seq.* Note, however, that a new regime is likely to be introduced in the near future by a revised Insolvent Partnerships Order.

[10] *e.g. Muir Hunter On Personal Insolvency*; *Palmer's Company Law* (24th ed.).

[11] See the Companies Act 1985, ss.665(1)(c), 666 (repealed by the Insolvency Act 1986, s.438, Sched. 12); Companies Act 1948, 398(1)(c), 399.

[12] As to when a partnership will be regarded as insolvent, see *Re Hough, The Independent*, April 23, 1990. Note, however, that this presupposes the existence of a partnership in law: *Re C. & M. Ashberg, The Times*, July 17, 1990.

[13] Insolvent Partnerships Order 1986, art. 7, applying the Insolvency Act 1986, Pt. V, with modifications. See further, *infra*, paras. 27–09 *et seq.*

[14] Insolvent Partnerships Order 1986, art. 8(1), applying the Insolvency Act 1986, ss.220, 221, with modifications; see further, *infra*, paras. 27–23 *et seq.* As to the position of an insolvent corporate partner in such a case, see *ibid.* art. 8(2) and *infra*, paras. 27–26 *et seq.*

[15] Insolvent Partnerships Order 1986, art. 13(1), applying the Insolvency Act 1986, s.264; see further, *infra*, paras. 27–45 *et seq.*

(d) where petitions for a bankruptcy order[16] are presented against one or more partners but not against others, no attempt being made to wind up the firm.[17]

The first two cases, more than either of the other two, typify the approach of the new legislation and will be considered together.

Banking and insurance partnerships

The court has jurisdiction to wind up an authorised banking **27–06** partnership as an unregistered company on a petition presented by the Bank of England.[18] A similar jurisdiction is exercisable in the case of a partnership carrying on insurance business, in the event of a petition being presented by the requisite number of policy holders or by the Secretary of State.[19] Neither of these statutory jurisdictions is affected by the Insolvent Partnerships Order 1986.[20]

2. INSOLVENCY INVOLVING THE WINDING-UP OF THE FIRM AS AN UNREGISTERED COMPANY

Firm wound up as an unregistered company

It goes almost without saying that a firm can only be wound up as **27–07** an unregistered company if, as a matter of law, a partnership actually exists. If two or more persons merely hold themselves out as partners,[21] there will be no partnership to be wound up.[22]

Where a firm is wound up as an unregistered company, the normal **27–08** legislation governing company insolvencies will apply subject only to the specific amendments introduced by the Insolvent Partnerships Order 1986[23] and any "necessary modifications" to the Rules

---

[16] See generally, the Insolvency Act 1986, ss.264 et seq.

[17] Insolvent Partnerships Order 1986, art. 15(3), preserving the creditor's rights in this respect. See further, infra, paras. 27–48 et seq.

[18] Banking Act 1987, s.92(1), (2). A former authorised partnership may be wound up in the same way: ibid. As to authorisation, see ibid. ss.8 et seq. (as amended); also the definitions in ibid. s.106(1). And see supra, para. 24–42.

[19] Insurance Companies Act 1982, ss.53, 54 (as amended by the Companies Consolidation (Consequential Provisions) Act 1985, Sched. 2; the Insolvency Act 1986, Sched. 14; the Insurance Companies (Amendment) Regulations 1990 (S.I. 1990 No. 1333), reg. 8(3); the Insurance Companies (Amendment) Regulations 1993 (S.I. 1993 No. 174), reg. 2(1)(c)). See also supra, para. 24–43.

[20] Insolvent Partnerships Order 1986, art. 15(3).

[21] As to holding out, see the Partnership Act 1890, s.14 and supra, paras. 5–43 et seq.

[22] Re C. & M. Ashberg, The Times, July 17, 1990.

[23] Insolvent Partnerships Order 1986, art. 7, Sched. 1 (winding up without concurrent petitions against two or more of the partners); art. 8(1)(b) (substituting the Insolvency Act 1986, s.221(1)), (2), Sched. 2 (winding up with concurrent petitions).

required to give effect thereto.[24] As already noted, a winding-up order may be obtained with or without concurrent petitions against two or more of the partners and the procedure and consequences will naturally differ according to the nature of the order sought.

A. WINDING-UP ORDER AGAINST FIRM WITHOUT CONCURRENT PETITIONS

Grounds for petition

27–09   For this purpose, the Insolvent Partnerships Order 1986 adds insolvent partnerships to the list of unregistered companies which may be wound up under the Act.[25] However, a petition to wind up such a partnership may only be presented on a limited number of grounds, namely:

(a)   if the firm has already been dissolved, whether or not its business is being carried on in the course of winding up its affairs;[26]

(b)   if it has ceased to carry on business without being dissolved;[27]

(c)   if it is unable to pay its debts;[28] or

(d)   on the "just and equitable" ground.[29]

27–10   *Firm's inability to pay its debts*: There are a number of circumstances in which a firm will be deemed unable to pay its debts, which are set out in the Act.[30] They may be summarised as follows:

(i)   where a creditor, to whom the firm is then indebted in a sum exceeding £750,[31] has served[32] a written demand[33] on

---

[24] *Ibid.* art. 5(1). In any given case, it may not be clear what those "necessary modifications" may be.

[25] *Ibid.* Sched. 1, para. 1, amending the Insolvency Act 1986, s.220(1).

[26] Insolvency Act 1986, s.221(5)(a). The current editor submits that the distinction between a partnership which has been dissolved and one which is "carrying on business only for the purpose of winding up its affairs" may be of little or no substance, save that the dissolved firm may not be able to take on any *new* business. See further, as to the authority and obligations of the members of a dissolved firm, the Partnership Act 1890, s.38, considered *supra*, paras. 13–64 *et seq*.

[27] Insolvency Act 1986, s.221(5)(a). *Cf.* the provisions of *ibid.* s.122(1)(d). And see further, as to the possible effects of a firm ceasing to carry on any business whatsoever, *supra*, para. 24–38.

[28] *Ibid.* s.221(5)(b).

[29] *Ibid.* s.221(5)(c).

[30] *Ibid.* ss.222–224.

[31] This sum may be increased: *ibid.* s.222(2).

[32] Service may be effected by leaving the demand at the firm's principal place of business, by delivering it to a partner or the firm's "manager or principal officer" (if any) or in such other manner as the court directs: *ibid.* s.222(1)(a).

[33] The demand must be in the prescribed form: see the Insolvency Rules 1986, Sched. 4, Form 4.1, as substituted by the Insolvency (Amendment) Rules 1987 (S.I. 1987 No. 1919), Sched., Pt. 2, para. 158(1), Pt. 5.

the firm and the sum due has not been paid, secured or compounded within three weeks;[34]

(ii)   where proceedings have been instituted against any partner for any debt or demand due[35] or claimed to be due from the firm or from that partner (in his capacity as a member of the firm) of which notice in writing has been served on the firm[36] and the firm has not within three weeks paid, secured or compounded for the debt or demand, had the proceedings stayed or satisfactorily indemnified the defendant partner "against the action or proceeding, and against all costs, damages and expenses to be incurred by him because of it";[37]

(iii)   where "execution or other process"[38] issued on a judgment[39] obtained against the firm or against any partner as such,[40] whatever the sum involved,[41] is returned unsatisfied;[42]

(iv)   where it is proved to the court's satisfaction that the firm is unable to pay its debts (whatever may be their amount) as and when they fall due;[43]

(v)   where it is proved to the court's satisfaction that the firm's liabilities, whether actual, contingent or prospective, exceed the value of its assets.[44]

---

[34] Insolvency Act 1986, s.222(1)(b).

[35] The expression used is merely "due" not "then due": cf. ibid. s.222(1).

[36] Ibid. s.223(a). And see supra, n. 32. Note that the subsection does not technically state by whom the notice is to be served.

[37] Ibid. s.223(b). The current editor doubts whether, in the normal case, such an indemnity would be appropriate, since the partner against whom the proceedings are instituted will have to bear his share of the liability: cf. ibid. s.221(10)(b)(i) (as added by the Insolvent Partnerships Order 1986, Sched. 1, para. 2), where the expression used is "reimbursement." The position may be otherwise in the case of a salaried partner who is entitled to an indemnity in any event: see further, supra, para. 20–06. Quaere, why would a creditor pursue a partner, when his ultimate aim is to wind up the firm? It is questionable whether this ground will in practice be relied on by petitioners.

[38] It should be noted that the service of a demand under ibid. s.222(1)(a) will not constitute execution or other process for these purposes.

[39] It may be that the court is entitled to enquire into the validity of the contract, etc., on which the judgment was obtained, as under the old law: see Ex p. Troup [1895] 1 Q.B. 404; Ex p. Beauchamp [1904] 1 K.B. 572; Re A Debtor [1927] 2 Ch. 367; cf. Re A Debtor [1929] 1 Ch. 125 (where the court refused to go behind the compromise); and see Bowes v. Hope Life Insurance and Guarantee Company (1865) 11 H.L.Cas. 389; Railway Finance Co. (1866) 14 W.R. 785; Ex p. Kibble (1875) 10 Ch. 373; Re Ex p. Banner (1881) 17 Ch.D. 480; Ex p. Lennox (1885) 16 Q.B.D. 315, explained in Ex p. Scotch Whisky Distillers Ltd. (1888) 22 Q.B.D. 83; Ex p. Central Bank of London [1892] 2 Q.B. 633; also Ex p. Revell (1884) 13 Q.B.D. 720; Ex p. Edwards (1884) 14 Q.B.D. 415; Ex p. Anderson (1885) 14 Q.B.D. 606. And see Brandon v. McHenry [1891] 1 Q.B. 538; Ex p. Lancaster [1911] 2 K.B. 981. Cf. the position where an application is made to set aside a statutory demand based on a judgment debt: Re A Debtor (No. 657/SD/91) [1992] S.T.C. 751; also para. 3 of the Practice Note (Bankruptcy: Statutory Demand: Setting Aside) (No. 1/87) [1987] 1 W.L.R. 113.

[40] Accordingly, the judgment against a partner must be obtained in respect of a partnership debt.

[41] In such a case, there is no prescribed minimum amount for the debt in question; cf. s.222(1)(a).

[42] Ibid. s.224(1)(a). As to the position in Scotland or Northern Ireland, see ibid. s.224(1)(b), (c).

[43] Ibid. s.224(1)(d). And note the decision in Taylors Industrial Flooring Ltd. v. M & H Plant Hire (Manchester) Ltd. [1990] BCC 44 (a decision under ibid. s.123(1)(e)); also Re Clemence plc (1992) 59 B.L.R. 56.

[44] Ibid. s.224(2).

In the latter case, the manner in which the firm's liabilities and assets are to be valued is not stated.

27–11 *Just and equitable ground*:   A winding-up order on this ground will in general be made on precisely the same basis as the court would order a dissolution of a solvent partnership under section 35(f) of the Partnership Act 1890.[45] However, where the petition is presented by one or more of the partners,[46] the court will seemingly be bound to refuse the order sought if it is satisfied that some other remedy is available to the petitioner and that he is acting unreasonably in seeking a winding-up order instead of pursuing that other remedy.[47]

Group and sub-partnerships

27–12 The grounds will be the same where a petition is to be presented against an insolvent member firm of a group partnership,[48] provided that the group partnership is not itself insolvent.[49]

In the case of a sub-partnership,[50] the solvency (or otherwise) of the head partnership will be irrelevant.[51]

Firm comprising minor or foreign partners

27–13 The current editor submits that there is no bar to a petition against a firm comprising minor or foreign partners.[52]

Who may present petition

27–14 A petition on the above grounds may be presented by:

　　(*a*) a creditor;[53]

---

[45] See *supra*, paras. 24–75 *et seq.*

[46] Leave may be required in such a case: see *infra*, para. 27–14.

[47] Insolvency Act 1986, s.125(2). *Cf.* the approach under the old bankruptcy legislation: *Ex p. Browne* (1810) 1 Rose 151; *Ex p. Christie* (1832) Mont. & Bl. 352; *Ex p. Johnson* (1842) 2 M.D. & D. 678; *Ex p. Phipps* (1844) 3 M.D. & D. 505; *Ex p. Upfill* (1866) 1 Ch. 439; *King v. Henderson* [1898] A.C. 720.

[48] See further, as to such partnerships, *supra*, paras. 11–20 *et seq.*

[49] As to the position where the group partnership is insolvent, see *infra*, para. 27–28.

[50] See, as to such partnerships, *supra*, paras. 5–75 *et seq.*

[51] See *infra*, para. 27–28.

[52] This is not a possibility catered for under the legislation.

[53] A contingent or prospective creditor or a creditor by assignment may present a petition: Insolvency Act 1986, ss.124(1) (as amended), 222(1). There would seem to be no reason why a creditor, who is not a member of the firm but has been held out as such or who was formerly a member thereof, should not petition as such: see *Ex p. Notley* (1833) 1 Mont. & Ayr. 46; *Ex p. Richardson* (1833) 3 D. & Ch. 244. See also *infra*, para. 27–48.

(b)   the liquidator of a present or former corporate partner;[54]

(c)   the trustee of a present or former bankrupt partner's estate;[55] or

(d)   the partnership itself, provided that there are eight or more partners.[56]

However, the *partners'* freedom to petition for the winding-up of their firm is more restricted. As in the case of a petition presented by the firm, there must be at least eight partners[57] or the petition must be presented with the leave of the court following the service on the firm of a written demand[58] in respect of a *joint* debt (or debts) exceeding £750 which, although then due from the firm, has been paid by the petitioning partner otherwise than out of partnership moneys.[59] The court will only grant such leave if the partner concerned has obtained a judgment or order entitling him to be reimbursed by the firm[60] and taken all reasonable steps[61] to enforce that judgment or order.[62] However, an individual partner may not present a *debtor's* petition[63] on the ground that the partnership is unable to pay its debts unless petitions are at the same time presented against the partnership and against all the other partners and those other partners are all willing to have insolvency orders made against them.[64] A similar restriction applies to a corporate partner.[65]

---

[54] *Ibid.* s.221(8) (as added by the Insolvent Partnerships Order 1986, Sched. 1, para. 2). In such a case, the petitioner's costs may, if the partnership assets ultimately prove to be insufficient, be treated as proper expenses in the liquidation of the corporate partner: *ibid.* s.221(11) (as added by *ibid.*).

[55] *Ibid.* As in the previous case, the trustee's costs as petitioner may ultimately be payable out of the bankrupt partner's estate, if the partnership's assets are insufficient.

[56] *Ibid.* s.221(10)(a) (as added by the Insolvent Partnerships Order 1986, Sched. 1, para. 2). In such a case, the consent of all the partners to the presentation of the petition must be presupposed, in the absence of a specific provision in the agreement entitling a majority to take such action unilaterally: see the Partnership Act 1890, s.24(8) and *supra*, paras. 15–05 *et seq.*, 24–31.

[57] *Ibid.*

[58] For the form of the demand, see the Insolvent Partnerships Order 1986, Sched. 3, Form 2. Note that the form requires the demand to be dealt with within 21 days, even though there is no reference to such a period in the relevant section of the Act: see the next footnote.

[59] *Ibid.* s.221(10)(b) (as added by the Insolvent Partnerships Order 1986, Sched. 1, para. 2). Although the subsection is expressed to be subject to *ibid.* ss.124(3) (as added by *ibid.* Sched. 2, Pt. II, para. 5) and 272 (as modified by *ibid.* Sched. 2, Pt. III, para. 8), it is difficult to see how these sections are relevant. Note also that there appears to be no mechanism for increasing the sum of £750.

[60] *Quaere*, can such an order ever be obtained without taking an account as between the partners? See further, *supra*, paras. 23–70 *et seq.*

[61] Other than insolvency proceedings.

[62] Once the partner has obtained leave, he can serve a petition on any of the grounds set out *supra*, para. 27–09. However, given the written demand procedure outlined in the text, he will almost inevitably petition on the basis of the firm's inability to pay its debts.

[63] See the Insolvent Partnerships Order 1986, Sched. 3, Form 7.

[64] Insolvency Act 1986, ss.221(10), 272 (as respectively added/substituted by the Insolvent Partnerships Order 1986, Sched. 1, para. 2, Sched. 2, Pt. III, para. 8).

[65] *Ibid.* ss.124(3), 221(10) (as respectively substituted/added by the Insolvent Partnerships Order 1986, Sched. 2, Pt. II, para. 5, Sched. 1, para. 2).

Form and service of petition

27–15   The petition will be in the normal form,[66] but the affidavit verifying its contents must include the full names and addresses of the partners, in so far as they are known to the petitioner.[67] Service will in general be effected at the firm's principal place of business[68] by handing the petition to a partner (including any person held out as such),[69] employee or other person authorised to accept service.[70]

Presentation of the petition will be to the High Court[71] or to a county court within whose insolvency district the firm has "a" principal place of business.[72]

Consequences of presentation of petition

Avoidance of transactions

27–16   Since the winding-up of a partnership is deemed to commence when the petition is presented,[73] any disposition of partnership property, transfer of shares or "alteration in the status of the [*partners*]" after that date is void unless sanctioned by the court.[74] This would clearly invalidate any agreement between the partners to treat a partnership asset as belonging to one or more of their number[75] and would also, seemingly, operate to freeze the membership of the firm so that no existing partner may retire or be expelled nor any new partner be admitted after the relevant date.[76] *A fortiori* in the case of an attempt to turn the firm into a limited partnership.[77]

---

[66] Insolvency Rules 1986, r. 4.7(1), Sched. 4, Form 4.2.

[67] Insolvent Partnerships Order 1986, art. 4. See, as to the form of the affidavit, the Insolvency Rules 1986, Sched. 4, Form 4.3.

[68] See the Insolvency Act 1986, s.221(3).

[69] For this purpose a partner is treated as an "officer and director" of the firm: Insolvent Partnerships Order 1986, art. 3(a). As to the position of persons held out as partners, see the Partnership Act 1890, s.14, *supra*, paras. 5–43 *et seq.* Note also, in this context, the decision in *Re C. & M. Ashberg*, *The Times*, July 17, 1990, noticed *supra*, para. 27–07.

[70] Insolvency Rules 1986, r. 4.8(3)(a), (b).

[71] Insolvency Act 1986, s.117(1).

[72] *Ibid.* ss.117(2), 221(12) (as added by the Insolvent Partnerships Order 1986, Sched. 1, para. 2). Note that the existence of more than one principal place of business appears to be contemplated: *cf. ibid.* s.117(6), the application of which is presumably (by implication) excluded.

[73] *Ibid.* s.129(2).

[74] *Ibid.* s.127. See, generally, as to the approach likely to be adopted by the court, *Re Burton & Deakin Ltd.* [1977] 1 W.L.R. 390; *Re Gray's Inn Construction Co. Ltd.* [1980] 1 W.L.R. 711 (both decisions under the Companies Act 1948, s.227); *S.A. & D. Wright Ltd.* [1992] BCC 503 (a decision under the Companies Act 1985, s.522); *Re Flint* [1993] Ch. 319 (a decision under the Insolvency Act 1986, s.284).

[75] See, as to such agreements, *supra*, paras. 18–43 *et seq.* and *infra*, paras. 27–102 *et seq.*

[76] Even if the incoming partner does not acquire any interest in the capital or assets of the firm, the creation of his profit share will almost inevitably involve a "transfer" of part of the existing partners' profit shares as well as a change in their status, *i.e.* when they become members of the "new" firm constituted following the incoming partner's admission.

[77] See generally, as to the formalities which would otherwise be required in order to effect such conversion, *infra*, paras. 29–01 *et seq.*

Stay of proceedings

An application to the court to stay any proceedings pending against **27–17** the firm or any member thereof may be made at any time after the presentation of the petition and prior to a winding-up order being made, by the firm itself or by any partner or creditor.[78]

Appointment of provisional liquidator

A provisional liquidator may be appointed following the presenta- **27–18** tion of the petition.[79] However, whilst the court is given power, in the case of a petition presented by the liquidator of a corporate partner or by the trustee of a bankrupt partner's estate, to appoint such liquidator/trustee to be the liquidator of the partnership, this power is only expressed to be exercisable where a winding-up order is made.[80] Nevertheless, it is apprehended that, in an appropriate case, such liquidator/trustee could theoretically be appointed as the provisional liquidator.

The winding-up order and its consequences

When it hears the petition, the court will have a wide discretion **27–19** when determining whether a winding-up order against the firm should be made.[81] The order itself will follow the same form as an order made against a company.[82]

Stay of proceedings and executions

Once a winding-up order has been made, proceedings may only be **27–20** commenced or continued against the firm[83] or any partner[84] in respect of a partnership debt if the leave of the court is obtained.

---

[78] Insolvency Act 1986, ss.126, 227. For these purposes a partner is clearly a "contributory": see *ibid.* s.226(1) and *infra*, paras. 27–60 *et seq.* Although *ibid.* s.227 refers to "actions or proceedings against any contributory", thus seemingly including actions in respect of a partner's *separate* debts, the current editor submits that it should not be so construed: *cf. ibid.* s.228, where the position is clear.

[79] *Ibid.* s.135(1), (2). As to the manner in which the application is made, see the Insolvency Rules 1986, r. 4.25.

[80] *Ibid.* s.221(9) (as added by the Insolvent Partnerships Order 1986, Sched. 1, para. 2).

[81] *Ibid.* s.125(1). Note, however, the restrictions on that discretion where a partner petitions on the just and equitable ground: *ibid.* s.125(2), noticed *supra*, para. 27–11.

[82] Insolvency Rules 1986, Sched. 4, Form 4.11.

[83] Insolvency Act 1986, s.130(2).

[84] *Ibid.* s.228. For these purposes a partner is clearly a "contributory": see *ibid.* s.226(1) and *infra*, para. 27–60. *Cf.* the terms of *ibid.* s.227: see *supra*, para. 27–17, n. 78.

There is an express restriction on all forms of execution against the partnership assets[85] but seemingly not against the partners' separate estates. Nevertheless, on the footing that execution in respect of a partnership debt amounts to a "proceeding,"[86] leave would be required even in the latter case.[87]

Subsequent insolvency proceedings against a partner

27–21 Although there is no restriction on insolvency proceedings brought against a partner in respect of his separate debts,[88] the Insolvent Partnerships Order 1986, Art. 14(1) provides as follows:

"(1) Where at any time after a winding-up or bankruptcy petition has been presented to the court against any insolvent member the attention of the court is drawn to the fact that the person in question is a member of an insolvent partnership,[89] the court may make an order as to the future conduct of the insolvency proceedings and any such order may apply any provisions of this Order with any necessary modifications."

The application of this article is somewhat unclear. The expression "insolvent member" is defined as a "member of an insolvent partnership, against whom an insolvency petition is being or has been presented,"[90] whilst "insolvency petition" is in turn defined in terms which include only a petition presented *in conjunction with a petition for the winding-up of the partnership.*[91] In the case presently supposed (*i.e.* a winding-up order previously made against the firm) the presentation of such a petition is an effective impossibility, so that the power would appear not to be exercisable by the court. This is perhaps consistent with the title to Part 4 of the Order.[92]

---

[85] *Ibid.* s.128. Although seemingly absolute in its terms, the section may be overridden by an order under *ibid.* s.130(2): see *The Constellation* [1966] 1 W.L.R. 272 (a decision under the Companies Act 1948, ss.228, 231).

[86] *Re Artistic Colour Printing Company* (1880) 14 Ch.D. 502, 505, *per* Jessel M.R.; *The Constellation, supra.* Note that it has been held that "proceedings" for the purposes of the Insolvency Act 1986, s.11(3)(d) must be of a legal or quasi-legal nature: *Bristol Airport plc v. Powdrill* [1990] Ch. 744.

[87] Insolvency Act 1986, s.228. It is submitted that proceedings by the liquidator in order to enforce a call on a partner *qua* contributory (see *infra*, para. 27–63) would also require leave: see *Williams v. Harding* (1866) L.R. 1 H.L. 9. *Sed quaere.*

[88] *Ibid.* s.228 will not apply in such a case; *per contra* if the proceedings are brought in respect of a partnership debt.

[89] This expression is not defined. See, however, *Re Hough, The Independent*, April 23, 1990; also *Re C. & M. Ashberg, The Times*, July 17, 1990.

[90] Insolvent Partnerships Order 1986, art. 2(1).

[91] *Ibid.* But note how the definition is set out in the original Order.

[92] *i.e.* "Insolvency Proceedings against members of Insolvent Partnership *not involving the Winding Up of the Partnership as an Unregistered Company*" (emphasis supplied).

It would seem to follow that, where an insolvency order is made against a partner in subsequent proceedings, his separate estate will in general be administered independently of the administration of the joint partnership estate.[93]

Administration of the joint partnership estate

The mechanics of such administration will be considered **27–22** hereafter.[94]

B. WINDING-UP ORDER AGAINST FIRM WITH CONCURRENT PETITIONS AGAINST THE PARTNERS

If an insolvent partnership[95] is to be wound up in this way, there **27–23** must be concurrent petitions[96] against at least *two* (but not necessarily all) of the partners.[97]

Grounds for petition against firm

As in the case previously considered, the Insolvent Partnerships **27–24** Order 1986[98] adds insolvent partnerships to the list of unregistered companies which may be wound up under the Act, although the court will only have jurisdiction in the case of a firm which has carried on business in England and Wales within three years of the presentation of the petition.[99] There is, however, only one ground on which such a petition may be presented, namely that the partnership is unable to pay its debts.[1]

Firm's inability to pay its debts. The circumstances in which a firm **27–25** will be *deemed* unable to pay its debts is limited to the single case[2]

---

[93] See *infra*, paras. 27–48 *et seq.*, 27–87.

[94] See *infra*, paras. 27–82 *et seq.*

[95] This procedure will not be possible if, in reality, no partnership exists: see *Re C. & M. Ashberg, The Times*, July 17, 1990, noticed *supra*, para. 27–07.

[96] Such petitions may either consist of a petition for a winding-up order against a corporate partner or a petition for a bankruptcy order against an individual partner: see the definition of insolvency petition in the Insolvent Partnerships Order 1986, art. 2(1).

[97] *Ibid.* art. 8(1).

[98] *Ibid.* art 8(1)(a), amending the Insolvency Act 1986, s.220(1).

[99] Insolvency Act 1986, s.117 (as added by the Insolvent Partnerships Order 1986, Sched. 2, Pt. I, para. 1). As to when a firm will be treated as having carried on business in England and Wales within the requisite period, note *Re A Debtor (No. 784 of 1991)* [1992] Ch. 554 (a decision under *ibid.* s.265(1)(c)(ii)), applying *Theophile v. Solicitor-General* [1950] A.C. 186.

[1] Insolvency Act 1986, s.221(5) (as substituted by the Insolvent Partnerships Order 1986, art. 8(1)(c)). *Ibid.* ss.223, 224 do not apply: Insolvent Partnerships Order 1986, Sched. 2, Pt. I, para. 18.

[2] *Cf.* the position where a petition is presented against the firm but not against any of the partners: see *supra*, paras. 27–10 *et seq.*

where a creditor, to whom the firm is indebted in a sum exceeding £750[3] then due, has served[4] written/statutory demands on the firm[5] and on two or more of the partners[6] (who need not be the partners against whom the petitions are presented) and the sum due has not been paid, secured or compounded to the "reasonable satisfaction of the creditor"[7] within three weeks of the date on which the last demand was served.[8] It must, however, be remembered that the firm's inability to pay its debts may be proved in some other way, without reliance on the foregoing deeming provision.[9]

Grounds for petition against corporate partner

27–26   If the court has jurisdiction to wind up the firm, it also has jurisdiction to wind up a corporate member thereof.[10] As in the case of the firm, a petition against such a partner may only be presented on the ground that it is unable to pay its debts.[11] There will be a deemed inability in three cases, namely:

---

[3] This sum may be increased: Insolvency Act 1986, s.222(2).

[4] Service may be effected by leaving the demand at the firm's principal place of business, by delivering it to a partner or any person having at the time of service control or management of the partnership business "there" [*i.e.* at the firm's principal place of business] or in such other manner as the court directs. The current editor submits that a valid demand may be served on a partner *otherwise* than at the firm's principal place of business, although the position is not entirely clear. *Cf.* the Insolvency Act 1986, ss.123(1), 268(3) (as respectively substituted by the Insolvent Partnerships Order 1986, Sched. 2, Pt. II, para. 4(a) and Pt. III, para. 5(d)), in both of which an additional "or" is inserted before the reference to a person having control or management of the partnership business. Service on a *corporate* partner must seemingly be effected in the manner set out in the former subsection, there being no other mode of service prescribed. Similarly, in a case where the creditor has obtained a judgment against the firm or (more unusually) against an individual partner in respect of a partnership debt and is entitled to issue execution or other process against the firm's property or the property of that partner in respect thereof, service may be effected on that partner in the manner set out in the latter subsection. Otherwise, it would seem that the Insolvency Rules 1986, r. 6.3, which requires the creditor, where practicable, to effect personal service of the demand (see, in particular, r. 6.3(2)) will apply in the case of an individual partner: see the Insolvent Partnerships Order 1986, art. 5(1).

[5] The demand served on the firm must be in Form 3 set out in the Insolvent Partnerships Order 1986, Sched. 3. Note, however, that this form requires amendment in the case of service on an individual: see the Practice Note (Bankruptcy: Prescribed Forms) (No. 2/88) [1988] 1 W.L.R. 557, para. 4.

[6] The demands served on the partners must also be in Form 3 set out in the Insolvent Partnerships Order 1986, Sched. 3. See, in the case of corporate partners, the Insolvency Act 1986, s.123(1) (as substituted by the Insolvent Partnerships Order 1986, Sched. 2, Pt. II, para. 4) and, in the case of individual partners, *ibid* s.268(1)(a), (3) (as substituted by the Insolvent Partnerships Order 1986, Sched. 2, Pt. III, para. 5(b), (d)).

[7] *Cf.* the Insolvency Act 1986, s.222(1)(b) which, in its original form, omits any reference to reasonableness.

[8] *Ibid.* s.222(1) (as substituted by the Insolvent Partnerships Order 1986, Sched. 2, Pt. I, para. 17).

[9] Note, however, that s.224(1)(d) of the Insolvency Act 1986 does not apply: Insolvent Partnerships Order 1986, Sched. 2, Pt. I, para. 17.

[10] Insolvency Act 1986, s.117 (as amended by the Insolvent Partnerships Order 1986, Sched. 2, Pt. I, para. 1 and read subject to *ibid.* Sched. 2, Pt. II, para. 2). Voluntary winding-up is not possible in these circumstances: see the Insolvency Act 1986 s.73 (as substituted by the Insolvent Partnerships Order 1986, Sched. 2, Pt. II, para. 1).

[11] Insolvency Act 1986, s.122 (as substituted by the Insolvent Partnerships Order 1986, Sched. 2, Pt. II, para. 3).

(a) where the relevant partnership debt is not paid, secured or compounded to the creditor's reasonable satisfaction following completion of the written/statutory demand procedure described in the preceding paragraph.

(b) where it is proved to the court's satisfaction that the corporate partner's liabilities, whether actual or contingent, exceed the value of its assets[12] or

(c) where the court has made a winding-up order against the firm.[13]

As in the case of the petition presented against the firm, actual inability may always be proved in some other way.

Foreign corporate partner

A concurrent petition may be presented against a corporate partner **27–27** registered outside England and Wales, provided that the court has jurisdiction to wind up the partnership.[14]

Group and sub-partnerships[15]

Where a group partnership is insolvent, each constituent firm will **27–28** be treated as a corporate member of the group for the above purposes.[16] If petitions are not to be presented against the partners, a winding-up order may be sought against the group partnership in the normal way.[17]

It is the view of the current editor that a sub-partnership will not fall to be similarly treated in the event of the insolvency of the head partnership.[18]

---

[12] *Ibid.* s.123(2).

[13] *Ibid.* s.123(1), (4) (as respectively substituted by the Insolvent Partnerships Order 1986, Sched. 2, Pt. II, para. 4(a), (b)).

[14] *Ibid.* s.117(1) (read subject to the Insolvent Partnerships Order 1986, Sched. 2, Pt. II, para. 2).

[15] See, as to such partnerships, *supra*, paras. 11–20 *et seq.*

[16] Insolvent Partnerships Order 1986, art. 12. Note that a petition to wind up one of the constituent firms without winding up the group partnership will proceed in the normal way: see *supra*, para. 27–09.

[17] See *supra*, paras. 27–09 *et seq.*

[18] To apply the Insolvent Partnerships Order 1986, art. 12 in such a case would involve ignoring the true nature of a sub-partnership: in a normal case, only one of the sub-partners will in fact be a member of the head partnership and it is only that sub-partner who will be liable to a creditor of the head partnership; *vis-à-vis* the sub-partnership, that creditor will be no more than a separate creditor of one of the sub-partners. There would seem to be little point in deeming that sub-partner to be a corporate partner (whether he be a company or an individual), unless the underlying intention is to render the sub-partnership itself as a member of the head partnership and liable to be wound up accordingly. *Semble* this cannot be the effect of art. 12. Note also that the same approach is, more logically, adopted in the case of any other body which can be wound up as an unregistered company under the Insolvency Act 1986, Pt. V. A petition to wind up a sub-partnership without winding up the head partnership will be no different from a petition against any other firm: see *supra*, para. 27–09.

Grounds for petition against individual partner

27–29   A petition for a bankruptcy order may only be presented against an individual partner in respect of one or more joint debts owed by his insolvent firm[19] if he appears unable to pay[20] those debts and they are liquidated, immediately due[21] and total £750 or more.[22] A partner will display such an apparent inability where, within the three weeks following completion of the written/statutory demand procedure described above,[23] the relevant debts are not paid, secured or compounded to the creditor's reasonable satisfaction and the demand against that partner has not been set aside[24] or where the court has made a winding-up order against the firm.[25]

Minor or foreign partners

27–30   A court which has jurisdiction to wind up the partnership will also have jurisdiction to hear a bankruptcy petition presented against a minor or foreign partner.[26]

Personal representatives

27–31   Where personal representatives carry on the deceased's business in the old firm name and, in the course of so doing, incur joint debts,

---

[19] Insolvency Act 1986, s.267(1) (as amended by the Insolvent Partnerships Order 1986, Sched. 2, Pt. III, para. 4(a)).

[20] *Ibid.* s.267(2)(c) (as amended by the Insolvent Partnerships Order 1986, Sched. 2, Pt. III, para. 4(c)).

[21] *Ibid.* s.267(2)(b) (as amended by the Insolvent Partnerships Order 1986, Sched. 2, Pt. III, para. 4(b)). It follows that future debts cannot found a petition: see *ibid.* s.267(2)(b) in its original form.

[22] *Ibid.* s.267(2)(a), (4). This sum may, of course, be increased: *ibid.*

[23] See *supra*, para. 27–25. Note that the three week period specified in the Insolvency Act 1986, s.286(1)(a) (as substituted by the Insolvent Partnerships Order 1986, Sched. 2, Pt. III, para. 5(b)) is measured from the date of service of the "relevant demand", which would appear to be a reference to the statutory demand. *Cf. ibid.*, s.221(1) (as substituted by the Insolvent Partnerships Order 1986, Sched. 2, Pt. III, para. 5(b)).

[24] Insolvency Act 1986, s.286(1)(a) (as substituted by the Insolvent Partnerships Order 1986, Sched. 2, Pt. III, para. 5(b)). *Quaere* whether a petition may properly be presented if there is an outstanding application to set aside the statutory demand served on the partner concerned at the end of the three week period specified in that subsection: see *ibid.* s.267(1)(d). As to the procedure for setting aside a statutory demand, see the Insolvency Rules 1986, rr. 6.4, 6.5; *Re A Debtor (No. 415–50–1993)* [1994] 1 W.L.R. 917; also the Practice Note (Bankruptcy: Statutory Demand: Setting Aside) (No. 1/87) [1987] 1 W.L.R. 113.

[25] Insolvency Act 1986, s.268(2) (as substituted by the Insolvent Partnerships Order 1986, Sched. 2, Pt. III, para. 5(d)). However, in practice, reliance on this subsection is unlikely to be possible, given the written/statutory demand procedure described at *supra*, para. 27–25, and the need to establish the individual partner's inability to pay the relevant debts at the time the petition is presented (*ibid.*, s.267(2)(c), as amended by the Insolvent Partnerships Order 1986, Sched. 2, Pt. III, para. 4(c)), which must be at the same time as the petition is presented against the firm: see *infra*, para. 27–34.

[26] See *ibid.* s.265 (as substituted by the Insolvent Partnerships Order 1986, Sched. 2, Pt. III, para. 2); *cf. ibid.* s.265 in its original form. It is assumed that, as under the Bankruptcy Act 1914, for a valid petition to be presented against a minor, it would be necessary to establish his liability for the debts and obligations of the firm: see, *Re A Debtor (No. 564 of 1949)* [1950] Ch. 282; also *Ex p. Jones* (1881) 18 Ch.D. 109; *Ex p. Margrett* [1891] 1 Q.B. 413; *Re Davenport* [1963] 1 W.L.R. 817. See also *supra*, paras. 4–07 *et seq.* R.S.C. Ord. 80 will apply in such a case: Insolvency Rules 1986, r. 7.51.

they cannot be treated as partners for insolvency purposes unless that is in fact the relationship between them.[27]

Who may present petitions

Petitions against the firm and against any corporate or individual **27–32** partners may obviously be presented by one or more of the firm's joint creditors.[28] However, a corporate or individual partner may present its or his own petition on the ground that the firm is unable to pay its debts, provided that petitions are presented against the firm and against all the other partners, individual or corporate, and those other partners are willing to have insolvency orders made against them.[29] Although it is not clearly so stated, the petition presented by such a partner appears to be a mere supplemental petition, *i.e.* it presupposes the presentation of the other petitions by a creditor; *sed quaere.*[30]

Form and service of petitions

The form of all the petitions referred to in the foregoing **27–33** paragraphs is prescribed by the Insolvent Partnerships Order 1986.[31] Service on the firm will generally be effected at its principal place of business[32] by handing the petition to a partner (including any person held out as such),[33] employee or other person authorised to accept service.[34] Service on a corporate or individual partner is effected in the normal way.[35]

---

[27] See *Re Fisher & Sons* [1912] 2 K.B. 491, noticed *supra,* para. 5–08, n. 18.

[28] See, as to the petition against the firm, the Insolvency Act 1986, s.124(1) (as substituted by the Insolvent Partnerships Order 1986, Sched. 2, Pt. I, para. 2), as to petitions against corporate partners, *ibid.* s.124(1) (as substituted by the Insolvent Partnerships Order 1986, Sched. 2, Pt. II, para. 5) and, as to petitions against individual partners, *ibid.,* s.264(1) (as substituted by the Insolvent Partnerships Order 1986, Sched. 2, Pt. III, para. 1(a)). Note that, in the latter case, the section somewhat oddly refers to the "individual's creditors", even though the petition may only be presented on the basis of a joint debt: see *ibid.* s.267(1)(a) (as substituted by the Insolvent Partnerships Order 1986, Sched. 2, Pt. III, para. 4(a)).

[29] See, as to a petition presented by a corporate partner, the Insolvency Act 1986, s.124(3) (as substituted by the Insolvent Partnerships Order 1986, Sched. 2, Pt. II, para. 5) and, as to a petition presented by an individual partner, *ibid.,* s.272 (as substituted by the Insolvent Partnerships Order 1986, Sched. 2, Pt. III, para. 8).

[30] If this were not so, it would be necessary to explain why the possibility of a partner presenting all the petitions is apparently not recognised by the Insolvency Act 1986, s.124(1) (as substituted by the Insolvent Partnerships Order 1986, Sched. 2, Pt. I, para. 2) or *ibid.,* s.264(1) (as substituted by the Insolvent Partnerships Order 1986, Sched. 2, Pt. III, para. 1(a)).

[31] See the Insolvent Partnerships Order 1986, Sched. 3, Forms 4, 6 and 7 (petition against the firm, a corporate partner and an individual partner respectively).

[32] Insolvency Act 1986, s.221(3).

[33] For this purpose a partner is treated as an "officer and director" of the firm: Insolvent Partnerships Order 1986, art. 3(a), *infra,* para. 27–58. See further, as to the position of persons held out as partners, *supra,* paras. 5–43 *et seq.* And note also, in this context, *Re C. & M. Ashberg, The Times,* July 17, 1990, noticed *supra,* para. 27–07.

[34] Insolvency Rules 1986, r. 4.8(3).

[35] *Ibid.* rr. 4.8 (corporate partners), 6.14 (individual partners).

27–34   The petitions must all be presented at the same time and to the same court.[36] In the case of a petition against an individual partner, it is provided that the court must have jurisdiction to wind up the partnership[37] as well as jurisdiction for the purposes of the bankruptcy provisions of the Insolvency Act 1986.[38] This will mean either the High Court[39] or a county court within whose insolvency district the firm has "a" principal place of business.[40]

Withdrawal of petitions and addition of parties

27–35   If the petitioner seeks to withdraw all the petitions which he has presented,[41] the court may permit a creditor of the firm to be substituted.[42]

Additional partners can, with the leave of the court, be added to the proceedings at any time after the presentation of a petition.[43]

Consequences of presentation of petitions

Consequences for the firm and any corporate partner

27–36   The position where a petition is presented for the winding-up of a partnership has already been noted.[44] A corporate partner against whom a petition is presented will be subject to the same regime.

---

[36] Insolvency Act 1986, s.124(2) (as substituted by the Insolvent Partnerships Order 1986, Sched. 2, Pt. I, para. 2 in the case of the petition against the firm and by *ibid.* Sched. 2, Pt. II, para. 5 in the case of the petition against a corporate partner), s.264(1A) (as added by the Insolvent Partnerships Order 1986, Sched. 2, Pt. III, para. 1(b) in the case of the petition against an individual partner).

[37] Insolvency Act 1986, s.265 (as substituted by the Insolvent Partnerships Order 1986, Sched. 2, Pt. III, para. 2). In order to have such jurisdiction, the partnership must have carried on business in England and Wales within the last three years: *ibid.* s.117(7) (as added by the Insolvent Partnerships Order 1986, Sched. 1, Pt. I, para. 1). Note, in this context, *Re A Debtor (No. 784 of 1991)* [1992] Ch. 554 (a decision under *ibid.* s.265(1)(c)(ii)), applying *Theophile v. Solicitor-General* [1950] A.C. 186.

[38] *Ibid.* s.117(8) (as added by the Insolvent Partnerships Order 1986, Sched. 2, Pt. I, para. 1). The reference to the "Parts in the Second Group of Parts of this Act" is to *ibid.* ss.252 *et seq.*

[39] *Ibid.* ss.117, 373.

[40] *Ibid.* s.117(9) (as added by the Insolvent Partnerships Order 1986, Sched. 2, Pt. I, para. 1), 373. See also *supra*, para. 27–15, n.72.

[41] *Ibid.* s.124(8) (as substituted by the Insolvent Partnerships Order 1986, Sched. 2, Pt. I, para. 2 in the case of the petition against the firm), s.124(7) (as substituted by the Insolvent Partnership Order Sched. 2, Pt. II, para. 5 in the case of the petition against a corporate partner) and s.264(1D) (as added by the Insolvent Partnerships Order Sched. 2, Pt. III, para. 1(b) in the case of the petition against an individual partner).

[42] *Ibid.* s.124(9) (as substituted by the Insolvent Partnerships Order 1986, Sched. 2, Pt. I, para. 2 in the case of the petition against the firm), s.124(8) (as substituted by the Insolvent Partnerships Order, Sched. 2, Pt. II, para. 5 in the case of the petition against a corporate partner) and s.264(1E) (as added by the Insolvent Partnerships Order, Sched. 2, Pt. III, para. 1 in the case of the petition against an individual partner). The substituted petitioner must already have been substituted in respect of the petition presented against the firm before he can be substituted in respect of the petitions against the corporate and individual partners.

[43] *Ibid.* s.124(4) (as substituted by the Insolvent Partnerships Order 1986, Sched. 2, Pt. I, para. 2 in the case of the petition against the firm), s.124(5) (as added by the Insolvent Partnerships Order Sched. 2, Pt. II, para. 5 in the case of the petition against a corporate partner) and s.264(1B) (as added by the Insolvent Partnerships Order Sched. 2, Pt. III, para. 1 in the case of the petition against an individual partner).

[44] See *supra*, paras. 27–16 *et seq.*

Consequences for an individual partner

An *individual* partner against whom a bankruptcy petition is **27–37** presented will be subject to a general restriction on his ability to dispose of property in his hands,[45] including any assets vested in him on trust for the firm.[46] An interim receiver of his estate may be appointed if that is necessary for the protection of his property.[47]

The insolvency orders and their consequences

Order against the firm

The court must hear the petition against the firm *before* the **27–38** petitions against the partners[48] and will have a general discretion in deciding whether or not to make the order sought.[49] This will also extend to any directions which the court may make as to the future conduct of insolvency proceedings against partners who are already subject to an insolvency order.[50] The order will follow the normal form.[51]

Order against the corporate and individual partners

If an order is made against the firm, the court seemingly has no **27–39** discretion when it subsequently hears a petition presented against a corporate partner and *must* make a winding-up order in respect of that partner.[52] The discretion is marginally greater when it hears a petition presented against an individual partner, since the court must first be satisfied that the relevant debt has not been paid, secured or compounded.[53] This was clearly established in *Re Marr*,[54] where the petitioner's debt was paid after a winding-up order had been made

---

[45] Insolvency Act 1986, s.284. See further *Re Flint* [1993] Ch. 319. *Cf. Re Palmer* [1994] 3 W.L.R. 420 (insolvency administration order following death of joint tenant).

[46] Insolvency Act 1986, s.284(6) (as amended by the Insolvent Partnerships Order 1986, Sched. 2, Pt. III, para. 11). *Per contra* in the case of other forms of trust property.

[47] Insolvency Act 1986, s.286. As to the manner in which the application is made, see the Insolvency Rules 1986, r. 6.51.

[48] Insolvency Act 1986, s.124(7) (as substituted by the Insolvent Partnerships Order 1986, Sched. 2, Pt. I, para. 2). Note, however, that all the petitions will normally be heard on the same day: *Re Marr* [1990] Ch. 773, 784C.

[49] Insolvency Act 1986, s.125(1).

[50] *Ibid.* s.125(2) (as substituted by the Insolvent Partnerships Order 1986, Sched. 2, Pt. I, para. 3).

[51] Insolvency Rules 1986, Sched. 4, Form 4.11.

[52] Insolvency Act 1986, s.125(2) (as substituted by the Insolvent Partnerships Order 1986, Sched. 2, Pt. II, para. 6). The court does, however, retain some discretion in the case of a limited partner: *ibid.* s.125(3) (as substituted by the Insolvent Partnerships Order 1986); see also *infra*, para. 33–07.

[53] Insolvency Act 1986, s.271(1), (2A) (as respectively amended and added by the Insolvent Partnerships Order 1986, Sched. 2, Pt. III, para. 7(a), (c)). Again, further discretion is retained in the case of a limited partner: *ibid.*, s.271(2B) (as added by the Insolvent Partnerships Order 1986). Note also that *ibid.*, ss.273, 274 do not apply in this case: Insolvent Partnerships Order 1986, Sched. 2, Pt. III, para. 9.

[54] [1990] Ch. 773, C.A.

against the firm. Because the order remained extant when the petitions against the two partners were heard, the registrar made bankruptcy orders against them both. Although the orders were, with some diffidence, confirmed by Mervyn Davies J.,[55] the Court of Appeal allowed the partners' appeals, adopting a purposive construction of the legislation and refusing to reject the irresistible inference that section 271(1) of the Insolvency Act 1986[56] was intended to apply. The justification for the stricter approach in the case of a corporate partner seemingly lies in the procedures required to be adopted *prior* to the presentation of the concurrent petitions which, taken together with the fact that an order has previously been made against the firm, presuppose the inability of the firm and its members to meet the debt in question;[57] *sed quaere.*

27-40   If the court has *declined* to make an order against the firm, it has discretion to dismiss any concurrent petition against an individual partner.[58] A similar discretion will, it is thought, exist on the hearing of a concurrent petition against a corporate partner.[59]

The orders made will be in the appropriate forms.[60]

Stay of proceedings and executions

27-41   As in the case of an order made against a firm *without* concurrent petitions against the partners, a winding-up order will operate to stay all existing and future proceedings, etc., against the firm and its members, including those partners in respect of whom no concurrent petitions have been presented.[61]

Subsequent insolvency proceedings against a partner

27-42   The obscure provisions of the Insolvent Partnerships Order 1986, Art. 14(1) have already been noted.[62] If the intention behind the article was to confer on the court power to give directions as to the

---

[55] [1990] Ch. 773, 777.

[56] As amended by the Insolvent Partnerships Order 1986, Sched. 2, Pt. III, para. 7(a).

[57] See, as to these procedures, *supra*, para. 27–25. See also the Insolvency Act 1986, s.123(4) (as substituted by the Insolvent Partnerships Order 1986, Sched. 2, Pt. II, para. 4(b)). Note that the distinction between the position of an individual and a corporate partner was not adverted to in *Re Marr* [1990] Ch. 773.

[58] Insolvency Act 1986, s.271(2) (as substituted by the Insolvent Partnerships Order 1986, Sched. 2, Pt. III, para. 7(b)).

[59] Insolvency Act 1986, s.125(1). Although there is no equivalent to s.271(2) (see *supra*, n.58), there would seem to be no reason to doubt the court's discretion: its existence would also seem to be implicit in *ibid.* s.125(2) (as substituted by the Insolvent Partnerships Order 1986, Sched. 2, Pt. II, para. 6).

[60] See, in the case of a corporate partner, the Insolvency Rules 1986, Sched. 4, Form 4.11 and, in the case of an individual partner, *ibid.* Forms 6.25 (creditor's petition), 6.30 (debtor's petition), as amended.

[61] Insolvency Act 1986, s.228, as to which see further, *supra*, para. 27–20. See also *ibid.* ss.130(2), 183 (in the case of insolvent corporate partners) and ss.285, 346 and 347 (in the case of insolvent individual partners).

[62] See *supra*, para. 27–21.

future conduct of insolvency proceedings brought against any partner in respect of whom a concurrent petition was *not* presented, it is at least doubtful whether that result has been achieved, given the definition of "insolvent member." Moreover, it is perhaps surprising that such an (assumed) power was included in Part 4 of the Order.[63]

Administration of the joint estate and separate estates

This subject will be considered in a subsequent section of this chapter.[64]   **27–43**

3. INSOLVENCY NOT INVOLVING WINDING UP THE FIRM AS AN UNREGISTERED COMPANY

In each of the following cases, insolvency proceedings will be initiated against one or more of the partners, either by a creditor or by the partners themselves and may lead to the firm being wound up, but not as an unregistered company.[65]   **27–44**

Joint debtor's petition presented by the partners

A joint debtor's petition may only be presented on the ground that the partnership is unable to pay its debts.[66] All the partners must be individuals[67] and concur in such presentation.[68] The petition will request the partners' trustee to wind up the firm's business and administer its assets.[69]   **27–45**

If a winding-up order has previously been made against the firm and this is drawn to the attention of the court at any time after the

---

[63] *i.e.* a Part entitled "Insolvency Proceedings against Members of Insolvent Partnership *not Involving the Winding Up of the Partnership as an Unregistered Company*" (emphasis added).

[64] See *infra*, paras. 27–82 *et seq.*

[65] Even where the proceedings do not in themselves involve a winding up of the firm, *e.g.* where a petition is presented against a single partner in respect of a joint or separate debt (see *infra*, para. 27–48), they may still cause the firm to be dissolved: see the Partnership Act 1890, ss.33(1), 35, considered *supra*, paras. 24–20, 24–39 *et seq.*

[66] Insolvency Act 1986, s.272 (as substituted by the Insolvent Partnerships Order 1986, art. 13(5)). In this case, there is no procedure for establishing a firm's *deemed* inability to pay its debts; *cf. ibid.* ss.222 *et seq.*, noticed *supra*, para. 27–09. And see the decision in *Taylors Industrial Flooring Ltd. v. M & H Plant Hire (Manchester) Ltd.* [1990] BCC 44 (a decision under the Insolvency Act 1986, s.123(1)(e); also *Re Clemence plc* (1992) 59 B.L.R. 56. *Semble*, a joint debtor's petition may not be presented where two or more persons merely hold themselves out as partners: see *Re C. & M. Ashberg, The Times*, July 17, 1990, noticed *supra*, para. 27–07.

[67] Insolvent Partnerships Order 1986, art. 13(1). This procedure is not available in the case of a limited partnership: *ibid.*

[68] *Ibid.* art. 13(2)(b).

[69] *Ibid.* art. 13(2)(a). The form of the petition is set out in *ibid.* Sched. 3, Form 8.

presentation of the joint petition, the court will have a discretion as to the future conduct of the proceedings.[70]

Minor or foreign partners

27–46   This procedure may seemingly be used in the case of a firm comprising a minor[71] or foreign partner.[72]

Jurisdiction

27–47   The court having jurisdiction will be determined in the manner described, *supra*, paragraph 27–34, although it will seemingly not be necessary to establish the court's jurisdiction to wind up the partnership.[73] If an order is made on the petition, it will not involve an order against the firm, even though a dissolution will be inevitable.[74]

Creditor's petition against one or more partners

27–48   Where a partnership debt remains unpaid, the creditor retains the option of presenting a petition against some or all of the partners without seeking to wind up the firm as an unregistered company. In such a case, the court may give directions as to the future conduct of the insolvency proceedings[75] and (*inter alia*) direct their consolidation.[76] Subject thereto, the Insolvent Partnerships Order 1986 will have no application and the petitioner's debt will be treated as the debt of the partner against whom the petition is presented.[77] The procedure in such a case will follow the normal course of insolvency proceedings against an individual or corporate partner and falls outside the scope of this work.[78]

---

[70] *Ibid.* art. 14(1): see *supra*, para. 27–21. Note that the court may apply any provision of the Order "with any necessary modifications".

[71] The provisions of R.S.C., Ord. 80 will apply: Insolvency Rules 1986, r. 7.51. See also *supra*, para. 4–09.

[72] See the Insolvency Act 1986, s.265 (as substituted by the Insolvent Partnerships Order 1986, Sched. 2, Pt. II, para. 2 and applied by *ibid.* art. 13(3)).

[73] Insolvent Partnerships Order 1986, art. 13(3), applying *ibid.*, art. 8(2) and the amendments to the Insolvency Act 1986 set out in Sched. 2, Pt. III "with the necessary modifications".

[74] See the Partnership Act 1890, s.33(1) and *supra*, paras. 24–20, 24–22 *et seq.* Even if there were some agreement purporting to negative the effects of a partner's bankruptcy (see *supra*, para. 10–33), the bankruptcy of *all* the partners must inevitably work a dissolution.

[75] Insolvent Partnerships Order 1986, art. 14(1), *supra*, para. 27–21.

[76] *Ibid.* art. 14(2).

[77] *Ibid.* art. 15(3). As to the methods of enforcing a judgment obtained against a firm, see R.S.C. Ord. 81, r. 5 and *supra*, paras. 14–89 *et seq.*

[78] See the standard works dealing with insolvency, *e.g. Muir Hunter on Personal Insolvency, Palmer's Company Law.*

Petition presented by one partner against another

In an appropriate case, a partner may present a petition against a **27–49** co-partner, provided that he can do so in the capacity of creditor.[79] If his claim is dependent on the taking of a partnership account,[80] he will not be in a position to petition until such time as the account has been concluded and the sum due to him ordered to be paid. In the normal course, an account will not be taken without dissolving the firm, so that the older cases dealing with petitions presented with a view to obtaining a dissolution are now unlikely to be of relevance in this context.[81]

Subsequent insolvency proceedings against a partner

Reference has already been made to the provisions of the Insolvent **27–50** Partnerships Order 1986, Article 14(1).[82] Given the definition of the expression "insolvent member," it is questionable whether that article confers any power on the court to give directions where a petition is presented against a partner in any of the ways described above, unless such petition has been preceded by concurrent petitions against the firm and against that partner. However, it should be noted that Article 14(2) provides as follows:

"(2) Where a bankruptcy petition has been presented against more than one individual in the circumstances mentioned in paragraph (1) above, the court may give such directions for consolidating the proceedings, or any of them, as it thinks just."

It is perhaps arguable that the reference to "the circumstances mentioned in paragraph (1)" does not import a reference to each individual partner's status as an "insolvent member," so that, in such a case, the power is exercisable where concurrent petitions have not

---

[79] See, for example, *Ex p. Notley* (1833) 1 Mont. & Ayr. 46, where the petitioning creditor had lent the bankrupt a sum of money on terms that he would receive interest and a share in the net profits of the bankrupt's business as long as the principal remained unpaid; by reason of this agreement, the petitioning creditor was liable to third parties as if he were a partner of the bankrupt (see, further, *supra*, paras. 5–32 *et seq.*) but was nevertheless able to petition on the basis of the principal sum outstanding together with certain arrears of interest. Similarly, in *Ex p. Richardson* (1833) 3 D. & Ch. 244 a member of a dissolved firm presented a petition against his former partner in respect of sums found due to him on the taking of an account together with other moneys borrowed from him after the dissolution. *Cf. Ex p. Gray* (1835) 2 Mont. & Ayr. 283. See also *Ex p. Nokes* (1801) and *Ex p. Maberley* (1808) 1 Mont. on Part., Note N, p. 62; *Windham v. Paterson* (1815) 2 Rose 466; *Ex p. Page* (1821) 1 Gl. & J. 100; *Hope v. Meek* (1855) 10 Ex. 842.

[80] See *supra*, para. 23–72. And see *Ex p. Notley* and *Ex p. Richardson, supra*; also *Re a Debtor, Debtor v. Brown*, unreported, November 29, 1985 (C.A.T. No. 787), [1986] C.L.Y. 131, where an adjournment of bankruptcy proceedings was refused because the debtor's claim for an account would not be completed within the foreseeable future.

[81] See the cases cited *supra*, para. 27–11, n.47.

[82] See *supra*, paras. 27–21, 27–42.

been presented; *sed quaere*. Consolidation with insolvency proceedings brought against a *corporate* partner would clearly not be
appropriate.

4. APPOINTMENT OF LIQUIDATORS AND TRUSTEES

Appointment of liquidator

Interim appointment

27–51   Where a firm is wound up as an unregistered company, whether or
not on a petition presented concurrently with petitions against two or
more of the partners,[83] the Official Receiver will normally act as
liquidator until such time as another person is appointed in his
place.[84] However, if the petition against the firm was presented by
the liquidator of a corporate partner or the trustee of a bankrupt
partner and there were *no* concurrent petitions, the court can appoint
the petitioner as liquidator, thus relieving the Official Receiver of his
duties.[85]

If a corporate partner is wound up on a separate or concurrent
petition, the Official Receiver will initially act as liquidator in the
normal way. This ensures that, in the latter case, the same person
will act as liquidator both of the firm and of any insolvent corporate
partner.

Subsequent appointment

27–52   When no concurrent petitions have been presented against the
partners, the Official Receiver has the normal discretion to call a
joint meeting of the creditors and contributories with a view to the
appointment of another liquidator in his place.[86] This option is
naturally not available when the liquidator or trustee of a corporate
or bankrupt partner has originally been appointed to act as
liquidator. If, on the other hand, orders on concurrent petitions have
been made against two or more partners,[87] the Official Receiver's
discretion is removed and he must call a meeting of the creditors of
the partnership *and of any insolvent partner* for the purpose of

---

[83] See *supra*, paras. 27–09 *et seq.*, 27–23 *et seq.*
[84] Insolvency Act 1986, s.136(2).
[85] *Ibid.* s.221(9) (as added by the Insolvent Partnerships Order 1986, Sched. 1, para. 2), applying
the provisions of *ibid.* s.140(3).
[86] *Ibid.* s.136(4), (5).
[87] Once an order has been made against the firm, orders on the petitions presented against any
corporate (but not individual) partners *must*, seemingly, be made: see *supra*, paras. 27–38, 27–39.

choosing a person to act as liquidator of the firm and as liquidator/trustee of any such partner.[88]

If a liquidator is not appointed at the relevant meeting, the Official Receiver must consider whether to apply for an appointment by the Secretary of State.[89]

Appointment of trustee

When a bankruptcy order is made against an individual partner, **27–53** the Official Receiver will act as his receiver and manager until such time as a trustee is appointed.[90] If the partner was not bankrupted on a concurrent petition,[91] the trustee will be appointed by a general meeting of the partner's creditors, unless the Official Receiver decides to act as trustee.[92] If there were concurrent petitions, the appointment will be made by the joint meeting of the creditors of the partnership and of any insolvent partner,[93] thereby ensuring that the assets of the firm and of the insolvent partners are administered by the same person.[94] A similar meeting will be held where an order is made on a joint debtor's petition presented by the partners,[95] even though the partnership is itself not ordered to be wound up.[96] This will again ensure that the joint and separate estates will be administered by the same trustee.

If a trustee is not appointed at the relevant meeting, the Official Receiver must consider whether to apply for an appointment by the Secretary of State.[97]

Conflicts of interest

Where a common liquidator/trustee appointed in any of the above **27–54** ways encounters a conflict of interest as between his various functions, he can apply to the court for directions and may be

---

[88] Insolvency Act 1986, s.136(4), (4A) (as substituted by the Insolvent Partnerships Order 1986, Sched. 2, Pt. I, para. 5(a)). *Ibid.* s.136(5), (6) are omitted in this case (see the Insolvent Partnerships Order 1986, Sched. 2, Pt. I, para. 5(b)). See also *ibid.* s.139 (as amended by the Insolvent Partnerships Order 1986, Sched. 2, Pt. I, paras. 7, 8). And see, as to the position *vis-à-vis* a corporate partner, *ibid.* s.136(4) (as substituted by the Insolvent Partnerships Order 1986, Sched. 2, Pt. II, para. 9(a)).
[89] Insolvency Act 1986, s.137(1), (2). In a case where concurrent petitions have been presented, *ibid.* subs. (2) is amended by the Insolvent Partnerships Order 1986, Sched. 2, Pt. I, para. 6(a).
[90] *Ibid.* s.287(1).
[91] See, as to this, *supra*, paras. 27–48, 27–49.
[92] Insolvency Act 1986, s.293.
[93] See *supra*, para. 27–52.
[94] Note that, in this case, the Insolvency Act 1986, s.293 is omitted: see the Insolvent Partnerships Order 1986, Sched. 2, Pt. III, para. 15.
[95] See *supra*, para. 27–45.
[96] This appears to be the effect of the Insolvent Partnerships Order 1986, art. 13(4). See also, *ibid.* art. 13(3), applying *ibid.* art. 8(2) and, thus, the amendments set out in *ibid.* Sched. 2, albeit with "the necessary modifications."
[97] Insolvency Act 1986, s.295. In a case where concurrent petitions have been presented, *ibid.* subss. (1), (4) are amended by the Insolvent Partnerships Order 1986, Sched. 2, Pt. III, para. 16.

replaced as liquidator of the firm or of any corporate partner and/or as trustee of any one or more of the bankrupt partners.[98]

Removal and resignation

27–55 Special provision is made for the removal and resignation of liquidators/trustees appointed pursuant to insolvency orders made on concurrent petitions.[99]

Meetings, etc.

27–56 The detailed provisions of the Insolvency Act 1986, as amended by the Insolvent Partnerships Order 1986, relating to meetings, the appointment of liquidation and creditors' committees and the release of liquidators and trustees is outside the scope of this work.[1]

5. STATUS AND DUTIES OF THE PARTNERS IN THE WINDING-UP OF A FIRM

Firm wound up as an unregistered company

27–57 Where a firm is wound up as an unregistered company, each partner will be treated as having a dual capacity, *i.e.* both as a "contributory"[2] and as an "officer and director." However, it is not only the current partners (in the true sense of that word) who will be so treated. Section 226 of the Insolvency Act 1986 in effect provides as follows:

> "(1) In the event of [*a firm*] being wound up, every person is deemed a contributory who is liable to pay or contribute to the

---

[98] Insolvency Act 1986, s.139(3) (as substituted by the Insolvent Partnerships Order 1986, Sched. 2, Pt. I, para. 8). See also the Insolvent Partnerships Order 1986, art. 13(3). For an example of a case in which a trustee in bankruptcy's duties as such conflicted with his duties as liquidator of an insolvent company, see *Re Corbenstoke (No. 2)* (1989) 5 BCC 767.

[99] Insolvency Act 1986, s.172 (as amended by the Insolvent Partnerships Order 1986, Sched. 2, Pt. I, para. 14 and Pt. II, para. 14), s.298 (as amended by the Insolvent Partnerships Order 1986, Sched. 2, Pt. III, para. 18). See also *ibid.* s.300 (as amended by the Insolvent Partnerships Order 1986, Sched. 2, Pt. III, para. 20). These provisions all apply, with the necessary modifications, where an order is made on a joint debtor's petition: see the Insolvent Partnerships Order 1986, art. 13(3).

[1] See generally, the Insolvent Partnerships Order 1986, Sched. 2, Pt. I, para. 10 (amending the Insolvency Act 1986, s.141), para. 13 (amending *ibid.* s.168), para. 15 (amending *ibid.* s.174), Pt. II, para. 13 (amending *ibid.* s.168), para. 15 (amending *ibid.* s.174), Pt. III, para. 19 (amending *ibid.* s.299), para. 21 (amending *ibid.* s.301).

[2] As applied to partnerships, the Insolvency Act 1986, s.79(1) provides that "the expression 'contributory' means every person liable to contribute to the assets of a [*firm*] in the event of it being wound up". *Quaere* will a partner against whom an insolvency order is made on a concurrent petition be treated as a contributory? It is thought not, since this would be inconsistent with the framework established under the Insolvent Partnerships Order 1986, *e.g.* how could the liquidator of the firm treat himself as a contributory *qua* liquidator/trustee of a corporate or bankrupt partner? *Per contra* where such a partner has previously been made subject to an insolvency order, when the relevant liquidator/trustee would presumably be treated as the contributory: see *infra,* para. 27–60.

payment of any debt or liability of the [*firm*], or to pay or contribute to the payment of any sum for the adjustment of the rights of members amongst themselves, or to pay or contribute to the payment of the expenses of winding up the [*firm*].

(2) Every contributory is liable to contribute to the [*firm's*] assets all sums due from him in respect of any such liability as is mentioned above."

The foregoing words are apt to include not only a person held out as a partner[3] but also an outgoing partner who remains directly liable to creditors of the firm[4] or who has (exceptionally) agreed to bear a share of a particular ongoing liability *vis-à-vis* his former partners.[5]

Equally, the Insolvent Partnerships Order 1986, Article 3 provides: **27–58**

"Where an insolvent partnership is being wound up under Part V of the Act as an unregistered company, any member or former member of the partnership or any other person who has or has had control or management of the partnership business—

(a) shall for the purposes of the provisions of the [*Insolvency Act 1986*] and the Company Directors Disqualification Act 1986 applied by this Order be deemed to be an officer and director of the company. . .".

It is doubtful whether a partner by holding out, who has at no time participated in the control or management of the firm's business,[6] could be treated as a partner for these purposes, even though he is deemed to be a contributory.

Firm not wound up as an unregistered company

Neither of the foregoing provisions will have any application where **27–59** an order is made on a joint debtor's petition or on a petition presented against one or more partners, even though the former will inevitably result in the firm being wound up.[7]

---

[3] See the Partnership Act 1890, s.14, considered *supra*, paras. 5–43 *et seq*. Where, on the other hand, persons merely hold themselves out as partners but no partnership in law exists, there is no firm to be wound up: see *Re C. & M. Ashberg, The Times*, July 17, 1990.

[4] See, in particular, the Partnership Act 1890, ss.9, 17(2), 36, *supra*, paras. 13–03 *et seq*., 13–42 *et seq*. and 13–74 *et seq*.

[5] For example, a partner might, as a condition of being permitted to retire on a date earlier than that permitted by the agreement, undertake a continuing obligation to contribute towards the firm's liability in respect of a particularly onerous asset, *e.g.* a lease of premises or equipment, even though he is not directly liable as a signatory thereto.

[6] It is frequently a feature of the terms on which so called "salaried partners" are engaged that they are not entitled to attend partners' meetings and so have no control whatsoever over the direction of the firm.

[7] See *supra*, paras. 27–44 *et seq*.

Partners as contributories

27–60   The liability of a solvent partner, as a contributory, to meet calls made by the liquidator of an insolvent firm represents a specialty debt accruing at the time that such liability commenced,[8] so that the limitation period is extended to 12 years.[9] If a partner dies or becomes bankrupt before or after his name has been placed on the list of contributories, his personal representatives or trustee[10] will be liable as contributories.[11] This will seemingly cover the case where a partner's death or bankruptcy precedes the order against the firm.

27–61   The measure of a partner's liability *qua* contributory will reflect his unlimited liability under the general law[12] and any adjustments necessary to ensure that an appropriate contribution is made by each partner.[13] A former partner's liability will be limited only to those debts, etc., incurred whilst he remained (or was held out) as a partner,[14] subject to account being taken of any right which he may have to an indemnity from the continuing partners.[15] On that footing, the current editor tentatively submits that the provisions of the Insolvency Act 1986 which establish the liability of the members of a company[16] are inapplicable to partners. If that were not the position, the liability attaching to a former partner (otherwise than pursuant to some express contractual arrangement with the continuing partners[17]) would be subject to three express qualifications, namely:

(1)   his liability would cease altogether one year after the date on which he ceased to be a partner;[18]

(2)   he would not be liable to contribute towards debts or liabilities incurred after he ceased to be a partner;[19]

(3)   he would not be liable to contribute unless the court were satisfied that the current partners could not contribute sufficient to satisfy the firm's debts and liabilities.[20]

---

[8] Insolvency Act 1986, s.80.

[9] Limitation Act 1980, s.8(1).

[10] It is assumed that this will include the liquidator of an insolvent corporate partner.

[11] Insolvency Act 1986, ss.81, 82, as applied by *ibid.* s.226(4).

[12] See *supra*, paras. 13–14, 13–15. But see *Investment and Advisory Service Ltd. v. Gray* [1990] BCLC 38, 42, *per* Morritt J.

[13] This is conceived to be the effect of the Insolvency Act 1986, s.226(1), (2), which states the primary liability of each partner under subs.(2) in terms of the qualifying liability identified under subs.(1).

[14] See *supra*, paras. 13–39 *et seq.*

[15] See *supra*, para. 10–207.

[16] Insolvency Act 1986, s.74.

[17] See *supra*, para. 27–57, n.5.

[18] Insolvency Act 1986, s.74(2)(a).

[19] *Ibid.* s.74(2)(b). This release would appear to be unaffected by any subsequent holding out; *sed quaere.*

[20] *Ibid.* s.74(2)(c).

Although the second and third qualifications would do no more **27–62** than endorse the normal limitations on an outgoing partner's liability, to which reference has been made above, the first would effect an arbitrary release from liability which would not only be alien to the very concept of partnership but which would also confer on such a partner more protection than would be available to a former member of a *solvent* firm.

The current editor does not consider that a partner's (or former partner's) liability *qua* contributory would be increased by seeking to treat him as a "director ... whose liability is under the Companies Act unlimited"[21] even if such an approach were permissible.[22]

Calls on contributories

The liquidator is responsible, under powers delegated to him by the **27–63** court,[23] for drawing up a list of the firm's contributories[24] and for making calls upon them in order to settle the firm's debts and liabilities.[25] He is also required to adjust the rights of the contributories *inter se* and may accordingly be obliged to return to a partner any sum which that partner has paid in excess of his due share, if the amount of that excess is in fact contributed by the other partners.[26] Enforcement of the payment required by a call is by order of the court[27] and will seemingly require leave.[28]

Partners as officers and directors

It has already been seen[29] that each partner is deemed to be an **27–64** officer and director of a firm which is being wound up as an unregistered company[30] for the purposes of certain provisions of the

---

[21] See *ibid.* s.75.

[22] It has already been seen (see *supra*, para. 27–58) that the Insolvent Partnerships Order 1986, art. 3(a) deems any partner or former partner to be an "officer and director", but it is submitted that this is not sufficient to bring him within the scope of the Companies Act 1985, s.306. *Semble* it would not in any event be possible to increase the liability of a former partner by treating him as a *present* director, unless he had continued to participate in the management of the firm, *e.g.* in the capacity of a consultant: there would be no legitimate warrant for limiting the application of *ibid.* s.75(2) in this way. But note, in this context, the distinction between *ibid.* s.74(2)(c) and s.75(2)(c).

[23] *Ibid.* s.160(b), (d); Insolvency Rules 1986, rr. 4.195, 4.202.

[24] Insolvency Act 1986, s.148; Insolvency Rules 1986, rr. 4.196 *et seq*. See in particular the Insolvency Rules 1986, r. 4.198, as to the procedure for notifying the contributories of their appearance in the list and for dealing with objections received in response thereto.

[25] Insolvency Act 1986, s.150; Insolvency Rules 1986, rr. 4.202 *et seq*. Note that a call may only be made with the consent of the liquidation committee or the court: Insolvency Rules 1986, rr. 4.203, 4.204.

[26] Insolvency Act 1986, s.154; Insolvency Rules 1986, rr. 4.221, 4.222.

[27] Insolvency Rules 1986, r. 4.205(2). It would seem that leave would also technically be required under the Insolvency Act 1986, s.228, since any attempt at enforcement would involve a "proceeding ... in respect of any debt of the [*firm*]"; see also *Williams v. Harding* (1866) L.R. 1 H.L. 9, as to the need for leave prior to commencing insolvency proceedings.

[28] *Ibid.* s.228: see *supra*, para. 27–20.

[29] See *supra*, paras. 27–57, 27–58.

[30] Insolvent Partnerships Order 1986, arts. 6, 7 and 8(1).

Insolvency Act 1986 and the Company Directors Disqualification Act 1986. Although the liability of a partner would prima facie not be increased if the liquidator were able to demonstrate to the court that he was guilty of fraudulent or wrongful trading,[31] it would enable the court to make a disqualification order against him,[32] thus seemingly preventing him from becoming a member of any other partnership during the period of the disqualification otherwise than with the leave of the court.[33] A similar order will be made if the court, on the application of the Secretary of State or (at his direction) the Official Receiver, is satisfied that a partner's conduct in that capacity makes him unfit to be concerned in the management of a company or firm.[34]

Although the position of a former partner is less clear,[35] it is submitted that a disqualification order can in appropriate circumstances be made against him.

Delivery up of partnership property

27-65   Where a winding-up order is made against a firm, whether or not there are concurrent petitions against two or more of the partners,[36] the authority of all the partners (solvent and insolvent) to bind the

---

[31] In essence, fraudulent trading involves a business being carried on with intent to defraud creditors or for a fraudulent purpose (Insolvency Act 1986, s.213), whilst wrongful trading connotes a business being carried on in the knowledge (actual or constructive) that an insolvent liquidation is unavoidable (*ibid.* s.214). See generally, as to the application of these sections in the case of an insolvent company, *Re A Company (No. 001418 of 1988)* [1990] BCC 526 (a decision under the forerunner of the Insolvency Act 1986, s.213, *i.e.* the Companies Act 1985, s.630); *Re Produce Marketing Consortium (No. 2)* [1989] BCLC 520 (a decision under the Insolvency Act 1986, s.214). *Quaere* could a finding of either sort against some (but not all) of the partners alter their respective liabilities *qua* contributories, notwithstanding their primary obligations under the partnership agreement and/or the Partnership Act 1890? It is thought not.

[32] Company Directors Disqualification Act 1986, s.10, as applied by the Insolvent Partnerships Order 1986, art. 6; also the Insolvent Companies (Disqualification of Unfit Directors) Proceedings Rules 1987 (S.I. 1987 No. 2030).

[33] Company Directors Disqualification Act 1986, s.1. The maximum period of disqualification is 15 years: *ibid.* s.10(2). If a person subject to such an order enters into partnership in contravention thereof, he will be "personally responsible for all the relevant debts of the [*firm*]": *ibid.* s.15(1). That liability is joint and several: *ibid.* s.15(3). Apart from the imposition of several liability (*cf.* the Partnership Act 1890, s.9, *supra*, paras. 13–03 *et seq.*), this would in practical terms seem to add little to the normal liability of a partner and represents only a minimal deterrent. However, there are criminal penalties: see the Company Directors Disqualification Act 1986, s.13.

[34] Company Directors Disqualification Act 1986, s.6, as applied by the Insolvent Partnerships Order 1986, art. 6. As to what amounts to unfitness for these purposes, see *ibid.* s.9, Sched. 1. In this case the minimum period of disqualification is two years and the maximum 15 years: *ibid.* s.6(4). See also the Insolvent Companies (Disqualification of Unfit Directors) Proceedings Rules 1987 (S.I. 1987 No. 2030). And see generally, as to the court's approach to such orders, *Re Lo-Line Electric Motors Ltd.* [1988] Ch. 477 (a decision under the Companies Act 1985, s.300(1)); *Re Cedac Ltd.* [1991] Ch. 402; *Re Sevenoaks (Stationers) Retail Ltd.* [1991] Ch. 164; *Re Polly Peck International plc (No. 2)* [1993] BCC 890 and other cases of that class.

[35] Whilst the Insolvent Partnerships Order 1986, art. 3(a) (see *supra*, para. 27–58) clearly applies to "any member *or former member*" (emphasis supplied), *ibid.* art. 6, which applies the relevant provisions of the Company Directors Disqualification Act 1986, refers only to "any member of the partnership," thus appearing to exclude former members. It is thought that a court would construe the word "member" in art. 6 as any member mentioned in art. 3(a), although the point is arguable.

[36] See *supra*, paras. 27–09 *et seq.*, 27–23 *et seq.*

firm or to dispose of its assets[37] is automatically terminated and each partner is obliged to deliver up to the liquidator any partnership property[38] in his hands.[39] A similar obligation is imposed on former partners. If such property is in the hands of a third party, *e.g.* a partner's spouse, the liquidator can apply to the court for an order for such delivery up.[40]

Where bankruptcy orders are made on a joint debtor's petition,[41] the partners will be subject to the same obligation as regards the trustee.[42]

Statement of affairs

Once a winding-up order has been made against a firm or a **27–66** provisional liquidator appointed,[43] the Official Receiver may require any of the partners or former partners to submit a statement of the firm's affairs, including particulars of its assets, debts and liabilities.[44] Where a winding-up order has been made against a corporate partner on a concurrent petition,[45] the statement in relation to that partner must show its interest in the partnership assets[46] and specify the debts and liabilities attributable to the joint and separate estates respectively.[47] A similar provision governs the statement in respect of an individual partner bankrupted on a concurrent petition[48] or on a joint debtor's petition.[49]

It is important to identify each partner's share in the partnership property, since it is only this share which vests in that partner's liquidator or trustee and which is primarily available to meet his separate debts.[50]

---

[37] In such a case, the Partnership Act 1890, s.38 clearly has no application: see *supra*, paras. 13–64 *et seq*.

[38] This expression is defined by reference to the Partnership Act 1890: see *ibid.* s.20, *supra*, paras. 18–03 *et seq*.

[39] Insolvent Partnerships Order 1986, art. 3(b). A similar obligation applies to any person "who has or has had control or management of the partnership business". In the case of an individual partner, there are no exceptions to the obligation to deliver up: Insolvency Act 1986, s.283(2) (as amended by the Insolvent Partnerships Order 1986, Sched. 2, Pt. III, para. 10).

[40] Insolvency Act 1986, s.237.

[41] See *supra*, para. 27–45.

[42] Insolvent Partnerships Order 1986, art. 13(3), applying *ibid.* art. 3(a) and the amendments to the Insolvency Act 1986 set out in *ibid.* Sched. 2 "with the necessary modifications".

[43] See *supra*, para. 27–18.

[44] Insolvency Act 1986, s.131(1), (2)(a).

[45] See *supra*, para. 27–39.

[46] See generally, as to the nature of a partner's interest in such assets, *supra*, paras. 19–02 *et seq*.

[47] Insolvency Act 1986, s.131(2)(a) (as amended by the Insolvent Partnerships Order 1986, Sched. 2, Pt. II, para. 7).

[48] *Ibid.* s.288(2)(a) (as amended by the Insolvent Partnerships Order 1986, Sched. 2, Pt. III, para. 12(b)).

[49] Insolvent Partnerships Order 1986, art. 13(3), applying *ibid.* art. 8(2) and, thus, Sched. 2, Pt. III, para. 12(a). See, as to such petitions, *supra*, para. 27–45.

[50] Each of the above cases presupposes the insolvency of the firm, so that the existence of a lien in favour of a solvent partner (see the Partnership Act 1890, s.39, *supra*, paras. 19–29 *et seq*.) will be academic. *Cf.* the position where the firm is *not* wound up, *infra*, para. 27–71.

6. SHARE OF AN INSOLVENT PARTNER WHEN FIRM NOT WOUND UP

Dissolution of firm and conduct of winding up

27–67   It has already been seen[51] that, in the absence of some other agreement, the bankruptcy of an individual partner or the winding-up and ultimate dissolution of a corporate partner will dissolve the firm. Thereafter the authority of the solvent partners to wind up the firm's affairs and to dispose of its assets will derive from the agreement or, more usually, from the Partnership Act 1890.[52] The insolvent partner will have no such authority, although his former partners may be liable for his acts on the basis of holding out.[53]

27–68   Since the insolvent partner's trustee or liquidator has no right to step into the shoes of the insolvent partner and to become a partner in his place, he will not be entitled to interfere in the winding-up of the partnership affairs,[54] unless the solvent partners are guilty of misconduct or they are all either dead or abroad.[55] Moreover, although the trustee or liquidator cannot compel the solvent partners to deliver up possession of the partnership books,[56] they can be summoned before the court for examination and ordered to produce the books for that purpose.[57]

Solvent partner acting as receiver

27–69   It follows from the foregoing that, if there is a dispute between the trustee or liquidator and the solvent partners as to the winding-up of the partnership affairs and there is no reason to impugn the conduct of the latter, the court may appoint one of them receiver of the partnership property.[58]

---

[51] Partnership Act 1890, s.33(1), *supra*, paras. 10–33, 11–11 and 24–25 *et seq.*

[52] *Ibid.* s.38, *supra*, paras. 13–64 *et seq.* And see, in particular, the following cases decided before the Act: *Fox v. Hanbury* (1776) Cowp. 445; *Harvey v. Crickett* (1816) 5 M. & S. 336; *Morgan v. Marquis* (1853) 9 Ex. 145; *Ex p Robinson* (1833) 3 D. & Ch. 376. Note the decision in *Ex p McGae* (1816) 19 Ves.Jr. 607, regarding the position where bills are accepted and notes issued in the name of a firm after the bankruptcy of one or more partners.

[53] Partnership Act 1890, s.38, proviso; *Thomason v. Frere* (1809) 10 East 418; *Lacy v. Woolcott* (1823) 2 D. & R. 458; *Craven v. Edmondson* (1830) 6 Bing. 734. See also *ibid.* s.14, *supra*, paras. 5–43 *et seq.*

[54] See *Francis v. Spittle* (1840) 9 L.J.Ch. 230.

[55] See, as to the latter eventualities, *Hankey v. Garratt* (1792) 1 Ves.Jr. 236; *Everett v. Backhouse* (1804) 10 Ves.Jr. 94; *Barker v. Goodair* (1805) 11 Ves.Jr. 78; *Dutton v. Morrison* (1810) 17 Ves.Jr. 193.

[56] *Ex p. Finch* (1832) 1 D. & Ch. 274. See also *Ex p. Good* (1882) 21 Ch.D. 868; *Re Burnand* [1904] 2 K.B. 68. And note the exceptional decision in *Davidson v. Napier* (1827) 1 Sim. 297.

[57] Insolvency Act 1986, ss.236, 366; Insolvency Rules 1986, rr. 9.1 *et seq.* See generally, *Cloverbay Ltd. v. Bank of Credit and Commerce International S.A.* [1991] Ch. 90. And see, under the old bankruptcy laws, *Ex p. Trueman* (1832) 1 D. & C. 464; also *Re Burnand, supra.*

[58] See *Ex p. Stoveld* (1823) 1 Gl. & J. 303; *Freeland v. Stansfield* (1854) 2 Sm. & G. 479; *Collins v. Barker* [1893] 1 Ch. 578.

Dealings with partnership land

If land is vested in the partners on trust for sale as a partnership **27–70** asset,[59] it is not entirely clear whether, on the insolvency of a partner, the trustee or liquidator takes his place as a joint tenant of the legal estate with the solvent partners, although the better view would seem to be that he does not.[60] Even if he did, the solvent partners could prima facie compel the trustee or liquidator to give effect to directions given pursuant to the authority conferred on them by the Partnership Act 1890.[61]

Rights in relation to insolvent partner's share

All that vests in the liquidator or trustee is the insolvent partner's **27–71** share in the partnership, subject to the liens and other rights of the solvent partners.[62] Accordingly, he can claim nothing until all the partnership debts have been paid and the accounts as between the partners duly settled.[63] However, unless the agreement so provides,[64] the solvent partners cannot insist on buying out the insolvent partner's share at a valuation;[65] that share can only be ascertained and paid out following a sale of the partnership assets and the application of the proceeds in the manner specified in section 44 of the Partnership Act 1890.[66] In settling the accounts between the solvent partners and the trustee or liquidator, the latter will, on

---

[59] Of course, the legal estate can only be vested in up to four partners: Law of Property Act 1925, s.34(2); Trustee Act 1925, s.34(2).

[60] It appears to have been conceded that the bankrupt remained a trustee in *Re Holliday* [1981] Ch. 405, 411. See also *Re Turner* [1974] 1 W.L.R. 1556.

[61] Partnership Act 1890, s.38, *supra*, paras. 13–64 *et seq.* Alternatively, an application could be made to the court under the Law of Property Act 1925, s.30; and see also *ibid.* s.26(3) (as substituted by the Law of Property (Amendment) Act 1926) and *Re Mayo* [1943] Ch. 302. Where the land is *not* a partnership asset, any application must necessarily be made under the Law of Property Act 1925. In such a case, the court might, in the exercise of its discretion, decline to compel the other partners to sell where the partnership continues as between them: see for example, *Re Turner* [1974] 1 W.L.R. 1556 (husband and wife); also *Re McCarthy* [1975] 1 W.L.R. 807, 809; *Re Densham* [1975] 1 W.L.R. 1519, 1531, *per* Goff J.; *Re A Debtor (No. 24 of 1971)* [1976] 1 W.L.R. 952; *Re Bailey (No. 25 of 1975)* [1977] 1 W.L.R. 278; *Re Holliday* [1981] Ch. 405; *Re Lowrie* [1981] 3 All E.R. 353; *Re Citro* [1991] Ch. 142.

[62] See the Partnership Act 1890, s.39, *supra*, paras. 19–29 *et seq.* See also *Anon.* (1700) 3 Salk. 61 and 12 Mod. 446; *West v. Skip* (1749) 1 Ves.Sen. 239; *Fox v. Hanbury* (1776) Cowp. 445; *Bolton v. Puller* (1796) 1 Bos. & Pul. 539; 1 Mont. Part., note P., p. 66; *Re Ward* [1985] N.Z.L.R. 352. And see also, generally, as to the nature of a partnership share, *supra*, paras. 19–01 *et seq.*

[63] *Richardson v. Gooding* (1693) 2 Vern. 293; *Gross v. Dufresnay* (1735) 2 Eq.Ca.Abr. 110, pl. 5; *West v. Skip* (1749) 1 Ves.Sen. 239 and (1750) 1 Ves.Sen. 456; *Taylor v. Fields* (1799) 4 Ves.Jr. 396; *Ex p. Terrell* (1819) Buck 345; *Holderness v. Shackels* (1828) 8 B. & C. 612; also *Re Ward*, *supra*, and see *supra*, para. 23–72.

[64] It is considered that such an agreement would be effective: see *Borland's Trustee v. Steel Bros. & Co. Ltd.* [1901] 1 Ch. 279 (a decision concerning a company); also *Collins v. Barker* [1893] 1 Ch. 578. Note, however, the decisions in *Wilson v. Greenwood* (1818) 1 Swan. 471 (where the circumstances were exceptional) and *Whitmore v. Mason* (1861) 2 J. & H. 204 (where no attempt was made to avoid the main valuation provision). And see *supra*, paras. 10–124, 10–125.

[65] But see *supra*, paras. 19–12, 23–182.

[66] See generally, *supra*, paras. 19–09, 25–39 *et seq.* And see also *Crawshay v. Collins* (1808) 15 Ves.Jr. 218, 229, *per* Lord Eldon; *Wilson v. Greenwood* (1818) 1 Swan. 471.

normal principles, be entitled to share in any capital profits
attributable to the partnership assets since the date of dissolution,[67]
together with interest or the share of *income* profits attributable to
the continued use of the insolvent partner's share.[68]

Expulsion prior to insolvency order

27–72   If the partnership agreement entitles the other partners to expel an
insolvent partner *before* a formal bankruptcy or winding-up order can
be made and thereupon to acquire his share, and that right is duly
exercised but the share has not been paid out at the date of the
order, what will vest in the trustee or liquidator is merely the right to
the relevant payment.[69] If the provision is framed as an automatic
accruer, thus representing a limitation inherent in the share itself,[70] it
is doubtful whether its operation could be avoided under section
127[71] or 284[72] of the Insolvency Act 1986; *per contra* in the case of
an option in favour of the continuing partners which is exercised after
the presentation of the petition.[73]

Charging order on share

27–73   It has already been seen that a charging order obtained by a
judgment creditor pursuant to section 23 of the Partnership Act 1890
prior to a partner's insolvency is not a completed execution for the
purposes of section 183 or 346 of the Insolvency Act 1986, and will
therefore not be enforceable against that partner's share in the
trustee's or liquidator's hands.[74]

7.   SET-OFF AND MUTUAL CREDIT

27–74 The equitable doctrine of set-off and mutual credit, which was
applied even before it was expressly recognised by the bankruptcy
legislation,[75] has been preserved under the Insolvency Act 1986 and

---

[67] *Barclays Bank Trust Co. Ltd. v. Bluff* [1982] Ch. 172, noticed *supra*, para. 25–27.
[68] Partnership Act 1890, s.42, *supra*, paras. 25–23 *et seq.*
[69] *Quaere*, can such an agreement be attacked as a fraud on the insolvency laws? See *supra*, paras. 10–124, 10–125.
[70] See further, *supra*, para. 10–122 and *infra*, paras. 35–19, 36–50.
[71] This section avoids any disposition of a corporate partner's property after the presentation of the winding up petition (see *ibid.* s.129(2)), unless the court orders otherwise: see also *supra*, para. 27–16. Note also the court's jurisdiction under *ibid.* s.423 (transactions defrauding creditors).
[72] This section similarly avoids any disposition of a bankrupt partner's property after the presentation of the petition (see subs.(3)), except to the extent that it is approved or ratified by the court. Again, the court's jurisdiction under *ibid.* s.423 should be noted.
[73] See *supra*, paras. 10–122 *et seq.*
[74] See *supra*, para. 19–50.
[75] See *Anon.* (1676) 1 Mod. 215; *Chapman v. Derby* (1689) 2 Vern. 117.

the rules made thereunder. Accordingly, set-off will be applied not only on the bankruptcy of an individual partner[76] or the winding-up of a corporate partner,[77] but also where a firm is wound up as an unregistered company, with or without concurrent petitions against two or more partners.[78]

Although a general consideration of the circumstances in which **27-75** cross demands may be set off against each other is strictly outside the scope of this work,[79] the following summary of the rule (taken from a formulation appearing in earlier editions) may be useful:

1. Both demands must be money demands[80] and the sum sought to be set off against the trustee or liquidator must be provable in the bankruptcy or liquidation;[81]
2. The demands must be mutual;[82]
3. The demands must have arisen before the creditor had notice of the presentation of the petition.[83]

Where those conditions are satisfied, set-off is mandatory.[84]

---

[76] Insolvency Act 1986, s.323. But note the apparent effect of the Insolvent Partnerships Order 1986, art. 15(3) in such a case: see *infra*, para. 27–79.

[77] Insolvency Rules 1986, r. 4.90. Somewhat surprisingly, the Insolvency Act 1986 itself contains no provision relating to set-off in the case of a liquidation.

[78] *Ibid.* See generally, as to the circumstances in which a firm may be so wound up, *supra*, paras. 27–07 *et seq.*

[79] See the notes to the Insolvency Act 1986, s.323 in *Muir Hunter on Personal Insolvency*; also (as to the old law) the 15th ed. of this work, at pp. 815 *et seq.*

[80] See *Rose v. Hart* (1818) 8 Taunt. 499; also *Palmer v. Day & Sons* [1895] 2 Q.B. 618; *Ellis & Co.'s Trustee v. Dixon Johnson* [1925] A.C. 489. And see *Ex p. Bolland* (1878) 8 Ch.D. 225; *Eberle's Hotels Co. v. Jonas* (1887) 18 Q.B.D. 459; *Great Eastern Ry. Co. v. Lord's Trustee* [1908] A.C. 109; *Re H.E. Thorne & Sons Ltd.* [1914] 2 Ch. 438. As to the position where part of a demand constitutes a preferential debt, see *Re Unit 2 Windows Ltd.* [1985] 1 W.L.R. 1383.

[81] Insolvency Act 1986, s.323(1), (4); Insolvency Rules 1986, r. 4.90(1), (4). As to the extent to which contingent claims may be set-off, see *Carreras Rothmans Ltd. v. Freeman Mathews Treasure Ltd.* [1985] Ch. 207; *Re Charge Card Services Ltd.* [1987] Ch. 150 (affirmed at [1989] Ch. 497).

[82] See *National Westminster Bank Ltd. v. Halesowen Presswork & Assemblies Ltd.* [1972] A.C. 785, H.L., affirming the judgment of Buckley L.J. on the set-off point, reported at [1971] 1 Q.B. 1. See also *Forster v. Wilson* (1843) 12 M. & W. 191; *British Guiana Bank v. Official Receiver* (1911) 104 L.T. 754; *Rolls Razor v. Cox* [1967] 1 Q.B. 552; *Carreras Rothmans Ltd. v. Freeman Mathews Treasure Ltd.* [1985] Ch. 207; *Re Charge Card Services Ltd.* [1987] Ch. 150 (affirmed at [1989] Ch. 497); *M.S. Fashions Ltd. v. Bank of Credit and Commerce International S.A.* [1993] Ch. 425. Note that a debt accruing after the bankruptcy or winding up order cannot be set off: see *Kitchen's Trustee v. Madders* [1949] Ch. 588; *Re A Debtor* [1956] 1 W.L.R. 1226. Cf. *Re A Debtor (No. 4 of 1951)* [1952] Ch. 192; *Re Eros Films* [1963] Ch. 565. Nor can there be a set off in the case of a secured debt which is not sought to be proved: *Re Norman Holding Co. Ltd.* [1991] 1 W.L.R. 10; cf. *M.S. Fashions Ltd. v. Bank of Credit and Commerce International S.A., supra*, at p.446B. And see also *Business Computers Ltd. v. Anglo-African Leasing Ltd.* [1977] 1 W.L.R. 578.

[83] Insolvency Act 1986, s.323(3); Insolvency Rules 1986, r. 4.90(3).

[84] *National Westminster Bank Ltd. v. Halesowen Presswork & Assemblies Ltd.* [1972] A.C. 785, H.L.; *British Eagle International Air Lines Ltd. v. Compagnie Nationale Air France* [1975] 1 W.L.R. 758, H.L.; *Willment Brothers v. North West Thames Regional Health Authority* (1984) 26 Build.L.R. 51; *Re Unit 2 Windows Ltd.* [1985] 1 W.L.R. 1383; *M.S. Fashions Ltd. v. Bank of Credit and Commerce International S.A.* [1993] Ch. 425; *Stein v. Blake* [1994] Ch. 16. See also *infra*, para. 27–81.

Joint debts cannot be set off against separate debts

27–76 It follows from the requirement for mutuality that a demand against a firm cannot in general be set off against a cross-demand by one or more of the partners or vice versa.[85] Thus, in *Watts v. Christie*,[86] bankers were indebted to A on his separate account but creditors of A & Co. on their joint account. Whilst the bankers were in financial difficulties (but before they had committed an act of bankruptcy, as the law then stood), A assigned to A & Co. the sum due to him on his separate account and directed the bankers to transfer that sum to the credit of A & Co., but this was not done. On the bankruptcy of the bankers, it was held that A & Co. could not set off what was due from them to the bankers against what was due from the bankers to A.

27–77 The position will be no different where a debt due to a firm is sought to be set off against a debt incurred by a partner who has acquired the firm's business on or following a dissolution.[87] Even if only one partner is insolvent and his separate estate is more than sufficient to pay his separate debts, a debt due to the firm cannot be set off against a debt due from him alone.[88]

27–78 The same principle will prevent a joint debt being split with a view to permitting a set-off. Thus, if A, B and C are jointly indebted to D, and D is separately indebted to them on several different accounts, the latter debts cannot be met by setting them off against A's, B's and C's respective proportions of the debt owing by them jointly to D.[89]

Insolvency of one or more partners

27–79 The Insolvent Partnerships Order 1986 expressly preserves the right of a creditor to petition for an insolvency order against an individual or corporate partner on the basis of a partnership debt without at the same time petitioning for the winding-up of the firm.[90] The Order provides that "in such a case the debt or debts [*of the insolvent partnership*] shall be treated as the debt or debts of the member in

---

[85] See *Re Pennington and Owen Ltd.* [1925] Ch. 825. The decision in *James v. Kynnier* (1799) 5 Ves.Jr. 108 is not inconsistent with this principle, being a case of payment rather than set-off. As to the position between solvent partners, see *supra*, paras. 14–78 *et seq.*
[86] (1849) 11 Beav. 546.
[87] *Ex p. Ross* (1817) Buck 125. The marginal note in this case is somewhat misleading.
[88] *Ex p. Twogood* (1805) 11 Ves.Jr. 517; and see *Re Jane* (1914) 110 L.T. 556, *supra*, para. 5–24, n.69. *Cf. Ex p. Edwards* (1745) 1 Atk. 100 and *Ex p. Quintin* (1798) 3 Ves.Jr. 248, which Lord Lindley regarded as unreliable authorities.
[89] *Ex p. Christie* (1804) 10 Ves.Jr. 105.
[90] *Ibid.* art. 15(3).

question."[91] The current editor considers that, whilst the effect of this provision might be to deem a joint debt to be a separate debt,[92] set-off in the type of case considered in the previous paragraph will still be impossible by reason of a failure to satisfy the mutuality requirement.

Set-off as between firm and partner

If, following a winding-up order being made against the firm,[93] the **27–80** court were prepared to treat the firm as an unlimited company for the purposes of section 149(2)(a) of the Insolvency Act 1986, a partner might be permitted to set off against sums due from him to the firm (otherwise than pursuant to a call by the liquidator) any sum due to him in respect of an "independent dealing or contract" with the firm;[94] *sed quaere.*

Agreements as to set-off

A bona fide agreement permitting a joint debt to be set off against **27–81** a separate debt, or vice versa, will be perfectly valid and binding as between the parties but of no effect on their insolvency.[95]

8. ADMINISTRATION OF THE ESTATES OF INSOLVENT FIRMS AND PARTNERS

The general principle: distinction between joint and separate debts and estates

Notwithstanding the introduction of a wholly new regime of **27–82** insolvency, the old rule governing the priority of debts as between the respective estates of an insolvent firm and an insolvent partner remains unchanged.[96] Indeed, the following statement of principle retains as much relevance today as when it was originally formulated by Lord Lindley:

> "In administering the estate of a bankrupt firm or of some or one only of its members, it is necessary to distinguish accurately, first,

---

[91] *Ibid.*

[92] *Quaere*, do the words "in such a case" refer only to the procedure for presenting the petition or do they have some wider meaning?

[93] See *supra*, paras. 27–07 *et seq.*

[94] Note that, even if a set-off were entertained, it would clearly not extend to sums due to a partner in that capacity, *e.g.* in respect of profits.

[95] *National Westminster Bank Ltd. v. Halesowen Presswork & Assemblies Ltd.* [1972] A.C. 785, H.L. and the other cases cited *supra*, para. 27–75, n.84. The position was formerly otherwise: see *Kinnerley v. Hossack* (1809) 2 Taunt. 170; *Vulliamy v. Noble* (1817) 3 Mer. 593; *Ex p. Flint* (1818) 1 Swan. 30; *Young v. Bank of Bengal* (1836) 1 Deac. 622.

[96] This approach seems likely to change under the forthcoming revised Insolvent Partnerships Order.

joint from separate estate; and, secondly, joint from separate debts: for the leading principle of administration is, if possible, to pay the debts of the firm (joint debts) out of the assets of the firm (joint estate), and the private debts of each partner (separate debts) out of his own private property (separate estate): in other words, to make each estate pay its own creditors."[97]

27–83   A clear and authoritative judicial recognition of this long established rule is to be found in *Ex p. Cook*,[98] where Lord King observed:

"It is settled, and is a resolution of convenience, that the joint creditors shall be first paid out of the partnership or joint estate, and the separate creditors out of the separate estate of each partner; and if there be a surplus of the joint estate, besides what will pay the joint creditors, the same shall be applied to pay the separate creditors; and if there be, on the other hand, a surplus of the separate estate beyond what will satisfy the separate creditors, it shall go to supply any deficiency that may remain as to the joint creditors."

The rule appeared in successive Bankruptcy Acts[99] and is now expressly preserved by articles 9 and 10 of the Insolvent Partnerships Order 1986.[1]

Insolvent Partnerships Order 1986

27–84   Article 9 of the Insolvent Partnerships Order 1986 establishes the priority of the expenses of insolvency proceedings and is in the following terms:

"*Priority of expenses of insolvency proceedings where insolvency orders are made in relation to an insolvent partnership.*
   9.—(1) The provisions of paragraphs (2) to (5) below shall apply as regards priority of expenses of insolvency proceedings, where insolvency orders are made in relation to an insolvent partnership, incurred up to and including the date of the appointment of a person to act as liquidator of the partnership and to act as the

---

[97] *Ex p. Elton* (1796) 3 Ves.Jr. 238, and see 1 Mont.Part. 110, Note 2D.
[98] (1728) 2 P.W. 500, applied in *Re Rudd & Son Ltd.* [1984] Ch. 237. See also *Ex p. Crowder* (1715) 2 Vern. 706; *Twiss v. Massey* (1737) 1 Atk. 67.
[99] See for example, the Bankruptcy Act 1883, s.40(3), 59; the Bankruptcy Act 1914, ss.33(6), 63. Note, however, that its existence, as a rule of convenience, was independent of those Acts: *Re Rudd & Son Ltd.* [1984] Ch. 237, 241, 242, *per* Nourse J.
[1] And see *Investments and Pensions Advisory Service Ltd. v. Gray* [1990] BCLC 38, 41, *per* Morritt J.

responsible insolvency practitioner in relation to any insolvent member against whom an insolvency order has been made.

(2) The joint estate of an insolvent partnership shall be applicable in the first instance in payment of the joint expenses of the insolvency proceedings in winding-up the partnership, and the separate estate of each insolvent member shall be applicable in the first instance in payment of the separate expenses of the insolvency proceedings relating to that member.

(3) Where the joint estate of the partnership is insufficient for the payment in full of the joint expenses of the insolvency proceedings in winding-up the partnership incurred up to and including the date mentioned in paragraph (1) above, the unpaid balance shall be apportioned equally between the separate estates of the insolvent members and form part of the expenses to be paid out of those estates.

(4) Where any separate estate of an insolvent member is insufficient for the payment in full of the expenses of the insolvency proceedings so incurred to be paid out of that estate, the unpaid balance shall form part of the expenses to be paid out of the joint estate of the partnership.

(5) Where after the transfer of any unpaid balance in accordance with the preceding paragraphs of this Article any estate is insufficient for the payment in full of the expenses to be paid out of that estate, the balance then remaining unpaid shall be apportioned equally between the other estates, and if after such an apportionment one or more estates are insufficient for the payment in full of the expenses to be paid out of those estates, the total of the unpaid balances of the expenses to be paid out of those estates shall continue to be apportioned equally between the other estates until provision is made for the payment in full of the expenses or there is no estate available for the payment of the balance finally remaining unpaid, in which case it abates in equal proportions between the estates which are then insufficient.

(6) The provisions of paragraphs (2) above and (7) and (8) below shall apply as regards priority of expenses of insolvency proceedings, where insolvency orders are made in relation to an insolvent partnership, incurred after the date of the appointment of a person to act as liquidator of the partnership and to act as the responsible insolvency practitioner in relation to any insolvent member against whom an insolvency order has been made.

(7) Where the joint estate of the partnership is insufficient for the payment in full of the joint expenses of the insolvency proceedings in winding-up the partnership incurred after the date mentioned in paragraph (6) above, the unpaid balance shall be apportioned between the separate estates of the insolvent members and form part of the expenses to be paid out of those estates in

such proportions as the liquidation committee established for the partnership and any corporate members sanctions or the court, on application by the liquidator of the partnership or any person interested, orders.

(8) With the sanction of the liquidation committee established for the partnership and any corporate member, or with the leave of the court obtained on application, the responsible insolvency practitioner may—

(*a*)   pay out of the joint estate of the partnership as part of the expenses to be paid out of that estate any expenses so incurred for any separate estate of an insolvent member; or

(*b*)   pay out of any separate estate of an insolvent member any part of the expenses so incurred for the joint estate of the partnership which affects that separate estate."

27–85   Article 10 then establishes the priority of debts as follows:

"*Priority of debts where insolvency orders are made in relation to an insolvent partnership.*

10.—(1) The provisions of this Article shall apply as regards priority of debts, where insolvency orders are made against an insolvent partnership and an insolvent member.

(2) The joint estate of an insolvent partnership shall be applicable in the first instance in payment of the joint debts due to the creditors of the partnership other than those to be postponed under section 3 of the Partnership Act 1890[2] or any provision of the Act[3] or any other Act, and the separate estate of each insolvent member shall be applicable in the first instance in payment of the separate debts of that member, other than those to be postponed as mentioned above.

(3) Any surplus remaining after the payment of the separate debts of any insolvent member out of his separate estate, in accordance with paragraph (2) above, shall, without the prior payment of any interest under section 189 or 328(4) of the Act, as the case may be, form part of the joint estate of the partnership and be applied in payment of the joint debts due to the creditors of the partnership.

(4) Any surplus remaining after the payment of the joint debts of the partnership out of its joint estate in accordance with paragraphs (2) and (3) above shall form part of the separate estate of each partner in proportion to the right and interest of each such partner in the joint estate:

---

[2] See *supra*, paras. 5–40 *et seq*.
[3] *i.e.* the Insolvency Act 1986: Insolvent Partnerships Order 1986, art. 2(1).

Provided that in the case of a partner against whom an insolvency order has not been made, before any part of the surplus shall form part of his separate estate interest shall be paid out of his share on the joint debts of the partnership to the creditors of the partnership, in pursuance of section 189 of the Act.

(5) Distinct accounts shall be kept of the joint estate and of the separate estate or estates.

(6) Subject to the provisions of this Article and of the Act and of any order made under it and of any other Act all debts of the partnership other than preferential debts rank equally between themselves. [4]

(7) Nothing in this Article shall alter the effect of section 3 of the Partnership Act 1890 or any rule of law.

(8) Neither the official receiver, the Secretary of State nor a responsible insolvency practitioner shall be entitled to remuneration or fees under the Insolvency Rules 1986, the Insolvency Regulations 1986 or the Insolvency Fees Order 1986 for his services in connection with the transfer of a surplus from a separate estate of an insolvent member to the joint estate or from the joint estate to a separate estate under this Article.

(9) If any two or more members of an insolvent partnership constitute a separate partnership, the creditors of such separate partnership shall be deemed to be a separate set of creditors and subject to the same statutory provisions as the separate creditors of any member of the insolvent partnership.

(10) Where any surplus remains after the administration of the estate of a separate partnership, the surplus shall be carried over to the separate estates of the partners in that partnership according to their respective rights and interests in it."

Scope of the Order

Articles 9 and 10 of the Insolvent Partnerships Order 1986 clearly **27–86** apply in any case where:

(*a*) insolvency orders are made against a firm and at least one partner[5]; or

---

[4] It would, however, seem that the rights of a creditor may be subordinated with his agreement: *Re Maxwell Communications Corporation plc* [1993] 1 W.L.R. 1402, distinguishing *National Westminster Bank Ltd. v. Halesowen Presswork & Assemblies Ltd.* [1972] A.C. 785, H.L. and *British Eagle International Air Lines Ltd. v. Compagnie Nationale Air France* [1975] 1 W.L.R. 758, H.L.

[5] The Insolvent Partnerships Order 1986, art. 9(1) and 10(1) appear to assume that such orders will be made on concurrent petitions presented against the firm and against two or more of the partners, *i.e.* pursuant to *ibid.* art. 8: see *supra*, paras. 27–23 *et seq.* However, the title to *ibid.* Pt. 3 is tantalisingly imprecise, *viz.*: "Winding up of Insolvent Partnerships *involving* Insolvency Petitions against two or more Insolvent Members" (emphasis supplied).

(*b*) an order is made on a joint debtor's petition presented by all the partners.[6]

The court also has power to apply those Articles (with any necessary modifications) where, following the presentation of a petition against a corporate or individual partner, it appears that such a partner is "a member of an insolvent partnership."[7] This will include a case where bankruptcy petitions are successively presented against a number of partners,[8] but the position where a winding up order has already been made against the firm is perhaps less clear.[9]

Cases falling outside scope of Order

27–87   The natural assumption underlying the Insolvent Partnerships Order 1986 is that, if Articles 9 and 10 do not apply, no question of priority as between the joint and separate estates will arise. Admittedly, there will be no question of apportioning the expenses of insolvency proceedings where the respective estates of an insolvent firm and of one or more insolvent partners are being separately administered,[10] but the current editor considers that the rule of convenience that the joint debts should principally be paid out of the joint estate and the separate debts out of the relevant separate estate, which exists independently of the insolvency legislation,[11] must still be applied. Moreover, even when administering the assets of an insolvent partnership or an insolvent partner, it will still be necessary to distinguish between those assets which belong to the firm and those which belong to one or more of the partners and, at least to an extent, between joint and separate debts.[12]

Joint and separate debts and estates

27–88   Given that, in any insolvency involving a partnership or a partner, it is necessary to distinguish between, on the one hand, the joint and separate debts and, on the other, the joint and separate estates, the current editor submits that the principles to be applied by the court will be the same as under the old bankruptcy laws. Accordingly, the following summary, adapted from material appearing in earlier editions of this work, will still be of relevance.

---

[6] *Ibid.* art. 13(3), applying *ibid.* arts. 9 and 10. As to such petitions, see *supra*, para. 27–45.

[7] *Ibid.* art. 14(1), (3). But see further, *supra*, para. 27–50.

[8] *Ibid.* art. 14(2), (3).

[9] See *supra*, para. 27–21.

[10] *e.g.* in any of the cases last supposed, assuming the court not to have exercised its power to apply the provisions of the Order.

[11] See *Re Rudd & Son Ltd.* [1984] Ch. 237, 242B, *per* Nourse J.

[12] This will be of particular relevance where any question of set-off arises: see *supra*, paras. 27–74 *et seq*. Note, in particular, the possible effect of the Insolvent Partnerships Order 1986, art. 15(3): see *supra*, para. 27–79.

(a) Joint and separate debts

Creditors may be divided into three classes, *viz.*:   **27–89**

(i)   The joint creditors[13] of the firm, to whom all the partners
      are jointly liable.[14]

(ii) The separate creditors of each partner, to whom only that
      partner is liable.

(iii) The joint and separate creditors, to whom the partners are
      at one and the same time liable both jointly and separately
      in respect of the same debt.[15]

The circumstances in which a debt can properly be regarded as a debt
of the firm were considered earlier in this work and reference should
be made thereto.[16] However, the following brief recapitulation may
be useful in the present context:

Original status of debt

Having regard to the joint nature of a partner's liability,[17] it can be **27–90**
said that, as a general rule, a debt of the firm will not also be the
separate debt of any partner, unless he has agreed to be severally
liable therefor.[18]

Dormant and apparent partners

Where a firm comprises two partners, one of whom actively **27–91**
participates in the business and the other of whom is dormant or
merely held out to the world as a partner,[19] a creditor of the firm will

---

[13] Although this expression is conventionally used, it is in truth something of a misnomer: joint
creditors, properly so called, are persons who are jointly entitled to the same debt, rather than, as
here, persons who have no such joint entitlement but who merely happen to have the same joint
debtors. A more accurate expression might perhaps be "joint estate creditors". The Insolvent
Partnerships Order 1986, art. 10 refers to "the creditors of the partnership": see *supra*, para. 27–85.

[14] Note that creditors may have a dual capacity as regards the firm and the partners. If four out
of five members of a firm are jointly liable to a creditor, he will be a separate creditor as regards
the firm, but may be a joint creditor as regards the four partners. See the Insolvent Partnerships
Order 1986, art. 10(9), *supra*, para. 27–85.

[15] A creditor who has obtained a judgment against several persons in respect of a joint debt can
levy execution against any one or more of them but who is not properly styled a joint and separate
creditor; he remains a joint creditor: see *Ex p. Christie* (1832) Mont. & Bl. 352. Under the old
bankruptcy law, no distinction was made between creditors to whom the partners were jointly
indebted in connection with the partnership business and other creditors to whom they were also
jointly indebted: see *Hoare v. Oriental Bank Corporation* (1877) 2 App.Cas. 589. It would seem
that this is no longer the position under the Insolvent Partnerships Order 1986, art. 10 (*supra*, para.
27–85), which refers to "the creditors of the partnership"; *sed quaere.*

[16] See *supra*, paras. 12–01 *et seq.* and 13–17 *et seq.*

[17] Partnership Act 1890, s.9: see *supra* paras. 13–03 *et seq.*

[18] See *Ex p. Dobinson* (1837) 2 Deac. 341; *Ex p. Carlisle Canal Co.* (1837) 2 Deac. 349; *Ex p.
Appleby* (1837) 2 Deac. 482; *Ex p. Benson* (1842) 2 M.D. & D. 750. See also, as to bills of
exchange, *Ex p. Wilson* (1842) 3 M.D. & D. 57; *Ex p. Flintoff* (1844) 3 M.D. & D. 726; *Re Clarke*
(1845) De Gex 153; *Ex p. Buckley* (1845) 14 M. & W. 469.

[19] See, further, the Partnership Act 1890, s.14, *supra*, paras. 5–43 *et seq.*

seemingly have a choice: he may treat the debt as a joint debt of both "partners" or as a separate debt of the partner who is the real or apparent proprietor of the business.[20]

Frauds and breaches of trust

27–92   Where a fraud or breach of trust can be imputed to a firm, the liability of the partners will be joint and several.[21]

Bills of exchange

27–93   Subject to questions of authority and notice,[22] bills drawn, indorsed or accepted in the name of a firm will give rise to a joint debt,[23] whilst those drawn, accepted or indorsed in the names of some, but not all, of the partners will not.[24] A separate creditor of one partner who takes the firm's bill in settlement of his debt must show that it was given with the authority of all the partners if it is to be treated as creating a joint debt.[25]

Money of which firm has had the benefit

27–94   A separate creditor cannot be treated as a joint creditor merely because the firm has had the benefit of the money in question, nor can a joint creditor be treated as the separate creditor of a partner because the latter has had such benefit.[26]

Loss of right to prove and conversion of joint and separate debts

27–95   A joint creditor who releases one of his debtors cannot subsequently prove against the estates of the others.[27] Moreover, if a

---

[20] See *Ex p. Hodgkinson* (1815) 19 Ves.Jr. 291; *Ex p. Norfolk* (1815) 19 Ves.Jr. 455; *Ex p. Law* (1839) 3 Deac. 541; *Ex p. Arbouin* (1846) De Gex 359. See also *Scarf v. Jardine* (1882) 7 App.Cas. 345, *supra*, paras. 5–62, 13–04. But note also, in this context, the decision in *Re C. & M. Ashberg, The Times*, July 17, 1990, noticed, *supra*, para. 27–07.

[21] See *supra*, paras. 13–12, 13–13. As to frauds, see *Ex p. Unity Joint-Stock Mutual Banking Association* (1858) 3 De G. & J. 63; *Ex p. Adamson* (1878) 8 Ch.D. 807. As to breaches of trust, see *Ex p. Poulson* (1844) De Gex 79; *Ex p. Barnewall* (1855) 6 De G.M. & G. 795. *Cf. Ex p. Geaves* (1856) 8 De G.M. & G. 291; *Ex p. White* (1871) L.R. 6 Ch. 397. And see also *Ex p. Burton* (1843) 3 M.D. & D. 364.

[22] See *Ex p. Holdsworth* (1841) 1 M.D. & D. 475; also *Rooth v. Quin* (1819) 7 Price 193. And see further, *supra*, paras. 12–147 *et seq.*

[23] *Ex p. Bushell* (1844) 3 M.D. & D. 615. And see *supra*, paras. 12–175 *et seq.*

[24] Bills of Exchange Act 1882, s.23; *Ex p. Bolitho* (1817) Buck 100. As to the position where the firm and the acceptor share the same name, see *Ex p. Law* (1839) 3 Deac. 541.

[25] Partnership Act 1890, s.7, *supra*, para. 12–148. And see *Ex p. Agace* (1792) 2 Cox 312; *Ex p. Bonbonus* (1803) 8 Ves.Jr. 540; *Ex p. Goulding and Davies* (1829) 2 Gl. & J. 118; *Ex p. Thorpe* (1836) 3 M. & A. 716; *Ex p. Austen* (1840) 1 M.D. & D. 247.

[26] *Ex p. Hunter* (1742) 1 Atk. 223; *Ex p. Wheatley* (1797) Cooke's *Bankruptcy Law* (8th ed.), p. 534; *Ex p. Peele* (1802) 6 Ves.Jr. 602; *Ex p. Hartop* (1806) 12 Ves.Jr. 349; *Ex p. Emly* (1811) 1 Rose 61; *Re Ferrar* (1859) 9 Ir.Ch. 289. See also *supra*, paras. 12–193 *et seq.*

[27] *Ex p. Slater* (1801) 6 Ves.Jr. 146. As to the discharge of a surety, see *Ex p. Webster* (1847) De Gex 414; *Re Darwen and Pearce* [1927] 1 Ch. 176. See also *supra*, paras. 13–94 *et seq.*

higher security is taken or judgment obtained in respect of a joint or separate debt, the right to prove against the relevant estate may be lost by virtue of the doctrine of merger.[28] Alternatively, that right may be lost if there is a substitution of debtors.[29]

Merger

Thus, by taking a separate bond from one partner to secure a debt 27-96 of the firm, the creditor will become entitled to a separate debt in place of that joint debt, which will prima facie be destroyed;[30] similarly, if a joint bond is taken to secure a separate debt. Whilst a judgment no longer *per se* has the same effect,[31] a joint judgment in respect of a joint and several debt will seemingly create a joint debt,[32] although a separate judgment in respect thereof will not have a corresponding effect.[33]

Position where additional security taken

Where a creditor obtains an *additional* security for a pre-existing 27-97 debt, in circumstances which do not give rise to a merger, he may still prove for his original debt if the additional security later becomes unavailable. Thus, a creditor who takes a joint bill for a separate debt[34] or vice versa[35] becomes, as he intended, a joint and separate creditor and may, if necessary, fall back on the original debt, unless the bill was taken in satisfaction thereof[36] or there has been a substitution of debtors.[37]

Substitution of debtors

A substitution of debtors can only be effected with the consent of 27-98 the relevant creditor. Accordingly if, following the dissolution of a partnership, one partner agrees to carry on its business and to pay its

---

[28] See further *supra*, paras. 13–130 *et seq.*
[29] See further *supra*, paras. 13–101 *et seq.*
[30] See *Ex p. Hernaman* (1848) 12 Jur. 643. See further, *supra*, para. 13–131.
[31] See the Civil Liability (Contribution) Act 1978, considered *supra*, paras. 13–05, 13–134, 20–16. As to the position before that Act, see *Kendall v. Hamilton* (1879) 4 App.Cas. 504.
[32] *Ex p. Christie* (1832) Mont. & Bl. 352. But this does not apply to breaches of trust in respect of which there is a joint and several liability: see *Re Davison* (1884) 13 Q.B.D. 50.
[33] *Drake v. Mitchell* (1803) 3 East 251; *Re Clarkes* (1845) 2 Jo. & La T. 212; *Ex p. Bate* (1838) 3 Deac. 358. And see *Ex p. Waterfall* (1851) 4 De G. & Sm. 199. See also *supra*, para. 13–135.
[34] *Ex p. Seddon* (1788) 2 Cox 49; *Ex p. Lobb* (1802) 7 Ves.Jr. 592; *Ex p. Hay* (1808) 15 Ves.Jr. 4; *Ex p. Kedie* (1832) 2 D. & Ch. 321; *Ex p. Meinertzhagen* (1838) 3 Deac. 101.
[35] *Ex p. Hodgkinson* (1815) 19 Ves.Jr. 291; *Bottomley v. Nuttall* (1858) 5 C.B. (N.S.) 122; *Keay v. Fenwick* (1876) 1 C.P.D. 745. See also *Ex p. Fairlie* (1830) Mont. 17; *Ex p. Raleigh* (1838) 3 M. & A. 670.
[36] See, generally, *Wegg Prosser v. Evans* [1895] 1 Q.B. 108.
[37] See *Ex p. Whitmore* (1838) 3 Deac. 365; also *Ex p. Kirby* (1819) Buck 511; *Ex p. Jackson* (1841) 2 M.D. & D. 146.

debts, the creditors of the firm do not become the separate creditors of that partner unless they accede to the arrangements made between the former partners[38] or, knowing of those arrangements, deal with that partner in such a way as to prejudice the rights of the others, thereby discharging them.[39] On the same basis, a separate debt existing before the creation of a partnership is not converted into a joint debt merely because the partners have agreed, as between themselves, to treat it as such.[40]

27–99 It is, as a general rule, easier for a separate creditor to establish a right to prove against the joint estate than it is for a joint creditor to establish a right to prove against a separate estate. This is because, in the former case, it is merely necessary to prove that *additional* persons have become liable to the creditor[41] whilst, in the latter, it must be shown that one of several debtors has alone agreed to undertake liability for the debt. The practical difficulty of establishing that a joint debtor's conduct is referable to his intention to take over sole liability for the debt rather than to the continuation of his existing joint liability should be self evident; if more is required, it is merely necessary to refer to the numerous cases in which just such an argument has failed.[42]

(b) Joint and separate estates

27–100 Since the doctrine of reputed ownership no longer has any place in insolvency law,[43] identification of the assets comprised in the joint

---

[38] Partnership Act 1890, s.17(2), (3): see *supra*, paras. 13–75 *et seq.*, 13–103. See also *Ex p. Freeman* (1819) Buck 471; *Ex p. Fry* (1821) 1 Gl. & J. 96; *Ex p. Appleby* (1837) 2 Deac. 482; *Ex p. Gurney* (1842) 2 M.D. & D. 541.

[39] *Rouse v. Bradford Banking Co.* [1894] A.C. 586. And see *supra*, paras. 13–98, 13–99.

[40] Partnership Act 1890, s.17(1): see *supra*, paras. 13–25 *et seq.* See also *Ex p. Jackson* (1790) 1 Ves.Jr. 130; *Ex p. Peele* (1802) 6 Ves.Jr. 602; *Ex p. Williams* (1817) Buck 13; *Ex p. Hitchcock* (1839) 3 Deac. 507; *Ex p. Parker* (1842) 2 M.D. & D. 511; *Ex p. Graham* (1842) 2 M.D. & D. 781; *Re Littles* (1847) 10 Ir.Eq. 275. As to the evidence necessary to show the creditor's accession to the new arrangement, see *Rolfe v. Flower* (1865) L.R. 1 P.C. 27; *Bilborough v. Holmes* (1876) 5 Ch.D. 255; *Scarf v. Jardine* (1882) 7 App.Cas. 345, noticed *supra*, paras. 5–62, 13–04. Lord Lindley also observed: "Mr. Cooke, indeed, lays it down that if new partners come into a firm, and it is agreed that the stock and debts of the old firm shall become those of the new firm, and the latter becomes bankrupt, the creditors of the old firm may prove against the joint estate of the new firm; and he cites *Ex p. Bingham* and *Ex p. Clowes* (1789) 2 Bro.C.C. 595 (Cooke's *Bankruptcy Law*, 534, 8th ed.). The facts of the first of these two cases are not stated. *Ex p. Clowes* was a very peculiar case, and if it was ever an authority for the doctrine that a separate debt can, as between the partners and the creditor, become a joint debt, or *vice versa*, without the privity of the creditor, the case must be considered as no longer law. See 1 Mont. Part., note 2 F., p. 117, in notes. Perhaps Mr. Cooke rested the right of proof on the absence of joint estate, as in *Ex p. Taylor* (1842) 2 M.D. & D. 753."

[41] A written agreement is not necessary: *Ex p. Lane* (1846) De Gex 300.

[42] See *Ex p. Fairlie* (1830) Mont. 17; *Ex p. Raleigh* (1838) 3 M. & A. 670; *Ex p. Smith* (1840) 1 M.D. & D. 165. See also *Bilborough v. Holmes* (1876) 5 Ch.D. 255 and the cases cited *supra*, para. 27–98, n.38. Cf. *Ex p. Bradbury* (1839) Mont. & C. 625. As to the position where there is no joint estate, see *Ex p. Taylor* (1842) 2 M.D. & D. 753 and *infra*, para. 27–133.

[43] See, formerly, the Bankruptcy Act 1914, s.38(c) and the 15th ed. of this work at pp. 844 *et seq.*

estate of the firm and the separate estates of the partners is dependent on the agreement of the partners, express or implied, and on the operation of the Partnership Act 1890.[44] Since this subject has already been considered in detail,[45] it is merely necessary to consider whether a notional joint estate can now be created by holding out and then to refer to the manner in which joint estate can be converted into separate estate and vice versa.

Joint estate created by holding out

Lord Lindley observed that: **27–101**

">... if A allows B to carry on business with his, A's, goods and on his, A's, behalf, although not in his name, but credit is given to them both on the supposition that they are partners, the property with which the business is carried on will be treated as the joint estate of the two, and not as the separate estate of A."[46]

This view was expressed against a background of the doctrine of reputed ownership,[47] which has not been preserved under the Insolvency Act 1986, and was, in any event, confined within narrow parameters.[48] The current editor considers that a similar approach could not be justified under the 1986 Act, since it specifically refers to "the joint estate of an insolvent partnership"[49] and a partnership by holding out is not a true partnership in the eyes of the law.[50] Even if that were not the case, the circumstances in which credit could be said to have been given in the manner contemplated by Lord Lindley must now be severely reduced, assuming compliance with the requirements of the Business Names Act 1985.[51]

Agreements converting joint into separate estate and vice versa

It has already been seen that a bona fide agreement between **27–102** partners to convert partnership property into the separate property of one of their number was, under the old bankruptcy laws, treated as

---

[44] *Ibid.* s.20, *supra*, para. 18–03.

[45] See *supra*, paras. 18–06 *et seq.*

[46] See *Re Rowland and Crankshaw* (1866) L.R. 1 Ch. 421; *Ex p. Hayman* (1878) 8 Ch.D. 11. In any such case, the respective interests of the partners in the apparent joint estate were ignored: see *Ex p. Hunter* (1816) 2 Rose 382.

[47] See then the Bankruptcy Act 1883, s.44(iii).

[48] See, as to the position where there are dormant or apparent partners, *supra*, para. 27–91.

[49] See, for example, the Insolvent Partnerships Order 1986, art. 10(2), *supra*, para. 27–85.

[50] The Partnership Act 1890, s.14 (see *supra*, paras. 5–43 *et seq.*) does not cause the person held out actually to be a partner but merely renders him *liable* as if he were: see *Hudgell Yeates & Co. v. Watson* [1978] Q.B. 451, 467, *per* Waller L.J.; also *Re C. & M. Ashberg, The Times*, July 17, 1990, noticed *supra*, para. 27–07.

[51] See generally, *supra*, paras. 3–24 *et seq.*

binding on a trustee in bankruptcy, provided that it preceded the commission of an act of bankruptcy.[52] The current editor suggests that the position will in general be the same under the new insolvency legislation, save that the relevant date will be the presentation of the petition.[53] Accordingly, the observations of Lord Lindley on the decision in *Ex p. Ruffin*[54] still hold good, *viz*.:

> "This case [*Ex p. Ruffin*] has been followed by many others, and it is therefore now beyond dispute that if a partnership is dissolved, and a *bona fide* agreement is come to between the partners, to the effect that what was the partnership property shall become the property of him who continues the business, and afterwards the firm or the continuing partner becomes bankrupt, that which was the partnership property cannot be distributed as the joint estate of the firm, but must be treated as the separate estate of the continuing partner.[55] The creditors of the firm have no lien on its property which can prevent the partners from bona fide changing its character, and converting it into the separate estate of one of them."[56]

This would seem to be the position even where the partnership liabilities exceed its assets at the time of the agreement.[57]

Exceptions to the general rule

27–103 However, there are three well established exceptions, in the face of which no such agreement can stand; they are as follows:

  1. Fraud, whether practised against a partner or against creditors;[58]

---

[52] See *supra*, paras. 18–43 *et seq*.

[53] Insolvency Act 1986, ss.127, 129(2) (winding up of firm or corporate partner), s.284, as amended, where appropriate, by the Insolvent Partnerships Order 1986, Sched. 2, Pt. III, para. 11 (bankruptcy of individual partner). In either case, the court could theoretically sanction the agreement, but it is difficult to imagine the circumstances where this would be appropriate.

[54] (1801) 6 Ves.Jr. 119. See also *supra*, para. 18–51.

[55] *Ex p. Titner* (1746) 1 Atk. 136; *Bolton v. Puller* (1796) 1 Bos. & P. 539; *Ex p. Fell* (1805) 10 Ves.Jr. 347; *Ex p. Williams* (1805) 11 Ves.Jr. 3; *Ex p. Clarkson* (1834) 4 D. & Ch. 56; *Ex p. Gurney* (1842) 2 M.D. & D. 541; *Ex p. Walker* (1862) 4 De G.F. & J. 509; *Re Simpson* (1874) L.R. 9 Ch. 572.

[56] *Ex p. Ruffin* (1801) 6 Ves.Jr. 119; *Ex p. Williams* (1805) 11 Ves.Jr. 3; *Stuart v. Ferguson* (1832) Hayes (Ir.Ex.) 452. *Cf.* the cases cited *infra*, para. 27–103, n.58. And see *supra*, para. 18–44.

[57] *Ex p. Peake* (1816) 1 Madd. 346; *Ex p. Clarkson* (1834) 4 D. & C. 56, 66, *per* Sir G. Rose; *Ex p. Walker* (1862) 4 De G.F. & J. 509; and see *Ex p. Carpenter* (1826) Mont. & MacA. 1. *Cf. Re Kemptner* (1869) 8 Eq. 286, where mala fides was proved.

[58] See *Anderson v. Maltby* (1793) 2 Ves.Jr. 244; *Ex p. Rowlandson* (1813) 2 V. & B. 172; *Ex p. Mayou* (1865) 4 De G.J. & S. 664; *Re Kemptner* (1869) 8 Eq. 286. *Cf. supra*, nn.56, 57; also *Pearce v. Bulteel* [1916] 2 Ch. 544. See further *supra*, para. 18–45. And see the Insolvency Act 1986, ss. 206, 207 (read with the Insolvent Partnerships Order 1986, art. 3(a)), 357; also *supra*, paras. 10–124 and 10–125, as to frauds on the insolvency laws.

2. Where the agreement remains executory;[59]
3. Where the former partnership property is still subject to the liens of the other partners.[60]

To these exceptions must be added the power of the court under the Insolvency Act 1986 to set aside any transaction entered into by partners in the period of five years (in the case of the conversion of separate into joint property)[61] or two years (in the case of the conversion of joint into separate property)[62] ending with the presentation of the relevant petition, if it was unsupported by consideration or otherwise at an undervalue.[63] A similar power is exercisable in the case of preferences to creditors, etc.,[64] although it is doubtful whether the statutory presumption of a desire to prefer[65] is applicable where an apparent preference is given by a partner to the *joint* creditors of the firm.[66] Equally, the 1986 Act confers a general power on the court to set aside transactions at an undervalue independently of the existence of any insolvency proceedings.[67]

Evidence of such agreements

The mere fact that a partnership has been dissolved or that a **27–104** partner has retired is not of itself sufficient evidence of an agreement to convert a partnership asset into the separate property of a

---

[59] *Ex p. Wheeler* (1817) Buck 25; *Ex p. Cooper* (1840) 1 M.D. & D. 358; *Ex p. Gurney* (1842) 2 M.D. & D. 541; *Re Kemptner* (1869) 8 Eq. 286; *Ex p. Wood* (1879) 10 Ch.D. 554; *Pearce v. Bulteel* [1916] 2 Ch. 544; *cf. Ex p. Clarkson* (1834) 4 D. & Ch. 56, 64, (*per* Erskine C.J.), 67 (*per* Sir G. Rose); also *Re Jane* (1914) 110 L.T. 556. See further, *supra*, para. 18–46.

[60] See *Ex p. Morley* (1873) L.R. 8 Ch. 1026; *Ex p. Dear* (1876) 1 Ch.D. 514; *Ex p. Manchester Bank* (1879) 12 Ch.D. 917 and, *sub nom. Ex p. Butcher* (1880) 13 Ch.D. 465. *Cf. Re Simpson* (1874) L.R. 9 Ch. 572. As to the partners' liens generally, see the Partnership Act 1890, s.39 and *supra*, paras. 19–28 *et seq.*

[61] Insolvency Act 1986, s.341(1)(a) (individual partner). The period will be only two years in the case of a corporate partner: *ibid.* s.240(1)(a).

[62] *Ibid.* s.240(1)(a).

[63] *Ibid.* ss.238(2), (4) (winding up), 339(1), (3)(a), (c) (bankruptcy). As to what transactions will be treated as at an undervalue, see *Re Kumar* [1993] 1 W.L.R. 224 and, as to the nature of the court's discretion, see *Re Paramount Airways Ltd.* [1993] Ch. 223, 239 *et seq.* See also, as to general assignments of book debts, the Insolvency Act 1986, s.344.

[64] *Ibid.* ss.239 (winding up), 340 (bankruptcy). As to the relevant periods in this case, see *ibid.* ss.240(1)(a), (b) (winding up), 341(1)(a), (b) (bankruptcy). And see, generally, *Re M.C. Bacon Ltd.* [1990] BCLC 324; *Re Beacon Leisure Ltd.* [1992] BCLC 565 (both decisions under *ibid.* s.239); *Re Ledingham-Smith* [1993] BCLC 635 (a decision under *ibid.* s.340).

[65] *Ibid.* ss.239(6) (winding up), 340(5) (bankruptcy). Partners will be treated as "connected with" the firm for the purposes of the former subsection and "associates" of each other for the purposes of the latter: see *ibid.* s.249 (read with the Insolvent Partnerships Order 1986, art. 3(a)) and s.435(3). And see, generally, as to this statutory presumption, *Re Beacon Leisure Ltd., supra*; *Re Ledingham-Smith, supra.*

[66] A partner is not treated as an associate of the *firm*, otherwise than in Scotland: Insolvency Act 1986, s.435(3).

[67] *Ibid.* ss.423–425. See, generally, *Arbuthnot Leasing International Ltd. v. Havelet Leasing Ltd. (No. 2)* [1990] BCC 636; *Chohan v. Saggar* [1992] BCC 306 and 750; *Agricultural Mortgage Corporation plc v. Woodward, The Times*, May 30, 1994.

continuing partner, since the asset might be in his hands simply for the purposes of winding up the affairs of the old firm.[68]

Priority of expenses

27–105 It has already been seen that, where insolvency orders have been made against the firm and against any one or more of the partners on concurrent petitions, the same person will in general act as liquidator of the partnership and of any corporate partner and as trustee of any bankrupt partner;[69] similarly in any case in which bankruptcy orders are made against all the partners on a joint debtor's petition[70] and in any other relevant case in which the provisions of the Insolvent Partnerships Order 1986 are applied by order of the court.[71] The expenses of the insolvency proceedings, both before and after such appointment, which are attributable to the joint and separate estates are paid out of those estates respectively.[72] If the expenses attributable to the joint estate cannot be met out of that estate, the balance is, as might be expected, apportioned between the separate estates of the partners.[73] More surprisingly, if expenses incurred *prior* to the appointment of the liquidator, etc., and attributable to a partner's separate estate cannot be met out of that estate, the balance is treated as an expense of the joint estate[74] and, if that is insufficient, seemingly apportioned between the separate estates of the other partners.[75] In this way, it would seem that the separate estate of one partner may be liable for expenses attributable to the separate estate of another.

Where the joint and separate estates are administered independently, no question of apportionment of expenses will arise.

Distinct accounts to be kept

27–106 Where the joint and separate estates are being administered by the same liquidator/trustee, he must keep distinct accounts of each estate.[76] This accords with the previous bankruptcy law.[77]

---

[68] *Ex p. Williams* (1805) 11 Ves.Jr. 3; *Ex p. Leaf* (1840) 4 Deac. 287; *Ex p. Cooper* (1840) 1 M.D. & D. 358.

[69] See *supra*, para. 27–52.

[70] See *supra*, para. 27–53.

[71] See *supra*, paras. 27–21, 27–41.

[72] Insolvent Partnerships Order 1986, art. 9(1), (2) (expenses prior to appointment of liquidator, etc.), (6) (expenses following appointment), *supra*, para. 27–84.

[73] *Ibid.* art. 9(3), (7), *supra*, para. 27–84. The precise manner in which expenses following the appointment of the liquidator, etc., will be apportioned is determined by the liquidation committee or the court.

[74] *Ibid.* art. 9(4), *supra*, para. 27–84.

[75] *Ibid.* art. 9(5), *supra*, para. 27–84.

[76] *Ibid.* art. 10(5), *supra*, para. 27–85.

[77] See *Ex p. Voguel* (1743) 1 Atk. 132; *Dutton v. Morrison* (1810) 17 Ves.Jr. 193; *Re Wait* (1820) 1 J. & W. 610. Note also *Ex p. Marlin* (1785) 2 Bro. C.C. 15.

Correcting mistakes, etc.

Where debts or expenses are paid out of the wrong estate, the **27–107** amount paid must be refunded by the estate which ought properly to have borne them.[78]

Priority and proof of debts

The general rule

It has already been seen that, where joint and separate estates are **27–108** being administered together[79] or independently,[80] questions of priority of debts will inevitably arise. In the former case, the Insolvent Partnerships Order 1986 clearly requires the joint estate to be applied in paying the joint debts and the separate estate of each partner to be applied in paying his separate debts.[81] Only the surplus joint estate remaining after payment of the joint debts will be available for transfer to the partners' respective separate estates and vice versa.[82] There can, of course, be no such transfer as between the *separate* estates. All the joint debts rank equally,[83] other than preferential debts,[84] those postponed under section 3 of the Partnership Act 1890[85] or under some other Act[86] and, seemingly, those postponed with the agreement of the creditor in question.[87]

Group and sub-partnerships

The creditors of a constituent firm of a group partnership[88] are, **27–109** *vis-à-vis* the group partnership, treated as *separate* creditors.[89]

---

[78] See *Re Hind & Sons* (1889) L.R. (Ir.) 23 Ch.D. 217.

[79] See *supra*, para. 27–86.

[80] See *supra*, para. 27–87.

[81] Insolvent Partnerships Order 1986, art. 10(2), *supra*, para. 27–85; see also the Insolvency Act 1986, s.189(6) (as added, in relation to the firm, by the Insolvent Partnerships Order 1986, Sched. 2, Pt. I, para. 16 and, in relation to a corporate partner, by *ibid.* Sched. 2, Pt. II, para. 16), s.328(6) (as added, in relation to an individual partner, by the Insolvent Partnerships Order 1986, Sched. 2, Pt. III, para. 23). And see *Investment and Pensions Advisory Service Ltd. v. Gray* [1990] BCLC 38, 41, *per* Morritt J.

[82] Insolvent Partnerships Order 1986, art. 10(3), (4), *supra*, para. 27–85. Note that interest is payable on a solvent partner's share of the joint debts: *ibid.* art. 10(4), proviso, applying the Insolvency Act 1986, s.189.

[83] Insolvent Partnerships Order 1986, art. 10(6), *supra*, para. 27–85.

[84] As to what debts are treated as preferential, see the Insolvency Act 1986, s.386, Sched. 6 (as amended).

[85] See *supra*, para. 5–40.

[86] Insolvent Partnerships Order 1986, art. 10(2), (7), *supra*, para. 27–85.

[87] See *Re Maxwell Communications Corporation plc* [1993] 1 W.L.R. 1042, distinguishing *Halesowen Presswork & Assemblies Ltd. v. National Westminster Bank Ltd.* [1972] A.C. 785 and *British Eagle International Airlines Ltd. v. Compagnie Nationale Air France* [1975] 1 W.L.R. 758, H.L.

[88] See further, as to such partnerships, *supra*, paras. 11–20 *et seq.*, 27–12 and 27–28.

[89] Insolvent Partnerships Order 1986, art. 10(9), *supra*, para. 27–85.

Accordingly, a share of any surplus arising in the joint estate of the group partnership will be transferred into the constituent firm's joint estate. Only if there is a surplus in the latter will there be a transfer into the separate estates of the members of that firm.[90]

The current editor considers that the same regime will not apply in the case of a sub-partnership between a partner and a third party.[91] Nevertheless, since a share of any surplus transferred to a sub-partner out of the joint estate of the head partnership will form part of the sub-partnership's joint estate rather than part of his separate estate, the ultimate result may be the same.

Relevance of pre-Insolvency Act 1986 law

27–110   The Insolvent Partnerships Order 1986 expressly preserves any rule of law applicable to the priority of debts.[92] It would seem to follow that the rules established under the old bankruptcy laws will continue to be of relevance both to independent and combined administrations.[93] As in previous editions of this work, these rules will be considered first in relation to proof against the joint estate and then in relation to proof against the separate estates.

A.   PROOF AGAINST THE JOINT ESTATE

27–111   This subject can best be analysed in terms of:

(*a*)   The rights of the joint creditors.
(*b*)   The rights of the partners.
(*c*)   The rights of their separate creditors.

(a)   Rights of the joint creditors

27–112   The general right of such creditors to be paid the entirety of their debts out of the joint estate has already been noticed[94] and does not require further elaboration. The joint debts will in general rank *pari*

---

[90] *Ibid.* art. 10(10), *supra*, para. 27–85.

[91] See further, as to such partnerships, *supra*, paras. 5–75 *et seq.*, 27–12, 27–28. *Quaere* whether, if two or more members of a single sub-partnership are (unusually) both members of the head partnership, it could be argued that, notwithstanding the interests of third parties, such members "constitute a separate partnership" for the purposes of *ibid.* art. 10(9)? The current editor considers that such a construction would not be permissible.

[92] *Ibid.* art. 10(7), *supra*, para. 27–85.

[93] Note that the courts are, in general, reluctant to follow rules developed under the old bankruptcy laws when applying the new insolvency legislation: see, for example, *Re A Debtor (No. 1 of 1987)* [1989] 1 W.L.R. 271; *Re Smith* [1990] 2 A.C. 215, 237–238; *Re M. C. Bacon* [1990] BCLC 324, 335, *per* Millett J.

[94] See *supra*, paras. 27–82, 27–83, 27–108.

passu,[95] unless they are preferential,[96] due under a contract to which section 3 of the Partnership Act 1890 applies[97] or are postponed by agreement.[98] Although debts due to a bankrupt partner's spouse will be postponed in administering his or her separate estate,[99] it is submitted that this will not affect the priority of a *joint* debt due to that spouse.[1]

Secured creditors

A secured creditor may in general realise his security and prove for **27–113** the balance of his debt or surrender his security and prove for the whole debt;[2] what he cannot do is both retain the benefit of the security and prove for the *whole* debt. However, under the old bankruptcy laws, there was an established exception to this rule, applicable only in the case of a partnership,[3] where the debt was payable out of one estate and the security derived from another.[4] Thus, a creditor of a bankrupt two partner firm, who held a security given by a larger firm of which those two partners were members, was entitled both to prove for the whole amount of the debt against the joint estate of the bankrupt firm and to retain the security given by the larger (solvent) firm.[5] The position was the same where a partner had mortgaged his own property to secure a joint debt.[6] However, that exception did not apply if, unbeknown to the creditor, the property over which the security was given in fact belonged to the

---

[95] Insolvent Partnerships Order 1986, art. 10(6), *supra*, para. 27–85; Insolvency Act 1986, ss.175, 189 (as amended by the Insolvent Partnerships Order 1986, Sched. 2, Pt. II, para. 16), s.328 (as amended by the Insolvent Partnerships Order 1986, Sched. 2, Pt. III, para. 23). But note also the power of the court to alter the priority of debts under *ibid.*, s.215(4), in the case of fraudulent or wrongful trading.

[96] As to what constitute preferential debts, see the Insolvency Act 1986, s.386, Sched. 6 (as amended). *Cf.* the position under the old law, as expounded in *Re Rudd & Sons Ltd.* [1984] Ch. 237.

[97] See *supra*, para. 5–40.

[98] See *Re Maxwell Communications Corporation plc* [1993] 1 W.L.R. 1042, distinguishing *National Westminster Bank Ltd. v. Halesowen Presswork & Assemblies Ltd.* [1972] A.C. 785, H.L. and *British Eagle International Air Lines Ltd. v. Compagnie Nationale Air France* [1975] 1 W.L.R. 758, H.L.

[99] Insolvency Act 1986, s.329.

[1] See *Ex p. Nottingham* (1887) 19 Q.B.D. 88 (a decision under the Married Women's Property Act 1882, s.3).

[2] Insolvency Rules 1986, rr. 4.88, 4.95 *et seq.* (winding up), 6.109, 6.115 *et seq.* (bankruptcy). See also the Insolvency Act 1986, ss.269(1), 383(2).

[3] See *Re A Debtor (No. 5 of 1967)* [1972] Ch. 197.

[4] See *Ex p. West Riding Union Banking Co.* (1881) 19 Ch.D. 105; *Ex p. Cocks, Biddulph & Co.* [1894] 2 Q.B. 256; also *Ex p. Brett* (1871) L.R. 6 Ch. 838.

[5] *Ex p. Bloxham* (1801) 6 Ves.Jr. 449; *Ex p. Parr* (1811) 1 Rose 76; *Ex p. Goodman* (1818) 3 Madd. 373; *Ex p. Sammon* (1832) 1 D. & C. 564; also *Ex p. Wilson* (1838) 2 Jur. 67; *Ex p. English and American Bank* (1868) L.R. 4 Ch.App. 49 (both cases involving a creditor of two firms which had engaged in a joint transaction).

[6] *Ex p. Peacock* (1825) 2 Gl. & J. 27; *Ex p. Adams* (1837) 3 M. & Ayr. 157; *Ex p. Groom* (1837) 2 Deac. 265; *Ex p. Caldicott* (1884) 25 Ch.D. 716; *Re Hind & Sons* (1889) L.R. (Ir.) 23 Ch.D. 217. See also *Ex p. Manchester and Liverpool District Banking Co.* (1874) 18 Eq. 249 and the cases cited in the next note.

estate out of which the secured debt was payable.[7] Numerous other examples may be imagined.[8] The current editor submits that the same exception continues to apply under the new insolvency legislation.

27–114   The foregoing exception will naturally not apply in the case of a creditor who has advanced money to a partner and taken a security from him, merely because the money has subsequently been applied for the firm's benefit: in such a case, there is clearly no joint debt payable out of the joint estate and the creditor has no *locus standi* against the firm.[9]

(b)   Rights of the partners

27–115 Lord Lindley stated that, subject to certain exceptions:

"... it is an established rule that a partner in a bankrupt firm shall not prove in competition with the creditors of the firm. They are, in fact, his own creditors, and he cannot be permitted to diminish the partnership assets to the prejudice of those who are not only creditors of the firm, but also of himself.[10] If, therefore, a partner is a creditor of the firm, neither he nor his separate

---

[7] *Ex p. Connell* (1838) 3 Deac. 201; *Ex p. Manchester and County Bank* (1876) 3 Ch.D. 481.

[8] The following passage (based on Lord Lindley's original formulation) appeared in earlier editions of this work: "Again, if A and B are partners, and A gives a separate security for a partnership debt and dies, and B becomes bankrupt, the creditor can prove against B's estate without giving up his security. [*Ex p. Bowden* (1832) *1 D. & Ch. 135*; *Ex p. Smyth (1839) 3 Deac. 597*]. So, where a creditor of a firm has a security belonging to the firm and also a separate covenant for payment by each partner, such creditor may, on the bankruptcy of the firm, retain his security and prove against the separate estates of the covenantors. [*Re Plummer (1841) 1 Ph. 56*]. So, too, if a creditor holds a security on the separate property of one partner for the joint debt of his firm, and has also the separate guarantee of that partner for the joint debt, he may prove against the separate estate of that partner, for the amount due under his guarantee without realising or accounting for the security, because the security is not a security for the partner's separate debt under the guarantee, but for the joint debt of the firm. [*Ex p. Manchester and Liverpool District Banking Co. [1924] 2 Ch. 199*]. Again, where a firm has assigned its property in trust for its creditors, whose rights against the separate estates of the partners are expressly reserved, a creditor who is both a joint and a separate creditor may claim the benefit of the assignment, and yet prove as a separate creditor against one of the firm if he becomes bankrupt. [*Ex p. Thornton (1858) 5 Jur. (N.S.) 212*; also *Ex p. Greaves (1856) 8 De G.M. & G. 291*]. Where, however, one partner only is bankrupt, and a joint creditor is secured by a mortgage of the bankrupt's separate estate, that creditor cannot prove as a separate creditor without giving up his security [*Ex p. West Riding Union Banking Co. (1881) 19 Ch.D. 105*]; and if the mortgage is a mere equitable mortgage giving the creditor no *locus standi* as a separate creditor and nothing more than a lien, he will not be a separate creditor of the bankrupt, or be allowed to prove against his separate estate at all. [*Ex p. Leicestershire Banking Co. (1846) 1 De Gex 292*; *Ex p. Lloyd (1838) 3 M. & A. 601*]." Note, however, that an equitable mortgage by deposit of title deeds may no longer be created: *United Bank of Kuwait v. Sahib, The Times,* July 7, 1994.

[9] *Ex p. Hunter* (1742) 1 Atk. 223; *Ex p. Emly* (1811) 1 Rose 61; *Lloyd v. Freshfield* (1826) 9 D. & R. 19. See also, *supra,* paras. 12–193 *et seq.*

[10] See *Ex p. Hargreaves* (1788) 1 Cox. 440; *Ex p. Reeve* (1804) 9 Ves.Jr. 588; *Ex p. Rawson* (1821) Jac. 274; *Ex p. Sillitoe* (1824) 1 Gl. & J. 374; *Ex p. Williams* (1843) 3 M.D. & D. 433; see also *Ex p. Mawde* (1867) 2 Ch. 550; *Ex p. Gliddon* (1884) 13 Q.B.D. 43.

creditors (for they are in no better position than himself) can compete with the joint creditors as against the joint estate. Lord Hardwicke, it is true, in *Ex p. Hunter*,[11] allowed this to be done; but that case has not, in this respect, been followed, and has long been considered as overruled."[12]

Holding out

A person who has rendered himself liable for joint debts on the **27-116** basis of holding out[13] will, as regards his ability to prove against the joint estate, be in no better position than a true partner.

Personal representatives of a deceased partner

Since a deceased partner's estate is liable for the debts of the **27-117** firm,[14] it follows from the general principle described above that, whilst such liability continues, his personal representatives will not be permitted to prove against the joint estate of the surviving partners for the amount due from them to his estate;[15] but, once such debts are paid or the estate freed from liability therefor,[16] such proof will be permitted.[17] Even then, the personal representatives may be prevented from proving in respect of any sum which they have brought into or left in the business as part of the deceased's capital. In such a case, their proof will in general only be admissible once all the debts contracted both before and after the death have been paid.[18] However, if that sum was brought into the business in breach of trust, it will not form part of the joint estate and proof will be

---

[11] (1742) 1 Atk. 223.

[12] *Ex p. Parker* (1780); *Ex p. Burrell* (1783); *Ex p. Pine* (1783), all cited in Cooke's *Bankruptcy Law* (8th ed.), p. 528; and see *Ex p. Harris* (1813) 1 Rose 438.

[13] See the Partnership Act 1890, s.14, *supra*, paras. 5–43 *et seq.*

[14] *Ibid.* s.9: see *supra*, paras. 13–03, 13–06 *et seq.*

[15] *Nanson v. Gordon* (1876) 1 App.Cas. 195; *Ex p. Blythe* (1881) 16 Ch.D. 620.

[16] *Ex p. Moore* (1826) 2 Gl. & J. 166. It is clear from the decision in *Ex p. Andrews* (1884) 25 Ch.D. 505 that the outstanding joint liabilities need not be paid: it is enough that there is no proof in respect of any of them. Note, however, that there was in that case no reason to suppose the debts ever would be proved.

[17] *Ex p. Edmonds* (1862) 4 De G.F. & J. 488; *Ex p. Executors of James Douglas* [1930] 1 Ch. 342.

[18] *Ex p. Butterfield* (1847) De Gex 570; *Ex p. Corbridge* (1876) 4 Ch.D. 246; see also *Ex p. Garland* (1804) 10 Ves.Jr. 110, where proof in respect of assets improperly employed in the business was admitted but proof in respect of assets properly employed rejected; *Ex p. Thompson* (1842) 2 M.D. & D. 761; *Scott v. Izon* (1865) 34 Beav. 434. *Cf. Ex p. Edmonds* (1862) 4 De G.F. & J. 488, where the money was continued in the business in the form of an interest bearing loan. Note that, in this case, the debts in respect of which the deceased's estate was liable had been paid, distinguishing it from *Nanson v. Gordon* (1876) 1 App.Cas. 195. See also *Ex p. Hill* (1837) 3 M. & A. 175; *Ex p. Crofts* (1837) 2 Deac. 102 (trust money lent to partners held to be provable as a joint debt); *Ex p. Executors of James Douglas* [1930] 1 Ch. 342. And note *Re Meade* [1951] Ch. 774, where an advance of money by the bankrupt's mistress to be employed in his business was held to be a contribution of capital and not a loan and so not provable.

allowed, even in competition with the joint creditors whose debts accrued during the deceased partner's lifetime;[19] *per contra*, if it was merely improperly *left* in the business.[20]

Two firms with common partner

27-118   The same principle may even be applied where a partner in one firm seeks to prove against the joint estate of another which shares a common partner. In this connection, Lord Lindley referred to the decision in *Ex p. Brown*,[21] the effect of which he summarised thus:

> "There, in substance, there were two firms, with a common partner, *viz.* A and B, and A and C: C had made himself separately liable for a debt owing by A and B; both firms became bankrupt. The principal creditor proved against C's separate estate, and received a dividend. A claim was then made on behalf of C's separate estate, to prove for the amount thus paid out of it against the joint estate of A and B. But it was held that this proof could not be allowed, for the principal creditor not having been paid in full, he had a right of proof against the joint estate of A and B, and that, consequently, C could not diminish that estate to his prejudice."

When a partner may compete with his own creditors

There are three established circumstances in which the principle under consideration will not apply, *viz.*:

(i)   *Fraud*

27-119 Where the separate property of one partner has been converted to the use of the firm by a fraud practised by the other partners, proof on behalf of his separate estate in competition with the joint creditors will be allowed in respect of such property.[22]

---

[19] *Ex p. Garland* (1804) 10 Ves.Jr. 110; *Ex p. Westcott* (1874) L.R. 9 Ch. 626. See also *supra*, paras. 26–23 *et seq.*

[20] The current editor submits that, in such a case, proof will not be allowed unless the debts of the firm contracted during the deceased partner's lifetime have been paid.

[21] (1842) 2 M.D. & D. 718; also *Ex p. Rawson* (1821) Jac. 274.

[22] *Ex p. Sillitoe* (1824) 1 Gl. & J. 374, 382, *per* Lord Eldon; also *Ex p. Harris* (1813) 1 Rose 437. *Quaere* whether, in such a case, it must be shown that there is an overall balance due to the defrauded partner on the taking of the partnership accounts before the proof will be allowed: see *Ex p. Maude* (1867) L.R. 2 Ch. 550 (a case of distinct trades: see *infra*, paras. 27–120 *et seq.*). As to the position where a partner fraudulently converts partnership property into his own separate property, see *infra*, para. 27–137.

(ii) *Distinct trades*

Lord Lindley summarised this exception in the following way: **27–120**

> "If one of two firms, carrying on distinct trades, becomes creditor
> of the other in the ordinary way of their trade, the creditor firm
> may prove against the joint estate of the debtor firm, in
> competition with its other joint creditors, although one or more
> persons may be partners in both firms."[23]

If the two firms merely have one or more partners in common, *e.g.*
one firm comprising A and B and the other comprising B and C,
either firm may in any event rank as a joint creditor of the other,
because the creditors of the one are not creditors of the other.[24]

Where, however, all the partners of one firm are partners of the **27–121**
other, *e.g.* one firm comprising A, B and C ("the ABC Partnership")
and the other comprising A and B ("the AB Partnership"), the
ability to prove will vary according to which firm is the creditor.
Whilst all the creditors of the ABC Partnership are inevitably
creditors of the AB partnership, the converse proposition does not
hold good. Consequently, although the ABC Partnership does not
compete with its own creditors if it seeks to prove against the joint
estate of the AB Partnership, the AB Partnership must necessarily do
so if it seeks to prove against the joint estate of the ABC partnership.
Although Lord Lindley pointed out that this had long been settled
law,[25] he went on:

> "However, it seems now settled that if the two trades are distinct,
> and if the larger firm has become indebted to the smaller in the
> regular way of their trades,[26] the smaller firm may prove, like any
> other joint creditor, against the joint estate of the larger. This was
> decided in *Ex p. Cook*,[27] where one partner, who carried on a
> separate business, was allowed to rank as a joint creditor against
> the joint estate of the firm of which he was a member, and which

---

[23] *Ex p. Cook* (1831) Mont. 228; also *Ex p. Ring* (1796), *Ex p. Freeman* (1796), *Ex p. Johns*
(1802), cited in Cooke's *Bankruptcy Law* (8th ed.), p. 534. *Cf. Ex p. Gliddon* (1884) 13 Q.B.D. 43.
It should be noted that Lord Lindley had earlier summarised this exception in these terms: "Where
there are two distinct trades, carried on by the firm, and by one or more of the members of it, *with
distinct capitals*" (emphasis supplied). The reference to distinct capitals is somewhat misleading: it
relates to the existence of two separate joint estates against which debts can be proved, rather than
to the manner in which each trade is financed.

[24] *Ex p. Thompson* (1834) 3 D. & Ch. 612.

[25] As to proof by the larger firm, see *Ex p. St. Barbe* (1805) 11 Ves.Jr. 413; *Ex p. Hesham* (1810)
1 Rose 146; *Ex p. Castell* (1826) 2 Gl. & J. 124; as to proof by the smaller firm, see *Ex p.
Hargreaves* (1788) 1 Cox 440; *Ex p. Adams* (1812) 1 Rose 305; *Ex p. Sillitoe* (1824) 1 Gl. & J. 374.

[26] This is essential: see also *infra*, paras. 27–139, 27–140.

[27] (1831) Mont. 228.

had become indebted to him in the ordinary way of their and his respective trades."

If this exception is to apply, two fundamental conditions must be fulfilled. First, there must be two distinct trades: if the smaller firm is merely a branch of the larger and is in truth carrying on a part of the latter's business, the condition will not be satisfied and the proof will be disallowed.[28] Secondly, the debt sought to be proved must have arisen from dealings between the two firms in the ordinary way of business,[29] and must *not* have been converted into a mere personal debt.[30]

27-122   However, even if these conditions are satisfied, it would seem that no proof will be allowed unless it can be shown that the partnership accounts have been taken and that a balance is due to the proving partner(s).[31]

(iii) *Discharge of bankrupt partner*

27-123 Where a partner has been discharged from bankruptcy[32] or has otherwise been discharged from the joint debts,[33] and has subsequently become a creditor of the firm,[34] he will no longer be a debtor *vis-à-vis* the joint creditors of the firm and will, accordingly, not be competing with his own creditors.

Partnership not yet commenced

27-124   Although it does not, unlike the cases considered in the preceding paragraphs, strictly represent an exception to the general principle, it should be noted that there is no restriction on the right of proof in the case of a person who merely *intends* to enter into partnership, provided that he has not already been held out as a partner and thereby rendered himself liable for the joint debts. This is illustrated by the decision in *Ex p. Turquand*[35] where, in substance, A had

---

[28] *Ex p. Hargreaves* (1788) 1 Cox 440.
[29] *Ex p. Sillitoe* (1824) 1 Gl. & J. 374; *Ex p. Williams* (1843) 3 M.D. & D. 433; also *Ex p. Maude* (1867) L.R. 2 Ch. 550.
[30] *Ex p. Kaye* (1892) 9 Morr. 269.
[31] *Ex p. Maude* (1867) L.R. 2 Ch. App. 550.
[32] See, as to the effect of such a discharge, the Insolvency Act 1986, s.281. And note also, as to the position between the partners, *Wood v. Dodgson* (1813) 2 M. & S. 195; and see *Wright v. Hunter* (1800) 1 East 20; *Ex p. Carpenter* (1826) Mont. & MacA. 1; *Aflalo v. Fourdrinier* (1829) 6 Bing. 306.
[33] *e.g.* by a compromise or by limitation. See *Ex p. Executors of James Douglas* [1930] 1 Ch. 342, 350, *per* Luxmoore J.; also *Ex p. Smith* (1884) 14 Q.B.D. 394.
[34] *Ex p. Atkins* (1820) Buck 479; *Ex p. Smith* (1884) 14 Q.B.D. 394.
[35] (1841) 2 M.D. & D. 339. See also *Ex p. Hickin* (1850) 3 De G. & Sm. 662; *Ex p. Davis* (1863) 4 De G.J. & Sm. 523. Note that, where money is advanced for a particular purpose which fails, it may, in appropriate circumstances, be claimed that the money is held upon a resulting trust for the person making the advance: see *Barclays Bank v. Quistclose Investments* [1970] A.C. 567; *Carreras Rothmans Ltd. v. Freeman Mathews Treasure Ltd.* [1985] Ch. 207.

agreed to enter into partnership with B and C, who were already carrying on business in partnership under the names B and C. A was to bring in a certain sum of cash and the firm name was to be altered to B, C & Co. A advanced the cash to B and C and the firm name was duly altered, but no partnership agreement was signed; A refused to proceed any further until he was satisfied as to B and C's solvency. There was no evidence of holding out. On B and C's bankruptcy, A was allowed to prove for the advance he had made.

(c) Rights of separate creditors

Lord Lindley observed that: 27–125

"The principle which prohibits a partner from competing with the joint creditors of the firm evidently has no application as between one partner and the separate creditors of his co-partners. Moreover, the lien which each partner has upon the assets of the firm[36] must be satisfied before any part of the joint estate can be divided amongst the members of the firm, or, which comes to the same thing, be carried to the account of their respective separate estates."[37]

The current editor submits that this still represents a correct statement of the position under the current insolvency legislation, albeit that a partner's lien will be unenforceable against the liquidator (and, in any event, largely irrelevant) where a firm is wound up as an unregistered company.[38] The Insolvent Partnerships Order 1986 expressly directs that any surplus in the joint estate should be carried to the partners' separate estates "in proportion to the right and interest of each ... partner in the joint estate."[39]

Where a partner's lien is exercisable, it may effectively prefer his 27–126 separate creditors over the separate creditors of any partner who cannot exercise such a lien.[40] If, in such a case, the joint estate is not sufficient to satisfy the lien, the deficiency will be provable against the separate estates of the other partners liable therefor.[41]

---

[36] See generally, as to this lien, *supra*, paras. 19–28 *et seq.*
[37] See *Ex p. Reeve* (1804) 9 Ves.Jr. 588; *Ex p. King* (1810) 17 Ves.Jr. 115; *Ex p. Reid* (1814) 2 Rose 84; *Ex p. Terrell* (1819) Buck 345; *Holderness v. Shackels* (1828) 8 B. & C. 612; *Fereday v. Wightwick* (1829) Tam. 250.
[38] See *supra*, para. 19–42.
[39] *Ibid.* art. 10(4), *supra*, para. 27–85. Note the terms of the proviso, which requires interest to be paid only on the *solvent* partners' shares of the joint debts.
[40] *Ex p. King, supra*; *Ex p. Reid* (1814) 2 Rose 84. As to the circumstances in which a partner may lose his lien, see *supra*, paras. 19–40, 19–41.
[41] *Ex p. King, supra*; *Ex p. Terrell* (1819) Buck 345; *Ex p. Watson* (1819) Buck 449; also *Ex p. Moore* (1826) 2 Gl. & J. 172.

Surplus of joint estate

27-127   When the surplus joint estate is divided between the partners'
separate estates, according to their respective entitlements,[42] it will
effectively cease to form part of the joint estate and thereafter be
comprised in those partners' separate estates. However, it is
submitted that, as under the old bankruptcy law,[43] joint estate which
is prematurely divided must be restored by the recipients.[44]

B.   PROOF AGAINST THE SEPARATE ESTATES

27-128 As in the case of proof against the joint estate, it is most convenient
to consider this subject under three headings, namely:

(*a*)   The rights of the separate creditors.
(*b*)   The rights of the joint creditors.
(*c*)   The rights of the partners.

(a)   Rights of separate creditors

27-129 It has already been seen that, where questions of priority arise, a
partner's separate debts are primarily payable out of his separate
estate.[45] Interest is not payable on such debts where the firm is
insolvent, unless there are independent administrations.[46]

A partner's separate debts will in general rank *pari passu*, unless
they are preferential[47] or due either to his spouse[48] or under a
contract to which section 3 of the Partnership Act 1890 applies[49] or
which provides for the creditor's rights to be postponed.[50]

---

[42] See, in particular, the Insolvent Partnerships Order 1986, art. 10(4), *supra*, para. 27-85.

[43] See *Ex p. Lanfear* (1813) 1 Rose 442.

[44] In the case of a firm wound up as an unregistered company, the partners would in any event
be liable to have calls made upon them in respect of any deficiency in the joint estate: see *supra*,
paras. 27-60 *et seq.*

[45] See *supra*, paras. 27-82, 27-85 *et seq.*

[46] Insolvent Partnerships Order 1986, art. 10(3), *supra*, para. 27-85. *Per contra* where that Order
does not apply: see *supra*, para. 27-87.

[47] Insolvency Act 1986, ss.175, 189 (as amended, where relevant, by the Insolvent Partnerships
Order 1986, Sched. 2, Pt. II, para. 16), s.328 (as amended, where relevant, by the Insolvent
Partnerships Order 1986, Sched. 2, Pt. III, para. 23). But see also, in the case of fraudulent and
wrongful trading, *ibid.* s.215(4). As to what debts are treated as preferential, see *ibid.* s.386, Sched.
6 (as amended).

[48] *Ibid.* s.329. This will seemingly not preclude a partner's spouse from proving against the joint
estate of the firm in respect of a loan to that partner and his/her co-partners jointly: see *Ex p.
Nottingham* (1887) 19 Q.B.D. 88 (a decision under the Married Women's Property Act 1882, s.3).

[49] See *supra*, paras. 5-40 *et seq.* And see also the Insolvent Partnerships Order 1986, art. 10(2),
(7), *supra*, para. 27-85.

[50] See *Re Maxwell Communications Corporation plc* [1993] 1 W.L.R. 1402, distinguishing
National Westminster Bank Ltd. v. Halesowen Presswork & Assemblies Ltd. [1972] A.C. 785, H.L.
and *British Eagle International Air Lines Ltd. v. Compagnie Nationale Air France* [1975] 1 W.L.R.
758, H.L.

Secured creditors

The rights of a secured creditor have already been noticed in **27–130**
relation to the joint estate.[51]

(b) Rights of joint creditors

Lord Lindley observed that, save in certain exceptional cases: **27–131**

"... the joint creditors of partners[52] are not entitled to payment
out of their separate estates, in competition with their separate
creditors."[53]

Before considering the exceptions to the general principle, it should
be noted that, where the joint and separate estates are being
administered independently, proof against both estates by a joint
creditor would seem to be possible.[54]

When joint creditors may compete with separate creditors

Under the old bankruptcy law, there were four cases in which such **27–132**
competition was allowed, notwithstanding the general principle to
which Lord Lindley referred. The current editor submits that these
exceptions are equally applicable under the current insolvency
legislation.[55]

(i)   *No joint estate*

Where there is no joint estate, the joint creditors are entitled to rank **27–133**
as separate creditors against the separate estates of the individual
partners;[56] *per contra* where there is a joint estate, however small.[57]

---

[51] See *supra*, paras. 27–113, 27–114.

[52] As to joint debtors who are not partners, see *Ex p. Crosfield* (1836) 1 Deac. 405; *Ex p. Buckingham* (1840) 1 M.D. & D. 235; *Ex p. Field* (1842) 3 M.D. & D. 95.

[53] Lord Lindley went on: "The Bankruptcy Act 1883 mentions no exceptions, and it has not yet been decided that there are any; owing to the language of section 59(1) it is doubtful whether they exist in cases where one partner only is bankrupt. But it would be strange if the exceptions existed (and it is apprehended that the first three do exist) where a separate estate is administered under a joint adjudication against a firm, and not where the separate property of one partner is administered under an adjudication against himself alone." The equivalent provision under the Bankruptcy Act 1914 was s.63(1).

[54] See the Insolvent Partnerships Order 1986, art. 15(3). See further, *supra*, para. 27–79.

[55] See, in particular, *ibid.* art. 10(7), *supra*, para. 27–85; also *supra*, para. 27–110.

[56] *Re Carpenter* (1890) 7 Morr. 270; *Re Budgett* [1894] 2 Ch. 557.

[57] *Ex p. Peake* (1814) 2 Rose 54; *Ex p. Harris* (1816) 1 Madd. 583; *Ex p. Kennedy* (1852) 2 De G.M. & G. 228. *Cf. Ex p. Birley* (1841) 2 M.D. & D. 354; *Ex p. Burdekin* (1842) 2 M.D. & D. 704. It would seem that the existence of joint property which is pledged for more than its value or which cannot, for any reason, be made available for the benefit of creditors will be ignored: *Ex p. Hill* (1802) 2 Bos. & Pul.N.R. 191, note; *Ex p. Peake, supra*; *Ex p. Geller* (1817) 2 Madd. 262; but see *Ex p. Clay* (1808) 1 Mont.Part. 132, note; *Ex p. Kennedy, supra*. A joint creditor holding such a pledge must sell it or have it valued before he can claim to rank as a separate creditor; until he has done so, he cannot say that there is no joint estate: see *Ex p. Smith* (1813) 2 Rose 63; *Ex p. Barclay* (1822) 1 Gl. & J. 272. In *Ex p. Hill, supra*, the pledge had been sold, and the creditor proved for the difference.

This exception might entitle a joint creditor to rank as a separate creditor of a single bankrupt partner,[58] if there are no apparent partners who are solvent.[59] For this purpose, no account will seemingly be taken of the existence of a dormant[60] or deceased[61] partner, even though he, or his estate, may be solvent. The position will be the same where a number of firms enter into partnership together and one becomes insolvent, save only that it will be necessary for the joint creditors of the main partnership to show that all the partners in the solvent firms are abroad before they can prove against the insolvent firm's joint estate.[62]

If it is doubtful whether any joint estate exists, an inquiry will be directed.[63]

27–134   *Firm wound up as unregistered company.*   In such a case, the liquidator has power to make calls on the partners *qua* contributories,[64] and may thereby himself constitute a joint estate where none previously existed.

27–135   *Subsequent realisation of joint estate.*   If joint creditors prove against the separate estate of a partner on the footing that there is no joint estate, but such an estate is subsequently realised, they must repay any dividend received.[65]

27–136   *Joint creditors paying separate creditors.*   Joint creditors can acquire a right to prove against the separate estate of any partner by paying his separate creditors the full amount of their provable debts.[66]

(ii)   *Fraud*

27–137   If a partner fraudulently converts partnership property to his own use, such property cannot properly be treated as part of his separate estate. Consequently, in such a case, proof on behalf of the joint

---

[58] See *Ex p. Hayden* (1785) 1 Bro.C.C. 454; *Ex p. Sadler* (1808) 15 Ves.Jr. 52; *Ex p. Bradshaw* (1821) 1 Gl. & J. 99; *Ex p. Bauerman* (1838) 3 Deac. 476.

[59] See *Ex p. Kensington* (1813) 14 Ves.Jr. 447; *Ex p. Janson* (1818) 3 Madd. 229. The latter case demonstrates that, for this purpose, a person is solvent if he is not bankrupt. As to the position where the solvent partner is not in this country, see *Ex p. Pinkerton* (1801) 6 Ves.Jr. 814, note.

[60] See *Ex p. Hodgkinson* (1815) 19 Ves.Jr. 291; *Ex p. Norfolk* (1815) 19 Ves. Jr. 455; *Ex p. Chuck* (1832) 8 Bing. 469.

[61] See *Ex p. Bauerman* (1838) 3 Deac. 476. The surviving partner's separate creditors cannot insist on the joint creditors proceeding first against the deceased partner's estate: see *Ex p. Kendall* (1811) 17 Ves.Jr. 514.

[62] *Ex p. Machel* (1813) 1 Rose 447; *Ex p. Nolte* (1826) 2 Gl. & J. 295.

[63] *Ex p. Birley* (1840) 1 M.D. & D. 387 and (1841) 2 M.D. & D. 354.

[64] See *supra*, paras. 27–60 *et seq.*

[65] See *Ex p. Willock* (1816) 2 Rose 392.

[66] See *Ex p. Chandler* (1803) 9 Ves.Jr. 35; *Ex p. Taitt* (1809) 16 Ves.Jr. 193.

estate (and, thus, the joint creditors) is admitted against the separate estate in competition with the separate creditors,[67] even though the value of the latter estate may not have been increased by the fraud.[68]

The mere fact that one partner is indebted to the firm is naturally **27–138** no proof of fraud; nor is a breach of the agreement, particularly if its provisions have habitually been ignored by the partners. What is required is an act tantamount to the theft of partnership property and a breach of good faith which has not been condoned by the other partners.[69] Any arrangement between the partners which results in the debt arising by reason of the fraud being treated as a mere matter of accounting between the partners will prevent any proof by the joint estate.[70]

(iii) *Distinct trades*

The circumstances in which a partner who carries on a distinct trade **27–139** will be permitted to prove against the joint estate of his firm in competition with the joint creditors have already been noticed.[71] On the same principle, the firm[72] or, if it is insolvent, the joint estate[73] will be permitted to prove against the separate estate of a partner in competition with his separate creditors, provided that he became indebted to the firm in the ordinary course of carrying on a similarly distinct trade.[74] Lord Eldon stated the principle thus: "... a joint trade may prove against a separate trade; but not a partner against a partner."[75]

An attempt to invoke this principle failed in *Ex p. Gliddon*,[76] **27–140** where there appeared to be two wholly independent firms but, in fact, one was no more than the agent of a partner in the other and there was no such trading between the two supposed firms as was necessary to create a provable debt.[77]

---

[67] *Ex p. Cust* (1774) Cooke's *Bankruptcy Law* (8th ed.), p. 531; *Ex p. Lodge and Fendal* (1790) 1 Ves.Jr. 166; *Ex p. Smith* (1821) 1 Gl. & J. 74; *Ex p. Watkins* (1828) Mont. & McA. 57. See also, as to the converse situation (*i.e.* where a partner's separate property is fraudulently converted to the use of the firm by his co-partners), *supra*, para. 27–119.

[68] *Lacey v. Hill* (1876) 4 Ch.D. 537, affirmed *sub nom. Read v. Bailey* (1877) 3 App.Cas. 94.

[69] See *Ex p. Yonge* (1814) 3 V. & B. 31; *Ex p. Smith* (1821) 1 Gl. & J. 74; *Ex p. Turner* (1833) 4 D. & Ch. 169; *Ex p. Crofts* (1837) 2 Deac. 102; *Ex p. Hinds* (1850) 3 De. G. & Sm. 613.

[70] See *Ex p. Turner* (1833) 4 D. & Ch. 169.

[71] See *supra*, paras. 27–120 *et seq.*

[72] *Ex p. Johns* (1802) Cooke's *Bankruptcy Law* (8th ed.), p. 534 and *Watson on Partnership*, p. 286; *Ex p. Hesham* (1810) 1 Rose 146; *Ex p. Castell* (1826) 2 Gl. & J. 124.

[73] *Ex p. St. Barbe* (1805) 11 Ves.Jr. 413.

[74] See *Ex p. Hargreaves* (1788) 1 Cox 440; *Ex p. Sillitoe* (1824) 1 Gl. & J. 382; *Ex p. Williams* (1843) 3 M.D. & D. 433; also *supra*, para. 27–121.

[75] *Ex p. St. Barbe* (1805) 11 Ves.Jr. 413, 414.

[76] (1884) 13 Q.B.D. 43.

[77] In fact, the real debt was owing by the principal behind the "agent" firm to himself and his co-partner.

(iv) *Petitioning creditor*

27–141 Where the petitioning creditor is a joint creditor, he will be permitted to prove in competition with the separate creditors.[78]

(c) **Rights of the partners**

27–142 One partner will not be permitted to prove against the separate estate of his co-partner if, by so doing, he will reduce the surplus available for transfer to the joint estate. Lord Lindley analysed the position in this way:

> "The principle that a debtor shall not be allowed to compete with his own creditors, is as strictly carried out in administering the separate estates of individual partners, as in administering the joint estate of a firm. The separate estate of each partner is liable to the debts of the firm, subject only to the prior claims of his separate creditors; whence it is obvious that one partner cannot compete with the separate creditors of his co-partner, without diminishing the fund which, subject to their claims, is applicable to the payment of the joint debts, and therefore of his own creditors. In other words, the rights of the joint creditors preclude one partner from ranking as a separate creditor of his co-partner, until the joint creditors are paid in full."[79]

The same rule will in general prevent the insolvent partner's firm proving a debt against his separate estate, since this would involve a proof by that partner and his co-partners.[80]

When co-partners can compete with separate creditors

27–143 Notwithstanding the rule described in the preceding paragraph, there are a number of circumstances in which a co-partner will be permitted to prove in competition with the separate creditors.

(i) *Joint creditors not prejudiced*

27–144 If it can be shown that proof by the co-partner will not involve competition with the joint creditors, there will be no reason to invoke the rule and competition with the separate creditors will be allowed.

---

[78] See *Ex p. Hall* (1804) 9 Ves.Jr. 349; *Ex p. Ackerman* (1808) 14 Ves.Jr. 604; *Ex p. De Tastet* (1810) 17 Ves.Jr. 247; *Ex p. Burnett* (1841) 2 M.D. & D. 357.
[79] See *Ex p. Collinge* (1863) 4 De G.J. & S. 533, where the result of such proof would have benefited the joint creditors; also *Ex p. Rawson* (1821) Jac. 274; *Ex p. Carter* (1827) 2 Gl. & J. 233; *Ex p. Ellis* (1827) 2 Gl. & J. 312; *Ex p. Robinson* (1834) 4 D. & Ch. 499; *Ex p. May* (1838) 3 Deac. 382.
[80] See *Ex p. Smith* (1821) 1 Gl. & J. 74; *Ex p. Turner* (1833) 4 D. & Ch. 169.

The fact that the latter will thereby be prejudiced is of no relevance, since the rule was not developed for their benefit. There will be no competition with the joint creditors in the following cases:

No joint debts. If there never were any joint debts or such joint **27–145** debts as there were have ceased to exist,[81] because they have been paid or satisfied, statute-barred or converted into separate debts,[82] proof will be allowed.[83] It is *not*, however, sufficient for the co-partner merely to offer an indemnity against such debts.[84]

Separate estate insolvent. If the separate estate is clearly insuffi- **27–146** cient to pay the separate debts, excluding that owed to the co-partner, there will be no possibility of any surplus being transferred to the joint estate for the benefit of the joint creditors and the co-partner's proof will be allowed.[85] No objection can be taken to such proof on the grounds that the dividends received will eventually go to swell the surplus of the co-partner's separate estate divisible among the joint creditors.[86]

Co-partner paying joint debts. If the co-partner has paid the joint **27–147** debts, he will be entitled to prove as a separate creditor for the amount of the share which the insolvent partner ought to have paid.[87]

Where the right to prove is established, it will generally be necessary to take the partnership accounts before the proof is admitted, since the alleged debt may in fact not exist.[88]

---

[81] It appears to be sufficient to show that the joint debts have not been, and are not likely to be, proved: see *Ex p. Andrews* (1884) 25 Ch.D. 505.

[82] See *Ex p. Grazebrook* (1832) 2 D. & Ch. 186.

[83] *Ex p. Grazebrook, supra; Ex p. Head* [1894] 1 Q.B. 638. See also *Ex p. Hall* (1838) 3 Deac. 125; *Ex p. Gill* (1863) 9 Jur.(n.s.) 1303. In *Ex p. Dodgson* (1830) Mont. & MacA. 445, there were no joint debts; similarly in *Ex p. Davis* (1863) 4 De G.J. & S. 523.

[84] *Ex p. Moore* (1826) 2 Gl. & J. 166. *Cf.* the earlier cases: *Ex p. Taylor* (1814) 2 Rose 175; *Ex p. Ogilvy* (1814) 2 Rose 177.

[85] *Ex p. Topping* (1865) 4 De G.J. & S. 551; *Ex p. Head* [1894] 1 Q.B. 638. See also *Ex p. Sheen* (1877) 6 Ch.D. 235, where the proof was by a person who had held himself out as a partner.

[86] *Ex p. Head, supra.*

[87] See *Wood v. Dodgson* (1813) 2 M. & S. 195; *Ex p. Watson* (1819) 4 Madd. 477; *Ex p. Carpenter* (1826) Mont. & MacA. 1. In the first two cases the partner who had paid the debts had retired and been indemnified against them by the bankrupt partner. It seemingly does not matter whether the debts were paid before or after the insolvency order: *ibid.* See also *Ex p. Young* (1814) 2 Rose 40; *Parker v. Ramsbottom* (1824) 3 B. & C. 257; *Moody v. King* (1825) 2 B. & C. 558. It should be noted that the amount provable is not calculated merely by reference to the partners' respective shares, with no account being taken of their ability to pay; rather, each partner is liable to contribute not only his own share of the debts but also a share of any amount due from the other partners, which they are unable to contribute, *i.e.* those who can pay must make up for those who cannot: see *Ex p. Hunter* (1820) Buck 552; *Ex p. Moore* (1826) 2 Gl. & J. 166; *Ex p. Plowden* (1837) 2 Deac. 456. *Cf.* the position when settling accounts as between partners: see *supra*, paras. 25–45 *et seq.*

[88] See *Ex p. Maude* (1867) L.R. 2 Ch.App. 550; and note *Ex p. Grazebrook* (1832) 2 D. & Ch. 186.

(ii) *Fraud*

27–148 The right of proof in the case of the fraudulent conversion of partnership property has already been noted.[89]

In addition, where a person is fraudulently induced to enter into partnership, he may prove against the separate estate of the person who practised the fraud for any amount paid to him as consideration for admission to the partnership.[90]

(iii) *Distinct Trades*

27–149 The circumstances in which proof for a debt contracted by a partner in the normal course of carrying on a distinct trade will be allowed have already been noted.[91]

Partnership not yet commenced

27–150 If a person intends to enter into partnership with another but does not ultimately do so, he may prove against the latter's separate estate for any advances he may have made in anticipation of such partnership, provided that he has not permitted himself to be held out as a partner.[92]

Surplus of separate estate

27–151 Once all his separate creditors have been paid, the surplus in a partner's separate estate will be transferred to the joint estate.[93] If he was in fact a member of several insolvent firms, that surplus must be divided between the various joint estates in proportion to the amount of the debts proved against each such estate.[94]

---

[89] *Ex p. Yonge* (1814) 3 V. & B. 31 and 2 Rose 40. See further, *supra*, paras. 27–137, 27–138.

[90] Lord Lindley observed that: "At one time it was supposed that when a person had been induced, by the fraud of another to join him in partnership, the former could not, on the bankruptcy of the latter, prove against his separate estate, for the amount paid to the bankrupt as a consideration for the partnership. This opinion was founded on the case of *Ex p. Broome* [*(1811) 1 Rose 69*]. There A was induced, by the false and fraudulent representations of B, to enter into partnership with him, and to pay him a considerable premium. Shortly afterwards B became bankrupt, and A sought to recover out of B's estate the amount of the premium paid as above mentioned. According to the report this was refused, upon the ground that, although A might be entitled to recover the money as between himself and B, yet he was liable with B to third persons, *viz.* the creditors of the firm. The report of this case, however, is not warranted by the order which was actually made in it. [*See the order in (1845) 1 Coll. 598.*] Indeed, the order expressly directed that A should be at liberty to prove against B's estate, and that A should be paid a dividend in respect of his proof, rateably with B's other creditors. This order is in conformity with the opinion expressed by Lord Thurlow in *Ex p. Lodge and Fendal* [*(1790) 1 Ves.Jr. 166*], and with the cases of *Hamil v. Stokes* [*(1817) 4 Price 161*] and *Bury v. Allen* [*(1845) 1 Coll. 589*]."

[91] See *Ex p. Maude* (1867) L.R. 2 Ch. 550; also *supra*, paras. 27–120 *et seq.*, 27–139, 27–140.

[92] *Ex p. Turquand* (1841) 2 M.D. & D. 339, *supra*, para. 27–124. Note also *Ex p. Megarey* (1845) De Gex. 167.

[93] See the Insolvent Partnerships Order 1986, art. 10(3), *supra*, paras. 27–85, 27–108.

[94] *Ex p. Franklyn* (1819) Buck 332.

C.   Proof Against Both Joint and Separate Estates

Rights of joint and separate creditors

It has already been seen that partners will only rarely be treated as **27–152** having undertaken joint and several liability to creditors of the firm, thus giving the latter the option of suing all the partners jointly or one or more of them separately.[95] Nevertheless, under the old bankruptcy law, special considerations affected the right of proof of such joint and separate creditors and it is possible that such considerations may still be of relevance under the current insolvency legislation.

The general rule

The general rule was formulated by Lord Lindley in this way: **27–153**

"... a person to whom the members of a firm are bound jointly and severally is not allowed in bankruptcy to rank as a creditor both against the joint estate and also against the separate estates, or any of them; he is compelled to elect whether he will rank as joint creditor or as a separate creditor.[96] If he elects to rank as a joint creditor he must, like other joint creditors, go in the first place against the joint estate, and he has no greater rights than they against the separate estates, or any of them; whilst, on the other hand, if he elects to rank as a separate creditor he must, like other separate creditors, confine himself in the first place to the separate estate, and he has no greater rights than they to the joint estate."[97]

An election was required even though the creditor became a joint creditor under one instrument and a separate creditor under another, provided that the debt was one and the same.[98] The position was, however, otherwise if the creditor could not properly be regarded as a joint and separate creditor. Thus, if, following a dissolution, one partner agreed to take over all the firm's debts, that arrangement would not affect a creditor of the firm unless he acceded to it: only when he had done so could he properly be treated as a separate creditor of that partner.[99]

---

[95] See *supra*, paras. 13–02 *et seq*.
[96] See *Ex p. Rowlandson* (1735) 3 P.W. 405; *Ex p. Banks* (1740) 1 Atk. 106; *Ex p. Bond* (1742) 1 Atk. 98; *Ex p. Bevan* (1804) 10 Ves.Jr. 106; *Ex p. Hay* (1808) 15 Ves.Jr. 4.
[97] *Ex p. Bevan* (1804) 10 Ves.Jr. 106; *Bradley v. Millar* (1812) 1 Rose 273.
[98] *Ex p. Hill* (1837) 2 Deac. 249.
[99] *Ex p. Freeman* (1819) Buck 471; *Ex p. Fry* (1821) 1 Gl. & J. 96; see also *supra*, paras. 27–98, 27–99.

27–154 Where an election was required to be made, the creditor was entitled to know how the joint and separate estates stood before being forced to make a binding election.[1]

Exceptions to the general rule

27–155 The general rule was originally subject to an exception in the case of separate trades[2] but was effectively abolished, as regards contracts, by the Bankruptcy Acts,[3] so much so that Lord Lindley observed:

> "The old rule against double proof still remains; but it is now subject to so large a class of exceptions as to render the rule itself practically of little consequence."

Accordingly, the application of the rule was in real terms confined to torts, frauds and breaches of trust.

Position under Insolvency Act 1986

27–156 In the absence of any equivalent provision in the Insolvency Act 1986 or the rules made thereunder, it is unclear whether the rule against double proof still exists. Even if it does, it is tentatively submitted that article 10(7) of the Insolvent Partnerships Order 1986[4] could not operate to revive its application as regards contracts; sed quaere.

Secured joint and separate creditors

27–157 Even where the rule against double proof applied, a joint and separate creditor with a security for his debt had two options, summarised by Lord Lindley in the following terms:

> "1. He may prove for his whole debt against the estate to which the security does not belong, and retain and make what he can of his security[5]; or

---

[1] Lord Lindley summarised the rights of the creditor thus: "... in order to make his election he must have a reasonable time to inquire into the state of the different funds. He is entitled to defer his election until a dividend is declared, or at least until the trustee is possessed of a fund to make a dividend": see Cooke's *Bankruptcy Law* (8th ed.), p. 275; *Ex p. Bond* (1742) 1 Atk. 98; *Ex p. Bentley* (1790) 2 Cox 218; *Ex p. Bolton* (1816) 2 Rose 389. It appears that the creditor ought properly to have proved against both estates, but elected before taking a dividend: *Ex p. Bentley* (1790) 2 Cox 218; and see also *Ex p. Bielby* (1806) 13 Ves.Jr. 70; *Ex p. Masson* (1811) 1 Rose 159; *Ex p. Dixon* (1841) 2 M.D. & D. 312. Presentation of a joint petition against a firm was regarded as a prima facie election to be treated as a joint creditor; *per contra* in the case of a separate petition against one of the partners: *Ex p. Bolton* (1816) 2 Rose 390, 391, *per* Lord Eldon; see also, as to withdrawing a joint proof, *Ex p. Chandler* (1884) 13 Q.B.D. 50.
[2] See *Ex p. Adam* (1813) 1 V. & B. 493; *Ex p. Bigg* (1814) 2 Rose 37.
[3] Bankruptcy Act 1861, s.152; Bankruptcy Act 1869, s.37; Bankruptcy Act 1883, Sched. II, r. 18; Bankruptcy Act 1914, Sched. 2, r. 19.
[4] See *supra*, para. 27–85.
[5] As in *Ex p. Groom* (1837) 2 Deac. 265; *Ex p. Bate* (1838) 3 Deac. 358; *Ex p. Smyth* (1839) 3 Deac. 597. Lord Lindley observed in a footnote at this point that "He can now, it is apprehended, prove against the other estate for the difference between his debt and the value of the security."

2. He may give up his security; prove for the whole debt due on it (*i.e.*, the whole secured debt) against the estate to which the security belongs, and then prove for the residue of his debt against the other estate: thus in fact splitting his demand and proving for part against the joint estate, and for the residue against the separate estates of the partners, or *vice versa*."[6]

9. VOLUNTARY ARRANGEMENTS WITH CREDITORS

The Insolvency Act 1986 contains detailed provisions governing **27–158** voluntary arrangements entered into by insolvent companies[7] and insolvent individuals,[8] whether before or after insolvency orders are made. These provisions will not only be of relevance where independent insolvency proceedings are taken against one or more corporate or individual partners, but also where the firm is wound up as an unregistered company and an insolvency order is made against at least one partner on a concurrent petition,[9] where all the partners present a joint debtors' petition[10] and in any other case in which the court has jurisdiction to order their application.[11] In each of the latter instances, references in the Act to the creditors of the relevant corporate or individual partner will include references to the creditors of the partnership.[12]

Somewhat surprisingly, in view of the general approach adopted by **27–159** the Insolvent Partnerships Order 1986, there appears to be no mechanism whereby an arrangement can be proposed by the partnership or by the partners, unless each individual partner applies for an interim order[13] and the directors or liquidator of each corporate partner take steps to propose an arrangement;[14] nor can any arrangement be confined solely to the firm's joint creditors.[15] This is a potentially serious omission, given that a partnership may now be wound up as an unregistered company *without* concurrent orders being made against the partners.[16]

---

[6] *Ex p. Ladbroke* (1826) 2 Gl. & J. 81; *Ex p. Hill* (1837) 2 Deac. 249.

[7] Insolvency Act 1986, Pt. I, ss.1 *et seq*.

[8] *Ibid.* Pt. VIII, ss.252 *et seq*.

[9] Insolvent Partnerships Order 1986, art. 11. See, as to the procedure on concurrent petitions, *supra*, paras. 27–23 *et seq*.

[10] *Ibid.* art. 13(4), applying *ibid.* art. 11 "with the necessary modifications." See further, as to this procedure, *supra*, para. 27–45.

[11] See *ibid.* art. 14(1) (*supra*, para. 27–21), which would seem to entitle the court to apply *ibid.* art. 11 "with any necessary modifications".

[12] *Ibid.* art. 11.

[13] See the Insolvency Act 1986, ss.252, 253. Note, as to the rights of a creditor who does not accept the voluntary arrangement, *Re A Debtor (No. 2389 of 1989)* [1991] Ch. 326.

[14] See the Insolvency Act 1986, ss.1, 2.

[15] See *ibid.* ss.1(1), 253(1).

[16] At the time of writing, it seems likely that this omission will be remedied in the forthcoming revised Insolvent Partnerships Order.

Part Six

LIMITED PARTNERSHIPS

CHAPTER 28

INTRODUCTION

Nature of limited partnership

The essence of limited partnership is the combination in a firm of **28–01** (1) one or more partners whose liability for the debts and obligations of the firm is unlimited and who alone are entitled to manage the firm's affairs, and (2) one or more partners whose liability for such debts and obligations is limited in amount and who are *excluded* from all management functions.[1]

Such partnerships were, however, unknown to the law of England prior to January 1, 1908, when the Limited Partnerships Act 1907 came into force.[2] Pollock went so far as to observe:

"The institution of partnership *en commandite*, or limited partnership, as we may call it in English, is unknown in the United Kingdom, and in these kingdoms alone, or almost alone, among all the civilised countries of the world."[3]

Origins of limited partnership

Limited partnership or partnership *en commandite* is said to have **28–02** had its origins in Italy during the Middle Ages, and to have developed from a practice adopted by the nobility, for whom it was at the time disgraceful or unlawful to engage directly in trade. They circumvented this inhibition by investing in commercial enterprises indirectly, through trusted merchants, on the understanding that they, whilst not in name parties, would receive a share of any profits *without* accepting any liability for losses beyond the amount of their contributions.[4]

Introduction of limited partnership into England

The possible introduction of limited partnership into the laws of **28–03** England was considered and discussed from time to time during the last century. In a Departmental Report on the Law of Partnership

---

[1] Note that in Germany and Switzerland, a limited partner *may* take part in the firm's management: see *supra*, para. 2–44.

[2] See *Coope v. Eyre* (1788) 1 H.Bl. 37, 48, *per* Lord Loughborough L.C.J.

[3] *Essays on Jurisprudence and Ethics* (1882), p. 100.

[4] *Ibid.*; Troubat's *Law of Commandatory and Limited Partnership in the United States* (1853), p. 34; Law Review, Vol. 17 (1852–53), p. 352. See also *Ames v. Downing* (1850) 1 Brad. (New York Surrogates' Court), 321 and 329; *Jacquin v. Buisson* (1855) 11 How. (New York) Practice Reports 385.

made by Mr. Bellenden Ker to the President of the Board of Trade on March 1, 1837, it was stated that it would not be expedient to recommend the introduction of partnership *en commandite* until further information as to the operation of the law in other states had been obtained. In 1851, a Select Committee of the House of Commons was appointed—

> "to consider the Law of Partnership and the expediency of facilitating the Limitation of Liability with a view to encourage useful enterprise and the additional Employment of Labour."

The committee made their report on July 8, 1851, and while expressing themselves in favour of an easier means of borrowing additional capital without risk to the lender beyond the amount of the sum advanced, did no more than recommend the appointment of a Royal Commission to consider the question of limited and unlimited liability of partners.[5]

Bovill's Act

28–04 The Companies Act 1862 probably eased some of the pressure in favour of the introduction of limited partnership and then, in 1865, the Act generally known as Bovill's Act[6] was passed. As has already been seen,[7] this Act provided that, in certain cases, the receipt of a share of profits would not of itself constitute the recipient a partner or render him liable as such, but did not go so far as to enable a person to become a partner and at the same time avoid unlimited liability. The Act was, of course, in substance only declaratory of the principle laid down by the House of Lords in *Cox v. Hickman*[8] but when it was first passed it was generally supposed to have had more far reaching effects[9] and was popularly known as the Limited Partnership Act.[10]

Partnership Act 1890

28–05 After Bovill's Act, further attempts were made to introduce limited partnership but without success.[11] The Partnership Act 1890, while it repealed and re-enacted Bovill's Act, albeit with some modifica-

---

[5] Report of Select Committee H. of C. 1851, No. 509, p. viii.
[6] Partnership Act 1865 (28 & 29 Vict. c.86).
[7] See *supra*, para. 5–37.
[8] (1860) 8 H.L.Cas. 267. See *supra*, paras. 5–34 *et seq*.
[9] See *Holme v. Hammond* (1872) L.R. 7 Ex. 218, 232, *per* Bramwell B.
[10] See *Syers v. Syers* (1876) 1 App.Cas. 174, in which the Act was so referred to both in the agreement under consideration and in the judgments.
[11] See Pollock, *Digest of the Law of Partnership* (10th ed.), Preface, pp. vii and viii.

tions,[12] did not touch on the question of limited partnership, which was only addressed in the Limited Partnerships Act 1907.[13]

Limited Partnerships Act 1907

The Limited Partnerships Act 1907 for the first time under English **28–06** law enabled a partnership to be formed which did not display three of the essential characteristics of an ordinary or general partnership, namely:

(1) the unlimited liability of every partner;[14]
(2) the implied authority of each partner to bind the firm in all matters within the ordinary scope of the partnership business,[15] and
(3) the right of each partner, subject to any contrary agreement, to take part in the management of that business.[16]

The policy of the Act is to give any number of persons not **28–07** exceeding 20[17] the freedom, subject to certain registration requirements,[18] to enter into partnership on terms that the liability of some of them (who are styled "limited partners") will be limited to the amount contributed by them in cash or property when the partnership was originally created. However, it is a fundamental and unalterable condition that the liability of at least one of the partners (styled a "general partner") should be unlimited. Moreover, during the continuance of the partnership, a limited partner has no implied authority to bind the firm[19] and may neither be repaid any part of his capital contribution nor take part in the management of the firm, potentially severe penalties being imposed in the case of contravention of the latter prohibitions.[20] As a result, the limited partner is forced to adopt an essentially passive role akin to that of the more traditional dormant partner.

Application of the Partnership Act 1890 and the general law

It is important to bear in mind that, subject to the provisions of the **28–08** Limited Partnerships Act 1907, limited partnerships are governed by

---

[12] *Ibid.* ss.2, 48.
[13] The introduction of limited liability was recommended in the Report of the Company Law Amendment Committee appointed in 1905. See 1906 Cd. 3052, para. 89.
[14] Partnership Act 1890, s.9: see *supra*, paras. 13–03 *et seq.*
[15] *Ibid.* s.5: see *supra*, paras. 12–02 *et seq.*
[16] *Ibid.* s.24(5): *supra*, paras. 15–05 *et seq.*
[17] This limit may now be exceeded in the case of certain professional firms: see *infra*, para. 29–02.
[18] See *infra*, paras. 29–17 *et seq.*
[19] See *infra*, paras. 30–04 *et seq.* Note, however, that there is seemingly no penalty attached if a limited partner is, by agreement, given power to bind the firm: see *infra*, para. 30–06.
[20] See *infra*, paras. 30–11 *et seq.*, 31–04 *et seq.*

the Partnership Act 1890 and the rules of law and equity applicable to ordinary partnerships.[21] As a result, a formal partnership agreement will usually be indispensable.[22]

Popularity of limited partnership

28–09 The limited partnership has never been a vehicle that has attracted public attention or, for that matter, notoriety. As a result, at any given time there are relatively few of such partnerships on the register.[23] Nevertheless, they have on occasion been employed for tax planning purposes[24] and continue to enjoy an unusual prominence in the field of venture capital.[25]

28–10 In earlier editions of this work, after referring to the relative simplicity with which business can be carried on through the medium of a limited liability company, an attempt was made to summarise the perceived advantages of limited partnership in the following terms:

> "It may, perhaps, therefore be urged that there is not now any useful purpose to be served by limited partnership, but the following points in favour of limited partnership may be noted. First, where use is made of the Limited Partnerships Act 1907 the attendant publicity will be much less than in the case of a private company formed under the Companies Acts[26]; secondly, a return of capital from a limited company is not in ordinary circumstances practicable,[27] but this can be effected in the case of a limited partnership[28]; thirdly, limited partnerships are taxed in the same way as ordinary partnerships and are not subject to corporation tax; and fourthly, trustees can, if they have sufficiently wide powers of investment, safely participate in a limited partnership since they are not exposed to unlimited personal liability. A fifth factor used to be the not inconsiderable expense of forming a limited company as compared with forming a limited partnership,

---

[21] Limited Partnerships Act 1907, s.7.

[22] See, for example, the *Encyclopedia of Professional Partnerships*, Precedent 4. And see also the 8th and 9th eds. of this work.

[23] The number on the Register has steadily increased in recent years and, as at February 14, 1994, stood at 1962 in respect of England and Wales. The figure for Scotland as at that date was even higher at 2075, but for Northern Ireland was merely 5.

[24] See *Reed v. Young* [1986] 1 W.L.R. 649 (H.L.). The particular device under consideration in that case is, in fact, nullified by the Income and Corporation Taxes Act 1988, s.117: see *infra*, para. 34–72.

[25] See [1987] S.T.I. 783.

[26] But see, in the case of *corporate* limited partnerships, the Unlimited Companies (Accounts) Regulations 1993 (S.I. 1993 No. 1820), noticed *supra*, para. 22–08.

[27] Note, however, that a company may now in certain circumstances purchase its own shares: see the Companies Act 1985, ss. 162 *et seq*.

[28] *Quaere* to what extent this is so: see *infra*, paras. 30–12, 31–09, 31–20, 31–21.

but since the advent of ready-made companies this factor is no longer valid."[29]

The current editor suggests that few of the foregoing "advantages" can be regarded as having any current significance;[30] indeed, the form of limited partnership most commonly encountered today is likely to be composed almost exclusively of limited liability companies.

---

[29] See the 15th ed. of this work at page 928.
[30] Note, however, that the tax "transparency" of a partnership is regarded as a significant advantage in the field of venture capital.

CHAPTER 29

NATURE, FORMATION, DURATION AND REGISTRATION
OF LIMITED PARTNERSHIPS

29–01 A limited partnership is not a legal entity like a limited company[1] but a form of partnership with a number of special characteristics introduced by the Limited Partnerships Act 1907. Although it is necessary to ensure strict compliance with the statutory conditions if the benefit of limited liability is to be obtained,[2] such a partnership is otherwise governed by the general law.[3]

1. NATURE, FORMATION AND DURATION

Number of partners

29–02   Limited partnerships, like ordinary partnerships,[4] must, in general, not consist of more than 20 persons.[5] However, by what is now section 717(1) of the Companies Act 1985,[6] this restriction does not apply to partnerships carrying on practice as solicitors, accountants or members of a recognised Stock Exchange, provided that all the partners or the firm (as the case may be) are appropriately qualified.[7] In addition, the Secretary of State has power, by regulation, to accord a similar exemption to limited partnerships carrying on other designated businesses.[8] This power has been exercised in relation to:

(i) partnerships carrying on the activities of surveying, auctioneering, valuing, estate agency, land agency, and estate

---

[1] See *Re Barnard* [1932] 1 Ch. 272.
[2] Limited Partnerships Act 1907, s.4(1).
[3] *Ibid.* s.7.
[4] See *supra*, paras. 4–27 *et seq.*
[5] Limited Partnerships Act 1907, s.4(2) (as amended by the Banking Act 1979, s.51(2), Sched. 7). A limit of 10 partners was formerly applied to banking partnerships: see further, as to such partnerships, *supra*, paras. 8–18 *et seq.* Note, however, that the employment of a trustee partner may enable the size restrictions to be circumvented and this device has had official blessing in the case of venture capital partnerships: see *supra*, para. 4–25.
[6] As amended by the Companies Act 1989, Sched. 19, para. 16 and the Companies Act 1989 (Eligibility for Appointment as Company Auditor) (Consequential Amendments) Regulations 1991 (S.I. 1991 No. 1997), reg. 2, Sched., para. 53(4).
[7] In the case of a solicitors' partnership, all the partners must be solicitors: Companies Act 1985, s.717(1)(a), (2) (as substituted by the Companies Act 1989, Sched. 19, para. 16(3)). In the case of an accountants' partnership, the firm must be eligible for appointment as a company auditor under the Companies Act 1989, s.25: Companies Act 1985, s.717(1)(b) (as amended by the Companies Act 1989 (Eligibility for Appointment as Company Auditor) (Consequential Amendments) Regulations 1991 No. 1997), reg. 2, Sched., para. 53(4). In the case of a stockbroking partnership, each partner must be a member of a recognised stock exchange: Companies Act 1985, s.717(1)(c), (3) (as substituted by the Companies Act 1989, Sched. 19, para. 16(3)).
[8] *Ibid.* s.717(1)(d) (as added by the Companies Act 1989, Sched. 19, para. 16(2)).

management, provided that not less than three-quarters of the partners are members of either the Royal Institution of Chartered Surveyors or the Incorporated Society of Valuers and Auctioneers and not more than one-quarter of them are limited partners within the meaning of the 1907 Act;[9]

(ii) partnerships of insurance brokers, where all the partners, both general and limited, are either registered insurance brokers or enrolled bodies corporate;[10]

(iii) stockbroking partnerships which are and carry on business as member firms of the International Stock Exchange.[11]

If the statutory prohibition is contravened, the partnership will naturally be illegal,[12] but the current editor apprehends that, in addition to the normal consequences of illegality,[13] the limited partners will forfeit their limited liability.

General partners

A limited partnership must consist of one or more general partners **29–03** and one or more limited partners.[14] Any partner who is not a limited partner must be a general partner[15] and will, like any member of an ordinary partnership, be personally liable for all the debts and obligations of the firm.[16]

Limited partners

A limited partner must make a contribution of capital[17] and will **29–04** not, subject to certain exceptions,[18] be liable for the debts and obligations of the firm beyond the amount so contributed.[19] The contribution must be made immediately upon entry into partnership[20]

---

[9] Limited Partnerships (Unrestricted Size) No. 1 Regulations 1971 (S.I. 1971 No. 782). These regulations were originally made under the Companies Act 1967, s.121(2) but must now be treated as made under the Companies Act 1985, s.717(1)(d): Interpretation Act 1978, s.17(2)(b); Companies Consolidation (Consequential Provisions) Act 1985, s.31(2), (11).

[10] Limited Partnerships (Unrestricted Size) No. 2 Regulations 1990 (S.I. 1990 No. 1580).

[11] Limited Partnerships (Unrestricted Size) No. 3 Regulations 1992 (S.I. 1992 No. 1027).

[12] See *supra*, paras. 4–30, 8–46.

[13] See *supra*, paras. 8–48 *et seq.*

[14] Limited Partnerships Act 1907, s.4(2).

[15] *Ibid.* s.3.

[16] *Ibid.* s.4(2).

[17] This is not as clearly expressed in the Act as it might be, *viz.* "limited partners ... shall contribute ... *a sum or sums of cash* as capital or property valued at a stated amount ..." (emphasis supplied): *ibid.* s.4(2). It is submitted that no logical distinction can be drawn between cash and other property, and that a contribution in either form will become part of the firm's fixed capital. It does not matter that the limited partner's contribution is of a nominal amount: see *Dickson v. MacGregor*, 1992 S.L.T. 83 (Land Ct.), where the contribution was a mere £10.

[18] See the Limited Partnerships Act 1907, ss.4(3), 5, 6(1).

[19] *Ibid.* s.4(2).

[20] But see further, *infra*, para. 30–10.

and may consist of cash[21] or property. Any contribution of property must be fairly and honestly valued, so that the requisite particulars can be submitted for registration purposes.[22]

Change in liability of partners

29-05   Provided that the partnership at all times comprises at least one general partner and one limited partner,[23] any partner is free to change his status from general to limited partner or vice versa.[24]

Capacity

29-06   Any person who has the capacity to become a partner in an ordinary firm[25] may enter into a limited partnership as either a general or a limited partner.

Although the Act of 1907 specifically provides that a body corporate may be a limited partner,[26] it does not extend the powers of such a body. Accordingly, whether it is strictly within the scope of a particular company's objects clause to become a limited partner will depend on the terms of its memorandum and articles of association.[27] There is no reason to suppose that a limited company cannot be a general partner;[28] indeed this is a common occurrence.

Business of the partnership

29-07   Any lawful business[29] which could be carried on by the members of an ordinary partnership without infringing any statute or rule of law may properly be carried on by a limited partnership. If it would be illegal for an unqualified person to be a member of the firm,[30] that illegality is unlikely to be cured by ensuring that he only participates in the business *qua* limited partner.

---

[21] A bank guarantee is not cash: *Rayner & Co. v. Rhodes* (1926) 24 Ll.L. Rep. 25.
[22] Limited Partnerships Act 1907, s.8(g). See also the Perjury Act 1911, s.5 and *infra*, para. 29–25. Capital duty is no longer payable in respect of a limited partner's capital contributions: see *infra*, para. 29–20.
[23] Limited Partnerships Act 1907, s.4(2).
[24] *Ibid.* ss.9(1)(g), 10; and see *infra*, paras. 29–27, 29–29, 29–30, 30–16.
[25] See *supra*, paras. 4–01 *et seq.*
[26] Limited Partnerships Act 1907, s.4(4).
[27] The *ultra vires* doctrine has now effectively been abolished: see *supra*, para. 4–19.
[28] See *supra*, para. 11–06. *Quaere*: could it be argued that, because the Limited Partnerships Act 1907, s.4(4) expressly authorises a body corporate to be a *limited* partner, there is an implication that such a body may not be a general partner? In the view of the current editor, such an argument would not be sustained.
[29] As to the meaning of the word "business," see the Limited Partnerships Act 1907, s.3, applying the Partnership Act 1890, s.45. As to what businesses are lawful, see *supra*, paras. 8–01 *et seq.*
[30] *e.g.* a dentists' partnership: see *supra*, para. 8–30. *Semble*, this is no longer the position in the case of a solicitors' partnership: see *supra*, para. 8–43.

Firm name

A limited partnership must have a firm name and that name and **29–08** any change in it must be registered.[31]

The name need not disclose the fact that the partnership is limited[32]: subject to the requirements of the Business Names Act 1985,[33] the members of such a partnership have the same right as the members of an ordinary partnership to trade under any name of their choosing.[34] However, they may not adopt a name in which "limited" or any contraction or imitation thereof appears as the last word.[35]

Use of limited partner's name: holding out

It might be thought that, if the firm name consists of or includes **29–09** the name of a limited partner, this is *per se* sufficient to render him liable as a general partner on the basis of holding out.[36] However, it is clear that, whilst the law recognises both ordinary and limited partnerships and requires the latter to be made up of two kinds of partner, it does not insist that a firm name must disclose its status or prohibit the inclusion of a limited partner's name therein. In that context, the current editor submits that there is no justification for suggesting that, as a general proposition of law, the mere use of a limited partner's name *must* involve a representation that he is a partner of one kind rather than another.

This conclusion is to a large extent confirmed by the provisions of **29–10** the Business Names Act 1985,[37] which applies equally to limited and ordinary partnerships. Thus, if a limited partnership has a place of business and carries on business in Great Britain under a name which does not consist of the surnames of *all* the partners (together with any permitted additions),[38] the name of each limited partner may be included in the firm name but must inevitably appear on all the firm's business letters and other documents, as well as in a notice displayed in the partnership premises.[39] Significantly, the Act makes no

---

[31] Limited Partnerships Act 1907, ss.3, 8, 9. See also *infra*, paras. 29–26, 29–27.

[32] The Bill for the Limited Partnerships Act 1907 originally contained a provision that the firm name should contain the words "limited firm" as the last words in the name, while the Bill introduced into the House of Lords in 1906 provided that the firm name should not include the name of a limited partner.

[33] See *supra*, paras. 3–24 *et seq.*; also *infra*, paras. 29–10 *et seq.*

[34] See the Limited Partnerships Act 1907, s.7 and *supra*, paras. 3–17 *et seq.*, 8–12.

[35] Companies Act 1985, s.34.

[36] See, generally, the Partnership Act 1890, s.14 and *supra*, paras. 5–43 *et seq.*

[37] See generally, *supra*, paras. 3–24 *et seq.*

[38] Business Names Act 1985, s.1.

[39] *Ibid.* s.4(1). A limited exemption is afforded to partnerships of 20 or more persons: *ibid.* s.4(3). It should also be noted that any customer of the partnership is entitled to request, and must be supplied with, a notice containing the names and addresses of all the partners: *ibid.* s.4(2).

provision for distinguishing between general and limited partners on such letters, etc.[40] and it cannot, in the current editor's view, be right that compliance with these statutory requirements will, of itself, expose a limited partner to a liability more extensive than that prescribed by the Limited Partnerships Act 1907, so long as the partnership is duly registered under that Act.[41]

29–11   The position may, however, be different if the limited partner was formerly a general partner or, indeed, the sole owner of the business, at least as regards any person who knew of his former status but has had no express notice of any change therein.[42]

29–12   In the absence of any authority on this point, a degree of caution is to be commended. Thus, any limited partner, irrespective of his previous status, would be well advised not to allow his name to appear in the firm name or on its business letters, etc., without some clear indication that he is a limited partner. What he cannot do is to compel his co-partners to omit all references to his name, since this would involve an offence under the Business Names Act 1985.[43]

Duration of limited partnership

29–13   The rules governing the duration of ordinary partnerships apply to limited partnerships.[44] Thus, if no fixed term is adopted, the partnership will be determinable by the general partners at any time on notice.[45] However, subject to any contrary agreement, such a notice may not be given by a limited partner[46] and, moreover, the death or bankruptcy of such a partner will not automatically dissolve the firm.[47]

Where a limited partnership is formed for a fixed term, that term must be specified in the statement to be delivered on registration[48] and notice must be given of any subsequent change therein.[49]

---

[40] Note, however, that the Secretary of State could in theory require a distinction to be drawn between general and limited partners in the notice to be displayed in the partnership premises pursuant to *ibid.* s.4(1)(b) or in any list of partners maintained under *ibid.* s.4(3), by means of regulations made under *ibid.* s.4(5).

[41] See also *infra*, paras. 29–17 *et seq.*

[42] See *infra*, paras. 29–29, 29–30.

[43] *Ibid.* s.4(6).

[44] Limited Partnerships Act 1907, s.7; Partnership Act 1890, ss. 32 *et seq.* See further *supra*, paras. 9–01 *et seq.*, 24–07 *et seq.*

[45] Partnership Act 1890, ss.26(1), 32(*c*); and see *supra*, paras. 9–01 *et seq.*, 24–10.

[46] Limited Partnerships Act 1907, s.6(5)(e). It is clear that the provisions of this paragraph can be overridden by agreement: see the opening words of *ibid.* s.6(5).

[47] *Ibid.* s.6(2). *Semble*, there is no reason why the agreement should not contain some contrary agreement. But *cf.* the terms of *ibid.* s.6(5).

[48] *Ibid.* s.8(e). If no definite term is fixed, the conditions of the existence of the partnership must be stated: see Form L.P.5 in the Appendix to the Limited Partnerships Rules 1907, *infra*, para. A4–04.

[49] Limited Partnerships Act 1907, s.9(e). See also *infra*, para. 29–26.

Continuation of partnership after expiration of term

An ordinary fixed term partnership which is continued after the **29–14** expiration of its term will be converted into a partnership at will; such a continuance will be presumed where the business is carried on by those partners who habitually acted therein without any settlement of the partnership affairs.[50] It would seem that this rule is equally applicable to limited partnerships,[51] so that a limited partner could find that a continuance of the business by the general partners has inadvertently deprived him of the protection of the Limited Partnerships Act 1907 by turning him into a general partner, unless the change in the term or character of the partnership has been duly registered.[52]

Agreement for limited partnership

Although an agreement for a limited partnership need not be in **29–15** any particular form, a formal deed or agreement is generally desirable.[53] Moreover, even if the initial agreement is oral, certain of its terms will inevitably have to be reduced to writing for registration purposes.[54]

Discrimination

Whilst it is unlawful to discriminate against a general partner (or a **29–16** proposed general partner) on the grounds of sex or race,[55] no sanctions are imposed in the case of discrimination against a limited partner.[56]

2. REGISTRATION

Limited partnerships must be registered as such in accordance with **29–17** the provisions of the Limited Partnerships Act 1907,[57] and the registrar of companies is required to keep an index of the names of such registered partnerships.[58]

---

[50] Partnership Act 1890, s.27: see *supra*, paras. 9–08, 10–16 *et seq.*
[51] Limited Partnerships Act 1907, s.7.
[52] See *infra*, paras. 29–26, 29–27.
[53] See further *infra*, para. 31–20.
[54] Limited Partnerships Act 1907, s.8.
[55] Sex Discrimination Act 1975, s.11 (as amended); Race Relations Act 1976, s.10. See also *supra*, paras. 8–08, 8–09.
[56] Sex Discrimination Act 1975, s.11(5); Race Relations Act 1976, s.10(4).
[57] Limited Partnerships Act 1907, s.5.
[58] Companies Act 1985, s.714(1)(d). As to the partners' freedom to adopt a name of their choice, see *supra*, paras. 29–08 *et seq.*

Time for registration

29–18   The Act does not state when a limited partnership must be registered; however, since the partnership will be deemed to be a general partnership until such time as it has been registered,[59] there will be little sense in commencing business before that process is complete.

Manner and place of registration

29–19   Registration is effected by posting or delivering a statement containing the prescribed particulars to the registrar of companies at the Companies Registration Office in that part of the United Kingdom in which the firm's principal place of business is situate or proposed to be situate.[60]

It is considered that a firm's principal place of business will be the place where its administrative headquarters are situated,[61] which is a question of fact. Accordingly, whilst the partners may designate a particular location as the principal place of business, that will not be conclusive. It is, perhaps, arguable that a firm may have more than one principal place of business located in different parts of the United Kingdom;[62] if that is in truth the position, registration in each such part of the United Kingdom would appear to be necessary.[63]

Statement to be registered

29–20   The statement to be registered must be signed by all the partners, both general and limited, and must contain the following particulars[64]:

(1) the firm name;
(2) the general nature of the business;

---

[59] Limited Partnerships Act 1907, s.5.

[60] *Ibid.* ss.8, 15; see also the Limited Partnerships Rules 1907, r.2, *infra*, para. A4–01. It would not seem to matter that a *proposed* principal place of business has not yet been established when registration is sought. There would also appear to be no objection to the principal place of business being relocated within *or outside* the U.K. after registration has taken place: see *infra*, para. 29–26, n. 76.

[61] See *De Beers Consolidated Mines Ltd. v. Howe* [1906] A.C. 455; *Palmer v. Caledonian Railway* [1892] 1 Q.B. 823.

[62] *e.g.* see the Insolvency Act 1986, s.221(2), (3).

[63] This appears to be contemplated by the wording of Limited Partnerships Act 1907, s.15. It is, however, understood that the correctness of this proposition is disputed by the Department of Trade and Industry.

[64] Limited Partnerships Act 1907, s.8; see also Form L.P. 5 in the Appendix to the Limited Partnerships Rules 1907, *infra*, para. A4–04. A fee of £2 must be paid: *ibid.* r.3(a).

(3) the principal place of business;[65]

(4) the full name of each partner;

(5) the term, if any, of the partnership and the date of its commencement;[66]

(6) a statement that the partnership is limited and the description of every limited partner as such; and

(7) the sum contributed by each limited partner and whether paid in cash or how otherwise.

Since the abolition of capital duty,[67] it is no longer necessary to state the amount of duty payable.[68]

Two firms with identical partners

There would seem to be no objection to the submission of separate **29–21** statements for registration purposes by two firms composed of the same partners, provided that the make-up of each firm is different, *i.e.* one or more of the general partners in the first firm are limited partners in the second or vice versa.[69] What is less clear is whether two identical firms are entitled to apply for separate registrations merely because their registered particulars will be different, *e.g.* where they each carry on distinct businesses or have a differing capital structure. Obviously any difficulties can be avoided by the simple expedient of introducing an additional general or limited partner into *one* of the firms.

Certificate of registration

The statement submitted by the partners must be filed by the **29–22** registrar, who must post a registration certificate to the firm.[70] The certificate is admissible as evidence in all legal proceedings, both civil and criminal,[71] but is not conclusive evidence that the partnership is registered in accordance with the provisions of the Act.

---

[65] See *supra*, para. 29–19.

[66] If no definite term is fixed, the "conditions of existence of the partnership" must be stated: see Form L.P. 5 in the Appendix to the Limited Partnership Rules 1907, *infra*, para. A4–04. It is assumed that this is the same thing as the "character" of the partnership, to which reference is made in the Limited Partnerships Act 1907, s.9(e).

[67] By the Finance Act 1988, s.141.

[68] See Form L.P. 5 in the Appendix to the Limited Partnerships Rules 1907, *infra*, para. A4–04.

[69] See, for example, *H. Saunders v. The Commissioners* (1980) V.A.T.T.R. 53, noticed *infra*, para. 37–08.

[70] Limited Partnerships Act 1907, s.13.

[71] *Ibid.* s.16(2).

Completion of registration

29–23   It is submitted that registration is complete as soon as the prescribed statement has reached the registrar; the filing of the statement and the issue of the certificate are ministerial acts, failure to perform which would not deprive a limited partnership of the benefit of the Act.

Effect of non-registration

29–24   A limited partnership which is not registered as such in accordance with the provisions of the Act is not illegal, but is deemed to be a general partnership and every limited partner is deemed to be a general partner.[72] It naturally follows that the benefits of limited liability will be lost.[73]

False statements

29–25   The current editor submits that a partnership will only be registered in accordance with the provisions of the Act if the particulars given in the statement submitted on registration are in substance true.[74] It is an offence to make or send for registration a statement which is *known* to be false.[75]

Registration of changes in limited partnerships

29–26   If, during the continuance of the partnership, there is any change in the particulars originally submitted on registration, a statement specifying the nature of the change must be posted or delivered to the registrar within seven days.[76]

The statement must be signed "by the firm"[77] and not by the partners: as a result, it is considered that a signature in the firm name

---

[72] *Ibid.* s.5.

[73] *Ibid.* s.4(2).

[74] But see *Re Blair Open Hearth Furnace Co.* [1914] 1 Ch. 390 (a decision on the provisions of the Companies (Consolidation) Act 1908 relating to the allotment of shares before the necessary statement in lieu of a prospectus had been filed); *National Provincial and Union Bank of England v. Charnley* [1924] 1 K.B. 431 (a decision under s.93 of that Act).

[75] Perjury Act 1911, s.5, replacing (as to England) the Limited Partnerships Act 1907, s.12: see *infra*, para. A3–11. As to Scotland, see the False Oaths Act 1933, s.2.

[76] Limited Partnerships Act 1907, s.9; see also Form L.P. 6 in the Appendix to the Limited Partnerships Rules 1907, *infra*, para. A4–05. This statement must also be filed by the registrar and a registration certificate sent to the firm: *ibid.* Note that it is seemingly possible to move the firm's principal place of business within *or outside* the U.K. without affecting the firm's registration, provided that the change is itself duly registered.

[77] Limited Partnerships Act 1907, s.9(1); also Form L.P. 6 in the Appendix to the Limited Partnerships Rules 1907, *infra*, para. A4–05.

by any person who has the requisite authority will be sufficient.[78] A limited partner seemingly does not possess such authority.[79]

Default in registration of changes

Failure to deliver such a statement will involve the commission of **29–27** an offence by the general partners, the penalty for which is a daily fine.[80] However, it is submitted that such a failure may have more serious implications for the limited partners, since a limited partnership which is not registered in accordance with the provisions of the Act is deemed to be a general partnership.[81] There would seem no logical reason to distinguish between an unregistered firm and a firm which is registered with inaccurate particulars, at least so long as the default continues. If the Act were construed in some other way, a limited partner would retain the benefit of limited liability notwithstanding major changes in the firm, of which there is no record on the register. These might (*inter alia*) include changes in the firm's name, duration or business[82] or in the nature and extent of one or more partners' liability.[83] On the other hand, the statutory penalty for non-registration is only sought to be imposed on the general partners and a limited partner seemingly has no power to sign the statement required to be submitted to the registrar.[84] If this is indeed the position, a limited partner should (where he is able)[85] refuse to agree to any such change, otherwise than on terms which will ensure that the change only takes effect, if at all, when particulars thereof have been registered.

Right to inspect statements

Any person has a right to inspect the statements filed by the **29–28** registrar and to require a certificate of the registration of any limited partnership or a certified copy of, or extract from, any registered

---

[78] Partnership Act 1890, s.6; Limited Partnerships Act 1907, s.7. *Cf. Rogers, Eungblut & Co. v. Martin* [1911] 1 K.B. 19.
[79] Limited Partnerships Act 1907, s.6(1).
[80] *Ibid.* s.9(2). It is also an offence knowingly to make or send a false statement: Perjury Act 1911, s.5 and *supra*, para. 29–25, n.75.
[81] Limited Partnerships Act 1907. s.5; *Rayner & Co. v. Rhodes* (1926) 24 Ll.L.R. 25, 27, *per* Wright J.
[82] Changes in the business may alter the general partners' implied authority to bind the firm: Partnership Act 1890, s.5. See also *supra*, paras. 12–02 *et seq.* and, *infra*, para. 30–01.
[83] The Limited Partnerships Act 1907, s.10 requires the change of a general into a limited partner to be advertised in the *Gazette*, and renders the change inoperative until it is so advertised. Although registration is not mentioned in that section, it is framed in negative terms; the current editor submits that the change will not in fact be operative until all the other requirements of the Act, including registration, have been satisfied.
[84] See *ibid.* s.6(1).
[85] See *ibid.* s.6(3) and *infra*, paras. 31–02 *et seq.*, 31–18 *et seq.*

statement on payment of the prescribed fee.[86] Such a certificate or certified copy or extract is admissible as evidence in all legal proceedings.[87] The right to inspect appears to carry with it the right to make plain copies or extracts.[88]

How far registration constitutes notice

29–29   Notwithstanding this general right of inspection, it is questionable whether, and if so to what extent, registration under the Limited Partnerships Act 1907 constitutes notice to third parties of the nature of the partnership or of its registered particulars. The Act itself suggests that registration will not in every case be sufficient notice of matters which require to be registered. Thus, where a general partner becomes a limited partner, the change in his status must be registered *and* immediately be advertised in the *Gazette*.[89] Even then, a *Gazette* notice is not always sufficient notice of a fact advertised therein.[90]

29–30   The current editor submits that, whilst registration may be sufficient notice of the registered particulars to any person who deals with the firm knowing it to be a limited partnership,[91] it may not be sufficient where the nature of the partnership is not known to him. Suppose that an existing firm is converted into a limited partnership without changing its name and that one or more of the existing partners become limited partners therein. Suppose further that the firm is duly registered and the change advertised in the *Gazette*, but no notice is given to the customers of the "old" firm, who remain totally unaware of the change. It is considered that such customers could properly hold any limited partner known to be a general partner in the "old" firm liable beyond the amount of his capital contribution in respect of liabilities incurred *after* the change.[92] On that basis, a general partner who becomes a limited partner should take care to ensure that specific notice of the change in his status is given to every existing customer of the firm.

---

[86] *Ibid.* ss.16(1), 17. As to the fees payable, see the Limited Partnerships Rules 1907, r.3, *infra*, para. A4–02.

[87] Limited Partnerships Act 1907, s.16(2).

[88] See *Mutter v. Eastern & Midlands Railway* (1888) 38 Ch.D. 92 (a decision on the Companies Clauses Act 1863, s.28). *Re Balaghat Gold Mining Co. Ltd.* [1901] 2 K.B. 665 appears to be distinguishable, since the section under consideration in that case (*i.e.* the Companies Act 1862, s.32) prescribed a payment to be made by any person requiring a copy; see, now, the Companies Act 1985, s.356 (as amended by the Companies Act 1989, ss.143(8), 212, Sched. 24).

[89] Limited Partnerships Act 1907, s.10. See further *supra*, para. 29–27, n.83.

[90] See *supra*, paras. 13–70 *et seq.*

[91] An analogy may perhaps be drawn with the principles enunciated in *Royal British Bank v. Turquand* (1856) 6 E. & B. 327, and other cases of that class.

[92] See the Limited Partnerships Act 1907, s.7; Partnership Act 1890, s.36(1). See also *supra*, paras. 13–43 *et seq.*

3. LIMITED PARTNERSHIPS AND THE FINANCIAL SERVICES ACT 1986

Definition of collective investment scheme

The Financial Services Act 1986 contains the following provision: **29–31**

"75.—(1) In this Act 'a collective investment scheme' means subject to the provisions of this section, any arrangements with respect to property of any description, including money, the purpose or effect of which is to enable persons taking part in the arrangements (whether by becoming owners of the property or any part of it or otherwise) to participate in or to receive profits or income arising from the acquisition, holding, management or disposal of the property or sums paid out of such profits or income.

(2) The arrangements must be such that the persons who are to participate as mentioned in subsection (1) above (in this Act referred to as 'participants') do not have day to day control over the management of the property in question, whether or not they have the right to be consulted or to give directions; and the arrangements must also have either or both of the characteristics mentioned in subsection (3) below.

(3) Those characteristics are—

(a) that the contributions of the participants and the profits or income out of which payments are to be made to them are pooled;[93]

(b) that the property in question is to be managed as a whole by or on behalf of the operator of the scheme."

It is, however, also provided that a collective investment scheme will not exist where each of the participants carries on a business other than investment business[94] and enters into the arrangements for "commercial purposes related to that business."[95] The Act also contains a number of other exceptions.[96]

---

[93] Where the pooling arrangements relate to separate parts of the property, they will only constitute a collective investment scheme if the participants can exchange rights in one part for rights in another: *ibid.* s.75(4).

[94] The view is expressed in the *Encyclopedia of Financial Services Law*, para. 2–246 that each of the participants must be carrying on the *same* business, although it is not clear whether this is taken to mean a joint business or merely a business of the same type. The current editor doubts that this restrictive interpretation is justified and suggests that the commercial purposes of each participant's business (whatever it may be) must be considered in isolation.

[95] Financial Services Act 1986, s.75(6)(b).

[96] *Ibid.* s. 75(5)–(7) (as amended by the Financial Services Act 1986 (Restriction of Scope of Act and Meaning of Collective Investment Scheme) Order 1990 (S.I. 1990 No. 349), Art. 6) and Sched. 1, paras. 34, 35 (as added by *ibid.* Art. 7) and, in the case of para. 35, as amended by the Financial Services Act 1986 (Restriction of Scope of Act and Meaning of Collective Investment Scheme) (No. 2) Order 1990 (S.I. 1990 No. 1493), Art. 2 and the Financial Services Act 1986 (Schedule 1 (Amendment) and Miscellaneous Exemption) Order 1991 (S.I. 1991 No. 1516), Art. 2).

Limited partnership as a collective investment scheme

29–32   Given the essential characteristics of a limited partnership[97] and, in particular, the exclusion of the limited partners from any participation in the management of its affairs,[98] there can, in the current editor's view, be little doubt that such a partnership will constitute a collective investment scheme, unless advantage can be taken of one of the exceptions set out in the Financial Services Act 1986.[99] However, it would seem that, in general, only the limited partners will be the participants in the scheme.[1]

It follows that—

(1)   the shares of the limited partners will constitute "units" in that scheme[2] and, thus, investments;[3]

(2)   the establishment, operation or winding up of the partnership will constitute investment business,[4] as will any dealings, etc. in relation to those "units";[5] and

(3)   advertisements may not in general be issued nor any advice given with a view to inviting third parties to participate in the partnership.[6]

Accordingly, the general partner(s) would apparently need to seek authorisation under the Act,[7] unless they are exempt[8] or the partnership is in fact managed by some other authorised person.[9]

---

[97] See *supra*, para. 28–01 and *infra*, paras. 30–01 *et seq.*, 31–02 *et seq.*

[98] Limited Partnerships Act 1907, s.6(1); also *infra*, para. 31–04.

[99] See *supra*, para. 29–31.

[1] Financial Services Act 1986, s. 75(2), *supra*, para. 29–31. But see *infra*, n.9.

[2] *Ibid.* s.75(8).

[3] *Ibid.* Sched. 1, para. 6. Note, in this context, the power of the Secretary of State to order the official listing of such investments: *ibid.* s.142(4).

[4] *Ibid.* Sched. 1, para. 16.

[5] *Ibid.* Sched. 1, paras. 12–15.

[6] *Ibid.* s.76. Note, however, the exception in *ibid.* s.76(2). Such advice may also properly be given *otherwise* than by way of business: *ibid.* s.3.

[7] As to authorisation, see *ibid.* ss. 3, 7 *et seq.* And see *supra*, paras. 8–33 *et seq.*

[8] *Ibid.* ss. 3, 35 *et seq.*

[9] It is, in practice, not uncommon to find that the general partner(s) will delegate the management of the partnership to a third party. *Semble*, in such a case the general partners would still be the "operator of the scheme" within the meaning of *ibid.* s.75(3)(b) and not a participant for the purposes of *ibid.* s.75(2). *Sed quaere*.

CHAPTER 30

THE RIGHTS AND OBLIGATIONS OF THE PARTNERS AS REGARDS THIRD PARTIES

1. THE AUTHORITY OF PARTNERS TO BIND THE FIRM

General partners

A general partner in a limited partnership has the same implied **30–01** authority to bind the firm as a member of an ordinary partnership: the limits of that authority will accordingly be determined by the nature of the business and the way in which it is usually carried on.[1] However, whilst such a partner has the exclusive right to manage the partnership business,[2] it is considered that he does not have power, without the consent of the limited partners, to *alter* the nature of that business in order to extend his authority.[3]

Provided that he does not become bankrupt, a general partner's **30–02** authority will continue after the dissolution of the firm for so long as is necessary to wind up its affairs and to complete any unfinished business;[4] indeed, in the absence of a court order to the contrary, it is the duty of a general partner to attend to such winding-up.[5]

Deeds

It is submitted that the Limited Partnerships Act 1907[6] so modifies **30–03** the general rule that a partner has no implied authority to bind his firm by deed[7] as to confer such authority on the general partner(s), provided that the deed in question is framed and executed in the appropriate manner.[8]

---

[1] Partnership Act 1890, s.5; Limited Partnerships Act 1907, s.7. See also *supra*, paras. 12–02 *et seq.*
[2] Limited Partnerships Act 1907, s.6(1).
[3] See *infra*, paras. 31–02, 31–03.
[4] Partnership Act 1890, s.38; Limited Partnerships Act 1907, s.7. See also *supra*, paras. 13–64 *et seq.*
[5] Limited Partnerships Act 1907, s.6(3).
[6] *Ibid.* s.6(1).
[7] See *supra*, paras. 12–63 *et seq.*
[8] See the Partnership Act 1890, s.6 and *supra*, paras. 12–171, 12–172. *Quaere*, does it matter that the partnership was not itself created by deed: see *supra*, para. 12–63.

Limited partners

The general rule

30–04   The Limited Partnerships Act 1907 provides that a limited partner has no power to bind the firm and may not take part in the management of the partnership business.[9]

It follows from the inability of a limited partner to bind the firm that any admission or representation which he may make will not be evidence against the firm[10] and, moreover, the firm will not automatically have notice of any matter of which he has notice.[11] It is also submitted that such a partner does not have the authority to sign the statement required to be submitted to the registrar following a change in the firm.[12]

30–05   If a limited partner purports to act on behalf of the firm, the firm will obviously not be bound but he may be liable in damages for breach of warranty of authority.[13] Save in exceptional circumstances, a partner so acting will not incur any liability if the person with whom he dealt knew of his lack of authority;[14] but, for this purpose, knowledge that he is a limited partner[15] would in itself appear to be insufficient, since he might have express authority to bind the firm.

Express authority

30–06   Notwithstanding the general statutory rule, it is submitted that a limited partner may be *expressly* authorised to act on behalf of the firm, either generally or for a particular purpose. In such a case, the firm will be bound by his acts within the scope of that authority, in the same way and to the same extent as it would be bound by the acts of any other agent. However, such a course is not without danger: if the limited partner, in pursuance of the authority conferred on him, performs some act which amounts to taking part in the management of the partnership business, he will forfeit the benefit of his limited liability for so long as such participation continues.[16]

---

[9] Limited Partnerships Act 1907, s.6(1).
[10] *Cf.* the Partnership Act 1890, s.15; and see *supra*, paras. 12–17 *et seq.*
[11] *Cf. ibid.* s.16; see also *supra*, paras. 12–21 *et seq.*
[12] Limited Partnerships Act 1907, ss.6, 9; see *supra*, para. 29–26.
[13] See *Collen v. Wright* (1857) 8 E. & B. 647; *Starkey v. Bank of England* [1903] A.C.114; *Yonge v. Toynbee* [1910] 1 K.B. 215.
[14] See *Halbot v. Lens* [1901] 1 Ch. 344.
[15] As to how far registration constitutes notice of the fact that a person is a limited partner, see *supra*, paras. 29–29, 29–30.
[16] Limited Partnerships Act 1907, s.6(1); see further *infra*, paras. 31–02 *et seq.*

2. THE LIABILITY OF PARTNERS FOR THE DEBTS AND OBLIGATIONS OF THE FIRM

A. GENERAL PARTNERS

As might be expected, the liability of a general partner for the debts **30–07** and obligations of a limited partnership is precisely the same as that of a member of an ordinary partnership.[17]

Retirement

In order to avoid the risk of continuing liability following the retirement of a general partner or the dissolution of the firm, it is advisable to advertise that fact *and* to notify all the firm's existing or "old" customers, as in the case of an ordinary partnership.[18] It would not on any footing be safe to rely on the firm's amended registration as sufficient notice to such customers.[19]

Change of liability

A general partner may become a limited partner at any time during **30–08** the continuance of the partnership, provided that there will still be at least one continuing general partner.[20] Such a change of status can be effected by a suitable arrangement[21] between the partners, but will not prejudice the rights of third parties in respect of the *past* debts and obligations of the firm, in respect of which the unlimited liability of the former general partner will continue. Moreover, such an arrangement will also not affect his liability for *future* debts and obligations until it has been advertised in the *Gazette*[22] and duly registered[23]; even then it may still be necessary to give express notice to the firm's existing customers.[24] Only when all these steps have been completed can he be assured of the benefits of limited liability.

Since the Business Names Act 1985 contains no provision requiring a distinction to be drawn between general and limited partners in a firm's business letters, etc., or in any notice or list required to be

---

[17] *Ibid.* ss.4(2), 7; and see *supra*, paras. 13–01 *et seq.*
[18] See *supra*, paras. 13–39 *et seq.*
[19] See *supra*, paras. 29–29, 29–30.
[20] See the Limited Partnerships Act 1907, ss.4(2), 9(1)(g).
[21] This is the expression used in *ibid.* s.10(1).
[22] *Ibid.* s.10.
[23] *Ibid.* s.9(1)(g); see also *supra*, para. 29–27. If the change of liability is registered within the permitted 7 days but is preceded by the *Gazette* notice, it will seemingly be effective from the date of the notice; *per contra*, perhaps, if a person dealing with the firm had not seen the notice but had inspected and relied upon the old registered particulars.
[24] See *supra*, para. 29–30.

displayed or made available,[25] no steps need be taken as a result of a mere change of liability.

B. LIMITED PARTNERS

(a) Extent and Duration of Liability

Extent of liability

30–09   Save in the cases noted hereafter,[26] the liability of a limited partner for the debts and obligations of the firm is limited to the amount of his contribution to the partnership,[27] however small,[28] but his liability for debts and obligations *vis-à-vis* third parties must be contrasted with the sharing of trading losses as between the partners themselves: as to the latter, there is no necessary limitation on his liability.[29]

A limited partner may increase the amount of his original contribution[30] which will inevitably entail a corresponding increase in his liability, even though this is not expressly stated in the Act.

30–10   Equally, there does not appear to be any objection to a limited partner making an initial contribution on becoming a partner and at the same time binding himself to make a further contribution at a later date. It is submitted that, if the agreement is bona fide, such a partner's liability will be restricted to the amount of his *current* contribution, no account being taken of any further contribution which has not yet fallen due.[31] *Per contra*, perhaps, if the agreement amounts to a deliberate attempt to evade the Act by so limiting his liability, whilst at the same time securing to him all the benefits which he would have enjoyed if the entirety of his contribution had been brought in from the outset.[32]

---

[25] *Ibid.* s.4. The Secretary of State does, however, have power to make regulations specifying the form of any such notice or list: *ibid.* s.4(5). See also *supra*, paras. 29–10 *et seq*.

[26] See *infra*, para. 30–11. To these exceptions should perhaps be added the illegality of the partnership: see *supra*, para. 29–07.

[27] Limited Partnerships Act 1907, s.4(2); and see *supra*, para. 29–04.

[28] See *Dickson v. MacGregor* 1992 S.L.T. 83 (Land Ct.), where the contribution was £10.

[29] *Reed v. Young* [1986] 1 W.L.R. 649. However, a limited partner is now restricted in the use he can make of such losses: see the Income and Corporation Taxes Act 1988, s.117 and *infra*, para. 34–72.

[30] Limited Partnerships Act 1907, s.9(1)(f).

[31] In such a case, particulars of the sum actually contributed will be given when the firm is registered: see *ibid.* s.8(g). Particulars of the subsequent contribution will be given when it is made: *ibid.* s.9(1)(f). *Quaere*, if the limited partner agrees to make a further contribution but fails to do so on the due date, should particulars be given to the registrar? It is thought that they should, and that the limit of his liability will be the amount of his agreed contribution, irrespective of whether it has in fact been contributed. It is, however, unclear how effect would be given to the increase in his liability in such a case: see *infra*, paras. 30–22 *et seq*. Presumably, it would be treated as analogous to a case of withdrawal of capital.

[32] *e.g.* an enlarged profit share. There would naturally be substantial problems of proof in such a case but, given the latitude afforded to them by the Act, it is hard to see why prospective partners should organise their affairs in this unnecessarily circuitous way.

A limited partner may not during the continuance of the partnership draw out or receive back any part of his contribution, although the penalty for a breach of this prohibition does not amount to a substantial deterrent.[33]

Forfeiture of limited liability

Notwithstanding the general limitation on his liability, there are **30–11** three circumstances in which a limited partner may face a liability for the debts and obligations of the firm beyond the amount of the contribution which he has invested in the firm. They are as follows:

(1) If the firm is not registered in accordance with the provisions of the Act,[34] a limited partner is deemed to be a general partner and, as such, his liability is unlimited.

(2) If he takes part in the management of the partnership business, a limited partner becomes liable as though he were a general partner for as long as such participation continues.[35]

(3) If, during the continuance of the partnership, he either directly or indirectly draws out or receives back any part of his contribution, the limited partner becomes liable up to the amount so drawn out or received back.[36]

Withdrawal of contribution

It appears that breach of the statutory prohibition on the **30–12** withdrawal of a limited partner's contribution during the continuation of the partnership is attended *only* by the sanction of liability for the debts and obligations of the firm up to the amount so drawn out or received back. If this is, indeed, the position, the Act provides no real deterrent to such withdrawals, since limited liability is, in effect, preserved at the original level. Although the current editor considers that the Act could, on its face, be construed in such a way as to impose on the limited partner both a liability up to the amount of the original contribution[37] and an *additional* liability in respect of the amount withdrawn,[38] *i.e.* an effective double penalty and a real disincentive to the early withdrawal of capital,[39] this would imply that a limited partner is in all cases personally liable up to the amount of his contribution, which does not appear to have been the legislative intention.[40]

---

[33] Limited Partnerships Act 1907, s.4(3). See further, *infra*, paras. 30–12 *et seq.*
[34] *Ibid.* s.5; and see *supra*, paras. 29–24, 29–27.
[35] *Ibid.* s.6(1). See further, *infra*, paras. 31–02 *et seq.*
[36] *Ibid.* s.4(3).
[37] *i.e.* under *ibid.* s.4(2).
[38] *i.e.* under *ibid.* s.4(3).
[39] If this *were* the correct construction, it is submitted that the additional liability would automatically cease once the improperly withdrawn contribution has been repaid to the firm.
[40] See *infra*, paras. 30–14, 30–22.

30–13   In the face of the above possibility, it is of importance to identify what types of payment received by a limited partner will fall to be treated as a return of contribution. In earlier editions of this work it was submitted that:

> "any payment to a limited partner which directly or indirectly comes out of his contribution, whether such payment takes the form of a payment of interest on his capital or of a share of profits or any other form, will be a receipt by him of a part of his contribution, and will render him liable for the debts of the firm up to the amount he has so received."

The current editor considers that, as a general proposition, this goes too far: it will be a question of fact in each case whether any particular payment must be treated as an effective repayment of capital. Payments out of profits, whether framed as interest on capital or otherwise, can rarely, if ever, be regarded as such; *per contra*, if there are no profits and interest on capital is (exceptionally) funded out of the capital itself. Even if the Act were interpreted in a less benign way, once a partner has received a share of profits equal to the amount of his contribution, the receipt of any further profit distributions would not *increase* his liability, *i.e.* he could not be regarded as having been repaid his capital several times over.

Lost capital

30–14   A limited partner will seemingly enjoy the full benefits of limited liability even where his original contribution has been lost in the course of carrying on the firm's business. Since the Act does not require the partners to replace any lost capital out of profits, the current editor submits that the subsequent receipt of a share of profits should not be regarded as a repayment of that lost capital.

A more cautious view was, however, expressed in the following passage taken from the original Supplement to this work on the Limited Partnerships Act 1907 but, unaccountably, omitted from later editions:

> "It is apprehended that under this sub-section a question may arise whether, when there have been capital losses, a limited partner who shares in a division of profits before the losses are made good will be drawing out or receiving back part of his contribution. The question would appear to be similar to that which arises under the Companies Acts where dividends have been paid without making good capital losses. The decided cases under the Companies Acts seem to show that, provided the business of the limited company is, having regard to all the circumstances, fairly conducted, there

may be cases in which it is not improper for the company to pay dividends notwithstanding that there have been losses of capital which have not been made good.[41]

In connection with this question a distinction has been drawn between 'fixed' and 'circulating' capital, the former being treated as a form of capital which need not be replaced before ascertaining profits available for dividend.[42]

The distinction, however, does not appear to have been universally accepted, nor is it one which is always easy of application,[43] and in any event, as in many businesses of the kind which are usually made the subject of partnerships, a great part of the capital is in its nature clearly 'circulating' rather than 'fixed,' a limited partner will in many cases certainly run the risk of being called upon to refund if he shares in a division of so-called profits, or receives interest on capital before capital losses have been made good."

Position following dissolution

It is considered that, for present purposes, a partnership will be **30–15** regarded as continuing until its affairs have been fully wound up or, at any rate, until all its debts and liabilities have been discharged.[44] It follows that the prohibition on the withdrawal of a limited partner's contribution will continue even after the dissolution of the firm.

Change of liability

If a limited partner becomes a general partner, particulars of the **30–16** change must be registered,[45] but no other formalities need be observed.[46] The former limited partner's liability for the debts and obligations of the firm incurred before he became a general partner will, in the normal way, be limited to the amount of his contribution,[47] but he will naturally have unlimited liability for all debts and obligations incurred after he gave up that status.

---

[41] The editors referred in particular to *Verner v. General and Commercial Investment Trust* [1894] 2 Ch. 239; *Barrow Haematite Steel Co.* [1900] 2 Ch. 846, affirmed at [1901] 2 Ch. 746; *Dovey v. Cory* [1901] A.C. 477.

[42] *Verner v. General and Commercial Investment Trust, supra,* p.266, *per* Lindley L.J.; *Dovey v. Cory, supra,* pp. 493, 494, *per* Lord Davey.

[43] *Dovey v. Corey, supra,* p. 487, *per* Earl of Halsbury L.C. and p. 494, *per* Lord Davey.

[44] See the Partnership Act 1890, s.38; the Limited Partnerships Act 1907, s.7. And see *supra,* paras. 13–64 *et seq.*

[45] Limited Partnerships Act 1907, s.9(1)(g).

[46] *Cf.* the position of a general partner who becomes a limited partner: see *supra,* para. 30–08.

[47] What will be the position if, following the change in his liability, he withdraws the contribution which he originally made as a limited partner? Will the Limited Partnerships Act 1907, s.4(3) still apply? It is thought not, since he will be withdrawing it in his capacity as a general partner; *sed quaere.*

Termination of liability as to future debts

30–17   The sections of the Act which prohibit the withdrawal of a limited partner's contribution during the continuance of the partnership[48] and provide that a limited partnership is not dissolved by the death or bankruptcy of such a partner[49] raise questions of considerable difficulty when considering the termination of liability. Neither section is expressed to be subject of any contrary agreement between the partners; in this respect, the latter section differs from the corresponding provision in the Partnership Act 1890.[50] Nevertheless, the terms upon which a partner may retire or otherwise cease to be a member of the firm, and the rights conferred on the personal representatives or trustee of a deceased or bankrupt partner in respect of his share, are matters which primarily affect the partners themselves and, as such, are in general left to their determination.[51] On that footing, the current editor submits that the partners may quite properly agree to permit the retirement of a limited partner and to accept that the death or bankruptcy of such a partner will cause the firm to be dissolved, either as between all of them or solely as regards that partner. It follows that, so long as any change in the firm is duly registered,[52] the liability of a limited partner can be terminated as regards future debts and obligations, notwithstanding the fact that the partnership continues as between the remaining partners and that the outgoing partner or his estate has drawn out or received back the value of his contribution. However, in the case of retirement,[53] registration of the change should also be supplemented by the usual *Gazette* and other notices.[54]

30–18   What is less clear is whether the former limited partner (or his personal representatives or trustee in bankruptcy) is, in the absence of agreement, *entitled* to withdraw his contribution until the partnership is terminated by effluxion of time or is otherwise dissolved. In earlier editions of this work, it was submitted that there is no such right and that such a partner's contribution will remain liable for the debts and obligations of the firm, whether incurred before or after his death or bankruptcy. The current editor questions the correctness of this proposition: if it is right that the Limited Partnerships Act 1907 does not prohibit the withdrawal of a *former*

---

[48] Limited Partnerships Act 1907, s.4(3).
[49] *Ibid.* s.6(2).
[50] See the Partnership Act 1890, s.33(1), *supra* para. 24–20; *cf.* the Limited Partnerships Act 1907, s.6(5).
[51] Partnership Act 1890, s.19; Limited Partnerships Act 1907, s.7.
[52] Limited Partnerships Act 1907, s.9(1)(d); Limited Partnerships Rules 1907, Appendix, Form L.P.6, Note (1), *infra*, para. A4–06. See further, *supra*, para. 29–26.
[53] Similar considerations will apply if a limited partner is expelled from the firm.
[54] Partnership Act 1890, ss.36, 37, *supra*, paras. 13–42 *et seq.*; see also *supra*, paras. 29–29, 29–30.

limited partner's contribution because, on his retirement, a new partnership comes into existence,[55] there can be no warrant for the continuing partners insisting on the retention of that contribution, save (perhaps) until the firm's registration has been duly amended.[56]

Assignment of share

The liability of a limited partner for future debts and obligations **30-19** may also be terminated by the assignment of his share, which will, in the absence of some contrary agreement, require the consent of the general partners.[57] However, his liability will continue until the assignment has been advertised in the *Gazette*[58] and duly registered.[59]

Termination of liability as to past debts

It has already been seen that the retirement, expulsion, death or **30-20** bankruptcy of a partner does not terminate his liability to creditors for the existing debts and obligations of the firm.[60] Therefore, if a former limited partner withdraws or receives back (or has previously withdrawn or received back) any part of his contribution, he or his estate will at the very least remain liable for such debts and obligations up to the original amount of that contribution.[61] The position is less clear where a limited partner assigns his share.[62] Earlier editions of this work contained the following analysis:

"In the case of assignment with the consent of the general partners, the limited partner will not, as a rule, withdraw any part of his contribution; he will receive the purchase-money (if any) for his share out of the pocket of the assignee and not from the partnership. In such case, therefore, he will not be responsible for the past debts and obligations of the firm unless before the assignment he has incurred liability beyond the amount of his contribution."

The current editor questions whether such an approach is **30-21** warranted by the terms of the Act itself: a limited partner's liability does not depend on withdrawal of his contribution[63] although it is, in general, limited to the amount thereof.[64] By assigning his share, he

---

[55] See *infra*, para. 31–21.
[56] Limited Partnerships Act 1907, s.9(1)(d).
[57] *Ibid.* s.6(5)(b).
[58] *Ibid.* s.10(1).
[59] See *ibid.* s.9(1)(d); and see *supra*, para. 29–27.
[60] See *supra*, paras. 13–74 *et seq.*, 26–14 *et seq.*
[61] It is considered that, in such a case, there will not even be the *theoretical* risk of additional liability noticed, *supra*, para. 30–12.
[62] Limited Partnerships Act 1907, s.6(5)(b). See also *infra*, paras. 31–16, 31–17.
[63] Note that, on one construction of the Limited Partnerships Act 1907, such withdrawal might result in *additional* liability: see *supra*, para. 30–12.
[64] *Ibid.* ss.4(2), 5, 6(1).

will certainly cease to be a limited partner and the assignee will become a limited partner in his place, but does it necessarily follow that a creditor will have a direct right of action against that assignee in respect of a debt or obligation incurred *prior* to the advertisement and registration of the change in the firm?[65] This will be of particular importance if the assignee has withdrawn any part of the assignor's original contribution. It is submitted that a clear statutory provision would be required to displace the liability of a former limited partner to such a creditor, which is not to be found in the Act.[66] It goes almost without saying that a suitable indemnity should be obtained from the assignee against the possibility of such continuing liability being imposed.[67]

(b) Nature of Liability

30-22 The Limited Partnerships Act 1907 does, with certain exceptions, take care to limit the liability of a limited partner to the amount of his contribution.[68] Somewhat surprisingly it contains no provision regulating proceedings by creditors of the firm nor any protection for the limited partners against any execution which may be levied against them by such creditors. The Act does not even *expressly* seek to modify the general law under which every partner is personally liable for the debts and obligations of the firm.[69] Nevertheless, it is with considerable diffidence submitted that a limited partner's position under the Act is analogous to that of a married woman who had, prior to the Law Reform (Married Women and Tortfeasors) Act 1935, contracted debts which could only be met out of her separate estate,[70] and that a creditor of the firm cannot obtain a personal judgment against such a partner or issue execution against him, unless he has incurred liability beyond the amount of his contribution. Some support for this view is to be found in the observations of Farwell J. in *Re Barnard*,[71] to the effect that there was no joint liability in the case of a bankrupt limited partnership comprising a single general partner, since only he was liable for its debts. The position of a former limited partner who has assigned his share to a third party may, however, be anomalous.[72]

---

[65] See generally, *supra*, paras. 13–24 *et seq.*
[66] Could it perhaps be argued that, since the assignee becomes entitled to all the rights of the assignor (Limited Partnerships Act 1907, s.6(5)(b)), he must also by implication assume all of his duties and obligations? Surely this represents an impermissible gloss on the Act.
[67] Note, however, that such an indemnity will normally be implied: see *supra*, para. 19–67.
[68] See *supra*, para. 30–11. However, subject to the prohibition against the withdrawal of a limited partner's contribution, it would seem that limited liability is *not* dependent on his contribution still being retained by or invested in the firm: see *supra*, para. 30–14 and *infra*, para. 31–09.
[69] Partnership Act 1890, ss.9, 10; Limited Partnerships Act 1907, s.7. See also *supra*, paras. 13–03 *et seq.*
[70] For a summary of the position prior to the 1935 Act, see the 14th ed. of this work, at pp. 60 *et seq.*
[71] [1932] 1 Ch. 269; see further *infra*, para. 33–08.
[72] See *supra*, para. 30–21.

Form of judgment

If the foregoing analysis is correct, it is considered that any **30–23** judgment against a firm must be framed in such a way as to ensure that each limited partner enjoys the benefit of the limited liability conferred on him by the Act.[73] No such protection is provided by the Rules of the Supreme Court,[74] which still appear to require amendment in this respect. Similar considerations naturally apply where judgment is to be entered directly against a limited partner.

Limited partner liable beyond the amount of his contribution

The position of a limited partner who falls to be treated as a **30–24** general partner, by reason of default in the registration of the partnership[75] or participation in the management of the partnership business,[76] or who becomes liable for the firm's debts and obligations by drawing out or receiving back any part of his contribution[77] will be very different from that of a normal limited partner.

In either of the two former cases, a creditor of the firm will have **30–25** all the remedies against the limited partner which would be open to him against a general partner and, save only as to debts and obligations incurred whilst the limited partner *did* continue to enjoy limited liability, any judgment against the firm or against the limited partner need take no special form.

The rights of a creditor in the latter case are less clear. It is **30–26** nevertheless submitted that any judgment obtained against the firm, whether in the firm name or in the names of the individual partners, should be framed so as to leave the creditor free to levy execution against the limited partner personally up to the amount of the contribution drawn out or received back and that such a judgment could found a petition for an insolvency order against the firm and/or against that partner.[78]

3. ACTIONS BY AND AGAINST PARTNERS

Since the Limited Partnerships Act 1907 does not seek to regulate the **30–27** form of an action by or against a limited partnership, such an action will not, in terms of the necessary parties, differ from an action by

---

[73] See, as to the execution of judgments against a firm, R.S.C. Ord. 81, r.5, *infra*, para. A2–13; C.C.R. Ord. 25, r.9; also *supra*, paras. 14–89 *et seq*. And see, as to the form of judgment against a firm where one partner is a minor, *Lovell v. Beauchamp* [1894] A.C. 607; also *supra*, para. 14–19.

[74] See *infra*, paras. A2–09 *et seq*.

[75] Limited Partnerships Act 1907, s.5. See also *supra*, para. 29–24.

[76] *Ibid.* s.6(1). See *infra*, paras. 31–02 *et seq*.

[77] *Ibid.* s.4(3). See *supra*, paras. 30–12 *et seq*. and *infra* paras. 31–09, 31–10.

[78] See *supra*, paras. 27–09 *et seq*. and *infra*, paras. 33–06, 33–07.

and against an ordinary partnership.[79] However, difficulties may in practice arise, particularly given the fact that the Rules of the Supreme Court[80] do not take account of the possibility that one or more of the partners may enjoy the benefit of limited liability.

Actions by the firm

It has already been seen that, under the general law, each partner has authority to bring an action on behalf of the firm.[81] It is, however, apprehended that a limited partner will not have such authority.[82] Nevertheless, a civil proceedings order[83] against such a partner will prevent the firm from instituting proceedings without the leave of the court.[84]

Actions against the firm

30–28   Actions may be brought against an ordinary partnership either in the firm name or in the names of the individual partners[85] and, under the general law, a managing partner has authority to acknowledge service on behalf of all the partners.[86] It is apprehended that a limited partnership may also be sued in the firm name or in the names of the partners, including the limited partners, but that a limited partner will have no authority to acknowledge service on behalf of his co-partners.[87]

Service of writ on limited partner

30–29   If an action is brought against a partnership in the firm name, the writ may be served on any one or more of the partners.[88] However, it is at least questionable whether service of the writ on a limited partner will constitute good service on the firm.[89]

---

[79] See *supra*, paras. 14–01 *et seq.*

[80] See R.S.C. Ord. 81, *infra*, paras. A2–09 *et seq.* Similarly in the case of the County Court Rules.

[81] See *supra*, paras. 12–35, 14–69 *et seq.*; also the Limited Partnerships Act 1907, s.6(5)(a).

[82] *Ibid.* s.6(1); see also *supra*, para. 30–04.

[83] See, as to such orders, the Supreme Court Act 1981, s.42 (as amended by the Prosecution of Offences Act 1985, s.24).

[84] *Mephistopheles Debt Collection Service v. Lotay, The Times,* May 17, 1994.

[85] See R.S.C. Ord. 81, rr. 1 *et seq., infra*, paras. A2–09 *et seq.*; C.C.R. Ord. 5, r.9(1). See also *supra*, paras. 14–03 *et seq.*

[86] See *supra*, paras. 14–18, 14–72; and see *Tomlinson v. Broadsmith* [1896] 1 Q.B. 386.

[87] See the Limited Partnerships Act 1907, s.6(1). And see *supra*, para. 30–04.

[88] See R.S.C. Ord. 81, r. 3, *infra*, para. A2–11; C.C.R. Ord. 7, r. 13. And see *supra*, paras. 14–13 *et seq.*

[89] However, a limited partner could obviously be given *express* authority to accept service: see *Kenneth Allison Ltd. v. A.E. Limehouse & Co.* [1992] 2 A.C. 105. As to the form of a judgment against a limited partnership, see *supra*, para. 30–23.

CHAPTER 31

THE RIGHTS AND OBLIGATIONS OF THE PARTNERS
BETWEEN THEMSELVES

It has already been seen that, in matters of internal regulation, the **31–01**
Partnership Act 1890 gives partners complete freedom to agree the
terms of their partnership[1] and that freedom is, with certain
exceptions, expressly preserved by the Limited Partnerships Act
1907.[2] However, if the members of a limited partnership do *not* reach
agreement on all aspects of their relationship, their mutual rights and
obligations will in general be governed by the provisions of the 1890
Act and the rules of law and equity applicable to ordinary
partnerships.[3] This may have consequences which the partners neither
intended nor foresaw, particularly as regards their profit shares,[4] the
division of surplus assets on a winding-up[5] and the ownership of
goodwill.[6]

1. THE MANAGEMENT OF THE PARTNERSHIP BUSINESS

General partners

The right to manage the partnership business is conferred on the **31–02**
general partners alone: any limited partner who seeks to participate
therein may do so only at the cost of forfeiting his limited liability.[7]
Moreover, a majority of the general partners may, subject to any
agreement between the partners (both general *and* limited), decide
any question arising in relation to ordinary matters connected with
the partnership business.[8] There can be little doubt that, in the
absence of some other agreement, a decision so taken will bind all
the partners, general and limited alike, even though the latter may
not have been consulted or given an opportunity of expressing their
views.[9] It is thus of particular importance that the general partners

---

[1] Partnership Act 1890, s.19: see *supra*, paras. 10–10 *et seq.*
[2] Limited Partnerships Act 1907, s.7.
[3] *Ibid.*
[4] See *infra*, para. 31–12.
[5] See the Partnership Act 1890, s.44; also *supra*, paras. 25–40 *et seq.*
[6] See *supra*, paras. 10–158 *et seq.*, 18–18.
[7] Limited Partnerships Act 1907, s.6(1).
[8] *Ibid.* s.6(5)(a). *Cf.* the Partnership Act 1890, s.24(8) and *supra*, paras. 15–05 *et seq.*
[9] In practice, any agreement overriding the provisions of the Limited Partnerships Act 1907,
s.6(5)(a) is likely to specify the manner in which the general partners may take such decisions (*e.g.*
by requiring something other than a simple majority), rather than giving the limited partners a right
to participate in the decision-making process, with the attendant risk of unlimited liability under
ibid. s.6(1).

exercise this power with the utmost good faith,[10] since any attempt at consultation with the limited partners might result in their direct or indirect participation in the management of the firm.

31-03   However, the current editor considers that the general partners' powers neither extend beyond the management of the partnership business nor authorise them to change that business without the consent of the limited partners. In the latter case, not only might a change in the business materially affect the extent of the general partners' implied authority to bind the firm,[11] but the limited partners could also properly say that they did not contribute capital to be applied for that purpose.[12] Similarly, the general partners cannot unilaterally change the terms of the partnership and, given the peculiar nature of a limited partner's position, his agreement to such a change could not be inferred merely from the conduct of the general partners.[13]

Limited partners

31-04   As noted above, a limited partner may not take part in the management of the partnership business,[14] either directly or indirectly: if he does so, he will be liable for all the debts and obligations of the firm incurred whilst his participation continues.[15] However, he enjoys a statutory right, exercisable either personally or by means of an agent, to inspect the partnership books,[16] to "examine into" the state and prospects of its business and to "advise with" the partners thereon.[17] It goes without saying that such rights, as well as any special powers conferred upon the limited partner by

---

[10] See supra, paras. 16-01 et seq.

[11] Partnership Act 1890, s.5: see supra, paras. 12-09 et seq.

[12] See supra, para. 15-10.

[13] Partnership Act 1890, s.19; see also supra, paras. 10-10 et seq.

[14] This expression is not defined. It is considered that any decision which constitutes an "ordinary matter connected with the partnership business" (see the Partnership Act 1890, s.24(8); the Limited Partnerships Act 1907, s.6(5)(a)) is likely to trespass into the field of management, whereas any decision relating to the terms or structure of the partnership (e.g. the nature of the business carried on, the admission of new partners, the profit sharing ratios) will not. Nevertheless, there is a substantial "grey" area in between.

[15] Limited Partnerships Act 1907, s.6(1). The current editor is of the opinion that such liability will not necessarily cease as soon as the limited partner withdraws from participation in management, at least so far as concerns any of "his" decisions which require to be implemented thereafter. Sed quaere.

[16] See supra, paras. 22-09 et seq.

[17] Limited Partnerships Act 1907, s.6(1). The current editor considers that the words "advise with" connote discussion and an interchange of views falling short of any attempt to influence management decisions. A similar view was expressed in the original Supplement to this work on the Limited Partnerships Act 1907, where the editors observed "... it will not be safe for a limited partner to take part in the actual determination of any question upon which he advises with his co-partners."

the agreement, must be exercised with particular care so as to avoid any suggestion of involvement in the management of the business.

2. THE CAPITAL OF LIMITED PARTNERSHIPS

Initial capital and change of liability

A limited partnership must, by definition, have a fixed capital **31–05** when it is established, since the Act requires the limited partners to contribute a sum of capital on entry, particulars of which must be delivered on registration.[18] However, there appears to be nothing in the Act which requires such capital, once contributed, to be retained by the limited partners: thus, like any other capital contribution, it may seemingly be divided between some or all of the partners in such proportions as they may agree.[19] By the same token, it would not seem to affect the limited partners' rights if their contributions are all lost in the course of carrying on the partnership business.[20]

A corresponding statutory obligation to contribute capital is not **31–06** imposed on the general partners, so long as they retain that status. Where, however, a general partner wishes to become a limited partner, he must at that stage make a capital contribution. If he has already made such a contribution *qua* general partner, then the amount thereof (or such part of it as still remains in the firm) may properly be treated as forming part (or the whole) of his contribution *qua* limited partner.[21]

Alteration of capital

Subject to the restrictions on the withdrawal of capital by limited **31–07** partners[22] and to compliance with the registration requirements,[23] the partners are free to alter the firm's capital at any time, whether by way of increase or decrease. The current editor does, however, submit that such a change would require the consent of all the partners,[24] save where it results from the admission of a new partner

---

[18] *Ibid.* ss.4(2), 8: see further *supra*, paras. 29–04, 29–20. It does not appear to matter that the contribution is of a nominal amount: see *Dickson v. MacGregor*, 1992 S.L.T. 83 (Land Ct.).

[19] See generally, *supra*, paras. 17–08 *et seq.* Details of such division would seemingly not require to be registered under the Limited Partnerships Act 1907, s.9(1)(f), on the footing that there is no alteration in "the sum contributed by any limited partner"; *sed quaere.*

[20] See *supra*, para. 30–14.

[21] The amount of his contribution in the latter capacity must, of course, be duly registered: *ibid.* s.9(1)(f).

[22] *Ibid.* s.4(3): see *infra*, para. 31–09.

[23] *Ibid.* s.9(1)(f).

[24] *Ibid.* s.7; see also *supra*, para. 17–10.

which, under the Act, does *not* require the limited partners' consent.[25]

31–08   As already noted,[26] there appears to be no objection to a limited partner making an initial capital contribution and at the same time agreeing to make a further contribution at a later date.

Withdrawal of capital

31–09   There is a strict statutory prohibition on the direct or indirect withdrawal of a limited partner's capital contribution whilst the partnership is continuing,[27] although there is no related requirement that such contribution must continue to be owned by the limited partner once it has been made.[28] Moreover, the prohibition is framed solely in terms of the limited partners. It would appear to follow that if, by the terms of the agreement or the general law, the whole or any part of a limited partner's contribution is treated as belonging to a general partner, the latter would, subject to obtaining his co-partners' consent, be free to withdraw it at any time without penalty to himself or to the limited partner.[29] This highlights the fundamental difference between a limited partnership and a limited company, since the general partners will remain personally liable for all the debts and obligations of the firm irrespective of the presence (or absence) of the partners' respective capital contributions.[30] It should also be noted that there is no restriction whatsoever on the members of an ordinary or limited partnership agreeing to convert the joint property of the firm into the separate property of one of their number or vice versa.[31]

31–10   If a limited partner *does* seek to withdraw his contribution, the current editor considers that the creditors of the firm could neither object to nor prevent such withdrawal.[32] Their real protection lies in that partner's liability for the debts of the firm up to the amount so withdrawn.[33]

---

[25] *Ibid.* s.6(5)(d).

[26] See *supra*, para. 30–10.

[27] Limited Partnerships Act 1907, s.4(3); see also *supra*, paras. 30–11 *et seq.*

[28] See *supra*, para. 31–05. As to the position where capital has been lost, see *supra*, para. 30–14.

[29] There is no legitimate warrant for an inference that the limited partners' contributions should at all times be available to the firm in the form of cash or assets, *e.g.* capital may quite properly be risked in the business or applied in meeting day to day expenses (including any payments due to the general partners).

[30] This will be the position whether those contributions have been withdrawn by the partners or lost in the course of carrying on the partnership business.

[31] See *supra*, paras. 18–43 *et seq.* But see also, in the case of insolvency, *supra*, paras. 27–102 *et seq.*

[32] See *supra*, para. 18–44.

[33] Limited Partnerships Act 1907, s.4(3). See further, *supra*, para. 30–12.

Interest on capital

In the absence of some specific agreement, a limited partner will **31–11** not be entitled to interest on his capital contribution.[34]

3. SHARES IN LIMITED PARTNERSHIPS

Quantum: profits and losses

The Limited Partnerships Act 1907 does not lay down how the **31–12** profits and losses of a limited partnership are to be shared between the partners. Those provisions of the Act which establish the extent of a limited partner's liability refer only to the debts and obligations of the firm[35] and, on that footing, in earlier editions of this work it was submitted that—

"the same limit of liability will apply in making good losses between the partners as in the payment of the creditors of the firm, for under the Partnership Act 1890 losses and deficiencies of capital are met in the same way as any other losses."[36]

However, in *Reed v. Young*[37] the House of Lords emphatically held that, so far as concerns *trading* losses, there is no warrant for this view.[38] It follows that a limited partner may be liable for losses over and above the amount of his capital contribution, and this must always be borne in mind, particularly since there are now strict rules governing the relief available in respect of such losses for tax purposes.[39]

Subject as aforesaid and in the absence of any express agreement **31–13** between the partners, the presumption of equality will apply to a limited partnership just as it applies to an ordinary partnership,[40]

---

[34] Partnership Act 1890, s.24(4); Limited Partnerships Act 1907, s.7; see also *supra*, paras. 17–13, 20–27 *et seq.*

[35] See the Limited Partnerships Act 1907, ss.4(2), (3), 6(1). *Ibid.* s.5 is expressed in more general terms, but *ibid.* s.4(2) defines the liability of a general partner solely by reference to the debts and obligations of the firm.

[36] See the Partnership Act 1890, s.44, *supra*, para. 25–40 *et seq.*

[37] [1986] 1 W.L.R. 649.

[38] *Quaere*, can a distinction be drawn between trading and other losses, with a view to distinguishing *Reed v. Young*? Although the *ratio decidendi* is strictly confined to the treatment of losses for tax purposes, the House of Lords took care to draw a distinction between accounting losses on the one hand and liabilities to third parties on the other. The current editor considers that all losses as between the partners must be treated as falling within the former category, so that any distinction would in real terms be illusory.

[39] See *infra*, para. 34–72.

[40] Partnership Act 1890, s.24(1); Limited Partnerships Act 1907, s.7; see also *supra*, paras. 19–19 *et seq.*, 20–04 *et seq.*

even though this will rarely, if ever, be what the partners intend.
Care should accordingly be taken to record the agreed profit and loss
shares, the nature of which are in the discretion of the partners
themselves.

31–14   Having regard to the liability imposed on a limited partner who
withdraws or receives back any part of his capital contribution during
the continuance of the partnership,[41] care must be taken to avoid an
inadvertent return of capital in the form of a supposed share of
profits, *e.g.* where partners' preferential "salaries" are payable
irrespective of the firm's profitability.[42]

Assignment: general partners

31–15   The assignment of a general partner's share is governed by the law
applicable to ordinary partnerships,[43] save that the assignee may
normally be admitted to the firm without the consent of the limited
partners.[44] Any such change in the firm would, of course, have to be
registered.[45]

Assignment: limited partners

31–16   Subject to any agreement between the partners, a limited partner
may, with the consent of the general partners, assign his share to a
third party.[46] The assignment must be registered[47] and notice thereof
given in the *Gazette*.[48] Until those formalities have been completed,
the assignment will be of no effect, at least as regards third parties.[49]
Thereafter, the assignee will become a limited partner in the place of
the assignor and enjoy all the rights which were available to him.[50]

31–17   However, the current editor submits that a limited partner has
another option if he does not wish to obtain (or cannot obtain) the
general partners' consent, namely to assign his share in such a way as

---

[41] Limited Partnerships Act 1907, s.4(3); see *supra*, paras. 30–11 *et seq*.

[42] See also *supra*, para. 30–13. As to what falls to be treated as profits, see *supra*, paras. 10–70, 21–02 and *infra*, para. 34–30.

[43] Partnership Act 1890, s.31; Limited Partnerships Act 1907, s.7; see also *supra*, paras. 19–59 *et seq*.

[44] Limited Partnerships Act 1907, s.6(5)(d). It is, of course, open to the partners to agree otherwise: see the opening words of *ibid*. s.6(5).

[45] *Ibid.* s.9(1)(d). See *supra*, paras. 29–26, 29–27.

[46] *Ibid.* s.6(5)(d). See also *supra*, para. 30–19.

[47] *Ibid.* s.9(1)(d). See also *supra*, paras. 29–26, 29–27.

[48] *Ibid.* s.10.

[49] *Ibid.* Note, however, that the penalty for failure to advertise applies only "for the purposes of this Act."

[50] *Ibid.* s.6(5)(b). See also, *supra*, paras. 30–20, 30–21.

to confer on the assignee the more limited rights specified in section 31 of the Partnership Act 1890.[51] Since, in such a case, the limited partner's liability would be unaffected and there would be no change in the firm's constitution,[52] neither advertisement nor registration would seem to be required.[53]

4. CHANGES IN LIMITED PARTNERSHIPS

Admission and retirement of partners

Subject to any agreement between the partners and to the statutory **31–18** restrictions on the size of limited partnerships,[54] one or more new general or limited partners may be introduced at any time without the consent of the limited partners,[55] even though the consent of all the general partners will normally be required.[56]

In those cases where the agreement does not permit a general or **31–19** limited partner to retire, *all* the partners' consent to any such retirement must be obtained.[57] Equally, a limited partner may, with the consent of the general partners, achieve the same result merely by assigning his share to a third party.[58]

Any change in the firm must be duly registered.[59]

Death or bankruptcy of a limited partner

In earlier editions of this work, successive editors advanced the **31–20** following view:

> "If a limited partner dies or becomes bankrupt during the continuance of the partnership, it is apprehended that, in the absence of any agreement to the contrary, the continuing partners will have the right to retain his contribution in the business until the partnership is terminated by effluxion of time or is otherwise dissolved,[60] for the limited partner has no right to withdraw his

---

[51] See *supra*, paras. 19–59 *et seq.*
[52] See *supra*, paras. 19–62 *et seq.*
[53] Limited Partnerships Act 1907, ss.9(1)(d), 10. Note in particular the words "for the purposes of this Act" in the latter section.
[54] See *supra*, para. 29–02.
[55] Limited Partnerships Act 1907, s.6(5)(d).
[56] Partnership Act 1890, s.24(7); Limited Partnerships Act 1907, s.7.
[57] See *supra*, paras. 24–79 *et seq.* And see also, as to the retirement of limited partners, *supra*, para. 30–17.
[58] Limited Partnerships Act 1907, s.6(5)(b): see *supra*, para. 31–16.
[59] *Ibid.* s.9(1)(d): see *supra*, paras. 29–26, 29–27.
[60] See *supra*, paras. 30–17, 30–18.

contribution[61] nor to determine the partnership,[62] nor is it determined by his death or bankruptcy.[63] If this be the true construction of the Act, his estate will doubtless be entitled until the partnership is determined to receive the share of profits or other pecuniary advantages to which he would have been entitled had he not died or become bankrupt,[64] but the position of his executor or administrator or his trustee in bankruptcy is far from clear. As his bankruptcy does not dissolve the partnership, it may be that the bankrupt will still continue to be a partner though his share will have passed to his trustee in bankruptcy.[65] In the case of his death the partnership, so far as he personally is concerned, must come to an end, and as the Act does not provide for his executor or administrator becoming a partner, and he may leave more executors than one, there is a difficulty in supposing that the Act intended them to become partners in his place; yet unless his legal personal representatives do become limited partners in his place it is difficult to see how the partnership could continue if, as might well be the case, the deceased was the only limited partner in the firm, for there cannot be a limited partnership without a limited partner,[66] and the partnership agreement *ex hypothesi* is for a limited partnership and not a general one. Until these difficulties have been removed by decisions of the court all that can be done is to insert such provisions in the partnership agreement to meet these events as will carry out the intention of the partners."

31–21   However, a reappraisal of the legal position produces a different and, in many ways, more attractive result. The fact that the death or bankruptcy of a limited partner will not dissolve the partnership is undeniable in the face of the specific terms of the 1907 Act.[67] It naturally follows that the estate of a deceased limited partner would not be entitled to force a sale of the partnership assets or a general winding up of its affairs,[68] but is it right to assume that the Act also intended to confer on a limited partnership what amounts to a legal personality separate and distinct from the partners who from time to time compose it? Yet, it is only if the partnership before and after a limited partner's death or bankruptcy can properly be regarded as one and the same legal entity that it can be argued, as in the passage

---

[61] Limited Partnerships Act 1907, s.4(3).

[62] *Ibid.* s.6(5)(e).

[63] *Ibid.* s.6(2).

[64] See, as to a limited partner's liability for losses, *supra*, paras. 31–12, 31–13.

[65] If this were the case, there would be little appreciable impact on the firm, since a limited partner is in any event prohibited from taking part in the management of its business and has no power to bind the firm: Limited Partnerships Act 1907, s.6(1).

[66] See *ibid.* s.4(2).

[67] *Ibid.* s.6(2).

[68] See generally, as to the position of an outgoing or deceased partner, *supra*, paras. 19–04 *et seq.*, 23–179 *et seq.*

quoted above, that his capital contribution cannot be withdrawn.[69] The current editor ventures to suggest that such an analysis cannot be correct, given that the Act specifically adopts the Partnership Act definition of the word "firm" as meaning the partners for the time being.[70] Although the word "partnership" is not itself defined, it should surely be treated as synonymous with "firm," so that the prohibition on a limited partner withdrawing his capital contribution "during the continuance of the partnership" applies only to the partnership of which he is a member; when he dies or retires, a different partnership comes into existence and the prohibition ceases to apply.[71]

Change of partner's status

So long as there continue to be at least one general and one limited **31–22** partner in the firm, a general partner may become a limited partner or vice versa.[72] However, the current editor considers that such a change of status may in general only be achieved with the consent of all the partners.[73]

It has already been seen that, in certain circumstances, a limited partner may be *deemed* to be a general partner,[74] but this will not involve a true change of status.

---

[69] If this argument is correct, what rights does a creditor whose debt was incurred after the date of death have against the estate of the deceased partner if the contribution is withdrawn in breach of the statutory prohibition? Surely there can be no privity with the personal representatives such as to give him a direct right of action.

[70] In *Jardine-Paterson v. Fraser* 1974 S.L.T. 93, 97, Lord Maxwell (considering the position of a general partnership in Scotland) observed "I am not satisfied that, as a matter of strict construction of the Partnership Act [*1890*], it necessarily follows that, because a partnership is not dissolved within the meaning of s.33, there is one continuing legal person before and after the death [*of the partner*]." After quoting from the Partnership Act 1890, s.4(1) and (2), he continued "The legal person is, therefore, the group of individuals who have entered into the partnership and prima facie one would think that a differently constituted group would be a different legal person. It is not clear to me why that prima facie view should not apply, even though the partners have agreed that their relationship *inter se* as partners should not be 'dissolved' by the death of one of their number." The position is *a fortiori* in the case of an English partnership which does not enjoy a separate legal personality. See also *Hadlee v. Commissioner of Inland Revenue* [1989] 2 N.Z.L.R. 447, 455, *per* Eichelbaum J. This aspect was not pursued on appeal: see [1993] A.C. 524.

[71] Note, however, the terms of the Limited Partnerships Act 1907, s.9(1) which requires any change in the partners "during the continuance of a limited partnership" to be duly registered.

[72] *Ibid.* ss.4(2), 9(1)(g); see also *supra*, para. 30–16.

[73] Note, however, the terms of *ibid.* s.6(5)(b), (d), which might in certain circumstances permit the general partners alone to consent to the change of status.

[74] *Ibid.* ss. 5, 6(1): see *supra*, paras. 29–24, 29–27, 30–11, 31–02, 31–04.

CHAPTER 32

DISSOLUTION AND WINDING-UP

1. DISSOLUTION OTHERWISE THAN BY THE COURT

Events giving rise to dissolution

32–01   A limited partnership will in general be dissolved by any event which would dissolve an ordinary partnership,[1] subject to certain specific exceptions which only relate to the limited partners. Thus the death or bankruptcy of a general partner will normally dissolve the partnership as regards all the partners.[2] Although such a dissolution can be avoided by agreement,[3] the death or bankruptcy of a *sole* general partner will inevitably affect the firm's status as a limited partnership, unless a new general partner is simultaneously admitted to the firm.[4]

The exceptions to the general rule stated above are as follows:

(1)   *Death or bankruptcy of a limited partner*

32–02   It is specifically provided by the Limited Partnerships Act 1907 that the death or bankruptcy of a limited partner will not dissolve the firm[5] and this is not in terms stated to be subject to any contrary agreement between the partners. Nevertheless, the current editor considers that such a qualification must be implied, so that either event *can* be treated as terminating the partnership if the partners so desire.[6]

(2)   *Dissolution notice served by limited partner*

32–03   Unless such a power is conferred on him by agreement, a limited partner is not entitled to dissolve the partnership by notice.[7]

---

[1] Limited Partnerships Act 1907, s.7; see generally, *supra*, paras. 24–04 *et seq.*
[2] Partnership Act 1890, s.33(1); Limited Partnerships Act 1907, s.7. See *supra*, paras. 24–20 *et seq.*
[3] See *supra*, para. 10–33.
[4] A limited partnership must at all times comprise at least one general partner: Limited Partnerships Act 1907, s.4(2). Note also *ibid.* s.6(3): see *infra*, para. 32–17.
[5] *Ibid.* s.6(2). *Cf.* the Partnership Act 1890, s.33(1), *supra*, paras. 24–20 *et seq.*
[6] See further, *supra*, paras, 30–17, 31–20.
[7] Limited Partnerships Act 1907, s.6(5)(e); *cf.* the Partnership Act 1890, ss.26(1), 32(c), *supra*, paras. 9–01 *et seq.*, 24–10 *et seq.*

(3) Charging order on limited or general partner's share

Subject to any contrary agreement, the other partners are not 32–04 entitled to dissolve the partnership merely because a limited partner has allowed his share to be charged for his separate debts.[8]

This may be contrasted with the position where a general partner 32–05 allows his share to be so charged: in such a case, the current editor submits that a limited partner may safely exercise (or join with the other partners in exercising) the option to dissolve the partnership which is conferred by the Partnership Act 1890,[9] without being treated as having taken part in the management of the partnership business[10] or as having attempted to serve a dissolution notice.[11]

2. DISSOLUTION BY THE COURT

A. JURISDICTION TO DISSOLVE A LIMITED PARTNERSHIP

The court's jurisdiction to dissolve and wind up a limited partnership 32–06 is in general no different from that exercisable in respect of an ordinary partnership.[12]

Winding up as an unregistered company

The Limited Partnerships Act 1907 originally appeared to preclude 32–07 the court from ordering the dissolution and winding up of a limited partnership otherwise than pursuant to the Companies Acts 1862 to 1900,[13] but the relevant subsection was subsequently repealed.[14] Thereafter, a limited partnership could be wound up in the same way as an ordinary partnership, *i.e.* in the exercise of the court's normal jurisdiction or pursuant to the Companies (Consolidation) Act 1908.[15] However, the latter option was removed with effect from January 1, 1914,[16] and this remained the position under the Companies Act 1948.[17]

---

[8] Limited Partnerships Act 1907, s.6(5)(c).
[9] s.33(2), *supra*, paras. 24–29 *et seq.*
[10] Limited Partnerships Act 1907, s.6(1): see *supra*, para. 31–04. Even if this were not the case, it is difficult to see what debts could have been incurred whilst the limited partner was so taking part.
[11] *Ibid.* s.6(5)(e), *supra*, para. 32–03.
[12] See generally *supra*, paras. 24–39 *et seq.*
[13] Limited Partnerships Act 1907, s.6(4).
[14] Companies (Consolidation) Act 1908, s.286.
[15] *Ibid.* ss.267, 268.
[16] Bankruptcy Act 1913, s.24.
[17] s.398. A limited exception was, however, introduced in the case of banking partnerships by the Banking Act 1979, s.18(2)(a). See, now, *infra*, para. 32–09.

32–08   The culmination of this troubled history is to be found in changes introduced under the new insolvency legislation.[18] Thus, a petition for the winding-up of a limited partnership as an unregistered company may now be presented with or without concurrent petitions against two or more of the partners.[19] The partners' ability to serve such petitions is however, restricted.[20]

Banking partnerships

32–09   A limited partnership which is a recognised bank or licensed deposit taker within the meaning of the Banking Act 1987, may be wound up by the court on a petition presented by the Bank of England.[21]

B.   GROUNDS FOR DISSOLUTION BY THE COURT

Mental disorder of a general or limited partner

32–10   In the case of a general partner's mental disorder, a judge of the Court of Protection will have power to dissolve the partnership under the Mental Health Act 1983 in the normal way.[22] However, the Limited Partnerships Act 1907 provides that the mental disorder of a *limited* partner is not a ground for dissolution by the court unless the patient's share "cannot be otherwise ascertained and realised."[23] The underlying assumption appears to be that such a partner will usually enjoy a right to have his share ascertained and realised without a dissolution, even though the Act does not expressly provide for this. In earlier editions of this work it was argued that such an assumption is inconsistent with section 4 of the Limited Partnerships Act 1907[24] but, in the current editor's view, this argument is at the very least questionable.[25] An explanation may be that the reference to the realisation of the limited partner's share is no more than an allusion to his power to assign his share with the consent of the general

---

[18] See the Insolvency Act 1986, s.420 and the Insolvent Partnerships Order 1986 (S.I. 1986 No. 2142).

[19] Insolvent Partnerships Order 1986, Arts. 7, 8(1). See further, *supra*, paras. 27–09 *et seq*. The expression "insolvent partnership" is not defined in the Order and is clearly apt to include a limited partnership. See also the Insolvency Act 1986, ss.125(3) (as substituted by the Insolvent Partnerships Order 1986, Sched. 2, Part II, para. 6), 271 (2B) (as added by *ibid*. Sched. 2, Pt. III, para. 7(c)), *infra*, para. 33–07.

[20] See *supra*, paras. 27–14, 27–32.

[21] Banking Act 1987, s.92. See also *supra*, para. 24–42.

[22] See the Mental Health Act 1983, s.96(1)(g) and *supra*, paras. 24–40, 24–49 *et seq*.

[23] Limited Partnerships Act 1907, s.6(2).

[24] See *supra*, para. 31–20.

[25] See *supra*, paras. 30–18, 31–21.

partners[26] or to those cases in which the agreement contains provision for the purchase of a mentally disordered partner's share.[27]

It would seem to follow from the foregoing that, if the other **32–11** partners are to avoid a general dissolution resulting from the mental incapacity of a limited partner, they must themselves purchase his share or arrange for its sale to a third party who is acceptable to them as a partner.

Other grounds affecting a limited partner

Where dissolution proceedings are brought by a limited partner or **32–12** are framed by reference to the conduct of or some other matter directly affecting such a partner, the exercise of the court's discretion will inevitably be influenced by his special status under the Act.[28] However, it does not follow that the court will necessarily be unsympathetic to such an application, as is evidenced by the decision in *Re Hughes & Co.*,[29] where an order appears to have been made on the "just and equitable" ground.

Winding up of corporate partner

The existence of a corporate partnership[30] is not expressly **32–13** contemplated by the Partnership Act 1890 or by the Limited Partnerships Act 1907, so that no statutory provision establishes the effect of a winding up order against a corporate partner. It is submitted that, in the event of a corporate *general* partner going into liquidation, the court would in all probability order a dissolution on the just and equitable ground;[31] *a fortiori* if it was the sole general partner.[32] Moreover, the dissolution of such a partner would almost inevitably bring about a dissolution of the firm, in the absence of some other agreement.[33] However, the same cannot be said of a corporate limited partner: in either of the above instances, there is perhaps little more than an arguable case for a dissolution on the just and equitable ground.[34]

---

[26] Limited Partnerships Act 1907, s.6(5)(b): see *supra*, para. 31–16.
[27] Such a construction would support the arguments advanced *supra*, paras. 30–18, 31–21.
[28] See, generally, the Partnership Act 1890, s.35, *supra*, paras. 24–39, 24–55 *et seq*.
[29] [1911] 1 Ch. 342, where a petition had been brought by the limited partner under the Companies (Consolidation) Act 1908). See also *Muirhead v. Borland*, 1925 S.C. 474 (Ct. of Session).
[30] See, as to the meaning of this expression, *supra*, para. 11–02.
[31] Partnership Act 1890, s.35(f); and see *supra*, paras. 24–25, 24–26, 24–75 *et seq*. The liquidation of a corporate partner by no means implies that it is insolvent: see *supra*, para. 11–12.
[32] A limited partnership must comprise at least one general partner: Limited Partnerships Act 1907, s.4(2).
[33] Partnership Act 1890, s.33(1); see also *supra*, para. 24–27.
[34] Since the dissolution of a company may be equated with the death of an individual, it might be argued that the Limited Partnerships Act 1907, s.6(2) (which prevents the death of a limited partner from automatically dissolving the firm) is effective to prevent such a dissolution being ordered; *sed quaere*.

32–14   It should be noted that special provisions apply under the new insolvency legislation in the case of a corporate partner which is wound up on a petition presented concurrently with a petition for the winding up of the firm.[35]

Insolvency

32–15   The grounds on which an insolvent partnership may be wound up as an unregistered company under the Insolvency Act 1986 are considered elsewhere in this work.[36]

3. WINDING-UP

32–16 When a limited partnership is dissolved, the task of winding up its affairs is entrusted to the general partners (or such of them as are solvent), unless the court directs otherwise.[37] Whilst a limited partner retains the right to apply for an order that the affairs of the partnership be wound up under the supervision of the court,[38] the current editor considers that such an application might not be entertained unless misconduct by the general partners or some other special circumstances could be shown to exist.

32–17   It goes almost without saying that, if the partnership is dissolved by the death or bankruptcy of a sole general partner or if, following a dissolution, the only solvent general partner dies or becomes insolvent before the winding-up is complete, the limited partners will have to make an immediate application to the court.[39]

---

[35] Insolvent Partnerships Order 1986, Art. 8(2), Sched. 2, Pt. II. See *supra*, paras. 27–23 *et seq.*
[36] See *supra*, paras. 27–09 *et seq.*
[37] Limited Partnerships Act 1907, s.6(3); see also the Partnership Act 1890, s.38, *supra*, paras. 13–64 *et seq.* As to bankruptcy, see *supra*, paras. 27–67 *et seq.*
[38] Partnership Act 1890, s.39, *supra*, paras. 19–29 *et seq.*
[39] *Quaere*, could it be argued that, in such a case, the Limited Partnerships Act 1907, s.6(3) does not apply, so that the limited partners are free to undertake the winding-up (albeit perhaps not in that capacity)?

CHAPTER 33

INSOLVENCY

1. APPLICATION OF INSOLVENCY LAWS TO LIMITED PARTNERSHIPS

THE Insolvency Act 1986, as applied to partnerships by the Insolvent **33–01** Partnerships Order 1986, does not in general distinguish between limited and ordinary partnerships, so that, as has already been seen,[1] an insolvent limited partnership may in appropriate circumstances be wound up as an unregistered company on the petition of the firm, one or more of the partners or a creditor.

Position of limited partners

It is consistent with the treatment of a partnership as an **33–02** unregistered company that the partners should in general be treated as its officers and directors.[2] However, in so doing, the insolvency legislation appears to ignore the peculiar status of the limited partner, who is precluded from participation in the management of the partnership business as a condition of retaining his limited liability.[3]

Thus, where an insolvent partnership is being wound up as an **33–03** unregistered company and there are no concurrent petitions against the partners, any "member or former member of the partnership or any other person who has or has had control or management of the partnership business" is deemed to be an officer and director of that "company."[4] It is not entirely clear whether the "control or management" requirement is applicable to the past and present members of the firm as well as to "any other person"; if its application is confined to the latter, a limited partner will seemingly fall to be treated as a director, even though he enjoys few of the attributes normally associated with such a position.[5] The uncertainty is further compounded by a supplemental provision which merely refers to "any member of the partnership," thus apparently treating all partners, both general and limited, indiscriminately.[6] However,

---

[1] See *supra*, paras. 27–08 *et seq.*
[2] See *supra*, paras. 27–58, 27–64.
[3] Limited Partnerships Act 1907, s.6(1): see *supra*, paras. 30–11, 31–04.
[4] Insolvent Partnerships Order 1986 (S.I. 1986 No. 2142), Art. 3(a). And see *supra*, para. 27–58.
[5] Equally, if the requirement is of general application, a dormant general partner would also be exempted from any notional director status. *Quaere* would a court readily countenance such a result?
[6] Insolvent Partnerships Order 1986, Art. 6, applying the Company Directors Disqualification Act 1986, ss.6–10, 15, 19(c), 20 and Sched. 1.

since the type of conduct likely to result in a disqualification or other order against a limited partner will usually denote prior participation in the management of the firm (with a consequent forfeiture of limited liability), the above question may in practice prove to be of largely academic interest.

33–04   Whether or not a limited partner falls to be treated as a director, he will be liable *qua* contributory to the extent that he has received back any part of his contribution[7] and, perhaps, even where his capital contribution continues to be held by the firm.[8] However, the current editor is of the opinion that this will not involve any alteration in the quantum of a current or former limited partner's liability, although the position is far from clear.[9]

Authority of limited partners

33–05   It is apprehended that, in the absence of express authority, a limited partner would have no power to act for the firm in insolvency proceedings.[10] Equally, if such authority were conferred on him, its exercise would prima facie not involve participation in the management of the firm, thus causing him to forfeit his limited liability.[11]

2. PETITIONS BY AND AGAINST LIMITED PARTNERS

Petitions by limited partners

33–06   The members of a limited partnership may not present a joint debtors' petition unless the firm is itself wound up as an unregistered company.[12]

Petitions against limited partners

33–07   Where concurrent petitions are presented against the firm and against two or more of the partners, a limited partner may secure a dismissal of the petition against him, even though an order is made against the firm,[13] if he either lodges in court "sufficient money or

---

[7] See, as to the effect of such withdrawal, the Limited Partnerships Act 1907, s.4(3) and *supra*, paras. 30–11 *et seq.*

[8] The Insolvency Act 1986, s.226(1) provides that "every person is deemed a contributory who is liable to pay or contribute to the payment of any debt or liability of the company"; see also *ibid.* s.79(1). A limited partner is so liable, but only to the extent of his contribution: Limited Partnerships Act 1907, s.4(2); see also *supra*, paras. 29–04, 30–09. But see also *infra*, para. 33–07.

[9] See *supra*, para. 27–61. As to the ability of a limited partner to retire from the firm, see *supra*, paras. 30–17, 30–18, 31–20, 31–21.

[10] See *supra*, paras. 12–36, 30–04.

[11] Limited Partnerships Act 1907, s.6(1). See *supra*, para. 30–06.

[12] Insolvent Partnerships Order 1986, Art. 13(1).

[13] As to the position in the case of an ordinary partnership, see *supra*, para. 27–39.

security ... to meet his limited liability for the debts and obligations of the partnership" or satisfies the court that he is no longer under any liability in respect of such debts and obligations.[14] The current editor submits that a limited partner should be able to satisfy the latter condition by demonstrating that he has neither withdrawn his capital contribution nor forfeited his limited liability.[15] If that is not, for whatever reason, possible, the petition will seemingly be dismissed only if the limited partner lodges in court a sum equal to the amount of his contribution, irrespective of whether he has previously sought to withdraw it from the firm.

3. ADMINISTRATION OF INSOLVENT PARTNERS' ESTATES

Joint and separate estates

As in the case of the old bankruptcy law, in the event of the **33–08** insolvency of a partnership, the joint debts are principally payable out of the joint estate and the separate debts out of the partners' respective separate estates.[16] It would thus seem that the decision *Re Barnard*[17] may still be in point. In that case, a bankrupt, Barnard, was the sole general partner in two limited partnerships known respectively as W. H. Barnard and the Scrap Metal Co. There was only one limited partner in the former firm, but three in the latter. Bills of exchange amounting to £9,869 were drawn on the Scrap Metal Co. and accepted by Barnard as managing partner. These bills were held by Martins Bank. In June, a receiving order was made against the first firm, W. H. Barnard, and Barnard was adjudicated bankrupt. In July, a receiving order was made against the second firm, Scrap Metal Co., and Barnard was again adjudicated bankrupt. Martins Bank lodged a proof for £9,869 in the second bankruptcy but later withdrew it and sought to prove their debt in the first. The trustee rejected the proof on the ground that Barnard was not a party to the bills. Farwell J. held that, in these circumstances, the receiving order against the firm, W. H. Barnard, operated against Barnard alone, that the signature of the Scrap Metal Co. to the bills was equivalent to Barnard's signature,[18] and that the bank was therefore entitled to prove in the bankruptcy of W. H. Barnard. He went on to point out that, as Barnard was the sole general partner in both firms,

---

[14] Insolvency Act 1986, ss.125(3) (as substituted, in the case of a corporate partner, by the Insolvent Partnerships Order 1986, Sched. 2, Pt. II, para. 6), 271(2B) (as added, in the case of an individual partner, by *ibid.* Sched. 2, Part. III, para. 7(c)).

[15] See the Limited Partnerships Act 1907, ss.4(3), 6(1), considered *supra,* paras. 30–11 *et seq.,* 31–02 *et seq.*

[16] See *supra,* paras. 27–82 *et seq.* Note that some inroads into this principle are likely to be made in the forthcoming revised Insolvent Partnerships Order.

[17] [1932] 1 Ch. 269.

[18] See the Bills of Exchange Act 1882, s.23(2). And see *supra,* para. 12–176.

there was technically no question of any joint liability but he nevertheless expressed the opinion that the assets of W. H. Barnard must first be applied in payment of that firm's debts and the surplus in repaying the limited partner's contribution; only the balance would form part of Barnard's separate estate applicable towards his own private debts and any other debts incurred by him on behalf of other limited partnerships. The assets of the Scrap Metal Co. fell to be applied in a similar way.

Part Seven

TAXATION

CHAPTER 34

INCOME TAX

1. INTRODUCTION

The development of partnership taxation

Reference has already been made earlier in this work to the fact **34–01**
that, under English law, a partnership generally has no legal status or
existence independently of the individual partners of which it is
composed; in fact the term "partnership" is nothing more than a
convenient method referring to the existence of two or more persons
who are carrying on a business in common with a view of profit.[1] The
rights and liabilities of a partnership are nothing more than the
aggregate of the rights and liabilities of the individual partners. In
theory, therefore, there is no reason why the ordinary rules as to the
taxation of the income of individuals should not apply to the taxation
of partnerships, with each partner being assessed to tax separately
from his co-partners. However, this would necessitate the dissection
of the partnership accounts and an apportionment of the overall
expenses and gross receipts amongst the individual partners in order
to determine their respective net incomes.[2] It was to avoid this
consequence that the Income Tax Act 1918 provided that where a
trade was carried on by two or more persons jointly, the tax was to
be computed and stated jointly and in one sum and was to be treated
as separate and distinct from any other tax chargeable on those
persons. It also provided for a joint assessment to be made in the
firm name. These provisions were subsequently re-enacted on three
occasions without alteration and are now contained in section 111 of
the Income and Corporation Taxes Act 1988. However, as part of the
wide ranging reforms introduced by the Finance Act 1994, that long-
standing approach has been abandoned in favour of the individual
assessment of each partner by reference to his share of the
partnership profits.[3] This new regime applies to all firms formed after
April 6, 1994[4] and will apply to *all* firms, whenever formed, as from
the tax year 1997/98.[5]

---

[1] See *supra*, paras. 3–01 *et seq.* For a recent reaffirmation of this principle in an income tax case,
see *MacKinlay v. Arthur Young McClelland Moores & Co.* [1990] 2 A.C. 239.
[2] This is, in fact, the approach adopted in New Zealand: see *Hadlee v. Commissioner of Inland
Revenue* [1993] A.C. 524, 528 (P.C.).
[3] See the Income and Corporation Taxes Act 1988, s.111, as substituted by the Finance Act
1994, s.215(1). See further *infra*, para. 34–06.
[4] This will include any firm in existence on that date whose trade is thereafter deemed to have
been discontinued by virtue of the provisions of *ibid.* s.113(1): see *infra*, para. 34–45.
[5] Finance Act 1994, ss.215(4), (5). See further *infra*, paras. 34–06 *et seq.*

34-02   Nevertheless, under both the old and new regimes the taxation of partnership income, *i.e.* the income of the individual partners which is derived from partnership activities, stands on a different footing from the taxation of income derived by them from other sources and thus requires special attention, albeit that the position is much simplified under the new regime. Firms comprising one or more corporate partners remain subject to special rules.[6]

34-03   The other distinctive feature of the old regime is to be found in the provisions which accord to a partnership a degree of continuity and recognition independent of its members, thus enabling its trade to be treated as continuing notwithstanding the admission or departure of a partner, provided that a suitable form of election is submitted.[7] Again, this will no longer be a feature of the new regime, under which each partner is deemed to carry on a separate trade, profession or business[8]: whilst he remains a member of the firm, the continuance of that deemed trade or profession will inevitably be unaffected by any change in its composition.[9]

34-04   The present code of income tax law for partnerships, which is substantially contained in the Taxes Management Act 1970, the Income and Corporation Taxes Act 1988, the Capital Allowances Act 1990 and the amending provisions of the Finance Act 1994, embodies a number of special rules and principles which are peculiar to partnerships within the meaning of the legislation.[10]

2. TAX TREATMENT OF PARTNERSHIPS

Partnerships and the Income and Corporation Taxes Act 1988

Firms in existence prior to April 6, 1994

34-05   The main statutory provisions governing the taxation of partnership income, apart from capital allowances, are those contained in Chapter VII of the Income and Corporation Taxes Act 1988. The first section of that Chapter is section 111, which will continue to apply to firms in existence on April 6, 1994 until the beginning of the tax year 1997/98[11] and provides as follows:

---

[6] See *infra*, paras. 34-80 *et seq.*

[7] See, *infra*, paras. 34-46 *et seq*. *Cf.* the position under the general law, *supra*, paras. 3-04, 3-06 *et seq.*, 14-48 *et seq.*

[8] Income and Corporation Taxes Act 1988, s.111(3), (5), as substituted by the Finance Act 1994, s.215(1).

[9] See also *ibid.* s.113(2), as substituted by the Finance Act 1994, s.216(1).

[10] It is proposed to consider only those rules and principles which are of particular importance in relation to partnerships. For all other matters, the reader is referred to the standard works on income tax, *e.g. Whiteman on Income Tax* (3rd ed.).

[11] Finance Act 1994, s.215(4)(a). Note, however, that the section will cease to apply if the firm's trade is deemed to be discontinued pursuant to the provisions of the Income and Corporation Taxes Act 1988, s.113(1): see *infra*, para. 34-45.

"Partnership assessments to income tax

111. Where a trade or profession is carried on by two or more persons jointly, income tax in respect thereof shall be computed and stated jointly, and in one sum, and shall be separate and distinct from any other tax chargeable on those persons or any of them, and a joint assessment shall be made in the partnership name."

The section does not purport to establish a definition of partnership for the purposes of the Taxes Act; nor is there any other provision in that Act or in any other taxing statute which defines partnership. Indeed, the word "partnership" itself appears only in the heading and, by way of a subsidiary reference to "the partnership name" at the end of the section. Thus, the only requirement for the application of section 111 appears to be the carrying on of a trade or profession (but not, in terms, a business)[12] by two or more persons jointly. This requirement will clearly cover a number of relationships which would not constitute partnerships within the meaning of the Partnership Act 1890[13] but, whilst the point is by no means free from doubt, it is

---

[12] *Quaere* is the word "trade" synonymous with "business," or is there an anomalous class of joint businesses (*e.g.* an investment business) which falls outside the scope of the section? The words "trade or profession" have appeared in successive Income Tax Acts, yet in other Acts, *e.g.* the Finance (No. 2) Act 1939, s.12(1) (excess profits duty), the words "trade or business" have been adopted. "Trade" is defined in the Income and Corporation Taxes Act 1988, s.832(1) as including "every trade, manufacture, adventure or concern in the nature of trade." Although it has been held, in relation to the forerunner of what is now the Companies Act 1985, s.715, that "business" has a more extensive meaning than "trade" (see *Harris v. Amery* (1865) L.R. 1 C.P. 148, 154, *per* Willes J.), decisions under the Taxes Acts do not appear to address the point: see, for example, *Ransom v. Higgs* [1974] 1 W.L.R. 1594 and the other cases collected in *Stroud's Judicial Dictionary* (5th ed.), pp. 2660, 2661; note also *Watts v. Hart* [1894] S.T.C. 548, where the two words appear to be used interchangeably. If and when the point arises for decision, it seems likely that the word "trade" would be construed liberally so as to avoid the creation of such an anomalous class; some support for that construction may be derived from the Income and Corporation Taxes Act 1988, s.112(2), which refers to the "trade or business" of a partnership firm; but *cf. ibid.* s.277(2). Nevertheless, until the point is actually decided, it is submitted that a real doubt remains. Under the new regime of partnership taxation, this doubt is removed: see *ibid.* s.111(5), as substituted by the Finance Act 1994, s.215(1) and reproduced *infra*, para. 34–06.

[13] Thus, it would appear possible for a "partnership" to exist within the meaning of the rubric to the Taxes Act 1988, s.111, even though there is no profit motive, as expressly required by the Partnership Act 1890, s.1(1): see, for example, *Morden Rigg & Co. and R.B. Eskrigge & Co. v. Monks* (1923) 8 T.C. 450, 463, *per* Lord Sterndale M.R; *Lindsay, Woodward & Hiscox v. C.I.R.* (1932) 18 T.C. 43, 58, *per* Lord Morison; *Dodd & Tanfield v. Haddock* (1963) 43 T.C. 229, 246, *per* Buckley J.; *cf.* the decision in *Three H. Aircraft Hire v. Customs & Excise Commissioners* [1982] S.T.C. 653 (in relation to value added tax) noticed *infra*, para. 37–01, n. 2. Although it is not easy to define the scope of s.111 with precision, the section is clearly capable of applying to all partnerships within the meaning of the Partnership Act 1890, subject only to the point discussed in the preceding footnote; it is outside the scope of this work to consider whether the section has any wider application. Note that the Revenue accept that a limited partnership established "for the purpose of raising funds for investment into companies" (*i.e.* venture capital) is a partnership for tax purposes but may, nevertheless, not be regarded as trading: see the Statement issued by the British Venture Capital Association on May 26, 1987.

submitted that a partnership which falls within the definition
contained in section 1(1) of that Act should be regarded as a
partnership for income tax purposes and, thus, liable to assessment
under section 111. It follows that, in considering authorities relating
to the income tax treatment of partnerships, care must be taken to
ascertain whether the particular "partnership" is in truth a
partnership within the meaning of the 1890 Act or merely falls within
the wide definition contained in section 111 or its predecessors.[14]

The above approach will cease to apply with effect from the
beginning of the tax year 1997/98, unless there is a deemed
discontinuance in the meantime.[15]

Firms formed on or after April 6, 1994 and all firms from 1997/98

34–06   In its amended form,[16] which applies to any firm whose trade,
profession or business was commenced on or after April 6, 1994,[17]
including a firm in existence prior to that date which has been the
subject of a deemed discontinuance after that date,[18] and to *all* firms
with effect from the tax year 1997/98,[19] section 111 the Income and
Corporation Taxes Act 1988 provides as follows:

"**111.**—(1) Where a trade or profession is carried on by two or
more persons in partnership, the partnership shall not, unless the
contrary intention appears, be treated for the purposes of the Tax
Acts as an entity which is separate and distinct from those persons.

(2) So long as a trade or profession ('the actual trade or
profession') is carried on by persons in partnership and each of
those persons is chargeable to income tax, the profits or gains or
losses arising from the trade or profession shall be computed for
the purposes of income tax in like manner as if the partnership
were an individual.

(3) A person's share of the profits or gains or losses of the
partnership which for any period are computed in accordance with
subsection (2) above shall be determined according to the interests
of the partners during that period; and income tax shall be
chargeable or, as the case may require, loss relief may be claimed
as if—

---

[14] See, for example, *Morden Rigg & Co. and R.B. Eskrigge & Co. v. Monks* (1923) 8 T.C. 450;
John Gardner & Bowring, Hardy & Co. Ltd. v. C.I.R. (1930) 15 T.C. 602; *cf. Pratt v. Strick* (1932)
17 T.C. 459.
[15] Finance Act 1994, ss.215(4), (5). As to the circumstances giving rise to a deemed
discontinuance, see the Income and Corporation Taxes Act 1988, s.113(1) and *infra*, para. 34–45.
[16] As substituted by the Finance Act 1994, s.215(1).
[17] *Ibid.* s.215(4)(b), (5). An exception is made in the case of firms to which the Income and
Corporation Taxes Act 1988, s.112(3) applies: *ibid.* See further, as to such firms, *infra*, para. 34–86
et seq.
[18] Income and Corporation Taxes Act 1988, s.113(1); see further *infra*, para. 34–45.
[19] Finance Act 1994, s.215(4)(a), (5).

(a) that share derived from a trade or profession ('the deemed trade or profession') carried on by the person alone;

(b) the deemed trade or profession was set up and commenced by him at the time when he became a partner or, where the actual trade or profession was previously carried on by him alone, the time when the actual trade[20] was set up and commenced; and

(c) the deemed trade or profession is permanently discontinued by him at the time when he ceases to be a partner or, where the actual trade of profession is subsequently carried on by him alone, the time when the actual trade or profession is permanently discontinued.

(4) Where—

(a) subsections (2) and (3) above apply in relation to the profits or gains or losses of a trade or profession carried on by persons in partnership, and

(b) other income accrued to those persons by virtue of their being partners,

that other income shall be chargeable to tax by reference to the same periods as if it were profits or gains arising from the trade or profession.

(5) Subsections (1) to (3) above apply, with the necessary modifications, in relation to a business as they apply in relation to a trade."[21]

It will be noted that, unlike its predecessor, the concept of partnership, albeit still not defined in the Act, is central to the application of the section. It must follow that any partnership within the meaning of the Partnership Act 1890 must necessarily be regarded as a partnership for the purposes of this section. Where, however, the firm comprises one or more corporate partners,[22] the majority of its provisions will not apply.[23]

The approach adopted by the new section 111 is still to treat the partnership as a separate person, but *only* for the purposes of computing the partnership profits.[24] Once the computation is complete and the share of each partner is determined,[25] he will be taxed thereon as if that share was derived from a separate trade, profession or business carried on by him.[26]

---

[20] The words "or profession" appear to have been accidentally omitted at this point.

[21] This subsection resolves a doubt which existed under the original s.111 and its predecessors: see *supra*, para. 34–05, n. 12.

[22] See *supra*, paras. 11–01 *et seq.*

[23] The corporate partners will, by definition, not be chargeable to income tax, as required by *ibid.* s.111(2). See further, *infra*, para. 34–80 *et seq.*

[24] *Ibid.* s.111(2). *Cf. ibid.* s.111(1).

[25] *Ibid.* s.111(3).

[26] *Ibid.* s.111(3)(a).

Partnership agreements and the Revenue

34–07　(a) *Existence of partnership.* It was originally thought that a determination as to the existence of a partnership involved a pure question of fact from which there could be no appeal[27] but, in view of the decision in *Keith Spicer Ltd. v. Mansell*,[28] it must now be recognised as involving a mixed question of law and fact. Thus, where the Commissioners[29] have made a finding that a partnership does or does not exist, an appeal will lie.[30]

34–08　As already noted,[31] in order to determine whether a partnership exists regard must be had to the substance of the transaction or the nature of the activity, rather than to its outward form.[32] If, on a true analysis, the relationship of partnership exists, an express agreement purporting to negative such existence will be of no effect. Thus, in *Weiner v. Harris*,[33] Cozens-Hardy M.R. observed:

> "It is quite plain that by the mere use of a well-known legal phrase you cannot constitute a transaction that which you attempt to describe by that phrase. Perhaps the commonest instance of all, which has come before the Courts in many phases, is this: Two parties enter into a transaction and say 'It is hereby declared that there is no partnership between us.' The court pays no regard to that. The Court looks at the transaction and says 'Is this, in point of law, really a partnership? It is not in the least conclusive that the parties have used a term or language intended to indicate that the transaction is not that which in law it is.' "[34]

34–09　Conversely, an attempt to dress up a transaction or activity in the form of a partnership, where one or more of the essential characteristics of that relationship are lacking, will be rejected as a

---

[27] See *Wood v. Duke of Argyll* (1844) 6 Man. & G. 928; *Lake v. Duke of Argyll* (1844) 6 Q.B. 477. And see *supra*, paras. 5–44, 7–16.

[28] [1970] 1 W.L.R. 333. See also *Morgan Rigg & Co. and R.B. Eskrigge & Co. v. Monks* (1923) 8 T.C. 450, 464, *per* Lord Sterndale M.R.

[29] The Commissioners will normally make the initial finding as to the existence (or non-existence) of a partnership: see, for example, *Alexander Bulloch & Co. v. I.R.C.* [1976] S.T.C. 514 and *Morden Rigg & Co. and R.B. Eskrigge & Co. v. Monks* (1923) 8 T.C. 450.

[30] Thus, in hearing the appeal, the court will be able to decide the question *de novo*: *Keith Spicer Ltd. v. Mansell* [1970] 1 W.L.R. 333. And see *C.I.R. v. Williamson* (1928) 14 T.C. 335. As to the authority of a single partner to appeal against a joint assessment, see *Re Sutherland & Partners' Appeal* [1994] S.T.C. 387.

[31] See *supra*, paras. 5–03 *et seq.*

[32] In *Pratt v. Strick* (1932) 17 T.C. 459, the vendor of a medical practice agreed to continue in the practice for a short period in order to introduce the purchaser to his patients. Notwithstanding the fact that the vendor and the purchaser had agreed to share both receipts and outgoings during that period, it was held that no partnership had been created.

[33] [1910] 1 K.B. 285, 290.

[34] See also *C.I.R. v. Williamson* (1929) 14 T.C. 335, 340, *per* the Lord President; *Reeves v. Evans, Boyce and Northcott Syndicate* (1971) 32 T.R. 483, 487, *per* Megarry J.; *Stekel v. Ellice* [1973] 1 W.L.R. 191, 199–200, *per* Megarry J.; *Alexander Bulloch & Co. v. I.R.C.* [1976] S.T.C. 514, 580, *per* the Lord President; *Newstead v. Frost* [1980] 1 W.L.R. 135; *Saywell v. Pope* [1979] S.T.C. 824.

mere sham.[35] Thus, in one case[36] a father owning two farms executed a deed of partnership whereby he was expressed to enter into partnership with his three sons. The deed provided for the signing of cheques by any of the partners, the sharing of profits, and the payment of rent to the father. In fact, however, they carried on as before, ignoring the terms of the deed. It was held that no partnership existed.[37]

It should be remembered in this context that it is not an essential **34–10** characteristic of the partnership relation (or of the carrying on of a trade by two or more persons jointly[38]) that all the partners must take an active part in the firm's affairs. Thus, there is no reason why a valid partnership should not exist between A, B and C when A is given the sole powers of management, B and C being merely dormant partners. Indeed, this situation is expressly provided for, in connection with limited partnerships, by sections 4 and 6 of the Limited Partnerships Act 1907, and there can be no doubt but that a limited partnership is a partnership for tax purposes.[39]

The continuing development of the so-called *Ramsay* principle[40] **34–11** has added a degree of uncertainty in this area. Nevertheless, if a *genuine* partnership is interposed as a pre-ordained step in an overall tax avoidance scheme, the current editor submits that a court could not properly ignore its existence, particularly if enduring rights and liabilities have been created as between the partners. *A fortiori* if liabilities to third parties have been incurred.[41]

(b) *Date of commencement or dissolution of the partnership.* It is **34–12** a general principle that a partnership deed cannot alter the past; whilst it may have effect as between the partners, the Revenue are

---

[35] *Cf. Martin v. Davies* [1952] C.P.L. 189 (an attempt to dress up a tenancy agreement as a purchase by instalments).

[36] *Dickenson v. Gross* (1927) 11 T.C. 614.

[37] See also *Alexander Bulloch & Co. v. I.R.C.* [1976] S.T.C. 514.

[38] See the Income and Corporation Taxes Act 1988, s.111, *supra*, para. 34–05; *Att.-Gen. v. Borrodaile* (1814) Price's Rep. 148; *J.J. Farrell v. The Sunderland Steamship Co. Ltd.* (1903) 4 T.C. 605.

[39] See, for example, the Income and Corporation Taxes Act 1988, s.117; also *Reed v. Young* [1986] 1 W.L.R. 649.

[40] See *W. T. Ramsay v. I.R.C.* [1982] A.C. 300; *Furniss v. Dawson* [1984] A.C. 474. However, a restrictive interpretation was placed upon these decisions by a majority of the House of Lords in *Craven v. White* [1989] A.C. 398; see also *Shepherd v. Lyntress Ltd.* [1989] S.T.C. 617; *Ensign Tankers (Leasing) Ltd. v. Stokes* [1992] 1 A.C. 655.

[41] See, for example, *Ensign Tankers (Leasing) Ltd. v. Stokes* [1989] 1 W.L.R. 1222, where Millett J. dismissed the Inspector's argument that the creation of two limited partnerships could be treated as a step in a larger transaction. He observed (at *ibid.* p. 1243) that "it logically is impossible at one and the same time to find that the partnerships were trading and that the transactions into which they entered had no commercial purpose." This part of the decision was not appealed from: see [1991] 1 W.L.R. 341, 357H. In such a case, it can clearly be said that the creation of the partnership serves a genuine business purpose *apart* from the avoidance of tax, so that one of the fundamental conditions laid down in both *Ramsay* and *Furniss*, *supra*, and confirmed by all members of the House of Lords in *Craven v. White*, *supra*, will inevitably not be satisfied.

quite entitled to ignore it and to look at the true position. Thus, a recital in such a deed that the partnership existed prior to the date of its execution is not conclusive.[42] What must be considered whenever the date of commencement of a partnership is called into question is whether a *de facto* partnership existed independently of the deed prior to its execution. As noted above, that question will involve a mixture of fact and law; the facts to be considered will include the provision (or absence of provision) for the sharing of profits and losses and the powers of management, etc., exercisable by the alleged "partners"; the questions of law will include the construction to be placed upon any written partnership agreement and the conclusions to be drawn from the facts as found.

34–13   In *Waddington v. O'Callaghan*,[43] a father had given instructions to his solicitors to draw up a deed taking his son into partnership in his own solicitor's practice as from the date of the instructions, subject to the terms of the partnership deed being agreed between himself and his son. It was held that no partnership existed prior to the date of execution of the deed. In arriving at this decision, the court had regard to the fact that no formal notice had been given to clients (although it appears to have been generally known that the partnership had been arranged), no alteration had been made in the name of the firm, and no joint banking account had been opened prior to the execution of the deed. In cases of this type it is immaterial that the profits have been divided as from the notional date of commencement.

34–14   Similar considerations may arise when the date of dissolution of a partnership is in issue. If, for example, some or all of the activities associated with a firm's business are seen to be continuing, it will be necessary to determine whether that firm has ceased to trade and is merely engaged in winding up its affairs following a dissolution or is, in reality, continuing to trade.[44] It should be noted that, in those cases where section 111 of the Taxes Act 1988 in its original form continues to apply,[45] activities carried out in the course of winding up the affairs of a dissolved firm may well, for tax purposes, be sufficient to amount to active trading.

---

[42] *Ayrshire Pullman Motor Services and D. M. Ritchie v. C.I.R.* (1929) 14 T.C. 754; *Reeves v. Evans, Boyce and Northcott Syndicate* (1971) 32 T.R. 483; also *Saywell v. Pope* [1979] S.T.C. 824.

[43] (1931) 16 T.C. 187. See also *Saywell v. Pope, supra*, where two partners attempted (unsuccessfully) to introduce their wives into the partnership with retrospective effect. In the course of his judgment in the latter case, Slade J. observed (at p. 835d): "Partnership accounts cannot operate to make persons partners retrospectively, any more than a written partnership agreement can so operate."

[44] *O'Kane (J. & R.) & Co. v. C.I.R.* (1922) 12 T.C. 303; *Hillerns & Fowler v. Murray* (1932) 17 T.C. 77; *Watts v. Hart* [1984] S.T.C. 548; *C. Connelly & Co. v. Wilbey* [1992] S.T.C. 783.

[45] See *supra*, para. 34–05.

(c) *Other agreements reached between partners.* It follows from **34–15** the foregoing that any agreement which seeks to alter a partners' status or entitlement *ex post facto* can quite properly be implemented as between the partners, whether for accounting purposes or otherwise, but will not bind the Revenue. Thus, where partners agreed to re-allocate the firm's income between themselves several years after it arose, so as to obtain the maximum benefit from available tax reliefs, the re-allocation was held to be of no effect *vis-à-vis* the Revenue.[46]

On the other hand, a bona fide agreement which governs the **34–16** partners' present and future relationship and which does not seek to have any retrospective effect will be equally valid as between the partners themselves and as between them and the Revenue, provided that its terms are adhered to. Thus, it is, for example, open to the partners to agree that the entirety of a capital allowance or balancing charge[47] accruing in respect of a particular partnership asset will be enjoyed or borne by one or more of their number; or even that one partner will indemnify the others against a particular partnership liability, without affecting the deductibility of that liability in computing the taxable profits of the firm.[48] Significant tax advantages can often be obtained from careful planning, coupled with the use of such agreements.[49]

3. METHOD OF ASSESSMENT

Returns, etc.

Position prior to 1996/97

It has already been seen that, until the tax year 1997/98, the profits **34–17** of a partnership which existed prior to April 6, 1994 will continue to be assessed jointly in one sum in the name of the firm, separately and distinctly from any other tax chargeable on the individual partners.[50]

---

[46] *Bucks v. Bowers* [1970] Ch. 431, 441, *per* Pennycuick J. If such an *ex post facto* re-allocation of profit is desired, particular care should be taken to provide for the incidence of the burden of tax, *i.e.* is the reallocated profit to be paid over subject to deduction of tax at the rate of the partner who is for tax purposes treated as entitled to it, or at the rate of the recipient partner, or subject to no deduction at all? If no specific provision is included, it may well be difficult to determine what deduction, if any, is to be made.

[47] There is no reason why the partnership agreement should not specifically allocate a capital allowance or balancing charge between the partners; in the absence of any such provision, the allowance or charge will prima facie be shared by the partners in their profit sharing ratios. See further, *infra*, para. 34–64.

[48] See *Bolton v. Halpern & Woolf* [1981] S.T.C. 14, where the indemnity was given by a retired partner.

[49] In such a way, it may be possible to depress the share of profits of one partner, and increase the share of another. This might formerly have been desirable with a view to increasing the amount of an outgoing partner's annuity for the purposes of what is now the Income and Corporation Taxes Act 1988, s.628: see further, *infra*, para. 34–95.

[50] See the Income and Corporation Taxes Act 1988, s.111 in its original form, *supra*, para. 34–05.

The Inspector of Taxes is given power to require any one or more of the partners to make and deliver a partnership return, together with such accounts and statements as may be required;[51] alternatively such a requirement may be imposed on any person identified in a notice given to all the partners.[52] The return must, *inter alia*, include the names and residences of each of the other partners,[53] as well as particulars of any disposals or acquisitions of partnership property during the year of assessment to which the return relates.[54] The responsibility for making partnership returns is no longer imposed on the "precedent partner" in the firm.[55]

Position with effect from 1996/97

34-18   As from the tax year 1996/97, a similar power will be conferred on what is styled "an officer of the Board".[56] In the case of a firm comprising individuals, the notice may not specify a date for the submission of the return which is earlier than January 1 next following the relevant year of assessment or, where the notice is given after October 31 in the next following year, the expiration of a period of 3 months after the date of the notice.[57] The return must also be accompanied by a partnership statement giving details of the firm's income or losses from each source and its charges on income in respect of each accounting period ending during the period covered by the return and specifying each partner's share of that income, loss or charge.[58]

Tax as a joint debt

Firms in existence prior to April 6, 1994

34-19   Until the new regime of partnership taxation comes into effect,[59] tax on trading income, when assessed, will continue to be a debt of

---

[51] Taxes Management Act 1970, s.9(1), (3), as substituted by the Finance Act 1990, s.90(1).

[52] *Ibid.* s.9(2), as substituted by the Finance Act 1990, s.90(1). The Inspector may proceed under either s.9(2) or (3): *ibid.* s.9(1). It does, however, appear that the power under *ibid.* s.9(2) will only be exercised against a partner or, where no partner is resident in the U.K., the agent, manager or factor of the firm in the U.K.: see the Statement of Practice (SP 4/91) entitled "Tax Returns" dated May 1, 1991, para. 9.

[53] *Ibid.* s.9(4), as substituted by the Finance Act 1990, s.90(1).

[54] *Ibid.* s.12(4), as amended by the Finance Act 1990, s.90(2)(c), Sched. 19, Pt. V.

[55] *Cf. ibid.* s.9(1) in its original form.

[56] *Ibid.* s.12AA(1)-(3), (6), (7), as added by the Finance Act 1994, s.184. Note also *ibid.* s. 42(6), (7), as substituted by the Finance Act 1994, Sched. 19, Pt. 1, para. 13.

[57] *Ibid.* s.12AA(4). In the case of a corporate partnership (*i.e.* a partnership comprising one or more companies), the date for submission must not be earlier than the first anniversary of the end of the relevant period or, where the notice is given more than 9 months after the end of the relevant period, the expiration of 3 months after the date of the notice: *ibid.* s.12AA(5). As to the penalties for failing to submit a return or for submitting an incorrect return, see *ibid.* ss.93A, 95A, as added by the Finance Act 1994, Sched. 19, Pt. 1, paras. 26, 28.

[58] *Ibid.* s.12AB(1), as added by the Finance Act 1994, s.185.

[59] *i.e.* until the tax year 1997/98, unless there is a deemed discontinuance of the firm's trade in the meantime: see *supra*, paras. 34–05, 34–06.

the partnership, for which all the partners will be jointly liable, whether they are true partners or merely held out as such.[60] Thus, any one or all of them may be sued for the whole of the amount of tax due but, as they are not severally liable, a release of one may be tantamount to a release of all, even though the Revenue's failure to join a partner as a party to the action will no longer *per se* release him from liability.[61] However, when a partner dies, his personal representatives will be released, unless the deceased was the last surviving member of the firm.[62]

The fact that the tax is a debt of the partnership should be **34–20** carefully borne in mind when, on a change of partners, the continuing partners undertake to satisfy all the liabilities of the old firm,[63] since this will, unless expressly or impliedly qualified, include a liability for tax on any share of profits previously received by the outgoing partner.[64] However, such an agreement will only have effect as between the continuing and the outgoing partners, and not as between them and the Revenue,[65] so that an outgoing partner will at all times remain directly accountable for the tax liabilities of the old firm, and cannot insist that the Revenue looks first to the continuing partners for settlement. In such circumstances, the outgoing partner will be forced to rely on the indemnities (if any) extracted from the continuing partners on his departure from the firm.[66]

It should be noted that the above provisions applied in the case of a partnership between a husband and wife, even before the introduction of the new regime of separate taxation.[67]

Tax on non-trading income, *e.g.* investment income, is in all cases assessed on the partners individually.

---

[60] Income and Corporation Taxes Act 1988, s.111; *Stevens v. Britten* [1954] 1 W.L.R. 1340. The liability of the partners for tax is joint but not several: see *Harrison v. Willis Bros.* [1966] Ch. 619. As to liability on the basis of holding out, note the apparent doubts expressed in Lawton, Goldberg & Fraser, *The Law of Partnership Taxation* (2nd ed.), para. 3.039. Note also that, as a partnership debt, tax represents something of an anomaly, since it will almost inevitably *not* be borne by the partners in their normal loss sharing ratios once account has been taken of the partners' respective shares in the relevant profits and their entitlement to reliefs, etc.: see the Income and Corporation Taxes Act 1988, s.277(1). This subsection will, with effect from the year 1997/98, be amended by the Finance Act 1994, s.215(3)(c).

[61] See the Civil Liability (Contribution) Act 1978, s.3; also *supra*, paras. 13–05, 20–16.

[62] *Harrison v. Willis Bros.* [1966] Ch. 619, 640, *per* Lord Denning M.R.

[63] Even if not express, such an obligation will normally be implied when a partner leaves a firm: see *supra*, para. 10–207.

[64] See *Stevens v. Britten* [1954] 1 W.L.R. 1340.

[65] See *supra*, para. 34–15. It should be noted that continuing partners may also be liable in respect of an assessment under the Taxes Management Act 1970, s.36 (as substituted by the Finance Act 1989, s.149(1)): *ibid.* s.36(2). With effect from the tax year 1996/97, this subsection is as substituted by the Finance Act 1994, Sched. 19, Pt. 1, para. 11(2): *ibid.* s.196, 199(2)(a).

[66] The value of such indemnities, whether express or implied, will inevitably depend on the resources available to the continuing partners.

[67] See the Income and Corporation Taxes Act 1988, s.279(4). That section ceased to have effect for the year 1990/91 and subsequent years: Finance Act 1988, s.32, Sched. 14, Pt. VIII. See, now, the Income and Corporation Taxes Act 1988, s.282A(4) (as inserted by the Finance Act 1988, s.34).

34-21   It is because of this joint liability that the majority of firms make provision in their agreements for tax reserves to be made out of each partner's profit share year by year and, moreover, for a suitable sum to be retained on account of tax whenever a partner leaves the firm.[68]

Firms formed on or after April 6, 1994 and all firms from 1997/98

34-22   Under the new regime of partnership taxation, tax on trading income will no longer be a debt of the partnership, so that each partner will only be liable in respect of the tax assessable on *his* share of the partnership profits, just as if he were carrying on a wholly separate trade.[69] Where non-trading income, *e.g.* investment income, accrues to the partners, each partner's share will be charged to tax by reference to the same periods as his share of the trading profits.[70]

Ascertainment and apportionment of profits

(a)   *Firms in existence prior to April 6, 1994: old regime*

34-23   Under the old regime of partnership taxation, which will only continue to apply up to the end of the tax year 1995/96,[71] the procedure for assessing the profits of a partnership to tax involve a number of distinct steps.[72] First, the relevant profits must be identified: these are the statutory, as opposed to the actual, profits of the firm for the year of assessment in question, by which is generally meant the profits made in the financial year of the partnership ending in the preceding year of assessment.[73] Those statutory profits must then be apportioned between the individual partners by reference to their respective shares[74] in that year of assessment, even though different shares may have been applied to such profits when they

---

[68] See *supra*, paras. 10–73, 10–208.

[69] Income and Corporation Taxes Act 1988, s.111(1)-(3), as substituted by the Finance Act 1994, s.215(1). See *supra*, para. 34–06. Note, however, that there is still the possibility of an assessment under the Taxes Management Act 1970, s.36 (as substituted by the Finance Act 1989, s.149(1)): *ibid.* s.36(2) (as substituted, with effect from the tax year 1996/97, by the Finance Act 1994, Sched. 19, Pt. 1, para. 11(2): *ibid.* s.196, 199(2)(a)).

[70] *Ibid.* s.111(4), as substituted by the Finance Act 1994, s.215(1). See also, *infra*, para. 34–28.

[71] Transitional provisions apply in the year 1996/97: see *infra*, para. 34–27.

[72] For a judicial summary of these steps, see *MacKinlay v. Arthur Young McClelland Moores & Co.* [1986] 1 W.L.R. 1468, 1474, 1475 (*per* Vinelott J.), as approved by the House of Lords at [1990] 2 A.C. 239, 249.

[73] As to the special treatment of profits on a commencement or cessation of the trade, see *infra*, paras. 34–39 *et seq.*

[74] As to what will be treated as comprised in a partner's share of profits, see *Lewis v. C.I.R.* (1933) 18 T.C. 174; *Arthur Young McClelland Moores & Co.* [1990] 2 A.C. 239, 249A-C; also *infra*, para. 34–30.

arose.[75] Each partner is entitled to set his personal reliefs, allowances and other deductions against such share, provided that it represents his main source of income.[76] This determines the tax chargeable by reference to each such share and, ultimately, the total tax assessable on the firm.[77]

It should, however, be noted that it is only possible to apportion **34–24** statutory profits where the partners were actually entitled thereto. If the partnership agreement specifically provides that the partners should not be entitled to a certain proportion of the profits, *e.g.* where they are expressed to be taken to a reserve in which no partner has a specific interest, it might be successfully argued that no apportionment is possible, so that tax can only be charged at the basic rate.[78] *Sed quaere.*

Where their entitlement in the relevant year of assessment is clear, **34–25** and apportionment has taken place on that basis, it is not open to the partners, otherwise than by way of an agreement *inter se*, subsequently to re-allocate those profits in a different manner, so as to obtain a greater benefit from the available reliefs.[79]

If the trade of a firm is deemed to be discontinued after April 6, **34–26** 1994, it will immediately lose the benefit of the preceding year basis of assessment.[80]

(b) *Firms in existence prior to April 6, 1994: transitional provisions*

Under the transitional provisions contained in the Finance Act **34–27** 1994, provided that the firm's trade continues to be carried on after April 5, 1997, in the year 1996/97 tax will be charged on the

---

[75] This will not always produce a fair or equitable result; if there has been such an alteration in the profit shares between the basis period and the relevant year of assessment, a partner may be deemed to receive a larger, or smaller, proportion of those profits than he did in fact receive. This may work a particular hardship where the profits of the basis period were abnormally high and, in such a case, some form of indemnity or what now tends to be styled an "equitable adjustment" may be required. See also the Income and Corporation Taxes Act 1988, s.277(2).

[76] *Ibid.* s.277. And see, as to the Revenue practice, *MacKinlay v. Arthur Young McClelland Moores & Co.* [1986] 1 W.L.R. 1468, 1475B (*per* Vinelott J.), as approved by the House of Lords at [1990] 2 A.C. 239, 249. Note also, as to the manner in which certain reliefs should be claimed as from the year 1996/97, the Taxes Management Act 1970, s. 42(6), (7) (as substituted by the Finance Act 1994, Sched. 19, Pt. 1, para. 13).

[77] It is thus desirable that the partners should make freely available any information necessary to ascertain the reliefs to which they are entitled.

[78] *Stocker v. C.I.R.* (1919) 7 T.C. 304; *Franklin v. C.I.R.* (1930) 15 T.C. 464; *Latilla v. C.I.R.* (1943) 25 T.C. 107, 116, *per* Lord Greene M.R.

[79] *Bucks v. Bowers* [1970] Ch. 431, 441, *per* Pennycuick J.

[80] Income and Corporation Taxes Act 1988, s.113(1). The partnership trade commenced after the deemed discontinuance will be taxed under the new regime: see *infra*, paras. 34–28, 34–42. And see the Inland Revenue Press Release "Self-assessment and simplification of personal tax" dated January 11, 1994, para. 28.

appropriate percentage[81] (in general, one half) of the aggregate of the profits of the accounting period ending in that year[82] and the profits of the immediately preceding accounting period.[83] Where, however, the former period is of more or less than 12 months' duration, the relevant period will be the 12 months ending on April 5, 1997.[84] If, on the other hand, tax was charged in the year 1995/96 on the profits of that year, *i.e.* on an actual basis, it follows that in 1996/97 it will be unnecessary to perform the above calculation and tax will be assessed on the basis of the 1996/97 profits.[85]

The Revenue have announced that attempts to avoid liability by manipulating these transitional provisions will be countered by anti-avoidance measures to be introduced in the Finance Act 1995,[86] although their precise scope and effect are not yet known.[87]

(c) *Firms formed on or after April 6, 1994 and all firms from 1997/98*

34–28   The intention behind the new regime of partnership taxation is to move onto a *current* year basis of assessment and to dispense with the preceding year basis and its attendant anomalies.[88] Thus, tax will now normally be assessed by reference to the profits of the basis period, *i.e.* the accounting period ending in the current year of assessment.[89] Where there is no such period, the relevant profits will be those of the year of assessment in question.[90]

It would seem that similar issues will arise in respect of partnership profits in which no partner has a specific interest as were discussed in

---

[81] As defined by the Finance Act 1994, Sched. 20, para. 2(5).

[82] This is defined as the "basis period": *ibid.* Sched. 20, para. 1(2)(a).

[83] *Ibid.* Sched. 20, para. 2(2); Income and Corporation Taxes Act 1988, s.60, as substituted by the Finance Act 1994, s.200. The earlier period is defined as the "relevant period" and must satisfy the conditions of the Finance Act 1994, Sched. 20, para. 2(5), *i.e.* it must begin immediately after the end of the period which was chargeable in the year 1995/96 and end immediately before the basis period for 1996/97. Note also that the profits for the basis period for the year 1997/98 which arise prior to April 6, 1997 are treated as an "overlap profit" and relieved accordingly: *ibid.* Sched. 20, para. 2(4); Income and Corporation Taxes Act 1988, s. 63A (as added by the Finance Act 1994, s. 205). See further *infra*, para. 34–60.

[84] Finance Act 1994, Sched. 20, para. 1(2)(b).

[85] *Ibid.* Sched. 20, para. 2(3). Where necessary, an apportionment of the firm's accounting profits will be made.

[86] Inland Revenue Press Release "Self-assessment and simplification of personal tax" dated January 11, 1994, para. 35.

[87] Some details have, however, been given in a Press Release "Self-assessment: transition to current year basis — anti-avoidance provisions" dated March 31, 1994. The relevant "trigger" events which will prima facie attract the application of the new provisions are likely to be a change or modification in the firm's accounting policies, transactions with connected persons, reciprocal or self-cancelling arrangements and changes in business behaviour: *ibid.* Naturally, it will be possible to escape such application by showing (*inter alia*) that obtaining a tax advantage was not the main benefit or one of the main benefits reasonably expected to arise from the trigger event or that such event arose out of a bona fide commercial transaction.

[88] See *supra*, paras. 34–23 *et seq.*

[89] Income and Corporation Taxes Act 1988, s.60(2), (3), as substituted by the Finance Act 1994, s.200.

[90] *Ibid.* s.60(1), as substituted by the Finance Act 1994, s.200.

relation to the old regime.[91] Moreover, *ex post facto* reallocation of profits as between partners will no more be possible under the new regime than it was under the old.[92]

Expenses

If one partner incurs expenses which are wholly and exclusively **34-29** referable to the performance of his partnership duties but which, under the partnership agreement, he is required to bear out of his own pocket, such expenses may, on general principles, be deducted by him from his share of the partnership profits both under the old and new regimes.[93] Such a situation will be encountered frequently in the case of medical partnerships, where partners may be required to use their private cars in the course of practice. To be deductible, the expenses must be referable to the relevant accounting year.[94] A partner will also be able to deduct from his share of the profits interest payable by him in respect of a loan obtained either:

(i)   to purchase a share in the partnership; or
(ii) to contribute capital or advance money to the partnership.[95]

However, no such relief is available in the case of a limited partner, whilst the relief may be restricted in the case of a partner who does not participate in the management of the firm and who is entitled to be wholly or partially indemnified or relieved from liability for the firm's debts and obligations.[96] Moreover, a return of capital which is not applied in repayment of the loan will reduce the amount of

---

[91] See *supra*, para. 34–24. Note that *ibid.* s.111(3), as substituted by the Finance Act 1994, s.215(1), requires a partner's share to be "determined according to the interests of the partners" during the relevant period.

[92] See *supra*, para. 34–25.

[93] See the Income and Corporation Taxes Act 1988, s.74(a). For the principles upon which such deductions will be allowed, see generally *Whiteman on Income Tax* (3rd ed.), Chap. 7. And note that an expense may still be deductible even where one or more of the partners are indemnified in respect of any liability associated therewith: *Bolton v. Halpern & Woolf* [1981] S.T.C. 14. As to the treatment of expenditure incurred by partners prior to the commencement of the partnership, see *infra*, para. 34–71.

[94] See *Stephenson v. Payne, Stone, Fraser & Co.* [1968] 1 W.L.R. 858.

[95] Income and Corporation Taxes Act 1988, ss.353 (as amended by the Finance Act 1994, s.81, Sched. 26, Pt. V(2)), 362(1). Full relief is only available if the partner has at all times been a member of the partnership and has not received a repayment of his capital: see *ibid.* s.362(2), 363(1). As to what will be treated as a return of capital for this purpose, see *ibid.* s.363(2). The Inspector may in certain circumstances seek to argue that such a repayment has been received where a partner is permitted to overdraw on his current account. Relief will, in any event, be withdrawn as soon as the partner ceases to be a member of the firm: see [1993] S.T.I. 298; however, by concession, the relief is continued following the incorporation of the partnership or a merger or demerger: Extra-Statutory Concession A43 (1994 Revision), reproduced at [1994] S.T.I. 723. No relief will be available if the partnership business consists of the occupation of commercial woodlands: see the Finance Act 1988, Sched. 6, para. 3(3)(b)(i), (4)(b).

[96] *Ibid.* ss.362(2)(a), 117(1). The expression "limited partner" in the former subsection is not defined: *cf. ibid.* s.171(2). It seems that a dormant partner who is not entitled to such an indemnity will enjoy unrestricted relief.

interest eligible for relief.[97] The Revenue have already announced that the Finance Act 1995 will contain anti-avoidance provisions designed to counter attempts to maximise interest relief claims in respect of the transitional tax year 1996/97.[98]

34–30   On the other hand, certain payments made to partners,[99] such as so called preferential "salaries" or interest on capital (but not, it is thought, interest on advances[1]), are not allowed as a deduction from the partnership profits because they represent payments for services rendered to the firm by a partner *in that capacity*.[2] It follows that such payments must be added back to the partnership profits and apportioned as an additional profit share to the partners in receipt thereof.[3] However, the position may be different in the case of other payments to partners, provided that the "wholly and exclusively" test[4] can be satisfied. Much will depend on the capacity in which any payment is received: rent receivable by a partner *qua* landlord is deductible,[5] but re-imbursement of removal expenses, which can only be received *qua* partner, will not.[6] Where a firm pays interest on a loan taken out by a partner in order to acquire premises occupied by the firm, the payment of such interest will, by concession, be regarded as rent and, thus, deductible in computing the partnership profits.[7]

---

[97] *Ibid.* s.363(1). See also *supra*, n. 95.

[98] See Inland Revenue Press Release "Self-assessment: transition to current year basis — anti-avoidance provisions" dated March 31, 1994, paras. 14, 15. See also *supra*, para. 34–27.

[99] For this purpose, it is immaterial whether the payments are made pursuant to the terms of a partnership agreement or otherwise.

[1] Such interest is expressly allowed by the Partnership Act 1890, s.24(3) and should accordingly be regarded as part of the cost of earning the (net) trading profit. If, however, in the absence of sufficient income, the burden of the interest is thrown on capital, it will clearly not be deductible: *Fitzleet Estates Ltd. v. Cherry* [1977] 1 W.L.R. 1345 (H.L.).

[2] See *Lewis v. C.I.R.* (1933) 18 T.C. 174; *MacKinlay v. Arthur Young McLelland Moores & Co.* [1990] 2 A.C. 239, 249C.

[3] Such payments accordingly cannot be assessed under Sched. E (nor can P.A.Y.E. be deducted) save, perhaps, in an exceptional case where a partner has performed services for a client of the firm, and the Revenue seek to assess any payment to him under Sched. E, on the basis that he is in truth a "worker" whose services have been supplied by an "agency" for the purposes of the Income and Corporation Taxes Act 1988, s.134. Where a salary is expressed to be payable to a partner *irrespective* of the firm's profitability and is duly paid in a year in which no profits are realised, it cannot properly be treated as a share of profits but must constitute capital in the hands of the recipient partner: see also *supra*, para. 34–29, n. 95. *Per contra* in the case of a salaried partner taxable under Sched. E. See generally, as to salaried partners, *supra*. para. 5–65.

[4] Income and Corporation Taxes Act 1988, s.74(a).

[5] *Heastie v. Veitch & Co.* [1934] 1 K.B. 535; see also the Statement of Practice entitled "Income Tax: Relief for Interest on Loans Used to Buy Land Occupied for Partnership Business Purposes" (SP4/85), para. 2. Care must, however, be taken to ensure that a tenancy does in fact exist: see, as to the possible difficulties, *supra*, para. 10–38.

[6] See *MacKinlay v. Arthur Young McLelland Moores & Co.* [1990] 2 A.C. 539. See also *Watson and Everitt v. Blunden* (1933) 18 T.C. 402.

[7] See the Statement of Practice (SP4/85) "Income tax: Relief for Interest on Loans Used to Buy Land Occupied for Partnership Business Purposes", para. 5. Although the "rent" will technically be taxable as such in the recipient partner's hands, it will be regarded as covered by the interest for which he is liable and which is eligible for relief under the Income and Corporation Taxes Act 1988, s.355(1)(b), (4) (as amended by the Finance Act 1994, Sched. 9, para. 4). *Per contra* if the loan is in fact taken out by the firm: see *R. v. Inspector of Taxes, ex p. Brumfield* [1989] S.T.C. 151.

Earned income[8]

A partner's share of the firm's trading profits, including any **34–31** preferential salary or interest on capital payable as a first or other charge on such profits, is payable in full without deduction of tax, and will be regarded as earned income, unless the recipient is a dormant or limited partner.[9] However, it cannot be assumed that all *non-trading* profits will be similarly treated. Clearly, profits derived from a combination of personal effort and property will constitute earned income, but the status of income derived from investments held by the firm is more doubtful. It was formerly provided that if the proceeds of sale of the investments would form part of the partnership profits, the income derived therefrom would not be regarded as investment income.[10] In the absence of even that ambivalent provision, the current editor considers that such income would, on normal principles, not qualify as earned income; *a fortiori*, in the case of dividends.[11]

Charges on income

Annual charges on income payable by the firm under deduction of **34–32** tax will be apportioned to the partners in their profit-sharing ratios, in the absence of any agreement to the contrary.[12] Each partner is treated as personally paying his apportioned part of the charge, and may use the entirety of his income, both earned and unearned, to frank that part.[13]

Directors' fees

Where the members of a professional partnership are in receipt of **34–33** directors' fees, those fees should properly be assessed on the

---

[8] Although a distinction is still drawn between earned income and unearned or investment income, it has become of less importance since the abolition of the investment income surcharge in 1984.

[9] The definition of "earned income" contained in the Income and Corporation Taxes Act 1988, s.833(4) (as amended) includes "income which ... is immediately derived by the individual from the carrying on or exercise by him of his trade ... in the case of a partnership, as a partner *personally* acting in the partnership" (emphasis added.) Since the dormant or limited partner is by definition not actively engaged in the partnership business, any profits received by him clearly cannot be treated as earned income.

[10] Finance Act 1971, s.32(4), partially reversing the decision in *Bucks v. Bowers* [1970] Ch. 431. The subsection did not provide that the income would qualify as earned income, but merely exempted it from the investment income surcharge.

[11] The Income and Corporation Taxes Act 1988, s.833(4)(c) (as amended by the Finance Act 1988, Sched. 14, Pts. IV, V) refers only to income chargeable under Sched. D, whilst dividend income is chargeable under Sched. F. It should be noted that interest earned by a firm of solicitors on moneys deposited in a client deposit account has been held not to be earned income, even though the account would not have existed if the profession of solicitors had not been carried on: *Northend v. White & Leonard and Corbin Greener* [1975] 1 W.L.R. 1037, following *Bucks v. Bowers, supra*, and *Pegler v. Abell* [1973] 1 W.L.R. 155.

[12] There would seem to be no reason why a charge on income should not be borne in shares specifically set out in the partnership agreement.

[13] See the Inland Revenue Press Release dated May 1957; also the final report, Royal Commission on the Taxation of Profits and Income, Cmnd. 9474, para. 513.

individual partners under Schedule E. However, under the old regime, the Revenue are prepared, by concession, to accept the inclusion of such fees in the firm's Schedule D assessment, provided that two conditions are satisfied. First, the directorships must be normal incidents of the profession in general as well as of the particular practice in question: secondly, the fees must be only a small part of the partnership profits and be pooled for division among the partners under the terms of the partnership agreement.[14] The firm must request such treatment and will be required to give an undertaking that the fees received in full will be included in the gross income or receipts of the basis period, whether or not the directorships are still held in the relevant year of assessment and whether or not the partners holding them are still members of the firm.

It would seem likely that a similar approach will be adopted under the new regime, albeit that there will no longer be a Schedule D assessment on the firm.[15]

Conventional or earnings basis of assessment

34–34   At the commencement of a partnership, care must be taken when choosing the accounting basis upon which the partnership profits will be calculated.[16] There are two possible bases: the conventional basis,[17] which excludes the value of work in progress, and the earnings basis.[18] The latter is normally adopted, but the Revenue may be prepared to accept the former where that is particularly appropriate.[19] It should, however, be noted that the Revenue will, in any event, generally insist that the earnings basis is adopted for the first three years of trading.[20] Any subsequent change from an earnings to a conventional basis will almost inevitably result in a degree of double taxation, since profits earned, but not received, before the change will already have come into charge to tax, yet will be included in the partnership profits when received. On the other

---

[14] Extra Statutory Concession A37 (1994 Revision). It is, however, understood that the Revenue do not in practice accept the availability of such concessionary treatment in the case of offices held by doctors. *Sed quaere* in the case of other professions.

[15] See *supra*, para. 34–06.

[16] This assumes that the Revenue will be prepared to accept that such a choice is available, which will not always be the case, particularly for a trading partnership: see the Inland Revenue Statement of Practice (A27) "Accounts on a Cash Basis" dated June 18, 1979.

[17] *i.e.* cash or bills delivered.

[18] The adoption of the earning basis will not always be disadvantageous: see, for example, *Symons v. Weeks* [1983] S.T.C. 195, where progress payments were payable to a firm of architects under long term contracts.

[19] The conventional basis is usually allowed for barristers and authors, but may also be considered appropriate in the case of certain professional firms, *e.g.* solicitors and accountants: see the Inland Revenue Statement of Practice (A27) "Accounts on a Cash Basis" dated June 18, 1979.

[20] *Ibid.* This practice will also apply where, under the old regime, a change in the partnership results in a deemed discontinuance under the Income and Corporation Taxes Act 1988, s.113(1). See further *infra*, para. 34–45.

hand, where there is a change from a conventional to an earnings basis, specific provision is made in the Taxes Act 1988 to prevent any profits or gains entirely escaping a charge to tax.[21]

In deciding between the conventional and the earnings basis, where **34-35** that choice is available, it is as well to bear in mind the possible complications which can result on a change in the firm. If a conventional basis has been adopted and the value of work in progress ignored, it may be difficult to compensate an outgoing partner for his share of that asset, otherwise than in a capital form.[22] In such cases, a specific provision in the agreement governing the treatment of work in progress will be essential.

Where an earnings basis is adopted, it will be necessary to decide **34-36** how work in progress is to be valued. The normal bases are "direct cost"[23] or "on cost,"[24] but, as alternatives, it would seem that either market value[25] or "accrued profit"[26] may be adopted. Where, however, a change in the basis of valuation is contemplated, *e.g.* from an on cost basis to an accrued profit basis, a substantial charge to tax may be thrown up.[27]

4. COMMENCEMENT, CESSATION AND CONTINUANCE

Although the Finance Act 1994 has introduced a simplified **34-37** framework for the taxation of incoming and outgoing partners, the old and infinitely more complex rules which govern the commencement and cessation of partnership trades will continue to apply to firms in existence on April 6, 1994 until the tax year 1997/98 and must therefore be considered in some detail.

---

[21] Income and Corporation Taxes Act 1988, s.104.

[22] If, in the case of a firm in existence prior to April 6, 1994, an election for continuance is submitted under *ibid.* s.113(2), the outgoing partner will not be able to receive any sums attributable to work in progress as a post cessation receipt; it follows that either a capital payment must be made to him or his annuity (if any) adjusted to reflect the value of his share in the work in progress. In such a case, it would seem that a charge to capital gains tax may be imposed on the outgoing partner: see *infra*, para. 35-18. And see further, as to annuities payable to outgoing partners, *infra*, paras. 34-92 *et seq*.

[23] *i.e.* taking into account only the labour and materials directly used on the work.

[24] *i.e.* taking into account the cost of labour and materials, together with a proportion of the general overheads of the firm.

[25] Market value would appear to be a possible basis for valuing work in progress, the point being left open by the House of Lords in *Duple Motor Bodies v. I.R.C.* [1961] 1 W.L.R. 739. Although Viscount Simonds (at pp. 748, 749) indicated that market value was an appropriate basis, Lord Reid (at p. 756) expressed the view that market value *in its ordinary sense* was not.

[26] *i.e.* increasing the value of work in progress by a proportion of the anticipated profit attributable thereto. This is contrary to the normal principle that profit is only taxable when it is received: see *Willingale v. International Commercial Bank Ltd.* [1978] A.C. 834; *Symons v. Weeks* [1983] S.T.C. 195; also *Gallagher v. Jones* [1993] S.T.C. 537; *R v. I.R.C., ex p. S.G. Warburg & Co. Ltd.* [1994] S.T.C. 518.

[27] See *Pearce v. Woodall-Duckham Ltd.* [1978] 1 W.L.R. 832.

Pre-trading expenditure

34-38   In certain circumstances, relief in respect of expenditure incurred by partners prior to the commencement of a partnership can be obtained; this relief is considered in more detail hereafter in connection with the treatment of losses.[28]

Taxation of new partnership

Firms in existence prior to April 6, 1994: tax years up to 1996/97

34-39   Under the old commencement rules which apply to firms formed prior to April 6, 1994,[29] the first assessment on a newly constituted partnership[30] is based on the actual adjusted profits made during the period from the date of commencement down to April 5 next following; the second assessment is based on the actual adjusted profits for the first 12 months' trading from the date of commencement; the third assessment is based on the firm's accounts for a complete period of 12 months ending in the preceding year of assessment.[31] The fourth and following assessments are based on the normal preceding year basis,[32] although partnerships which carry on a trade of farming or market gardening have the right, within certain limits, to average the profits of two consecutive years of assessment.[33]

34-40   The firm does, however, have an option to be assessed for the second and third years of assessment on the actual profits for those years. Such option must be exercised by giving notice to the Inspector of Taxes within seven years after the end of the second year of assessment.[34] If the election is made, and subsequently proves disadvantageous to the firm, it may be revoked by notice in writing given to the Inspector within six years after the end of the third year of assessment, whereupon the original assessments will be restored.[35]

34-41   Clearly, the above provisions worked most favourably, from the partnership's point of view, where the profits earned in the first year

---

[28] See *infra*, para. 34–71.

[29] See the Finance Act 1994, ss.201, 218(1)(a).

[30] Note that, under the new regime, assessments are no longer made on the partnership but on the individual partners thereof: see *supra*, para. 34–06.

[31] Income and Corporation Taxes Act 1988, s.60(2), (3), 61(1)-(3).

[32] *Ibid.* s.60(1).

[33] *Ibid.* s.96. No claim may be made in respect of a year of assessment in which the trade is, or by virtue of *ibid.* s.113(1) is treated as, set up and commenced or permanently discontinued: *ibid.* s.96(4)(b). Otherwise, the claim must be made within two years of the end of the second year of assessment to which the claim relates, by all the partners who are individuals: *ibid.* s.94(6)(b), (8). Where there is a change in the constitution of the firm, and a continuance election is submitted under *ibid.* s.113(2), the claim must be made by all the individuals who were partners during the years of assessment in question or, if they are dead, by their personal representatives: *ibid.* s.94(6).

[34] *Ibid.* s.62(2).

[35] *Ibid.* s.62(3).

of trading were low, but the Revenue keep a careful watch on attempts to reduce the amount of such profits by artificial means.[36]

Although special commencement rules formerly applied where partners decided not to submit a continuance election following a change in the firm,[37] in the case of a change after April 6, 1994 the new regime of partnership taxation will now apply to the trade deemed to have been commenced by each of the partners.[38]

Firms formed on or after April 6, 1994 and all firms from 1997/98

It has already been seen that, under the new regime of partnership **34-42** taxation, each partner is deemed to carry on a separate trade from that carried on by his co-partners.[39] It follows that, when a new partner joins an existing firm or where two or more persons enter into partnership for the first time, each of them will be treated as having set up a new trade and be assessed to tax under the (revised) opening rules.[40] Thus, the first assessment on a partner, in respect of the year in which he joined the firm,[41] will be based on his share of the partnership profits for that year;[42] the second assessment will be based on his share of profits for the accounting period ending in the next year[43] or, if that period is of less than 12 months' duration, the 12 month period beginning on the date he became a partner.[44] Thereafter, the basis period will be determined in the usual way.[45]

Averaging of profits is still available in the case of partnerships carrying on the trade of farming or market gardening, although the relief will now be claimed separately by each partner.[46]

Overlap profits. If, as a result of the application of the above **34-43** commencement rules, an amount of profits is included in the computation for two successive years of assessment,[47] relief is given

---

[36] See, for example, *Stephenson v. Payne, Stone, Fraser & Co.* [1968] 1 W.L.R. 858.

[37] Income and Corporation Taxes Act 1988, ss.61(4) (as amended by the Finance Act 1988, Sched. 13, para. 2), 62(4). See further, *infra*, para. 34-50.

[38] See the Finance Act 1994, ss.215(4)(b), (5)(a), 218(1)(b); also *supra*, para. 34-06 and *infra*, para. 34-42.

[39] See *supra*, para. 34-06.

[40] Income and Corporation Taxes Act 1988, ss.61, 111(3)(a), as respectively substituted by the Finance Act 1994, ss.201, 215(1).

[41] This is styled the "commencement year": *ibid.* s.60(5), as substituted by the Finance Act 1990, s.200.

[42] *Ibid.* s.60(1), as substituted by the Finance Act 1994, s.201.

[43] *Ibid.* s.60(3)(a), as substituted by the Finance Act 1994, s.200.

[44] *Ibid.* s.61(2)(a), as substituted by the Finance Act 1994, s.201.

[45] *Ibid.* s.60(2), (3), as substituted by the Finance Act 1994, s.200.

[46] *Ibid.* s.96(6), as amended by the Finance Act 1994, s.216(3)(a). Where the first of the years of assessment to which the claim relates is the year 1996/97 or any subsequent year, the relief must be claimed not later than 12 months after January 31 next following the end of the second such year: *ibid.* s.96(8), as amended by the Finance Act 1994, Sched. 19, Pt. II, para. 37. See also *supra*, para. 34-39.

[47] *e.g.* where the accounting period ending in the year of assessment after that in which the trade was commenced is of less than 12 months' duration: see *ibid.* s.61(2)(a), as substituted by the Finance Act 1994, s.201.

in respect of these so-called "overlap profits"[48] by deducting them from the profits of the basis period for the year of assessment in which the trade is discontinued[49] or, where the basis period for any year of assessment is of *more* that 12 months' duration,[50] by deducting a proportion from the profits of that basis period.[51]

Taxation of discontinued partnership

Firms in existence prior to April 6, 1994: tax years up to 1996/97

34–44   Where a partnership permanently ceases to trade,[52] *e.g.* on or following a dissolution,[53] the following cessation provisions apply. The assessment for the year in which the permanent discontinuance occurs is based on the actual (adjusted) profits for the period beginning April 6 immediately preceding the discontinuance and ending on the date of the discontinuance.[54] The assessment for the penultimate year will be based on the adjusted profits of the preceding year, save that where the aggregate of the profits of each of the two preceding years ending on April 5 prior to the year of assessment in which the discontinuance occurs exceeds the aggregate of the amounts on which the partnership has been charged for each of such preceding years, the Revenue is required to reopen both (and not merely one of) such preceding years and to make an assessment on the actual profits of each such year.[55]

34–45 *Deemed discontinuance on change of partners.*   A change in the partnership, whether caused by the departure of an existing partner or the admission of a new partner, will technically involve the dissolution of the old firm and the creation of a new firm, even though the partners may have agreed between themselves that their partnership is to continue.[56] This approach is reflected in section 113(1) of the Taxes Act 1988, which provides that the partnership trade is deemed to have been permanently discontinued on the date

---

[48] This expression is defined by *ibid.* s.63A(5), as added by the Finance Act 1994, s.205.

[49] *Ibid.* s.63A(3)(a), as added by the Finance Act 1994, s.205.

[50] See *ibid.* s.62(2)(b), as substituted by the Finance Act 1994, s.202.

[51] *Ibid.* s.63A(1), (2), as added by the Finance Act 1994, s.205.

[52] This will be a pure question of fact: see *O'Kane (J. & R.) & Co. v. C.I.R.* (1922) 12 T.C. 303; *Hillerns & Fowler v. Murray* (1932) 17 T.C. 77; *Laycock v. Freeman Hardy & Willis Ltd.* [1939] 2 K.B. 1; *Watts v. Hart* [1984] S.T.C. 548; *C. Connelly & Co. v. Wilbey* [1992] S.T.C. 783 (a decision under the Finance Act 1981, Sched. 9, para. 21); *Maidment v. Kibby* [1993] S.T.C. 494.

[53] See *supra*, para. 34–14.

[54] Income and Corporation Taxes Act 1988, s.63(1)(a).

[55] *Ibid.* s.63(1)(b) (as amended by the Finance Act 1988, Sched. 3, para. 3); and see also, as to the mandatory nature of this provision, *Baylis v. Roberts* [1989] S.T.C. 693. Any adjustment to the profits made under *ibid.* s.96 (see *supra*, para. 34–39, n. 33) will be ignored for this purpose: *ibid.* s.96(5)(b).

[56] See, generally, the decision of the House of Lords in *C.I.T. v. Gibbs* [1942] A.C. 402.

of the change, so that the cessation and commencement provisions of the Act can be applied as from such date.[57]

Election to be assessed on continuing basis. However, such a **34–46** deemed discontinuance may well work unfairly where, in reality, the partnership is continuing. Thus, in order to provide an element of continuity, section 113(2) of the Taxes Act 1988 permits the partners to elect to be assessed on a continuing basis, provided that at least one of their number is a member of both the old and the new firms. It should be noted that this condition will be fulfilled where a sole proprietor takes another person into partnership with him.

The election must be made within two years[58] from the date of the **34–47** change by giving written notice to the Inspector of Taxes. Elections given out of time will rarely be accepted.[59] The notice must be signed by all the living members of both the old and new firms and, in the case of a deceased partner, by his personal representatives. In the case of a firm comprising more than 50 partners,[60] the Revenue have stated that they will accept a so-called "blanket election" which will apply to *all* changes in the firm, provided that new partners add their names to the election and the partners indemnify the Board of Inland Revenue against any loss of tax which may result from a failure to comply with the strict requirements of the legislation.[61] Such a blanket election may be withdrawn at any time.[62]

A continuance election, once submitted, may be revoked by a similar notice given to the Inspector within two years.[63]

If an election is submitted, the assessment for the year in which the **34–48** change in the firm takes place will be made on the same basis as if

---

[57] The section presupposes that the same trade is carried on before and after the change: *Laycock v. Freeman Hardy & Willis Ltd.* [1939] 2 K.B. 1; *Maidment v. Kibby* [1993] S.T.C. 494. If the trade is of a different nature, there will be an *actual* as opposed to a deemed discontinuance. Care must obviously be taken to ensure that a change in the firm, and thus a discontinuance for tax purposes, does not come about unwittingly: see, for example, *Hudgell Yeates & Co. v. Watson* [1978] Q.B. 451, noticed *supra*, para. 8–43. It should also be noted that the discontinuance provisions will not be applied where a husband and wife carry on a business in partnership, and one succeeds to the whole of the business on the death of the other, no election for continuance being submitted under the Income and Corporation Taxes Act 1988, s.113(2): see Extra-Statutory Concession A7 (1994 Revision). Where the Concession applies, the losses and capital allowances to be carried forward are restricted to the share appropriate to the surviving partner.

[58] The period under the predecessor of *ibid.* s.113(2) (*i.e.* the Income and Corporation Taxes Act 1970, s.154(2)), was originally one year, but was increased to two years by the Finance Act 1971.

[59] As to the exceptional circumstances in which a late election *may* be accepted, see [1992] S.T.I. 989; also [1993] S.T.I. 298. In most cases it will be desirable for a form of election to be prepared and signed by all the partners as soon as possible after the change, even if it is ultimately decided that it should not be submitted.

[60] Similar treatment is accorded to firms comprising *less* than 50 partners, provided that at least 20 of them are not resident in the U.K. immediately after the first change.

[61] Extra Statutory Concession A80 "Blanket partnership continuation elections", reproduced *infra*, para. A6–05.

[62] *Ibid.*

[63] See the Inland Revenue Statement of Practice (A4) "Partnerships: Change in Membership," first published January 17, 1973 and reproduced *infra*, para. A6–01. This time limit will also be strictly applied by the Revenue.

there had been no such change, but tax will be assessed and charged on the members of the old and the new firms separately. Apportionment as between those members will be made on such basis as may be just,[64] although time apportionment will normally be applied. Account will be taken not only of the share of the profits to which each partner was entitled but also of the length of time for which he was a member of the firm during the year. In the event of a dispute as to the apportionment, there is a right of appeal to the General or Special Commissioners, with a right of appeal from their decision on a question of law to the High Court.[65]

34-49   In some cases, to submit a continuance election under section 113(2) may be of advantage to the continuing partners but not to an outgoing partner. It is thus desirable that the partnership agreement contains a specific provision requiring such a partner, or his personal representatives, to join in such an election if requested to do so by the continuing partners.[66] The usual corollary is for the continuing partners to indemnify the outgoing partner or the personal representatives against any additional liability to tax which may result from the submission of the election.[67]

34-50 *Failure to elect for continuance.*   Where a continuance election could be submitted following a change in the firm, but the partners decide not to do so, special commencement rules apply when taxing the "new" partnership.[68] This will result in the application of the normal preceding year basis being deferred until the fourth year of assessment following that in which the change occurred, subject to the right of the partners to elect to defer such application for a further two years.[69] However, these rules can only apply in the case of a deemed discontinuance prior to April 6, 1994.[70]

34-51 *Desirability of submitting continuance election.*   The question whether a continuance election should be submitted in any given case will ultimately depend upon a number of factors, including the profit trends of the business. Although, as a general rule, a continuance will

---

[64] Income and Corporation Taxes Act 1988, s.113(3)(a).

[65] *Ibid.* s.113(5).

[66] Such a provision is included in most partnership agreements as a matter of course: see further, *supra*, para. 10–211. Of course, such a provision will be redundant as from the year 1997/98.

[67] Although it is often imagined that such an indemnity will cover any additional liability thrown up in the event of a permanent discontinuance within the same year of assessment or within either of the two following years (see further, *infra*, para. 34–52), such a discontinuance could not in fact produce an *additional* liability over and above that which would be chargeable if no election had been submitted. Note also that an additional capital gains liability may be thrown up: see *supra*. para. 10–212.

[68] Income and Corporation Taxes Act 1988, s.61(4) (as amended by the Finance Act 1988, Sched. 13, para. 2).

[69] *Ibid.* s.62(4).

[70] Where the discontinuance occurred *after* that date, the new regime of partnership taxation will apply: see the Finance Act 1994, s.215(4)(b), (5)(a), 218(1)(b); also *supra*, paras. 34–06, 34–42.

be desirable where the profits are rising and are expected to continue to do so after the change, sustained profitability may well depend on whether the firm is contemplating taking on (or has just taken on) additional highly-paid staff.[71] Account must also be taken of the transitional provisions which will apply in respect of the year 1996/97.[72] It certainly cannot be assumed in all cases that the submission of an election will automatically be beneficial.

Change followed by cessation. Where there is a change in the firm **34–52** followed by a discontinuance (actual or deemed) within the same year, or within the following two years of assessment, and a continuance election was submitted in respect of the first change, but not in respect of the second, the Revenue may, in applying the discontinuance provisions, effectively ignore the first change and raise an additional assessment under section 63 of the Taxes Act 1988. Thus, an additional assessment under that section may be made on persons who were partners prior to the first change, in respect of periods prior to that change, as if they had remained partners down to the date of the discontinuance.[73] It should, however, be noted that this provision can only apply where a continuance election was submitted in respect of the first change. Thus, an outgoing partner who desires to safeguard his own position, could, unless he is bound by a specific provision in the partnership agreement, refuse to sign the election or only agree to sign it on being given an indemnity from the continuing partners against any future liability under this provision. The normal form of indemnity afforded to outgoing partners in consideration of their joining in the election will not cover such a liability.[74]

Death of a partner. In the case of the death of a partner who would **34–53** otherwise be chargeable under the provisions of section 113 of the Taxes Act 1988, the tax can be assessed on his personal representatives and constitutes a debt due from and payable out of his estate.[75] However, an assessment can only be made within three years of the year of assessment in which such partner died.[76]

---

[71] *e.g.* a salaried professional assistant. When determining whether to elect for a continuance, it is as well to bear in mind that an incoming partner could be employed as a salaried assistant for a period prior to the date of his admission, thus depressing the profits in that period. Equally, the dangers presented by the decision in *Stephenson v. Payne, Stone, Fraser & Co.* [1968] 1 W.L.R. 858 should not be ignored; note also the (as yet unspecified) anti-avoidance provisions due to be introduced in the Finance Act 1995: see *supra*, para. 34–27. As to salaried "assistants" and salaried "partners," see *Stekel v. Ellice* [1973] 1 W.L.R. 191; also *supra*, para. 5–65.

[72] See *supra*, para. 34–27.

[73] Income and Corporation Taxes Act 1988, s.113(3)(b).

[74] Since the charge will be by reference to the actual profits prior to the change, there can be no additional liability over and above that which would have been payable had no continuance election been submitted: see further, *supra*, paras. 10–211, 10–212.

[75] Income and Corporation Taxes Act 1988, s.113(6).

[76] Taxes Management Act 1970, s.40(1); and see *Harrison v. Willis Bros.* [1966] Ch. 619.

34–54 *Merger of two partnerships.* Where two partnerships carrying on different trades merge, the new combined business will in all probability represent a synthesis of those trades and may, as such, be unrecognisable as a continuation of either. If, on a true analysis, both of the former trades have been discontinued and a wholly new trade commenced, the cessation and commencement rules must be applied in the normal way.[77] Where, however, the merged trades are of the same general nature, it may be possible to identify both trades as continuing, albeit in a merged form. The present practice of the Revenue[78] is to accord three options to the partners in the merged firm: they may accept the application of the cessation and commencement rules to each of the trades, submit a continuance election under section 113(2) of the Taxes Act 1988 in respect of only one trade, or submit elections in respect of both trades. In the intermediate case, an apportionment of the profits of the merged trade will be required when applying the commencement rules.[79]

Naturally, whether there has been a succession in any case will be a question of fact, although in this context the Revenue will apparently not regard the disparity between the size of the old and new firms as significant.[80]

34–55   If one of the merged firms has to change its accounting basis to accord with the other, there might be an immediate additional liability under section 104(4) of the Taxes Act 1988 in respect of the debtors and/or work in progress of that firm;[81] concessionary "top-slicing" relief is no longer available.[82] This is a factor which should be taken into account when a merger is considered.

34–56 *Hiving-off operations and demergers.* Section 113 of the Income and Corporation Taxes Act 1988 is concerned only with changes in the persons carrying on a trade—not with changes in the quantum of the trade being carried on. Thus, the fact that some part, or even a major part, of a trade is hived-off to another entity will not bring about a cessation in relation to the remainder of that trade, provided

---

[77] Where the merger occurs after April 6, 1994, the new commencement rules, etc. will apply: see *supra*, paras. 34–06, 34–42.

[78] See the Inland Revenue Statement of Practice (SP9/86) "Income Tax: Partnership Mergers and Demergers" dated December 10, 1986, para. 3, reproduced *infra*, para. A6–03. The Revenue formerly took the view that, as a matter of law, no election was possible in such a case, although an election was generally allowed "by concession." The current editor considers that this view was based on an incorrect interpretation of the law, which seems to be recognised by the current practice.

[79] It is assumed that this practice will continue to apply in the period prior to the introduction of the new regime of partnership taxation in 1997/98.

[80] Inland Revenue Statement of Practice (SP9/86) "Income Tax: Partnership Mergers and Demergers", para. 4, *infra*, para. A6–03.

[81] See *supra*, para. 34–34.

[82] The former Extra-Statutory Concession A18 was withdrawn with effect from the 1988/89 tax year.

that the scale of the hiving-off operation is not such that there is in reality no part of the original trade remaining.[83] Of course, the entity which carries on the hived- off part of the trade, if newly created, will be separately taxed under the normal commencement rules.[84]

Where partners wish to dissolve their firm and to divide the business between them, it will be a question of fact whether any of the "demerged" firms has in truth succeeded to the business of the original firm. Only where there is such a succession will a continuance election be possible;[85] otherwise, the old business will be treated as permanently discontinued. In such a case, the safer course might perhaps be to initiate a hiving-off operation prior to the dissolution, so as to ensure that an election can be submitted in respect of the business that remains. However, for the reasons discussed in the preceding paragraph, there will obviously be a limit to the amount of the business which can be successfully hived-off without jeopardising the availability of the election. The Revenue will closely scrutinise any demerger which appears to have been engineered for fiscal reasons.[86] **34–57**

Firms formed on or after April 6, 1994 and all firms from 1997/98

Under the new regime of partnership taxation, when a partner leaves an existing firm,[87] whether with a view to setting up some other business, joining another firm or retiring completely, the trade which he is deemed to carry on[88] will be treated as permanently discontinued.[89] Similarly, where a partnership is dissolved and its business ceases to be carried on.[90] Provided that he does not leave the firm in the same year that he joined it or in the next following year, the basis period for the year of the discontinuance will be the period which began immediately after the end of the previous basis period and ended on the date of the discontinuance.[91] If he joins the firm in one year and leaves it in the next, the basis period will be the **34–58**

---

[83] See, for example, *Seaman v. Tucketts Ltd.* (1963) 41 T.C. 422; also *Whiteman on Income Tax* (3rd ed.), para. 5–05.

[84] In the case of a commencement prior to April 6, 1994, see *supra*, paras. 34–39 *et seq.*; in the case of a commencement thereafter, see *supra*, para. 34–42.

[85] See the Inland Revenue Statement of Practice (SP9/86) "Income Tax: Partnership Mergers and Demergers", para. 5, *infra*, para. A6–04.

[86] *Ibid.* para. 6, *infra*, para. A6–04.

[87] Whether by reason of death, retirement or expulsion.

[88] Income and Corporation Taxes Act 1988, s.111(3)(a), as substituted by the Finance Act 1994, s.215(1). See *supra*, para. 34–06.

[89] *Ibid.* s.111(3)(c), as substituted by the Finance Act 1994, s.215(1). There is no scope for the service of a continuation election in such a case, even if a partner retires and takes an ascertainable part of the former partnership trade with him into a new firm/sole trade.

[90] It does not necessarily follow that the partnership trade (and thus the deemed trade of each individual partner) will necessarily cease at the moment of dissolution: see *supra*, para. 34–14.

[91] Income and Corporation Taxes Act 1988, s.63(b), as substituted by the Finance Act 1994, s.204.

period which began immediately after the end of that first year and ended on the date of the discontinuance.[92]

As under the old regime, where a partner dies, an assessment can be made on his personal representatives.[93]

34–59 However, it is expressly provided that a change in the firm will not result in a permanent discontinuance of its trade, provided that at least one partner remains a member of the firm both before and after the change.[94] It follows that a change in the firm cannot result in a discontinuance of the trades deemed to be carried on by each of the continuing partners.

34–60 *Overlap profits.* In the event of a discontinuance of his deemed trade, a partner will be entitled to deduct any unrelieved overlap profits[95] from his share of profits in the basis period for the year of assessment in which the discontinuance occurs.[96] In the case of a firm in existence prior to April 6, 1994, such overlap profits will include any share of profits in respect of the basis period for the year 1997/98 which arose *prior* to April 6, 1997.[97]

Post-cessation receipts

34–61 Post-cessation receipts of a trade which is permanently discontinued, or deemed to be permanently discontinued under section 113(1) of the Taxes Act 1988,[98] are liable to tax and are assessable under Case VI of Schedule D on the members of the old firm in accordance with sections 103–105 of that Act.[99]

If, in the case of a deemed discontinuance, the right to such receipts is assigned to the new firm, they must be included in the profits of that firm, and are not assessable on the members of the old firm under sections 103 and 104.[1] The Act provides for a deduction to be made in computing the profits of the new firm for debts taken over by it which are subsequently proved to be bad, in so far as they have not already been allowed to the old firm.[2]

---

[92] *Ibid.* s.63(a), as substituted by the Finance Act 1994, s.204.
[93] *Ibid.* s.60(4), as substituted by the Finance Act 1994, s.200.
[94] *Ibid.* s.113(2), as substituted by the Finance Act 1994, s.216(1).
[95] As to the meaning of this expression, see *ibid.* s.63A(5), as added by the Finance Act 1994, s.205. See also *supra,* para. 34–43.
[96] *Ibid.* s.63A(3)(a), as added by the Finance Act 1994, s.205.
[97] Finance Act 1994, Sched. 20, para. 2(4).
[98] Such a deemed discontinuance can now only arise where the firm was in existence prior to April 6, 1994 and the change occurs prior to the tax year 1997/98: see the Finance Act 1994, ss.215(4)(a), 216(1).
[99] Income and Corporation Taxes Act 1988, s.110(2). For the taxation of post-cessation receipts generally, see *Whiteman on Income Tax* (3rd ed.), paras. 6–27 *et seq.*
[1] *Ibid.* s.106(2).
[2] *Ibid.* s.89.

Trading stock[3]

On a permanent discontinuance (including a deemed discon- **34-62** tinuance)[4] trading stock is dealt with as follows: if the trading stock is sold to another United Kingdom trader who is able to deduct the purchase price as an expense in computing his profits, then the amount of such purchase price will be treated as part of the trading profits of the former partnership or, in the case of the new regime of partnership taxation, of its former members;[5] in any other case, a sum equal to the open market value of the stock must be brought into account.[6]

Stock relief may no longer be claimed.[7]

Work in progress[8]

The work in progress of a professional firm is treated in the same **34-63** way as trading stock in the event of a discontinuance,[9] *viz.* the actual amount realised (if any) forms part of the profits of the old firm or, in the case of the new regime of partnership taxation, of the former members of that firm[10] if the work in progress is transferred in such circumstances that its value can be deducted as an allowable expense in the accounts of the new firm; otherwise the open market value of such work in progress is brought into account.[11]

However, the partners in the old firm may elect, by notice in writing sent to the Inspector of Taxes within 12 months of the discontinuance, that the actual cost of the work in progress be credited in the accounts up to the date of the discontinuance, and that any sums received from the new firm in excess of such actual cost be treated as a post-cessation receipt and taxed under section 103 of the Taxes Act 1988.[12] Under the new regime of partnership taxation, all the members of the old firm must agree to make such an election.[13]

---

[3] This expression is defined in *ibid.* s.100(2). See also *Reed v. Nova Securities Ltd.* [1985] 1 W.L.R. 193.

[4] *Ibid.* s.102(2). As to when there can now be such a deemed discontinuance, see *supra*, para. 34-61, n. 98.

[5] See *ibid.* s.111(3)(c), as substituted by the Finance Act 1994, s.215(1).

[6] *Ibid.* s.100(1).

[7] This relief was abolished by the Finance Act 1984, s.48, although the availability of unused relief is preserved by the Income and Corporation Taxes Act 1988: see *ibid.* s.96(7)(c), Sched. 30, para. 18.

[8] This expression is defined in the Income and Corporation Taxes Act 1988, s.101(3).

[9] The discontinuance may be actual or deemed: *ibid.* s.102(2). As to when there can now be a deemed discontinuance, see *supra*, para. 34-61, n. 98.

[10] See *ibid.* s.111(3)(c), as substituted by the Finance Act 1994, s.215(1).

[11] *Ibid.* s.101(1). Note also the decision in *Symons v. Weeks* [1983] S.T.C. 195.

[12] Ibid. s.101(2). As to the manner in which relief is to be claimed as from 1996/97, see the Taxes Management Act 1970, s. 42(2), (6), (7)(a) (as substituted by the Finance Act 1994, Sched. 19, Pt. 1, para. 13).

[13] Income and Corporation Taxes Act s.111(2) (as substituted by the Finance Act 1994, s.215(1)) provides that the profits or gains of a trade or profession carried on by two or more persons in partnership are to be computed as if the partnership were an individual. It would follow that it is not open to one partner unilaterally to insist that his share of the profits should be computed in some different way. This is confirmed by the terms of the Taxes Management Act 1970, s. 42(2), (6), (7)(a) (as substituted by the Finance Act 1994, Sched. 19, Pt. 1, para. 13), which applies as from the year 1996/97.

5. CAPITAL ALLOWANCES AND LOSSES

Capital allowances

34–64   In normal circumstances, expenditure on capital items will be incurred by the firm and, under the old regime of partnership taxation,[14] capital allowances will be claimed and received by it.[15] It would seem that the position will be the same under the new regime, notwithstanding the fact that each partner is deemed to carry on a separate trade.[16] It follows that, in the absence of some specific provision in the agreement, the benefit of such allowances will under both the old and new regimes, ultimately be shared between the partners in their normal profit sharing ratios.[17] There are, however, restrictions on the use which may be made of certain allowances by limited and other partners.[18]

34–65   Where, under the old regime, there is a change in the firm which brings about a deemed discontinuance under section 113(1) of the Taxes Act 1988,[19] there will generally be a discontinuance for the purposes of capital allowances.[20] On such a deemed discontinuance, there will be a deemed sale to the new firm of the property used by the old firm at its open market value, and a balancing charge will be incurred · on the residual value of the relevant capital items.[21] However, in the case of machinery and plant, this result can be avoided by submitting a suitable form of election[22] and, in the case of other assets, by electing for them to be taken over by the new firm at their written down values.[23] No difficulties arise where the old and

---

[14] See *supra*, para. 34–05.

[15] *i.e.* under the Income and Corporation Taxes Act 1988, s.111. Such allowances will be claimed by the firm on normal principles.

[16] *Ibid.* s.111(2), (3)(a) (as substituted by the Finance Act 1994, s.215(1)); Capital Allowances Act 1990, s.140(2), (3) (as substituted by the Finance Act 1994, s.211(1)).

[17] If the capital and income profit sharing ratios differ, the former should normally be applied. Equally, there would seem to be no reason why the partners should not agree to share capital allowances in some other way. Indeed, such an agreement may be advantageous: see further, *supra*, para. 34–16.

[18] Income and Corporation Taxes Act 1988, s.117(1), as amended by the Capital Allowances Act 1990, Sched. 1, para. 8(8), restricting the application of s.141 of the 1990 Act. See also *infra*, para. 34–72.

[19] Such a deemed discontinuance can now only arise where the firm was in existence prior to April 6, 1994 and the change occurs prior to the tax year 1997/98: see the Finance Act 1994, ss.215(4)(a), 216(1).

[20] Capital Allowances Act 1990, s.161(9). There are, however, certain specific provisions in the capital allowances legislation which provide that a deemed discontinuance should not be treated as a discontinuance for the purposes of capital allowances: see, for example, *ibid.* s.134(4).

[21] *Ibid.* ss.78(1), 152(1). Note that the new firm will not be afforded any first year or initial allowance on the deemed purchase (*ibid.* s.78(1), 152(2)), although few such allowances in any event now exist. See also *infra*, para. 34–73.

[22] *Ibid.* s.77(3)-(5).

[23] *Ibid.* s.158 (as amended by the Finance Act 1993, s.117). See also the Finance Act 1994, s.119(1).

the new partners submit a continuance election under section 113(2) of the Taxes Act 1988.[24] In the case of firms formed after April 6, 1994, such a deemed discontinuance cannot now arise;[25] moreover, the possibility of such a discontinuance will be removed in the case of *all* other firms as from the tax year 1997/98.[26]

Machinery and plant. Particular attention should be drawn to the **34–66** provisions relating to machinery and plant contained in section 65 of the Capital Allowances Act 1990. The effect of section 65(1) is to permit a claim for capital allowances where capital expenditure on machinery or plant to be used for the purposes of the firm is incurred by one or more of the partners personally. In such circumstances, for the purposes of claiming capital allowances, the machinery or plant is treated as partnership property, but the allowances, will only be claimable by and for the benefit of those partners who actually incurred the expenditure.[27] Such treatment will not, however, be available where those partners have leased the machinery or plant to the firm, or have otherwise received any consideration for its use, if that consideration has been deducted in computing the profits or gains of the firm.[28] Although this provision affords considerable assistance to partners, there would still appear to be a number of anomalies which are not at present covered by the legislation.[29] It would seem that this section will continue to have effect under the new regime of partnership taxation, even though each partner is deemed to carry on a separate trade of his own; *sed quaere*.[30]

Where a sale or gift of machinery or plant used for partnership **34–67** purposes is made by one or more partners to other partners, there will be no balancing allowance or balancing charge provided that the machinery or plant continues to be used by the firm.[31] Thus, where an outgoing partner assigns his share in such machinery or plant to an incoming partner or to the continuing partners, no adverse consequences will result.[32]

---

[24] *Ibid.* s.78(3), (4), 152(3).

[25] See the Income and Corporation Taxes Act 1988, s.113(2), as substituted by the Finance Act 1994, s.216(1); Finance Act 1994, s.215(4)(b), 5(a). See also *supra*, para. 34–59.

[26] See the Finance Act 1994, s.215(4)(a).

[27] Nothing in the Capital Allowances Act 1990, s.65(1) alters the incidence of any allowance, but merely enables such allowance to be claimed by the firm.

[28] *Ibid.* s.65(3).

[29] Thus, where machinery or plant is owned by the firm, but not all of the partners are entitled to share in its capital assets, *ibid.* s.65(1) will prima facie not apply, and it might be difficult for the firm to claim the allowances. Arguments in favour of such a claim do, however, exist: see Lawton, Goldberg and Fraser, *The Law of Partnership Taxation* (2nd ed.), paras. 2.048 *et seq.* Be that as it may, so long as each partner has some, albeit small, share in the firm's capital assets, the requirements of the section would appear to be satisfied.

[30] See the Income and Corporation Taxes Act 1988, ss.111(2), (3)(a), as substituted by the Finance Act 1994, s.215(1).

[31] Capital Allowances Act 1990, s.65(2).

[32] As to the treatment of shares in machinery or plant, see *ibid.* s.83(4). The position is the same for the purposes of capital gains tax: see *infra*, para. 35–13.

Losses

34–68   Where losses are made in any period of assessment, they will be
allocated between the partners in accordance with the terms of the
partnership agreement[33] or, alternatively, in the shares in which they
were actually borne.[34] In ascertaining the amount of each partner's
share of any loss, account must be taken of any preferential salary or
other entitlement which will, in practice, shift the entire burden of
that loss onto the other partners.[35] Once the allocation as between
partners has taken place, each partner will be able to utilise his share
of the loss in the same way as any other trading loss by setting it
against his income from other sources[36] or against his capital gains,[37]
carrying it forward to set against his future shares of profit[38] or,
under the new regime of partnership taxation,[39] setting it against his
income in the *previous* year.[40]

34–69   A partner has a further option in respect of losses sustained in the
year of assessment in which a trade is first carried on or in any of the
following three years: he may claim to carry back his share to set

---

[33] Losses may, of course, be borne in different proportions to the profit sharing ratios: see,
generally, *supra*, paras. 20–05 *et seq.*

[34] As to the position under the new regime of partnership taxation, see the Income and
Corporation Taxes Act 1988, ss.111(2), (3), as substituted by the Finance Act 1994, s. 215(1). See
also *supra*, para. 34–06.

[35] Thus, where a partner is entitled to his salary irrespective of the firm's profitability, he will
only have sustained a loss to the extent (if at all) that his apportioned share of the partnership loss
exceeds the amount of his salary. For a general discussion of this problem, see Lawton, Goldberg
and Fraser, *The Law of Partnership Taxation* (2nd ed.), para. 2.070.

[36] See, as regards firms in existence prior to April 6, 1994 until the tax year 1996/97, the Income
and Corporation Taxes Act 1988, ss.380(1), 383. As regards firms formed on or after that date and
all firms with effect from 1996/97, see *ibid.* s.380(1)(a), as substituted by the Finance Act 1994,
s.209(1) and amended, in respect of the years 1994/95 and 1995/96, by the Finance Act 1994, Sched.
20, para. 8. In either case, the trade must have been carried on on a commercial basis and with a
view to the realisation of profit in the year in which the loss was incurred: *ibid.* s.384(1), as
amended, in the case of firms formed on or after April 6, 1994 and all firms as from the year
1997/98, by the Finance Act 1994, s.214(1)(c). And see generally *Whiteman On Income Tax* (3rd
ed.). Chap. 10. The following additional restrictions on the availability of this relief should be
noted: *ibid.* s.117 (limited and non-participating partners: see further, *infra*, para. 34–72); *ibid.*
s.384(6) (as amended, in the case of firms formed on or after April 6, 1994 and all firms as from
the year 1997/98, by the Finance Act 1994, s.214(2)), (7), read subject to *ibid.* subs. (10) (as
amended by the Capital Allowances Act 1990, Sched. 1, para. 8(14)) and the Capital Allowances
Act 1990, s.142 (capital allowances on machinery and plant); Income and Corporation Taxes Act
1988, s.399(2) (partnerships dealing in commodity futures). And see, as to Case VI losses, *ibid.*
s.392.

[37] Finance Act 1991, s.72, as amended by the Taxation of Chargeable Gains Act 1992, Sched. 10,
para. 23 and, in the case of firms formed on or after April 6, 1994 and all firms with effect from
1997/98, by the Finance Act 1994, Sched. 26, Pt.V(24).

[38] Income and Corporation Taxes Act 1988, s.385(1), as substituted, in the case of firms formed
on or after April 6, 1994 and all firms with effect from 1997/98, by the Finance Act 1994, s.209(4).

[39] In this respect, the new regime applies to any firm formed on or after April 6, 1994 (including
a firm in existence prior to that date whose trade is deemed to have been permanently discontinued
thereafter under the Income and Corporation Taxes Act 1988, s.113(1)) and to all firms with effect
from the year 1996/97: Finance Act 1994, s.218(1).

[40] Income and Corporation Taxes Act 1988, s.380(1)(b), as substituted by the Finance Act 1994,
s.209(1) and amended, in respect of the years 1994/1995 and 1995/96, by *ibid.* Sched. 20, para. 8.

against his income for the three years of assessment preceding the year in which the losses were sustained.[41]

For the purposes of these reliefs, where the old regime of **34–70** partnership taxation continues to apply,[42] changes in the firm are ignored, whether or not an election is made under section 113(2) of the Taxes Act 1988, provided that the partner claiming the relief was a partner both before and after the change.[43] Under the new regime, there is no need for such an express provision, since each partner is deemed to carry on a separate trade of his own.[44]

Pre-trading expenditure

Where a partner has, within seven years of the commencement of a **34–71** partnership, incurred expenditure for the purposes of its business, and that expenditure would have constituted an allowable deduction if incurred after that time, he can claim to have it treated as a loss sustained in the year of assessment in which the partnership (and thus, under the new regime, his deemed trade[45]) commenced.[46] Such a loss can then be relieved in the same way as any other loss which might have been sustained in that year.[47]

Limited and non-participating partners

A partner who is either a limited partner within the meaning of the **34–72** Limited Partnerships Act 1907,[48] or who has no right to participate in the management of the firm and is entitled to be wholly or partially indemnified or relieved from liability for its debts and obligations,

---

[41] Income and Corporation Taxes Act 1988, s.381, as amended, in the case of firms formed on or after April 6, 1994 and all firms as from 1996/97, by the Finance Act 1994, s.209(2). The relief must be claimed within two years and is only available if the loss was sustained during a period in which the trade was being carried on on a commercial basis and in such a way that profits could reasonably be expected to be realised in that period or within a reasonable time thereafter: *ibid.* s.381(1), (4). It is not, however, possible to apportion a loss so that a part is relieved under this section, whilst the remainder is relieved under some other section, *e.g. ibid.* s.380: see *Butt v. Haxby* [1983] S.T.C. 239. As to the restrictions on the availability of such relief, see *supra*, para. 34–68, n. 36.

[42] *i.e.* in the case of firms in existence prior to April 6, 1994 until the year 1997/98: Finance Act 1994, s.215(4)(a). Note that where such a firm is subject to an actual or deemed discontinuance after April 6, 1994, the new regime will apply with immediate effect: *ibid.* ss.215(4)(b), (5)(a), 218(1)(b).

[43] Income and Corporation Taxes Act 1988, ss.380(3), 381(6), 384(5), 385(5). Each of these subsections will cease to apply as from 1997/98: Finance Act 1994, ss.215(4)(a), 216(3)(b)-(e), Sched. 26, Pt. V(24).

[44] Income and Corporation Taxes Act 1988, ss.111(3)(a), 113(2), as respectively substituted by the Finance Act 1994, ss.215(1), 216(1).

[45] *Ibid.* s.111(3)(a), as substituted by the Finance Act 1994, s.215(1).

[46] *Ibid.* s.401 (as amended by the Finance Act 1993, s.109). This relief will naturally not be available if the expenditure is already allowable as a deduction: *ibid.* s.401(1)(b).

[47] A separate claim for relief under the Income Tax Acts will, however, be required in respect of the deemed loss: *ibid.* s.401(2).

[48] See generally, *supra*, paras. 29–03 *et seq.*

even though he in other respects enjoys the attributes of a full partner,[49] may not set his share of any loss against income derived from non-partnership sources[50] to the extent that it exceeds the aggregate amount of his capital contribution[51] and any undrawn profits for the time being left in the firm.[52] Similar restrictions apply to the reliefs in respect of certain capital allowances[53] and (in the case of persons other than limited partners) in respect of interest payable on loans taken out in order to acquire a partnership share or otherwise to fund a capital contribution or advance.[54]

Losses and unrelieved capital allowances on a partnership change: old regime

34-73   Where, in the case of a firm in existence prior to April 6, 1994,[55] no continuance election is submitted pursuant to section 113(2) of the Taxes Act 1988 following a change in the firm,[56] a continuing partner is able to carry forward his share of losses from the old firm to set against his share of profits in the new firm, until such losses have been fully relieved.[57] Any unused capital allowances at the time of the change would be treated as losses sustained in the part of the year prior to the change.[58] He may also, on making the appropriate claim, set his losses, including unrelieved capital allowances treated as such,[59] against his total income in the year of assessment in which the

---

[49] See the definition of "limited partner" in the Income and Corporation Taxes Act 1988, s.117(2).

[50] *i.e.* under the new regime of partnership taxation, the loss can only be set against the income of the trade which he is deemed to carry on by virtue of *ibid.* s.111(3)(a), as substituted by the Finance Act 1994, s.215(1).

[51] Such contribution must not, however, have been directly or indirectly withdrawn: see *ibid.* s.117(3)(a). In fact, a limited partner is technically not entitled to withdraw any part of his capital: see the Limited Partnerships Act 1907, s.4(3), considered *supra*, paras. 30–12 *et seq.*

[52] Income and Corporation Taxes Act 1988. s.117(1) (as amended by the Capital Allowances Act 1990, Sched. 1, para. 8(8)), (3). This section and its predecessor (the Finance Act 1985, s.48, Sched. 12) reversed the effects of the decision in *Reed v. Young* [1986] 1 W.L.R. 649, in which the House of Lords had held that the Limited Partnerships Act 1907, s.4(2) did not apply to trading losses, as distinct from ordinary debts and liabilities. See further, *supra*, para. 30–09. A similar restriction applies to the use of loans by a *corporate* partner: Income and Corporation Taxes Act 1988, s. 118 (as amended by the Capital Allowances Act 1990, Sched. 1, para. 8(9) and the Finance Act 1991, Sched. 15, para. 4).

[53] *Ibid.* s.117(1); Capital Allowances Act 1990, s.141.

[54] Income and Corporation Taxes Act 1988, ss.353 (as amended by the Finance Act 1994, s.81, Sched. 26, Pt. V(2)), 362(1), 117(1) (as amended by the Capital Allowances Act 1990, Sched. 1, para. 8(8)): see further, *supra*, para. 34–29. A true limited partner would appear to be entitled to no relief in respect of such interest.

[55] But not after the tax year 1997/98: Finance Act 1994, ss.215(4)(a), 216(1).

[56] See *supra*, paras. 34–46 *et seq*. In the case of a deemed discontinuance *prior* to April 6, 1994, the modified cessation and commencement rules would have applied to the new firm: see *supra*, para. 34–50.

[57] Income and Corporation Taxes Act 1988, s.385(5)(a). Losses sustained in that part of a year of assessment which falls before the change may be set against profits realised in the remainder of the year as if it were a subsequent year: *ibid* s.385(5)(b). The entire subsection will cease to have effect with effect as from the year 1997/98: Finance Act 1994, s.216(3)(e), Sched. 26, Pt. V(24).

[58] *Ibid.* s.385(5)(c). But see the previous note.

[59] *i.e.* under *ibid.* s.383. This section ceases to apply as from the tax year 1997/98: Finance Act 1994, s.214(1)(b), Sched. 26, Pt. V(24).

loss was incurred, and, if necessary, against such income in the next following year of assessment, but no further.[60] This right can, however, only be claimed where it is shown that, for the year of assessment in which the loss is claimed to have been sustained, the trade was being carried on on a commercial basis and with a view to the realisation of profits.[61]

Although a continuing partner may in this way be protected where **34–74** a continuance election is not submitted, an outgoing partner does not enjoy such a favoured position where such an election *is* submitted. Thus he will be unable to set his share of partnership losses against his total income in the year following the year of his departure, since at the time when such a claim would fall to be made he will no longer be carrying on the trade.[62]

Accordingly, any losses sustained by him in the year of assessment during which he left the firm, together with any losses carried forward from previous years, may be wholly lost, unless they can be set against his share of the partnership profits or his other income for that year. Of course, he may not have been required to bear a share of any losses incurred during that year, in which case the continuing partners will carry such losses forward on normal principles. The benefit of unrelieved capital allowances may also be lost if the outgoing partner's share of profits is not sufficiently large to cover them, unless he has assigned his share in the capital assets concerned to one or more of the continuing partners, thus allowing them to carry the allowances forward.[63]

It follows from the potentially disadvantageous consequences which **34–75** the submission of a continuance election may have for an outgoing partner that such a partner who has large unrelieved losses may well not sign such an election willingly. In such circumstances, it may be necessary to consider whether it is appropriate to afford to such a partner some form of compensation in addition to the usual indemnity.[64]

---

[60] Income and Corporation Taxes Act 1988, s.380(1), (2). Some measure of protection against the loss of unrelieved current capital allowances on a cessation is afforded by Extra-Statutory Concession A8 (1994 Revision). Note that, as from the year 1996/97, *ibid.* s.380(1), (2) are as substituted by the Finance Act 1994, s.209(1).

[61] *Ibid.* s.384(1), as amended with effect from the year 1997/98 by the Finance Act 1994, s.214(1)(c). A more rigorous test is, however, provided in the case of farmers and market gardeners: *ibid.* s.397 (as amended by the Capital Allowances Act 1990, Sched. 1, para. 8(18), the Finance Act 1991, Sched. 15, para. 10 and, as from the year 1997/98, the Finance Act 1994, s. 214(3)) may prevent a loss from being so relieved if a loss was incurred in the trade in each of the previous five years.

[62] *Ibid.* s.380(2) (in its unamended form) requires that the trade should be "still carried on by him in the year for which the claim is made." This will clearly exclude the outgoing partner. Obviously, there is no possibility of carrying forward his losses under *ibid.* s.385.

[63] See the Capital Allowances Act 1990, s.65(2) (machinery and plant). As to the capital gains tax consequences, see *infra*, paras. 35–13 *et seq.*

[64] See further, as to the desirability of submitting a continuance election, *supra*, para. 34–51.

Similar problems do not arise under the new regime of partnership taxation.[65]

Terminal loss relief

34-76 Where, under the old regime,[66] no continuance election is submitted following a change in the firm, a partner who ceases trading (and therefore does not continue as a member of the new firm)[67] will be entitled, as an alternative to any other form of relief,[68] to claim carry-back terminal loss relief under section 388 of the Taxes Act 1988, *i.e.* he can set his terminal loss against the share of partnership profits[69] on which he has been assessed in the three years of assessment immediately preceding the year in which the discontinuance occurred.[70] The same relief is available under the new regime to a partner who leaves a firm and whose deemed trade is thereupon treated as permanently discontinued.[71] Obviously the relief is also available under both regimes where the partnership trade is permanently discontinued, *e.g.* following a dissolution.[72]

34-77 The terminal loss will in all cases comprise:

(i) any loss sustained by the partner in question in the year of the discontinuance;[73] and

(ii) any loss sustained by him in the part of the preceding year beginning 12 months before the date of the discontinuance.[74]

However, in the case of firms in existence prior to April 6, 1994, the terminal loss incurred in any year prior to 1997/98 will also comprise:

(iii) the relevant capital allowances[75] for that year; and

---

[65] *Cf.* the Income and Corporation Taxes Act 1988, s.380(1), (2), as substituted by the Finance Act 1994, s.209(1). See also *supra*, paras. 34–06, 34–58.

[66] The old regime applies to any firm in existence prior to April 6, 1994 which has not been subject to a discontinuance or a deemed discontinuance thereafter, but only until the year 1997/98.

[67] Income and Corporation Taxes Act 1988. s.389(4)(a). Needless to say, if there is a permanent discontinuance of the trade *otherwise* than on a change in the firm, all the partners will be entitled to the relief.

[68] *Ibid.* s.388(2).

[69] The profits may be either notionally increased or decreased by virtue of *ibid.* s.388(4), (5).

[70] *Ibid.* s.388(1). The relief will be given so far as possible against a later rather than an earlier year: *ibid.* s.388(3).

[71] *Ibid.* as amended by the Finance Act 1994, s.209(6). See also, as to a partner's deemed trade, *ibid.* s.111(3)(a), as substituted by the Finance Act 1994, s.215(1).

[72] *Ibid.* in its original form and as amended; see also, under the new regime, *ibid.* s.111(3)(c), as substituted by the Finance Act 1994, s.215(1). It does not necessarily follow that any trade will immediately be discontinued in the event of a dissolution: see *supra*, para. 34–14.

[73] *Ibid.* s.388(6)(a).

[74] *Ibid.* s.388(6)(c).

[75] The relevant capital allowances of any year of assessment are defined so as to exclude any allowances carried forward from an earlier year: *ibid.* s.388(7). This definition ceases to have effect, as from the year 1997/98: Finance Act 1994, s.214(1)(d), Sched. 26, Pt. V(24).

(iv) the same fraction of the relevant capital allowances for the preceding year beginning 12 months before the date of the discontinuance as the part thereof beginning 12 months before the discontinuance is of a year.[76]

Successive changes in firm: old regime

If, under the old regime, there is a change in the firm, followed by **34-78** a further change or a permanent discontinuance, a partner who was a member of both the old and the new firms on the first change, and who claims terminal loss relief on the second change, will be able to carry back his terminal loss beyond the first change in order to obtain full relief.[77] Where the second change occurs within 12 months of the first change, the latter will be ignored when calculating his terminal loss.[78]

Partnership business transferred to a company

Where a partnership business is transferred to a company in **34-79** consideration solely or mainly of the issue of shares in that company to the former partners, any unrelieved loss of the firm (but excluding unrelieved capital allowances) may be carried forward and set off by those partners in reduction of the tax payable by them on income derived from the company to which the business was transferred.[79] Such losses must first be set against income assessable on the partners, *e.g.* directors' fees and other earned income, and only the balance set against other income, *e.g.* dividends.[80] Any change in the firm prior to the transfer can, under the old regime, be ignored, provided that the partner claiming the relief was a member of both the old and the new firms.[81]

The relief can be claimed for any year of assessment throughout which the claimant is the beneficial owner of the shares allotted to him, and throughout which the company carries on trading,[82] but the claim must be submitted within six years after the end of the year of assessment to which it relates.

---

[76] See *ibid.* s.388(6)(b), (d). Both paragraphs cease to have effect as from the year 1994/95 in the case of firms formed on or after April 6, 1994 and, in the case of all firms, as from the year 1997/98: Finance Act 1994, s.214(1)(d), Sched. 26, Pt. V(24).

[77] Income and Corporation Taxes Act 1988, s.389(4)(b). In the case of a firm in existence prior to April 6, 1994, this subsection is, as from the year 1997/98, substituted by the Finance Act 1994, s.216(4).

[78] Income and Corporation Taxes Act 1988, s.389(4)(b)(i), (ii). By virtue of this provision the entirety of the relevant capital allowances in the preceding year of assessment may be treated as part of the terminal loss. And see the preceding note.

[79] *Ibid.* s.386(1), applying *ibid.* s.385 (excluding subs. (5)).

[80] *Ibid.* s.386(2).

[81] *Ibid.* s.386(4), restricting the application of *ibid.* s.385(5). This subsection ceases to have effect as from the year 1997/98: Finance Act 1994, s.216(3)(f), Sched. 26, Pt. V(24).

[82] *Ibid.* s.386(1)(b).

6. PARTNERSHIPS WITH CORPORATE MEMBERS

34-80 Special rules for the taxation of partnerships with one or more corporate members are contained in sections 114 and 115 of the Taxes Act 1988.[83]

Computation of partnership profits or losses

Stage 1—Partnership profits/losses

34-81 For Revenue accounting purposes, the profits (or losses) of the partnership must be computed, in the first instance, just as if the firm were a company, except that at this stage:

(*a*) distributions are disregarded;[84]

(*b*) charges on income, capital allowances and balancing charges, losses incurred in other accounting periods, and pre-trading expenditure are disregarded;[85] and

(*c*) any changes in the persons carrying on the trade are disregarded, save that where there is a change in the corporate partners, and after the change there is no corporate partner who was a member of both the old and the new firms, the trade is treated as having been transferred to another company.[86]

The Inspector of Taxes may determine by whom the partnership return is to be submitted and the information to be contained therein.[87]

Stage 2—Corporate partner's profit share

34-82 Having ascertained the profits (or losses) of the partnership, the corporate partner's share of those profits (or losses) is determined in the usual way, *i.e.* in accordance with the partnership agreement. At this stage, the corporate partner's share of all items falling under

---

[83] In the case of firms formed on or after April 6, 1994 and all firms as from the year 1997/98, these sections are amended by the Finance Act 1994, s.215(2), (3)(a), (b), Sched. 26, Pt.V(24).

[84] Thus, no advance corporation tax will be payable in respect of any payment made to the partners.

[85] Income and Corporation Taxes Act 1988, s.114(1)(b). Relief in respect of these items is of necessity dealt with separately as between the company partners and the individual partners, in view of the different principles applying to corporation tax.

[86] Income and Corporation Taxes Act 1988, s.114(1)(c).

[87] Taxes Management Act 1970, s.9(1)–(3), (6), as substituted by the Finance Act 1990, s.90(1). *Cf. ibid.* s.9(4) in its original form. With effect from the year 1996/97 see *ibid.* s.12AA(1)–(3), (5), (6), as added by the Finance Act 1994, s.184. See also, *supra*, para. 34–17, 34–18.

group (b) above (charges on income, capital allowances and balancing charges, losses incurred in previous accounting periods, and pre-trading expenditure[88]) is brought into account.[89] Corporation tax is then chargeable on the resulting share of profits as if those profits were derived from a trade carried on by the company alone in its corresponding accounting period or periods, and an assessment is made on the company accordingly.[90] The company's corresponding accounting period or periods means the period or periods which comprise the accounting period of the partnership. Where necessary an apportionment between corresponding accounting periods may be made.[91]

Stage 3—Individual partner's profit share

An individual partner's share of profits or losses will be ascertained **34–83** in the same way and then adjusted so as to bring into account his share of all items excluded from the partnership computation under group (b) above and an assessment to income tax made accordingly.[92] Under the old regime, which continues to apply to firms in existence prior to April 6, 1994 but only until the end of the year 1996/97,[93] where there are two or more individual partners, a joint assessment in the firm name will be made on them under section 111 of the Taxes Act 1988, as if they were the only partners.[94]

So far as concerns the individual (*i.e.* non-company) members of a firm formed prior to April 6, 1994, the discontinuance provisions of section 113(1) of the Taxes Act 1988 do not apply, unless there is a change amongst those individual partners. If there is such a change, the right to elect for assessment on a continuing basis is until the tax year 1997/98 exercisable as if the individuals were the only partners.[95] Thus, a corporate partner is not required to join in the election.

---

[88] Such expenditure may be treated as incurred on the day on which the trade is first carried on by the company partner: Income and Corporation Taxes Act 1988, s.401(1), as amended by the Finance Act 1993, s.109(1).

[89] But note the possible effects of *ibid.* s.116, considered *infra.* para. 34–85.

[90] This treatment now broadly accords with that applicable to individual partners under the new regime: see the Income and Corporation Taxes Act 1988, s.111(3), as substituted by the Finance Act 1994, s.215(1). See also *supra*, para. 34–06.

[91] *Ibid.* s.114(2), as amended, in the case of firms formed on or after April 6, 1994 and all firms as from the year 1997/98, by the Finance Act 1994, s.215(2)(b).

[92] *Ibid.* s.114(3), as amended in the case of firms formed on or after April 6, 1994 and all firms as from the year 1997/98 by the Finance Act 1994, s.215(2)(c), (3)(a), Sched. 26, Pt. V(24). The assessment will be made on the normal preceding/current year basis (depending on which regime applies), unless the commencement or cessation provisions apply. It should be noted that, in the case of a corporate partnership, the individual partners' shares of any capital allowances are given effect to not by reference to a basis period, but by reference to the accounting period of the partnership.

[93] See the Finance Act 1994, s.215(4), (5).

[94] Income and Corporation Taxes Act 1988, s.114(4), applying *ibid.* s.111. This subsection ceases to have effect as from 1997/98: Finance Act 1994, s. 215(3)(a), Sched. 26, Pt. V(24).

[95] *Ibid.* s.114(3)(b). As from the year 1997/98, this paragraph ceases to have effect: Finance Act 1994, s.215(3)(a), Sched. 26, Pt. V(24).

Relief for losses

34-84   The individual partners' shares of any partnership losses will be relieved in the normal way[96] and there is now no restrictions on their ability to carry back terminal losses under sections 388 and 389 of the Taxes Act 1988.[97] Although the regime governing the relief of a corporate partner's share of any such loss is broadly the same,[98] in lieu of terminal loss relief such a partner may carry the loss back to be set against its profits in the three preceding accounting periods.[99]

Anti-avoidance provisions

34-85   Where any arrangement exists which results in a share of a partnership profit or loss being transferred to a corporate partner in return for a payment,[1] comprehensive anti-avoidance provisions effectively prevent that corporate partner from setting its share of the loss or any charges on income against any income other than its share of the partnership profits and, indeed from setting any other trading losses or reliefs against that share.[2] Further, capital allowances will not be deductible in computing the corporate partner's share of profits,[3] and advance corporation tax cannot be set against the corporation tax payable in respect of that share.[4] There are no corresponding provisions relating to individual partners.

7. PARTNERSHIPS CONTROLLED ABROAD

Residence of all-individual partnerships

34-86   Where the control and management[5] of a firm's trade or business is situated outside the United Kingdom, that trade or business is

---

[96] See *supra*, paras. 34–68 *et seq.*; also, generally, *Whiteman On Income Tax* (3rd ed.), Chap. 10.

[97] The Income and Corporation Taxes Act 1988, s. 114(3)(c), which appeared to restrict that right to cases where the departure of the individual partners coincided with the departure of *all* the corporate partners, was repealed by the Finance Act 1991, Sched. 15, para. 3. Note that, in the case of firms formed on or after April 6, 1994, and all firms as from the year 1997/98, the Income and Corporation Taxes Act 1988, s. 114(3) is amended by the Finance Act 1994, s. 215(2)(c), (3)(a). See further, as to terminal loss relief, *supra*, paras. 34–76, 34–77.

[98] See, generally, the Income and Corporation Taxes Act 1988, s. 114(2) (as amended in the case of firms formed on or after April 6, 1994, and all firms as from the year 1997/98, by the Finance Act 1994, s. 215(2)(b)), 393 (as amended by the Finance Act 1990, s. 99(2), Sched. 19, Pt. V and the Finance Act 1991, Sched. 19, Pt. V), 393A(1)(a) (as added by the Finance Act 1991, s. 73(1)). Note also, as to the position of a corporate *limited* partner (as defined in *ibid.* s. 117(2)), the terms of *ibid.* s. 118 (as amended by the Capital Allowances Act 1990, Sched. 1, para. 8(9) and the Finance Act 1991, Sched. 15, para. 4). See also, *supra*, para. 34–72.

[99] *Ibid.* s.393A(1)(b), (2) (as added by the Finance Act 1991, s. 73(1)). *Ibid.* s.394 (terminal loss relief) was repealed by the Finance Act 1991, Sched. 20, Pt. V.

[1] Whether that payment is made by or to the company partner: Income and Corporation Taxes Act 1988, s.116(1).

[2] *Ibid.* s.116.

[3] *Ibid.* s.116(5), amending the application of *ibid.* s.114(1), (2).

[4] *Ibid.* s.116(2)(d).

[5] The question of where the control and management of a trade is situated is a pure question of fact: see *Padmore v. I.R.C.* [1989] S.T.C. 493; also *Colquhoun v. Brooks* (1889) 14 App. Cas. 493; *Ogilvie v. Kitton* (1905) 5 T.C. 338; *Mitchell v. Egyptian Hotels Ltd.* [1915] A.C. 1022; *Unit Construction Co. Ltd. v. Bullock* [1960] A.C. 351.

deemed to be carried on by persons resident outside the United Kingdom and, moreover, the firm itself is deemed to be non-resident, notwithstanding the fact that some of the partners may be resident and some of the firm's trading operations carried on in the United Kingdom.[6]

However, if such a deemed non-resident firm carries on trading operations within the United Kingdom, then tax is chargeable on the profits of such operations to the same extent as, and no further than, an individual trader resident abroad would be chargeable in respect of trading operations by him within the United Kingdom.[7] The firm will be so chargeable even though one or more of the partners is resident in the United Kingdom.

A United Kingdom resident partner of a deemed non-resident firm **34–87** will be taxed under Case V of Schedule D on his share of the partnership profits, although that share will be computed in accordance with the rules of Cases I and II of that Schedule.[8] Even though a double tax agreement between the United Kingdom and the firm's country of residence might in its terms exempt his share from liability to United Kingdom tax, that agreement will be ignored when determining such a partner's tax liability.[9]

Assessment

Where such a deemed non-resident firm is chargeable to tax in **34–88** respect of profits derived from trading operations in the United Kingdom, the assessment will be made on the firm in the name of any partner resident in the United Kingdom.[10] The person

---

[6] Income and Corporation Taxes Act 1988, s.112(1). It should be noted that this provision will also apply for capital gains tax purposes: see further, *infra*, para. 35–01. It should not, however, be assumed that a foreign partnership will automatically be treated as a partnership for income tax purposes: see *Dreyfus v. C.I.R.* (1929) 14 T.C. 560, a case concerning a French société en nom collectif, which, by reason of its corporate status (see *supra*, para. 2–39) was held not to be a partnership for tax purposes; *cf. Padmore v. I.R.C.* [1989] S.T.C. 493 (partnership formed under Jersey law).

[7] *Ibid.* s.112(2).

[8] *Ibid.* s.65(3) as amended, in the case of firms formed on or after April 6, 1994 and in respect of all firms as from the year 1997/98, by the Finance Act 1994, s.207(2), (6), Sched. 26, Pt.V(24). Note that in its unamended form, the subsection excludes the operation of *ibid.* ss.60–63 and 113, but in its amended form *applies ibid.* ss.60–63A and 113 (as themselves respectively amended, substituted or added by the Finance Act 1994, ss.200–205, 216(1), (2)). The potential application of *ibid.* s.111 (in its original form) to overseas partnerships is in doubt: *per* Browne-Wilkinson J. in *Newstead v. Frost* [1978] 1 W.L.R. 511, 519 (a decision in relation to the Income and Corporation Taxes Act 1970, s.152). *Semble*, s.111 (as substituted by the Finance Act 1994, s.215(1)) does not apply to such partnerships: see the Finance Act 1994, s.215(4), (5)(b). *Sed quaere.*

[9] Income and Corporation Taxes Act 1988, s.112(4). This section and its predecessor (the Income and Corporation Taxes Act 1970, s.153(4), as added by the Finance (No. 2) Act 1987, s.62(1)) reversed the effects of the decision in *Padmore v. I.R.C.* [1987] S.T.C. 36, affirmed at [1989] S.T.C. 493.

[10] Income and Corporation Taxes Act 1988, s.112(3). *Cf.* the approach adopted under the new regime of partnership taxation: *ibid.* s.111, as substituted by the Finance Act 1994, s.215(1). See *supra*, para. 34–06.

responsible for submitting the partnership return will be such partner or other person as the Inspector of Taxes may require.[11] The return must, *inter alia*, declare the name and residence of each partner.[12]

Residence of mixed company/individual partnership

34–89   Where the control and management of the trade or business of a firm is situated abroad, but one or more of the partners is a company resident in the United Kingdom, the firm will be deemed to be non-resident as regards the individual, but not the corporate, partners.[13] Accordingly, a corporate partner will be assessed to corporation tax in respect of the entirety of its share of the partnership profits.[14]

8.   PAYMENTS TO OUTGOING PARTNERS AND THEIR DEPENDANTS

Consultancy agreements

34–90   Where an outgoing partner enters into a consultancy agreement or similar arrangement with the continuing partners, under which he will continue to provide his services to the firm in return for a fee or other payment, the tax treatment of such remuneration will in large measure depend on whether the consultancy can in truth be said to represent, in whole or in part, consideration for the acquisition of his share. If it was entirely independent of such acquisition, and the outgoing partner provides genuine services to the firm which are not rewarded by a grossly disproportionate payment, his remuneration will constitute earned income in his hands[15] and will be deductible in computing the partnership profits.[16] Where, however, there is a direct or, possibly, indirect connection between the consultancy and the acquisition of the outgoing partner's share, the "remuneration" will not be wholly referable to the services he provides and will neither constitute earned income in his hands nor be deductible by the continuing partners.[17]

---

[11] Taxes Management Act 1970, s.9(1)-(3), as substituted by the Finance Act 1990, s.90(1). With effect from the year 1996/97, see *ibid.* s.12AA(1)-(3), as added by the Finance Act 1994, s.184. And see *supra*, paras. 34–17, 34–18.

[12] *Ibid.* s.9(4)(a). With effect from the year 1996/97, see *ibid.* s.12AA(6)(a), as added by the Finance Act 1994, s.184.

[13] Income and Corporation Taxes Act 1988, ss.112(6), 115(4), (5).

[14] *Ibid.* s.8(1).

[15] This is now of less importance, since the abolition of the investment income surcharge: see further, *supra*, para. 34–31.

[16] Provided that the continuing partners can show that the remuneration was wholly and exclusively laid out for the purposes of the partnership business: Income and Corporation Taxes Act 1988, s.74(a). Whether the consultancy fee is taxable under Sched. D or Sched. E will, of course, depend on the consultant's precise status, *i.e.* independent contractor or employee.

[17] See *Hale v. Shea* [1965] 1 W.L.R. 290. See also *Bucks v. Bowers* [1970] 1 Ch. 431; *Pegler v. Abell* [1973] 1 W.L.R. 155; *Lawrance v. Hayman* [1976] S.T.C. 227. In these circumstances, the remuneration would clearly *not* satisfy the requirements of the Income and Corporation Taxes Act 1988, s.74(a).

Accordingly, with a view to ensuring that any such remuneration **34–91** paid to an outgoing partner *cannot* be treated as consideration for the acquisition of his share, it may be desirable to keep the consultancy agreement wholly separate from any other agreement and, if necessary, incorporated in a separate document. As an alternative, a partner who wishes to render consultancy services might prefer to continue as an active partner, albeit on a part-time basis and with a reduced profit share.[18]

Whether a particular payment is to be regarded as earned income is not a pure question of fact, but rather a question of law based upon inferences to be drawn from the facts,[19] so that an appeal will lie from any determination by the Commissioners.

Partnership annuities and other payments

In order to determine the tax treatment of any payments received **34–92** by an outgoing partner, or by his widow or dependants, *otherwise* than pursuant to a consultancy agreement as described above, it is necessary to determine whether those payments are of an income or capital nature, since dissection may well not be possible.[20] In many cases, the true nature will appear from the terms of the contractual arrangement under which the payments are made, and this will normally bind the Revenue.[21] If the payments have the nature of capital, no income tax considerations will arise;[22] if, on the other hand, they are of an income nature, it is necessary to consider their status in the outgoing partner's hands and, moreover, whether they are deductible by the continuing partners.

Normally, an annuity payable to an outgoing partner (or his widow **34–93** or dependants) which is made in consideration of his past services or in return for the acquisition by the continuing partners of his share in the partnership, will be taxed by deduction under section 348 or 349

---

[18] Care must be taken to ensure that such a partner does not effectively become a dormant partner, *i.e.* he must be "personally acting in the partnership": see *ibid.* s.833(4)(c), as amended by the Finance Act 1988, Sched. 14, Pts. IV and V. It should at the same time be remembered that, by continuing as a partner, he will remain fully liable for the firm's debts, etc.

[19] Per Walton J. in *Lawrance v. Hayman* [1976] S.T.C. 227, 239.

[20] As to the possibility of dissecting a payment into its capital and income elements, see *I.R.C. v. Church Commissioners for England* [1977] A.C. 329.

[21] See, generally, *I.R.C. v. Church Commissioners for England, supra*; but *cf. C.I.R. v. Ledgard* (1937) 21 T.C. 129; *C.I.R. v. Mallaby-Deeley* (1938) 23 T.C. 153; *C.I.R. v. Hogarth* (1940) 23 T.C. 491. Account must also be taken of the application of the *Ramsay* principle in this context: see, in particular, *I.R.C. v. Moodie* [1993] 1 W.L.R. 266 (H.L.), declining to follow *I.R.C. v. Plummer* [1980] A.C. 896; also, *supra*, para. 34–11.

[22] Thus, the outgoing partner may receive a lump sum and himself purchase an annuity or, alternatively, the continuing partners may agree to pay a lump sum by instalments with interest on the balance from time to time outstanding. The capital element in either case would not be income taxable in the hands of the outgoing partner, and the continuing partners could obtain relief in respect of any interest payments under the Income and Corporation Taxes Act 1988, s.362. Such a payment would, however, attract a charge to capital gains tax, if made in consideration of the assignment by the retiring partner of his share in the partnership to the continuing partners: see further, *infra*, para. 35–15.

of the Taxes Act 1988, and will constitute a charge on income which is deductible by the continuing partners.[23] Further, such annual payments, provided they are made under the terms of the partnership agreement and under a liability incurred for full consideration[24] or pursuant to a bona fide commercial transaction,[25] will not be affected by section 674A[26] or 683 of the Taxes Act 1988, which would otherwise cause the annual payments to be treated as the income of the continuing partners.[27] Equally, those sections will not apply where the payments are made in consideration of the acquisition of the whole or part of the partnership business,[28] or where the entitlement to the annuity devolves upon the outgoing partner's death, provided that it does not continue for more than 10 years after the date on which he ceased to be a member of the firm.[29] When a continuing partner himself retires (or is expelled), and his obligations under the terms of the annuity agreement are assumed by an incoming partner, the requirements of the sections will seemingly be treated as satisfied as regards such incoming partner.[30]

34–94   It should also be noted that annual payments will not be deductible even for the purposes of *basic rate* tax, unless they represent "a payment made for bona fide commercial reasons in connection with [an] individual's trade profession or vocation."[31] However, the current editor submits that the latter test must, by definition, be

---

[23] The charge will normally be deducted first from partnership income, and then in the manner most favourable to each partner: *ibid.* s.835(4).

[24] *Ibid.* s.683(1)(a), as amended by the Finance Act 1988, Sched. 3, para. 20(2). Annuities payable under this section will not be affected by the anti–avoidance provisions contained in *ibid.* s.125: *ibid.* s.125(3)(a).

[25] See *Bulmer v. I.R.C.* [1967] Ch. 145; *I.R.C. v. Plummer* [1980] A.C. 896 (but see *I.R.C. v. Moodie* [1993] 1 W.L.R. 266, H.L.); also *I.R.C. v. Levy* [1982] S.T.C. 442. The presence of the commercial element should prevent the application of the *Ramsay* principle: see *Craven v. White* [1989] A.C. 398; also *supra*, para. 34–11. However, in the case of such a transaction, which will, by definition, not fall within the Income and Corporation Taxes Act 1988, ss.674A(1)(a), (2) (as added by the Finance Act 1989, 109(1)) or 683(1)(a), (6)(a), the payment of an annuity under a liability incurred for a consideration in money or money's worth might conceivably attract the anti–avoidance provisions contained in *ibid.* s.125. This would prevent the continuing partners from deducting the annuity from their own incomes: *ibid.* s.125(1). It would thus seem desirable that any annuity arrangement should, as a matter of course, be incorporated in the partnership agreement (or in a supplementary agreement) so as to ensure that *ibid.* ss.674A(1)(a), 683(1)(a) apply, thus excluding *ibid.* s.125(1): *ibid.* s.125(3)(a), as amended by the Finance Act 1989, s.109(2).

[26] As added by the Finance Act 1989, 109(1).

[27] Under the Income and Corporation Taxes Act 1988, s.674A, the annual payments would be treated as the income of the continuing partners for *all* purposes, whereas under *ibid.* s.683 they would only be treated as their income for the purposes of higher rate tax.

[28] *Ibid.* ss.674A(2), 683(6)(a) (as amended by the Finance Act 1988, Sched. 3, para. 29(3)). The exception will apply where the annual payments benefit either a former member of the partnership, or the widow, widower, or dependants of a deceased former member. *Ibid.* s.125 will not apply: *ibid.* s.125(3)(a), as amended by the Finance Act 1989, s.109(2).

[29] *Ibid.* ss.674A(2), 683(8). The current editor submits that this subsection (and its restrictions) will only apply where the annuity devolves upon persons *other* than the retired partner's widow or dependants.

[30] *Ibid.* ss.674A(2), 683(7). *Quaere* does the incoming partner truly incur a liability "in connection with an acquisition from a partnership" as required by the subsection?

[31] *Ibid.* s.347A(1), (2)(c) (as inserted by the Finance Act 1988, s.36(1)).

satisfied in the case of any annuity excepted from the application of section 674A or 683, and this has been confirmed by the Revenue.[32]

Whilst, the annuity will, in the above way, be deductible by the continuing partners, it will usually be treated as investment income in the hands of the retiring partner.[33]

Income and Corporation Taxes Act 1988, section 628[34]

This section, which is of reduced importance since the abolition of **34–95** the investment income surcharge,[35] allows partnership annuities to be treated as earned income within certain limits. In order to qualify for such treatment, the annuity must represent income in the recipient's hands[36] and be payable:

(a) on a partner's retirement (through age or ill health)[37] or on his death,

(b) under the terms of the partnership agreement, a supplemental partnership agreement or an agreement made with an individual who acquires all or part of the partnership business,[38] and

(c) for the benefit of the outgoing partner, or his widow[39] or dependants.

Where the above conditions are satisfied, the annuity will be treated as earned income provided that it does not exceed the specified limit of 50 per cent of the average share[40] of profits or gains of the

---

[32] See the I.C.A.E.W. Memorandum (TR739) on the Finance (No. 2) Bill 1988, para. 9, reproduced at [1989] S.T.I. 78.

[33] *Hale v. Shea* [1965] 1 W.L.R. 290; *Pegler v. Abell* [1973] 1 W.L.R. 155; *Lawrance v. Hayman* [1976] S.T.C. 227. Moreover, where the annuity is paid as consideration for the disposal by the outgoing partner of his share in the partnership, the capital value of the annuity will be subject to capital gains tax: see the Taxation of Chargeable Gains Act 1992, s.37(3). A certain degree of relief is, however, afforded by para. 8 of the Inland Revenue Statement of Practice "Capital Gains Tax: Partnerships" (D12) dated January 17, 1975; see further, *infra*, paras. 35–24 *et seq.*, A6–14, A6–19.

[34] This section falls within Pt. XIV, Chap. III of the Act. It should be noted that the first section in that Chapter (s.618, as amended by the Finance Act 1988, s.54(2)(a)(i)) provides that "Nothing in this Chapter shall apply in relation to ... a contract made ... on or after 1st July 1988." The word "contract" is not defined; it is assumed that it must be taken as a reference to retirement annuity contracts and not to other annuity arrangements: *cf.* the Finance Act 1987, s.54(a), where no such confusion arose. If not, the prospective amendment contained in the Finance Act 1988, Sched. 3, para. 19 served no purpose.

[35] By the Finance Act 1984, Sched. 7.

[36] See the cases cited *supra*, para. 34–92, n. 21.

[37] The current editor considers that a partner expelled on the grounds of ill health would be regarded as having "retired" for this purpose; *sed quaere*.

[38] Presumably where another firm acquires all or part of the partnership business, that firm will be treated as a collection of individuals for the purposes of this relief.

[39] This will include a widower: see the Income and Corporation Taxes Act 1988, s.628(1), as amended by the Finance Act 1988, Sched. 3, para. 19.

[40] The partner's share of profits or gains in respect of any year is the share which fell to be included in the return of his income for that year: Income and Corporation Taxes Act 1988, s.628(2)(a).

outgoing partner during the best three[41] of the last seven years of assessment during which he was required to devote substantially the whole of his time to his partnership duties.[42] If there has been any increase in the retail prices index over those seven years, the outgoing partner's share of profits or gains during each such year may be notionally increased for the purposes of the calculation.[43] Moreover, the specified limit, and thus the annuity, may be increased in line with increases in the retail prices index in the years of assessment following the partner's retirement or death, thereby affording some measure of protection against the effects of inflation.[44] Any excess over the specified limit will be treated as investment income.

Other arrangements

34-96   In lieu of partnership annuities, which are problematic not only in terms of taxation[45] but also in terms of their long term effect on the firm,[46] partners will often make provision for death or retirement on an individual basis, whether by way of endowment or life assurance, retirement annuity premiums[47] or contributions under approved personal pension arrangements.[48] However, this is largely a matter of individual financial planning, the further consideration of which is out of place in a work of this nature.[49]

---

[41] The best three years are the years in which the partner's share of profits was the highest: *ibid.* s.628(2)(d).

[42] *Ibid.* s.628(1), (2). The deductibility of such payments in the continuing partners' hands should not be affected by *ibid.* s.125, since the annuity will almost certainly fall within *ibid.* s.674A(a), (2) (as added by the Finance Act 1989, s.109(1)) or 683(1)(a) or (6)(a): see *ibid.* s.125(3)(a), as amended by the Finance Act 1989, s.109(2).

[43] *Ibid.* s.628(3). The notional increase is measured by reference to the difference between the retail prices index in the December of the year of assessment in question and the retail prices index in the December of the last of the seven years.

[44] *Ibid.* s.628(4). The permitted increase in any year of assessment following the retirement is measured by reference to the increase in the retail prices index in the December of the previous year of assessment over the retail prices index in the December of the year of assessment during which the partner concerned ceased to be a member of the firm.

[45] Thus, where an annuity is payable in consideration of the disposal of an outgoing partner's share, it would seem that a charge to both income tax *and* capital gains tax (on the capitalised value of the annuity) could be incurred: see *supra*, para. 34–94, n. 33. It should be noted that the Inland Revenue Statement of Practice "Capital Gains Tax: Partnerships" (D12) dated January 17, 1975, para. 8 (*infra*, para. A6–14) assumes that a charge to capital gains tax will be imposed *whenever* an annuity is payable to a retiring partner, whether or not in consideration of a disposal of his share. As discussed *infra*, para. 35–27, the current editor does not consider this "blanket" approach to be justifiable and the practice should, where appropriate, be resisted. In any event, if a double charge to tax is to be avoided, it would seem desirable that any annuity should be kept wholly separate from the consideration given for the disposal of the outgoing partner's share.

[46] The payment of such annuities to retired partners can lead to a high degree of resentment on the part of the continuing partners, who may (justly or unjustly) feel that their efforts are merely serving to benefit persons who contribute nothing to the success of the business: see further the *Encyclopedia of Professional Partnerships*, Precedent 2, Art. 6–06, notes.

[47] See the Income and Corporation Taxes Act 1988, s.618 *et seq.*

[48] See *ibid.* ss.630 *et seq.*

[49] Note, however, that inheritance tax considerations may arise in relation to such schemes: see further, *infra*, para. 36–37.

CHAPTER 35

CAPITAL GAINS TAX

1. INTRODUCTION

No special code for disposals of partnership assets

The considerations which led to the introduction of a special code **35–01** for the taxation of partnership income[1] were never regarded as significant when taxing capital gains realised on the disposal of a partnership asset. Accordingly, section 59 of the Taxation of Chargeable Gains Act 1992 provides as follows:

"**59.** Where 2 or more persons carry on a trade or business in partnership—
(a) tax in respect of chargeable gains accruing to them on the disposal of any partnership assets shall, in Scotland as well as elsewhere in the United Kingdom, be assessed and charged on them separately, and
(b) any partnership dealings shall be treated as dealings by the partners and not by the firm as such, and
(c) section 112(1) and (2) of the Taxes Act[2] (residence of partnerships) shall apply in relation to tax chargeable in pursuance of this Act as it applies in relation to income tax."[3]

Thus, no attempt is made to treat a partnership as a separate entity for the purposes of capital gains tax, even in Scotland where, under the general law, a partnership is a legal person distinct from its members.[4]

---

[1] See *supra*, para. 34–01. Of course, the Finance Act 1994 has introduced a new regime which is more comparable with that considered in the present chapter: see *supra*, para. 34–06.

[2] See, as to this section, *supra*, paras. 34–86 *et seq.*

[3] The practical application of the Income and Corporation Taxes Act 1988, s.112 to capital gains tax is at the very least obscure: see *Whiteman on Capital Gains Tax* (4th ed.), paras. 29–49 *et seq.* Thus, it might be argued that the effect of the section is to deem a resident (but not ordinarily resident) partner of a foreign partnership to be non-resident, and thus permit him to escape a charge to capital gains tax on a disposal of a partnership asset situated abroad; however, it is doubtful whether such a proposition can properly be supported by the words: "... the trade or business shall be deemed to be carried on by persons resident outside the United Kingdom, and the partnership shall be deemed to reside outside the United Kingdom, notwithstanding the fact that some of the members of the partnership are resident in the United Kingdom and that some of its trading operations are conducted within the United Kingdom." The residence of the partnership itself is clearly irrelevant for capital gains tax purposes, and the mere fact that the business is deemed to be carried on by persons resident outside the United Kingdom would not appear to deem any particular partners to be non-resident.

[4] Partnership Act 1890, s.4(2).

35–02   However, it would not be right to class the above approach as a success in fiscal terms: indeed, so extensive have been the potential anomalies over the years[5] that the taxation of partnership gains has in large measure had to be regulated by extra-statutory means. Thus, on January 17, 1975, the Inland Revenue, following discussions with both the Law Society and the Allied Accountancy Bodies, issued a Statement of Practice entitled "Capital Gains Tax: Partnerships," which has subsequently been extended on two separate occasions.[6] Although the published practice has not resolved all the potential problems and is, in some respects, open to objection, the clarification which it affords is to be welcomed. Whether a taxpayer may at some future date mount a successful challenge to that practice remains to be seen.[7]

Although the remainder of this chapter is to a large extent written by reference to the Revenue practice, every effort has been made to indicate where that practice does not accord with the strict law or is otherwise less than satisfactory.

2. DISPOSALS OF PARTNERSHIP ASSETS OR OF SHARES THEREIN

35–03 A clear distinction must be drawn between the following types of disposal:

A.   disposals of partnership assets to third parties;
B.   disposals of partnership shares;
C.   distribution of partnership assets amongst the partners.

Each of these categories will now be considered in turn.

A.   DISPOSALS OF PARTNERSHIP ASSETS TO THIRD PARTIES

35–04 For the purposes of capital gains tax, partnership property is treated in the same way as any other property jointly owned by two or more persons, *i.e.* regard is had to the effect of a disposal on the persons

---

[5] The provision now to be found in the Taxation of Chargeable Gains Act 1992, s.59 was originally contained in the Finance Act 1965, s.45(7) and then in the consolidating Capital Gains Tax Act 1979, s.60.

[6] The full text of the Statement of Practice (D12) is reproduced *infra*, paras. A6–06 *et seq.* and the subsequent extensions thereof (SP1/79 and SP1/89), which were issued on January 12, 1979 and February 1, 1989, are reproduced *infra*, paras. A6–19 *et seq.* And see also, generally, [1975] B.T.R. 87. The Revenue have confirmed that Statement D12 will apply to limited partnerships in the venture capital field: see the Statement issued by the British Venture Capital Association on May 26, 1987.

[7] See in particular *infra*, para. 35–13.

beneficially entitled.[8] The Revenue practice is to regard each partner as entitled to a fractional share of each partnership asset, thus ignoring his true entitlement, namely the right to a proportion of the surplus remaining after the realisation of all the partnership assets and the payment of all the partnership debts and liabilities.[9] It follows that, when a firm disposes of one of its assets, each partner is treated as having disposed of the entirety of his fractional share therein.[10]

Given the above approach, it is obviously necessary to identify the **35–05** size of each partner's fractional share of any given asset. In this respect, the Revenue practice does go some way towards recognising the true *legal* nature of a partnership share, by allocating the disposal proceeds between the partners in the ratio of their shares in asset surpluses at the time of the disposal.[11] If, as will usually be the case, those shares are laid down in the original partnership agreement or in some other supplementary agreement, that will be the end of the matter. However, in the absence of any such specific provision, the allocation of the proceeds will follow the actual destination of the surplus as shown in the partnership accounts.[12] The acquisition cost of an asset is allocated in the same way, although it may fall to be readjusted in the event of a subsequent alteration in the sharing ratios.[13]

---

[8] There is thus a direct analogy with the Taxation of Chargeable Gains Act 1992, s.60 (which governs the position of nominees and bare trustees). The current editor submits that the settled property provisions of the Act cannot apply, since the partners are together absolutely entitled to each partnership asset: see *Kidson v. Macdonald* [1974] Ch. 339; also *Booth v. Ellard* [1980] 1 W.L.R. 1443; *Jenkins v. Brown* [1989] 1 W.L.R. 1163.

[9] See Statement D12, para. 1, *infra*, para. A6–07. For this purpose, the market value of a partner's fractional share in any particular asset suffers no discount by reason of its size: *ibid*. Thus, where a firm owns all the issued shares in a company, the value of the holding of a partner with a one-tenth share would be one-tenth of the value of the partnership's 100 per cent. holding. As to the precise nature of a partner's share, see *supra*, paras. 19–01 *et seq*. And note also the Taxation of Chargeable Gains Act 1992, s.163(8).

[10] Similarly, where there is a part disposal of an asset, there will be a part disposal of each partner's fractional share.

[11] Statement D12, para. 2, *infra*, para. A6–08. Difficult questions may, however, arise where, under the terms of the partnership agreement, all future capital profits attributable to a particular asset are expressed to belong to one partner. It would seem that, consistently with the Revenue practice, such a partner should thereafter be treated as owning the asset. What, then, is the position if that asset was introduced into the partnership by the other partners, their capital accounts being credited with its full market value? Are those partners to be deemed to have disposed of the asset at such a value? Since they will have received full consideration (*i.e.* the credit in their capital accounts), no hold over relief under the Taxation of Chargeable Gains Act 1992, s.165 would be available. This argument is by no means straightforward, but might be adopted by the Revenue in an appropriate case; see also Statement D12, para. 5, considered *infra*, para. 35–17. Accordingly, where partners wish to adopt such a course, it may, perhaps, be preferable to proceed in stages: on Day 1, the partners who own the asset can introduce it into the partnership on terms that all capital profits attributable thereto will belong to them alone, so that they will be treated as continuing to own the asset. Then, on Day 2, the capital profit sharing ratios can be altered so as to ensure that the other partner becomes entitled to all such capital profits; this step will not involve any disposal: see Statement D12, para. 4, considered, *infra*, para. 35–13. As to the treatment of damages or compensation received by a firm, see Extra Statutory Concession D33 (1994 Revision), para. 12.

[12] Regard will, of course, be had to any agreements outside the accounts.

[13] See further *infra*, para. 35–14.

35–06   A firm might, in consequence, seek to avoid any charge to tax on a
disposal of its assets by establishing a capital profits account or
reserve into which all capital gains are to be paid, no provision being
made as to the respective entitlements of the partners thereto.[14] The
adoption of such a device is, however, anticipated by the Revenue
practice: in the absence of any specified asset-surplus sharing ratios,
the proceeds will be allocated in accordance with the ordinary profit-
sharing ratios.[15]

Reliefs available on disposal of partnership assets

35–07   (i) *"Roll-over" relief.*   Where the proceeds from the disposal[16] of
any assets which were throughout the period of ownership[17] used
only for the purposes of a trade are applied in or towards the
acquisition of other assets taken in and used only for the purposes of
the trade,[18] then "roll-over" relief may be available under section 152
of the Taxation of Chargeable Gains Act 1992. Both the assets
disposed of and the assets acquired[19] must fall within the specified
classes (but not necessarily the same class),[20] and the new assets must

---

[14] Statement D12, para. 2, *infra*, para. A6–08.

[15] *Ibid.* This to an extent anticipates the treatment of such a capital fund in the event of a
dissolution: see the Partnership Act 1890, s.44(b), para. 4. The practice is, however, questionable
given that, until a dissolution or other distribution, no-one is legally entitled to the present
enjoyment of the fund: see *Whiteman on Capital Gains Tax* (4th ed.), paras. 29–06, 29–07. And see
Stocker v. C.I.R. (1919) 7 T.C. 304; *Franklin v. C.I.R.* (1930) 15 T.C. 464; *Latilla v. C.I.R.* (1943)
25 T.C. 107, 116, *per* Lord Greene M.R.

[16] This will include the consideration deemed to be realised on a disposal of an asset by way of
gift, but *not* on a deemed disposal and reacquisition of the same asset: see the Institute of Taxation
paper dated October 31, 1991, para. 1.6, reproduced at [1991] S.T.I. 1098.

[17] This will not include any period of ownership prior to March 31, 1982: Taxation of Chargeable
Gains Act 1992, s.152(9).

[18] The assets acquired must immediately be taken into use in the trade if the relief is to be
available: *Campbell Connelly & Co. Ltd. v. Barnett* [1994] S.T.C. 50.

[19] The asset acquired may be a further interest in an asset which is already in use for the
purposes of the trade: Extra-Statutory Concession D25 (1994 Revision).

[20] The specified classes, as set out in the Taxation of Chargeable Gains Act 1992, s.155, are as
follows:

     1.   *Head A.*   Buildings or land used and occupied only for the purposes of the trade (save,
     in general, where the trade is one of land dealing or developing, or of providing services for
     the occupier of land in which the trader is interested: see *ibid.* s.156(2));
     Head B.   Fixed plant or machinery;
     2.   Ships, aircraft and hovercraft;
     3.   Satellites, space stations and spacecraft;
     4.   Goodwill;
     5.   Milk and potato quotas;
     6.   Ewe and suckler cow premium quotas (as introduced by the Finance Act 1993,
     s.86(1), (4)).

In *Anderton v. Lamb* [1981] S.T.C. 43, the scope of Class 1, Head A above was considered when a
taxpayer sought to rollover gains realised on the sale of part of a farm into houses constructed for
the occupation of two of his partners (who were also his sons). Goulding J. rejected the claim to
relief on the ground that the houses were not occupied for the purposes of the trade, since it was
not essential to the management of the farm that the partners should live in the houses, nor were
they expressly required to do so under the terms of the partnership agreement. An appeal against
that judgment was apparently settled by agreement: *The Times*, April 28, 1982. See also, as to the
scope of Class 1, Head B, *Williams v. Evans* [1982] 1 W.L.R. 972. Note that the Revenue do not
regard the decision in *Faulks v. Faulks* [1992] 15 E.G. 15 (noticed, *supra*, paras. 18–21, 18–59) as
having called into question the existence of Class 5 independently of Class 1: see [1993] S.T.I. 294.
and [1994] S.T.I. 664. For the treatment of assets which have been only partially used for the
purposes of the business, see the Taxation of Chargeable Gains Act 1992, s.152(6), (7). And as to
gains rolled over into depreciating assets, see *ibid.* s.154; also [1993] S.T.I. 892 and Extra-Statutory
Concession D45 (1994 Revision).

be acquired[21] within the period beginning twelve months prior to the disposal of the old assets and ending three years after that disposal.[22] Where only part of the proceeds are so applied, partial relief will be available.[23] The relief operates by treating the consideration for the disposal of the old assets as of such an amount as will secure neither a gain nor a loss on the disposal, and reducing the acquisition cost of the new assets by such part of the actual consideration received on the disposal of the old assets as exceeds the deemed consideration substituted therefor.[24] In this way, the charge to capital gains tax can be deferred until such time as assets are finally disposed of and the proceeds are not reapplied for business purposes.[25]

In the case of a disposal of partnership assets, the relief will only **35–08** be available to the extent that each partner has an interest both in the assets disposed of and in the assets acquired. If, between disposal and acquisition, a partner's share in asset surpluses is reduced, *e.g.* on the introduction of a new partner, the relief will be restricted to his reduced share of the acquisition cost of the new assets,[26] and any excess will attract a charge to tax. The incoming partner will obviously not be in a position to claim the relief. Similarly, if a partner retires between disposal and acquisition, no relief will be available in respect of his share of the disposal proceeds.

The relief is available to persons who carry on more than one trade, either successively or at the same time.[27]

(ii) *Retirement relief.* This relief, which may be available on the **35–09** disposal of partnership assets, is considered later in this chapter.[28]

(iii) *"Hold over" relief.* This relief may only be claimed where, **35–10** *otherwise* than under a bargain at arm's length,[29] an individual

---

[21] This will include an unconditional contract for the acquisition.

[22] Taxation of Chargeable Gains Act 1992, s.152(3), (4). The Revenue do, however, have discretion to allow the relief even when the strict time limits are not adhered to: see further the Institute of Taxation paper dated October 31, 1991, paras. 1.2 *et seq.*, reproduced at [1991] S.T.I. 1097.

[23] Taxation of Chargeable Gains Act 1992, s.153(1).

[24] *Ibid.* s.152(1).

[25] It should, however, be borne in mind that a claim to "roll-over" relief will result in any future indexation allowance under *ibid.* ss.53 (as amended by the Finance Act 1994, s. 93(1)–(3), 54 in respect of the new asset being calculated by reference to its notional (*i.e.* reduced) acquisition cost and not to its actual cost.

[26] This appeared from the Inland Revenue Booklet C.G.T. 8 (1980), para. 295, although this booklet has now been withdrawn.

[27] Taxation of Chargeable Gains Act 1992, s.152(8); also the Statement of Practice "Roll-over relief for replacement of business assets: trades carried on successively" (SP8/81) dated September 18, 1981. See further the Institute of Taxation papers dated May 11, 1990 (reproduced at [1990] S.T.I. 446) and October 31, 1991, para. 5 (reproduced at [1991] S.T.I. 1099).

[28] Taxation of Chargeable Gains Act 1992, s.163, Sched. 6. See *infra*, paras. 35–21 *et seq.*

[29] A transaction will be treated as otherwise than by way of a bargain at arm's length where there is a disposal between connected persons: *ibid.* s.18(1), (2). Partners are treated as connected persons, except in relation to disposals of partnership assets pursuant to bona fide commercial arrangements: *ibid.* s.286(4). Of course, where there is a disposal otherwise than by way of a bargain at arm's length which confers a gratuitous benefit on another, that disposal, whilst attracting capital gains tax relief, will also be likely to constitute a potentially exempt transfer for the purposes of inheritance tax, as to which see *infra*, para. 36–02. Such a transfer may, however, qualify for 100 per cent. agricultural property/business relief: see *infra*, paras. 36–13 *et seq.*

disposes of an asset (or an interest in an asset) used for the purposes of his trade, profession or vocation or of agricultural property eligible for inheritance tax relief.[30] The transferee must, however, be a United Kingdom resident.[31] The relief operates in much the same way as "roll-over" relief, in that the transferor's chargeable gain and the transferee's acquisition cost are both reduced by the amount of "held-over gain," which will in most cases be the amount of the chargeable gain itself.[32] Both the transferor and the transferee must claim the benefit of the relief.[33] In those cases in which retirement relief is applied automatically,[34] there may be no gain to hold over.[34a] Accordingly, if it is desired to preserve the right to retirement relief for a future occasion and merely to hold over the gain, it may be necessary so to structure the disposal that the conditions for the application of the former relief are deliberately not met.[35]

B. DISPOSALS OF PARTNERSHIP SHARES

The general treatment of dealings between partners

35–11   Whilst capital gains tax is normally charged by reference to the actual proceeds realised on the disposal of an asset, there are two occasions on which market value will be substituted, namely:

---

[30] Taxation of Chargeable Gains Act 1992, s.165(1), (5), Sched. 7, para. 1; and see [1989] S.T.I. 845. Relief is also available in the case of any disposal of assets (business or non-business) on which an immediate charge to inheritance tax is imposed, *i.e.* principally transfers into or out of discretionary trusts: *ibid.* s.260. The more generalised form of "hold-over" relief, which was available in respect of disposals made prior to March 14, 1989, pursuant to the provisions of the Finance Act 1980, s.79, was abolished by the Finance Act 1989, s.124(1).

[31] Taxation of Chargeable Gains Act 1992, s.166(1).

[32] *Ibid.* s.165(4). Where, however, actual consideration is given and received, and that consideration exceeds the allowable deductions on the disposal, then the "held-over gain" will be reduced by the amount of that excess: *ibid.* s.165(6), (7). If the consideration is incapable of being valued, and market value is substituted pursuant to *ibid.* s.17(1)(b), the current editor submits that relief will still be available; note, however, that a contrary view is expressed in *Whiteman on Capital Gains Tax* (4th ed.), para. 29–38. If part of the gain is relieved under *ibid.* Sched. 6 (retirement relief), the "held-over gain" will again be reduced: *ibid.* Sched. 7, para. 8(1). Any available indexation allowance under *ibid.* ss.53 (as amended by the Finance Act 1994, s. 93(1)–(3)), 54 will operate so as to reduce the amount of the "held-over gain," but the corollary is that any future indexation allowance will be calculated by reference to the transferee's notional (*i.e.* reduced) acquisition cost.

[33] *Ibid.* s.165(1)(b). It is therefore possible for a transferee, who does not wish to acquire the asset at a low base cost, to frustrate the application of the relief by refusing to make the claim therefor. In order to avoid such a situation, the transferor and the transferee should expressly agree whether or not such a claim is to be submitted before the disposal takes place.

[34] *i.e.* where the transferor has attained the age of 55: *ibid.* Sched. 6, para. 5(2).

[34a] But see the Statement of Practice "Valuation of assets in respect of which capital gains tax gifts holdover relief is claimed" (SP8/92), paras. 14, 15.

[35] See, for example, *McGregor v. Adcock* [1977] 1 W.L.R. 864, where retirement relief was denied on the disposal of part of a farm on the ground that the disposal in no way affected the taxpayer's farming business; similarly in *Atkinson v. Dancer* [1988] S.T.C. 758 and *Pepper v. Daffurn* [1993] S.T.C. 466. See also *infra,* paras. 35–21 *et seq.*

(a) where the asset was acquired or disposed of otherwise than by way of a bargain made at arm's length; or

(b) where the asset was acquired or disposed of wholly or partly for a consideration that cannot be valued.[36]

A disposal will be treated as a transaction otherwise than by way of a bargain at arm's length where the parties are "connected persons."[37] Partners are normally treated as connected,[38] except in relation to acquisitions or disposals of partnership assets pursuant to bona fide commercial arrangements.[39] The latter exception will, however, only apply where there is no other connection between the partners.[40]

On the admission of a new partner, the existing partners will often **35–12** wish to ensure that he becomes entitled to a share of the partnership assets; they will achieve this by reducing their own shares in order to create the incoming partner's share. Equally, partners may merely wish to rearrange their asset sharing ratios as between themselves, without admitting a new partner. In either case, any partner whose share is decreased will be treated as having disposed of part of that share. The rules described in the previous paragraph will apply to that disposal in the following way. If the consideration for the re-arrangement is capable of being valued, tax will be charged by reference thereto, unless the partners can be treated as connected persons.[41] If, on the other hand, the consideration *cannot* be valued, e.g. where it is represented by an incoming partner's agreement to devote his whole time to the partnership business, then market value will be substituted, irrespective of any connection between the partners.[42] Of course, where the disposal is otherwise than under a bargain at arm's length, "hold over" relief can normally be claimed

---

[36] Taxation of Chargeable Gains Act 1992, s.17(1).

[37] *Ibid.* s.18(1), (2).

[38] For the meaning of "connected persons" see, generally, *ibid.* s.286.

[39] *Ibid.* s.286(4). Although it will be a question of fact in each case, dealings between partners will usually involve such an arrangement: see, for example, the decisions in *Att.-Gen. v. Boden* [1912] 1 K.B. 539 and *Att.-Gen. v. Ralli* (1936) 15 A.T.C. 523, considered *infra*, paras. 36–05 *et seq.*

[40] *i.e.* by virtue of *ibid.* s.286(2), (8). Note that, in Statement D12, para. 7, *infra*, para. A6–13, the Revenue assume that an uncle and nephew are connected persons, but this is not warranted by the terms of the Act. *Cf.* the terms of the Inheritance Tax Act 1984, s.270 (as amended by the Taxation of Chargeable Gains Act 1992, Sched. 10, para. 8(12)).

[41] The Revenue will in general be bound to accept the value of a consideration honestly agreed between the parties to a bargain at arm's length: see *Stanton v. Drayton Commercial Investment Co. Ltd.* [1983] A.C. 501.

[42] Taxation of Chargeable Gains Act 1992, s.17(1)(b). The current editor is of the opinion that if, in such a case, no bona fide commercial arrangement were involved, "hold-over" relief could be claimed under *ibid.* s.165; however, a contrary view is expressed in *Whiteman on Capital Gains Tax* (4th ed.), para. 29–38.

under section 165 of the Taxation of Chargeable Gains Act 1992, thus effectively deferring any charge to tax until a subsequent disposal of the share, in respect of which the relief is not available.[43]

Whilst the foregoing represents the strict legal position, it must be read subject to the Revenue practice, the application of which may lead to some surprising results.

Revenue practice: rearrangement of shares without payment

35–13   Where no monetary consideration is given on a rearrangement of shares, the practice is to treat the consideration as the appropriate fraction of the current balance sheet value of each chargeable asset owned by the firm.[44] Thus, assuming no previous revaluation of those assets to have been reflected in the partnership accounts, the Revenue will regard the disposal as having been made for a consideration equal to the disposing partner's acquisition cost together with any available indexation allowance,[45] and neither a chargeable gain nor an allowable loss will result.[46] Any actual, non-monetary consideration, e.g. a covenant by the incoming partner to devote his whole time to the partnership business, will be ignored. Herein lies the danger of this extra-statutory form of "hold over" relief: the incoming partner may well have given full consideration for the acquisition of the share, yet he will acquire it at a low base cost and thereby store up a potentially large chargeable gain for the future. In such a case, there would seem to be every incentive for such a partner to reject the practice and to contend that his acquisition cost should be the market value of the share as at the date of his admission to the firm. Although the practice is not stated to be optional, the current editor regards it as unlikely that the Revenue would object if the partners *invited* a charge to tax, so as to prevent the incoming partner's acquisition cost, and thus any future indexation allowance,[47] being maintained at an artificially low level.[48]

---

[43] See further, as to this relief, *supra*, para. 35–10. And see the preceding footnote.

[44] Statement D12, para. 4, *infra*, para. A6–10. See further, *supra*, para. 35–05.

[45] By the Extension of the Statement of Practice "Capital Gains Tax—Partnerships" (SP1/89) dated February 1, 1989 (reproduced *infra*, paras. A6–20 *et seq.*), any disposal to which Statement D12, para. 4 applies qualifies as a no gain/no loss disposal within the Taxation of Chargeable Gains Act 1992, s.55(5), although a special rule applies to shares changing hands between April 6, 1985 and April 6, 1988.

[46] Note that, quite apart from the Revenue practice, where an indexation allowance exceeds the unindexed gain, an allowable loss will no longer be produced: Taxation of Chargeable Gains Act 1992, s.53(1) (as amended by the Finance Act 1994, s.93(1)). Similarly, no allowance will be available in respect of a loss-making disposal: *ibid.* s.53(2A) (as added by the Finance Act 1994, s.93(3)). A measure of transitional relief is afforded by the Finance Act 1994, s. 93(ii), Sched. 12.

[47] Under the Taxation of Chargeable Gains Act 1992, ss.53, 54. Note the amendments to s.53 contained in the Finance Act 1994, s.93(1)-(3).

[48] This aspect should, where necessary, be explained to an incoming partner, so as to avoid later recriminations. There is a marked contrast in a case where hold-over relief is claimable under the Taxation of Chargeable Gains Act 1992, s.165, since there the incoming partner can refuse to join in a claim for the relief, if it is against his interests so to do: *ibid.* subs. (1)(b).

Where the practice does apply, a partner whose share is reduced **35–14** will naturally suffer a like reduction in his acquisition cost, that reduction being taken over as the acquisition cost of the partner whose share is created or increased. The part disposal rules for apportionment of acquisition costs do not apply, and all calculations are made on a fractional basis.[49]

Although the operation of the practice in many respects parallels (and, to an extent, duplicates) the effect of "hold over" relief under section 165 of the Taxation of Chargeable Gains 1992,[50] its application is not restricted on that account.

Revenue practice: rearrangement of shares coupled with a payment

Where one partner makes a payment to another in consideration of **35–15** a reduction in the latter's share, that payment will be treated as consideration for the disposal and charged to tax accordingly.[51] Where the payment represents consideration for an asset which appears in the firm's balance sheet, the appropriate fractional share of the acquisition cost can be deducted in order to arrive at the chargeable gain; where, however, the asset does not appear therein, as will usually be the case with goodwill, there may be no relevant acquisition cost,[52] unless the asset was held on March 31, 1982 and is thus eligible for rebasing.[53] The amount of the payment will, of course, form part of the acquisition cost of the share of the partner making the payment.

It has already been seen that, where partners fall to be treated as **35–16** connected persons in relation to a disposal,[54] market value should strictly be substituted for any consideration actually given. However, in the case of a rearrangement of partnership shares between

---

[49] Statement D12, para. 4, *infra*, para. A6–10.

[50] See further, *supra*, para. 35–10.

[51] Statement D12, para. 6, *infra*, para. A6–12. Where the consideration consists of a fractional share in an asset which is introduced into the firm, *e.g.* by an incoming partner, roll-over relief under the Taxation of Chargeable Gains Act 1992, s.152 may be available: see further, as to this relief, *supra*, paras. 35–07, 35–08.

[52] If the partners write off goodwill in the balance sheet, this will not of itself create either a chargeable gain or an allowable loss; however, if the partners then rearrange their shares, there will be a disposal of goodwill and an allowable loss will arise. Alternatively, it could be argued that the value of the goodwill becomes negligible as soon as it is written off, so as to permit a claim for an allowable loss under the Taxation of Chargeable Gains Act 1992, s.24(2). The latter argument has apparently not found favour with the General Commissioners: see (1980) 77 L.S.Gaz. 127 and (1982) 79 L.S.Gaz. 257; but see also the cases discussed in Eastaway and Gilligan, *Tax and Financial Planning for Professional Partnerships* (2nd ed., 1986) pp. 98–105.

[53] Taxation of Chargeable Gains Act 1992, s.35 (as amended). Note that, where a partner has made an election under *ibid.* s.35(5) in respect of his fractional share of the partnership assets, the election will not automatically apply to assets held by him in his personal capacity and vice versa: *ibid.* s.35(7); Statement of Practice "Rebasing Elections" (SP4/92) dated May 14, 1992, para.10(a); also ICAEW Memorandum TR854, paras. 9, 10, reproduced at [1991] S.T.I. 1117.

[54] See *supra*, para. 35–11.

connected persons which is effected either gratuitously or for a consideration of less than market value, the Revenue will not seek to substitute market value if similar terms would have been negotiated between parties at arm's length.[55] In any other case, it would seem that market value *must* be substituted since there can, by definition, have been no bona fide commercial arrangement and the partners will be connected in that capacity, if in no other.[56]

Revenue practice: revaluation of partnership assets

35-17   The seemingly innocuous process of revaluing partnership assets may, under the Revenue practice, throw up an unexpected charge to tax but only if the revaluation is reflected in the partnership accounts.[57] The revaluation and the consequent adjustments in the accounts will not themselves attract such a charge, but the Revenue will regard any partner whose share in the revalued assets is subsequently reduced as having made a disposal of part of his fractional interest therein for a consideration equal to the like part of the increased value shown in the accounts and tax will be charged accordingly.[58] The justification for imposing a charge in these circumstances is, in the Revenue's words, that the reduction in such a partner's share would otherwise "reduce his potential liability to capital gains tax on the eventual disposal of the assets without an equivalent reduction of the credit he has received in the accounts." The current editor submits that this reasoning is essentially flawed, since there will in reality be no question of such a partner *avoiding* a chargeable gain on a subsequent disposal: he will deduct from his share of the consideration his fractional share of the acquisition cost, and no account will be taken of balance sheet values. Moreover, why should the partner whose share is increased have his acquisition cost artificially augmented? The net position is likely to be the same, whether the tax is collected from one partner or the other.[59] In this respect, the practice should, perhaps, not be accepted.

---

[55] Statement D12, para. 7, *infra*, para. A6-13. *Quaere*, is this practice of any real significance given the availability of hold-over relief under the Taxation of Chargeable Gains Act 1992, s.165?

[56] *Ibid.* ss.17(1)(a), 18(1), (2), 286(4). Hold over relief would be available in such a case: see *supra*, para. 35-10.

[57] It is a commonly held misconception that, having had partnership assets revalued, *e.g.* on the retirement of a partner, the partnership accounts must necessarily be adjusted so as to incorporate the revised figures. It will frequently be desirable merely to alter the capital profit sharing ratios in order to reflect the revaluation, rather than to court a charge to tax under the Revenue practice.

[58] Statement D12, para. 5, *infra*, para. A6-11. See the criticisms of this practice set out in [1975] B.T.R. 87. *Quaere* could a partner faced with such a charge not seek to hold over the gain under the Taxation of Chargeable Gains Act 1992, s.165? There is certainly no "actual" consideration for the purposes of *ibid.* s.165(7)(a), although the deemed consideration does not strictly fall within the parenthetical words "(as opposed to the consideration equal to the market value which is deemed to be given by virtue of section 17(1))."

[59] *Per contra* if only some of the partners are higher rate taxpayers: see *ibid.* s.4.

It may be noted that this charge on "balance sheet gains" will be in addition to any charge on the *actual* consideration received on the rearrangement.[60]

Entire disposal of partnership share

Where a partner retires (or is expelled) from the firm and disposes **35-18** of the entirety of his share to the continuing partners, the tax treatment will broadly accord with the position on a rearrangement of partnership shares. Thus, if no payment is made to the outgoing partner and the Revenue practice is accepted[61] or, where appropriate, hold over relief is claimed,[62] no chargeable gain will be realised on the disposal. If, on the other hand, such a payment is made, otherwise than by way of an annuity (within the limits specified by the Revenue),[63] a charge to tax will be almost inevitable.[64]

The position is less straightforward when, under the terms of the **35-19** partnership agreement, the share of an outgoing or deceased partner is expressed to accrue to the continuing partners.[65] It is theoretically possible to argue that, quite apart from the Revenue practice (or, indeed, any available claim to hold over relief[66]), there will be no charge to tax when an outgoing partner's share accrues pursuant to such a provision,[67] whether or not any payment falls to be made to him at that stage. The current editor submits that, on a true analysis, the bundle of rights comprised in such a partner's share either becomes valueless when he ceases to be a partner or, where a payment falls to be made on the accruer, effectively contracts into the right to that payment.[68] Similarly, the prospect of a corresponding increase in value is inherent in the bundles of rights which make up the shares of the continuing partners. Thus, when the outgoing partner leaves the firm, it can be contended that there is neither a disposal by him nor an acquisition by the continuing partners, so that tax cannot be charged, irrespective of any payment which falls to be

---

[60] Statement D12, para. 6, *infra*, para. A6-12.

[61] There are, however, objections to the practice: see *supra*, para. 35-13.

[62] Taxation of Chargeable Gains Act 1992, s.165: see *supra*, para. 35-10.

[63] The treatment of such annuities (whether or not coupled with a cash payment) is governed by Statement D12, para. 8 (*infra*, para. A6-14), as extended by the Inland Revenue Statement of Practice dated January 12, 1979 (SP1/79) (*infra* para. A6-19): see further, *infra*, paras. 35-24 *et seq.*

[64] As to the availability of hold-over relief where actual consideration is given, see the Taxation of Chargeable Gains Act 1992, s.165(7). And see *supra*, para. 35-10, n. 32.

[65] See, for example, *Att.-Gen. v. Boden* [1912] 1 K.B. 539; *Att.-Gen v. Ralli* (1936) 15 A.T.C. 523, noticed *infra*, paras. 36-05 *et seq.*

[66] Taxation of Chargeable Gains Act 1992, s.165. See *supra*, para. 35-10.

[67] There will, in any event, be no charge to tax if the share accrues on death: *ibid.* s.62(1).

[68] See further, *infra.*, paras. 36-20, 36-29, 36-30, 36-48, 36-50, 36-56.

made by the latter.[69] Equally, it would seem to follow from the fact that the share of the outgoing partner merely becomes valueless or, where a payment falls to be made, assumes a fixed value, that the accruer is not an "occasion of the entire loss, destruction, dissipation or extinction" of the share.[70] Perhaps the share should more properly be treated as a wasting asset,[71] thus precluding any claim to a capital loss when its value becomes negligible;[72] however, this analysis is not without difficulty.[73]

Retirement in anticipation of emigration

35–20   Tax is, in general, chargeable only in respect of gains accruing to a person in a year of assessment during any part of which he is resident or ordinarily resident in the United Kingdom.[74] Accordingly, if an outgoing partner is intending to take up permanent residence abroad, no tax will normally be chargeable on gains realised by him on the disposal of his share if he defers that disposal until the financial year *following* that in which he retired and became non-resident.[75]

Relief available on retirement of partner

35–21   Where a partner disposes of his partnership share in exchange for a cash or other consideration, he may be able to take advantage of the "retirement" relief afforded by the Taxation of Chargeable Gains Act 1992.[76] Although the forerunner of this relief was only available to persons who had attained the age of 60,[77] the qualifying age now stands at 55[78] and relief is also available in the case of retirement

---

[69] The current editor submits that such a payment cannot properly be regarded as compensation for the loss or depreciation of the share, thus attracting a charge to tax under the Taxation of Chargeable Gains Act 1992, s.22(1)(a): since the right to the payment itself forms part of the share, it surely cannot at the same time constitute compensation for its loss or depreciation. It should also be noted that *ibid.* s.30 (value shifting and tax-free benefits) could in theory apply in the case of a tax avoidance scheme which incorporates an accruer provision; however, in most cases it should be possible to show that the main purpose of the arrangement was not the avoidance of tax: see *ibid.* s.30(4); also *Att.-Gen. v. Ralli* (1936) 15 A.T.C. 523, 526, *per* Lawrence J., *infra*, para. 36–06.

[70] See *ibid.* s.24(1). Even if this subsection did apply, the share could still arguably be treated as a wasting asset (see *infra*) in order to determine its value at the moment of extinction; if it were not so treated, a substantial allowable loss would prima facie be realised on the disposal.

[71] *Ibid.* s.44; and see, generally, *Whiteman on Capital Gains Tax* (4th ed.), paras. 8–70 *et seq.*

[72] *i.e.* on a claim being made under *ibid.* s.24(2).

[73] *e.g.* can it be established that the share has a predictable life not exceeding 50 years? This may be possible if the partnership agreement makes provision for the compulsory retirement of partners on the grounds of age or if the partnership is for a fixed term, but may be extremely difficult in other cases. Perhaps the life of the share might be ascertained by reference to the predictable expectation of life interests in settled property: see *ibid.* s.44(1)(d).

[74] *Ibid.* s.2(1); see also *ibid.* s.10.

[75] *Quaere*, what is the effect of the Partnership Act 1890, s.43 in such a case? The right of a partner to retain his share *in specie* following his retirement will in general depend on the terms of the partnership agreement. See also *supra*, paras. 19–10 *et seq.*, 19–41, 23–33, 26–04.

[76] Taxation of Chargeable Gains Act 1992, ss.163, 164, Sched. 6 (as amended).

[77] Capital Gains Tax Act 1979, s.124 (now repealed).

[78] Taxation of Chargeable Gains Act 1992, s.163(1)(a).

under that age on the grounds of ill-health.[79] For the purposes of the relief, a partner is treated as disposing of the whole or part of his fractional share in the partnership assets,[80] but he must have owned that share throughout[81] the period of at least one year ending with the date of the disposal.[82] The amount of the relief is dependent on the length of time the partner has owned his share. Thus, full relief of £250,000 plus one half of any gains between £250,000 and £1 million is available where the share has been held for 10 or more years; for lesser periods of ownership, the relief is scaled down by 10 per cent. for each full year.[83]

Relief is also afforded to a partner who, as part of his "withdrawal **35–22** ... from participation in the business carried on by the partnership",[84] disposes of his share and, by what is styled an "associated" disposal, also disposes of an asset which was being used for the purposes of that business immediately before he ceased to be a partner,[84a] provided that the asset has been used for the purposes of that business or of some other business carried on by him (either alone or in partnership) during the whole or a part of his period of ownership.[85] Where the asset has not been so used throughout such period, or where a rent or other consideration has been paid in respect of such use, the relief will be appropriately restricted.[86]

The relief available to a partner who attains the age of 55 is **35–23** applied automatically by the Revenue and, in an appropriate case, care should be taken to ensure that it is not unintentionally exhausted

---

[79] *Ibid.* s.163(1)(b), Sched. 6, paras. 3(1), 5(4).

[80] *Ibid.* s.163(8). Given the terms of the subsection, it is assumed that a disposal of even a small part of a partner's fractional share in the partnership assets will be treated as a disposal of part of a business. *Per contra* in the case of the disposal of a specific partnership asset: see generally, *McGregor v. Adcock* [1977] 1 W.L.R. 864; *Atkinson v. Dancer* [1988] S.T.C. 758; *Pepper v. Duffurn* [1993] S.T.C. 466; also the I.C.A.E.W. Memorandum TR 667, paras. 16 *et seq.*, reproduced at [1987] S.T.I. 647.

[81] See *Davenport v. Hasslacher* [1977] 1 W.L.R. 869.

[82] Taxation of Chargeable Gains Act 1992, s.163(3). As to the availability of the relief where the business has not been owned for the requisite period, but has either replaced some other business or been acquired from a spouse, see *ibid.* Sched. 6, paras. 14, 16; also Extra-Statutory Concession D48 announced on April 14, 1994 and reproduced at [1994] S.T.I. 514.

[83] *Ibid.* Sched. 6, para. 13(1), as amended by the Finance Act 1994, s.92(1).

[84] The withdrawal must comprise the material disposal of business assets referred to in the Taxation of Chargeable Gains Act 1992, s. 164(7); *Clarke v. Mayo* [1994] S.T.C. 570. Consistently therewith, it would seem that the reference is *ibid.* s.164(7)(a) to "*a* withdrawal" (emphasis supplied), the current editor doubts whether this implies that a partial withdrawal may be sufficient to qualify for the relief; *sed quaere.*

[84a] See *Clark v. Mayo, supra.*

[85] *Ibid.* s.164(6)-(8). This element of the relief to an extent runs parallel to that afforded on the disposal of assets in use for the purposes of a business at the time at which it ceased to be carried on, albeit subject to different conditions: see *ibid.* s.163(2)(b), (4).

[86] *Ibid.* Sched. 6, para. 10. If the rent paid is clearly less than a market rent, it would seem that a larger fraction of the gain will qualify for the relief. The position was the same under the Capital Gains Tax Act 1979, s.124: see the Inland Revenue Statement of Practice "Capital Gains Tax: Retirement Relief" (D5), first published January 4, 1973. *Quaere* why this approach has been adopted: if the asset has been used for the purposes of the partnership business, why should the payment of a rent affect the partners' entitlement to the relief?

in franking a gain which could more advantageously be relieved by a claim to relief under some other section.[87] On the other hand, any gains which cannot be so relieved may be the subject of a claim to hold over relief.[88]

Partnership annuities

35–24   Although reference has already been made to the tax treatment of a straightforward capital payment made to an outgoing partner, if financial provision is made for such a partner by means of an annuity (whether in lieu of, or in addition to, such a payment), different questions will arise. Although there is no doubt that the capitalised value of an annuity given as consideration for the disposal of an outgoing partner's share can be taken into account in computing any gains,[89] if the annuity does not in fact represent such consideration and is to be paid independently of the disposal, it should, as a matter of strict law, be ignored.

35–25   It is in the above context that the Revenue practice must be considered. If the firm buys a purchased life annuity for the benefit of the outgoing partner, the actual cost of the annuity will be treated as the consideration for the disposal of his share. If, on the other hand, the firm itself agrees to pay the annuity, its capitalised value will be taken into account, but only if it can be regarded as more than a reasonable recognition of the outgoing partner's past contribution of work and effort to the firm.[90] It will not be so regarded if the outgoing partner has been a partner for at least 10 years[91] and the annuity does not represent more than two-thirds of his average share of profits[92] in the best three of the last seven years in which he was required to devote substantially the whole of his time to partnership activities. If he has been a partner for less than 10 years, the relevant fraction of his average share of profits is determined in accordance with a graduated scale, varying between 1/60th (after one to five years) and 32/60ths (after nine years).[93]

35–26   Although the application of the above practice was originally denied where the annuity was payable *in addition* to a lump sum, the Revenue now accept that, even in such a case, the capitalised value

---

[87] Taxation of Chargeable Gains Act 1992, Sched. 6, para. 5(2); see also *supra*, para. 35–10.
[88] *Ibid.* s.165(3)(a), (6).
[89] *Ibid.* s.37(3).
[90] Statement D12, para. 8, *infra*, para. A6–14.
[91] This may include any period during which the outgoing partner was a member of another firm which merged with the firm from which he retires.
[92] In assessing such share, no account will be taken of capital allowances or charges.
[93] See the Table set out in Statement D12, para. 8, *infra*, para. A6–14.

of the annuity can be left out of account, so long as the aggregate of the annuity and one-ninth of the lump sum does not exceed the appropriate fraction of the outgoing partner's average share of profits during the relevant years.[94] The lump sum itself will naturally continue to be taxable in the outgoing partner's hands.

Where, under the practice, the purchase cost or the capitalised value of the annuity is treated as consideration for the disposal of the outgoing partner's share, it will naturally constitute allowable expenditure on the acquisition of the share by the continuing partners.[95]

It will perhaps be apparent that there is an assumption underlying **35–27** the whole of the Revenue practice, namely that any annuity paid to an outgoing partner is inevitably given by way of consideration for the disposal of his share. The current editor submits that such an assumption is wholly unwarranted since there is no *necessary* connection between the annuity and the disposal, even though in practice such a connection will frequently exist. In this respect, the practice is potentially misleading and should be approached with caution; in an appropriate case, where the independent nature of the annuity arrangements is clear, the application of the practice (and of the underlying assumption) should be resisted.

Mergers and "roll-over" relief

Where two firms merge, and their respective assets are combined **35–28** in the new merged firm, the partners of each constituent firm will, on a true analysis, have disposed of a proportionate part of their shares in the assets of that firm in return for an appropriate share in the assets of the other firm, and tax will be charged by reference to the actual value of that consideration, although "roll-over" relief under section 152 of the Taxation of Chargeable Gains Act 1992 may be available.[96] The Revenue practice in relation to mergers involves an application of the same principles as are applied to changes in the partners' sharing ratios, *i.e.* where no actual consideration is paid outside the accounts (and where no "balance sheet gain" is treated as realised),[97] neither a chargeable gain nor an allowable loss will result.[98] Even if a chargeable gain is thrown up, "roll-over" relief will still be available to the extent that the consideration received is actually rolled over into assets brought into the merged firm. The

---

[94] See the Statement of Practice (SP1/79) dated January 12, 1979, *infra*, para. A6–19.
[95] Statement D12, para. 8, *infra*, para. A6–14.
[96] See further, *supra*, paras. 35–07, 38–08.
[97] See *supra*, para. 35–17.
[98] Statement D12, para. 9, *infra*, para. A6–15.

practice would, in this respect, appear to be beneficial, since it is now possible to effect a merger without incurring a charge to tax and without any necessary reliance on a claim to "roll-over" relief. Nevertheless, objection may still be taken to the basis upon which the practice is formulated.[99]

C. DISTRIBUTION OF PARTNERSHIP ASSETS AMONGST PARTNERS

35–29 Except in the case of a limited partnership,[1] there is nothing to prevent partners agreeing to distribute partnership assets between themselves whilst the partnership is continuing, although such a distribution will more commonly be encountered following a dissolution. In either case, each partner will exchange his fractional share in the entirety of the distributed assets for absolute ownership of such of those assets as are received by him. Equally, if specific assets are appropriated to an outgoing partner in satisfaction of his share in the remaining assets, each of the continuing partners will be treated as disposing of his fractional share in the specific assets in exchange for a disposal by the outgoing partner of his fractional share in the remaining assets. Although a partner to whom such a distribution is made may, in terms of value, receive no more than his existing entitlement, there is nothing in the Taxation of Chargeable Gains Act 1992 which prevents tax being charged on an exchange of assets,[2] and this much is clearly recognised by the Revenue practice. However, under that practice, the recipient of a distribution will (correctly) not be treated as having disposed of his fractional share in the assets distributed to him, even though there can be no doubt that the other partners have disposed of their shares in those assets.[3]

35–30 The practice requires the chargeable gain on such a distribution to be calculated in the following way[4]: the gain attributable to each partner (including the partner receiving the asset) is first calculated on the basis of a disposal at current market value. The fractional share of the gain deemed to have been realised by those partners who give up their interests in the asset will be chargeable to tax in the normal way, but no such charge will be imposed on the remainder of the gain, which will be attributed to the recipient partner. The corollary is, of course, that such part of the gain will be deducted from the market value of the asset in order to determine the latter's

---

[99] See *supra*, para. 35–13.
[1] See the Limited Partnerships Act 1907, s.4(3); and see further *supra*, paras. 30–11 *et seq.*, 31–09.
[2] But see *infra*, para. 35–33.
[3] Statement D12, para. 3, *infra*, para. A6–09.
[4] *Ibid.*

acquisition cost. The operation of the practice may be illustrated by the following simple example. A firm comprises four equal partners and owns an asset which was originally acquired for £8,000 but now has market value of £24,000. That asset is distributed *in specie* to one partner, A, in satisfaction of his share on a dissolution. The total gain on the deemed disposal is £16,000, of which £12,000 is apportioned to the other three partners and charged to tax accordingly. A's acquisition cost will be the market value (£24,000) less the amount of his gain (£6,000 − £2,000 = £4,000), *i.e.* £20,000. A similar computation will be made when a loss arises on the distribution.

The illogicality of the practice will be self evident: having properly **35–31** accepted that the recipient partner is not to be regarded as having disposed of his fractional share in the asset, the entirety of the practice is dependent upon his being deemed to have made just such a disposal and to have realised a gain thereon. This is a further example of the Revenue treating a gain as having been realised when no disposal has in fact taken place,[5] and again the practice must be open to challenge. It should also be noted that its application is not restricted to dissolutions: an attempt could in theory be made to apply it to the purchase of partnership assets by a partner pursuant to a bona fide commercial arrangement,[6] although this should be strenuously resisted.

Where partners are treated as having disposed of their shares in **35–32** land or other qualifying assets on such a distribution, the Revenue are prepared, by concession, to allow claims for "roll-over" relief,[7] provided that the partnership is dissolved immediately thereafter.[8] It is, of course, questionable whether this condition can be justified, given that the partnership "trade" and any new trade carried on by an individual partner will be treated as one and the same for the purposes of the relief, whether or not the firm is dissolved.[9]

A more fundamental objection to the latter concession and, **35–33** indeed, to the entirety of the Revenue practice in this area is the underlying assumption that a partition of land or other assets as

---

[5] The first example was discussed *supra*, para. 35–17, in relation to Statement D12, para. 5.

[6] See the Taxation of Chargeable Gains Act 1992, s.286(4); also *supra*, para. 35–11.

[7] Under *ibid.* s.152: see further, *supra*, paras. 35–07, 35–08. Note also that, in such a case, some measure of hold-over relief may also be available: see *supra*, para. 35–10.

[8] Extra-Statutory Concession D23 (1994 Revision) entitled "Relief for the replacement of business assets: partition of land on the dissolution of partnership." *Quaere*, would the Revenue permit the partners to take advantage of Extra-Statutory Concession D26 (1994 Revision), relating to exchanges of joint interests, which applies to land and to milk or potato quota associated therewith? It is assumed not, as long as the partnership continues. If, however, the land were partitioned following the dissolution and winding up of the firm, there would seem to be no reason why the Concession should not apply.

[9] See the Taxation of Chargeable Gains Act 1992, s.152(8).

between partners must *necessarily* involve capital gains tax disposals by them. In *Jenkins v. Brown*,[10] Knox J. held that a partition of land as between beneficial co-owners did *not* involve such a disposal and the same reasoning would seem to apply in the case of a partition of land or other assets as between partners, provided that each "pool" of like assets is divided strictly in accordance with their fractional shares therein. The position will obviously be otherwise if shares in one type of asset are exchanged for shares in another.[11]

3. ADMINISTRATION AND COMPUTATION

Information about chargeable gains

35–34   Section 12(4)(a) of the Taxes Management Act 1970[12] requires any partnership return[13] to contain particulars of "any disposal of partnership property" during any period covered by the return, as if the partnership were liable to tax on any chargeable gain accruing thereon.[14] The subsection appears to draw a distinction between a disposal of partnership property and a disposal of a share or shares therein, which somewhat ironically runs directly counter to the express provisions of section 59 of the Taxation of Chargeable Gains Act 1992,[15] whereby all "partnership dealings" (*i.e.* disposals of partnership property) are to be treated as dealings by the partners and not by the firm as such. Nevertheless, the duty is strictly defined: if anything less than the entirety of the partners' shares in a given partnership asset are disposed of, the responsibility for submitting the return will fall on the individual partners.[16]

35–35   Under the regime of self assessment due to be introduced by the Finance Act 1994 with effect from the tax year 1996/97,[17] it seems likely that a similar requirement will be imposed in relation to the new form of partnership return,[18] although it would seem that the contents of the partnership *statement* to be included in that return are

---

[10] [1989] 1 W.L.R. 1163.

[11] See *supra*, para. 35–29.

[12] As amended by the Finance Act 1990, s.90(2)(c), Sched. 19, Pt. V.

[13] *i.e.* a return made pursuant to the Taxes Management Act 1970, s.9(2) and/or (3) (as substituted by the Finance Act 1990, s.90(1)).

[14] The return must also contain particulars of any acquisition of partnership property: *ibid.* s.12(4)(b).

[15] See *supra*, para. 35–01.

[16] See the Taxes Management Act 1970, ss.7 (as substituted by the Finance Act 1988, s.120 and amended by the Finance (No. 2) Act 1992, s.19(1)), 8, 12(1) (as respectively substituted/amended by the Finance Act 1990, s.90(1), (2)(a)).

[17] Finance Act 1994, ss.178 *et seq.* See also, *supra*, para. 34–18.

[18] Taxes Management Act 1970, s.12AA(7) (as substituted by the Finance Act 1994, s.184(7)). The return will only have to include such information if the notice under *ibid.* s.12AA(2) or (3) so requires.

confined solely to the firm's income and will, therefore, not contain any reference to its supposed chargeable gains.[19]

Computation of gains

No particular difficulties of computation arise in relation to **35–36** partnerships,[20] save in two specific cases where the Revenue have seen fit to publish their practice. Those cases are as follows, namely:

(a) Partnership shares acquired in stages

Where a partner has acquired his share in stages[21] prior to March 31, **35–37** 1982, the automatic rebasing as at that date will in general obviate any need to consider the former pooling rules which would otherwise have applied thereto.[22] Where, on the other hand, the share has been acquired in whole or in part *since* that date,[23] it would seem that the identification provisions contained in the Taxation of Chargeable Gains Act 1992 must be applied.[24] Thus, on a disposal of a partnership asset, each partner's fractional share therein will be identified first with any part of such share acquired within the period of 10 days ending with the disposal date, then with any part acquired on or after April 6, 1982, then with any part acquired between April 5, 1964 and April 6, 1982, and lastly with any other part, on a "last in, first out" (L.I.F.O.) basis. However, again by reason of the automatic rebasing, there may in practice be no need to distinguish between shares of the latter two classes, save to the extent that they were acquired between April 1 and April 5, 1982.[25]

Consistently with the original published practice of the Revenue,[26] it would appear that a reasonably sympathetic attitude may be

---

[19] See *ibid.* s.12AB(1)(a)(i) (as substituted by the Finance Act 1994, s.185).

[20] See, generally, the Taxation of Chargeable Gains Act 1992, Pt. II.

[21] *i.e.* in one or more of the manners considered *supra*, paras. 35–13 *et seq.*

[22] Taxation of Chargeable Gains Act 1992, s.35 (as amended). See, as to the position where the share was acquired in whole or in part prior to April 6, 1965, *ibid.* Sched. 2, para. 18 and Statement D12, para. 10, *infra*, para. A6–16. The applicable rule is now "last in, first out" (L.I.F.O.) but, under the original provisions successively contained in the Finance Act 1965, Sched. 6, para. 26 and the Capital Gains Tax Act 1979, Sched. 5, para. 13, the rule was "first in, first out" (F.I.F.O.): this is reflected in Statement D12, para. 10. L.I.F.O. was first introduced by the Finance Act 1982, Sched. 13, para. 11.

[23] Note that acquisitions between April 1 and 5, 1982, form part of the 1965–1982 pool and are not rebased.

[24] Taxation of Chargeable Gains Act 1992, ss.104, 107. It is thought that the definition of "securities" in *ibid.* s.104(3) is prima facie apt to cover the fractional shares which go to make up a partnership share, albeit that its application is not without difficulty.

[25] *Ibid.* s.107(3)-(9).

[26] Statement D12, para. 10, *infra*, para. A6–16. A clear example of a case where the old F.I.F.O. rule would have been inappropriate was where, on the retirement of a partner, his share was acquired by the continuing partners but, shortly thereafter, a new partner was admitted and the shares were immediately rearranged in order to give him the share of the retired partner. In such circumstances L.I.F.O. would have been more apposite; under the new rules, L.I.F.O. would now be applied in any event. See also [1975] B.T.R. 87 (where the old rules are considered).

adopted where the application of the above rules will produce an unreasonable result.

(b) Shares held as partnership assets

35–38 Where a firm holds securities[27] which are eligible for a pooling election,[28] and a partner also hold such securities in his own right, the Revenue would appear to accept that he can submit separate elections *qua* partner[29] and *qua* individual; it follows that an election submitted in one capacity will not apply to securities held in another.[30] This accords with the published practice under the old pooling provisions,[31] as well as with the current attitude towards rebasing elections.[32] By the same token, the Taxation of Chargeable Gains Act 1992 makes clear that securities of the same class will only be regarded as a single asset if they are held by the same person *in the same capacity*.[33]

---

[27] As to the meaning of this expression, see the Taxation of Chargeable Gains Act 1992, s.104(3); also *supra*, para. 35–37, n. 24.

[28] See *ibid.* s.109(4) (pre-1982 share pools) or Sched. 2, para. 4(2) (quoted securities held on April 6, 1965).

[29] *i.e.* in respect of his fractional share in the firm's holding: see *supra*, para. 35–04, n.9.

[30] See the Taxation of Chargeable Gains Act 1992, Sched. 2, para. 4(10)(a). This sub-paragraph also applies to an election under *ibid.* s.109(4): *ibid.* s.109(5).

[31] Statement D12, para. 11, *infra*, para. A6–17.

[32] Taxation of Chargeable Gains Act 1992, s.35(5), (7) and the Statement of Practice "Rebasing Elections" (SP4/92), dated May 14, 1992, para. 10(a). And see also ICAEW Memorandum TR854, paras. 9, 10, reproduced at [1991] S.T.I. 1117.

[33] Taxation of Chargeable Gains Act 1992, s.104(1), Sched. 2, para. 4(3). And see also *ibid.* ss.105(1), 107(2), 108(2).

CHAPTER 36

INHERITANCE TAX

1. INTRODUCTION

UNLIKE capital transfer tax,[1] inheritance tax is primarily chargeable **36–01** on death, since the majority of *inter vivos* transfers of value[2] are now treated as potentially exempt and only come within the charge to tax if the transferor fails to survive for seven years.[3] However, the reintroduction of the estate duty concept of a "benefit reserved" (now styled a "gift with a reservation")[4] has complicated the relative simplicity of the new regime and effectively removed a number of the tax planning options formerly presented within the confines of a partnership.

Arm's length transactions

The essence of the charge to inheritance tax in respect of an *inter* **36–02** *vivos* disposition is a transfer of value conferring a gratuitous benefit on another. If, in such a case, the transfer is made by an individual in favour of another individual or a favoured trust,[5] it will qualify for potentially exempt status[6] and will only come into the charge to tax in the event of the transferor's death within seven years;[7] in any other case, it will be chargeable to tax forthwith.[8]

Where, on the other hand, it can be shown that a particular **36–03** disposition was *not* accompanied by any donative intent and that the transferor and the transferee were not "connected" or, even if they were, that the transaction was of a normal commercial nature, there will be no transfer of value by reference to which a charge to tax can be imposed nor, indeed, any gift with a reservation.[9] This important

---

[1] The structure of capital transfer tax was radically altered, and its name changed to inheritance tax, by the Finance Act 1986. As a result, what was formerly the consolidating Capital Transfer Tax Act 1984 is now conventionally referred to as the Inheritance Tax Act 1984: see the Finance Act 1986, s.100(1)(a).

[2] See, as to the meaning of this expression, the Inheritance Tax Act 1984, s.3.

[3] *Ibid.* s.3A(1), (4) (as inserted by the Finance Act 1986, Sched. 19, para. 1).

[4] Finance Act 1986, s.102, Sched. 20. See further *infra*, paras. 36–40 *et seq.*

[5] *i.e.* an "interest in possession" trust, an accumulation and maintenance trust or a disabled trust: Inheritance Tax Act 1984, s.3A(1) (c), (2) (as inserted by the Finance Act 1986, Sched. 19, para. 1 and amended by the Finance (No. 2) Act 1987, s.96(2)).

[6] *Ibid.* s.3A(1).

[7] *Ibid.* ss.3A(4), (5), 4(1).

[8] *Ibid.* s.2.

[9] See the Finance Act 1986, s.102(1); note also *ibid.* Sched. 20, para. 6.

principle is embodied in section 10(1) of the Inheritance Tax Act 1984,[10] which provides:

"(1) A disposition is not a transfer of value if it is shown that it was not intended, and was not made in a transaction intended, to confer any gratuitous benefit on any person and either—

(a) that it was made in a transaction at arm's length between persons not connected with each other, or

(b) that it was such as might be expected to be made in a transaction at arm's length between persons not connected with each other"[11]

The connected persons provisions of the Taxation of Chargeable Gains Act 1992[12] are, with certain extensions, applied for this purpose.[13] Thus, partners will normally be treated as connected persons, except in relation to bona fide commercial arrangements;[14] even then, the exception will only apply if they are not otherwise connected.[15]

36–04 Provided that a substantial element of reciprocity can be shown, it should be possible to justify most transactions between partners both as bona fide commercial arrangements and as arm's length transactions. The reciprocity test can, in particular, be satisfied by establishing that full consideration has been given and received, even though not in a monetary form. In this connection, a number of estate duty cases decided under section 3 of the Finance Act 1894[16] are of direct relevance.

36–05 In *Att.-Gen. v. Boden*,[17] a father entered into partnership with his two sons and the partnership agreement provided that, on the death of the father, his share was to accrue to the other partners, subject to the payment by them of its full value, but ignoring goodwill. For their part, the sons agreed to devote as much time and attention to the

---

[10] Formerly the Capital Transfer Tax Act 1984: see *supra*, para. 36–01, n. 1.

[11] See further, as to this limb, *I.R.C. v. Spencer-Nairn* [1991] S.T.C. 60.

[12] s.286; see further *supra*, para. 35–11.

[13] Inheritance Tax Act 1984, s.270 (as amended by the Taxation of Chargeable Gains Act 1992, Sched. 10, para. 8(12)). The definition of "relative" in the Taxation of Chargeable Gains Act 1992, s.286(8) is extended to include an uncle, aunt, nephew and niece.

[14] Taxation of Chargeable Gains Act 1992, s.286(4).

[15] *e.g.* pursuant to *ibid.* s.286(2). And note, in particular, the extended meaning of "relative" for inheritance tax purposes: see *supra*, n.13.

[16] This section, so far as material, provided as follows: "Estate duty shall not be payable in respect of property passing on the death of the deceased by reason only of a bona fide purchase from the person under whose disposition the property passes ... where such purchase was made ... for full consideration in money or money's worth paid to the vendor ... for his own use or benefit."

[17] [1912] 1 K.B. 539. But note the Irish case of *Re Clark* (1906) 40 I.L.T. 117, considered *infra*, para. 36–30, n.8.

partnership business as its proper conduct required and further agreed not to engage in any other trade or business without the father's consent. The father, on the other hand, was bound to give only so much time and attention to the business as he thought fit. In deciding whether estate duty should be paid in respect of the goodwill which accrued to the sons on the father's death, Hamilton J. held that (1) having regard to the sons' obligations under the agreement, the father's share in goodwill had passed to them by reason only of a bona fide purchase for full consideration in money's worth and was accordingly not dutiable; and (2) whilst the goodwill was of little real value, the covenant on the part of the sons to give their full time and attention to the partnership business was both capable of being, and was in fact, adequate consideration for the father's share therein. In the course of his judgment, Hamilton J. observed:

"Furthermore, the question whether full consideration was given or not may no doubt be solved by putting a value on the property which passed on the one side, and weighing against it the money value of the obligations assumed on the other; but that is not the only method of solving the question. Another method is by looking at the nature of the transaction and considering whether what is given is a fair equivalent for what is received; and that is the way in which the question should be approached in this case."[18]

Whilst part of the decision in this case was disapproved by the Privy Council in *Perpetual Executors & Trustees Association of Australia Ltd. v. Commissioner of Taxes of Australia*,[19] no adverse comment was made as to that part of *Boden's* case which turned on the application of section 3 of the 1894 Act.

A further illustration of the reciprocity principle can be seen in **36–06** *Att.-Gen. v. Ralli*,[20] where Sir Lucas Ralli (the father) had in 1920 entered into a partnership agreement with his son, Strati Ralli, and a third party for carrying on the old established family business of merchant bankers. The nature of the business made it necessary that large reserves should be maintained and it was provided in a collateral partnership agreement that, on the retirement or death of one of the partners, his interest in the partnership reserves should entirely cease and become vested in the continuing or surviving partner or partners without any payment or liability to account whatsoever. Sir Lucas retired in 1931 and in fact died 18 days later. The Crown claimed that the vesting of the reserves on Sir Lucas'

---

[18] [1912] 1 K.B. 539, 561.
[19] [1954] A.C. 114.
[20] (1936) 15 A.T.C. 523.

retirement was a gift which, having occurred less than three years before his death, was dutiable; in fact, the reserves in question were stated to be "very substantial" but Lawrence J., in holding that Sir Lucas' share of the reserves was not chargeable to estate duty, concluded:

> "The substance of the matter here, in my opinion, is not a gift. I think that the transaction carried out by the collateral agreement in 1920 was an ordinary commercial arrangement entered into between the three partners for valuable consideration, it had none of the elements of a gift in it. All partners were treated equally. It was in the interests of the partnership in this great business that large reserves should be carried in the business. It was in the interests of the partnership that on the retirement or death of any of the partners these reserves should not be depleted by his being paid out his share of the reserves. It therefore appears to me that it was ordinary business wisdom to provide, as the collateral agreement does provide, that the interest of the partners in the reserves should pass to the surviving partners. That was not intended to be a gift. It was not a gift. It was an ordinary business arrangement, and it applied equally to all the partners. The consideration moving from the one partner to the other was the undertaking of each partner to be a partner on those terms, one of which was that his interest in the reserves should pass to his partners if he retired or died." [21]

It should be noted that the decision of Lawrence J., to the effect that there had been no gift but merely a business arrangement, was quite apart from his (almost subsidiary) decision that the exemption contained in section 3 of the Finance Act 1894 applied. [22]

36–07 Whilst a *Boden* and *Ralli* argument will not be sustainable in all cases, it should be possible to establish that a disposition which forms part of a bona fide business arrangement falls within section 10(1) of the Inheritance Tax Act 1984 and thus does not constitute a transfer of value. The argument is equally applicable where the partners are connected otherwise than as partners, although it may be that much more difficult to prove bona fides in such a case. Practical applications of the argument will be considered later in this chapter.

By way of contrast, it should be noted that, if advantage is to be taken of the exemption from the reservation of benefit provisions involving the occupation of land or the possession of chattels, [23] it is

---

[21] *Ibid.* p. 526.
[22] *Ibid.* pp. 527–528.
[23] Finance Act 1986, Sched. 20, para. 6(1)(a); and see [1993] S.T.I. 1410. See further, *infra*, paras. 36–40 *et seq.*

necessary to show that full consideration *in money or money's worth* was received.[24]

2. EXEMPTIONS AND RELIEFS

Before considering the various circumstances in which a partner **36–08** may make a transfer of value for the purposes of inheritance tax, it will be convenient to outline the various exemptions and reliefs which are available.

Transfers between spouses

Any transfer of value will be exempt if it consists of a direct **36–09** transfer of property to the transferor's spouse or if, as a result of the transfer, the value of the spouse's estate is increased, *e.g.* where the transfer is made in favour a third party on terms that the third party will secure a benefit of corresponding value for the spouse.[25] In the latter case, the exemption will be limited to the amount of such increase. However, care must be taken to ensure that a subsequent disposal by the spouse is not treated as an associated operation, thus forfeiting the benefit of the initial exempt transfer.[26]

Annual exemptions

Transfers of value in any year are exempt to the extent that the **36–10** values transferred do not in the aggregate exceed £3,000.[27] Any unused part of the exemption may be carried forward to the next year, but no further.[28] Although the Inheritance Tax Act 1984 appears to provide that potentially exempt transfers are in the first instance left out of account for the purposes of this exemption and that, if they subsequently prove to be chargeable, such tranfers are to be treated as made *after* any other transfers of value in the year in question,[29] this is inconsistent with an earlier section the Act.[29a] The

---

[24] Of course, if property is transferred under an arm's length bargain and, pursuant thereto, possession or enjoyment is retained by the transferor, there will have been no gift, so that the presence or absence of a consideration in money or money's worth will be irrelevant.

[25] Inheritance Tax Act 1984, s.18(1). And see, as to the treatment of transfers of value arising out of loans, *ibid.* s.29(2).

[26] See *ibid.* s.268 and, generally, Foster, *Inheritance Tax*, para. C1.16. Note also that the principles developed in *W.T. Ramsay Ltd. v. I.R.C.* [1982] A.C. 300 and subsequent cases (see *supra*, para. 34–09) may apply to an inheritance tax avoidance scheme: see *I.R.C. v. Fitzwilliam* [1993] 1 W.L.R. 1189 (where, on the facts, all the steps in the scheme could not be shown to be pre-ordained).

[27] *Ibid.* s.19(1).

[28] *Ibid.* s.19(2).

[29] *Ibid.* s.19(3A) (as inserted by the Finance Act 1986, Sched. 19, para. 5).

[29a] *Ibid.* s. 3A(1)(b) (as added by the Finance Act 1986, Sched. 19, para. 1).

Revenue practice is in fact to apply the exemption to transfers in the order in which they are made, whether they are chargeable or potentially exempt.[29b] It follows that, in some cases, the exemption will be lost if the transferor lives for seven years after making a potentially exempt transfer to which that exemption is allocated.

Exemption is also conferred on outright gifts in any one year to any one person, if the value of the gift(s) does not exceed £250.[30] This exemption is in addition to the £3,000 annual exemption.

These exemptions may be of value when it is desired to alter the capital or asset sharing ratios in a firm without consideration and without incurring even a potential charge to tax.

Normal expenditure out of income

36–11   A transferor who wishes to take advantage of this exemption must show:

(a)   that the transfer of value was part of his normal expenditure,
(b)   that it was actually made out of his income (if necessary taking one year with another);[31] and
(c)   that, after allowing for all other items of normal expenditure, he had sufficient income remaining to maintain his usual standard of living.[32]

Where, however, the transfer of value consists of a loan of money or other property,[33] the transferor must show merely that the transfer is a normal one on his part and that requirement (c) above is satisfied.[34] Whether any particular expenditure or transfer can be regarded as normal for the transferor will clearly involve a question of fact, although, as with the corresponding estate duty exemption, the test would appear to be qualitative rather than quantitative;[35] as a result, it cannot properly be said that any recurring item of expenditure will *necessarily* be treated as normal, or that any non-recurring item will not.

[29b] See further, as to this practice, Foster *Inheritance Tax*, para. C3.22.

[30] Inheritance Tax Act 1984, s.20. The exemption will not apply in the case of a gift which forms part of a larger gift.

[31] It is thus possible to aggregate more than one year's income in order to show that a particular item of expenditure falls within the exemption: this might be of particular relevance where the transferor's income fluctuates from year to year.

[32] Inheritance Tax Act 1984, s.21(1). It should be noted that the exemption is available "to the extent that" the conditions can be satisfied, so that only part of an item of expenditure may qualify as exempt.

[33] Such transfers are taxable on normal principles: see *infra*, para. 36–38. Formerly, they were subject to their own specific regime: see the Finance Act 1976, s.115 (now repealed).

[34] Inheritance Tax Act 1984, s.29(4).

[35] See, generally, *Att.-Gen.* for *Northern Ireland v. Heron* [1959] T.R. 1 (C.A.) (Northern Ireland).

This exemption may be of particular relevance where annuities are paid to outgoing partners or their dependants, otherwise than pursuant to the partnership agreement. [36]

Dispositions allowable for income tax

Any disposition which is allowable in computing the transferor's **36–12** profits for the purposes of income tax, [37] or which would be so allowable if those profits were sufficient and fell to be so computed, will not be treated as a transfer of value. [38]

Agricultural property relief

Relief is afforded whenever the whole or part of the value **36–13** transferred by a transfer of value is attributable to the agricultural value [39] of agricultural property, [40] provided that one of two conditions is satisfied. [41] Thus, to qualify for the relief the agricultural property must either have been occupied by the transferor for the purposes of agriculture throughout the period of two years ending with the date of the transfer, or owned by him throughout the period of seven years ending with that date and occupied (by him or another) for the purposes of agriculture throughout that period. [42] Where the property constitutes a replacement for other property, the former condition may still be satisfied if the transferor can show that he occupied the original property and the replacement property [43] for an aggregate period of at least two years within the five years ending with the date of the transfer. [44] Otherwise, he must show that the original property and the replacement property were owned and occupied (by him or another) for the purposes of agriculture, for an aggregate period of at least seven years within the 10 years ending with the date of the transfer. [45] In either case, the relief will not

---

[36] But note the possible income tax implications attendant on the payment of an annuity in such circumstances: see *supra*, paras. 34–93 *et seq.*

[37] If the disposition is only partly allowable, then the allowable part will be treated as a separate disposition: Inheritance Tax Act 1984, s.12(5).

[38] *Ibid.* s.12(1). As to dispositions which represent contributions to a retirement benefit scheme, see *ibid.* s.12(2) (as amended).

[39] The "agricultural value" of agricultural property is the value which the property would have if it were subject to a perpetual covenant prohibiting its use otherwise than as agricultural property: *ibid.* s.115(3).

[40] The expression "agricultural property" is defined in *ibid.* s.115(2); note also *ibid.* s.115(4). See, generally, *Starke v. I.R.C.* [1994] 1 W.L.R. 888. Any part of the value of the land attributable to milk quota will qualify for the relief: see [1993] S.T.I. 295.

[41] *Ibid.* s.116(1). The relief is only available in respect of agricultural property situated in the U.K., the Channel Islands or the Isle of Man (*ibid.* s.115(5)), but is denied where the property is subject to a binding contract for sale: *ibid.* s.124(1). See further *infra*, para. 36–20, n. 76.

[42] *Ibid.* s.117. As to the position where the transferor became entitled to the property on the death of another person, see *ibid.* s.120.

[43] Any number of replacements, direct or indirect, may apparently be taken into account for these purposes.

[44] Inheritance Tax Act 1984, s.118(1).

[45] *Ibid.* s.118(2).

exceed what it would have been if the replacement had not been
made and, for this purpose, changes resulting from the formation,
alteration or dissolution of a partnership will be disregarded.[46]

36–14   Where either condition is satisfied, the relief is given by means of a
percentage reduction in the value attributable to the agricultural
value of the agricultural property.[47] The appropriate reduction is now
100 per cent if the transferor's interest in the property immediately
before the transfer carried the right to vacant possession or the right
to obtain it within the next 12 months, and in certain other
transitional cases;[48] otherwise the reduction is 50 per cent.[49] Given
that the maximum rate of relief amounts to a complete exemption
from tax, a partner who owns agricultural land which is *not* to
become a partnership asset should no longer proceed by way of a
lease to the firm, since he will thereby limit himself to a 50 per cent
reduction in the *tenanted* value of the land, when full relief in respect
of the *vacant possession* value could have been secured by granting
his co-partners a non-exclusive, terminable licence to occupy the
land.[50]

This relief is not dependent on a claim being made and will be
applied in priority to business relief.[51]

Potentially exempt transfers

36–15   Where agricultural property is the subject of a potentially exempt
transfer,[52] that property, or some other agricultural property which
replaces it,[53] must be retained by the transferee and occupied (by
him or by another) for the purposes of agriculture, if the continued
availability of relief is to be secured against the possibility that the
transferor will die within seven years of the original transfer.[54]

---

[46] *Ibid.* s.118(3), (4).
[47] The relief is given before the deduction of any exemptions; *cf.* the former position under the
Finance Act 1975, Sched. 8, para. 1(1) (now repealed).
[48] See, as to these transitional cases, the Inheritance Tax Act 1984, s.116(2)(b), (3)–(5).
[49] *Ibid.* s.116(2) (as amended by the Finance (No. 2) Act 1992, Sched. 14, para. 4). For this
purpose, the interest of a joint tenant or tenant in common will carry the right to vacant possession
(or the right to obtain it) if the interests of all the joint tenants or tenants in common together
carry that right: *ibid.* s.116(6).
[50] As to the effect of such a licence: see *supra*, para. 10–38. And see also the *Encyclopedia of
Professional Partnerships*, Pt. 6.
[51] Inheritance Tax Act 1984, s.114(1). In the case of the deemed transfer on death, the relief is,
in effect, applied *after* the deduction of any available exemptions: *ibid.* s.39A (as inserted by the
Finance Act 1986, s.105).
[52] *Ibid.* s.3A (as inserted by the Finance Act 1986, Sched. 19, para. 1).
[53] *Ibid.* s.124B(1), (3) (as inserted by the Finance Act 1986, Sched. 19, para. 22). The
replacement property must normally be acquired within 3 years after the disposal of the original
property: *ibid.* s.124B(2)(a), (8) (as amended by the Finance Act 1994, s.247(2)).
[54] *Ibid.* ss.124A(1), (3), 124B(3) (as inserted by the Finance Act 1986, Sched. 19, para. 22).
Similarly, in the case of a chargeable transfer made within seven years of the transferor's death:
ibid. s.124A(2). If the transferee predeceases the transferor, the conditions must be satisfied on *his*
death: *ibid.* ss.124A(4), 124B(4).

Business relief

This relief is available where the whole or part of the value **36–16**
transferred by a transfer of value is attributable to the value of
"relevant business property," provided that certain conditions can be
satisfied.[55] Relevant business property includes property consisting of
a business or an interest in a business, and any land or building,
machinery or plant which immediately before the transfer was used[56]
wholly or mainly for the purposes of a business carried on by a
partnership of which the transferor was a member,[57] but does not
include a business which consists wholly or mainly of dealings in
securities, stocks or shares, land or buildings or making or holding
investments.[58]

For the relief to apply, it must be shown that the relevant business **36–17**
property was owned by the transferor throughout the two years
immediately preceding the transfer[59] or that it replaced other
property and both the original and the replacement property were so
owned for periods together comprising at least two years out of the
five years immediately preceding the transfer.[60] In the case of
replaced property, the relief will not exceed what it would have been
if the replacement had not been made and, for this purpose, changes
resulting from the formation, alteration or dissolution of a
partnership will be disregarded.[61]

Where the above conditions are satisfied, the relief is given by way **36–18**
of a percentage reduction in the value attributable to the relevant
business property.[62] The appropriate reduction is 100 per cent. in the
case of a business or an interest in a business, and 50 per cent. in the
case of any land or building, machinery or plant used for the
purposes of a business.[63] The value attributable to a business or an
interest in a business, is ascertained by valuing the assets used in the

---

[55] *Ibid.* s.104(1).

[56] User under the terms of a lease would appear to qualify.

[57] Inheritance Tax Act 1984, s.105(1). It should be noted that where relief is claimed in respect of
any land, building, machinery or plant, it is also necessary to show that the transferor's interest in
the business is itself relevant business property: *ibid.* s.105(6). Where the value of milk quota is not
reflected in the value of the land to which it is attached, it should normally qualify for business
relief: see [1993] S.T.I. 295. Any property subject to a binding contract for sale is, with two limited
exceptions, incapable of constituting relevant business property: *ibid.* s.113. See also *infra*, para.
36–20.

[58] *Ibid.* s.105(3).

[59] *Ibid.* s.106.

[60] *Ibid.* s.107(1). Ownership may apparently be traced through any number of replaced
properties.

[61] *Ibid.* s.107(2), (3).

[62] Although the relief was formerly given, in the case of the deemed transfer on death, *before* the
deduction of any available exemptions, this is no longer the position: *ibid.* s.39A (as inserted by the
Finance Act 1986, s.105).

[63] *Ibid.* s.104(1) (as amended by the Finance (No. 2) Act 1992, Sched. 14, para. 1).

business (including goodwill[64] but excluding any excepted assets[65]) reduced by the aggregate amount of any liabilities incurred for the purposes of the business.[66] The relief is applied automatically, but only to the extent that agricultural property relief is not available.[67]

Potentially exempt transfers

36–19   Where relevant business property is the subject of a potentially exempt transfer,[68] that property, or some other property which replaces it,[69] must be retained by the transferee in the form of relevant business property, if the continued availability of the relief is to be secured against the possibility that the transferor will die within seven years of the original transfer.[70]

Scope of the relief

36–20   The relief should be available in the case of most dispositions of partnership shares, provided that the investment side of the partnership business (if any) has not assumed too dominant a position. It has, however, been announced that the relief will be denied on the death of a partner if, under the terms of the partnership agreement (or some other agreement), the surviving partners are *obliged* to purchase his share.[71] In the Revenue's view, such an agreement amounts to a binding contract for the sale of the share, so that it is incapable of constituting relevant business property at the date of death.[72] An unexercised option in favour of the surviving partners is obviously not regarded in the same way,[73] but the status of automatic accruer provisions is less clear. Since the prospect of the accruer and the resulting right to any cash payment are at all times inherent in the share itself,[74] the current editor

---

[64] As to the valuation of goodwill, see *infra*, paras. 36–69, 36–70.

[65] Excepted assets, as defined in *ibid.* s.112(2), are those which have neither been used wholly or mainly for the purposes of the business throughout the whole or the last two years of the transferor's ownership nor been required for future use in the business.

[66] *Ibid.* s.110.

[67] *Ibid.* s.114(1).

[68] *Ibid.* s.3A (as inserted by the Finance Act 1986, Sched. 19, para. 1).

[69] *Ibid.* s.113B(1), (3) (as inserted by the Finance Act 1986, Sched. 19, para. 21). The replacement property must normally be acquired within 3 years after the disposal of the original property: *ibid.* s.113B(2)(a), (8) (as amended by the Finance Act 1994, s.247(1)).

[70] *Ibid.* ss.113A(1), (3), 113B(3) (as inserted by the Finance Act 1986, Sched. 19, para. 21). Similarly, in the case of a chargeable transfer made within seven years of the transferor's death: *ibid.* s.113A(2). If the transferee predeceases the transferor, the conditions must be satisfied on *his* death: *ibid.* ss.113A(4), 113B(4).

[71] See the Inland Revenue Statement of Practice (SP12/80) dated October 13, 1980 and entitled "Business Relief from Capital Transfer Tax: 'Buy and Sell Agreements' ", reproduced *infra*, paras. A6–23 *et seq.*

[72] Inheritance Tax Act 1984, s.113.

[73] See, as to such provisions *infra*, para. 36–31.

[74] See further *infra*, paras. 36–29, 36–50.

submits that such a provision cannot properly be treated as a contract for its sale, and thus business relief should be available;[75] however, this appears not to be accepted by the Capital Taxes Office.[76] In any event, the outcome is in practice likely to depend on the construction of the particular accruer provision adopted.

Other exemptions and reliefs

There are a number of other miscellaneous exemptions and reliefs **36–21** which do not appear to be of any special interest in relation to partnerships and will thus not be further referred to.[77]

3.   CHARGEABLE TRANSFERS

In considering the impact of inheritance tax on partnerships, it is **36–22** necessary to identify the possible tax charges which may result at each of the following stages in the life of a firm:

A. formation,
B. continuation,
C. the retirement of a partner,
D. the death of a partner,
E. dissolution.

A.   FORMATION OF A PARTNERSHIP

Where, as will usually be the case, the intending partners are not **36–23** already connected persons,[78] the formation of a partnership will not attract an actual or potential tax charge unless, exceptionally, one of those partners intends to confer a gratuitous benefit on another.[79] It

---

[75] See (1981) 78 L.S.Gaz. 480 (which supports this conclusion, albeit without disclosing any reasoning).

[76] See the exchange of correspondence reproduced at [1984] S.T.I. 651 *et seq.*; also *McCutcheon on Inheritance Tax* (3rd. ed.), paras. 14–31 *et seq.* and an article at (1992) 89 L.S. Gaz., November 4, p. 30. Even if the accruer provision *were* capable of amounting to a contract for the sale of the deceased partner's share, it might in theory be possible to argue that the contract does not become binding until the partner has actually died *i.e.* after the deemed disposal under the Inheritance Act 1984, s.4(1); however, such an argument will be resisted by the C.T.O., who will refer to the provisions of *ibid.* s.3(4): see [1984] S.T.I. 653, 654. And see also *infra*, para. 36–56. *Semble*, a similar point does not arise in relation to *ibid.* s.124, since relief is only denied by that section where there is a binding contract for the sale of the agricultural property itself.

[77] It should, however, be noted that woodlands relief under the Inheritance Tax Act 1984, s.125 would appear not to be available in respect of a deceased partner's share, since he is never "beneficially entitled" to any asset owned by the firm: *ibid.* s.125(1)(b). For a discussion of this problem, see Lawton, Goldberg and Fraser, *The Law of Partnership Taxation* (2nd ed.), paras. 15.024–15.026. But note also, in this context, *Gray v. I.R.C.* [1994] S.T.C. 360, 377.

[78] An incoming partner will not normally be connected with the members of an existing firm: see *infra*, para. 36–45, n. 58.

[79] Inheritance Tax Act 1984, s.10(1)(a).

follows that there will, in such circumstances, be no scope for any partner later being treated as having made a gift with a reservation.[80] On the other hand, where one or more of the partners *are* already connected,[81] a disposition of assets as between them will only be ignored for tax purposes if the partnership agreement as a whole could properly be regarded as an arm's length transaction in the absence of that connection.[82] This test will be easier to satisfy if at least one of the partners has no existing connection with the others, since it will then be possible to demonstrate that the same terms have been offered to connected and non-connected partners alike.

Particular attention must be paid to the following aspects on the formation of a partnership.

Capital and capital profits

36–24 A partner who contributes capital on his entry into a partnership will only be treated as having made a transfer of value if, under the terms of the agreement, he is effectively deprived of the whole or part of that contribution but does not receive a corresponding benefit of sufficient value to satisfy the normal arm's length test.[83] A simple example of such a case would be where the agreement requires partners to contribute capital unequally but provides that it is to be *owned* by them in equal shares.[84] Such an arrangement might, perhaps, be justified commercially by adjusting the capital and/or income profit sharing ratios in favour of the partners who thereby give up part of their contributions. How far it would be possible to rely on a *non-monetary* benefit, such as a covenant on the part of the other partners to devote their whole time to the partnership business, will depend on the particular circumstances, but there would seem to be no reason in principle why a suitable analogy should not be drawn with the estate duty decisions in *Att.-Gen. v. Boden*[85] and *Att.-Gen. v. Ralli*[86] noticed above.[87]

---

[80] There can by definition be no "gift" for the purposes of the Finance Tax Act 1986, s.102 and Sched. 20 if there is no donative intent. Note, however, that the word "gift" is not defined.

[81] Inheritance Tax Act 1984, s.270 (as amended by the Taxation of Chargeable Gains Act 1992, Sched. 10, para. 8(12)), applying and extending the Taxation of Chargeable Gains Act 1992, s.286; see also *supra*, para. 35–11.

[82] See the Inheritance Tax Act 1984, s.10(1)(b). See further *supra*, paras. 36–02 *et seq.*

[83] See *supra*, paras. 36–02 *et seq.*

[84] This may be the result if the partners have not agreed any capital sharing ratios: see the Partnership Act 1890, s.24(1), considered *supra*, paras. 17–08, 17–09. It could, of course, be argued that, even though each partner's contribution is fully recognised and preserved under the agreement, his estate is nevertheless reduced because his right to call for the return of his capital is effectively deferred until his death or retirement or the ultimate dissolution of the firm; however, the current editor considers that any such reduction would clearly fall within the Inheritance Tax Act 1984, s.10(1), *supra*, para. 36–02.

[85] [1912] 1 K.B. 539.

[86] (1936) 15 A.T.C. 523.

[87] See *supra*, paras. 36–05 *et seq.* Both were cases where the share of a deceased or retiring partner accrued to the continuing partners; see also the Irish decision of *Re Clark* (1906) 40 I.L.T. 177, considered *infra*, para. 36–30, n.8.

Any transfer of value which does arise in this way will, of course, be treated as potentially exempt unless the recipient is a company or a non-favoured trust.[88] As a result, no tax will normally be payable unless the transferor dies within seven years.[89] It should, however, be noted that it is now the Revenue practice to apply the annual exemption[90] so as to frank part of what would otherwise qualify as a potentially exempt transfer,[91] which may result in an effective loss of that exemption if the transferor survives for the full seven year period. Where it is *not* possible to follow the "potentially exempt transfer" route, gradual transfers of capital utilising the annual and normal expenditure out of income exemptions[92] may still be advantageous.[93]

Where an intending partner wishes from the outset to make gifts of **36–25** capital (and in particular where his life expectancy is in doubt), he should almost as a matter of course ensure that, under the terms of the partnership agreement, he is excluded from any share in future *capital* profits; such a provision will not in itself involve a transfer of value, since there will be no present reduction in the value of his estate, other than a loss of the prospect of future profit.[94]

The current editor submits that the Capital Taxes Office could not, **36–26** in any of the above instances, successfully argue that the transferee of the share of capital (or capital profits) has not bona fide assumed possession and enjoyment thereof or, for that matter, that he does not enjoy the share to the entire exclusion of the donor.[95] On that footing, the share will not be deemed to form part of the transferor's estate in the event of his death.[96]

---

[88] Inheritance Tax Act 1984, s.3A(1)(c), (2) (as inserted by the Finance Act 1986, Sched. 19, para. 1 and amended by the Finance Act 1987, s.96(2)).

[89] *Ibid.* s.3A(4).

[90] *Ibid.* s.19. See *supra*, para. 36–10.

[91] It is by no means clear whether this practice has any legislative authority: *cf. ibid.* ss. 3A(1)(b) and 19(3A) (as respectively inserted by the Finance Act 1986, Sched. 19, paras. 1 and 5). See further *supra*, para. 36–10 and Foster, *Inheritance Tax*, para. C3.22.

[92] *Ibid.* ss. 19–21. See *supra*, paras. 36–10, 36–11.

[93] In such a case, business relief or agricultural property relief (as to which see *supra*, paras. 36–12 *et seq.*) may also be available and can be deducted *before* applying the annual exemptions.

[94] But see, as to the possible capital gains tax consequences of such a provision, *supra*, para. 35–05, n.11. *Cf.* the position where there is an *existing* fund of capital profits: see *infra*, para. 36–47.

[95] Finance Act 1986, s.102(1). And see *Re Nichol* [1931] N.Z.L.R. 718; *Baron-Hay v. Commissioner of Probate Duties* [1968] W.A.L.R 81. *Quaere* whether, in the case of capital profits, it might be argued that it is possible to "look through" to the underlying assets producing those profits (see *Burdett-Coutts v. I.R.C.* [1960] 1 W.L.R 1027), an approach which appears to have been endorsed by the Court of Appeal in *Gray v. I.R.C.* [1994] S.T.C. 360, 377 in relation to the valuation of property on death. If the argument were sustained, there would be a clear gift with a reservation: see *Chick v. Commissioner of Stamp Duties* [1958] A.C. 435 *infra*, para. 36–42. *Cf. Munro v. Commissioner of Stamp Duties* [1934] A.C. 61 *infra*, para. 36–41. But note that the future profits have never formed part of the transferor's estate. And see also an article at (1992) 89 L.S. Gaz., May 6, p. 27.

[96] Finance Act 1986, s.102(3).

Goodwill[97]

36–27   Given that goodwill may ultimately prove to be one of the firm's most valuable assets, care must be taken to ensure that its value is not further inflated for tax purposes by the imposition of an *unnecessary* restriction on competition by outgoing partners.[98] This may be of particular importance if it is not proposed to include any provision for the accruer of goodwill on death, so that the full value of a deceased partner's share therein will form part of his estate.[99] *Per contra*, if such a provision is to be included; indeed the restriction may, in such a case, form an integral part of an arm's length transaction between the intending partners.[1] An unwanted restriction can, of course, subsequently be released or varied by agreement between the partners.

Accruers and options

36–28   A properly drawn partnership agreement will in general entitle the continuing partners to acquire an outgoing partner's share by means of an automatic accruer or the exercise of an option.[2] The inclusion of either type of provision may in certain circumstances give rise to an immediate transfer of value which will, however, normally be potentially exempt.

Accruer clauses

36–29   Where (exceptionally) the partnership agreement provides for the accruer of an outgoing partner's share without payment,[3] there would at first sight appear to be an immediate reduction in the estate of each partner who contributes capital, since he will effectively exchange his absolute entitlement to such capital for a partnership share which will automatically cease to have any value when he dies or leaves the firm.[4] However, so long as the provision is of general application, such reduction should be offset by the prospect of benefiting from the accruer of the other partners' shares, at least

---

[97] See generally, as to goodwill *supra*, paras. 10–154 *et seq.*
[98] See *infra*, paras. 36–69, 36–70. And see generally, as to such restrictions, *supra*, paras. 10–180 *et seq.*
[99] See further *infra*, para. 36–54.
[1] As in *Att.-Gen. v. Boden* [1912] 1 K.B. 539. However, it is at least arguable that the accruer provision should be left out of account in valuing the share of the deceased partner: see *infra*, para. 36–56.
[2] See, generally, as to such provisions, *supra*, paras. 10–121 *et seq.*
[3] This assumes that the outgoing partner will not even be entitled to the return of his capital contribution, which would be very rare.
[4] Where it is provided that a nominal sum will be paid to the outgoing partner (or his estate) on the accruer, it would seem that, when the share accrues, its value must equal that nominal sum. Although the current editor does not consider that the accruer provision will constitute an exclusion or restriction of the partner's right to dispose of his share for the purposes of the Inheritance Tax Act 1984, s.163(1), the contrary view is tenable: see *infra*, para. 36–56. *Quaere*, could the existence of such a provision affect the availability of business relief on the death of a partner? See further *supra*, para. 36–20.

where all the partners contribute capital and enjoy broadly similar life expectancies.[5] On this footing, there would be no transfer of value, even if the agreement as a whole does not satisfy the arm's length test under section 10(1) of the Inheritance Tax Act 1984. If, on the other hand, one of the partners is much older than the others or, by reason of ill health, has a shorter life expectancy, the existence of the accruer must reduce the value of his estate; similarly, perhaps, where all the partners are of a comparable age but some of them do *not* contribute capital. To avoid a transfer of value in such a case, it would be necessary to justify the accruer as an integral part of an arm's length transaction, by demonstrating that sufficient (but not necessarily monetary) consideration has been provided by the other partners.[6]

Where the agreement provides for a substantive payment to be **36–30** made on the accruer, there will only be scope for an immediate transfer of value (albeit potentially exempt) if that payment does not equate to the amount of the relevant partner's capital contribution or, in the case of a pre-existing partnership, the then value of his share.[7] Any shortfall must be justified on an arm's length basis in the manner described above.

The current editor submits that precisely the same reasoning applies where the entirety of a partner's share, and not merely his share of goodwill, is expressed to accrue to the continuing partners.[8]

Option clauses

If the agreement gives the continuing partners an option to acquire **36–31** an outgoing partner's share at full market value, there will prima

---

[5] Any shortfall might itself be justified under *ibid.* s.10(1).

[6] See *Att.-Gen. v. Boden* [1912] 1 K.B. 539; *Att.-Gen. v. Ralli* (1936) 15 A.T.C. 523, noticed *supra*, paras. 36–05 *et seq.*

[7] *e.g.* it is conventionally provided that an outgoing partner will be repaid his capital and current accounts, even though the partnership assets may not be revalued for the purpose; see further *supra*, paras. 10–128 *et seq.*

[8] It should, however, be noted that attempts have been made to confine the decisions in *Att.-Gen. v. Boden* [1912] 1 K.B. 539 and *Att.-Gen. v. Ralli* (1936) 15 A.T.C. 523 solely to the accruer of goodwill. The Irish case of *Re Clark* (1906) 40 I.L.T. 117 is usually cited in support of such an argument. This case did in fact turn upon the application of the Finance Act 1894, s.3 and involved facts remarkably similar to those in *Att.-Gen. v. Boden* save that, on the death of the father, not only did his share in the goodwill of the partnership business pass to his two sons without payment, but also his share in its capital, stock in trade and other assets. The Irish Court (consisting of Palles L.C.B., Johnson and Keeny JJ.) held that there was no sufficient consideration provided by the sons to support the contention that they had given full consideration in money or money's worth for the father's share. It is, however, submitted that the findings of the court were unsatisfactory: in the course of his judgment (with which the other two judges merely concurred), Palles L.C.B. referred to the obligation of the sons to give their full time and attention to the partnership business (the father not being so bound) and observed that, while this might constitute consideration for the purposes of a contract, he did "not look upon that as coming within the intention of these Acts": see *ibid.* p. 120. The detailed and carefully reasoned judgment of Hamilton J. in *Att.-Gen. v. Boden* would appear to be more convincing: see *supra*, para. 36–05.

facie be no decrease in the value of any partner's estate[9] nor any immediate transfer of value. Where, however, the option price represents anything less than the amount of a given partner's capital contribution (or, in the case of an existing firm, the market value of his share as at the date of the agreement), there would appear to be an immediate reduction in the value of his estate and he will be treated as having made a potentially exempt or other transfer of value unless that reduction is fully compensated by the prospect of exercising similar options in respect of the other partners' shares or the agreement as a whole can be justified on the usual arm's length basis.[10] The position is, in this respect, broadly comparable with that discussed above in relation to accruers.[11]

The existence of such an option will normally be reflected in any subsequent valuation of a partner's share for inheritance tax purposes.[12]

Annuities

36–32   Where the partnership agreement provides for the payment of annuities to outgoing partners or their widows or dependants, it is necessary to determine whether the inclusion of such provision, or the payment of an annuity pursuant thereto, will constitute a transfer of value, albeit potentially exempt. The relevant considerations in the case of annuities payable to outgoing partners are in fact very different to those applicable to annuities payable to widows or dependants.

Annuities payable to outgoing partners

36–33   If the annuity is payable under the terms of the partnership agreement and that agreement was itself a commercial transaction, neither the incorporation of the annuity provision nor the subsequent

---

[9] Such modest reduction in value as there may be should be capable of being justified under the Inheritance Tax Act 1984, s.10(1). Otherwise it might be franked by one of the available exemptions: see further *supra*, paras. 36–08 *et seq.* As to the application of the annual exemption to a transfer which would otherwise qualify as potentially exempt, see *supra*, para. 36–24.

[10] The amount of any potentially exempt transfer will be reduced by any available exemptions: see the preceding footnote.

[11] Thus, the principle underlying *Att.-Gen. v. Boden* [1912] 1 K.B. 539 and *Att.-Gen. v. Ralli* (1936) 15 A.T.C. 523 will apply; but note, however, the decision in *Re Clark* (1906) 40 I.L.T. 117, considered *supra*, para. 36–30, n.8.

[12] The current editor suggests that, in valuing a partnership share which is subject to an accruer, all that falls to be valued is the bundle of rights which comprise that share: see *infra*, paras. 36–50, 36–56. On the other hand, in valuing a share which is subject to an option, the provisions of the Inheritance Tax Act 1984, s.163(1) will need to be taken into account: see *infra*, paras. 36–51. 36–57.

payment of the annuity will involve a potentially exempt transfer, since the requirements of section 10(1) of the Inheritance Tax Act 1984 will be satisfied.[13] This was confirmed by the Capital Taxes Office under the capital transfer tax regime and the same principles naturally apply to inheritance tax.[14] It follows that each partner will be free to dispose of his annuity as he sees fit, *e.g.* by assigning it to his spouse,[15] without imposing the risk of liability on his co-partners.

Annuities payable to widows or dependants

The potential tax consequences of including provision in the **36–34** partnership agreement for the payment of annuities to the widows or dependants of outgoing partners vary according to whether (*a*) the annuity will be enforceable by the recipient(s) or by the deceased partner's personal representatives[16] and (*b*) consideration in money or money's worth[17] was given therefor.

If the annuity is enforceable and each partner receives full **36–35** consideration for the inclusion of the provision in the agreement, no transfer of value will be involved when the agreement is entered into[18] or when the annuity is paid.[19] On the other hand, if the annuity is unenforceable[20] or there is a total absence of consideration, the agreement itself will not involve any adverse tax consequences,[21] but each partner will inevitably make a potentially exempt transfer as and when any annuity payment is made, unless that transfer is wholly or partially franked by one of the available

---

[13] See generally *supra*, paras. 36–02 *et seq.*

[14] See the letter published at (1975) 72 L.S.Gaz. 699.

[15] And thus taking advantage of the spouse exemption: Inheritance Tax Act 1984, s.18: see *supra*, para. 36–09.

[16] See generally, as to the enforceability of annuities, *Re Miller's Agreement* [1947] Ch. 615; *Beswick v. Beswick* [1968] A.C. 58; also *supra*, paras. 10–149 *et seq.*

[17] For the purposes of the Inheritance Tax Act 1984, s.5(5).

[18] It is submitted that, in such a case, there will be no reduction in the value of any partner's estate. Although the existence of the prospective liability to pay the annuity will be taken into account in valuing each such estate, provided that the consideration is in money or money's worth (see *ibid.* s.5(5)) the reduction in value attributable thereto should be balanced by such consideration.

[19] Since the annuity will be paid pursuant to an enforceable obligation incurred for full consideration.

[20] It is generally undesirable to permit a partner's widow or dependants to enforce an annuity provision directly, since this will greatly restrict the continuing partners' freedom of action and may necessitate the widow or dependants being made parties to any subsequent variation of the partnership agreement. However, a wholly unenforceable annuity will be fairly rare in practice; it is more likely to be encountered when an annuity provision is introduced on an ad hoc basis after a partner has retired or died. Note also the income tax position, considered *supra*, paras. 34–92 *et seq.*

[21] If the annuity is unenforceable, then obviously there will be no liability and thus no reduction in the value of any partner's estate. If, on the other hand, no consideration is received for the inclusion of the annuity provision, then under the Inheritance Tax Act 1984, s.5(5), the existence of the liability will not be taken into account in valuing any such estate.

exemptions.[22] Less straightforward is the case of the enforceable annuity provision in respect of which each partner has received only *partial* consideration.[23] As in the previous case, no partner will be regarded as having made a potentially exempt transfer on entering into the agreement,[24] but it is certainly arguable that, if no other exemptions are available,[25] there will be such a transfer when the annuity is paid, at least to the extent that consideration was not given at the time of the original agreement. Whilst it should be possible to defeat such an argument by contending that the agreement as a whole constituted an arm's length bargain between the partners for the purposes of section 10(1) of the Inheritance Tax Act 1984, that contention is not without difficulty.[26]

36–36   Where it is intended to provide annuities for outgoing partners and their widows and dependants, it will generally be desirable to have separate annuities payable to each potential recipient, so as to ensure that the value of a widow's or dependant's annuity does not form part of the outgoing partner's estate in the event of his death.[27] It is also undesirable, in cases where no consideration is to be given for the annuity provision, for the annuity to be charged on any of the partnership assets, since otherwise the settlement provision contained in the Inheritance Tax Act 1984 will apply.[28]

Partnership assurance schemes

36–37   Where the partnership agreement establishes an assurance scheme, with life assurance policies being effected by each partner on terms that the policy moneys will be held on trust for the other partners,

---

[22] *e.g.* the annual and normal expenditure out of income exemptions: *ibid.* ss.19 *et seq.* See further *supra*, paras. 36–10, 36–11. As to the application of the annual exemption to transfers which would otherwise be potentially exempt, see *supra*, paras. 36–10, 36–24.

[23] This will be the most common case, since part of the consideration received for the inclusion of the annuity provision will usually consist of the value of the right to the annuity which will become comprised in the estate of each partner's wife or dependants. *Quaere*: can such consideration received by a third party be taken into account under *ibid.* s.5(5)? It is thought not.

[24] Under *ibid.* s.5(5) a liability may only be taken into account "to the extent that it was incurred for a consideration in money or money's worth." To that extent only, there should be no effective reduction in the value of any partner's estate: see *supra*, n.18. The balance of the liability, in respect of which no consideration is received, will be discounted.

[25] See *supra*, n.22.

[26] There is no doubt that the C.T.O. is prepared to accept that a partnership agreement as a whole does constitute a commercial transaction: see the letter printed at (1975) 72 L.S. Gaz. 699. However, an agreement to pay an annuity to a third party must necessarily involve an element of gratuity. In those circumstances, it might in theory be difficult to show that the inclusion of the annuity provision "was not intended, and was not made in a transaction intended, to confer any gratuitous benefit on any person": see the Inheritance Tax Act 1984, s.10(1) and, *supra*, para. 36–02. It is thought that the C.T.O. may well in practice not take this point.

[27] Where a partner (or former partner) dies, the right to the annuity must be valued immediately prior to his death, and the value of a continuing annuity will clearly be higher than an annuity ceasing on death. Where, of course, the annuity is payable in favour of the deceased partner's widow, the spouse exemption will apply: Inheritance Tax Act 1988, s.18.

[28] *Ibid.* s.43(2)(c).

then the payment of each premium will constitute a potentially exempt transfer (or, where appropriate, a chargeable transfer),[29] unless the scheme as a whole can be justified as forming part of an arm's length commercial transaction between the partners.[30] Furthermore, the trusts of the policy moneys would prima facie constitute settlements for tax purposes, thus attracting the application of either the discretionary trust or the "interest in possession" trust regime established under the Inheritance Tax Act 1984, according to the nature of those trusts.[31] It is doubtful whether the general principle that a bona fide commercial transaction does not constitute a settlement can be invoked in this context,[32] but the Capital Taxes Office is prepared by "concession" not to treat the trusts of such policy moneys as settlements provided that the policies were effected prior to September 15, 1976 and the trusts have not been varied since that date.[33] Whether a taxpayer will, by invoking the above principle, be able to establish that, as a matter of law, the same treatment can be accorded to trusts of policies *irrespective* of the date on which they were effected remains to be seen.

Other types of partnership assurance schemes[34] do not appear to give rise to any particular difficulties and thus do not merit further consideration.[35]

Property of a partner used by the firm

There is no specific provision governing the treatment of free loans **36–38** of money or other property by one partner in favour of his co-partners and such loans accordingly fall to be taxed on normal principles.[36] Thus, where an intending partner owns property which is to be used or occupied by the firm, but which is not to form part of

---

[29] See *ibid.* s.3A(1)(c), (2) (as inserted by the Finance Act 1986, Sched. 19, para. 1 and amended by the Finance (No. 2) Act 1987, s.96(2)).

[30] *i.e.* within *ibid.* s.10(1). Where that subsection does not apply, it may be possible to show that one of the normal exemptions applies: see *supra*, paras. 36–10 *et seq.* The balance of any transfer will be potentially exempt. See further, as to the application of the annual exemption to a potentially exempt transfer, *supra*, paras. 36–10, 36–24.

[31] See *ibid.* Pt. III, Chaps. II and III.

[32] See, for example, the approach adopted in *Re A.E.G. Unit Trust* [1957] Ch. 415; also *Bulmer v. I.R.C.* [1967] Ch. 145; *I.R.C. v. Plummer* [1980] A.C. 896; *I.R.C. v. Levy* [1982] S.T.C. 442; *cf. I.R.C. v. Moodie* [1993] 1 W.L.R. 266 (H.L.). Note, however, that the view is expressed in Foster, *Inheritance Tax*, para. E1.12, n.2 that the principles established in the income tax cases do not apply to inheritance tax.

[33] See Extra-Statutory Concession F10 (1994 Revision).

[34] *e.g.* under the Income and Corporation Taxes Act 1988, ss. 630 *et seq.*

[35] See generally, Foster, *Inheritance Tax*, paras. E6.36, E6.37.

[36] Early in the capital transfer tax regime, such loans were governed by the detailed provisions of the Finance Act 1976, ss.115, 116, but both sections were later repealed. However, by *ibid.* s.115(7), it was provided that such provisions should not apply to loans by a partner (including a recently retired partner) or his spouse to the firm.

its assets, he will make a potentially exempt transfer (or, where appropriate, a chargeable transfer) to the extent that the value of the consideration received falls short of the diminution in the value of his estate which results from permitting such use, unless he can show that the arrangement forms part of an arm's length transaction,[37] or that one of the available exemptions applies.[38] However, so long as he ensures that he has power to terminate the arrangement at any time, there should be no significant diminution in his estate; *per contra*, perhaps, if he expressly or impliedly binds himself to permit the firm or his co-partners to enjoy continued use or occupation for a fixed period.[39] In the latter case, any transfer of value may well involve a gift with a reservation;[40] if so, the entire value of the property may in any event continue to form part of his estate.

36–39   Where premises used by the firm are owned by *all* the partners in their personal capacities, either as joint tenants or as tenants in common, no transfer of value will be involved no matter how long such user continues since, in the absence of an ouster, one co-owner is not entitled to demand rent from another, even though that other is in occupation of the entirety of the jointly owned premises.[41] The position will be unaffected if one or more of the co-owners leaves the firm but retains his interest in the premises; difficulties will only arise in the event of a partner's (or ex-partner's) death or the admission of a new partner who does not immediately acquire some interest in the premises.[42] Different principles apply in the case of personalty.[43]

---

[37] *i.e.* within the Inheritance Tax Act 1984, s.10(1).

[38] See generally *supra*, paras. 36–08 *et seq.*

[39] As to the ways in which a firm can be permitted to use or occupy property owned by one of the partners, see *supra*, paras. 10–38, 18–33; also the *Encyclopedia of Professional Partnerships*, Pt. 6. It should be noted that the grant of a tenancy of agricultural property at a rack rent will not be treated as a transfer of value: Inheritance Tax Act 1984, s.16.

[40] Finance Act 1986, s.102, Sched. 20. Note also *ibid.* Sched. 20, para. 6 and the exchange of correspondence reproduced at (1988) 85 L.S.Gaz., June 1, pp. 49 *et seq.* And see also *infra*, paras. 36–40 *et seq.*

[41] *A.E. Jones v. F. W. Jones* [1977] 1 W.L.R. 438; *Suttill v. Graham* [1977] 1 W.L.R. 819; *Dennis v. McDonald* [1982] Fam. 63; and see *supra*, para. 5–09, n.30.

[42] Whilst a continuing or outgoing partner cannot expect any payment from the other tenants in common unless there has been an ouster, as soon as a third party is let into occupation, a free loan will potentially be made in his favour, which could result in a tax charge. Whilst the continuing partners could doubtless rely on the Inheritance Tax Act 1984, s.10(1) to negative even a potentially exempt transfer, that option will not generally be available to an outgoing partner. It would accordingly seem desirable in such circumstances for some form of payment to be made to the outgoing partner, either by the incoming partner or by the firm. Neither course is, however, likely to be entirely satisfactory: if the incoming partner makes the payment, it will prima facie not be a deductible expense; on the other hand, if the payment is made by the firm, each of the co-owning partners will strictly make a potentially exempt transfer in favour of the outgoing partner. *Quaere* whether the Revenue would seek to take such a point given the amounts likely to be involved.

[43] The principle enunciated in *A. E. Jones v. F. W. Jones* [1977] 1 W.L.R. 438 does not apply to personalty. It may thus be necessary for the firm to make a payment to the outgoing partner, so as to avoid a charge to tax being imposed upon him. The problems discussed in the preceding footnote would not appear to arise. As between themselves and the incoming partner, the continuing partners should be able to rely on the Inheritance Tax Act 1984. s.10(1).

Reservation of benefit

Where property is to be used or occupied by the firm pursuant to **36–40**
an arrangement of the type discussed above and that property or an
interest therein has been acquired by one partner from another by
way of gift[44] at any time within the previous seven years, questions of
reservation of benefit will inevitably arise, unless full consideration in
money or money's worth is given by the firm or by the donor
partner.[45]

In considering whether it can be shown that the donee partner **36–41**
bona fide assumed possession and enjoyment of the property
immediately after the gift or that, throughout the relevant seven year
period, he enjoyed the property to the entire exclusion of the donor
partner or of any benefit to him by contract or otherwise,[46] reference
can conveniently be made to three Privy Council decisions under
legislation equivalent to the old estate duty regime, from which the
present gift with a reservation concept was derived. Thus, in *Oakes v.
Commissioner of Stamp Duties of New South Wales*[47] the owner of
certain grazing land had executed a declaration of trust under which
he held the land upon trust for himself and his four children as
tenants in common in equal shares. It was held (*inter alia*) that the
mere fact that he continued to be interested in the land *qua* tenant in
common did not involve a reservation of benefit out of the beneficial
interests in that land which he had given to his children. A similar
approach was adopted in *Munro v. Commissioner of Stamp Duties*,[48]
where a father owned certain land from which he carried on business
in partnership with his sons, the firm occupying the land as his tenant
or licensee. He subsequently transferred the land to his sons by way
of gift, subject to the firm's occupation rights, and the firm thereafter
continued in occupation as before. The Privy Council held that there
was no reservation of benefit but rather an absolute gift of a limited
interest in the land, *i.e.* the freehold subject to the firm's subsisting
rights of occupation. The principle underlying both of these decisions

---

[44] Finance Act 1986, s.102(1). The word "gift" is not defined. It should be noted that the section
applies only where the original gift was made after March 18, 1986: *ibid.*
[45] *Ibid.* Sched. 20, para. 6(1)(a).
[46] *Ibid.* s.102(1)(a), (b); see further [1993] S.T.I. 1409 and an article at (1992) 89 L.S. Gaz., May
6, p.27. Note the limited statutory exception in the case of land set out in *ibid.* Sched. 20, para.
6(1)(b).
[47] [1954] A.C. 57.
[48] [1934] A.C. 61. *Cf. Re Nichols* [1975] 1 W.L.R. 534. And see *Re Nichol* [1931] N.Z.L.R. 718;
Baron-Hay v. Commissioner of Probate Duties [1968] W.A.L.R. 81. Although the decision in
Kildrummy (Jersey) Ltd. v. I.R.C. [1990] S.T.C. 657 should, perhaps, be noted in this context, it
seems doubtful to what extent (if at all) it is applicable under English law: see (1991) 88 L.S. Gaz.,
July 10, p. 36; (1992) 89 L.S. Gaz., May 6, p.31.

has effectively been accepted by the Inland Revenue as applicable to inheritance tax.[49]

36–42   By way of contrast, in *Chick v. Commissioner of Stamp Duties*,[50] a father had transferred certain land to one of his sons by way of gift. He subsequently entered into partnership with that son and another son, it being agreed that the partnership business should be carried on on the partners' respective landholdings. The Privy Council held that, during the requisite period, the father was not excluded from possession and enjoyment of the land which he had given to his son, even though he provided full consideration for his subsequent occupation thereof, in the form of the land which he made available for occupation by the firm. Although such a result could not be reached under the present legislation, since there is a statutory exception where occupation is retained or assumed for full consideration in money or money's worth,[51] the decision remains a stark warning of the attendant dangers where such consideration is not, for whatever reason, provided.

36–43   Where there is a gift with a reservation and the reserved benefit subsequently terminates during the lifetime of the donor partner, *e.g.* on his retirement, he will be treated as having made a potentially exempt transfer at that stage;[52] if the benefit terminates by reason of his death, the property will be treated as forming part of his estate.[53] Where a charge is imposed, agricultural property or business relief should in general be available.[54]

B.   Continuation of a Partnership

36–44 When considering the tax position during the currency of a partnership, it is necessary to distinguish between a transfer of value made by all the partners in favour of a third party with whom they are not connected,[55] and a transfer of value made by one partner in favour of another.

---

[49] See the letter reproduced in (1988) 85 L.S.Gaz., June 1, p. 50.

[50] [1958] A.C. 435.

[51] Finance Act 1986, Sched. 20, para. 6(1)(a). This provision mirrors the Finance Act 1959, s.35(2). See also the letter from the Inland Revenue reproduced in (1988) 85 L.S. Gaz., June 1, p.50; also [1993] S.T.I. 1410 and an article at (1992) 89 L.S. Gaz., May 6, p.31.

[52] Finance Act 1986, s.102(4). And see [1993] S.T.I. 1410.

[53] *Ibid.* s.102(3).

[54] *Ibid.* Sched. 20, para. 8 (as amended).

[55] See as to the meaning of "connected persons," the Inheritance Tax Act 1984, s.270 (as amended by the Taxation of Chargeable Gains Act 1992, Sched. 10, para. 8(12)) applying and extending the Taxation of Chargeable Gains Act 1992, s.286. See also *supra*, para. 36–03.

Where a gratuitous transfer is effectively made by the firm (*i.e.* all **36–45** the partners acting together), which reduces the value of each partner's share,[56] tax will be chargeable on normal principles, unless (as will usually be the case) each partner's transfer qualifies in the first instance as potentially exempt.[57] If an incoming partner is not already connected with the existing partners,[58] the tax considerations on his admission to the firm will be broadly identical to those discussed in relation to the formation of a partnership.

On the other hand, when considering transfers between the **36–46** partners, it must be borne in mind that they and their spouses will be connected persons "except in relation to acquisitions or disposals of partnership assets pursuant to bona fide commercial arrangements."[59] Where, as will usually be the case,[60] the partners are treated as connected, if the requirements of section 10(1) of the Inheritance Tax Act 1984 are to be satisfied, it must be shown that the transfer was made without any gratuitous intent, and was "such as might be expected to be made in a transaction at arm's length between persons not connected with each other."[61]

The tax consequences of a re-arrangement of the capital sharing **36–47** ratios, and of the introduction into the partnership agreement of provision for the payment of annuities to outgoing partners and their widows or dependants have already been considered in relation to the formation of partnership, and reference should be made thereto.[62] However, one point which is frequently overlooked on the admission

---

[56] On a true analysis, no partner has an immediate or ascertainable beneficial interest in any asset owned by the firm, but merely a right to a proportionate part of the surplus remaining after the realisation of all the partnership assets, and the payment of all the partnership debts and liabilities: see generally, *supra*, paras. 19–01 *et seq.* Accordingly, when an asset owned by the firm is the subject of a gratuitous transfer, the value transferred by each partner will be the amount by which his share has been devalued, subject to the availability of agricultural property or business relief: see *supra*, paras. 36–13 *et seq.* Note, however, that in *Gray v. I.R.C.* [1994] S.T.C. 360, 377, the Court of Appeal held that partners must be treated as owning undivided shares in the partnership assets, at least for valuation purposes.

[57] Inheritance Tax Act 1984, s.3A (as inserted by the Finance Act 1986, Sched. 19, para. 1). And see as to the availability of agricultural property/business relief, *supra*, paras. 36–15, 36–19.

[58] This will generally be the position, unless he is related to one or more of the existing partners within the meaning of the Taxation of Chargeable Gains Act 1992, s.286(2), (8), as extended by the Inheritance Tax Act 1984, s.270.

[59] Taxation of Chargeable Gains Act 1992, s.286(4). However, this exception will only apply where the partners are *not* otherwise related.

[60] Since the transfers will rarely concern "partnership assets" (in which no partner has an immediate or ascertainable beneficial interest: see *supra*, para. 36–45, n.56), but will rather concern partnership shares, which are by definition *not* partnership assets: see further Lawton, Goldberg and Fraser, *The Law of Partnership Taxation* (2nd. ed.), para. 14.074. *Cf.* the capital gains tax position, where each partner is treated as having a direct interest in each partnership asset: see *supra*, para. 35–04.

[61] Inheritance Tax Act 1984, s.10(1)(b). The test would appear to be an objective one and the burden of satisfying it is imposed on the taxpayer.

[62] See *supra*, paras. 36–24 *et seq.*, 36–32 *et seq.*

of a new partner to an existing firm is the ownership not of the firm's capital but of its capital *profits*. Such profits will in general be divisible in the ordinary profit sharing ratios,[63] so that an incoming partner who becomes entitled to a share of profits may at the same time automatically become entitled to a share of any existing unrealised capital profits. Therein lies the potential for a wholly inadvertent transfer of value: if the assets of the firm appear in its balance sheet at a historic, written down value, there may be a very substantial "hidden" fund of capital profits so that the acquisition of even a small share therein might result in a significant reduction in the value of the existing partners' shares.[64] To avoid such a consequence, it will be necessary either to justify the partnership agreement as a whole as an arm's length transaction,[65] or to ensure that the existing partners reserve those capital profits to themselves.[66]

36–48   It has been seen[67] that the inclusion in a partnership agreement of a provision for the automatic accruer of the share of an outgoing partner or an option in favour of the continuing partners to acquire such share may have possible tax implications. Similar considerations will arise where either type of provision is introduced by way of variation of an existing agreement: on the introduction of an automatic accruer, each partner will exchange the bundle of rights which comprise his share for a bundle of rights which will become valueless in the event of his departure from the firm,[68] whilst on the introduction of an option exercisable at anything less than market value, there will be an immediate reduction in the value of each partner's share.[69] In either case, a potentially exempt transfer (or,

---

[63] See *supra*, para. 17–05.

[64] Where the capital profit sharing ratios are *deliberately* varied without at the same time altering the income profit sharing ratios, it might be argued that a partner whose capital profit share is reduced has made a gift with a reservation for the purposes of the Finance Act 1986, s.102(1): see an article at (1992) 89 L.S. Gaz. 27. Such an argument presupposes a direct correlation between a partner's income and capital profit sharing entitlements in all cases which is, in the current editor's view, wholly unjustified. Nevertheless, there may be cases in which such a correlation does exist, *i.e.* where the majority of the profits are produced by the firm's capital assets without any expenditure of time or effort by the partners. *Quaere* whether there would be a gift with a reservation if the incoming partner were to take on liability for a share of the firm's existing debts as part of such an arrangement. The current editor believes that, in most cases, the Inheritance Tax Act 1984, s.10(1) would apply so as to negative any donative intent.

[65] And thus within *ibid.* s.10(1): see further *supra*, paras. 36–02 *et seq.*

[66] This can be done in one of two ways: specific capital profit sharing ratios can be introduced with respect of certain assets or those assets can be revalued and the surplus on the revaluation credited to the capital/current accounts of the existing partners. However, the latter course may have adverse capital gains tax implications: see *supra*, para. 35–17. There is seemingly no objection to the incoming partner being given a share of *future* capital profits: see as to this, *supra*, para. 36–25.

[67] See *supra*, para. 36–28 *et seq.*

[68] Where a payment falls to be made in respect of the accruer, the bundle of rights comprised in the outgoing partner's share will seemingly assume the value of that payment. The current editor submits that the accruer provision will *not* constitute an exclusion or restriction of the partner's right to dispose of his share for the purposes of the Inheritance Tax Act 1984, s.163(1): see further *infra*, para. 36–56.

[69] See *supra*, para. 36–31.

where appropriate, a chargeable transfer) will be made by each partner when the accruer or option is first introduced, unless it can be shown:

(a) that the reduction in the value of his estate is offset by corresponding benefits conferred on him as part of the variation, e.g. the prospect of benefiting from an accruer/option to acquire the other partners' shares or, perhaps, compensation in the form of a new annuity entitlement;[70]

(b) that the variation can be brought within section 10(1) of the Inheritance Tax Act 1984;[71] or

(c) (where relevant) that one of the available exemptions applies.[72]

The effect of such a provision on a subsequent valuation of a partner's share is considered further below.[73]

C. The Retirement of a Partner

Where, as will often be the case, the agreement provides for the **36–49** partnership to continue following a partner's retirement[74] and for his share to be acquired at market value by the continuing partners,[75] no tax considerations will arise, unless the outgoing partner forgoes some part of his accrued entitlement. Of course, if he chooses to make a gratuitous assignment of his share to the continuing partners, an actual or potential charge to tax will be imposed on normal principles.[76]

More complex is the situation where, under the terms of the agreement,[77] the continuing partners are entitled to acquire the outgoing partner's share, either by way of automatic accruer or

---

[70] See supra, paras. 36–29 et seq.

[71] See supra, para. 36–02.

[72] See supra, para. 36–08 et seq.

[73] See infra, paras. 36–50, 36–51, 36–55 et seq.

[74] Where there is no such provision, the partnership may be dissolved on the retirement, unless it is argued that the concept of retirement necessarily implies the continuation of the firm: see further supra, paras. 23–180, 24–14. As to the possible tax consequences of a dissolution, see infra, para. 36–61. Similar considerations may conceivably arise in the case of a partner's expulsion or compulsory retirement.

[75] See generally, as to such provisions, supra, paras. 10–121 et seq. And see also supra, para. 36–28.

[76] In an appropriate case, the outgoing partner will be able to take advantage of any available exemptions or reliefs: see supra, paras. 36–08 et seq. As to business relief, see the Inland Revenue Statement of Practice (SP12/80) dated October 13, 1980 reproduced infra, paras A6–23 et seq.; also [1984] S.T.I. 651 et seq. See further supra, para. 36–20.

[77] This will include any collateral agreement, or subsequent deed of variation: see for example, Att.-Gen. v. Ralli (1936) 15 A.T.C. 523, where the provision for accruer was introduced by a collateral agreement.

option, for a consideration which represents *less* than the market value of that share.[78]

Accruer clauses

36–50   The current editor submits that, on a true analysis, no tax consequences should arise in such a case, since the retirement is merely an occasion on which a decrease in the value of the outgoing partner's share and an increase in the value of the continuing partners' shares, which were at all times respectively inherent in those shares, take effect.[79] Thus, whilst there is an admitted reduction in the value of the outgoing partner's estate on his retirement, he cannot be treated as having made a potentially exempt (or chargeable) transfer.[80]

Option clauses

36–51   If no consideration in money or money's worth was originally given for the grant of the option, its existence cannot be taken into account when valuing the outgoing partner's share at the date of exercise.[81] As a result, where the option price remains pegged at a low figure but the market value of the share has increased significantly since the date of grant, an exercise of the option may involve the outgoing partner incurring a *further* actual or potential charge to tax, over and above that incurred when he originally entered into the agreement.[82] On the other hand, where, as will normally be the case,[83] consideration was given for the grant of the option, its existence will be reflected in any valuation of the outgoing partner's share;[84] as a result, the value of his share at the date of exercise is likely to approximate closely to the option price.[85]

---

[78] This is a fairly common scenario, particularly in professional partnerships where an outgoing partner tends to receive no more than the balance standing to the credit of his current and capital accounts at the date of his departure.

[79] The current editor considers that an accruer provision does not constitute an exclusion or restriction of the outgoing partners's right to dispose of his share for the purposes of the Inheritance Act 1984, s.163(1), although just such a view is advanced in *Dymond's Capital Taxes*, paras. 9.215, 9.227. See also *infra*, para. 36–56.

[80] Since there will be no "disposition" for the purpose of *ibid.* s.3(1). As to the possible tax consequences of entering into an agreement containing an accruer provision, see *supra*, paras. 36–29, 36–30.

[81] *Ibid.* s.163(1)(a). An allowance will, however, be made for any value transferred at the date of grant: *ibid.* s.163(1)(b). Moreover, the option will only be left out of account on the *first* chargeable transfer after that date: *ibid.* s.163(1), (3).

[82] Where the market value has remained approximately constant, no charge should be incurred, since the value transferred as a result of the exercise of the option will already have suffered tax: *ibid.* s.163(1)(b). See further, as to the original transfer, *supra*, para. 36–31.

[83] *i.e.* where the original agreement constituted an arms's length transaction with no gratuitous element, for the purposes of *ibid.* s.10(1).

[84] *Ibid.* s.163(1)(a).

[85] The current editor submits that the value of the share will reduce progressively as the retirement date, and thus the date of exercise, approaches.

Annuities

If an annuity is payable to the outgoing partner under the terms of **36–52** an agreement which constituted an arm's length transaction within section 10(1) of the Inheritance Tax Act 1984,[86] no actual or potential charge to tax will arise.[87] If, however, the continuing partners voluntarily decide to pay such an annuity following a partner's retirement, they will each be regarded as making a series of potentially exempt transfers, unless those payments are franked by any available exemptions[88] or they are supported by full consideration, *e.g.* where the outgoing partner takes an annuity in lieu of a part of his share.[89]

Continuing use of outgoing partner's property

Where the outgoing partner, either alone or jointly with his co- **36–53** partners, owns property which is used or occupied by the firm, continuance of that arrangement following his retirement may involve possible tax consequences, the nature of which have already been discussed.[90]

D. The Death of a Partner

On the death of a partner, his share will normally[91] form part of his **36–54** estate, and tax will be charged on normal principles by reference to the transfer of value deemed to have been made immediately prior to his death.[92] His estate will also be treated as comprising any property which is subject to a reservation of benefit in his favour,[93] as well as the appropriate percentage of the value transferred by any potentially exempt transfers made within the previous seven years.[94] The usual

---

[86] See generally *supra*, paras. 36–02 *et seq.*, 36–33.

[87] See the letter from the Revenue reproduced at (1975) 72 L.S. Gaz. 699.

[88] *e.g.* the annual or normal expenditure out of income exemption: see *supra*, paras. 36–10, 36–11. As to the application of the annual exemption to transfers which are potentially exempt, see *supra*, paras 36–10, 36–24.

[89] See generally *supra*, para. 36–35. Such an annuity would not be deductible by the continuing partners for income tax purposes, and would be treated as investment income in the hands of the recipient: see *supra*, paras. 34–92 *et seq.* Moreover, capital gains tax would be chargeable by reference to the value of the right to the annuity: see *supra*, paras. 35–24 *et seq.*

[90] See *supra*, paras. 36–38, 36–39.

[91] Unless, of course, the deceased partner had disposed of his share during his lifetime. The position where the share is subject to an automatic accruer is considered further below, but note the views expressed in Lawton Goldberg and Fraser, *The Law of Partnership Taxation* (2nd ed.), paras. 14.084 *et seq.*

[92] Inheritance Tax Act 1984, s.4(1). Note, in this context, the decision in *Gray v. I.R.C.* [1994] S.T.C. 360, *infra*, para. 36–72.

[93] Finance Act 1986, s.102(3).

[94] Inheritance Tax Act 1984, s.3A(4), 7(4) (as respectively inserted by the Finance Act 1986, Sched. 19, paras. 1, 2).

exemptions and reliefs will be available, *i.e.* principally, in this context, business relief[95] and/or (if appropriate) agricultural property relief.[96]

Valuation of share

36–55   Although this subject is considered more fully elsewhere in this chapter,[97] it is of particular relevance in the present context to note the effect of an accruer or option provision contained in the partnership agreement.[98]

Accruer clauses

36–56   Consistently with the views already expressed,[99] the current editor considers that the share of a deceased partner which is expressed to accrue to the surviving partners without payment[1] will automatically cease to have any value on his death.[2] It follows that, when the share falls to be valued for tax purposes immediately *prior* to the date of death, account must be taken of the limited nature of the rights comprised therein: on that footing, given the imminence of death, the share can have no significant value.[3] This argument is in no way dependent on the provisions of section 171 of the Inheritance Tax Act 1984 (which permits account to be taken of changes in value occurring *by reason* of the death), but is framed solely by reference to limitations which are at all times inherent in the share itself.[4] Nevertheless, it could, perhaps, be argued[5] that the accruer constitutes an exclusion or restriction of the deceased partner's right to dispose of his share, so that its existence can only be taken into account to the extent that consideration was given for its introduction.[6] Therein lies a possible danger in cases where it cannot

---

[95] See *supra*, paras. 36–16 *et seq.* But note, that the C.T.O. may seek to deny the availability of the relief, depending on the terms of the agreement: see *supra*, para. 36–20.

[96] See *supra*, paras. 36–13 *et seq.*

[97] See *infra*, paras. 36–67 *et seq.*

[98] As to the position of a partner entering into an agreement containing such a provision, see *supra*, paras. 36–28 *et seq.*

[99] See *supra*, paras. 36–29, 36–50.

[1] It should make no difference whether the accruer provision is contained in the original agreement or introduced by way of subsequent variation; note, however, the views expressed in Lawton, Goldberg and Fraser, *The Law of Partnership Taxation* (2nd ed.), paras. 14.084 *et seq. Quaere* will business relief be available in respect of the share? See *supra*, para. 36–20.

[2] The potential decrease in value on the death is inherent in the bundle of rights which comprise the share. It is submitted that the view adopted by some commentators, to the effect that an accruer provision introduces an element of survivorship into the partnership, is misconceived.

[3] Where a payment falls to be made to the deceased partner's estate on the accruer, the value of the share immediately prior to the death should closely approximate the value of the payment.

[4] This is perhaps the mirror image of an argument advanced by the C.T.O. as set out at [1984] S.T.I. 653, 654. As to the difficulties presented by s.171, see *infra*, n.7.

[5] See for example, *Dymond's Capital Taxes*, paras. 9.215, 9.227.

[6] Inheritance Tax Act 1984, s.163(1).

be shown that the original agreement constituted an arm's length transaction between the partners.[7]

Option clauses

Where the surviving partners have an option to acquire a deceased **36–57** partner's share, a valuation of that share immediately prior to the date of death will only reflect the existence of the option to the extent that consideration was given for it.[8] In the absence of any such consideration, the option will be disregarded but an allowance will be made for any value transferred when it was originally granted.[9]

Other valuation considerations

In accordance with the normal statutory rule,[10] when a deceased **36–58** partner's share is valued immediately prior to his death, account will be taken of any increase or decrease in value resulting therefrom, other than a decrease attributable to the termination of an interest on his death or the passing of an interest by survivorship.[11] This may be of considerable importance where the death of a partner will have an adverse impact on the firm's business, *e.g.* if its goodwill is largely dependent upon his continued involvement.[12]

Annuities

Where, on the death of a partner, an annuity becomes payable to **36–59** his widow or dependants, there should be no adverse tax consequences so far as concerns the surviving partners, so long as

---

[7] This will be especially in point where the intending partners were already connected persons and thus had difficulty satisfying the conditions of *ibid.* s.10(1): see generally *supra*, paras. 36–02, 36–45. Even if the accruer provision *were* to amount to an exclusion or restriction of a partner's right to dispose of his share, so that its existence must be left out of account by virtue of *ibid.* s.163(1), it could still arguably be taken into account indirectly under *ibid.* s.171, on the basis that a decrease in the value of the share will occur on the death when the accruer operates. It should, however, be noted that a decrease in value cannot be taken into account under that section if it consists of "the termination on the death of any interest": *ibid.* s.171(2). Whether it can be said that a partner's interest in his share terminates as a result of an accruer is not clear. In *Att.-Gen. v. Boden* [1912] 1 K.B. 539, Hamilton J. held that the father's interest in goodwill, which was subject to such a provision, was an "interest ceasing on the death" for the purposes of the Finance Act 1894, s.2(1)(b): see *ibid.* p. 556. The decision in *Att.-Gen. v. Ralli* (1936) 15 A.T.C. 523 is not inconsistent therewith: see *ibid.* pp. 526–527. However, the judgment of Hamilton J. was criticised by the Privy Council in *Perpetual Executors & Trustees Association of Australia Ltd. v. Commissioner of Taxes of Australia* [1954] A.C. 114, 131. The current editor submits that the application of s.171 can be supported on one of two bases, namely (a) that the deceased partner's interest does not terminate on death, but merely becomes valueless (or, where a payment falls to be made on the accruer, merely assumes the value of that payment), or (b) that his interest in the share does not terminate but the share itself ceases to exist. It must, however, be appreciated that the *Boden* decision does present considerable difficulties with regard to either argument.

[8] Inheritance Tax Act 1984, s.163(1)(a). See also *supra*, para. 36–51.

[9] *Ibid.* s.163(1)(b).

[10] *Ibid.* s.171(1). And see *supra*, para. 36–56, n.7.

[11] *Ibid.* s.171(2).

[12] See further, as to the valuation of goodwill, *infra*, paras. 36–69, 36–70.

they can show that the annuity is enforceable and that either (1) full consideration was received by each partner when the annuity provision was originally introduced or (2) the agreement under which the annuity is to be paid constituted an arm's length transaction between the partners.[13] If those conditions cannot be satisfied,[14] each annuity payment will involve a potentially exempt transfer by the surviving partners.[15]

Partnership assurance schemes

36–60 Where the firm has established such a scheme, under which each partner insures his own life for the benefit of his co-partners,[16] it must be ascertained whether the trusts of the policy moneys constitute a settlement for tax purposes[17] and whether each of the other partners has an interest in possession therein.[18] If so, then the estate of a deceased partner will be treated as comprising that part of each policy in which his interest in possession subsisted.[19]

E. DISSOLUTION OF A PARTNERSHIP

36–61 It is the current editor's view that substantial tax complications are unlikely to arise on the dissolution of a partnership, which will normally involve a realisation of its assets, the discharge of its liabilities, and the payment to each partner of his full entitlement by way of a distribution of surplus cash or, in an appropriate case, of assets *in specie*.[20] On that basis, no reduction in the value of a partner's estate should be anticipated. Of course, if one partner gratuitously transfers or forgoes some part of his entitlement in favour of another, tax will be chargeable on normal principles.

It might, however, usefully be observed that goodwill is often of little or no value on a dissolution.[21]

---

[13] See the letter from the Revenue reproduced in (1975) 72 L.S. Gaz. 699. But note the difficulties discussed *supra*, para. 36–35, n.26.

[14] See *supra*, para. 36–35.

[15] A transfer will only be treated as potentially exempt to the extent that no other exemptions are available, *e.g.* the annual or normal expenditure out of income exemption: see *supra*, paras. 36–10, 36–11. But note that the position is less than clear so far as concerns the annual exemption: see *supra*, paras. 36–10, 36–24.

[16] See *supra*, para. 36–37.

[17] Where the policies were effected as part of a commercial transaction prior to September 15, 1976, and the trusts thereto have not been varied since that date, such trusts will not be treated as creating a settlement: see Extra-Statutory Concession F10 (1994 Revision). And see, as to the meaning of "settlement" for these purposes, the Inheritance Tax Act 1984, s.43(2); also *supra*, para. 36–37.

[18] See *ibid*. ss.49, 50.

[19] *Ibid*. ss.4(1), 5(1), 49(1). *Ibid*. s.167(1) does not apply on death: *ibid*. s.167(2)(a).

[20] See the Partnership Act 1890, ss.39, 44; also generally *supra*, paras. 19–29 *et seq.*, 25–39.

[21] *i.e.* where the valuation is on a "break up" basis: see *infra*, para. 36–68.

4. FOREIGN ELEMENT

Excluded property

Tax is actually or potentially chargeable in respect of all gratuitous **36–62** transfers of assets made by persons who are domiciled in the United Kingdom,[22] wherever such assets are situated. Thus, where a member of a foreign firm is domiciled in the United Kingdom, he will be chargeable in respect of any disposition which has the effect of reducing the value of his share.[23] Where, however, a non-domiciled individual owns property situated outside the United Kingdom, that property will be treated as "excluded property,"[24] and will be left out of account in computing the value transferred by an *inter vivos* disposition[25] or on the deemed transfer on death.[26] It is accordingly of considerable importance to ascertain whether a non-domiciled partner's share does indeed constitute excluded property.

Situs of a partnership share

The situs of a partnership share will largely depend on the nature **36–63** of the individual partners' interests in its assets. It has already been seen[27] that, under English law, a partner does in one sense have a beneficial interest in the capital and assets of the firm but that it should, on a true analysis, be expressed in terms of his right to a proportion of the net surplus remaining after realisation of all the partnership assets and payment of all its debts and liabilities. As a result, if the proper law governing the partnership[28] is English law or, in this respect, is similar to English law, the share will be treated as situate in the country in which the firm's principal place of business is located.[29] However, it should be noted that a firm which carries on a number of distinct businesses in different countries may conceivably have more than one principal place of business.[30]

---

[22] Certain persons are deemed to have a U.K. domicile for the purposes of the tax: Inheritance Tax Act 1984, s.267 (as amended by the Finance Act 1993, s.208(3), Sched. 23, Pt. V.). See generally *McCutcheon on Inheritance Tax* (3rd ed.), paras. 15–10 *et seq.*

[23] It does not for this purpose matter that the share is treated as situate outside the U.K.

[24] Inheritance Tax Act 1984, s.6(1).

[25] *Ibid.* s.3(2).

[26] *Ibid.* s.5(1).

[27] See *supra*, paras. 19–01 *et seq.* Note, however, that in *Gray v. I.R.C.* [1994] S.T.C. 360, 377, the Court of Appeal rejected an analysis of a partnership share in these terms when valuing it for the purposes of capital transfer tax on death.

[28] As to the method of determining the proper law governing a partnership agreement, see the Contracts (Applicable Laws) Act 1990 and Dicey and Morris, *The Conflict of Laws* (12th ed.) Chap. 32. Briefly, the proper law will be the system of law which the parties have chosen to govern their agreement or, where there is no such clear intention, the system of law with which the agreement is most closely connected.

[29] *Laidlay v. Lord Advocate* (1890) 15 App. Cas. 468; *Beaver v. Master in Equity of Victoria* [1895] A.C. 251 (P.C.); *Commissioner of Stamp Duties v. Salting* [1907] A.C. 449.

[30] *Beaver v. Master in Equity of Victoria, supra.* However, the mere fact that the firm carries on business in more than one country does not *ipso facto* mean that the business should be so treated: this will be a question of fact in each case.

36–64 Where the proper law governing the partnership gives each partner a *direct* interest in the firm's assets, it will be necessary to consider each item of property separately, in order to ascertain the situs of a partner's share therein.[31] In the case of an interest in land, the situs will depend on where the land itself lies,[32] whereas the situs of an interest in a chattel will be determined according to its current location.[33] Goodwill is normally located in the same place as the firm's principal place of business.[34]

36–65 It obviously follows from the foregoing that a non-domiciled partner in a foreign partnership who nevertheless has an identifiable beneficial interest in land situate in the United Kingdom will be chargeable to tax in respect of any disposition affecting the value of that interest.

Gift by foreign firm of United Kingdom property

36–66 Where a foreign firm makes a gratuitous disposition of property situate in the United Kingdom, thereby reducing the value of each partner's share, a partner will seemingly be treated as having made a transfer of value to the extent of such reduction, notwithstanding the fact that his share is not, for the reasons discussed above, situated in the United Kingdom.[35]

5. VALUATION AND ADMINISTRATION

Valuation of partnership shares

36–67 The value of a partnership share, like any other asset, will be the price which that share might reasonably be expected to fetch if sold in the open market at the relevant time.[36] However, it has already been seen that there are a number of complications in and about the valuation process, other than those presented by the peculiar nature

---

[31] As to the situs of particular items of property, see generally, Dicey and Morris, *The Conflict of Laws* (12th ed.), Chap. 22, and especially pp. 922 *et seq*.

[32] *Re Hoyles* [1911] 1 Ch. 179; *Re Berchtold* [1923] 1 Ch. 192; *Philipson-Stow v. I.R.C.* [1961] A.C. 727; *Haque v. Haque (No. 2)* (1965) 114 C.L.R. 98.

[33] *Gammell v. Sewell* (1860) 5 H. & N. 728; *Re Haig* (1922) 17 A.T.C. 635.

[34] *I.R.C. v. Muller & Co.'s Margarine Ltd.* [1901] A.C. 217; *B.J. Reuter Co. Ltd. v. Mulhens* [1954] Ch. 50, 94–95, *per* Romer L.J.

[35] Since the property transferred will not be "excluded property" for the purposes of the Inheritance Tax Act 1984, s.6(1). For a discussion of this and another somewhat anomalous problem (*i.e.* a charge to tax imposed upon a non-domiciled partner whose share is situate outside the U.K. when the firm makes a gift of assets situate *outside* the U.K.) see Lawton, Goldberg and Fraser, *The Law of Partnership Taxation* (2nd ed.), paras. 15.045, 15.046.

[36] *Ibid.* s.160. The price will not, however, suffer any reduction on the ground that the whole property is to be placed on the market at the same time: *ibid*. It is considered that all valuations must take place on this statutory basis, even where some other basis is established under the agreement: see *Gray v. I.R.C.* [1994] S.T.C. 360, noticed *infra*, para. 36–72; also the estate duty cases of *I.R.C. v. Crossman* [1937] A.C. 26 and *Lynall v. I.R.C.* [1972] A.C. 680.

of the share itself.[37] Thus, an exclusion or restriction on the right to dispose of a share may only be taken into account to the extent that its introduction was supported by consideration, although due allowance will be made for any value transferred at that time.[38] Further, where the valuation falls to be made immediately prior to the death of a partner,[39] account must be taken of any increase or decrease in value which may result from the death.[40]

The actual valuation of a share will normally be by reference to the **36–68** value of the underlying assets of the firm, which will in turn depend upon whether the valuation is made on a "going concern" or "break up" basis.[41] Whilst a detailed consideration of the principles governing such valuations lies outside the scope of this work, some reference should be made to the valuation of goodwill, which may be one of the firm's most important assets,[42] as well as to the value of agricultural tenancies.

Valuation of goodwill

The value of goodwill is dependent on a number of factors. First **36–69** and foremost, the goodwill itself may be of such a nature as to attract a high or a low value, *e.g.* the goodwill of a firm of medical practitioners providing general medical services under the National Health Service cannot lawfully be sold[43] and therefore has no disposable value. Equally, whatever the type of business, a large proportion of the firm's goodwill may rely on the continued presence of a particular partner. A further factor may be the presence or absence of a restriction on competition by outgoing partners: if such partners can immediately set up a similar business in the same area as the firm, this may significantly depress the value of its goodwill.[44]

Where goodwill has a value, the actual method of valuation will be **36–70** determined by the size of the business and the type of goodwill involved. Certain trades and professions have particular customary methods of valuing goodwill,[45] whereas, in valuing the goodwill of a

---

[37] It has, for example, been noted that a share may comprise a bundle of rights with inherent limitations, which must be reflected in any valuation: see *supra*, para. 36–56.

[38] Inheritance Tax Act 1984, s.163, considered *supra*, paras. 36–51, 36–56 *et seq.*

[39] *i.e.* pursuant to *ibid.* s.4(1).

[40] Inheritance Tax Act 1984, s.171, considered *supra*, para. 36–58.

[41] Thus, on a "break up" basis, goodwill is unlikely to have any significant value (and may, indeed, be completely valueless) and certain assets used by the firm may fall to be ignored: see, for example, *Eardley v. Broad*, *The Times*, April 28, 1970 and (1970) 215 E.G. 823. And see, generally, *Dymond's Capital Taxes*, paras. 23.430 *et seq.*

[42] See generally, as to goodwill, *supra*, paras. 10–154 *et seq.*

[43] National Health Service Act 1977, s.54, Sched. 10. This prohibition has not, however, extinguished the goodwill: *Whitehill v. Bradford* [1952] Ch. 236; *Kerr v. Morris* [1987] Ch. 90. But see *supra*, paras. 6–05 *et seq.*, 23–198.

[44] See generally, as to such restrictions and the protection of goodwill in the absence thereof, *supra*, paras. 10–168 *et seq.*, 10–180 *et seq.*

[45] See Foster, *Inheritance Tax*, para. H3.51.

large firm, one of the two recognised methods, *i.e.* "total capitalisation"[46] and "super profits,"[47] will normally be adopted. All the circumstances must be considered before it is possible to determine which method will be appropriate in a given case and reference should be made to the standard works in relation thereto.[48]

Valuation of agricultural tenancies

36–71   An agricultural tenancy will rarely be freely assignable,[49] the Capital Taxes Office insist that, consistently with the principles enunciated in *I.R.C. v. Crossman*,[50] such a tenancy may have a substantial value. This approach is well exemplified by the decision in *Baird's Executors v. I.R.C.*,[51] albeit that the case concerned the status of such a tenancy in Scotland.[52] Whilst there must be some doubt as to the value which could properly be ascribed to such a tenancy on the death of a *sole* tenant,[53] a tenancy which is vested in the names of up to four partners but held on behalf of the firm would clearly have a market value.[54]

Aggregation of tenancy and freehold

36–72   Special account must also be taken of the position where one of the partners is both a co-tenant *and* the freeholder. In *Gray v. I.R.C.*[55] Lady Fox was the freehold owner of a substantial farm as well as a

---

[46] *i.e.* the average annual profit yield multiplied by the appropriate number of years' purchase, less the net value of the tangible trading assets. See, generally, *Findlay's Trustees v. I.R.C.* (1938) 22 A.T.C. 437.

[47] *i.e.* the average assumed yield attributable to the tangible assets added to a sum representing reasonable remuneration for the partners, the "super profit" thus found being multiplied by the appropriate number of years' purchase, In *Findlay's Trustees v. I.R.C.*, *supra*, the expert witnesses did not consider the super profits method appropriate for valuing a share in the goodwill of a partnership owning a newspaper.

[48] Foster, Inheritance Tax, paras. H3.53 *et seq.*; *Dymond's Capital Taxes*, paras. 23.400 *et seq.*; *McCutcheon on Inheritance Tax* (3rd. ed.), para. 13–27. See also *supra*, paras. 10–175 *et seq.*

[49] As to the position where there is no tenancy agreement or where the agreement contains no express restriction on assignment, see the Agricultural Holdings Act 1986, s.6(1), Sched. 1, para. 9.

[50] [1937] A.C. 26. See also *Alexander v. I.R.C.* [1991] S.T.C. 112, which concerned a residential lease.

[51] 1991 S.L.T. 9 (Lands Trib.). In this case the tenancy was treated as having a value equal to 25 per cent. of the vacant possession value of the land. Although it is clear that there is no such thing as a *standard* percentage of the vacant possession premium or value to be taken in this context, it would seem that the District Valuer is likely to use such a percentage as a starting point for negotiation: see (1992) 89 L.S. Gaz., March 18, p. 15.

[52] Special considerations apply to such tenancies, as evidenced by the provisions of the Inheritance Tax Act 1984, s.177.

[53] In such a case, the prospect of the landlord being able to recover possession of the land (as to which see the Agricultural Holdings Act 1986, s.26(2), Sched. 3, Pt. 1, Case G) must be taken into account pursuant to the Inheritance Tax Act 1984, s.171. *Semble*, any right to succession under the Agricultural Holdings Act 1986, Pt. IV does not form part of the deceased tenant's estate. See also (1990) 87 L.Z. Gaz., November 14, at p.26.

[54] Note, however, that, in a recent decision, *Executors of J.H. Walton v. C.I.R.* (unreported), the Lands Tribunal declined to ascribe a *substantial* value to a partner's interest in an unassignable tenancy: see (1994) Farm Tax Brief 17 *et seq.* See also an article at (1990) 87 L.S.Gaz. November 14, p.23. *Cf. Baird's Executors v. I.R.C.*, *supra*.

[55] [1994] S.T.C. 360.

member of a partnership which was the tenant of that farm. She had a 92.5 per cent. interest in the partnership at the date of her death and the Court of Appeal had regard to the fact that she could have exercised a contractual power under the partnership agreement to dissolve the firm on 6 months' notice and thereupon acquired the remaining partners' shares, with a view to selling the farm with vacant possession. Since it had to be assumed that her partnership share could be sold to a third party,[56] it followed that a combined sale of the share and the freehold reversion would produce a greater price than if each were sold separately. On that basis, it was held that, in valuing Lady Fox's estate,[57] the share and the freehold reversion could properly be aggregated so as to achieve a value which more closely approximated to the vacant possession value of the farm.

Reliefs

Once the value of the share has been ascertained, it may be **36-73** reduced for the purposes of the tax by any available agricultural property or business relief,[58] or a combination of the two.[59]

Administration

The administration of the tax does not appear to give rise to any **36-74** particular problems in relation to partnerships, since any charge is levied by reference to transfers of value made or deemed to have been made by the individual partners and any returns must be delivered by those partners personally.[60]

Payment of tax by instalments

Partnership share

Where any of the tax payable in respect of a transfer of value **36-75** deemed to have been made on death[61] is attributable to the value of a business or an interest in a business, (which will clearly include a share in a partnership), an election may be made to pay the tax by ten yearly instalments.[62] A similar right of election is available where

---

[56] *Ibid.* p.378.

[57] *i.e.* pursuant to what is now the Inheritance Tax Act 1984, ss.160, 171.

[58] See generally, *supra*, paras. 36–13 *et seq*. But note, in particular, the effect of the Inheritance Tax Act 1984, s.39A (as inserted by the Finance Act 1986, s.105).

[59] See *ibid.* s.114(1).

[60] See *ibid.* ss. 216 *et seq*.

[61] *i.e.* pursuant to *ibid.* s.4(1).

[62] *Ibid.* s.227(1)(a), (2)(c). Note, however, that the election will not always be available where additional tax becomes payable on the death in respect of an *inter vivos* transfer made within the previous seven years: *ibid.* s.227(1A)(b), (1C) (as inserted by the Finance Act 1987, Sched. 8, para. 15).

the transfer of value was made as a result of an *inter vivos* disposition, *provided that the tax is borne by the donee.*[63] For these purposes, the value of a business means its net value, which is to be ascertained by deducting the aggregate amount of any liabilities incurred for the purposes of the business from the value of the assets used in the business (including goodwill);[64] an interest in a business will be valued in the same way, no account being taken of any assets or liabilities other than those which would be taken into account in ascertaining the net value of the business itself.[65]

36–76   Where an election is made, the first instalment is due (in the case of a chargeable transfer on death) six months after the end of the month in which the death occurred[66] or (in the case of an *inter vivos* transfer) at the time the tax would have been due if it were not payable by instalments.[67] Interest on each instalment is only payable from the date when that instalment falls due.[68]

Forfeiture of the right to elect

36–77   Notwithstanding such an election, the whole or an appropriate proportion of the tax outstanding which is attributable to a partnership share will become immediately payable on the occurrence of any one of the following events:

  (i)   a subsequent sale of the share,[69] *e.g.* where the continuing partners exercise an option to acquire an outgoing partner's share;[70]
  (ii) the payment of any sum, pursuant to the partnership agreement or otherwise, in satisfaction of the whole or any part of the share, otherwise than on sale, *e.g.* where the share automatically accrues to the continuing partners and a

---

[63] *Ibid.* s.227(1)(b), (2)(c). The availability of the right to elect cannot be guaranteed where a potentially exempt transfer proves to be chargeable: *ibid.* s.227(1A)(a), (1C) (as inserted by the Finance Act 1987, Sched. 8, para. 15). In the case of a transfer into settlement, see *ibid.* s.227(1)(c).

[64] *Ibid.* s.227(7)(a), (b).

[65] *Ibid.* s.227(7)(c). Thus, a right to an annuity on retirement (which clearly forms part of the bundle of rights which comprise the share) would be ignored; on the other hand, the liability to pay an annuity to a former partner *will* be taken into account.

[66] *Ibid.* s.227(3)(a).

[67] *Ibid.* s.227(3)(b). This will generally be six months after the end of the month in which the chargeable transfer was made or, in the case of such a transfer made between April 5 and October 1, on April 30 in the next year: *ibid.* s.226(1). However, in the case of a potentially exempt transfer which proves to be chargeable, the due date will be six months after the end of the month in which the transferor's death occurs: *ibid.* s.226(3A) (as inserted by the Finance Act 1986, Sched. 19, para. 30).

[68] *Ibid.* s.234(1).

[69] *Ibid.* s.227(4), (6)(a).

[70] See further, as to the implications of granting such an option, *supra*, para. 36–31, 36–51, 36–57.

payment falls to be made by them to the outgoing partner or his estate;[71]

(iii) a subsequent chargeable transfer in relation to the share (other than a deemed transfer on death), if the transfer giving rise to the instalment election was itself made otherwise than on death.[72]

It is, of course, questionable to what extent the statutory conversion of an outgoing partner's share into a debt will result in forfeiture of the instalment election.[73] However, there is no certain method of avoiding this consequence, save to provide that such a partner's share will accrue to the continuing partners without payment.[74]

Land

A similar right to pay tax by instalments is available where any of **36–78** the tax payable is attributable to the value of land of any description, wherever situated.[75] However, save in the case of agricultural land, interest on the unpaid portion of the tax will be added to each instalment.[76]

A gratuitous transfer of land owned and used by a firm for the **36–79** purposes of its business will naturally reduce the value of each partner's share[77] and that reduction in value, if chargeable, will itself qualify for an instalment election as a transfer of an interest in a business.[78] Since the latter election will avoid the payment of interest, otherwise than on overdue instalments,[79] it will rarely be beneficial to submit an election on the former basis, save in the case of agricultural land or land which is not used in the business.[80]

---

[71] *Ibid.* s.227(6)(b). This will cause a deemed sale at the time of payment.

[72] *Ibid.* s.227(5)(a) (as amended by the Finance Act 1986, Sched. 19, para. 31(2)). Note also that, in the case of a settled partnership share, any outstanding tax will become payable forthwith if the share ceases to be comprised in the settlement: *ibid.* s.227(5)(b).

[73] Partnership Act 1890, s.43: see *supra*, paras. 19–41, 23–33, 26–04.

[74] See also the *Encyclopedia of Professional Partnerships*, Pt. 6, where the possibility of overcoming the problem by means of a right to nominate a successor partner is considered.

[75] Inheritance Tax Act 1984, s.227(1), (2)(a).

[76] *Ibid.* ss.227(3), 233; the exemption contained in *ibid.* s.234 applies only to shares, securities, businesses, interests in businesses and property eligible for relief under *ibid.* Chap. II, Pt. V (agricultural property relief). See further, as to the latter relief, *supra*, paras. 36–13 *et seq.*

[77] As already noted, a partner has no immediate or ascertainable beneficial interest in the land, but merely a right to a proportion of the surplus remaining after the realisation of all the partnership assets and the payment of all its debts and liabilities: see further, *supra*, paras. 19–01 *et seq.*, 36–45. But see *Gray v. I.R.C.* [1994] S.T.C. 360, 377.

[78] See *supra*, para. 36–75.

[79] Inheritance Tax Act 1984, s.234(1).

[80] Land which is not so used will be ignored when ascertaining the net value of a business, and thus of a share therein: see *ibid.* s.227(7)(b); also *supra*, para. 36–75.

CHAPTER 37

VALUE ADDED TAX

1. REGISTRATION

37-01 VALUE Added Tax is chargeable on any taxable supply[1] of goods or services in the United Kingdom made by a taxable person "in the course or furtherance of any business[2] carried on by him," on the acquisition in the United Kingdom of any goods from another member State of the E.C. and on the importation of goods from outside the E.C.[3] A taxable person is any person who is or is required to be registered under the Value Added Tax Act 1983.[4]

Taxable supplies in the United Kingdom

37-02 A liability to be registered will arise if, at the end of any month, the value of a person's taxable supplies during the period of one year ending on that date exceeds the prescribed amount[5] or if, at any

---

[1] A taxable supply is a supply of goods or services made in the U.K., other than an exempt supply: Value Added Tax Act 1983, ss.(2) (as amended by the Finance (No. 2) Act 1992, Sched. 18, Pt. V(1)), 48(1). As to exempt supplies, see *ibid.* s.17, Sched. 6 (as amended). If the consideration for an apparent supply of services is a share of profits, it will be a question of fact whether a partnership does in fact exist; the mere receipt of a profit share will not in itself be decisive: see *Strathearn Gordon Associates v. Customs and Excise Commissioners* (1985) V.A.T.T.R. 79; *Keydon Estates v. The Commissioners* (LON/88/125) [1990] S.T.I. 179; *Fivegrange Ltd. v. The Commissioners* (LON/89/1631) [1990] S.T.I. 966; *cf. Stephanie A. Manuel t/a Stage Coach Centre for the Performing Arts v. The Commissioners* (LON/90/807) [1992] S.T.I. 47. Note also *Alberni String Quartet v. Customs and Excise Commissioners* (1990) 3 V.A.T.T.R. 166. And see generally, as to the possible implications of profit sharing arrangements, *supra*, paras. 5–20 *et seq.*

[2] "Business" includes any trade, profession or vocation: *ibid.* s.47(1). The definition is a wide one, but it has been held that a business carried on in partnership within the meaning of the Partnership Act 1890, s.1(1) will not *necessarily* constitute a business for this purpose: see *Three H. Aircraft Hire v. Customs and Excise Commissioners* [1982] S.T.C. 653, where a partnership which owned and, through a company, hired out an aircraft was held not to be carrying on a business and thus could not be registered for the tax. However, the decision was an exceptional one: in the vast majority of cases there will be no question of a partnership business not being regarded as a business for value added tax purposes: see *ibid.* p.660, *per* Webster J. And see generally, *Processed Vegetable Growers Association Ltd. v. Customs and Excise Commissioners* (1973) 1 V.A.T.T.R. 87; *Coleman v. The Commissioners* (1976) V.A.T.T.R. 24; *Border Flying Company v. The Commissioners* (1976) V.A.T.T.R. 132; *Customs and Excise Commissioners v. Morrison's Academy Boarding Houses Association* [1978] S.T.C. 1; *The National Water Council v. Customs and Excise Commissioners* [1979] S.T.C. 157; *Customs and Excise Commissioners v. Lord Fisher* [1981] S.T.C. 238; *Customs and Excise Commissioners v. Apple and Pear Development Council* [1985] S.T.C. 383 (C.A.), [1986] S.T.C. 92 (H.L.) and [1988] S.T.C. 221 (European Court of Justice); *Gubby v. Customs and Excise Commissioners* [1987] 3 C.M.L.R. 742; *Neuvale Ltd. v. Customs and Excise Commissioners* [1989] S.T.C. 395.

[3] Value Added Tax Act 1983, s.1, as amended by the Finance (No. 2) Act 1992, Sched. 3, para. 2. See further, as to the scope of the tax in such cases, *ibid.* ss.2A, 2B, as added by the Finance (No. 2) Act 1992, Sched. 3, para. 3.

[4] *Ibid.* s.2C(1), as added by the Finance (No. 2) Act 1992, Sched. 3, para. 3.

[5] *Ibid.* Sched. 1, para. 1(1)(a), as substituted by the Finance Act 1990, s.10(2) and amended by the Value Added Tax (Increase of Registration Limits) (No. 2) Order 1993 (S.I. 1993 No. 2953), Art. 2(a). Currently, the limit stands at £45,000. As to the position of a transferee of a business as a going concern, see *ibid.* Sched. 1, para. 1(2), (3) (as amended).

time, there are reasonable grounds for believing that the value of such supplies during the ensuing 30 days will exceed that amount.[6] In the former case, it may, however, be possible to avoid registration by demonstrating that the value of such supplies in the *forthcoming year*[7] will not exceed a (lesser) prescribed amount.[8] In addition, where a person qualifies for the flat-rate scheme for farmers, certain supplies of goods and services will be disregarded for registration purposes.[9]

The option of voluntary registration is open to any person who is *not* liable to be registered, provided that he can satisfy the Commissioners that he makes, or intends to make, taxable supplies[10] or supplies which would be taxable supplies if made in the United Kingdom.[11]

Supplies from other E.C. states

A person who is not required to register on account of the value of **37–03** his taxable supplies[12] will nevertheless be liable to be registered if:

(a) the value of his relevant supplies[13] since January 1 in any year exceed the prescribed amount;[14]

(b) he makes a relevant supply of any value after having exercised an option under the laws of any member state of the E.C. in which he is taxable to treat relevant supplies made by him as made *outside* that state and those supplies involve the removal of goods from that state;[15] or

---

[6] *Ibid.* Sched. 1, para. 1(1)(b), as substituted by the Finance Act 1990, s.10(2) and amended by the Value Added Tax (Increase of Registration Limits) (No. 2) Order 1993, Art. 2(a). The prescribed amount is currently £45,000.

[7] This will be the year commencing at the time when registration would otherwise have been necessary.

[8] *Ibid.* Sched. 1, para. 1(3), as amended by the Value Added Tax (Increase of Registration Limits) (No. 2) Order 1993, Art. 2(b). The prescribed amount is currently £43,000.

[9] *Ibid.* s.37B, as added by the Finance (No. 2) Act 1992, s.16(1). See also the Value Added Tax (Flat-rate Scheme for Farmers) Regulations 1992 (S.I. 1992 No. 3103); the Value Added Tax (Flat-rate Scheme for Farmers) (Designated Activities) Order 1992 (S.I. 1992 No. 3220); the Value Added Tax (Flat-rate Scheme for Farmers) (Percentage Addition) Order 1992 (S.I. 1992 No. 3221).

[10] Value Added Tax 1983, Sched. 1, para. 5, as substituted by the Finance Act 1988, s.14(1) and amended by the Finance (No. 2) Act 1992, Sched. 3, para. 53. Note that the option of voluntary registration is now open to doctors and dentists practising within the National Health Service: see [1993] S.T.I. 536.

[11] *Ibid.* Sched. 1, para. 5A, as substituted by the Finance Act 1988, s.14(1) and amended by the Finance (No. 2) Act 1992, Sched. 3, para. 53, Sched. 18, Pt. V(1).

[12] See *supra*, para. 37–02.

[13] As to the meaning of this expression, see *ibid.* Sched. 1A, para. 10, as added by the Finance (No. 2) Act 1992, Sched. 3, para. 59.

[14] *Ibid.* Sched. 1A, para. 1(1), as added by the Finance (No. 2) Act 1992, Sched. 3, para. 59. The prescribed amount is currently £70,000.

[15] *Ibid.* Sched. 1A, para. 1(2), as added by the Finance (No. 2) Act 1992, Sched. 3, para. 59. Note that, in such a case the liability to be registered will continue for so long as the option is in force: *ibid.* para. 2(2).

(c) he makes a supply of goods which satisfies the specified conditions.[16]

Voluntary registration is available to any person who can satisfy the Commissioners either that he intends to make relevant supplies to which such an option will relate, irrespective of whether it has already been exercised,[17] or that he intends to make supplies of goods which satisfy the specified conditions.[18]

Acquisitions from other E.C. states

37–04 In addition, a person who is not otherwise liable to be registered will become so liable if at the end of any month the value of his relevant acquisitions[19] since January 1 of that year exceeds the prescribed amount[20] or there are reasonable grounds to believe that the value of such acquisitions during the ensuing 30 days will exceed that amount.[21]

A person who can satisfy the Commissioners that he makes or intends to make relevant acquisitions may at any time apply for voluntary registration.[22]

Notification and registration

37–05 A person who becomes liable to be registered must notify the Commissioners of Customs and Excise, although the time limit for such notifications varies according to the circumstances which gave rise to that liability,[23] as does the date from which the registration will have effect.[24] Until registration has taken place, that person will

---

[16] *Ibid.* Sched. 1A, para. 1(3), as added by the Finance (No. 2) Act 1992, Sched. 3, para. 59.
[17] *Ibid.* Sched. 1A, para. 4(1)(a)(i), (ii), as added by the Finance (No. 2) Act 1992, Sched. 3, para. 59.
[18] *Ibid.* Sched. 1A, para. 4(1)(a)(iii), as added by the Finance (No. 2) Act 1992, Sched. 3, para. 59.
[19] As to the meaning of this expression, see *ibid.* Sched. 1B, para. 11, as added by the Finance (No. 2) Act 1992, Sched. 3, para. 59.
[20] *Ibid.* Sched. 1B, para. 1(1), as added by the Finance (No. 2) Act 1992, Sched. 3, para. 59 and amended by the Value Added Tax (Increase of Registration Limits) (No. 2) Order 1993 (S.I. 1993 No. 2953), Art. 3. The prescribed amount is currently £45,000.
[21] *Ibid.* Sched. 1B, para. 1(2), as added by the Finance (No. 2) Act 1992, Sched. 3, para. 59 and amended by the Value Added Tax (Increase of Registration Limits) (No. 2) Order 1993, Art. 3.
[22] *Ibid.* Sched. 1B, para. 4(1), (2), as added by the Finance (No. 2) Act 1992, Sched. 3, para. 59.
[23] *Ibid.* Sched. 1, paras. 3(1), 4(1), 4A(1) (as respectively substituted by the Finance Act 1990, s.10(6)), Sched. 1A, para. 3(1), Sched. 1B, para. 3(1) (as respectively added by the Finance (No. 2) Act 1992, Sched. 3, para. 59). See further *infra*, para. 37–29, as to the form of notification.
[24] *Ibid.* Sched. 1, paras. 3(2), 4(2), 4A(2) (as respectively substituted by the Finance Act 1990, s.10(6)), Sched. 1A, para. 3(2), Sched. 1B, para. 3(2), (3) (as respectively added by the Finance (No. 2) Act 1992, Sched. 3, para. 59).

be in the highly disadvantageous position of an unregistered taxable person.[25]

Registration of partnerships

The Value Added Tax Act 1983 makes specific provision for the **37–06** registration of partnerships,[26] but the application of that provision, as in the case of its predecessor,[27] is not without difficulty. Under the heading "Partnerships," section 30 of the Act now provides:

"(1) The registration under this Act of persons carrying on a business in partnership [or carrying on in partnership any other activities in the course or furtherance of which they acquire goods from other member States] may be in the name of the firm; and no account shall be taken, in determining for any purpose of this Act whether goods or services are supplied to or by such persons [or are acquired by such persons from another member State], of any change in the partnership.

(2) Without prejudice to section 36 of the Partnership Act 1890 (rights of persons dealing with firm against apparent members of firm) until the date on which a change in the partnership is notified to the Commissioners, a person who has ceased to be a member of a partnership shall be regarded as continuing to be a partner for the purposes of this Act and, in particular, for the purpose of any liability for tax on the supply of goods or services by the partnership [or on the acquisition of goods by the partnership from another member State].

(3) Where a person ceases to be a member of a partnership during a prescribed accounting period (or is treated as so doing by virtue of subsection (2) above) any notice, whether of assessment or otherwise, which is served on the partnership and relates to, or to any matter arising in, that period or any earlier period during the whole or part of which he was a member of the partnership shall be treated as served also on him.

(4) Without prejudice to section 16 of the Partnership Act 1890 (notice to acting partner to be notice to the firm) any notice,

---

[25] Thus, the unregistered taxable person must account for tax on taxable supplies made by him, but cannot issue valid tax invoices in respect of those supplies: see the Value Added Tax (General) Regulations 1985 (S.I. 1985 No. 886), regs. 12, 13 (as substituted by the Value Added Tax (General) (Amendment) (No. 4) Regulations 1992 (S.I. 1992 No. 3102) regs. 8, 9 and, in the case of reg. 13, amended by the Value Added Tax (General) (Amendment) (No. 3) Regulations 1993 (S.I. 1993 No. 856), reg. 3). He may also be liable for interest and penalties: Finance Act 1985, ss.15, 18 (as amended). Note, however, the decision in *Smith v. The Commissioners* (LON/90/1094) [1991] S.T.I. 149, which was an exceptional case.

[26] This presupposes the existence of a partnership in the true sense: see, for example, *Britton v. Customs and Excise Commissioners* (1986) V.A.T.T.R. 209, where it was held that a husband and wife were *not* partners in a shopfitting business.

[27] Finance Act 1972, s.22, as amended by the Finance Act 1982, s.16.

whether of assessment or otherwise, which is addressed to a partnership by the name in which it is registered by virtue of subsection (1) above and is served in accordance with this Act shall be treated for the purposes of this Act as served on the partnership and, accordingly, where subsection (3) above applies, as served also on the former partner.

(5) Subsections (1) and (3) above shall not affect the extent to which, under section 9 of the Partnership Act 1890, a partner is liable for tax owed by the firm; but where a person is a partner in a firm during part only of a prescribed accounting period his liability for tax on the supply by the firm of goods or services during that accounting period [or on the acquisition during that period by the firm of any goods from another member State] shall be such proportion of the firm's liability as may be just."[28]

It is clear from the terms of the section that the Commissioners have a discretion as to whether or not to effect the registration in the name of the firm. It is thus technically open to them to require the firm to be registered under the names of the individual partners,[29] although it is thought that this discretion will rarely be exercised.

37–07   Certain implications of the predecessor to section 30 were considered by the Divisional Court in *Customs and Excise Commissioners v. Glassborow*.[30] In that case, a husband and wife, Mr. and Mrs. Glassborow, carried on an estate agent's business in partnership under the name "Bertram & Co.," and a wholly separate land developer's business in partnership under the name "Glassborow & Glassborow." Application was made to the Commissioners for registration in respect of each separate partnership, but the Commissioners, having registered Mr. and Mrs. Glassborow under the name "Glassborow & Glassborow," refused a second registration under the name "Bertram & Co." The Divisional Court upheld that refusal, holding that the section was a permissive and procedural section, and that the persons who were registered for value added tax purposes were Mr. and Mrs. Glassborow, and not the business carried on by them in partnership. In the course of his judgment

---

[28] The words in square brackets in subss. (1), (2) and (5) were inserted by the Finance (No. 2) Act 1992, Sched. 3, para. 31.

[29] Where the firm is registered in the names of the individual partners, the latter part of s.30(1) (no account being taken of changes in the partnership) will still apply; but see further, *infra*, para. 37–09. An individual partner may, of course, still be separately registered in respect of any business carried on by him either alone or in partnership with others.

[30] [1975] Q.B. 465. See also *Miller v. The Commissioners* (1977) V.A.T.T.R. 241; *Customs and Excise Commissioners v. Evans* [1982] S.T.C. 342 (although the main part of this decision has now been statutorily overruled: see *infra*, para. 37–33); also *Michaelis v. The Commissioners* (LON/90/925) [1991] S.T.I. 427.

(with which Lord Widgery C.J. and Boreham J. agreed) May J. made the following observations on the treatment of partnerships for registration purposes:

"By virtue of section 19 of the Interpretation Act 1889[31] the word 'person' in Part I of the [*Finance*] Act of 1972 must, unless a contrary intention appears, be construed as including an unincorporated body of persons, which more often than not will be the persons trading in partnership ... However, although we frequently use the words 'a partnership' as a collective label for the individuals who trade together in partnership, this is in my view strictly erroneous, save as a convenient shorthand. One cannot equate the word 'partnership' with the word 'person' in section 4[32] of and Schedule 1[33] to the Act of 1972 by virtue of section 19 of the earlier Act of 1889. It will be noticed that in section 22(1)[34] of the Finance Act 1972 the draftsman has been careful and, as I think, accurate in the words he has used.

"With this concept in mind it was conceded ... on behalf of the commissioners, and I think rightly conceded, that A carrying on business on his own account is for the purposes of the Act a different 'person' from A and B carrying on business in partnership. Similarly the 'person' comprising A, B and C trading in partnership is different from that comprising A, B and D so trading, because the two bodies of persons are different: they consist of different individuals ...

... notwithstanding the provisions of the Interpretation Act 1889, I think that in the particular context of the opening words of section 22(1) which I have quoted it is impossible to read the word 'persons' other than in its ordinary and natural meaning, that is to say individuals in the plural, and that consequently, although Glassborow and Glassborow has been registered as a firm name the persons who have in truth registered under Part I of the Act are those carrying on business in partnership as such, namely, Mr. and Mrs. Glassborow. That being so, the registration is apt to cover the taxable activities of these two individuals trading alternatively as Bertram & Co. In my judgment section 22 is permissive and procedural only, and once a firm name has been registered, the effect of the registration is as though the names of all the individuals trading under that name from time to time were recorded."[35]

---

[31] See, now, the Interpretation Act 1978, Sched. 1.
[32] Now the Value Added Tax Act 1983, s.2(2).
[33] Now the Value Added Tax Act 1983, Sched. 1 (as amended).
[34] Now the Value Added Tax Act 1983, s.30(1), *supra*, para. 37–06.
[35] [1975] Q.B. 465, 473E–H, 474C–E. See also *Glasse Brothers v. The Commissioners* (LON/88/917) [1989] S.T.I. 619.

37–08   On the other hand, in *H. Saunders v. The Commissioners*,[36] it was held that separate registrations *were* appropriate in the case of two limited partnerships between a Mr. Saunders and a Mr. Sorrell, since in the first partnership Mr. Saunders was the general partner and Mr. Sorrell the limited partner, whilst in the second those roles were reversed. However, the current editor submits that this decision was exceptional and explicable only by reference to the particular attributes of limited partnership.[37]

37–09   The implications of the *Glassborow* decision must be considered whenever questions of registration arise as regards persons carrying on business in partnership. There should be little difficulty where only one firm is involved, since it will be treated as a separate "person" in order to determine whether its taxable supplies, etc.[38] exceed the prescribed limits.[39] If those limits are exceeded, registration is applied for, and will normally be granted, in the firm name.[40] Unexpected complications may, however, arise where a number of firms have one or more members in common. This may be illustrated by supposing the existence of two separate firms, the first comprising A, B and C (the ABC partnership) and the second comprising A, B, C and D (the ABCD partnership). So long as the constitution of each firm remains unchanged, they will, on the above principles, be treated as separate "persons" for registration purposes. If D retires from the ABCD partnership[41] at a time when neither the ABC partnership nor the ABCD partnership is registered, it will be necessary to aggregate the taxable supplies, etc. of the two firms in order to determine whether A, B and C (as persons carrying on business in partnership) are obliged to register.[42] If registration is necessary, it may either be in the name of ABC or ABCD.[43] On the other hand, if both the ABC partnership and the ABCD partnership are already registered and notification is given of D's retirement,[44]

---

[36] (1980) V.A.T.T.R. 53.
[37] Had Mr. Saunders and Mr. Sorrell retained the same roles in both partnerships, the decision would in all probability have been different. See generally, as to limited partnerships, *supra*, paras. 29–01 *et seq*.
[38] See *supra*, paras. 37–02 *et seq*.
[39] *Customs and Excise Commissioners v. Glassborow* [1975] Q.B. 465; *Border Flying Company v. The Commissioners* (1976) V.A.T.T.R. 132, 139; *J. Procter (Waddington) Ltd. v. The Commissioners* (1976) V.A.T.T.R. 184, 195; *Miller v. The Commissioners* (1977) V.A.T.T.R. 241.
[40] Nevertheless, the form VAT 2, which must accompany the application, will contain the names, addresses and signatures of each partner: see further, *infra*, para. 37–29. It has already been noted that, in an appropriate case, the Commissioners could insist that the firm is registered in the name of the individual partners: see *supra*, para. 37–06.
[41] The same questions will inevitably arise if D dies or, indeed, if he, for whatever reason, joins the ABC partnership.
[42] *J. Procter (Waddington) Ltd. v. The Commissioners* (1976) V.A.T.T.R. 184, 195.
[43] But not in both: see *Customs and Excise Commissioners v. Glassborow* [1975] Q.B. 465. It would seem to be open to the partners to decide under which name to apply for registration.
[44] See *infra*, para. 37–11.

the Commissioners could cancel the registration of either firm, and require A, B and C to continue both businesses under a single registration.[45] If only the ABC partnership is registered, the business of the ABCD partnership will be covered by the ABC partnership's registration and tax must be charged on all taxable supplies made by it.[46]

It naturally follows that the status of a firm's registration (or non-registration) may need to be reviewed following any change in its membership, depending on the nature of the partners' other business interests.[47]

Attempts to avoid registration

Given the position set out above, it might be thought that registration could be avoided by fragmenting a business whose turnover is likely to exceed the registration limits into a number of "separate" partnership businesses, none of which have a complete identity of partners. However, if the Commissioners are satisfied that this is the main reason for the fragmentation exercise, and that each firm is making taxable supplies whilst carrying on activities which should properly be regarded as a single business, they may direct that all the firms should be treated as a single taxable person for registration purposes,[48] thereby constituting a deemed global partnership comprising all the members of the constituent firms.[49] If any of those firms is already registered, its registration will be cancelled.[50] Supplementary directions may be issued if the existence of other elements of the fragmented business come to the attention of the Commissioners at a later date.[51]

Such a direction can equally well be made where one or more parts of the fragmented business are carried on by individuals or

37–10

---

[45] It is understood that the Commissioners *will* in practice cancel one of the registrations. It should be noted that this is the position, notwithstanding the express terms of the Value Added Tax Act 1983, s.30(1), which directs that no account is to be taken of any changes in a partnership.

[46] *J. O. W. & E. M. Harris t/a Advanced Structural Maintenance & Repair Co. and Harris & Harris v. The Commissioners,* (CAR/76/220).

[47] Where two firms have identical partners and thus a single registration, a change resulting from the departure of one partner from, or the admission of a new partner to, one of those firms will automatically cause them to become separate taxable persons and their respective taxable supplies, etc. will no longer fall to be aggregated.

[48] Value Added Tax Act 1983, Sched. 1, para. 1A(1), as added by the Finance Act 1986 s.10(1) and amended by the Finance (No. 2) Act 1992, Sched. 3, para. 49(1). And see *Lewis v. The Commissioners* (MAN/88/260) [1989] S.T.I. 271; *Jervis v. The Commissioners* (MAN/88/596) [1989] S.T.I. 784; *Chamberlain v. Customs and Excise Commissioners* [1989] S.T.C. 505; *West End Health and Fitness Club v. The Commissioners* (EDN/89/70) [1989] S.T.I. 869; *Horsman v. The Commissioners* (1990) V.A.T.T.R. 151; *Hundsdoerfer v. The Commissioners* (1990) V.A.T.T.R. 158. The same result could also perhaps be achieved by applying the principles enunciated in *W. T. Ramsay Ltd. v. I.R.C.* [1982] A.C. 300 and *Furniss v. Dawson* [1984] A.C. 474; but see also *Customs and Excise Commissioners v. Faith Construction Ltd.* [1990] 1 Q.B. 905 and *supra,* para. 34–11.

[49] *Ibid.* para. 1A(7)(e).

[50] *Ibid.* para. 1A(5).

[51] *Ibid.* para. 1A(4).

companies, *e.g.* if a partnership is dissolved by agreement and its assets distributed *in specie* between the former partners in such a way as to permit the various elements of the business to be carried on by them.

Changes in the firm

37–11   Once a firm has registered, no account is in general taken of any subsequent change in its members.[52] This will apply equally whether registration is in the name of the firm or in the names of the individual partners, although in the latter case the current editor understands that an appropriate amendment will be made in the registration to delete or add the name of the outgoing/incoming partner.[53] It should, however, be noted that such a change may in certain circumstances cause a firm's registration to be cancelled,[54] as well as affecting the registrability of other businesses carried on by the partners.[55]

37–12   Even though changes in the firm are ignored for registration purposes, the partners must within 30 days notify the Commissioners of:

   (i)   any change in the name or trading name of the firm;
   (ii) any change in the name and/or address of any of the partners;
   (iii) any change in the composition[56] of the firm;
   (iv) any change in the address of its principal place of business; and

---

[52] *Ibid.* s.30(1), *supra*, para. 37–06. As to the liability of partners in respect of tax following a change, see *ibid.* s.30(2), (3), considered *infra*, para. 37–33.

[53] The Commissioners will, as a matter of practice, require a fresh form VAT 2 to be completed.

[54] *Customs and Excise Commissioners v. Glassborow* [1975] Q.B. 465. See also *Weakley v. The Commissioners* (LON/2/73/14S); 93 Taxation 343. And see *supra*, para. 37–09.

[55] Particular care must be taken to ensure that the business of one firm has not been brought under the registration of another, thus requiring tax to be charged on all its supplies, etc.: see *J. O. W. & E. M. Harris t/a Advanced Structural Maintenance & Repair Co. and Harris & Harris v. The Commissioners* (CAR/76/220), *supra*, para. 37–09.

[56] The Commissioners only require notification where the change in composition involves a change in the identity of the partners, as opposed to a mere change in their capital or asset-surplus sharing ratios. Where two firms merge but only one firm is registered, there will be a change in the composition of the registered firm which must be duly notified. Where, however, both firms are registered, the position is more complex, although much will depend on the precise manner in which the merger is effected. The current editor considers that a merger is likely to bring about a change in the composition of each firm, so that two separate notifications are required. Thereafter, the registration of one of the merged firms must be cancelled. There would seem to be no reason why representations should not be made to the Commissioners as to which registration should be cancelled and which preserved: if no representations are made, the decision will be left to the discretion of the Commissioners. *Quaere*, in the case of a limited partnership, whether the Commissioners should be notified when a general partner becomes a limited partner or vice-versa, having regard to the decision in *H. Saunders v. The Commissioners* (1980) V.A.T.T.R. 53, noticed *supra*, para. 37–08.

(v) the dissolution of the firm.[57]

The notification procedure, and the possible consequences of failure to comply therewith, will be considered further below.[58]

Cancellation of registration

The registration of a firm may now only be cancelled in a limited **37–13** number of circumstances.[59] The firm itself may request such cancellation, if it ceases to be liable to be registered.[60] Alternatively, the Commissioners may initiate the cancellation, if they are satisfied that the firm has ceased to be registrable[61] or that it was not

---

[57] Value Added Tax (General) Regulations 1985 (S.I. 1985 No. 886), reg. 4(2), as substituted by the Value Added Tax (General) (Amendment) (No. 4) Regulations 1992 (S.I. 1992 No. 3102), reg. 4(a); Customs and Excise Notice No. 700, paras. 93, 94 (1991 Revision). In view of the terms of the latter Notice it is, perhaps, arguable that notification does not need to be given immediately following the date of dissolution, but only when the business is discontinued at or prior to the conclusion of the winding-up process. Written notification is, in any event, mandatory: *The Bengal Brasserie v. The Commissioners* (LON/90/604) [1991] S.T.I. 662.

[58] See *infra*, paras. 37–29, 37–30.

[59] *Cf.* the Value Added Tax Act 1983, Sched. 1, paras. 7 *et seq.* in their original form.

[60] *Registration pursuant to ibid. Sched. 1:* see *ibid.* para. 8A (as substituted by the Finance Act 1988, s.14(6) and amended by the Finance (No. 2) Act 1992, Sched. 3, para. 56). A firm will cease to be liable to be registered if the Commissioners are satisfied that it is not otherwise registrable under the Act (*ibid.* para. 8A(1A), as added by the Finance (No. 2) Act 1992, Sched. 3, para. 56) and it has ceased to make taxable supplies or the value of its taxable supplies in the ensuing year will not exceed £45,000: *ibid.* paras. 1B (as added by the Finance (No. 2) Act 1992, Sched. 13, para. 50), 2(1) (as substituted by the Finance Act 1987, s.14(3) and amended by the Finance (No. 2) Act 1992, Sched. 3, para. 51 and the Value Added Tax (Increase of (Registration Limits) (No. 2) Order 1993 (S.I. 1993 No. 2953), Art. 2(b)). The registration will be cancelled with effect from the date of the request or such later date as may be agreed: *ibid.* para. 8A(1). *Registration pursuant to ibid. Sched. 1A:* The procedure is by no means clear in this instance. The only provision authorising the cancellation of a registration on request is contained in *ibid.* para. 6(1) (as added by the Finance (No. 2) Act 1992, Sched. 3, para. 59), which applies where a registered person is able to satisfy the Commissioners that "he is not liable to be so registered", not that he has *ceased* to be liable to register. Yet if this paragraph is intended to cover the case of a person who was not liable to register *ab initio*, the difference of wording between that sub-paragraph and *ibid.* para. 6(2)(a) is inexplicable. Be that as it may, a firm will cease to be liable to be registered if the value of its relevant supplies in the year ending on the previous December 31 did not exceed £70,000 and did not include any supplies satisfying the conditions specified in *ibid.* para. 1(3) and the Commissioners are satisfied that both requirements will continue to be met in the current year: *ibid.* para. 2(1), as added by the Finance (No. 2) Act 1992, Sched. 3, para. 59. *Per contra*, if an option of the type specified in *ibid.* para. 1(2) is in force: *ibid.* para. 2(2). See also *supra*, para. 37–03. If *ibid.* para. 6(1) applies, the registration will be cancelled with effect from the date of the request or such later date as may be agreed. *Registration pursuant to Sched. 1B:* Again the procedure is uncertain. The wording of *ibid.* para. 6(1) (as added by the Finance (No. 2) Act 1992, Sched. 3, para. 59) follows that adopted in *ibid.* Sched. 1A, para. 6(1), *supra*; *cf. ibid.* Sched. 1B, para. 6(2), (3). A firm will cease to be liable to be registered if the value of its relevant acquisitions in the year ending on the previous December 31 did not exceed £45,000 and the Commissioners are satisfied that the value of such acquisitions in the current year will not exceed that amount, unless there are reasonable grounds for believing that the value of such acquisitions will exceed that figure in the ensuing period of 30 days: *ibid.* para. 2, as added by the Finance (No. 2) Act 1992, Sched. 3, para. 59 and amended by the Value Added Tax (Increase of Registration Limits) (No. 2) Order 1993, Art. 3. If *ibid.* para. 6(1) applies, the registration will be cancelled with effect from the date of the request or such later date as may be agreed.

[61] *Registration pursuant to the Value Added Tax Act 1983, Sched. 1:* see *ibid.* para. 9, as substituted by the Finance Act 1988, s.14(6) and amended by the Finance (No. 2) Act 1992, Sched. 3, para. 57. As to when a firm will cease to be registrable, see *supra*, n. 60. The registration will be cancelled with effect from the date on which the firm ceased to be registrable or such later date as may be agreed: *ibid.* para. 9(1). *Registration pursuant to ibid. Sched. 1A: ibid.* para. 6(3), as added by the Finance (No. 2) Act 1992, Sched. 3, para. 59. As to when a firm will cease to be registrable

—continued on page 1022

registrable on the date when it was originally registered.[62] In addition, a firm's registration may be cancelled where there is already a subsisting registration in respect of a firm comprising the same persons[63] or where a direction is made by the Commissioners which has the effect of treating a number of notionally separate firms or persons as a single taxable person.[64]

2. TAXABLE SUPPLIES

37–14 The general treatment of taxable supplies of goods and services made by a firm is no different to that applied to any other taxable person and accordingly falls outside the scope of this work. It should, however, be noted that prior to January 1, 1978, tax was only chargeable on taxable supplies made "in the course of a business" but, after that date, was chargeable on taxable supplies made "in the course or furtherance of a business."[65] The additional words are of a very general and imprecise nature, and the scope of the tax at that stage appears to have been considerably enlarged.[66] Thus, the

---

—continued from page 1021

see *supra*, n. 60. In this case, the Commissioners' power is only exercisable where the proposed supplies have not been made or the place of supply option has not been exercised by the date specified in the original request for registration or where there is a contravention of any condition attached to the registration; the registration will, in general, be cancelled with effect from that specified date or the date of the contravention, as the case may be: *ibid.* para. 6(3); but see also *ibid.* para. 7(3), as added by the Finance (No. 2) Act 1992, Sched. 3, para. 60. *Registration pursuant to ibid. Sched. 1B:* see *ibid.* para. 6(2), as added by the Finance (No. 2) Act 1992, Sched. 3, para. 59. As to when a firm will cease to be registrable, see *supra*, n. 59. The registration will be cancelled with effect from the date on which the firm ceased to be registrable or such later date as may be agreed: *ibid.* The power is also exercisable where the proposed acquisitions have not been made by the date specified in the original request for registration or where there is a contravention of any condition attached to the registration: *ibid.* para. 6(4), as added by the Finance (No. 2) Act 1992, Sched. 3, para. 59. In such a case, the registration will, in general, be cancelled with effect from that specified date or the date of the contravention (as the case may be): *ibid. Notifications:* Note that, if the firm ceases to make or to have the intention to make taxable supplies, the Commissioners must be notified: *ibid.* para. 7, as substituted by the Finance Act 1988, s.14(5) and amended by the Finance (No. 2) Act 1992, Sched. 3, para. 54. A similar requirement applies in the case of registration under *ibid.* Scheds. 1A and 1B: see *ibid.* Sched. 1A, para. 5, Sched. 1B, para. 5 (as respectively added by the Finance (No. 2) Act 1992, Sched. 3, para. 59).

[62] *Registration pursuant to ibid. Sched. 1:* see *ibid.* para. 10, as substituted by the Finance Act 1988, s.14(6). *Registration pursuant to ibid. Sched. 1A:* see *ibid.* para. 6(2), as added by the Finance (No. 2) Act 1992, Sched. 3, para. 59. In the case of registration under *ibid.* para. 4, it must also be shown that the firm had no intention to make the supplies in question: *ibid. Registration pursuant to ibid. Sched. 1B:* see *ibid.* para. 6(3), as added by the Finance (No. 2) Act 1992, Sched. 3, para. 59. In the case of registration under *ibid.* para. 4(2), it must also be shown that the firm had no intention to make relevant acquisitions: *ibid.* Where the Commissioners proceed under any of the above provisions, the registration is cancelled retrospectively.

[63] *Customs and Excise Commissioners v. Glassborow* [1975] Q.B. 465. And see *supra*, para. 37–07.

[64] Value Added Tax Act 1983, Sched. 1, para. 1A, as added by the Finance Act 1986, s.10(1). See further, *supra*, para. 37–10.

[65] Finance Act 1972, s.2(1), as substituted by the Finance Act 1977. See now the Value Added Tax Act 1983, s.2(1).

[66] In *Re Ward* [1941] Ch. 308 the word "furtherance" was considered to be synonymous with "advancement": *ibid.* p. 311, *per* MacKinnon L.J. However, this case concerned a charitable bequest, and too much reliance cannot be placed thereon in the present context. Equally, in *Express Newspapers Ltd. v. McShane* [1980] A.C. 672 and *Duport Steels Ltd. v. Sirs* [1980] 1 W.L.R. 142 it was held that the expression "in . . . furtherance" in the Trade Union and Labour Relations Act 1974, s.13(1) contemplated a subjective test. See also *R.H.M. Bakeries (Northern) Ltd. v. Customs and Excise Commissioners* [1979] S.T.C. 72, and generally, Avery Jones, *Encyclopedia of Value Added Tax*, para. 2–202/1.

tribunal has held that a firm of solicitors makes a taxable supply "in the course of a business" when paying moneys into a client's deposit account, but not when paying moneys into the firm's own deposit account, even if that account is treated as a reserve fund, which may be called on in the event of a cash flow problem.[67] The current editor considers that the Commissioners could now contend that payments into such an account, whilst not made "in the course of a business," are made "in the furtherance of a business," since the maintenance of such a reserve is clearly beneficial to the business. On that footing, the payments would constitute taxable supplies. However, the point is arguable, given the imprecision of the words "in the furtherance of a business."

It is nevertheless of importance to refer to a number of specific transactions to which a firm or its members may be party, in order to identify whether a taxable supply is involved and, if so, its potential effect on the firm's registrability.[68]

Offices held by partners

The Value Added Tax Act 1983, s. 47(4) provides as follows: **37–15**

"(4) Where a person, in the course or furtherance of a trade, profession or vocation, accepts any office,[69] services supplied by him as the holder of that office are treated as supplied in the course or furtherance of the trade, profession or vocation."

The subsection only applies to an office and *not* to a position which has the nature of employment. Thus, a partner in a firm of solicitors who also held a part-time appointment as a salaried solicitor to a borough council was held to be an employee and, thus, not supplying services to the council.[70]

Whether an office held by an individual partner will involve the **37–16** firm, as opposed to that partner, making a taxable supply will be a question of fact in each case. However, it should be noted that the Commissioners formerly adopted a fairly generous approach in determining what offices were held "in the course of a trade,

---

[67] *Hedges and Mercer v. The Commissioners* (1976) V.A.T.T.R. 146.

[68] For example, the value of the supplies made by a firm during the course of winding up its affairs may be sufficient to exceed the prescribed limits, and thus to render the firm a taxable person. Equally, it would seem that any value attributable to the sale of the partnership assets will be ignored for this purpose: see *infra*, para. 37–19, n. 88.

[69] There is no longer any exemption for public offices: *cf.* the original provision contained in the Finance Act 1972, s.45(3), as considered in *Hempsons v. The Commissioners* (1977) V.A.T.T.R. 73. It follows that the fees of a Commissioner for Oaths are subject to the tax: see the replies of the Customs and Excise to the comments of the Consultative Committee of Accountancy Bodies on the Finance Bill 1977, reproduced at [1977] S.T.I. 276, 278. See also (1979) 76 L.S.Gaz. 1151.

[70] *Lean and Rose v. The Commissioners* (1974) 1 V.A.T.T.R. 7.

profession or vocation,"[71] and did not regard the fact that the office-holding partner accounted to the firm for any fees received as in itself decisive.[72] Although it must be recognised that almost any benefit which accrues to a firm from an office held by one of the partners[73] will or may further the partnership business, thus supporting an argument that the firm has made a taxable supply,[74] it would seem that the Commissioners are unlikely to depart from their former practice in applying section 47(4). This is to a large extent borne out by the terms of the joint Statement issued by the Law Society and H.M. Customs and Excise in 1979,[75] wherein it is stated that an office will be regarded as held in the course of a profession if the professional skills of the office-holder are exercised in the performance of the duties of the office, whilst an office will be regarded as held in the *furtherance* of a profession if possession of professional skills was a factor in the appointment or acceptance of the office was likely to enhance the reputation of the individual or firm concerned. Moreover, the Customs and Excise are apparently prepared to accept that there is no taxable supply by the firm, even if the office-holder accounts to it for his fees, provided that three conditions are satisfied, namely that:

(a) the office-holding has been arranged with the individual partner concerned and there is no written agreement between the firm and the organisation in which the office is held;

(b) the office-holding arises from some personal, family or significant financial interest of the partner in that organisation, rather than from his professional qualifications or interest; and

(c) the duties of the office do not involve significant use of the skills which the partner currently employs in practising his profession (unless such services are separately charged for by the firm).[76]

In addition, there may be no taxable supply where the office is accepted by a prospective partner *before* the commencement of the partnership business.[77]

---

[71] See the original terms of the Finance Act 1972, s.45(3).

[72] See [1976] S.T.I. 107. It is understood that the principles there set out did not constitute the *official* view of the Commissioners. As to the effect of the office-holder making use of partnership facilities as a matter of convenience, see *Hempsons v. The Commissioners* (1977) V.A.T.T.R. 73, 92–93.

[73] The benefit may be tangible (*e.g.* fees) or intangible (*e.g.* general goodwill).

[74] It seems that the Commissioners did not intend to introduce a substantial change of practice, otherwise than in relation to public offices: see the replies of the Customs and Excise to the comments of the C.C.A.B. on the Finance Bill 1977, reproduced at [1977] S.T.I. 276, 278.

[75] (1979) 76 L.S.Gaz. 1151. The Statement is entitled "V.A.T. and Public Offices," but deals only with the position of solicitors. It does, however, provide a clear indication of the approach likely to be adopted by the Customs and Excise where offices are held by partners in other spheres.

[76] *Ibid.* para. 8.

[77] *Gardner v. Customs and Excise Commissioners* (1989) V.A.T.T.R. 132.

Use of partnership property by the partners

A supply of services will be treated as made by a firm whenever **37–17** goods or land[78] held or used by it for the purposes of its business are used or made available to a partner for his own personal benefit, rather than for business purposes.[79] Such a supply will automatically be treated as made in the course or furtherance of the business, if it would not otherwise be so treated.[80] The tribunal analysed this type of supply in *Border Flying Co. v. The Commissioners*,[81] where a group of five businessmen had formed a consortium to acquire an aircraft both for their own use and for public hire. Having found them to be partners, the tribunal went on to hold that each partner had a direct beneficial interest in the aircraft.[82] On that basis, whenever one partner chose to use the aircraft for his own private purposes, the other partners were treated as temporarily releasing (and therefore supplying) their beneficial interests to him and, moreover, he was treated as having supplied his own beneficial interest to himself. In the circumstances, it was clear that those supplies were made in the course of the firm's business.[83]

The above decision is unsatisfactory, since the tribunal treated each **37–18** partner as having a direct beneficial interest in the aircraft, without considering whether that conclusion was justifiable in law, given the true nature of a partnership share.[84] On that footing it is open to challenge, even though there is now no doubt that a taxable supply occurs whenever a partner uses a partnership asset for his own purposes.[85] However, the decision has more serious implications in another context which will be referred to hereafter.[86]

---

[78] Value Added Tax Act 1983, Sched. 2, para. 8, as added by the Finance Act 1989, para. 11(c).

[79] *Ibid.* Sched. 2, para. 5(3). However, no such supply will be treated as made where credit for the input tax on the goods in question could not be obtained under *ibid.* ss.14, 15: *ibid.* Sched. 2, para. 5(3A), as added by the Finance Act 1993, s.47(4). The value of the supply would appear to be its open market value, unless it forms part of a bona fide commercial arrangement between the partners: see *ibid.* Sched. 4, para. 1, as amended by the Finance Act 1987, s.17(1); Income and Corporation Taxes Act 1988, s.839(4).

[80] Value Added Tax Act 1983, Sched. 2, para. 5(4)(b).

[81] (1976) V.A.T.T.R. 132. This decision was, of course, reached before the introduction of the revised provisions which are now contained in the Value Added Tax Act 1983, Sched. 2, para. 5(3). *Cf.* the decision in *Three H. Aircraft Hire v. Customs and Excise Commissioners* [1982] S.T.C. 653, noticed *supra*, para. 37–01, n. 2.

[82] (1976) V.A.T.T.R. 132, 138.

[83] *Ibid.* pp. 137–138. As has been noted, such a supply would now automatically be treated as made in the course or furtherance of the business: Value Added Tax Act 1983, Sched. 2, para. 5(4)(b).

[84] *i.e.* an entitlement to a share in the surplus remaining after the realisation of all the partnership assets and the payment of all partnership debts and liabilities: see further, *supra*, paras. 19–04 *et seq.* It should be noted that the approach adopted by the tribunal mirrors the Revenue's treatment of disposals by partners for the purposes of capital gains tax (see *supra*, paras. 35–04 *et seq.*) and the approach adopted by the court in *Gray v. I.R.C.* [1994] S.T.C. 360, 377, noticed *supra*, para. 36–72.

[85] Value Added Tax Act 1983, Sched. 2, para. 5(3).

[86] *i.e.* the potential charge to tax on the transfer of a partnership share: see *infra*, paras. 37–24 *et seq.*

Sales of partnership assets

Goods

37–19   A supply of goods is made whenever goods forming part of the assets of a business are transferred or disposed of so as no longer to form part of those assets[87] and that supply will automatically be treated as made in the course or furtherance of the business.[88] The only exceptions relate to small gifts and gifts of industrial samples.[89]

Accordingly, whenever a firm disposes of such an asset, a taxable supply will be made, unless the asset is exempt[90] or otherwise outside the scope of the tax.

Goodwill

37–20   It has been seen[91] that goodwill will usually be an asset of the firm, but it is questionable whether it can properly be described as "goods."[92] Nevertheless, in 1982 H.M. Customs and Excise announced that they will treat all sales of goodwill as taxable supplies, whether the goodwill takes some tangible form, *e.g.* a list of customers, or not.[93]

Sale of partnership business as a going concern

37–21   The tax treatment of a sale of an entire business as a going concern gave rise to considerable difficulties prior to the introduction of what is now section 47(6) of the Value Added Tax Act 1983,[94] which provides:

---

[87] Value Added Tax Act 1983, Sched. 2, para. 5(1) (as amended by the Finance Act 1989, Sched. 3, para. 11(b)), which effectively enacts the decision in *H. B. Mattia Ltd. v. The Commissioners* (1976) V.A.T.T.R. 33. Note also that, where goods forming part of the assets of the business are sold by a third party under a power exercisable by him (*e.g.* as mortgagee), a taxable supply will be treated as made in the course or furtherance of that business: *ibid.* para. 6. As to the position where the goods are merely *removed* to another member State of the E.C. in the course or furtherance of the business, see *ibid.* para. 5A, as added by the Finance (No. 2) Act 1992, Sched. 3, para. 60(1).

[88] *Ibid.* Sched. 2, para. 5(4). However, it would seem that H.M. Customs and Excise are prepared to disregard such a supply when calculating the value of taxable supplies for registration purposes: see H.M. Customs and Excise V.A.T. Leaflet No. 700/1/94, para. 7.

[89] Value Added Tax Act 1983, Sched. 2, para. 5(2); also *ibid.* para. 5(2A), as added by the Finance Act 1993, s.47(3).

[90] See, as to exempt supplies, *ibid.* s.17 (as amended by the Finance (No. 2) Act 1992, Sched. 3, para. 18), Sched. 6 (as amended).

[91] See *supra*, paras. 10–41, 10–158 *et seq.*, 18–18.

[92] The expression "goods" is not defined in the Value Added Tax Act 1983, although several provisions expressly treat certain types of supply as a supply of goods, *e.g.* see *ibid.* Sched. 2. paras. 2, 3, 4 (as amended). It is submitted that, where no such provision applies, "goods" should be given its usual meaning, *i.e.* tangible chattels or choses in possession (as opposed to choses in action).

[93] H.M. Customs and Excise Press Release dated December 10, 1982, reproduced at [1982] S.T.I. 554. Formerly, goodwill was treated as outside the scope of the tax unless it took some tangible form: see, for example, the decision in *J. Procter (Waddington) Ltd. v. The Commissioners* (1976) V.A.T.T.R. 184.

[94] The predecessor of this subsection was the Finance Act 1972, s.45(6) (as added by the Finance Act 1977). In *J. Procter (Waddington) Ltd. v. The Commissioners, supra*, the tribunal had

"(6) The disposition of a business as a going concern, or of its assets or liabilities (whether or not in connection with its reorganisation or winding up), is a supply made in the course or furtherance of the business."

The subsection requires the disposition to be treated as a "supply," but not necessarily as a "taxable supply."[95] It would accordingly still seem necessary to dissect the business into its constituent elements in order to determine which of its assets are exempt or outside the scope of the tax[96] and whether there has been a taxable supply of goods or services. Furthermore, a supply will, in any event, only be treated as made where the business assets are transferred by a taxable person to a purchaser who is not, and does not as a result of the transfer become, a taxable person and who could not, for whatever reason, use the assets in carrying on the same kind of business, whether as a new business or as part of an existing business.[97]

For registration purposes, the purchaser will be treated as having carried on the business before as well as after the transfer.[98]

---

previously held that the sale of a business as a going concern was a taxable supply in the course of the business, since the business of a taxable person falls to be treated as the management of all the businesses which he carries on: *ibid.* p. 195. The decision is an unsatisfactory one, and may still give rise to considerable difficulties: see further, *infra,* para. 37–28.

[95] This expression is defined in the Value Added Tax Act 1983, s.2(2) as "a supply of goods or services made in the United Kingdom other than an exempt supply."

[96] For an example of the dissection which is required, see *J. Procter (Waddington) Ltd. v. The Commissioners* (1976) V.A.T.T.R. 184. It should, however, be noted that goodwill is no longer treated as outside the scope of the tax (see *supra,* para. 37–20) and that the general exemption in respect of land has been severely curtailed and may now, in any event, be waived within certain limits: Value Added Tax Act 1983, Sched. 6, Group 1 (as substituted by the Finance Act 1989, Sched. 3, para. 4(1) and amended by the Value Added Tax (Construction of Dwellings and Land) Order 1990 (S.I. 1990 No. 2553), Art. 3 and the Value Added Tax (Buildings and Land) Order 1991 (S.I. 1991 No. 2569), Art. 2), Sched. 6A, para. 2(1) (as substituted by the Finance Act 1989, Sched. 3, para. 6(2) and amended by the Value Added Tax (Buildings and Land) Order 1991, Arts. 3–8). It may well be desirable, when drawing up a contract for the sale of a business as a going concern, to apportion the purchase price between the various assets sold, so that, subject to the apportionment being shown to be genuine, the dissection process will be simplified.

[97] The Value Added Tax (Special Provisions) Order 1992 (S.I. 1992 No. 3129), Art. 5(1) in general prevents a supply of goods or services being treated as made on the sale of a business as a going concern where the business assets are transferred by a taxable person to another taxable person (or a person who immediately becomes a taxable person as a result of the transfer); see also *Customs and Excise Commissioners v. Dearwood Ltd.* [1986] S.T.C. 327; *Rakshit v. The Commissioners* (LON/87/716) [1989] S.T.I. 114; *Conard Systems and Engineering Ltd. v. The Commissioners* (MAN/89/23) [1990] S.T.I. 49; *Chevenings Ltd. v. The Commissioners* (LON/89/733) [1990] S.T.I. 841; *ECSG Ltd. v. The Commissioners* (LON/88/580) [1990] S.T.I. 873 (transfer following cessation of trading by insolvent firm); *The Golden Oak Partnership v. The Commissioners* (LON/90/958) [1992] S.T.I. 491 (sale of partially developed land); *cf. McMichael v. The Commissioners* (LON/88/98) [1990] S.T.I. 128. Note, however, the exception in the case of certain categories of land and buildings: *ibid.* para. 5(2). There is now *no* specific provision covering the sale of a business by any person (other than a taxable person) to another person: *cf.* the Value Added Tax (Special Provisions) Order 1977, Art. 12, which was revoked by the Value Added Tax (Special Provisions) Order 1981 (S.I. 1981 No. 1741), Art 3(1). However, it is thought that, by implication, such a sale would not involve a supply of goods or services for the purposes of the tax, provided that the transferee is going to carry on the same kind of business as that carried on by the transferor and thus should, in most cases, not have the effect of turning an otherwise non-taxable person into a taxable person.

[98] Value Added Tax Act 1983, s.33(1)(a); see also *ibid.* Sched. 1, para. 1(2), (3), as added by the Finance Act 1990, s.10(2) and amended by the Value Added Tax (Increase of Registration Limits) (No. 2) Order 1993 (S.I. 1993 No. 2953), Art. 2. In addition the Commissioners may make

—continued on page 1028

Partnership ceasing to be a taxable person

37–22 The circumstances in which the Commissioners may cancel the registration of a firm which ceases to be a taxable person have already been noticed.[99] In such a case, any goods forming part of its assets will, in general, be treated as supplied in the course or furtherance of its business immediately before the firm lost that status.[1] An exception is, however, made where the business is transferred as a going concern to another taxable person[2] or is temporarily carried on following the death, bankruptcy or incapacity of all the partners,[3] or where the tax on the deemed supply would not exceed £250.[4]

Dissolution of the partnership

37–23 A taxable supply of all the goods owned by a partnership will be almost inevitable in the event of a general dissolution.[5] It has already been seen[6] that the sale of a partnership asset, or of the partnership business as a going concern, may be treated as a taxable supply. In addition, the Act specifically provides that anything done in connection with the termination or intended termination of a business is treated as done in the course or furtherance of that business[7]: there can accordingly be no doubt that all supplies of goods and services made whilst the firm's affairs are being wound up will be taxable.[8]

—continued from page 1027
provision, by regulation, for securing continuity in the application of the Act: *ibid.* s.33(2) and (3). The current regulations are to be found in the Value Added Tax (General) Regulations 1985 (1985 No. 886), reg. 4(4)–(8) (as substituted/amended by the Value Added Tax (General) (Amendment) (No. 4) Regulations 1992 (S.I. 1992 No. 3102), reg.4(a)). Note also the decision in *Ponsonby v. Customs & Excise Commissioners* [1988] S.T.C. 28.

[99] See *supra*, para. 37–13.

[1] Value Added Tax Act 1983, Sched. 2, para. 7(1). Note that certain goods may be excepted: *ibid.* para. 7(2), as amended by the Finance (No. 2) Act 1992, Sched. 3, para. 60(2). The deemed supply will be at open market value: *ibid.* s.10(3).

[2] *Ibid.* Sched. 2, para. 7(1)(a). Note, however, that such a transfer may itself be treated as a taxable supply: see *supra*, para. 37–21.

[3] *Ibid.* Sched. 2, para. 7(1)(b); Value Added Tax (General) Regulations 1985 (S.I. 1985 No. 1650), reg. 11(1). Such treatment is, however, in the discretion of the Commissioners: *ibid. Semble*, the position will be the same in the event of the firm being wound up as an unregistered company (as to which see *supra*, paras. 27–08 *et seq.*): but note the terms of *ibid.* reg. 11(3), as inserted by the Value Added Tax (General) Regulations 1985, reg. 7.

[4] Value Added Tax Act 1983, Sched. 2, para. 7(1)(c).

[5] This will be so whether or not any *actual* supplies are made in the course of winding up the firm's affairs.

[6] See *supra*, paras. 37–19 *et seq.*

[7] Value Added Tax Act 1983, s.47(5). It would seem that no change of practice was contemplated when the wording of the original section (Finance Act 1972, s.45(5)) was amended: see the replies of the Customs and Excise to the comments of the Consultative Committee of Accountancy Bodies on the Finance Bill 1977, reproduced at [1977] S.T.I. 276, 278.

[8] In the absence of a specific provision, it might have been argued that there can be no supply in the course or furtherance of a business when the supply is made purely with a view to winding that business up. As to the continuing authority of the partners to make supplies in the course of winding up the firm's affairs, see the Partnership Act 1890, s.38, considered *supra*, paras. 13–64 *et seq.*

Any remaining goods owned by the firm will in any event be the subject of a deemed supply immediately before the firm ceases to be a taxable person,[9] even though it may only have become such a person by reason of supplies made in the course of the winding-up.[10]

Once the final deemed supply of all the firm's goods has been made, any subsequent supply of those goods will not be taxable,[11] unless it is made in the course or furtherance of a *new* business carried on by the partners in respect of which they are required to be registered.

Transfers of partnership shares

The question whether tax should be charged on the transfer of a **37–24** partnership share[12] raises an issue of considerable complexity, but will be of no direct concern to the partnership, since the taxable supply (if any) will be made by the transferor partner, who may or may not already be a taxable person in his own right.[13]

In this context, it would seem that a distinction must be drawn between cases where the share is transferred to another partner or partners, *e.g.* to a continuing or incoming partner, and cases where it is transferred to a third party who is not and does not become a partner.

Transfers to another partner or partners

Even if the transfer of a partnership share does constitute a supply **37–25** of goods or services made in the course or furtherance of a business,[14] the current editor submits that no tax is properly chargeable thereon. Section 30(1) of the Value Added Tax Act 1983 specifically provides that "no account shall be taken, in determining

---

[9] Value Added Tax Act 1983, Sched. 2, para. 7(1): see *supra*, para. 37–22.

[10] Save in certain cases where the partnership business is sold as a going concern (as to which see *supra*, para. 37–21, n. 97), the sale of any goods which it owns may itself cause the value of its supplies to exceed the prescribed limits: see *supra*, paras. 37–19, 37–20.

[11] See *Marshall v. The Commissioners* (1975) V.A.T.T.R. 98.

[12] There can, of course, be no supply if there is no transfer; thus, even if tax is chargeable on the transfer of a share from one partner to another, the current editor suggests that there can be no taxable supply where a partner retires and, under the terms of the partnership agreement, his share is expressed to accrue to the continuing partners. In such circumstances it is submitted that the share of the retiring partner merely becomes valueless, whilst the shares of the continuing partners enjoy an inbuilt increase in value; at no stage is there either a transfer or a supply. See further, *supra*, paras. 35–19, 36–50, 36–56.

[13] The partnership (*i.e.* the individuals carrying on business in partnership) is a separate "taxable person": see *supra*, para. 37–06 *et seq.* Thus, even though each individual partner may be deemed to be registered where the partnership is registered in the firm name (see *Customs and Excise Commissioners v. Glassborow* [1975] Q.B. 465), that registration will only apply to the partnership business and will not cover a business carried on by a partner on his own account.

[14] The current editor doubts whether a share is within the scope of the tax: see further, *infra*, para. 37–27.

for any purpose of this part of this Act whether goods or services are supplied to or by such persons [*i.e. persons carrying on business in partnership*] ... of any change in the partnership."[15] The purpose behind the section is by no means clear,[16] but one effect of the quoted words would appear to be that any change in a firm, whether resulting from the admission or retirement of a partner or from a mere change in capital or asset-surplus sharing ratios, cannot give rise to a supply of goods or services. It is considered that such a result is both desirable and correct.[17]

Transfers to third parties

37–26   Where a share is transferred to a third party who does not become a partner,[18] section 30(1) of the Value Added Tax Act 1983 cannot apply and tax is potentially chargeable. However, such a charge will only be imposed if the transfer constitutes a taxable supply of goods or services made in the course or furtherance of a business carried on by the transferor partner.

37–27   In order to determine whether this condition is satisfied, it is first necessary to ascertain whether the transfer of a share can be treated as a taxable supply of goods or services. It has already been seen[19] that, on a true analysis, a partner's share is represented by his right to a proportion of the surplus remaining after all the partnership assets have been sold, and all the partnership debts and liabilities discharged. Given the nature of the entitlement, it is submitted that such a share cannot easily be treated as either "goods" or "services,"[20] and should properly be regarded as outside the scope of

---

[15] See further, *supra*, paras. 37–06 *et seq.*

[16] Could it seriously be argued that the entire subsection deals only with the mechanics of registration, and contains no general exemption for supplies between partners? It is thought not. *Cf.* the Finance Act 1972, s.22(1) in its original unamended form.

[17] It is at the same time recognised that the Value Added Tax Act 1983, s.30(1) is open to a less generous interpretation, thus admitting an argument that tax is chargeable on the transfer of a share from one partner to another. Were such an argument to be pursued, it would raise considerations identical to those set out *infra*, paras. 37–27, 37–28, although the current editor submits that no charge to tax can in any event arise where the share of a retiring partner is expressed to accrue to the continuing partners: see *supra*, para. 37–24, n. 12. Note also that the Commissioners could treat the value of any supply as the open market value of the share transferred, unless the transfer was made pursuant to a bona fide commercial arrangement: Value Added Tax Act 1983, s.10(2), (5), Sched. 4, para. 1, as amended by the Finance Act 1987, s.17(1); Income and Corporation Taxes Act 1988, s.839(4).

[18] *e.g.* where the share is transferred to trustees.

[19] See generally, *supra*, paras. 19–04 *et seq. Cf.* the approach of the court in *Gray v. I.R.C.* [1994] S.T.C. 360, 377.

[20] Although neither expression is defined in the Value Added Tax Act 1983 or the regulations made thereunder, the current editor submits that (subject to the express provisions of *ibid.* Scheds. 5, 6 and 6A) "goods" should be given its normal meaning, *i.e.* tangible chattels or choses in possession, except in those cases which involve a *deemed* supply of goods; on the other hand, whilst in normal usage the expression "services" implies that something must be "done," the Act treats the assignment of any right as a supply of services (see *ibid.* s.3(2)(b)), which is prima facie apt to cover the transfer of a partnership share.

the tax.[21] Nevertheless, in at least one case[22] the Tribunal has been prepared to hold that each partner has a direct beneficial interest in a particular partnership asset, thus laying the foundation for an argument that a partner's share should be treated as a composite bundle of such interests. On that footing, it would be possible to dissect the share into those interests which subsist in goods owned by the firm and those which subsist in other assets.[23] A transfer of the former could clearly constitute a supply of services, provided that consideration is received.[24]

If it can be shown that a partnership share is within the scope of **37–28** the tax and that it is the subject of a taxable supply, tax will only be chargeable if that supply was made by the partner concerned "in the course or furtherance of any business carried on by him."[25] Whilst it is arguable that a partner does not carry on any business in relation to his share, it must be recognised that his share can itself be regarded as a business carried on by him.[26] On that basis, any

---

[21] Even if this argument were not sustained, the transfer would only involve a taxable supply if a consideration is received: *ibid.* s.3(2); but note the terms of *ibid.* s.3(4). And see the reply of the Customs and Excise to the comments of the Consultative Committee of Accountancy Bodies on the Finance Bill 1977, reproduced at [1977] S.T.I. 276–277.

[22] *Border Flying Co. v. The Commissioners* (1976) V.A.T.T.R. 132, 138. See also *supra*, para. 37–17.

[23] It should be noted that a partner's interest in goodwill would apparently now be taxable: see the Customs and Excise Press Release dated December 10, 1982, reproduced at [1982] S.T.I. 554; see also *supra*, para. 37–20. So far as concerns his interest in any land owned by the firm, it will be necessary to establish whether (1) the land falls within one of the exceptions to the Value Added Tax Act 1983, Sched. 6, Group 1 (as substituted by the Finance Act 1989, Sched. 3 para. 4(1) and amended by the Value Added Tax (Construction of Dwellings and Land) Order 1990 (S.I. 1990 No. 2553), Art. 3 and the Value Added Tax (Buildings and Land) Order 1991 (S.I. 1991 No. 2569), Art. 2) or (2) a waiver under *ibid.* Sched. 6A, para. 2(1) (as added by the Finance Act 1989, Sched. 3, para. 6(2)) is in effect.

[24] It is provided that the transfer of an undivided share in goods is a supply of services: Value Added Tax Act 1983, Sched. 2, para. 1(1)(a). Although *ibid.* s.3(2), which requires consideration to be given for a supply of services, takes effect subject to the provisions of that Schedule, the current editor submits that this does not dispense with the need for consideration in the absence of a clear statutory direction: *cf.* Sched. 2, para. 5(1), as amended by the Finance Act 1989, Sched. 3, para. 11(b). It is doubted whether reliance could ever be placed on the Value Added Tax (Special Provisions) Order 1992 (S.I. 1992 No. 3129), Art. 5, which prevents a supply of business assets from constituting a supply of goods or services where the business is transferred as a going concern by a taxable person either to another taxable person or to a person who immediately becomes a taxable person as a result of the transfer, provided that the assets are to be used by the transferee in carrying on the same kind of business as that carried on by the transferor: see further, *supra*, para. 37–21. Given the nature of the business which the transferor partner will be regarded as carrying on (as to which, see *infra*, para. 37–28) and the fact that the transferee will, *ex hypothesi*, not become a partner, it is difficult to see how the latter condition could be fulfilled: note also, in this context, the implications of the decision in *Customs and Excise Commissioners v. Dearwood* [1986] S.T.C. 327. The position of a non-taxable person who transfers a business as a going concern is no better: even though Art. 5 contains no provision specifically governing such a case, it is apparent that, in order to avoid the transfer of the business assets being treated as a supply for registration purposes, the latter condition must still be fulfilled and the same difficulty will arise.

[25] Value Added Tax Act 1983, s.2(1).

[26] Such an argument could derive some support from the decision in *J. Procter (Waddington) Ltd. v. The Commissioners* (1976) V.A.T.T.R. 184. In that case, the Tribunal decided that the business of a taxable person may comprise the management of one or more different and diversified businesses: *ibid.* p. 195. Thus, it could be said that one of the businesses carried on by a partner is the business which he carries on in partnership with his fellow partners.

disposition of the share "as a going concern" would automatically be treated as a supply in the course or furtherance of the business.[27] As a result, tax would have to charged on the transfer if the transferor partner is, or will as a result of the transfer become, a taxable person.

It will be apparent from the foregoing that the transfer of a partnership share to a third party gives rise to a number of (as yet) unresolved problems and it cannot be stated with any degree of certainty that such a transfer will *not* involve a taxable supply.[28]

3. ADMINISTRATION

Although the administration of value added tax gives rise to few specific problems in its application to partnerships, certain points do merit particular mention.

Notification by partners

37–29   Reference has already been made to the circumstances in which partners must give a notification to the Commissioners, *e.g.* of their liability to be registered or of a change in or affecting the firm.[29] The Commissioners have wide powers to specify (a) the form of any notification to be given under Schedule 1 to the Value Added Tax Act 1983,[30] and (b) by what persons anything required to be done under that Act is to be done where a business is carried on in partnership.[31] Thus, regulations provide that the notification by a partnership of its liability to be registered must include, on the form VAT 2,[32] the name, address and signature of each partner.[33] Moreover, it is the joint and several liability of all the partners to give any notice required to be given for the purposes of the Act or the regulations, although there will be sufficient compliance if one of the partners gives such notice.[34]

---

[27] Value Added Tax Act 1983, s.47(6): see further, *supra*, para. 37–21. As already noted, it may be necessary to dissect the share into its component elements in order to determine on which of those elements tax should be charged; see also *supra*, paras. 37–19, 37–20.
[28] Should the Commissioners seek to impose a charge, it would clearly be advantageous to the transferor partner to contend that his share comprises a bundle of direct beneficial interests in each partnership asset, since in this way the full value of the share may not be subject to tax.
[29] See *supra*, para. 37–12.
[30] Value Added Tax Act 1983, Sched. 1, para. 14; also Sched. 1A, para. 9, Sched. 1B, para. 10 (as respectively added by the Finance (No. 2) Act 1992, Sched. 3, para. 59).
[31] *Ibid.* s.31(2).
[32] See the Value Added Tax (General) Regulations 1985 (S.I. 1985 No. 886), Sched. 1, Form No. 2.
[33] *Ibid.* reg. 4(1), as substituted by the Value Added Tax (General) (Amendment) (No. 4) Regulations 1992 (S.I. 1992 No. 3102), reg. 4(a).
[34] *Ibid.* reg. 9(1).

Failure to notify change in firm

An outgoing partner will continue to be treated as a partner, and **37–30** will be liable as such, until such time as the Commissioners have been duly notified of the change in the firm.[35]

Signature on forms

The Commissioners will seemingly require that any return or form **37–31** which falls to be signed by the firm is signed by one of the partners in his own name, rather than in the firm name.[36] The justification for this requirement appears to lie in the need to identify the actual individual who appended the signature.

Notices to partners

Any notice, whether of assessment or otherwise, addressed to a **37–32** firm by the name in which it is registered and served in accordance with Part I of the Value Added Tax Act 1983[37] will be treated as served not only on the firm but also on any former partner, if it relates to, or to any matter arising in, the prescribed accounting period[38] during which he ceased to be a member of the firm, or any earlier period during the whole or part of which he was such a member.[39]

Liability for tax

The liability of partners for tax due in respect of taxable supplies **37–33** made in the course or furtherance of the partnership business is expressly laid down by reference to section 9 of the Partnership Act 1890, and is not affected by the provisions of section 30(1) or (3) of

---

[35] Value Added Tax Act 1983, s.30(2), *supra*, para. 37–06; and note *The Bengal Brasserie v. The Commissioners* (LON/90/604) [1991] S.T.I. 662. Since the subsection is expressed to be without prejudice to the Partnership Act 1890, s.36 (see *supra*, paras. 13–42 *et seq.*), it seemingly can have no application to deceased partners: see subs. (3) of the latter section. *Sed quaere* in the case of bankrupt partners.

[36] See the reply of the Customs and Excise to item 10(b) of the Memorandum of Comments of the Allied Accountancy Bodies submitted in January 1974, reproduced at [1974] S.T.I. 133, 137. This requirement is in marked contrast to the express provisions of the Partnership Act 1890, s.6: see *supra*, paras. 12–161 *et seq.*

[37] See, in particular, the Value Added Tax Act 1983, s.46, as amended by the Finance (No. 2) Act 1992, Sched. 3, para. 43.

[38] See, as to the meaning of this expression, *ibid.* s.14(1) (as amended by the Finance Act 1987, s.11(1)), Sched. 7, para. 2 (as amended); Value Added Tax (General) Regulations 1985, reg. 58(1) (as amended).

[39] Value Added Tax Act 1983, s.30(3), (4), *supra*, para. 37–06. However, it does not follow that an outgoing partner will necessarily fall to be treated as such: this will depend on whether the appropriate notification has been given to the Commissioners: see *ibid.* s.30(2) and *supra*, para. 37–30. As to the position prior to the introduction of the above subsections (and their predecessors), see *Customs and Excise Commissioners v. Evans* [1982] S.T.C. 342.

the Value Added Tax Act 1983.[40] Thus, whilst he is alive, each partner will be liable jointly with his fellow partners for tax due in respect of any prescribed accounting period during which he remained a partner; after his death, his estate will be severally liable therefor.[41] Where a partner dies or leaves the firm in the middle of a prescribed accounting period, an appropriate apportionment will be made,[42] provided that, in the latter case only, the Commissioners have been duly notified of the change in the firm.[43] If the proper notification has not been given, the outgoing partner will remain liable jointly with his former partners for all tax subsequently due until such time as the default is remedied, at which point he will be deemed to have retired. An apportionment will only be appropriate in respect of the prescribed accounting period in which fell the date of such *deemed* retirement.

---

[40] *Ibid.* s.30(5), as amended by the Finance (No. 2) Act 1992, Sched. 3, para. 31(3): see *supra*, para. 37–06.

[41] Partnership Act 1890, s.9: see *supra*, paras. 13–03, 13–06 *et seq.*

[42] Value Added Tax Act 1983, s.30(5) (as amended). The apportionment will be on such a basis "as may be just."

[43] *Ibid.* s.30(2) (as amended by the Finance (No. 2) Act 1992, Sched. 3, para. 31(2)): see *supra*, para. 37–30. It is submitted that the subsection has no application to deceased partners; *sed quaere* in the case of bankrupt partners.

CHAPTER 38

STAMP DUTY

THE 1980s saw the abolition of capital duty[1] and the *ad valorem* **38-01**
charge on voluntary dispositions,[2] as well as the removal of a
significant number of the fixed heads of duty,[3] but a far more radical
change was introduced by the Finance Act 1991.[4]

Property exempt from *ad valorem* duty

The Finance Act 1991 abolished the charge to *ad valorem* duty **38-02**
under most of the remaining heads[5] so far as concerns "exempt
property," which comprises property *other than* land, an interest in
the proceeds of the sale of land held on trust for sale and a licence to
occupy land.[6] It follows that duty can no longer be charged on
goodwill.[7] Where duty would be chargeable under the heading
"conveyance or transfer on sale"[8] and part of the property in
question consists of exempt property, the consideration is apportioned as between the exempt and non-exempt elements and only
that attributable to the latter is chargeable.[9]

Stamp duty and partnership transactions

This development has greatly simplified the treatment of partner- **38-03**
ship transactions and, in many cases, stamp duty considerations will
no longer arise. Nevertheless, in those cases in which non-exempt
property[10] is involved, it may be necessary to analyse the
circumstances in which a charge to *ad valorem* duty can be imposed.

---

[1] Capital duty, which was levied on certain transactions affecting "capital companies" under the
Finance Act 1973, was abolished by the Finance Act 1988, s.141. The statutory definition of
"capital company" specifically included limited (but not ordinary) partnerships: Finance Act 1973,
s.29(1)(b).
[2] This head of charge, which was introduced by the Finance (1909–1910) Act 1910, s.74, was
abolished by the Finance Act 1985, s.82.
[3] Finance Act 1985, s.85(1), Sched. 24, amending the Stamp Act 1891, Sched. 1.
[4] Finance Act 1991, ss.110, 111.
[5] *Ibid.* s.110(1)-(3). The headings include a "Conveyance or Transfer on Sale" and a
"Conveyance or Transfer of any kind not hereinbefore described". Duty is no longer charged under
the head "Exchange or Excambion": Finance Act 1994, s.241(3).
[6] Finance Act 1991, s.110(5).
[7] As to the former position, see *Potter v. C.I.R.* (1854) 10 Ex. 147; *Troup v. C.I.R.* (1891) 7
T.L.R. 610; *Benjamin Brooke & Co. Ltd. v. C.I.R.* [1896] 2 Q.B. 356; *West London Syndicate v.
C.I.R.* [1898] 2 Q.B. 507; *I.R.C. v. Muller & Co.'s Margarine Ltd.* [1901] A.C. 217; *Eastern
National Omnibus Co. Ltd. v. I.R.C.* [1939] 1 K.B. 161.
[8] Stamp Act 1891, Sched. 1.
[9] Finance Act 1991, s.111. The consideration will be apportioned "on such basis as is just and
reasonable": *ibid.* s.111(2)(a).
[10] As to what property qualifies as exempt, see *ibid.* s.110(5) and *supra*, para. 38–02.

These can most conveniently be considered in the context of the following four stages in the life of a firm:

(1) formation;
(2) alteration of partners' shares;
(3) retirement and admission of partners;
(4) dissolution.

However, in each case, one overriding principle must be borne in mind, namely that *ad valorem* duty will only be chargeable by reference to the consideration apportioned to non-exempt property[11] where a deed or other document is brought into existence[12]: if this formality can be dispensed with,[13] duty can still be avoided.

(1) *Formation of a Partnership*

38–04 A partnership agreement which does not operate to convey or transfer any non-exempt property will not be chargeable to *ad valorem* duty nor, if it is under seal, will it attract a deed stamp.[14] This will include the normal case of an agreement under which a partner contributes a sum of capital represented in whole or in part by non-exempt property, even if he does not receive a credit in his capital account equivalent to the full value of that property, since there will in such a case be nothing resembling a "conveyance or transfer on sale."[15] However, the position may be otherwise if that partner's capital contribution is demonstrably credited to another partner's capital account as the purchase price for a share in the firm;[16] *a fortiori* if such "capital" is immediately withdrawn by that other partner under the terms of the agreement.

(2) *Alteration of Partners' shares*

38–05 Where, unusually, one partner purchases part of another partner's share whilst the partnership is continuing, there will be a conveyance or transfer on sale and *ad valorem* duty will be chargeable on any

---

[11] Finance Act 1991, s.111. See also, *supra*, para. 38–02, n. 9.

[12] See the judgment of Darling J. in *Garnett v. C.I.R.* (1899) 81 L.T. 633, 637.

[13] Thus, it may be possible to prove that land has become an asset of a firm even though the partnership agreement has not been reduced to writing: see *supra*, paras. 7–01 *et seq.* Prior to the Finance Act 1991, when all forms of property were dutiable, movable property, such as machinery and plant, could be passed by delivery.

[14] This head of duty was abolished by the Finance Act 1985, s.85(1), Sched. 24.

[15] Stamp Act 1891, s.1, Sched. 1. Indirect support for this proposition may be drawn from *Mcleod v. I.R.C.* (1885) 22 S.L.R. 674, noticed *infra*, para. 38–09.

[16] In such a case, the supposed capital contribution would amount to no more than a colourable device to avoid stamp duty. The court would look to the substance of the transaction (*i.e.* a sale) and charge duty accordingly: see, for example, *Ingram v. I.R.C.* [1986] Ch. 585, where Vinelott J. applied the principles enunciated in *W. T. Ramsay Ltd. v. I.R.C.* [1982] A.C. 300 and *Furniss v. Dawson* [1984] A.C. 474 to a stamp duty avoidance transaction. But note also that inroads have recently been made into those principles: see *supra*, para. 34–11.

deed or document by which that transaction is effected, to the extent that the consideration is apportioned to non-exempt property.[17] It would seem that the position will now be the same where the re-arrangement involves an effective exchange,[18] although the limits of the charge are by no means clear.[19]

(3) *Retirement and Admission of Partners*

Outgoing partners

Where an outgoing partner assigns his share and interest in the **38–06** firm to his co-partners in return for a payment, which will often be computed by reference to the balances due to him on capital and current account adjusted by reference to the market value of the partnership assets,[20] there will clearly be a sale for stamp duty purposes and any document evidencing the assignment will be charged to *ad valorem* duty by reference to that part of the consideration which is apportioned to non-exempt property.[21] Given the nature of non-exempt property,[22] the current editor submits that it is unlikely to be possible to prove that an assignment of such property was completed *before* any document is brought into existence with a view to avoiding the charge to duty.[23]

If, however, the outgoing partner does not, as such, assign his **38–07** share to his co-partners,[24] but merely withdraws the amount due to him on account of capital and undrawn profits and gives a receipt

---

[17] Finance Act 1991, s.111.

[18] Finance Act 1994, s.241. Care should, in practice, be taken to avoid an exchange of interests in land, since both transfers will be dutiable: *ibid.*; and see also [1994] S.T.I. 419, 518.

[19] *Quaere*, where a partner accepts a diminution in his entitlement to income profits in exchange for a greater share of capital profits, can *ibid.* s.241 apply? Given the true nature of a partnership share (see generally, *supra*, paras. 19–02 *et seq.*), can a partner be said to have an interest in any land owned by the firm? Even if he can, does the consideration consist of or include "any property" for the purposes of *ibid.* s.241(1)(a)? If, as the current editor would submit, the section does not apply, it would seem that a fixed duty of 50p might be payable under the head "Conveyance or Transfer of any kind not hereinbefore described": Stamp Act 1891, s.1, Sched. 1; and see *Littlewoods Mail Order Stores Ltd. v. I.R.C.* [1963] A.C. 135. *Semble*, apart from the Finance Act 1994, s.241, duty could not be charged under the head "Conveyance or Transfer on Sale" (Stamp Act 1891. ss.1, 54, Sched. 1). Note that there is no longer a charge to duty under the head "Exchange or Excambion": Finance Act 1994, s.241(3).

[20] See, generally, *supra*, paras. 10–128 *et seq.*

[21] Under the head "Conveyance or Transfer on Sale": Stamp Act 1891, s.1, Sched. 1; Finance Act 1991, s.111. See *Christie v. C.I.R.* (1866) L.R. 2 Ex. 46; *Phillips v. C.I.R.* (1867) L.R. 2 Ex. 399; *Garnett v. C.I.R.* (1899) 81 L.T. 633; also *Potter v. C.I.R.* (1854) 10 Ex. 147. Alternatively, any contract or agreement for sale may attract an *ad valorem* charge: Stamp Act 1891, s.59.

[22] *i.e.* land, an interest in land and a licence to occupy land: Finance Act 1991, s.110(5).

[23] See the Law of Property Act 1925, ss.52, 53. The position may be otherwise on the *creation* of a partnership: see *supra*, paras. 7–02 *et seq.* For an example of the dangers of bringing a document into existence, see *Garnett v. I.R.C. supra*; see also, generally, *Grey v. C.I.R.* [1960] A.C. 1.

[24] Note, however, that, in the case supposed, he will inevitably relinquish his share in the partnership on his retirement so that, on one view, there will be an assignment: see, for example, *Gray v. Smith* (1880) 43 Ch.D. 208; and see *supra*, para. 10–207.

therefor, it is the view of the current editor that there will, on a true analysis, be no sale so that a charge to *ad valorem* duty cannot be imposed. This may be so even if a deed or other document is brought into existence contemporaneously or otherwise.[25]

Incoming partners

38–08 Where an incoming partner purchases a share in the firm on his admission,[26] there will clearly be a conveyance on sale and any deed or document by which it is effected it will be chargeable to *ad valorem* duty to the extent that the consideration is apportioned to non-exempt property.[27] However, if the existing assets of the firm comprise such property and the incoming partner merely contributes capital, in the form of cash or a specific asset, and receives an appropriate credit in his capital account, there will normally be no question of a sale and no duty can be charged. As already noted, the position may be otherwise where the value of the incoming partner's contribution is credited to the capital account of one or more of the existing partners.[28] Equally, if the incoming partner provides a non-tangible, but otherwise valuable, consideration for his share,[29] then it would seem that a charge to *ad valorem* duty could, in theory, be imposed.[30]

(4) *Dissolution of Partnership*

38–09 Where the terms of dissolution involve one or more of the partners' shares being bought out by the others, then any deed or document effecting the dissolution will, if any part of the consideration is apportioned to non-exempt assets, be chargeable to *ad valorem* duty as a conveyance or transfer on sale.[31] If, on the other hand, each partner merely takes out a sum of cash, then there will be no sale and no duty can be charged.[32] The intermediate position is where the assets are divided between the partners *in specie*: in such a case, a

---

[25] See *Garnett v. C.I.R.* (1899) 81 L.T. 633, 637, *per* Darling J.; *cf. Fleetwood-Hesketh v. C.I.R.* [1936] 1 K.B. 351. See also *supra*, para. 10–206.

[26] Instances in which an incoming partner will buy his way into a firm are becoming increasingly rare, particularly in the professional sphere.

[27] In such a case, duty will be charged under the head "Conveyance or Transfer on Sale": Stamp Act 1891, s.1, Sched. 1; Finance Act 1991, s.111.

[28] Since the admission of an additional partner in law results in the creation of a new partnership, the relevant considerations will be the same as those set out *supra*, para. 38–04.

[29] *e.g.* by undertaking to devote his whole time to the partnership business. The current editor submits that such an undertaking would effectively amount to valuable consideration: see *Att.-Gen. v. Boden* [1912] 1 K.B. 539 and *Att.-Gen. v. Ralli* (1936) 15 A.T.C. 523, considered *supra*, paras. 36–05 *et seq.*

[30] *Quaere* whether, in the circumstances supposed in the preceding note, any attempt would be made to impose a charge.

[31] See the cases cited *supra*, para. 38–06, n. 21.

[32] *Garnett v. C.I.R.* (1899) 81 L.T. 633; *Fleetwood-Hesketh v. C.I.R.* [1936] 1 K.B. 351. And see *supra*, paras. 10–206, 38–04.

fixed duty of 50p will prima facie be imposed,[33] even though one or more of the partners may receive part of his entitlement in cash.[34]

If the dissolution is not effected by a deed or other document, then **38–10** no duty will in any circumstances be payable, although the scope for such avoidance in the case of non-exempt property is minimal in the face of the strict requirements of the Law of Property Act 1925.[35] Even if that difficulty could be overcome, the parties might still wish to bring some documentary evidence of the dissolution into existence, *e.g.* with a view to restricting competition on the part of one or more of the former partners. In such a case, great care would have to be taken to ensure that the dissolution had already been effected (and could be proved to have been effected) prior to the document coming into existence; otherwise a recital or other reference in the document to the manner in which the partnership assets had been distributed between the partners might cause it to be stampable.[36]

---

[33] Under the head "Conveyance or Transfer of any kind not hereinbefore described": Stamp Act 1891, s.62, Sched. 1. *Aliter*, if the partnership assets only comprise exempt property: Finance Act 1991, s.110(1), (3)(b), (4), (5). *Quaere* whether, to the extent that the partnership assets comprise non-exempt property, *ad valorem* duty would be chargeable on any equality money paid: see the Stamp Act 1891, ss.1, 73, Sched. 1: also *supra*, para. 38–05, n. 19. And see *Jopling v. C.I.R.* [1940] 2 K.B. 282.

[34] See *Mcleod v. I.R.C.* (1885) 22 S.L.R. 674; *cf. Christie v. C.I.R.* (1866) L.R. 2 Ex. 46; *Phillips v. C.I.R.* (1867) L.R. 2 Ex. 399; *Troup v. C.I.R.* (1891) 7 T.L.R. 610; *Garnett v. C.I.R.* (1899) 81 L.T. 633; also *Potter v. C.I.R.* (1854) 10 Ex. 147.

[35] ss.52, 53. And see *Gray v. Smith* (1880) 43 Ch.D. 208 (a case of retirement) noticed, *supra*, para. 10–207. *Cf.* the position on the *creation* of a partnership: see *supra*, paras. 7–02 *et seq.*

[36] See in particular, *Garnett v. C.I.R.* (1899) 81 L.T. 633.

APPENDICES

PARTNERSHIP ACT 1890

A1–01

53 & 54 Vict. c. 39

ARRANGEMENT OF SECTIONS

Nature of Partnership

Relations of Partners to Persons dealing with them

Relations of Partners to one another

An Act to declare and amend the Law of Partnership

[August 14, 1890.]

Nature of Partnership

Definition of partnership

A1–02   1.—(1) Partnership is the relation which subsists between persons[1] carrying on a business[2] in common with a view of profit.[3]

(2) But the relation between members of any company or association which is—

(a) Registered as a company under the Companies Act 1862 or any other Act of Parliament for the time being in force and relating to the registration of joint stock companies; or

(b) Formed or incorporated by or in pursuance of any other Act of Parliament or letters patent, or Royal Charter; or

---

[1] By the Interpretation Act 1978, Sched. 1, person includes a corporation.
[2] For the definition of business, see s.45, *infra*, para. A1–46.
[3] See *supra*, paras. 2–01 *et seq.*

(c) A company engaged in working mines within and subject to the jurisdiction of the Stannaries[4]:

is not a partnership within the meaning of this Act.[5]

Rules for determining existence of partnership

2. In determining whether a partnership does or does not exist regard shall **A1–03** be had to the following rules[6]:

(1) Joint tenancy, tenancy in common, joint property, common property or part ownership does not of itself create a partnership as to anything so held or owned, whether the tenants or owners do or do not share any profits made by the use thereof.[7]

(2) The sharing of gross returns does not of itself create a partnership, whether the persons sharing such returns have or have not a joint or common right or interest in any property from which or from the use of which the returns are derived.[8]

(3) The receipt by a person of a share of the profits of a business is prima facie evidence that he is a partner in the business, but the receipt of such a share, or of a payment contingent on or varying with the profits of a business does not of itself make him a partner in the business; and in particular—

(a) The receipt by a person of a debt or other liquidated amount by instalments or otherwise out of the accruing profits of a business does not of itself make him a partner in the business or liable as such:

(b) A contract for the remuneration of a servant or agent of a person engaged in a business by a share of the profits of the business does not of itself make the servant or agent a partner in the business or liable as such[9]:

(c) A person being the widow or child of a deceased partner, and receiving by way of annuity a portion of the profits made in the business in which the deceased person was a partner, is not by reason only of such receipt a partner in the business or liable as such:

(d) The advance of money by way of loan to a person engaged or about to engage in any business on a contract with that person that the lender shall receive a rate of interest varying with the profits, or shall receive a share of the profits arising from carrying on the business, does not of itself make the lender a partner with the person or persons carrying on the business or liable as such. Provided that the contract is in writing, and signed by or on behalf of all the parties thereto:

(e) A person receiving by way of annuity or otherwise a portion of the profits of a business in consideration of the sale by him of the goodwill of the business is not by reason only of such receipt a partner in the business or liable as such.[10]

---

[4] s.23 applies to these companies: see *infra*, para. A1–24.

[5] See *supra*, paras. 2–22 *et seq.*

[6] See *supra*, paras. 5–01 *et seq.*

[7] See *supra*, paras. 5–08 *et seq.*; see also s.20(3), *infra*, para. A1–21.

[8] See *supra*, paras. 5–11, 5–15 *et seq.*

[9] This paragraph and paras. (c), (d) and (e) and s.3 are substantially re-enactments of ss.2, 3, 1 and 4 of Bovill's Act.

[10] See *supra*, paras. 5–20 *et seq.*

Postponement of rights of person lending or selling in consideration of share of profits in case of insolvency

A1–04   **3.** In the event of any person to whom money has been advanced by way of loan upon such a contract as is mentioned in the last foregoing section,[11] or of any buyer of a goodwill in consideration of a share of the profits of the business, being adjudged a bankrupt, entering into an arrangement to pay his creditors less than [one hundred pence][12] in the pound, or dying in insolvent circumstances, the lender of the loan shall not be entitled to recover anything in respect of his loan, and the seller of the goodwill shall not be entitled to recover anything in respect of the share of profits contracted for, until the claims of the other creditors of the borrower or buyer for valuable consideration in money or money's worth have been satisfied.[13]

Meaning of "firm"

A1–05   **4.**—(1) Persons who have entered into partnership with one another are for the purposes of this Act called collectively a firm, and the name under which their business is carried on is called the firm-name.[14]

(2) In Scotland a firm is a legal person distinct from the partners of whom it is composed, but an individual partner may be charged on a decree of diligence directed against the firm, and on payment of the debts is entitled to relief *pro rata* from the firm and its other members.

Relations of Partners to Persons dealing with them

Power of partner to bind the firm

A1–06   **5.** Every partner is an agent of the firm and his other partners for the purpose of the business of the partnership; and the acts of every partner who does any act for carrying on in the usual way business of the kind carried on by the firm of which he is a member, bind the firm and his partners, unless the partner so acting has in fact no authority to act for the firm in the particular matter, and the person with whom he is dealing either knows that he has no authority, or does not know or believe him to be a partner.[15]

Partners bound by acts on behalf of firm

A1–07   **6.** An Act or instrument relating to the business of the firm and done or executed in the firm-name, or in any other manner showing an intention to bind the firm, by any person thereto authorised, whether a partner or not, is binding on the firm and all the partners.

Provided that this section shall not affect any general rule of law relating to the execution of deeds or negotiable instruments.[16]

---

[11] *Quaere*, does this only apply to a contract in writing signed by the parties? See *supra*, para. 5–41.

[12] Substituted by the Decimal Currency Act 1969, s.10(1).

[13] See *supra*, paras. 5–40 *et seq*.

[14] See *supra*, paras. 3–01 *et seq*. For the rules governing actions in the High Court by and against partners in the firm name, see *infra*, paras. A2–09 *et seq*. And see, generally, *supra*, paras. 14–03 *et seq*.

[15] See *supra*, paras. 12–01 *et seq*.; see also s.8, *infra*, para. A1–09.

[16] See *supra*, paras. 12–63 *et seq*., 12–160 *et seq*.

Partner using credit of firm for private purposes

7. Where one partner pledges the credit of the firm for a purpose **A1–08** apparently not connected with the firm's ordinary course of business, the firm is not bound, unless he is in fact specially authorised by the other partners; but this section does not affect any personal liability incurred by an individual partner.[17]

Effect of notice that firm will not be bound by acts of partner

8. If it has been agreed between the partners that any restriction shall be **A1–09** placed on the power of any one or more of them to bind the firm, no act done in contravention of the agreement is binding on the firm with respect to persons having notice of the agreement.[18]

Liability of partners

9. Every partner in a firm is liable jointly with the other partners, and in **A1–10** Scotland severally also, for all debts and obligations of the firm incurred while he is a partner and after his death, his estate is also severally liable in a due course of administration for such debts and obligations, so far as they remain unsatisfied but subject in England or Ireland to the prior payment of his separate debts.[19]

Liability of the firm for wrongs

10. Where, by any wrongful act or omission of any partner acting in the **A1–11** ordinary course of the business of the firm, or with the authority of his co-partners, loss or injury is caused to any person not being a partner in the firm, or any penalty is incurred, the firm is liable therefor to the same extent as the partner so acting or omitting to act.[20]

Misapplication of money or property received for or in custody of the firm

11. In the following cases; namely—   **A1–12**
  (a) Where one partner acting within the scope of his apparent authority receives the money or property of a third person and misapplies it; and
  (b) Where a firm in the course of its business receives money or property of a third person, and the money or property so received is misapplied by one or more of the partners while it is in the custody of the firm;
the firm is liable to make good the loss.[21]

Liability for wrongs joint and several

12. Every partner is liable jointly with his co-partners and also severally for **A1–13** everything for which the firm while he is a partner therein becomes liable under either of the two last preceding sections.[22]

---

[17] See *supra*, paras. 12–147 *et seq.*
[18] *Ibid.*
[19] See *supra*, paras. 13–02 *et seq.*
[20] See *supra*, paras. 12–88 *et seq.* The liability under this section is joint and several: see s.12, *infra.*
[21] See *supra*, paras. 12–105 *et seq.*
[22] See *supra*, para. 13–12.

Improper employment of trust property for partnership purposes

A1–14   **13.** If a partner, being a trustee, improperly employs trust property in the business or on the account of the partnership, no other partner is liable for the trust property to the persons beneficially interested therein:
Provided as follows:

(1)   This section shall not affect any liability incurred by any partner by reason of his having notice of a breach of trust; and
(2)   Nothing in this section shall prevent trust money from being followed and recovered from the firm if still in its possession or under its control.[23]

Persons liable by "holding out"

A1–15   **14.**—(1) Every one who by words spoken or written or by conduct represents himself, or who knowingly suffers himself to be represented, as a partner in a particular firm, is liable as a partner to any one who has on the faith of any such representation given credit to the firm, whether the representation has or has not been made or communicated to the person so giving credit by or with the knowledge of the apparent partner making the representation or suffering it to be made.
(2) Provided that where after a partner's death the partnership business is continued in the old firm-name, the continued use of that name or of the deceased partner's name as part thereof shall not of itself make his executors or administrators estate or effects liable for any partnership debts contracted after his death.[24]

Admissions and representations of partners

A1–16   **15.** An admission or representation made by any partner concerning the partnership affairs, and in the ordinary course of its business, is evidence against the firm.[25]

Notice to acting partner to be notice to the firm

A1–17   **16.** Notice to any partner who habitually acts in the partnership business of any matter relating to partnership affairs operates as notice to the firm, except in the case of a fraud on the firm committed by or with the consent of that partner.[26]

Liabilities of incoming and outgoing partners

A1–18   **17.**—(1) A person who is admitted as a partner into an existing firm does not thereby become liable to the creditors of the firm for anything done before he became a partner.[27]

---

[23] See *supra*, paras. 12–133 *et seq.*
[24] See *supra*, paras. 5–43 *et seq.* See also ss.36, 38, *infra*, paras. A1–37, A1–39.
[25] See *supra*, paras. 12–17 *et seq.*
[26] See *supra*, paras. 12–20 *et seq.*
[27] See *supra*, paras. 13–25 *et seq.*

(2) A partner who retires from a firm does not thereby cease to be liable for partnership debts or obligations incurred before his retirement.[28]

(3) A retiring partner may be discharged from any existing liabilities, by an agreement to that effect between himself and the members of the firm as newly constituted and the creditors, and this agreement may be either express or inferred as a fact from the course of dealing between the creditors and the firm as newly constituted.[29]

Revocation of continuing guaranty by change in firm

18. A continuing guaranty or cautionary obligation given either to a firm or **A1–19** to a third person in respect of the transactions of a firm is, in the absence of agreement to the contrary, revoked as to future transactions by any change in the constitution of the firm to which, or of the firm in respect of the transactions of which, the guaranty or obligation was given.[30]

Relations of Partners to one another

Variation by consent of terms of partnership

19. The mutual rights and duties of partners whether ascertained by **A1–20** agreement or defined by this Act may be varied by the consent of all the partners and such consent may be either express or inferred from a course of dealing.[31]

Partnership property

20.—(1) All property and rights and interests in property originally brought **A1–21** into the partnership stock or acquired, whether by purchase or otherwise, on account of the firm, or for the purposes and in the course of the partnership business, are called in this Act partnership property, and must be held and applied by the partners exclusively for the purposes of the partnership and in accordance with the partnership agreement.[32]

(2) Provided that the legal estate or interest in any land, or in Scotland the title to and interest in any heritable estate, which belongs to the partnership shall devolve according to the nature and tenure thereof, and the general rules of law thereto applicable, but in trust, so far as necessary, for the persons beneficially interested in the land under this section.[33]

(3) Where co-owners of an estate or interest in any land, or in Scotland of any heritable estate, not being itself partnership property are partners as to profits made by the use of that land or estate, and purchase other land or estate out of the profits to be used in like manner, the land or estate so purchased belongs to them, in the absence of an agreement to the contrary, not as partners, but as co-owners for the same respective estates and interests as are held by them in the land or estate first mentioned at the date of the purchase.[34]

---

[28] See *supra*, paras. 13–74 *et seq.*; see also s.38, *infra*, para. A1–39.

[29] See *supra*, paras. 13–102 *et seq.*

[30] See *supra*, paras. 3–43 *et seq.* This is a re-enactment of the Mercantile Law Amendment (Scotland) Act 1856, s.4 and the Mercantile Law Amendment Act 1856, s.7, as repealed by the Partnership Act 1980, s.48.

[31] See *supra*, paras. 10–10 *et seq.*

[32] See *supra*, paras. 18–03 *et seq.*; see also ss.29, 30, *infra*, paras. A1–30, A1–31.

[33] See *supra*, paras. 18–03 *et seq.*

[34] See *supra*, paras. 18–03 *et seq.*; see also s.2(1), *supra*, para. A1–03.

Property bought with partnership money

A1–22 21. Unless the contrary intention appears, property bought with money belonging to the firm is deemed to have been bought on account of the firm.[35]

Conversion into personal estate of land held as partnership property

A1–23 22. Where land or any heritable interest therein has become partnership property, it shall, unless the contrary intention appears, be treated as between the partners (including the representatives of a deceased partner), and also as between the heirs of a deceased partner and his executors or administrators, as personal or movable and not real or heritable estate.[36]

Procedure against partnership property for a partner's separate judgment debt

A1–24 23.—(1) [...][37] a writ of execution[38] shall not issue against any partnership property[39] except on a judgment against the firm.[40]

(2) The High Court, or a judge thereof, [...][41] or a county court, may, on the application by summons of any judgment creditor of a partner, make an order charging[42] that partner's interest in the partnership property and profits with payment of the amount of the judgment debt and interest thereon, and may by the same or a subsequent order appoint a receiver of that partner's share of profits (whether already declared or accruing), and of any other money which may be coming to him in respect of the partnership, and direct all accounts and inquiries, and give all other orders and directions which might have been directed or given if the charge had been made in favour of the judgment creditor by the partner,[43] or which the circumstances of the case may require.

(3) The other partner or partners shall be at liberty at any time to redeem the interest charged, or in case of a sale being directed, to purchase the same.

(4) This section shall apply in the case of a cost-book company as if the company were a partnership within the meaning of this Act.

(5) This section shall not apply to Scotland.[44]

Rules as to interest and duties of partners subject to special agreement

A1–25 24. The interests of partners in the partnership property and their rights and duties in relation to the partnership shall be determined, subject to any agreement express or implied between the partners, by the following rules:

---

[35] See paras. 18–07 et seq.

[36] See supra, paras. 19–15 et seq.

[37] The words "After the commencement of this Act," which originally appeared at this point, were repealed by the Statute Law Revision Act 1908.

[38] As to the meaning of this expression, see R.S.C. Ord. 46, r. 1.

[39] See s.20, supra, para. A1–21.

[40] For execution when judgment is obtained against a firm in the firm-name, see R.S.C. Ord. 81, r. 5, infra, para. A2–13. and see further, supra, paras. 14–89 et seq.

[41] The reference to the Chancery Court of the County Palatine of Lancaster, which formerly appeared at this point, was repealed by the Courts Act 1971, Sched. 11, Pt. II.

[42] Such an order gives the other partners an option to dissolve the firm, see s.33(2), infra, para. A1–34.

[43] See, as to the rights of a mortgagee, s.31, infra, para. A1–32.

[44] See supra, paras. 19–43 et seq.

(1)   All the partners are entitled to share equally in the capital and profits of the business, and must contribute equally towards the losses whether of capital or otherwise sustained by the firm.[45]

(2)   The firm must indemnify every partner in respect of payments made and personal liabilities incurred by him—

     (a)   In the ordinary and proper conduct of the business of the firm; or

     (b)   In or about anything necessarily done for the preservation of the business or property of the firm.[46]

(3)   A partner making, for the purpose of the partnership, any actual payment or advance beyond the amount of capital which he has agreed to subscribe is entitled to interest at the rate of five per cent. per annum from the date of the payment or advance.[47]

(4)   A partner is not entitled, before the ascertainment of profits, to interest on the capital subscribed by him.[48]

(5)   Every partner may take part in the management of the partnership business.[49]

(6)   No partner shall be entitled to remuneration for acting in the partnership business.[50]

(7)   No person may be introduced as a partner without the consent of all existing partners.[51]

(8)   Any difference arising as to ordinary matters connected with the partnership business may be decided by a majority of the partners, but no change may be made in the nature of the partnership business without the consent of all existing partners.[52]

(9)   The partnership books[53] are to be kept at the place of business of the partnership (or the principal place, if there is more than one), and every partner may, when he thinks fit, have access to and inspect and copy any of them.[54]

Expulsion of partner

25. No majority of the partners can expel any partner unless a power to do **A1–26** so has been conferred by express agreement between the partners.[55]

Retirement from partnership at will

26.—(1) Where no fixed term has been agreed upon for the duration of the **A1–27** partnership, any partner may determine the partnership[56] at any time on giving notice of his intention so to do to all the other partners.[57]

(2) Where the partnership has originally been constituted by deed, a notice in writing, signed by the partner giving it, shall be sufficient for this purpose.[58]

---

[45] See *supra*, paras. 17–08 *et seq.*, 19–18 *et seq.*; see also s.44, *infra*, para. A1–45.
[46] See *supra*, paras. 20–03 *et seq.*
[47] See *supra*, para. 20–32.
[48] See *supra*, paras. 17–13, 20–28, 20–29.
[49] See *supra*, paras. 15–01 *et seq.*
[50] See *supra*, paras. 20–40 *et seq.*
[51] See *supra*, paras. 15–10, 19–56, 19–57.
[52] See *supra*, paras. 15–05 *et seq.*
[53] For the duty to keep accounts, see s.28, *infra*, para. A1–29.
[54] See *supra*, paras. 22–09 *et seq.*
[55] See *supra*, paras. 24–84 *et seq.*
[56] The heading to this section is somewhat misleading, since the power is to *dissolve* the firm, not to retire from it.
[57] See *supra*, paras. 9–01, 24–10 *et seq.* See also s.32, *infra*, para. A1–33.
[58] See *supra*, para. 24–15.

Where partnership for term is continued over, continuance on old terms presumed

A1–28 **27.**—(1) Where a partnership entered into for a fixed term is continued after the term has expired, and without any express new agreement, the rights and duties of the partners remain the same as they were at the expiration of the term, so far as is consistent with the incidents of a partnership at will.

(2) A continuance of the business by the partners or such of them as habitually acted therein during the term, without any settlement or liquidation of the partnership affairs, is presumed to be a continuance of the partnership.[59]

Duty of partners to render accounts, etc.

A1–29 **28.** Partners are bound to render true accounts and full information of all things affecting the partnership to any partner or his legal representatives.[60]

Accountability of partners for private profits

A1–30 **29.**—(1) Every partner must account to the firm for any benefit derived by him without the consent of the other partners from any transaction concerning the partnership, or from any use by him of the partnership property name or business connexion.

(2) This section applies also to transactions undertaken after a partnership has been dissolved by the death of a partner, and before the affairs thereof have been completely wound up, either by any surviving partner or by the representatives of the deceased partner.[61]

Duty of partner not to compete with firm

A1–31 **30.** If a partner, without the consent of the other partners, carries on any business of the same nature as and competing with that of the firm, he must account for and pay over to the firm all profits made by him in that business.[62]

Rights of assignee of share in partnership

A1–32 **31.**—(1) An assignment by any partner of his share in the partnership, either absolute or by way of mortgage or redeemable charge, does not, as against the other partners, entitle the assignee, during the continuance of the partnership, to interfere in the management or administration of the partnership business or affairs, or to require any accounts of the partnership transactions, or to inspect the partnership books, but entitles the assignee only to receive the share of profits to which the assigning partner would otherwise be entitled, and the assignee must accept the account of profits agreed by the partners.[63]

(2) In case of a dissolution of the partnership, whether as respects all the partners or as respects the assigning partner, the assignee is entitled to

---

[59] See *supra*, paras. 10–16 *et seq.*

[60] See *supra*, paras. 16–01 *et seq.*, 22–09 *et seq.* For custody of books and rights of inspection, see s.24(9), *supra*, para. A1–25.

[61] See *supra*, paras. 16–08 *et seq.*

[62] *Ibid.*

[63] As to whether an assignment of a share will give grounds for a dissolution under s.35(f), see *supra*, para. 24–77.

receive the share of the partnership assets to which the assigning partner is entitled as between himself and the other partners, and, for the purpose of ascertaining that share, to an account as from the date of the dissolution.[64]

Dissolution of Partnership, and its consequences

Dissolution by expiration of notice

32. Subject to any agreement between the partners, a partnership is **A1-33** dissolved—

(a) If entered into for a fixed term, by the expiration of that term[65];

(b) If entered into for a single adventure or undertaking, by the termination of that adventure or undertaking;

(c) If entered into for an undefined time, by the partner giving notice to the other or others of his intention to dissolve the partnership.

In the last-mentioned case the partnership is dissolved as from the date mentioned in the notice as the date of dissolution, or, if no date is so mentioned, as from the date of the communication of the notice.[66]

Dissolution by bankruptcy, death, or charge

33.—(1) Subject to any agreement between the partners, every partnership **A1-34** is dissolved as regards all the partners by the death or bankruptcy[67] of any partner.[68]

(2) A partnership may, at the option of the other partners, be dissolved if any partner suffers his share of the partnership property to be charged under this Act for his separate debt.[69]

Dissolution by illegality of partnership

34. A partnership is in every case dissolved by the happening of any event **A1-35** which makes it unlawful for the business of the firm to be carried on or for the members of the firm to carry it on in partnership.[70]

Dissolution by the court

35. On application by a partner the Court[71] may decree a dissolution of the **A1-36** partnership in any of the following cases:

(a) [Repealed by the Mental Health Act 1959, Sched. 8][72]

(b) When a partner, other than the partner suing, becomes in any other way permanently incapable of performing his part of the partnership contract[73]:

(c) When a partner, other than the partner suing, has been guilty of such conduct as, in the opinion of the Court, regard being had to the nature of the business, is calculated to prejudicially affect the carrying on of the business[74]:

---

[64] See *supra*, paras. 19–59 *et seq.*
[65] See s.27, *supra*, para. A1–28, as to the position where the partnership is continued *after* the term.
[66] See *supra*, paras. 24–07 *et seq.*
[67] For meaning of bankruptcy as applied to Scotland, see s.47, *infra*, para. A1–48.
[68] See *supra*, paras. 10–33, 24–20 *et seq.*
[69] See *supra*, paras. 24–29 *et seq.*; and see s.23, *supra*, para. A1–24.
[70] See *supra*, paras. 8–48, 24–34 *et seq.*
[71] For the definition of court, see s.45, *infra*, para. A1–46 and *supra*, paras. 24–44, 24–45.
[72] See *supra*, paras. 24–49 *et seq.*
[73] See *supra*, paras. 24–55 *et seq.*
[74] See *supra*, paras. 24–59 *et seq.*

(*d*)   When a partner, other than the partner suing, wilfully or persistently commits a breach of the partnership agreement, or otherwise so conducts himself in matters relating to the partnership business that it is not reasonably practicable for the other partner or partners to carry on the business in partnership with him[75]:

(*e*)   When the business of the partnership can only be carried on at a loss[76]:

(*f*)   Whenever in any case circumstances have arisen which, in the opinion of the Court, render it just and equitable that the partnership be dissolved.[77]

Rights of persons dealing with firm against apparent members of firm

A1–37   **36.**—(1) Where a person deals with a firm after a change in its constitution he is entitled to treat all apparent members of the old firm as still being members of the firm until he has notice of the change.

(2) An advertisement in the *London Gazette* as to a firm whose principal place of business is in England and Wales, in the *Edinburgh Gazette* as to a firm whose principal place of business is in Scotland, and in the [*Belfast*][78] *Gazette* as to a firm whose principal place of business is in Ireland, shall be notice as to persons who had no dealings with the firm before the date of the dissolution or change so advertised.

(3) The estate of a partner who dies, or who becomes bankrupt, or of a partner who, not having been known to the person dealing with the firm to be a partner, retires from the firm, is not liable for partnership debts contracted after the date of the death, bankruptcy, or retirement respectively.[79]

Right of partners to notify dissolution

A1–38   **37.** On the dissolution of a partnership or retirement of a partner, any partner may publicly notify the same, and may require the other partner or partners to concur for that purpose in all necessary or proper acts, if any, which cannot be done without his or their concurrence.[80]

Continuing authority of partners for purposes of winding up

A1–39   **38.** After the dissolution of a partnership the authority of each partner to bind the firm, and the other rights and obligations of the partners, continue notwithstanding the dissolution as far as may be necessary to wind up the affairs of the partnership, and to complete transactions begun but unfinished at the time of the dissolution, but not otherwise.

Provided that the firm is in no case bound by the acts of a partner who has become bankrupt; but this proviso does not affect the liability of any person who has after the bankruptcy represented himself or knowingly suffered himself to be represented as a partner of the bankrupt.[81]

---

[75] See *supra*, paras. 24–66 *et seq.*
[76] See *supra*, paras. 24–73, 24–74.
[77] See *supra*, paras. 24–75 *et seq.*
[78] A reference to the *Belfast Gazette* is substituted for the *Dublin Gazette* by virtue of the General Adaptation of Enactments (Northern Ireland) Order 1921 (S.R. & O. 1921 No. 1804), Art. 7(a).
[79] See *supra*, paras. 13–41 *et seq.*; see also s.14, *supra*, para. A1–15, as to liability by holding out.
[80] See *supra*, paras. 13–41 *et seq.*
[81] See *supra*, paras. 10–160, 13–64 *et seq.*

Rights of partners as to application of partnership property

39. On the dissolution of a partnership every partner is entitled, as against **A1–40** the other partners in the firm, and all persons claiming through them in respect of their interests as partners, to have the property of the partnership[82] applied in payment of the debts and liabilities of the firm, and to have the surplus assets after such payment applied in payment of what may be due to the partners respectively after deducting what may be due from them as partners to the firm[83]; and for that purpose any partner or his representatives may on the termination of the partnership apply to the Court[84] to wind up the business and affairs of the firm.[85]

Apportionment of premium where partnership prematurely dissolved

40. Where one partner has paid a premium to another on entering into a **A1–41** partnership for a fixed term, and the partnership is dissolved before the expiration of that term otherwise than by the death of a partner, the Court[86] may order the repayment of the premium,[87] or such part thereof as it thinks just, having regard to the terms of the partnership contract and to the length of time during which the partnership has continued; unless

(a) the dissolution is, in the judgment of the Court, wholly or chiefly due to the misconduct of the partner who paid the premium or,

(b) the partnership has been dissolved by an agreement containing no provision for a return of any part of the premium.[88]

Rights where partnership dissolved for fraud or misrepresentation

41. Where a partnership contract is rescinded on the ground of the fraud or **A1–42** misrepresentation of one of the parties thereto, the party entitled to rescind is, without prejudice to any other right, entitled—

(a) to a lien on, or right of retention of, the surplus of the partnership assets, after satisfying the partnership liabilities, for any sum of money paid by him for the purchase of a share in the partnership and for any capital contributed by him, and is

(b) to stand in the place of the creditors of the firm for any payments made by him in respect of the partnership liabilities, and

(c) to be indemnified by the person guilty of the fraud or making the representation against all the debts and liabilities of the firm.[89]

Right of outgoing partner in certain cases to share profits made after dissolution

42.—(1) Where any member of a firm has died or otherwise ceased to be a **A1–43** partner, and the surviving or continuing partners carry on the business of the firm with its capital or assets without any final settlement of accounts as between the firm and the outgoing partner or his estate, then, in the absence of any agreement to the contrary, the outgoing partner or his estate is

---

[82] See ss.20, 21, 29 and 30, *supra*, paras. A1–21, A1–22, A1–30, A1–31.
[83] As to the rules governing the distribution of assets, see s.44, *infra*, para. A1–45 and, as to the right of lien where the partnership contract is rescinded for fraud, see s.41, *infra*, para. A1–42.
[84] See s.45, *infra*, para. A1–46 and *supra*, paras. 24–44, 24–45.
[85] See *supra*, paras. 19–28 *et seq*.
[86] See s.45, *infra*, para. A1–46 and *supra*, paras. 24–44, 24–45.
[87] In cases of fraud, see s.41, *infra*.
[88] See *supra*, paras. 25–09 *et seq*.
[89] See *supra*, paras. 23–52 *et seq*.

entitled at the option of himself or his representatives to such share of the profits made since the dissolution as the Court may find to be attributable to the use of his share of the partnership assets, or to interest at the rate of five per cent. per annum on the amount of his share of the partnership assets.

(2) Provided that where by the partnership contract an option is given to surviving or continuing partners to purchase the interest of a deceased or outgoing partner, and that option is duly exercised, the estate of the deceased partner, or the outgoing partner or his estate, as the case may be, is not entitled to any further or other share of the profits; but if any partner assuming to act in exercise of the option does not in all material respects comply with the terms thereof, he is liable to account under the foregoing provisions of this section.[90]

Retiring or deceased partner's share to be a debt

A1–44   **43.** Subject to any agreement between the partners, the amount due from surviving or continuing partners to an outgoing partner or the representatives of a deceased partner in respect of the outgoing or deceased partner's share is a debt accruing at the date of the dissolution or death.[91]

Rule for distribution of assets on final settlement of accounts

A1–45   **44.** In settling accounts between the partners after a dissolution of partnership the following rules shall, subject to any agreement, be observed:

(a)   Losses, including losses and deficiencies of capital, shall be paid first out of profits, next out of capital and lastly, if necessary, by the partners individually in the proportion in which they were entitled to share profit:

(b)   The assets of the firm including the sums, if any, contributed by the partners to make up losses or deficiencies of capital, shall be applied in the following manner and order:

1.   In paying the debts and liabilities of the firm to persons who are not partners therein:

2.   In paying to each partner rateably what is due from the firm to him for advances as distinguished from capital:

3.   In paying to each partner rateably what is due from the firm to him in respect of capital:

4.   The ultimate residue, if any, shall be divided among the partners in the proportion in which profits are divisible.[92]

Supplemental

Definitions of "court" and "business"

A1–46   **45.** In this Act, unless the contrary intention appears,
The expression "court" includes every court and judge having jurisdiction in the case[93];
The expression "business" includes every trade, occupation, or profession.[94]

---

[90] See *supra*, paras. 25–23 *et seq.*
[91] See *supra*, paras. 19–41, 23–33, 26–04. *Quaere*, does s.9, *supra*, para. A1–10 apply in such a case?
[92] See *supra*, paras. 25–40 *et seq.* And see also s.24(1), (3) *supra*, para. A1–25. As to the right of a partner to have the assets applied in accordance with this section, see s.39, *supra*, para. A1–40.
[93] See *supra*, paras. 24–44, 24–45.
[94] See *supra*, para. 2–02.

Saving for rules of equity and common law

46. The rules of equity and of common law applicable to partnership shall **A1–47** continue in force except so far as they are inconsistent with the express provisions of this Act.

Provision as to bankruptcy in Scotland

47.—(1) In the application of this Act to Scotland the bankruptcy of a firm **A1–48** or of an individual shall mean sequestration under the Bankruptcy (Scotland) Acts, and also in the case of an individual the issue against him of a decree of *cessio bonorum.*
(2) Nothing in this Act shall alter the rules of the law of Scotland relating to the bankruptcy of a firm or of the individual partners thereof.

Repeal

48. [*Repealed by the Statute Law Revision Act* 1908]   **A1–49**

Commencement of Act

49. [*Repealed by the Statute Law Revision Act* 1908]

Short Title

50. This Act may be cited as the Partnership Act 1890.

SCHEDULE

[*Repealed by the Statute Law Revision Act* 1908]

RULES OF THE SUPREME COURT, ORDERS 43 and 81

(a) Order 43[1]

Accounts and Inquiries

Summary order for account

A2–01   **1.**—(1) Where a writ is indorsed with a claim for an account or a claim which necessarily involves taking an account, the plaintiff may, at any time after the defendant has acknowledged service of the writ or after the time limited for acknowledging service, apply for an order under this rule.

(1A) A defendant to an action begun by writ who has served a counterclaim, which includes a claim for an account or a claim which necessarily involves taking an account, on—

  (*a*)   the plaintiff, or
  (*b*)   any other party, or
  (*c*)   any person who becomes a party by virtue of such service may apply for an order under this rule.

(2) An application under this rule must be made by summons and, if the Court so directs, must be supported by affidavit or other evidence.

(3) On the hearing of the application, the Court may, unless satisfied that there is some preliminary question to be tried, order that an account be taken and may also order that any amount certified on taking the account to be due to either party be paid to him within a time specified in the order.

Court may direct taking of accounts, etc.

A2–02   **2.**—(1) The Court may, on an application made by summons at any stage of the proceedings in a cause or matter, direct any necessary accounts or inquiries to be taken or made.

(2) Every direction for the taking of an account or the making of an inquiry shall be numbered in the judgment or order so that, as far as may be, each distinct account and inquiry may be designated by a number.

Directions as to manner of taking account or making inquiry

A2–03   **3.**—(1) Where the Court orders an account to be taken or inquiry to be made it may by the same or a subsequent order give directions with regard to the manner in which the account is to be taken or vouched or the inquiry is to be made.

(2) Without prejudice to the generality of paragraph (1), the Court may direct that in taking an account the relevant books of account shall be evidence of the matters contained therein with liberty to the parties interested to take such objections thereto as they think fit.

---

[1] As amended by R.S.C. (Writ and Appearance) 1979 (S.I. 1979 No. 1716); R.S.C. (Amendment No. 2) 1982 (S.I. 1982 No. 1111); R.S.C. (Amendment No. 3) 1982 (S.I. 1982 No. 1786).

Account to be made, verified, etc.

4.—(1) Where an account has been ordered to be taken, the accounting **A2–04** party must make out his account and, unless the Court otherwise directs, verify it by an affidavit to which the account must be exhibited.

(2) The items on each side of the account must be numbered consecutively.

(3) Unless the order for the taking of the account otherwise directs, the accounting party must lodge the account with the Court and must at the same time notify the other parties that he has done so and of the filing of any affidavit verifying the account and of any supporting affidavit.

Notice to be given of alleged omissions, etc. in account

5. Any party who seeks to charge an accounting party with an amount **A2–05** beyond that which he has by his account admitted to have received or who alleges that any item in his account is erroneous in respect of amount or in any other respect must give him notice thereof stating, so far as he is able, the amount sought to be charged with brief particulars thereof or, as the case may be, the grounds for alleging that the item is erroneous.

Allowances

6. In taking any account directed by any judgment or order all just **A2–06** allowances shall be made without any direction to that effect.

Delay in prosecution of accounts, etc.

7.—(1) If it appears to the Court that there is undue delay in the **A2–07** prosecution of any accounts or inquiries, or in any other proceedings under any judgment or order, the Court may require the party having the conduct of the proceedings or any other party to explain the delay and may then make such order for staying the proceedings or for expediting them or for the conduct thereof and for costs as the circumstances require.

(2) The Court may direct any party or the official solicitor to take over the conduct of the proceedings in question and to carry out any directions made by an order under this rule and may make such order as it thinks fit as to the payment of the official solicitor's costs.

Distribution of fund before all persons entitled are ascertained

8. Where some of the persons entitled to share in a fund are ascertained, **A2–08** and difficulty or delay has occurred or is likely to occur in ascertaining the other persons so entitled, the Court may order or allow immediate payment of their shares to the persons ascertained without reserving any part of those shares to meet the subsequent costs of ascertaining those other persons.

Guardian's accounts

9. [*This rule is not material in the present context and has, therefore, been omitted.*]

(b) Order 81[2]

Partners

Actions by and against firms within jurisdiction

A2–09   1. Subject to the provisions of any enactment, any two or more persons claiming to be entitled, or alleged to be liable, as partners in respect of a cause of action and carrying on business within the jurisdiction may sue, or be sued, in the name of the firm (if any) of which they were partners at the time when the cause of action accrued.

Disclosure of partners' names

A2–10   2.—(1) Any defendant to an action brought by partners in the name of a firm may serve on the plaintiffs or their solicitor a notice requiring them or him forthwith to furnish the defendant with a written statement of the names and places of residence of all the persons who were partners in the firm at the time when the cause of action accrued; and if the notice is not complied with the Court may order the plaintiffs or their solicitor to furnish the defendant with such a statement and to verify it on oath or otherwise as may be specified in the order, or may order that further proceedings in the action be stayed on such terms as the Court may direct.

(2) When the names of the partners have been declared in compliance with a notice or order given or made under paragraph (1), the proceedings shall continue in the name of the firm but with the same consequences as would have ensued if the persons whose names have been so declared had been named as plaintiffs in the writ.

(3) Paragraph (1) shall have effect in relation to an action brought against partners in the name of a firm as it has effect in relation to an action brought by partners in the name of a firm but with the substitution, for references to the defendant and the plaintiffs, of references to the plaintiff and the defendants respectively, and with the omission of the words "or may order" to the end.

Service of writ

A2–11   3.—(1) Where by virtue of rule 1 partners are sued in the name of a firm, the writ may, except in the case mentioned in paragraph (3), be served—

    (*a*)   on any one or more of the partners, or

    (*b*)   at the principal place of business of the partnership within the jurisdiction, on any person having at the time of service the control or management of the partnership business there; or

    (*c*)   by sending a copy of the writ by ordinary first-class post (as defined in Order 10, rule 1(2)) to the firm at the principal place of business of the partnership within the jurisdiction,

and subject to paragraph (2) where service of the writ is effected in accordance with this paragraph, the writ shall be deemed to have been duly served on the firm whether or not any member of the firm is out of the jurisdiction.

(2) Where a writ is served on a firm in accordance with sub-paragraph (1)(*c*)—

---

[2] As amended by R.S.C. (Amendment No. 4) 1971 (S.I. 1971 No. 1269); R.S.C. (Amendment No. 2) 1979 (S.I. 1979 No. 402); R.S.C. (Writ and Appearance) 1979 (S.I. 1979 No. 1716); R.S.C. (Amendment No. 4) 1980 (S.I. 1980 No. 2000); R.S.C. (Amendment No. 2) 1981 (S.I. 1982 No. 1111); R.S.C. (Amendment No. 2) 1983 (S.I. 1983 No. 1181).

(a)   the date of service shall, unless the contrary is shown, be deemed to be the seventh day (ignoring Order 3, rule 2(5)) after the date on which the copy was sent to the firm; and

(b)   any affidavit proving due service of the writ must con tain a statement to the effect that—

> (i)   in the opinion of the deponent (or, if the deponent is the plaintiff's solicitor or an employee of that solicitor, in the opinion of the plaintiff) the copy of the writ, if sent to the firm at the address in question, will have come to the knowledge of one of the persons mentioned in paragraph (1)(a) or (b) within 7 days thereafter, and
>
> (ii)   the copy of the writ has not been returned to the plaintiff through the post undelivered to the addressee.

(3) Where a partnership has, to the knowledge of the plaintiff, been dissolved before an action against the firm is begun, the writ by which the action is begun must be served on every person within the jurisdiction sought to be made liable in the action.

(4) Every person on whom a writ is served under paragraph (1)(a) or (b) must at the time of service be given a written notice stating whether he is served as a partner or as a person having the control or management of the partnership business or both as a partner and as such a person; and any person on whom a writ is so served but to whom no such notice is given shall be deemed to be served as a partner.

Acknowledgment of service in action against firm

4.—(1) Where persons are sued as partners in the name of their firm, **A2–12** service may not be acknowledged in the name of the firm but only by the partners thereof in their own names, but the action shall nevertheless continue in the name of the firm.

(2) Where in an action against a firm the writ by which the action is begun is served on a person as a partner, that person, if he denies that he was a partner or liable as such at any material time, may acknowledge service of the writ and state in his acknowledgment that he does so as a person served as a partner in the defendant firm but who denies that he was a partner at any material time.

An acknowledgment of service given in accordance with this paragraph shall, unless and until it is set aside, be treated as an acknowledgment by the defendant firm.

(3) Where an acknowledgment of service has been given by a defendant in accordance with paragraph (2), then—

(a)   the plaintiff may either apply to the Court to set it aside on the ground that the defendant was a partner or liable as such at a material time or may leave that question to be determined at a later stage of the proceedings;

(b)   the defendant may either apply to the Court to set aside the service of the writ on him on the ground that he was not a partner or liable as such at a material time or may at the proper time serve a defence on the plaintiff denying in respect of the plaintiff's claim either his liability as a partner or the liability of the defendant firm or both.

(4) The Court may at any stage of the proceedings in an action in which a defendant has acknowledged service in accordance with paragraph (2), on the application of the plaintiff or of that defendant, order that any question as to the liability of that defendant or as to the liability of the defendant firm be tried in such manner and at such time as the Court directs.

(5) Where in an action against a firm the writ by which the action is begun is served on a person as a person having the control or management of the

partnership business, that person may not acknowledge service in the action unless he is a member of the firm sued.

Enforcing judgment or order against firm

A2–13   **5.**—(1) Where a judgment is given or order made against a firm, execution to enforce the judgment or order may, subject to rule 6, issue against any property of the firm within the jurisdiction.

(2) Where a judgment is given or order made against a firm, execution to enforce the judgment or order may, subject to rule 6 and to the next following paragraph, issue against any person who—

    (*a*)   acknowledged service of the writ in the action as a partner, or

    (*b*)   having been served as a partner with the writ of summons failed to acknowledge service of it in the action, or

    (*c*)   admitted in his pleading that he is a partner, or

    (*d*)   was adjudged to be a partner.

(3) Execution to enforce a judgment or order given or made against a firm may not issue against a member of the firm who was out of the jurisdiction when the writ of summons was issued unless he—

    (*a*)   acknowledged service of the writ in the action as a partner, or

    (*b*)   was served within the jurisdiction with the writ as a partner, or

    (*c*)   was, with the leave of the Court given under Order 11, served out of the jurisdiction with the writ, as a partner;

and, except as provided by paragraph (1) and by the foregoing provisions of this paragraph, a judgment or order given or made against a firm shall not render liable, release or otherwise affect a member of the firm who was out of the jurisdiction when the writ issued.

(4) Where a party who has obtained a judgment or order against a firm claims that a person is liable to satisfy the judgment or order as being a member of the firm, and the foregoing provisions of this rule do not apply in relation to that person, that party may apply to the Court for leave to issue execution against that person, the application to be made by summons which must be served personally on that person.

(5) Where the person against whom an application under paragraph (4) is made does not dispute his liability, the Court hearing the application may, subject to paragraph (3), give leave to issue execution against that person, and, where that person disputes his liability, the Court may order that the liability of that person be tried and determined in any manner in which any issue or question in an action may be tried and determined.

Enforcing judgment or order in actions between partners

A2–14   **6.**—(1) Execution to enforce a judgment or order given or made in—

    (*a*)   an action by or against a firm in the name of the firm against or by a member of the firm, or

    (*b*)   an action by a firm in the name of the firm against a firm in the name of the firm where those firms have one or more members in common,

shall not issue except with the leave of the Court.

(2) The Court hearing an application under this rule may give such directions, including directions as to the taking of accounts and the making of inquiries, as may be just.

Attachment of debts owed by firm

A2–15   **7.**—(1) An order may be made under Order 49, rule 1, in relation to debts due or accruing due from a firm carrying on business within the jurisdiction notwithstanding that one or more members of the firm is resident out of the jurisdiction.

(2) An order to show cause under the said rule 1 relating to such debts as aforesaid must be served on a member of the firm within the jurisdiction or on some other person having the control or management of the partnership business.

(3) Where an order made under the said rule 1 requires a firm to appear before the Court, an appearance by a member of the firm constitutes a sufficient compliance with the order.

Actions begun by originating summons

8. Rules 2–7 shall, with the necessary modifications, apply in relation to an **A2–16** action by or against partners in the name of their firm begun by originating summons as they apply in relation to such an action begun by writ.

Application to person carrying on business in another name

9. An individual carrying on business within the jurisdiction in a name or **A2–17** style other than his own name, may whether or not he is within the jurisdiction be sued in that name or style as if it were the name of a firm, and rules 2 to 8 shall, so far as applicable, apply as if he were a partner and the name in which he carries on business were the name of his firm.

Applications for orders charging partner's interest in partnership property

10.—(1) Every application to the Court by a judgment creditor of a partner **A2–18** for an order under section 23 of the Partnership Act 1890 (which authorises the High Court or a judge thereof to make certain orders on the application of a judgment creditor of a partner, including an order charging the partner's interest in the partnership property), and every application to the Court by a partner of the judgment debtor made in consequence of the first-mentioned application must be made by summons.

(2) A master or the Admiralty Registrar or a [district judge][3] may exercise the powers conferred on a judge by the said section 23.

(3) Every summons issued by a judgment creditor under this rule, and every order made on such a summons, must be served on the judgment debtor and on such of his partners as are within the jurisdiction or, if the partnership is a cost book company, on the judgment debtor and the purser of the company.

(4) Every summons issued by a partner of a judgment debtor under this rule, and every order made on such a summons, must be served—

(*a*) on the judgment creditor, and

(*b*) on the judgment debtor, and

(*c*) on such of the other partners of the judgment debtor as do not join in the application and are within the jurisdiction or, if the partnership is a cost book company, on the purser of the company.

(5) A summons or order served in accordance with this rule on the purser of a cost book company or, in the case of a partnership not being such a company, on some only of the partners thereof, shall be deemed to have been served on that company or on all the partners of that partnership, as the case may be.

---

[3] The original reference to the district registrar falls to be construed as a reference to the district judge by virtue of the Courts and Legal Services Act 1990, s.74(3).

A3–01   **LIMITED PARTNERSHIPS ACT 1907**

7 Edw. 7, c. 24

ARRANGEMENT OF SECTIONS

SECT.
1. Short title.
2. Commencement of Act.
3. Interpretation of terms.
4. Definition and constitution of limited partnership.
5. Registration of limited partnership required.
6. Modifications of general law in case of limited partnerships.
7. Law as to private partnerships to apply where not excluded by this Act.
8. Manner and particulars of registration.
9. Registration of changes in partnerships.
10. Advertisement in Gazette of statement of general partner becoming a limited partner and of assignment of share of limited partner.
11. *Ad valorem* stamp duty on contributions by limited partners.
12. Making false returns to be misdemeanour.
13. Registrar to file statement and issue certificate of registration.
14. Register and index to be kept.
15. Registrar of joint stock companies to be registrar under Act.
16. Inspection of statements registered.
17. Power to Board of Trade to make rules.

An Act to establish Limited Partnerships.

[August 28, 1907.]

Short title

A3–02   **1.** This Act may be cited for all purposes as the Limited Partnerships Act 1907.

Commencement of Act

    2. [. . .]¹

Interpretation of terms

A3–03   **3.** In the construction of this Act the following words and expressions shall have the meanings respectively assigned to them in this section, unless there be something in the subject or context repugnant to such construction:—

---

¹ This section was repealed by the Statute Law Revision Act 1927.

"Firm," "firm name," and "business" have the same meanings as in the Partnership Act 1890:

"General partner" shall mean any partner who is not a limited partner as defined by this Act.[2]

Definition and constitution of limited partnership

4.—(1) [...][3] limited partnerships may be formed in the manner and **A3–04** subject to the conditions by this Act provided.

(2) A limited partnership shall not consist [...][4] of more than twenty persons, and must consist of one or more persons called general partners, who shall be liable for all debts and obligations of the firm, and one or more persons to be called limited partners, who shall at the time of entering into such partnership contribute thereto a sum or sums as capital or property valued at a stated amount, and who shall not be liable for the debts and obligations of the firm beyond the amount so contributed.[5]

(3) A limited partner shall not during the continuance of the partnership, either directly or indirectly, draw out or receive back any part of his contribution, and if he does so draw out or receive back any such part shall be liable for the debts and obligations of the firm up to the amount so drawn out or received back.[6]

(4) A body corporate may be a limited partner.[7]

Registration of limited partnership required

5. Every limited partnership must be registered as such in accordance with **A3–05** the provisions of this Act, or in default thereof it shall be deemed to be a general partnership, and every limited partner shall be deemed to be a general partner.[8]

Modifications of general law in case of limited partnerships

6.—(1) A limited partner shall not take part in the management of the **A3–06** partnership business, and shall not have power to bind the firm:

Provided that a limited partner may by himself or his agent at any time inspect the books of the firm and examine into the state and prospects of the partnership business, and may advise with the partners thereon.[9]

If a limited partner takes part in the management of the partnership business he shall be liable for all debts and obligations of the firm incurred while he so takes part in the management as though he were a general partner.[10]

---

[2] See *supra*, paras. 29–03 *et seq.*

[3] The words "From and after the commencement of this Act", which originally appeared at this point, were repealed by the Statute Law Revision Act 1927.

[4] The words "in the case of a partnership carrying on the business of banking, of more than ten persons, and, in the case of any other partnership", which appeared at this point, were repealed by the Banking Act 1979, s.51(2), Sched. 7.

[5] See *supra*, paras. 29–02 *et seq.*, 30–09, 30–10, 31–05.

[6] See *supra*, paras. 30–11 *et seq.*, 31–09, 31–10, 31–20, 31–21.

[7] See *supra*, para. 29–06.

[8] See *supra*, paras. 29–17 *et seq.*

[9] See *supra*, para. 31–04.

[10] See *supra*, paras. 30–11, 31–02, 31–04.

(2) A limited partnership shall not be dissolved by the death or bankruptcy of a limited partner, and the lunacy of a limited partner shall not be a ground for dissolution of the partnership by the court unless the lunatic's share cannot be otherwise ascertained and realised.[11]

(3) In the event of the dissolution of a limited partnership its affairs shall be wound up by the general partners unless the court otherwise orders.[12]

(4) [*Repealed by the Companies (Consolidation) Act 1908, s.286, Sched. 6, Part I.*]

(5) Subject to any agreement expressed or implied between the partners—

(a)   Any difference arising as to ordinary matters connected with the partnership business may be decided by a majority of the general partners[13];

(b)   A limited partner, may with the consent of the general partners, assign his share in the partnership, and upon such an assignment the assignee shall become a limited partner with all the rights of the assignor[14];

(c)   The other partners shall not be entitled to dissolve the partnership by reason of any limited partner suffering his share to be charged for his separate debt[15];

(d)   Any person may be introduced as a partner without the consent of the existing limited partners[16];

(e)   A limited partner shall not be entitled to dissolve the partnership by notice.[17]

Law as to private[18] partnerships to apply where not excluded by this Act

A3–07   7. Subject to the provisions of this Act, the Partnership Act 1890, and the rules of equity and of common law applicable to partnerships, except so far as they are inconsistent with the express provisions of the last-mentioned Act, shall apply to limited partnerships.[19]

Manner and particulars of registration

A3–08   8. The registration of a limited partnership shall be effected by sending by post or delivering to the registrar at the register office in that part of the United Kingdom in which the principal place of business of the limited partnership is situated or proposed to be situated[20] a statement signed by the partners containing the following particulars:

(a)   The firm name;
(b)   The general nature of the business;
(c)   The principal place of business;
(d)   The full name of each of the partners;

---

[11] See *supra*, paras. 31–20, 31–21, 32–01 *et seq.*
[12] See *supra*, paras. 32–16, 32–17.
[13] See *supra*, paras. 31–02, 31–03.
[14] See *supra*, paras. 30–19, 31–16, 31–17.
[15] See *supra*, para. 32–04.
[16] See *supra*, para. 31–18.
[17] See *supra*, para. 32–03.
[18] The word "private" is apparently used because ordinary partnerships need not be registered.
[19] See *supra*, para. 28–08.
[20] See *supra*, para. 29–19. And note that, by the Government of Ireland (Companies, Societies etc.) Order 1992 (S.R. & O. 1922 No. 184), Art. 9(a), this section has effect as regards Northern Ireland as if for the words "to the registrar at the register office in that part of the United Kingdom in which the principal place of business of the limited partnership is situated or proposed to be situated" there were substituted "to the registrar of companies at his office".

(e) The term, if any, for which the partnership is entered into, and the date of its commencement;
(f) A statement that the partnership is limited, and the description of every limited partner as such;
(g) The sum contributed by each limited partner, and whether paid in cash or how otherwise.[21]

Registration of changes in partnerships

9.—(1) If during the continuance of a limited partnership any change is **A3–09** made or occurs in—
(a) the firm name,
(b) the general nature of the business,
(c) the principal place of business,
(d) the partners or the name of any partner,
(e) the term or character of the partnership,
(f) the sum contributed by any limited partner,
(g) the liability of any partner by reason of his becoming a limited instead of a general partner or a general instead of a limited partner,
a statement, signed by the firm, specifying the nature of the change shall within seven days be sent by post or delivered to the registrar at the register office in that part of the United Kingdom in which the partnership is registered.

(2) If default is made in compliance with the requirements of this section each of the general partners shall, on conviction under [the Magistrates Courts Act 1980],[22] be liable to a fine not exceeding one pound for each day during which the default continues.[23]

Advertisement in *Gazette* of statement of general partner becoming a limited partner and of assignment of share of limited partner

10.—(1) Notice of any arrangement or transaction under which any person **A3–10** will cease to be a general partner in any firm, and will become a limited partner in that firm, or under which the share of a limited partner in a firm will be assigned to any person, shall be forthwith advertised in the *Gazette*, and until notice of the arrangement or transaction is so advertised the arrangement or transaction shall, for the purposes of this Act, be deemed to be of no effect.[24]

(2) For the purposes of this section, the expression "the *Gazette*" means—

In the case of a limited partnership registered in England, the *London Gazette*;
In the case of a limited partnership registered in Scotland, the *Edinburgh Gazette*;
In the case of a limited partnership registered in Ireland, the [*Belfast*] *Gazette*.[25]

---

[21] See *supra*, paras. 29–17 *et seq.*
[22] These words are substituted by virtue of the Interpretation Act 1978, s.17(2)(a).
[23] See *supra*, para. 29–27.
[24] See *supra*, paras. 29–29, 29–30, 30–08, 30–16.
[25] A reference to the *Belfast Gazette* is substituted for the *Dublin Gazette* by virtue of the General Adaptation of Enactments (Northern Ireland) Order 1921 (S.R. & O. 1921 No. 1804), Art. 7(a).

Ad valorem stamp duty on contributions by limited partners

A3–11   11. [*Repealed by Finance Act 1973, Sched. 22.*]

Making false returns to be misdemeanour

12. [*This section was repealed as to England*[26] *by the Perjury Act 1911, s.17, and replaced by s.5 of that Act which, so far as material, provides as follows:*

"5. *If any person knowingly and wilfully makes (otherwise than on oath) a statement false in a material particular, and the statement is made*
. . .
(b) *in an abstract, account, balance sheet, book, certificate, declaration, entry, estimate, inventory, notice, report, return, or other document which he is authorised or required to make, attest, or verify, by any public general Act of Parliament for the time being in force;*
. . .
he shall be . . . liable on conviction thereof on indictment to imprisonment . . . for any term not exceeding two years, or to a fine or to both such imprisonment and fine."]

Registrar to file statement and issue certificate of registration

A3–12   13. On receiving any statement made in pursuance of this Act the registrar shall cause the same to be filed, and he shall send by post to the firm from whom such statement shall have been received a certificate of the registration thereof.[27]

Register and index to be kept

A3–13   14. At each of the register offices hereinafter referred to the registrar shall keep, in proper books to be provided for the purpose, a register and an index of all the limited partnerships registered as aforesaid, and of all the statements registered in relation to such partnerships.

Registrar of joint stock companies to be registrar under Act

A3–14   15. The registrar of joint stock companies shall be the registrar of limited partnerships, and the several offices for the registration of joint stock companies in London, Edinburgh, and Dublin shall be the offices for the registration of limited partnerships carrying on business within those parts of the United Kingdom in which they are respectively situated.[28]

---

[26] As to Scotland, the section was repealed by the False Oaths (Scotland) Act 1933, s.8 and replaced by *ibid.* s.2.

[27] See *supra*, para. 29–22.

[28] See *supra*, para. 29–19. Note that, by the Government of Ireland (Companies, Societies etc.) Order 1992 (S.R. & O. 1922 No. 184), Art. 9(b), this section has effect as regards Northern Ireland as if the following section were substituted: "The registrar of companies shall be the registrar of limited partnerships, and the office for the registration of companies in Belfast shall be the office for the registration of limited partnerships."

Inspection of statements registered

16.—(1) Any person may inspect the statements filed by the registrar in the **A3–15** register offices aforesaid, and there shall be paid for such inspection such fees as may be appointed by the Board of Trade,[29] not exceeding [five pence] for each inspection; and any person may require a certificate of the registration of any limited partnership, or a copy of or extract from any registered statement, to be certified by the registrar, and there shall be paid for such certificate of registration, certified copy, or extract such fees as the Board of Trade may appoint, not exceeding [ten pence] for the certificate of registration, and not exceeding [two and a half pence] for each folio of seventy-two words, or in Scotland for each sheet of two hundred words.[30]

(2) A certificate of registration, or a copy of or extract from any statement registered under this Act, if duly certified to be a true copy under the hand of the registrar or one of the assistant registrars (whom it shall not be necessary to prove to be the registrar or assistant registrar) shall, in all legal proceedings, civil or criminal, and in all cases whatsoever be received in evidence.[31]

Power to Board of Trade to make rules

17. The Board of Trade[32] may make rules (but as to fees with the **A3–16** concurrence of the Treasury) concerning any of the following matters:

    (a)   The fees to be paid to the registrar under this Act, so that they do not exceed in the case of the original registration of a limited partnership the sum of two pounds, and in any other case the sum of [twenty five pence][33];

    (b)   The duties or additional duties to be performed by the registrar for the purposes of this Act;

    (c)   The performance by assistant registrars and other officers of acts by this Act required to be done by the registrar;

    (d)   The forms to be used for the purposes of this Act;

    (e)   Generally the conduct and regulation of registration under this Act and any matters incidental thereto.[34]

---

[29] Now the Department of Trade and Industry.
[30] As amended by the Decimal Currency Act 1969, s.10(1).
[31] See *supra*, para. 29–28.
[32] Now the Department of Trade and Industry.
[33] As amended by the Decimal Currency Act 1969, s.10(1).
[34] As to the regulations made under this section, see *infra*, paras. A4–01 *et seq.*

A4–01 THE LIMITED PARTNERSHIPS RULES 1907[1]

1. "The Act" means the Limited Partnerships Act 1907.

2. Whenever any act is by the Act directed to be done to or by the registrar such act shall be done in England to or by the Registrar of Joint Stock Companies[2] or in his absence to or by such person as the Board of Trade[3] may for the time being authorise; in Scotland to or by the existing Registrar of Joint Stock Companies of Scotland; and in Ireland to or by the existing Assistant Registrar of Joint Stock Companies for Ireland[4] or by such person as the Board of Trade may for the time being authorise in Scotland or Ireland in the absence of the registrar; but in the event of the Board of Trade altering the constitution of the existing Joint Stock Companies Registry Office such act shall be done to or by such officer or officers and at that place or places with reference to the local situation of the principal place of business of the limited partnership to be registered as the Board of Trade may appoint.

A4–02 **3.** The fees to be paid to the registrar under the Act shall be as follows:—

    (*a*) on the original registration of a limited partnership the sum of two pounds,

    (*b*) [*Revoked by the Limited Partnerships (Amendment) Rules 1972, Rule 2.*]

    (*c*) by any person inspecting the statements filed by the registrar in the register office the sum of [five pence] for each inspection.

    (*d*) by any person requiring a certificate of the registration of any limited partnership or a certified copy of or extract from any registered statement the sum of [ten pence] for each certificate and for a certified copy or extract the sum of [two and a half pence] for each folio of 72 words or in Scotland for each sheet of 200 words.[5]

A4–03 **4.** The forms in the appendix hereto with such variations as the circumstances of each case may require shall be the forms to be used for the purposes of the Act.

Appendix[6]

A4–04   FORMS TO BE USED FOR THE PURPOSES OF THE ACT AND FOR THE PURPOSES OF SECTION 47 OF THE FINANCE ACT 1973[7]

Registration No ....   Form No. L.P.5
                                  (Registration fee £2)
                                  (Capital duty also payable)[8]

---

[1] S.R. &. O. 1907 No. 1020, dated December 17, 1907, and made under the Limited Partnerships Act 1907, s.17, *supra*, para. A3–16. The Rules were amended by the Limited Partnerships (Amendment) Rules 1972 (S.I. 1972 No. 1040) and the Limited Partnerships (Amendment) Rules 1974 (S.I. 1974 No. 560).

[2] Now the registrar of companies: Companies Act 1985, s.705.

[3] Now the Department of Trade and Industry.

[4] As to Northern Ireland, note the terms of the Government of Ireland (Companies, Societies etc.) Order 1992 (S.R. & O. 1922 No. 184), Arts. 5, 6.

[5] The words in square brackets were substituted by the Decimal Currency Act 1969, s.10(1).

[6] This appendix was substituted by the Limited Partnerships (Amendment) Rules 1974 (S.I. 1974 No. 560).

[7] This section was repealed by the Finance Act 1988, Sched. 14, Pt. XI.

[8] Capital duty was abolished by the Finance Act 1988, s.141.

LIMITED PARTNERSHIPS ACT 1907

Application for Registration of a Limited Partnership and
Statement of particulars and of the amounts contributed
(in cash or otherwise) by the Limited Partners
(Pursuant to Section 8 of the Limited Partnerships Act 1907
and Section 47 of the Finance Act 1973)

Name of firm or partnership ....
We, the undersigned, being the partners of the above-named firm, hereby
apply for registration as a limited partnership and for that purpose supply the
following particulars:

The general
nature of
the business

The principal
place of
business

The term, if any, for which
the partnership is entered into

If no definite term, the conditions
of existence of the partnership

Date of commencement

The partnership is limited and the full name and address of each of
the partners are as follows:
General partners

Limited partners	Amounts Contributed (1)	Capital duty payable (2)
	Total	

Signatures of all ⎫
the partners   ⎭

Date ....

Presented by:
Presentor's reference:

NOTES

(1) State amount contributed by each limited partner, and whether paid in cash, or how otherwise.

(2) The capital duty is £1 for every £100, or part of £100, contributed by each limited partner.

A4–05 Registration No. ....   Form No. L.P.6

LIMITED PARTNERSHIPS ACT 1907

Statement specifying the nature of a change in the
Limited Partnership
and Statement of increase in the amount contributed (in cash
or otherwise) by limited partners
(Pursuant to section 9 of the Limited Partnerships Act 1907
and Section 47 of the Finance Act 1973[9])

Name of firm or partnership ....

Notice is hereby given that the changes specified below have occurred in this limited partnership:

(please see Notes overleaf)

(a) The firm name	Previous name
	New name
(b) General nature of the business	Business previously carried on
	Business now carried on

---

[9] This section was repealed by the Finance Act 1988, Sched. 14, Pt. XI.

(c) Principal place of business	Previous place of business New place of business
(d) Change in the partners or the name of a partner (Note 1)	
(e) Term or character of the partnership (Note 2)	Previous term New term
(f) Change in the sum contributed by any limited partner (Note 3) (particulars of any increase in capital contributions must be provided at (h) overleaf)	
(g) Change in the liability of any partner by reason of his becoming a limited instead of a general partner, or vice versa	

(h) Statement of increase in capital contributions

Names of Limited Partners	Increase or additional sum now contributed (If otherwise than in cash, that fact, with particulars, must be stated)	Total amount contributed (If otherwise than in cash, that fact, with particulars, must be stated)	Capital duty payable on increase, etc.

Total Capital duty payable

Signature of firm ....
Date ....

Presented by:
Presentor's reference:

A4–06   (1) Changes brought about by death, by transfer of interests, by increase in the number of partners, or by change of name of any partner, must be notified here.

(2) If there is, or was, no definite term, then state against "previous term" the conditions under which the partnership was constituted and against "new term" the conditions under which it is now constituted.

(3) Any variation in the sum contributed by any limited partner must be stated at (*f*) overleaf. A statement of any increase in the amount of the partnership capital, whether arising from increase of contributions, or from introduction of fresh partners must also be made at (*h*) above. Capital duty is payable at £1 for every £100, or part of £100, on any increase in the amounts of contributions made, in cash or otherwise, by a limited partner.[10]

(4) Each change must be entered in the proper division (*a*), (*b*), (*c*), (*d*), (*e*), (*f*) (*g*) or (*h*), as the case may be. Provision is made in this form for notifying all the changes required by the Act to be notified, but it will frequently happen that only one item of change has to be notified. In any such case, the word "Nil" should be inserted in the other divisions.

(5) The statement must be signed at the end by the firm, and delivered for registration within seven days of the change or changes taking place.

---

[10] Capital duty was abolished by the Finance Act 1988, s.141.

APPENDIX 5

E.C. COMPETITION LAW

I. EUROPEAN COMMUNITY TREATY

ARTICLE 85

1. The following shall be prohibited as incompatible with the common **A5–01** market: all agreements between undertakings, decisions by associations of undertakings and concerted practices which may affect trade between Member States and which have as their object or effect the prevention, restriction or distortion of competition within the common market, and in particular those which:
- (a) directly or indirectly fix purchase or selling prices or any other trading conditions;
- (b) limit or control production, markets, technical development, or investment;
- (c) share markets or sources of supply;
- (d) apply dissimilar conditions to equivalent transactions with other trading parties, thereby placing them at a competitive disadvantage;
- (e) make the conclusion of contracts subject to acceptance by the other parties of supplementary obligations which, by their nature or according to commercial usage, have no connection with the subject of such contracts.

2. Any agreements or decisions prohibited pursuant to this Article shall be **A5–02** automatically void.

3. The provisions of paragraph 1 may, however, be declared inapplicable in the case of:
    —any agreement or category of agreements between undertakings;
    —any decision or category of decisions by associations of undertakings;
    —any concerted practice or category of concerted practices;
which contributes to improving the production or distribution of goods or to promoting technical or economic progress, while allowing consumers a fair share of the resulting benefit, and which does not:
- (a) impose on the undertakings concerned restrictions which are not indispensable to the attainment of these objectives;
- (b) afford such undertakings the possibility of eliminating competition in respect of a substantial part of the products in question.

II. COUNCIL REGULATION 17 OF FEBRUARY 6, 1962
FIRST REGULATION IMPLEMENTING ARTICLES 85 AND 86 OF THE TREATY

ARTICLE 1

Basic Provision

Without prejudice to Articles 6, 7 and 23 of this regulation, agreements, **A5–03** decisions and concerted practices of the kind described in Article 85(1) of the Treaty and the abuse of a dominant position in the market, within the

1075

meaning of Article 86 of the Treaty, shall be prohibited, no prior decisions to that effect being required.

ARTICLE 2

Negative Clearance

A5–04   Upon application by the undertakings or associations of undertakings concerned, the Commission may certify that, on the basis of the facts in its possession, there are no grounds under Article 85(1) or Article 86 of the Treaty for action on its part in respect of an agreement, decision or practice.

ARTICLE 3

Termination of Infringements

A5–05   1. Where the Commission, upon application or upon its own initiative, finds that there is infringement of Article 85 or Article 86 of the Treaty, it may by decision require the undertakings or associations of undertakings concerned to bring such infringement to an end.
2. Those entitled to make application are:
   (*a*)   Member States;
   (*b*)   natural or legal persons who claim a legitimate interest.
3. Without prejudice to the other provisions of this regulation, the Commission may, before taking a decision under paragraph (1), address to the undertakings or associations of undertakings concerned recommendations for termination of the infringement.

ARTICLE 4

Notification of New Agreements, Decisions and Practices

A5–06   1. Agreements, decisions and concerted practices of the kind described in Article 85(1) of the Treaty which come into existence after the entry into force of this regulation and in respect of which the parties seek application of Article 85(3) must be notified to the Commission. Until they have been notified, no decision in application of Article 85(3) may be taken.

A5–07   2. Paragraph (1) shall not apply to agreements, decisions or concerted practices where:
   (i)   the only parties thereto are undertakings from one Member State and the agreements, decisions or practices do not relate either to imports or to exports between Member States;
   (ii)   not more than two undertakings are party thereto, and the agreements only:
       (*a*)   restrict the freedom of one party to the contract in determining the prices for or conditions of business on which the goods which he has obtained from the other party to the contract may be resold; or
       (*b*)   impose restrictions on the exercise of the rights of the assignee or user of industrial property rights—in particular patents, utility models, designs or trade marks—or of the person entitled under a contract to the assignment, or grant, of the right to use a method of manufacture or knowledge relating to the use and to the application of industrial processes;

(iii) they have as their sole object:
  (*a*) the development or uniform application of standards or types;
  [(*b*) joint research and development;
  (*c*) specialisation in the manufacture of products, including agreements necessary for the achievement thereof;
      —where the products which are the object of specialisation do not, in a substantial part of the common market, represent more than 15 per cent. of the volume of business done in identical products or those considered by the consumers to be similar by reason of their characteristics, price and use, and
      —where the total annual turnover of the participating undertakings does not exceed 200 million units of accounts.

These agreements, decisions and concerted practices may be notified to the Commission].[1]

ARTICLE 5

Notification of Existing Agreements, Decisions and Practices

1. Agreements, decisions and concerted practices of the kind described in **A5–08** Article 85(1) of the Treaty which are in existence at the date of entry into force of this regulation and in respect of which the parties seek application of Article 85(3) shall be notified to the Commission [before November 1, 1962].[2] [However, notwithstanding the foregoing provisions, any agreements, decisions and concerted practices to which not more than two undertakings are party shall be notified before February 1, 1963].[3]

2. Paragraph (1) shall not apply to agreements, decisions or concerted practices falling within Article 4(2); these may be notified to the Commission.

ARTICLE 6

Decisions Pursuant to Article 85(3)

1. Whenever the Commission takes a decision pursuant to Article 85(3) of **A5–09** the Treaty, it shall specify therein the date from which the decision shall take effect. Such date shall not be earlier than the date of notification.

2. The second sentence of paragraph (1) shall not apply to agreements, decisions or concerted practices falling within Article 4(2) and Article 5(2), nor to those falling within Article 5(1), which have been notified within the time limit specified in Article 5(1).

ARTICLE 7

Special Provisions for Existing Agreements, Decisions and Practices

1. Where agreements, decisions and concerted practices in existence at the **A5–10** date of entry into force of this regulation and notified [within the limits specified in Article 5(1)][4] do not satisfy the requirements of Article 85(3) of

---

[1] The words in square brackets were added by Reg. 2822/71.
[2] The words in square brackets were substituted by Reg. 59, Art. 1(1).
[3] The words in square brackets were added by Reg. 59, Art. 1(2).
[4] The words in square brackets were added by Reg. 59, Art. 1(3).

the Treaty and the undertakings or associations of undertakings concerned cease to give effect to them or modify them in such manner that they no longer fall within the prohibition contained in Article 85(1) or that they satisfy the requirements of Article 85(3), the prohibition contained in Article 85(1) shall apply only for a period fixed by the Commission. A decision by the Commission pursuant to the foregoing sentence shall not apply as against undertakings and associations of undertakings which did not expressly consent to the notification.

2. Paragraph (1) shall apply to agreements, decisions and concerted practices falling within Article 4(2) which are in existence at the date of entry into force of this regulation if they are notified [before January 1, 1967].[5]

ARTICLE 8

Duration and Revocation of Decisions under Article 85(3)

A5–11   1. A decision in application of Article 85(3) of the Treaty shall be issued for a specified period and conditions and obligations may be attached thereto.

2. A decision may on application be renewed if the requirements of Article 85(3) of the Treaty continue to be satisfied.

A5–12   3. The Commission may revoke or amend its decision or prohibit specified acts by the parties:
   (*a*)   where there has been a change in any of the facts which were fundamental in the making of the decision;
   (*b*)   where the parties commit a breach of any obligation attached to the decision;
   (*c*)   where the decision is based on incorrect information or was induced by deceit;
   (*d*)   where the parties abuse the exemption from the provisions of Article 85(1) of the Treaty granted to them by the decision.
   In cases to which sub-paragraphs (*b*), (*c*) or (*d*) apply, the decision may be revoked with retroactive effect.

ARTICLE 9

Powers

A5–13   1. Subject to review of its decision by the Court of Justice, the Commission shall have sole power to declare Article 85(1) inapplicable pursuant to Article 85(3) of the Treaty.

2. The Commission shall have power to apply Article 85(1) and Article 86 of the Treaty; this power may be exercised notwithstanding that the time limits specified in Article 5(1) and in Article 7(2) relating to notification have not expired.

3. As long as the Commission has not initiated any procedure under Articles 2, 3 or 6, the authorities of the Member States shall remain competent to apply Article 85(1) and Article 86, in accordance with Article 88 of the Treaty; they shall remain competent in this respect notwithstanding that the time limits specified in Article 5(1) and in Article 7(2) relating to notification have not expired.

---

[5] The words in square brackets were substituted by Reg. 118/63.

ARTICLE 10

Liaison with the Authorities of the Member States

1. The Commission shall forthwith transmit to the competent authorities of **A5–14** the Member States a copy of the applications and notifications together with copies of the most important documents lodged with the Commission for the purpose of establishing the existence of infringements of Articles 85 or 86 of the Treaty or of obtaining negative clearance or a decision in application of Article 85(3).

2. The Commission shall carry out the procedure set out in paragraph (1) in close and constant liaison with the competent authorities of the Member States; such authorities shall have the right to express their views on that procedure.

3. An Advisory Committee on Restrictive Practices and Monopolies shall be consulted prior to the taking of any decision following upon a procedure under paragraph (1), and of any decision concerning the renewal, amendment or revocation of a decision pursuant to Article 85(3) of the Treaty.

4. The Advisory Committee shall be composed of officials competent in the **A5–15** matter of restrictive practices and monopolies. Each Member State shall appoint an official to represent it who, if prevented from attending, may be replaced by another official.

5. The consultation shall take place at a joint meeting convened by the Commission; such meeting shall be held not earlier than 14 days after dispatch of the notice convening it. The notice shall, in respect of each case to be examined, be accompanied by a summary of the case together with an indication of the most important documents, and a preliminary draft decision.

6. The Advisory Committee may deliver an opinion notwithstanding that some of its members or their alternates are not present. A report of the outcome of the consultative proceedings shall be annexed to the draft decision. It shall not be made public.

ARTICLE 11

Requests for Information

1. In carrying out the duties assigned to it by Article 89 and by provisions **A5–16** adopted under Article 87 of The Treaty, the Commission may obtain all necessary information from the Governments and competent authorities of the Member States and from undertakings and associations of undertakings.

2. When sending a request for information to an undertaking or association of undertakings, the Commission shall at the same time forward a copy of the request to the competent authority of the Member State in whose territory the seat of the undertaking or association of undertakings is situated.

3. In its request the Commission shall state the legal basis and the purpose of the request and also the penalties provided for in Article 15(1)(*b*) for supplying incorrect information.

4. The owners of the undertakings or their representatives and, in the case **A5–17** of legal persons, companies or firms, or of associations having no legal personality, the persons authorised to represent them by law or by their constitution, shall supply the information requested.

5. Where an undertaking or association of undertakings does not supply the information requested within the time limit fixed by the Commission, or supplies incomplete information, the Commission shall by decision require the information to be supplied. The decision shall specify what information is required, fix an appropriate time limit within which it is to be supplied and indicate the penalties provided for by Article 15(1)(*b*) and Article 16(1)(*c*) and the right to have the decision reviewed by the Court of Justice.

6. The Commission shall at the same time forward a copy of its decision to the competent authority of the Member State in whose territory the seat of the undertaking or association of undertakings is situated.

ARTICLE 12

Inquiry into Sectors of the Economy

A5–18 **1.** If in any sector of the economy the trend of trade between Member States, price movements, inflexibility of prices or other circumstances suggest that in the economic sector concerned competition is being restricted or distorted within the common market, the Commission may decide to conduct a general inquiry into that economic sector and in the course thereof may request undertakings in the sector concerned to supply the information necessary for giving effect to the principles formulated in Articles 85 and 86 of the Treaty and for carrying out the duties entrusted to the Commission.

2. The Commission may in particular request every undertaking or association of undertakings in the economic sector concerned to communicate to it all agreements, decisions and concerted practices which are exempt from notification by virtue of Article 4(2) and Article 5(2).

A5–19 **3.** When making inquiries pursuant to paragraph (2), the Commission shall also request undertakings or groups of undertakings whose size suggests that they occupy a dominant position within the common market or a substantial part thereof to supply to the Commission such particulars of the structure of the undertakings and of their behaviour as are requisite to an appraisal of their position in the light of Article 86 of the Treaty.

4. Article 10(3) to (6) and Articles 11, 13 and 14 shall apply correspondingly.

ARTICLE 13

Investigations by the Authorities of the Member States

A5–20 **1.** At the request of the Commission, the competent authorities of the Member States shall undertake the investigations which the Commission considers to be necessary under Article 14(1) or which it has ordered by decision pursuant to Article 14(3). The officials of the competent authorities of the Member States responsible for conducting these investigations shall exercise their powers upon production of an authorisation in writing issued by the competent authority of the Member State in whose territory the investigation is to be made. Such authorisation shall specify the subject-matter and purpose of the investigation.

2. If so requested by the Commission or by the competent authority of the Member State in whose territory the investigation is to be made the officials of the Commission may assist the officials of such authority in carrying out their duties.

ARTICLE 14[6]

Investigating Powers of the Commission

1. In carrying out the duties assigned to it by Article 89 and by provisions **A5–21** adopted under Article 87 of the Treaty, the Commission may undertake all necessary investigations into undertakings and associations of undertakings. To this end the officials authorised by the Commission are empowered:

    (*a*)   to examine the books and other business records;

    (*b*)   to take copies of or extracts from the books and business records;

    (*c*)   to ask for oral explanations on the spot;

    (*d*)   to enter any premises, land and means of transport of undertakings.

2. The officials of the Commission authorised for the purpose of these investigations shall exercise their powers upon production of an authorisation in writing specifying the subject-matter and purpose of the investigation and the penalties provided for in Article 15(1)(*c*) in cases where production of the required books or other business records is incomplete. In good time before the investigation, the Commission shall inform the competent authority of the Member State in whose territory the same is to be made, of the investigation and of the identity of the authorised officials.

3. Undertakings and associations of undertakings shall submit to investigations ordered by decision of the Commission. The decision shall specify the subject-matter and purpose of the investigation, appoint the date on which it is to begin and indicate the penalties provided for in Article 15(1)(*c*) and Article 16(1)(*d*) and the right to have the decision reviewed by the Court of Justice.

4. The Commission shall take the decisions referred to in paragraph 3 after **A5–22** consultation with the competent authority of the Member State in whose territory the investigation is to be made.

5. Officials of the competent authority of the Member State in whose territory the investigation is to be made may, at the request of such authority or of the Commission, assist the officials of the Commission in carrying out their duties.

6. Where an undertaking opposes an investigation ordered pursuant to this Article, the Member State concerned shall afford the necessary assistance to the officials authorised by the Commission to enable them to make their investigation. Member States shall, after consultation with the Commission, take the necessary measures to this end before October 1, 1962.

ARTICLE 15

Fines

1. The Commission may by decision impose on undertakings or **A5–23** associations of undertakings fines of from one hundred to five thousand units of account, where, intentionally or negligently:

    (*a*)   they supply incorrect or misleading information in an application pursuant to Article 2 or in a notification pursuant to Articles 4 or 5; or

---

[6] See, as to the scope of this Article, *A.M. & S. Europe Ltd. v. Commission of the European Communities* [1983] Q.B. 878.

(b) they supply incorrect information in response to a request made pursuant to Article 11(3) or (5) or to Article 12, or do not supply information within the time limit fixed by a decision taken under Article 11(5); or

(c) they produce the required books or other business records in incomplete form during investigations under Article 13 or 14, or refuse to submit to an investigation ordered by decision issued in implementation of Article 14(3).

A5–24 2. The Commission may by decision impose on undertakings or associations of undertakings fines of from one thousand to one million units of account, or a sum in excess thereof but not exceeding 10 per cent of the turnover in the preceding business year of each of the undertakings participating in the infringement where, either intentionally or negligently:

(a) they infringe Article 85(1) or Article 86 of the Treaty; or

(b) they commit a breach of any obligation imposed pursuant to Article 8(1).

In fixing the amount of the fine, regard shall be had both to the gravity and to the duration of the infringement.

3. Article 10(3) to (6) shall apply.

4. Decisions taken pursuant to paragraphs (1) and (2) shall not be of a criminal law nature.

A5–25 5. The fines provided for in paragraph (2)(a) shall not be imposed in respect of acts taking place:

(a) after notification to the Commission and before its decision in application of Article 85(3) of the Treaty, provided they fall within the limits of the activity described in the notification;

(b) before notification and in the course of agreements, decisions or concerted practices in existence at the date of entry into force of this regulation, provided that notification was effected within the time limits specified in Article 5(1) and Article 7(2).

6. Paragraph (5) shall not have effect where the Commission has informed the undertakings concerned that after preliminary examination it is of opinion that Article 85(1) of the Treaty applies and that application of Article 85(3) is not justified.

ARTICLE 16

Periodic Penalty Payments

A5–26 1. The Commission may by decision impose on undertakings or associations of undertakings periodic penalty payments of from fifty to one thousand units of account per day, calculated from the date appointed by the decision, in order to compel them:

(a) to put an end to an infringement of Article 85 or 86 of the Treaty, in accordance with a decision taken pursuant to Article 3 of this regulation;

(b) to refrain from any act prohibited under Article 8(3);

(c) to supply complete and correct information which it has requested by decision taken pursuant to Article 11(5);

(d) to submit to an investigation which it has ordered by decision taken pursuant to Article 14(3).

2. Where the undertakings or associations of undertakings have satisfied the obligation which it was the purpose of the periodic penalty payment to

enforce, the Commission may fix the total amount of the periodic penalty payment at a lower figure than that which would arise under the original decision.

3. Article 10(3) to (6) shall apply.

ARTICLE 17

Review by the Court of Justice

The Court of Justice shall have unlimited jurisdiction within the meaning of **A5–27** Article 172 of the Treaty to review decisions whereby the Commission has fixed a fine or periodic penalty; it may cancel, reduce or increase the fine or periodic penalty payment imposed.

ARTICLE 18

Unit of Account

For the purposes of applying Articles 15 to 17 the unit of account shall be **A5–28** that adopted in drawing up the budget of the Community in accordance with Articles 207 and 209 of the Treaty.

ARTICLE 19

Hearing of the Parties and of Third Persons

1. Before taking decisions as provided for in Articles 2, 3, 6, 7, 8, 15 and **A5–29** 16, the Commission shall give the undertakings or associations of undertakings concerned the opportunity of being heard on the matters to which the Commission has taken objection.

2. If the Commission or the competent authorities of the Member States consider it necessary, they may also hear other natural or legal persons. Applications to be heard on the part of such persons shall, where they show a sufficient interest, be granted.

3. Where the Commission intends to give negative clearance pursuant to Article 2 or take a decision in application of Article 85(3) of the Treaty, it shall publish a summary of the relevant application or notification and invite all interested third parties to submit their observations within a time limit which it shall fix being not less than one month. Publication shall have regard to the legitimate interest of undertakings in the protection of their business secrets.

ARTICLE 20

Professional Secrecy

1. Information acquired as a result of the application of Articles 11, 12, 13 **A5–30** and 14 shall be used only for the purpose of the relevant request or investigation.

2. Without prejudice to the provisions of Articles 19 and 21, the Commission and the competent authorities of the Member States, their officials and other servants shall not disclose information acquired by them as a result of the application of this regulation and of the kind covered by the obligation of professional secrecy.

3. The provisions of paragraphs (1) and (2) shall not prevent publication of general information or surveys which do not contain information relating to particular undertakings or associations of undertakings.

ARTICLE 21

Publication of Decisions

A5–31 **1.** The Commission shall publish the decisions which it takes pursuant to Articles 2, 3, 6, 7 and 8.

2. The publication shall state the names of the parties and the main content of the decision; it shall have regard to the legitimate interest of undertakings in the protection of their business secrets.

ARTICLE 22

Special Provisions

A5–32 **1.** The Commission shall submit to the Council proposals for making certain categories of agreement, decision and concerted practice falling within Article 4(2) or Article 5(2) compulsorily notifiable under Article 4 or 5.

2. Within one year from the date of entry into force of this regulation, the Council shall examine, on a proposal from the Commission, what special provisions might be made for exempting from the provisions of this regulation agreements, decisions and concerted practices falling within Article 4(2) or Article 5(2).

ARTICLE 23

Transitional Provisions Applicable to Decisions of Authorities of the Member States

A5–33 **1.** Agreements, decisions and concerted practices of the kind described in Article 85(1) of the Treaty to which, before entry into force of this regulation, the competent authority of a Member State has declared Article 85(1) to be inapplicable pursuant to Article 85(3) shall not be subject to compulsory notification under Article 5. The decision of the competent authority of the Member State shall be deemed to be a decision within the meaning of Article 6; it shall cease to be valid upon expiration of the period fixed by the authority but in any event not more than three years after the entry into force of this regulation.

Article 8(3) shall apply.

2. Applicants for renewal of decisions of the kind described in paragraph (1) shall be decided upon by the Commission in accordance with Article 8(2).

ARTICLE 24

Implementing Provisions

A5–34 The Commission shall have the power to adopt implementing provisions concerning the form, content and other details of applications pursuant to Article 2 and 3, and of notifications pursuant to Articles 4 and 5, and concerning hearings pursuant to Article 19(1) and (2).

ARTICLE 25[7]

1. As regards agreements, decisions and concerted practices to which **A5–35** Article 85 of the Treaty applies by virtue of accession, the date of accession shall be substituted for the date of entry into force of this regulation in every place where reference is made in this regulation to this latter date.

2. Agreements, decisions and concerted practices existing at the date of accession to which Article 85 of the Treaty applies by virtue of accession shall be notified pursuant to Article 5(1) or Article 7(1) and (2) within six months from the date of accession.

3. Fines under Article 15(2)(*a*) shall not be imposed in respect of any act **A5–36** prior to notification of the agreements, decisions and practices to which paragraph (2) applies and which have been notified within the period therein specified.

4. New Member States shall take the measures referred to in Article 14(6) within six months from the date of accession after consulting the Commission.

[5. The provisions of paragraphs (1) to (4) above still apply in the same way in the case of accession of the Hellenic Republic, the Kingdom of Spain and of the Portuguese Republic.][8]

This Regulation shall be binding in its entirety and directly applicable in all Member States.

---

[7] This Article was added by the Act annexed to the Treaty of Accession.

[8] This paragraph was originally added by the 1979 Act of Accession of the Hellenic Republic, and replaced by the Act of Accession of the Kingdom of Spain and the Portuguese Republic.

INLAND REVENUE STATEMENTS OF PRACTICE AND CONCESSIONS

I. Income Tax

STATEMENT OF PRACTICE (A4)

PARTNERSHIPS—CHANGE IN MEMBERSHIP (*January 17, 1973*)

A6–01   Where there is a change in the persons carrying on a trade, profession or vocation involving:

(*a*)   a change in the membership of a partnership,

(*b*)   a sole trader entering into partnership with one or more partners, or

(*c*)   a partnership being dissolved and the business being carried on by one partner as a sole trader,

the parties may elect under section 154(2) ICTA 1970[1] to have the profits of the business taxed as though it continued. In the absence of such an election the business has to be treated as ceasing and a new business as set up and commencing. The time limit for making this election was extended from 1 year to 2 years by Section 17 FA 1971 and this has lengthened the period during which there may be uncertainty as to the basis of assessment for the years immediately before and immediately after the change.

Where an election is to be made it would save work in both accountants' and Tax Offices if it could be made early enough to prevent the Inspector of Taxes having first to make assessments applying the cessation and commencing provisions and then to revert later to the continuing basis of assessment. The Board of Inland Revenue would welcome co-operation from accountants in achieving this end.

It is recognised that in some cases the decision whether or not to make an election is delayed in order to estimate more accurately the trend of profits after the partnership change. The Board think it might be helpful, and lead to an earlier election in such cases, if it were more widely known that it is the practice of Inspectors to accept a revocation of an election under Section 154(2) *provided* that the notice of revocation, signed by all the interested parties, is given before the expiry of the 2 year time limit for making the election.

STATEMENT OF PRACTICE (SP9/86)

INCOME TAX: PARTNERSHIP MERGERS AND DEMERGERS
(*December 10, 1986*)

A6–02   1. This statement explains the basis on which the Inland Revenue apply the provisions of Section 154 of the Income and Corporation Taxes Act 1970[2]

---

[1] Now the Income and Corporation Taxes Act 1988, s.113(2). As to the changes introduced by the Finance Act 1994, see *supra*, paras. 34–58, 34–59.

[2] Now the Income and Corporation Taxes Act 1988, s.113. As to the changes introduced by the Finance Act 1994, see *supra*, paras. 34–58, 34–59.

(change in ownership of trade, profession or vocation) to mergers and demergers of partnership businesses. In the following paragraphs, the word "business" means trades, professions or vocations carried on in partnership.

Mergers

2. When two businesses which are carried on in partnership and which are **A6–03** different in nature merge, it may be that the result of the merger is a new business, different in nature from either of the previous businesses. Whether this is so is a question of fact to be determined according to the circumstances of each case. Where it is the case, the old businesses will have been permanently discontinued, and a new business commenced; Section 154 ICTA 1970[3] will therefore not apply and the normal commencement and cessation provisions will apply to each business respectively.

3. However, where two partnership businesses in different ownership carrying on the same sort of activities are merged and then carried on by the joint owners in partnership, the total activities of both businesses may continue, even though in a merged form *i.e.* the new partnership may succeed to the businesses of the old partnerships. In that event the partners have the following options:

(*a*) Section 154(1) ICTA 1970[4] applies to both businesses so that the cessation and commencement provisions are deemed to apply to both;

(*b*) an election under Section 154(2) ICTA 1970[5] is made in respect of one business, and the cessation and commencement provisions are deemed to apply to the other;

(*c*) elections are made in respect of both businesses.

4. Where (*b*) applies, it will be necessary to apportion the profits of the combined business to apply the commencement provisions to the business in respect of which no election is made. It will of course be a question of fact whether succession has occurred and in this connection disparity in size between the old partnerships will not of itself be a significant matter.

Demergers

5. When a business carried on in partnership is divided up, and several **A6–04** separate partnerships are formed, it will again be a question of fact, to be determined according to the circumstances in each case, whether any of the separate partnerships carries on the same business as was carried on previously by the original partnership. It might be that one of the businesses carried on after the division was so large in relation to the rest as to be recognisably "the business" as previously carried on; but that will frequently not be the case, and if it is not the case an election under Section 154(2)[6] will not be possible.

6. The Inland Revenue would want to look carefully at any case where it was claimed that a demerger of a partnership had occurred but it appeared that the demerger was more apparent than real, and that the demerger seemed to have taken place for fiscal reasons. The Revenue might wish to argue that in such a case the same trade was being carried on after the demerger as before, that a Section 154(2)[7] election could be made, and that Section 47 Finance Act 1985[8] therefore applied.

---

[3] Now the Income and Corporation Taxes Act 1988, s.113.
[4] Now the Income and Corporation Taxes Act 1988, s.113(1).
[5] Now the Income and Corporation Taxes Act 1988, s.113(2).
[6] Now the Income and Corporation Taxes Act 1988, s.113(2).
[7] Now the Income and Corporation Taxes Act 1988, s.113(2).
[8] Now *ibid.* ss. 61, 62. As to the changes introduced by the Finance Act 1994, see *supra*, paras. 34–58.

Extra-Statutory Concession A80

Blanket Partnership Continuation Elections

A6–05 Where a trade or profession is carried on in partnership, under TA 1988 s. 113(1) a change in the membership of the partnership is treated for income tax purposes as the cessation of one trade or profession and the commencement of another. However TA 1988 s. 113(2)[9] permits the partners to elect for this rule to be set aside and for the trade or profession to be treated as continuing (provided as least one person who carried on the trade or profession before the change continues to do so after the change).

Under TA 1988 s. 113(2) the election must be signed jointly in respect of each change by all those who were partners both before and after the change. However by concession the Board of Inland Revenue will accept an election as covering all future changes in respect of a particular partnership until such time as the partners (or any partner) give notice that they wish to withdraw from the arrangement, provided that:—

   (i)   the firm in question has not less than 50 partners or, if less than 50, at least 20 who are not resident in the U.K., immediately after the first change,

  (ii)   new partners add their names to the election and

 (iii)   the Board of Inland Revenue is indemnified by the persons who were partners immediately before the first change, and by any person joining the partnership on the occasion of that change, or later, against any loss of tax which might arise from a claim by a partner or former partner that the election does not comply strictly with the provisions of TA 1988 s.113(2) and that s.113(1) should therefore have been applied to the particular change or changes.

II. Capital Gains Tax

Statement of Practice (D12)

Capital Gains Tax: Partnerships (*January 17, 1975*)

A6–06   The Board of Inland Revenue have had discussions with the Law Society and the Allied Accountancy Bodies on the capital gains tax treatment of partnerships. This statement sets out a number of points of general practice which have been agreed.

1. *Nature of the asset liable to tax*

A6–07   Section 45(7), Finance Act 1965[10] treats any partnership dealings in chargeable assets for capital gains tax purposes as dealings by the individual partners rather than by the firm as such. Each partner has therefore to be regarded as owning a fractional share of each of the partnership assets and not for this purpose an interest in the partnership.

Where it is necessary to ascertain the market value of a partner's share in a partnership asset for capital gains tax purposes, it will be taken as a fraction of the value of the total partnership interest in the asset without any discount for the size of his share. If, for example, a partnership owned all the issued shares in a company, the value of the interest in that holding of a partner with a one-tenth share would be one-tenth of the value of the partnership's 100 per cent holding.

---

[9] As to the changes introduced by the Finance Act 1994, see *supra*, paras. 34–58, 34–59.
[10] Now the Taxation of Chargeable Gains Act 1992, s.59.

2. *Disposals of assets by a partnership*

Where an asset is disposed of by a partnership to an outside party each of **A6–08** the partners will be treated as disposing of his fractional share of the asset. Similarly if a partnership makes a part disposal of an asset each partner will be treated as making a part disposal of his fractional share. In computing gains or losses the proceeds of disposal will be allocated between the partners in the ratio of their shares in asset surpluses at the time of the disposal. Where this is not specifically laid down the allocation will follow the actual destination of the surplus as shown in the partnership accounts; regard will of course have to be paid to any agreement outside the accounts. If the surplus is not allocated among the partners but, for example, put to a common reserve, regard will be had to the ordinary profit-sharing ratio in the absence of a specified asset-surplus-sharing ratio. Expenditure on the acquisition of assets by a partnership will be allocated between the partners in the same way at the time of the acquisition. This allocation may require adjustment, however, if there is a subsequent change in the partnership sharing ratios (see paragraph 4).

3. *Partnership assets divided in kind among the partners*

Where a partnership distributes an asset in kind to one or more of the **A6–09** partners, for example on dissolution, a partner who receives the asset will not be regarded as disposing of his fractional share in it. A computation will first be necessary of the gains which would be chargeable on the individual partners if the asset had been disposed of at its current market value. Where this results in a gain being attributed to a partner not receiving the asset the gain will be charged at the time of the distribution of the asset. Where, however, the gain is allocated to a partner receiving the asset concerned there will be no charge on distribution. Instead, his capital gains tax cost to be carried forward will be the market value of the asset at the date of distribution as reduced by the amount of his gain. The same principles will be applied where the computation results in a loss.

4. *Changes in partnership sharing ratios*[11]

An occasion of charge also arises when there is a change in partnership **A6–10** sharing ratios including changes arising from a partner joining or leaving the partnership. In these circumstances a partner who reduces or gives up his share in asset surpluses will be treated as disposing of part or the whole of his share in each of the partnership assets and a partner who increases his share will be treated as making a similar acquisition. Subject to the qualifications mentioned at 6 and 7 below the disposal consideration will be a fraction (equal to the fractional share changing hands) of the current balance sheet value of each chargeable asset provided that there is no direct payment of consideration outside the partnership. Where no adjustment is made through the partnership accounts (for example, by revaluation of the assets coupled with a corresponding increase or decrease in the partner's current or capital account at some date between the partner's acquisition and the reduction in his share) the disposal is treated as made for a consideration equal to his capital gains tax cost and thus there will be neither a chargeable gain nor an allowable loss at that point. A partner whose share reduces will carry forward

---

[11] This paragraph must be read with and subject to the Further Extension of the Statement of Practice (SP1/89) issued on February 1, 1989, which is reproduced *infra*, paras. A6–20 *et seq*.

a smaller proportion of cost to set against a subsequent disposal of the asset and a partner whose share increases will carry forward a larger proportion of cost.

The general rules in paragraph 7 of Schedule 6, Finance Act 1965[12] for apportioning the total acquisition cost on a part disposal of an asset will not be applied in the case of a partner reducing his asset-surplus share. Instead, the cost of the part disposed of will be calculated on a fractional basis.

5. *Adjustments through the accounts*

A6–11 Where a partnership asset is revalued a partner will be credited in his current or capital account with a sum equal to his fractional share of the increase in value. An upward revaluation of chargeable assets is not itself an occasion of charge. If, however, there were to be a subsequent reduction in the partner's asset-surplus share, the effect would be to reduce his potential liability to capital gains tax on the eventual disposal of the assets without an equivalent reduction of the credit he has received in the accounts. Consequently at the time of the reduction in sharing ratio he will be regarded as disposing of the fractional share of the partnership asset represented by the difference between his old and his new share for a consideration equal to that fraction of the increased value at the revaluation. The partner whose share correspondingly increases will have his acquisition cost to be carried forward for the asset increased by the same amount. The same principles will be applied in the case of a downward revaluation.

6. *Payments outside the accounts*

A6–12 Where on a change of partnership sharing ratios payments are made directly between two or more partners outside the framework of the partnership accounts, the payments represent consideration for the disposal of the whole or part of a partner's share in partnership assets in addition to any consideration calculated on the bases described in 4 and 5 above. Often such payments will be for goodwill not included in the balance sheet. In such cases the partner receiving the payment will have no capital gains tax cost to set against it unless he made a similar payment for his share in the asset (for example, on entering the partnership) or elects to have the market value at 6 April 1965 treated as his acquisition cost. The partner making the payment will only be allowed to deduct the amount in computing gains or losses on a subsequent disposal of his share in the asset. He will be able to claim a loss when he finally leaves the partnership or when his share is reduced provided that he then receives either no consideration or a lesser consideration for his share of the asset. Where the payment clearly constitutes payment for a share in assets included in the partnership accounts, the partner receiving it will be able to deduct the amount of the partnership acquisition cost represented by the fraction he is disposing of. Special treatment, as outlined in 7 below, may be necessary for transfers between persons not at arm's length.

7. *Transfers between persons not at arm's length*

A6–13 Where no payment is made either through or outside the accounts in connection with a change in partnership sharing ratio, a capital gains tax

---

[12] Now the Taxation of Chargeable Gains Act 1992, s. 42.

charge will only arise if the transaction is otherwise than by way of a bargain made at arm's length and falls therefore within section 22(4)(a) Finance Act charge will only arise if the transaction is otherwise than by way of a bargain made at arm's length and falls therefore within section 22(4)(a) Finance Act 1965,[13] as extended by paragraph 17(2) of Schedule 7 Finance Act 1965,[14] for transactions between connected persons. Under paragraph 21(4) of that Schedule[15] transfers of partnership assets between partners are not regarded as transactions between connected persons if they are pursuant to bona fide commercial arrangements. This treatment will also be given to transactions between an incoming partner and the existing partners.

Where the partners (including incoming partners) are connected other than by partnership (for example, father and son) or are otherwise not at arm's length (for example, uncle and nephew) the transfer of a share in the partnership assets may fall to be treated as having been made at market value. Market value will not be substituted, however, if nothing would have been paid had the parties been at arm's length. Similarly if consideration of less than market value passes between partners connected other than by partnership or otherwise not at arm's length, the transfer will only be regarded as having been made for full market value if the consideration actually paid was less than that which would have been paid by parties at arm's length. Where a transfer has to be treated as if it had taken place for market value, the deemed disposal proceeds will fall to be treated in the same way as payments outside the accounts.

8. *Annuities provided by partnerships*[16]

A lump sum which is paid to a partner on leaving the partnership or on a **A6–14** reduction of his share in the partnership represents consideration for the disposal by the partner concerned of the whole or part of his share in the partnership assets and will be subject to the rules in 6 above. The same treatment will apply when a partnership buys a purchased life annuity for a partner, the measure of the consideration being the actual cost of the annuity.

Where a partnership makes annual payments to a retired partner (whether under covenant or not) the capitalised value of the annuity will only be treated as consideration for the disposal of his share in the partnership assets under paragraph 2(3) of Schedule 6, Finance Act 1965,[17] if it is more than can be regarded as a reasonable recognition of the past contribution of work and effort by the partner to the partnership. Provided that the former partner had been in the partnership for at least 10 years an annuity will be regarded as reasonable for this purpose if it is no more than two-thirds of his average share of the profits in the best 3 of the last 7 years in which he was required to devote substantially the whole of his time to acting as a partner. In arriving at a partner's share of the profits regard will be had to the partnership profits assessed before deduction of any capital allowances or charges. The 10 year period will include any period during which the partner was a member of another firm whose business has been merged with that of the present firm. For lesser periods the following fractions will be used instead of the two-thirds:

---

[13] Now the Taxation of Chargeable Gains Act 1992, s.17(1)(a).
[14] Now *ibid*. s.18(2).
[15] Now *ibid*. s.286(4).
[16] This paragraph must be read with and subject to the Extension of the Statement of Practice (SP1/79) issued on January 12, 1979, which is reproduced *infra*, para. A6–19.
[17] Now the Taxation of Chargeable Gains Act 1992, s. 37(3).

Complete years in partnership	Fraction
1–5	1/60 for each year
6	8/60
7	16/60
8	24/60
9	32/60

Where the capitalised value of an annuity is treated as consideration received by the retired partner, it will also be regarded as allowable expenditure by the remaining partners on the acquisition of their fractional shares in partnership assets from him.

9. *Mergers*

A6–15   When the members of two or more existing partnerships come together to form a new one, the capital gains tax treatment will follow the same lines as that for changes in partnership sharing ratios. If gains arise for reasons similar to those covered in 5 and 6 above, it may be possible for rollover relief under section 33, Finance Act 1965,[18] to be claimed by any partner continuing in the partnership in so far as he disposes of part of his share in the assets of the old firm and acquires a share in other assets put into the "merged" firm. Where, however, in such cases the consideration given for the shares in chargeable assets acquired is less than the consideration for those disposed of, relief will be restricted under section 33(2).[19]

10. *Shares acquired in stages*

A6–16   Where a share in a partnership is acquired in stages wholly after 5 April 1965, the acquisition costs of the various chargeable assets will be calculated by pooling the expenditure relating to each asset. Where a share built up in stages was acquired wholly or partly before 6 April 1965 the rules in paragraph 26 of Schedule 6, Finance Act 1965,[20] will normally be followed to identify the acquisition cost of the share in each asset which is disposed of on the occasion of a reduction in the partnership's share; *i.e.* the disposal will normally be identified with shares acquired on a "first in, first out" basis. Special consideration will be given, however, to any case in which this rule appears to produce an unreasonable result when applied to temporary changes in the shares in a partnership, for example those occurring when a partner's departure and a new partner's arrival are out of step by a few months.

11. *Elections under Schedule 11 to the Finance Act 1968*[21]

A6–17   Where the assets disposed of are quoted securities eligible for a pooling election under Schedule 11, Finance Act 1968, partners will be allowed to make separate elections in respect of shares or fixed interest securities held by the partnership as distinct from shares or securities which they hold on a personal basis. Each partner will have a separate right of election for his proportion of the partnership securities and the time limit for the purposes of Schedule 11 will run from the earlier of—

(a)   the first relevant disposal of shares or securities by the partnership, and

---

[18] Now *ibid.* ss.152–158.
[19] Now *ibid.* s.153(1).
[20] Now *ibid.* Sched. 2, para. 18.
[21] Now the Taxation of Chargeable Gains Act 1992, Sched. 2, para. 4.

(*b*)   the first reduction of the particular partner's share in the partnership assets after 19 March 1968.

Where this time limit expired before today, the Board will consider sympathetically a request for extension within the next two years if the liability has not been finally determined and the tax paid.

12.   *Transitional arrangements*

The practices set out in this statement will be applied to all capital gains **A6–18** tax assessments after today. Where tax liabilities have already been settled on other reasonable bases the assessments will not be upset. Often gains and losses on previous disposals will have been computed on a different basis and the acquisition costs allocated as a result to partners to set against future disposals will be different from those which would have arisen had the new practices been followed. Such costs will only be recalculated in exceptional circumstances.

EXTENSION OF STATEMENT OF PRACTICE (SP1/79)

CAPITAL GAINS TAX—PARTNERSHIPS (*January 12, 1979*)

Paragraph 8 of the Statement of Practice issued by the Board of Inland **A6–19** Revenue on January 17, 1975 explains the circumstances in which the capitalized value of an annuity paid by a partnership to a retired partner will not be treated as consideration for the disposal of his share in the partnership assets. The Board have now agreed that this practice will be extended to certain cases in which a lump sum is paid in addition to an annuity. Where the aggregate of the annuity and one-ninth of the lump sum does not exceed the appropriate fraction (as indicated in the Statement) of the retired partner's average share of the profits, the capitalized value of the annuity will not be treated as consideration in the hands of the retired partner. The lump sum, however, will continue to be so treated.

This extension of the practice will be applied to all cases in which the liability has not been finally determined at the date of this Notice.

FURTHER EXTENSION OF STATEMENT OF PRACTICE (SP1/89)

CAPITAL GAINS TAX—PARTNERSHIPS (*February 1, 1989*)

Rebasing

The Board of Inland Revenue have agreed that a disposal of a share of **A6–20** partnership assets to which paragraph 4 of the Statement of Practice of 17 January 1975 [Statement D12] applies so that neither a chargeable gain nor an allowable loss accrues (before indexation, for disposals before 6 April 1988) may be treated for the purposes of FA 1988 s.96, Sch. 8[22] as if it were a no gain/no loss disposal within FA 1988 Sch. 8 para. 1.

Deferred charges

A disposal of a share of partnership assets to which paragraph 4 of the **A6–21** Statement of Practice of 17 January 1975 [Statement D12] applies so that neither a chargeable gain nor an allowable loss accrues (before indexation, for disposals before 6 April 1988) may be treated for the purposes of FA 1988 s.97, Sch. 9[23] as if it were a no gain/no loss disposal within FA 1988 Sch. 8 para. 1.[24]

---

[22] Now the Taxation of Chargeable Gains Act 1992, s.35, Sched. 3.
[23] Now the Taxation of Chargeable Gains Act 1992, s.36, Sched. 4.
[24] Now *ibid.* Sched. 3, para. 1.

Indexation

A6–22 When, on or after 6 April 1988, a partner disposes of all or part of his share of partnership assets in circumstances to which paragraph 4 of the Statement of Practice of 17 January 1975 [Statement D12] applies so that neither a chargeable gain nor an allowable loss accrues, the amount of the consideration will be calculated on the assumption that an unindexed gain will accrue to the transferor equal to the indexation allowance, so that after taking account of the indexation allowance, neither a gain nor a loss accrues.

Where a partner disposes on or after 6 April 1988 of all or part of his share of partnership assets, and he is treated by virtue of this Statement as having owned the share on 31 March, 1982, the indexation allowance on the disposal may be computed as if he had acquired the share on 31 March 1982. A disposal of a share in a partnership asset on or after 31 March 1982 to which paragraph 4 of the Statement of Practice of January 17 1975 [Statement D12] applies so that neither a chargeable gain nor an allowable loss accrues may be treated for the purposes of FA 1985 s.68(7)[25] as if it were a no gain/no loss disposal within FA 1985 s.68(7A)[26]. A special rule will however apply where the share changed hands on or after 6 April 1985 (1 April, in the case of an acquisition from a company) and before 6 April 1988: in these circumstances the indexation allowance will be computed by reference to the 31 March 1982 value but from the date of the last disposal of the share before 6 April 1988.

III. Inheritance Tax

STATEMENT OF PRACTICE (SP12/80)

BUSINESS RELIEF FROM CAPITAL TRANSFER TAX[27]: "BUY AND SELL" AGREEMENTS (*October 13, 1980*)

A6–23 The Inland Revenue understand that it is sometimes the practice for partners or shareholder directors of companies to enter into an agreement (known as a "Buy & Sell" Agreement) whereby, in the event of the death before retirement of one of them, the deceased's personal representatives are obliged to sell and the survivors are obliged to purchase the deceased's business interest or shares, funds for the purchase being frequently provided by means of appropriate life assurance polices.

In the Inland Revenue's view such an agreement, requiring as it does a sale and purchase and not merely conferring an option to sell or buy, is a binding contract for sale within paragraph 3(4) of Schedule 10 to the Finance Act 1976.[28] As a result the capital transfer tax[29] business relief will not be due on the business interest or shares. (Paragraph 3(4) provides that where any property would be relevant business property for the purpose of business relief in relation to a transfer of value but a binding contract for its sale has been entered into at the time of the transfer, it is not relevant business property in relation to that transfer).

---

[25] Now the Taxation of Chargeable Gains Act 1992, s.55(5).
[26] Now the Taxation of Chargeable Gains Act 1992, ss.35(3)(*d*), 55(5).
[27] Capital transfer tax was redesignated as inheritance tax by the Finance Act 1986.
[28] Now the Inheritance Tax Act 1984, s.113. It should be noted that the rate of business relief is now, in general, 100 per cent: *ibid.* s.104(1)(*a*), as amended by the Finance (No.2) Act 1992, Sched. 14, para. 1.
[29] Now inheritance tax: see *supra*, n.27.

1994 No. 2421   A7–01

INSOLVENCY

THE INSOLVENT PARTNERSHIP ORDER 1994

Made 13th September 1994

Laid before Parliament 16th September 1994

Coming into force 1st December 1994

ARRANGEMENT OF ARTICLES

PART I

General

PART II

Voluntary Arrangements

PART III

Administration Orders

PART IV

Creditors' etc. Winding-up Petitions

PART V

Members' Petitions

The Lord Chancellor, in exercise of the powers conferred on him 420(1) and (2) of the Insolvency Act 1986[1] and section 21(2) of the Company Directors Disqualification Act 1986[2] and of all other powers enabling him in that behalf, with the concurrence of the Secretary of State, hereby makes the following Order:—

Part I

General

Citation, commencement and extent

1.—(1) This Order may be cited as the Insolvent Partnerships Order 1994 **A7–02** and shall come into force on 1st December 1994.

(2) This Order—
  (a) in the case of insolvency proceedings in relation to companies and partnerships, relates to companies and partnerships which the courts in England and Wales have jurisdiction to wind up; and
  (b) in the case of insolvency proceedings in relation to individuals, extends to England and Wales only.

(3) In paragraph (2) the term "insolvency proceedings" has the meaning ascribed to it by article 2 below.

Interpretation: definitions

2.—(1) In this Order, except in so far as the context otherwise requires— **A7–03**
    "the Act" means the Insolvency Act 1986;
    "agricultural charge" has the same meaning as in the Agricultural Credits Act 1928[3];
    "agricultural receiver" means a receiver appointed under an agricultural charge;

---

[1] 1986 c. 45.
[2] 1986 c. 46; the amendments to section 21(2) made by the Companies Act 1989 (c. 40) are not relevant for the purposes of this Order.
[3] 1928 c. 43.

"corporate member" means an insolvent member which is a company;

"the court", in relation to an insolvent partnership, means the court which has jurisdiction to wind up the partnership;

"individual member" means an insolvent member who is an individual;

"insolvency order" means—

(a) in the case of an insolvent partnership or a corporate member, a winding-up order; and

(b) in the case of an individual member, a bankruptcy order;

"insolvency petition" means, in the case of a petition presented to the court—

(a) against a corporate member, a petition for its winding up by the court;

(b) against an individual member, a petition for a bankruptcy order to be made against that individual,

where the petition is presented in conjunction with a petition for the winding up of the partnership by the court as an unregistered company under the Act;

"insolvency proceedings" means any proceedings under the Act, this Order or the Insolvency Rules 1986[4];

"insolvent member" means a member of an insolvent partnership, against whom an insolvency petition is being or has been presented;

"joint bankruptcy petition" means a petition by virtue of article 11 of this Order;

"joint debt" means a debt of an insolvent partnership in respect of which an order is made by virtue of Part IV or V of this Order;

"joint estate" means the partnership property of an insolvent partnership in respect of which an order is made by virtue of Part IV or V of this Order;

"joint expenses" means expenses incurred in the winding-up of an insolvent partnership or in the winding-up of the business of an insolvent partnership and the administration of its property;

"limited partner" has the same meaning as in the Limited Partnerships Act 1907[5];

"member" means a member of a partnership and any person who is liable as a partner within the meaning of section 14 of the Partnership Act 1890[6];

"officer", in relation to an insolvent partnership, means—

(a) a member; or

(b) a person who has management or control of the partnership business;

"partnership property" has the same meaning as in the Partnership Act 1890;

"postponed debt" means a debt the payment of which is postponed by or under any provision of the Act or of any other enactment;

"responsible insolvency parctitioner" means—

(a) in winding up, the liquidator of an insolvent partnership or corporate member; and

(b) in bankruptcy, the trustee of the estate of an individual member,

---

[4] S.I. 1986/1925, amended by S.I. 1987/1919, S.I. 1989/397, S.I. 1991/495 and S.I. 1993/602.
[5] 1907 c. 24.
[6] 1890 c. 39.

and in either case includes the official receiver when so acting;

"separate debt" means a debt for which a member of a partnership is liable, other than a joint debt;

"separate estate" means the property of an insolvent member against whom an insolvency order has been made;

"separate expenses" means expenses incurred in the winding-up of a corporate member, or in the bankruptcy of an individual member; and

"trustee of the partnership" means a person authorised by order made by virtue of article 11 of this Order to wind up the business of an insolvent partnership and to administer its property.

(2) The definitions in paragraph (1), other than the first definition, shall be added to those in section 436 of the Act.

(3) References in provisions of the Act applied by this Order to any provision of the Act so applied shall, unless the context otherwise requires, be construed as references to the provision as so applied.

(4) Where, in any Schedule to this Order, all or any of the provisions of two or more sections of the Act are expressed to be modified by a single paragraph of the Schedule, the modification includes the combination of the provisions of those sections into the one or more sections set out in that paragraph.

Interpretation: expressions appropriate to companies

3.—(1) This article applies for the interpretation in relation to insolvent **A7–04** partnerships of expressions appropriate to companies in provisions of the Act and of the Company Directors Disqualification Act 1986 applied by this Order, unless the contrary intention appears.

(2) References to companies shall be construed as references to insolvent partnerships and all references to the registrar of companies shall be omitted.

(3) References to shares of a company shall be construed—
  (a) in relation to an insolvent partnership with capital, as references to rights to share in that capital; and
  (b) in relation to an insolvent partnership without capital, as references to interest—
    (i)   conferring any right to share in the profits or liability to contribute to the losses of the partnership, or
    (ii) giving rise to an obligation to contribute to the debts or expenses of the partnership in the event of a winding-up.

(4) Other expressions appropriate to companies shall be construed, in relation to an insolvent partnership, as references to the corresponding persons, officers, documents or organs (as the case may be) appropriate to a partnership.

Part II

Voluntary Arrangements

Voluntary arrangement of insolvent partnership

4.—(1) The provisions of Part I of the Act shall apply in relation to an **A7–05** insolvent partnership, those provisions being modified in such manner that, after modification, they are as set out in Schedule 1 to this Order.

(2) For the purposes of the provisions of the Act applied by paragraph (1), the provisions of the Act specified in paragraph (3) below, insofar as they

relate to company voluntary arrangements, shall also apply in relation to insolvent partnerships.

(3) The provisions referred to in paragraph (2) are—
(a) section 233 in Part VI,
(b) Part VII, with the exception of section 250,
(c) Part XII,
(d) Part XIII,
(e) sections 411, 413, 414 and 419 in Part XV, and
(f) Parts XVI to XIX.

Voluntary arrangements of members of insolvent partnership

A7–06   **5.**—(1) Where insolvency orders are made against an insolvent partnership and an insolvent member of that partnership in his capacity as such. Part I of the Act shall apply to corporate members and Part VIII to individual members of that partnership, with the modification that any reference to the creditors of the company or of the debtor, as the case may be, includes a reference to the creditors of the partnership.

(2) Paragraph (1) is not to be construed as preventing the application of Part I or (as the case may be) Part VIII of the Act to any person who is a member of an insolvent partnership (whether or not a winding-up order has been made against that partnership) and against whom an insolvency order has not been made under this Order or under the Act.

PART III

Administration Orders

Administration order in relation to insolvent partnership

A7–07   **6.**—(1) The provisions of Part II of the Act shall apply in relation to an insolvent partnership, certain of those provisions being modified in such manner that, after modification, they are as set out in Schedule 2 to this Order.

(2) For the purposes of the provisions of the Act applied by paragraph (1), the provisions of the Act specified in paragraph (3) below, insofar as they relate to administration orders, shall also apply in relation to insolvent partnerships.

(3) The provisions referred to in paragraph (2) are—
(a) section 212 in Part IV.
(b) Part VI,
(c) Part VII, with the exception of section 250,
(d) Part XIII,
(e) sections 411, 413, 414 and 419 in Part XV, and
(f) Parts XVI to XIX.

PART IV

Creditors' etc. Winding-up Petitions

Winding up of insolvent partnership as unregistered company on petition of creditor etc. where no concurrent petition presented against member

A7–08   **7.**—(1) Subject to paragraph (2) below, the provisions of Part V of the Act shall apply in relation to the winding-up of an insolvent partnership as an unregistered company on the petition of a creditor, of a responsible insolvency practitioner of the Secretary of State, where no insolvency petition is presented by the petitioner against a member or former member of that partnership in his capacity as such.

(2) Certain of the provisions referred to in paragraph (1) are modified in their application in relation to insolvent partnerships which are being wound up by virtue of that paragraph in such manner that, after modification, they are as set out in Part I of Schedule 3 to this Order.

(3) The provisions of the Act specified in Part II of Schedule 3 to this Order shall apply as set out in that Part for the purposes of section 221(5) of the Act, as modified by Part I of that Schedule.

Winding up of insolvent partnership as unregistered company on creditor's petition where concurrent petitions presented against one or more members

8.—(1) Subject to paragraph (2) below, the provisions of Part V of the Act **A7–09** (other than sections 223 and 224), shall apply in relation to the winding-up of an insolvent partnership as an unregistered company on a creditor's petition where insolvency petitions are presented by the petitioner against the partnership and against one or more members of former members of the partnership in their capacity as such.

(2) Certain of the provisions referred to in paragraph (1) are modified in their application in relation to insolvent partnerships which are being wound up by virtue of that paragraph in such manner that, after modification, they are set out in Part I of Schedule 4 to this Order.

(3) The provisions of the Act specified in Part II of Schedule 4 to this Order shall apply as set out in that Part for the purposes of section 221(5) of the Act, as modified by Part I of that Schedule.

(4) The provisions of the Act specified in paragraph (5) below, insofar as they relate to winding up of the companies by the court in England and Wales on a creditor's petition, shall apply in relation to the winding-up of a corporate member or former corporate member (in its capacity as such) of an insolvent partnership which is being wound up by virtue of paragraph (1).

(5) The provisions referred to in paragraph (4) are—
  (a) Part IV,
  (b) Part VI,
  (c) Part VII, and
  (d) Parts XII to XIX

(6) The provisions of the Act specified in paragraph (7) below, insofar as they relate to the bankruptcy of individuals in England and Wales on a petition presented by a creditor, shall apply in relation to the bankruptcy of an individual member or former individual member (in this capacity as such) of an insolvent partnership which is being wound up by virtue of paragraph (1).

(7) The provisions referred to in paragraph (6) are—
  (a) Part IX (other than sections 269, 270, 287, 297), and
  (b) Parts X to XIX.

(8) Certain of these provisions referred to in paragraphs (4) and (6) are modified in their application in relation to the corporate or individual members or former corporate or individual members of insolvent partnerships in such manner that, after modification, they are as set out in Part II of Schedule 4 to this Order.

(9) The provisions of the Act applied by this Article shall further be modified so that references to a corporate or individual member include any former such member against whom an insolvency petition is being or has been presented by virtue of this Article.

PART V

Members' Petitions

Winding up of insolvent partnership as unregistered company on member's petition where no concurrent petition presented against member

A7–10   9. The following provisions of the Act shall apply in relation to the winding-up of an insolvent partnership as an unregistered company on the petition of a member where no insolvency petition is presented by the petitioner against a member of that partnership in his capacity as such—

(a)   sections 117 and 221, modified in such manner that, after modification, they are as set out in Schedule 5 to this Order; and

(b)   the other provisions of Part V of the Act, certain of those provisions being modified in such manner that, after modification, they are as set out in Part I of Schedule 3 to this Order.

Winding up of insolvent partnership as unregistered company on member's petition where concurrent petitions presented against all members

A7–11   10.—(1) The following provisions of the Act shall apply in relation to the winding-up of an insolvent partnership as an unregistered company on a member's petition where insolvency petitions are presented by the petitioner against the partnership and against all its members in their capacity as such—

(a)   sections 117, 124, 125, 221, 264, 265, 271 and 272 of the Act, modified in such manner that, after modification, they are as set out in Schedule 6 to this Order; and

(b)   sections 220, 225 and 227 to 229 in Part V of the Act, section 220 being modified in such manner that, after modification, it is as set out in Part I of Schedule 4 to this Order.

(2) The provisions of the Act specified in paragraph (3) below, insofar as they relate to winding up of companies by the court in England and Wales on a member's petition, shall apply in relation to the winding-up of a corporate member (in its capacity as such) of an insolvency partnership which is wound up by vistue of paragraph (1).

(3) The provisions referred to in paragraph (2) are—

(a)   Part IV,

(b)   Part VI,

(c)   Part VII, and

(d)   Parts XII to XIX.

(4) The provisions of the Act specified in paragraph (5) below, insofar as they relate to the bankruptcy of individuals in England and Wales where a bankruptcy petition is presented by a debtor, shall apply in relation to the bankruptcy of an individual member (in his capacity as such) of an insolvent partnership which is being wound up by virtue of paragraph (1).

(5) The provisions referred to in paragraph (4) are—

(a)   Part IX (other than sections 273, 274, 287, and 297), and

(b)   Parts X to XIX.

(6) Certain of the provisions referred to in paragraphs (2) and (4) are modified in their application in relation to the corporate or individual members of insolvent partnerships in such manner that, after modification, they are as set out in Part II of Schedule 4 to this Order, save that the provisions on summary administration of a debtor's estate shall apply in relation to the individual members of insolvent partnerships in such manner that, after modification, those provisions are as set out in Schedule 7 to this order.

Insolvency proceedings not involving winding up of insolvent partnership as unregistered company where individual members present joint bankruptcy petition

11.—(1) The provisions of the Act specified in paragraph (2) below shall **A7–12** apply in relation to the bankruptcy of the individual members of an insolvent partnership where those members jointly present a petition to the court for orders to be made for the bankruptcy of each of them in his capacity as a member of the partnership, and the winding up of the partnership business and administration of its property, without the partnership being wound up as an unregistered company under Part V of the Act.

(2) The provisions referred to in paragraph (1) are—

(a) Part IX (other than sections 273, 274 and 287), and

(b) Parts X to XIX,

insofar as they relate to the insolvency of individuals in England and Wales where a bankruptcy petition is presented by a debtor.

(3) Certain of the provisions referred to in paragraph (1) are modified in the application in relation to the individual members of insolvent partnerships in such manner that, after modification, they are as set out in Schedule 7 to this Order.

PART VI

Provisions Applying in Insolvency Proceedings in Relation to Insolvent Partnerships

Winding up of unregistered company which is a member of insolvent partnership being wound up by virtue of this Order

12.—(1) Where an insolvent partnership or other body which may be **A7–13** wound up under Part V of the Act as an unregistered company is itself a member of an insolvent partnership being so wound up, articles 8 and 10 above shall apply in relation to the latter insolvent partnership as though the former body were a corporate member of that partnership.

Deposit on petitions

13.—(1) Where an order under section 414(4) or 415(3) of the Act **A7–14** (security for fees) provides for any sum to be deposited on presentation of a winding-up or bankruptcy petition, that sum shall, in the case of petitions presented by virtue of articles 8 and 10 above, only be required to be deposited in respect of the petition for winding up the partnership, but shall be treated as a deposit in respect of all those petitions.

(2) Production of evidence as to the sum deposited on presentation of the petition for winding up the partnership shall suffice for the filing of an insolvency petition against an insolvent member.

Supplemental powers of court

14.—(1) At the end of section 168 of the Act there shall be inserted the **A7–15** following subsections:—

"(5A) Where at any time after a winding-up petition has been presented to the court against any person (including an insolvent partnership or other body which may be wound up under Part V of the Act as an unregistered company), whether by virtue of the provisions of the Insolvent Partnerships Order 1994[7] or not, the attention of the court is drawn to the fact that the person in question is a member of an insolvent partnership, the court may make an order as to the future conduct of the insolvency proceedings and any such order may apply any provisions of that Order with any necessary modifications.

(5B) Any order or directions (5A) may be made or given on the application of the official receiver, any responsible insolvency practitioner, the trustee of the partnership or any other interested person and may include provisions as to the administration of the joint estate of the partnership, and in particular how it and the separate estate of any member are to be administered.

(5C) Where the court makes an order under section 72(1)(a) of the Financial Services Act 1986[8] or section 92(1)(a) of the Banking Act 1987[9] for the winding-up of an insolvent partnership, the court may make an order as to the future conduct of the winding-up proceedings, and any such order may apply any provisions of the Insolvent Partnerships Order 1994 with any necessary modifications.".

(2) At the end of section 303 of the Act there shall be inserted the following subsections:—

"(2) Where at any time after a bankruptcy petition has been presented to the court against any person, whether under the provisions of the Insolvent Partnerships Order 1994 or not, the attention of the court is drawn to the fact that the person in question is a member of an insolvent partnership, the court may make an order as to the future conduct of the insolvency proceedings and any such order may apply any rovisions of that Order with any necessary modifications.

(2B) Where a bankruptcy petition has been presented against more than one individual in the circumstances mentioned in subsection (2A) above, the court may give such directions for consolidating the proceedings, or any of them, as it thinks just.

(2C) Any order or directions under subsection (2A) or (2B) may be made or given on the application of the official receiver, any responsible insolvency practitioner, the trustee of the partnership or any other interested person and may include provisions as to the administration of the joint estate of the partnership, and in particular how it and the separate estate of any member are to be administered.".

Meaning of "act as insolvency practitioner"

A7–16   **15.**—(1) After section 388(2) of the Act there shall be inserted the following—

"(2A) A person acts as an insolvency practitioner in relation to an insolvent partnership by acting—
(a)   as its liquidator, provisional liquidator or administrator, or
(b)   as trustee of the partnership under article 11 of the Insolvent Partnerships Order 1994, or

---

[7] S.I. 1994/2421.
[8] 1986 c. 60.
[9] 1987 c. 22.

(c)   as supervisor of a voluntary arrangement approved in relation to it under Part I of this Act.".

(2) In section 388(3) the words "to a partnership and" shall be omitted.

Part VII

Disqualification

Application of Company Directors Disqualification Act 1986

16. Where an insolvent partnership is wound up as an unregistered **A7–17** company under Part V of the Act, the provisions of sections 6 to 10,[10] 15, 19(c) and 20 of, and Schedule 1[11] to, the Company Directors Disqualification Act 1986 shall apply, certain of those provisions being modified in such manner that, after modification, they are as set out in Schedule 8 to this Order.

Part VIII

Miscellaneous

Forms

17.—(1) The forms contained in Schedule 9 to this Order shall be used in **A7–18** and in connection with proceedings by virtue of this Order, whether in the High Court or a county court.

(2) The forms shall be used with such variations, if any, as the circumstances may require.

Application of subordinate legislation

18.—(1) The subordinate legislation specified in Schedule 10 to this Order **A7–19** shall apply as from time to time in force and with such modifications as the context requires for the purpose of giving effect to the provisions of the Act and of the Company Directors Disqualification Act 1986 which are applied by this Order.

(2) In the case of any conflict between any provision of the subordinate legislation applied by paragraph (1) and any provision of this Order, the latter provision shall prevail.

Supplemental and transitional provisions

19.—(1) This Order does not apply in relation to any case in which a **A7–20** winding-up or a bankruptcy order was made under the Insolvent Partnerships Order 1986[12] in relation to a partnership or an insolvent member of a partnership, and where this Order does not apply the law in force immediately before this Order came into force continues to have effect.

(2) Where the winding-up or bankruptcy proceedings commenced under the provisions of the Insolvent Partnerships Order 1986 were pending in

---

[10] Section 8 of the Company Directors Disqualification Act 1986 was amended by section 198 of the Financial Services Act 1986, section 55(b) of the Criminal Justice (Scotland) Act 1987 (c. 41), section 145(b) of the Criminal Justice Act 1988 (c. 33) and section 79 of the Companies Act 1989.

[11] Schedule 1 to the Company Directors Disqualification Act 1986, was amended by sections 23 and 139(4) of, paragraph 35(1) and (3) of Schedule 10 to, the Companies Act 1989.

[12] S.I. 1986/2142.

relation to a partnership or an insolvent member of a partnership immediately before this Order came into force, either—

(a) those proceedings shall be continued, after the coming into force of this Order, in accordance with the provisions of this Order, or

(b) if the court so directs, they shall be continued under the provisions of the 1986 Order, in which case the law in force immediately before this Order came into force continues to have effect.

(3) For the purpose of paragraph (2) above, winding-up or bankruptcy proceedings are pending if a statutory or written demand has been served or a winding-up or bankruptcy petition has been presented.

(4) Nothing in this Order is to be taken as preventing a petition being presented against an insolvent partnership under—

(a) section 53 or 54 of the Insurance Companies Act 1982[13] (winding up: insurance companies),

(b) section 72(2)(d) of the Financial Services Act 1986 (winding up: investment business),

(c) section 92 of the Banking Act 1987 (winding up: authorised institutions), or

(d) any other enactment.

(5) Nothing in this Order is to be taken as preventing any creditor or creditors owed one or more debts by an insolvent partnership from presenting a petition under the Act against one or more members of the partnership liable for that debt or those debts (as the case may be) without including the others and without presenting a petition or the winding up of the partnership as an unregistered company.

(6) Bankruptcy proceedings may be consolidated by virtue of article 14(2) above irrespective of whether they were commenced under the Bankruptcy Act 1914[14] or the Insolvency Act 1986 or by virtue of the Insolvent Partnerships Order 1986 or this Order, and the court shall, in the case of proceedings commenced under or by virtue of different enactments, make provision for the manner in which the consolidation proceedings are to be conducted.

REVOCATION

A7–21   **20.** The Insolvent Partnerships Order 1986 is hereby revoked.

Mackay of Clashfern, C.

Dated 8th September 1994

I concur, on behalf of
the Secretary of State

Neil Hamilton
Parliamentary Under-Secretary of State for
Corporate Affairs, Department of Trade
Dated 13th September 1994   and Industry.

---

[13] 1982 c. 50. Sections 53 and 54 were amended by section 439(2) of, and Schedule 14 to, the Insolvency Act 1986 and by S.I. 1989/2405. Section 54 was also amended by section 30 of, and Schedule 2 to, the Companies Consolidation (Consequential Provisions) Act 1985 (c. 9), and by S.I. 1990/1333.

[14] 1914 c. 59.

INDEX

[References preceded by the letter A are to the statutory and other materials contained in the Appendices.]

1107

ACCOUNTS—*cont.*
  dissolution—*cont.*
    adjustments to, 22–06, 25–39 *et seq.*
      A1–45
    distinct, 13–85, 27–106
    duty to keep, 22–09 *et seq.*, A1–29
      corporate partnerships, 10–59, 11–16,
        22–08
    errors, 10–62, 23–109
    estoppel, creating, 13–123
    evidence, as, 23–126
    failure to keep, 22–11
    false, 12–100, 23–56
    final adjustment, 22–06, 25–39 *et seq.*,
      A1–45
    form of, 22–07
    fraud, 10–06, 10–62, 12–100, 23–56,
      23–108
    goodwill, 10–63
    group, 22–08
    inquiries, 23–78, A2–03
    inspection, 22–12 *et seq.*, 23–97 *et seq.*,
      27–68. *See also* DISCOVERY;
      DOCUMENTS; *and* INSPECTION.
    corporate partnerships, 22–08
    interim, 10–59n
    interrogatories as to, 23–96
    just allowances, 23–123
    liquidator, kept by, 27–106
    management, 10–59n
    mistake, 23–109
    mode of keeping, 22–02 *et seq.*
    partner, rendered by, 12–34
    partnership agreement, 10–59 *et seq.*,
      10–133 *et seq.*, 22–12, 22–14
    period, of, 23–124, 23–125
    preparation of, 10–61
      corporate partnerships, 10–59, 11–16,
        22–08
    private book, kept in, 22–12, 23–127
    production, 23–97 *et seq.*, 23–127
    receivers, access to, 23–174
    re-opening, 10–62, 23–107 *et seq.*,
      23–124
    revaluation reserve, 22–04
    scope of, 23–76
    settled. *See* SETTLED ACCOUNT.
    signature of, 10–61, 10–64
    solicitors, 12–137
    summary order for, 23–78
    surcharging and falsifying, 23–109
    taking, 23–121 *et seq.*, 26–39
    tax reserve, 22–04
    trustee in bankruptcy, kept by,
      27–106
    undue influence, 23–109
    unintelligible, 22–11
    valuation of share by reference to,
      10–133 *et seq.*
    waiver, 23–114
    withholding, 22–11

ACCOUNTS—*cont.*
  work-in-progress, 10–61, 21–04, 34–34
    et seq., 34–63
  See also ACCOUNT, RIGHT TO;
    ACCOUNT STATED; ACTIONS FOR
    ACCOUNT; BOOKS; *and* SETTLED
    ACCOUNT.

ACCRUER,
  goodwill, of, 10–122, 10–164, 36–27,
    36–30
  share in partnership, of,
    capital gains tax, 35–19
    expulsion, on, 11–13, 10–125, 27–72
    inheritance tax, 36–05 *et seq.*, 36–28
      et seq., 36–48 *et seq.*, 36–56,
      A6–23
    insolvent partner, 10–125, 27–72
    value added tax, 37–24n

ACKNOWLEDGMENT,
  agent, by, 13–138
  authority of partners, 13–139
  continuing partners, by, 13–139
  continuing partnership, 13–138
  dissolution, after, 13–139
  limitation of actions, 13–137, 23–35 *et
    seq.*
  one partner, by, 13–137, 13–138
  service of writ, of, 14–18, 14–72, 14–89,
    23–78, 30–28, 30–29, A2–12
  surviving partners, by, 13–138, 13–139

ACTIONS,
  account, for. *See* ACTIONS FOR
    ACCOUNT.
  accrual. *See* LIMITATION OF ACTIONS.
  acknowledgment of service, 14–18,
    14–72, 14–89, 23–78, A2–12
  judgment in default of, 14–20
  managing partner, by, 14–18, 14–72,
    30–27
  administration, for, 26–09 *et seq.*, 26–17
    et seq. See also ESTATES OF
    DECEASED PARTNERS.
  agreements for partnership, 23–194
  aliens, against, 14–04, 14–05. *See also*
    ALIENS.
  apportionment, for, 8–52 *et seq.*
  authority of partners, 12–35, 12–36,
    14–28, 14–69 *et seq.*, 30–27. *See
    also* AUTHORITY OF PARTNERS.
  bankrupt partners, against, 14–59,
    27–17, 27–20, 27–41
  contribution, for. *See* CONTRIBUTION.
  co-owners, between, 5–09
  costs. *See* COSTS.
  defences, 14–60 *et seq. See also*
    DEFENCES.
  discovery, 23–93 *et seq. See also*
    DISCOVERY.

LIEN—*cont.*
  partners, of—*cont.*
    loss of, 19–32, 19–40 *et seq.*
    mortgagee's lien, distinguished from, 19–32
    nature of, 19–28
    private debts, for, 19–38
    property subject to, 19–31, 19–32
    purchasers, enforceability against, 19–35 *et seq.*
    registration, 19–30n
    retirement, 19–28 *et seq.*
    stock-in-trade, 19–31, 19–35, 19–37
    trustee in bankruptcy, against, 27–71
  rescission of agreement for partnership, on, 23–52, 23–53, A1–42
  outgoing partners, of, 10–209, 19–28 *et seq.*, 27–102 *et seq.*, A1–40
  solicitors, of, 3–49, 23–120

LIMITATION OF ACTIONS,
  account, actions for, 23–35 *et seq.*
  acknowledgment, 13–137 *et seq.*, 23–36
  agreed accounts, 23–37, 23–38
  appropriation of payments, 13–81
  arbitrations, 10–238, 23–42
  breach of trust, 23–39
  concealment, 23–39
  continuing partnerships, 23–31, 23–32
  contribution, right to, 20–17
  contributories, calls on, 27–60
  deed, where, 23–34
  dissolution, 13–139, 23–32 *et seq.*
  estate of deceased partner, against, 13–139, 26–16
  fiduciary relationships, 23–41
  forfeiture of share, 23–32
  fraud, 23–39
  laches, 23–17 *et seq. See also* LACHES.
  land, 23–41
  lien of partners, 19–32, 19–41
  outgoing partners, between, 23–33, 23–34
  partners, between, 23–31 *et seq.*
    part-payment, 13–137 *et seq.*, 23–40
  receiver, by, 23–40
  specialty, 23–34
  surviving partners, between 23–32, 23–33
  time, running of, 23–31
    acknowledgment, effect of, 13–138, 13–139, 23–36
    agreements as to, 23–37
  trusts, 23–41
  winding up, after completion of, 23–38

LIMITED PARTNERS,
  actions by and against, 30–27 *et seq.*
  admissions, 30–04
  assignees from, 30–20, 30–21

LIMITED PARTNERS—*cont.*
  assignment of share, 30–19, 31–16, 31–17
  authority, 29–26, 30–04 *et seq.*, 30–27, 31–04, 33–05
  books, inspection by, 31–04
  capacity, 29–06
  civil proceedings order against, 30–27
  companies as, 29–06
  contributions, 28–07, 29–04, 30–09 *et seq.*, 31–05 *et seq.*, A3–04
    loss of, 30–14, 31–05
    withdrawal, 28–07, 30–10, 30–12 *et seq.*, 30–21, 31–09, 31–10, 31–14, 31–20, 31–21, A3–04
  contributories, as, 33–04
  corporate, 32–13, 32–14
  death, 29–13, 30–17 *et seq.*, 31–20, 31–21, 32–02, A3–06
  directors, treated as, 33–02 *et seq.*
  disabilities affecting, 30–27
  discrimination against, 29–16
  general partners,
    becoming, 30–08, 30–16, 31–22
    death of sole, 32–01
    deemed to be, 29–27, 30–11, 30–24, 30–25, 31–22, A3–05
  holding out, 29–09 *et seq.*
  income tax, 34–29, 34–31, 34–72
  insolvency, 29–13, 30–17 *et seq.*, 31–20, 31–21, 32–02, 33–01 *et seq.*, A3–06
    administration of estates, 33–08
    joint and separate estates, 33–08
    petitions,
      against, 33–07
      by, 33–06
      dismissal, 33–07
  insolvent firm, where, 33–02 *et seq.*
  interest on capital, 30–13
  judgment against, 30–23
  liability, 13–14, 29–04, 29–24, 30–05, 30–09 *et seq.*, 33–02 *et seq.*
    changes in, 29–05, 29–14, 30–08, 30–16
    insolvency, 33–02 *et seq.*
    limit of, 30–09, 30–10
    nature of, 30–22 *et seq.*
    non-registration, effect of, 29–27
    termination of, 30–17, 30–18
  losses,
    sharing, 31–12, 31–13
    use of, 34–72
  management, exclusion from, 29–32, 30–04, 30–11, 30–24, 30–25, 31–02, 31–04, 33–02, 33–05, A3–06
  mental disorder, 32–10, 32–11, A3–06
  names, use of, 29–09 *et seq.*
  number of, 29–02
  obligations of, 30–01 *et seq.*
  outgoing, liability of, 30–21
  payments to, 30–13 *et seq.*